CONTRACT LAW IN IRELAND

EIGHTH EDITION

ROBERT CLARK

Barrister at Law (King's Inns)
Professor Emeritus, School of Law, UCD.
Consultant to Arthur Cox, London and Dublin

ROUND HALL

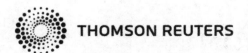

THOMSON REUTERS

Published in 2016 by
Thomson Reuters Ireland Limited
(Registered in Ireland, Company No. 416940.
Registered Office and address for service: 43 Fitzwilliam Place, Dublin 2)
trading as Round Hall

Typeset by Carrigboy Typesetting Services
Printed by CPI Group (UK) Ltd, Croydon, CR0 4YY

ISBN 9780414056367

A catalogue record for this book is available from the British Library

Thomson Reuters and the Thomson Reuters Logo are trademarks of
Thomson Reuters.

Round Hall ® is a registered trademark of Thomson Reuters Ireland Limited.

To Alice

Table of Contents

Contents

Preface

The Irish legal landscape is quite unrecognisible to that which existed in 1982 when the first edition of this book appeared. In that year, the Oireachtas passed 29 statutes, most of which were modest in terms of subject matter and length. Some 389 statutory instruments were made. In 2015, 66 statutes were enacted with 642 statutory instruments being laid. The number of ordinary judges of the High Court has risen from "not more than fourteen" to 37 in the same period. It is to be assumed that this increase in legislative output and judicial brainpower (at least in a quantative sense) necessarily reflects a society and an economy that is more complex, diverse and in need of greater regulatory intervention than hithertofore. Contract law in Ireland in the 1980s was largely rooted in case law and common law, and equitable doctrines. Statute law had little to say with even the Sale of Goods and Supply of Services Act 1980 being the exception to Freedom of Contract. Even in the last few years the situation has changed insofar as legislation such as the Construction Contracts Act 2013 and the Assisted Decision-Making (Capacity) Act 2015 introduce mandatory mechanisms that are not only welcome but overdue. The Criminal Justice (Spent Convictions and Certain Disclosures) Act 2016 is hopefully a harbinger of legislation to overhaul insurance contract law along the lines of the Law Reform Commission Report from 2014.

Case law in Ireland also reflects the trend evident elsewhere in terms of public law intervention in contractual matters, as well as judicial control in relation to discretionary aspects of contractual performance. Supreme Court guidance in relation to statutory illegality is perhaps the highlight for Irish legal scholars (if not for students who may be examined on this subject). It would be a welcome development if at some stage the Supreme Court could undertake a rationalisation of the law of promissory estoppel and bargain theory, but I suspect that the "fools rush in ..." dictum applies here.

I wish to thank the library staff in UCD and the IALS for help and assistance as well as providing warmth and light over the winter months. As usual the personnel in Round Hall have been terrific and I am grateful to colleagues in Arthur Cox for advice, information and assistance, especially Pearse Ryan, Audrey Keogh, Louise McDonnell, Miriam Dunne and Chris Bollard. Thanks for the support of my wonderful wife Alice, the mainstay of my existence, goes without saying.

ROBERT CLARK
Mount Merrion
August 19, 2016

Table of Cases

IRELAND

NORTHERN IRELAND

EUROPEAN

UNITED KINGDOM

Table of Cases

Table of Cases

SCOTLAND

AUSTRALIA

CANADA

Table of Cases

NEW ZEALAND

UNITED STATES

Table of Cases

OTHER

Table of Legislation

Post–1922 Acts

Court Rules

Statutory Instruments

EUROPEAN

Directives

Regulations

ENGLAND AND WALES

Acts

NORTHERN IRELAND

SCOTLAND

CANADA

NEW ZEALAND

UNITED STATES

INTERNATIONAL TREATIES, LEGISLATION AND CONVENTIONS

OTHER

BILLS

Part 1

Formation of a Binding Contract

1 The Rules of Offer and Acceptance

Introduction

1–01 The primary characteristic of a binding contract is one of bargain. Generally, the common law rules on the enforceability of promises entitle members of society to expect that a promise will be enforced by the courts or made the subject of monetary compensation because the promise was made in the context of an exchange relationship. In other words, the common law does not normally make a promise binding as a contract simply because the promise was made. By the same token, once a promise is made in return for another promise or some requested action, it is generally unnecessary for the promise to be made or evidenced in writing.

1–02 There are, of course, several circumstances in which the bargain model is not truly applicable. In many instances the contract is not the result of a negotiated bargain, as in the case of public utility companies such as the electricity and communications industries where the terms of supply are fixed either by legislation or standard contracts which leave little or no room for variation. The contract may be implied by virtue of a long term familiarity with the activities of a regulatory body that sets out rules and procedures for individuals or associations; see *Modahl v British Athletic Federation*[1] where continued participation at athletics meetings organised by clubs and associations operating under the rules of the British Athletic Federation ripened into a contract between plaintiff and defendant, there being no basis at all for an express contract. The bargain model is also incapable of explaining several situations where the courts have upheld a contract while at the same time finding it difficult or even unnecessary to locate a true exchange between the parties. In general, however, the common law recognises enforceable contractual arrangements are in place even when the agreement is purely verbal and the terms of the contract have not been reduced into writing. A striking illustration of this kind of agreement is provided by the case of *Pernod Ricard & Comrie Plc v FII Fyffes Plc*.[2] The defendants were the registered owners of shares in Irish Distillers Plc. The plaintiffs placed a general offer to purchase the shares owned or controlled by the defendants, this agreement being verbally negotiated over a two-day period, the parties eventually reaching agreement on price and the method of payment and shaking hands on the deal. Costello J. rejected submissions that the agreement was conditional on a written contract being executed, observing:

---

[1] [2002] 1 W.L.R. 1192. See generally, *Chitty on Contracts*, edited by H.G. Beale, 32nd edn. (London: Sweet & Maxwell, 2015), Vol.1, paras 2-001–2-167.

[2] Unreported, High Court, October 21, 1988. On negotiations concluded by shaking hands on the deal, see *Murphy v O'Toole and Sons Ltd* [2014] IEHC 486.

"It is true that no written form of irrevocable undertaking had been produced for the defendant's inspection at that time [of agreement] and that it was understood that one would be executed [the following day]. But the contract which the parties had entered into was not required by law to be in writing and the execution of a written document was not made a condition precedent to the defendant's liability under the agreement; it was merely a means of implementing a concluded bargain."

The Supreme Court[3] upheld Costello J. and decreed specific performance of a multi-million pound take-over transaction even though no contemporaneous document evidencing the agreement existed.

Prima Facie Rules of Interpretation

1–03 In some circumstances, however, there are formal statutory requirements which must be complied with if a contract is to be enforceable and it is increasingly common to require written documents if consumer transactions are to be enforced. In general, however, the common law system utilises a minimal number of formal devices.

1–04 The absence of any general requirement that contracts be in a written form should not be confused with the desirability of documentation. In *Donnelly v Woods*,[4] Charleton J. gave a very cogent summary of the reasons which underpin the requirement that essential terms be agreed and, preferably, documented. Donnelly claimed that he had been engaged to provide specialist services to the defendant, a developer who proposed to develop land for a housing project. Due to financial and planning difficulties, the work was never completed. Donnelly claimed for fees due under an agreement that had been verbally struck some 12 years previously. Donnelly gave evidence that as a financial consultant engaged to raise funding, he normally charged 10 per cent of the fee. Charleton J. found that the evidence had not established, as a probability, that such a fee had been arranged and that no clear terms existed in relation to Donnelly's duties. Charleton J. observed:

"The essential aspect of a contract is that the parties come together and agree what their obligations are. Not every single issue as to liability and performance needs to be foreseen and provided for. To dismiss a contractual claim on the basis of a missing term would be to undermine the business efficacy which the courts are obliged to give to commercial transactions on the basis that reasonable people will conclude a contract where what is essential to their obligations is defined and agreed. Certain matters will be essential. This depends on the nature of the obligations

---

[3] Unreported, Supreme Court, November 11, 1988.
[4] [2012] IEHC 26; *Bergin v Walsh* [2015] IEHC 594.

being undertaken through contract by the parties. In a contract for the sale of land, for instance, it is essential to nominate the parties, to sufficiently describe the land by reference to its location and the interest in it that is being disposed of and the price that is to be paid. Often times, much more than such bare terms will be specified by reference to fixed contracts published by professional bodies which are in each individual sale adapted to the needs of the vendor and the purchaser. Building and engineering bodies also publish standard form contracts and continually refine these based on experience; these documents will be replete with detail. Whereas this is desirable in avoiding all kinds of disputes later on, what is essential is that the parties to an agreement should not be left in doubt as to the substance of what they are to do in discharge of the obligation created by the contract.

Here, there is a problem. The nature of the services provided by the plaintiff to the defendant and his partner are left uncertain due to lack of documentation. This is compounded by an understandable vagueness in evidence by all of the parties who gave testimony; after the lapse of up to twelve years. If people put their obligations in writing, even through the exchange of letters, then there is at least something to refresh the memory and there may also be the clarity that written language can bring to the definition of obligations. All of that is absent in this case. The court is left uncertain as to the nature of the professional services provided by the plaintiff; what exactly this consisted of; how many hours were involved; and what the hourly rate of charge would be."

Conversely, the verbal or written understanding may lead a court to conclude that the parties intended a signed contract to constitute *the contract*. Where signature is a *sine qua non* to the conclusion of a binding contract, specific difficulties arise where no definitive, universal signed text exists. The English decision in *Koenigsblatt v Sweet*[5] suggests that when there are multiple parties involved in the execution of signatures to the contract, any problems about subsequent alterations and corrections can be resolved through ratification and that position holds true in respect of defective (i.e. missing) signatures. In a case arising out of s.1(3) of the Law of Property (Miscellaneous Provisions) Act 1989 (for which there is no equivalent Irish provision) an English High Court judge[6] has remarked, *obiter*, that on virtual signing of documents, that is, solicitors for the parties are not all together and each forwards pre-signed copies to be attached to the final draft, s.1(3) is not satisfied. This dictum has led Irish solicitors to either give proxy consents to lawyers attending the closing of a contract or arrange for physical copies to be completed at

---

[5] [1923] 2 Ch. 314.
[6] Judgment of Underhill J. in *R (Mercury) v HMRC* [2008] EWHC 2721 (Admin). See generally Scottish Law Commission, *Review of Contract Law*, Discussion Paper No. 154 on Formation of Contracts (March 2012). Many of the doubts about this subject have been addressed in legislation: execution of documents and nominees and electronic documents are treated in the Legal Writings (Counterparts and Delivery)(Scotland) Act 2015.

different times, and other methods of closing transactions upon signature have been evolved. It is important, as a counterweight to fraud and mistake, that contract documentation is uniform and that a definitive version is signed, even by a simple electronic signature.[7] In the absence of any statutory mandatory rule, the courts strive to give effect to the objectively ascertained intention of contracting parties.

1–05 As a result, it has become necessary to create rules on the formation of contracts that enable judges to view everyday incidents and actions as having legal consequences. The rules of offer and acceptance, for example, are designed to determine whether the parties have reached agreement on the subject matter, price, and other material terms, or whether the parties remain locked in negotiation, still edging their way towards agreement.

1–06 Many contractual relationships are forged almost instantaneously. By stepping on a bus or buying a newspaper or a lottery ticket,[8] for example, we enter into a contract, and in this context it seems artificial to isolate these transactions into separate stages. Lord Wilberforce remarked during a complex dispute where it seemed obvious to him that a bargain should be enforced that the only problem was to make the facts amenable to the rules on formation.

> "It is only the precise analysis of this complex of relations into the classical offer and acceptance with identifiable consideration that seems to present difficulty, but this same difficulty exists in many situations of daily life, *e.g.* sales at auction, supermarket purchases; boarding an omnibus; purchasing a train ticket, tenders for the supply of goods; offers of rewards; acceptance by post … These are all examples which show that English law, having committed itself to a rather technical and schematic doctrine of contract, in application takes a practical approach, often at the cost of forcing the facts to fit uneasily into the marked slots of offer, acceptance and consideration."[9]

A most useful summary of the cases[10] in which traditional offer and acceptance analysis does not assist in locating a binding contract is found in the judgment of Heydon J.A. in the New South Wales Court of Appeal decision in *Brambles*

---

[7] Electronic Commerce Act 2000 ss.2 and 13.

[8] *Carroll v An Post National Lottery Co* [1996] 1 I.R. 443.

[9] *New Zealand Shipping Co Ltd v AM Satterthwaite & Co Ltd (The Eurymedon)* [1974] 1 All E.R. 1015 at 1020; applied in *Kuzmanovski v New South Wales Lotteries Corp* [2010] FCA 876 in which the recipient of a winning lottery ticket purchased by his wife as a birthday present was able to enforce a contract.

[10] e.g. Mass transportation contracts, *MacRobertson Miller Airline Services v CST* (1975) 133 C.L.R. 125; contracts formed by conduct, *Clarke v Dunraven* [1897] A.C. 59; contracts for the sale of land, *Eccles v Bryant & Pollock* [1948] Ch. 93; long term but evolving commercial transactions, *Integrated Computer Services Pty v Digital Equipment Corp* (Aust) (1988) 5 B.P.R. 11 at 110.

Holdings Ltd v Bathurst City Council.[11] Heydon J.A. opined that if it is not possible to identify an offer and acceptance, a contract may nevertheless be inferred, notwithstanding, for example, a rejection or counter-offer:

> "[I]t is relevant to ask; in all the circumstances can an agreement be inferred? Has mutual assent been manifested? What would a reasonable person in the position of [each of the parties to the putative contract] think as to whether there was a concluded bargain?"[12]

Later Australian cases, the most important decisions being from the New South Wales Court of Appeal, revolve around the issue of whether the silence of an offeree may, implicitly or by inference, be capable of forming a binding contract. In *Kriketos v Livschitz*,[13] an offeree who did not respond to the last of three letters that constituted a series of negotiations was held not to be bound by a contract. Applying the three questions[14] that had been mandated in earlier case law—"did the parties arrive at a consensus?; (if they did) was it such a consensus as was capable of forming a binding contract?; and (if it was) did the parties intend that the consensus at which they arrived should constitute a binding contract?"—the New South Wales Court of Appeal concluded that, on an objective basis, there was insufficient evidence of a final agreement, criticising the finding of the judge at first instance who inferred a contract because the evidence was consistent with the offeror's arguments. It must be pointed out that these Australian precedents must be treated with caution because of the liberal use of post-contractual conduct as an aid to interpretation, a position both English and Irish law does not generally countenance.

1–07 The New Zealand courts have also endorsed a more flexible approach based on factual analysis of the evidence on an objective basis[15] and in *Apple Corps v Apple Computer Inc,*[16] a jurisdiction case, this greater flexibility of approach has led one English judge to contemplate that a contract may be concluded in two places rather than one. But decisions of this kind, in Irish and English case law, are the exception rather than the rule and tried and tested methods are preferred. The most authoritative statement in favour of the traditional offer and acceptance approach being the correct analysis in England

---

[11] (2001) 53 N.S.W.L.R. 153 at 176–179.

[12] (2001) 53 N.S.W.L.R. 153 at 179; *Air Great Lakes Pty Ltd v K.S. Easter (Holdings) Pty Ltd* [1985] 2 N.S.W.L.R. 309. See also *Integrated Computer Services Pty Ltd v Digital Equipment Corp (Aust) Pty Ltd* (1988) 5 B.P.R. 11; *Empirnall Holdings Pty Ltd v Machon Paul* (1988) 14 N.S.W.L.R. 523; *Hendriks v McGeoch* [2008] NSWCA 53; *Laidlaw v Hillier Hewitt Elsley Pty* [2009] NSWCA 44; *Ostron Pty v Rose Dion Pty* [2015] NSWSC 643.

[13] [2009] NSWCA 96; *A&M Green Investments Pty Ltd v Progressive Pod Properties Pty Ltd* [2011] NSWSC 502.

[14] *Air Great Lakes Pty Ltd v K.S. Easter (Holdings) Pty Ltd* [1985] 2 N.S.W.L.R. 309 per Mahoney J.A. at 326.

[15] *GHP Piling Ltd v Leighton Contractors Pty Ltd* [2012] 3 N.Z.L.R. 255, citing *Wilmott v Johnson* [2003] 1 N.Z.L.R. 649.

[16] [2004] EWHC 768 (Ch).

and Wales comes from the English Court of Appeal in *Tekdata Interconnections Ltd v Amphenol*,[17] a battle of the forms case. Both sides agreed that a contract was in existence but the question was, did the purchase order with terms on the reverse side from Tekdata apply, or was the contract constituted by Amphenol's acknowledgment of the purchase order, those forms containing an exception clause for the benefit of Amphenol? The trial judge found that while the battle of the forms favoured Amphenol, the commercial context—a long running supply contract of component parts for aircraft, the need for clarity on performance standards—favoured the conclusion that Tekdata's terms should apply. The Court of Appeal held that the trial judge was incorrect in departing from a standard offer and acceptance analysis, repeating that set rules were to be deployed in answering battle of the forms issues. Longmore L.J. said that the offer and acceptance approach could be displaced if the evidence clearly discloses a clear course of dealing between the parties. Dyson L.J. agreed:

> "[T]he rules which govern the formation of contracts have been long established and they are grounded in the concepts of offer and acceptance. So long as that continues to be the case, it seems to me to be that the general rule should be that the traditional offer and acceptance analysis is to be applied in battle of the forms cases. That has the great merit of providing a degree of certainty which is both desirable and necessary in order to promote effective commercial relationships."

Offer

1–08 An offer may be defined as a clear and unambiguous statement of the terms upon which the offeror is willing to contract, should the person or persons to whom the offer is addressed decide to accept. Should the terms proposed be imprecise, no offer will be held to have been made. In *Hoare v Allied Irish Banks Plc*,[18] a letter written by the defendant to customers who had defaulted on various loans stipulated that if a series of actions were undertaken the bank "is willing to show a level of forbearance" vis-à-vis various breaches and arrears. Charleton J. said that the letter did not contain a definite offer but was an intimation that the defendant would "do its best" to see you through the next year. Statements of this kind, Charleton J. observed, might ground an estoppel (see chapter 2) but not a contract.

1–09 It is important to distinguish an offer from a statement made without intending that a contract will result if the person to whom it is made indicates assent to those terms. Such statements are often called "an invitation to treat". In such a case the courts often view the response itself to be an offer which

---

[17] [2009] EWCA Civ 1209; *Trebor Bassett Holdings Ltd v ADT Fire and Security Plc* [2011] EWHC 1936 (TCC).
[18] [2014] IEHC 221.

can in turn be accepted or rejected. The distinction is not always easy to draw but litigation has produced a series of *prima facie* rules which are approximate guides to the student.

(1) Auction sales

1–10 Under s.58(2) of the Sale of Goods Act 1893, a sale by auction is complete when the auctioneer announces its completion, normally by the fall of the hammer. It is clear then that it is the bidder who makes the offer and that the offer is accepted or rejected by the auctioneer. The auctioneer who announces that a sale will take place at a certain time does not make an offer to sell goods which will be accepted by arriving at the saleroom. The auctioneer then cannot be liable in contract if the sale does not take place: see *Harris v Nickerson*.[19] On the other hand, an announcement by an auctioneer that a sale will take place "without reserve" may give rise to liability if bidding commences but the auctioneer refuses to sell to the highest bidder.

1–11 By announcing that he will sell to the highest bidder the auctioneer is said to make an offer which is accepted by attending the sale and bidding, although the person making the highest bid at the time of refusal to sell is thought to be the only person entitled to recover damages: see *Tully v Irish Land Commission*.[20] Therefore, the statement that goods will be sold "without reserve" has two consequences; it invites persons to make offers to purchase the property or the goods in question and it constitutes an offer made by the auctioneer for which he will be liable in damages should he refuse to knock down the goods after bidding has started. Of course if the auctioneer has been authorised to sell "without reserve" and the refusal to sell is the result of the owner's change of mind, the auctioneer should be indemnified by the owner for any damages he has had to pay. The declaration that the sale will be "without reserve" prohibits direct bidding by the owner and indirect bidding by or on behalf of the owner. In *Tkachuk Farms Ltd v Le Blanc Auction Service Ltd*,[21] the owner of farm equipment contracted with an auctioneer on terms that the sale would take place without reserve but the owner was promised a guaranteed sum. The sale did not go well with total sums raised falling below the guaranteed price. Both under the basic principles of contract law and the terms of the contract, bidding by the owner's nephew, in breach of contract, was held to entitle the auctioneer to rescind the contract, thereby avoiding an obligation to pay the shortfall between the sum raised ($387,000) and the guaranteed price ($577,500).

1–12 On the measure of damages that may be recovered, the leading English case of *Warlow v Harrison*[22] indicates that the correct approach to

---

[19] (1873) L.R. 8 Q.B. 286.
[20] (1961) 97 I.L.T.R. 174.
[21] [2007] 2 W.W.R. 662, following, *inter alia, Proctor v Almansask Distributors Ltd* (1984) 37 Alta L.R. (2d) 164.
[22] (1859) 1 E. & E. 309.

be adopted is to measure the difference between the highest bona fide bid, made presumably by the plaintiffs, and the price at which the hammer falls. This will not, however, always be possible (for example, where the goods are withdrawn) and other cases, such as the leading Australian case of *Ulbrick v Laidlaw*,[23] lend support for the view that damages will tend to be nominal. Another approach would require the court to speculate on the full market value of the property in question and award the difference between this figure and the plaintiff's bid.

1–13 It was just such an award that was made in the most recent English case on this point. In *Barry v Davies*,[24] the Court of Appeal considered a claim brought by the only bidder at a "without reserve" sale of engineering equipment with a list price value of £28,000. The plaintiff bid £400 but the auctioneer withdrew the goods rather than knock them down at obvious undervalue. The auctioneer could not do this because no power to bid had been reserved by the owner.[25] The Court of Appeal awarded damages of £27,600 to the plaintiff. Because on the facts of this case there was only one bidder, the case leaves open the question of whether there is a contract between the highest bona fide bidder and the auctioneer or between the auctioneer and all persons who attend and bid on the strength of the auctioneer's offer.

1–14 In the case of online auctions, it is generally agreed that they differ significantly from auctions that have evolved and been recognised by the Sale of Goods Act 1893. Essentially the parties to an online auction are bound by the contractual terms which the service provider (for example eBay) imposes upon participants and these will differ from one "auction house", or selling platform, to another. For example, the rules may exclude certain kinds of goods (e.g. narcotics, firearms) or deny the bidder a right to withdraw a bid. Australian case law holds that an online auction does create direct contractual relations between the seller and a successful bidder on the auction site terms: *Smyth v Thomas*.[26] However, the Consumer Rights Directive[27] does not use the terminology of an online auction but regards such transactions as a distance contract concluded by way of an online platform. Public auctions are not equated with distance contracts concluded by way of an online platform in certain respects.[28]

(2) Display of goods

1–15 In the case of *Minister for Industry and Commerce v Pim*,[29] a coat was displayed in a shop window with a notice declaring the cash price and

---

[23] [1924] V.L.R. 247.

[24] [2001] 1 All E.R. 944; Carter (2001) 17 J.C.L. 69.

[25] On which, see *Commerce Commission v Grenardier Real Estate Ltd* [2004] 2 N.Z.L.R. 186.

[26] [2007] NSWSC 844.

[27] Directive 2011/83/EU [2011] OJ L304/64.

[28] *e.g.* Article 16(k) excepts contracts concluded by way of public auction from the arts 9 to 15 rights of withdrawal. On transposition see the European Union (Consumer Information, Cancellation and Other Rights) Regulations 2013 reg.13 (SI No. 484 of 2013).

[29] [1966] I.R. 154.

indicating that credit terms were available. It was an offence to offer for sale goods on credit terms without specifically setting out those terms and the shopkeeper was prosecuted. The prosecution failed. It was held that to display goods with a price tag is not to offer them for sale. This display constitutes an invitation to treat, an action tantamount to inviting offers from members of the public. This rule is said to protect shopkeepers who would otherwise be obliged to sell goods to anyone who saw them in the window and came into the shop demanding that they can be purchased. If this represented the law a shopkeeper who had already sold the goods to another person would be obliged to sell them a second time, making him liable in contract or tort to the first buyer.

1–16 On the other hand, if I camp outside a department store for three days waiting for the January sale to commence in the hope of purchasing a furniture suite displayed in the window with a sale tag of €5 attached, it would be monstrous if the salesman could lawfully refuse to sell it to me when the sale began. Remember that these are only prima facie rules and in such a case the display would be regarded as an offer; see the American case of *Lefkowitz v Gt. Minneapolis Surplus Store*.[30] In the leading English case of *Pharmaceutical Society v Boots Cash Chemists*,[31] the Court of Appeal held that when a shopper takes goods from a shelf he does not accept an offer made by the storekeeper when he displays the goods. The acts of appropriation and approaching the cash desk constitute an offer by the prospective purchaser which is accepted by the cashier.

1–17 Many of these cases are not contract cases at all but are criminal prosecutions for misleading advertising. Some statutes make it an offence to "expose for the purpose of sale" which would catch acts of display: see *Minister for Industry and Commerce v Pim* itself. Section 1 of the Registration of Potato Growers and Potato Packers Act 1984, for example, defines "sell" so as to include "agree to sell, expose for sale, invite an offer to buy and offer to sell".

(3) Advertisements

1–18 In most cases an advertisement is considered to be an invitation to treat, so if an advertisement for goods appears in a newspaper, a person writing to order those goods cannot sue in contract if the vendor replies that he is out of stock and cannot meet the order. The rationale behind this rule is the same as that mentioned in relation to display of goods cases. In the English case of *C.A. Norgren Co v Technomarketing*,[32] Walton J. refused to make out a committal order against one of the defendants for allegedly breaching an undertaking given to the High Court that the defendants would not "make, offer for sale, sell or distribute"

---

[30] 86 N.W. 2d 689 (1957).
[31] [1953] 1 Q.B. 401; see Munday, "Fisher v Bell Revisited: Misjudging the Legislative Craft" [2013] C.L.J. 50.
[32] *The Times*, March 3, 1983.

items that were the subject of copyright. The defendants had distributed a price list and brochure which included an item covered by the undertaking. Walton J. upheld the contention of the defendant that, in general terms, the distribution of advertising material constituted an invitation to treat and was not an offer.

1–19 Consumer protection legislation in Ireland, however, would make a person who invites offers by way of false or misleading statements as to price liable under the civil law and guilty of a criminal offence; see generally Pt 3 of the Consumer Protection Act 2007. Specific legislation is in force[33] which requires the supplier of credit facilities in respect of goods, services, accommodation, or facilities of any description, to provide information on the annual percentage rate of charge applicable to the goods, etc., in question.

1–20 An advertisement will, however, be considered to be an offer if the court is convinced that it is seriously intended to be binding should persons come forward prepared to act on it. Such contracts are known as *unilateral* contracts. In normal cases where a contract exists both parties are bound. These contracts are called *bilateral* contracts. On the other hand, an advertisement may bind the party issuing the advertisement without creating any concurrent obligation upon any other person. The leading English case of *Carlill v Carbolic Smoke Ball*[34] is an example of a unilateral contract in which an advertisement was declared to be an offer. The defendants manufactured a proprietary medicine that was advertised to be so efficient that should anyone catch influenza after purchasing and using it they would be entitled to £100. As a mark of the manufacturer's sincerity, the advertisement continued, £1,000 was deposited with a bank to meet any claims. Mrs Carlill read the advertisement, used the medicine but caught influenza nevertheless. The advertisement was held to be an offer and Mrs Carlill entitled to £100.

1–21 An interesting, if somewhat inconclusive, illustration of this analysis can be found in the case of *Kennedy v London Express Newspapers*.[35] Readers of the *Daily Express* were invited to become registered readers of the newspaper and induced to do so by an offer of free accident insurance for the year 1929. The plaintiff's wife was registered in 1929 and the offer was renewed for the year 1930, by advertisement in the newspaper, registration not being needed if the reader was registered during 1929. The plaintiff's wife died in an accident during 1930 and the plaintiff sought to recover the insurance payable under an alleged contract but the defendant claimed that one of the conditions had not been met by the deceased, that is, taking the newspaper on a daily basis. The defendants conceded that their advertisements constituted an offer to Mrs Kennedy, which in order to be validly accepted, required Mrs Kennedy to register and take the newspaper on a daily basis. Kennedy C.J. held that

---

[33] Consumer Credit Act 1995 s.31.
[34] [1893] 1 Q.B. 256.
[35] [1931] I.R. 532; *Lowden v Accident Insurance Co* (1904) 43 I.L.T.R. 277.

the contract had been formed in Ireland, the valid act of acceptance being the placing of an order with a local newsagent.

1–22 Two further cases, possessing superficially similar facts but differing conclusions, are instructive. In the first case, *Wilson v Belfast Corp*,[36] an unauthorised newspaper report which indicated that the council would pay half wages to any employee who enlisted during the Great War was held incapable of being an offer. An advertisement in similar terms, posted by the employer on his own premises, was held in *Billings v Arnott*[37] to be an offer which was accepted by an employee when he enlisted. The defendants argued that when their representative attempted to dissuade the employee from enlisting this was not sufficient to constitute a retraction of the offer. The important point to note about *Wilson v Belfast Corp* is that the newspaper report was not intended to be the medium by which the local authority intended to communicate with its employees and, as such, it would be premature to characterise a preliminary initiative of this kind as an offer. In the case of *Tansey v The College of Occupational Therapists Ltd*,[38] the plaintiff unsuccessfully attempted to build a contract between herself and the defendant by utilising the *Carlill* decision. Ms Tansey had enrolled as a student at St Joseph's College, Dún Laoghaire, in the hope that she would successfully complete a course of study which would result in the award of a Diploma by the defendant, a professional body that set an examination for students and recognised, *inter alia*, St Joseph's College as a competent institution to educate students. Ms Tansey, upon enrolment, was given a handbook which stated that students would have a right to sit two repeat examinations if unsuccessful. There were disputed facts about whether the handbook had been amended by an erratum slip but the repeat rule was revised so as to give one repeat examination only. The plaintiff claimed that the defendant had a contractual relationship with the plaintiff, concluded via the agency of St Joseph's College, after the plaintiff had offered to enrol as a student in the college. The plaintiff contended that her offer was accepted by the defendant when its agents handed her a copy of the defendant's manual, the contract being concluded on the terms of the (unamended) manual. Murphy J. rejected this submission, holding that *Carlill* did not assist the plaintiff because she was not aware of any offer made by the defendant when she enrolled in the college in respect of multiple rights of examination re-sits. The manual, as such, was intended to convey information and not to constitute an offer to contract. Similarly, an estate agent who "cold called" the defendant to advise that a property was on the market could not rely upon a statement that a fee would be charged if the introduction led to a contract to purchase the property. The information could have provided the basis of a later contract but not be the contract itself; see *Lady Manor Ltd v Fat Cat Café Bars (No.2)*.[39] Statements of information, however, will not always possess this neutral

---

[36] (1921) 55 I.L.T.R. 205.
[37] (1945) 80 I.L.T.R. 50.
[38] Unreported, High Court, August 27, 1986.
[39] [2001] 2 E.G. 88; *Ove Arup & Partners International v Mirant Pacific* [2004] B.L.R. 49.

quality. In contrast, a majority of the English Court of Appeal, in *Bowerman v Association of British Travel Agents Ltd*,[40] held that a notice displayed on the premises of ABTA holiday tour operators could constitute an offer made by ABTA, so that when a specific ABTA member became insolvent ABTA was held bound by a statement in the notice that clients would be completely reimbursed for wasted expenditure. Acceptance of the offer was constituted by booking a holiday through an ABTA member. While the notice was held to be a mixture of "information, promise, disclaimer and reassurance", the majority of the Court of Appeal held that, on this point, the specific promise was clear enough so as to come within the *Carbolic Smoke Ball* case. Hirst L.J. dissented, viewing the entire notice as descriptive rather than contractual in character.

(4) Tenders

1–23 When a manufacturer or a local authority issues advertisements soliciting tenders, whether it be to supply goods or build a school for example, the advertisement is an invitation to treat. The tender setting out the terms upon which the supplier or builder is prepared to contract constitutes an offer. There is no obligation upon the offeree to accept any of the tenders unless he has promised in the statement inviting tenders to accept the lowest figure. In these instances the situation is amenable to the collateral contract analysis that is found in auction sales "without reserve", and, as the "sealed bid" case of *Harvela Investments Ltd v Royal Trust Co of Canada and Outerbridge*[41] illustrates, there can be a substantial remedy in appropriate circumstances. Here, the first defendant invited the plaintiff and the second defendant to submit sealed bids to purchase shares which the first defendant held as trustee, offering to accept the highest bid. The second defendant made a bid which was lower than that of the plaintiff but he added a referential clause, i.e. he agreed to pay $101,000 more than any higher bid submitted, if any. The first defendant accepted the referential bid. In the House of Lords the plaintiff was able to overturn the sale. The first defendant, in promising to sell to the highest bidder, was not simply issuing an invitation to tender—an invitation to negotiate. As Lord Diplock said, the statement was a unilateral or "if" contract issued to the two potential bidders. There was thus an obligation to sell to the highest bona fide bidder. In these circumstances, the referential bid was not acceptable because the unilateral contract was to invite fixed bids rather than "auction-type" bids.

1–24 The decision in *Harvela*[42] was reached by virtue of the essential nature of the sealed referential bidding process and the interpretation of the call

---

[40] *The Times*, November 24, 1995; see also *Royal & Sun Alliance Life Assurance Australia Ltd v Feeney* (2001) 80 S.A.S.R. 229.

[41] [1986] A.C. 207, followed in *Smart Telecom v RTE* [2006] IEHC 176.

[42] In *Howberry Lane Ltd v Telecom Éireann* [1999] 2 I.L.R.M. 232, Morris P. did not refer to *Harvela*, and, it is submitted, the argument put to Morris P. was an implied term argument based on Canadian case law. In *Howberry* the vendors also reserved the right to withdraw at anytime, unlike *Harvela*.

itself.[43] The Supreme Court of Canada in *M.J.B. Enterprises Ltd v Defence Construction (1951) Ltd*[44] has crafted a more broad principle. Here, in response to an invitation to tender, containing a privilege clause that "the lowest or any tender may not be accepted", the plaintiff submitted a bid to the defendant. The defendant accepted the tender, which contained a term inconsistent with the terms of the call itself, denying the contract to the plaintiff who would otherwise have submitted the lowest bid. The call to tender was held to constitute an offer, accepted by submission of bids. The Supreme Court of Canada reasoned that the invitation to tender impliedly obliged the defendant to consider only compliant bids (which the successful tender was not). Decisions like this take the law of tenders some distance away from the basic rule that an offeree is free to accept, reject or ignore an offer,[45] but the Supreme Court of Canada declined to imply a term that the lowest compliant bid had to be accepted. The leading English case, *Blackpool and Fylde Aero Club v Blackpool Borough Council*,[46] similarly does not require the contract to be awarded to a disappointed or outraged bidder, for example, but there are some interesting recent developments where the fault line between common law duties, public procurement and judicial review is located.

1–25 While an analysis of public procurement rules are outside the scope of a general text such as this, it is clear that the *Blackpool* case has led to the emergence of a duty for the inviter to act fairly and in good faith, vis-à-vis tenderers. This is not such a duty as to require the tenderer to act judicially: *Pratt Contractors Ltd v Transit New Zealand*,[47] but there are a number of Northern Ireland cases in which remedies such as *certiorari* have been granted so as to set aside the award of the contract: *Natural World Products Ltd v ARC 21*,[48] for example. The perspective here is not so much on the position of the tenderer but whether the authority has acted reasonably or not.[49]

1–26 In some instances the bidder does not, however, have all the advantages of a unilateral offeror, who is normally free to retract his bid at any time prior to acceptance. In many tender documents there may be a clause which forbids retraction by the bidder at any time after it has been delivered, or opened, as

---

[43] Note that in *Harvela* implied term arguments were raised by counsel for the appellants but the House of Lords did not resort to them, relying instead on *South Hetton Coal Co v Haswell, Shotton and Easington Coal & Coke Co* [1898] 1 Ch. 465.

[44] (1999) 170 D.L.R. (4th) 577.

[45] Causation will still need to be satisfied, see *R. v Martel Building Ltd* (2000) 193 D.L.R. (4th) 1.

[46] [1990] 3 All E.R. 25.

[47] [2003] UKPC 83.

[48] [2007] NIQB 19; *Deane Public Works Ltd v Northern Ireland Water Ltd* [2009] NI Ch 8; *Resource (NI) v Northern Ireland Courts and Tribunal Service* [2011] NIQB 121.

[49] *Fairclough Building Ltd v Borough Council of Port Talbot* (1992) 62 B.L.R. 82; *Harman CFEM Facades (UK) Ltd v Corporate Officer* (1997) 67 Con. L.R. 1; *Easycoach Ltd v Department for Regional Development* [2012] NIQB 10.

the case may be. These clauses have been held effective in the Supreme Court of Canada.[50]

1–27 However, these decisions are exceptional, in the sense that both *Ron Engineering* and *MJB Enterprises Ltd v Defence Construction (1951) Ltd*[51] hold that the question whether the parties intend to commence a contractual relationship by the submission of a bid, and the terms of any such relationship, are governed by the terms and conditions of the call for tenders and it may be that the call itself makes it clear that no contractual relationship of any kind is anticipated before the person issuing the call accepts one of the tenders. However, there may still be room for implied terms, whether by custom or usage or by virtue of either the express terms of the call documents, or judicial doctrine.

1–28 Again the Canadian courts have been active in identifying an implied term, necessary to protect the integrity of the bidding system, that there should be a "duty to treat all bidders equally but still with due regard for the contractual terms incorporated into the tender call".[52] However, the liberal use of implied terms tends to remove a discretion that traditional contract theory provides to the offeree, superimposing an obligation to act reasonably in an objective sense or, more seriously, imposing duties to assist or co-operate. Such duties are incompatible with *caveat emptor* and the economic self-interest that drives individuals to contract in the first place, as well as being very difficult to define or operate.[53]

1–29 The Supreme Court of Canada, in *Double N Earthmovers Ltd v Edmonton*,[54] divided on the factual issues about whether there had been an acceptance of a non-compliant bid, and while the case is one in which discussion centred on the scope of the duty to investigate whether a bid was compliant or not, all justices reaffirmed the notion that implied duties can be limited or displaced by careful drafting of the tender documents and by "substantial compliance". In *GHP Piling Ltd v Leighton Contractors Pty Ltd*[55]

---

[50] *R., in Right of Ontario v Ron Engineering & Construction* (1981) 119 D.L.R. (3d) 267; *Calgary v Northern Construction* [1988] 2 W.W.R. 193; *Toronto Transit Commission v Gottardo Construction Ltd* (2005) 257 D.L.R. (4th) 539.

[51] [1999] 1 S.C.R. 619.

[52] *Martselos Services Ltd v Artic College* (1994) 111 D.L.R. (4th) 65 at 71 per Vertes J.A. See in England, *Harmon C.F.E.M. Facades v House of Commons* (1999) 67 Con. L.R. 1, discussed by Craig at (2003) 19 Const. L.J. 237.

[53] It should be noted that in *Howberry Lane Ltd v Telecom Éireann* [1999] 2 I.L.R.M. 232, Morris P. declined to follow Canadian jurisprudence on the liberal use of implied terms as not representing the law in Ireland.

[54] [2007] S.C.C. 3.

[55] [2012] NZHC 1695; *Prime Commercial Ltd v Wool Board Disestablishment Co Ltd* [2006] NZCA 295. For some recent Canadian developments see *Budget Rent a Car of BC Ltd v Vancouver International Airport Authority* [2009] BCCA 22; *Trevor Nicholas Construction Co v Canada* (2010) 328 D.L.R. (4th) 665; *Manitoba Eastern Star Chalet Inc. v Dominion*

the New Zealand High Court stressed that the tendering process in respect of sub-contracts is likely to be a more informal one in contrast to negotiation of head contracts. In a helpful judgment, Asher J. opined that the factors that may indicate the existence of a formal contract process (i.e. a Contract A, to use the Canadian terminology) include requirements of the tenderer to register a tender, pay a deposit or comply with detailed specifications for a tender; on the part of the invitor any stated methodology for processing tenders or assessing the tender, a statement indicating that the most compliant tender will be accepted, and a general atmosphere of formality, may be expected to create the existence of a preliminary tender contract, as distinct from leaving the invitor freedom of manoeuvre. Other recent Canadian cases suggest that there appears to be a trend away from readily inferring the existence of a Contract A and Contract B analysis.

(5) Agreement on price in sale of land cases

1–30 As the decision of the UK Supreme Court in *RTS Flexible Systems Ltd v Molkerei Alois Müller GmbH*[56] illustrates, in all commercial contracts, including sales and construction contracts, the general principles relating to formation are clear. A court must look to the intention of the parties, assessed objectively, on what each has said and written. As in *RTS*, one party may, belatedly, argue that no contract was agreed but where, as in *RTS*, a price has been agreed, work has commenced and the principle commercial terms are identifiable via a chain of correspondence, the court may find a "no contract" solution to be (in Lord Clarke's speech in *RTS*) "unconvincing".

1–31 While it is sometimes said that there is no difference in approach to be adopted in various kinds of negotiation, some judges do qualify this to a limited extent: see *Bigg v Boyd-Gibbins Ltd.*[57] Practical considerations may come into the equation. Given that contracts for the sale of land are often negotiated over a prolonged period of time and given that conveyancing practice is often complicated and protracted, it is sometimes stated that there is a presumption against mere agreement on price constituting a binding contract. *Harvey v Facey*[58] is the case most often cited in this respect. The appellants telegraphed "will you sell us Bumper Hall Pen Telegram lowest cash price". The respondents telegrammed "Lowest cash price for Bumper Hall Pen £900". The appellants replied that they would pay that price. The appellants' action failed. The Privy Council held that the respondents' telegram was only a statement of the price they would be prepared to accept should they decide later to sell. The view that even agreement on the price will not of itself provide prima facie evidence of the existence of a contract was reaffirmed by Finnegan J. in

---

Construction Co (2011) MBQB 320. Note the use of the unconscionable bargain doctrine, e.g. *Rankin Construction Inc. v Quinn* [2013] ONSC 139.

[56] [2010] UKSC 14; *Sony/ATV Music Publishing LLC v WPMC Ltd* [2015] EWHC 1853 (Ch).
[57] [1971] 2 All E.R. 183.
[58] [1893] A.C. 552.

McGill Construction v McKeon.[59] Agreement on a price of €3.6 million for development lands was reached, but related matters such as disposal of a show house, a deposit and a closing date, were not agreed. Critically, the matter was complicated with the need to agree on mechanisms for share transfers in order to resolve taxation issues and as the evidence indicated that such matters might have gone on for some time, no concluded contract was held to exist. If the correspondence is clear and unequivocal, however, there is no reason why the courts will not hold an agreement to have been made although enforceability will depend on compliance with the Statute of Frauds (Ireland) 1695 or s.51 of the Land and Conveyancing Law Reform Act 2009.

1–32 The action in *Harvey v Facey* failed because there was no indication that the sellers wanted to assent to a sale of their property. The negotiations were still in their early stages. In the leading Irish case of *Boyers & Co v Duke*,[60] the plaintiff wrote asking for the lowest quotation the defendants could make for 3,000 yards of canvas. The defendants wrote that the lowest price was 4⅝ d. per yard. The plaintiffs replied that they would accept this "offer". The defendants then realised that they had underestimated the price and refused to make up the fabric at the price quoted. Lord O'Brien C.J., following *Harvey v Facey*, said of the plaintiffs' second letter that "it is not the acceptance of an offer because the letter to which it was a reply was a quotation and not an offer". It should be noted that the purported letter of acceptance itself recognised that no binding contract was concluded by it because the plaintiffs gave the names of referees who would vouch for their commercial reliability.

Acceptance

1–33 The response to the offer may, at first blush, be equivocal. But as two recent cases show, on close analysis, a court might find that the response is a rejection of the offer. In *Bonner Properties v McGurran Construction Ltd*.[61] Deeny J. held that when a response to an inquiry about the alteration of proposed terms consisted of a new term, previously not the subject of discussion between the parties, a statement that this unilateral alteration "is not acceptable to our client" was a rejection of the new term which had the effect of terminating the offer. Deeny J. wrote that "to say that one does not accept something is merely a less stark way of saying one rejects it". Similarly, in *Grant v Bragg*,[62] the English Court of Appeal had to examine a chain of six emails. In the second of the emails the statement, "I am not ready to transfer" was held to be a rejection of the buyer's offer. On this basis the Court of

---

[59] [2004] IEHC 88; *JC v WC* [2004] 2 I.R. 312. *An Cumann Peile Boitheimeach Teoranta v Albion Properties Ltd* [2008] IEHC 447.
[60] [1905] 2 I.R. 617.
[61] [2008] NI Ch 16.
[62] [2009] EWCA Civ 1228. For a straightforward example of a contract concluded by the exchange of emails see *Immingham Storage Co v Clear Plc* [2011] EWCA Civ 89.

Appeal held the trial judge had fallen into error by holding that the first and sixth emails could constitute a valid offer and acceptance as the second email had the effect of nullifying the first email. Neuberger M.R. said that the trial judge "went wrong by just ignoring the intermediate four emails".

1–34 Acceptance may be defined as a final and unequivocal expression of agreement to the terms of an offer. To acknowledge that an offer has been received is not to accept the offer. In one English case an offer to build a freight terminal was made by tender. The offeror, who quoted two prices in the alternative, was told that his offer had been accepted. The "acceptor", however, did not indicate which price he was prepared to accept. It was held that the acceptance was invalid: see *Lind v Mersey Docks & Harbour Board*.[63]

1–35 Acceptance is divided into two constituent parts.

(1) The fact of acceptance

1–36 It is particularly obvious that acceptance may take place by performing a stipulated or requested action if the offer is a unilateral contract. So in *Billings v Arnott*[64] the offer to pay half of any employee's wages who joined the defence forces was accepted by Billings when he performed the action requested. In commercial life offers are often accepted, not by stating "I agree" or "I accept", but by performance. An offeror who posts a letter asking for goods to be supplied will often find his offer has been accepted when the delivery van arrives to transfer the goods themselves. However, objective conduct which indicates consent will not always be operative. If, for example, B knows that, despite A's conduct indicating assent, A has no intention to contract, A is not bound. B knows the truth of A's actual intention; see *Airways Corp of New Zealand v Geyserland Airways Ltd*.[65] There is more recent judicial support for the view that if one side to a negotiation does not intend a concluded agreement to be legally binding while the other side is aware of this absence of legal intent, the objective theory of contracting will not apply.[66] Knowledge that A may not be able to perform, however, is not the same thing.[67]

1–37 A person may be bound by his conduct if, objectively speaking, that person conducts himself or herself in such a way that the conduct would indicate to a reasonable person that he or she intends to be bound. In general

---

[63] [1972] 2 Lloyd's Rep. 234. In some instances offer and acceptance requirements are not applied mechanistically. Offer and acceptance may be constituted by the offeree responding to an email in the same manner and collating bank details as requested, even if express confirmation or agreement to terms in the offer itself is not mentioned: *Ashton v Pratt* [2015] NSWCA 12.

[64] (1945) 80 I.L.T.R. 50.

[65] [1996] 1 N.Z.L.R. 116 at 125, followed in *Transpower New Zealand v Meridian Energy* [2001] 3 N.Z.L.R 700.

[66] *Maple Leaf Macrovolatility Master Fund v Rouvroy* [2009] EWHC 257 (Comm), but doubted in the Court of Appeal.

[67] *Society of Lloyds v Twinn*, *The Times*, April 4, 2000.

terms subjective intent will not persuade a court to hold that no contract exists, nor that the contract may be amended because of mistake.[68] As a general rule, acceptance may often take place by the offeree acting in response to the offer in the manner stipulated; see the English case of *Howard Marine Dredging v A. Ogden*[69] and the older Irish case of *Saunders v Cramer*.[70] In these circumstances a distinction must be drawn between acceptances which take place in the context of a unilateral offer, as distinct from an offer which is bilateral in form—that is, where the offeror is requesting a promise or undertaking as distinct from the thing itself. The leading Irish case is *Brennan v Lockyer*.[71] An offer was posted in which the applicant requested certain benefits be made available to him by his trade union through enrolment. The union sent a certificate of enrolment which was posted in London and which arrived in Dublin, the certificate recording the fact of enrolment in London. The question arose whether the contract was completed in London, when the certificate was despatched, or in Dublin, when it was communicated to the union member. A distinction was drawn between an acceptance in relation to an offer asking for information and an offer that requests an act be done. When the acceptance consists of a promise this must be validly communicated, but if the offeror requests action, such as the posting of goods, no further communication is necessary. The proposition that an offer can be accepted by conduct has been recently reaffirmed by Deeny J. in *Hamilton v Judge*.[72] The negotiation of a contract for the purchase of commercial property was followed by the return of a draft contract by the purchaser's solicitor to the vendor's solicitor. Deeny J. treated this action as an offer and after approving a statement from *Chitty on Contracts*, namely, that, "an offer may be accepted by conduct; and this has never been thought to give rise to any difficulty where the conduct takes the form of a positive act", the learned judge held that by silence, and by standing by whilst the vendor auctioned goods and chattels, with a view to winding up the vendor's business, the purchaser had tacitly accepted the vendor's offer.

1–38 Where the offer takes place within a bilateral contract framework, the courts are less willing to dispense with the communication of acceptance requirement, because absence of a final communication is often indicative of the parties still being locked in negotiation. In *Anglia Television v Cayton*,[73] it was held that before an offer could be accepted by conduct there must be some unequivocal offer which exists in a form capable of being accepted. There must also be subsequent conduct by way of acceptance which is exclu-

---

[68] *Smith v Hughes* (1871) L.R. 6 Q.B. 597.

[69] [1978] 2 W.L.R. 515.

[70] (1842) 5 I.Eq.R. 12. On acceptance of a contract by carrying out work requested in an offer, see *John G. Burns Ltd v Grange Construction and Roofing* [2013] IEHC 284.

[71] [1932] I.R. 100; *Clarke v Gardiner* (1861) 12 I.C.L.R. 472.

[72] [2009] NI Ch 4. The Northern Ireland Court of Appeal, in dismissing an appeal from Deeny J.'s judgment ([2010] NICA 49) expressed no opinion on this point. See also *Londonderry Port and Harbour Commissioners v WS Atkins* [2011] NIQB 74.

[73] *The Independent*, February 14, 1989.

sively applicable to the offer. The litigation involved a dispute between Anglia Television and other television companies who had allegedly interfered in contractual arrangements to allow Anglia Television to show the Bruno v Tyson fight in 1989. The action failed because documents that were alleged to record the terms of the contract were inconsistent with the alleged contract. The court held that the subsequent conduct in question, namely, accepting fee payments, were just as consistent with one-off payments for other bouts as an alleged contract to screen the fight.

1–39 Where, however, subsequent conduct can be added so as to show prejudicial reliance by the alleged offeree this will raise the likelihood that a contract by conduct will be imputed, as in the older Irish case of *McEvoy v Moore*.[74] A request or instruction to undertake building work, which is accepted by compliance with this request, will create a contract and the law will imply into it an obligation to pay a reasonable sum for the work; see *ACT Construction Ltd v E Clarke & Sons (Coaches) Ltd*.[75] This will be so even if there is no entire contract, or the agreement has yet to be put into formal shape, or the price has not been agreed. Ultimately the issue is whether the offeree intended to accept the offer. In the case of *Parkgrange Investments Ltd v Shandon Park Mills Ltd*,[76] Carroll J. held that there was no contract, despite the fact that the offeree signed a draft agreement. Carroll J. accepted the offeree's evidence that he signed the document as a preparatory measure, intending to use the document to obtain a capital gains tax clearance certificate if the offeree should at a later date resolve to accept the offer.

1–40 In some cases the courts have held that a contract exists because the parties have conducted themselves so as to indicate that they believed a contract existed. Where *animus contrahendi* is present the difficulty of accommodating the conventional rules on offer and acceptance will not always prove insurmountable. In *Western Electric Ltd v Welsh Development Agency*,[77] the plaintiff failed to reply to the defendant's letter containing an offer and prescribed form of acceptance but instead began to perform under the terms of the offer. The court held that, by its conduct, the plaintiff was offering to contract on the terms of the earlier letter written by the defendant. The defendant, in turn, by its acquiescence, was held to have accepted this offer. While this conclusion is difficult to reconcile with the rule which allows an offeree the power to decide whether to decline or accept an offer—or indeed ignore it altogether—the result was a just one on the facts of the case.

1–41 Sometimes the form of the offer may, by implication, be prescribed by the terms of the invitation to treat. In *Harvela Investments Ltd v Royal Trust Co of*

---

[74] (1902) 36 I.L.T.R. 99.
[75] (2002) 85 Con. L.R. 1.
[76] Unreported, High Court, May 2, 1991.
[77] [1983] Q.B. 796.

Canada and Outerbridge,[78] the vendors of shares invited bids from a small group of interested parties, promising to sell to the highest bidder. The bids, to be made by way of sealed offers, would all be opened together, at which time the highest bidder would be known. The second defendant made a fixed bid and a referential bid, i.e. agreed to pay either a fixed amount but, in the event that this bid was "topped" by another bidder, he agreed to pay $101,000 more than the highest rival bid. The House of Lords held that the vendor could not accept the referential bid and that the highest bona fide bidder was entitled to receive the shares.

Counter-offers

1–42 If a valid acceptance exists then the acceptor must be prepared to accept the terms proposed. As Murphy J. said in *Tansey v The College of Occupational Therapists Ltd*[79]:

> "[I]t is difficult to conceive of an acceptance which would itself prescribe conditions. Ordinarily a communication in the course of negotiations leading to a contract which contains conditions not previously agreed by the party to whom the communication is addressed will fall to be treated as a new or counter-offer rather than an acceptance."

If the response by the offeree is not a clear and unconditional acceptance of the offer, the response itself may be described as a counter-offer which in turn may be accepted or ignored by the person to whom it is addressed. In *Swan v Miller*,[80] the defendants offered to sell their interest in a lease for £4,750 plus ground rent of £50. The plaintiffs replied that they would pay £4,450. This response to the defendants' offer was a counter-offer and, as such, was not itself capable of producing a binding contract.

1–43 The rules on counter-offers have another consequence. If an offer is met with a counter-offer then this response has the same effect as a rejection of the first offer. If the counter-offer is in turn refused, the initial offer cannot now be accepted. If A offers to sell iron to B for €100 and B replies with an offer to purchase for €90 which A refuses, B cannot now hold A to his offer to sell for €100. The case of *Wheeler v Jeffrey*[81] provides an excellent illustration of this. The parties were negotiating a contract under which the plaintiffs were to act as agent to sell the defendants' goods. During correspondence no mention of a commencement date was made. On June 10, the plaintiffs wrote "we agree to carry on your agency as from 1st July next". On June 12, the defendants wrote indicating their acceptance. The issue was whether a contract was formed on June 10 or 12. The Court of Appeal, reversing the Kings Bench Division, held the contract was formed on June 12. As Lord Chancellor Campbell pointed out, the mention of a commencement date added a new term to the

---

[78]   [1986] A.C. 207, followed in *Smart Telecom v RTE* [2006] IEHC 176.
[79]   Unreported, High Court, August 27, 1986.
[80]   [1919] 1 I.R. 151.
[81]   [1921] 2 I.R. 395; *Shepherd Homes Ltd v Encia Remediation Ltd* (2007) 110 Con. L.R. 90.

negotiations. But for this, the letter of June 10 would have been an acceptance, the law implying commencement within a reasonable time. It was possible for the defendants to reply that July 1 was not acceptable and, had they done so, there would have been no contract, in the absence of some later agreement.

1–44 However, the courts are quite sensitive to commercial practice and, rather than oblige the parties to recommence negotiations whenever a somewhat ambiguous response is made by an offeree, the courts do at least strive to keep the offer open if the offeree's response can be characterised as one in which the offeree seeks clarification or additional information from the offeror, although the boundary between a request for additional terms and an implied or express counter-offer is at times difficult to draw. If the offeree, however, is presented with a written offer and the offeree adds in additional material which has been negotiated, but omitted from the document, and the offeree then signs that document, as requested, the case of *Lynch v The Governors, etc. of St. Vincent's Hospital*[82] is authority for the proposition that this is a valid acceptance. If, however, the offeree adds new terms which have not been settled by antecedent negotiations, then the leading case of *Gt. Northern Railway Co v Witham*[83] is still operative and the offeree's response will be a counter-offer.

1–45 Of course, it becomes particularly difficult to tell when an offer or counter-offer has been made when negotiations consist of each party sending printed forms back and forth. This problem has been discussed by the English Court of Appeal in *Butler Machine Tool Co v Ex-Cell-O Corp*.[84] The sellers of a machine tool quoted a price of £75,000, the offer including a price variation clause under the terms of which the price would rise if costs rose for the sellers before delivery, which was to take place 10 months later. The buyers responded by placing an order on the foot of their own documentation which did not permit a price variation. The sellers did not reject this but returned a portion of the buyers' printed form acknowledging the contract took place on the buyers' conditions. The Court of Appeal held for the buyers; the sellers' quotation was held to be an offer. The buyers' response was a counter-offer which was accepted by returning the slip. The fact that the sellers included a covering letter which reasserted their own terms of contract applied was ignored.

1–46 In a most helpful judgment in *Butler Machine Tool Co v Ex-Cell-O Corp*, Lord Denning M.R. stressed that there are no hard and fast results in "battle of

---

[82] Unreported, High Court, July 31, 1987.
[83] (1873) L.R. 9 C.P. 16.
[84] [1979] 1 W.L.R. 401; *Buchanan v Brook Walker & Co* [1988] N.I. 116; *Stryker Corp v Sulzer Metco AG* [2006] IEHC 60; *Tekdata Interconnections Ltd v Amphenol* [2009] EWCA Civ 120. Post-*Tekdata* case law in England (*Transformers and Rectifiers Ltd v Needs Ltd* [2015] EWHC 269 (TCC)) and Northern Ireland (*John Graham Construction Ltd v Lowry Piling Ltd* [2015] NIQB 40) emphasises that if inadequate notice is given of the existence of terms, the terms of neither side will apply. *John Graham Construction* illustrates that where there is no consistent cause of dealing to fill the documentary void, the applicable contract terms may be a separate and highly speculative exercise.

the forms" cases. In *Chichester Joinery v John Mowlem*,[85] the *Butler* case was distinguished. Mowlem was the successful main contractor for a construction project. The plaintiff, Chichester Joinery, tendered for sub-contracting work and its tender followed upon a written statement, dated March 14, by Mowlem, which set out his requirements. Mowlem added that acceptance by Chichester Joinery of the proposed contract would be on Mowlem's terms and conditions as set out on the form and that any delivery made would constitute an acceptance of the order. Chichester Joinery responded by agreeing to the contract, in writing dated April 30, "subject to the conditions overleaf". It was held that, at this point, there was no contract—the Chichester Joinery letter was a counter-offer which destroyed the offer of March 14. However, when Chichester Joinery later delivered goods that were in accordance with the needs of Mowlem and Mowlem accepted the goods, the last act, the acceptance of the goods, was held to be an acceptance of the printed terms of Chichester Joinery, despite the earlier inconclusive "battle of the forms".

1–47 It is widely felt that the counter-offer rules are likely to result in a holding that no contract exists at all. Other solutions have been suggested; the United States Uniform Commercial Code, s.2–207 provides that an acceptance is effective even if it contains additional or different terms to those offered or agreed upon unless acceptance is expressly made conditional on assent to those new terms. The section goes on to specify that, as between merchants, new terms become part of the contract unless, *inter alia*, these terms materially alter the original offer. For an analysis of British legislation that also attempts to deal with the counter-offer in the context of international sales, see the discussion in the *Butler Machine Tool* case. It is doubtful whether this kind of solution is really much of an improvement. There are problems of definition involved here that seem to be as difficult as the counter-offer rule itself. In any event, the fact that the counter-offer rules are surmounted where necessary— see *Butler Machine Tool Co v Ex-Cell-O Corp* itself—and the possibility that a contract will result from the conduct of the parties, make a finding that no contract exists rather unlikely. Even if this does happen, relief by way of restitution is available.

(2) Communication of acceptance

1–48 Once it is established that the offeree intends to accept the offer he generally has to go further and communicate his acceptance to the offeror.[86] The offeror may stipulate that it will be enough to communicate acceptance to an agent or he may dispense with, or "waive," the need for communication. This is impliedly the case when the offer is an offer to enter into a unilateral contract. Mrs Carlill did not have to inform the Carbolic Smoke Ball Company that she intended to purchase and use its medicine; the employee in *Billings*

---

[85] (1987) 42 Build. L.R. 100; *Percy Trentham v Archital Luxfer Ltd* [1993] 1 Lloyd's Rep. 25.
[86] *Embourg Ltd v Tyler Group* [1996] 3 I.R. 480.

v Arnott[87] did not have to inform his employer that he intended to enlist. In these cases the act of acceptance and performance are one and the same. The application of this "waiver" principle arose in a somewhat novel form in the case of *Commerce Commission v Telecom Mobile Ltd.*[88] Telco wished to sell mobile phones to consumers of a rival company, engaging the defendants to sell via a call centre. Interested responses were forwarded to Telco who undertook a credit check of the customer, and if approved, a phone and contract documents were sent out by post, the external packaging indicating that opening of the box constituted an acceptance of Telco's terms and conditions. The defendants sought to avoid liability for ongoing anti-consumer business practices by arguing that as the contract was concluded in the call centre, the relevant statutes did not apply. The New Zealand Court of Appeal held that the contract was not formed in the call centre. The defendants had no authority to bind Telco. Telco offered to provide services by mailing out the phone, along with the conditions of contract, and the offer was accepted by opening the package. It is noteworthy that the Court of Appeal was critical of pushing the application of *Brinkibon* (see para.1–52) too far, especially if a literal application undermined consumer credit legislation.[89]

1–49 It should be noted that the offeror can only waive the need for acceptance to be communicated to him; he cannot oblige the offeree to respond to the offer by stipulating that failure to communicate rejection of the offer shall be deemed consent. This is illustrated by the facts of *Russell & Baird v Hoban.*[90] The defendant in Castlebar negotiated with the plaintiffs to purchase oatmeal. He asked the plaintiffs' manager if they could supply a fixed amount. The plaintiffs' manager, on his return to Dublin, sent a note indicating that they could supply that amount. The note provided that "if this sale note be retained beyond three days after this date, it will be held to have been accepted by the buyer". The Court of Appeal held that there was no contract. Ronan L.J. observed: "[n]o man can impose such conditions upon another. The document is conclusive evidence against the parties who sent it, that it was an offer which required acceptance." Because the defendant decided not to respond, there was no contract.

1–50 So the practice of inertia-selling, that is, posting unsolicited goods to members of the public and obliging them to return them within a certain period of time, or, in default, pay the price, is both a dubious commercial practice and is outside established principles of law. In the Republic, s.47 of the Sale of Goods and Supply of Services Act 1980 deems such a delivery a gift in

---

[87] (1945) 80 I.L.T.R. 50.

[88] [2006] 1 N.Z.L.R. 190. The time at which contracting parties may be contractually bound is a matter that can be determined by the parties. A particular usage within a specific market or commercial sector may provide a basis for resolving a dispute about the effective time a contract was concluded: *Molton Street Capital LLP v Shooters Hill Capital Partners LLP* [2015] EWHC 3419 (Comm).

[89] [2006] 1 N.Z.L.R. 190 at 199 per William Young J.

[90] [1922] 2 I.R. 159.

certain cases—see S.I. No. 484 of 2013, implementing Directive 2011/83/EU on Consumer Rights and amending s.47.

1–51 For acceptance to be effective the general rule is that the offeror is bound when he (or his agent for the purpose of receipt of acceptance) learns from the offeree of his acceptance. At that moment a contract springs into existence. This general rule was once illustrated by Lord Denning by two hypothetical examples. A is in communication with B, both parties standing on opposite banks of a river. A shouts an offer to B; B shouts his reply but this is drowned out either by an aeroplane flying overhead or by the sound of rushing water. B must repeat his reply before any contract can result. The second example extends this rule into modern means of communication. A telephones an offer to B, B replies but the line goes dead. If B intends to accept he must repeat his words of acceptance, the contract being concluded when A hears them. The point is not as metaphysical as it sounds because important jurisdictional questions may depend on where a contract is concluded. In the leading English case of *Entores Ltd v Miles Far East Corp*,[91] an offer sent by telex from the plaintiff's offices in London to the defendant in Amsterdam was accepted by telex. The only problem concerned where the contract came into existence. The Court of Appeal held the contract was concluded in London when notice of acceptance was received there.

1–52 In *Brinkibon Ltd v Stahag Stahl und Stahlwarenhandelgesellschaft GmbH*,[92] the House of Lords approved the *Entores* decision while at the same time indicating that the general rule will not prove dispositive in all cases where actual communication by telex is not instantaneous. If the general rule should prove inconvenient or inappropriate, as where the telex is sent by or to an agent with limited authority, or where the telex arrives outside office hours, for example, then it seems likely that the general rule will not be automatically applicable. Lord Wilberforce said of these and other problematic situations: "[n]o universal rule can cover all such cases; they must be resolved by reference to the intentions of the parties, by sound business practice and in some cases by a judgment where the risks should lie." The general rule was held to apply to transmission of an acceptance, signed in Ontario and returned to the offeror by fax machine, the offeror being in Italy. The Ontario Court of Appeal, applying *Brinkibon*, declined an invitation to hold the case governed by the postal rule and held that the Ontario courts had no jurisdiction over this contract; see *Eastern Power Ltd v Azienda Comunale Energia & Ambiente*.[93]

---

[91] [1955] 2 Q.B. 327. For an Irish case which appears to apply this case, see the Supreme Court's judgment in *Unidare Plc and Unidare Cable Ltd v James Scott Ltd*, unreported, Supreme Court, May 8, 1991.

[92] [1983] 2 A.C. 34.

[93] (1999) 178 D.L.R. (4th) 409. For a recent Ontario decision on contract formation and call centres, see *Ontario College of Pharmacists v 1724665 Ontario Inc* (2013) 360 D.L.R. (4th) 299.

1–53 In practical terms the use of new information technology in the ordering and distribution of goods and services will no doubt raise the applicability of this general rule. Many companies and groups of companies active in manufacturing and assembly industries utilise computer networks which automatically review and order goods for the workplace when stocks fall to a predetermined level. The rules governing electronic data exchange and contract formation are under review by various international agencies[94] and the rather flexible approach taken in *Brinkibon* may still prove to be serviceable in this context also.

Acceptance by post
1–54 The general rule, which determines that a contract comes into being when the offeror learns of acceptance, does not apply where the parties intend that acceptance is to be communicated by post, neither party stipulating that acceptance is only to be valid when the offeror receives notification thereof. The so-called "postal rule" indicates that a contract is concluded when the offeree posts the letter of acceptance. This rule, which was established in England as early as 1818,[95] has not found universal acceptance; German law, for example, holds acceptance to be effective when brought to the place of business of the offeror. The Irish courts, however, have followed the English rule. In *Sanderson v Cunningham*,[96] the plaintiff, through a Dublin insurance broker, sent in a proposal for an insurance policy. This constitutes an offer by the prospective insured. The defendant company in London decided to issue a policy which it posted to the plaintiff's agent. The plaintiff read the policy and indicated his assent by signing it. The plaintiff, who wished to sue the defendant in Ireland, could only commence proceedings if the contract was concluded in Ireland. The claim failed. The Court of Appeal in Ireland held that the contract was concluded by posting it in London.

1–55 Not all the cases in which the issue of formation of a contract by the use of the postal services possess a transnational dimension. The case of *Dooley v Egan*[97] may be prosaic but it illustrates the rule admirably. The defendants, based in Cork, sent a postcard to the plaintiff to inquire whether the plaintiff could supply them with a medical cabinet. By letter posted in Dublin, the plaintiff on June 22 stated that it could supply an enclosed list of goods at fixed prices, the "quotation" being for immediate acceptance only. The defendants on June 24 replied by ordering two medical cabinets, not one. The plaintiff on June 26 replied with its own letter in which the plaintiff agreed to supply two

---

[94] The Electronic Commerce Act 2000 reflects a number of EU electronic commerce and electronic signature Directives, as well as the 1996 UNCITRAL Model Law on Electronic Commerce. See Kelleher and Murray, *Information Technology Law in Ireland*, 2nd edn (Dublin: Tottel, 2007); Smith, *Internet Law and Regulation*, 4th edn (London: Sweet & Maxwell, 2007), Chs 9 and 10; Lloyd, *Information Technology Law*, 7th edn. (Oxford: OUP 2014), Pt IV.

[95] *Adams v Lindsell* (1818) 1 B. & Ald. 681; Winfield, "Some Aspects of Offer and Acceptance" (1939) 55 L.Q.R. 499.

[96] [1919] 2 I.R. 234. Contrast *O'Leary v Law Integrity Ins.* [1912] 1 I.R. 479. An attempt to similarly displace the postal rule failed in *Kelly v Cruise Catering Ltd* [1994] 2 I.L.R.M. 394.

[97] (1938) 72 I.L.T.R. 155.

medical cabinets. The issue was whether the contract was formed in Dublin or Cork. Meredith J. held that the letter of the plaintiff of June 22 was an offer, notwithstanding the nomenclature of "quotation". The reply of the defendants, posted in Cork, was not an acceptance, but a counter-offer which was accepted in Dublin on June 26 when the plaintiff posted the letter of acceptance. The contract was formed in Dublin.

1–56 The postal rule has been heavily criticised as leading to injustice. The well-known English case of *Household Fire Insurance v Grant*[98] illustrates this point graphically. Grant issued an offer to take an insurance policy. The company posted an acceptance. The letter never arrived. Grant was held liable to pay the premiums. The rule has been said to rest upon the unsatisfactory theory that a letter handed to the postal authorities amounts to communication to an agent. This of course ignores the fact that the "agent" is unaware of what the letter contains. Even if the postal agency knows that the letter contains a reply to an offer, the agency presumably has not opened the letter to discover its contents.

1–57 In truth, the rule is one of convenience. It is said to be convenient for two reasons. First, the now obsolete practice of recording the date of issue of letters in office ledgers indicated to the nineteenth century judges that a letter had at least been posted. The fact of posting was easier to verify than the non-arrival of the letter. Secondly, the postal rule, while it seems to unduly favour the offeree, is rational enough, for if another rule applied the offeree could not rely on his act of acceptance. He would have to contact the offeror to ensure that his letter had actually arrived before he could safely assume that a contract had resulted, and act accordingly. Indeed, it has been argued that the rule does not in fact unduly favour the offeree. In *Household Fire Insurance v Grant* it was pointed out that the offeror can stipulate for receipt of the acceptance, thereby protecting himself from the perils of an inefficient postal service. This was successfully achieved by the defendant in *Holwell Securities v Hughes*,[99] when the contract provided that if the plaintiff wished to exercise an option to purchase a house owned by the defendant, this had to be done "by notice in writing" within six months. Shortly before the time elapsed, the plaintiff posted a letter which did not arrive. The English Court of Appeal held that while the parties intended the postal service to be the means of communication, the words of the agreement indicated that the defendant was only bound when the letter arrived. The postal rule was displaced and it mattered not that the defendant had been told by his own solicitor who had received a copy of the letter of acceptance that the plaintiff was about to exercise the option. Lawton L.J. in the English Court of Appeal stated that not only will the rule not apply where the offeror specifies that acceptance must reach him, "[i]t probably does not operate if its application would produce manifest inconvenience and absurdity". The implications of this dictum have yet to be fully explored.

---

[98] (1879) L.R. 4 Ex. 216.
[99] [1974] 1 W.L.R. 155: see, however, *Hippodrome Night Club v Sean Quinn Properties*, unreported, High Court, December 13, 1989 (notice in right of pre-emption case).

1–58 In essence the postal rule will be quite easily displaced if the language of the offer is incompatible with that rule. In *Nunin Holdings Property v Tullamarine Estates Property*,[100] the plaintiff was held by the terms of his offer, namely, that he would be bound "upon receipt by us of an identical contract". The posting of that identical contract did not conclude the matter so when the defendants, in the period between posting and delivery, telephoned to revoke their posted acceptance, that revocation was held effective.

1–59 The courts may decide not to apply the postal rule for reasons other than a desire to avoid injustice between the parties. In *Apicella v Scala*,[101] the plaintiffs in England sued the defendant who had purchased Irish sweepstake tickets as part of an alleged partnership arrangement. One of the tickets drew first prize. Meredith J. considered whether the worldwide distribution of tickets could be considered an offer, accepted when the counterfoils are posted back to the organisers of the sweepstake. The learned judge concluded that:

> "The ticket is not an offer. It, with the attached counterfoil, is more like a proposal form, and an offer is first made by forwarding the counterfoil with the price of the ticket, the ticket being retained by the purchaser. If the offer is accepted the price of the ticket is retained and an official receipt is forwarded, the contract is thus concluded."[102]

In rejecting the postal rule in this context, Meredith J. was concerned to permit the organisers the freedom to regulate the number of tickets included in the draw, and more importantly, to ensure that the organisers did not envisage breaches of the domestic law of other states in which lotteries are illegal.

> "If the transmission of the counterfoils was illegal in a particular country, and if the encouragement of breaches of the law of that country were resented, the Management Committee might decide to refuse all counterfoils transmitted from that country."

In short, the postal rule will not be allowed to operate so as to breach principles of international law such as the rule relating to comity of nations: contrast the approach taken in *Stanhope v Hospitals Trust (No.2)*.[103]

1–60 The old Irish case of *Clarke v Gardiner*[104] decided that where a letter of offer arrives from an offeror and the offeree validly accepts by despatching the goods by courier, the offeror cannot validly withdraw the offer before the goods arrive, the Court of Common Pleas holding that if a letter of acceptance

---

[100] [1994] 1 V.R. 74; *Elizabeth City Centre Property v Corralyn Property* (1994) 63 S.A.S.R. 235.
[101] (1931) 66 I.L.T.R. 33.
[102] (1931) 66 I.L.T.R. 33 at 40.
[103] [1936] Ir.Jur.Rep. 25.
[104] (1861) 12 I.C.L.R. 472.

cannot be retracted before it arrives then conduct amounting to acceptance cannot be treated any differently. However, Christian J. stated *obiter* that if the act of acceptance is countermanded (e.g. by the offeree repossessing goods before they are delivered to the offeror and before the offeror learns that the offeree intended to accept) he was of the view that there would be no contract.

1–61 No modern Irish court has considered whether a letter of acceptance which has been posted can be rendered ineffective if the offeree changes his mind before the letter arrives. If this issue arises in the near future, Lawton L.J.'s dictum in *Holwell Securities v Hughes* may help allow the offeree to retract, for unless there is proof of loss to the offeror, no hardship would be produced by such a result.[105] *Nunin Holdings Property v Tullamarine Estates Property*[106] holds that revocation can be effective in these circumstances but, in that case, the postal rule itself was displaced by the terms of the offer.

1–62 In cases where there is a prescribed method of acceptance, whether it be the post, hand-delivery, or a facsimile machine, to give but three examples, the question of whether another method may be utilised may arise. It is reasonably clear that where some other method is used but the acceptance is not as expeditious as the stipulated method and it arrives after arrival via the stipulated method could have been anticipated, then the offeror is not bound and can ignore the purported acceptance, although there is no clear case law on this point. But if the method used is more expeditious (e.g. the offeror requests a reply by motor cycle courier and it is instantly faxed or emailed instead) it would be necessary for the offeror to have insisted upon the stated method only, in the clearest terms, for the acceptance to be defeated. In *Staunton v Minister for Health*,[107] a method of acceptance was stated to have been laid down by the offeror, that is, signature of a contract document. It was held that a verbal acceptance was adequate. The Northern Ireland case of *Walker v Glass*[108] more directly addresses this question for, in considering whether a purported acceptance which was not in precise compliance with the offer, Lord Lowry said that the essential test was whether the method used was as beneficial to the offeror as the method stated. The rules on precise modes of acceptance do not always apply fully. Where commercial documents are prepared by the offeree and they are not satisfied, the conduct of the offeree (when at odds with the document) may be either an acceptance by conduct of the offer or may bind the offeree as a waiver.[109]

---

[105] See Fried, *Contract as Promise* (Cambridge, Mass.: Harvard University Press, 1981), pp.52–53.

[106] [1994] 1 V.R. 74; see also *Trans-Pacific Trading v Rayonier Canada* [1998] 9 W.W.R. 266.

[107] Unreported, High Court, February 21, 1986.

[108] [1979] N.I. 129.

[109] *Carlyle Finance Ltd v Pallas Industrial Finance* [1999] 1 All E.R. (Comm.) 659; *MSM Consulting Ltd v United Republic of Tanzania* [2009] EWHC 121 (Q.B.); *Reveille Independent LLC v Anontech International (UK) Ltd* [2015] EWHC 726 (Comm); *Civil and Allied Construction Pty Ltd v A1 Quality Concrete Tanks Pty Ltd* [2015] VSCA 75.

1–63 A further problem that may arise from time to time is whether an offer may be accepted by an offeree who is unaware of the existence of the offer. The situation that is likely to produce this set of circumstances is encapsulated in the reward cases—instances where a felon is captured but the person who is responsible for effecting this (an informant for example) is unaware of the existence of a reward offer.[110] Oblique Irish authority against the existence of such a contract is provided by Kenny J. in *Tully v Irish Land Commission*[111] and, more recently, by Murphy J. in *Tansey v College of Occupational Therapists Ltd.*[112] This issue arose in England in *Inland Revenue v Fry*.[113] A taxpayer wrote a letter offering to settle a tax liability of £113,000 by giving a cheque for £10,000. The cheque was processed but the case worker who later read the letter indicated that the payment could be regarded as a payment "on account" or a replacement cheque would be issued to the taxpayer. The taxpayer argued that in processing the cheque, the offer had been accepted. The argument was rejected on the ground that at the time the Inland Revenue had cashed the cheque it was unaware of the offer and the conduct pointed to by the taxpayer was not a valid acceptance. The policy implications of a contrary decision are obvious.

Offer and Acceptance and Electronic Contracts

1–64 The transmission of information or data over a telecommunications network, as part of the contracting process, is a matter of considerable economic importance and is subject to numerous levels of regulation. It may be, for example, that advertising material that is communicated by email will itself be illegal. Such messages, called "commercial communications" in the relevant legislation,[114] must be clearly marked by the service provider with information as prescribed being attached. Unsolicited commercial communications ("spam") originated with a relevant service provider must also clearly and unambiguously be marked as an unsolicited commercial communication.[115] Non-compliance by an Irish service provider is a breach of criminal law.

1–65 Moving on to the question of where and when a contract is concluded electronically, the answer to this question depends on how the communications are phrased, whether prescribed modes of acceptance exist and whether any statutory rules are in place. While the *Brinkibon* decision affords some general guidance, experience to date shows that most web-based disputed contracts produce issues of formation, intention to create legal relations and contractual mistake. Basic principles of offer and acceptance have featured in several accounts of errors being made in relation to goods and services available in

---

[110] *R. v Clarke* (1927) 40 C.L.R. 227.
[111] (1961) 97 I.L.T.R. 174.
[112] Unreported, High Court, August 27, 1986.
[113] [2001] S.T.C 1715, applying *Re Broderick* [1986] N.I.J.B. 36.
[114] S.I. No. 68 of 2003, art.8, giving effect to the Electronic Commerce Directive (Directive 2000/31/EC).
[115] S.I. No. 68 of 2003, art.9.

websites although, to date, these disputes have not produced a judgment. For instance, Argos advertised television sets at £2.99 when the intended price was £299.[116] Thai Air also advertised "free flights" with only taxes to pay when the value of the ticket was £6,200,[117] and Amazon UK offered iPAQ pocket personal computers for £7 (usual price £275).[118] All three companies refused to honour confirmatory emails sent to customers as contractually binding although one company, Kodak, honoured orders placed for EasyShare cameras at £100 when the normal price was £329.[119] Kodak has done so on the basis of a "goodwill" gesture rather than by acknowledging liability. Online platforms that provide intermediary services on behalf of e-commerce sellers may also create difficulties for those sellers. In one recent situation, Amazon used defective software in relation to pricing mechanisms that resulted in goods being sold to buyers for 1p, a fraction of the value of goods.[120]

1–66 The Electronic Commerce Act 2000 (the "2000 Act"), legislation based upon the UNCITRAL Model Law on Electronic Commerce adopted in 1996, is noteworthy in making provision in respect of the legal enforceability of electronic contracts.[121] Sections 20 and 21 of the 2000 Act also contained provisions regulating the acknowledgment of receipt of an electronic communication and the time and place of receipt of electronic communications, but these provisions have been supplanted by a later text, the European Communities (Directive 2000/31/EC) Regulations 2003.[122] Article 14 provides that notwithstanding the 2000 Act, where the recipient of the services places his or her order through electronic means, the relevant service provider is to acknowledge receipt of the order without undue delay and by electronic means. The regulations provide that the order and the acknowledgment of receipt are deemed to be received when the parties to whom they are addressed are able to access them. So, for example, if an order is placed with the person placing the order providing an email address, the acknowledgment is effective when it first becomes accessible by that person—a solution consistent with *Brinkibon*. The regulations also provide that the service provider must give the user of the service "appropriate, effective and accessible technical means" to correct errors made by the user in inputting the order (such as a "pop-up" statement of the order prior to electronic dispatch of the order). These rules apply in

---

116 "Argos refuses to part with £3 TV sets", *The Times*, September 9, 1999. For an Irish example, see "Mispriced television orders cancelled", *The Irish Times*, March 3, 2013.
117 "£6,400 tickets for free?", *The Times*, May 3, 2003.
118 "£6,400 tickets for free?", *The Times*, May 3, 2003.
119 Wise [2002] C.L.S.R 280; Rodgers [2002] Business L.R. 112; see generally Nolan, p.61 in Burrows and Peel (eds), *Contract Formation and Parties* (Oxford: OUP, 2010).
120 See *http://www.uncitral.org* Daily Telegraph December 16, 2014, "Amazons accidental 1p bargain bonanza".
121 Electronic Commerce Act 2000 ss.19 and 22.
122 S.I. No. 68 of 2003. For the transposition of the Consumer Rights Directive 2011/83/EU, in particular the cancellation right for off-premises contracts and distance contracts, as well as the provisions relating to contracts for the sale to consumers of digital content (see the Directive, recital 19), see S.I. No. 484 of 2013.

business-to-consumer contracts, but also in business-to-business contracts. However, business-to-business parties can "contract-out" of these provisions. These rules apply to electronic transactions that are interactive such as web-based contracts, but in the case of individual communications (such as an email communicating an offer or an acceptance which is not part of a relevant services operation, within the Electronic Commerce Directive) these rules do not apply. Neither the 2000 Act or the EC (Directive 2000/31/EC) Regulations 2003 address the question whether the message being transmitted is an offer or an acceptance: the neutral phrases "order" and "acknowledgement" are not necessarily the same as "offer" and "acceptance". The order, for example, could well be an acceptance if the website contains a unilateral offer, so the way the website is constructed and the sequence in which the contract process is rolled out will be of critical importance.

1–67 Where errors and misrepresentations have occurred, there have been a number of well-publicised instances where websites and the booking process have thrown up a number of situations where the choice for the seller or service provider has been to deny that a contract exists or honour the apparent promise. Some businesses, as a matter of commercial expediency, may resolve any disputes, for which the business is culpable, in favour of the customer. In April 2008, Aer Lingus advertised a USA seat sale in which business class seats valued at €1,775 each way were snapped up by several hundred customers at €5 each. While the airline initially took the view that the mistake must have been an obvious unilateral mistake (and the offer was thus void),[123] the company ultimately compromised by offering to accommodate all buyers in economy class.[124] This decision appears to have been reached because some buyers had opted for €5 economy class tickets (the mistake was not so obvious here) and because a number of "follow on" bookings (cars, connecting flights) had been made by the purchasers. Perhaps the most compelling circumstance of all would be the email confirmation order and the debiting of the customer credit card; Aer Lingus may well have formed the view that a court would not be sympathetic to a defendant that was the primary author of its own misfortune.

1–68 While legislation has sought to promote "technological neutrality", in the courts, the earlier principles of law have been found to be readily applicable to the online world. In *Ryanair Ltd v Billigfluege de GmbH*,[125] Ryanair sought

---

[123] See "Aer Lingus €5 bargain buy turn out not to be the ticket", *The Irish Times*, April 18, 2008.

[124] "Aer Lingus to reinstate €5 tickets—but in economy class", *The Irish Times*, April 19, 2008. See *Chwee Kin Keong v Digilandmall.com* [2006] 1 L.R.C. 37.

[125] [2010] IEHC 47; see also *Century 21 Canada Ltd Partnership v Rogers Communications* [2011] BCSC 1196. See also *Ryanair v Club Travel* [2012] IEHC 165; *Ryanair v On the Beach Ltd* [2013] IEHC 124. In *Ryanair Ltd v Billigfluege.de GmbH* and *Ryanair Ltd v On the Beach Ltd* [2015] IESC 11, the Supreme Court distanced itself from Hanna J.'s use of orthodox contract principles to resolve jurisdiction issues, preferring Laffoy. J.'s reasoning in *On the Beach*. This is not to say that Hanna J.'s analysis can be faulted and the Supreme

to bring a German website proprietor before the Irish courts, arguing that the extraction of data from Ryanair websites for competing commercial reasons was in breach of Ryanair's terms and conditions and actionable in contract. The defendant contested the effect of an exclusive jurisdiction clause in those Ryanair terms and conditions on the basis that the defendant was not required to click any "accept" button before accessing the Ryanair site although the terms and conditions were available via a clearly marked hyperlink. Some earlier cases had drawn distinctions between "click-wrap" consent and so called "browse-wrap" terms that do not seek the user's acceptance of terms prior to website use.[126] Hanna J., applying both standard contractual principles and ECJ jurisprudence on the Brussels Regulation said that the search is for consensus and, in particular, the need to establish that reasonable conspicuous notice of the existence of the terms has been given, and that there has been assent to the terms in question. The fact that the defendants here had not given consent to the terms was not dispositive. Hanna J. said:

> "The defendants claim that they never consented to the Terms of Use or entered into any agreement with the plaintiff. The plaintiff says this is not the case and that at all material times its Terms of Use governed its relationship with the defendants. As regards whether or not the Terms of Use were binding on the defendant, it is a well established general principle of law that parties to a contract cannot be bound by terms which they have not had an opportunity of reading prior to making the contract. That is not to say that a party will not be bound because they have not read the terms—they will only escape being bound if they can show they were not afforded a reasonable opportunity to read the term in question before entering into the contract."

Hanna J. went on to distinguish the facts of this case from *Thornton v Shoe Lane Parking*[127] on the basis that the terms were clearly accessible at all times via the hyperlink whereas the terms in *Thornton* were difficult to locate and onerous. Hanna J. found the necessary element of assent from the fact that the defendant's repeatedly "screen-scraped" data from the Ryanair site for the defendant's own commercial use:

> "In this case, we are dealing with commercial entities and the existence and effect of the website's Terms of Use are clear and unambiguous. If you use the site, you agree not to breach its terms and if you do so, the exclusive jurisdiction clause set out in the Terms of Use make it clear that Ireland is the appropriate jurisdiction for the purpose of litigating any disputes that may arise as a result."

Court pointed out that factual differences between the way Billigfluege and On the Beach interacted with consumers may, at any later trial, produce different conclusions. See Charleton J.'s judgment at [2015] IESC 11 at paras 8, 11 and 18 in particular.

[126] *Caspi v Microsoft Corp* 732 A. 2d 528 (1999); *Specht v Netscape* 306 F. 3d 17 (2002).
[127] [1971] 2 Q.B. 163.

If the terms are not clear and unambiguous, then it may be expected that they will not be incorporated into the contract; *eBay International AG v Creative Festival Entertainment Pty Ltd*[128] It is to be expected that where the contract is between a commercial entity and a person negotiating for non-business purposes, the reasonable notice and assent provisions will be more strictly policed than in business-to-business contracts.[129] Recent US case law, for example, has imposed high assent requirements if consumers are to be bound by mandatory arbitration provisions and it is clear that *post hoc* unsolicited emails and "browse-wrap" contracts are not likely to suffice for these purposes. The US case law is usefully examined by the Second Circuit Appeal Court decision in *Schabel v Trilegiant*.[130]

1–69 The CJEU, in *EI Majdoub v CarsOnTheWeb.Deutschland GmbH*,[131] and by the Ninth Circuit Court of Appeals Opinion in *Nguyen v Barnes & Noble Inc.*[132] for the purposes of the Brussels Regulation has ruled that a click wrap consent to a jurisdiction clause in a contract between two car dealers will constitute consent to the sellers terms and conditions. In this case the communication requirement, in writing or other durable medium, was met even though no effort was made to print off the contract. Click consent will suffice as long as there is the possibility of obtaining a durable record of the transaction. The CJEU however contrasted the position under the Brussels Regulation with the now defunct Distance Contracts Directive 97/7/EC. A hyperlink will not suffice in a consumer transaction under that Directive because a "written confirmation" or confirmation in another durable medium available and accessible is required under the Consumer Rights Directive I, Directive 2011/83/EC. Directive 97/7/EC has been replaced by Directive 2011/83/EC, transposed by S.I. No.484 of 2013.

Termination of an Offer

1–70 An offer may be incapable of producing a contract for a variety of reasons.

(1) Revocation

1–71 It is established that an offer can be revoked or withdrawn at any time before it is validly accepted. In cases where the offer is to enter into a bilateral contract, that is, a contract to which both parties are bound, it should

---

[128] [2006] 170 F.C.R. 450. See also *Evagora v eBay Australia and New Zealand Pty Ltd* [2001] VCAT 49 on eBay terms and conditions.
[129] While pleaded in tort, this makes the majority decision of the English Court of Appeal, in *Patchett v Swimming Pool & Allied Trades Associates Ltd* [2009] EWCA Civ 717, even more incredible—a collateral contract argument should have been used by the plaintiffs.
[130] 697 F. 3d 110 (2012).
[131] Case C-322/14.
[132] 763 F. 3d 1171 (2014). For post-formation but pre-performance notices which may be effective see *Tompkins v 23andMe.Inc* 2014 WL2903752 (N.D. Cal. June 25, 2014).

be remembered that acceptance has two elements: (a) the intention to accept; and (b) communication of acceptance. In the case of *The Navan Union v McLoughlin*,[133] the defendant submitted a tender to the plaintiffs, a poor law authority. The guardians met amongst themselves and agreed to accept the defendant's tender but before acceptance was communicated to McLoughlin, he revoked his offer. Because the plaintiffs had not validly accepted the defendant's offer, he was held to be entitled to withdraw it.

1–72 For revocation to be effective, the offeror need only show that, at the time of purported acceptance, the offeree knows that the subject matter is no longer available to the offeree. This follows from the much criticised English case of *Dickinson v Dodds*.[134] Dodds offered to sell his house to Dickinson for an agreed sum. The offer was to remain open "until Friday, June 12th 9.00 a.m.". On the Thursday, Dickinson was told that the house may have been sold to a third party. This information was communicated to Dickinson by a man called Barry who had not been authorised by Dodds to communicate this information to Dickinson. Dickinson handed a letter of acceptance to Dodds before the deadline set. The Court of Appeal held that because Dickinson had notice of the sale, even if the informant was not the offeror or an agent, the offer then became incapable of acceptance. Dickinson could not obtain the property or damages.

1–73 It seems that Dickinson intended to purchase before he learnt of the intervening sale. Had he given even a nominal consideration then the promise to keep the offer open until Friday would have been binding. In the US, a promise to keep an offer open is described as a "firm offer" and it cannot be revoked. The English Law Commission, in a 1975 Working Paper, suggested that the law be changed to make a promise such as that made by Dodds binding if it is deliberately meant and made in the course of business.[135]

1–74 It should also be noted that a letter of revocation does not become effective by posting it. In other words, the postal rule does not apply to letters revoking an offer. That letter only becomes effective when it arrives. This is established by the English case of *Byrne v Van Tienhoven*.[136] Actual knowledge seems to be the critical factor in these revocation cases. In *Himmelman v Pare Estate*,[137] a Nova Scotia case, the issue was whether a counter-offer, made in writing, had to be revoked in writing. The defendants in a telephone con-

---

[133] (1855) 4 I.C.L.R. 451. For post-formation but pre-performance notices which may be effective, see *Tompkins v 23andMe.Inc* 2014 WL2903752 (N.D. Cal. June 25, 2014).

[134] (1876) 2 Ch.D. 463. On the capacity of an agent who communicates an offer to receive notice of revocation, see *CF Asset Finance Ltd v Okonji* [2014] EWCA Civ 870.

[135] Working Paper No. 60. This has not been acted upon by the UK Parliament. Working Paper No. 60. This has not been acted upon by the UK Parliament. For "firm offer" case law in England, see *Proton Energy Group SA v Lietuva* [2013] EWHC 2872 (Comm) and *Glencore Energy Ltd v Cirrus Oil Services Ltd* [2014] EWHC 87 (Comm).

[136] (1880) 5 C.P.D. 344.

[137] (2001) 197 N.S.R. (2d) 374.

versation indicated to the plaintiffs that the counter-offer had been withdrawn. Later the same day the plaintiff, by fax, purported to accept the counter-offer. The Nova Scotia Supreme Court held that the counter-offer could be revoked orally or in writing at any time prior to acceptance.

1–75 The important decision of Lord Lowry C.J. in the Northern Ireland case of *Walker v Glass*[138] provides an excellent analysis of the basic rules on offer and acceptance. Walker wished to purchase an estate owned by Glass and to this end persuaded Glass to consider selling it to him. The parties contracted solicitors to draw up a form of offer in which Glass offered to sell the estate for £400,000, a deposit of £40,000 being payable. The offer was declared to be open for acceptance until March 13, 1979. Acceptance was prescribed; Walker had to sign a form of acceptance and forward the deposit before that date. On March 1, Walker notified Glass of his intention to buy but failed to forward the deposit until March 12. In the meantime, Glass had "revoked" the offer. Walker's action for specific performance failed. Despite the statement to the contrary in the offer, revocation could be effective at any time before acceptance. Walker argued that the offer had been effectively accepted on March 1. By communicating acceptance before the purported withdrawal on March 2, this effectively "froze" the transaction which was concluded on payment of the deposit. Lord Lowry C.J. refused to accept this theory. He noted that the prescribed mode of acceptance had to be satisfied. Payment of the deposit was not a neutral act, as counsel for Walker contended, because the failure to proceed would result in any deposit paid being forfeited by the seller.

1–76 If the offer is an offer to enter into a unilateral contract then difficulties may arise in regard to revocation. If, as we said earlier, acceptance and performance are one act and if revocation is possible before it is accepted then it should follow that an offer of this nature can be revoked any time until completion, even if the offeree has started to accept by performance. If I offer a man €2,000 to walk from Cork to Dublin, can I revoke the offer when I see him on the outskirts of Kildare Town?

1–77 An affirmative answer would be clearly unjust but finding a jurisprudential basis for denying the offeror the right to revoke is difficult. If the offeror revokes before the offeree starts to perform, no injustice results. However, the English Court of Appeal, in dealing with the more difficult problem of revocation after performance has commenced, has decided that an offer to enter into a unilateral contract is subject to an implied obligation "that [the offeror] would not render the performance by [the offeree] of the acts necessary for acceptance impossible ... and ... that the [offeror] could not withdraw ... once [the offeree] ... embarked on those acts", per Buckley L.J. in *Daulia Ltd v Four Millbank Nominees*.[139]

---

[138] [1979] N.I. 129.
[139] [1978] Ch. 231 at 245.

1–78 Although conclusive English authority on this point is of fairly recent origin, the Australian courts, since the 1860 case of *Abbott v Lance*,[140] have held the offer irrevocable once performance has commenced. The High Court of Australia in a decision in 1987 has confirmed this rule; see *Pavey and Matthews Pty Ltd v Paul*.[141] There is some slight Irish authority on the point, for the Supreme Court followed *Offord v Davies*,[142] a leading early English authority, in *O'Connor v Sorahan*,[143] but the point remains open in Irish law.

(2) Rejection of the offer

1–79 Clearly his refusal to accept the offer will make it impossible for the offeree, in the absence of a fresh offer, to change his mind and later accept. As we have seen, if a counter-offer is made by the offeree in response to an offer this has the effect of destroying the first offer. Such drastic consequences have been criticised and the courts often give the offeree's response a neutral effect by characterising it as a request for information—which does not destroy the offer—rather than a counter-offer. If this is the case then the offer can be validly accepted. The recent case of *Dany Lions Ltd v Bristol Cars*[144] provides an excellent illustration of how a judge may chacterise a rather ambiguous statement in this way The court may also describe the added term as of importance to the offeree only which he can also waive; see the decision of the House of Lords in the Irish case of *Maconchy v Trawer*.[145]

(3) Lapse of time

1–80 If the offeree does not respond quickly to the offer he may find his tardiness will prevent him from being able to accept the offer. The offeror may expressly stipulate that the offer is for immediate acceptance only as was the case in *Dooley v Egan*.[146] If the offeror is silent on the method of communicating acceptance the courts may hold that the medium of communication used indicates that acceptance take place immediately. An offer posted by airmail or sent by telegram from Australia to Dublin could not be validly accepted by sending a reply by surface mail. In all other cases acceptance must take place within a reasonable time. The commodity in question will be an important factor here because acceptance of an offer to purchase perishable goods or a commodity that fluctuates wildly in price such as oil or shares may have to take place earlier than a similar offer to purchase land. In *Commane v*

---

[140] (1860) Legges N.S.W.R. 1283.
[141] (1987) 162 C.L.R. 221; *Lyndel Nominees Pty Ltd v Mobil Oil Australia Ltd* (1997) 37 I.P.R. 599.
[142] (1862) 12 C.B. (n.s.) 748.
[143] [1933] I.R. 591 at 599–560 per Kennedy C.J.
[144] [2013] EWHC 2997 (Q.B.).
[145] [1894] 2 I.R. 663.
[146] (1938) 72 I.L.T.R. 155. "Firm offer" usage in some sectors may indicate that the offer will be irrevocable by the offerors when a specific deadline is set and that it will be incapable of acceptance (i.e. the offer will lapse) when that deadline expires: *Glencore Energy Ltd v Cirrus Oil Services Ltd* [2014] EWHC 87 (Comm).

Walsh,[147] O'Hanlon J. stated that an offer was open for acceptance until it was withdrawn or until it would be unreasonable to hold the offeror to it any longer because of the length of time which had elapsed without acceptance. After citing the leading case of *Ramsgate Hotel Co v Montefiore*,[148] O'Hanlon J. held that the casual approach of the parties in relation to closing a contract for the sale of land, allied to an understanding that the transaction would be attended with a considerable amount of delay, meant that an offer to transfer part of the property in a separate transaction could still be accepted four months after it had been made.

1–81 However, the courts will require compelling evidence before holding that the offeror was prepared to indulge the offeree, even in land transactions. The words of Carroll J. in *Parkgrange Investments Ltd v Shandon Park Mills Ltd*[149] are cautionary indeed:

> "[A] purchaser who does not accept a contract as proferred runs the risk that his counter offer will not be accepted. A purchaser who ignores a time limit for accepting an offer runs the risk that it will lapse."

Similarly, if an offeree is engaged in negotiations to settle complex matters and the offeree engages in delay and brinkmanship, to such an extent that the offeror terminates subsisting contractual arrangements on the basis of breach of contract, the offeree should infer from this that the effect is to render an unaccepted offer incapable of being accepted: *APRA v Monster Communications Property Ltd.*[150]

1–82 In some exceptional cases the interval between the making of an offer and a valid acceptance can be remarkably protracted. In the Manitoba case of *Earn v Kohut*,[151] the defendant was being sued in a civil claim arising out of an incident in which he shot the plaintiff. Just prior to sentencing, in relation to criminal charges brought in respect of the same incident, the defendant offered to settle the civil action, a factor that was relevant as a mitigating factor at the sentencing hearing. Discussions between the lawyers ensued and the plaintiff purported to accept the defendant's offer some two-and-a-half years later, shortly after the limitation period had expired in respect of the tort claim. In these exceptional circumstances, Beard J. held there was acceptance within a reasonable time. At the sentencing hearing the defendant's counsel had pledged the defendant's remorse and an intention to compensate the plaintiff. The defendant had subsequently reaffirmed this intention via counsel, and the defendant had been imprisoned for three years so the issue of payment only arose upon release of the defendant shortly before the purported acceptance.

---

147 Unreported, High Court, May 3, 1983.
148 (1866) L.R. 1 Ex. 109; *Dencio v Zivanovic* (1991) 105 F.L.R. 117.
149 Unreported, High Court, May 2, 1991.
150 (2006) 71 I.P.R. 212.
151 (2002) 164 Man.R. (2d) 50.

(4) Death

1–83 There is one recent Australian case which is destined to be followed in later judgments. In *Smith v Woods*[152] the parties to a dispute entered into mediation proceedings to settle outstanding issues. Woods responded to an offer by making a counter-offer, via his solicitor, which the offeror's solicitor left with his four clients for their consideration. On the morning of March 13 the solicitors, by telephone, established that all four of the offerors' clients had accepted the counter-offer and they agreed to finalise the necessary settlement documentation. Later that same day the offerors and both legal teams were told that Woods had died early on the morning of March 13. The Supreme Court of Victoria held that the death of Woods did not revoke the counter-offer; save in cases where the offeree knows of the death, automatic termination of an offer should not arise. As in this case, the offer made did not involve anything personal to be undertaken by the offeror and, on an objective basis, the estate stood to benefit from the proposed settlement agreement.

1–84 With the exception of *Re Whelan*[153] there are no Irish cases which discuss whether an offeror's death before acceptance can make it impossible to accept the offer, so as to hold the estate of the deceased liable. Even the English cases are unclear on this question. *Re Whelan* holds that where a surety dies and the bank acquires knowledge of the death of the surety, via formal or informal means, the bank cannot continue to advance monies supported by the surety. Knowledge will end the standing offer. However, it is possible for the contract to expressly stipulate a particular kind of notice be served and, absent such notice, the death and knowledge of the surety may not terminate the standing offer; see *Coulthart v Clementson*.[154] Death may, of course, terminate a contractual obligation through the doctrine of frustration but we will deal with this later.

Ambiguous, Illusory and Uncertain Contract Terms

1–85 If the parties have concluded negotiations then they will consider agreement to have been reached. It often becomes apparent later that the parties have not reached agreement on every important issue or it may be that the contract document is unclear on certain matters. It is suggested that there are several distinct problems here.

1–86 A contract term may be ambiguous, that is, capable of being interpreted in two or more ways. The courts do not readily hold that the doubts surrounding the negotiations must lead to the contract being deprived of all effect. In *E.S.B.*

---

[152] [2014] VSC 646, applying *Fong v Cilli* (1968) 11 F.L.R. 495 and limiting Mellish L.J.'s dicta in *Dickinson v Dodds* which is to the contrary effect.

[153] [1897] 1 I.R. 575.

[154] (1879) 5 Q.B.D. 42 per Bowen L.J., applied in *Ronan v ANZ Banking Group* (2000) 2 V.R. 523.

v Newman,[155] the plaintiffs supplied electricity to a Mrs Waddington at four different premises in Dublin. The defendant who had agreed to indemnify Mrs Waddington, was sued by the plaintiffs for the total sum due on all four "accounts". The defendant pleaded that the contract of indemnity applied only to one of the four premises. Judge Davitt held that the word "accounts" was ambiguous because it could apply either to all four premises or the periodic accounts submitted in relation to one of them. Judge Davitt refused to hold that no contract existed; he instead admitted parol evidence to show that the indemnity was intended only to apply to one of the premises.

1–87 Just as a contract term may be capable of more than one meaning so too can a contract term be devoid of any meaning. This kind of term is called an illusory promise. Here words are used which show that the "promisor" has attempted to give himself a discretion to perform by qualifying his promise so much that it has no promissory content at all. In *Spreadex Ltd v Cochrane*,[156] an online betting company sought to impose liability upon one of its account holders for accumulated losses incurred when a young boy, the son of the account holder's girlfriend, gained access to the account and incurred losses of around £100,000. The account holder successfully argued that a term in the standard conditions that sought to impose liability for unauthorised trading was not enforceable because other terms rendered the contract illusory (e.g. "we have the right at our absolute discretion to refuse to accept part or all of any bet"). Instances of illusory promises are most frequently found in the context of clauses exempting a promisor from liability when in breach of a promise. In the leading Australian case of *MacRobertson Miller Airlines v Commissioners of State Taxation*,[157] an airline company promised to fly a passenger from X to Y but reserved for itself the power to cancel any flight, ticket or booking. This promise was held by the High Court of Australia to be illusory. The airline had given itself a discretion to perform or decline to do so. Promises "to deliver goods if I feel like it" or to supply "all the petrol you may require if I am not liable for non delivery" are also illusory. In *Provincial Bank of Ireland v Donnell*[158] a guarantor's promise to provide security for her husband's bank account in consideration of "advances ... that might hereafter be made" was held illusory. The bank retained an absolute discretion on whether future advances would be made or not. On the other hand, in the case of *O'Mullane v Riordan*[159] a purchaser of land agreed to pay £1,500 an acre or such larger sum as the purchaser later stipulated. McWilliam J. held that this promise was not illusory. The purchaser was obliged to pay a minimum of £1,500 per acre even though this sum could be varied upwards

---

[155] (1933) 67 I.L.T.R. 124.
[156] [2012] EWHC 129 (Comm).
[157] (1975) 133 C.L.R. 125.
[158] (1932) 67 I.L.T.R. 142, followed in *McKay v National Australia Bank Ltd* [1998] 1 V.R. 173. See also *ACC Bank v Dillon* [2012] IEHC 474.
[159] Unreported, High Court, April 20, 1978.

by the purchaser at his discretion. Similarly, in *Rooney v Byrne*[160] a promise to purchase a house "subject to getting an advance on the property" was held not to give the promisor an election whether to apply for the loan or advance. O'Byrne J. held the promisor was obliged to make reasonable efforts to secure an advance on reasonable terms. To similar effect is the more recent decision in the South Australian case of *Smith v Pisani*[161] where "a subject to finance" clause was held not to create a total discretion to proceed with a land purchase. The buyer was obliged not to refuse to accept an offer of available finance if this would be unreasonable. Similar reasoning, as part of a process of interpreting the contract, can be found in the New Zealand case of *Lerner v Schiehallion Nominees*[162] on "subject to survey".

1–88 In many contractual arrangements the parties seek to build into the agreement some degree of flexibility so that the agreement can be adjusted if certain contingencies occur. Obvious instances of this kind arise when one party is obliged to make periodic monetary payments over a prolonged period of time. The contract may be drafted in a way that allows the payee to adjust payments due if interest rates, taxation rates or other costs rise. Is such an agreement void for uncertainty? The English Court of Appeal in *Lombard Tricity Finance Ltd v Paton*[163] held that a credit agreement which allowed the credit supplier to vary the interest rate payable, on notification to the borrower, was lawful as being an express term which was drafted in plain terms. Clauses of this kind are in common use in Irish commercial contracts. Leasing contracts, for example, often contain clauses giving the lessor of movables the right to adjust rental rates if there should be adverse movements in relation to interest rates, capital allowances and other factors.

1–89 If a promise lacks any substance the courts may do one of two things; first the court can look to see if the promisee subsequently performs and permit him to recover the remuneration promised. So, if I ask someone to deliver a ton of coal indicating that in return "I may pay you €500" the supplier who delivers coal will be entitled to recover the sum in question. This is necessary to prevent unjust enrichment. A slight variation from this position will occur if one negotiating party embarks upon either design acts (*EMOR Drake & Scull v Sir Robert McAlpine*)[164] or performance (*Peregrine Systems v Steria Ltd*).[165] The court may hold that failure to agree on terms which are essential to the project does not prevent payment in respect of either preparatory or preliminary acts. In *Peregrine Systems* a computer programme was never completed by the programmer but it was held that the programmer had never promised to complete a viable program for the contract price; rather, the promise was to

---

[160] [1933] I.R. 609.
[161] (2001) 78 S.A.S.R. 548, following *Meehan v Jones* (1982) 149 C.L.R. 571.
[162] [2003] 2 N.Z.L.R. 671.
[163] [1989] 1 All E.R. 918. See now S.I. No. 27 of 1995.
[164] (2004) 98 Con. L.R. 1.
[165] [2005] EWCA Civ 239.

do £200,000 of development work, even if a finished product was not created. Secondly, the court may delete or sever the illusory promise from the contract and enforce the rest of it. In *Mackie v Wilde and Longin*,[166] the Supreme Court, however, refused to sever a vague promise that the plaintiff would agree with the defendant that only 25 annual fishing permits and "a few" day tickets would be issued. The vagueness of the "a few" day tickets was held fatal to the entire agreement although the Supreme Court declined to explain why severance was an inappropriate response to this situation.

1–90 A vague or uncertain contract can exist in a variety of forms. In *Central Meat Products v Carney*,[167] an action was brought to prevent the sale of cattle by the defendant to third parties, the plaintiff claiming that he had concluded an agreement with the defendant which provided that all the cattle the defendant acquired for canning purposes would be sold to the plaintiff. Overend J. held that there was no agreement capable of being enforced. There was no clear acceptance, nor was there agreement on important issues including price variation clauses and insurance arrangements.

1–91 The line of authority set in train in England in *Pagnan* (see para.1–93) and in several Australian and New Zealand cases, which permits a court to hold that some terms that remain to be resolved may not preclude a finding that an enforceable contract exists, was examined by Edwards J. in *An Cumann Peile Boitheimeach Teoranta v Albion Properties Ltd*.[168] A complex and lengthy set of negotiations over a development project that lasted for over four years broke down: the defendant submitted that there was nevertheless a concluded agreement, characterising unresolved issues relating to the negotiation and conclusion of wayleaves, easements and leases, as minor matters. Edwards J., relying in particular on evidence concerning the need for legal and engineering matters of some importance to be formalised prior to construction held that no concluded agreement was reached—any contract was void for uncertainty.[169] Joint ventures to develop a business opportunity that fails to come to fruition will simply fall away and the courts will not substitute some arrangement that was not intended in lieu of the inchoate joint venture: see *Sweeney v Lagan Developments Ltd*.[170]

1–92 In cases where the contractual arrangement seems to lack clarity on the meaning to be attached to essential terms, or in cases where the contract is

---

[166] [1998] 2 I.R. 578. In *Mackie v Wilde and Longin*, the Supreme Court did not refer to the general policy objective of trying to uphold a lease or conveyance wherever possible. Contrast *Hackney LBC v Thompson* [2001] L. & T.R. 69 (payment of a "due proportion" not void for uncertainty).

[167] (1944) 10 Ir.Jur.Rep.34. *Cosmoline Trading v DH Burke and Son Ltd* [2006] IEHC 38.

[168] [2008] IEHC 447.

[169] Reliance was placed in particular on the High Court decision in *Dore v Stephenson*, unreported, High Court, April 24, 1980 and Blanchard J.'s speech in *Electricity Corp of New Zealand v Fletcher* [2001] NZCA 289.

[170] [2007] NICA 11.

silent altogether, there are a number of devices and techniques that can be used by the courts to ascertain the intention of the parties, in the objective sense. In cases where the clause is part of a contract which in previous years has been adequately performed, a vague clause which relates to future supplies may provide appropriate points of clarification. So, in *Hillas & Co Ltd v Arcos Ltd*,[171] a contractual option for the sale of timber, being described as "100,000 standards", was given greater precision by reference to the fuller description of the goods found in the contract relating to the previous growing season. However, if there is no previous course of dealing between the parties, or the clause in question purports to refer to a set of criteria or situation which is not uniform within the industry, or has not been delimited or defined by a course of dealing between the parties, then the clause may be incapable of being given any meaning; see *Scammell v Ouston*.[172] Additionally, the courts may opt to fill in gaps by reference to the standard of reasonableness. This is quite common in cases where the contract is silent altogether and the contract does not purport to provide machinery which will somehow produce a result (e.g. an arbitration clause). The general power of the courts to imply terms so as to give the contract the efficacy it must be assumed the parties intended, does not subvert the general principle of private autonomy.

1–93 A most important decision of the English Court of Appeal stresses a fundamental distinction to be drawn between terms which are essential and terms which are non-essential. While this dichotomy is not new, the Court of Appeal, in *Pagnan Sp.A. v Feed Products Ltd*,[173] built upon it to stress the difference between instances where the parties have reached agreement on essential terms, and the evidence suggests that the parties intended and believe they have made a binding contract, and instances where the parties have not reached agreement on terms which they do not regard as essential to a binding agreement. In this latter situation there can be no enforceable contract. However, in the Court of Appeal the situation before the court was said to be a somewhat intermediate one: the parties had intended to continue to negotiate on some inessential or incidental matters. The issue before the court was whether their intention was that until these matters were resolved there was no binding contract. Each case depends on its facts, objectively ascertained. In some instances it may be clear that the parties may intend not to be bound unless this incidental matter is agreed, as in *Love and Stewart v Instone*.[174] In other cases it may be evident that the parties may intend to be bound forthwith, notwithstanding the need to agree further terms or carry out some formality such as executing a formal document. Where this does not happen it is only because the outstanding matter not agreed upon results in an uncertain or unworkable contract. So, in *Pagnan Sp.A. v Feed Products Ltd*, the agreement on parties, price, identity and quality of goods and terms of shipment were

---

[171]   [1932] Com.Cas. 23.
[172]   [1941] A.C. 251.
[173]   [1987] 2 Lloyd's Rep. 601.
[174]   (1917) 33 T.L.R. 475. *Birse Construction Ltd v St. David Ltd* (2000) 78 Con. L.R. 121.

held to constitute a binding contract, notwithstanding the existence of later negotiations and subsequent failure to agree on loading rate, demurrage, and despatch and carrying charges. Each case is said to depend and turn on its own facts.[175] Even employment contracts to work on a casual or required basis may appear to contain enough promissory content to give rise to legally enforceable mutual obligations; see *Carmichael v National Power Plc.*[176]

1–94 To similar effect is the decision of Carroll J. in *Parkgrange Investments Ltd v Shandon Park Mills Ltd.*[177] The failure of a contract for the sale of an interest in land to record an undertaking by the vendor to exercise best efforts to arrange the transfer of a policy of insurance to the purchaser did not undermine the validity of the contract: "the agreement about insurance was peripheral".

Agreements to agree in the future

1–95 The decision of the Court of Appeal in *Pagnan Sp.A. v Feed Products Ltd*[178] re-emphasises the importance of interpreting contracts in their entirety and the fact that the process of interpretation is intended to give effect to the intentions of the parties. As such, reasonable persons are taken to have intended their agreements to have reasonable effect. While it is possible for the parties to stipulate that until every detail is negotiated the agreement is unenforceable, the courts are now less willing to hold that the failure to agree an outstanding matter will result in the contract being void for uncertainty. Certainly, the following words of Lord Dunedin in *May & Butcher v The King*[179] are no longer to be taken literally:

"[T]o be a good contract there must be a concluded bargain, and a concluded contract is one which settles everything that is necessary to be settled and leaves nothing to be settled by agreement between the parties."[180]

In sale of goods cases, if the parties fail to agree on a price and they have not covenanted that they will negotiate on price at some future date, s.8(2) of the Sale of Goods Act 1893 intervenes to require the payment of a reasonable

---

175 *Granit S.A. v Benship International* [1994] 1 Lloyd's Rep. 526; *The Gladys (No. 2)* [1994] 2 Lloyd's Rep. 402. An "objective appraisal" of the language used—a "firm offer" seeks to infer the offeror wants only an acceptance or rejection in reply—and the market itself will be dispositive. See the oil spot market case of *Proton Energy Group SA v Lietuva* [2013] EWHC 2872 (Comm) and *Glencore Energy Ltd v Cirrus Oil Services Ltd* [2014] EWHC 87 (Comm).

176 *The Times*, April 2, 1998.

177 Unreported, High Court, May 2, 1991. Similarly, in *Danbywiske v Donegal Investment Group plc* [2015] IEHC 126, heads of an agreement, drafted by lay persons but recording all the essential terms, was held to constitute a binding agreement, notwithstanding the fact that the execution of the terms would be effected by later formal documents.

178 [1987] 2 Lloyd's Rep. 601.

179 [1934] 2 K.B. 17n.

180 [1934] 2 K.B. 17n.

price. However, if the agreement is executory, that is, it must be performed at some future date, there may be considerable difficulty in enforcing such an undertaking. If the contract is outside the 1893 Act, a building contract or sale of land, for instance, failure to agree on a price may be fatal as was the case in *Courtney & Fairbairn v Tolaini Brothers (Hotels)*,[181] an English Court of Appeal decision. In this case a builder provided finance to a developer in return for a promise that he would be awarded the construction contract itself, on the basis that the developer's quantity surveyor would negotiate a fair and reasonable contract sum. The plaintiff argued that while he had not entered into a binding contract to build, the defendant had broken a contract to negotiate. The theory that someone can "contract to make a contract" was rejected by the Court of Appeal, primarily because the damages to be awarded are too uncertain. Who can tell if the negotiations will be successful? The *Tolaini Brothers* case was subsequently followed in the British Columbia case of *Mannpar Enterprises Ltd v Canada*[182] when a mining renewal clause allowing renewal "for a further five year period subject to satisfactory performance and renegotiation of the royalty rate and annual surface rental" was held to be a bare agreement to negotiate and void for uncertainty. In this decision the British Columbia Court refused to imply a duty to negotiate in good faith in order to repair the deficiencies in the wording of the clause. In *Walford v Miles*[183] the House of Lords reaffirmed the view that there cannot be a contract requiring the parties to negotiate in good faith because the right of each party to withdraw at any time from the negotiations is simply incompatible with such a contract; Lord Ackner observed that it was quite impractical to expect the courts to police such an inherently vague agreement of the kind contended for. Lord Ackner, however, did indicate that a contract to use best endeavours may be enforceable and it has been held that if an enforceable contract exists but other covenants which lack precision are identified, the *Courtney & Fairbairn* case does not prevent a court from implying a further term that the parties will negotiate in good faith about future terms to be inserted into a written agreement; see *Donwin Productions v E.M.I. Films*.[184]

"Endeavours" clauses

1–96 The distinction drawn between best endeavours to secure a defined object, such as to achieve planning permission, which is enforceable, and a general duty to use best endeavours to agree, which is not, was endorsed by

---

[181] [1975] 1 All E.R. 716.

[182] (1997) 33 B.C.L.R. (3d) 203; *PP (Portage) Holdings Inc. v 346 Portage Avenue Inc.* (1999) 177 D.L.R. (4th) 359.

[183] [1992] 2 A.C. 128; *Arnold v Northern Bank* [1995] N.I.J.B. 55; *Walford v Miles* has been adopted by the New Zealand courts: *Wellington City Council v Body Corporate 51702 (Wellington) Ltd* [2002] 3 N.Z.L.R. 486.

[184] *The Times*, March 9, 1984. See also *Renard Constructions ME Pty Ltd v Minister of Public Works* (1992) 33 Con. L.R. 72 at 112–113; *Philips Electronique Grand Public S.A. v British Sky Broadcasting Ltd* [1995] E.M.L.R. 472. Recent case law has distinguished *Walford v Miles* when the issue is whether a time limited obligation in a dispute resolution clause requiring the parties to seek to resolve a dispute via friendly discussions is enforceable:

the Court of Appeal in *Little v Courage Ltd.*[185] It is evident that in cases of this kind the court will make a finding that the parties have reached a definite agreement, with an identifiable consideration and that the parties are required to negotiate further, often incidental terms in good faith. It may be that the parties have the benefit of a number of specific terms or benchmarks against which the "good faith" negotiations are to proceed (*Coal Cliff Collieries Pty v Sijehama Pty Ltd*[186]) or a specific reference point such as "market rate" is laid down in the contract (*Empress Towers Ltd v Bank of Nova Scotia*[187]) or a methodology such as alternative dispute resolution ("ADR") (*Cable & Wireless Plc v IBM (UK) Ltd*[188]).

1–97 It must be said that the cases here have an *ad hoc* quality about them. The most important recent English case is *Jet2.com Ltd v Blackpool Airport Ltd.*[189] In 2005, Jet2, a low-cost airline, signed a contract for 15 years with Blackpool Airport. There were only two clauses, clause 1 requiring the airport and Jet2 to "co-operate together and use their best endeavours to promote" Jet2 services. After four years Jet2 complained that it was being denied out-of-hours (i.e. late evening/early morning) departure slots in breach of this clause because the airport found it uneconomic to keep facilities open at such times. While the defendants argued that the "co-operation and promote" clause was too uncertain to have any meaning, a very strong Court of Appeal found otherwise. This was a case where a contract was in existence. The commercial context was relevant and informative. Low-cost airlines in the summer months expect access to out-of-normal-hours facilities. The word "promote" meant something more than "market" and the contract itself had clauses that dealt separately with marketing activities. This part of clause 1 could be given the meaning of a promise by the airport to "advance" Jet2's interests. On the "best endeavours" part of the clause, the Court of Appeal divided the cases into ones which were unenforceable because the lack of objective criteria made it impossible to define what it was the parties had contracted about, and cases where the promise was detailed and capable of being given a meaning by reference to a reasonableness standard.[190] Longmore L.J. summarised his view thus:

United Group Rail Services Ltd v Rail Corporation New South Wales [2009] NSWCA 177, followed in *Emirates Trading Agency LLC v Prime Minesal Exports Private Ltd* [2014] EWHC 2104 (Comm).

[185] (1994) 70 P. & C.R. 469; *Wellington City Council v Body Corporate 51702 (Wellington) Ltd* [2002] 3 N.Z.L.R. 486; McLauchlan, 'The Justiciability of an Agreement to Negotiate in Good Faith" (2003) 20 N.Z.U.L.R. 265.

[186] (1991) 24 N.S.W.L.R. 1, cited in *Alcatel Australia v Scarcella* (1998) 44 N.S.W.L.R 349, the N.S.W.C.A. therein sanctioning the development of a broader duty of good faith.

[187] (1990) 73 D.L.R. (4th) 400; contrast *P.P. (Portage) Holdings Inc. v 346 Portage Avenue Inc.* (1999) 177 D.L.R. (4th) 359.

[188] [2002] 2 All E.R. (Comm.) 1041.

[189] [2012] EWCA Civ 417.

[190] *Jet2.com* has been cited and applied by the High Court in Northern Ireland: see *McDonald v McKenna* [2012] NI Ch 24.

"As both Moore-Bick and Lewison LJJ agree, the object of the best endeavours will always be important in deciding whether the commitment is to be legally enforceable. An agreement to use best endeavours to reach an agreement may be unenforceable as an agreement to agree as effectively held in *Little v Courage Ltd* (1995) 70 P & CR 469, but even in such a case the matter may not be completely beyond argument since a best endeavours obligation might at least be held to import an agreement to negotiate in good faith, as to which see *Petromec Inc. v Petroleo Brasiliero* [2006] 1 Lloyds's Rep 121 paras 125–121. No doubt, damages for breach of such an obligation could be problematic."

The Court of Appeal was, however, unclear about how far the person under the duty is required to go vis-à-vis prejudicing his or her own commercial interests in order to meet the "reasonable or best endeavours" obligation and it is noteworthy that the Court of Appeal agreed with the trial judge in declining to give an order clarifying the boundary between the breach and compliance. In cases of this kind this will be a difficult question, as will the issue of the most appropriate remedy. Where the complainant is seeking some form of declaratory relief, these facts may not be all that critical.

1–98 In *Lambert v HTV Cymru*,[191] the assignee of copyright in cartoon characters was contracted to "use all reasonable endeavours" to obtain future book rights for the assignor in subsequent dealings in the characters. It was held that this clause was not void for uncertainty. In *Rhodia International Holdings Ltd v Huntsman International LLC*,[192] a dispute over the obligations of parties to a novation agreement centred upon the meaning to be attached to an obligation on each party to "use reasonable endeavours" to obtain the necessary third party novation consents. It was held that the obligation to use reasonable endeavours is less onerous than an obligation to use best endeavours, and while the distinction appears to be rooted in the notion that best endeavours may require conduct that may be commercially prejudicial to the bound party (where as reasonable endeavours do not), the usefulness of *Rhodia* lies in the fact that the obligation is tagged onto a series of steps or benchmarks, which, if they are not attained, will facilitate the court in finding that the obligee has not met whatever standard is set. Most courts will seek to give a clause a purpose whenever possible.[193] But judicial activism has its limits, even if the court is willing to co-operate. In *Shaker v Vistajet Group Holding SA*,[194] a letter of intent was executed to confirm that the defendant had agreed to sell an aircraft to the plaintiff for $23 million (US). A deposit of $3.55 million was paid. The letter stated that the parties agreed to proceed in good faith and to use reasonable endeavours to execute the transaction documents

---

[191] *The Times*, March 17, 1998.
[192] [2007] 2 All E.R. (Comm.) 577, following *Jolley v Carmel Ltd* [2000] 2 E.G.L.R. 153; *Yewbelle Ltd v London Green Developments Ltd* [2007] EWCA Civ 475.
[193] *BBC Worldwide Ltd v Bee Load Ltd* [2007] EWHC 134 (Comm).
[194] [2012] EWHC 1329 (Comm).

but were not bound to execute those documents. The letter of intent provided that the deposit would be returned as long as good faith and reasonable endeavours had been demonstrated. The transaction was not completed and the defendant refused to return the deposit. Assuming that the good faith/ reasonable endeavours clause stood as a condition precedent to the return of the deposit, Teare J. held that English law does not recognise a bare contractual promise to use reasonable endeavours because there are no objective criteria by which a court can decide whether a party has acted reasonably. Similarly, a good faith obligation is unworkable as being "inherently inconsistent with the position of a negotiating party". The same barriers prevent the enforceability of a condition precedent of this kind. Teare J. went on to observe that the fact that the parties had agreed to such a condition precedent did not mean it was enforceable, as a matter of policy, driven by the difficulty of policing such a condition precedent, absent objective criteria.[195]

Other repairing techniques

1–99 Another way of trying to compel another person to conclude a deal is found in so-called lock-out agreements, that is, an agreement whereby one party agrees not to negotiate with others in relation to a proposed transaction. While these agreements are invalid if no fixed limit is set by the contract, these agreements have been held to be legally effective in other circumstances.[196] In *Triatic Ltd v Cork County Council*,[197] the plaintiffs sought to develop State-owned lands under the control of the defendants and obtained an undertaking that the defendant would "deal exclusively" with the plaintiff "in regard to the submission of a comprehensive development plan" for the lands for six months. The six-month deadline was extended for a further 12 months, but the proposals that were initially put forward were unacceptable and incomplete and eventually the defendant decided to advertise for development proposals some 30 months after commencement of the negotiations. Laffoy J., following Lord Ackner's approach in *Walford v Miles*, found that here, there was a valid "lock-out" agreement, that is, the defendant was required to negotiate any deal only with the plaintiff during this period. Laffoy J., however, found that the lock-out agreement did not require that the defendant (and indeed the plaintiff) were required to negotiate until they reached a concluded agreement. The period of negotiations in this situation were set by the defendant's initial letter and the verbal extensions; once these expired, any continuing talks were negotiations *simpliciter*. It was not necessary for Laffoy J. to rule on the questions whether the defendant could have terminated negotiations during the lock-out period if, for example, it was clear that the negotiations were unlikely to be positive or some other objectively justifiable reason came

---

[195] See *Petromec v Petroleo Brasileiro* [2006] 1 Lloyd's Rep 121, distinguished on its facts. Teare J. nevertheless recognised the force of Longmore L.J.'s dicta in that case that it is "a strong thing to declare unenforceable a clause into which the parties have deliberated, and expressly entered".

[196] *Walford v Miles* [1992] 2 A.C. 128; *Pitt v PHH Asset Management Ltd* [1993] 4 All E.R. 961.

[197] [2006] IEHC 111; *Ryan v FAS* [2015] IEHC 777.

into play, such as the subsequent insolvency of the other party. Laffoy J. also found that, on the facts, the defendant's had acted bona fide in relation to both the negotiations and the decision to re-advertise.

1–100 One way of avoiding the consequences of *Courtney & Fairbairn*, and other situations in which parties fail to reach complete agreement, is for them to create some method or machinery for resolving any disagreement. However, a general arbitration clause may be allowed to function once a contract has come into existence, but according to *May & Butcher v The King*,[198] a general clause cannot repair a failure to agree on price when the contract contemplated that price would be a matter of mutual agreement as between the parties. Section 8(1) of the Sale of Goods Act 1893 suggests a similar solution in cases where the parties to a contract for the sale of goods intended to reach agreement.

1–101 Notwithstanding *May & Butcher v The King*, many more English cases demonstrate a greater judicial willingness to find that the parties have created an enforceable contract (see, for example, *Beer v Bowden*[199]) or, alternatively, that they have done enough to allow the courts to effectively repair any defects that the agreement itself contains. The leading case is *Sudbrooke Trading Estate v Eggleton*.[200] Under the terms of a lease, the lessees were entitled to exercise an option to purchase the reversion at a valuation to be agreed by two valuers. The valuers were to be nominated, one by the lessor, the other by the lessee. In default of agreement by the valuers the price was to be settled by an umpire appointed by the valuers. The lessor refused to appoint his valuer and therefore claimed the contract was unenforceable, citing authorities for the proposition that where an agreement is incomplete because something further has to be done, the court is powerless. The House of Lords, however, by a majority of four to one resisted this contention on the ground that some decisions show that when a contract is agreed at a "fair valuation" there is an enforceable contract. Their Lordships described the machinery for valuation in the present case as a non-essential term and interpreted the clause so that the price would be a fair price. Specific performance of the agreement was decreed. In the case of *Voest Alpine Intertrading v Chevron Int Oil Co*,[201] Hirst J. went further and held that where an arbitration clause is found in the contract, and the contract has been carried into effect, the court may itself rule on what is a reasonable price for the commodity in question. However, it remains a question of interpretation whether the parties have intended the valuation to be at a fair and reasonable price. Should the arbitrator be named, or the criteria be a subjective valuation, it may not be possible to operate the *Sudbrooke* analysis, helpful though it may be. This point is made eloquently by the decision in *Lonergan v McCartney*.[202] Here, an option clause in respect of

---

[198] [1934] 2 K.B. 17n.
[199] [1981] 1 W.L.R. 522.
[200] [1982] 3 W.L.R. 315; *The Didymi* [1988] 2 Lloyd's Rep. 108.
[201] [1987] 2 Lloyd's Rep. 547.
[202] [1983] N.I. 129.

the purchase of "premises" was held void for uncertainty; the valuer could not be sure whether the valuation process was to be the full value of the premises, or the landlord's interest. Other factors influencing "value" such as renewal rights under statute and the possible relevance of the tenant's improvements made the clause unworkable in the view of Gibson L.J. However, Carswell L.J. in the later case of *North Down Hotels Ltd v Province-Wide Filling Stations Ltd*[203] was able to distinguish *Lonergan v McCartney* on the ground that Carswell L.J. was being invited to repair defective valuing machinery in respect of the reversionary interest in property and while such a process would not be easy, the issue of fixing a value was something that a competent professional would be able to resolve on objective grounds.

1–102 Murphy J. in *Bula Ltd v Tara Mines Ltd*[204] has mapped out the option that faces a court in the Republic of Ireland in relation to this issue. The dispute related to the enforceability of a co-operation clause in a mining lease, the lease containing a general arbitration clause. Murphy J. summarised the issue thus:

> "It was contended by the defendants that this clause was void for uncertainty. It was said that it was no more than an agreement to agree and that such a concept is a contradiction in terms. But the defendants went even further, relying on the decision of Lord Denning M.R. and the Court of Appeal in *Courtney & Fairbairn Ltd v Tolaini Brothers (Hotels) Ltd* [1975] 1 W.L.R. 297. They contended that the law does not recognise a contract to negotiate and adopted the language of Lloyd J. in *The 'Scaptrade'* [1981] 2 Lloyd's Rep. 425 at p.432 in the following terms:
>
>> '... for an agreement to seek a mutually acceptable conclusion is like an agreement to agree, or an agreement to negotiate. It is a thing writ in water. It confers no rights or obligations of any kind; see *Courtney Faibairn Ltd v Tolaini Bros. (Hotels) Ltd* [1975] 1 W.L.R. 297.'
>
> Moreover, the defendants in this regard can find further support from the decision in the *Cadbury Ireland Ltd* case [1982] I.L.R.M. 77 where Barrington J. found a particular clause in issue as being unenforceable because at best it involved a 'commitment to enter into honest negotiations'—see page 85.
>
> Notwithstanding the impressive arguments adduced by the defendants in this regard it does seem to me that consideration must still be given to the observations (albeit *obiter*) of Lord Wright in *Hillas & Co. Ltd v Arcos Ltd* (1932) 147 L.T. 503 at p.515 when he said:
>
>> 'There is then no bargain except to negotiate, and negotiations may be fruitless and end without any contract ensuing; yet even then,

---

203 [1993] N.I. 261.
204 [1987] I.R. 95.

in strict theory, there is a contract (if there is good consideration) to negotiate, though in the event of repudiation by one party the damages may be nominal, unless a jury think that the opportunity to negotiate was of some appreciable value to the injured party.'

This is of course the view which the Court of Appeal rejected in the *Courtney & Fairbairn Ltd* case [1975] 1 W.L.R. 297 but it does offer the bones of an argument which, as I understand it, the plaintiffs seek to couple with the arbitration clause in the present case. As I understand it it is their argument that the facts are such that reasonable negotiation would necessarily produce a viable solution and that the arbitration clause is capable of procuring reasonableness in the negotiations if duly held." [205]

Aggressive interpretation of commercial negotiations

1–103 The trend before the English courts is to interpret agreements so as to produce a positive rather than a negative interpretation, a point emphasised by Ralph Gibson L.J. in *Corson v Rhuddlan B.C.*[206] Nevertheless, even when the more liberal approach outlined by the House of Lords in *Sudbrooke*, and subsequently adopted by the Privy Council in the New Zealand case of *Money v Ven-Lu-Ree Ltd*[207] is adopted, there will still be instances where a contract cannot be pieced together. Many illustrations can be found in sale of land transactions. Failure to agree on the period for which a lease is to run will be fatal (*Lindsay v Lynch*[208]) as will failure to reach agreement on the commencement of the lease.[209] When the agreement is executory there is less likelihood of the agreement being carried into effect because there is less incentive for the courts to try and salvage an agreement than in cases where the agreement has been acted upon; see Denning M.R. in *Sykes (Wessex) Ltd v Fine Fare Ltd.*[210] Some judges support a radical approach to defeating issues of uncertainty of terms when the purported contract is set out in documentary form. Even if a chain of correspondence does not cumulatively create a clear offer and acceptance there is some support for the view that the courts may be driven to conclude that if there exists agreement on essential terms a contract should result, at least in cases where the parties have actually completed their intended project.[211] Using standard principles of construction it may be possible for an enterprising judge to prevent a contract from being void for uncertainty by using a variety of techniques. In *Covington Marin Corp v*

---

[205] [1987] I.R. 95 at 102.

[206] [1989] 59 P. & C.R. 185.

[207] [1989] 3 N.Z.L.R. 129.

[208] (1804) 2 Sch. & Lef. 1.

[209] *Kearns v Manning* [1935] I.R. 869. Failure to agree on payment of a deposit, when clearly an important matter, will also be fatal: *Boyle and Boyle v Lee and Goyns* [1992] I.L.R.M. 65.

[210] [1967] 1 Lloyd's Rep. 53; *Sri Apparal Ltd v Revolution Workwear Ltd* [2013] IEHC 289.

[211] *Clarke v Dunraven* [1897] A.C. 59; *Gibson v Manchester City Council* [1979] 1 All E.R. 972, as discussed in *Marist Bros. Community v Harvey Shire* (1994) 14 W.A.R. 69. See also *Regalian Properties Plc v London Dockland Development Corp* [1995] 1 All E.R. 1005. *Crystal Palace FC (2000) Ltd v Dowie* [2008] EWHC 240 (Q.B.).

Xiamen Shipbuilding Industry Corp,[212] a written offer setting out alternative provisions was held to have been accepted by the offeree identifying which proposed provisions the offeree wished to accept. The failure by the parties to agree on other material provisions did not prevent the contract from having an immediate existence. Langley J. held that a provision that stated that failure to agree on these matters would trigger immediate termination was not evidence and that until those terms were agreed, no contract could subsist; rather the clauses indicated that there was an agreement that was subject to a number of conditions subsequent. Langley J., however, reaffirmed the view that agreements to agree are unenforceable in English law. Even if the negotiations continue to take place, especially in the light of commercial or financial difficulties experienced, the court may hold that an agreement was reached, this being replaced by a number of later agreements which vary or replace the earlier contract.[213]

1–104 Even if the agreement is void for uncertainty there is the possibility that any work done, on request, by one party for another, will have to be paid for on the basis of *quantum meruit*. In England this is recognised by *British Steel Corp v Cleveland Bridge and Engineering Co Ltd*[214] and the Irish case of *Folens v Minister for Education*[215] provides clear support in Ireland for this basic principle of quasi-contract, or restitution.

1–105 These difficult issues of formation were examined by the English Court of Appeal in *Mamidoil-Jetoil Greek Petroleum Co S.A. v Okta Crude Oil Refinery A.D.*[216] Jetoil contracted with Okta under a 1993 agreement, placing its crude oil with Okta for processing. The agreement was carried out until 1998 when Okta was acquired by a Jetoil facility at Okta. The argument that succeeded at trial was that of two inconsistent clauses, one of which required a handling fee to be renegotiated after the end of 1994, the other stating the contract was for a 10-year-period, the failure to negotiate the handling fee meant that the contract was void for uncertainty.[217] After an exhaustive review of the authorities, the Court of Appeal set forward the following approach to issues of uncertainty:

> "Each case must be decided on its own facts and on the construction of
> its own agreement. Subject to that:

---

[212] [2006] 1 Lloyd's Rep. 745; *Stewart v Stewart Estate* (2005) 239 N.S.R. (2d) 187; *Mitsui Babcock Energy Ltd v John Brown Engineering* (1996) 51 Con. L.R. 129.
[213] *Sydenhams (Timber Engineering) v CHG Holdings* (2007) 112 Con. L.R. 49.
[214] [1984] 1 All E.R. 504. *Hescorp Italia SpA v Morrison Construction Ltd* (2000) 75 Con. L.R. 51; *Countrywide Communications Ltd v Pathway Ltd* [2000] C.L.C. 324. *Whittle Movers Ltd v Hollywood Express Ltd* [2009] EWCA Civ 1189; *RTS Flexible Systems Ltd v Molkerei Alois Miller GmbH* [2010] UKSC 14.
[215] [1984] I.L.R.M. 265; contrast *Malcolm v University of Oxford* [1994] E.M.L.R. 17.
[216] [2001] 2 Lloyd's Rep. 76.
[217] Note the use of an implied term in *Mamidoil*, per Rix L.J. at 92 on the reasonable fee issue.

'to be agreed' in relation to an essential term is likely to prevent any contract coming into existence, on the ground of uncertainty. This may be summed up by the principle that 'you cannot agree to agree'. Similarly, where no contract exists, the absence of agreement on essential terms of the agreement may prevent any contract coming into existence, again on the ground of uncertainty.

However, particularly in commercial dealings between parties who are familiar with the trade in question, and particularly where the parties have acted in the belief that they had a binding contract, the courts are willing to imply terms, where that is possible, to enable the contract to be carried out.

Where a contract has once come into existence, even the expression 'to be agreed' in relation to future executory obligations is not necessarily fatal to its continued existence.

Particularly in the case of contracts for future performance over a period, where the parties may desire or need to leave matters to be adjusted in the working out of their contract, the courts will assist the parties to do so, so as to preserve rather than destroy bargains, on the basis that what can be certain is itself certain. *Centum est quod certum redid potest.*

This is particularly the case where one party has either already had the advantage of some performance which reflects the parties' agreement on a long-term relationship, or has had to make an investment premised on that agreement.

For these purposes, an express stipulation for a reasonable or fair measure or price will be a sufficient criterion for the courts to act on. But even in the absence of express language, the courts are prepared to imply an obligation in terms of what is reasonable.

Such implications are reflected but not exhausted by the statutory provision for the implication of a reasonable price ... in ... the Sale of Goods Act ...

The presence of an arbitration clause may assist the courts to hold a contract to be sufficiently certain or to be capable of being rendered so, presumably as indicating a commercial and contractual mechanism, which can be operated with the assistance of experts in the field, by which the parties, in the absence of agreement, may resolve their dispute."[218]

Applying these principles to the case at bar, the Court of Appeal noted that the contract had subsisted for almost 10 years. The contract contained an arbitration clause, which was undoubtedly of a commercial character, that the parties had a long-established familiarity with each other and with the commercial

---

[218] Per Rix L.J. at 89–90, Waterhouse J. and Schiemann L.J. agreeing. See also *MRI Trading AG v Erdnet Mining Corporation LLC* [2013] EWCA Civ 156 on the use of Rix L.J.'s guidelines. In *Simms Construction Ltd v GR Homes Ltd* [2012] NIQB 73 Coughlin L.J. endorsed them as affording solutions in a complex construction dispute.

arrangements, as between themselves. A critical fact was that the handling fee had been agreed over the years. In essence, the Court of Appeal held that even if there was a difficulty in agreeing the handling fee, an English court would intervene and fix the fee for the parties if sufficient objective criteria were in place in order for the court to do so.[219] The owners of Okta were thus obliged to pay Jetoil a reasonable price for oil processing for the remainder of the contract period.[220] Nevertheless, there are cases where the courts will decline the invitation to take on the task of repairing defective agreements. If there is, for example, a clause which requires the property to be valued by "an independent chartered accountant" and it is clear that this is intended to be an essential term in the contract, the essential term must be observed,[221] so *May & Butcher Ltd v The King* is not entirely devoid of authority. In *Willis Management (Isle of Man) Ltd v Cable and Wireless Plc*,[222] employees of Willis were implicated in fraudulent practices that were prejudicial to Cable and Wireless. In order to avoid being joined in proceedings, Willis negotiated an understanding that he would contribute towards sharing responsibility for Cable and Wireless' losses, the Willis lawyer making it clear that Willis would pay its share and this would be discussed by all the parties in good faith. At first instance the agreement was held to constitute an agreement to pay a fair share. The Court of Appeal disagreed, finding that there was no unqualified commitment by Willis to pay a fair share. The parties were to discuss the issue of what would be a fair share and agree accordingly. This was a different matter to a bare agreement to pay a fair share of Cable and Wireless' losses. In the latter case the court could fix the sum in question, but in the first case the parties had reserved this function for themselves; Rix L.J. specifically distinguished the situation in *Willis* from *Mamidoil*.

"Subject to Contract"

1–106 Where two persons seemingly conclude negotiations for the sale of land either or both of them may wish to protect themselves by stipulating that in certain instances the agreement will not be binding. The owner may want to reserve for himself the right to accept a better offer, for example; the purchaser, on the other hand, may want to ensure that he has the money to pay for the property and permit himself to withdraw without being liable for breach of contract. Each could stipulate that agreement is conditional on such and such an eventuality. In *O'Mullane v Riordan*,[223] the purchaser agreed to buy subject to planning permission being obtained. In such cases until planning

---

[219] See [2001] 2 Lloyd's Rep. 76 at 91(vi).
[220] For subsequent proceedings on a *force majeure* argument, see [2003] 1 Lloyd's Rep 1.
[221] *Gillat v Sky Television* [2000] 1 All E.R. (Comm.) 461; contrast *Re Malpass* [1985] Ch. 42. In *Gillat* "open market value" was said to cover a number of methodologies; see p.473 of the judgment.
[222] [2005] 2 Lloyd's Rep. 597; *United Guild Developments Ltd v Iskandar* (2007) 254 N.S.R. (2d) 263.
[223] Unreported, High Court, April 20, 1978.

permission is given the contract is said to exist but it is unenforceable. If planning permission is not given the purchaser is not bound to purchase but he can waive this term (if property values have risen he may do this) at which point the contract becomes enforceable.[224]

1–107 Instead of inserting a specific stipulation into the contract, lawyers, estate agents and others may use the expression, "subject to contract". This formula has been interpreted to mean that until the formal contract is signed by both parties (the normal Irish practice), or until contracts are exchanged (the conventional practice in England), no contract of sale exists.[225] The English authorities are summarised by Lord Denning in the leading case thus: "[t]he effect of the words 'subject to contract' is that the matter remains in negotiation until a formal contract is executed."[226]

1–108 The Irish courts have also ruled that if the phrase is used by the parties during negotiations then there is no contract until exchange of contracts or signature by both parties takes place. The leading Irish case is *Thompson v The King*.[227] After a series of offers, rejections and counter-offers, the plaintiff received a telegram from the defendant stating "will accept subject to contract … £24,200 for Waterford factory". Three days later the plaintiff responded by telegram "we accept your offer … at £24,200". The negotiations then broke down and the plaintiff sought specific performance of the contract, which the plaintiff contended had been formed following this exchange of telegrams. After considering the effect of the words "subject to contract", the Kings Bench Divisional Court held that there was no concluded contract. The words used and surrounding circumstances deferred the contractual obligation until a formal contract was settled, accepted and executed (per Gibson J.). This was not a case where the parties intended there and then to be bound, the further contract only being a matter of form which did not pre-empt a finding of contractual intention.

1–109 While the "subject to contract" usage generally developed to protect purchasers from entering into "open", legally binding contracts, *Thompson v The King* illustrates the point that the usage can be utilised by either party. It follows, therefore, that if a property owner offers to sell "subject to contract", "acceptance" by the offeree will simply mark a step in the march towards a binding contract. If the offeree, on the other hand, introduces the term "subject to contract", his response is not a counter-offer requiring the offeror to respond,

---

[224] *Malone v Elf Investments*, unreported, High Court, December 7, 1979.

[225] In real property transactions the exchange of contracts will not, when the court is not persuaded that a concluded contract exists, bring a contract into existence: *Embourg Ltd v Tyler Group* [1996] 3 I.R. 480; *Greenband Investments v Bruton* [2009] IEHC 67. In Northern Ireland, see *Hamilton v Judge* [2010] NICA 49.

[226] *Tiverton Estates Ltd v Wearwell* [1975] Ch. 146.

[227] [1920] 2 I.R. 365; *BBS Merchandising v Urban Regeneration Agency* [2006] EWHC 2754 (Ch).

but of course the point is of little importance given that either party can refuse to proceed.

1–110 There are important differences between the Irish and English cases on the question of "subject to contract" agreements. First, suppose the words are added by the solicitor for the purchaser in a letter "confirming" that agreement has been reached "subject to contract". Suppose also neither the vendor nor the purchaser used the words when he was discussing details of the sale. Under English law the "subject to contract" letter cannot satisfy the statute requiring a memorandum in writing evidencing the agreement. The Irish courts, in contrast, have permitted the vendor to introduce parol evidence to show that oral agreement was reached. The letter containing the "subject to contract" phrase will not be allowed to operate because it was added after the oral agreement had been struck. This important difference between the English and Irish position was established by *O'Flaherty v Arvan Property*[228] and *Casey v Irish Intercontinental Bank*.[229] In the *O'Flaherty* case, the purchasers of property were handed a receipt for the deposit which contained all the material terms, adding "subject to contract". The plaintiffs successfully argued that at the time of negotiation nothing was said about the sale being "subject to contract". McWilliam J. ordered that the sale be completed. This decision meant that Irish solicitors, auctioneers and others could not rely on this phrase to protect their clients if they attempted to add the "subject to contract" formula after oral negotiations between the principals had ended, the principals having themselves failed to use the phrase. Secondly, there is Irish authority for the view that the phrase "subject to contract" may be ignored if, within the context of the contract in question, it is a meaningless phrase. The decision of the Supreme Court in *Kelly v Park Hall Schools*[230] proved to be a controversial one and it may rest on its own particular facts. Nevertheless, the Supreme Court in that case was prepared to scrutinise the negotiations to see if all the terms had been settled and, if so, "subject to contract" added in any letter was to be treated as if it were an ambiguous or meaningless phrase. In the Supreme Court case of *McCarthy v O'Neill*,[231] Henchy J. said "subject to contract" normally means that "a full contract" has yet to be agreed, which, in the author's view, is a mistaken interpretation of the older cases.

1–111 There are several subsequent High Court cases which reassert the orthodox view, namely, that "subject to contract" agreements cannot be enforced simply by admitting parol testimony about the circumstances surrounding the bargain. The *Tiverton* case has been followed by Keane J. in

---

[228] Unreported, High Court, November 3, 1976. While the Supreme Court overruled McWilliam J. in a judgment delivered on July 21, 1977, this point was not at issue.
[229] [1979] I.R. 364; for an interesting follow-up case, see *Park Hall School Ltd v Overend* [1987] I.R. 1.
[230] [1979] I.R. 340.
[231] [1981] I.L.R.M. 443.

Mulhall v Haren[232] and in *Dorene Ltd v Suedes (Ireland) Ltd.*[233] Costello J. held that a "subject to contract" acceptance meant that the parties were still in negotiation; "... there was no legally binding agreement". Indeed, in the Circuit Court case of *Cunningham v Maher*,[234] Judge Sheridan, after describing the "quite bewildering number of recent Irish cases touching upon the question arising out of oral agreements made subject to contract", held that, faced with a set of irreconcilable authorities, he preferred to follow *Tiverton* and *Mulhall v Haren*.

1–112 The Supreme Court, in *Boyle and Boyle v Lee and Goyns*,[235] has reconsidered *Kelly v Park Hall School* and *Casey v Irish Intercontinental Bank*. The soundness of both cases was doubted by Finlay C.J., Hederman J. concurring, and by McCarthy J. These judges observed that, insofar as *Kelly* contemplated the introduction of parol evidence to gainsay the "subject to contract" correspondence, it should not be followed, and similar observations were made about the decision in *Casey*. O'Flaherty J. observed that both *Kelly* and *Casey* turned on their own special facts.[236] Thus, it seems the Supreme Court, having approved of both *Tiverton* and Keane J.'s masterly review of the law in *Mulhall v Haren*, has brought Irish law back into the fold of orthodoxy.

1–113 Only in the most exceptional cases will "subject to contract" be ignored. If the words appear by mistake (*Michael Richards Properties v Corporation of Wardens of St. Saviours, Southwark*[237]) and do not reflect the intention of the parties (see *Guardian Builders Ltd v Patrick Kelly*[238]) they will be ignored. If, on the true construction of the contract, the words were not intended to render the agreement still under negotiation, a binding contract will be upheld, as in the English case of *Alpenstow Ltd v Regalian Properties Ltd.*[239] In that case the "subject to contract" formula was held irreconcilable with an express obligation to close the sale within a stipulated period. One problem that may arise because of the considerable delay that can occur before completion of a real property transaction arose in *Tevanan v Norman Brett (Builders) Ltd.*[240] Suppose the parties reach an agreement which is labelled "subject to contract". Some time later the agreement is replaced by another, which is not stated to be "subject to contract". The general position will be that the two agreements will

---

[232] [1981] I.R. 364.

[233] [1981] I.R. 312.

[234] Unreported, Circuit Court, March 1983.

[235] [1992] I.L.R.M. 65.

[236] Egan J. did not consider the "subject to contract" issue in detail, but the learned judge approved of both *Tiverton* and *Mulhall v Haren*.

[237] [1975] 3 All E.R. 416.

[238] Unreported, High Court, March 31, 1981.

[239] [1985] 1 W.L.R. 721.

[240] (1972) 223 E.G. 1945; *Sherbroke v Dipple* (1980) 225 E.G. 1203. While "without prejudice" negotiations may need to be viewed within the factual matrix and are thus not as compelling as "subject to contract", there are cases where the use of that phrase will prevent an enforceable contract from coming into existence until all terms are agreed with all parties: *Globe Entertainments Ltd v The Pub Pool Ltd (In Receivership)* [2015] IEHC 115.

generally be governed by the "subject to contract" stipulation unless the later agreement is expressly or impliedly nullified.

Where "subject to contract" is not used in negotiations

1–114 Usages similar to a "subject to contract" stipulation have evolved elsewhere. In relation to charter party agreements, it is common for negotiations to be concluded in a variety of ways, one of which might consist of an agreement "subject to details" or on the foot of an agreement listing makers that require further discussion and the conclusion of negotiations. In *The Lisheen Mine v Mullock and Sons (Shipbrokers) Ltd*[241] Cregan J. held that an exchange of emails that identified agreed terms but was headed as being "subject to details" had the same effect in Irish law as the usage has in English law: no agreement exists until there exists a concluded charterparty agreement (preferably in the form of a written contract in standard form). Cregan J. noted that "subject to details" agreements had the same effect as a "subject to contract" stipulation. The "subject to contract" usage is simply a convenient and shorthand method of indicating that the agreement is not to have legal effect until signature of the contract (or an exchange of contracts) takes place. There are other ways of negating contractual effect. In *Brien v Swainson*,[242] the cases were said by Chatterton V.C. to divide into two classes:

> "First, where there is a complete agreement signed by the parties containing their actual contract. If there be a concluded agreement, it will be specifically enforced, though by its terms it contemplates some more formal contract being entered into. The other class is where the terms are to a greater or lesser extent contained in a duly signed writing, but expressed in that writing to be liable to be modified or added to, by a future contract then in the contemplation of the parties."[243]

If the "subject to contract" formula is not used the correspondence may make it quite clear that only upon exchange of contracts in some form will a contract come into existence; see *Kelly v Irish Landscape Nursery*.[244] The courts will honour such an intent. The exact meaning of such a conditional statement is a matter of interpretation. In the case of *Irish Mainport Holdings Ltd v Crosshaven Sailing Centre Ltd*,[245] the words "my Board have agreed in principle" were held not to prevent a concluded agreement coming into existence. Keane J. held these words could not be equated with the words "subject to contract".

---

[241] [2015] IEHC 50.
[242] (1877) 1 L.R. (Ir.) 135.
[243] (1877) 1 L.R. (Ir.) 135 at 139–140.
[244] [1981] I.L.R.M. 433.
[245] Unreported, High Court, October 14, 1980. *Rossiter v Miller* (1878) 3 App. Cas. 1124; *Harvey Shopfitters Ltd v ADI Ltd* [2003] 2 All E.R. 982; *Bryen & Langley v Boston* [2005] B.L.R. 508; *Mi-Space (UK) Ltd v Bridgewater Civil Engineering Ltd* [2015] EWHC 3360 (TCC).

1–115 The contrasting decision of Keane J. in *Silver Wraith Ltd v Siúicre Éireann cpt*[246] provides a most useful illustration of this process of interpretation. The defendants wrote, "the following terms are acceptable subject to full lease being agreed". The letter went on to set out the terms. In considering whether this constituted evidence of a concluded agreement between the parties, Keane J. noted that the question was what the phrase used suggested in relation to the contracting state of mind of the parties. Keane J. noted that here the phrase made the existence of a full lease a condition of the agreement. The defendants were lay persons, not qualified lawyers, and they could not be expected to be legally bound to a complex lease transaction of the kind anticipated, without resorting to legal advice and assistance.

1–116 Although the phrase will normally be encountered in land contracts, the "subject to contract" usage has been found to be part of general commercial practice and its effect has similar consequences: a "subject to contract" offer prevents the communication from being an offer. However, unlike land contracts, the "subject to contract" stipulation can be overridden by less formal means—no written contract executed by the parties is required. In *Confetti Records v Warner Music UK Ltd,*[247] "subject to contract" negotiations to sample a sound recording were followed by the despatch of a CD containing the music and an invoice; Lewison J. held that this was an offer from the putative licensor that was accepted by conduct.[248]

1–117 In *RTS Flexible Systems Ltd v Molkerei Alois Müller GmbH,*[249] a written term in a construction contract that required both parties to execute a written contract was treated as a "subject to contract" clause, the UK Supreme Court taking a pragmatic view because, in Lord Clarke's words:

> "[A]ny other conclusions makes no commercial sense. RTS could surely not have refused to perform the contract as varied pending a formal contract being signed and exchanged … if one applies the standard of the reasonable honest businessman suggested by Steyn J. [in *Percy Trentham*] … he would have concluded that the parties intended that the work be carried out for the agreed price on the agreed terms, including the terms as varied … without the necessity for a formal written agreement which had been overtaken by events."

---

[246] Unreported, High Court, June 8, 1989.
[247] [2003] E.C.D.R. 336; in computer contracts this usage is less common; see Chapman [2004] C.T.L.R. 141. In relation to patent licences, see *QR Licences Ltd v BTG International Ltd* [2005] F.S.R. 909.
[248] Lewison J. also held that an estoppel operated against the owner of copyright in the music.
[249] [2010] UKSC 14; *Biebers v Teathers* [2014] EWHC 4205 (Ch).

Gazumping

1–118 Conveyancing practice in both England and Ireland can leave the purchaser at the mercy of the vendor in a rising market. The long interval which can sometimes occur between a "subject to contract" agreement being struck, and contracts being sent out (much less signed) may give rise to temptation for the vendor in the form of subsequent higher offers. A debate has opened in England about ways of reducing this temptation by making much of the preparatory conveyancing material available at the time the property is put up for sale, thus speeding up the process. Some commentators favour adoption of Scottish conveyancing practices where steps of this kind are the norm. In Ireland, particularly within the Dublin area, there is widespread concern about the re-emergence of gazumping, particularly in relation to a number of well-publicised accounts in which first-time buyers in particular have put "booking deposits" down for a house in a new development but have not signed a contract. When at a later stage the process has moved on to putting the arrangement on a contractual footing, these purchasers have sometimes found the price has been raised by the developer—in one case from £69,000 to £89,000 within a nine-month period.[250] An unsuccessful Fine Gael Private Members' Bill, the Home Purchasers (Anti-Gazumping) Bill 1998,[251] sought to address problems of this kind by making the payment of a booking deposit by the purchaser of residential property an event which was to trigger a number of legal obligations for a vendor. Delivery of a contract and supporting documents to the purchaser must take place within 14 days of payment, and for a further 14 days of receipt of those documents the vendor is precluded from selling the property to a third party. Should the purchaser sign the contract and return it along with a sum of money that brings the payments received by the vendor up to 10 per cent of the purchase price, this will conclude the contract of purchase, and only on default by the purchaser at the end of this 14-day grace period may the vendor sell the property to a third party. The booking deposit must, however, be returned. This proposal sought to address a specific problem but through the criminal law and this was widely regarded as an unacceptable aspect of the legislative proposal. Nor did the proposal have much to do with "subject to contract" agreements where no deposit is paid, and some professional bodies such as the Irish Auctioneers and Valuers Institute suggested[252] other solutions, such as making the issuing of a contract by a vendor legally binding if returned by a purchaser without significant alteration within two weeks. It is not clear to this writer how such a proposal would have significantly improved matters, for the difficulty often arises simply because documents may issue from the vendor somewhat tardily, if at all. Conveyancing practice itself cannot always be adjusted to make up for the

---

250 See "Order restrains company from selling house", *The Irish Times*, July 21, 1998.
251 Hayes, "The Home Purchasers (Anti-Gazumping) Bill 1998" (1998) 3(3) C.P.L.J. 48.
252 "Auctioneers' body suggests law change", *The Irish Times*, July 29, 1998.

frailty of human nature.[253] The Law Reform Commission, in a 1999 Report,[254] reviewed the "subject to contract" usage in the light of these developments. A number of possible reforms were considered, including legislation to make booking deposits the basis of a legally enforceable contract. This proposal was rejected as being legally impractical and doubtful in terms of the Constitution. A further approach canvassed by the Law Reform Commission was the possibility that, in cases of gazumping, the disappointed party should be able to obtain damages to compensate for out-of-pocket expenses but this option was rejected on the ground that this would not provide a satisfactory solution to the problem.[255] The Law Reform Commission came out against any legislative response to gazumping by recommending that purchasers be made better aware of the legal consequences of the booking deposit system. The Law Reform Commission also suggested that a statutory form of deposit receipt be devised, failure to comply being a breach of criminal law. The basic difficulty for the Law Reform Commission was in trying to find a remedy in respect of the abuse of a contractual practice that, of its nature, is generally of strong practical value for a purchaser, and it was felt that any reform would only make matters worse.

1–119 There are occasions on which politicians put forward proposals for anti-gazumping legislation or Dáil motions calling for national housing policies to protect consumers in this sphere of property law.[256] However, the Land and Conveyancing Law Reform Act 2009 has not addressed this question and given the limited number of property sales since the property market collapsed after 2008, the gazumping issue is not currently a matter of any general concern.

---

[253] Wylie, *Conveyancing Law*, 3rd edn (Dublin: Butterworths, 2005).

[254] *Report on Gazumping* (LRC 59–1999).

[255] The possibility that damages for expectation loss could be awarded was also rejected on the ground that such a new tort would engender considerable uncertainty on issues relating to quantum, but more particularly, this tort would undermine the law of contract.

[256] e.g. Home Purchasers (Anti-Gazumping) Bill 1998: see a Dáil Supplementary Order Paper with a proposal in the name of several Labour deputies, dated November 21, 2006.

2 The Doctrine of Consideration

Introduction

2–01 If it is clear that one party has made a promise to another person who in turn has assented to it, to the knowledge of the promisor, there is at first sight no reason why the Irish courts should refuse to enforce the promise. Yet this would make all promises enforceable and legal historians have pointed out that no legal system has enforced a promise simply upon proof that it was made.

2–02 The English common law recognised a promise to be enforceable if the promisee provided something in exchange for the promise—a *quid pro quo*—or if the promise was contained in a deed under seal. The first route to enforcement helps form the basis of the modern doctrine of consideration. The alternative, obtaining the assent of the promisor to a deed under seal, is not as difficult or technical as it sounds. Once the seal is affixed (and this is often done by placing a red sticker on the paper or simply drawing a circle with L.S. stamped on it) the deed takes effect on delivery. In this context the word "delivery" is interpreted very liberally; see the leading Irish case of *Evans v Gray*.[1] It seems that the promisor does not even have to sign the document. A solemn verbal declaration that "I deliver this as my act and deed" traditionally sufficed.[2] The law relating to the use of sealed documents as a means of transferring property or enforceable obligations has been reviewed by the Supreme Court of Canada in *Friedmann Equity Developments Inc. v Final Note Ltd*.[3] In this case the court declined to strike down what the court described as "the sealed contract rule" as anachronistic, holding that it continues to prove useful in several respects. In particular, in the *Friedmann* case the rule ensures that liability is restricted by the party sealing the deed to those persons named in the deed. Furthermore, once the promise is recorded in a deed under seal, extrinsic evidence is only admissible if the deed is itself ambiguous; see *Romaine Estate v Romaine*.[4] Whether the instrument is a deed under seal and operative, as such, depends ultimately on whether the matter of the instrument intended to execute it under seal and make it a deed; even novel seals such as a soot mark or a finger impression may as a matter of law be valid, but such radical departures from standard sealing practices are likely to raise the issue

---

[1] (1882) 9 L.R. (Ir.) 539; *Bolton MBC v Torkington* [2004] 3 All E.R. 411.
[2] See Law Reform Commission of British Columbia, *Report on Deeds and Seals* (1988) at 6: "The seal at that time (early 14th century) was merely a means of 'signing' used by a person who was illiterate … the royal courts required that agreements be in writing and 'signed' by using the seal."
[3] (2000) 188 D.L.R. (4th) 269.
[4] (2001) 205 D.L.R. (4th) 321.

of determining the maker's intention.[5] These and other benefits of adopting "the sealed contract rule" are, however, not as important as the fact that once the sealing requirements are met the seal becomes a symbol that the promise was seriously meant: the need for consideration is thus dispensed with. Deeds under seal are mostly used in family or partnership transactions.[6] In *Drimmie v Davies*[7] two partners exchanged promises and recorded these promises in a deed under seal. The Irish Court of Appeal held that adopting this form made it unnecessary to decide if consideration was present. The boundaries between customary practices that continue out of inertia—"we have always done it this way"—and mandatory requirements are ill-drawn. Where the transaction involves the purchase of land and or an interest in land[8] the law requires that a deed be drawn up as this is the only way of creating or conveying a legal estate or interest in land; Land and Conveyancing Law Reform Act 2009 (the "2009 Act") ss.62 and 63. Many of the requirements in relation to deeds and the need for the sealing of documents are both unclear and anachronistic and s.64 of the 2009 Act makes a number of welcome adjustments to the law, based in the main on the Law Reform Commission's Report from 1998.[9] Rules on sealing and authority to deliver a deed, by deed are abolished. In normal business practice people do not execute deeds under seal; so if a promise is enforceable the promisee must show that he has provided consideration in exchange for the promise. It is through the doctrine of consideration that the common law identifies promises that are to be enforced simply because they have been made. At the heart of the doctrine of consideration is the idea of mutuality of obligation but, as the authors of *Corbin on Contracts* declare, the notion of mutuality can be vague:

> "Mutuality of obligation should be used solely to express the idea that each party is under a legal duty to the other; each has made a promise and each is an obliger. This is the meaning with which the term is commonly used. There are cases, however, in which it is otherwise defined. In order to save the supposed requirement of 'mutuality' it is

---

5 Hoat, "The Sealing of Documents—Fact or Fiction" (1980) 43(4) M.L.R. 415; Fridman (2002) 81 Can. B.R. 219. On the overlap between enduring powers of attorney and contracts see the recent Tasmanian Case of *Lincolne v Williams* [2008] 18 Tas. R. 76.

6 But for an example of where a deed under seal was intended in a commercial contract, see *Galliard Homes Ltd v J. Jarvis* (1999) 71 Con. L.R. 219. Even if a promise is executed in a deed, there may be circumstances where the promisee may wish to establish consideration was provided in order to avail of a range of equitable remedies by sidestepping the equitable maxim that equity will not come to the aid of a volunteer: see *Dome Resources NL v Silver* [2008] NSWCA 322.

7 [1899] 1 I.R. 176 at 186. Even when a deed is executed, courts will have little difficulty in establishing the existence of consideration as a matter of fact: *Bank of Scotland v Foster* [2014] NICA 18.

8 Apart from the conveyances themselves there is often a spillover effect. Related transactions such as debentures secured on land, chattel mortgages etc. are commonly executed by deed, with or without a seal, whether a mandatory statutory requirement or not. See now s.64 of the 2009 Act.

9 *Report on Land Law and Conveyancing Law* (LRC 56-1998). On the demise of the seal in Irish law see Woods (2014) 53 Ir. Jur. 190.

sometimes declared that it means nothing more than that there must be a sufficient consideration. Even though one of the parties has made no promise and is bound by no duty, the contract has sufficient mutuality if he has given an executed consideration."[10]

The consideration doctrine is at times ambiguous; in the above extract *Corbin* is contrasting the classical exchange model with situations where one person makes a promise—the unilateral contract—and, because it is foreseeable that the promisee will rely on the promise, that promise may itself be binding. This will be particularly so if the promise contains a request that the person or persons to whom the promise is addressed do some act stipulated by the promisor; see *Carlill v Carbolic Smoke Ball Co*.[11] But commercial convenience has also led the courts to hold that an implied request may be attributed to the promisor (or, to put it another way, the person addressed has impliedly promised to do or abstain from doing something) and in such cases the promise will be held binding upon proof that the promise caused the other party to provide an executed consideration; see *Commodity Broking Co v Meehan*[12] discussed below. Perhaps the most striking examples of the limits of the consideration requirement appear in cases where a charitable donation is requested and promised but the donor is unable to honour this promise. Can the donee raise the promise to the status of a binding contractual undertaking? Two Canadian cases, *Dalhousie College v Boutilier Estate*,[13] as recently applied in *Brentford General Hospital Foundation v Canada Trust Co*,[14] suggest that a court will be unwilling to infer a contract in the absence of some request being made by the donee. In the *Brentford* case funding cutbacks by a provincial government led the Brentford Hospital authorities to fundraise amongst its benefactors. One philanthropist, Mrs Marquis promised to give $1 million. The hospital suggested that it would name the critical care unit after herself and her husband. Mrs Marquis died having made a donation of $200,000. The estate was held not liable in contract to pay the balance. The donee had not bartered for the critical care unit to be named after her. Consideration would have been present if she had stipulated that her donation was contingent upon the dedication of the unit to herself and her husband. The surrounding circumstances did not suggest any implied request or understanding existed from which the court could infer the presence of consideration.

2–03 The common law and the insistence on utilising an external test of contractual intention, the doctrine of consideration, stands in marked contrast with the position of most other legal systems which do not require an additional

---

[10] Section 152.
[11] [1893] 1 Q.B. 256.
[12] [1985] I.R. 12.
[13] [1934] 3 D.L.R. 593.
[14] (2003) 67 O.R. (3d) 432. The process of inferring the presence of consideration may make the promise enforceable in contract but other difficulties may remain. The court may have to determine issues other than the existence of a contract and consideration such as whether the transfer is a gift or a bailment; *Day v Harris* [2013] EWCA Civ 191.

substantive element before holding a promise to be enforceable. For many other legal systems the question whether a promise is enforceable is answered by the test of whether there was a deliberate and voluntary undertaking by the promisor. The law of Scotland, for example, adopts such a position but many promises must be formally reduced into writing, and in Scotland and elsewhere a writing requirement is often insisted upon as a measure of the promisor's intention to be bound by the promise. Critics of the common law system point out that if other legal systems can function without the consideration requirement the common law should be revised. The attacks on the bargain model of consideration in particular come from a variety of philosophical positions and, as such, these commentators point out that the bargain model lacks historical legitimacy, is conceptually uncertain, and fails to explain a diverse body of case law that throws up exceptions and qualifications to the bargain model, exceptions that make the bargain a quite inaccurate means of explaining why and when a promise is enforceable as a contract.[15]

2–04 In general, however, the doctrine of consideration enables the courts to discriminate between promises that are enforceable as contracts and promises that may be binding through some other legal concept. For example, if I promise to give my car to X the promise alone cannot lead to X successfully suing for delivery. X has provided nothing for my promise. Suppose I deliver the car to X. My action will make it difficult if not impossible for me to recover the vehicle but it is the transfer of possession allied with my gratuitous promise that makes it impossible to recover the vehicle. Even so, there is still no contract. I have made a promise but the promise is to be seen as a promise of a gift. Until delivery of the promised item the promisee has no right to performance, merely a hope or expectation which the courts will not, of itself, realise for the promisee. Suppose, however, I promise to give my car to the first person to pay or offer to pay €500 for it. Here the promise has an entirely different quality. My promise is allied to a request: I stipulate that in return for my promise I require something to be done in exchange. On performance of the act, or when performance is promised, a bargain springs into existence. The opening sentence to this book drew attention to bargain as the primary characteristic of a contract; it is through the doctrine of consideration that the distinctive features of the common law model of contract take shape. A striking illustration of the difference between motive and exchange is afforded by the controversial English case of *Taylor v Dickens*.[16] Here an elderly lady promised that she would leave her house to the plaintiff who was her part-time gardener. The plaintiff later indicated that he would not take payment for his gardening services. It was held that there was no contract, the court observing that there "was no offer, no acceptance, no exchange of promises, no mutually binding obligations".

---

[15] e.g. Fried, *Contract as Promise* (Cambridge, Mass.: Harvard University Press, 1981); Atiyah, *Essays on Contract* (Oxford: Clarendon, 1986); Wright, "Ought the doctrine of Consideration to be abolished from the Common Law?" (1936) 49 Harv. L.R. 1225; and McFarlane and Sales, "Promises, Detriment and Liability: Lessons from Proprietary Estoppel" (2015) 131 L.Q.R. 610.

[16] [1998] 3 F.L.R. 455; heavily criticised in *Gillett v Holt* [2000] 2 All E.R. 289 to the extent that it must be regarded as overruled on the estoppel issue at least.

2–05 The best definition of consideration is that of Sir Frederick Pollock who argued that consideration is the price a promisee pays in return for a promise.

> "An act or forbearance of the one party, or the promise thereof, is the price for which the promise of the other is bought, and the promise thus given for value is enforceable."

In commenting on this definition in a famous article,[17] Lord Wright indicated that this definition stresses that the act or forbearance must first be of value, something which in a materialistic sense can be given a price by the courts. The act or forbearance must also be purchased:

> "[I]t is done or suffered by the one party at the request of the other: it is a matter of mutuality, not a motive or emotion of affection, benevolence bounty or charity which from their nature must be personal to the promisor … the test of contractual intention is thus external, objective, realistic."[18]

Conventional case law affirms that the orthodox view of consideration retains its essential vitality. Where one party bargains for a promise which is given and it is evident that the promise is of value to the promisee, in most cases the law will also regard the promised exchange as creating a contract in the absence of some compelling policy to the contrary; *O'Keeffe v Ryanair Holdings Plc*.[19] Nevertheless the courts will retain the power to rule that a promised exchange does not have value in the eyes of the law, as in the unusual case of *O'Neill v Murphy*[20] when it was held that parish building undertaken as part of an exchange in which the consideration moving from the parish was the saying of prayers for the benefit of the builder and his family, was held not to be a good and valuable consideration in the eyes of the law. Conventional case law in Ireland also requires the element of mutuality referred to by Lord Wright if a promise is to be contractually enforceable: it is not, as the law in Ireland currently stands, possible to enforce one promise as a contract simply by showing that but for the promise of another the promisee would have followed a course of conduct which would have been different to that followed as a result of the promise. This point can be made clear by a simple example.

2–06 I promise X that on her birthday next week I will give her my car. My promise is conditional on her reaching her next birthday. However, my failure to honour the promise will not be actionable because it is simply a promise to

---

17 Wright (1936) 49 Harv. L.R. 1225.
18 Wright (1936) 49 Harv. L.R. 1225 at 1227. On the distinction between motive and promise see *Thomas v Thomas* (1842) 2 Q.B. 851. In *Akazawa v Firestone and Firestone* [1992] I.L.R.M. 31, Morris J. found that a written promise was unenforceable for want of consideration: "it was a voluntary document given by Mr Firestone in the hope of cementing business relationships"; [1992] I.L.R.M. 31 at 48.
19 [2003] 1 I.L.R.M. 14 at 25.
20 [1936] N.I. 16; *Allied Irish Banks Plc v Fagan*, unreported, High Court, November 10, 1995.

make a gift. Suppose X now informs me that she has given away her bicycle because she expected me to honour my promise. To be sure, "the price she has paid" for my promise is loss of her bicycle; she has not, however, provided consideration. My own promise caused this to occur but I did not request or stipulate that before X could acquire my car she had to transfer her bicycle. It may be that X will receive some limited compensation through other means—negligent mistatement, or restitution, for example—of estoppel but she cannot satisfy the needs of the conventional doctrine of consideration. On the other hand, an inducement that causes a person to commit resources in the understanding that the person making the promise will continue to contract with that person in the future goes beyond a mere expectation.[21]

Historical Antecedents

2–07 While it is clear that executory transactions in which each party assumes a duty to the other have been enforceable since the seventeenth century and the decision in *Slade's* case,[22] it is by no means established that the bargain model has long represented the basic or fundamental premise upon which enforceable contracts are formed. Simpson, in his analysis of the evolution of consideration,[23] advances the view that equitable and common law concepts of consideration were far from identical, and that the origins of consideration in *assumpsit* are traceable back to canon law or civil law. Atiyah argues strenuously that the bargain model was never representative of equitable practice and that equity generally recognised a promise to be enforceable when the promisee relied upon it. These views at least serve to point to the diversity of view, and uncertainty, that still surround the consideration doctrine. In any event, it is reasonably clear that since the eighteenth century the English and Irish courts have rejected the view that a gift made in consideration of natural love and affection, even within the context of a family unit, can be enforceable as a contract. A twentieth century illustration of this is found in the case of *Re Wilson, Grove-White v Wilson*.[24] Johnston J. held that an agreement for a valuable consideration cannot be sustained where a father makes over property to a son "for natural love and affection" and then gives an allowance to the son to assist in maintaining that property, following *Lee v Matthews*[25] and disapproving *Price v Jenkins*.[26] The doctrine of consideration is foreign to many legal systems including that of Scotland which historically is closer to the Roman law tradition than that of the common law world. If a Scottish court is convinced that a promise is seriously meant then the fact that it was not given in the context of a bargain will not prevent enforcement of the promise. Lord

---

[21] *Hennigan v Roadstone Wood Ltd* [2015] IEHC 326.
[22] (1602) 46. Rep. 91a.
[23] Simpson, *A History of the Common Law Contract* (Oxford: Clarendon, 1975).
[24] [1933] I.R. 729.
[25] (1880) 6 L.R. (Ir.) 530.
[26] (1876) 5 Ch.D. 619.

Mansfield was undoubtedly the most influential figure in moulding modern English commercial law and his Scottish ancestry no doubt helps explain his attempts during the eighteenth century to uproot the doctrine of consideration. One attack mounted against the doctrine occurred in a series of cases in which Lord Mansfield argued that a promise to pay an antecedent debt, the debt itself being unenforceable, would be supported by moral consideration alone. If an infant, a discharged bankrupt or a married woman promised to pay a debt incurred during infancy, bankruptcy or coverture respectively, this promise would be void. However, Lord Mansfield argued a subsequent promise would be enforceable for this promise, in his view, should be both morally and legally binding. The "moral consideration" theory was dismissed as alien to English law in *Eastwood v Kenyon*.[27] It is also clear that the moral consideration theory at no time formed part of the jurisprudence developed by the Irish courts. In *Ferrar v Costelloe*[28] the Irish Court of Exchequer held that a married woman who promised to be jointly and severally liable upon a bill of exchange signed with her husband could not be liable upon a new promise made after her husband died and the disability of coverture ended. Brady L.C. noted that *Eastwood v Kenyon* went "a great way to overrule this doctrine of moral obligation". Richards C.B. in *Bradford v Roulston*[29] also rejected the moral obligation theory.

2–08 The doctrine of consideration is not as irrational as many of its critics have argued. It is through the doctrine that the courts often satisfy themselves that a promise was in fact seriously meant. This has been described as "the deliberative function".[30] By adopting the form of an exchange of promises this ritual should indicate to a court that each intended to be bound. Whether other forms of ritual evidencing intent should be permitted this effect, such as recording a promise in writing, is another question. Several American jurisdictions enforce promises evidenced in this fashion and several commentators, including Lord Wright, have been attracted to such a reform. However, *Canadian Taxpayers Federation v Ontario*[31] attests that no degree of legal formalism will persuade a court to find a contract exists where to do so would fly in the face of common experience, common sense, or public policy considerations. Ontario legislation required taxation adjustments to follow a citizen's referendum. During an election campaign in the Province, the Liberal Party leader signed a "Taxpayer Protection Promise" not to introduce new taxes without voter approval. Almost inevitably on these facts, the Liberal Party was elected and it sought to amend the referendum legislation to allow introduction of a new health levy. One of the questions that arose was whether the written

---

[27] (1840) 11 A. & E. 458. For an excellent historical analysis see *McMeel, Pillans v Van Mierop* in Mitchell and Mitchell, *Landmark Cases in the Law of Contract* (Oxford: Hart Publishing, 2008), p.23.

[28] (1841) 4 I.L.R. 425.

[29] (1858) 8 I.R.C.L. 468.

[30] Fuller, "Consideration and Form" (1941) 41 Col. L.Rev. 799.

[31] (2004) 73 O.R. (3d) 621.

promise, made at a press conference, to no-one in particular, was enforceable. The Ontario High Court held that it was not. Rouleau J. said: "it is not the role of the courts ... To intervene to enforce such promises and pledges ... The remedy is for the electorate to consider and weigh the record of each candidate and party at the time of voting and in the intervening period."[32]

Adequacy and Sufficiency of Consideration

2–09 If the terms of the bargain are unduly favourable to one of the parties in the sense that the price paid by him is disproportionate to that which he obtains in return, the consideration may be said to be inadequate. Nevertheless, it is axiomatic that the courts will not investigate the adequacy of the consideration. If a landowner wishes to let his property for a handful of peppercorns or give an option to purchase his estate for one euro that is his affair. The attitude of the courts was neatly summed up by Manners L.C. in *Grogan v Cooke*[33]: "If there be a fair and bona fide consideration the Court will not enter minutely into it, and see that it is full and ample." So if the bargain is an honest one it will be enforced, even if one party gets more from the bargain than the other. There is more recent authority on this question. In *Kennedy v Kennedy*,[34] a case in which there was no allegation of improper pressure or disparity of intellect on either side, Ellis J. remarked that "once there is consideration its adequacy in this sort of case is irrelevant to its validity and enforceability". This basic rule of contract law was illustrated by the 1996 sale of Irish Steel Ltd to a foreign consortium for a payment of one pound; the transaction involved a number of collateral undertakings that made the overall bargain a balanced one but the central issue, about the transfer of ownership in the assets of the company, is in point.[35] Disparity of the exchange will, however, be an important factor in alerting the courts to the possibility of fraud or the existence of an unconscionable or improvident bargain, considered later in this book. Indeed, the enforceability in equity of a contract entered into with a person who is mentally incapable of looking after business affairs and is unable to understand the transaction will turn upon whether the transaction is "fair and bona fide". In the leading Irish case of *Hassard v Smith*[36] Vice Chancellor Chatterton indicated that to satisfy this test the consideration paid must be an ample or fair price.

2–10 The operation of this procedure is well illustrated by the decision of Lynch J. in *Noonan (A Ward of Court) v O'Connell*.[37] An application was

---

[32] (2004) 73 O.R. (3d) 621 at 638.
[33] (1812) 7 Ball & B. 234.
[34] Unreported, High Court, January 12, 1984.
[35] See the annotation to the Irish Steel Limited Act 1996, in *Irish Current Law Statutes Annotated* (Dublin: Round Hall Sweet & Maxwell, 1996).
[36] (1872) 6 I.R. Eq. 429.
[37] Unreported, High Court, April 10, 1987.

brought to set aside the transfer of farmland owned by the plaintiff which was made at a time when the plaintiff was suffering from senile dementia, the defendant being a relative of the plaintiff. The transfer had been supervised by a solicitor and had been drafted so as to record the transaction as a sale of land for 50 pence. After finding that there was gross inequality in the position of plaintiff and defendant, and that the transaction had not been clearly explained to the plaintiff, the weaker party, Lynch J. dealt with the contention that the transaction was one of sale rather than a gift transfer: "On its face it is a purely voluntary transfer and of course the reference to fifty pence consideration is a complete anachronism and does not constitute any consideration." Had the transfer been freely agreed between parties standing on equal terms the form may have been recognised as a valid contract. Leases for peppercorn or nominal rents are still recognised as valid although even these transactions may be overturned if improvident or unconscionable.

2–11 Nevertheless, the provision of tokens or vouchers will not always constitute consideration. In the case of *Lipkin Gorman v Karpnale*[38] the House of Lords rejected the argument that when a casino provided a gambler with gaming chips, the provision of chips constituted a valuable consideration. The chips remained the property of the casino and were simply a convenient device to enable gaming to be conducted.

2–12 The leading English textbook writers, however, indicate that while consideration need not be adequate it must be sufficient. This means that before the consideration promised can support a counter promise it must not run foul of a series of rules designed to indicate when a promise will not suffice in law. These rules are often dictated by the needs of public policy. While the Irish courts have not as yet ruled conclusively on sufficiency the decision of the Northern Ireland Court of Appeal in *O'Neill v Murphy*[39] provides a useful illustration of a case in which the alleged consideration was held to be insufficient. A builder executed work for the parish next to the one in which he resided; an allegation of undue influence on the part of the religious advisor of the builder was countered by an argument based on contract; the builder had agreed to do the work in consideration of prayers being said for his intentions. It was held that there was no consideration in law for the builder's work. Andrews L.J. said that "while it is clear that the courts will not interfere with the exercise of free will and judgement of the parties by enquiry into the adequacy of consideration, it is necessary that it should be sufficient in law. Thus, neither a mere voluntary courtesy nor some act already executed will suffice". The promise must be within the legal capacity of the promisor or be *nudum pactum*. A promise by the Government not to legislate for three years on a particular matter, in this case tobacco advertising, in consideration for agreement on marketing restrictions for tobacco products from the tobacco

---

[38] [1991] 3 W.L.R. 10.
[39] [1936] N.I. 16.

industry, was not enforceable. The Government could not contract so as to bind Parliament from abstaining to exercise the legislative function; *Rothmans v Attorney-General*.[40] There are a number of basic rules to be satisfied if public policy is not to defeat a contractual claim.

2–13 First of all, a promise in exchange for performing a duty already imposed by the general law, such as answering a subpoena, would not be enforceable. Public agencies and citizens should perform their public or statutory duties without hoping for or encouraging payment. The owner of a burning building who promises to pay €1,000 to a group of firemen if they save the premises could only be sued on this promise if the firemen's actions went beyond those required or expected of public service firemen.

2–14 The leading English case is the decision of the House of Lords in *Glasbrook Bros Ltd v Glamorgan County Council*.[41] The appellants sought police protection of their coal mine and its equipment during the currency of a strike. In the view of the police authority the mine could be adequately protected by patrolling the mine and its environs. The appellants sought a standing guard and, as such, the police authority "lent" constables for this purpose and imposed a charge. The House of Lords held that the practice was both legal and done for a valuable consideration, although several members of the House indicated that if the measures were taken after the police authority had formed the view that these measures were necessary for the maintenance of property and keeping the peace, then no charge could be levied. Here, however, no such opinion had been formed and the police officers had been billeted at the mine in order to meet the wishes of the appellants.

2–15 In the case of *Harris v Sheffield United Football Club*,[42] however, the Court of Appeal had to consider whether a professional football club could be liable for the cost of the internal and external policing of its stadium by members of the South Yorkshire Police Force. The club argued that these charges, in the unfortunately violent climate of the 1980s, were not recoverable because the prospects of crowd misbehaviour and the attendant risk to property and persons made the provision of policing services an essential part of the duty owed by the Police Authority to the public generally. The Court of Appeal rejected this view. Given the fact that the premises were, by and large, private premises, the fact that the event, a football match, had been privately organised, and the strain that resulted on scarce resources (constables were often off-duty and were required at weekends) meant that these services were special police services and overtime payments and other expenses were recoverable from the football club. However, it has been decided in *West Yorkshire Police Authority v Reading Festival*[43] that if the police seek reimbursement in contract then

---

[40] [1991] 2 N.Z.L.R. 323; *Canadian Taxpayers Federation v Ontario* (2004) 73 O.R. (3d) 621.
[41] [1925] A.C. 270.
[42] [1987] 2 All E.R. 836.
[43] [2006] 1 W.L.R. 1005.

the person to whom the services are provided must have made a request for services, express or implied.

2–16 The English Court of Appeal, in *Leeds United Football Club v West Yorkshire Police*[44] has reiterated the importance of distinguishing policing services that take place to prevent crime and disorder and protect life and property, and other services (special police services). As a basic rule a charge can be made for special police services. Football matches played in the main on private land will generally be events that will be classified as involving special police services except where the police are summoned to deal with actual or imminent violence. In regard to the policing of football matches in the sense of pre- and post-match activities on public land the Court of Appeal applied the same guiding principle: are policing services necessary to prevent and detect crime and/or protect life and property? No simple answer is available, but the Court of Appeal held that, save for the area immediately around the stadium, policing in "the extended footprint" of streets around the ground is provided in furtherance of the duty owed to the public and are not special police services.

2–17 The only Irish case in which this kind of argument has directly arisen is *McKerring v Minister for Agriculture*.[45] The case arose out of a dispute between the Minister and the plaintiff farmer in respect of grant payments under the Tuberculosis and Brucellosis Eradication Scheme. The plaintiff had been disallowed payment because of non-compliance with the rules and one issue that arose was whether the scheme was a discretionary scheme or one in which payment was made under contract. Although the point was not a contentious one, O'Hanlon J. wondered whether merely complying with the scheme as was required by statute could not constitute consideration moving from the plaintiff. O'Hanlon J. found that the plaintiff did provide consideration:

> "[I]t appears to me that there is sufficient consideration involved in strict compliance with all the conditions, even though *some of them* may be a matter of legal obligation as well." (emphasis added)

Secondly, performance of a duty already owed *to the promisor* may constitute consideration although the limits of this doctrine have yet to be established. The older cases, *Stilk v Myrick*[46] and *Hartley v Ponsonby*[47] suggest that only if the initial contract is discharged can a second promise be actionable by a party who in substance performs the duty owed under the first contract. The

---

[44] [2013] EWCA Civ 115. The Court of Appeal pointed out that the club in question had fans with a poor record in relation to football-related violence and that the protection of persons in public areas who had no involvement in the football matches was an important policing consideration.

[45] [1989] I.L.R.M. 82: see also *Rooney v Minister for Agriculture and Food, Irish Times Law Report*, February 3, 1992.

[46] (1809) 2 Camp. 317; Luther (1999) 19 L.S. 526.

[47] (1857) 7 E. & B. 872. See, however, *The Sansone* (1851) 3 Ir. Jur. Rep. (o.s.) 258.

view is supported in the Irish case of *Farrington v Donoghue*.[48] More recently, however, it has been suggested that generally a promise to perform an existing duty is sufficient consideration for a promise; see *Williams v Williams*.[49] The case of *Williams v Williams* concerned the enforceability of a promise made in a maintenance agreement whereby the husband promised to pay £1 10s. per week to his wife if she would maintain herself and for as long as she lived apart from him. The majority of the Court of Appeal were able to find a sufficient consideration to the husband from the fact that, during her "desertion" from him, he was no longer bound to maintain her and that she could have resumed cohabitation with him or sought maintenance if he refused to accept her offer to return. Denning L.J., while attracted to such sophistry, took a more forthright view, stating *obiter*:

> "I agree that in promising to maintain herself whilst she was in desertion, the wife was only promising to do that which she was already bound to do. Nevertheless, a promise to perform an existing duty is, I think, sufficient consideration to support a promise, so long as there is nothing in the transaction which is contrary to the public interest."[50]

In *McHugh v Kildare County Council*,[51] the plaintiff entered into a written agreement that he would transfer 20 per cent of his lands to the defendant if the council re-zoned the remainder of his lands. The plaintiff subsequently resiled from the agreement on the basis, *inter alia*, that no consideration moved to him, arguing that the defendant owed an existing legal duty to consider rezoning applications. Gilligan J. brushed this defence aside, approving Denning L.J.'s dicta in *Ward v Byham*,[52] where the Lord Justice had earlier said much the same as he did in *Williams v Williams*.[53]

2–18 These two lines of authority have been fully discussed in *North Ocean Shipping v Hyundai*.[54] Mocatta J. suggested that if the duty owed arises under statute then performance of that duty will be consideration for a promise. The point can be illustrated from Irish statute law. Under the old Poor Laws (which have been supplanted by provisions in the Social Welfare Consolidation Act 2005 s.345) the mother of an illegitimate child had a statutory duty of support.

---

[48] (1866) I.R. 1 C.L. 675. However, see *Pordage v Canter* (1854) 6 Ir. Jur. Rep. (o.s.) 246 where additional consideration was provided by the mother's promise to remain chaste.

[49] [1957] 1 W.L.R. 148. *Airways Corp of New Zealand v Geyserland Airways Ltd* [1996] 1 N.Z.L.R. 116 also points to very little by way of additional consideration being necessary to render the promise enforceable, following *Williams v Williams*.

[50] [1957] 1 W.L.R. 148 at 150–151. Internal family promises may be policed to ensure a substantive transaction took place: *MC (A Ward) v FC* [2013] IEHC 272.

[51] [2006] 1 I.R. 100.

[52] [1956] 1 W.L.R. 496.

[53] [1956] 2 All E.R. 318 at 319: "I have always thought that a promise to perform an existing duty or the performance of it shall be regarded as good consideration because it is a benefit to the person to whom it is given."

[54] [1978] 3 All E.R. 1170.

Should the father promise to pay a fixed sum every week the mother would on this modern line of authority be able to recover, even though she owes a statutory duty to do that requested by the promisor. If, however, the duty owed springs from *contract* it cannot provide consideration for a promise. In the *North Ocean Shipping* case a shipbuilding company was promised an increase in the price payable for building the vessel. Mocatta J. held the promise enforceable because, on the facts, additional consideration was provided for the increased price but was clearly of the view that unless the additional element was present, the discharge of an existing contractual duty owed by the promisee is an insufficient consideration. O'Hanlon J. in *Kenny v An Post*[55] has also reiterated the orthodox view said to be laid down in *Stilk v Myrick*.[56]

2–19 This entire area of law has been thrown into confusion by the decision of the Court of Appeal in *Williams v Roffey Brothers & Nicholls (Contractors) Ltd*.[57] The defendant was a contractor who awarded a sub-contract for joinery work to the plaintiff. The contract and sub-contract involved the refurbishment of the roof and interior of some 27 flats and the price agreed involved a payment of £20,000 impliedly payable in stages as work progressed. After the roof and nine flats had been totally refurbished and the remaining 18 flats had been partially refurbished, the plaintiff approached the defendant seeking additional payments because the plaintiff had seriously underestimated the cost of carrying out the work and this, allied to his failure to properly supervise his workmen, made it difficult for him to complete for the agreed amount without facing financial difficulties. The plaintiff, having received interim payments totalling £16,200 and having brought his difficulties to the attention of the defendant, obtained a promise that upon completion of the work he would be paid a further £10,300. The plaintiff's representative persuaded the defendant that it was in its own interests that its subcontractor should not be held to perform for too low a price for, in Glidewell L.J.'s words, the main contractor "will never get the job finished without paying more money". In response to the plaintiff's action on the promise the defendant, relying on *Stilk v Myrick*, argued that because the plaintiff was only promising to do that which he was bound to do for the defendant anyway, the promise to pay an additional amount was unenforceable for want of consideration.

2–20 Notwithstanding the decision in *Stilk v Myrick*, and the reaffirmation of the proposition that "consideration" remains a fundamental requirement before a contract not under seal can be enforced, the Court of Appeal took, in the words of Russell L.J., a "pragmatic approach" to the relationship between the parties. Consideration could be found in the fact that a haphazard system of

---

[55] [1988] J.I.S.L.L. 187.
[56] (1809) 2 Camp. 317; *South Caribbean Trading Ltd v Trafigura Beheer BV* [2005] 1 Lloyd's Rep. 128.
[57] [1990] 1 All E.R. 512, followed in *Newsmasters v Ranier* [1992] 2 N.Z.L.R. 68; *Musumeci v Winadell Pty* (1994) 34 N.S.W.L.R. 723; *Simon Container Machinery Ltd v Emba Machinery A.B.* [1998] 2 Lloyd's Rep. 429; *Teat v Willcocks* [2013] NZCA 162; *Kain v Wynn Williams Co* [2013] 1 N.Z.L.R. 498.

payment was replaced by a more structured payment system and the plaintiff had provided consideration by giving the defendant grounds for believing that the work would be completed without interruption by reason of insolvency or other difficulty, a very real benefit from promisor to promisee for the construction contract contained a penalty clause which would have operated against the defendant in the event of any delay. In the leading judgment Glidewell L.J. stated that the law supported the following propositions:

> "(i) if A has entered into a contract with B to do work for, or to supply goods or services to, B in return for payment by B and (ii) at some stage before A has completely performed his obligations under the contract B has reason to doubt whether A will, or will be able to, complete his side of the bargain and (iii) B thereupon promises A an additional payment in return for A's promise to perform his contractual obligations on time and (iv) as a result of giving his promise B obtains in practice a benefit, or obviates a disbenefit, and (v) B's promise is not given as a result of economic duress or fraud on the part of A, then (vi) the benefit to B is capable of being consideration for B's promise, so that the promise will be legally binding."[58]

The application of such a controversial and difficult proposition not only threatens to further undermine the bargain theory; it also makes the boundary between promissory estoppel and consideration even more difficult to draw. Perhaps a more rational response would have required the Court of Appeal to negative the consideration argument that the plaintiff successfully utilised, and to address the issues from a promissory estoppel perspective. The *Roffey Brothers* case has been held to apply only in cases where the promise by A consists of rendering services to B in return for B's promise of additional payment. The decision in *Re Selectmove*[59] makes it clear that *Roffey Brothers* does not change the rule that payment of part of a liquidated debt will not constitute consideration for a promise to forego the remainder of the amount due.

2–21 Thirdly, performance of a duty owed *to someone other than the promisor* may support a promise. Students will find the application of the old case of *Scotson v Pegg*[60] by the Privy Council in 1974 in *The Eurymedon*[61] case instructive. Simply put, if A owes a contractual duty to marry B and a third party (the father of B perhaps) promises to pay A €10,000 after the ceremony, A can enforce this promise. While it is no longer possible to sue in the

---

[58] [1990] 1 All E.R. 512 at 521–522; *Fitzsimons v Value Homes* [2006] IEHC 146; *Process Automation Inc. v Norstream Intertec* (2010) 321 D.L.R. (4th) 724 notes the statutory change made in Ontario.

[59] [1995] 2 All E.R. 531, followed by Keane J. in *Truck and Machinery Sales Ltd v Marubeni Komatsu Ltd*, unreported, High Court, February 23, 1996. See also *Musumeci v Winadell Pty Ltd* (1994) 34 N.S.W.L.R. 723.

[60] (1861) 6 H. & N. 295.

[61] *New Zealand Shipping Co Ltd v AM Satterthwaite & Co Ltd (The Eurymedon)* [1975] A.C. 154.

Republic of Ireland for breach of promise to marry, the cause of action having been abolished by the Family Law Act 1981, *Saunders v Cramer*[62] is an Irish authority in favour of this rule. Indeed, there are several mid-nineteenth century Irish cases which demonstrate that if a promise of this kind is evidenced in writing, so as to satisfy the requirements of s.2 of the Statute of Frauds 1695, the argument that the engaged couple could not provide consideration for a third party promise by marrying, was never raised.[63] Some explanation for this can be found in the leading English case of *Shadwell v Shadwell*.[64] Here the plaintiff's uncle, upon learning of his nephew's engagement, wrote promising to assist the nephew upon commencement of his married life by providing him with £150 yearly until such time as the nephew's annual earnings at the Chancery bar reached 600 guineas. An action to enforce the promise against his uncle's executors was successful. One of the justifications advanced by Earle C.J. was the accrual of a benefit to the uncle in such a situation, saying that a marriage may be a matter of interest to a near relative. In his dissenting judgment Byles J. pointed out that there was no evidence to support the view that the marriage resulted in any personal benefit to the plaintiff's uncle, and it is submitted that this dissenting judgment provides a clearer analysis of the case, if we are concerned to retain the view that consideration must consist of some tangible exchange between the parties and is not to include cases of supposed psychological gratification. In *Pitts v Jones*[65] the English Court of Appeal has indicated that a court should not rely too heavily on evidence given by a party on subjective motivation at the time of a negotiation. The fact that the promisee did not have in mind the benefit afforded to the promisor does not mean that consideration is absent. The critical point here is that the promise made induced the promisee to co-operate with the promisor by forebearing to withdraw earlier consents and assent to a new proposed course of action. A court may resort to an implied promise in order to secure that the consideration requirement is satisfied. This can produce marginal decisions. In *Dome Resources NL v Silver*[66] the managing director of a mining company stepped down from that post, the company being aware that he was unhappy with his retirement package. Silver was asked to remain as a non-executive director of the company because of his knowledge of the business affairs of that company. Variations to his retirement package were made. The New South Wales Court of Appeal rejected an argument that the variation was unsupported by consideration and that Silver was merely doing what he had earlier contracted to do, that he was not obliged to serve for any period and that Silver was free to leave the day after the variation was executed. The variation was held to

---

62 (1842) 5 I. Eq. R. 12.
63 *O'Sullivan v O'Callaghan* (1849) 2 Ir. Jur. 314; *Arthure v Dillon* (1849) 2 Ir. Jur. 162.
64 (1860) 9 C.B. (N.S.) 159.
65 [2008] 1 All E.R. 941.
63 [2008] NSWCA 322; see also *Tinyow v Lee* [2006] NSWCA 60. Contrast *Atco Controls Ltd v Newtronics Pty Ltd* [2009] VSCA 238. A letter of comfort promising financial support to a subsidiary company was held to be unsupported by consideration, the Victoria Court of Appeal being unable to imply a term as to how long the promise was to last for and in which trading circumstances it would apply.

be supported by consideration in the form of an implied promise that Silver was obliged to continue to serve as a director for a reasonable time, absent any material change in circumstances. The New South Wales Court of Appeal saw no reason to distinguish between orthodox consideration principles and a *Roffey Bros* "practical benefit" test.

2–22 Finally, consideration will not be present when the promise, express or implied, relates to conduct on the part of the promisor which is seen by the court as being socially or ethically unacceptable, whether within the context of a family arrangement[67] or a broader commercial context. In *Borrelli v Tring*[68] a settlement agreement was held not to be binding on liquidators who were being obstructed by the promisee who was not acting bona fide: "all he was offering to do was to cease acting in bad faith and to do what he should have done in the first place." Situations of this kind almost invariably shade into areas of undue influence, unconscionability or duress.

The Rule against Past Consideration

2–23 Because the common law recognises that contracts are enforced in order to carry into effect the expectations of the parties responsible for creating them, there are instances where a contract will be held to exist where neither party has attempted to perform his respective promises. If A agrees to purchase six tons of coal from B in six months time and to pay a price of €100 a ton, a contract exists as from the exchange of promises. The consideration provided is the promised act of each; in this bilateral contract the consideration is said to be executory. While neither party has performed as yet, both parties are said to have provided consideration by their exchange of promises. Should *one* party perform (for example, when A forwards the price of the coal to B) the consideration by A is executed and he can of course maintain an action against B in the event of delivery.

2–24 Professor Atiyah in his book, *Promises, Morals and Law*[69] challenged the view that bilateral executory contracts, that is, cases in which the parties have simply exchanged promises without either party having acted to implement the exchange, often are not, and should not be, given the same weight and importance as executed or completed exchanges. This argument has been repudiated by the Court of Appeal in *Centrovincial Estates Plc v Merchant Investors Assurance Co Ltd*.[70] The lessee of a building was informed by the lessor that following upon the operation of a rent review clause the rent due for the future would be reduced. The lessor asked the lessee to indicate acceptance of this

---

[67] *White v Bluett* (1853) 23 L.J. Ex. 36; *MC (a Ward) v FC* [2013] IEHC 272.
[68] [2010] UKPC 21.
[69] (Oxford: Clarendon, 1981).
[70] [1983] Com. L.R. 158; *Redevco UK v WH Smith Plc* [2008] NIQB 116.

offer which the lessee promptly did. The lessor then discovered that the rent review had been incorrectly carried out and he sought to retract the accepted offer by arguing that where an offer is accepted the offer can be withdrawn by the offeror if the offeree has not suffered a detriment, and in this case, neither side had acted upon the offer. The Court of Appeal, allowing the lessee's appeal, held the offer, once validly accepted, could not be withdrawn save in instances of operative mistake. In the Court of Appeal Slade L.J. pointed out that the offeree had given consideration when he gave the promise requested and that it was irrelevant whether or not the offeree had changed his position beyond giving the promise requested by him.

2–25 It is well established, however, that if a promise is made after some gratuitous act has been performed by the promisee the subsequent promise is not supported by consideration. The benefit conferred before the promise was made cannot be said to have been made by reference to an antecedent promise. We have already seen that promises are not enforced because they satisfy a test of causation; if I promise to give my house to my brother because he paid my hospital bill during an earlier illness my promise was the result of a benefit already conferred. Nevertheless, it was not given in the context of an exchange of promises so no bargain or contract will result. Here the consideration is said to be past consideration which is no consideration at all.

2–26 The leading English case is *Roscorla v Thomas*.[71] The plaintiff purchased a horse for £30 from Thomas who, following the sale, warranted the horse "free from vice". The horse bit and was therefore not as warranted. The action failed; the pleadings clearly indicated that the sale had been completed when the warranty was given. Roscorla then had provided no consideration; the promise to pay the purchase price was not given in exchange for the warranty sued upon. The courts, however, do not sit over the negotiations ready to record and examine the exchange of promises second by second. In *Smith v Morrison*[72] the Irish Queens Bench Division distinguished *Roscorla v Thomas*. It was pleaded that the sale of a horse took place contemporaneously with the giving of the warranty. It was held that if this be so the promise will not be held to have been given for a past consideration.

2–27 The wording of the promise will no doubt provide guidance on this; the past tense will indicate that the promised act has already been performed but parol evidence is admissible to show whether the consideration is past or not. In *Bewley v Whiteford*[73] the Court of Exchequer indicated that if after hearing parol testimony the court is in doubt whether the consideration is wholly executed (past) or executory then an action on the promise will not succeed; see also *Gorrie v Woodley*.[74] On this matter of evidence, the leading

---

[71] (1842) 3 Q.B. 234.
[72] (1846) 10 I.L.R.C.L. 213.
[73] (1832) Hayes 356.
[74] (1864) 17 I.C.L.R. 221.

English case is *Re McArdle*.[75] The plaintiffs were promised a sum of money "in consideration of your carrying out certain alterations and improvements" to property in which the promisors had an interest. Upon proof that the words indicated work that had already been done, rather than work that had yet to be completed, the action upon the promise failed. Another difficulty that a plaintiff may face is that promises given by members of a family may be held unenforceable for lack of legal intent—see Ch.3.

2–28 The leading Northern Irish case is *Provincial Bank of Ireland v Donnell*,[76] a decision of the Northern Ireland Court of Appeal. The bank sued the defendant on a deed (not under seal) in which she agreed to provide security for her husband's overdraft in consideration of "advances heretofore made or that might hereafter be made". The action failed. The consideration stated here was either past or illusory; the advances that had earlier been made were a past consideration while the advances that "might hereafter be made" gave the bank a total discretion whether it would provide advances or not. The promises then should have been recorded in a deed under seal in order to render them enforceable. Commercial organisations do enter into illusory contracts every day. A licence to manufacture goods, subject to a detailed evaluation of the product and market may reserve a total discretion to perform the agreement because of the want of consideration provided by the licensee: *Stabilad Ltd v Stephens & Carter Ltd (No.2)*.[77] There may be statutory provisions that authorise a different construction; see s.288 of the Companies Act 1963 and *Re Daniel Murphy Ltd*.[78]

2–29 A promise made after the promisee has conferred a benefit upon another person may be enforceable if the court is able to bring the case within the seventeenth century English case of *Lampleigh v Braithwait*.[79] This case holds that while a past consideration will not of itself provide support for an implied promise to pay, it may support a subsequent express promise made by the beneficiary. The rule itself, which predates *Lampleigh v Braithwait* was applied by the Court of Exchequer in *Bradford v Roulston*.[80] Roulston was employed by Bradford to find a purchaser for Bradford's boat. A third party agreed to purchase the vessel but when the bill of sale was to be completed the purchaser did not have sufficient funds to pay the purchase price. Bradford was about to withdraw from the transaction when he was asked by Roulston to sign. Bradford signed the bill of sale. After the bill of sale was signed Roulston promised in writing that he would ensure payment of the balance the following day. Roulston was sued on this promise. The consideration provided—signature of the bill of sale by Bradford—was clearly past. Pigot

---

[75] [1951] Ch. 669.
[76] (1932) 67 I.L.T.R. 142; contrast *Northern Bank Ltd v Quinn and Quinn* [2014] IEHC 310.
[77] [1999] 2 All E.R. (Comm.) 651.
[78] [1964] I.R. 1.
[79] (1615) Hob. 105.
[80] (1858) 8 I.R.C.L. 468; *ACC Bank v Mullee and Mullee* [2014] IEHC 553.

C.B. stated in his speech, however, that "[w]here there is a past consideration, consisting of a previous act done at the request of the defendant, it will support a subsequent promise; the promise being treated as coupled with the previous request". The fact that the plaintiff was out of pocket was significant. In the majority of these cases existence of a benefit conferred upon the defendant tends to explain why the plaintiff succeeds. In this instant case, Bradford was held entitled to claim the sum promised because he had signed the bill of sale at Roulston's behest. What is important here is that when the requested act is provided, the parties must not have intended the act to be gratuitous. Evidence that the parties intended the promise to be compensable at some later date will be necessary. In fact in *Bradford v Roulston* the defendant may well have uttered his promise to pay the plaintiff when the bill of sale was to be signed but the plaintiff chose to rely on the promise in the letter because had he relied exclusively on the earlier oral promise he may have encountered problems in relation to the Statute of Frauds 1695. In *Pao On v Lau Yiu Long*[81] Lord Scarman summarised the exception to the rule against past consideration thus:

> "The act must have been done at the promisor's request, the parties must have understood that the act was to be remunerated either by a payment or the conferment of some other benefit, and payment, or the conferment of a benefit, must have been legally enforceable had it been promised in advance."[82]

An illustration of this principle not being satisfied can be found in the old Irish case of *Morgan v Rainsford*[83] decided in 1845. Specific performance of a promise was sought, the promise being "in consideration of the permanent improvements you have made and have promised to make". The action failed; the reference to past improvements was held to be an invalid consideration and the reference to future improvements was too vague. The failure to specify these improvements meant that that part of the alleged consideration was void for uncertainty. It may be difficult for the plaintiff to satisfy the second of Lord Scarman's three conditions if a family relationship or a close friendship subsists between the parties for the court may conclude that the plaintiff's conduct was motivated by factors other than the expectation of remuneration.[84]

Consideration must Move from the Promisee

2–30 Where the contract is executory the bargain may remain to be performed yet the exchange of promises gives each party the right to seek and obtain performance or monetary compensation. If A promises to buy coal from

---

[81] [1979] 3 All E.R. 65; *Classic Maritime Inc. v Lion Diversified Holdings* [2009] EWHC 1142 (Comm).

[82] [1979] 3 All E.R. 65 at 74.

[83] (1845) 8 Ir. E.R. 299.

[84] *Sim Tony v Lim Ah Ghee* [1995] 4 L.R.C. 377.

B tomorrow, paying €100 for the goods, each is a promisor and each is a promisee. A has given his promise to pay €100 and has received B's promise to deliver and vice versa. The nineteenth century authorities indicate that consideration exists where the promisee, the party seeking enforcement, can point to performance of a detrimental act (or the promise thereof) on the part of the promisee; see *Lowry v Reid*.[85] Alternatively, if the promisor has received a requested benefit from the promisee, consideration is present. The essential requirement is that the promisee must have provided the benefit or incurred the detriment, as the case may be.

2–31 Take the facts of *McCoubray v Thompson*.[86] AG owned land, goods and chattels worth £196 which he intended to transfer to M and T, share and share alike. T wanted the land to himself and it was agreed that in consideration for AG transferring everything to T, T would pay M £98, half the value of the property. T defaulted and was sued by M. Clearly the defendant had made a promise; it was also addressed to both AG and M, so they constituted joint promisees. Applying the rule requiring consideration to move from the promisee, however, it is clear that M had no cause of action in contract. He had made no promise in return for T's own promise to pay £98; the sole consideration for T's promise moved from AG. Monaghan C.J. held that where three parties join in an allegedly tripartite contract such as this the plaintiff must be able to show that *he* has provided consideration in some sense.

2–32 In *Barry v Barry*[87] a similar transaction was held to give a valid cause of action. Under the terms of his father's will the defendant was to receive the family farm if he promised to pay, personally, legacies to members of the family, including the plaintiff, a younger brother. If the defendant was unwilling to do this the legacy was to be payable from the land. The defendant promised to be personally liable to pay the legacies, whereupon the executors permitted him to use the farm. The promise was addressed to the executors and the plaintiff. When the defendant defaulted the plaintiff sued claiming the defendant was personally bound by his promise. The Court of Appeal held that consideration had moved from the promisee. The defendant by his promise led the plaintiff to give up any right to have the legacy realised out of the property; by forbearing to exercise rights over the estate at the implied request of the defendant the promisee had provided consideration. The difference between this case and *McCoubray v Thompson* is that McCoubray had no rights at all, however ill-defined, over the property which he could give up or refrain from exercising, so consideration could not be provided from this source. Commercial convenience often requires the judiciary to ease the task of a plaintiff in seeking to enforce a promise which the plaintiff has acted upon

---

[85] [1927] N.I. 142; *ACC Bank Plc v Kelly* [2011] IEHC 7.
[86] (1868) 2 I.R.C.L. 226.
[87] (1891) 28 L.R. (Ir.) 45.

to the plaintiff's detriment. For example, in *Moss v 158339 Canada Inc.*,[88] the plaintiff was a property management company which was entitled to profit sharing benefits in respect of property it managed on behalf of the defendant company. These entitlements could be secured by way of a mortgage. Payment was to be made by the owners of the corporate defendant by its shareholders, A and Z. A and Z negotiated that if the plaintiff agreed to surrender the mortgage power, and reduce its assessment of the sum due to $162,500 from $175,000, the corporate defendant would pay the amount of $162,500 in full settlement. The corporate defendant, by Board decision, resolved to pay the agreed amount. The Manitoba Court of Appeal held that the plaintiff's surrender of its claims constituted consideration and it mattered not that the plaintiff (the promisee) may not have provided consideration to the corporate defendant, the promisor. A and Z had received the benefits requested and the Manitoba Court of Appeal affirmed the view that consideration flowing to a third person not a party to a contract may be a valid consideration as between the parties to the contract.

2–33 A distinction, however, is to be drawn between cases where the promisor makes a promise to two persons, in circumstances where both promisees are intended to benefit, either jointly or severally, but only one promisee will actually provide the necessary exchange. It is hardly surprising that the courts will not provide a promisor with a defence to an action on the promise in such circumstances, for the application of a strict consideration requirement here would prove commercially inconvenient in many everyday contexts. So, although the joint promisee should provide consideration before he can enforce this promise, it has been recognised that this may be inconvenient if a joint bank account is opened but one of the parties does not intend to provide consideration by paying funds into the account. Could a bank refuse to pay him funds held in the account on the grounds that it has no contract with this person because he has not provided consideration? It seems not. See the opinions of the members of the House of Lords in *McEvoy v Belfast Banking Co Ltd*[89] and the controversial Australian case of *Coulls v Bagot's Trustee*,[90] criticised by Coote.[91] Notwithstanding these criticisms by Professor Coote, Brennan J., in the High Court of Australia's decision in *Thomas v Hollier*,[92] seemed prepared to apply this reasoning to the case at the bar but found that this doctrine was not satisfied by the facts of the case before him.

Compromise of a Claim

2–34 It is well established that an undertaking not to continue civil litigation or an agreement to compromise a claim will provide consideration for the promise of another. Indeed, the courts view it as in the public interest to

---

[88] [2004] 1 W.W.R. 201.
[89] [1935] A.C. 24; *Lynch v Burke* [1995] 2 I.R. 159.
[90] [1967] A.L.R. 385.
[91] [1978] C.L.J. 301.
[92] [1984] A.L.R. 39.

encourage out-of-court settlement of civil disputes. In *Taylor v Smyth*[93] Lardner J. said:

> "[I]t is also well established that where proceedings between parties are settled by an agreement to compromise, the agreement to compromise constitutes a new and independent contract between the parties made for good consideration and the original rights of the parties and causes of action become superceded by the compromise agreement."[94]

A difficulty may arise, however, if the claim that one party agrees to give up subsequently turns out to have had little or no chance of success. The promisor who is sued upon this agreement to compromise may argue that the claim was so vacuous and of such doubtful validity that it cannot provide consideration for his own promise.

2–35 The courts, however, refuse to hold that because the earlier cause of action had no chance of success the compromise is invalid. It is the legitimacy of the compromise that must be assessed. If both parties, however, know that the initial claim was invalid then the compromise too will fail. This view was taken by Palles C.B. in *O'Donnell v O'Sullivan*.[95] The parties agreed to compromise a claim for £137 by the defendant paying £75. During the trial it became clear that the original debt was a gambling debt, unenforceable at law. While this fact alone did not make the compromise invalid for want of consideration the fact that both parties knew this to be so did. Chief Justice Baron declared, "[i]t is settled law that unless there is a reasonable claim which is bona fide intended to be pursued the settlement of that claim cannot be good consideration for a compromise".

2–36 In general, the compromise must satisfy three conditions:

(1) the initial claim must have been reasonable and not vexatious or frivolous;
(2) the plaintiff must have had an honest belief in the chances of its success; and
(3) the party contending that the compromise is valid must not have withheld or suppressed facts that would have shown the claim in a truer light.

The third condition is normally broken by a defendant who threatens an action while suppressing facts which clearly show that the claim would no doubt fail. In the case of *Leonard v Leonard*[96] a claim was compromised between two half-brothers who each claimed entitlement to an estate. The plaintiff agreed to compromise his claim because he had been advised that on the facts the claim was not certain to succeed. The defendant, however, had withheld information

---

[93]   [1990] I.L.R.M. 377.
[94]   [1990] I.L.R.M. 377 at 389, citing, *inter alia, Green v Rozen* [1955] 2 All E.R. 797; *O'Mahony v Gaffrey* [1986] I.R. 36.
[95]   (1913) 47 I.L.T.R. 253.
[96]   (1812) 2 Ball & B. 171.

from the plaintiff which suggested that the claim would indeed succeed. The compromise was held invalid because the defendant had exploited the plaintiff's ignorance of all the facts.

2–37 Part of the reason why bona fide compromises of doubtful claims have been upheld can be attributed to the view that it is for the parties to make their own bargain. Indeed, there is a considerable body of support for the view that when the consideration requested by the promisor is the surrender or delivery of a document, the contractual compromise is valid, notwithstanding the fact that the document is worthless. As long as the transaction is an arm's length commercial transaction the instructive New Zealand case of *Veitch v Sinclair*[97] supports the proposition, but if the surrender takes place in circumstances where the policy of the law is to protect one of the parties, the compromise may not be valid. So in *O'Reilly v Connor; O'Reilly v Allen*[98] the Court of Kings Bench refused to uphold the validity of a compromise in which the plaintiff accepted a compromise of an unenforceable claim against a borrower, the plaintiff alleging that the later compromise allowed him to sue on a promissory note. Barton J. distinguished this situation from the leading English case of *Haigh v Brooks*[99] on the ground that this transaction was a loan transaction subject to strict statutory provisions to protect borrowers from oppressive practices.

2–38 Professor Kelly has convincingly argued that just as the surrender of a case of action may constitute a valuable consideration, so too may the surrender of a defence to an action.[100]

Forbearance—Promise and Fact

2–39 A promise to abstain from doing something will in many cases be as valuable to the promisee as a positive action. Pollock's definition of consideration refers to forbearance *or the promise thereof* as capable of supporting another promise. Forbearance to make an offer to purchase property because of an understanding that another person, the promisee, will negotiate on behalf of both of them will be consideration, as in *Conroy v Fitzpatrick*,[101] where the plaintiff succeeded by showing that but for the defendant's undertaking to negotiate to buy property in their joint names the plaintiff would have acted for himself. The Canadian courts, in contrast, generally still insist upon the "traditional" requirements that trigger the application of promissory estoppel such as the need for the parties to be in some pre-existing legal relationship and the denial of promissory estoppel as a cause of action:

---

[97] [1975] 1 N.Z.L.R. 264.
[98] (1904) 38 I.L.T.R. 21.
[99] (1839) 10 Ad. & El. 309.
[100] (1964) 27 M.L.R. 540.
[101] Unreported, High Court, December 18, 2003, following *McGillicuddy v Joy* [1959] I.R. 189.

see, for example, *Brentford General Hospital Foundation v Canada Trust Co*[102] the facts of which are given at para.2–02 above. In the American case of *Hamer v Sidway*[103] an uncle promised his nephew $5,000 if he refrained from drinking, using tobacco, swearing or gambling until 21. The nephew met these conditions and was successful in an action for the promised sum. He had a legal privilege to do these things and the acts of forbearance, requested by his uncle, provided consideration for the promise. The court was satisfied that the promise was seriously meant; it had been earnestly repeated before assembled members of the family.

2–40 Any expressly requested forbearance then will provide consideration. If I indicate I wish to leave my job and my employer promises me €10,000 if I remain in his employment for another six weeks this will be good consideration for although I will be performing the same tasks as before my forbearance will entitle me to claim the sum promised after performance.

2–41 The most common act of forbearance to come before the courts arises in cases where a promise is given in return for a promise not to enforce a legal remedy. In the leading English case of *Cook v Wright*[104] parish trustees threatened the occupant of a house with proceedings unless he signed promissory notes. Under a local Act of Parliament rates could be levied on owners in order to maintain local services. An action on the notes succeeded because the trustees had provided consideration by refraining to take proceedings to recover the rates due. Incidentally, the claim by the defendant that he was not the owner and therefore not liable to pay the rate failed; as we have seen it was enough for the trustees to have a reasonable belief that proceedings would have been successful.

2–42 If the promise has to be recorded in writing so as to satisfy the Statute of Frauds 1695 the courts have held that the consideration should be stated in the alleged memorandum. It is sufficient if the consideration is stated, expressly or impliedly, on the memorandum itself. In *Hibernian Gas Co v Parry*[105] a hotel business fell into receivership, one of the creditors being the plaintiff company. The plaintiffs were owed £32 for gas supplied. The receiver executed a document in favour of the company promising to pay all sums due six months hence. The consideration for this promise was not expressly stated on the memorandum (a contract of guarantee requiring a memorandum) but the Court of Exchequer unanimously held the receiver liable on his promise. Pennefather B. pointed out that the memorandum implicitly recorded two requested acts in the form of forbearance for the £32 due and continued supply of gas for the future. When the company agreed to these terms a contract was concluded, for as Brady C.B. observed, if the company sought to recover sums

---

[102] (2003) 67 O.R. (3d) 432, following *Reclamation Systems Inc. v Rae* (1996) 27 O.R. (2d) 419.
[103] (1891) 124 N.Y. 583.
[104] (1861) 1 B. & S. 559.
[105] (1841) 4 I.L.R. 453.

due before the six-month period elapsed the action would not have succeeded. Students should contrast the terms of the promise given here with those in the earlier English case of *Wood v Benson*[106] where part of a similar guarantee was held to infringe the rule against past consideration.

2–43 The context within which the promise was made may assist the court in finding consideration for a seemingly gratuitous promise. In *Blandford & Houdret Ltd v Bray Travel Holdings Ltd & Hopkins*[107] the plaintiff sought to recover on a guarantee, executed by the second defendant in favour of the plaintiff, in which the second defendant promised to pay debts of the first defendant already due to the plaintiff. While the instrument itself did not specify the consideration provided by the plaintiff—Gannon J. stated that on its face consideration was past—the facts revealed that the guarantee was given on the understanding that the plaintiff impliedly promised to forbear from exercising his right to withhold future services from the first defendant, something the plaintiff was entitled to do under the contract when payments were not made. In *O'Keeffe v Ryanair Holdings Plc*,[108] Kelly J. identified a new form of forbearance consideration. In return for the defendant's promise to give the plaintiff "free flights for life" the plaintiff agreed to participate in a number of press and television media events as the "Ryanair one millionth passenger". Kelly J. found that:

> "[T]he participation of the plaintiff in the publicity generated on the day in question was regarded as being of value by the defendant and I see no reason why the law should not regard it as likewise being of value. *The surrender by the plaintiff of her anonymity and privacy* and her active participation in the generation of publicity that was created on the day in question in my view amounted to a real consideration and sufficient to support a contract." (emphasis added)[109]

So if Ms O'Keeffe had only allowed her name to be used in Ryanair promotions she would still have provided consideration.

2–44 Many of the leading cases concern undertakings given by a debtor to a creditor whereby the debtor undertakes to provide security for the debt. The question often arises: what consideration moves from the creditor to the debtor in such a context? A typical case is provided by *Re Montgomery*[110] where a

---

[106] (1831) 2 C. & J. 94; *GMAC Commercial Credit Development Ltd v Sandhu* [2006] 1 All E.R. (Comm.) 268.

[107] Unreported, High Court, November 11, 1983. On consideration via the assignment of debts see *O'Malley v Law Society of Ireland* [1999] 1 I.R. 162.

[108] [2003] 1 I.L.R.M. 14.

[109] [2003] 1 I.L.R.M. 14 at 25. See also Kelly J. at 24 where he takes the view that the promise to participate in the photocall was the critical feature. See also *Canadian Taxpayers Federation v Ontario* (2004) 73 O.R. (3d) 621.

[110] (1876) 10 Ir.Rep.Eq. 479.

creditor was able to establish forbearance as consideration for promises by the defendant to meet trading debts incurred by the defendant's father while operating the family business. The role of forbearance as part of the doctrine of consideration takes on a very controversial aspect when it is said that a promise may be supported simply upon proof that the promisor relied upon the promise. At this point the entire bargain theory of consideration begins to split at the seams. The leading English case of *Alliance Bank Ltd v Broom*[111] was applied by the House of Lords in *Fullerton v Bank of Ireland*.[112] The bank wrote a letter to Colonel Stevenson, drawing his attention to the fact that his account was overdrawn. The client responded that he would provide title deeds to property as security. The Law Lords held that the consideration provided for this promise was the restraint and patience displayed by the bank in not immediately calling in the overdraft: "such forbearance in fact although there was no agreement by the bank to forbear suing Colonel Stevenson for any indefinite period was sufficient consideration to support his promise to give the security."[113]

2–45 In *Commodity Broking Co v Meehan*[114] the defendant, sole beneficial owner of all shares in P. Ltd, ran up a large account with the plaintiffs in the name of the company. When the account reached an indebtedness of £36,000 the defendant was asked to give a personal guarantee; he refused but promised to pay off the debt at the rate of £1,000 per month. He failed to honour this promise and in reply to an action on the promise pleaded an absence of consideration. After reviewing the English authorities and in particular *Alliance Bank Ltd v Broom*[115] Barron J. held that it was not necessary to find that the parties had reached an actual agreement not to sue upon the debt. Barron J. stated, "[t]he better view is that where a request express or implied to forbear from bringing proceedings induces such forbearance this amounts to good consideration". On the facts before him Barron J. found that there was no consideration. The plaintiff company had abstained from seeking a remedy from P. Ltd because the company was insolvent and the exercise would have been pointless: see also Denning L.J. in *Combe v Combe*.[116] However, where the evidence establishes that the promise actually induced forbearance the courts will readily infer a tacit promise from the promisee that will provide the requisite consideration. In *Techform Products v Wolda*[117] the defendant invented a hinge while employed as a consultant with the plaintiff. The plaintiff presented the defendant with a document assigning the intellectual property rights in the invention to the plaintiff, the plaintiff signing under protest. The

---

[111] (1864) 2 Dr. & Sm. 289.
[112] [1903] A.C. 309.
[113] [1903] A.C. 309 at 315. Forbearance may *a fortiori* be provided by the offeree forbearing to sue after receipt of the offer before communicating acceptance of the offer: *Earn v Kohut* (2002) 164 Man. R. (2nd) 50.
[114] [1985] I.R. 12; *Western Surety Co v Hancan Holdings Ltd* [2007] 6 W.W.R. 630.
[115] (1864) 2 Dr. & Sm. 289.
[116] [1951] 2 K.B. 215.
[117] (2001) 206 D.L.R. (4th) 170, following *Maguire v Northland Drug Co* [1935] 2 D.L.R. 521.

Ontario Court of Appeal reversed the finding of the trial judge, who had held there was no consideration for the assignment. The Court of Appeal reasoned that the evidence disclosed that if the defendant had not signed the document his contract would have been lawfully terminated some six months later. By signing the document the defendant was implicitly being promised retention in employment for a reasonable period and in fact his job continued for a further four years.[118] In the New Zealand case of *Attorney-General for England and Wales v R*,[119] the appellant, serving member of special services involved in the *Bravo Two Zero* operation in the first Gulf War, was presented with a document preventing him from writing about his experiences during that time, it being made known to him that if he did not sign then there was a probability that he would be returned to his unit. Upon signature he retained his post with Special Services. Applying *Alliance Bank v Broom*, the New Zealand Court of Appeal held that there had been consideration in the form of actual forbearance moving from the Crown to the appellant. The Privy Council upheld this view[120] and also considered that the appellant had received a practical benefit sufficient to ground the enforceability of his promise not to publish his memoirs.

2–46 Some cases are even more difficult to reconcile with the orthodox doctrine of consideration. It has been convincingly argued by Professor Atiyah in his book *Rise and Fall of Freedom of Contract*[121] that in certain types of transaction no exchange exists but, nevertheless, the courts have held a promise enforceable through the concept of contract, largely because the promisee has or may have relied upon the promise. This is particularly so, Atiyah points out, in relation to promises made to an engaged couple. The likelihood that these persons may rely on the promise—buy expensive furniture, rent or buy a house—in a way they would not have done if the promise had not been made explains the decision in many cases, amongst them *Shadwell v Shadwell*[122] and the Irish case of *Saunders v Cramer*.[123] In *Moore v Kelly*,[124] Ronan L.J. remarked that the cases support the proposition that, "[i]f there is an honest family transaction a slight legal consideration is sufficient to take the case out of the category of voluntary deeds". So it is certainly arguable that in certain types of relationship the courts may impose qualitively different standards before the promise can be enforced, standards that may not be as exacting as in other areas of human or commercial relationships. Consideration may not be one doctrine but in fact several doctrines.

---

[118] The facts raise issues of duress, discussed in Ch.12. *Wolda* was distinguished in *Hobbs v TDI Canada* (2005) 246 D.L.R. (4th) 43, where an employee signed a document waiving rights to sales commission; no promise to retain the employee was made or capable of being implied so consideration was absent.

[119] [2002] 2 N.Z.L.R. 91.

[120] [2003] UKPC 22.

[121] (Oxford: Clarendon Press, 1979), at pp.457–458.

[122] (1860) 9 C.B. (N.S.) 159.

[123] (1842) 5 I.Eq.R. 12.

[124] [1918] 1 I.R. 169.

2–47 Atiyah has argued that in cases where a promise was made in order to induce the promisee into a course of action which causes the promisee to act, thereby incurring a liability that would not otherwise have arisen, the courts of equity, certainly by the beginning of the nineteenth century, regarded the promise as enforceable. Atiyah gives as an illustration the decision of Lord Eldon in *Crosbie v McDougall*.[125] In the case of *Wilcocks v Hennyngton*[126] Sugden L.C. approved *Crosbie v McDougall* but on the facts before him was unable to find any altered change of position.

Payment of an Existing Debt

2–48 The rule in *Pinnel's* case,[127] as laid down by the English Court of Common Pleas, dictates that if a liquidated sum is owed by A to B, a promise by B to take a lesser sum in full satisfaction of the larger debt will not bind B. After receipt he can immediately sue for the balance because the debtor has only performed part of a contractual duty already owed to the creditor. In other words, the creditor's promise is unenforceable for lack of consideration. In *O'Neill v Murphy*[128] the rule in *Pinnel's* case was described by Andrews L.J. as a landmark "too firmly fixed in our law to be shaken".

2–49 The decision of the House of Lords in *Foakes v Beer*[129] places the consideration doctrine at the forefront of promises to make, and also discharge, contracts. In this case Beer, a judgment creditor in the sum of £2,090, gave Foakes a promise that if he paid £500 and the balance by instalments, she would not "take any proceedings whatever on the judgment". Judgments carried interest and the issue arose whether her promise estopped Beer from seeking the interest. Interpreting the agreement as if it impliedly contained a promise to forego interest, the House of Lords held that the interest could be recovered because Beer's promise to forego interest was unsupported by consideration. The decision is a harsh and somewhat mechanical one and it fails to meet commercial expectations and commercial practice. As we shall see, the issue of reconciling this case with promissory estoppel remains problematical in English and Irish law.

2–50 Other jurisdictions, however, have been more forthright in addressing the venerable line of authority that starts with the dictum in *Pinnel's* case. In Canada, the New Brunswick Court of Appeal has held that the rule in *Pinnel's* case had to be qualified in the light of the need to produce a more

---

[125] (1806) 13 Ves. 148.
[126] (1855) 5 I.Ch.R. 38.
[127] (1602) 5 Co.Rep. 117a. See Kane (2014) 37 D.U.L.J. 79.
[128] [1936] N.I. 16. See also *Ferguson v Davies* [1997] 1 All E.R. 315.
[129] (1884) 9 App. Cas. 605. See also *Riordan v Carroll* [1996] 2 I.L.R.M. 263, and *Inland Revenue v Fry* [2001] S.T.C. 1715.

reasoned result according with day-to-day business practice.[130] A bank agreed to accept $1,000 in full discharge of a judgment debt awarded against a debtor for $3,780, this agreement being confirmed in writing by the bank. At first instance the settlement was held not to be binding, following *Pinnel's* case. On appeal, consideration was held to be present. Angers J.A. declared:

> "[I]t cannot be denied that a financial institution, of its own accord and knowing all the consequences of its action, entered into an agreement by which it agreed to waive the priority of a judgment in its favour in return for part payment of the debt due to it. This agreement constituted full satisfaction. The consideration for the Caisse Populaire was the immediate receipt of payment and the saving of time, effort and expense."[131]

However, in these islands, *Foakes v Beer* has yet to be directly challenged and some courts[132] are constrained by the doctrine of *stare decisis* in finding ways around such an illogical proposition.

2–51 If, however, a new element is introduced into the relationship the promise will be binding; there will be both agreement (accord) and consideration (satisfaction) for the promise to release the debtor from his obligation to pay the larger debt. So, if instead of paying €10 I pay by giving an object, this new element will suffice regardless of the worth of the object. It is established that payment by cheque is not a new element. Alternatively, payment of the lesser sum before the date due or in a different place to that previously agreed will suffice.

2–52 Although this rule was not applied by the House of Lords until 1884 it has been accepted and (reluctantly) acted upon by the courts for centuries. In *Drogheda Corp v Fairtlough*[133] premises were demised in 1820 for a period of 99 years to a local clergyman. The Corporation in 1837 passed a resolution agreeing to reduce the rent as a gesture to the tenant but before this could be done the clergyman died. The Corporation decided to carry out the resolution and in 1842 the old lease was surrendered and a new lease executed for the remainder of the 99-year period, rent reduced from £11 9s. 8d. per annum to £5 6s. per annum. The rent was paid at the new rate until 1854 when the Corporation sued for the arrears of rent calculated at the original higher rate from 1842 until 1854. The action succeeded. Lefroy C.J. indicated that payment of a lesser sum under a parol agreement rather than one by deed cannot at common law be deemed any satisfaction of a larger, liquidated sum unless some collateral advantage, however small, is given. In this case there

---

[130] *Robichaud v Caisse Populaire* (1990) 69 D.L.R. (4th) 589.
[131] (1990) 69 D.L.R. (4th) 589 at 595.
[132] *Re Selectmove* [1995] 2 All E.R. 531; *Collier v P & M J Wright (Holdings) Ltd* [2008] 1 W.L.R. 643.
[133] (1858) 8 Ir.C.L.R. 98.

was no collateral advantage. "What is the consideration which the corporation received for this agreement? They received a less rent; but upon the other hand the tenant was allowed to keep in his pocket the balance of the greater rent." This common law decision directly confronts the modern cases on promissory estoppel but before we turn to this difficult problem two exceptions to the rule that payment of a smaller sum is not sufficient consideration should be noted. These cases represent a significant exception to the rule that consideration must move from a promisee.

(1) Compositions with creditors

2–53 Suppose X, a trader, has a large number of creditors but lacks the financial resources to pay them. He faces bankruptcy and the creditors run the risk of being paid little or nothing. It will be in the interest of all concerned for the creditors to agree to take less than that due. This agreement or composition is a valid way of ensuring that payment of the lesser sum will bind a creditor. So in *Morans v Armstrong*[134] a partner in the plaintiff firm agreed to take 6s. 8d. in the pound on sums due the firm. When the money was tendered it was refused. An action to recover the original sum due failed.

(2) Payment by a third party

2–54 In *Lawder v Peyton*[135] the administrator of a creditor's estate sought execution over the property of the defendant who owed a debt of £534, £268 of which had been paid, not by the defendant but by a third party on the defendant's behalf. It was held that to permit recovery of the entire sum after payment would be a fraud upon the defendant. Although both this case and *Morans v Armstrong*, above, seem based on the desire to prevent fraud it is doubtful whether it is the defendant who is defrauded. In these cases it seems more likely that the third parties involved are the sole victims. This alternative reasoning has been selected to justify similar rules developed by the English judges.[136]

Promissory or Equitable Estoppel

2–55 The doctrine of estoppel is historically a common law doctrine. In the case of *Jorden v Money*[137] the House of Lords declared the doctrine to apply only to cases where the statement made is one of existing fact. If, therefore, I say "X does not owe me €100" I will at common law be prevented or estopped from denying the truth of this declaration. If, however, I say "you owe me €11 but pay me €6; I do not intend at any time to recover the balance", estoppel

---

[134] (1840) Arm. Mac. Og. 25. See LRC 100, *Report on Personal Debt Management and Debt Enforcement* (2010).
[135] (1877) 11 I.R.C.L. 41.
[136] *Welby v Drake* (1825) 1 C. & P. 557; *Cook v Lister* (1863) 13 C.B. (N.S.) 543.
[137] (1845) 5 H.L.Cas. 185.

will not operate. My statement is one of intention, not fact. So, if we return to *Drogheda Corp v Fairtlough*, at para.2–52 above, we can see that those facts fall into the second category. In the case of *Munster & Leinster Bank v Croker*,[138] Black J. upheld the view that estoppel cannot operate on statements of intention. The really significant feature of *Jorden v Money* is the extension of this distinction into cases where the power of a court of equity to prevent a promisor from going back on a promise is being invoked by the promisee. In *Jorden v Money* the promisor led the promisee to believe that she would not seek to recover a debt, in consequence of which the promisee took on family commitments which he submitted he would not otherwise have done if the promisor had not given a voluntary undertaking not to seek to recover the debt in the future. The promisee sought a declaration that the debt was irrecoverable but failed on the ground that the doctrine of estoppel by representation only operated on statements of existing fact and not statements of law. In a vigorous dissenting judgment Lord St. Leonards argued that equitable case law would be operative in such a situation as the one before the House of Lords, but this approach did not find favour with the House.

2–56 Where the traditional, i.e. *Jorden v Money*, approach is applied, the effect of the estoppel is exclusionary. The promisor is estopped from pleading or introducing facts which vary or contradict the representation already made. So while the estoppel can be used to provide the representee with a defence, or can be used in an ancillary way if the representee has an independent cause of action, it is rarely available to give the representee a cause of action, except in exceptional instances, such as giving a tenancy by estoppel; see *Ramsden v Dyson*.[139]

2–57 There are nevertheless some excellent instances of an estoppel by representation being used to overcome some formidable obstacles to a plaintiff's success in litigation. In *McNeill v Miller*[140] the plaintiff left his motor car with the defendants for repair. The plaintiff was told that the defendants had insurance cover and, acting on this, the plaintiff did not obtain separate insurance. The vehicle was destroyed by fire and the plaintiff sued on the misrepresentation of fact, for it transpired that no cover was available. The defendants were held to be estopped from denying that the motor car was insured for the plaintiff. Wright J. observed that the general principle of estoppel applied notwithstanding the absence of a contract to insure.

2–58 Nevertheless it is clear that the line of equitable authority commencing with *Hughes v Metropolitan Railway Co*[141] threatens this limited view of the estoppel doctrine. In that case it was said by Lord Cairns L.C., an Irishman, that:

---

[138] [1940] I.R. 185.
[139] (1866) L.R. 1 H.L. 129; *JC v WC*, unreported, High Court, December 19, 2003.
[140] [1907] 2 I.R. 328.
[141] (1877) 2 App.Cas. 439.

"It is the first principle upon which all courts of equity proceed that if parties who have entered into definite and distinct terms involving certain legal results ... afterwards by their own act ... enter upon a course of negotiations which has the effect of leading one of the parties to suppose that the strict legal rights arising under the contract will not be enforced or will be kept in suspense ... the person who otherwise might have these rights will not be allowed to enforce them where it would be inequitable, having regard to the dealings which have thus taken place between the parties."[142]

This line of authority, if carried to its logical conclusion, would mean that the dicta in *Pinnel's* case[143] would be bad law and that all promises and not merely those made in the context of a pre-existing contractual relationship are enforceable if the promise is seriously meant and the other party acts on it, even in a way not stipulated or requested by the promisor. In short, the rule in *Drogheda Corp v Fairtlough*, *Jorden v Money*, and the entire bargain doctrine of consideration would be swept aside. This movement towards making a non-bargain promise enforceable began in earnest after the judgment in *Central London Property Trust v High Trees House*.[144] In that case Denning J. (as he then was) stated *obiter* that he would apply Lord Cairn's principle to hold a landlord estopped from going back on a promise to reduce the rent.

2–59 The facts of the *High Trees* case are instructive and straightforward. High Trees House, a London block of flats, was the subject of a 99-year lease, the rent being £2,500 per annum. After the outbreak of the Second World War it became extremely difficult to let the flats so the lessee agreed to pay half the annual rent for as long as war conditions lasted. By the terms of the agreement the full rent would become payable when war conditions ended. By the beginning of 1945 the flats were all let and the receiver of the landlord company sought to recover rental arrears for the last half of 1945, effectively testing the basis for mounting a more extensive action. Denning J. held that while the terms of the agreement meant that the landlord was clearly entitled to succeed on this claim he stated *obiter* that the landlord could not succeed if he sought to resile from the agreement to take half the rental for the duration of the war. Relying on *Hughes v Metropolitan Railway* and other cases[145] in which representations of future intention have been held to restrain a landlord from relying on strict legal rights against a tenant, Denning J. indicated that these cases were applicable to promises generally and that in his view the proper principle to apply is that "a promise intended to be binding, intended to be acted on, and in fact acted on, is binding so far as its terms properly apply". This principle is of great scope and has been cited with approval in several

---

[142] (1877) 2 App.Cas. 439 at 448.
[143] (1602) 5 Co.Rep. 117a.
[144] [1947] K.B. 130.
[145] *Birmingham and District Land Co v London and North Western Rly* (1888) 40 Ch.D. 268.

Irish cases. One of the most important decisions on the *High Trees* principle is that of Barron J. in *Kenny v Kelly*.[146] The applicant sought, by way of judicial review, a declaration that she was entitled to a place as an undergraduate Arts degree student at University College Dublin. As a transferring student from Trinity College Dublin, the applicant was of the belief that her application had been successfully processed by the defendant and that she had been given a right to defer taking up her place for one academic year. On the facts Barron J. found that such an assurance had been given and that she acted upon the assurance by making part payment of fees; citing Denning J. in *High Trees* Barron J. said that in that case "the essence of promissory estoppel was said to be a promise intended to be binding intended to be acted upon, and in fact acted upon".

2–60 Many judges and academic commentators have struggled to reconcile promissory estoppel with both consideration theory and accepted equitable principles. One school, for example, draws a distinction between promissory estoppel and proprietary estoppel, indicating that cases of promissory estoppel will sometimes afford a party a defence in a contractual context but that such an estoppel cannot create new rights or independent causes of action. Proprietary estoppel, however, may create new rights where it would be unjust or unconscionable for equity not to intervene, but this will only occur when the subject matter of the estoppel is real property. At the other extreme are commentators and judges who suggest a more universal approach is needed, the view being taken that illogical and fragmented categories should not be utilised just to preserve the bargain theory of consideration, for example.

Orthodox views of equitable estoppel

2–61 In later cases the English courts have attempted to limit the *High Trees* case to promises made, first, to suspend and not to give up altogether a legal right, the right to resile from the statement being available where reasonable notice is given; see *Ajayi v R. T. Briscoe (Nigeria) Ltd*.[147] Secondly, the estoppel can only operate where a pre-existing legal relationship can be shown as between the parties; see *Combe v Combe*.[148] A third limitation remains to be considered by the House of Lords. Is it necessary for the party pleading the estoppel to show that the promise caused the promisee to act to his or her detriment? Lord Denning rejected this as an essential requirement, e.g. *Brikom Investments Ltd v Carr*,[149] but there are cases in which the courts have emphasised that if promissory estoppel is to apply there must be evidence that the promise has caused the person pleading estoppel to act in a certain way; see

---

[146] [1988] I.R. 457; *Noonan v O'Connell*, unreported, High Court, April 10, 1987.
[147] [1964] 1 W.L.R. 1326; *Offredy Developments Ltd v Steinback* (1971) 221 E.G. 963; *North Down Hotels Ltd v Province-Wide Filling Stations Ltd* [1993] N.I. 261.
[148] [1951] 2 K.B. 215.
[149] [1979] Q.B. 467; *Walmsley v Acid Jazz Records* [2001] E.C.D.R. 29.

The Scaptrade.[150] Indeed in *McCambridge v Winters*,[151] Murphy J. adopted as a correct statement of the law in Ireland an observation made by Diplock J. in *Lowe v Lombank Ltd*[152] in which Diplock J. held that for an estoppel to apply the representation made must be intended to be acted upon and in fact acted upon by the representee to his detriment: see also Costello J. in *Industrial Yarns Ltd v Greene*.[153] In *North Down Hotels Ltd v Province-Wide Filling Stations Ltd*[154] Carswell L.J. insisted that detriment was an essential requirement under *Hughes v Metropolitan Railway*. The learned judge continued by holding that a tenant who was seeking to exercise an invalid option clause by appointing a valuer and preparing for an arbitration procedure did not thereby act to his detriment; the tenant "has not altered its position in doing so, merely incurred expenditure". With respect, this seems to be a very artificial view of what is needed to satisfy the detriment requirement and it may be better to regard the case as turning upon a finding that the *degree* of reliance was insufficient to make it inequitable to hold the landlord to honour his representation. A fourth limit holds that promissory estoppel cannot confer upon the party pleading estoppel a cause of action where none existed before: see Birkett L.J.'s "shield and sword" metaphor in *Combe v Combe*.[155] In *Chartered Trust Ireland Ltd v Healy*,[156] Barron J. applied the shield and sword metaphor so as to deny a remedy in damages to the plaintiff who had purchased a motor vehicle in circumstances where the contract of sale itself was void. Because the contract was void the estoppel could not operate so as to confer a cause of action. However, the estoppel can be used to defeat a claim, or, in exceptional cases, may be used in an ancillary manner by a plaintiff who has been led to believe that a particular defence will not be asserted by the defendant. In this sense the estoppel operates in an exclusionary manner, as in *Traynor v Fegan*[157] when the statements made by the defendant's solicitors in respect of whether service of proceedings would be accepted on behalf of the client were held to operate an estoppel, denying the defendant the right to plead non-compliance with the Statute of Limitations 1957; see also *Incorporated Food Products Ltd (In Liquidation) v Minister for Agriculture*.[158] In this writer's view the limitation seems a rather unsatisfactory one for if the whole basis of promissory estoppel is a desire to avoid the inequitable and unfair consequences that may follow from the non-observance of promises that are meant to be binding and acted

---

[150] [1983] 1 All E.R. 301; *South Caribbean Trading Ltd v Trafigura Beheer BV* [2005] 1 Lloyds Rep. 128.

[151] Unreported, High Court, August 28, 1984.

[152] [1960] 1 W.L.R. 196.

[153] [1948] I.L.R.M. 15; *Morrow v Carty* [1957] N.I. 174.

[154] [1993] N.I. 261. It may be that detriment is an essential proof where promissory estoppel is pleaded but that it is not necessary in instances of proprietary estoppel when unconscionability is the central focus. Even this distinction is highly artificial.

[155] [1951] 2 K.B. 215.

[156] Unreported, High Court, December 10, 1985; *Zurich Bank v McConnon* [2011] IEHC 75.

[157] [1985] I.R. 586.

[158] Unreported, High Court, June 6, 1984.

upon, it seems vital that a flexible system of remedies, including damages, be available to the courts.

2–62 It is also clear from the cases that before an estoppel can operate there must be a clear and unambiguous statement of fact or intention; a vague statement cannot be used to justify imposing an estoppel upon the person making that vague or ambiguous statement: see *Woodhouse Ltd v Nigerian Produce Ltd.*[159] For this reason Ellis J. held in *Keegan & Roberts Ltd v Comhairle Chontae Átha Cliath*[160] that alleged assurances given could not create an estoppel. *Odyssey Pavillion LLP v Marcus Ward Ltd*[161] provides a good example of a classical promissory estoppel situation. Sheridan was the moving force behind the Odyssey Millennium project in Belfast, letting two of the units in 1999. Under the terms of the lease standard rental provisions were imposed on the tenants, one of whom was Marcus Ward Ltd, a company in the Sheridan Group. Curistan, the controlling mind behind both the landlord and the tenant companies, formulated as a policy that Sheridan would not charge or seek to recover rent from Marcus Ward Ltd until such time as that company was acquired by a third party. Following the trading difficulties of the Odyssey Millennium project Sheridan assigned all rental arrears due to it from its tenants, one of whom was Marcus Ward Ltd, in April 2009. Girvan L.J. found that while Curistan's own mental processes could not constitute the basis for grounding an adjustment in the contractual rights of Sheridan in respect of rents due, there was a sufficient basis for holding that Sheridan had made a promise or representation not to enforce its strict legal rights. Girvan L.J rejected the argument that the nature of the promise or representation must have the same degree of certainty as would be needed to give it contractual effect if it were to be supported by consideration. Perhaps rather less controversially, Girvan L.J argued that the focus is not on the intention of the representor who grants forbearance but on the conduct of that party and its effects on the position of the other party. Girvan L.J also restated the orthodox view that for promissory estoppel to operate there must be in place, at the time the promise was made, a legal relationship giving rise to rights and duties between the parties. As these factors were satisfied Girvan L.J went on to consider whether the representation had demonstrated a significant reliance and change of position in the way that Marcus Ward Ltd had operated its business. Girvan L.J. found this to be the case although, significantly, there was no discussion about whether the reliance needed to be detrimental reliance. The court held that as Sheridan had made this representation in 2000—a representation that was ratified through conduct when rent was neither offered nor requested—it could only be resiled from when the third party interest in the unit came into

---

[159] [1972] A.C. 741; *North Down Hotels Ltd v Province-Wide Filling Stations Ltd* [1993] N.I. 261; *National Asset Loan Management v Downes* [2014] IEHC 71; *Hoare v Allied Irish Banks* [2014] IEHC 221.

[160] Unreported, High Court, March 12, 1981.

[161] [2011] NI Ch 10.

existence, as intended. As Sheridan could not have obtained arrears of rent for that period, neither could the assignee, on the foot of the promissory estoppel.

2–63 The clearest and most rational statement on the application of promissory estoppel to contemporary commercial conditions is to be found in s.90(1) of the US Restatement of Contracts (2nd):

> A promise which the promisor should reasonably expect to induce action or forbearance on the part of the promisee and which does induce such action or forbearance is binding if injustice can be avoided only by enforcement of the promise. The remedy granted for breach may be limited as justice requires.

Section 90 does not dispense with the consideration doctrine. Contracts remain enforceable as contracts if consideration is present. Section 90 is often likely to be invoked in cases where a conditional contract exists and the promisee relies on assurances that are not actionable in contract but loss results from foreseeable reliance.[162] The flexibility of the remedy is an essential feature of s.90; normally the measure of damages will be gauged by reference to the losses incurred and not the benefit promised. In the Minnesota case of *Grouse v Group Health Plan, Inc.*[163] the plaintiff relied upon a promise of a job offer by giving notice to his employer and turning down another job offer. He was then injured when the offer was withdrawn following a reference given to the defendant. The loss suffered, rather than the benefit anticipated, was the basis of assessment in *Grouse*. On the other hand, in Illinois promissory estoppel was held to be an affirmative cause of action entitling a promisee to recover damages when a prospective business associate raised from preliminary statements of intention that the representee reasonably relied upon: *Newton Tractor Sales v Kubota Tractor Corp.*[164] US states are divided on key issues of this kind, notwithstanding the powerful persuasive pull of s.90(1) of the US Restatement.

2–64 The Australian courts have followed the general approach adopted by the English judiciary. Attempts have been made in the Australian courts to explore promissory estoppel and its relationship with older cases and in particular the link between promissory estoppel—which applies to promises of fact and future intention—and the older case of *Jorden v Money*[165] in which the majority of the House of Lords limited estoppel to statements of fact. In *Reed v Sheehan*[166] and in *Legione v Hateley*[167] approval of the limited doctrine of promissory estoppel, enunciated in the Privy Council in *Ajayi v R. T. Briscoe*

---

[162] *Hoffman v Red Owl Stores Inc.* 133 N.W. 2d. 267 (1965); Craswell 48 Stan. L.R. 481 (1996).
[163] 306 N.W. 2d 114 (1981).
[164] 906 N.E. 2d 520 (2009). The judgment presents powerful counterweights to enforceability of promises via promissary estoppel in commercial negotiations.
[165] (1845) 5 H.L.Cas. 185.
[166] [1982] F.L.R. 206.
[167] (1983) 57 A.L.J.R. 292.

(Nigeria) Ltd[168] was given by the Federal Court of Australia and the High Court of Australia respectively. It is significant, however, that in *Legione v Hateley* the members of the High Court of Australia refused to decide whether promissory estoppel should be limited to cases where there is a pre-existing legal relationship. The decision of the High Court of Australia in *Waltons Stores (Interstate) v Maher*[169] unequivocally rules that promissory estoppel may be pleaded by a plaintiff when no pre-existing legal relationship exists and that the promissory estoppel principle may give a cause of action to the promisee. In this case negotiations for the sale of real property were at an advanced stage and prospective lessors undertook site clearance and construction work in the belief that a draft contract had been executed. The lessees were aware of the lessors' state of mind but withdrew from the transaction, some 40 per cent of the construction work stipulated in the lease having been completed. The lessors could not sue in contract but brought an action pleading promissory estoppel. The basic factor stressed by the members of the court was the unconscionable behaviour of the lessees in failing to disabuse the lessors of their mistaken belief and their willingness to allow the lessors to expend monies when the lessees knew there was a prospect of the lease not being signed. This case is of great importance, not least because several of the judges stressed that the basis of the decision was promissory estoppel rather than proprietary estoppel and all members of the court were anxious to adopt a unitary view of the estoppel doctrine rather than the more fragmented perspective of some judges who emphasise the different nature of the various estoppels. Both *Waltons Stores* and *Verwayen* have been frequently cited and discussed in a number of Australian intellectual property cases and it appears from the discussion in those cases that giving a successful plaintiff a cause of action is not a difficulty for the Australian courts; see *Lyndel Nominees Pty Ltd v Mobil Oil Australia Ltd*,[170] *EOS Australia Pty Ltd v Expo Tomei Pty*[171] and *Australian Olympic Committee Inc. v Big Fights Inc.*[172] One commentator has written that in the decision handed down in *Giumelli v Giumelli*[173] the High Court of Australia has abolished the distinction between proprietary and promissory estoppel.[174] Recent Australian case law[175] suggests that promissory estoppel may be invoked in relation to pre-contractual statements by which the person making the representation induced the representee to enter into a contract. The sellers of the development land promised that if the development did not go ahead in certain circumstances "you don't have to buy and you'll get your money back". Relying on this oral assurance clause the buyers paid a deposit and lent money

---

[168] [1964] 1 W.L.R. 1326.
[169] (1988) 76 A.L.R. 513; *Austotel Ltd v Franklins Selfserve Pty* (1989) 16 N.S.W.L.R. 582; *Commonwealth v Verwayen* (1990) 64 A.L.J.R. 540; *Lyndel Nominees Pty Ltd v Mobil Oil Australia Ltd* (1997) 37 I.P.R. 599.
[170] (1997) 37 I.P.R. 599.
[171] (1998) 42 I.P.R. 277.
[172] (1999) 46 I.P.R. 53.
[173] (1999) 161 A.L.R. 437.
[174] Wright (1999) 115 L.Q.R. 476.
[175] *Saleh v Romanous* [2010] NSWCA 274.

to the sellers but the development did not proceed. Holding that the contract contained an entire agreement clause and that the parol evidence rule together meant the seller's promise was not actionable in contract, there was sufficient Australian and English authority[176] to allow the buyers to recover their deposit and monies advanced to the sellers. However, in that situation the New South Wales Court of Appeal indicated that promissory estoppel was only to be used to act as a restraint on the enforcement of rights.[177] In *Ashton v Pratt*,[178] a case where a former escort agreed to become the mistress of a billionaire in exchange for money, property and a trust fund, the New South Wales Court of Appeal noted the tension between *Waltons Stores* and cases such as *Saleh v Romanous*. The fact that insufficient acts of detrimental reliance were put before the court and that the New South Wales Court of Appeal found that any agreement that could have been made out would have been void for uncertainty meant that the ideological aspects of promissory estoppel did not require to be addressed. It will be necessary to establish proprietary estoppel if a promise to transfer a benefit to the promisee is to be recoverable under Australian law.[179] Irish law shares a similar perspective, although there are isolated decisions that suggest otherwise.

2–65 In *Folens v Minister for Education*,[180] McWilliam J. seemed prepared to allow the plaintiff to recover compensation for wasted pre-contractual expenditure, incurred at the behest of the defendant, but held that he was unable to do so because the *High Trees* principle required a definite commitment or representation be made, and, on the facts, no commitment or representation had been made. This is a somewhat oblique authority on this matter, however. The decision of Kenny J. in *Revenue Commissioners v Moroney*[181] is of greater importance. The learned judge held that a father who had obtained his two sons' signatures to a deed by promising them that at no time would they be expected to pay the consideration stated in the deed, would be estopped, under *High Trees*, from reneging on his promise. Kenny J. not only implicitly rejected

---

[176] Reliance on *Bank Negara Indonesia v Hoalim* [1973] 2 M.L.J. 3 (a Privy Council case) is misplaced as there was a pre-existing relationship—a landlord and tenant case. *Saleh v Romanous* (leave to appeal to the High Court of Australia refused) looks more like an evidential estoppel case rather than an injurious reliance case (i.e. Lord Diplock per *The Hannah Blumenthal*). This completely radical position taken by the Australian courts is evident from *Bushby v Dixon Homes Du Pont Pty Ltd* (2010) 78 N.S.W.L.R. 111, when the court was asked to decide if promissory estoppel could afford a defence as well as a cause of action (i.e. provide a shield as well as a sword)!

[177] See also *DHJPM Pty Ltd v Blackthorn Resources Ltd* [2011] NSWCA 348.

[178] [2015] NSWCA 12.

[179] *Sidhu v Van Dyke* [2014] HCA 19. The balance between granting expectation-based remedies as distinct from reliance-based orders is very well drawn by the New Zealand Court of Appeal in *Wilson Parking New Zealand Ltd v Fanshawe 136 Ltd* [2014] NZCA 407. The Court observed that "the court should grant expectation-based relief where the minimum equity will not be satisfied by anything less than enforcing the promise."

[180] [1984] I.L.R.M. 265. Contrast *McCarron v McCarron*, unreported, Supreme Court, February 13, 1997, a proprietary estoppel case where expenditure of money and/or erection of buildings were held not to be the sole criteria for establishing a proprietary estoppel.

[181] [1972] I.R. 372.

Jorden v Money, for the father's promise referred to his future intention, he also expressly rejected the view that estoppel only suspends a legal right and that for the estoppel to operate there must exist a legal relationship at the time the promise was made. In the Supreme Court the appeal was dismissed but the members of the Supreme Court used the parol evidence rule to explain the facts before them and declined to comment on *High Trees*.

2–66 In the present writer's view it is a mistake to see the *High Trees* case as presenting the courts with the problem of reconciling the authorities in such a way as to leave *Jorden v Money* and the bargain theory of consideration intact. Lord Denning M.R. once wrote: "[w]e are approaching a state of affairs which Ames regarded as desirable, namely that any act done on the faith of a promise should be regarded as sufficient consideration to make it binding".[182] Some 28 years later Lord Denning viewed the cases on estoppel in his book, *The Discipline of Law*, as abolishing "the doctrine of consideration in all but a handful of cases".[183] While it is doubtful that the present English cases go so far, the implications of equitable or promissory estoppel are profound; are we not in fact returning to Lord Mansfield's moral obligation theory? This is certainly the case if the courts favour the view that the estoppel will be upheld even in the absence of proof that the promisee has acted to his detriment; in such a situation the estoppel would be truly promissory. Some support for this view can be found in *Waltons Stores (Interstate) v Maher*[184] when several members of the court indicated that a detrimental change of position is not needed to ground the estoppel, whether proprietory or promissory. Brennan J., for example, stated that the person pleading estoppel can successfully do so when that person "acts or abstains from acting in reliance on the assumption or expectation" created by the promisor. The emphasis on the unconscionable conduct of the promisor rather than the detrimental reliance of the promisee is a striking feature of this case. It is certainly true that emphasis is placed on the unconscionable consequences of the representation by many judges and that some progress could be made by adopting the term "equitable estoppel" as a unifying concept that, for example, sees detrimental reliance as an aspect of unconscionability.[185]

2–67 In Ireland, the development of the concept of promises being enforceable because of the legitimate expectation that the promise creates seems likely to deepen the conceptual confusion between promissory estoppel as a private law device, based perhaps on detrimental reliance as in s.90 of the US Restatement (2nd), and the much looser and, frankly, inflexible concept of legitimate expectation, as a source of actionable right,[186] which stands apart from existing

---

[182] (1951) 15 M.L.R. 1 at 9–10.

[183] (London: Butterworth, 1979), p.223.

[184] (1988) 76 A.L.R. 513.

[185] Lunney [1992] Conv. 230; Halliwell, "Estoppel: unconscionability as a cause of action" [1994] *Legal Studies* 15. In Australia it is possible to identify something of a retreat from the position outlined by Brennan J. in *Waltons Stores. Ashton v Pratt* [2015] NSWCA 12 traces the fault lines very well.

[186] The basis seems to be *Amalgamated Investment Property Co v Texas Commerce International*

civil law concepts such as contract, unjust enrichment, actionable misrepresentation and promissory estoppel, to name but a few. In Ireland, severance of the link between legitimate expectation and injurious reliance seems to have already taken place.[187]

2–68 At the present time, Irish law remains rooted in a rather orthodox view of promissory estoppel. In *The Barge Inn Ltd v Quinn Hospitality Ireland Operations 3 Ltd*,[188] Finlay Geoghegan J. was required to consider whether promissory estoppel could apply in a case where trading difficulties experienced by a tenant lead to a promised rent reduction. The learned judge took the six factor summary of the relevant principles as stated by McDermott in *Contract Law* (2001) to be representative of Irish law. The key ingredients are:

> "(a) the pre-existing legal relationship between the parties;
> (b) an unambiguous representation;
> (c) reliance by the promisee (and possible detriment);
> (d) some element of unfairness and unconscionability;
> (e) that the estoppel is being used not as a cause of action, but as a defence; and
> (f) that the remedy is a matter for the Court."

This judgment has proved to be influential in a number of later cases.[189] There can be no doubt, however, that in the long term significant changes are in the wind. In *The Hannah Blumenthal*[190] Lord Diplock stated:

> "[T]he rule that neither party can rely on his own failure to communicate accurately to the other party his own real intention by what he wrote or said or did, as negativing the consensus ad idem, is an example of a general principle of English law that injurious reliance on what another person did may be a source of legal rights against him. I use the broader expression 'injurious reliance' in preference to 'estoppel' so as to embrace all circumstances in which A can say to B, 'you led me reasonably to believe that you were assuming particular legally enforceable obligations to me,' of which promissory or *High Trees* estoppel (see *Central London Property Trust Ltd v High Trees House Ltd* [1947] K.B. 130) affords another example, whereas 'estoppel,' in the strict sense of the term, is an exclusionary rule of evidence, though it may operate so as to affect substantive legal rights inter partes."[191]

Bank Ltd [1982] Q.B. 84.
[187] *Webb v Ireland* [1988] I.R. 353; *Duggan v An Taoiseach, Members of the Government and Thomas Gerard Fahy* [1989] I.L.R.M. 710. See generally Mee (1998) 33 Ir. Jur. 187.
[188] [2013] IEHC 387.
[189] *NALM v Kelleher* [2015] IEHC 169; *Harrahill v Swaine* [2015] IECA 36; *Gladney and Others v P O'M.* [2015] IEHC 718; *Sheehan v Breccia* [2016] IEHC 67.
[190] [1983] 1 All E.R. 34.
[191] [1983] 1 All E.R. 34 at 49.

Proprietary estoppel

2–69 Irish judges, however, are not, it seems, attracted to "injurious reliance" but there are a number of recent estoppel cases where broader approaches to the enforcement of non-contractual statements relating to land are evident. Some of these cases are instances which are traditionally to be regarded as proprietary estoppel cases. The decision of Costello J. in *In the matter of JR*[192] asserts that the distinction between promissory estoppel and proprietary estoppel remains valid. In the former case, Costello J. opined that estoppel will not result in the creation of a right or interest in land but, rather, the representee obtains a personal right which can operate against the representor. In cases of proprietary estoppel, however, the representation relates to the creation of rights in the representee and in equity a species of constructive trust is imposed to prevent the representor from relying on his legal rights when it is unconscionable so to do. While Costello J. relied upon statements in Snell's *Principles of Equity* and English case law to justify this distinction, the underlying principles upon which the court intervenes under both these varieties of estoppel are fundamentally the same and it is not clear how such a distinction can be justified by reference to the consequences, or range of remedies, available to counterbalance the unfairness or unconscionability that the representor's statement or conduct has produced. Nevertheless the distinction could have interesting consequences. Promissory estoppel, as a personal right against the representation, does not appear to be affected by any underlying illegality as the Privy Council's decision in *Maharaj v Chand*[193] demonstrates, and in *Daly v Minister for the Marine*[194] the Supreme Court appeared to be willing to enforce the Minister's promise despite the illegal nature of the promisee's acts, had such acts been adduced.

2–70 In *Gillett v Holt*[195] the English Court of Appeal has produced a splendid analysis of the critical aspects to a claim brought in proprietary estoppel. The case concerned a married couple who, to quote Robert Walker L.J., devoted the best years of their lives to working for Mr Holt and his company, showing loyalty and devotion to his business interests, his social life and his personal wishes, on the strength of clear and repeated assurances that the farm on which they both worked would be left to Gillett and his family upon Holt's death. The trial judge had found that Holt had not made an irrevocable promise and that the salary paid to Gillett as farm manager over the years was not so low as to amount to unconscionable conduct by Holt, thus raising the equity. On both these critical points the Court of Appeal reversed the trial judge. The argument derived from *Taylor v Dickens*,[196] a decision that puts forward the view that a promise that is initially unsupported by consideration remains revocable, was

---

[192] [1993] I.L.R.M. 657; Delany, "Is there a future for Proprietary Estoppel as we know it?" (2009) 31 D.U.L.J. (ns) 440.
[193] [1986] A.C. 898.
[194] [2001] 3 I.R. 513.
[195] [2000] 2 All E.R. 289; *Little v Maguire* [2007] NI Ch 7.
[196] [1998] 3 F.C.R. 455.

criticised on the basis that it ignores the entire thrust of proprietary estoppel; it is the detrimental reliance that renders the promise irrevocable. On the second point, the Court of Appeal said the trial judge had considered detriment from too narrow a perspective:

> "[T]he detriment need not consist of the expenditure of money or other quantifiable financial detriment, so long as it is something substantial. The requirement must be approached as part of a broad inquiry as to whether repudiation of an assurance is or is not unconscionable in all the circumstances."[197]

Proprietary estoppel cases in recent years have become increasingly frequent, with rural Ireland (on both sides of the border) creating both the themes and the persona. The case of the returning emigrant,[198] the youngest sibling who stays at home on the farm to look after the ageing parents,[199] as well as the relative who takes up the running of the family farm,[200] have all been litigated. There has even been a case of a long-running romance between a young woman and an older man who gave the woman to believe that there would be property rights afforded to her when the time came.[201] These proprietary estoppel cases attest to the fact that the estoppel is made out even if there is scant evidence of clear oral representations, the core issue being whether it is equitable to allow the person who has made the promise or assurance, such as it is, to resile from it. In *Murphy v Rayner*,[202] an English case, an elderly and vulnerable man was induced to make promises in response to fraudulent statements. It was held not to be inequitable to allow the promises to be unenforceable. There is often great difficulty in relation to the remedy—a limited interest or an outright conveyance is often the choice and the Northern Ireland Chancery Division has followed the view that the court should strive to develop the minimum equity to do justice: *Kinney v McKittrick*.[203] These decisions are helpful even if the various judgments in the pronouncements of the House of Lords in *Thorner v Major*[204] do nothing to resolve the conflicts between the terminology and taxonomy in this branch of law—as Lord Walker of Gestingthorpe there acknowledged.

---

[197] Per Robert Walker L.J. at [2000] 2 All E.R. 289 at 308. See also *Campbell v Griffin* [2001] W.T.L.R. 981 and *Flinn v Flinn* [1999] 3 V.R. 712 in which the first instance decision in *Gillett v Holt* was not followed by the Victoria Court of Appeal.

[198] *McDermott v McDermott* [2008] NI Ch 5.

[199] *Re Estate of Johnston* [2008] NI Ch 11.

[200] *Dolan v Reynolds* [2011] IEHC 334; *Kinney v McKittrick* [2011] NI Ch 24; *Naylor v Maher* [2012] IEHC 408.

[201] *Mulholland v Kane* [2009] NI Ch 9.

[202] [2011] EWHC 1 (Ch).

[203] [2011] NI Ch 24.

[204] [2009] 1 W.L.R. 776; *Henry v Henry* [2010] UKPC 3; Piska (2009) 72 M.L.R. 998; *Thorner v Major* has proved influential in Australia, suggesting that the distinction between promissory estoppel and proprietary estoppel should be maintained: *Ashton v Pratt* [2015] NSWCA 12. See also *Sidhu v Van Dyke* [2014] HCA 19.

2–71 One Irish case, *An Cummann Peile Botheimeach Teoranta v Albion Properties Ltd*,[205] attests to the use of proprietary estoppel in commercial contracts. As part of the defendants plan to redevelop the Phibsboro Shopping Centre in 2002, the plaintiffs agreed to sell a small parcel of land to the defendants. Heads of Agreement were drawn up in February 2003 and later proved the subject of revisions. The defendants paid tranches of the consideration as "goodwill gestures" to the plaintiffs on several occasions, as well as a non-refundable deposit. Difficulties with maps and lack of certainty on what precisely the land in question was, as well as disagreements on works prevented the negotiations from being concluded. In May 2006 negotiations ceased altogether. Edwards J. held that the matters to be agreed and executed by the parties prevented a finding that a concluded contract was ever in place. However, applying proprietary estoppel principles, Edwards J. held that it would be unconscionable for the plaintiff not to transfer the lands in question to the defendant. There were repeated assurances over several years that the deed would go ahead; over €1 million had been transferred on a goodwill basis at a time when the plaintiffs were in a dire financial state and there were strenuous efforts made by the defendants to close the transaction and meet the needs of the plaintiff. Edward J. declared that the plaintiffs held the lands in question upon a constructive trust for the benefit of the plaintiffs.

The Importance of Words and Conduct in Grounding an Estoppel

2–72 In *McMullan Brothers Ltd v McDonagh*,[206] the Supreme Court was required to consider whether a lessor who had placed the obligation onto the lessee to maintain equipment located on the premises could be estopped from enforcing these covenants by either words or conduct. In these situations the terminology used in recent times has included the notions of estoppel by representation as distinct from a representation by convention. In the first situation a representation may be made which may be held to bind the person who has made it. The representation may not be limited to verbal statements. In *Smith v Ireland*,[207] Finlay P. endorsed the following statement on the scope of equitable estoppel:

> "Short of an actual promise, if he, by his words or conduct, so behaves as to lead another to believe that he will not insist on his legal rights knowing or intending that the other will act on that belief—and he does so act, that again will raise an equity in favour of the other, and it is for the court to say in what way the equity may be satisfied."[208]

---

[205] [2008] I.E.H.C. 447.
[206] [2015] IESC 19.
[207] [1983] I.L.R.M. 300, quoting from Lord Denning MR's judgment in *Crabb v Arun District Council* [1976] 1 Ch. 179 at 188.
[208] [1976] 1 Ch. 179 at 188. See *In the matter of JR* [1993] I.L.R.M. 657 on flexibility of remedies.

An estoppel may also arise, not from words or conduct, but because the parties have agreed to conduct themselves by reference to some agreed or assumed state of affairs. This is described as an estoppel by convention. Both estoppels can overlap. Charleton J. in *McMullen Brothers* found that there was no basis for either an estoppel by representation or an estoppel by convention but his obiter comments on the scope of the estoppels provides a helpful summary of these forms of estoppel.[209]

The Relationship between Common Law and Equitable Estoppel

2–73 The important decision of the English Court of Appeal, in *Collier v P & M J Wright (Holdings) Ltd*,[210] may spark some efforts amongst the English judiciary to resolve the conflict between orthodox bargain theory and promissory estoppel. The facts raise a standard example of adequacy of consideration. C was one of a three-person partnership that ceased trading, owing large sums to the defendant. The defendant promised that if C paid one-third of the debt it would not pursue C for any of the remaining debt. Was this promise binding? Applying *Pinnel's* case, *Foakes v Beer* and *Re Selectmove*, the Court of Appeal held that this was simply an example of a promisee paying a lesser sum than the sum due to the promisor. The Court of Appeal declined the opportunity to carve out an exception to *Pinnel's* case by distinguishing this situation from the earlier precedents, but, demonstrating considerable courage, the Court of Appeal held that equitable considerations made this a situation where promissory estoppel could well prevail. The Court of Appeal took the view that this was in many ways the converse situation to that which arose in *D.C. Builders v Rees*,[211] that is, in this situation equity favoured the enforcement of the promise to take a lesser sum in discharge of the greater debt. This decision is limited in scope because all the Court of Appeal was asked to decide was whether C had an arguable case; nor does the factual situation raise broader issues relating to the remedies available vis-à-vis the estoppel. The problem of reconciling the conventional wisdom on the need for consideration to be present if a promise is to be enforceable with equitable development remains.

The Irish decisions that have considered the rule in *Pinnel*'s case in recent years however have continued to apply that reasoning.[212] In a series of cases involving payment of taxes to the Revenue Commissioners, several High Court judges[213] and the Court of Appeal[214] have observed that *Pinnel*'s case

---

[209] [2015] IESC 19, paras 26–32. See also *National Asset Loan Management Ltd v McMahon and Others* [2014] IEHC 71.

[210] [2008] 1 W.L.R. 643.

[211] [1966] 2. W.L.R. 288.

[212] See the masterly treatment of Finlay Geoghegan J. in *The Barge Inn Ltd v Quinn Hospitality Ireland Operations 3 Ltd* [2013] IEHC 387 (a rent reduction case).

[213] e.g. Fullam J. in *NALM v Kelleher* [2015] IEHC 169.

[214] *Harrahill v Swaine* [2015] IECA 36; *Gladney and Others v P.O'M.* [2015] IEHC 718.

and *Foakes v Beer* are binding so any adjustments in the law will require a clear ruling from the Supreme Court.

Legitimate expectation

2–74 In order for promises to be enforceable in contract a litmus test of consideration is necessary. For a promise to be enforceable in equity the estoppel principle requires detrimental reliance and/or unconscionability to be shown, although the precise scope of the broad equitable estoppel, and the specific varieties of the estoppels, await a definitive statement by the highest appellate courts in various jurisdictions. In Ireland, as elsewhere, the possibility that decisions taken by public bodies may be the subject of judicial review has produced a further line of complication in the form of the concept of legitimate expectation. The principle emerged in English and Irish law through cases which indicated that a public body could in certain circumstances be bound to follow certain procedural steps (e.g. consult or negotiate) when that public body has either done so in the past or has indicated to the person in question that such a procedure would be followed in the instant case. The idea that such a benefit or advantage may be obtained via a "legitimate expectation", which may not be the same thing as something obtained via contract or a representation, was accepted by the House of Lords in *Council of Public Service Unions v Minister for the Civil Service*.[215] The obligation to follow settled or agreed procedures has been accepted and extended by both the Irish and the UK courts. The leading Irish case is *Webb v Ireland*.[216] Here the plaintiffs, the finders of the Derrynaflan Hoard, were told by the Director of the National Museum that in response to their act of depositing the Hoard with the National Museum the plaintiffs would be "honourably treated". The Supreme Court extended the notion so as to include the legitimate expectation that a financial payment would be made, observing that such a payment was an aspect of the plaintiffs being "honourably treated". In giving his judgment Finlay C.J. had this to say of the concept itself in *Webb v Ireland*:

> "[T]he doctrine of 'legitimate expectation' sometimes described as 'reasonable expectation' has not in those terms been the subject matter of any decision of our courts. However, the doctrine connoted by such expressions is but an aspect of the well recognised equitable concept of promissory estoppel ... whereby a promise or representation as to intention may in certain circumstances be held binding on the representor or promisor."[217]

Later courts have continued to emphasise the links with promissory estoppel, the most striking example of which is probably the decision in *Association of*

---

[215] [1985] 1 A.C. 374. See Biehler, "Legitimate Expectation—An Odyssey" (2013) 2 Ir. Jur. 40 for a general treatment of the topic.

[216] [1988] I.R. 353; [1988] I.L.R.M. 565.

[217] [1988] I.R. 353 at 384, citing Denning M.R. in the *Texas Commerce* case. See generally Delany, "The Doctrine of Legitimate Expectation in Irish Law" (1990) 12 D.U.L.J. 1 and also (2009) 31 D.U.L.J. (ns) 440.

General Practitioners v Minister for Health[218] in which O'Hanlon J. indicated that legitimate expectation cannot create a cause of action for the concept is only an aspect of promissory estoppel, citing *Combe v Combe*.[219] That this view retains a degree of judicial support is evident from the decision of Hough J. in *Hennessey v St Gerard's School*.[220] In this case it was held that the plaintiff, a probationary teacher, was entitled to a right to a hearing before the school Board of Governors in advance of a decision being made to dismiss her for unsatisfactory performance. Hough J. reaffirmed the view that legitimate expectation was merely a part of promissory estoppel, and the plaintiff's right arose under the law of contract, promissory estoppel and legitimate expectation. It is significant that Hough J. identified the plaintiff's forbearance to exercise alternative dispute resolution procedures as the necessary consideration, or detrimental reliance, in relation to the first two causes of action, but the case here on those two causes of action is weak because no promise was made to the plaintiff vis-à-vis any right to be heard. In a recent article[221] Professor Delany explores the impact of legitimate expectation as a procedural or substantive remedy and she clearly favours the view that, *prima facie*, promises or representations made by public authorities should be honoured, via legitimate expectation.

Legitimate Expectation—The *Triatic* Decision

2–75 The decision of the Supreme Court in *Glencar Exploration Plc v Mayo County Council (No. 2)*[222] has added a further twist to the difficult question of resolving private law and public law mechanisms for recognising whether promises, understandings and objectively reasonable expectations should be recognised and vindicated in the courts. The decision taken by the Supreme Court in *Daly*, considered below, was based on the need for a representee to demonstrate reliance if legitimate expectation could be used to overreach administrative powers as well as possibly property rights and contractual freedoms. However, the *obiter* dicta of Fennelly J. in *Glencar (No. 2)* have suggested[223] that if a claim is brought, based upon a perceived failure of a public authority, three conditions must be met:

(1) the public authority must have made or adopted a position amounting to a promise or representation about how it will act in an identifiable area of its activity;

(2) the representation must have been addressed or conveyed, directly or indirectly, to an identifiable person or group affected actually or potentially so as to form part of a transaction definitely entered into, or a relationship

---

[218] [1995] 2 I.L.R.M. 481; see also *Garda Representative Association v Ireland* [1989] I.R. 193.
[219] [1951] 2 K.B. 215.
[220] *Irish Times Law Report*, March 13, 2006.
[221] [2007] 29 D.U.L.J. 423.
[222] [2002] 1 I.R. 84.
[223] [2002] 1 I.R. 84 at 162–163.

between that person or group and the public authority, and the person or group has acted on the faith of the representation;

(3) the representation must create an expectation reasonably entertained by the person or group that the public authority will abide by the representation to the extent that it will be unjust to permit the local authority to resile from it.

While nothing turns upon the observation of Hough J. in *Hennessy v St. Gerard's School*[224] in which the learned judge saw no reason to confine legitimate expectation to instances where the representor was a public authority, it is submitted that the decision of Laffoy J. in *Triatic Ltd v Cork County Council*[225] suggests that it may be legitimate to consider whether the public authority in question engaged in what may be considered to be its essentially regulatory, or public functions, or whether the activity is best regarded as commercial in nature. Here, negotiations to secure the sale of property with development potential failed to reach fruition, and the plaintiff developers sought damages for wasted fees, expenditure and time spent in negotiations, invoking legitimate expectation and, belatedly, a collateral contract argument. While Laffoy J. found that there was no representation given that the plaintiff would be permitted to negotiate exclusively with the defendants until an agreement was reached, Laffoy J. went on to approve submissions counsel made for the defendant that there are strong public policy considerations why the court should not extend legitimate expectation into the area of negotiations, on the basis that to do so will engender considerable uncertainty. After noting that the failure to agree a contract would have invited the plaintiffs to come to the court seeking the court to do the impossible, "order litigants or negotiating parties to agree the terms of a complex property development and acquisition transaction", Laffoy J. went on to identify the most compelling policy reason why legitimate expectation is an inappropriate doctrine in this context:

> "[T]here is a large grain of truth in the suggestion made on behalf of the defendant that in this case the plaintiff is seeking to extend the notion of legitimate expectation to insulate it from ordinary commercial risks which are inherent in negotiations ... the dealings between the parties in this case were essentially commercial in nature and ... the doctrine of legitimate expectation could only come into play because one of the parties in the commercial negotiations was a public body."

It remains to be seen whether negotiations *qua* public authority, acting as a public authority, and negotiations that are to be regarded as commercial, or governed by private law considerations, will form a part of future judicial developments in this critical area of the law of obligations.

---

[224] *Irish Times Law Report,* March 13, 2006; *McEneaney v Cavan and Monaghan Education and Training Board* [2014] IEHC 423.

[225] [2006] IEHC 111.

Application of Glencar (No. 2)

2–76 While Fennelly J. labelled his remarks in *Glencar (No. 2)* as being "essentially provisional" in nature, and while it is clear that these remarks were delivered *obiter* dicta, they have been followed by Macken J. in *Dunleavy v Dún Laoghaire–Rathdown County Council*.[226] In this case the plaintiffs were tenants of the defendant who had been locked in negotiation with the defendants over the sale to them of maisonettes, in accordance with statutory powers afforded to the defendants to sell those properties to tenants. Negotiations commenced in 1979 but legal difficulties meant that the power to sell was only clarified by Statutory Instrument in 1995. Macken J. held that legitimate expectation arose from this time and she gave a declaratory judgment holding that qualified tenants had a legitimate expectation to purchase as of the 1995 valuation of those properties. Macken J. also indicated that promissory estoppel could also be invoked by the plaintiffs although again there was no effort to distinguish or tease out the doctrinal differences, if any. Macken J. applied the Fennelly J. three-fold test and found that the first test was satisfied by a number of direct intimations to the plaintiffs that the scheme was likely to go ahead; the plaintiffs relied upon the representations, particularly by spending money on maintaining and improving their properties and not moving into other accommodation (some of which would have been available for purchase also) so the second factor was satisfied, while the third factor necessitated the plaintiffs to be entitled to the 1995 rather than the 1979 price, as a matter of justice.

2–77 It must be said that it is only to be expected that concepts of this kind will be the subject of different judicial interpretations and that conflicting judgments will exist until the concept is bedded down. It is evident, however, that legitimate expectation is a feature of Irish public law. In the case of *Re La Lavia*[227] the Supreme Court reaffirmed the decision in *Webb v Ireland* but found on the facts that no legitimate expectation arose. In this case the finders of three Spanish Armada wrecks claimed entitlement in law to monies for the discovery of that wreck site and artefacts. The Supreme Court distinguished *Webb* on the ground that in that case there was an express promise while in the instant case the applicants were maintaining title and negotiating with the State for a finder's reward, a somewhat contradictory position for them to maintain. Similarly, in *Daly v Minister for the Marine,* the Supreme Court emphasised the expectation must be a legitimate one. If the applicant has acted improperly, by exploiting an obvious error, for example, the expectation may not be legitimate.[228]

---

[226] [2005] IEHC 381.
[227] [1996] 1 I.L.R.M. 194. See also *Duff v Minister for Agriculture*, unreported, Supreme Court, March 4, 1997.
[228] [2001] 3 I.R. 513.

2–78 The possibility that a legitimate expectation may involve the acquisition of a tangible benefit in the form of a substantive right was affirmed by Hamilton P. in *Duggan v An Taoiseach, Members of the Government and Thomas Gerard Fahy*.[229] Here civil servants were held to have a legitimate expectation that their work in the farm tax office would last until such time as the work of that office was terminated under statute. This expectation was frustrated by an unlawful Government decision to terminate the work of that office and the applicants were held entitled to damages to vindicate the legitimate expectation in question. *Duggan v An Taoiseach* was explained as turning upon its own facts in the decision of the Supreme Court in *Glencar Exploration Plc v Mayo County Council (No. 2)*,[230] a case in which developers sought compensation for a mining ban. Even if the developers had been able to make out a legitimate expectation, the Supreme Court held that damages would not be available. Keane C.J. wrote:

"[D]amages would not be available for its breach in the absence of a subsisting contractual or equivalent relationship. The cases in which damages have been awarded such as *Webb* ... *Duggan* ... are distinguishable from this case because the applicants there were in long term contractual or equivalent relationships with the respondents and the wrongs done were akin to a breach of contract."[231]

The "equivalent relationship" in *Webb* appears to be one in which protracted negotiations were in train, negotiations that were not specific enough to precisely locate contractual terms. At least on the issue of remedies *Webb* seems to be a relatively rarefied situation and it can be expected that the courts will close off this route to damages wherever possible; see *Re La Lavia*.

2–79 While most of the cases in which legitimate expectation has been pleaded involve situations where a citizen is seeking to obtain some benefit or privilege such as a tax refund, a licence or legal aid (and thus are not contract situations) the "legitimate expectation" has been used in order to forestall the exercise of contractual rights or discretions. In *Donegal County Council v Porter*[232] the blanket dismissal of part-time firemen by the County Council when they reached 55 years of age was held incompatible with a legitimate expectation that such employees could continue to work until 60 if they were fit enough. Flood J. said that fitness could have been assessed via a medical examination so there was no countervailing consideration that could

---

[229] [1989] I.L.R.M. 710. Contrast *Egan v Minister for Defence*, unreported, High Court, November 24, 1988 and *White v Glackin*, unreported, High Court, May 19, 1995. The view that legitimate expectation confers procedural reliefs rather than substantive benefits in monetary terms was reiterated by Murphy J. in his dissenting judgment in *Coonan v Attorney General* [2002] 1 I.L.R.M. 295 at 301.

[230] [2002] 1 I.R. 84.

[231] [2002] 1 I.R. 84 at 109. This is no longer so after the *Lett* case considered below.

[232] Unreported, High Court, July 12, 1993. See also *Navan Tanker Services v Meath County Council*, unreported, High Court, December 13, 1996.

have justified denial of such an expectation.[233] However, *Eogan v University College Dublin*[234] indicates that if the employer is open and transparent about policies of this kind, and if the policy is rational and persons affected have the opportunity to comment on any scheme proposed, then any finding of arbitrary or oppressive conduct by a public body will not be sustainable by a court. Legitimate expectation has been pleaded in relation to the operations of professional or regulatory bodies such as the Medical Council[235] and the Law Society.[236] The universities[237] have also been considered to be within the scope of judicial review via legitimate expectation and the courts have indicated that the concept of a public body is broadly judged. If the body makes the decision pursuant to a statute, if the decision maker is performing a duty relating to a matter of particular and immediate public concern, if the decision relates to an employment contract and the employee invokes statutory protections which are thus public rights, and finally, if the decision maker depends on statute or legislative or governmental rights, and support for its continued exercise of powers, then such factors will influence the decision to trigger judicial review.[238]

Legitimate expectation as a cause of action that sounds in damages

2–80 The issue of the appropriate remedy to be available to a plaintiff who successfully invokes legitimate expectation arose in *Atlantic Marine Supplies Ltd v Minister for Transport*.[239] The plaintiff complained that for many years the Minister for Transport had not rigorously enforced statutory rules and a code of practice imposing on fishing vessels the obligation to carry inflatable life rafts that met a certain standard (many vessels carried life rafts that were compatible with lower standards relating to yachts). The plaintiff provided safety equipment for fishing craft and had to maintain its own certification requirements as well as significant commercial expenditure. The plaintiff argued that in failing to enforce safety requirements, the Minister had not acted in accordance with the position he had adopted when promulgating the relevant statutory code. Clarke J. agreed and also thought that the second *Glencar* requirement, that the relevant representation had been conveyed to an identifiable group of persons was also satisfied, being both fishermen and allied entities such as the plaintiff. Clarke J. also found that there was a reasonable expectation created in that identifiable group that the Minister would undertake that the code would be "reasonably enforced". While there were no countervailing policy considerations to negative the legitimate expectation, Clarke J. found that because the code was only in place on a

---

[233] Contrast *Egan v Minister for Defence*, unreported, High Court, November 24, 1988.
[234] [1996] 2 I.L.R.M. 303.
[235] *Phillips v Medical Council* [1991] 2 I.R. 115.
[236] *Abrahamson v Law Society of Ireland* [1996] 2 I.R. 481. See also *Geoghegan v Institute of Chartered Accountants in Ireland* [1995] 3 I.R. 86.
[237] *Kenny v Kelly* [1988] I.R. 457; *Eogan v University College Dublin* [1996] 2 I.L.R.M. 303.
[238] Per Shanley J. in *Eogan v University College Dublin* [1996] 2 I.L.R.M. 303 at 309.
[239] [2010] IEHC 104.

mandatory basis for four years and because there was evidence of some level of enforcement—material compliance—damages were not an appropriate remedy. In contrast, in *Lett & Co v Wexford Borough Council* the High Court[240] and the Supreme Court[241] endorsed the view that where the legitimate expectation is that a benefit will be secured, the court will endeavour to realise that benefit or to compensate the applicant, whether by an order of mandamus or by an award of damages provided that to do so was lawful. However, the Supreme Court viewed Clarke J.'s award of €1.15 million as being over generous, even allowing for the difficulty of the task and the lack of reliable evidence on future loss. The Supreme Court endorsed Lord Justice Scarman's view that the court should award "the minimum equity to do justice to the plaintiff". The Supreme Court reduced the award to €650,000.

2–81 On the level of principle, however, the Supreme Court adopted a very forthright view of how compensation should be approached in legitimate expectation cases. O'Donnell J. said that Clarke J. was required to characterise the plaintiff's claim in a rather artificial way because of doubts about the availability of damages arising out of legitimate expectation.

> "However, if the claim is understood as a claim for damages, then much of this difficulty disappears ... by analogy with the position in estoppel in private law, the issue for the court is that once a legitimate expectation or estoppel has been identified it is necessary to make good the equity so found, and that in such circumstances again in principle, the court can make an order, whether characterised as damages or restitution, in order to make good the breach identified."

Thus, in brief, legitimate expectation is a cause of action that may exceptionally lead to the award of damages assessed on a conservative basis.

The Supreme Court ruling in Daly v Minister for the Marine[242]

2–82 In this case the Supreme Court gave a strong and clear view on the requirements of promissory estoppel. The case concerned a dispute between the owner of a fishing vessel and the Minister for the Marine in respect of the entitlement of the owner of the fishing vessel to sell the vessel on and avail of a departmental scheme regulating marine fisheries policy. In particular, the Department had mistakenly sent the owner of the vessel a letter, dated October 1, 1993, indicating that the scheme was open to him. Claims under both legitimate expectation and promissory estoppel were brought against the Department. In giving judgment for a very strong five-member Supreme Court,[243] Fennelly J. described this as a "daring submission" and rejected the

---

[240] [2007] IEHC 195.
[241] [2012] IESC 14.
[242] [2001] 3 I.R. 513.
[243] Keane C.J., and Denham, Murphy and Geoghegan JJ. concurring.

argument outright. However, it is submitted that it is not clear what the nature of the acts of reliance the promisee must adduce if the estoppel is to work. Fennelly J., it appears, was prepared to countenance both a narrow perspective and a broader one at the same time. In respect of the narrower view, which requires detrimental reliance, Fennelly J. cited with approval Griffin J.'s speech in *Doran v Thompson*[244] and the speech of Kenny J.[245] where both judges stressed that the view in *Snell's Principles of Equity* that there must be evidence of the promisee "altering his position to his detriment" is applicable. On the other hand, Fennelly J. only speaks of the promisee's need to show reliance. But, it is submitted, the judgment, read on the whole, presents a narrow perspective on promissory estoppel, requiring a clear and unambiguous representation by the promisor inducing detrimental reliance by the promisee:

> "It is the fact that it would be unconscionable for one party to be permitted to depart from a position, statement or representation upon which the other party has acted to his detriment that justifies the courts in intervening to restrain him from doing so. If the recipient of a promise or representation is to be dispensed from any obligation to demonstrate reliance, the doctrine would be more than exceptionally generous. It would be a virtually ungovernable new force affecting potentially not only equity but the laws of contract and property and, as here, the exercise of administrative powers."[246]

Applying this test to the facts of the case at bar, the Supreme Court held that while the necessary representations had been made to the promisee, no acts of reliance had been shown by the promisee. This retreat to a very orthodox position is in many ways to be welcomed. As we shall see, this case helps to distinguish promissory estoppel from legitimate expectation without eliminating the overlap between them.

2–83 By grafting on to the *Daly* decision the more flexible but at the same time intelligible principles to be found in *Gillett v Holt*, especially on the issue of the estoppel conferring rights of action, Irish law could develop a workable equitable doctrine that would soften the harsher effects of bargain theory and consideration. In addition, recent cases suggest that the use of constructive trusts to create property rights may increasingly be used.[247]

The relationship between promissory estoppel and legitimate expectation

2–84 Despite some observations to the effect that legitimate expectation is simply an aspect of promissory estoppel there are some signs that there are

---

[244] [1978] I.R. 223 at 230; *Flynn v National Asset Loan Management Ltd* [2014] IEHC 408.
[245] [1978] I.R. 223 at 233.
[246] [2001] 3 I.R. 513 at 529.
[247] *Kelly v Cahill* [2001] 2 I.L.R.M. 205; *Byrne v Byrne*, unreported, High Court, December 11, 2003; *JC v WC*, unreported, High Court, December 19, 2003; *McDermott v McDermott* [2008] NI Ch 5; *MC (A Ward) v FC* [2013] IEHC 272.

significant differences between these concepts. We have seen that while a legitimate expectation operates only vis-à-vis public bodies, the concept of a public body is broad indeed. Thus, sometimes estoppel and legitimate expectation are pleaded in the alternative, e.g. *Kenny v Kelly*.[248]

2–85 While detrimental reliance appears to be an essential proof in cases of promissory estoppel this has been doubted in relation to legitimate expectation.[249] The scope of legitimate expectation, as a public law concept, has been narrowly drawn by the Supreme Court in *Daly v Minister for the Marine*[250] where Fennelly J. contrasted the legitimate expectation notion from promissory estoppel as turning on the need to see that administrative powers are not used unfairly. As such, Fennelly J. said legitimate expectation may operate in circumstances where detrimental reliance in the estoppel sense may not be made out. But Fennelly J. did seem to place legitimate expectation firmly in the administrative law camp only, with private law obligations being governed by promissory estoppel. Orthodox estoppel theory also seems to require that a pre-existing legal relationship should subsist so that the estoppel may only operate within such a context, but no such prior relationship needs to exist between a citizen and a public body or a government department,[251] for example. It is also likely that legitimate expectation may operate by way of a practice or failure within the public body which may stop short of a promise or representation[252] and that while promissory estoppel may not be used to interfere with a minister's powers under statute, some Irish cases indicate that the legitimate expectation argument may prevail in such a context,[253] although there are several cases which go against this argument[254] where the expectation in question is substantive rather than procedural. In *Galvin v Chief Appeals Officer*,[255] for example, Costello P. declined to allow the plaintiff to obtain a social welfare pension, despite procedural irregularities, because the plaintiff's contribution record meant that he was not legally entitled as a matter of substantive statutory entitlement.

2–86 However, the recognition in the *Letts* case that citizens who act upon assurances, or a state of affairs, that State agencies have created or allowed to develop, within the *Glencar* guidelines may recover financial compensation is welcome, insofar as it clarifies the legitimate expectation range remedies.

---

[248] [1988] I.R. 457.

[249] *Attorney-General of Hong Kong v Ng Yeun Shiu* [1983] 2 A.C. 629; in *Abrahamson v Law Society of Ireland* [1996] 2 I.R. 481, McCracken J. doubted whether reliance was an aspect of legitimate expectation.

[250] [2001] 3 I.R. 513.

[251] *Cosgrove v Legal Aid Board*, unreported, High Court, October 17, 1990; *Re La Lavia* [1996] 1 I.L.R.M. 194.

[252] *Ghneim v Minister for Justice, The Irish Times,* September 2, 1989.

[253] *Conroy v Garda Commissioner* [1989] I.R. 140.

[254] *Tara Prospecting Ltd v Minister for Energy* [1993] I.L.R.M. 771; *Abrahamson v Law Society of Ireland* [1996] 2 I.L.R.M. 481; *Galvin v Chief Appeals Officer*, unreported, High Court, June 27, 1997.

[255] Unreported, High Court, June 27, 1997.

Where there is no State agency involved, however, or the agency is acting in a commercial context, the law of contract appears to be the sole source of redress under *Triatic* reasoning. Despite the actions of the Australian courts in pushing promissory estoppel forward there is no sign that the Irish courts will follow suit. As Irish law currently stands, the compensatory possibilities for a person asserting equitable or proprietary estoppel are much better than utilising a promissory estoppel argument.

3   Intention to Create Legal Relations

Introduction

3–01 It is possible for the parties to negotiations to stipulate that, when the negotiating process is at an end, and the parties have apparently reached agreement on essential matters, any resultant agreement is not to be legally enforceable. This may be because each side wishes to reserve the right to reconsider his or her position; any agreement reached in such circumstances will be seen as some kind of half-way-house between preliminary, inchoate negotiations and a legally enforceable contract. The business usage that most clearly illustrates this is the "subject to contract" agreement in land transactions. O'Flaherty J. in *Boyle and Boyle v Lee and Goyns*[1] has reminded us of the fact that "the historic purpose of the phrase 'subject to contract' was to keep negotiations in train and to allow either party to *resile* from the agreement made". A more general issue is whether it can be said that there is a specific requirement that enforceability of a contract will depend in part upon proof that a legally enforceable agreement was intended.

3–02 It is thus established that negotiations which meet the requirements of offer, acceptance and consideration may fail to be enforceable at common law as a contract because it is said that there was an absence of legal intent. This view has been challenged by several commentators who point out that it is only through the application of the doctrine of consideration itself that the common law distinguishes enforceable promises from non-enforceable promises. The need to show legal intent is said to be an interloper, of foreign extraction, which may be a legitimate requirement in civil law jurisdictions where no doctrine of consideration exists, but it is quite superfluous to the needs of the common law.

3–03 Professor Williston put forward this argument very strongly:

> "[T]he views of parties as to what are the requirements of a contract, as to what mutual assent means, or consideration, or what contracts are enforceable without a writing, and what are not, are wholly immaterial ... [in this context] the law not the parties fixes the requirements of a legal obligation."[2]

---

[1]   [1992] I.L.R.M. 65.
[2]   This quotation is from *Williston on Contracts* (1957), s.3, pp.20–21. See now Williston, *A Treatise on the Law of Contract*, 4th edn (Eagan, MN: West, 1990), s.3.5.

It is evident that Williston's views are shared by many scholars,[3] who point out that an additional test of legal intent, based on the desires and beliefs of the parties, objectively determined, seems to be largely unnecessary, given that the bargain theory of consideration is the common law test of contractual intention. Nevertheless, it is clear that under the private autonomy principle the parties are free to enter into arrangements and yet declare that these arrangements are not to be the subject of enforceable contractual rights. Furthermore, the courts, by using ordinary rules of construction, are free to conclude that some exchanges are not intended to be legally enforceable, even if there is a certainty and a finality about the negotiations. Sometimes legal intent questions overlap with the more common and fundamental problem of uncertainty of terms and it must be conceded that, at times, consideration[4] and uncertainty of terms[5] problems are not clearly distinguished by the judges. Indeed, general consider-ations of public policy also underline situations where a court concludes that a promise was not attended by intention to create legal relations. In *Robinson v Commissioners of Customs & Excise*,[6] an informant sought to recover monies he claimed to be due in respect of information provided about persons who had evaded taxes, it being the practice of the Revenue to provide a reward. Brown J. held the claim to be ill-founded because of lack of legal intent as the contract would be contrary to public policy. Brown J. no doubt had in mind the likelihood that all kinds of "bogus" information would be given on the off-chance that a person's tax affairs were not in order.

3–04 Even though many of the legal intent cases can be argued away on alternative grounds there are several which can only be explained on the basis of lack of intent. No matter what objections may be levied against the legal intent requirement it has now taken root in English and Irish law.

Family Arrangements

3–05 In *Leahy v Rawson*,[7] O'Sullivan J. said that the presumption against an intention to create legally binding arrangements "appears to apply only to the closest family kinships such as parent and child and spouses. Where it applies there is only a presumption of fact which can be rebutted but the onus is on the claimant to rebut". In that case the presumption did not arise as between an arrangement between the plaintiff and her partner's brother relating to domestic building work.

---

[3]   e.g. Hepple, "Intention to Create Legal Relations" (1970) 28 C.L.J. 122; Unger, "Intent to Create Legal Relations, Mutuality and Consideration" (1956) 19 M.L.R. 96; Stoljar, "Enforcing Benevolent Promises" (1989) 12 Syd. L.R. 17.

[4]   e.g. *Balfour v Balfour* [1919] 2 K.B. 571.

[5]   *Carthy v O'Neill* [1981] I.L.R.M. 443.

[6]   *The Times*, April 28, 2000. Similar public policy dimensions may arise where the underlying transaction involves immoral objectives (*Ashton v Pratt (No.2)* [2012] NSWSC 3) (on appeal, in *Ashton v Pratt* [2015] NSWCA 12 the NSWCA did not make a finding on the morality issue but found the agreement void for uncertainty and not intended to have legal effect) or the court suspects unconscionable behaviour (*MC (A Ward) v FC* [2013] IEHC 273).

[7]   Unreported, High Court, January 14, 2003.

3–06 In *Mackay v Jones*[8] the plaintiff's uncle promised that if the plaintiff, then a boy of 14, came to live with him and looked after the farm he would, on death, convey it to the boy by will. On the death of the promisor the property was bequeathed to a third party. Judge Deale in the Circuit Court refused to characterise the promise as absolutely binding; it was said to be an agreement to work in the expectation that the legacy would be given. This case can only be explained as one where the court refused to find that the promisor intended his promise to be binding. In contrast, the Supreme Court in *McCarron v McCarron*[9] ordered specific performance of an agreement on the basis that the plaintiff had worked long hours for the deceased, without reward, for 16 years. Compensation had been promised in the form of promises to make the young man rich one day. The courts are wary of readily inferring agreements in the absence of some proof of prejudicial or detrimental reliance,[10] although in appropriate cases there are Irish decisions that demonstrate a willingness to grant equitable relief when the facts are persuasive enough, even absent a contract.

3–07 The leading case on family arrangements in English law is that of *Balfour v Balfour*.[11] In that case, Atkin L.J. stated *obiter* that contracts between husband and wife are not intended to be attended by legal consequences. In *Courtney v Courtney*[12] an agreement made between a husband and wife who had decided to solve their matrimonial differences by living apart was upheld as legally binding. Although *Balfour v Balfour* was distinguished in *Courtney* as applicable only to executory contracts, it is established that where the parties have not been living together amicably, any agreement made between them falls outside *Balfour v Balfour*; otherwise separation agreements would not be enforceable. It has been suggested that if the parties in *Balfour v Balfour* had done anything to indicate that they intended the promise to be legally enforceable, by getting a solicitor to draw up an agreement, for example, the presumption against enforcing an arrangement between husband and wife would be inapplicable. Note that in *Courtney v Courtney* the promises were made with the sanction of the local priest and this seems to have indicated to the court that the arrangement was seriously meant. See also *Hamer v Sidway*[13] where the fact that a promise was repeated before others at a family gathering was another indication of legal intent.

3–08 The decision of the Supreme Court in *Rogers v Smith*[14] illustrates that when a family arrangement is made the terms agreed are often ambiguous. Members of a family do not always haggle and bargain with the intensity of

---

8   (1959) 93 I.L.T.R. 117; *Baldwin v Lett*, unreported, High Court, February 1, 1971.
9   Unreported, Supreme Court, February 13, 1997. See also *JC v WC* [2004] 2 I.R. 312, distinguishing *Jones v Padavatton* [1969] 1 W.L.R. 328.
10 See the unreported cases discussed in *JC v WC* [2004] 2 I.R. 312.
11 [1919] 2 K.B. 571; *Shortall v White* [2007] NSWCA 372; there may also be certainty of terms issues as in *Ward v Ward* (2011) 332 D.L.R. (4th) 537.
12 (1923) 57 I.L.T.R. 42; see *Pettitt v Pettitt* [1970] A.C. 777.
13 (1891) 124 N.Y. 583.
14 Unreported, Supreme Court, July 16, 1970.

dealers at a horse fair. In *Rogers v Smith* a mother promised her son that the cost of supporting her would be recoverable from her estate following her death. The Supreme Court refused to hold this promise was seriously intended. It was made in the most general terms; the "promisee" also gave evidence that if the promise had not been made he would have supported the "promisor" anyway.

3–09 In contrast, however, the case of *Hynes v Hynes*[15] illustrates that an agreement between two brothers will be enforced, notwithstanding a plea that the blood relationship between the parties, and other circumstances, would indicate an absence of legal intent. In this case an agreement between the plaintiff and defendant, transferring a business owned and run by the plaintiff to the defendant, was held enforceable; the case is consistent with the English case of *Jones v Padavatton*[16] in which Salmon L.J. indicated that the test for determining the enforceability of a family arrangement was objective; would a reasonable person, when the court looks at this agreement and its surrounding circumstances, have intended to create a legally binding agreement?

3–10 The factors that will influence a court when a plea of lack of intent is raised within a family context are numerous. The degree of closeness within the family relationship may be extremely relevant. Husband-and-wife and parent-and-child arrangements will be obviously very compelling relationships if in the individual case there is the degree of love and affection present that, in an ideal world, one would expect to see in every such relationship; parents are, however, no more immune from falling out with their children than a wife may be with her husband, and vice versa. Another factor that has proved influential, even where the blood or marriage link has not been very strong[17] (e.g. uncle and nephew), is the extent to which the promisee has acted in reliance. Moving from one continent to another,[18] or from one end of the country to the other,[19] or disposing of property as a result of a promise,[20] may indicate a degree of seriousness and deliberateness of purpose. Conversely, if the course of action taken was not momentous or prejudicial, or if the promisee would have acted in a similar way even without the promise sought to be enforced,[21] an absence of legal intent may be inferred. If the promise is vague or hastily made a plea of absence of legal intent may be more readily inferred than in cases where the promise is specific and reduced into writing. These factors are approximate guides only, however.

---

[15] Unreported, High Court, December 21, 1984. In *Conroy v Fitzpatrick*, unreported, High Court, December 18, 2003, the parties were in evidence described as being "like brothers" but their agreement to buy property was no "mere social arrangement".

[16] [1969] 1 W.L.R. 328.

[17] *Parker v Clark* [1960] 1 All E.R. 93.

[18] *Jones v Padavatton* [1969] 1 W.L.R. 388. Contrast *Ronowska v Kus* [2012] NSWSC 280, following *Tadrous v Tadrous* [2010] NSWSC 1388. In *Ronowska v Kus*, proprietary estoppel was established by the plaintiff, following *Jennings v Rice* [2002] EWCA Civ 159.

[19] *Parker v Clark* [1960] 1 All E.R. 93.

[20] *Parker v Clark* [1960] 1 All E.R. 93.

[21] *Rogers v Smith*, unreported, Supreme Court, July 16, 1970.

3–11 Another way of approaching the issue of legal intent was demonstrated by Fruman J. in the Alberta case of *Beaudoin v Waters*,[22] which involved an action to recover the value of building work undertaken by the plaintiff on the defendant's home while they were involved in a relationship. Fruman J. thought that imposing the presumption in respect of a married couple upon lovers was an "overstatement", but looking at the circumstances, she said the conduct of the parties was equally consistent with the services being rendered out of friendship or another affinity as it was with a contract. Fruman J. dismissed the claim:

> "Had they wanted to properly document their contractual arrangements they had ample opportunity to do so. Human emotions being somewhat predictable, people who are closely connected should take extra care to properly document their business arrangements in contemplation of the day that the romance dies and with it, the willingness to pay."[23]

In *Shortall v White*[24] the New South Wales Court of Appeal has similarly observed that the principle in *Balfour v Balfour* will normally apply to parties in a cohabitation relationship, as well as the parties to a marriage, but that this is "not the case once the relationship breaks down".

3–12 Even when cohabitation is not intended, private understandings may exist. In the controversial case of *Ashton v Pratt*[25] the New South Wales Court of Appeal held that promises made to the plaintiff, an escort, were not intended to be legally binding. The plaintiff was told that if she provided sexual favours and did not return to escort work, becoming the mistress of the promisor, she would benefit from gifts, a generous allowance and a Trust Fund. When the promisor (a billionaire) died not all of these promises had been fulfilled. Looking at all the objective circumstances—the vague nature of the promises sought and given, the failure to document or record the transaction in particular, and the "inherent improbability that a person in the position of Mr. Pratt would bind himself to make significant payments in consideration of a promise that was essentially unenforceable [for uncertainty]" led the Court to conclude no contractual obligations existed.

Commercial Agreements

3–13 The UK Supreme Court has recently explained its position in legal intent cases. In *RTS Flexible Systems Ltd v Molkerei Alois Müller GmbH*[26] a letter of intent, executed so as to allow the negotiation of a fuller and much more complete agreement, with detailed schedules, expired, but the detailed draft

---

[22] (1998) 203 A.R. 1.
[23] (1998) 203 A.R. 1 at 10. Direct evidence, if uncontradicted, can also be compelling as in *Ashton v Pratt (No.2)* [2012] NSWSC 3, affirmed on appeal: [2015] NSWCA 12.
[24] [2007] NSWCA 372.
[25] [2015] NSWCA 12.
[26] [2010] UKSC 14; *McCabe Builders (Dublin) Ltd v Sagamu Developments* [2009] IESC 31.

agreement and schedules were never executed. Work on the project, however, commenced. Lord Clarke, giving judgment for the entire Supreme Court said:

> "The general principles are not in doubt. Whether there is a binding contract between the parties and, if so, upon what terms depends upon what they have agreed. It depends not upon their subjective state of mind, but upon a consideration of what was communicated between them by words or conduct, and whether that leads objectively to a conclusion that they intended to create legal relations and had agreed upon all the terms which they regarded or the law requires as essential for the formation of legally binding relations. Even if certain terms of economic or other significance to the parties have not been finalised, an objective appraisal of their words and conduct may lead to the conclusion that they did not intend agreement of such terms to be a precondition to a concluded and legally binding agreement."

This statement is not innovative and does not make new law but, rather, it represents a short and cogent statement on the approach to be adopted. The most enduring and oft cited dictum in this area of law is to be found in a 1964 English Case.

3–14 In *Edwards v Skyways Ltd*,[27] the question arose whether an agreement negotiated between an employer and an employee relating to the terms upon which the contract of employment could be consensually terminated was attended by an intention to create legal relations. Megaw L.J. stated:

> "Where the subject matter of the agreement is not domestic or social, but is related to business affairs, the parties may, by using clear words, show that their intention is to make the transaction binding in honour only and not in law, and the courts will give effect to the expressed intention …
>
> In the present case the subject matter of the agreement is business relations, not social or domestic matters. There was a meeting of minds—an intention to agree. There was admittedly consideration for the defendant company's promise. I accept the propositions of counsel for the plaintiff that in a case of this nature the onus is on the party who asserts that no legal effect was intended and the onus is a heavy one. Counsel for the plaintiff also submitted, with the support of the well known textbooks on the law of contract, (*Anson* and *Cheshire and Fifoot*), that the test of intention to create or not to create legal relations is 'objective'."[28]

This dictum has been cited with approval by Irish courts on several occasions.[29]

---

27 [1964] 1 All E.R. 494.
28 [1964] 1 All E.R. 494 at 499–500. The onus of proof applies in this way to both bilateral and unilateral contracts: *Desdner Kleinwort Ltd v Attrill* [2013] EWCA Civ 394.
29 e.g. *O'Rourke v Talbot Ireland Ltd* [1984] I.L.R.M. 587.

3–15 It is important to note that the objective test applies with even greater force to cases where business transactions are set out in documentary form. The search here is for the meaning the document conveys to a "reasonable addressee" and, while no Irish court has looked at the *Belize*[30] line of authority yet, there is no reason to think this will not be influential in Ireland. This case is fully considered in Ch.6.

3–16 If the parties are commercial organisations or business persons then it is to be presumed that the contract will be attended by legal intent. The leading English case on honour clauses, *Rose and Frank Co v Crompton*[31] would no doubt be followed in Ireland. Readers should note that on the facts of *Rogers v Smith*[32] it might have been possible to characterise the contract as a commercial one between the plaintiff and his father; this would have pointed towards enforcement. In *Apicella v Scala*[33] an arrangement between plaintiff and defendant designed to enable all parties to take a share in sweepstake tickets to be purchased by the defendant was described as "a conditional or revocable decision"; even though Meredith J. would have found consideration to be present the absence of any intention to conclude a bargain was fatal to the plaintiff's action in contract.

3–17 In more recent times the courts have been prepared to uphold as contracts arrangements to purchase lottery tickets, or participate in gambling transactions, on the ground that the arrangement before the court has been specific and deliberately entered into with a view to sharing both the risks and the profits, if any. The leading English case is *Simpkins v Pays*.[34] Readers of a newspaper were invited to take part in a competition, paying a fee of about five pence for each attempt. The defendant was the owner of a residence which she shared with her granddaughter and a paying boarder, the plaintiff. These three persons regularly competed but there were no specific agreed rules on completion of the entry and payment of postage and the entry fee. Each selected an entry each week and on one occasion the defendant's granddaughter won £750. The plaintiff successfully brought an action to recover £250. Sellers J. said that the issue of who actually paid the entry fee was not the central issue but rather the question of whether this was a syndicate in which risks and profits were to be shared. It may have been a very loose syndicate but it was seriously intended so to be. Sellers J. rejected the argument that because the arrangement involved a granddaughter and grandmother it was not supported by legal intent. To similar effect is a recent decision handed down in the Liverpool County Court in which an understanding that a mother and daughter would share their respective bingo winnings with each other was held to be an enforceable contract.[35] In Ireland, there have been several cases in which

---

30   *AG of Belize v Belize Telecom* [2009] UKPC 10.
31   [1923] 2 K.B. 261; *Sadler v Reynolds* [2005] EWHC 309 (Q.B.).
32   Unreported, Supreme Court, July 16, 1970.
33   (1931) 66 I.L.T.R. 33.
34   [1955] 1 W.L.R. 975.
35   "Bingo daughter must pay mother", *The Times*, February 3, 2001.

injunctive relief has been obtained to prevent the National Lottery from paying the entire amount of winnings on a lottery ticket to the holder of the ticket on the basis, *inter alia,* that the ticket had been purchased as part of a structured pooling arrangement between persons. Each case, however, must be judged on its own facts, but it can hardly be doubted that pooling arrangements of this kind should really be regarded as *prima facie* contractual, given the potential for great financial enrichment for the participants. The leading Irish case is *Horan v O'Reilly and Others.*[36] Horan claimed a one-fifth share in a winning national lottery ticket which the four defendants contested. The parties were a syndicate under which one O'Brien was responsible for collecting the stake and buying the tickets. Horan had a history of tardiness in making his contributions which was indulged in by O'Brien, the controlling person in the consortium. Four months after Horan last contributed his share of the stake, a ticket, purchased by reference to four contributions only, was successful. The Supreme Court held that the original contract was not varied by O'Brien's indulgence of Horan's periodic payments and the oral agreement required a weekly contribution. At the time the winning ticket was purchased, Horan was no longer a member of the consortium. Horan's action failed.

3–18 In recent years the Australian courts have distanced themselves from utilising presumptions, favouring the view that while classifying a contract as a commercial one as between the parties may readily lead to a conclusion that legal effect was intended,[37] the same is not the case where, for example, the facts are that a body established to regulate social, cultural, professional or religious interests, on a not-for-profit basis, operates via rules drawn up for this purpose.

3–19 In *Ermogenous v Greek Orthodox Community of SA Inc.*,[38] the High Court of Australia indicated that, at best, presumptions do no more than invite attention to the question of which party is to bear the onus of proof. In *Shahid v College of Dermatologists*,[39] legal intent was held to be absent from the appeal mechanisms laid down by a medical body on the basis that there was no commercial operation undertaken by the medical body and the body in question had neither an intention to be legally bound nor an intention to contract with a person in the position of the plaintiff, a person who did not seek membership of the medical body. This approach relies upon both objective and subjective factors to be assessed but the overall test is objective.[40]

---

[36] [2008] IESC 65.

[37] *Toll (FGCT) Pty Ltd v Alphapharm Pty* (2004) 210 C.L.R. 165. Regulatory consequences may follow if one of the parties at least misjudges the contractual status of any framework agreement or letter of intention: *Australian Securities and Investments Commission v Fontescue Metals Group Ltd* [2011] FCAFC 19 appeal dismissed [2013] HCA 34.

[38] (2002) 209 C.L.R. 95; *Plenty v Seventh-Day Adventist Church* [2006] SASC 361.

[39] (2007) 72 I.P.R. 555. Contrast cases where there is a contract in place: *Palmer v East & North Hertfordshire NHS Trust* [2006] EWHC 1997 (Q.B.).

[40] *Kovan Engineering (Aust) Pty v Gold Peg International Pty* (2006) 234 A.L.R. 241.

3–20 If the court establishes that, on its true construction, an alleged agreement was not intended to have legal consequences as a contract then it may be that what would otherwise appear to be a commercial contract will be denied the status of an enforceable contract. In *Cadbury Ireland Ltd v Kerry Co-operative Creameries Ltd*[41] an agreement under which the defendant had effectively promised to continue to supply milk to the plaintiff company, when the defendant acquired a small creamery that had previously supplied milk to the plaintiffs, was held not capable of enforcement. Despite the presumption and despite the apparent solemnity with which the clause was drafted and inserted into the agreement a closer scrutiny of the circumstances of the case convinced Barrington J. that this agreement was non-contractual. The clause itself was unspecific; the parties themselves had not relied upon it to determine their rights and obligations after the agreement was signed, choosing instead to negotiate subsequent contracts for the supply of milk. The agreement was a statement in which all involved had evinced an intention to subsequently draw up clear and binding agreements and, in the absence of any later agreements, this provision itself lacked any real status in a legal sense. A similar situation is provided by *Cunard Steamship Co v Revenue Commissioners*[42] where a booking arrangement was denied the status of a contract because it was intended that a subsequent contract would be made. These cases are very exceptional ones and it is true to say that, generally, a plea of absence of legal intent will be given short shrift; witness Barron J.'s decision in *Commodity Broking Co v Meehan*.[43] In *Bowerman v Association of British Travel Agents Ltd*[44] the majority of the Court of Appeal held that a notice produced by the defendant and displayed in premises run by members of the Association was to be given legal effect. Hobhouse L.J. in particular remarked that the defendants had intended to publish the notice and reasonable persons reading it would regard the notice as having legal consequences. The fact that the defendants privately did not intend to expose themselves to legal liability was held to be irrelevant in such a context.

Discretionary payments in employment contracts

3–21 The issue of whether discretionary payments envisaged during a contract of employment, or severance packages contemplated by an employee upon leaving employment, are the subject of contractual entitlements raises diverse questions in employment law. One of them, however, is that of legal intent. Did an employer make a promise that the employer is contractually bound to perform? The cases generally provide an affirmative answer, either through the court holding there was an express term, or implied obligations, to be met. In recent years the contentious subject of bonus payments to persons employed in the financial services sector has been controversial. Particular attention has

---

[41] [1982] I.L.R.M. 77; *Tolan v Connacht Gold* [2016] IECA 131.
[42] [1931] I.R. 287.
[43] [1985] I.R. 12.
[44] *The Times*, November 24, 1995.

been paid by the courts to the right of employees to recover bonus payments as a matter of contractual entitlement. A bonus will form part of the employee's remuneration, and any effort by the employer will have to be the subject of both sufficient notice (*Finnegan v JE Davy*[45]) given in circumstances where the employee may be said to have accepted the change.[46] Can the difficulty for an employer in lawfully imposing unilateral changes in the terms and conditions of employment be overcome by declaring that the payment is not to be surrounded by legal consequences, particularly by labelling the payment as discretionary? The test is based upon standard rules, i.e. the court is concerned with objective criteria and not statements about what each party actually intended, and the onus rests upon the party seeking to displace the default position, that is, that legal intention is assumed. The context is all-important here, and in these bonus cases there is ample space for judicial differences of view. But what is not in doubt is the fact that a discretionary bonus promise is not an illusory promise.

3–22 In *Khatri v Cooperatieve Centrale*[47] Jacob L.J. said that the employer claimed that under:

> "… the contract in question the claimant's entitlement to a bonus was discretionary. Before I go further I should say a word about discretionary bonuses generally since their widespread existence forms part of the background matrix. The authorities establish that even where an employee's contract says that he is entitled to a bonus on a purely discretionary basis that does not mean the employer is entirely free to decide whether to pay a bonus or not. On the contrary, in making his decision whether to pay a bonus, and if so how much, the employer must act in a rational and fair manner. The test is essentially one of *Wednesbury* unreasonableness, (see *Horkulak v Cantor Fitzgerald* [2005] ICR 402, [2004] E.W.C.A. Civ. 1287 and *Keen v Commerzbank* [2007] ICR 623, [2006] E.W.C.A. Civ. 1536)."

The employer who undertakes to staff that they shall be eligible for consideration for a bonus payment will be held to have made a promise that has contractual force, even though the payment itself may not be capable of being computed.[48] It follows from the circumstances surrounding the employment relationship—particularly the employer's duty to act in good faith and not capriciously—that a discretionary bonus does not allow an employer to decide to reduce or withhold any payment altogether. The employer must not act irrationally or perversely

---

[45] [2007] IEHC 18.

[46] *Selectron Scotland v Roper* [2004] I.R.L.R. 4; *Attrill v Dresdner Kleinwort Ltd* [2012] EWHC 1189 (Q.B.) affirmed on appeal. It will be difficult to infer employee assent to continuing in the same work, especially when the change in terms is to the detriment of the employee.

[47] [2010] I.R.L.R. 715.

[48] *Clark v Nomura* [2000] I.R.L.R. 766; *Horkulak v Cantor Fitzgerald* [2004] EWCA Civ 1287; *Keen v Commerzbank AG* [2007] I.C.R. 623.

when exercising the discretion in relation to the bonus payment.[49] This test has been approved in Northern Ireland in *Shimmons v PricewaterhouseCoopers LLP*[50] where the Employment Appeals Tribunal (EAT) found that custom and practice in making payments over several years—statements that were consistent with entitlement, a detailed set of rules to assist in the calculation— pointed to the discretionary payment being an implied term in the contract of employment. In the most important recent case, *Attrill v Dresdner Kleinwort Ltd*,[51] the plaintiffs had been in receipt of annual bonus payments for many years. The employer was acquired by another bank, the acquired bank assuring employees that the payments would be made the following year. Many employees remained in employment on the strength of the promise. There were arguments about the vagueness of the answers and absence of legal intent but Owen J. not only held that the statements made were binding, later efforts by the Board to depart from the promise because the bank was in a far worse state than had been anticipated, post-Lehman Brothers, did not bring the position within a clause which allowed reduced payments due to "additional material deviations" from the assumed state of affairs of the merged bank.

3–23 Each clause will need to be interpreted in context and there is English authority for allowing an entire agreement clause to effectively limit the scope of undertakings and employee expectations. It was held in this case that government funding cuts may justify a decision not to provide bonus payments, as long as there is no conduct which can be characterised as arbitrary or capricious: *The Equality and Human Rights Commission v Earle*.[52] Payments already earned are clearly payable and cannot be withheld upon the employee later leaving employment.[53]

3–24 Even clauses which seek to carve out for the employer a discretion to cap the bonus will be restrictively interpreted. If, for example, the clause refers to "exceptional circumstances", this will be viewed as instances of misconduct or breach of duty rather than the employer's alarm at the size of the bonus that will be payable to a highly motivated and successful employee: *GX Networks Ltd v Greenland*.[54] Where the contract of employment is clearly drafted in the sense that the bonus clause provides that payment of the bonus is dependent upon the individual employee meeting performance standards that have either demonstrably not been met, or the contract affords the employer a wide discretion in respect of the employee evaluation, a different result will follow. In subjective assessment clauses of the latter kind, the discretion will have to

---

[49] *Horkulak v Cantor Fitzgerald* [2004] EWCA Civ 1287 per Potter L.J.
[50] [2011] NIIT 02645 10IT.
[51] *Attrill v Dresdner Kleinwort Ltd* [2012] EWHC 1189 (Q.B.), affirmed at [2013] EWCA Civ 394; see the severance package decision in *Fish v Dresdner Kleinwort Ltd* [2009] EWHC 2246 (Q.B.).
[52] [2014] I.R.L.R. 845; see also *Brogden v Investec Bank plc* [2014] EWHC 2785 (Comm).
[53] *Gunning v Coilte* [2015] IEHC 44.
[54] [2010] EWCA Civ 784.

be shown to have been exercised irrationally or in a bad faith, perhaps, if the employee is to succeed. This onus will rest on the employee according to the *Keen* case,[55] as followed in *Humphreys v Norilsk Nickel International (UK) Ltd*.[56] There have been issues about whether a bonus will be payable if the employee leaves employment before the date of assessment and in *Rutherford v Seymour Pierce Ltd*.[57] Coulson J. said that no implied term to that effect could be said to exist in that particular contract. Where, however, the contract is clear in express terms, as in *King v Royal Bank of Canada Ltd*[58] an English EAT held that the contract may require the claimant to show employee status on the relevant date. The only decision within this jurisdiction is a remarkable one. In *Simpson v Torpey*[59] an employer had promised a bonus to an employee but no decision had been made on the bonus criteria or whether a bonus should be paid. Clarke J. said a greatly reduced bonus of €50,000 (one-sixth of the maximum amount) would have been a reasonable amount for the employer to have estimated and Clarke J. ordered this amount to be paid on the basis of the *Rutherford* case. While the English cases suggest that the court must fix the bonus as part of its role in providing a remedy, it is unusual to find judges making decisions by putting themselves in the shoes of a contracting party and asking, what figure would this contracting party have arrived at, acting rationally and in good faith, with the figure not being fixed at the bottom end of the possible spectrum?[60]

Religious issues and legal intent

3–25 The question whether a spiritual adviser or priest from a wide range of religious churches, faith groups, sects or creeds may be engaged in contractual relationships with the church and/or its "administrative" structures has been much litigated in recent years in several jurisdictions. While English law initially started with a presumption against the relationship between a minister and the church being attended by an intention to create legal relations,[61] the law is now settled that no such presumption is to be employed and that the court is required to consider the nature of the obligation.[62] There is a substantial body

---

[55] *Keen v Commerzbank* [2007] I.C.R. 623 per Mummery L.J. In *Keen* the complaint was about the amount of the bonus, not the non-payment of a bonus.

[56] [2010] EWHC 1867 (Q.B.) (non-payment for poor performance). In *Humphreys* the employee was engaged to make forecasts which turned out to contain "serious inaccuracies" and it was a "performance bonus".

[57] [2010] EWHC 375 (Q.B.).

[58] [2011] UKEAT 0333.

[59] [2011] IEHC 343; *Clark v BET Plc* [1997] I.R.L.R. 348.

[60] While the case is a severance payments case, the reasoning on intention to create legal relations and consideration in *Korner up v Raytheon Canada Ltd* (2007) 282 D.L.R. (4th) 434—see Madame Justice Bourne's compelling arguments on earlier Canadian case law—mirrors that of Owen J. in *Attrill*. The English Court of Appeal has held that the bonus payment cases also apply in respect of commission payments as part of the *Braganza v BP Shipping Ltd* [2015] UKSC 17 mechanism. See *Hills v Niksun Inc* [2016] EWCA Civ 115.

[61] *President of the Methodist Conference v Parfitt* [1984] I.C.R. 176; *Diocese of Southwark v Coke* [1988] I.C.R. 140; *Singh v Gurn Nanak Gundwara* [1990] I.C.R. 209.

[62] *Percy v Church of Scotland* [2006] 2 A.C. 28; *New Testament Church of God v Stewart* [2007] EWCA Civ 1004.

of Canadian case law[63] that indicates that promises made between husband and wife are not intended to have legal consequences on the basis that motivation may be faith-based rather than an act of volition.[64]

Letters of Intent/Letters of Comfort[65]

3–26

"Letters of intent come in all sorts of forms. Some are merely expressions of hope; others are firmer but make it clear that no legal consequences ensue; others presage a contract and may be tantamount to an agreement 'subject to contract'; others are contracts falling short of the full-blown contract that is contemplated; others are in reality that contract in all but name. There can therefore be no prior assumptions such as looking to see if words such as 'letter of intent' have or have not been used. The phrase 'letter of intent' is not a term of art. Its meaning and effect depend on the circumstances of each case."[66]

This helpful summary of the law governing letters of intent, a phrase that is sometimes used interchangeably with that of letter of comfort, stresses that there are no *a priori* rules that are of any real assistance. Most of the questions that arise revolve around the search for legal certainty and an intention to be legally bound by the document(s) in question. Most of the cases concern letters of intent but we will first of all consider letters of comfort. This expression as a term of art is applied to an undertaking given by a government, or a state agency, or by a company, in respect of some related or subsidiary body, and which sets out a particular set of circumstances, or gives an assurance that the government, state agency or company intends to maintain or adopt a position in relation to that related or subsidiary body. However, if the assurance leads the party to whom it is given to adopt a certain course of action, trade with or supply credit to the subsidiary body, for example, is the assurance to be seen as promissory or a declaration of intent that is not actionable? The leading English case is *Kleinwort Benson Ltd v Malaysia Mining Corp Bhd*.[67] The defendant owned a subsidiary company that traded in tin on the London Metal Exchange. The defendant sought a credit facility for the subsidiary, giving an undertaking that "it is our policy to ensure that the business [of the subsidiary] is at all times in a position to meet its liabilities to you". The assurance had

---

[63] e.g. *Bruker v Morrovitz* (2006) 259 D.L.R. (4th) 55.
[64] See also discussion on art.9 of the European Convention on Human Rights in *Stewart* [2007] EWCA Civ 1004.
[65] For a review of the leading cases, see Trichardt (2001) 9 J.I.B.F.L. 416 and Clarke (2004) 4 J.I.B.F.L. 136.
[66] His Honour Judge Humphrey Lloyd Q.C. in *ERDC Group Ltd v Brunel University* [2006] B.L.R. 255 at 265. See also *Danbywiske Ltd v Donegal Investment Group Plc* [2015] IEHC 126.
[67] [1989] 1 All E.R. 785; *Chemco Leasing S.p.a. v Rediffusion* [1987] 1 F.T.L.R. 201; *Bank of New Zealand v Ginivan* [1991] 1 N.Z.L.R. 178.

been given after the defendant had refused to give a formal guarantee on behalf of the subsidiary. When the tin market collapsed the plaintiff sued on the assurance, the subsidiary having gone into liquidation. Hirst J., relying upon the concept of legal intent and the presumption that commercial undertakings are enforceable, held that the letter of comfort was actionable. The Court of Appeal overruled Hirst J., declaring that the undertaking itself was a statement of existing fact and that as it was not a misrepresentation of existing fact it was not actionable. The undertaking was drafted in a way that segregated it from other promissory undertakings, and, although the arguments of counsel had changed somewhat since the first instance hearing before Hirst J., the Court of Appeal held that Hirst J. had been incorrect in viewing the promise as governed by the *Edwards v Skyways*[68] presumption: indeed, their Lordships viewed the case as depending on whether there was any promise at all in respect of future policy changes.

3–27 There is a considerable degree of uncertainty surrounding letters of comfort. If the letter can be viewed as merely an acceptance of an offer, then any cautionary or ambivalent language will not prevent a court from holding that there is legal intent, as in *Wilson Smithett & Cape (Sugar) Ltd v Bangladesh Sugar and Food Industries Corp.*[69] The document, however, must be interpreted in its entirety. In the Victorian case of *Commonwealth Bank of Australia v T.L.I. Management Property Ltd*[70] a letter of comfort given by a company to confirm that it would take over another company, subject to shareholders' permission, was held not to constitute an undertaking, but rather was merely a non-binding expression of intention. Had the words "we agree", "we promise" or "we undertake" been used then a contrary decision may well have resulted. The *ad hoc* nature of the cases has been criticised by one Australian judge, on the ground that considerable uncertainty is engendered by the notion that some business transactions, even though no honour clause is attached thereto, may "reside in a twilight zone of merely honourable engagement".[71] However, in *Australia European Finance Corp v Sheahan*[72] Rodgers C.J. was himself criticised for subjecting the clauses in *Banque Brussels Lambert* to the kind of minute textual analysis that he himself had complained about when he was reviewing earlier cases, including *Commonwealth Bank of Australia v T.L.I. Management Property Ltd.* However, in *Australia European Finance Corp v Sheahan* the clauses under review were clearly tentative and non-promissory in

---

[68] [1964] 1 W.L.R. 349.

[69] [1986] 1 Lloyd's Rep. 378.

[70] [1990] V.L.R. 510.

[71] Rogers C.J. in *Banque Brussels Lambert v Australian National Industries Ltd* (1989) 21 N.S.W.L.R. 502; see Tyree, "Southern Comfort" (1990) 2 J.C.L. 279. In *Australian European Finance Corp Ltd v Sheahan* (1993) 60 S.A.S.R. 187 the letter of comfort was clearly ambiguous on matters of detail and *Kleinwort* was applied. Although Matheson J. "distinguished" *Banque Brussels Lambert* he was clearly not impressed by that decision. See Clarke, "Enforceable Obligations in Comfortletters in Australia" (2004) 4 J.I.B.F.L. 136 for a review of comfort letters in Australia.

[72] (1993) 60 S.A.S.R. 187.

tone and it was not necessary for Matheson J. in that case to really distinguish the lines of authority. In deciding whether legal consequences were intended, some collateral transactions between the parties may also be conclusive. In *Atco Controls Property Ltd (In Liquidation) v Newtronics Pty Ltd*[73] the Victoria Court of Appeal considered that Atco had not given binding letters of support in respect of Newtronics, a subsidiary company. Letters of support were provided to the auditors of Newtronics' accounts for some but not all of the accounting years between 1994 to 2000 in respect of Newtronics' trading losses. While most of the evidence as to intention was equivocal, the court held the letters were not legally binding because of parallel documents executed which were incompatible with such a conclusion. No valid consideration for any such promise was evident.

3–28 A letter of intent, in contrast to a comfort letter, is one in which a person or company seeks to induce another entity to undertake work or incur expenditure, while denying or limiting liability to that other entity, often by insisting that liability turns on concluding a formal contract at a later date. In *AC Controls Ltd v BBC*[74] several of the letters of intent cases[75] were summarised as giving rise to the following principles:

"1. A document called or treated by the parties as a letter of intent may, on analysis, give rise to a binding contract, if that is the effect of the language of the parties when objectively construed. That contract is one in which pending the entering into of a formal contract governing the whole of the project, the parties have assumed reciprocal obligations towards each whose content is defined by the terms of the document.

2. Alternatively, the document may, on an objective construction of its terms, give rise to an 'if' contract whereby one party makes a standing offer to the other that if it carries out the defined performance of services, that other party will be remunerated for that performance. However, no obligation to perform is created and the reciprocal obligation to remunerate is limited by the express and implied terms of that offer.

3. It is possible for a contract to come into being without the conclusion of the formalities of the signing and execution of formal contract documents if a transaction is fully performed and all obstacles to the formation of a contract are removed in the negotiations and during the performance of the contract.

4. In construing and giving effect to the language of the letter of intent, it is necessary to take into account the factual background out of which the letter of intent arose."[76]

---

[73] [2009] V.S.C.A. 238.
[74] (2002) 89 Con. L.R. 52 per Judge Thornton Q.C.
[75] Specifically *Turriff Construction Ltd v Regalia Knitting Mills Ltd* (1971) 9 B.L.R. 20; *British Steel Corp v Cleveland Bridge & Engineering Co* [1984] 1 All E.R. 504; *Pagnan SpA v Feed Products Ltd* [1987] 2 Lloyd's Rep. 601; *Kleinwort Benson Ltd v Malaysia Mining Corp* [1989] 1 All E.R. 785; *G. Percy Trentham Ltd v Archital Luxfer Ltd* (1992) 63 B.L.R. 44.
[76] (2002) 89 Con. L.R. 52 at 71.

Construction contracts are often formed against the backdrop of letters of intent. It is common to find that the prospective commissioner issues a letter of intent seeking a contractor to commence work on behalf of the commissioner while not necessarily giving the contract to the (putative) contractor. Just such a situation arose in *Galliard Homes Ltd v J. Jarvis*.[77] Galliard Homes sought to induce J. Jarvis to commence the interior fitting out of apartments built for it by writing "in the event we do not enter into a formal contract you will be reimbursed all fair and reasonable costs". Work was undertaken, no formal contract was concluded and the work undertaken by J. Jarvis was unpaid for, the argument being put by Galliard Homes that the issue of value should be sent to arbitration because no contract existed and no separate agreement to arbitrate had been made. The *quantum meruit* nature of the letter of intent[78] provided the basis of the claim brought by the contractor. Normally, however, the letter of intent will at some stage be superseded by a contract, particularly if the letter of intent is given at a preliminary stage in a large construction project involving a number of contractors. In *RTS Flexible Systems Ltd v Molkerei Alois Müller*[79] the UK Supreme Court held that when work commenced on a construction project on the basis of a two-month long letter of intent, subsequently verbally extended for a further two-month period, the fact that the total price had been agreed, and instalments paid to the contractor, and that the essential terms had been negotiated in correspondence between the lawyers on each side (save for failure to obtain a parent company guarantee and some immaterial details) meant that a written contract (subsequently varied) was in existence in the form of the draft text that was never executed.[80] The parties were also held to have waived a requirement that a formal contract was to be signed by both parties. The general position in relation to letters of intent that seek to authorise work, materials or services pending the conclusion of a later contract is that such letters will be viewed as contracts in themselves as long as objective assent is present.[81] In *ERDC Group Ltd v Brunel University*,[82] the defendant sought to commission the plaintiff to start construction on a new sports hall but as it did not have the necessary planning permissions the work commenced on foot of letters of intent. The parties had agreed a pricing formula and a draft standard industry contract formed the basis of negotiations, but no contracts were ever signed. The plaintiff sought payment *quantum meruit* which the defendant resisted on the basis that contractual terms governed the building work and there was evidence that the parties had intended these terms to be legally binding. The judge viewed the letters issued by the defendant, some of which were actually later signed by the plaintiff, as

---

[77] (1999) 71 Con. L.R. 219 (House of Lords refused Galliard permission to appeal).

[78] As distinct from a *quantum meruit* claim per se.

[79] [2010] UKSC 14.

[80] The Supreme Court applied *Pagnan* and *Percy Trentham v Archital Luxfer Ltd* [1993] 1 Lloyd's Rep. 25, holding that the *Pagnan* guidelines apply where the court is considering whether a contract was concluded in correspondence as well as by oral communications and conduct.

[81] *Durabella Ltd v J. Jarvis* (2001) 83 Con. L.R. 145, especially at 150–151.

[82] [2006] B.L.R. 255.

being instances of unilateral or "if" contracts. It was also possible for the court to find sufficient certainty of terms and while there were blanks or omissions in the "remarkably thorough" letters of intent, His Honour Judge Humphrey Lloyd Q.C. said there was nothing in the letters or anything missing from them "that prevents an effective contract or which cannot be supplied by interpretation or implication".[83]

3–29 In *AC Controls Ltd v BBC*[84] the defendants sought to commission a centralised computerised security system for its buildings but because of internal auditing and budgetary considerations it did so by writing two letters of intent, the first seeking to obtain design and survey work, at a "cap" of £250,000, a second letter one month later giving the plaintiffs instructions to proceed with the project, the cap being raised to £500,000 while at the same time advising that a formal contract would be issued. No contract was ever agreed and the plaintiffs sued in *quantum meruit*; the defendants argued that the "cap" of £500,000 was the scope of their liability. Judge Thornton Q.C. held that both letters were "if" contracts or unilateral offers which, on being accepted by the plaintiffs created contractual obligations on both sides. The effect of the "caps", in the judge's view, were to give the BBC the right to terminate the contract when the expenditure limit was reached. The "cap" did not give the BBC the right not to pay for work that had been completed by the plaintiff in accordance with the general instruction to proceed with the work.

3–30 In *Orion Insurance Plc v Shere Drake Insurance Ltd*[85] the plaintiffs were held to have proved, on the balance of probabilities, that an agreement entered into in 1975 by two insurance companies and signed by both parties, was not intended to have legal consequences. The agreement was in the nature of an estimate of future liabilities and was made in circumstances where future events could make the calculations entirely inappropriate. Despite the fact of the agreement and signature of a document containing these terms by both parties, Hirst J. found the agreement was in the nature of a "gentleman's agreement". Hirst J. stressed that the onus was a heavy one, and that the degree of probability varied, depending on the nature of the context and the allegation of lack of intent. It is doubtful whether the courts are acting wisely in reaching decisions of this kind and it is preferable for the courts to insist on express disclaimers, by way of honour clauses, before decisions of the kind reached in *Orion Insurance* become more frequent.

---

[83]   [2006] B.L.R. 255 at 266.
[84]   (2002) 89 Con. L.R. 52.
[85]   [1990] 1 Lloyd's Rep. 465. Investment and shareholder service agreements are commonly the subject of litigation that centre on issues of intention to create legal relations and whether the terms that have been agreed are sufficiently certain to constitute an agreement: e.g. *Dhanani v Crasnianski* [2011] EWHC 926 (Comm); *Barbudev v Eurocom Cable Management Bulgaria Eood* [2012] EWCA Civ 548; *Hughes v Pendragon Sabre Ltd* [2016] EWCA Civ 18 (a sale of goods case), distinguishing *Dhanani v Crasnianski*.

Side Letters

3–31 Just as parties may use a letter of intent as a means of giving them the space to negotiate a formal contract, it is often the case that a contract may have been agreed only to be supplemented by another text, a side letter. In *Barbudev v Eurocom Cable Management Bulgaria Eood*[86] the English Court of Appeal listed four factors which indicated to that court that a side letter to a separate agreement was in its own terms sufficient to demonstrate an intention to create legal relations:

1. the letter was drafted by a leading international law firm;
2. the language contained therein, e.g. one of the paragraphs started "in consideration of you agreeing to enter into";
3. references to specific statute law and references to English law as the applicable law;
4. one clause in particular was clearly intended to be legally enforceable "whatever might be the status of other parts of the letter".

Collective Agreements

3–32 Two issues should be kept apart. First of all, collective agreements may be a valid source of contractual terms if they are subsequently incorporated into individual contracts of employment: see *N.C.B. v Galley*.[87] So in the EAT case of *Lynch & O'Brien v Goodbody Ltd*[88] the appellants had been dismissed according to the terms of an agreement struck between union and management governing procedures for dismissal. Applying the dictum in the leading English case of *Blackman v P.O.*[89] it was held that the appellants were dismissed by reason of the union/management agreement and not because of redundancy. More recently, the English EAT has held that while the terms of a redundancy clause found in a collective agreement may be binding in honour only, if those terms find their way into the individual contract of employment they become binding: see *Marley v Forward Trust Group*,[90] applying *Robertson v B.G.C.*[91]

3–33 This line of case law, however, is not to be taken too far. In *Kenny v An Post*[92] a group of postal sorters claimed that a work practice giving the plaintiffs a casual break at a fixed time, during which they would be paid,

---

[86] [2012] EWCA Civ 548.
[87] [1958] 1 W.L.R. 16; *Alexander v Standard Telephones and Cables Ltd (No.2)* [1991] I.R.L.R. 286; *Molloy v IMPACT*, unreported, High Court, June 15, 1995. The conditions necessary to satisfy an incorporation question were discussed in *Joel v Cammell Laird (Ship Repairers)* [1969] I.T.R. 206, applied in *O'Connell v Building and Allied Trade Unions* [2014] IEHC 360.
[88] M24/1978.
[89] [1974] I.C.R. 151.
[90] [1986] I.C.R. 891.
[91] [1983] I.C.R. 351.
[92] [1988] J.I.S.L.L. 187.

was a contractual entitlement. The practice had been developed following the act of a supervisor which had not been authorised by the higher echelons of management. O'Hanlon J. held that the supervisor had no authority to bind the defendant employer but implicitly drew a distinction between *ad hoc* variations in work practices and more formal collective agreements on terms and conditions. In respect of the former, O'Hanlon J. said "where a particular change in the terms of employment is intended to be regarded as binding contractually the parties should take some positive steps to achieve this object".

3–34 The second issue is whether breach of a disputes procedure by unions or management will be a breach of contract rendering the party in breach liable in the ordinary courts. Following the decision in *Ford v A.E.U.W.*[93] the common law position in England is often said to be that a collective agreement between trade unions and employers or employers' organisations is not enforceable in the courts. In *Ford*, however, it was held that this particular agreement was not intended to have legally enforceable consequences[94]; Otto Kahn Freund argued that a collective agreement resembles an industrial "peace treaty" rather than a contract. The view that collective agreements are not enforceable at common law is of fairly recent origin; Kahn Freund himself argued[95] that, in general, such agreements are contractually enforceable: contrast his later views, cited in *Ford v A.E.U.W.*

3–35 Irish case law provides support for the views that, at common law, the collective agreement may be enforceable in the ordinary courts: see *McLoughlin v G.S. Ry. Co.*[96] In *Ardmore Studios v Lynch*[97] the plaintiffs, who owned a film studio, entered into an agreement with a trade union that electricians would be drawn only from a "seniority list" of union electricians. The plaintiffs hired electricians not on the list. The plaintiffs sought an injunction to restrain the defendants from picketing their premises. The company argued that the agreement had been terminated before the electricians who had been the cause of the dispute had been hired. Budd J. gave the plaintiffs an interlocutory injunction, refusing to decide whether the agreement was binding. McLoughlin J. at trial of the action declared *obiter* that in his view the agreement was not binding *because of uncertainty of terms*. In other words, had the agreement been clear and specific the collective agreement would have possessed contractual effect.

3–36 In Ireland the Supreme Court has unanimously endorsed the view that collective agreements can be binding in the ordinary courts. In *Goulding*

---

[93]   [1969] 1 W.L.R. 339.
[94]   Hepple (1970) 28 C.L.J. 122.
[95]   (1940) 4 M.L.R. 225 and (1943) 6 M.L.R. 112. See generally Wedderburn, *The Worker and the Law*, 3rd edn (Harmondsworth, Middlesex: Penguin, 1986), Ch.4; in the UK the common law position has been vitiated by statute: *Selwyn's Law of Employment,* 17th edn (Oxford: OUP, 2013), Chs 3 and 22.
[96]   [1944] I.R. 479; see Kerr, p.668 in Regan, *Employment Law* (Dublin: Tottel, 2009).
[97]   [1965] I.R. 1.

Chemicals Ltd v Bolger[98] trade union members refused to accept the terms of a redundancy scheme agreed between their employer and the unions. Picketing commenced in breach of the redundancy agreement. While the Supreme Court advanced the view that unauthorised industrial action by the union members did not involve a breach of contract on their part (there being no evidence that the agreement was incorporated into their contract), the agreement did bind the unions and union officials. O'Higgins C.J. said that in this situation *Edwards v Skyways*[99] indicated that the agreement was binding; Kenny J. went so far as to state that *Ford* was wrongly decided in the light of *Edwards v Skyways*. Kenny J. approved Megaw J.'s dictum in *Edwards* that the onus of showing absence of legal intent is a heavy one. While the Supreme Court's observations on the point were delivered *obiter*, *Ford* is clearly not good law in Ireland if it is held to be authority for the proposition that all collective agreements are unenforceable. Nevertheless the *Report of the Commission of Inquiry on Industrial Relations* found that both sides of industry were generally against legal enforcement of collective agreements and recommended that it would not be advisable to make collective agreements legally binding by statute.[100]

3–37 In general, collective agreements are (often deliberately) loosely drafted and ambiguous in their terms, so in practice the agreement may fail to satisfy the requirements as to certainty of terms. The court may also find that the agreement itself contains language that reflects the intent that the agreement is to have an aspirational quality, as in *Kaur v MG Rover Ltd*,[101] where a collective agreement stipulated that "there will be no compulsory redundancy". This statement was held not to be incorporated into individual contracts of employment because the agreement also provided that "employment with the company is in accordance with and, *where appropriate* [emphasis added by Keane J.] subject to collective agreements".[102] The judges, as in *Kaur*, also reserve the right to rule on whether the term is an appropriate one to include in a collective agreement. But in some situations, and in particular where the law of mistake is pertinent, a plea of absence of legal intent may be defeated. This point has in a sense been made already: issues of legal intent are resolved by reference to objective factors; what the parties said, did and wrote may overcome an objection that the defendant did not intend to be bound. In *O'Rourke v Talbot Ireland Ltd*[103] a "guarantee" that there would be no redundancies amongst foremen in the defendant's works was given to an

---

[98] [1977] I.R. 211. In *Reilly v Drogheda Borough Council* [2008] IEHC 357, Laffoy J. held that a collective agreement seeking to reduce a contractual entitlement to work from 65 years of age to 58, did not bind the individual employee because of lack of notice about the terms of the collective agreement varying individual contracts of employment. See the more ambiguous facts in *Murdock v South Eastern Education and Library Board* [2010] NI Ch 18 and English cases cited therein.

[99] [1964] 1 W.L.R. 349.

[100] (1981) (Pl. 114), para.764.

[101] [2005] I.R.L.R. 40.

[102] [2005] I.R.L.R. 40 at 44.

[103] [1984] I.L.R.M. 587.

ad hoc negotiating committee, in writing, by the management. In response to a claim for damages for breach of the agreement the employer claimed the statement was not intended to be binding. While this may have been the case, the plaintiffs, to the knowledge of the defendant's negotiating representatives, believed they had been given a legally enforceable "guarantee" and for this reason Barrington J. held that the objective test of intention had been met and that the presumption had not been rebutted.

3–38 This case does not run contrary to the *Ford* case in England—Barrington J. referred to the fact that the plaintiffs had negotiated for themselves and not through union representatives. Indeed the case provides some degree of support for the essentially pragmatic line taken in *Ford* for, speaking of the productivity agreements negotiated by the union and employer in *O'Rourke v Talbot Ireland Ltd*, Barrington J. found that these agreements were not intended to be binding. The experience in England suggests that certain types of obligation—normally relating to pay, health and safety, hours of work— are likely to be legally enforceable but that other terms—creche facilities and productivity agreements—are unlikely to be given legal effect. Obviously each agreement must be interpreted against the industrial relations context in which it was devised, but a very helpful indication of the approach that may be adopted is found in the judgment of a very strong Court of Appeal in *Wandsworth LBC v D'Silvia*.[104] In this case the employer had developed a code of practice in respect of short-term sickness absence by employees. In 1995 the employer announced changes to the code, particularly in respect of medical examinations of absent employees that were less favourable to the employee than hithertofore. The employees objected and before both the industrial tribunal and the EAT the code was held to be a part of their conditions of employment, the terms of which could not be varied unilaterally by the employer. The Court of Appeal, allowing the appeal, said that the code was not contractual but was a statement explaining to supervisors and employees what could be expected to happen in the event of sickness absence. The code was not a disciplinary code and did not seek to impact on contractual rights: employees were entitled to rely on statutory protection by way of unfair dismissal legislation. Nevertheless, in Ireland, Pt III of the Industrial Relations Act 1946 (the "1946 Act") for the first time made provision for a method of enforcing all the terms in certain kinds of collective agreements. Agreements relating to wages and conditions of employment, defined as an "employment agreement", could be registered and enforced by the Labour Court under the

---

[104] [1998] I.R.L.R. 193. Contrast *Stewart v Department of Finance and Personnel* [2012] NIQB 43, where a code was accepted by both parties to have contractual effect. That code related to "core" terms of pay and overtime working: Millett L.J. and Robert Walker L.J. In *Department for Transport v Sparks* [2016] EWCA Civ 360 a short term absence policy in a stall handbook was held to be incorporated into employment contracts, the Wandsworth case being distinguished on the facts. See also *Romero v Farstad Shipping (Indian Pacific) Pty Ltd* [2014] 315 A.L.R. 243 where the Full Federal Court of Australia held a workplace harassment policy was contractual rather than being aspirational and formed a part of the employee's contract of employment.

terms of s.32 of the 1946 Act. If the agreement was vague and ambiguous the registrar refused to register it. The agreement could be varied or cancelled with the consent of all parties to the registered employment agreement.[105]

3–39 The conditions relating to pay and other contractual terms were rarely updated when improvements were negotiated and the principal reason why the agreements were registered at all was to make the disputes procedures contained therein legally binding. The *Report of the Commission of Inquiry on Industrial Relations* noted that these provisions are not particularly useful but no real changes (or even outright repeal) were recommended.[106] The essentially pragmatic nature of the industrial relations agreement is highlighted by the controversy surrounding the TEAM Aer Lingus letters of comfort which were negotiated by Aer Lingus, the TEAM unions and the Irish Congress of Trade Unions in 1990. This agreement, which all sides recognised as legally binding, gave TEAM workers contractual rights to sue Aer Lingus should Aer Lingus seek to change conditions of employment or transfer TEAM employees without their consent.[107] These contractual terms, set out in a "letter of comfort" were part of the items for negotiation between TEAM workers and Aer Lingus in relation to plans to restructure and sell off the TEAM maintenance division of Aer Lingus, and attempts to buy out these letters of comfort[108] were successful in 1998. However, subsequent difficulties in relation to the aircraft maintenance business meant that these agreements became the subject of litigation between Aer Lingus and the workers in question: see *King v Aer Lingus Plc.*[109]

3–40 The status of agreements found to be analogous to collective agreements are similarly uncertain. The Supreme Court, in *Irish Pharmaceutical Union v Minister for Health and Children*,[110] had to consider whether two memoranda of agreements that set out the terms of concluded negotiations between the Minister for Health and the Irish Pharmaceutical Union could either be legally binding as between the parties or take effect by incorporation into contractual arrangements between the Minister and individual pharmacists. While the Supreme Court appears to have endorsed the trial judge's view that negotiations of this kind could be regarded as analogous to collective agreements struck between an employer and trade unions, there was no definitive statement made in respect of the legal status of such an agreement, in either sense. Fennelly J. wrote:

---

[105] See *Reilly v Drogheda Borough Council* [2008] IEHC 357, the 2002 Collective Agreement was not registered under the 1946 Act.

[106] (Pl. 114), para.770. In *McGowan v Labour Court & Ors* [2013] IESC 21 the Supreme Court has held that Pt III of the 1946 Act is unconstitutional, having regard to Art.15.2.1° of the Constitution of Ireland.

[107] The text of the agreement is found on the "Business This Week" page of *The Irish Times*, November 28, 1997.

[108] See "TEAM Workers have one week to accept", *The Irish Times*, July 21, 1998.

[109] [2002] 3 I.R. 381 and [2005] 4 I.R. 310.

[110] [2010] IESC 23.

"Both parties have accepted that collective bargaining agreements are not, generally speaking binding contracts *inter partes* and impose no contractual obligations on the parties thereto. This is clear, it is said, from the case law of our Courts (see *Kenny v An Post* [1988] I.R. 285). So far as I can ascertain, however, the question as to whether a collective bargaining type arrangement, however it is defined, is legally enforceable, even *inter partes*, has not been definitively determined in this jurisdiction. Nevertheless, the dominant view appears to be that both parties to a collective bargaining type arrangement do not intend to create legal relations (see decision of Barrington, J. in *O'Rourke v Talbot Ireland Limited* [1984] I.L.R.M. 587, a case which does not appear to be very different from the decision in *Transport Salaried Staffs' Association and Others v Coras Iompair Eireann* [1965] I.R. 180). Both parties accept that the 1971 and 1996 Memoranda are not legally binding or enforceable, *inter partes*, the legal basis for this position appearing to be the fact that the parties did not so intend. I do not think it necessary, for the reasons next dealt with, to make any definitive ruling on this issue generally, as it is not the basis for the appeal."

Similar reasoning has been expressed in relation to the justiciability of the Croke Park Agreement (Public Service Agreement 2010/2014). In *Hollard v Athlone Institute of Technology*[111] Hogan J. held individuals could not invoke its "terms" directly.

---

[111] [2011] IEHC 414.

4 Formal and Evidentiary Requirements

Introduction

4–01 In this Chapter we will consider those contracts which can only be enforced if the contract itself is reduced into written form or if the contract (which may have been struck orally) is evidenced in writing. The notion that a contract should be in documentary form and signed by the parties is at the heart of the law relating to contracts of specialty. However, communications in electronic form are an essential part of commercial life and efforts to update formal requirements so as to recognise the legal validity of these communications have been a significant feature of Irish law. The Electronic Commerce Act 2000 (the "2000 Act") defines "writing" so as to include electronic modes of representing or reproducing words in visible form.[1] The 2000 Act also provides that information is not to be denied legal effect, validity or enforceability solely on the grounds that it is wholly or partly in electronic form[2] and the 2000 Act also provides that an electronic contract shall not be denied legal effect, validity or enforceability solely because it is wholly or partly in electronic form or has been concluded, in whole or in part by an electronic communication.[3] The conclusion of contracts for the creation or acquisition of an interest in land may, after the commencement of the 2000 Act, be concluded electronically, i.e. may be achieved through email, for example, and solicitors in particular must be wary of negotiating or communicating information electronically in case a memorandum for the Statute of Frauds 1965 (the "1695 Statute") or the Land and Conveyancing Law Reform Act 2009 (the "2009 Act") is created[4] unwittingly.

4–02 There are a diverse number of specific statutory provisions which may require a contract to be set out in writing before that contract can be enforced by way of an action. For example, contracts which seek to create a trust in consideration of marriage must be evidenced by a writing signed by the person entitled to declare a trust.[5] Provisions of this kind may be seen as anachronistic and it is noteworthy that in the case of the example just given

---

[1] Electronic Commerce Act 2000 s.2(2).
[2] Electronic Commerce Act 2000 s.9.
[3] Electronic Commerce Act 2000 s.19(1).
[4] Electronic Commerce Act 2000 s.10(1)(b): see Brennan, "Trouble down the line" [2001] *Law Society Gazette* 18 (June). It has been recently held that an email communicating an offer may constitute a memorandum if verbally accepted, subject to a signature being found which authenticates the text: *J. Pereira Fernandes v Mehta* [2006] 1 All E.R. (Comm.) 885; ditto on email acceptance: *Orton v Collins* [2007] 3 All E.R. 863.
[5] Sections 2 and 4 of the Statute of Frauds 1695. The Electronic Commerce Act 2000 does not apply to certain transactions, including testamentary dispositions or trusts: see s.10.

the law in Northern Ireland no longer requires an agreement of this kind to be reduced into writing. There is, however, a trend towards reassessing the utility of formal requirements because of the fact that procedural methods, that is, an insistence that before certain contracts or obligations are enforceable there should be clear written evidence of assent and voluntariness on the part of all persons privy to the agreement, provide a most useful function when there is a risk of extreme prejudice to one party if the contract should be freely enforceable. Irish statute law has been reinvigorated recently by consumer protection measures which give the Irish consumer some redress against prejudicial or unfair contracts by the expedient of requiring certain kinds of agreement to be set out in writing, and in some cases, giving one of the parties a right to cancel contracts. Nevertheless, Ní Shuilleabháin,[6] in a very penetrating analysis of the law relating to formalities in contract law, paying particular attention to the 1695 Statute, makes a number of suggestions about how rules relating to specific formalities may be adjusted to both improve the application of a formality requirement and avoid the kind of unjust result that cases such as *Pitts v Jones*[7] can throw up. While she considers that the 1695 Statute protections are probably better left in place vis-à-vis contracts for the sale of an interest in land and that the English Law of Property (Miscellaneous Provisions) Act 1989 is not a desirable legal transplant, suggestions in relation to confining the guarantee requirement to gratuitous and non-business promises appear entirely sensible. Ní Shuilleabháin also recommends the repeal of s.4 of the Sale of Goods Act 1893 (the "1893 Act") and although she says nothing in particular about the two other remaining provisions in s.2 of the 1695 Statute (contracts not to be performed within one year and contracts in consideration of marriage) one may conclude that these provisions should, in her view, also be consigned to legal history.

4–03 For the sake of completeness it is important to point out that there is no general requirement, whenever a formal document is contractually required, that the instrument be witnessed. In *Maple Leaf Macro Volatility Master Fund Ltd v Rouvroy*[8] a formal contract was sent to the defendants for signature. The defendants duly signed and returned the document but they argued, inter alia, that there was no binding agreement because their signatures had not been witnessed. There was no evidence to support a signature requirement nor any understanding that the defendants could have believed that this was a requirement for validity. (There are, however, witnessing requirements in relation to deeds—s.64 of the 2009 Act.) A similar argument was also unsuccessful in *Ulster Bank Ireland Ltd v Roche and Buttimer.*[9] A standard form bank guarantee was completed—a space on the form requiring completion before a witness; the guarantors argued that the failure to witness the signature by a bank official in some way raised a duty to advise the guarantor. As the

---

6   (2005) 27 D.U.L.J. 113.
7   [2008] 1 All E.R. 941.
8   [2009] EWHC 257 (Comm), affirmed at [2009] EWCA Civ 1334.
9   [2012] IEHC 166.

defendants admitted the document contained their signature, the purpose behind this witnessing part of the document (i.e. non-repudiation by the signor) did not arise. Conversely, signature with reservations attached tends to be ineffective; see the important guarantee case of *Alonso v SRS Investments (WA) Pty Ltd*.[10]

Contracts that must be Evidenced in Writing

4–04 Section 2 of the 1695 Statute[11] provides in part:

> [N]o action shall be brought ... whereby to charge the defendant upon any special promise to answer for the debt, default or miscarriage of another person, or to charge any person upon any agreement made upon consideration of marriage, or upon any contract or (*sic*) sale of lands, tenements or hereditaments or any interest in or concerning them, or upon any agreement that is not to be formed within the space of one year from the making thereof, unless the agreement upon which such action shall be brought, or some memorandum or note thereof, shall be in writing, and signed by the party to be charged therewith, or some other person thereunto by him lawfully authorised.

As a result of Sch.2, Pt 1 of the 2009 Act, the words "or upon any contract or sale of lands, tenements, or hereditaments, or any interest in or concerning them" were repealed with effect from December 1, 2009. Section 51(1) provides a new formulation of this, the most important part of s.2 of the 1695 Statute[12]:

> Subject to subsection (2), no action shall be brought to enforce any contract for the sale or other disposition of land unless the agreement on which such action is brought, or some memorandum or note of it, is in writing and signed by the person against whom the action is brought or that person's authorised agent.

Subsection 51(2) provides:

> Subsection (1) does not affect the law relating to part performance or other equitable doctrines.

This is a more minimalist approach than that adopted in England and Wales in the Law of Property (Miscellaneous Provisions) Act 1989. That Act requires the contract to be in writing and dispenses with the part performance doctrine. The Law Reform Commission had considered reform of this part of Irish

---

[10] [2012] WASC 168.

[11] 7 Will. 3, c.12 based upon the provisions of s.4 of the English Statute of Frauds 1677 (29 C.II, c.3).

[12] *Reform and Modernisation of Land Law and Conveyancing Law* (LRC 74–2005), p.163. See also LRC CP 34–2004, para.8.03.

contract law and decided that, until e-conveyancing mechanisms were fully in place facilitating electronic conveyancing without the use of paper and documents, it was more appropriate to retain the substance of the existing law, including part performance and other equitable reliefs.

(1) Contracts to pay for the debt, etc. of another

4–05 In *Actionstrength Ltd v International Glass Engineering SOA*,[13] the plaintiffs were sub-contractors engaged by I., the main contractor on a construction contract between I. and S.G. I. fell behind in payments to the plaintiffs and the plaintiffs threatened to walk off the site. S.G. promised that they would ensure that the plaintiffs received any monies due from I. under the sub-contract. On the basis of this promise the plaintiffs provided labour for a further month. I. went into liquidation so the plaintiffs proceeded against S.G. The House of Lords held that the promise by S.G. was unenforceable as being an oral contract of guarantee. It is clear that their Lordships viewed the statutory requirement as anachronistic.

4–06 Before such a contract falls within the 1695 Statute it is essential to show that the contract is one of guarantee and not one of indemnity. The classical example of a contract of guarantee arises where A asks B to supply goods to C, a trader, adding that if C does not pay up then B, the supplier, can turn to A for payment. In such a case it can be seen that both C and A are liable to pay; C is described as the principal debtor, A the guarantor. A's promise is said to be a collateral promise, the consideration for it being B's act of supplying goods to the principal debtor; see the decision of the Court of Common Pleas in *Bull v Collier*[14] and that of the Court of Exchequer in *Fennel v Mulcahy*.[15] At times, however, it is difficult to decide whether the promise made is a personal promise which is enforceable because it has induced forbearance amounting to consideration, or because the promisee can produce a memorandum. Sometimes the distinction is not clearly brought out in litigation. In the 1908 case of *Dunville & Co v Quinn*[16] a solicitor acting for the vendor of a hotel wrote to a creditor of the vendor who was pressing for payment of a debt, "I will pay you the amount of your account out of the proceeds of sale". This induced forbearance on the part of the creditor but when the proceeds were disbursed to other creditors, to the exclusion of the promisee, the creditor successfully brought an action against the solicitor who was held personally liable on this undertaking.

4–07 In the case of the *Maria D.*[17] the House of Lords considered whether the alleged guarantor could adduce evidence to show that the guarantee was signed in some capacity other than that of guarantor. In that case, the charterer

---

[13] [2003] B.L.R. 207.
[14] (1842) 4 Ir.L.R. 107.
[15] (1845) 8 Ir.L.R. 434.
[16] (1908) 42 I.L.T.R. 49.
[17] [1991] 3 All E.R. 758.

of a vessel negotiated with the charterparty by way of an agent who affixed his name to the charter, the charter containing an undertaking by the agent that the agent would be liable for demurrage and freight. It was not clear whether this undertaking had been given by the agent personally or as guarantor of the principal. It was not disputed that there had been a previous oral agreement between the agents and the shipowners. In these circumstances the House of Lords held that signature by the agent was binding and it mattered not whether the agent signed as agent or in a personal capacity; see *Re Hoyle*[18] which was followed on this point. While the words "debt or default" refer to contractual liabilities which the main debtor owes to the creditor, the 1695 Statute also extends into promises to answer for the "miscarriage" of another. Therefore, a promise to meet tortious obligations must be made in a written contract or evidenced in writing, as in *Kirkham v Marter*.[19] Here the defendant orally promised to compensate the plaintiff, who had suffered loss as a result of the negligence of the defendant's son. The action failed for non-compliance with the 1695 Statute.

4–08 On the other hand, if the promise made envisages the promisor being solely liable to pay the debt then it is said to be an original promise and not a collateral one. This is a contract of indemnity and no memorandum is necessary here; the promisor can be liable on the oral promise. In *Barnett v Hyndman*[20] the plaintiff argued that as a bill of exchange had been accepted by one Moore, he was therefore liable on it. The bill had been dishonoured. The plaintiff was asked to relinquish his claim against Moore by the defendant who promised to give half the sum due and another note for the balance. The plaintiff agreed but payment was not made. The defendant was held liable on his promise; by dropping the claim against Moore the plaintiff provided consideration for the defendant's promise that he alone would meet the debt. It should be noted that the cause of action was the tort of deceit. In *Pitts v Jones*,[21] the English Court of Appeal has also endorsed the view that if the negotiations can be classified as one transaction and the obligation to pay arises as an incident to a central object of the contract or transaction, the obligation is likely to be an indemnity, but if the obligation is the central object sought, it is likely to be a guarantee. This rather opaque test is a difficult one to understand as well as apply.

4–09 The Law Reform Committee of South Australia[22] has not been alone in regarding this indemnity/guarantee dichotomy as "a disgrace to the law and

---

[18] [1893] 1 Ch. 84.

[19] (1819) 2 B. & Ald. 613.

[20] (1840) 3 Ir.L.R. 109; *Scottish and Newcastle Plc v Raguz* [2003] EWCA Civ 1070, applying *Yeoman Credit Ltd v Latter* [1961] 1 W.L.R. 828.

[21] [2008] 1 All E.R. 941.

[22] 34th Report (1975). In Australia generally, see Carter, *Contract Law in Australia*, 6th edn (Sydney: LexisNexis, 2012), para.9–07. Ní Shuilleabháin, "Formalities of Contracting A Cost Benefit Analysis of Requirements that Contracts be Evidenced in Writing" (2005) 27 D.U.L.J. 113 favours confining the requirement to gratuitous promises made outside the course of a business.

a trap for the unwary". This distinction between contracts of guarantee and contracts of indemnity is both difficult to apply and at times arbitrary in its consequences. However, when the choice has arisen between abolition of the writing requirement and retention, most jurisdictions have retained it. In some of the Canadian provinces, most notably British Columbia, the writing requirement has been extended into contracts of indemnity, thereby effecting a most welcome extension of requirements of form into contracts where the promisor may often act impulsively and without any obvious benefit accruing.

4–10 The existing requirement in respect of contracts of guarantee has several exceptions. The first arises in cases where the law of agency recognises the status of a *del credere* agent, that is, an agent who gets a higher commission for ensuring that his principal is paid by the other contracting party. A second exception is also found in agency law. It is established that if the promise is made in the context of a larger contract (an agent's promise to pay sums due to his principal, for example), because such a promise is given in the context of agency, the 1695 Statute does not apply. Nor does the 1695 Statute apply to cases where the liability arises on an implied promise or an account stated: see *Wilson v Marshall*.[23] A further exception arises if the guarantor enjoys rights over property and makes a promise to a third party in order to free the property from an encumbrance.[24] In *GMAC Commercial Credit Development Ltd v Sandhu*,[25] the English High Court has held that rectification of a defective memorandum of guarantee is possible. Here a guarantee was defective insofar as it contained a clause that was void for uncertainty and the document, as such, was tainted by mutual mistake. Following *Whiting v Diver Plumbing & Heating Ltd*,[26] the court saw no reason to confine the application of rectification to contracts for the sale of an interest in land.[27] Thus, rectification of a document that fails to reflect the common intention of the parties to bring it into line with that common intention, and enforcement of that rectified memorandum, will subvert many non-compliant memorandum defences. The New Zealand *Whiting* decision is particularly compelling because here the court repaired the memorandum by inserting the name of the principal debtor, this having been omitted at the time of drafting.

(2) An agreement made in consideration of marriage

4–11 This provision does not require a contract of marriage to be evidenced in writing; the old practice of members of a family agreeing to transfer property or a sum of money to an engaged couple has to be evidenced in writing before the promise can be enforced: see the judgment of Sugden L.C. in *Saunders v Cramer*.[28] This part of the 1695 Statute is of little importance today and the

---

[23] (1866) I.R. 2 C.L. 356.
[24] *Fitzgerald v Dressler* (1859) 7 C.B.N.S. 374.
[25] [2006] 1 All E.R. (Comm.) 268.
[26] [1992] 1 N.Z.L.R. 560.
[27] The leading case is *United States of America v Motor Trucks Ltd* [1924] A.C. 196.
[28] (1842) 5 I.Eq.R. 12.

English counterpart has been repealed. The Law Reform Commissions for Ontario, South Australia and Manitoba, amongst others, recommended the repeal of this kind of provision from the law in force in those jurisdictions.

4–12 Despite the quaintness of this requirement there are isolated cases in which the defence may prevail. In *The Goods of Leslie Good, Deceased*[29] the applicant sought Letters of Administration over the estate of her deceased father in order to take an action against her stepmother so as to enforce an alleged contract between the deceased and the applicant's stepmother. The applicant claimed that, by agreement, the deceased and the applicant's stepmother had contracted that, upon their respective deaths, property would pass back to the children of each of the parties by their previous marriages and would not devolve under the intestacy provisions found in s.67 of the Succession Act 1965. Hamilton P., relying on s.4 (*sic*) of the 1695 Statute, noted that the applicant was seeking to enforce a verbal agreement made, inter alia, in consideration of marriage, and because the applicant did not suggest or claim that the agreement was in writing, nor evidenced by a memorandum, the application failed.

(3) Contracts for the sale of lands or an interest therein

4–13 This very important part of s.2 has been considered by the Irish courts in a great many cases. Apart from contracts for the sale of freehold interests, contracts of assignment, leases and grants of incorporeal hereditaments, the sale of things attached to the land may also involve the sale of an interest in land and therefore fall within s.2. In *Mackie v Wilde and Longin*[30] an alleged agreement in relation to the allocation of fishing rights over a river was clearly held to require the parties to comply with the 1695 Statute. A conacre letting of land, that is, one under which certain grazing rights are transferred to another, does not create an interest in land and, as Wylie argues, should not be within the 1695 Statute.[31] If, however, the contract is for the sale of crops or the natural products of the land it is arguable whether, in each individual case, the contract is for the sale of goods or for the disposition of an interest in land.

4–14 However, it was held in *Scully v Corboy*[32] that a letting of meadowing is a contract for the sale of goods under s.62 of the 1893 Act, and that payment on account is part payment within s.4. Wylie remarks of this part of s.2 that, "it is clear from the voluminous case law on the section that it applies to contracts for sale in the widest sense". Nevertheless there are inevitably going to be instances where the transaction will be marginal. One such example is found in *Guardian Builders Ltd v Sleecon Ltd and Berville Ltd*.[33] The plaintiff wished to purchase a building site but following advice on the best way of avoiding

---

[29] Unreported, High Court, July 14, 1986.
[30] [1998] 2 I.R. 578.
[31] *Irish Conveyancing Law*, 4th edn. (Haywards Heath: Bloomsbury Professional, 2016).
[32] [1950] I.R. 140; *Dunne v Ferguson* (1832) Hayes 521.
[33] Unreported, High Court, August 18, 1988.

stamp duty and obtaining tax benefits, was advised to purchase the second defendant company, the owners of the site, and a wholly-owned subsidiary of the second defendant. In dealing with the question of whether the contract was a contract for the sale of shares or, in reality, a contract for the sale of land, Blayney J., obiter, indicated that on the facts of this case the transaction would not be within the 1695 Statute. Where land is held by a corporate body the purchase of the shares of that body does not vest in the purchaser an actual interest in the land. Blayney J. distinguished the case at bar from *Boyce v Greene*[34] on the ground that the property in that case was held by a partnership and the purchase of shares in the partnership vested in the purchaser an interest in land owned by the partnership.

(4) Contracts not to be performed within one year

4–15 In order to eliminate the possibility of cases being decided on the strength of oral testimony which may be deficient simply because of the interval between formation of a bargain and the litigation, the 1695 Statute required such contracts to be evidenced in writing. In *Tierney v Marshall*[35] the plaintiff alleged that it had been agreed between himself and the defendant landlord that the rent payable by the plaintiff would not be paid over to the defendant but would be set off against sums due to the plaintiff as arrears of wages earned while in the defendant's employment. The plaintiff claimed that this oral agreement made the defendant's landlord's acts of distress unlawful. The rent payable was £17 per annum; sums due were in excess of £200. For the set-off to operate then the contract would run for 12 years before the arrears would be paid. It was the view of the court that the contract was intended to run for more than one year and because it was not evidenced in writing, was unenforceable. Similarly, in *Naughton v Limestone Land Co Ltd*[36] an oral contract of employment which was to run for four years was held unenforceable without a memorandum of agreement. In the case of *In the Goods of Leslie Good, Deceased*,[37] the facts of which are set out above in relation to contracts in contemplation of marriage, Hamilton P., alternatively, held that because either party could survive the making of the contract for more than one year, the contract was caught by this part of s.2 of the 1695 Statute. One need only look to the facts of *Donnelly v Woods*[38] to see how prudent the drafters of the 1695 Statute were on this point, at that time, but the arbitrary and anachronistic nature of this provision cannot be contested in this day and age.

4–16 It is established, however, that if at the time the contract is struck the parties intend it to be performed within one year, the 1695 Statute does

---

[34] (1826) Batty 608.
[35] (1857) 7 I.C.L.R. 308.
[36] [1952] Ir.Jur.Rep. 19.
[37] Unreported, High Court, July 14, 1986.
[38] [2012] IEHC 26, discussed on the opening pages of this book.

not apply. If the contract is to be performed within one year by one of the parties, as would be the case if A promised to convey Whiteacre to B next week in return for B's promise to support A for life, the 1695 Statute does not apply; see *Murphy v O'Sullivan*.[39] In the case of *Hynes v Hynes*[40] a plea that a contract for the transfer of a business from one brother to another was unenforceable for want of a memorandum was rejected. Barrington J., looking at the situation prevailing at the time of agreement, held that there was no intention on either side that the agreement should not be completed within the space of one year; the intention was that the agreement would be implemented immediately and that completion take place as soon as possible. In such a case it is immaterial whether the agreement is, in fact, completed within one year or not. It does not suffice for there merely to exist the possibility that one party may perform within the one-year period: *Farrington v Donoghue*.[41] In this case the contract will be unenforceable unless there is a memorandum. If the contract is terminable at will, *Dublin Corp v Blackrock Commissioners*[42] holds the contract is outside the 1695 Statute.

4–17 If, however, the employee performs his part of the bargain he may be entitled to reasonable remuneration by making a claim in *quantum meruit* as occurred in *Savage v Canning*.[43] This case concerned an action to recover £500 due for work and labour carried out on foot of a contract that could not be enforced because of non-compliance with the 1695 Statute. An action in quantum meruit was permitted because the plaintiff had done everything necessary under the contract. The *quantum meruit* remedy should be noted because in cases of part performance the plea may not be available, even in cases of substantial or complete performance by the plaintiff of his obligations, unless a plea of specific performance would have been available to each contracting party, a proposition established by *Crowley v O'Sullivan*.[44]

4–18 It is established in *Naughton v Limestone Land Co*[45] that the courts will not sever the contract and allow an action in contract to lie for the first year of the oral contract.

(5) Contracts for the sale of goods in excess of £10

4–19 By virtue of Sch.1 to the Euro Changeover (Amounts) Act 2001 this figure of £10 is converted to €12. Section 13 of the 1695 Statute declares that such contracts cannot be enforceable unless the buyer: (i) accepts and receives part of the goods sold; or (ii) he gives something in earnest to bind the bargain; or (iii) the buyer makes part payment. In all other cases a memorandum must

---

[39] (1866) 11 Ir.Jur.(N.S.) 111.
[40] [1984] IEHC 48; *Donnelly v Woods* [2012] IEHC 26.
[41] (1866) I.R. 1 C.L. 675.
[42] (1882) 16 I.L.T.R. 111.
[43] (1867) I.R. 1 C.L. 432.
[44] [1900] 2 I.R. 478.
[45] [1952] Ir.Jur.Rep. 19.

exist. This section was substantially repeated by s.4 of the 1893 Act and although the 1893 Act did not expressly repeal s.13 of the 1695 Statute the courts seem to have regarded the 1893 Act as effecting an implied repeal. Section 13 of the 1695 Statute was eventually repealed by the Statute Law Revision (Pre-Union Irish Statutes) Act 1962 s.1 and Schedule.

4–20 The three alternatives that present a means of enforcing the contract where no memorandum exists hinge upon the conduct of the buyer. "Acceptance and receipt" was considered in *Hopton v McCarthy*.[46] A coach-builder in Tipperary ordered materials from the plaintiff in England but he refused to proceed with the transaction when he learnt that the price payable was three times that indicated during negotiations. The seller sent the materials by rail. They were held in the carrier's warehouse awaiting collection by the defendant. The acceptance and receipt formula did not apply here because the defendant had not actually received them: delivery into the custody of a carrier was held not to satisfy this requirement because the carrier was not authorised to accept them for the defendant.

4–21 In most cases where the question of acceptance and receipt arises this will be a relatively easy requirement to satisfy; witness the decision of the Supreme Court in *Tradax (Ireland) Ltd v Irish Grain Board Ltd*[47] affirming the decision of Gannon J. in which the learned judge held that, by accepting 1,871 tonnes of grain out of a total of 12,000 tonnes due under the contract, the defendant could not plead the absence of a memorandum under s.4 of the 1893 Act.

4–22 The buyer can also be held liable if at the time of the bargain something in earnest is given. This ancient and obscure provision would be satisfied if the buyer gave his business card, for example, as a gesture of his good faith. The modern practice, for example, in ordering goods by giving a credit card number over the telephone could conceivably be regarded as the giving of something in earnest, even if the credit card holder does not sign the transaction docket.

4–23 For part payment to have been made it is essential that the payment be tendered and accepted. To post a cheque which is immediately returned uncashed will not satisfy the part payment provision. It was argued in the case of *Kirwan v Price*[48] that when the buyer offered the cash price payable for a horse which he had orally agreed to buy (the seller declining to proceed with the sale at the agreed price), this constituted "something given in earnest". The Circuit Court judge refused to accept the argument, indicating that while the distinction between part payment and tendering of something in earnest is not clear, acceptance by the seller is essential to both. If the contract is marginal

---

[46] (1882) 10 L.R.(Ir.) 266.
[47] [1984] I.R. 1.
[48] [1958] Ir.Jur.Rep. 56.

in the sense that it may be either a contract for the sale of goods or an interest in land it seems that the party arguing for enforcement may stand a greater chance of success if he argues that it is a contract for the sale of goods. The decision in *Scully v Corboy*[49] held a letting of meadowing to be a contract for the sale of goods and because there were acts of part payment the absence of a memorandum was not fatal under s.4. Had the court decided otherwise the action would have failed because payment of part of the price in a contract for the sale of an interest in land does not readily satisfy the doctrine of part performance; see *Clinan v Cooke*.[50] The retention of s.4 of the 1893 Act is anachronistic and provides a technical and unmeritorious defence to executory contracts, regardless of the transaction type or status of the buyer. It has been repealed in most other jurisdictions, including the UK in 1954. In Australia there is a $20 threshold in Tasmania and Western Australia but the requirement has been repealed in other States.

The Requirements of the 1695 Statute and Section 51 of the 2009 Act

(1) The memorandum

4–24 It is not necessary for the memorandum to have been specifically drafted as a memorandum before the 1695 Statute can be satisfied. Letters written by solicitors, estate agents and others setting out the terms of the agreement have been held to constitute a memorandum even though the solicitor did not intend the document to take on the character of such an instrument. Other instruments that have been held to suffice include auctioneer's sale books, cheques for a deposit and receipts, all of which were not intended to *evidence* the contract. Indeed, in *Tradax (Ireland) Ltd v Irish Grain Board Ltd*[51] the Supreme Court upheld the decision of the judge at the first instance in which it was held that a letter written by the defendant's agent in which the agent repudiated the contract could constitute a memorandum of agreement because it set out all the material terms of the oral agreement.

4–25 The only compelling requirement is that the memorandum should have come into existence before the commencement of the action brought to enforce the contract in question. So, in one case,[52] an action was brought in the name of a plaintiff who sought specific performance against the defendant. The defendant filed a defence in which it was asserted that a contract existed but that a company other than the plaintiff was the purchaser. The plaintiff then sought to amend the writ and statement of claim so as to instate the company as plaintiff. Leave was granted. The defendant's pleadings were

---

[49] [1950] I.R. 140.
[50] (1802) 1 Sch. & Lef. 22.
[51] [1984] I.R. 1.
[52] *Farr, Smith & Co v Messers Ltd* [1928] 1 K.B. 397.

regarded as being a sufficient memorandum of the alleged agreement between the company and the defendant for, in essence, the amendment of the writ and statement of claim, constituted commencement of a new action.

4–26 Some memoranda actually pre-date the conclusion of the contract itself. There are several cases[53] which indicate that a letter of offer may be a valid memorandum even though the offer, ipso facto, does not acknowledge the existence of a contract. In *J. Pereira Fernandes v Mehta*,[54] the appellant directed a member of staff to send an email in which the appellant offered to meet the debts of a company of which the appellant was a director, if the respondent would adjourn proceedings it had brought against the company. The respondent verbally accepted the offer and adjourned the proceedings. It was held that the verbal acceptance, which the appellant accepted had occurred, was sufficient to render the written offer the necessary memorandum for the purposes of the 1695 Statute.[55] Irish law is of the same effect and there is Supreme Court authority on this very point. In *Boyle and Boyle v Lee and Goyns*,[56] O'Flaherty J. defended this "anomalous" exception of a written offer being accepted orally as turning on the fact that "once there is an oral acceptance of a written offer it is at that moment that a contract comes into existence and, therefore, the note or memorandum becomes relevant". The general rule, however, is neatly illustrated by a recent decision of Costello J. In *Globe Entertainments Ltd v The Pub Pool (In Receivership)*[57] the Plaintiff sought to rely upon an email in which the receiver of a company recommended that an offer be accepted, subject to conditions. This was the last document signed by the alleged vendor. The argument failed because a recommendation to sell is not evidence of an agreement to sell. Without subsequent communications evidencing an agreement, the memorandum simply does not exist.

(2) Contents of the memorandum

4–27 The memorandum must contain the names of both parties to the contract or describe them in such a way as to make it possible to identify them. This provision is, like other parts of the 1695 Statute, read liberally, the courts preferring to find a contract to be enforceable than unenforceable. In *Bacon & Co v Kavanagh*[58] the words "you" and "your employment" in a contract of guarantee were held to be sufficiently clear to identify the party charged after surrounding circumstances were adverted to. In *Guardian Builders Ltd v Patrick Kelly & Park Avenue Ltd*,[59] Costello J. stated that the test was whether

---

[53] e.g. *Reuss v Picksley* (1866) L.R. 1 Ex. 342.
[54] [2006] 1 All E.R. (Comm.) 885.
[55] Applying Devlin J. in *Parker v Clark* [1960] 1 All E.R. 93. In *Mehta* the court expressly reserved its position where there was a dispute on whether the written offer had actually been accepted.
[56] [1992] I.L.R.M. 65.
[57] [2015] IEHC 115.
[58] (1908) 42 I.L.T.R. 120.
[59] Unreported, High Court, March 31, 1981.

the parties can be readily identified. In that case the name of the plaintiff company was misstated and the reference to the buyer failed to refer to the corporation involved, referring only to the person of the first defendant. It was held nevertheless to be sufficient to enable the court to identify the parties. The words used may not be such as to identify one of the parties but if proof of identity from an external source is possible the memorandum may suffice. Thus, in *Rossiter v Miller*[60] it was held that if an agent signs qua agent for "the owner," parol evidence to prove the identity of the owner will perfect the memorandum.

4–28 If all the essential matters have been agreed then the court will hold that there is an oral contract, and will then proceed to consider whether there is an adequate memorandum. It is of course essential that there be agreement on the property to be transferred and that this description finds its way into the memorandum. In some instances the memorandum may refer only to the seller's property but, if this can be readily identified, then the contract will be enforceable. Should the memorandum fail to refer to the entire property and omit to mention a small offshore island of little value, for example, then the defect may be waived at the option of the purchaser, as in *Barrett v Costello*.[61]

4–29 It is also necessary for the contract to state the consideration. In *Lynch v O'Meara*[62] Butler J. held that it is not necessary to add whether the mode of payment will be in cash or by cheque.[63] However, if the parties refer to the balance payable after the purchaser has paid a deposit, in a manner that makes the reference misstate the total consideration, the memorandum will be defective. In *Black v Grealy*,[64] where just such a situation arose, Costello J. said:

> "[I]n the circumstances of the present case the document relied on does not omit the consideration—it contains a figure for the consideration for the sale which the evidence establishes is the balance of the purchase price … it is not apt to describe the resultant written document as a memorandum 'of' the parties' oral agreement (as it does not properly state the full consideration for the sale); rather, it is a memorandum which is 'in accordance with' one of the stipulations of the oral agreement—which is not the same thing."

---

[60] (1878) 3 App.Cas. 1124.
[61] Unreported, High Court, July 13, 1973. It may be that a number of defects are evident. Is it clear that the vendor is the person having legal title? What if the vendor is in receivership? Have the parties agreed upon a closing date and is this stated in the memorandum: *Globe Entertainments Ltd v The Pub Pool (In Receivership)* [2015] IEHC 155.
[62] Unreported, High Court, October 23, 1973.
[63] In *Aga Khan v Firestone and Firestone* [1992] I.L.R.M. 31 Morris J. held that the allocation of relevant parts of consideration to components of the bargain is not necessary as an essential matter.
[64] Unreported, High Court, November 10, 1977; *Maloney v O'Connor* [2015] IEHC 678.

The Supreme Court, in *Godley v Power*,[65] affirmed the view that the memorandum must recite the property, the parties and the price. If these three material terms are set out then most contracts will be enforceable unless on the evidence it is clear that the parties intended additional provisions to be essential terms. Failure to add these material terms will result in the memorandum being defective.

4–30 Two distinct problems must be distinguished here. First of all, the parties may fail to agree on additional terms that the courts consider to be essential before a contract can be said to exist at all. Here the contract is void for uncertainty. In *Supermacs Ireland Ltd & McDonagh v Katesan (Naas) Ltd & Sweeney*[66] the Supreme Court has clarified the law[67] by stating that the failure of the parties to agree a deposit is not per se fatal to the existence of a concluded agreement. If the evidence disclosed that the parties intended to, at a later date, agree upon the amount of a deposit in express terms there may be no concluded contract but this is not necessarily so.

4–31 This is to be contrasted with the case of an agreement struck on all essential terms, the parties failing to record these terms in the memorandum. Here the contract is unenforceable unless some other means of enforcement exists. The distinction between certainty of terms and the adequacy of the memorandum is fundamental. This question arose in the case of *Supermacs Ireland Ltd and McDonagh v Katesan (Naas) Ltd & Sweeney*.[68] The plaintiffs alleged a binding agreement to purchase six fastfood restaurants from the defendants. The defendants sought to strike out the claim, arguing, *inter alia*, that no concluded agreement had been struck on the size of the deposit, counsel for the defendant submitting that in *Boyle and Boyle v Lee and Goyns*[69] the Supreme Court held that the failure to agree a deposit in a land purchase agreement was such as to render the agreement void for uncertainty. The Supreme Court distinguished the instant case on the ground that, in *Boyle*, the evidence indicated that the parties had left it to their solicitors to agree a deposit and that failure to agree a material term of this kind was in the case fatal. In *Boyle* the Supreme Court did not hold that agreement on a deposit was essential for a contract to come into existence. Geoghegan J. in particular stressed in *Supermacs* that when the case came to trial it was possible that

---

[65] (1961) 95 I.L.T.R. 135. The Northern Ireland Court of Appeal has recently reaffirmed that failure in the documentation to identify the price will mean that the Statute of Frauds is not satisfied: *Hamilton v Judge* [2010] NICA 49, overruling Deeny J. on this point.

[66] [2000] 4 I.R. 273.

[67] Doubts arose due to the dicta of Finlay C.J. in *Boyle & Boyle v Lee & Goyns* [1992] 1 I.R. 555 at 571. The position has been codified by s.51(3) of the Land and Conveyancing Law Reform Act 2009 which provides that, for the avoidance of doubt, "but subject to an express provision in the contract to the contrary, payment of a deposit in money or money's worth is not necessary for an enforceable contract".

[68] [2000] 4 I.R. 273.

[69] [1992] 1 I.R. 555. See Maddox and Canny, "Enforcing Contracts for the Sale of Land: Have the Courts Retreated from *Boyle v Lee and Goyns*" (2005) 12 C.L.P. 3.

the court could find that the parties intended to be contractually bound by a particular deposit yet to be negotiated, having been agreed, and if this were so the contract would be void for uncertainty.[70] However, Geoghegan J. also remarked that there were at least four other possible findings that would not make the plaintiff's action unsustainable.

4–32 There may be circumstances in which both these defects coincide. In *Guardian Builders Ltd v Sleecon Ltd and Berville Ltd*[71] the plaintiff purchaser sought specific performance of an agreement to purchase land by way of a share purchase of the company owning the land. The plaintiff alleged that the oral agreement involved a covenant that there would be an indemnity for any tax losses that could not be transferred to the plaintiff upon acquisition and, further, the plaintiff sought specific performance of the alleged agreement and was not prepared to take the property unless the indemnity accompanied the property. Blayney J. held that the evidence did not establish any concluded oral agreement, much less an agreement upon an indemnity being available to the plaintiff from the defendants. Further, any such agreement would be unenforceable for the alleged memorandum omitted to mention the indemnity in question.

4–33 If the contract is for the sale or transfer of a leasehold interest in land it is well established that unless the parties agree on the date of commencement the contract is void; see *Kerns v Manning*.[72] If the contract is divisible then failure to agree may not always be fatal. In *Godley v Power*[73] a contract to sell a leasehold interest in a pub with stock-in-trade was held not to be void because the parties had not agreed on the price of stock-in-trade. The majority of the Supreme Court held the contract for stock-in-trade to be a separate collateral contract.

4–34 On the other hand, a memorandum that fails to record all agreed terms is not defective for only essential terms need be included. The decisions of Lord MacDermott in *Stinson v Owens*[74] and Gannon J. in *Black v Kavanagh*[75] show that only terms thought to be material by the parties are essential. The courts are prepared to indicate that unless there is clear evidence to the contrary, it is not essential for the memorandum to state whether a deposit is payable. Nor is the closing date normally a material term. It is also unnecessary to state the nature of the interest sold if on the evidence both parties know what this is. Another factor that may sometimes be a material term is whether the property, if rented out to a third party or owner-occupied, is to be given with vacant possession

---

[70] See the same judge's decision in *Shirley Engineering Ltd v Irish Telecommunications Investments*, unreported, High Court, December 2, 1999.

[71] Unreported, High Court, August 18, 1988. See also *JC v WC*, unreported, High Court, December 19, 2003.

[72] [1935] I.R. 869.

[73] (1961) 95 I.L.T.R. 135.

[74] (1973) 24 N.I.L.Q. 218.

[75] (1973) 108 I.L.T.R. 91.

and when vacant possession is to be given. While this may normally be envisaged to be material, as in *Hawkins v Price*,[76] there may be circumstances where it will not be so; see *Doherty v Gallagher*.[77] Certain apparent gaps in the memorandum may be repaired by judicial ingenuity. In some cases the courts will imply terms into both the contract and the memorandum. In *Kelly v Park Hall School*[78] a failure to agree on the date for signing the contract was not fatal, the Supreme Court implying that this will take place within a reasonable time. Similarly in *Barrett v Costello*[79] the failure of the parties to discuss a completion date was held to be no obstacle to enforcement, for completion will impliedly take place within a reasonable time.

4–35 The decision of Costello J. in *Guardian Builders Ltd v Patrick Kelly & Park Avenue Ltd*[80] illustrates the extent to which the materiality of terms is a question of fact. If the parties discuss a variety of matters—the provision of roads, date for possession, for example—but no agreement has been made, then the action cannot fail because of non-compliance with the 1695 Statute. It may be that the contract is void for uncertainty—no agreement has been reached—but this is a distinct matter. *Guardian Builders* also illustrates another point; if important matters have not in fact been discussed then they cannot possibly be material terms as long as the parties, price and property have been identified by the memorandum.

(3) Signature

4–36 The memorandum should be signed by the person to be charged or his agent. "Signature" has been interpreted very loosely and it has been held that a rubber stamp, typed words or an illiterate's mark may suffice. In the Supreme Court decision in *Casey v Irish Intercontinental Bank*[81] a solicitor who instructed a secretary to type a letter setting out the material terms of the memorandum on headed notepaper was held to adopt the heading as his signature, so even if he fails personally to sign the letter a signed memorandum will exist. On the other hand, the initials of a solicitor added as a reference were held not to constitute a signature in *Kelly v Ross & Ross*.[82] In *Maloney v O'Connor*,[83] Barrett J. thought that this decision was incorrect but in any event was able to distinguish the case before him from *Kelly v Ross & Ross*. The signature was "Ger"—being the short form of "Geraldine"—by which the individual in question was generally known.

---

[76] [1947] Ch. 645.
[77] Unreported, High Court, June 9, 1975.
[78] [1979] I.R. 340. This case also has been held to be authority for the proposition that even if there is no clear statement in the memorandum on title, evidence that the parties knew what title was being transferred will suffice. See also *Greenband Investments v Bruton* [2009] IEHC 67.
[79] Unreported, High Court, July 13, 1973.
[80] Unreported, High Court, August 18, 1988.
[81] [1979] I.R. 364.
[82] Unreported, High Court, April 29, 1980.
[83] [2015] IEHC 678.

4–37 It is established that if the "signature" is added as a point of information rather than a means of authenticating the document this will not be a valid signature for the purpose of the 1695 Statute; see *McQuaid v Lynam*.[84] If initials are included at the foot of the page where the signature is normally to be found this may satisfy the 1695 Statute. Three recent English cases have considered this point in some detail. In *J. Pereira Fernandes v Mehta*,[85] the appellant sent an email offering to act as a guarantor but he defaulted and defended his position by arguing that when his email address was automatically inserted into the email header, this could not constitute a signature. The English High Court rejected the respondent's argument that intention was irrelevant and that all that mattered was the fact that the name of the sender appeared because it was well known that when sending an email the sender is automatically identified. Following *Caton v Caton*,[86] it was held that where a "signature" appears in a document incidentally, with no intention to authenticate the document being evinced, the document will not be signed for the purposes of the 1695 Statute. In *Orton v Collins*,[87] the court had to deal with a situation where a solicitor sent an email setting out the terms of an acceptance, adding at the foot, "yours faithfully" and "Putsmans", the name of the firm. Peter Prescott Q.C., sitting as a Deputy Judge of the High Court, distinguished these facts from the *Mehta* case:

> "I have no doubt that its purpose would be recognised throughout the profession. Anyone would think: 'Putsmans are signing off on this document'."[88]

In *Golden Ocean Group Ltd v Salgaocar Mining Industries PVT Ltd*[89] correspondence in the form of a thread of emails were held to constitute the memorandum necessary to enforce a contract of guarantee. The last document, an email signed by "Guy", was argued not to be intended to authenticate the memorandum, being intended as a salutation delivered in a "matey" or familiar fashion. The Court of Appeal held there was a sufficient signature. Similarly, in *Bassano v Toft*[90] a typed loan agreement form which was sent by pressing an "I accept" button was held to constitute the signature of a form of acceptance in a prescribed form for consumer credit purposes. In particular the word "I" could identify the signer, applying *In Re Cook*.[91]

4–38 *Golden Ocean* is also an important case on the authority of a shipping agent to send a communication which may constitute the statutory

---

[84] [1965] I.R. 564.
[85] [2006] 1 All E.R. (Comm.) 885.
[86] (1867) L.R. 2 H.L. 127.
[87] [2007] 3 All E.R. 863.
[88] [2007] 3 All E.R. 863 at 868.
[89] [2012] EWCA Civ 265.
[90] [2014] EWHC 377 (Q.B.).
[91] [1960] 1 All E.R. 689 (signature of "your loving mother").

memorandum. The authority of an agent to execute a memorandum is a rather complex issue.

4–39 For a detailed account of the complex problem of the authority of an estate agent to bind his principal, students should examine Wylie, *Irish Conveyancing Law*.[92] In general terms, however, the capacity of professional persons to bind others who employ them to assist in obtaining a purchaser of real property is not in dispute; an auctioneer appointed for the purpose of finding a purchaser has the implied authority to write a letter setting out the terms of the oral agreement, particularly if the principal is aware that the agent intends to write such a letter and says nothing (*Guardian Builders Ltd v Patrick Kelly & Park Avenue Ltd*[93]) and implied authority to execute a memorandum is also vested in a solicitor engaged to assist in the sale or purchase. Auctioneers expressly engaged to sell property by public auction similarly have implied authority to execute a memorandum. The authority of the auctioneer will ultimately turn on any express agreement between the parties, as in *Lynch v Bulbulia*.[94] An estate agent, in contrast to an auctioneer, has no implied authority to accept an offer on behalf of the principal, nor has the estate agent any implied authority to execute a memorandum on behalf of the principal. No ostensible authority can arise in these circumstances either, according to a long line of cases that is exemplified by the decision of Hamilton J. in *Aherne v Gilmore*.[95] However, in *Ballyowen Castle Homes Ltd v Collins*[96] the evidence persuaded Keane J. that the defendant vendor had not given her estate agent express or implied authority to accept an offer and that the defendant accepted the offer on her own behalf. The circumstances surrounding the transaction indicated that it was part of the estate agent's function to find a buyer at a satisfactory price and write letters confirming any agreement reached. Again, the facts of each case will determine the scope of the agent's authority.

(4) Joinder of documents

4–40 It is established that a memorandum may be made up of two or more documents. If only one of the documents is signed, however, difficulties will arise because it is said that signature must authenticate the entire memorandum. If at the time of signature the other document does not exist it is illogical to hold the signature to refer to that document. The leading case on joinder of documents is *McQuaid v Lynam*.[97]

---

[92]   3rd edn (Dublin: Butterworths, 2005), paras 3.05 to 3.09. (A 4th edition is about to appear.)
[93]   Unreported, High Court, August 18, 1988.
[94]   Unreported, High Court, July 25, 1980.
[95]   Unreported, High Court, June 19, 1981.
[96]   Unreported, High Court, June 26, 1986.
[97]   [1965] I.R. 564; *Irvine v Dare* (1849) 2 Ir.Jur.(o.s.) 205. *Supermacs Ireland Ltd & McDonagh v Kateson (Naas) Ltd & Sweeney* [2000] 4 I.R. 273; *Globe Entertainments Ltd v The Pub Pool (In Receivership)* [2015] IEHC 115.

4–41 In *Golden Ocean Group Ltd v Salgaocar Mining Industries PVT Ltd*[98] the English Court of Appeal has affirmed that joinder of documents, in the form of an email thread of concluded negotiations, and the individual messages, may form a composite memorandum, there being no single document rule in respect of contracts of guarantee. In *Globe Entertainments Ltd v The Pub Pool (In Receivership)*[99] Costello J. was prepared to accept that preliminary documents and a chain of emails could constitute a memorandum of agreement.

4–42 The Irish courts have followed the English practice of requiring the signed document expressly or impliedly to refer to the other documents. In *Kelly v Ross & Ross*,[100] McWilliam J. held that particulars and conditions of sale, drawings, a solicitor's attendance dockets, an estate agent's day book and correspondence—a total of nine items in all—could not collectively or individually constitute one memorandum because the signed documents (which did not contain all material terms) did not refer to the other documents submitted in evidence.

(5) "Subject to contract"

4–43 The English authorities show that if a document contains the hallowed phrase, "subject to contract", that document cannot constitute a memorandum because the memorandum must acknowledge that an oral contract exists. We saw at the end of Ch.1 that "subject to contract" will normally be taken to mean that the parties are still negotiating and have yet to reach an agreement.

4–44 Although there is no statutory authority to support the position, some modern Irish cases indicate important differences in approach to the "subject to contract" formula. If oral negotiations have been concluded without the phrase being used, a solicitor who adds the "subject to contract" formula in correspondence will not prevent a court from finding that an oral contract has been struck. Furthermore, the letter written will be held to constitute a memorandum even though the "subject to contract" phrase is thought to indicate that no contract exists. This unhappy conclusion is the result of the decision of the Supreme Court in *Kelly v Park Hall Schools*.[101] The parties orally agreed to contract for the sale of land. The defendant's solicitor wrote, "I confirm that we have agreed terms 'subject to contract'…". The defendants refused to proceed and were held liable. The Supreme Court held that the letter acknowledged that an oral contract had been struck; this suggests that a memorandum cannot exist unless it acknowledges the existence of a contract. The Supreme Court, however, seems to have decided that over 100 years of conveyancing practice must be disregarded when the court further held that in this context the words "subject to contract" were ambiguous and that they do not deny the

---

[98] [2012] EWCA Civ 265.
[99] [2015] IEHC 115.
[100] Unreported, High Court, April 29, 1980.
[101] [1979] I.R. 340: see generally [1984] *Conveyancer* 173 and 254.

existence of a contract; the words were seen as meaningless. This decision has been critically examined by Keane J. in *Mulhall v Haren*[102] where the learned judge (who was incidentally the defendant's counsel in the *Park Hall Schools* case) went some way towards re-establishing orthodoxy by "distinguishing" *Park Hall* as depending on its own special facts. The *Park Hall* case makes it difficult for lawyers and auctioneers to know how they can protect their client and it makes it possible for oral testimony to override written documents, something the 1695 Statute was designed to prevent. In fact the *Park Hall Schools* case was described by Circuit Court Judge Sheridan in *Cunningham v Maher*[103] as having been "distinguished out of existence" and the orthodox view, namely, that the memorandum must itself acknowledge the existence of a contract, has been re-emphasised in several recent Irish cases; see *Carthy v O'Neill*,[104] *Barry v Buckley*[105] and *Kelly v Irish Landscape Nursery Ltd*.[106]

4–45 The Supreme Court in *Boyle and Boyle v Lee and Goyns*[107] has repudiated any tendency, inherent in the *Park Hall* case, to weaken the proposition that a memorandum of agreement must, directly or by implication, acknowledge the existence of a contract. O'Flaherty J. and Egan J. confined *Park Hall* to its own special facts. McCarthy J. was of the view that *Park Hall* and indeed *Casey v Irish Intercontinental Bank* should not be followed. Finlay C.J., Hederman J. concurring, also agreed that *Casey v Irish Intercontinental Bank*, like *Park Hall*, is not to be regarded as good law. All members of the Supreme Court approved of Keane J.'s approach to this problem in his judgment in *Mulhall v Haren*. However, the Supreme Court, in *Jodifern Ltd v Fitzgerald*,[108] while reaffirming the potency of the "subject to contract" formula when used at the head of a document, left open the probative value of a similar phrase used in the text of a document, Barron J. remarking that in this latter context the meaning and context of the phrase may be open to a process of construction. See also the discussion by Deeny J. in the Northern Ireland case of *Bonner Properties Ltd v McGurran Construction Ltd*.[109]

(6) Non-compliance—common law consequences

4–46 While the contract caught by the 1695 Statute will be unenforceable at common law for want of a memorandum, it is important to note that the 1695 Statute will not be interpreted so as to render the contract void. If, following an oral contract the purchaser has paid a deposit, then the vendor may retain the deposit and plead the oral agreement as a defence to an action for restitution.[110]

---

[102] [1981] I.R. 364.
[103] Unreported, Circuit Court, March 1983.
[104] [1981] I.L.R.M. 443.
[105] [1981] I.R. 306.
[106] [1981] I.L.R.M. 433.
[107] [1992] I.L.R.M. 65. See Maddox and Canny (2005) 121 C.L.P. 3.
[108] [2000] 4 I.R. 273.
[109] [2008] NI Ch 16.
[110] *Thomas v Brown* (1876) 1 Q.B.D. 714.

Similarly in the case of *Re a Debtor (No. 517 of 1991)*[111] the applicant had agreed to guarantee the debts of a company. The creditor had orally agreed that monies advanced by the debtor to a third party should go towards the reduction of the debtor's liability on the guarantee. The creditor claimed this oral agreement was unenforceable. However, Ferris J. held that the oral agreement could nevertheless be utilised as a defence. In *Flynn v National Asset Loan Management Ltd*[112] the validity of a signed document as part of a conveyancing transaction was called into question when it emerged that a contract of sale and assignment were actually signed much later than the dates as stated on the documents. Cregan J. held that this was not intended to mislead or defraud. The signatures could, under common law principles, take effect from the day of its date rather than the date of execution when, as here, the agreement is intended to reduce into writing a prior oral agreement.

Equitable Means of Enforcing the Contract—Part Performance

4-47 The historical justification for the 1695 Statute—the prevalence of fraudulent and perjured evidence being adduced before the common law courts and the jury—was never an attractive argument for the courts of equity. The weight of academic opinion tends towards the view that it was never the intention of Parliament to inhibit equitable methods of enforcement of a contract. Corbin explains that the 1695 Statute was intended to limit the power of juries to decide cases when rules of evidence were unclear and jurors could act on local knowledge or prejudices, judges being unable to curb such excesses. Courts of Equity resolved, therefore, to apply the 1695 Statute less strictly, for this and other reasons, despite the silence of the 1695 Statute on executed transactions:

> "[I]t is established law that, after certain kinds of part performance by a purchaser, the court will specifically enforce the vendor's promise to convey land, and there are numerous cases giving the same remedy to a vendor on similar grounds. By a course of judicial development, the statute has become inapplicable in these cases, in spite of the fact that they are clearly included within its words. Part performance of a contract for the transfer of land may not, properly speaking, 'take the case out of the statute," but it may be of such a character that it will take the statute out of the case."[113]

However, not all judges favoured a very expansive role for equity and Lord Redesdale, for example, opined in *Lindsay v Lynch*[114] that had equity not granted relief the practice of concluding parol agreements would have been

---

[111] *The Times*, November 25, 1991.
[112] 2014] IEHC 408.
[113] *Corbin on Contracts* (Virginia: Lexis, 1997), Vol.4, para.18.1; see also Costigan, "Dale and Authorship of the Statute of Frauds" (1913) 26 Harv. L.R. 329.
[114] (1804) 2 Sch. & Lef. 1 at 5.

eliminated and the more satisfactory practice of reducing the agreement into writing would have emerged. In any event, there is a considerable volume of case law which points to a number of methods of persuading a court, by way of equitable jurisdiction, to grant a remedy on the contract, notwithstanding non-compliance with the 1695 Statute.

4–48 The doctrine of part performance is the most obvious route leading to enforcement of a contract which fails to satisfy the formal requirements of the 1695 Statute. Although the precise basis of this equitable doctrine is disputed it seems that the acts of part performance raise an equity in favour of the plaintiff, an equity which the courts should enforce. This view was forcefully expressed by Lord Reid in *Steadman v Steadman*[115] and it has the support of the two leading Irish cases, *Hope v Lord Cloncurry*[116] and *Lowry v Reid*.[117]

4–49 In *Lowry v Reid*, Andrews L.J. wrote:

"[T]he doctrine is a purely equitable one. Its underlying principle is that the court will not allow a Statute which was passed to prevent fraud to be made itself an instrument of fraud. In other words, the court disregards the absence of that formality which the Statute requires when insistence upon it would render it a means of effecting, instead of a means of averting, fraud. The question in each case is, whether the plaintiff has an equity arising from part performance which is so affixed upon the conscience of the defendant that it would amount to fraud on his part to take advantage of the fact that the contract is not in writing. The right to relief vests not so much on the contract as on what has been done in pursuance or in execution of it."[118]

In an important article, Coughlan and Bently[119] have refined the argument found in *Lowry v Reid* and have suggested that unconscionable conduct lies at the heart of the doctrine of part performance. This link between this ancient equitable doctrine and more recent phenomena such as proprietary estoppel is to be welcomed as marking a significant advance in understanding the judicial basis of many contemporary developments in equity.

4–50 A contrasting view of the rationale behind the part performance doctrine tends to focus on the evidentiary role of the writing requirement; the doctrine of part performance repairs the formal defect that arises where no memorandum exists and, for this reason, the evidence furnished by the acts of the parties should be unequivocal. In the opinion of Lord O'Hagan in

---

[115] [1976] A.C. 536.
[116] (1874) I.R. 8 Eq. 555.
[117] [1927] N.I. 142.
[118] [1927] N.I. 142 at 154–155.
[119] (1988) 23 Ir. Jur. (N.S.) 38.

Maddison v Alderson,[120] the acts of part performance "must be sufficient of itself and without any other information or evidence, to satisfy a court, from the circumstances it has created and the relations it has formed; that they are only consistent with the assumption of the existence of a contract".

4–51 It is often also argued that the acts of part performance must, on the facts, be only compatible with a contract for the sale of land and such a title as that alleged. It is clear that if the strict standards of Lord O'Hagan were insisted upon the doctrine would be virtually impossible to satisfy and for this reason a practical compromise has been effected (see Lord Simon in *Steadman v Steadman*) between these two theories. In recent times the courts have indicated that part performance will have been satisfied if, on the balance of probabilities, the acts of part performance have been carried out by the person alleging that the contract is not enforceable and that these acts of part performance are consistent with a contract for the sale of land; see *Re Gonin*.[121] In the case of *Silver Wraith Ltd v Siúicre Éireann*[122] Keane J., obiter, indicated that the test to be applied is whether, as a matter of probability, the plaintiff can establish that the acts of part performance can be held unequivocally referable to the type of contract alleged. In *Mackie v Wilde and Longin*[123] Barron J. addressed many of the central points that surround the scope of part performance. Barron J. cited with approval the words of Lord Simon of Glaisdale in *Steadman v Steadman* and Andrews L.J. in *Lowry v Reid*, and *Fry on Specific Performance*. The doctrine requires that the courts should investigate the acts of part performance to see if they refer to some contract; if those acts prove the existence of some contract and are consistent with the contract alleged then the acts of part performance should suffice. However, Barron J. stressed that "ultimately the court is seeking to ensure that a defendant is not, in relying upon the Statute, breaking faith with the plaintiff". Barron J. took the view that:

> "[W]hat is essential is that
> (1) there was a concluded oral contract;
> (2) that the plaintiff acted in such a way that showed an intention to perform that contract;
> (3) that the defendant induced such acts or stood by while they were being performed; and
> (4) it would be unconscionable and a breach of good faith to allow the defendant to rely upon the terms of the Statute of Frauds to prevent performance of the contract."

Barron J. also expressed the view that the court should take evidence of what was agreed and then look to the conduct of the parties to establish acts of part performance: classical formulations suggest that the sequence of events should

---

[120] (1883) 8 App.Cas. 467.
[121] [1977] 3 W.L.R. 379.
[122] Unreported, High Court, June 8, 1989.
[123] [1998] 2 I.R. 578; *Claystone Ltd v Larkin* [2007] IEHC 89.

be the first reference point, but Barron J. rejected this approach, opining that "it is more logical to find out what the parties agreed since, in the absence of a concluded agreement, there is no point in seeking to find acts of part performance". The judgment of Barron J., with which Hamilton C.J. and Barrington J. concurred, is of the first importance in presenting a contemporary foundation for resolving part performance disputes.

4–52 The most important effect of *Steadman v Steadman* has been to compel the lower courts to revise the long-established proposition which declares that payment of money can never, of itself, constitute an act of part performance; see *Clinan v Cooke*.[124] In *Steadman v Steadman*, the House of Lords indicated that if on the facts the payment is referable to a contract for the disposition of an interest in land and if the payee accepts the money, e.g. by cashing a cheque, then it may in these circumstances be inequitable to allow the payee to rely on non-compliance with the 1695 Statute; see *P. M. Howlin v Thomas F. Power (Dublin) Ltd*[125] and *Re Irish Commercial Society*.[126] For an illustration of the circumstances in which payment of money may satisfy the doctrine of part performance see the decision of Kilner Brown J. in *Cohen v Nessdale Ltd*,[127] later affirmed by a unanimous Court of Appeal on another point.[128]

4–53 The classic act of part performance is entry into possession of the land with the agreement or acquiescence of the defendant; see *Kennedy v Kennedy*.[129] In *Starling Securities v Woods*[130] entry onto the site and demolition of derelict property was held to constitute part performance and in *W. P. McCarter & Co v Roughan*[131] the plaintiff purchaser's act of moving into possession, allied with incurring expenditure on the building, with the consent of the vendor, was held to constitute part performance. In the majority of cases the plaintiff will seek to adduce multiple acts of part performance, as in the case of *Howe v Hall*.[132] Here the payment of an increased rent and the draining of agricultural land and planting of the land were held to be compelling and consistent acts of part performance; see also *Lanyon v Martin*.[133] In a landmark Supreme Court decision on part performance, *McCarron v McCarron*,[134]

---

[124] (1802) 1 Sch. & Lef. 22.
[125] Unreported, High Court, May 5, 1978; Tompkin (1978) 13 Ir.Jur. 343.
[126] Unreported, High Court, February 12, 1987.
[127] [1981] 3 All E.R. 118.
[128] [1982] 2 All E.R. 87.
[129] Unreported, High Court, January 12, 1984; *Rainsford v Eager* (1853) 3 Ir.Jur. (o.s.) 240; *Steven's Hospital v Dyas* (1864) 15 Ir.Ch.R. 405.
[130] Unreported, High Court, May 24, 1977.
[131] [1986] I.L.R.M. 447.
[132] (1870) 4 I.Rep.Eq. 242. Conversely, the defendant may seek to isolate one contract covering a number of properties by arguing that there are multiple contracts and that acts of part performance cannot create an "across the board" equity: *Supermacs Ireland Ltd & McDonagh v Katesan (Naas) Ltd & Sweeney* [2000] 4 I.R. 273 at 282.
[133] (1884) 13 L.R.Ir. 297.
[134] Unreported, Supreme Court, February 13, 1997: contrast *JC v WC*, unreported, High Court, December 19, 2003.

the court was persuaded by evidence pertaining to the relationship between the parties and the quality of the acts done by the plaintiff. The judgment of Murphy J. indicates that, despite the terse nature of the oral exchanges that were brought into evidence, the quality of the res gestae persuaded the court that some bargain of the kind alleged was struck; such a paucity of evidence on the oral bargain could be explained away by cultural and sociological factors that would be unfamiliar to many in the Irish business community, for example. The acts of part performance consisted of work done around the farm rather than work done in relation to land and/or buildings. A recent Northern Ireland case also involved a novel set of res gestae. In *Hamilton v Judge*[135] the acts of part performance were acts undertaken by the vendor who, following the sale, cleared the land of business chattels, allowed bore hole drilling to facilitate construction work, the purchaser being aware of these and other actions undertaken on foot of the contract. The Northern Ireland Court of Appeal granted specific performance in favour of the vendor. In giving judgment for the court, Higgins L.J. said:

> "We agree with the trial judge that these acts were sufficient acts of part performance. Anyone who had knowledge of the exchange of contracts, witnessed the auction of the stock with a view to winding down the business and observed the digging of the bore holes in the yard by the appellant would have concluded that he had a contract giving him some interest in the properties. It is clear that the respondents in winding down the business, selling the contents and allowing holes to be dug altered their position such that it would be a fraud in the appellant to take advantage of the fact that the memoranda signed by the appellant and sent to the respondents' solicitor for completion, omitted the price. The more so as this was done because there was an issue as to how *the* price (my emphasis) would be subdivided between the memoranda, about which the appellant's solicitor needed to speak to the appellant and about which the appellant's solicitor sought the views of the respondents' solicitor."

Although Deeny J. had gone further and included the fact that there was an exchange of contracts amongst the list of relevant actions, it remains to be seen how subsequent courts will treat such an exchange as acts of part performance. This may depend on how the *General Conditions of Sale of the Law Society of Northern Ireland* come to be interpreted.[136] Whether part performance applies to land transactions remains moot. The scope of application for the doctrine of part performance is a matter of uncertainty. See *Crowley v O'Sullivan*[137] which puts forward a broad view of part performance.

---

[135] [2010] NICA 49.

[136] [2010] NICA 49; see paras 19 and 31 of Higgins L.J.'s judgment.

[137] [1900] 2 I.R. 478. Lord Hoffmann in *Actionstrength* was clearly of the view that part performance does not operate in relation to contracts of guarantee: see [2003] B.L.R. 207 at 212.

Other Equitable Devices

4–54 The precise limits of the doctrine of part performance remain unsettled in English law. There are suggestions in a handful of Irish cases that failure to satisfy the 1695 Statute and the doctrine of part performance may not always be fatal. Given that the 1695 Statute was designed to counteract conveyancing malpractices and other frauds it would be ironic if a person could shelter behind the strict letter of that Statute and avoid liability for breach of contract. This irony has not escaped the judges. It has been said that the courts will not allow the 1695 Statute to be used as "an engine of fraud" and, while this helps explain the doctrine of part performance, the matter does not end there.

4–55 In *Doherty v Gallagher*[138] the purchaser agreed to give the vendor a reasonable time to clear the land of his, the vendor's, cattle. This material term was not mentioned in the memorandum. Finlay P. awarded specific performance nevertheless, declaring that where there is a danger of encouraging fraud by a strict interpretation of the 1695 Statute this should be avoided if possible. Similarly, a trustee cannot plead the strict requirements of the 1695 Statute if to do so would permit him to commit a fraud; see *McGillycuddy v Joy*.[139] In *Conroy v Fitzpatrick*[140] the parties agreed to purchase a house in equal shares but the defendant covertly negotiated the sale to himself only. There was no memorandum of agreement, but Lavan J., applying *McGillycuddy v Joy*, held that the defendant was bound to exercise legal ownership in favour of the plaintiff:

> "[F]or the defendant to deny the existence of that trust is a fraud and the Statute of Frauds does not prevent proof of such fraud."

Conroy also recognises the so-called *Pallant v Morgan*[141] equity. Here, a court of equity will impose a constructive trust if A acts unconscionably in his dealings with B; A will hold property in trust for B even in circumstances where a contract or agreement to purchase property jointly is unenforceable for lack of certainty or the absence of an intention to create legal relations would preclude the grant of specific performance. If there is a mistake in the memorandum in circumstances where rectification is not possible an oral agreement may be enforced regardless of the memorandum's deficiencies. Indeed, the *Pallant v Morgan* equity does not require an agreement to exist, but rather, it is enough to show either a benefit to the acquiring party and/ or a detriment to the non-acquiring party, and that it is inequitable that

---

[138] Unreported, High Court, June 9, 1975.
[139] [1959] I.R. 189; *Ballyowen Castle Homes v Collins*, unreported, High Court, June 26, 1986; *Kavanagh v Delicato*, unreported, High Court, December 20, 1996.
[140] Unreported, High Court, December 18, 2003; *Shiel v McKeon* [2006] IEHC 194.
[141] [1953] Ch. 43; *Banner Homes Plc v Luff Developments Ltd* [2000] Ch. 372.

the understanding or arrangement is not enforced.[142] In *Black v Grealy*[143] Costello J. stressed that for the 1695 Statute to be held inapplicable it must be proved that the defendant would thereby perpetrate a fraud. In that case, the defendant, Grealy, was responsible for the memorandum for it was prepared expressly in accordance with his wishes and for his benefit.

4–56 In *Black v Grealy*, Costello J., obiter, observed that a distinct plea of estoppel may also be utilised in appropriate cases, for the learned judge said:

> "[T]here may well be cases (and this could be one of them) where a party, expressly agreeing to accept the adequacy of a memorandum of an oral agreement, is in subsequent proceedings estopped from alleging its inadequacy."

Indeed, there are instances of an estoppel being successfully utilised when the estoppel relates to whether or not a memorandum exists as a matter of fact. In *Thwaites v Ryan*[144] Fullagar J. observed that the traditional view of estoppel prevented equitable estoppel from being utilised when the representation related to matters of intention. However, this may not be dispositive if reliance is induced. The most recent English case in which this point had been considered sets forth the view that there must be clear evidence of a change of position by the promisee or a holding-out by the promisor which may trigger the estoppel. In *Actionstrength v International Glass Engineering SpA*,[145] an oral promise was made but there were no other representations as to the legally binding nature of the undertaking. Lord Clyde, with whom the other Law Lords concurred, said that in order to be estopped from invoking the Statute of Frauds there should be some additional encouragement or inducement; merely keeping the workforce on the site was not necessarily an indication that the promisee was relying on the undertaking. In *Actionstrength* the promise related to future action but this was not regarded as a barrier to a successful estoppel plea.

4–57 *Black v Grealy* also supports a further ground for avoiding the 1695 Statute. Several cases indicate that it is established that if a term orally agreed is inserted into a memorandum, the term being for the benefit of one party alone, and the term cannot be implemented, compliance with the term may be waived. In *Barrett v Costello*[146] Kenny J. stressed that:

> "[T]he note in writing for the purposes of the Statute of Frauds has to be of the contract sued on, not the contract made and the plaintiff may

---

[142] *Shiel v McKeon* [2006] IEHC 194. The leading recent English decision is *Yeoman's Row Management Ltd v Cobbe* [2008] 1 W.L.R. 1752.
[143] Unreported, High Court, November 10, 1977.
[144] [1984] V.R. 85.
[145] [2003] B.L.R. 207.
[146] Unreported, High Court, July 13, 1973.

waive a term which is wholly in his favour and which is not referred to in the memorandum."

In *Healy v Healy*[147] the plaintiff agreed to purchase land for £46,000. The memorandum inaccurately stated the consideration to be £40,000. The plaintiff was able to enforce the oral contract by unilaterally waiving the mistake in the memorandum and agreeing to pay the £46,000 orally agreed. Similarly, if the memorandum fails to record a material term it will be defective but enforceable through waiver; see the English case of *Martin v Pyecroft*[148] which has been cited with approval in several Irish cases.

4–58 If the waiver is to be effective, however, the party who seeks to waive the omitted term must show that the oral term, whilst a material term, was inserted into the agreement for that person's benefit alone. So, in *Anom Engineering Ltd v Thornton*[149] specific performance of a contract for the sale of land was decreed in favour of the plaintiff purchaser because the omitted material term, which related to the plaintiff's right to obtain a water and sewage supply, was for the plaintiff's benefit alone. On the other hand, if the omitted term was part of the oral bargain and for the benefit of both parties, or solely for the benefit of the party resisting an action on foot of the oral contract, waiver will not be possible; see *Tiernan Homes Ltd v Fagan*.[150]

Further Reform of the 1695 Statute

4–59 The 2009 Act, insofar as it retains the substance of the provisions that evolved in order to apply (and indeed step around) the 1695 Statute, looks to be something of a transitional measure awaiting the wholesale adoption of e-conveyancing. To date, no significant case law has emerged to suggest that the courts will view s.51 of the 2009 Act as being anything other than a reiteration of those parts of s.2 of the 1695 Statute in more modern language. It is noteworthy that the Sales Law Review Group in its 2011 Report on the legislation governing the sale of goods and supply of services concluded that repeal of the £10 memorandum provision "is long overdue".[151] The same may be said of the writing requirement in s.2 of the 1695 Statute vis-à-vis contracts in consideration of marriage and contracts not to be performed within one year. There is considerable support for the retention of the writing requirement in respect of contracts of guarantee and it is arguable that the distinction between contracts of guarantee and contracts of indemnity should be abrogated and the writing requirement be broadened to apply also to indemnities.[152]

---

[147] Unreported, High Court, December 3, 1973.
[148] (1852) 2 D.M. & G. 785.
[149] Unreported, High Court, February 1, 1983.
[150] Unreported, Supreme Court, July 23, 1981.
[151] Prn. A11/1576: go to *http://www.enterprise.gov.ie/publications.*
[152] Judicial support can be gleaned from *Actionstrength Ltd v International Glass Engineering SOA* [2003] B.L.R. 207 and *Golden Ocean Group Ltd v Salgaocar Mining Industrial PVT Ltd* [2012] EWCA Civ 265.

Corporations

4–60 At common law a contract was enforceable against or by a corporation only if the contract was executed under the common seal. The rule was never absolute, however. In *Donovan v South Dublin Guardians*[153] it was held that if work was ordered, carried out and accepted by a statutory corporation, the work being within the scope of its objects, the absence of a contract under seal was no defence if the corporation was sued; similarly if it was the corporation that was endeavouring to sue upon the contract.[154]

4–61 The Companies Act 2014 affects a substantial change to Irish law insofar as the company, if a private company limited by shares—a Ltd—is registered under Pt 2 of the Act.[155] Such a company will have full and unlimited capacity to carry or undertake any transaction as if the company were a natural person —see s.38 of the 2014 Act. The 2014 Act abolishes the ultra vires rule in this context. The company will generally act through its board of directors—see s.158(1) of the 2014 Act—and changes to the Act make authorisation of persons who are not directors possible under s.39(1) of the 2014 Act and registration of this may be made. Difficulties of authority will remain an issue. Difficulties can arise when individuals on behalf of a company sign the contract without a clear statement of capacity. In one important recent English case, where the Court of Appeal was required to stretch the formalities provisions in s.44(4) of the Companies Act 2006, Mummery L.J. said:

> "From a practical point of view it may just be worth stating the obvious: expensive and long drawn-out litigation about the execution of a document by a company can be avoided by taking more care over compliance with the formalities at the time of execution by, for example, adding words that expressly state the capacity in which an individual is signing a document to which a company is a party."[156]

Contracts that are Unenforceable or Void unless Recorded in Writing

4–62 As a result of the Consumer Credit Act 1995 (the "1995 Act") there are significant changes to the law governing credit agreements. The new law now regulates credit agreements and makes significant changes to moneylending agreements and hire-purchase agreements. We will begin to summarise the law by looking at the old and the new law relating to hire-purchase agreements.

---

[153] (1904) N.I.J.R. 106.
[154] (1882) 16 I.L.T.R. 111.
[155] Conroy, *The Companies Act 2014: An Annotation* (Dublin: Round Hall, 2013).
[156] *Williams v Redcard Ltd* [2011] EWCA Civ 466.

Hire-Purchase—the old law

4–63 Under the Hire-Purchase Acts 1946–1980 contracts which failed to meet the terms set out in s.3 of the Hire-Purchase Act 1946 were generally held to be unenforceable by the owner: s.3(2) has been discussed by Carroll J. in *Henry Forde & Son Finance Ltd v John Forde & General Accident Fire and Life Assurance Co.*[157] Strictly speaking, non-compliance with the Hire-Purchase Acts did not make the contract of hire-purchase void but unenforceable and the fact that most lending institutions used standard documents which comply with the statutory requirements in terms of format, made the most likely cause for default non-signature of the document. However, there was no statutory power given to the court to ignore the non-signature, even if the court could be persuaded that the hirer was not prejudiced, whereas non-compliance with other requirements could be ignored in cases of non-prejudice to the consumer; see the proviso to s.3(2). In the *Forde* case Carroll J. said:

> "[T]he legislature considered it was essential for the enforcement of a hire purchase agreement that a note or memorandum should be signed by the hirer and by or on behalf of all other parties to the agreement."

Hire-Purchase—the new law

4–64 It should be noted that s.11(d) of the Electronic Commerce Act 2000 specifically provides that the consumer protection provisions set out in the 1995 Act are not to be prejudiced by anything in the 2000 Act. This means that electronic communications under the 2000 Act cannot be invoked to satisfy the mandatory provisions in relation to consumer credit transactions. However, the English Courts have recently ruled that consumer credit transactions may, in appropriate circumstances, be concluded by electronic means: *Bassano v Toft*.[158]

4–65 A hire-purchase agreement,[159] when the hirer is a consumer and where made after May 13, 1996, is regulated by the 1995 Act. Sections 58–62 of the 1995 Act set out information requirements that must be made to the hirer in the form of statements concerning hire-purchase price, cash price, the amount of each instalment, number of instalments, names and addresses of the parties, and costs and penalties. A waivable 10-day cooling-off period must be stated in the agreement. The hirer must sign the agreement. If the agreement is not signed by the hirer and a copy given to the hirer or delivered to the hirer the agreement is not enforceable. Other failures to satisfy the 1995 Act may lead a court to declare the agreement to be valid notwithstanding, if the failure was not deliberate, did not prejudice the hirer and it would be

---

[157] Unreported, High Court, June 13, 1986.
[158] [2014] EWHC 377 (Q.B.).
[159] See Bird, *Consumer Credit Law* (Dublin: Round Hall Sweet & Maxwell, 1998); Donnelly and White, *Consumer Law: Rights and Regulation* (Dublin: Round Hall, 2014), paras 8–99 to 8–116; see also *ACC Loan Management Ltd v Browne* [2015] IEHC 722.

just and equitable for the court to make the agreement enforceable. The 1995 Act also regulates credit agreements made by a consumer. Similar obligations to those noted above in relation to information requirements, signature and form of agreement are imposed upon the creditor in ss.29–39. The decision of Charleton J. in *Friends First Finance Ltd v Lavelle*[160] provides important guidance on the relationship between the way in which a court may exercise its discretion, where applicable. Consumer hire agreements are also regulated in the 1995 Act in this way (ss.84–91).

Contracts Negotiated Away from Business Premises

4–66 The prospect of consumers being pressured into agreeing to purchase goods and services by way of high pressure and other unscrupulous sales techniques has long been of concern to the courts and the legislature, and the unconscionable bargain doctrine and various measures of statutory protection have been utilised to protect the public. A most significant measure of consumer protection is to be found in the European Communities (Cancellation of Contracts Negotiated Away from Business Premises) Regulations 1989.[161] In essence, a contract negotiated away from the business premises of a trader must provide a right to cancel the contract within a minimum period of seven days from the making of the contract. To this end the trader must provide a written notice of the cancellation right, as prescribed by the Regulations. Upon exercise of the right the contract is void. Failure to provide the cancellation notice makes the contract void also.

Distance Contracts

4–67 In the case of contracts that are negotiated at a distance—by post, telephone, fax, electronic mail and so on—the supplier who provides goods or services under an organised distance sales scheme is obliged to provide the consumer with a prescribed amount of information both prior to the making of the contract and during performance of the contract, and at the latest at the time of delivery of the goods. The relevant legislation, the European Communities (Protection of Consumers in respect of Contracts made by means of Distance Communication) Regulations 2001[162] came into effect on May 15, 2001. This information may be made available in writing or, in certain instances, in "durable form" such as in electronic form on a website, for example. Other rights such as a cooling-off period are provided to the

---

[160] [2013] IEHC 201; see also *AIB v Higgins* [2010] IEHC 219.
[161] S.I. No. 224 of 1989, implementing Council Directive 85/577 of December 20, 1985 to protect the consumer in respect of contracts negotiated away from business premises [1985] OJ L372/31, replaced by the Consumer Rights Directive (2011/83), see below.
[162] S.I. No. 207 of 2001, implementing Council Directive 97/7 of May 20, 1997 [1997] OJ L144/19 (the "Distance Contracts Directive").

consumer. Non-compliance may constitute the basis for a criminal prosecution and the contract will be unenforceable to the supplier against the consumer. The Distance Contracts Regulations have been repealed and replaced, with effect from 13 June 2014 in respect of contracts concluded after that date, by the European Union (Consumer Information, Cancellation and Other Rights)—Regulations 2013 which are intended to transpose the Consumer Rights Directive.[163] Allied to these Regulations are the provisions of the European Communities (Directive 2000/31/EC) Regulations 2003,[164] which regulate the provision of online services made available in Ireland by Irish service providers, with effect from February 24, 2003. The Regulations provide that distance communication of services (for example, the provision of computer programs or music online) is to be regulated with the service provider making information about the service easily, directly and permanently accessible to recipients of the service. The Regulations also make provision for the labelling of online advertising, for example, including spam, and provide requirements in relation to the acknowledgment of the placing of an order by electronic means. Non-compliance with the various provisions found in the Regulations involves criminal liability but the effect on the validity of any contract is not stated in the Regulations. The online sale of most financial services such as life insurance and pension products is also the subject of regulation under another EU Directive.[165] The deadline for transposition of the Distance Financial Services Directive was October 9, 2004, but S.I. No. 853 of 2004 transposed the Directive with effect from February 15, 2005.

Consumer Rights

4–68 Both the Contracts Negotiated Away from Business Premises Regulations and the Distance Contracts Regulations have been superseded by a new Directive, the Consumer Rights Directive.[166] The Directive repeals Directive 85/577 and Directive 97/7 and seeks to lay down standard rules for what are described as "the common aspects of distance and off-premises contracts".[167] Because of the possibility that consumers may increasingly be able to, and choose to, access information online or via mobile commerce technologies, the Directive requires traders to provide information before the consumer is bound. Chapter 11 of the Directive sets out a general requirement to provide consumers with information, other than in the case of a distance or an off-premises contract, "in a clear and comprehensible manner, if that

---

[163] S.I. No. 484 of 2013, implementing Council Directive 2011/83 of 25 October 2011 [2011] OJ L 304164 (the Consumer Rights Directive).

[164] S.I. No. 68 of 2003, implementing Council Directive 2000/31 of June 8, 2000 [2000] OJ L178/1 (the "Electronic Commerce Directive").

[165] 2002/65.

[166] Council Directive 2011/83 of October 25, 2011 [2011] OJ L304/64.

[167] Directive 2011/83, recital 2.

information is not already apparent from the contract".[168] In practice, this general requirement will be satisfied when the consumer deals with a trader on the trader's premises—the information will be "apparent" from the context. Chapter III sets out consumer information requirements in respect of distance and off-premises contracts between a trader and a consumer. In regard to off-premises contracts, the trader must give the information to the consumer on paper, or, if the consumer agrees, "on another durable medium" such as accessible web pages or SMS message.[169] The trader must also provide the consumer with a copy of any signed contract on paper, or, if the consumer agrees, on another durable medium.[170] Article 8 of the Directive sets out requirements of form in respect of distance contracts. Here, the provisions are more flexible, recognising that, while there is a basic requirement that the information is to be provided in plain intelligible language, the fact that information technology now offers widely different communications possibilities, the means and details to be provided are to be appropriate. For example, a consumer who buys goods or services by mobile phone can be given bare details of the transaction and have remaining details accessible via a link to a website or delivered to an email address.[171] Distance contracts concluded by telephone may be made the subject of signed consents under national law.[172] The Directive harmonises the right of withdrawal from distance and off-premises contract and communication of the right of withdrawal within 14 days of the controlling event (see art.9(2): the right of withdrawal); in the case of a trader who has not provided this information the withdrawal period runs for 12 months from the date of the conclusion of the contract (service contracts).[173] Exercise of the right of withdrawal does not require a specific formality to be satisfied but the Directive does include a Model Withdrawal Form in Annex 1. Transposition has been effected by S.I. No. 484 of 2013.

Regulatory Powers under the Sale of Goods and Supply of Services Act 1980

4–69 There are a number of provisions in the Sale of Goods and Supply of Services Act 1980 that enable the ministerial control of consumer contracts to be exercised. Section 51 enables the Minister to, by order, require the seller of specified classes of goods and services to include specified particulars in a specified class of contract or in any guarantee, notice or other writing. Non-compliance is to constitute a criminal offence. Section 52 also enables ministerial control of standard form contracts used in the course of business in sales, hire purchase, letting of goods and supply of services in the sense that

---

[168] Article 5.
[169] Article 7(1).
[170] Article 7(2).
[171] Article 8(4).
[172] Article 8(6). There is also an information confirmation provision in art.8(7).
[173] Article 10.

the trader must clarify use of such contracts. Section 53 is intended to allow the Minister to regulate the print size deployed by traders in printed contracts, guarantees and other documents. Although the section 53 power has not been exercised, there was a public consultation in recent times to consider measures to ensure documentation in a contract is legible and intelligible.[174] Section 54 goes even further than the earlier three sections. Section 54 provides:

> The Minister may by order provide, in relation to goods or services of a class described in the order, that a contract (being a contract for the sale of goods, an agreement for the letting of goods, otherwise than in a hire-purchase agreement or a consumer-hire agreement, or a contract for the supply of a service) shall, where the buyer, hirer or recipient of the service deals as consumer, be in writing and any contract of such class which is not in writing shall not be enforceable against the buyer or hirer or recipient of the service.

This useful method of controlling high pressure sales techniques in which the consumer is unaware of the finer details of the suppliers' conditions of supply is rather vague. Does the consumer have to sign the contract? The section does not expressly state this. To date, no orders have been made but work is in progress on preparing legislative controls on the, to date, entirely unregulated area of leasing contracts; see the facts of *O'Callaghan v Hamilton Leasing (Ireland) Ltd*[175] In the meantime, see the recent decision of the High Court in *Flynn v Dermot Kelly Ltd*,[176] where, in the absence of lessee protection legislation, a collateral contract was imposed upon the supplier of goods.

4–70 In the 2011 *Report of the Sales Law Review Group* two recommendations were made in relation to consumer contracts, guarantees and associated documents. These were:

> "Regulations governing print size and related presentational issues in consumer contracts should be introduced. The content of such Regulations should be determined after consultation with business and consumer interests.
>
> The Minister for Enterprise, Trade and Innovation should be empowered to make regulations requiring the issue of a receipt in consumer transactions. The scope and manner of application of such a requirement should be the subject of consultation with business and consumer interests."[177]

---

[174] Department of Jobs, Enterprise and Innovation Consultation, February 2013.
[175] [1984] I.L.R.M. 146. The law relating to finance leasing is considered by the author in *Pacta Leasing 1991 Report—Ireland*, pp.90–144 (Pacta Sophia-Antipolis, 1992).
[176] [2007] IEHC 103.
[177] Prn.A11/1576, recommendation at para.13.50. Chapter 13 of the Report contains a much broader analysis of documentary failings or misuse in consumer transactions.

Contracts between Suppliers and Relevant Grocery Goods Undertakings

4–71 For many years the producers of goods intended for consumption have agitated for fairer prices to be payable to those producers who retail such goods to the public in Ireland. The Consumer Protection Act 2007, as amended by the Competition and Consumer Protection Act 2014, now requires that a relevant grocery goods undertaking shall ensure that all of the terms and conditions of a grocery goods contract to which it is a party are expressed in clear understandable language and recorded in writing and that a copy of that contract shall be signed and returned by each party to the contract.

Part 2

Construction of a Contract

5 Express Terms

Introduction

5–01 Even if both parties to a dispute agree that a contract has been concluded the court will still have to determine what obligations each party has consented to. The statements made by each of them will be of paramount importance in limiting the scope of the bargain. Not every statement made will form part of the contract, however. A variety of reasons why this must be so will be evident to the reader. First, the statement may be made during preliminary negotiations when each party may be seeking to establish the best bargain possible, and if every statement made were contractual, the contract would probably contain inconsistent and contradictory terms on essential matters. Secondly, the parties may also not intend certain statements to be contractual; for example, laudatory claims about the goods may be an effective part of sales hype and uttered in circumstances where no reasonable person could believe the statement was seriously meant and intended to be relied upon. Sales "puffs" of this kind are at times difficult to disentangle from claims by the seller about the efficacy of goods, and the more specific the assertion, the more likely it is that the statement will be given contractual status. A third reason why a statement may be denied contractual effect can be said to be the result of a process of interpretation. The contract itself may contain other terms that are incompatible with the term alleged. The most obvious example of such a term is an exclusion clause, considered later in Ch.7. Conversely, the express term may be too imprecise. As we have seen in Ch.1, contracting parties who hit a wall during negotiations may insert "best or reasonable endeavours" or good faith obligations in the hope that some meaning may be extracted by a court. Recent English law indicates that the express duty to act in good faith takes its meaning from its commercial context—generally a duty to observe reasonable commercial standards of fair dealing and act consistently with the agreed commercial purpose.[1]

5–02 There are examples where express obligations in commercial contracts to act in good faith with one another may be viewed as providing an additional or supplementary basis for arguing there exists a fiduciary or other reputable duty that is breached, for example, by not disclosing objectively relevant matters: *Horn v Commercial Acceptances Ltd.*[2] That duty is not breached purely by establishing dishonesty and there is strong support in English law for the view that where the party alleged to be acting in bad faith cannot be shown to have believed that he or she was acting dishonestly, a breach of that duty

---

[1]   See *Compass Group v Mid Essex NH Trust* [2012] EWHC 781 (Ch).
[2]   [2011] EWHC 1757 (Ch), affirmed on narrower grounds at [2012] EWCA Civ 958.

cannot arise.[3] Although these recent cases suggest that there has been some significant movement in the courts, there remains the fundamental proposition that a promise to negotiate in the hope of concluding a future agreement, "in good faith" will not give rise to any enforceable obligations: *Barbudev v Eurocom Cable Management Bulgaria*.[4] Good faith has been examined in recent Australian case law and it has been equated with an honest standard of conduct.[5] It is noteworthy that where the "obligation" is not part of an agreed contract, the most recent utterances of the High Court of Australia have suggested that failure to reach an agreement will not be actionable as a breach of contract via an implied term.[6]

The Basic Distinction

5–03 A distinction must be drawn between representations that do not have contractual effect and those that do. The former are called "mere representations" while the latter are often described as "warranties". In this context the word warranty is used in the neutral sense of "contractual" term rather than as a technical expression denoting a term, breach of which gives rise to a remedy in damages.[7]

5–04 The evolution of the law on warranties and mere representations is closely linked with the law of evidence and now outdated rules of pleading. A person who claimed that he had contracted because the other party represented a state of affairs existed which subsequently turned out to be untrue could recover only if the word "warrant" or similar phrases had been used. The courts moved towards protecting a purchaser by discarding such a rule; as Lefroy B. remarked in the 1843 case of *Scales v Scanlan*:

> "To make a warranty it is not necessary that the word 'warrant' or 'warranty' should be used. There was a time in the law when it was otherwise ... but it has been long since well settled, that words of affirmation, affirming a matter of fact, on the faith of which the party contracts, are as competent to make a warranty as any strict technical term."[8]

---

[3] *Medforth v Blake* [2000] Ch. 86; *Niru Battery Manufacturing Co v Milestone Trading Ltd* [2003] EWCA Civ 1446, applied by Smith J. in *Horn v Commercial Acceptances* [2011] EWHC 1757 (Ch).

[4] [2012] EWCA Civ 548. See also *Carillion Construction Ltd v Hussain* [2013] EWHC 685 (Ch) (a letter of comfort case).

[5] *United Group Rail Services Ltd v Rail Corp of New South Wales* [2009] NSWCA 177; *Macquarie International Health Clinic Pty v Sydney South West Area Health Service* [2010] NSWCA 268; *Strzelecki Holdings Pty Ltd v Cable Sands Pty* [2010] WASCA 222. Australian case law after *Macquarie International Health Clinic Pty* has not developed further.

[6] e.g. *Campbell v Backoffice Investments Pty* [2009] HCA 25.

[7] Sale of Goods Act 1893 s.11.

[8] (1843) 6 I.L.R.C.L. 432 at 457.

Scales v Scanlan was followed by Gilligan J. in *Carey v Independent Newspapers Ltd.*[9] In this case Gilligan J. indicated that the significance of the representation to the eventual entry of the parties into a contract is of relevance in deciding whether the statement is a warranty or not. In *Carey* the plaintiff was promised that she could work from home for part of her working day, a relevant consideration due to child-minding responsibilities. But for this statement she would not have taken up the defendant's offer. Gilligan J. followed an earlier Northern Ireland case[10] in which a collateral warranty was inferred from the circumstances in which negotiations had commenced, the court in that case considering it unlikely that the plaintiffs would have changed position merely upon a reasonable expectation that the defendants would carry out their promise.

5–05 Nevertheless, if a person simply affirms his belief to be "such and such" in circumstances that make it apparent that he does not take any responsibility for the accuracy of it then such a statement may be held to be an affirmation rather than a warranty. To state that a car is believed to be a 1948 model when it is in fact a 1939 model may be held to be a non-contractual affirmation or representation if the seller advises the buyer to verify this statement. Indeed, the seller may not be liable in contract if the purchaser is a motor dealer who had the resources available to check the year of manufacture and the seller is an individual lacking any professional skill, honestly believing the car to be as stated; see *Oscar Chess Ltd v Williams*.[11] In the English case of *Hummingbird Motors v Hobbs*[12] Hobbs sold a motor vehicle to Hummingbird Motors for £2,700. Hobbs had purchased the vehicle at a car auction for £2,275, the odometer reading 34,900 miles. When completing the transaction Hobbs signed the plaintiff's standard form which contained a declaration that the odometer reading was correct to the best of the seller's knowledge and belief. In fact the vehicle had done 80,000 miles. The Court of Appeal held that there was no warranty by Hobbs for there was no reasonable basis for Hummingbird Motors to believe that the seller here was making a contractual promise. Of course, if the sale was by Hobbs in circumstances where the history of the vehicle could have been known to Hobbs—he was selling as the first and only registered owner of the vehicle, for example—a warranty could be inferred. On the whole the Irish courts have been less troubled by the affirmation/warranty dichotomy than their English brethren. In *McGuiness v Hunter*[13] the defendant, who owned a horse, told the plaintiff, a prospective purchaser, that "the horse is all right and I know nothing wrong about him". The plaintiff purchased the horse which soon afterwards died. Counsel for the plaintiff conceded that the words "is all right" amounted to a promissory statement and that if they had not been uttered the remainder of the statement

---

9 [2003] IEHC 67; *King v Aer Lingus Plc* [2002] 3 I.R. 481.
10 *Gill v Cape Contracts Ltd* [1985] I.L.R. 49.
11 [1957] 1 W.L.R. 370.
12 [1986] R.T.R. 276.
13 (1853) 6 Ir. Jur. (o.s.) 103; *Murphy v Hennessey* (1897) 3 I.L.T. 404.

would only amount to an affirmation. The statement was held to be a warranty. In *Schawel v Reade*[14] the owner of a horse informed the plaintiff's agent, who was about to inspect the animal, that "you need not look for anything; the horse is perfectly sound. If there was anything the matter with the horse I should tell you". The agent broke off his inspection, the horse was purchased and later turned out to suffer from an eye defect that made it unsuitable for the purchaser's purpose. The Court of Appeal in Ireland held the statement to be merely an affirmation; the House of Lords unanimously reversed this decision. Had *McGuiness v Hunter* been cited before the Irish Court of Appeal (which it was not), it is suggested that the purchaser would have there succeeded; the statement in *Schawel v Reade* seems to be a more obvious warranty than the words uttered in *McGuinness v Hunter*.

5–06 The courts often ask whether the representee acted on the faith of the truth of the statement rather than whether the representor intended the statement to be a warranty, the latter being a metaphysical test at the best of times. The modern law is admirably summarised by Kenny J. in *Bank of Ireland v Smith*.[15] After discussing the older English case law he said: "The modern cases, however, show a welcome tendency to regard a representation made in connection with a sale as being a warranty unless the person who made it can show that he was innocent of fault in connection with it". Indeed, in the 1886 case of *Cobden v Bagnell*[16] a father who stated an honest belief that his daughter was entitled to an estate under a complicated settlement was held not liable because the statement was found to be a reasonable but mistaken interpretation of the effect of the instrument. The test is not entirely new it seems.

The Interpretation of a Contract—The Hoffmann Analysis

5–07 Apart from deciding what statements are to be included within the contract, which is the purpose behind filtering through the written and verbal statements made prior to the conclusion of the contract, the judges are required to decide what the contract actually means. This is essentially done by undertaking a rigorous analysis of the words used, viewed on an objective basis within the context of the factual matrix against which the contract was concluded. This is no longer to be an exercise in giving a literal or strained interpretation of a contract. Given the fact that words rarely if ever are capable of yielding up only one meaning this will not be a precise or scientific exercise. Lord Clarke, in giving the judgment of the UK Supreme Court in *Rainy Sky SA v Kookmin Bank*,[17] summarised the earlier English jurisprudence succinctly:

---

[14] [1913] 2 I.R. 81; contrast *Routledge v McKay* [1954] 1 W.L.R. 615.
[15] [1966] I.R. 646; *John O'Donoghue & Co v Collins*, unreported, High Court, March 10, 1972.
[16] (1886) 19 L.R. (Ir.) 150.
[17] [2011] 1 W.L.R. 2900; *Flynn v Breccia* [2015] IEHC 547; *Luxor Investments Ltd v Beltany Property Finance Ltd* [2015] IEHC 316. In Northern Ireland see *CSS Surveying Ltd v Enterprise Managed Services Ltd* [2013] NIQB 80.

"The language used by the parties will often have more than one potential meaning. I would accept the submission made on behalf of the appellants that the exercise of construction is essentially one unitary exercise in which the court must consider the language used and ascertain what a reasonable person, that is a person who has all the background knowledge which would reasonably have been available to the parties in the situation in which they were at the time of the contract, would have understood the parties to have meant. In doing so, the court must have regard to all the relevant surrounding circumstances. If there are two possible constructions, the court is entitled to prefer the construction which is consistent with business common sense and to reject the other."

In particular, Lord Clarke approved the following observation from Lord Reid in *Schuler AG v Wickman Tools*[18]:

"The fact that a particular construction leads to a very unreasonable result must be a relevant consideration. The more unreasonable the result, the more unlikely it is that the parties can have intended it, and if they do intend it the more necessary it is that they shall make that intention abundantly clear."

It is the speech of Lord Hoffmann in *Investors Compensation Scheme v West Bromwich Building Society*[19] that is most closely identified with the "new" process of interpretation and it is to this line of case law that we now turn.

5–08 Lord Hoffmann laid down a basic principle and five rules in the *West Bromwich* case:

"I should preface my explanation of my reasons with some general remarks about the principles by which contractual documents are nowadays construed. I do not think that the fundamental change which has overtaken this branch of the law, particularly as a result of the speeches of Lord Wilberforce in *Prenn v Simmonds* [1971] 3 All ER 237 at 240–242, [1971] 1 WLR 1381 at 1384–1386 and *Reardon Smith Line Ltd. v Hansen-Tagen, Hansen Tangen v Sanko Steamship Co* [1976] 3 All ER 570, [1976] 1 WLR 989, is always sufficiently appreciated. The result has been, subject to one important exception, to assimilate the way in which such documents are interpreted by judges to the common sense principles by which any serious utterance would be interpreted in ordinary life. Almost all the intellectual baggage of legal interpretation has been discarded. The principles may be summarised as follows:

1. Interpretation is the ascertainment of the meaning which the document would convey to a reasonable person having all the background

[18]   [1974] A.C. 235.
[19]   [1998] 1 W.L.R. 896 at 912–913.

knowledge which would reasonably have been available to the parties in the situation in which they were at the time of the contract.

2. The background was famously referred by Lord Wilberforce as the 'matrix of fact', but this phrase is, if anything, an understated description of what the background may include. Subject to the requirement that it should have been reasonably available to the parties and to the exception to be mentioned next, it includes absolutely anything which would have affected the way in which the language of the document would have been understood by a reasonable man.

3. The law excludes from the admissible background the previous negotiations of the parties and their declarations of subjective intent. They are admissible only in an action for rectification. The law makes this distinction for reasons of practical policy and, in this respect only, legal interpretation differs from the way we would interpret utterances in ordinary life. The boundaries of this exception are in some respects unclear. But this is not the occasion on which to explore them.

4. The meaning which a document (or any other utterance) would convey to a reasonable man is not the same thing as the meaning of its words. The meaning of the words is a matter of dictionaries and grammars; the meaning of the document is what the parties using those words against the relevant background would reasonably have been understood to mean. The background may not merely enable the reasonable man to choose between the possible meanings of words which are ambiguous but even (as occasionally happens in ordinary life) to conclude that the parties must, for whatever reason, have used the wrong words or syntax (see *Mannai Investment Co Ltd v Eagle Star Life Assurance Co Ltd.* [1997] 2 WLR 945).

5. The 'rule' that words should be given their 'natural and ordinary meaning' reflects the common sense proposition that we do not easily accept that people have made linguistic mistakes, particularly in the formal documents. On the other hand, if one would nevertheless conclude from the background that something must have gone wrong with the language the law does not require judges to attribute to the parties an intention which they plainly could not have had."

The extent to which the "old baggage" referred to by Lord Hoffmann has been "swept away" is somewhat controversial. Most judicial opinion sees Lord Hoffmann's speech as setting forth a restatement rather than a revolution. Judicial practice continues to rely on both the pre-*West Bromwich* and post-*West Bromwich* lines of authority in respect of articulating how judges are to approach matters of contractual interpretation. It is clear that while Lord Hoffmann's speech in *West Bromwich* has, according to Lewison, drawn attention to the fact that the search is for objective meaning rather than the actual intention of the parties, Lord Hoffmann's "refocusing of attention on the impression made by the words on the reader, rather than on the intended message of the writer is a departure from the traditional formulation of the aim of interpretation, namely to ascertain the presumed intention of the parties".[20] A close analysis of recent English and Irish case law suggests that there is a strong level of continuity of approach. In *Hickey v HSE*[21] Finlay Geoghegan J. endorsed *Igote v Badsey Ltd* in which Murphy J., for the Supreme Court, applied *Prenn v Simmonds* and *Reardon Smith Line v Yngvar Hansen-Tangen*. In *McAleenan v AIG (Europe) Ltd*[22] the same judge endorsed the *West Bromwich* dicta.[23] Similar examples are found in judgments from other High Court judges such as Charleton J.[24] In the Irish Supreme Court itself,[25] it is beyond question that judicial agreement on the universality of the *West Bromwich* dicta exists, even if the Irish Supreme Court is not entirely clear on the relationship between the *West Bromwich* guidelines and *contra proferentem* interpretation.

5–09 Perhaps the most important pre-*West Bromwich* statement on the search for the objective meaning and commercial common sense approach is to be found in Finlay C.J.'s speech in *Marathon Petroleum (Ireland) Ltd v Bord Gais Éireann*.[26] In this case the Supreme Court rejected a literal approach to the interpretation of words used. After holding that the clause in question was ambiguous the Chief Justice said that in cases involving contradictory clauses:

"... my obligation is to seek in the terms of the entire agreement evidence of the real intention of the parties and that if I can find it, that should prevail over the ordinary meaning of the words."

---

[20] *The Interpretation of Contracts*, 5th edn (London: Sweet & Maxwell, 2011), para.103. In this paragraph Lewison refers to rules excluding negotiations and evidence of subjective intent as being consistent with the philosophy of searching for an objective meaning. The exclusionary rules and Hoffmann principles are essentially pragmatic and are intended as a means of allowing judges to shorten expensive litigation. The dangers of relying on post-contractual statements after the dispute arose and allowing in pre- and post-contractual oral testimony at trial are obvious and many statements deprecating judicial slackness during the trial of the action can be identified, e.g. *Igote Ltd v Badsey Ltd* [2001] 4 I.R. 511 per Murphy J. and *Tekdata Interconnections Ltd v Amphenol Ltd* [2009] EWCA Civ 1209 per Dyson L.J.

[21] [2008] IEHC 290.

[22] [2010] IEHC 128.

[23] See also *O'Rourke v Considine* [2011] IEHC 191.

[24] *McCabe Builders (Dublin) Ltd v Sagamu Developments Ltd* [2007] IEHC 391, appeal allowed on another point; *Irish Bank Resolution Corp Ltd v Cambourne Investments Inc.* [2012] IEHC 262; *Ickendel Ltd v Bewley's Cafe Grafton St Ltd* [2013] IEHC 293.

[25] *EMO Oil Ltd v Sun Alliance & London Insurance Co* [2009] IESC 2 (insurance policy); *Viridian Power v Commissioner for Energy Regulation* [2012] IESC 13 (code of practice relating to statute-based licences); *Marlan Homes Ltd v Walsh* [2012] IESC 23 (mortgage agreement); *ICDL GCC Foundation FZ–LLC v European Computer Driving Licence Foundation Ltd* [2012] IESC 55 (an education and training licence).

[26] [1986] IESC 6. Recent Supreme Court decisions appear to allow the court to look for objective meaning/the factual matrix even when ambiguity or contradictory meanings are absent. The Australian courts still require ambiguity before the factual matrix is admissible.

The speech is, strictly speaking, to be seen as incompatible with *West Bromwich* because the search should always be for the ordinary meaning of words and not the actual intention of the parties. The speech lends some support for the fifth principle in *West Bromwich*, however.

5–10 The meaning to be attributed to words and phrases found in the contract in question has featured as a prominent part of the Lord Hoffmann analysis. The phrase "gross negligence", for example, has been the subject of differing judicial views.[27] The words "qualified electrician" were considered under the Hoffmann approach in *Strothers (M&E) Ltd v Leeway Strothers Ltd*[28] as was the phrase "subject lands" in a complex land transaction executed in contemplation of future mortgage funding.[29] It is often evident that the parties may have intended a formula which they then (imperfectly) reduce into a written text: even in those cases the "issue of construction boils down to the objective assessment of the meaning which the parties intended to convey by the use of those words".[30] As the dissent of Carnwath L.J. in that case attests, it is easier to state the nature of the exercise than to produce a clear and definitive result. There can be a fine line between interpreting a contract in a way that fixes a meaning that is commercially sensible and adjusting the meaning to improve the contract. Bargains may be bad, unwise or improvident and the Irish courts in recent years have had many occasions to enforce large investment contracts that have turned out badly for one or both sides. The speech of Lord Wilberforce in *Prenn v Simmonds*[31] has been cited with approval in England and Ireland on numerous occasions:

> "The time has long since passed when agreements, even those under seal, were isolated from the matrix of facts in which they were set and interpreted purely on internal linguistic considerations ... we must ... inquire beyond the language and see what the circumstances were with reference to which the words were used, and the object appearing from those circumstances, which the person using them had in view."

At the same time the Supreme Court, in *Marlan Homes Ltd v Walsh*[32] has warned against too much emphasis being placed on interpreting a clause so as

---

[27] *Sucden Financial Ltd v Fluxo-Cane Overseas Ltd* [2010] EWHC 2133 (Comm); *Camerata Property Inc. v Credit Suisse Securities (Europe) Ltd* [2011] EWHC 479 (Comm); *Weavering Macro Fixed Income Fund Ltd v PNC Global Investment Security (Europe) Ltd* [2012] IEHC 25; *ICDL GCC Foundation FZ–LLC v European Computer Driving Licence Foundation Ltd* [2012] IESC 55.

[28] [2011] N.I.Q.B. 35.

[29] *Marlan Homes Ltd v Walsh* [2009] IEHC 135. Clarke J.'s decision was reversed at [2012] IESC 23.

[30] Lord Neuberger in *Pink Floyd Music Ltd v EMI Records Ltd* [2010] EWCA Civ 533 at para.30 (meaning of phrase "at source" in a valuation clause viewed in a technologically volatile market).

[31] [1971] 1 W.L.R. 1381.

[32] [2012] IESC 23.

to give effect to commercial efficacy, approving the advice of Lord Mustill in *Charter Reinsurance v Fagan*:

> "There comes a point at which the court should remind itself that the task is to discover what the parties meant by what they have said, and that to force upon the words a meaning they cannot fairly bear is to substitute for the bargain actually made one which the court believed could better have been made. This is an illegitimate role for a court. Particularly in the field of commerce, where the parties need to know what they must do and what they can insist on not doing, it is essential for them to be confident that they can rely on the court to enforce the contract according to its terms."[33]

A Movement away from "Commercial Common Sense" and Surrounding Circumstances

5–11 Speaking for the majority of the UK Supreme Court in *Arnold v Britton*[34] Lord Neuberger stressed that the focus should be on the terms of the contract rather than any immediate resort to commercial common sense and surrounding circumstances, the effect of which Lord Neuberger criticised as undervaluing the importance of the language which is to be construed, observing that "unlike commercial common sense and surrounding circumstances, the parties have control over the language they use in a contract." Lord Neuberger went on to stress the importance of grammar and syntax of the central provisions in the contract; the worse their drafting, the more readily can the court depart from their natural meaning. Judges should not, he said, search for or construct drafting infelicities to justify a departure from the natural meaning of the words used. Lord Neuberger also cautioned against applying commercial common sense with hindsight; the fact that a provision has turned out badly, or even disastrously, is not to provide a reason for departing from the natural language: "commercial common sense is only relevant to the extent of how matters would or could have been perceived by the parties" at the date the contract was made. Lord Neuberger also pointed out that contracting parties make bad or imprudent bargains, but this is no basis for avoiding the natural meaning of the words used. "The purpose of interpretation is to identify what the parties have agreed, not what the court thinks that they should have

---

[33] [1997] A.C. 313 at 388. Cases which mandate the commercially sensible construction under *Mannai Investments* include *BNY Trust Co v Treasury Holdings* [2007] IEHC 271; *Danske Bank v Durcan New Homes* [2009] IEHC 278; *AIB v Galvin* [2011] IEHC 314; *McDonald v McKenna* [2012] NI Ch 24; *Dunnes Stores v Holtgen Ltd* [2012] IEHC 93; and *Ickendel Ltd v Bewley's Cafe Grafton St Ltd* [2013] IEHC 293. The recent decision on *Compass Group UK v Mid Essex HS Trust* [2012] EWHC 781 (Q.B.) deals with the commercially sensible interpretation of "co-operate with each other in good faith".

[34] [2015] UKSC 36.

agreed".[35] If a particular result is to be inferred, appropriate commercial terminology is to be expected.[36] The correction of mistakes by construction, or to be more accurate, reading into words an expression or meaning that the parties must have intended, is a noteworthy aspect of the Hoffmann approach. This can include inserting words into a clause which was obviously omitted by mistake. In *Quick Draw LLP v Live Events*[37] a pledge clause preventing subsequent dealings in the security failed to include a "not". Deputy Judge Aplin Q.C. corrected the clause as a typographical mistake. The correction of typographical errors can result in the names of different parties being entered onto deeds, as in *Moorview Developments Ltd v First Active Plc*[38] as well as contracts; see *Bank of Scotland Plc v Fergus*.[39]

5–12 Later English cases have continued to stress the unreliability of "business common sense". In *Wood v Sureterm District Ltd*[40] Clarke L.J. said

> "What is business common sense may depend on the standpoint from which you ask the question. Further the court will not be aware of the negotiations between the parties. What may appear, at least from one side's point of view, as lacking in business common sense, may be the product of a compromise which was the only means of reaching agreement …".[41]

Error Correction by Interpretation

5–13 Lord Hoffmann's rules 4 and 5 suggest a court will not be required to impose a result that the parties cannot have intended.

5–14 In *The Seashell of Lisson Grove Ltd v Aviva Insurance Co*,[42] a case concerning an express clause that was intended to qualify the common law rule that allows an insurer to avoid an insurance contract for any breach of warranty, it was clear to the court that the clause intended to limit the common law rule so as to allow avoidance only when the loss has been caused by the

---

[35] [2015] UKSC 36 at paras 17–20. This text paraphrases the sense of four of seven factors stressed by Lord Neuberger. All seven factors are extremely helpful.

[36] In *Hannon v BQ Investments Ltd* [2009] IEHC 191, a clause was not held to involve a condition precedent as traditional language (e.g. "subject to", "if") was not deployed in the contract.

[37] [2012] EWHC 2105 (Ch).

[38] [2010] IEHC 275.

[39] [2012] IEHC 131; *Point Village Development v Dunnes Stores* [2012] IEHC 482; *Byrne v Killoran* [2014] IEHC 328.

[40] [2015] EWCA Civ 839.

[41] [2015] EWCA Civ 839 at para.29. See also *Persimmon Homes Ltd v Ove Arup* [2015] EWHC 3753 (TCC); *Grove Developments Ltd v Balfour Beatty Regional Construction Ltd* [2016] EWHC 168 (TCC).

[42] [2011] EWHC 1761 (Comm).

breach, but the court still had to infer the degree of loss: was all or any of the loss recoverable?

5–15 The courts do not readily infer that something has gone wrong with the language. In *ING Bank NV v Ros Roca SA*[43] the English Court of Appeal observed that whatever competing interpretation was put forward had difficulties in terms of syntax but intention was clear enough: the trial judge had opted to reinterpret the clauses in the light of unforeseen consequences not anticipated by the parties which is not part of the Hoffmann scheme. It must be evident what correction must be made.

5–16 It may be that the court may reach the same result by way of alternative devices such as finding that a collateral contract exits, as in *AIB v Galvin Developments (Killarney) Ltd.*[44]

5–17 The Hoffmann approach gathers up two exclusionary rules, namely that the factual matrix does not include post-contractual conduct, nor does the court allow in pre-contractual negotiations and subjective intent, save in cases where rectification is sought.[45] The prohibition against the use of anything said or done after the contract was made as an aid to construction, which represented the law in both Ireland and England prior to *West Bromwich*[46] has recently been endorsed by the Northern Ireland Court of Appeal in *Clinton v Department of Employment and Learning.*[47]

5–18 The second exclusionary rule was re-considered by the House of Lords in *Chartbrook Ltd v Persimmon Homes Ltd.*[48] Lord Hoffmann reaffirmed this rule but indicated (after a review of academic literature and the law in some other jurisdictions which were generally critical of this position) that some exceptions to this rule were possible under case law[49] as well as to establish that a fact which may be relevant as background was known to the parties, or to establish a claim for rectification or estoppel (per Lord Hoffmann in *Chartbrook* who described such instances as being instances that operate outside the exclusionary rule whilst not being exclusions!) It will be interesting to see if the UK judiciary (Scottish law included) and the Irish courts continue

---

43 [2011] EWHC Civ 353.
44 [2011] IEHC 314. See also *Ulster Bank v Acheson* [2011] NIQB 33, following *Vodafone Ltd v GNT Holdings (U.K.) Ltd* [2004] EWHC 1526 (Q.B.).
45 See *Ted Baker Plc v Axa Insurance UK Plc* [2012] EWHC 1406 (Comm).
46 See the Supreme Court decision in *Re Wogans Ltd* [1993] 1 I.R. 157; *James Millar & Partners v Whitworth Street Estates* [1970] A.C. 572.
47 [2012] NICA 48; on preliminary negotiations see *McDonald v McKenna* [2012] NI Ch 24.
48 [2009] 1 A.C. 1101; see *The Leopardstown Club v Templeville Developments* [2010] IEHC 152, reversed on another point at [2015] IECA 164. See also *Knockacummer Wind Farm Ltd v Cremins* [2016] IEHC 95.
49 e.g. *The Karen Ottmann* [1976] 2 Lloyd's Rep. 708 ("an illegitimate extension of the private dictionary principle"). Perhaps *contra proferens* interpretation is not quite so illegitimate as we had thought: *Nobahar-Cookson v The Hut Group* [2016] EWCA Civ 128.

to operate both or either exclusionary rules.[50] Several members of the current UK Supreme Court have expressed reservations about excluding negotiations as inadmissible background.

5–19 Should Lord Hoffmann's approach become universally adopted (which of course it will not) then part of the "old baggage" that will be consigned to oblivion include interpretive devices such as maxims of interpretation, e.g. the *contra proferens* and *exclusio unius* maxims, as well as the parol evidence rule and language devices such as the collateral contract. On the assumption that these mechanisms will retain some vitality for some time to come,[51] we will now turn to examine them.

The Parol Evidence Rule

5–20 This controversial rule of evidence is designed to deal with problems that arise from attempts to introduce testimony about the terms agreed upon where the parties have subsequently executed a written document setting out their contract. The rule was stated in absolute terms by Lord Morris in *Bank of Australasia v Palmer*[52]: "parol testimony cannot be received to contradict, vary, add to or subtract from the terms of a written contract or the terms in which the parties have deliberately agreed to record any part of their contract". At first blush the rule is a harsh one for it would exclude all parol evidence which was not incorporated into the written document. It is apparent that the rule is capable of causing injustice. The rule was designed to prevent litigation from being protracted, the theory being that if parol testimony was excluded and the attention of the jury (whose task was to decide issues of fact, including contract terms) focused on the written document alone then civil trials would be shorter and less expensive. One sixteenth-century English judge observed that it was "better to suffer mischief to one man than an inconvenience to many".[53] Nevertheless, it is doubtful if litigation was shortened by the rule; indeed, the fact that the court heard the evidence and then decided whether to rule it admissible means that the rule often had the contrary effect. In any event, the decline of the institution of the jury in civil cases renders the rule out of date. It is nevertheless recited by the judges and relied upon by them even today. In *Macklin & McDonald v Greacen & Co*[54] the Supreme Court held that a contract, expressed to be one for the sale of the licence of licensed

---

[50] See the Scottish Law Commission, *Discussion Paper on Interpretation of Contract* [2011] SLC 147 and the 2012 Consultation Paper No. 154 on the *Formation of Contract*.

[51] The Latin maxim, *noscitur a sociis*, was approved and applied by O'Donnell J. in *ICDL GCC Foundation FZ–LLC v European Computer Driving Licence Foundation Ltd* [2012] IESC 55. For recent continuing Irish endorsement of the *contra proferens* approach see the Supreme Court in *McMullan Brothers Ltd v McDonagh* [2015] IESC 19; *LSREF III Achill Investments Ltd v Corbett* [2015] IEHC 652; *McGrath v Danske Bank* [2015] IEHC 712.

[52] [1897] A.C. 540.

[53] See *Waberley v Cockerel* (1542) 1 Oy. 51a.

[54] [1983] I.R. 61.

premises, could not be varied by reference to parol evidence, for the contract had been reduced into writing and, as such, the contract was unenforceable for the licence was inalienable from the premises in question. In the absence of a claim for rectification of the contract, in which case parol evidence would be admissible, the parol evidence rule was imposed with full force by the Supreme Court. The English Law Commission, in a important review of the operation of the parol evidence rule,[55] concluded that, despite calls for the abolition of the rule, it was a convenient procedural device, if properly understood by the judiciary. In the view of the Law Commission, abolition of the rule was unnecessary and undesirable. The rule, however, has never been applied absolutely and we shall now consider the many exceptions to it.

(1) To establish the limits of the contract

5–21 The parol evidence rule can only apply if an attempt is made to seek to add to, vary or contradict a contract. The rule is not infringed if the party seeking to introduce parol testimony is trying to show that there was no contract at all (see *Pym v Campbell*[56]) or show that there were two distinct contracts, one written and the other oral. This may prove a useful technique. In *Carrigy v Brock*[57] a deed of assignment failed to mention that Brock was to pay a sum of money to Carrigy. This promise had been recorded in a memorandum of agreement. When Carrigy sought to recover, the defendant pleaded the parol evidence rule. The defence failed for, as Pigot C.B. said, the plaintiff was trying to recover on a separate contract—it would now be called a collateral contract—and was not trying to establish that this promise contained in the memorandum should vary the deed of assignment. Pigot C.B. called the defendant's attempt to invoke the parol evidence rule "a solecism of language".

5–22 A more recent illustration is afforded by the decision of the Court of Appeal in *Haryanto v E.D. & F. Man Sugar Ltd.*[58] The defendant sought to argue that documents which set out contractual terms were not actionable because the documents merely set out the terms that would bind the parties should they, at a later date, conclude a contract. In the light of evidence that a contract was intended, the court ruled that documents that look like contracts are intended to be contracts. In cases of this kind the rule is essentially a convenient but misleading rationalisation of the decision. The court does hear the evidence, *de bene esse*, but rejects it in the light of the balance of probability and contradictory evidence that a contract, in particular terms, was intended.

---

[55] Law Com. No. 154.
[56] (1856) 6 El. & Bl. 370.
[57] (1871) I.R. 5 C.L. 501.
[58] [1986] 2 Lloyd's Rep. 44.

(2) To explain the circumstances surrounding an agreement

5–23 In *Harries v Hardy*[59] a ship-repairer brought an action against B and C, who, along with A, were the registered owners of the vessel under bills of sale. The action, brought to recover the cost of repairs carried out on the vessel failed because B and C were able to introduce parol evidence to show that the bills of sale were executed as mortgages. B and C were not liable as they were mortgagees, not owners. Similarly, in *Revenue Commissioners v Moroney*,[60] the Supreme Court admitted parol evidence to show that an apparent sale was in fact intended to be a transfer by way of gift. In *Ulster Bank v Synnott*[61] the defendant deposited stock certificates with his bank as security "against acceptances made" on the defendant's account. Because the phrase "against acceptances made" could refer to either acceptances which had been heretofore made, or acceptances made during the currency of the security, parol evidence was admissible to determine whether the parties intended to cover future as well as past acceptances. The circumstances indicated that future acceptances would also be covered by the security in question. In *Grahame v Grahame*[62] parol evidence was held to be admissible to show why a guarantee was executed; the purpose of admitting parol testimony was explained in this case as putting the court as nearly as possible in the position of the parties when entering into the agreement. More recently, in *Cuffe v CIÉ and An Post*[63] the Supreme Court took cognisance of the intended purpose behind a contractual risk allocation clause, holding that in the light of the limited purpose of that clause there was no room for viewing the clause as having a wider import, especially when that construction would have been particularly onerous and inconsistent with the limited purpose behind the agreement itself.

5–24 A more controversial application of this exception can be found in some of the "subject to contract" cases. There are decisions which hold that parol evidence is admissible to explain that an alleged oral agreement was struck by the parties in circumstances where neither the offer nor the acceptance was "subject to contract". The Supreme Court in *Casey v Irish Intercontinental Bank*[64] held that parol evidence, when accepted by the courts, will indicate that a later "subject to contract" memorandum will be regarded as an authorised variation of the oral agreement. It is submitted that the position thus adopted is both incompatible with earlier cases, which do not envisage such a departure from the rule, and undesirable in policy terms, for the memorandum necessary for the purposes of the Statute of Frauds 1695 is surely the best evidence

---

[59] (1851) 3 Ir. Jur. (o.s.) 290.
[60] [1972] I.R. 372.
[61] (1871) 5 I.R. Eq. 595.
[62] (1887) 19 L.R. (Ir.) 249.
[63] Unreported, Supreme Court, October 22, 1996; see also *Bank of Ireland v McCabe and McCabe*, unreported, High Court, March 30, 1993 where Flood J. concluded that the evidence admitted did not alter the prima facie meaning of the document.
[64] [1979] I.R. 364.

available of what was agreed. In *Boyle and Boyle v Lee and Goyns*[65] a majority of the Supreme Court were of the view that *Casey* should not be followed by any future court. O'Flaherty J. and Egan J. confined the decision in *Casey* to its own facts and thus effectively distinguished it out of existence.

(3) To explain the subject matter of the contract

5–25 In *Chambers v Kelly*[66] a contract was concluded for the sale of "all the oaks now growing on your lands called Greenmount near Enniscorthy, together with all other trees growing through the oak plantations and mixed with the said oak". The plaintiff vendor successfully contended that the parties had designated part of the plaintiff's land to be the oak plantation so that the felling of oak trees on other parts of the plaintiff's land constituted a breach of contract. A literal interpretation of the written document would produce a different result. Furthermore, the words "all other trees" were limited to larch trees, this being part of the oral contract.

5–26 It is said that parol evidence is only admissible if the contract itself is ambiguous. This view was categorically rejected by Chatterton V.-C. in *Ulster Bank v Synnott*[67] but it was applied in the Circuit Court case of *Oates v Romano*.[68] A hairdresser, employed by the plaintiff, agreed not to serve in "a like business" when he left the plaintiff's employment. The plaintiff attempted to adduce parol evidence that "like business" meant a specific type of hairdressing establishment catering for the needs of the more affluent sector of Dublin society. The clause was not intended to prevent the defendant from working as a hairdresser in all salons. The Circuit Court judge held the rule to be that parol evidence was not admissible if the contract was on its face unambiguous. This case must be regarded as wrongly decided. On the other hand, the court will understandably be reluctant to adduce parol evidence if this serves to render the terms of an otherwise unambiguous contract uncertain. In *Kinlen v Ennis U.D.C.*[69] the House of Lords refused to allow a tender to be admitted in evidence when the contract itself was at variance with a tender. Lord Buckmaster pointed out that preliminary documents and discussions which are intended to be gathered up in the contract are inadmissible unless the contract is ambiguous. There are obvious dangers in admitting into evidence a tender which is itself ambiguous but in exceptional cases the tender has been admitted in the interpretation or construction of a contract that is itself unclear. In *H.A. O'Neill Ltd v John Sisk & Son Ltd*[70] one price variation clause forming part of the conditions of tender was admitted to vary the standard form price clause in the contract document because there was a sufficient cross-reference

---

[65] [1992] I.L.R.M. 65.
[66] (1873) 7 I.R.C.L. 231.
[67] (1871) 5 I.R. Eq. 595.
[68] (1950) 84 I.L.T.R. 161.
[69] [1916] 2 I.R. 299.
[70] Unreported, Supreme Court, July 30, 1984.

in the conditions of tender to a subsequent contract document. In the leading English case of *Prenn v Simmonds*[71] Lord Wilberforce stressed that the courts no longer interpret a contract by reference to internal linguistic considerations, isolated from the matrix of facts in which the clauses of the agreement are set. In cases where there may be inconsistency as between clauses in an agreement it is likely that during trial of an action the court "may well … think it proper to admit evidence of the factual matrix", to use Lord Wilberforce's words, in which the agreement was set, and which may assist the court in arriving at a construction of the clause.[72] Lord Hoffmann, in *Investors Compensation Scheme Ltd v West Bromwich Building Society*[73] has emphasised that the courts are to assimilate the way that commercial documents are to be interpreted by the judges to the common sense principles by which any serious utterance would be interpreted in everyday life. This means that, except for rules which exclude from the consideration of the courts any statements about subjective belief or intention, and the inadmissibility of preliminary negotiations or post-contractual conduct,[74] there are very few *a priori* rules of interpretation which are exclusionary in nature and that issues of this kind are broadly matters of impression for the judge. The *West Bromwich* case[75] itself provides a number of illustrations but in the context of the parol evidence rule one is particularly apposite. In this case the issue was whether mortgage investors had assigned all their rights to damages and financial compensation to a compensation fund. The assignment, in one clause only, was drafted so as to indicate only a partial assignment had been effected. However, in the view of the majority of the House of Lords, it was relevant to consider the explanatory note, intended to interpret a complex legal document to a layperson. This note clearly indicated that the assignment of rights to damages and financial compensation was total and could legitimately be used in ascertaining the intention of the parties and interpreting the contract itself.

5–27 The general view in respect of reading clauses in a contract *contra proferentem*,[76] that is, against the party who "puts the clause forward", is that the approach works most reliably in respect of one-sided or exempting provisions in a contract. In other cases, the extent to which this canon of construction will be applied is uncertain. In *Analog Devices BV v Zurich Insurance*,[77] Kelly J. adopted Lord Hoffmann's analysis in *West Bromwich* and at the same time interpreted exclusion clauses in a contract of insurance *contra proferens*; following earlier Irish precedents on the use of *contra proferens* interpretation

---

[71] [1971] 1 W.L.R. 138; *Reardon Smith Line Ltd v Yngvar Hansen-Tangen* [1976] 1 W.L.R. 989.

[72] *LAC Minerals Ltd v Chevron Mineral Corp of Ireland and Ivernia West Plc*, unreported, High Court, August 6, 1993 per Keane J.

[73] [1998] 1 All E.R. 98.

[74] *Re Wogans Ltd* [1993] 1 I.R. 157; *JD Brian Ltd (No.2)* [2012] 1 I.L.R.M. 50.

[75] [1998] 1 All E.R. 98.

[76] See Lewison, *The Interpretation of Contracts*, 5th edn (London: Sweet & Maxwell, 2011), para.7.07 for the meaning of this phrase.

[77] Unreported, High Court, November 20, 2002.

in insurance cases. The Supreme Court dismissed the appeal, approving Kelly J.'s use of the *contra proferentem* principle and *West Bromwich*.[78]

5–28 The Supreme Court, in *Kramer v Arnold*,[79] considered obiter applying the maxim to a deposit clause but indicated that the clause cannot be made to yield a meaning contrary to the intention of the parties. More recently, Mance L.J., in *Sinochem International Oil London Co v Mobile Sales and Supply Corp*,[80] in interpreting a payments clause, described the *contra proferentem* rule as "a rule of last resort".[81] It is also necessary to subordinate the *contra proferentem* approach to the *West Bromwich* analysis. Once an ambiguity is detected in the contract the court should, first of all, look to the context within which the contract was formed in conjunction with any permissible aids to interpretation. In *McGeown v Direct Travel Insurance*,[82] Auld L.J., in giving judgment in the Court of Appeal remarked that a too "early recourse to the *contra proferentem* rule" runs the danger of "creating" an ambiguity where there is none[83] and recent case law on rent review clauses also point away from *contra proferentem* interpretation of such clauses: *Belfast Fashions v Wellworth Properties Ltd*.[84] This marginalisation of *contra proferens* interpretation is well advanced in the UK.

5–29 There is a little support for this view in the most recent Supreme Court case on the point: *ICDL GCC Foundation FZ-LLC v European Computer Driving Licence Foundation*.[85] O'Donnell J. said that:

> "[T]he principle of interpretation contra proferentem, may usefully be applied not just to exemption clauses but to a contract in general, but normally only as a last resort in the case of ambiguity, and not as a general approach. As has been observed, the purpose of the principle is to resolve ambiguity not to create it."[86]

(4) Mistake

5–30 If the contract document contains a mistake it is clearly possible to adduce parol testimony if the remedy sought is rectification: see *Macklin &*

---

[78] [2005] 1 I.R. 274.
[79] [1997] 3 I.R. 43; *Igote Ltd v Badsey Ltd* [2001] 4 I.R. 511; *Boyle v Whitevale Ltd, Irish Times Law Report*, October 20, 2003.
[80] [2000] 1 All E.R. (Comm.) 474.
[81] [2000] 1 All E.R. (Comm.) 474 at 483.
[82] [2004] 1 All E.R. (Comm.) 609.
[83] [2004] 1 All E.R. (Comm.) 609 at 615, citing *R. v Personal Investment Authority Ombudsman Bureau* [2002] Lloyd's Rep. 41 at 43 per Langley J.
[84] [2004] NIQB 42.
[85] [2012] IESC 550.
[86] Fennelly J., however, used both ordinary principles of construction and the *contra proferens* rule in a "belt and braces" approach to specific clauses in a licence agreement. The fact that the three other judges, Hardiman, McKechnie and MacMenamin JJ., concurred with the Chief Justice suggests that the application of *contra proferens* to all clauses once the clause is found to be ambiguous remains the position in Irish law: see also Clarke J. in *ICDL* [2011] IEHC 343 and in *Danske Bank v McFadden* [2010] IEHC 116.

McDonald v Greacen & Co.[87] In *Investors Compensation Scheme Ltd v West Bromwich Building Society*,[88] Lord Hoffmann indicated that in such a case it is not possible to adduce evidence of preliminary negotiations and declarations of subjective intent. This limitation to rectification actions is "for reasons of practical policy and, in this respect only, legal interpretation differs from the way we would interpret utterances in ordinary life".[89]

(5) The consideration

5–31 If a contract is silent on the consideration to be provided parol evidence will be admissible to prove the price payable: see *Jeffcott v North British Oil Co*,[90] as well as to help the court decide whether the price has in fact been paid: *Revenue Commissioners v Moroney*.[91] If one party has waived the right to payment of part of the price, or indeed any other term, evidence of this will also be admissible according to *Greenham v Gray*.[92]

5–32 Parol evidence can be admitted to show that the consideration stated in a memorandum, which apparently satisfies the Statute of Frauds 1695, is accurate. So in *Black v Grealy*[93] evidence was admissible to show that a memorandum which stated the consideration to be £40,000 was inaccurate, the court holding that parol evidence established that the price agreed was £46,000, the figure of £40,000 being the balance due after a deposit of £6,000 was paid.

(6) Custom

5–33 If the parties to a contract recognise that a particular trade custom exists then the parties will be permitted to adduce parol testimony to bring this custom to the attention of the court. In *Wilson Strain Ltd v Pinkerton*[94] a bread rounds-man who sold bread on credit terms was able to adduce evidence to show that it was an almost universal practice in the bakery industry in Belfast for the employer to take over outstanding debts when a roundsman left employment, rather than hold the roundsman personally liable. Clearly the unreasonableness of the view that the employee was himself liable influenced the court. If, however, the contract itself clearly provides another rule then the custom cannot be admissible; see *Malcolmson v Morton*.[95] Should the contract be silent the

---

[87] [1983] I.R. 61.
[88] [1998] 1 All E.R. 98.
[89] [1998] 1 All E.R. 98 at 114. See *Static Control Components (Europe) Ltd v Egan* [2004] 2 Lloyd's Rep. 429, for a compelling example of this, applying *West Bromwich*.
[90] (1873) I.R. 8 C.L. 17.
[91] [1972] I.R. 372.
[92] (1855) I.C.L.R. 50. In *Boyle and Boyle v Lee and Goyns* [1992] I.L.R.M. 65, Finlay C.J. left open the question of whether *Casey v Irish Intercontinental Bank* [1979] I.R. 364 can still be an authority on waiver of rights and admissibility of evidence.
[93] Unreported, High Court, November 10, 1977.
[94] (1897) 31 I.L.T.R. 86. Contrast *Joynson v Hunt & Son* (1905) 21 T.L.R. 692.
[95] (1847) 11 Ir. L.R. 230.

position will be otherwise. In *Page v Myer*[96] a custom peculiar to the grain trade was held admissible because the express terms of the contract did not cover the point in question. In exceptional cases it is not necessary for both parties to know of the existence of the custom or trade practice; see *King v Hinde*.[97]

(7) Where the written document is not the entire contract

5–34 Wedderburn, in an important article[98] argued that the parol evidence rule is little more than "a self-evident tautology". If the contract document is intended to be the entire contract parol evidence will not be admissible. If, however, the written document is not intended to be the entire contract but is to be supplemented by parol evidence then parol evidence will be admissible. The rule then, provides us with a presumption—a document that looks like a contract will be presumed to be the entire contract unless evidence to the contrary is forthcoming. The validity of this observation is graphically illustrated by the judgment of Wilson J. in *Howden v Ulster Bank*.[99] The plaintiffs ordered a ship to be built by a Larne shipyard which went bankrupt shortly before the vessel was completed. The plaintiffs sued to recover damages for wrongful detention of the vessel by the trustee in bankruptcy who claimed that the ship formed part of the assets of the bankrupt. The issue turned on whether property in the vessel remained with the defendants or whether it passed to the plaintiffs on payment of the price by instalments. A memorandum of agreement indicated that title remained in the defendants but Wilson J. found for the plaintiffs after hearing oral testimony: "parol evidence of a verbal transaction is not excluded by the fact that a writing was made concerning or relating to it unless such writing was in fact the transaction itself and not merely a note or memorandum of it or a portion of the transaction". In *Clayton Love v B + I Transport*,[100] Davitt P. held that parol evidence of the terms of a telephone conversation between the parties could be added to a written contract so as to form one contract, partly written and partly oral. Although the Supreme Court reversed Davitt P.'s judgment on another issue this view of the limits of the parol evidence rule was undisturbed.

5–35 If there is a contradiction between a written contract and an oral promise the courts will not enforce the oral promise, choosing instead the terms of the written document if they have been expressly drafted by one of the parties and agreed to. If, however, the written term is on a printed, standard form document the English case of *Evans v Merzario*[101] suggests that the oral promise is to be given preference. A recent English case applying the *Merzario* decision is instructive. In *BCT Software Solutions Ltd v Arnold Laver*,[102] a software

---

[96] (1861) 6 Ir. Jur. Rep. (N.S.) 27.
[97] (1883) 12 L.R. (Ir.) 113.
[98] (1959) 17 C.L.J. 58.
[99] [1924] I.R. 117.
[100] (1970) 104 I.L.T.R. 157.
[101] [1976] 1 W.L.R. 1078.
[102] [2002] 2 All E.R. (Comm.) 85.

supply company changed its standard business conditions so as to make all software licenses fully integrated with support obligations. Prior to this change software licensees could take a package without purchasing support services. The new conditions were in force when sales personnel sold a package to the defendants, the staff involved on both sides agreeing that the licence was independent of support obligations. Notwithstanding a cross-reference on the order form to these conditions, they were held to be inapplicable to the extent that the conditions were inconsistent with the expressly agreed verbal terms.

5–36 It should be noted that although the exceptions to the rule are so numerous and well established that it is doubtful whether any real injustice is caused by the rule, if it is applied properly, cases like *Oates v Romano* (discussed above at para.5–26) show that judges who do not properly understand the role of the rule *as a presumption* may fall into error. The English Law Commission concluded that on balance legislative amendments or outright repeal of the parol evidence rule would be likely to cause greater confusion than enlightenment and that clarifying the law and re-education of the legal profession "is a more satisfactory means of achieving justice than any attempt to legislate".[103]

Collateral Contracts

5–37 The partly-written, partly-oral contract seems to take effect as one contract. Nevertheless, certain judges take the view that the strict terms of the parol evidence rule can be evaded by holding that *two* contracts may come into existence. Indeed, one leading Irish judge, Murphy J., in *Cotter v Minister for Agriculture*[104] observed that where a collateral agreement is established "it is hardly an exception at all" to the parol evidence rule. The facts of *Webster v Higgin*[105] are instructive. The plaintiff inspected a vehicle owned by the defendants and was told by one of their employees, "if you buy the Hillman we will guarantee that it's in good condition and that you will have no trouble with it". An exclusion clause attempted to nullify this promise by excluding all warranties. Lord Greene M.R. held that this promise was a *collateral* warranty which was not covered by the exclusion clause in the contract document. This approach was subsequently approved by O'Hanlon J. in *Fitzpatrick v Harty & Ballsbridge International Bloodstock Sales Ltd*.[106] The case concerned an action for the price of a horse purchased by the first defendant at a sale. The condition of sale limited the buyer's right to claim damages or rescind the contract should the horse turn out to be unsound. The defendant refused to pay the price when a veterinary surgeon found the horse to be unsound. O'Hanlon

---

[103] Law Com. No. 154, para.3.7.
[104] Unreported, High Court, November 15, 1991.
[105] [1948] 2 All E.R. 127; *Hughes v Pendragon Sabre Ltd* [2016] EWCA Civ 18.
[106] Unreported, High Court, February 25, 1983.

J. held that the conditions of sale applied "unless there were some collateral contract made outside the terms of the conditions of sale". While the issue of whether an employee has the status to give a warranty may arise and may turn upon each individual case there is a general inclination towards holding that employees at the time of sale do have the authority to give express warranties; see *Rooney v Fielden*[107] when Palles C.B. held an employee had the authority to warrant the condition of a cow to be sold.

5–38 Consideration must exist before this second or collateral contract can be enforced. In *Webster v Higgin* consideration is provided by entering the main contract of purchase. Similarly, a landlord who promises to repair drains if the promisee signs a lease which is silent on this obligation to repair will be liable on this collateral contract. By signing the lease the promisee provides consideration for his prospective landlord's promise.[108]

5–39 The most significant Irish collateral contract case in recent years is *AIB v Galvin Developments (Killarney) Ltd.*[109] This is just one of many cases in which banks have sought to enforce loan agreements by developers who have defaulted on the loan, with personal guarantees also being called in where such exist. In most instances the terms of the loan agreement and/or the guarantee are enforceable in their own terms,[110] but in the *Galvin* case the personal guarantee documentation signed by the Galvin Brothers was inconsistent with the heads of agreement and bank sanction documentation. The land, Coolegreen, was to be co-owned by the Galvins and another development company and the understanding was that the guarantee would only relate to the Galvins' 50 per cent interest in the land being purchased by way of the loan, while the guarantee as signed covered the entire advance made to the Galvins. Finlay Geoghegan J. found that the Heads of Agreement, executed before and with the intention of setting out the relationship between the Galvins and AIB, constituted a collateral contract that could alter the relationship between the Galvins, GDK, the defendant company and the bank. The learned judge said:

> "The Heads of Terms, in my judgment, were a representation by AIB that subject to two conditions, it would make facilities available, on the terms and conditions indicated or any variation agreed to the five named persons as joint venturers in the Coolegrean project for purchase and development. The two conditions were formal approval by AIB and the issuance of a formal letter of sanction. The representations were intended to induce the potential borrowers to continue in negotiations with AIB to obtain the facilities referred to therein. In particular, as already stated, the proposal for funding was sought on the basis of a

---

[107]   (1899) 33 I.L.T.R. 100.
[108]   *De Lasalle v Guildford* [1901] 2 K.B. 215; *Record v Bell* [1991] 4 All E.R. 471.
[109]   [2011] IEHC 314.
[110]   e.g. *Anglo Irish Bank Corp v Collins* [2011] IEHC 385; *ACC Bank Plc v Kelly* [2011] IEHC 7; *ACC Bank v Dillon* [2012] IEHC 474.

50/50 recourse to the parties to the joint venture. The representation made by AIB in the Heads of Terms that it was prepared to make facilities available with a limited 50% recourse to each party to the joint venture was intended to and did induce the parties to continue in negotiations with AIB. This was known to AIB to be a fundamental term as far as the Galvin Brothers were concerned."

Finlay Geoghegan J. also approved earlier judicial criticisms that the phrase "collateral contract" was not entirely accurate—the contract was more like a preliminary contract in a sense.[111] Clearly the fact that the relationship between the bank and the Galvins, in historical terms, had often limited the right to recover on loans made to the Galvins' precise interest in the property was significant in persuading the court that the standard terms in the guarantee be ignored. In contrast, in *Ulster Bank Ireland Ltd v Deane*[112] the case concerned an action brought by the bank to enforce a loan facility extended to the defendants, two property developers. The loan agreement, on its face, was a standard demand loan which could allow the bank to recover at any time. The defendants argued that the understanding was that the loan would only be repayable on the sale by the defendants of a specific property. McGovern J. held that oral evidence that was being submitted to support this claim could not be admitted to breach the parol evidence rule and that, unlike *AIB v Galvin Developments (Killarney) Ltd*, there was no side letter or Heads of Agreement documents to support a collateral contract.

5–40 In most cases it makes no difference if the promise is enforced either as a collateral warranty, i.e. it forms part of one contract, or if it takes effect as a separate or collateral contract. There are nevertheless circumstances in which it is prudent to plead a separate contract, particularly if the main contract contains an exclusion clause or jurisdiction clause. In *Michelstown Co-operative Society Ltd v Société des Produits Nestlé SA*[113] the Supreme Court, reversing Egan J., found that the first defendant company could, acting with two related companies, enter into a collateral contract with the plaintiff company. The case involved a written licensing agreement whereby the plaintiff would manufacture yoghurt under the Chambourcy trademark owned by the first defendant. This written agreement, governed by Swiss law, was not actionable in the Irish courts. However, evidence was adduced to show that there was an arguable case that the plaintiff had entered into an oral collateral contract under the terms of which the plaintiff would be supplied with yoghurt from a UK company until such time as the plaintiffs completed their own production unit, and that the plaintiff would be given exclusive distributorship rights in the yoghurt so supplied. This separate collateral contract could be the

---

[111] Citing Cooke J. in *Industrial Steel Plant Ltd v Smith* [1980] 1 N.Z.L.R. 545.
[112] [2012] IEHC 248; *Redfern v O'Mahony* [2010] IEHC 253; *Tennants Building Products Ltd v O'Connell* [2013] IEHC 197; *Irish Bank Resolution Corporation Ltd v McCaughey* [2014] IEHC 230.
[113] [1989] I.L.R.M. 582.

subject of an action before the Irish courts, notwithstanding the fact that the main licensing contract was governed by Swiss law.

5–41 The collateral contract device may prove useful in overcoming what would otherwise prove insurmountable hurdles. Take a case where the plaintiff is unable to show that consideration has moved from him, the promisee. There is clear English authority to support the proposition that if the manufacturer of goods gives a warranty to X that the goods manufactured are suitable for a particular purpose and X induces Y to purchase and use those goods, then X may sue the manufacturer if the use occasions loss to X; see *Shanklin Pier Ltd v Detel Products*.[114] In *McCullough Sales Ltd v Chetham Timber Co Ltd*[115] McCullough's sold building materials to Chetham, who, in turn, complained that these materials were unfit for their purpose. Doyle J., finding for Chetham, stated obiter that it was possible that McCullough's may have a cause of action against the manufacturers of the building materials if the manufacturer made representations to McCullough's which caused McCullough's in turn to represent or warrant the goods to Chetham. Doyle J., citing *Shanklin Pier*, stated that this case "followed a venerable line of authority" and the learned judge clearly approved of this principle. Collateral contract arguments are frequently deployed to create liability where the court considers it just to do so. In *Flynn v Dermot Kelly Ltd*,[116] F took a tractor from DKL, a dealer, who arranged a finance lease whereby DKL sold the tractor to NH Finance, the second defendant. Because the plaintiff did not deal as a consumer and there was no contract of sale, liability under statute[117] could not be made out against NH Finance. However, O'Neill J. concluded that:

> "[T]he commercial reality of this transaction dictates the existence of a collateral contract between the plaintiff and the first named defendant [DKL] whereby the first named defendant agreed to sell the tractor to the second named defendant in consideration of the plaintiff entering into the leasing agreement with the second named defendant … as this was a contract for the supply of a new tractor, necessarily, there was implied into that contract between the plaintiff and the first named defendant a condition that the [tractor] was of merchantable quality and free from defects which would render it dangerous or unfit for its intended purpose."[118]

One may readily see why O'Neill J. was prepared to make up for the non-application of statutory terms by imposing similar common law duties in respect of machinery, such as farm tractors. But the test is one of commercial

---

[114]   [1951] 2 K.B. 854.
[115]   Unreported, High Court, February 1, 1983.
[116]   [2007] IEHC 103.
[117]   Sale of Goods and Supply of Services Act 1980 s.13; Consumer Credit Act 1995 s.76.
[118]   [2007] IEHC 103 per O'Neill J.

reality seen in the light of the status of the parties. In this case the plaintiff was not legally advised before making the contract.

5–42 In *Fuji Seal Europe Ltd v Catalytic Combustion Corp*,[119] the *Shanklin Pier* decision was distinguished from the facts of that case. Fuji approached C, an American company who said that E, a European subsidiary of C, would meet Fuji's contractual needs. Fuji contracted with E but when the product supplied proved defective, Fuji sought to sue C, not E. Significantly, Fuji did not seek a parent company guarantee. Jackson J. said that in *Shanklin* the main contractor and the plaintiff (the recipient of the contractual warranty) were at arm's length. Here, it would have been possible for Fuji to obtain a parent company guarantee and Jackson J. remarked that it was not appropriate for the court "to supplement the contractual arrangements which experienced and well advised commercial parties choose to make".

5–43 Should a contract for the sale of land be unenforceable because the memorandum is defective, it may be possible to remedy the situation by holding that there are in fact two contracts. In *Godley v Power*[120] the Supreme Court held that a contract for sale of a public house plus stock in trade was in fact two contracts. The memorandum setting out the terms of the sale of the premises did not recite the terms of the contract for sale of stock in trade. By holding that the stock was the subject of a collateral contract which, by definition, did not have to be included in the memorandum, the sale of the pub was enforceable. A similar problem may arise if a contract is void for illegality; English case law suggests that, notwithstanding this, a separate collateral contract will be valid.[121]

5–44 The most important use to which the collateral contract—described by Roskill L.J. in *Merzario* as "a lawyer's device"—can be put is to avoid the common law rule that a mere representation cannot lead to an award of damages. In order to avoid this rule it is increasingly common to plead that the statement made is independent or collateral to the main contract. While this practice may not now be as important, given the limited statutory reform effected in the Republic by the Sale of Goods and Supply of Services Act 1980, the collateral contract remains a useful part of a contract lawyer's armoury.

---

[119] [2005] EWHC 1659 (TCC).
[120] (1961) 95 I.L.T.R. 135; contrast *Aga Khan v Firestone and Firestone* [1992] I.L.R.M. 31.
[121] *Strongman (1945) Ltd v Sincock* [1955] 2 Q.B. 525.

6 Implied Terms

Introduction

6–01 Contractual obligations may arise as a result of circumstances other than express agreement between the parties. In general, it is accepted that terms may be implied through the operation of certain common law doctrines, custom and practice, the operation of statute law rather than judicial intervention, and the 1937 Constitution.

Implied Terms at Common Law

6–02 We have already seen that not everything stated, before or at the time of agreement, will necessarily form part of the contract. In this Chapter we will consider the converse proposition: can the courts hold the bargain to include terms or obligations not expressly stated? The question is a difficult one to answer. While it is clear that additional terms may be read into the contract the circumstances in which the implication may be made are not the subject of universal agreement amongst the judiciary. Traditionally, the courts do not relish implying terms into a bargain because this results in a modification of the contract as struck by the parties. The courts ofttimes shelter behind the maxim that "it is for the parties to strike a bargain; the judiciary serve merely to enforce it". On the other hand, some judges take the view that it is in the interests of justice for the courts to take a more active role. Lord Denning M.R. supported this view of the judicial function and he argued that the courts may imply a term into a bargain simply because it is reasonable to do so. The House of Lords have rejected this view as "undesirable and way beyond sound authority": per Lord Wilberforce in *Liverpool City Council v Irwin*.[1] In *Dakota Packaging Ltd v AHP Manufacturing B.V.*[2]—the most important recent Supreme Court pronouncement on the question of when an Irish court

---

[1] [1977] A.C. 239. See generally, *Chitty on Contracts*, edited by H.G. Beale, 32nd edn, (London, Sweet & Maxwell, 2015), Vol 1, paras 14-001–14-035. For important periodical literature see Phang, "Implied Terms, Business Efficacy and the Officious Bystander—A Modern History" [1998] J.B.L. 1; Davies, "Recent Developments in the Law of Implied Terms" [2010] L.M.C.L.Q. 140; McCaughren, "Implied Terms: The Journey of the Man on the Clapham Omnibus" [2011] C.L.J. 607; Hooley, "Implied Terms after *Belize Telecom*" [2014] C.L.J. 315. Insofar as these articles reflect English law developments, note that the UKSC has ruled that nothing in *Attorney General of Belize v Belize Telecom* [2009] 1 W.L.R. 1988 should be seen as undermining the central role of the business efficacy and officious bystander tests. See *Marks and Spencer plc v BNP Paribas Securities Services Trust Company (Jersey) Ltd* [2015] UKSC 72.
[2] [2004] IESC 102.

will imply terms into a contract—Fennelly J., giving judgment for the entire court, said obiter, "the courts do not have 'a broad discretion' to imply terms. It is not enough that a term to be implied is 'fair and reasonable'." As we shall see, the developments in England and Wales in regard to the contextual approach to the interpretation of contracts ushered in via the *West Bromwich* decision and its aftermath has and will have consequences for other aspects of contract law where the focus is upon giving effect to the intention of the parties when that intention is not crystal clear from words used. The rules relating to rectification for mistake and the ability of a court to imply terms are just two obvious examples. However, for the moment, Irish courts continue to operate the tried and trusted rules, uninfluenced by cases in England, that begin with *Attorney General of Belize v Belize Telecom*.[3] It is to the accepted rules that we now turn.

6–03 In *Tradax (Ireland) Ltd v Irish Grain Board Ltd*,[4] O'Higgins C.J. said that the power to imply terms "must, however, be exercised with care. The courts have no role in acting as contract makers, or as counsellors, to advise or direct which agreement ought to have been made by two people, whether businessmen or not, who chose to enter into contractual relations with each other". In the same case McCarthy J. said, "[i]t is not the function of a court to write a contract for parties who have met upon commercially equal terms; if such parties want to enter into unreasonable, unfair or even disastrous contracts, that is their business, not the business of the Courts".

6–04 Nevertheless, if the courts start from the premise that the parties are reasonable persons who wish to act reasonably and facilitate the commercial interests of the other party, a considerable amount can be inserted into the agreement by way of implied terms. What is important, however, is the test used by the judge in the case at bar.

6–05 In recent years the Supreme Court has had occasion to discuss the juridical basis upon which implied terms are inserted into a contract by the judiciary. In *Sweeney v Duggan*[5] Murphy J. observed:

> "There are at least two situations where the courts will, independently of statutory requirement, imply a term which has not been expressly agreed by the parties to a contract. The first of these situations was identified in the well-known *Moorcock* case (1889) 14 PD 64 where a term not expressly agreed upon by the parties was inferred on the basis of the presumed intention of the parties. The basis for such a presumption was explained by MacKinnon LJ in *Shirlaw v Southern Foundries (1926) Ltd.* [1939] 2 KB 206 at p.227 in an expression, equally memorable, in the following terms:

---

[3] [2009] 1 W.L.R. 1988. In Northern Ireland, see *McDonald v McKenna* [2012] NI Ch 24.
[4] [1984] I.R. 1; *R(M) v R(T)* [2006] 3 I.R. 449.
[5] [1997] 2 I.L.R.M. 211 at 216; *Meridian Communications Ltd v Eircell Ltd* [2002] 2 I.R. 17.

'*Prima facie* that which in any contract is left to be implied and need not be expressed is something so obvious that it goes without saying; so that, if while the parties were making their bargain, an officious bystander were to suggest some express provision for it in their agreement, they would testily suppress him with a common, "Oh, of course".'

In addition there are a variety of cases in which a contractual term has been implied on the basis, not of the intention of the parties to the contract but deriving from the nature of the contract itself. Indeed in analysing the different types of case in which a term will be implied Lord Wilberforce in *Liverpool City Council v Irwin* [1977] AC 239 preferred to describe the different categories which he identified as no more than shades on a continuous spectrum."

(1) The officious bystander test—obligations tacitly assumed

6–06 It is clear that if a term is so obvious that it goes without saying that the bargain is subject to this unstated term then it will be included in the contract. This proposition is most clearly articulated in the judgment of MacKinnon L.J. in *Shirlaw v Southern Foundries (1926) Ltd*[6] quoted immediately above. This test is extremely narrow. The court must find that *both* parties had the term contended for in mind when they contracted. The facts of *Kavanagh v Gilbert*[7] may make this test clearer. The plaintiff sued an auctioneer who had agreed to sell the plaintiff's farm by auction. A bid was accepted by the auctioneer but no binding contract was concluded because the auctioneer failed to draft a memorandum of agreement. While the contract was silent on this point an officious bystander who interjected: "surely the auctioneer will have to fill out a memorandum after the sale", would incur the wrath of both parties in the manner predicted by McKinnon L.J. It was held that there was an implied obligation placed on the auctioneer that he would use care and skill in concluding a binding contract.

6–07 Not every situation, however, will be as straightforward as *Kavanagh v Gilbert*. Recent English case law points up judicial reluctance to imply terms in less than obvious cases.[8] In *Times Newspapers v Weidenfeld & Nicholson*

---

[6] [1939] 2 K.B. 206 at 227.
[7] (1875) I.R. 9 C.L. 136. For a recent discussion on the notion that a reasonable person would consider a facet of a contractual relationship to include certain possibilities as being within the contractual nexus, see Hardiman J.'s judgment in *Viridian Power v Commissioner for Energy Regulation* [2012] IESC 13, discussing *Hall v Brooklands Racing Clubs* [1931] K.B. 205. *Hickey v HSE* [2008] IEHC 290 provides an interesting example where breach of an implied term was pleaded but, on construction, an express term covering the situation was established. In contrast, the fact that a judge finds that an obligation may necessarily be imported into an agreement may not be permissible if unsupported by reasoning along conventional lines—see *Irish Pharmaceutical Union v Minister for Health* [2010] IESC 23 (overruling Clarke J.).
[8] *Philips Electronique Grand Public S.A. v British Sky Broadcasting Ltd* [1995] E.M.L.R.

Ltd,[9] the defendants purchased publication rights of Edward Heath's memoirs, selling serialisation rights in those memoirs to *The Times*. After a considerable delay in receiving the manuscript the defendants cancelled the contract with Edward Heath. Later, *The Times* purchased serialisation rights in the memoirs from another publisher at a higher price. Implied terms that would have had the effect of preventing the defendant from terminating the publishing contract were held not to be a part of the serialisation agreement because those implied terms were inconsistent with the express terms permitting the defendants to cancel the author's contract. Bell J. also doubted whether both parties would have agreed that each or either term contended for was a part of the contract if it had been put to them before conclusion of the contract. If the written contract has complex and detailed terms this may also be held to negative an argument that the parties also intended other unwritten obligations to be contained in their bargain.[10]

6–08 However, if in a particular industry, trade or profession a standard practice or dispute procedure is the norm, the fact that a written contract has been agreed which fails to refer to this matter will not preclude a successful implied term argument. Indeed, it may be that the express terms of a contract will be capable of being interpreted so as to yield the obligation contended for, or, in the alternative, the court may uphold an implied term argument. In one Canadian software supply case[11] the contract expressly required the buyer to "confirm that the software meets the specifications". The British Columbia Court of Appeal held that on its construction the clause required the buyer to approve the specifications; alternatively, an implied term was needed to give business efficacy. In the Northern Ireland case of *Extrudakerb (Maltby Engineering) Ltd v Whitemountain Quarries Ltd*[12] the failure by the parties to a building sub-contract to make express reference to an arbitration clause when agreeing to be bound by standard industrial conditions was held not to be fatal to the contractor's contention that the arbitration clause was part of the contract. Carswell L.J. observed that if the officious bystander had asked the parties whether they considered the arbitration clause would apply in the event

---

472. The implied term will only be capable of supporting express obligations if the express obligation can be made out, as a matter of interpretation: see *Peregrine Systems Ltd v Steria* [2005] EWCA Civ 239; applied in *Anglo Irish Bank Corporation v Conway* [2014] NIQB 42 (Weatherup J.). In *Flynn v Breccia Ltd* [2015] IEHC 547 Houghton J. refused to imply a term that one party could take steps to prevent the performance—there were two aspects of this duty—but the argument was rejected on the basis that the term(s) were not obvious. The facts did however justify accepting a "good faith" implied term.

9   [2002] F.S.R. 463.

10 *Bedfordshire C.C. v Fitzpatrick Contractors* (1998) 62 Con. L.R. 65.

11 *Bridgesoft Systems Corp v British Columbia* (1998) 60 B.C.L.R. 246; *Stabilad Ltd v Stephens and Carter (No.2)* [1999] 1 All E.R. (Comm.) 651.

12 *The Times*, July 10, 1996; *Lynch Roofing Systems (Ballaghaderreen) Ltd v Christopher Bennett and Son (Construction) Ltd* [1999] 2 I.R. 450. Recent decisions suggest that after the Arbitration Act 2010 these earlier "incorporation by reference" cases may be unreliable, e.g. *Mount Juliet Properties Ltd v Melcarne Developments Ltd* [2013] IEHC 286. See Dowling-Hussey and Dunne, *Arbitration Law* (Dublin: Thomson Round Hall, 2008).

of the dispute, the answer would have been clear that the question would have been answered in the affirmative: both were experienced and knowledgeable persons who were aware of the standard terms used in their industry. On the other hand, if the response of one of the parties at least would have been one of bemusement because the term in question would have been unknown to that person, the contention will fail. If the court concludes that one of the parties would have rejected the term contended for then no implication will be made. So, the Supreme Court in *Carna Foods Ltd v Eagle Star Insurance Co*[13] declined to impose on an insurer an obligation to disclose reasons for a refusal to renew a policy because if this had arisen as an issue at formation the insurer would have declined to contract at all. In *Sweeney v Duggan*[14] an employer was held not to be under a similar implied duty to inform employees about the employer's insurance cover for his workers, for the reason that the contract worked effectively and that if such a term was under discussion prior to agreement it would have either been rejected or only agreed upon after much negotiation. If the term contended for is inconsistent with a statutory provision and cannot therefore be lawfully conceded then the term will not be implied: *Sullivan v Southern Health Board*.[15] Similarly, in the Australian case of *Spira v Commonwealth Bank of Australia*[16] an implied duty not to threaten to breach a contract was denied contract status. The New South Wales Court of Appeal indicated that because such conduct was itself probably a repudiatory or anticipatory breach, as well as tortious, there was no "gap" to be filled by such an implied term.

6–09 The English case of *The Moorcock*[17] is also said to be a case supporting the view that only if the court draws the conclusion that each party intended such and such a term to form part of their bargain can a term be implied. Bowen L.J. in giving judgment in that case, however, stated that, "[t]he law is raising an implication from the presumed intention of the parties with the object of giving the transaction such efficacy as both parties must have intended that at all events it should have". This test is extremely ambiguous. It is a wider test than the officious bystander test for it is doubtful whether the facts of *The Moorcock* would fall within MacKinnon L.J.'s test. At its widest *The Moorcock* has been used to support the view that a reasonable term may be implied in the contract. Many judges have said that Bowen L.J. did not mean to go that far. Nevertheless *The Moorcock* was applied by a majority of the Irish Court of Appeal in the 1904 case of *Butler v McAlpine*.[18] The facts of this case, which superficially at least resemble those of *The Moorcock* itself,

---

[13]   [1997] 2 I.L.R.M. 499.
[14]   [1997] 2 I.L.R.M. 211. *Sweeney v Duggan* has also been held to be authority for the view that an implied term cannot contradict an express term: *Barry v Medical Defence Union* [2005] IESC 41.
[15]   Unreported, Supreme Court, July 30, 1997.
[16]   (2003) 57 N.S.W.L.R. 544.
[17]   (1889) 14 P.D. 64.
[18]   [1904] 2 I.R. 445.

involved a contract under which a wharf owner was to allow a shipowner to unload a cargo at his wharf. The vessel was damaged when, at low tide, it came to rest on a sack of concrete that had previously fallen onto the riverbed. The Court of Appeal by a majority held there was an implied duty upon the wharf owner to take reasonable care that the berth was reasonably safe for the barge to lie in. While the members of the Court of Appeal refused to be drawn upon the question of how far Bowen L.J.'s test is to apply, there have been several later cases, including decisions of the Supreme Court in which Bowen L.J.'s speech has been approved. In agency contracts, the law relating to implied terms has often supplemented the express contractual terms: *The Moorcock* was considered in this context by the Supreme Court in *Ward v Spivack Ltd*[19] which held that sales agents could not obtain the benefit of commission after the termination of a contract on the basis of an implied term. Maguire C.J. held that it is not for the courts to use the implied term as a means of making a new contract for the parties.

6–10 In commercial contracts the courts often present the test in *The Moorcock* in a different way: is it necessary to imply this term into the contract so as to give the contract the business efficacy both parties must have intended it to have? This business efficacy test has been considered in several Irish cases. In *O'Toole v Palmer*,[20] Palmer, an auctioneer, agreed with O'Toole that if O'Toole was able to find a purchaser willing to buy Vesey's land, then Palmer would agree to share the five per cent commission fee so long as the fee was paid by the purchaser. O'Toole introduced a client of his to Palmer and the sale was completed. The purchaser, however, did not agree to pay the commission and Palmer closed the sale without the commission having been paid. O'Toole sued Palmer claiming that by closing the sale without obtaining the agreement of the purchaser to pay a commission Palmer had broken an implied term that he would not prevent the plaintiff from earning his remuneration. Gavan Duffy J. dismissed the action: "I do not think there is any necessity to imply a term for the purpose of giving the contract a business efficacy. Here the terms are clearly expressed in writing and the plaintiff has undertaken an ordinary business risk." Similarly in *Tradax (Ireland) Ltd v Irish Grain Board Ltd*[21] a majority of the Supreme Court held that an obligation could not be imposed by way of an officious bystander test upon the defendants to open a letter of credit. Despite the considerable volume of evidence which supported the view that in the industry in question this practice was normally to be expected, O'Higgins C.J., who gave the leading judgment, found that the officious bystander test was not satisfied because, on the facts, there was no evidence that the parties intended that this be done.

6–11 Regardless, therefore, of what test is operated, evidence that the agreement would never have been reached on the implied term in question

---

[19] [1957] I.R. 40.
[20] [1945] Ir.Jur.Rep. 59; *The County Homesearch Co v Cowham* [2008] EWCA Civ 26.
[21] [1984] I.R. 1.

should normally be dispositive. Nevertheless, in *Dakota Packaging v Wyeth Medica Ireland*,[22] Peart J. implied a term into a supply contract which required the defendant to afford 12 months' notice of any intention to transfer the packaging requirements of the defendant elsewhere, the defendant being required during this period to take a proportion of the plaintiff's product during the notice period.[23] This was a very controversial decision in the light of evidence from the defendant that it would not have agreed to any notice agreement. The contract of supply was based on individual orders and was not concluded under an "umbrella" agreement of any kind. The agreement was also not to be seen as one of distributorship. Nevertheless, Peart J. was persuaded that the relationship built up over the years by the parties and the benefits of some degree of continuity of supply justified a notice requirement on a "business efficacy" basis.[24] On appeal, the Supreme Court[25] allowed the appeal. While Peart J. had found that there was no contract between the parties, other than in respect of individual sales contracts—indeed Peart J. "studiously even elaborately" avoided using the words "contract" or "agreement" in favour of referring to a "relationship"—he had fallen into error in implying into a "relationship" or "arrangement" an implied term when no contract subsisted. Fennelly J., in giving judgment for the Supreme Court noted that "the courts will not lightly infer terms", particularly where, as in the instant case, the judge had difficulty in formulating the term with sufficient precision.[26]

6–12 This decision is perhaps the most visible demonstration by an Irish judge of the extent to which implied duties of co-operation may be imposed upon a commercial entity who, in the traditional way of things was able to organise business affairs by reference to commercial self-interest. It also emphasises the growing tendency for courts to view commercial relationships as being co-operative rather than antagonistic; the defendants in *Dakota* took the view that they had no long-term contractual relationship, so the idea that this relationship had "gaps" or omissions, to be filled in via judicial activism should not have arisen.

6–13 Litigation concerning the ability of an agent to recover fees alleged to be due is a rich source of learning on the law relating to express terms and implied terms. In *Murphy Buckley & Keogh v Pye (Ireland)*[27] the defendants engaged the plaintiffs to sell a factory in Dundrum on a sole-agency basis. The defendants later sold the premises to a purchaser not introduced by the plaintiffs. The plaintiffs

---

[22] Unreported, High Court, October 10, 2003.
[23] This situation is not to be confused with instances where duties of co-operation are imposed to realise completion of an installation contract: *Anglo Group Plc v Winther Browne & Co* (2000) 72 Con. L.R. 119.
[24] Citing in particular *Martin Baker Aircraft Co Ltd v Canadian Flight Equipment* [1955] 2 All E.R. 722 at 733 per McNair J.
[25] [2005] 2 I.R. 54.
[26] e.g. What quantity of goods did Wyeth have to buy? At what price? See, for an English parallel with the view of the Supreme Court, *Baird Textiles Holdings Ltd v Marks and Spencer Plc* [2002] 1 All E.R. (Comm.) 737.
[27] [1971] I.R. 57.

were unable to claim that the contract impliedly prevented the defendants from finding a purchaser; not only was such a term inconsistent with the presumed intent of the parties, the contract expressly provided that the auctioneer's fee was only payable on completion of a transaction involving a purchaser introduced by the plaintiffs. The auctioneer was only entitled to recover advertising expenses. In his carefully structured judgment Henchy J. stressed that these sole-agency cases depend very much upon their own facts, an observation that is graphically illustrated in *G.F. Galvin (Estates) Ltd v Hedigan*.[28] An estate agent claimed he was entitled to a fee for land sold by the defendant. The defendant had engaged the agent to lobby councillors to facilitate the rezoning of farmland to an industrial use and had promised to pay a fee upon the successful conclusion of this process. Costello J. held that the case was distinguishable from *Murphy Buckley & Keogh v Pye (Ireland)* because here the agent undertook to find a seller and carry on other activities and, in these circumstances, some obligation requiring the landowner to compensate the agent, should the landowner sell the land himself, was to be implied. On the facts, however, the landowner was not liable in contract because the "business efficacy" and "officious bystander" tests only required this implied term to be imposed for a limited time and the sale was effected after the time elapsed.

6–14 The business efficacy test will not be utilised to undo an agreement which is enforceable as it stands. In *Aga Khan v Firestone and Firestone*[29] it was submitted that the court should imply into a contract for the sale of lands (the contract being enforceable under the Statute of Frauds 1695) a term that it was only to be carried into force when a formal contract had been executed. Morris J. observed that the essence of *The Moorcock* was a desire to prevent the failure of the contract. The term sought to be introduced would have the contrary effect and Morris J. refused to imply it.

(2) Terms implied by law

6–15 Even though the courts have not carved out for themselves a sweeping power to insert terms into a bargain simply because the judge feels it reasonable to do so, there are well-established instances of legal duties being imposed upon contracting parties when it is clear that the parties themselves have not anticipated the dispute. In other words, a term will be implied at law because it is felt necessary to do so. In the English case of *Tournier v National Provincial & Union Bank of England*,[30] Atkin L.J. stated that in appropriate cases the court may, as a matter of law, impose implied obligations upon a party to a contract. This statement was applied by the Northern Ireland Court of Appeal in *Potter v Carlisle & Cliftonville Golf Club Ltd*.[31] A golfer who was struck in the eye by a ball hit by another golfer was held unable to recover

---

[28] [1985] I.L.R.M. 295.
[29] [1992] I.L.R.M. 31.
[30] [1924] 1 K.B. 461.
[31] [1939] N.I. 114.

damages against the defendant. By paying his green fee and walking onto the first tee the plaintiff was held to have impliedly contracted to take the course as he found it, provided it was free from unusual dangers or traps, and also to accept the risks of the game as between himself and the defendant club.

6–16 These duties often arise as incidents of well-recognised legal relation-ships. In *Sweeney v Duggan*[32] Murphy J. explained that whether an implied term is inserted into a contract as a matter of law, or presumed intention, there are common features:

> "Whether a term is implied pursuant to the presumed intention of the parties or as a legal incident of a definable category of contract it must be not merely reasonable but also necessary. Clearly it cannot be implied if it is inconsistent with the express wording of the contract and furthermore it may be difficult to infer a term where it cannot be formulated with reasonable precision."

In essence, cases where presumed intention is not the basis for the implication of a term turn upon the existence of a defined relationship and a test of necessity. Should the evidence indicate that a term was missing because of the complexity of the issue then there can be no room for a term under either category; see *Ali v Christien Salvesen Food Services Ltd*.[33] A landlord, for example, owes an implied duty to allow the tenant quiet possession of the demised premises. So, if a landlord fails to keep parts of a building well maintained, causing a nuisance to spread to property leased to tenants, the tenants have a cause of action even in the absence of an express covenant requiring the landlord to repair and maintain the exterior of the building; see *Byrne v Martina Investments Ltd*.[34] A particular difficulty arises where a contract for the sale of a house or for the lease of unfurnished premises is silent upon the condition of the property. The English common law rule provided that if a house was sold or let unfurnished and it turned out to be defective the purchaser could not recover on an implied warranty. It has been the view of many judges and commentators that Davitt P. in *Brown v Norton*[35] held this rule applicable in Ireland too. A close reading of the case discloses that Davitt P. held that on the sale of a house there is no *rule of law* that the premises will be fit for the purpose of occupation but there may still be room for an implied term. The Supreme Court held in *Siney v Dublin Corp*[36] that when Dublin Corporation let a new unfinished flat to the plaintiff it was liable in contract when it transpired that the flat was badly ventilated, causing damp which damaged the plaintiff's belongings. The Supreme Court pointed out that the case depended upon the specific fact that Dublin Corporation was under

---

[32] [1997] 2 I.R. 531, *Glenavon Football and Athletic Club Ltd v Lowry, Irish Times Law Report*, September 7, 1992.
[33] *The Times*, October 29, 1996.
[34] [1984] 3 J.I.S.L.L. 116.
[35] [1954] I.R. 34.
[36] [1980] I.R. 400.

a statutory obligation under the Housing Act 1966 as a housing authority, (which would not operate in private sector letting contracts). In *Coleman & Coleman v Dundalk U.D.C.*[37] the Supreme Court extended *Siney* by holding that a statutory housing authority cannot evade the obligation to ensure that the house was fit for human habitation by executing a lease rather than a tenancy agreement. *Siney* has been applied by a unanimous Supreme Court in *Burke v Corporation of Dublin*.[38] The defendant was sued in its capacity as a housing authority for the city of Dublin under which it provided housing to the various plaintiffs. The heating system provided solid fuel central heating and was found to be inefficient and unhealthy, causing physical damage to the personal belongings of one plaintiff and inducing bronchitis in another. There is a further significant extension of *Siney* in this case. One of the plaintiffs, while initially a tenant, had purchased the house from the housing authority and was therefore the owner of the fee simple at the time when proceedings commenced. However, the Supreme Court affirmed the view of Blayney J. at first instance where the learned judge had held that, because the sale and transfer of ownership had taken place under the Housing Act 1966, the implied duty could still arise. The Supreme Court, however, declined to decide on the position of a purchaser who, unlike the plaintiff in question, was not a tenant but nevertheless purchased property from a statutory housing authority. While the courts are constrained by authority to uphold the application of the *caveat emptor* principle in landlord and tenant contracts, there are other decisions which indicate that the immunity of the landlord will be narrowly interpreted. In England the decision in *Western Electric v Welsh Development Agency*[39] illustrates that the old common law immunity from liability will not be extended into commercial property lettings.

6–17 If the vendor of property is also in the process of building the house there will be an implied term that the house will be built in an efficient manner and that it will be inhabitable; see *Morris v Redmond and Wright*.[40] In the Northern Ireland case of *McGeary v Campbell*[41] this implied term was extended to apply to work completed before and after the contract of purchase is concluded; see also *Corrigan v Crofton & Crofton*[42] where the defendant builder conceded that, following *Brown v Norton*, it was bound by an implied term that the work be carried out in a good and workmanlike manner and with sound and suitable materials. In general, however, the vendor of a house is not to be taken to impliedly warrant the fitness of a house. In *Curling v Walsh*,[43] Hamilton P. rejected the view that upon the sale of a house the vendor is taken to impliedly warrant that the premises are in a good and habitable state of repair and free from any structural defect.

---

[37] Unreported, Supreme Court, July 17, 1985.
[38] [1991] I.R. 341.
[39] [1983] Q.B. 796.
[40] (1935) 70 I.L.T.R. 8.
[41] [1975] N.I. 7.
[42] [1985] I.L.R.M. 189.
[43] Unreported, High Court, October 23, 1987.

6–18 Lord Wilberforce pointed out that terms implied without reference to the intention of the parties are implied in order to make the existing contractual relationship work efficiently. The test then is necessity, not reasonableness. A contract to let premises in a multi-storey apartment building will not be effective unless the tenant can gain access to the apartment. The letting contract will include an obligation at law obliging the lessor to do everything reasonable to maintain and repair the stairways, lifts and escalators not included in the lease; see *Liverpool City Council v Irwin*.[44] A contract under the terms of which property is to be refurbished on behalf of one party, the other party being in possession, involves an implied term that the parties will facilitate completion of the work. In particular, the court will infer the buyer is under a duty to facilitate access to the site by the seller's construction team.[45] In these cases the relationship will be an important factor in the process. In *Mediterranean Salvage and Towage Ltd v Seamar Trading*[46] a voyage charter party giving the charterers the right to nominate a berth was silent on the question of whether the berth was safe or not. The charterer nominated a berth at Chekka in the Lebanon. The vessel was damaged because of an underwater projection at the berth. The English Court of Appeal refused to hold that the charterer was under an absolute duty to nominate a safe berth as a matter of implied contract. No such term was necessary: the contract, absent an express term, could still work. The loss was to lie where it fell. Significantly, no cases could be found which suggested support for such a duty despite hundreds of years of shipping litigation. Similarly, in *Chantry Estates v Anderson*[47] efforts to read into an option agreement certain implied terms restraining the option holder from making independent commercial decisions during the option period were unsuccessful. Jacob L.J. said:

> "[W]hen one approaches this option agreement one asks and is required to ask whether in its provisions as to the option period must mean what is contended for by the proposed implied terms. (*sic*) And I simply do not see why it must. It works perfectly well without it … the [written] agreement allows Chantry to make planning applications, to pursue planning applications to its best advantage solely to see whether it is worth exercising the option …".

Contracts of employment also contain terms that are imposed by operation of law. The duty of an employer to provide a safe system of work arises almost without question in many personal injury actions; see *McCann v Brinks Allied Ltd*.[48] There is considerable litigation on establishing the precise scope of contractual rights on other matters, particularly termination of a contract.

---

[44] [1977] A.C. 239.
[45] *Airscape Ltd v Heaslon Properties Ltd* [2008] IEHC 82.
[46] [2009] EWCA Civ 531.
[47] [2010] EWCA Civ 316.
[48] [1997] 1 I.L.R.M. 461. See also the post-traumatic stress disorder cases of *Murtagh v Minister for Defence* [2008] IEHC 292 and *McClurg v Chief Constable of the RUC* [2009] NICA 33.

In the case of *Royal Trust Co of Canada (Ireland) Ltd v Kelly*,[49] Barron J. stated that the basic rule in relation to contracts of employment is that "it is an implied term of every contract of employment other than for a fixed period that it can be terminated upon reasonable notice". In *Carvill v Irish Industrial Bank*[50] the plaintiff served as managing director of the defendant company. By resolution of the board the plaintiff was discharged from his post and from the board of the company. He successfully contended that he had been discharged from a contract of employment in such a way as to breach the employer's obligation to give a reasonable period of notice. Given the position of the plaintiff, his length of service and other factors, a reasonable period of notice was calculated at one year. Similar obligations are imposed by law on the employee. He has an obligation to faithfully serve his employer so if he "moonlights" by working for a rival concern he will break this implied term. In the Northern Ireland case of *A.F. Associates v Ralston*[51] the defendants, prior to terminating their contracts of employment with the plaintiff company, started a business in direct competition with the plaintiff by canvassing clients of the plaintiff company. It was held that the defendants were in breach of an implied obligation not to use their employer's time in furthering their own interests. In the Tasmanian case of *Orr v University of Tasmania*[52] a university professor who seduced a student was held to be in breach of the implied obligation to faithfully serve his employer and could be summarily dismissed. As we will see in a moment, there are also constitutional and statutory considerations which apply in employment contracts.

6–19 Perhaps the most interesting line of authority in the area of implied terms in contracts of employment is that which begins with the case of *Woods v WM Car Services (Peterborough) Ltd.*[53] This case is authority for the proposition that employers will not, without reasonable cause, act in a manner calculated to destroy the relationship of confidence and trust between employer and employee. Such a broad duty to act in good faith has been utilised by the English Court of Appeal[54] and in the case of *Imperial Group Pension Trust Ltd v Imperial Tobacco Ltd.*[55] Browne-Wilkinson V.-C. held that this implied term could inhibit the right of a company to exercise control over a company pension fund by declining to agree to allow an increase in pensions payable

---

[49] Unreported, High Court, February 27, 1989. The general rule that employment contracts are normally terminable upon giving reasonable notice has been reaffirmed by the Supreme Court in *Sheehy v Ryan* [2008] IESC 14, the Supreme Court regarding *McCelland v Northern Ireland General Health Services Board* [1957] 1 W.L.R. 594, as turning upon the meaning of the express term, "permanent" in the contract of employment. In the context of university tenure, see *Cahill v Dublin City University* [2007] IEHC 20, another case on express/statutory terms.

[50] [1968] I.R. 325.

[51] [1973] N.I. 229; *Cranleigh Precision Engineering v Bryant* [1965] 1 W.L.R. 1293.

[52] [1956] Tas. S.R. 155.

[53] [1981] I.R.L.R. 347.

[54] *Lewis v Motorworld Garages Ltd* [1985] I.R.L.R. 465.

[55] [1991] 2 All E.R. 597; *Spring v Guardian Assurance* [1994] 3 All E.R. 129.

out of the trust. So, if the company refused to allow such an increase because it wished to pressure employees into abandoning rights in the pension fund, such a collateral purpose would not be in accordance with a duty to act in good faith. While this duty may generally be expected to be invoked in favour of the employee, there are instances where the employee may be under such a duty.[56] In *Malik v BCCI*,[57] Lord Steyn, in giving judgment on behalf of the House of Lords, approved the development of a mutual duty of trust and confidence. In *University of Nottingham v Eyett (No.1)*,[58] the limit of the duty was under discussion. Here an employee requested information on pension entitlements if he retired on a certain date. He was not told that if he retired on the next possible date, one month later, his pension would be appreciably better. The duty was held not to have been broken by failure to advise. The plaintiff had been supplied with information which would have disclosed the information had he properly consulted the data and the employer was unaware of his lack of knowledge on these points. Irish courts have applied the *Malik* implied term.[59] In *McGrath v Trintech Technologies*,[60] the term was recognised but found not to have been breached by seeking to make the employee redundant during an illness. Most of the cases have been ones where the claim pushes the boundaries of other employment laws such as the right to terminate the contract[61] or cease to pay sick pay after a reasonable time.[62] On the other hand, an employer's conduct that was seen as bullying,[63] or which deprived the employee of meaningful or satisfying employment for which she had been engaged, was found to have breached this term in the contract.[64] Should the employee make reasonable efforts to meet the requirements of the employer during a period of suspension, the duty will clearly be relevant, as in *Palmer v East and North Hertfordshire National Trust*,[65] where the employer, in not expediting the retraining of a suspended employee, was held to have been in breach of the duty. More prosaic implied terms such as the duty to provide sick pay for a reasonable time are obviously less controversial.[66]

6–20 The power of an employer to terminate a contract of employment is also the subject of implied terms under both common law, statute and

---

[56] *Carr v Minister for Education* [2001] 2 I.L.R.M. 272.

[57] [1998] A.C. 20.

[58] [1999] 2 All E.R. 437.

[59] [1998] A.C. 20.

[60] [2004] IEHC 342; *Berber v Dunnes Stores* [2009] IESC 10.

[61] *Mahalingham v HSE* [2005] IEHC 186.

[62] *Mullarkey v Irish National Stud* [2004] IEHC 116.

[63] *Quigley v Complex Tooling and Moulding* [2009] IESC 526. Bullying in the workplace and in disciplinary proceedings is actionable as breach of the implied term of trust and confidence; *Sweeney v Ballinteer B.O.M.* [2011] IEHC 131; *Kelly v Bon Secours Health System Ltd* [2012] IEHC 21; *Praxis Care Group v Hope* [2012] NICA 8; *Ruffley v Board of Management of St. Anne's School* [2014] IEHC 235.

[64] *Cronin v eircom* [2006] IEHC 380.

[65] [2006] EWHC 1997 (Q.B.).

[66] *Charlton v Aga Khan*, unreported, High Court, December 22, 1998; *Rooney v Kilkenny* [2001] E.L.R. 129. Contrast *Mullarkey v Irish National Stud* [2004] IEHC 116.

the Constitution. These matters are addressed more specifically later in this chapter but the power of a court to imply a term permitting an employer the right to terminate a contract of employment upon giving reasonable notice was rejected in *Grehan v North Eastern Health Board*.[67] Because the contract contained express terms on this point, business efficacy did not require an additional term to be implied. An invalid notice of termination (e.g. because of breach of an implied term giving fair procedures) may in some instances be the subject of interlocutory relief[68] if the employee is held to be an office holder or exceptional circumstances exist. In general, however, common law requirements of reasonable notice remain if a contract of employment is to be lawfully terminated, i.e. the employer is not to be liable for wrongful dismissal. The Supreme Court in *Sheehy v Ryan*[69] has recently had occasion to revisit this subject in some detail. In that case, the Supreme Court was required to decide whether the plaintiff could establish a right to "pensionable" employment, i.e employment until 65 years of age, but concluded that the contract, which was made up by express oral terms and implied terms, was subject to the ordinary rule that, in the absence of express agreement to the contrary, a contract of employment is terminable upon the giving of reasonable notice. The cases, however, show that the decision may go in favour of the employee if the express terms of the contract favour the employee. There will be no room for an implied term if the contract deals with the issue, as a matter of interpretation.[70]

6–21 Contracts of agency are also terminable upon giving reasonable notice, according to *Ward v Spivack Ltd*.[71] Sometimes, however, matters such as the method of termination and the effect of termination on related rights, such as future commission payments, are a fruitful source of litigation. For example, if the contract has been executed and partially performed, and the contract is silent on the method of termination then the courts will have to imply terms which will safeguard the legitimate interests of both parties. The leading authority here is the judgment of Finlay P. in *Irish Welding v Philips Electrical (Ireland) Ltd*.[72] The defendants appointed the plaintiffs to be sole agents for the sale of electrodes manufactured by the defendants. The defendants supplied electrodes to another wholesaler whereupon the plaintiffs sought an injunction to restrain the defendants. The defendants denied that this agreement prevented them from supplying electrodes to third parties and they purported to immediately terminate the agreement. Finlay P. considered the question of whether and how the contract could be terminated. The plaintiffs argued it was not terminable at all. Finlay P., after referring to the complex chain of distributors built up by the

---

[67] [1989] I.R. 422.

[68] *Hill v C.A. Parsons* [1972] Ch. 305; *Fennelly v Assicurazioni Generali Spa* (1985) 3 I.C.T.R. 73; *Moore v Xnet Information Systems* [2002] 2 I.L.R.M. 278.

[69] *Sheehy v Ryan* [2008] IESC 14, following *Walsh v Dublin Health Board* (1965) 98 I.L.T.R. 82 and *Dooley v Great Southern Hotel* [2001] E.L.R. 340.

[70] *Barry v Medical Defence Union* [2005] IESC 41.

[71] [1957] I.R. 40.

[72] Unreported, High Court, October 8, 1976; see also *McGahan v Bioengineering Development*, unreported, High Court, February 17, 1995.

plaintiffs, said it was "quite unreal to suggest that it could possibly have been within the contemplation of either party that the other should be entitled to terminate the agreement instantly and without notice". Finlay P. held that the contract should be viewed as terminable after a reasonable period of time, in this case nine months; see also *Lennon v Talbot Ireland Ltd.*[73]

6–22 Before the contract will be held to be terminable by giving reasonable notice the court will have to consider whether such a power is compatible with the intention of the parties. This is to be assessed by reference to the background against which the contract was formed and the intention of the parties, ascertained by reference to objective manifestations of intent. After all, it is possible for persons to contract and undertake to do things that are extremely burdensome, or indeed impossible, if this intention can be detected by the courts. In *Watford Borough Council v Watford RDC*[74] the parties, in 1963, reached an agreement whereby each party would discharge statutory duties to provide burial grounds. The 1963 agreement, which resulted in cost sharing, proved to be quite onerous and the defendant, in 1984, purported to terminate the agreement, claiming that it was subject to an implied term that it could be ended by either party upon giving reasonable notice. This was rejected. There was no reason why a contract, entered into in order to meet a statutory obligation, could not run in perpetuity. There was no evidence to support the defendant's argument that the parties intended the agreement to be unilaterally terminable. A similar conclusion was reached, by a slightly different route, in *Harrods Ltd v Harrods Buenos Aires Ltd.*[75] The plaintiffs, by agreement between 1911 and 1914, established the first defendant with the object of allowing it to trade in South America. This intention was clear from the documents and surrounding circumstances and, further, was subject to an implied contract between the plaintiff and the first defendant which permitted the defendant to carry on business under the name "Harrods" anywhere in South America. That contract was irrevocable.

The Control of Contract-based Discretions on a Contracting Party

6–23 The English Courts have imposed implied terms which require a decision maker who exercises a discretion on behalf of one contracting party to do so in a way which does not abuse power. This will be particularly so when the contracting parties do not possess parity of bargaining power. Cases such as *Paragon Finance plc v Nash*[76] represent early examples of this position. The majority of the UK Supreme Court, in *Braganza v B.P. Shipping Ltd*[77] has

---

[73] Unreported, High Court, December 20, 1985; *O & E Telephones v Alcatel Business Systems*, unreported, High Court, May 17, 1995.
[74] *The Times*, December 18, 1987.
[75] *The Times*, June 1, 1998. See also *Power Co v Gore* [1997] 1 N.Z.L.R. 537 and *Bobux Marketing v Raynor Marketing* [2002] 1 N.Z.L.R. 506.
[76] [2002] 1 W.L.R. 685; *Socimer Bank v Standard Bank* [2008] B.L.R. 1304.
[77] [2015] UKSC 17.

moved the duty of a contractual decision maker into line with both limbs on *Wednesbury*. *Braganza* concerned an employment contract with the decision maker being the employer. Lady Hale, who gave the leading judgment, regarded employment contracts as being different from ordinary commercial contracts and observed that any employer must exercise decision making powers in accordance with the implied obligation of trust and confidence. How discretionary powers in commercial contracts will be constrained must await further developments via case law[78] but some tentative Irish cases do exist.

6–24 *Portsmouth City Council v Ensign Holdings Ltd*[79] provides an example of how an argument that a specific long term "relational" contract[80] may contain good faith obligations will be processed by a court. Here, the contract contained a specific good faith obligation in regard to how performance shortcomings would be valued and processed, but the English High Court did not accept that this could justify a free standing implied term being read into the contract generally. The Court reaffirmed the standard view that English law does not recognise a general duty to perform a contract in good faith but nevertheless viewed the express term under review as being subject to an implied term and that assessment powers would be undertaken honestly and on proper grounds. Edwards-Stuart J. repeated earlier observations from English judges[81] that discretionary powers are not to be exercised in a manner that is "arbitrary, irrational or capricious".

6–25 The fact that the parties have entered into an agreement under which they are subject to continuing and recurring obligations has been recognised in Ireland as an appropriate basis upon which implied duties may be imposed. In *Royal Trust Co of Canada (Ireland) Ltd v Kelly*[82] the plaintiff had dismissed the staff of its Irish operation. As a financial institution the plaintiff had provided mortgage finance to these employees on preferential rates. The issue arose whether the termination of the contract of employment could take effect without prejudice to the rights of the employees to preferential mortgage finance until the redemption of the loan. The defendants submitted that while the mortgage contract contained a term obliging the employee to repay the loan on cessation of employment, the mortgage should be subject to an implied term that cessation of employment should not be the result of the voluntary act of the plaintiff bank in closing its operations in Ireland. More specifically, it

---

[78] *Arbuthnott v Bonnyman* [2015] EWCA Civ 536.
[79] [2015] EWHC 3320 (TCC).
[80] The phrase "relational contracts" is most frequently identified with Professor Ian Macneil. See *The New Social Contract* (Yale 11P: New Haven 1980). Relational theory suggests, inter alia, that the contracts are not discrete transactions but depend on a range of norms, such as reciprocity, planning for the future, reading contracts against a social matrix and cooperative risk sharing.
[81] Specifically the line of authority affirmed in *Mid Essex Hospitals Services NHS Trust v Compass Group* [2013] EWCA Civ 200. Edwards-Stuart J. was rather lukewarm in his support of some of Leggatt J.'s views on relational contracts in *Yam Seng PTE Ltd v International Trade Corporation Ltd*. See [2015] EWHC 3320 (TCC) at paras 85–90.
[82] Unreported, High Court, February 27, 1989.

was submitted on behalf of the defendants that the loan contract contained an implied term whereby the plaintiff would not do anything to prevent the loan from being fully redeemed and closure of the Irish operation breached such a duty. Barron J. indicated that the cases,

"... establish that a party to a contract cannot voluntarily create conditions which will prevent the performance of the contract. So where A contracts with B to catalogue his library, he cannot sell his books before B commences work. Where A agrees to assign a leasehold interest to B and to obtain the necessary consent of the lessor, he cannot refuse to seek such consent. The rule is analogous to the rule in property law that a grantor cannot derogate from his own grant".

The English Court of Appeal, however, in *Paragon Finance Ltd v Nash*[83] has intervened in relation to the question whether a lender has an implied duty to exercise its discretion to fix interest rates reasonably. The Court of Appeal so held, in the sense that the lender is bound to meet the *Wednesbury*[84] standard. A fortiori, the lender cannot act dishonestly, for an improper purpose, capriciously or arbitrarily and the Court of Appeal has confirmed that this implied term is rooted in principles of fair dealing[85] and is independent of reliefs afforded through consumer credit legislation.

In *Flynn v Breccia Ltd*[86] complex arguments were raised within the context of a shareholder's agreement to the effect that all shareholders were bound by mutual duties of good faith and fair dealing not to alienate the holdings of other shareholders other than under the terms of the agreement. After reciting the general approach to be adopted in the process of interpreting the express terms of a contract, Houghton J. passed on to consider whether implied terms could arise, in particular duties of good faith. The judgment of Leggatt J. in *Yam Seng Pte Ltd* was cited and extensively discussed, as was most of the relevant case law from England and Wales and Ireland. Applying the guidelines that have emerged from the case law, in the light of the relationship between the parties, the open-ended nature of the contract, a common purpose in ensuring that the medical facility which was at the heart of the transaction retained its

---

[83] [2002] 1 W.L.R. 685; Peden, "Policy Concerns Behind the Implication of Terms in Law" (2001) 117 L.Q.R. 459. In Northern Ireland *Paragon v Nash* was followed in *Swift 1st Ltd v McCourt* [2012] NI Ch 33, Horner J. saying that limitations on a power to adjust mortgage interest rates should be implied "to give effect to the reasonable expectations of both parties. The rate of interest should not be set dishonestly, for an improper purpose, capriciously or arbitrarily when varied by the [lender]". However, on the facts, this clause, allowing variation to reflect changes in the cost of funds, did not contravene the implied term.

[84] *Associated Provincial Picture Houses Ltd v Wednesbury Corp* [1948] 1 K.B. 223.

[85] See Dyson L.J. in *Broadwick Financial Services Ltd v Spencer* [2002] 1 All E.R. (Comm.) 446 at 464; *Socimer Bank v Standard Bank* [2008] Bus. L.R. 1304; *Deutsche Bank (Suisse) Ltd v Khan* [2013] EWHC 482 (Comm). See also *Hamsart 3147 Ltd v Boots UK Ltd* [2013] EWHC 3251 (Pat); Lord Sumption's obiter statements in *British Telecommunications Plc v Telefonica O2 UK Ltd* [2014] UKSC 42; *Globe Motors Inc v TRW Lucas Varity Electric Steering Ltd* [2016] EWCA Civ 396.

[86] [2015] IEHC 547.

ethos, as well as mutual duties as between the parties; just such a duty could be made out by Houghton J.

6–26 In *Royal Trust Co of Canada (Ireland) Ltd v Kelly*, Barron J., it is submitted, was moving towards the view that in the contract in question the lender was also bound not to act capriciously.[87] While Barron J. felt unable to accept that any such implied term could be upheld, mainly because the contract of employment itself was terminable upon giving reasonable notice, there is a substantial body of case law which upholds the existence of this principle in contracts which are not real property transactions. In an English case a soccer club agreed to pay a transfer fee of £200,000 for a player, with an additional sum being payable if he scored 20 goals. The player was transferred to another club before he had a reasonable time to score the goals. This was held to breach an implied term; see *Bournemouth A.F.C. v Manchester United*.[88]

Good Faith Obligations as Implied Terms

6–27 There are isolated instances of cases where an Irish court has held that an express contract is the subject of implied duties to act in good faith. A purchaser who enters into a "subject to finance" agreement is not free to withdraw from the transaction or refuse to take a commercially satisfactory finance package when offered,[89] for example. There are also a number of situations in which Irish courts have held that statutory bodies[90] and State agencies[91] are constrained by duties to act fairly in relation to the exercise of powers to terminate a contract. The decision of Peart J. in *Dakota Packaging Ltd v Wyeth Medica Ireland*[92] is the clearest Irish case which supports the view that powers of termination in a private law setting may also need to be exercised by reference to a reasonable notice standard. It is submitted that Irish courts have tended to utilise concepts such as unconscionable bargain in order to relieve one contracting party from the consequences of *mala fides* performance by the other.[93]

---

[87] A contract to confer a discretion upon one of the parties must not be exercised "arbitrarily, capriciously or unreasonably"; *Abu Dhabi National Tanker Co v Products Star Ltd* [1993] 1 Lloyd's Rep. 397 per Leggatt L.J., followed in *Societa Esplosivi Industriali SpA v Ordnance Technologies UK* [2004] 1 All E.R. (Comm.) 619. See also *T Mobile (UK) v Bluebottle Investments S.A.* [2003] Info. T.L.R. 264.

[88] *The Times*, May 22, 1980; *Fraser v Thames Television* [1983] 2 W.L.R. 917; *CEL Group v NedLloyd Lines* [2004] 1 All E.R. (Comm.) 689.

[89] *Rooney v Byrne* [1933] I.R. 609; see also Australian cases such as *Zieme v Gregory* [1963] V.R. 214 and *Smith v Pisani* (2001) 78 S.A.S.R. 548.

[90] *Zockoll v Telecom Éireann* [1998/9] Info. T.L.R. 349. Note that in this report Kelly J. is described as one of Her Majesty's judges of the Queen's Bench Division! See also *Fluid Power Technology Co v Sperry Rand (Ireland) Ltd*, unreported, High Court, February 22, 1985.

[91] By way of legitimate expectation case law. See also *Tierney v An Post* [2000] 2 I.L.R.M. 214.

[92] Unreported, High Court, October 10, 2003, reversed on another point at [2005] 2 I.R. 54.

[93] *Grealish v Murphy* [1948] I.R. 35. See Ch.13 below.

6–28 In England the decision of the House of Lords in *Walford v Miles*[94] is regarded as being the bulwark against which good faith implied term arguments will fail. It is certainly the case that in *Walford* the implied term argument was unsuccessful because the good faith dimension was said to be "inherently repugnant to the adversarial position of the parties when involved in negotiations".[95] It is also clear that in *Howberry Lane Ltd v Telecom Éireann*,[96] Morris P. rejected a line of Canadian cases in respect of tenders that are, in reality, implied good faith cases on the basis that these decisions did not represent the law in Ireland. There is no doubt that public procurement negotiations must be conducted under good faith standards and the law in Northern Ireland is quite specific on this point (e.g. *Deane v Northern Ireland Water*[97]). Although the Irish and the English courts have not supported a freestanding implied good faith obligation, in English law there are instances where contracting parties may be placed under duties to warn the other contracting party of difficulties,[98] and professionals may be under good faith obligations in respect of the discharge of functions and contractual duties.[99] Covenants to act in good faith can spring out of declarations that an agreement has been reached in good faith.[100]

6–29 In other Commonwealth jurisdictions the position is all the more uncertain given the multiplicity of State and provincial jurisdictions that exist. In Australia, for example, the role of good faith in Australian contract law has been said to be "in a state of utter confusion".[101] The authors of this important article argue that recent Australian decisions suggest that the duty of good faith should be seen as an inherent part of contract law and that good faith appears as a requirement to act honestly (rather than reasonably), without an intention to cause harm, and to perform the contract with due regard to the substance rather than the form of the bargain. In rejecting the view that the duty also includes a duty to act reasonably on the grounds that this goes too far and imposes upon a contracting party an obligation that is hostile to the institution of contract itself, the authors echo part of Lord Ackner's objections to the putative implied term in *Walford*, and the authors also cite the views of Kirby J. in *Royal Botanic Gardens and Domain Trust v South Sydney Council*,[102] in which the learned

---

94 [1992] 2 A.C. 128.
95 [1992] 2 A.C. 128 per Lord Ackner at 138.
96 [1999] 2 I.L.R.M 232; *Triatic Ltd v Cork County Council* [2006] IEHC 111.
97 [2009] NI Ch 8; *Easycoach v Department for Regional Development* [2012] NIQB 10.
98 e.g. *Plant Construction Plc v Clive Adams Associates (No.2)* [2000] B.L.R. 137; *J.H. Ritchie Ltd v Lloyd Ltd* [2007] UKHL 9. Contrast express terms on reasonable and best endeavours; *Rhodia International Holdings Ltd v Huntsman International* [2007] EWHC 292 (Comm); *Yewbelle Ltd v London Green Developments Ltd* [2007] EWCA Civ 475.
99 *Hadjipanayi v Yeldon* [2001] B.P.I.R. 487 (receiver). *Ultraframe (UK) v Tailored Roofing Systems* [2004] 2 All E.R. (Comm.) 296.
100 *Haines v Carter* [2001] 2 N.Z.L.R. 167. Berg (2003) 119 L.Q.R. 357 suggests that "best endeavours to agree" and "good faith" agreements preclude resort to adversarial models of negotiation.
101 Carter and Peden, "Good Faith in Australian Contract Law" (2003) 19 J.C.L. 155.
102 (2002) 186 A.L.R. 289 at 311–312; see Carter and Stewart, "Intepretation, Good Faith and the 'True Meaning' of Contracts: The Royal Botanic Decision" (2002) 18 J.C.L. 182.

judge saw good faith obligations as in conflict with "fundamental notions of *caveat emptor* that are inherent (statute and equitable intervention apart) in common law conceptions of economic freedom". Australian courts have developed a strong line of case law, particularly in New South Wales, in which good faith obligations have been implied in the performance of a contract, as well as in relation to the negotiation and termination of contracts.[103] The scope of the duty, the issue of whether breach of good faith is a "stand alone" right to damages, and the impact of any such duty or right to damages on established law are all matters yet to be resolved by the High Court of Australia. In Canada too there are several "good faith" decisions relating to the performance of contracts,[104] and in relation to certain kinds of tender transactions traditionally suggested limited scope for implied terms.[105]

The landmark decision of the Supreme Court of Canada in *Bhasin v Hrynew*[106] directs that there is now required to exist a duty of honest contractual performance in all Canadian Contracts based on "an organizing principle of good faith". In writing for the entire Supreme Court of Canada, Cromwell J. wrote

"This means simply that parties must not lie or otherwise knowingly mislead each other about matters directly linked to the performance of the contract. This does not impose a duty of loyalty or of disclosure or require a party to forego advantages flowing from the contract; it is a simple requirement not to lie or mislead the other party about one's contractual performance."

This duty is reflected in other doctrines such as unconscionability and in existing case law relating to employment contracts and long term relational contracts such as dealership and franchise agreements, the court said. Like English decisions, the exercise of contractual discretion is constrained by a duty to act in good faith, narrow though this duty may be.

6–30 Even in single-jurisdiction countries such as New Zealand, the law is uncertain indeed.[107] Insofar as Irish judges have had occasion to consider this point, there appears to be a considerable degree of reluctance to embrace a "modish" and ill-defined concept and it is suggested that the alternative to

---

[103] e.g. *Renard Constructions ME Pty Ltd v Minister for Public Works* (1992) 26 N.S.W.L.R 234; *Alcatel Australia Ltd v Scarcella* (1998) 44 N.S.W.L.R 349; *Burger King v Hungry Jack's Pty Ltd* [2001] NSWCA 187. See the Privy Council's view on New South Wales law in *Dymocks Franchise Systems (N.S.W.) Pty v Todd* [2002] UKPC 50.

[104] e.g. *Le Mesurier v Andrus* (1986) 25 D.L.R. (4th) 424; O'Byrne (1995) 74 Can. B.R. 70.

[105] See Ch.1; decisions like *Mannpar Enterprises Ltd v Canada* (1999) 173 D.L.R. (4th) 243 and the Supreme Court of Canada decision in *Martel Building v Canada* (2000) 193 D.L.R. (4th) 1, suggest there is no general duty to negotiate in good faith. See also *Peel Condominium Corp v Cam Valley Homes* (2001) 196 D.L.R. (4th) 621; *Amber Contracting Ltd v Halifax* (2010) 312 D.L.R. (4th) 398.

[106] (2014) 381 D.LR (4th) 1.

[107] See McLauchlan, 'The Justiciability of an Agreement to Negotiate in Good Faith" (2003) 20 N.Z.U.L.R. 265.

lacing contracts with ancillary good faith obligations by way of implied terms, i.e. recognition that contract law is permeated with notions of honesty and hostility to capricious conduct by contracting parties, is to be preferred. Many existing doctrines such as economic duress, improvident and unconscionable bargains already achieve the same results in Irish contract jurisprudence.

Implied duties to co-operate

6–31 In *Airscape Ltd v Heaslon Properties Ltd*[108] the plaintiffs successfully sought an order declaring that the defendants were in repudiatory breach of contract. The defendants had effectively purchased an industrial site from the plaintiffs under a contract that required development of the site to be undertaken by the plaintiffs. The plaintiffs complained that the defendants had breached implied obligations not to unreasonably delay or unreasonably withhold its co-operation for the carrying out of works. Edwards J. found the implied term was established under the business efficacy test. Another way of explaining the basis of such decisions is known as the rule in *Mackey v Dick*[109]:

> "[A]s a general rule … where in a written contract it appears that both parties have agreed that something should be done, which cannot effectively be done unless both concur in doing it, the construction of the contract is that each agrees to do all that is necessary to be done on his part for the carrying out of that thing, though there may be no express words to that effect."

6–32 Courts will be circumspect in allowing this rationale to readily apply to the case at bar.[110]

Service contracts

6–33 While employment contracts and agency contracts[111] are instances where the contractual relationship itself creates implied duties, there are other instances where implied obligations will arise, even if the contract is a one-off or isolated transaction. The provider of a service, whether it be surgical or dental services,[112] the provision of false teeth, as in *Samuels v Davis*[113] or information to subscribers to a wire service, as in *Allen v Bushnell T.V. Co and Broadcast News Ltd*,[114] must exercise reasonable care and skill in discharging the contract. Contracts for legal services are generally accepted to require the

---

[108] [2008] IEHC 82.

[109] (1881) 6 App. Cas. 251 at 263.

[110] *Secured Income Real Estate (Australia) Ltd v St. Martins Investments Pty* [1979] HCA 51; *Campbell v Backoffice Investments Pty Ltd* [2009] HCA 25. See the treatment of the two cross appeal implied terms in *Swallow Falls Ltd v Monaco Yachting & Technologies* [2014] EWCA Civ 186.

[111] *Wong Me Wan v Kwan Kin Travel Services Ltd* [1995] 4 All E.R. 745.

[112] *Murphy v King* [2011] NIQB 1.

[113] [1943] K.B. 526.

[114] (1968) 1 D.L.R. (3d) 534.

lawyer to act on behalf of a client with reasonable skill and care and give fair, full, frank and honest advice to the client: *Strydom v Veadside Ltd.*[115] In the leading case of *Norta Wallpapers (Ireland) Ltd v John Sisk & Son (Dublin) Ltd*[116] the Supreme Court had to consider the liability of a contractor to the employer when defective materials are used by a sub-contractor. Henchy J. had this to say about the state of the law:

> "I conceive the law of the land to be that, unless the particular circumstances give reason for its exclusion, there is implied into the contract a term to the effect that the contractor will be liable to the employer for any loss or damage suffered by him as a result of the goods, materials or installations not being fit for the purpose for which they were supplied."[117]

Similarly, a subscriber to a mobile phone contract received abusive phone calls and text messages when pornographic images and texts that had purportedly been sent from her mobile phone provoked a reaction from other mobile users. Because the evidence indicated that the subscriber was out of credit at the time and the evidence established that the error was due to technical problems with a free sms promotion, damages were awarded for breach of contract.[118]

A new emphasis on the document—Belize Telecom

6–34 A recent decision of the Privy Council has drawn together older and more recent judicial opinions to emphasise that the search is not for the actual intention of the parties. In *Attorney General of Belize v Belize Telecom*[119] the Privy Council addressed the question from the perspective of Lord Hoffmann's strictures in *Investors Compensation Scheme Ltd v West Bromwich Building Society*.[120] The case concerned the question of what implication should be made in respect of articles of association of a company when directors of a company were appointed by virtue of a specified shareholding, the holder of the shareholding in question being in default and the shares seized. Did the appointment of two special directors by that defaulting shareholder end or could those directors remain in office? The articles of association were silent and as the shareholder was no longer able to exercise powers of termination, it was necessary to arrive at a solution. Giving judgment, the Privy Council stressed that the process was not one in which a court added anything to

---

[115] [2009] EWHC 2130 (Q.B.); *Outlet Recording Co v Barry F. Thompson* [2011] NIQB 24. On financial services see *ABN AmroBank v Bathurst Regional Council* [2014] FCAFC 65.

[116] [1978] I.R. 114.

[117] [1978] I.R. 114 at 123. Implied terms about construction contracts requiring work to be carried out in a good and workmanlike manner, using suitable materials, are found in most systems, e.g. *Mack v Stuike* (1963) 43 D.L.R. (2d) 763 and *Maisonneuve v Burley* (2001) 211 Sask. R. 100.

[118] See "Teenager gets €7,500 after 'bug' sent porn images from her phone", *Irish Times*, July 31, 2004.

[119] [2009] 2 All E.R. 1127; Lowe and Loi, "The Many 'Tests' for Terms Implied in Fact: Welcome Clarity" (2009) 125 L.Q.R. 561.

[120] [1998] 1 All E.R. 98.

the contract; in most cases Lord Hoffmann said when an instrument does not expressly provide for what is to happen when an event occurs, the usual inference is that nothing is to happen. However, in some cases a "reasonable addressee" would conclude from the instrument that, on its terms, and (consistent with the other provisions of the instrument, when read against the relevant background), the instrument provides "that something is to happen ... to affect the rights of the parties ... the implication of the Term is not an addition to the instrument. It only spells out what the instrument means". Lord Hoffmann referred to earlier tests such as the business efficacy test and that of the officious bystander, remarking that they emphasise the need for the court to be satisfied that the proposed implication spells out what the contract would reasonably be understood to mean. But the dangers of invoking such tests, Lord Hoffmann said, is that they tend to focus on what the parties would have done had their attention been drawn to the omissions. That, Lord Hoffmann said, is irrelevant. It is the intention of the parties, determined objectively, from the express terms read against the relevant background "that is relevant". Lord Hoffmann stressed that this is not new law, approving the speech of Lord Simon of Glaisdale in *BP Refinery (Westernport) Pty Ltd v Shire of Hastings*,[121] who, when giving the majority view of the law on behalf of the Privy Council, said the following tests must be satisfied:

> "(1) it must be reasonable and equitable; (2) it must be necessary to give business efficacy to the contract, so that no term will be implied if the contract is effective without it; (3) it must be so obvious that 'it goes without saying'; (4) it must be capable of clear expression; (5) it must not contradict any express term of the contract."

Some commentators have taken the view that Lord Hoffmann's speech may result in fewer cases being decided in favour of making an implication, and Professor Davies in particular[122] argues that the Hoffmann approach is misguided and that the traditional tests operate more effectively to limit insertion of implied terms into a contract. We must see how the Irish courts will react.[123] In *Belize* itself the Privy Council concluded that the instrument meant that if the shareholding was no longer viable then the directors appointed to represent the relevant shareholder interests had no role to play. The Privy Council stressed that there could be no reliance on extrinsic facts known only to a few individuals. The implication made here was "based upon the scheme of the articles themselves, and, to a very limited extent, such background as was apparent from the memorandum of association and everyone in Belize would have known, namely that the telecommunications scheme had been a state monopoly and that the company was part of a scheme of privatisation".[124]

---

[121] (1977) 180 C.L.R. 266. See also Bingham M.R.'s speech in *Philips Electronique Grand Public SA v British Sky Broadcasting Ltd* [1995] E.M.L.R. 472.

[122] [2010] L.M.C.L.Q. 140.

[123] Some of the key cases relied on in *Belize* have been followed—see *O'Connor v McNamara* [2009] IEHC 190, for an example.

[124] [2009] 2 All E.R. 1127 at 1137.

Later English cases have discussed *Belize* with varying degrees of judicial enthusiasm.[125]

6–35 In *Marks and Spencer plc v BNP Paribas Securities Trust Company (Jersey) Ltd*[126] the UK Supreme Court has not only affirmed the pre-Belize orthodoxy, namely, that implied terms may arise from the express terms and surrounding circumstances will do so because of business necessity and obviousness, the Supreme Court has rejected Lord Hoffmann's view that implied terms are to be found through a process of interpretation. Writing for himself and Lords Sumption and Hodge, Lord Neuberger said

> "it is only after the process of construing the express words is complete that the issue of an implied term fails to be considered. Until one has decided what the parties have expressly agreed, it is difficult to see how one can set about deciding whether a term should be implied and if so what term."

Terms Implied under Statute

6–36 Several common law obligations have been codified into statutes which form part of a contractual relationship. The most important example of this is presented by the implied obligations arising under the Sale of Goods Act 1893 and the Republic's Sale of Goods and Supply of Services Act 1980. Common law obligations requiring the seller of goods to supply goods which are of merchantable quality and which are fit for the purpose for which they are intended are part of the 1893 Act (s.14). These obligations could formerly be excluded if the parties so agreed but this is no longer possible in consumer sales after the 1980 Act. The important subject of statutory implied terms under the Sale of Goods Acts 1893–1980 is considered in Chs 8 and 9.

6–37 The employment contract provides another rich source of statutory implied terms. The obligation on an employer to provide holiday pay stems from statute and not a contract expressly struck by the parties. There are important restrictions on the freedom of an employer to dismiss his employees without giving a minimum period of notice. An employee dismissed after 13 weeks of employment but before two years' service is entitled to one week's notice or wages in lieu thereof. This sliding scale progresses until workers who

---

[125] *Mediterranean Salvage & Towage Ltd v Seamar Commerce and Trading Inc.* [2009] EWCA Civ 531; *Crema v Cenkos Securities Plc* [2010] EWCA Civ 1444 (an important case on evidence of market practice known to the "reasonable addressee"); *Great Elephant Corp v Trafigura Beheer BV* [2012] EWHC 1745 (Comm) (per Teare J., "implied terms spell out the terms which the parties have agreed"). In *Societe Generale London Branch v Geys* [2012] UKSC 63, Lady Hale pointed out that the analysis in *Belize* did not affect cases where terms are implied into a particular relationship (e.g. employer and employee).

[126] [2015] UKSC 72.

have served for more than 15 years are entitled to eight weeks' notice. These provisions, to be found in s.4 of the Minimum Notice and Terms of Employment Act 1973, cannot be excluded by agreement. They are a minimum requirement and can be expanded by agreement or by circumstances. The 1968 case of *Carvill v Irish Industrial Bank*,[127] would not be decided differently today. The most recent enhancement of workers' notice rights is found in the Terms of Employment (Information) Act 1994, while the Protection of Employees (Temporary Agency Work) Act 2012 gives notice of terms and other important rights to generally vulnerable classes of workers.

6–38 Statute also provides for implied terms to exist in landlord and tenant agreements. See, for example, the power of a housing authority to pass bye-laws under s.70 of the Housing Act 1966 to impose minimum standards for rented property within its functional area, subsequently adjusted by s.18 of the Housing (Miscellaneous Provisions) Act 1992. Sections 12 and 16 of the Residential Tenancies Act 2004 also set out obligations upon landlords and tenants in respect of the occupation of a dwelling and payment of rent respectively.

6–39 However, statutory authority for a particular practice, or the provision of a service, may preclude an argument based on implied contract. In *Monaghan Board of Health v O'Neill*[128] the plaintiff provided hospital services for an elderly indigent person in pursuance of a statutory duty to maintain sick or feeble persons resident within its functional area. The plaintiff later sought to obtain a contribution from that person. It was held that the statutory obligation meant that there was no basis at common law for an implied term that money spent would be recoverable.

6–40 As we shall see, Constitutional rights to fair procedures may also be invoked against state bodies in particular. These overlap with some statutory obligations that arise directly from primary legislation or codes of practice drawn up thereunder. In *Flynn v National Asset Loan Management Ltd*[129] duties of transparency and key principles in the NAMA code under ss.11 and 35 were successfully invoked to challenge substantive and procedural shortcomings in the affairs of a family whose outstanding loans were abruptly called in by the defendant statutory agency. With the proliferation of statutes which contain express references to obligations to provide codes of good practice[130] it is to be expected that there will be many cases on the effect that non-compliance with a code may have on the enforceability of other contractual obligations, especially when the agency in question is in default.

---

[127] [1968] I.R. 325.
[128] (1934) 68 I.L.T.R. 239; *Gilheaney v Revenue Commissioners*, unreported, High Court, October 4, 1995. The possibility that an implied term will interfere with fundamental freedoms will be a strong disincentive to any such court: *Flynn v Breccia* [2015] IEHC 547.
[129] [2014] IEHC 408.
[130] See generally *Atlantic Marine Supplies Ltd v Minister for Transport* [2010] IEHC 104.

Financial institutions that are bound to observe Central Bank codes have been able to enforce transactions.[131]

Terms Implied under the Constitution

6–41 Important differences between Irish contract law and English contract principles arise because of the operation of the 1937 Constitution which sets out certain fundamental freedoms, absent from the English common law. The Constitution has proved important in employment law and its impact on principles of contract has, in this respect, proved substantial.

6–42 Sub-articles 40.6.1°iii and 40.6.2° have been interpreted as conferring upon citizens the right not only to form associations and unions but an implicit right not to join—a right of disassociation—see *Educational Co of Ireland Ltd v Fitzpatrick (No.2)*.[132] The Supreme Court has ruled in *Meskell v C.I.É.*[133] that this right of disassociation must be respected by an employer, even if the employer threatens to exercise his common law right of dismissal in a manner permissible at common law. Meskell was employed as a bus conductor. C.I.É. offered Meskell a new contract of employment which would oblige him to join and maintain membership of a trade union. Failure to assent would lead, after a reasonable period of notice, to termination of his employment. Meskell objected in principle and, following his refusal and dismissal, sued, alleging an actionable conspiracy by the unions and C.I.É. to infringe his constitutional right of disassociation. Walsh J. in the leading judgment, held that the fact that a person seeks to exercise a common law right in such a way as to dissuade a citizen from exercising a constitutional right "must necessarily be regarded as an abuse of the common law right because it is an infringement, and an abuse, of the Constitution which is superior to the common law and which must prevail if there is a conflict between the two".[134] In other words, if a statutory provision can override a common law right (or even an express agreement) then a right implied under the Constitution must, a fortiori, take priority over this common law right. Damages will also be recoverable for infringement of this constitutional right even if no other cause of action would appear to exist; per Walsh J. in *Meskell v C.I.É.*

6–43 Article 40.3 has been held to require that procedures and machinery established to reach decisions which effect the rights or liabilities of citizens must be fair. These procedures must allow a party to be heard if he is accused

---

[131] e.g. *AIB v Ryan* [2015] IEHC 260; *Irish Life and Permanent v Dunne* [2015] IESC 46; *Untoy v GE Capital Woodchester Ltd* [2015] IEHC 557.
[132] [1961] I.R. 345. See on the public/private law divide, Hogan and Morgan, *Administrative Law in Ireland*, 4th edn (Dublin: Round Hall, 2012), Ch.17.
[133] [1973] I.R. 121.
[134] [1973] I.R. 121 at 135.

of breach of contract. In *Glover v B.L.N.*[135] an employee was summarily dismissed for alleged misconduct. Clause 12(*c*) of the contract provided he could be so dismissed without compensation for serious misconduct. Walsh J. held:

> "This procedure was a breach of the implied term of the contract that the procedure should be fair, as it cannot be disputed, in the light of so much authority on the point, that failure to allow a person to meet the charges against him and afford him an adequate opportunity of answering them is a violation of an obligation to proceed fairly."[136]

The obligation, which modifies the employer's common law right to dismiss an employee by reasonable notice does not extend to all employees, but the applicability of this constitutional obligation has been consistently stated by the Irish courts to depend on whether the employee enjoys the status of office-holder.[137] However, the Supreme Court, in *Gunn v Bord an Choláiste Náisiúnta Ealaíne is Deartha*[138] held that termination of employment must take place in accordance with the principles of natural and constitutional justice and that these principles, when applicable, operate without regard to the status of the person who seeks to invoke them. Therefore, if a person is accused of wrongdoing, that person must be given details of the charge against him.[139]

> "Dismissal from one's employment for alleged misconduct with possible loss of pension rights and damage to one's good name, may, in modern society, be disastrous for any citizen. These are circumstances in which any citizen, however humble, may be entitled to the protection of natural and constitutional justice."[140]

The same holds true in respect of disciplinary proceedings for breach of turf club rules,[141] or those of the Gaelic Athletic Association[142] and the Irish Road Haulage Association.[143] There are suggestions that in the event that a breach of constitutional rights has taken place, in a contractual setting, damages awarded purely on a contract basis may not be enough to vindicate the constitutional rights of the injured party.[144] However, there is a line of authority that draws

---

[135] [1973] I.R. 388; *Mooney v An Post* [1998] 4 I.R. 288; *Moore v Xnet Information Systems Ltd* [2002] 2 I.L.R.M. 278. Recent cases affirm that the standard is fair procedures, not perfect procedures: *Rowland v An Post* [2011] IEHC 272; *Boyle v An Post* [2015] IEHC 589.

[136] [1973] I.R. 388 at 425–426; contrast *Rowland v An Post* [2011] IEHC 272.

[137] *Garvey v Ireland* (1979) 113 I.L.T.R. 61; *O'Reilly v Minister for Industry and Commerce* [1994] E.L.R. 48; *Burke v The Courts Service* [2013] IEHC 377.

[138] [1990] 2 I.R. 168.

[139] *N.E.E.T.U. v McConnell* [1983] I.L.R.M. 422; *Gallagher v Corrigan*, unreported, High Court, February 1, 1988.

[140] Per Barrington J. in *Mooney v An Post* [1998] 4 I.R. 288 at 298; *Dooley v Great Southern Hotels* [2001] E.L.R. 430.

[141] *Bolger v Osborne* [2000] 1 I.L.R.M. 250; *O'Connell v Turf Club* [2015] IESC 57.

[142] *Barry v Ginnity*, Irish Times Law Report, June 6, 2005.

[143] *McMahon v Irish Road Haulage Association* [2009] IEHC 145.

[144] *McMahon v Irish Road Haulage Association* [2009] IEHC 145 per Laffoy J.

a distinction between suspension in relation to a disciplinary process and paid leave from employment pending an investigation into circumstances being completed.[145]

6–44 The procedures for investigation of these allegations must take place as soon as is reasonably practicable.[146] Sometimes constitutional rights and contractual rights may reinforce each other. The decision of the Supreme Court in *McAuley v Commissioner of An Garda Síochána*[147] held that when a trainee garda was the subject of a disciplinary procedure, the requirements of the disciplinary code and his constitutional rights to constitutional justice had not been satisfied. In particular the plaintiff had not been provided with the evidence against him, nor was the decision to terminate his employment implemented in a lawful manner. In these circumstances the plaintiff was entitled to damages for breach of constitutional rights and breach of contract. On the other hand, it has been said that not every disciplinary process must be conducted in the same way and that any process in place must be fair—it does not have to be perfect—and implemented in a fair manner.[148]

6–45 Apart from the obligation to give an employee the right to be heard— see *Allied Irish Banks v Lupton*[149]—the Constitution and principles of natural justice also extend a right to be heard by an impartial tribunal. If the members of the disciplinary board are clearly not impartial then the rule *nemo iudex in causa sua* is infringed; see *National Engineering & Electrical Trade Union v McConnell*.[150] However, a citizen cannot use the Constitution to frustrate an employer, for example, from investigating allegations of misconduct or dishonesty and the use of allegations of past misconduct may well be relevant in this regard; see *Maher v Irish Permanent Plc*.[151]

6–46 While the provisions of Art.40.3 do not seem to do very much more than articulate the rules of natural justice that had already emerged in English administrative law, there are important practical results which flow from the argument that the Constitution has integrated principles of natural justice into the scheme of human rights guaranteed by the Constitution. These issues are explored by Hogan and Whyte.[152]

6–47 There are other aspects to the Constitution that may in the future be developed. Statute law has, however, an important role to play in the form of employment equality legislation, the central piece of legislation being the Employment Equality Act 1998. The Equal Status Act 2000 also provides

---

[145] *Quirke v Bord Lúthchleas na hÉireann* [1988] I.R. 83; *Higgins v Bank of Ireland* [2013] IEHC 6.
[146] *Flynn v An Post* [1987] I.R. 68.
[147] Unreported, Supreme Court, February 15, 1996.
[148] *Short v Royal Liver Assurance Ltd* [2008] IEHC 332; *Higgins v Bank of Ireland* [2013] IEHC 6.
[149] (1984) 3 J.I.S.L.L. 107.
[150] [1983] I.L.R.M. 422.
[151] Unreported, High Court, October 7, 1997.
[152] (1984) 19 Ir.Jur. 315 and *The Irish Constitution*, 4th edn (Dublin: Butterworths, 2003).

protection against discrimination in respect of the provision of goods and services, education, accommodation, and membership, etc. in respect of registered clubs[153]: *Equality Authority v Portmarnock Golf Club*.[154]

6–48 The Irish courts, however, have not readily taken the view that the equality provisions in Art.40.1 will intervene in the trading activities of citizens or the terms upon which those persons are employed; see *Murtagh Properties Ltd v Cleary*.[155] Thus in *Devaney v Minister for Agriculture*[156] an attempt to challenge a contractual term, which required Department of Agriculture inspectors to provide their own transport, as unconstitutional because only persons who could afford to run a car would be eligible for appointment was rejected as incompatible with the pronouncement of Kenny J. in *Murtagh Properties v Cleary* on the scope of Art.40.1:

> "[T]his article is not a guarantee that all citizens shall be treated by the law as equal for all purposes but it means that they shall, as human persons be held equal before the law. It relates to their essential attributes as persons, those features which make them human beings. It has, in my opinion, nothing to do with their trading activities or with the conditions on which they are employed."[157]

Nevertheless Kenny J. did go on to consider whether Art.40.1 could be infringed if a trade union pressured (by mounting a picket) an employer into dismissing someone on the ground of sex and concluded that such pressure would breach a citizen's right to earn a livelihood. Whether pressure mounted by A against B, requiring B to discontinue providing C, a self-employed female jobbing builder, with work, because A has a prejudice against women working outside the home, would infringe the Constitution must be an open question.

6–49 The Supreme Court in *Tierney v Amalgamated Society of Woodworkers*[158] held that the defendant union was free to decide whether it would permit the applicant to become a member of the trade union or not and that Art.40.6.1° iii extended to citizens a collective right to form unions and not an individual right which would require a union to accept a citizen's offer to become a member of that union. Even if the refusal prevented the applicant from taking up employment, thereby impeding the applicant from earning a livelihood— where a pre-entry closed shop operated—it seems that there is no remedy

---

[153] See *Joyce v Madden* [2004] 1 I.L.R.M. 277, in which a traveller refused service in a hotel succeeded under this legislation.
[154] [2009] IESC 73.
[155] [1972] I.R. 330.
[156] Unreported, High Court, March 22, 1979.
[157] [1972] I.R. 330 at 335–336.
[158] [1959] I.R. 254; see *Irish Municipal Public & Civil Trade Union v Ryanair Ltd* [2006] IEHC 118 invoking unsuccessfully Art.40.6.1°iii and the European Convention on Human Rights, discussed in Forde and Byrne, *Industrial Relations Law*, 2nd edn (Dublin: Round Hall, 2010), Ch.3.

unless perhaps the reason for refusal is itself discriminatory. In such a case it may be possible to invoke the provisions of the Employment Equality Act 1998. However, the right to earn one's living has been identified as a personal right, which is inherent in Art.40.3. For a discussion of the nature of this right, and the fact that the right may exist in two provisions in Art.40.3, see *Cafolla v O'Malley*.[159] Related to the right to earn a living are rights to enjoy the provisions of a subsisting contract of employment. In *Re Article 26 and the Employment Equality Bill 1996*,[160] however, many of the provisions in relation to age and disability discrimination were upheld, but in respect of obligations imposed on employers, such provisions in the Bill were struck down as unfairly transferring the cost of socially desirable objectives onto one particular group.

6–50 These implied fundamental freedoms are not absolute, however. If the parties agree in circumstances where it is clear that each is in a position to freely negotiate and that each understands the bargain then it may be possible for a citizen to waive a constitutional right of disassociation or a guarantee as to fair procedures.[161] In certain cases a constitutional right may have to take its place within a hierarchy of constitutional rights. Further, a contract may have a significant role in determining such a hierarchy. In *Oblique Financial Services Ltd v The Promise Production Co*[162] the various defendants, some of whom had covenanted to keep a secret while the others intended to publish the secret, could not assert an unlimited right to freedom to communicate information under Art.40.3.1°. Such a right could be qualified by other legal constraints such as the duty to observe confidentiality, whether owed by the defendants in contract or as a matter of moral obligation.

Judicial Review of Administrative Action

6–51 The *Braganza* decision[163] in England draws an analogy with the possible abuse of powers by persons who have obtained contractual discretions and the dangers that citizens may be the subject of unreasonable conduct or decisions by public bodies. Irish law has recently seen an explosion in judicial review litigation concerning the exercise of powers by statutory bodies in particular when the consequences for individuals are potentially or actually detrimental to those interests. The majority judgment in *Braganza* indicated that there has been a convergence of judicial review rules and common law controls over the

---

[159] [1985] I.R. 486.
[160] [1997] 2 I.R. 321.
[161] *Murphy v Stewart* [1975] I.R. 97; *Quinn v Honorable Society of Kings Inns* [2004] IEHC 220; *Dellway Investments v NAMA* [2011] IESC 14; Kerr and Whyte, *Irish Trade Union Law* (Abingdon: Professional Books, 1985), pp.31–33. See generally on waiver Hogan and Morgan, *Administrative Law*, 4th edn (Dublin: Round Hall, 2012), paras 11.96–11.100.
[162] [1994] I.L.R.M. 74. See generally Lavery, *Commercial Secrets* (Dublin: Round Hall Sweet & Maxwell, 1997). See also *Campbell v Frisbee* [2002] E.M.L.R. 31.
[163] *Braganza v BP Shipping Ltd* [2015] UKSC 17.

exercise of contract-created discretion.[164] Irish law continues at this time to focus on constitutional protection of judgmental rights.

Constitutional guarantees of fair procedures have developed from the two basic principles of natural justice, *audi alteram partem* and *nemo iudex in causa sua*. Later cases have created general principles of constitutional justice based upon specific articles in the Constitution and these two examples of natural justice. In *State (Furey) v Minister for Defence*[165] McCarthy J. said that in his view the two principles of natural justice, as they pre-existed the Constitution, are now part of the human rights guaranteed by the Constitution. As we have seen, early case law has recognised that in certain kinds of contractual settings these principles can be invoked even when the contracting parties are not in any sense public bodies, e.g. an employer fails to give an employee a right to address allegations of wrongdoing before the employer purports to terminate a contract of employment for misconduct. In general terms, however, the extent to which the duty can extend into all contracts has not been squarely addressed until recently. For example, in *Carna Foods v Eagle Star*[166] the judge at first instance, McCracken J., rejected an argument that an insurance company was required to follow constitutional requirements as to fair procedures before refusing to renew insurance cover. The Supreme Court upheld this decision. However, McCracken J. indicated that "where a decision is taken to exercise a function in the public realm, the person affected is entitled to know the reasons for the decision. This is because statutory powers must be determined and exercised reasonably". It follows from the extensive case law in Ireland on the judicial review of administrative action that where a public body makes a decision, of a public nature, there must be some degree of participation in arriving at those decisions by persons who will be affected by that decision. This applies to decisions of all kinds and not just discretionary aspects of an administrative process. For example, the Financial Services Ombudsman, charged under statute with resolving disputes between insurance companies and insured persons, should confine decisions to matters properly within his statutory remit: *Lyons v Financial Services Ombudsman*[167]; *Lyons v Financial Services Ombudsman*.[168] Because fair procedures cannot be precisely defined it is hardly surprising that the principle will impact on contractual rights. So, in *Haughy v Moriarty*,[169] the plaintiff was said to have rights of privacy vis-à-vis his contractual relationship with his bankers and decisions of the High Court in respect of discovery applications made by the Moriarty Tribunal required the plaintiff to be notified and heard before orders of discovery were made. A central theme in judicial review proceedings is to consider whether a person is likely to be "affected" by any decision made, and it is clear from recent

---

[164] Particularly through the application of both limbs of *Associated Provincial Picture Houses Ltd v Wednesbury Corporation* [1948] 1 K.B. 223 at 233–234, Greene M.R.

[165] [1988] I.L.R.M. 89. See also *State (Irish Pharmaceutical Union) v EAT* [1987] I.L.R.M. 36.

[166] [1995] 1 I.R. 526, affirmed [1997] 2 I.L.R.M. 499.

[167] [2011] IEHC 454.

[168] [2012] IEHC 92.

[169] [1999] 3 I.R. 1.

judicial developments that a person will be "affected" by a decision when the possible consequences of the decision will have ramifications for the way in which any contractual rights are exercised.

6–52 In what is clearly the leading case of *Dellway Investments v National Asset Management Agency*,[170] the Supreme Court has followed earlier judicial views that constitutional guarantees as to fair procedures in respect of property rights must be viewed as including "rights other than ownership of immovables, such as contractual rights".[171] In this case the complaint was made in respect of decisions of the National Asset Management Agency (NAMA) (under the National Asset Management Agency Act 2009) to exercise its discretion under s.84(1) to acquire eligible bank assets. The application for judicial review was brought by property developer Patrick McKillen who argued, in essence, that the assets being acquired were significant blue chip properties, the majority of which were abroad, rather than Irish properties that were themselves the subject of impaired loans. Mr McKillen's arguments were underpinned by economic testimony that in compulsory acquisitions cases of this kind the asset was generally obtained at undervalue. Further, in this specific instance, NAMA was not required to obtain the best possible price for the asset (unlike a mortgagee taking possession of a security). The perception that NAMA was a "bad bank" was said to undermine Mr McKillen's prestige and commercial status and business credibility. As Murray C.J. said:

> "It is well to underline at this point that the rights and interests involved in this case are property rights and interests derived from the ownership of certain properties by the appellants and related contractual rights, which, but for the provisions of the Act, they would normally be entitled to manage and deal with as they saw fit, within the ordinary parameters of the law. Persons in the position of the appellants would, but for the provisions of the Act, by reason of the rights and interests vested in them as owners of the development land in question, normally be entitled, as of right, to independently manage their affairs related to those properties, including negotiating with private institutions with whom they have credit facilities. It is in this sense that reference is made to rights and interests."

The legislation in question afforded banks that were caught up in the financial crisis with rights of representation but NAMA had afforded borrowers such as Mr McKillen and his companies no such opportunity to be heard. All six judges found that this was a breach of constitutional justice. While the rights in question are subject to exceptions such as emergencies no such exception applied and NAMA's own operational tardiness was noted by several of the

---

[170] [2011] IESC 14.
[171] *East Donegal Co-Operative Mart Ltd v Attorney General* [1970] I.R. 317 per O'Keeffe P. at 332.

judges. Fennelly J. found that NAMA had to function under quite different considerations to an "ordinary" commercial bank:

"The central point is, in my view, that the transfer to NAMA puts the appellants and Mr. McKillen in a fundamentally different situation. NAMA, a statutory body, with statutory powers and objectives replaces his banks with which he has had, up to now, a commercial relationship. His long-term business model is not compatible with NAMA's statutory remit, which is essentially short-term. Where NAMA is in a position to rely on default by any of the appellants under their loan agreements, it is not only likely to but obliged to take action in pursuance of its statutory objectives, where a bank either would, or at least might, not do so. The consequence of an acquisition decision is to make a substantial change in the way in which the appellants are in a position to exercise their property rights. Their ability to manage their properties independently is reduced."

The right to be afforded to the complainant was a right to be heard before a decision was made in respect of any acquisition decision by NAMA of any loans previously made to the complainant. In *Treasury Holdings v National Asset Management Agency*[172] Finlay Geoghegan J. pushed out the boundaries even further. Here, Treasury had already found that NAMA had acquired some bank assets in the form of Treasury debts and Treasury had submitted a business plan to NAMA for consideration in respect of those assets. NAMA nevertheless decided to exercise enforcement rights, arguing that as these were rooted in commercial arrangements between the parties, the decision was not amenable to judicial review. Thus, no right to be heard before NAMA made the decision to enforce those (contractual) rights existed. The learned judge found the decision, rooted in statute rather than being purely a commercial arrangement, could be reviewed and that a right to be heard existed, even post-acquisition of the asset by NAMA.[173]

Human rights/international standards

6–53 It is an increasingly common feature of Irish jurisprudence for the judges to set Irish law against standards of international human rights jurisprudence: see, for example, Macken J. in *Dellway*. Difficult questions about the boundary between purely commercial activities and statutory functions (e.g. *Triatic Ltd v Cork County Council*[174]) as well as the characterisation of the decision maker

---

[172] [2012] IEHC 297; *Dagenham Yank Ltd v Irish Bank Resolution Corporation* [2014] IEHC 192.

[173] An important consideration here is whether there are adequate rights of appeal to challenge a decision in a more orthodox way: *NAMA v Barden* [2013] IEHC 32; *NAMA v Cullen* [2013] IEHC 121; *Flynn v National Asset Management Ltd* [2014] IEHC 408; see also *Rehab Group v Minister for Justice and Equality* [2014] IEHC 312.

[174] [2006] IEHC 111.

as a public authority for judicial review purposes (e.g. *Bloxham Irish Stock Exchange*[175]) are to be expected to arise.

6–54 There are cases[176] from the European Court of Human Rights that clearly indicate that art.8 of the European Convention on Human Rights—the right to privacy—for example, will prevent an employer from monitoring an employee's telephone, email and internet usage, especially if contractual and data protection requirements are not observed. The *Copland* decision is of particular interest because the European Court of Human Rights specifically invoked the UK domestic law *Malik*[177] implied term to support its view that the UK had breached the employment rights of the plaintiff. In 2006 the Dublin Circuit Court awarded damages when audio or video surveillance, or both, was used by the landlord to monitor the activities of 10 tenants.[178] Domestic case law is also starting to reflect human rights legislation[179] and statutory contractual rights tensions.

Custom

6–55 It is possible for terms to be implied into contracts because of the commercial or local backcloth against which a contract is to take effect. Customs within a trade or industry can become part of the contract; in *Taylor v Hall*[180] an alleged custom in the building industry was rejected as inconsistent with the evidence adduced. In a leading early-twentieth century Irish case the courts had to consider whether a particular practice in relation to the costs of unloading ships had become binding customs in the port in question.[181] The essential issues to be established are whether the practice can be shown to exist in the trade or locality, and that the parties have relied upon it. If these two points can be satisfied then the custom will generally be part of the contract unless it is excluded by an express term, or a term which is part of the contract and which is inconsistent with the custom in question.

---

[175] [2013] IEHC 301.

[176] e.g. *Halford v UK* (1997) 24 E.H.R.R. 523; *Copland v UK* [2007] 45 E.H.R.R. 37. Article 8 cases in Ireland have focused on housing procedures: e.g. *Webster v Dún Laoghaire Rathdown County Council* [2013] IEHC 119; *Lattimore v Dublin City Council* [2014] IEHC 233. On remedies contrast *Lattimore* with *Pullen v Dublin City Council* [2008] IEHC 379.

[177] *Malik v BCCI* [1998] A.C. 20. The *Malik* implied term has not found favour in Australia. See *Australia Commonwealth Bank v Barker* [2014] 253 CLR 169, thus questioning the human rights credentials of *Malik* itself.

[178] See "Landlord is ordered to pay students €115,000 in damages", *The Irish Times*, November 14, 2007.

[179] *Donegan v Dublin City Council* [2012] IESC 18; *Dellway Investments and Others v NAMA* [2011] IESC 14 (art.6); *Comcast Int Holdings v Minister for Public Enterprise and Others* [2012] IESC 50 (art.6).

[180] (1869) I.R. 5 C.L. 477. See the inconclusive case of *Murphy v O'Toole* [2014] IEHC 486 (is shaking hands in agricultural machinery circles in order to conclude a deal a trade custom?).

[181] *Gallagher v Clydesdale Shipowners Co* [1908] 2 I.R. 482.

6–56 In the case of *O'Reilly v Irish Press*[182] Maguire P. indicated that for a custom to be established there must be an element of notoriety or general acquiescence to it. The alleged custom was that chief sub-editors in a newspaper were entitled to six months' notice:

> "[A] custom on usage of any kind is a difficult thing to establish ... I have to be satisfied that it is so notorious, well known and acquiesced in that in the absence of agreement in writing it is to be taken as one of the terms of the contract between the parties."

No such custom was established by the plaintiff in this case. On the other hand, in *Carroll v Dublin Bus*,[183] the plaintiff returned to work as a driver for Dublin Bus. He established that the custom and practice was to facilitate drivers who had returned to work after illness with a light or rehabilitation route, where possible. Clarke J. held that when the plaintiff was not allocated such a route, for no good reason, the defendant had breached the contract of employment.

6–57 The difficulty of establishing, on the balance of probabilities, a trade custom is illustrated by *Eastwood v Ryder*.[184] It was alleged by the first plaintiff, a publisher, that there was an implied custom in the newspaper and periodical publishing industry that serialised extracts from a book, published in the plaintiff's magazine, would be true and not libellous. Michael Davies J. held that, after hearing expert testimony, this custom could not be established. The situation could be dealt with by way of an express indemnity but the contract between the defendant author and the first plaintiff did not deal with this kind of problem by way of an express indemnity, while the contract between the defendant and the second plaintiff, the book publisher, did contain such an indemnity. One further illustration is provided by *O'Connail v The Gaelic Echo (1954) Ltd*,[185] when a journalist recovered holiday pay on proof that it was a custom in Dublin that such payments were made to journalists. Similarly, local agricultural customs often become part of the agreement as an implied term. See, for example, the Ulster tenant's right of sale. Terms implied by way of custom are often found in landlord and tenant contracts and custom is a most fruitful basis for legislative action in this area of law. Many statutory obligations in landlord and tenant law are codifications of customary law.[186]

---

[182] (1937) I.L.T.R. 194.
[183] [2005] IEHC 278.
[184] *The Times*, July 28, 1990.
[185] (1958) 92 I.L.T.R. 156.
[186] Wylie, *Irish Land Law*, 5th edn (Haywards Heath: Bloomsbury Professional 2013), para.1.44; Residential Tenancies Act 2004; Lyall, *Land Law in Ireland*, 3rd edn (Dublin: Round Hall, 2010), Ch.21.

7 The Exemption Clause

Introduction

7–01 An exemption clause is a contractual term by which one party attempts to cut down either the scope of his contractual duties or regulate the other party's right to damages or other possible remedies for breach of contract. So in a *non-consumer* contract for the sale of goods any attempt by the seller to exclude implied obligations as to merchantability can be interpreted as effectively removing any obligation to supply merchantable goods; under the Sale of Goods Act 1893 (the "1893 Act"), as amended in the Republic by the Sale of Goods and Supply of Services Act 1980 (the "1980 Act"), such an attempt to eliminate this obligation must be shown to be fair and reasonable: see ss.14(2) and 55(4). One party may not attempt to eliminate the other's rights altogether but simply require any complaints about defective performance to be lodged within a set period, say within 14 days; failure to satisfy this term will result in loss of any cause of action. Alternatively, the seller may limit the damages recoverable to a fixed sum, e.g. €50. In *Leonard v Gt. Northern Ry. Co*[1] the plaintiff sent a consignment of turkeys by rail. On arrival, four were missing. Under the terms of the contract set out on the forwarding note the plaintiff was required to notify the carrier of loss within three days. The plaintiff's claim was dismissed because of failure to comply with the notice provision. There is no doubt about the increasing willingness of the English courts in particular to allow the parties who are negotiating complex commercial contracts to employ risk allocation mechanisms and limit or exclude common law reliefs and remedies as long as the contractual provisions employed to do so are clearly drafted. In *Persimmon Homes Ltd v Ove Arup*[2], for example, Stuart-Smith J. refused to accept a technically ingenious restriction on the scope of a general disclaimer of liability. Similarly, in *Fujitsu Services Ltd v IBM UK Ltd*[3] a damages cap and exclusion of lost profits provision that was individually negotiated and which applied to both parties was upheld. Once the process of interpretation of limiting clauses is directed at seeking to establish what the ordinary meaning of the words used, in context, actually is, objectively speaking, there can be no room for strained meanings, identifying dubious ambiguity or hostile interpretation. But the facts of each case will be different and judicial views may differ.

7–02 If the clause negatives a right to performance it is said to have *substantive* effect; if the clause regulates entitlement to damages it is

---

[1] (1912) 46 I.L.T.R. 220.
)15] EWHC 357(TCC).
)14] EWHC 752 (TCC).

236

procedural; only failure to satisfy the procedural steps laid down results in loss of the right to damages.[4] It may be, that in exceptional cases, a clause that looks like an exemption clause will be classified in another way, such as a clause identifying which of the parties must insure against a category of loss. In *Casson v Ostley P.J. Ltd*[5] a clause in a building contract sought to place upon the client an obligation to insure and the clause contained exculpatory words. Property was destroyed by fire caused by the builder's negligence and in an action for damages for breach of contract the builder sought to rely on the clause. The Court of Appeal, giving the clause a purposive construction, held it was not intended to operate as a disclaimer in any sense and the builder was held liable, the clause not being sufficiently strong to overcome what Sedley L.J. described as "the law's disinclination to let people contract out of the consequences of their own neglect".

Substantive or Procedural?

7–03 It can sometimes prove difficult to decide whether the exemption clause has substantive or procedural effect. In *British Leyland Exports Ltd v Brittain Group Sales Ltd*[6] a contract for the supply of motor vehicles to the defendants in kit form included a clause which provided that while the sellers would endeavour to meet orders placed they "shall not be liable for any failure, delay or error in delivery, or any consequential loss therefrom, however caused". O'Hanlon J. held that while this clause did not exclude the sellers' primary obligation to deliver complete and satisfactory kits, the clause did limit the buyer's remedies, by excluding the general secondary obligation to pay damages when defective kits were provided. With respect, this analysis seems to this writer to ignore the fact that the clause was in fact designed to limit the obligations on the sellers to meet orders where possible and effectively ensure that complete kits were provided. On this analysis there could be no room for a finding that the implied obligation excluded the claim for damages; the exclusion clause excluded the implied obligation and, ipso facto, there was no contractual right which could bring the secondary obligation to pay damages into play.

7–04 There are several English cases in which the courts have suggested that the effect of an exemption clause is to qualify or limit the scope of the contractual duties one party is to perform. In *Kenyon Son and Craven Ltd v Baxter Hoare & Co Ltd*[7] the defendant operated a warehouse and undertook

---

[4] The development of this analysis is generally attributed to Coote, *Exception Clauses* (London: Sweet & Maxwell, 1964). See generally Lawson, *Exclusion Clauses and Unfair Contract Terms,* 10th edn (London: Sweet & Maxwell, 2012) and *Chitty on Contracts*, edited by H.G. Beale, 32nd edn (London: Sweet & Maxwell, 2015), Vol.1 paras 15-001–15-061.

[5] [2003] B.L.R. 147.

[6] [1981] I.R. 35.

[7] [1971] 2 All E.R. 708. On the meaning of "wilful misconduct" see *Laceys Footwear Ltd v Bowler, The Times,* May 12, 1997.

to store peanuts owned by the plaintiff. This contract of bailment was concluded on the foot of the defendant's standard conditions of business. One of the clauses provided that the defendant was not to be liable for loss or damage to goods unless such loss or damage was due to wilful neglect or default. The peanuts were damaged by rats and although the defendant had been negligent it had not acted with wilful neglect or default. Donaldson J. held that the clause was effective. It provided the defendant with a complete answer to the action because the clause made it clear that the defendant was not undertaking to excuse reasonable care and skill. The clause also excluded the ordinary duty of a bailee for reward. This approach to the interpretation of the exemption clause is based on the assumption that the court should read the contract in its entirety and that a limitation of liability clause cannot merely limit liability but can also limit the duty undertaken by the person relying on the clause.

7–05 It must, however, be conceded that there are other views of the role of an exemption clause. Some judges hold that the clause merely operates as a defence to liability and that the approach to be adopted in the interpretation of an exemption clause is to leave the clause to one side and then interpret the contract so as to see what the parties have undertaken. The clause is then examined to see if it provides a defence to the plaintiff's action. The best example of such a process is the judgment of Denning L.J. in *Karsales (Harrow) Ltd v Wallis*.[8] This theoretical debate does have some important practical consequences, as we shall see.

7–06 The exemption clause possessing substantive effect is designed to allocate risk between contracting parties—should goods stored with a bailee under a bailment contract be destroyed while in his possession, the bailee may have anticipated this possibility and by contract transferred risk to the owner. In principle there is no reason why this should not be permitted where the bailee has not acted fraudulently or deliberately destroyed the goods. Difficulties arise when the party invoking the exemption clause is in a stronger bargaining position and has exploited this by including a draconian provision which, on its face, protects him in every situation. The courts and the legislature have dealt with such instances of abuse of freedom of contract in different ways. This Chapter is concerned with the judicial response to exemption clauses, and while the author concedes that no neat demarcation can exist here, the legislative method of countering abuse of superior bargaining power (and in particular the exemption clause) is considered in the next chapter.

7–07 While most exemption clauses are written statements which are found either in the contract document itself, or in standard conditions of contract, there are instances where one party may verbally limit the scope of his contractual duty. In *Hughes v J.J. Power Ltd and Colliers Ltd*[9] the plaintiff

---

[8]   [1956] 1 W.L.R. 936.
[9]   Unreported, High Court, May 11, 1988.

took a tractor engine to the second defendant, a motor engineer, in order to have the engine serviced. The work to be done was somewhat difficult due to certain defects in the engine and the second defendant indicated that he would do the work but that the work would be done at the owner's risk. Blayney J. held that the effect of this statement was that the second defendant would not be liable for any physical damage caused during the necessary work and that a term to this effect was to be imported into the contract. This case provides a neat illustration of the fact that clauses which exclude a particular duty are essentially concerned with risk transfer or risk allocation.

7–08 The distinction between procedural and substantive clauses has been, in general, overlooked but some residual effects can occasionally be detected. There have been a number of situations where the proferens has been successful in arguing that a specific provision in a contract is not an exclusion clause. We consider these cases generally later on in this chapter in relation to entire agreement clauses, but essentially the argument presented here is that the contract is intended to identify the contractual nexus in a particular way. In other words, despite appearances the objective is not to sell goods that are subject to the implied terms in the Sale of Goods and Supply of Services Act 1893–1980. A contract to sell a second hand motor vehicle to a collector who wishes to use the exceptionally well preserved body panels and coachwork to restore another vehicle would afford an example. Many of the cases involve financial services contracts where the service provider seeks to limit or exclude liability for services to be rendered.[10] The utility of provisions of this kind lie in the fact that the assumed state of affairs by which the parties are contracting can operate as an estoppel (the precise nature of which is contentious) but the assumed state of affairs may prevent a court from implying common law implied terms, implied representations and statutory implied terms into any contract that has come into existence. There may also be grounds for holding that an inference is to be drawn that the parties are agreed that some statutory relief is not to be available in the circumstances of that case, e.g. under s. 46 of the Sale of Goods and Supply of Services Act 1980, or that the provisions in question are fair and reasonable under the statutory test.

7–09 Before an exemption clause (also known as an exclusion or exculpatory clause) will be permitted to take effect, it must pass two tests. First of all, the provision upon which the party asserting it seeks to rely (the proferens) must be incorporated into the contract. Secondly, as a matter of construction, the clause must cover the events that have occurred. We will deal with these issues separately.

---

[10] *Tudor Grange Holdings v Citibank* [1992] Ch.53 at 65-66; *Springwell Navigation Corporation v JP Morgan Chase Bank* [2010] EWCA Civ 1221; *Crestsign Ltd v National Westminster Bank plc* [2014] EWHC 3043 (Ch).

Incorporation

(1) Basic rules

7–10 The Irish judges, like their English brethren, have struggled with the problem of incorporation because the tests advanced have varied from time to time. This is particularly so when it is clear that the party against whom the clause is asserted has not read the exempting provision. In one early Irish case the plaintiff was held bound by an exempting provision printed on a railway ticket which exempted the company from liability should passengers be injured. The plaintiff was bound because he was said to have had the means of discovering the clause, that is, constructive notice: *Johnson v Gt. Southern & W. Ry.*[11] Three years later the English Court of Appeal decided the leading case of *Parker v S.E. Railway.*[12] In cases where someone is given a ticket or document which sets out or refers to limiting conditions to be read elsewhere the proferens will be able to rely on the terms if he can show that the other party read them or that he, the proferens, did everything reasonable to bring the clause to the attention of the public. Several questions were set out in *Parker v S.E. Railway* which the court should ask; these questions can be paraphrased in the following way:

(1) Did the party know of the conditions? If so he is bound.[13]

(2) Was notice given? If not the other party is not bound.[14]

(3) If notice was given but the other party did not know the notice contained writing he will not necessarily be bound.[15]

(4) If he did know there was writing on the document then the court must ask whether reasonable notice of the conditions has been given. If the other party knows the ticket contained not merely writing but conditions he will be bound even if he is unaware of the precise terms.[16]

The reasonableness test marks an improvement on the earlier *Johnson* case but there are still difficult issues of fact to be resolved. In the case of *Richardson Spence & Co v Rowntree*[17] the House of Lords applied the approach outlined earlier in *Parker*. The plaintiff was a passenger on a steamer travelling from Liverpool to Philadelphia. The plaintiff was given a folded ticket, no writing being visible in this form. The ticket when opened had a great many conditions, one of which limited liability for personal injury or loss of baggage to $100. The plaintiff never read the ticket. The plaintiff was injured whilst on the vessel. At first instance Bruce J. left three questions to the jury:

---

[11] (1874) I.R. 9 C.L. 108.
[12] (1877) 2 C.P.D. 416. *Shepherd Homes Ltd v Encia Remediation Ltd* [2007] EWHC 70 (TCC).
[13] (1877) 2 C.P.D. 416.
[14] *Roche v Corke, Blackrock and Passage Railway* (1889) 24 L.R. (Ir.) 250.
[15] The inquiry then passes to examine whether reasonable notice was given.
[16] *Taggart v Northern Counties Ry.* (1898) 32 I.L.T. 404.
[17] [1894] A.C. 297.

(1) Did the plaintiff know that there was writing on the ticket? This question was answered in the affirmative.

(2) Did the plaintiff know the writing contained conditions relative to the contract of carriage? This was answered in the negative.

(3) Did the defendants do what was reasonably sufficient to give the plaintiff notice of these conditions? This question was answered in the negative.

The High Court, Court of Appeal and House of Lords held that in the light of these findings the limitation clause was not available to the defendant. This decision was applied in *Ryan v Great Southern & Western Ry.*[18] in 1898. The plaintiff's baggage had been lost by the defendant. The terms of the plaintiff's ticket referred to standard conditions which were available for inspection. Upon finding that the plaintiff was unaware that the ticket contained limiting conditions of contract it was further held that insufficient notice had been given of the term. However, the case of *Taggart v Northern Counties Ry.*,[19] also decided in 1898, illustrates the fact that if the plaintiff is found to know that the ticket or contract document contains contractual conditions, the plaintiff will be bound even if he is unaware of the precise terms of contract.

7–11 The Irish courts have not laid down exacting standards which a proferens must meet before the limiting term will be incorporated. In the case of *Early v Gt. Southern Ry.*[20] the plaintiff was given an excursion ticket which, on its face, referred the passenger to the company's special conditions containing the limiting provisions. The plaintiff was injured. Notwithstanding the fact that the conditions were not available for inspection at this particular booking office the defendants were held entitled to rely on this clause. At times the judges display a quite unrealistic view of the problems confronting the person who contracts with a service provider, particularly when a monopoly is enjoyed by that provider. In *Shea v Great Southern Ry.*[21] the plaintiff took a bicycle onto a crowded bus. The bus ticket referred to a notice excluding liability for theft. The plaintiff was held bound by the notice. Judge Davitt said that the plaintiff was "at liberty to get off the bus or remove his bicycle".

7–12 If the proferens wants to be sure that the clause will be incorporated into the contract he should obtain the signature of the other party to a contract document setting out the term; see *Duff v Gt. Northern Railway*.[22] On signature the other party will be bound, even if the document is unread and the terms are set out in miniscule print. In the leading English case of *L'Estrange v F. Graucob*[23] the Court of Appeal reaffirmed the statement made in the *Parker*

---

[18] (1898) 32 I.L.T.R. 108.
[19] (1898) 32 I.L.T. 404. See also, *Balmoral Group Property Ltd v Borealis UK* [2006] EWHC 1900 (Comm) (invoice known to contain conditions and initialled by recipient).
[20] [1940] I.R. 414.
[21] [1944] Ir. Jur. Rep. 26.
[22] (1878) 4 L.R. (Ir.) 178.
[23] [1934] 2 K.B. 394.

case about the effect of signature; only if the signature is obtained by fraud or misrepresentation will the contract be held not to include a limiting clause. While this proposition has never been expressly overruled in England it must be considered as having been much qualified by the more recent English, Irish and Canadian cases. Speaking obiter, in *AGM Londis plc v Gorman's Supermarket Ltd*,[24] Barrett J. said

> "it can be argued that a signature cannot be treated, *ipso facto* in all instances and every circumstance, and without further consideration, to bind a significantly weaker party to every detail of contractual dealings which he genuinely purports not to understand and which the stronger counterparty admits were complicated by its own actions."

(2) The time at which notice was given

7–13 The general rule is that notice of a limiting clause, given after the contract is concluded, cannot bind the other party. In *Sproule v Triumph Cycle Co*[25] the plaintiff approached an agent of the defendants with a view to buying a motor cycle. He did not read a catalogue which attempted to limit the defendants' obligations to replacement of defective parts for three months after purchase. This "guarantee" was also set out on a card attached to the bike although this was not handed to the plaintiff and read by him until after the sale had been concluded. The plaintiff was held entitled to rely on s.14(1) of the 1893 Act. Moore C.J. held the guarantee ineffective because it was not read until after the contract had been concluded. It should be noted that when the case does not involve a railway ticket the onus on the proferens is greater when he alleges incorporation has occurred. In the well-known English case of *Olley v Marlborough Court Ltd*[26] the defendant let a hotel room to a husband and wife. At the time of checking into the hotel, the defendants obtained payment in advance for a one-week stay. On arriving in the hotel room, the husband and wife for the first time were made aware in the form of a printed notice that the hotel proprietor sought to exclude liability for theft or loss of articles of property unless handed to the hotel management for safekeeping. The wife left the hotel room and left the key downstairs in reception. The key was taken by a thief who stole her furs. The defendant unsuccessfully pleaded the notice excluding liability. The majority of the Court of Appeal held that the notice was not part of the contract because the contract had been formed at the reception desk prior to entry into the room. In *Thornton v Shoe Lane Parking Ltd*[27] Denning M.R. used the same line of reasoning in the context of a contract whereby the plaintiff was permitted to use the defendants' multi-storey car park. Entry was effected by way of an automatic barrier, the barrier being

---

)5.

. The importance of drawing attention to disclaimers in "battle of the forms" ically illustrated by *Noreside Construction Ltd v Irish Asphalt Ltd* [2014] IESC

532; *Jayaar Impex Ltd v Toaken Group* [1996] 2 Lloyd's Rep. 437.
163.

operated through a ticket machine. While the ticket contained a notice that the ticket was issued subject to conditions displayed on the premises, actual notice of the terms could only be given to members of the public after entry into the building. Denning M.R. opined that the offer was made via the terms stated on the outside of the building and that the offer was accepted by approaching the barrier and taking the ticket: the contract was concluded on terms which did not include the terms found within the building. In contrast, however, in *Brady v Aer Rianta*, the printed conditions were set out on the ticket and the terms were actually displayed on a notice board outside the entrance to the car parking area at Dublin Airport. Butler J. held that in these circumstances the contract was concluded before the plaintiff entered the parking area and the defendant had given reasonable notice of a limitation clause prior to the contract being formed. This reasoning has been followed in *O'Beirne v Aer Rianta*.[28]

7–14 Two Irish cases that, at first sight, seem to be inconsistent with this reasoning are *Knox v Gt. Northern Railway*[29] and *Slattery v C.I.É.*[30] Both cases concerned contracts to transport a horse, the horse being injured as a result of the defendant's employee's negligence. In *Slattery v C.I.É.* the plaintiff signed a consignment note which stated that delivery would take place at the owner's risk. This note was not signed until after the injury to the horse had occurred and after the journey had been completed: this was an oversight on the defendant's part. The defendant was held to be entitled to rely on the document as setting out the terms of the agreement. It should be noted that in this case, as in *Knox*, the plaintiff envisaged that the contract document had still to be completed; as Holmes J. said in *Knox*: "It is neither illegal, unreasonable nor unusual, for the terms of a contract to be reduced to writing after the performance of the services contracted for has been begun." If this was a case of the proferens attempting to add an exempting clause when a written or oral contract had already been completed, as occurred in *Olley v Marlborough Court Ltd,* such an attempt would no doubt fail in Ireland. In *Noreside Construction Ltd v Irish Asphalt Ltd*[31] the Supreme Court upheld Finlay Geoghegan J.'s view that documents in the form of delivery dockets could not provide notice of terms that could alter one central or master contract because the dockets came too late in time. The dockets merely recorded facts relating to delivery. There was no attempt to alter terms (e.g. on price) and, as such, these dockets filled in a narrative relating to performance of the master contract rather than being indicative of a number of distinct contracts.

---

[28] Judgment of Barrington J., delivered ex tempore on May 20, 1987. The earlier judgment of Butler J. in *Brady v Aer Rianta* was delivered in 1974 but is undated.

[29] [1896] 2 I.R. 632.

[30] (1972) 106 I.L.T.R. 71.

[31] [2014] IESC 68. See the earlier case of *Moynihan v Crowley & Warren & Co* [1958] Ir. Jur. Rep. 21.

(3) Incorporation—new wine in old bottles?

7–15 It is not too much of a generalisation to say that when the courts were faced with the problem of counteracting exemption clauses in circumstances where the agreement had not been freely negotiated or consented to, or where the result of allowing the exemption clause to operate was repugnant to the court's sense of justice and fair play, the most natural response was to require the clause itself to be couched in the clearest possible terms. At times this led to the most artificial distinctions imaginable; witness the attempt of counsel in *Ailsa Craig Fishing Co Ltd v Malvern Fishing Co*[32] to argue that the word "default" would allow the proferens to rely on an exemption clause if he attempted to discharge his contractual duty and failed, but that the clause would not be operative if there was a total failure to attempt performance. The House of Lords on several occasions has urged judges to resist "the temptation to resort to the device of ascribing to the words appearing in exemption clauses a tortured meaning": per Lord Diplock in *Ailsa Craig*, above. While the primary reason for this appeal to abandon the covert but unsatisfactory approach of giving plain words a strained and at times fanciful meaning is the fact that the legislators have intervened, another factor that must be considered is the greater awareness amongst the judiciary that the proferens was, under the old incorporation tests, given too much latitude. The proferens can no longer assume that the exemption clause will be readily admitted to the contract. The realisation that the rules on incorporation were framed during the heyday of freedom of contract and that these rules were often totally inappropriate, even at that time, has transformed the approach of the judges to questions of incorporation. As the judge in *Hollingworth v Southern Ferries Ltd*[33] put it:

> "Although the principles enunciated in *Parker* and reaffirmed subsequently have remained constant and do remain constant, the application of those principles have (*sic*) altered considerably in recent years. There is increased consciousness of the need to protect consumers."[34]

Sometimes protection is afforded by adopting the view that before a particular clause can be incorporated the proferens must show that the other party should have normally encountered a clause of this type and scope. In *Thornton v Shoe Lane Parking Ltd*[35] a clause on a ticket issued from an automatic vending machine was denied effect by holding that it had not been incorporated into the contract. The ticket attempted to exclude liability, not simply for the theft of the car and/or its contents; but also for liability for personal injury to the consumer, even if caused by the negligence of company employees. Sufficient notice of this particular clause had not been given. Factors such as

---

[32] [1983] 1 W.L.R. 964. See also *Photo Production Ltd v Securicor Transport Ltd* [1980] 2 W.L.R. 283; *George Mitchell (Chesterhall) Ltd v Finney Lock Seeds Ltd* [1983] 2 A.C. 803; *Bovis Construction (Scotland) Ltd v Whatlings Construction Ltd* (1995) 46 Con. L.R. 103.
[33] [1977] 2 Lloyd's Rep. 70.
[34] [1977] 2 Lloyd's Rep. 70 at 78 per Deputy Judge Ogden.
[35] [1971] 2 Q.B. 163.

the size of the print, whether the clause was clearly set out, the kind of risk or liability it excluded or limited, were not generally relevant under the *Parker* tests and they were clearly irrelevant if the contract was signed. The decision of the Court of Appeal in *Interfoto Picture Library Ltd v Stiletto Visual Programmes Ltd*,[36] while not ostensibly concerned with exemption clauses, is a landmark decision on the issue of incorporation of contractual terms, when not specifically drawn to the attention of the other party. The defendant, an advertising agency, obtained photographs from the plaintiff, a company that operated a photographic library. The photographs were to be used in preparing an advertising campaign, but the photographs were not actually used in the campaign. The parties had not dealt with each other before and the photographs were supplied on foot of a delivery note which set out conditions of contract in some detail. These terms were probably not read. One of the terms provided that if not returned after 14 days a fee of £5 per day per photograph would be charged. By oversight the defendant held onto the transparencies for a further 14 days and was sent an invoice for the charges calculated under this condition: some £3,783.50. The defendant disputed the charge. The Court of Appeal held that the condition was not part of the contract because its existence had not been drawn to the attention of the defendant. Dillon L.J. said:

> "It is in my judgment a logical development of the common law into modern conditions that it should be held, as it was in *Thornton v Shoe Lane Parking Ltd.*, that, if one condition in a set of printed conditions is particularly onerous or unusual, the party seeking to enforce it must show that that particular condition was fairly brought to the attention of the other party."[37]

This line of authority was endorsed by Costello J. in *Carroll v An Post National Lottery Co.*[38] After finding that the plaintiff was aware that his lottery playslip contained conditions, even though the plaintiff did not read them, Costello J. considered that the defendant had to establish that where other contracting parties habitually did not read those conditions the party using such conditions "must show that it has been fairly and reasonably brought to the other party's attention". Costello J. stressed that this requirement was based on both contractual principles and the concept of fair dealing, as articulated by Bingham L.J. in the *Interfoto* case. Costello J. concluded obiter that on the facts before him, the particular clauses relied upon by the defendants were able to satisfy this reasonableness requirement.

7–16 So then, the narrow rules on incorporation have in recent years broadened into a general analysis of whether it is fair that the term is included.

---

[36] [1988] 1 All E.R. 348. See Bradgate, "Unreasonable Standard Terms" (1997) 60(4) M.L.R. 582.

[37] [1988] 1 All E.R. 348 at 352.

[38] [1996] 1 I.R. 443. *McCabe Builders (Dublin) Ltd v Sagamu Developments Ltd* [2007] IEHC 391, appeal allowed on another point: [2009] IESC 31.

This principle is, of course, not simply concerned with consumer protection. In *Kaye v Nu Skin*[39] Kitchin J. considered that both the standard incorporation tests and the residual issue that Bingham M.R. approved in *Interfoto*—whether it would be fair to hold the clause binding—required the clause to be held inapplicable. The defendant was a young woman, inexperienced in business and the clause was both an onerous one and at odds with the way in which the parties had conducted themselves prior to concluding the contract. This question has been extensively reviewed by the Supreme Court in *Noreside Construction Ltd v Irish Asphalt Ltd*[40] and *James Elliott Construction Ltd v Irish Asphalt Ltd*.[41] Both cases concerned issues of incorporation but the central question was whether delivery dockets, signed when the buyer's "agent" authorised delivery of materials onto various building sites, could form part of the contract. In these cases the delivery dockets simply referred to the seller's conditions which were available on request. The Supreme Court indicated that notice of the terms themselves needed to be given; a cross reference of this kind would not be adequate notice given the broad scope of the clause and its effects.

7–17 If the rules are not unusual or onerous—for example, the rules in a newspaper "scratchcard" sales promotion scheme—it will be relatively easy for the proferens to satisfy the reasonableness standard.[42] Even if the clauses are sweeping in their consequences a proferens should be able to overcome the incorporation hurdle by exercising thought and care. In *Amiri Flight Authority v BAE Systems Plc*[43] the defendants sought to exclude liability through a disclaimer set out at the end of the substantive provisions, the disclaimers in fact being separately set out because the contract document was in reality a number of distinct contracts. The exclusion was set out in capital letters and the positioning of the exclusion was such that Tomlinson J. could see "no basis on which it can be said that the clause has not fairly and reasonably been brought to the attention of the buyer".[44] Where, however, the clause effectively takes away a buyer's common law and statutory rights where the consequences of breach are potentially horrific, a different result will follow. In *James Elliott Construction Ltd v Irish Asphalt Ltd*[45] Charleton J. found that reasonable notice had not been given of a disclaimer that was both onerous in its terms and highly prejudicial to the buyer. The clause, which sought to exclude liability for building aggregate which was used as hardcore, defects being catastrophic for the structure built upon this material,

---

[39] [2011] 1 Lloyd's Rep. 40.
[40] [2014] IESC 68.
[41] [2014] IESC 74.
[42] *O'Brien v MGN Ltd* [2002] C.L.C. 33.
[43] [2003] 1 Lloyd's Rep. 50, overruled by the Court of Appeal at [2003] 2 Lloyd's Rep. 767 on another point.
[44] [2003] 1 Lloyd's Rep. 50 at 59; *Maxitherm Boilers Pty Ltd v Pacific Dunlop* [1998] 4 V.R. 559.
[45] [2011] IEHC 269.

"... is a highly onerous clause and one which would otherwise not be expected. It would leave the builder to lose his reputation and possibly his profit, and more, should the material turn out not only to be of bad quality but also to be actively dangerous to the contemplated construction project. Therefore, it was entirely reasonable for Irish Asphalt to set out its terms and conditions from the very start. This it failed to do; though that is probably what it would have done had office systems been reliable".

Delivery dockets provided to the buyers' "deliveries" staff did not incorporate the clause as such staff were not responsible for negotiating contracts. Absent actual knowledge being provided to the buyers prior to the first delivery, a clause of this kind, poorly communicated to the buyer, would rarely pass muster, Charleton J. clearly felt. The Supreme Court upheld Charleton J.'s reasoning on the incorporation question.[46]

7–18 No direct attack has been launched on the rule that signature of the contract, in the absence of fraud or misrepresentation, will incorporate the clause. This proposition, stated in *Parker* and reaffirmed in England in *L'Estrange v F. Graucob*[47] and *Curtis v Chemical Cleaning and Dyeing Co*[48] has horrific results in cases where the proferens is allowed to utilise the signature rule in cases of personal injury or death, as the case of *Delaney v Cascade River Holdings Ltd*[49] illustrates. Cases such as *Crocker v Sundance Northwest Resorts Ltd*,[50] in which signature was held by the Supreme Court of Canada not to indicate assent to the terms proposed, are much to be preferred. Even in non-personal injury cases signature has been held to be inconclusive. For example, in two Canadian cases the consumer could not reasonably have expected this kind of clause to be included in the contract where the clause was tucked away in small print: see *Tilden Rent-A-Car Co v Glendenning*[51] followed in *Tilden Rent-A-Car Co v Chandra*.[52] In *Le Mans Grand Prix Circuits Pty Ltd v Iliadis*,[53] a majority of the Victoria Court of Appeal held that a disclaimer signed by the plaintiff prior to participating in a promotional race at a go-kart track was not binding. There was no evidence of a commercial dealing between the parties, no fee was paid, and the participants believed they were signing a registration and licensing form rather than a contractual disclaimer. In the absence of any attempt to point out the nature of the document or explain the effect of the disclaimer, the plaintiff's right to recover for the defendant's negligence was not affected.

---

[46] [2014] IESC 74.
[47] [1934] 2 K.B. 394.
[48] [1951] 1 K.B. 805.
[49] [1983] 44 B.C.L.R. 24.
[50] [1988] 1 S.C.R. 1186. In *Crocker* the plaintiff was in an inebriated condition. More recent Canadian cases place great importance on signature in the context of hazardous sporting activities (e.g. *Loychuk v Cougar Mountain Adventures* [2012] BCCA 193).
[51] (1978) 83 D.L.R. (3d) 400.
[52] (1984) 150 D.L.R. (3d) 685.
[53] [1998] 4 V.R. 661; *Alameddine v Glenworth* (2015) 324 A.L.R. 355.

7–19 In Ireland there has not yet been any direct assault on the signature rule but in the case of *Regan v The Irish Automobile Club Ltd*[54] Lynch J. noted that while the plaintiff had signed a release form which waived the liability of the defendant, it was also established by the evidence that the plaintiff was aware of the fact that she had signed a document that restricted her rights in the event of accidental injury. Also, in *O'Connor v First National Building Society*[55] the plaintiff's signature on a house loan application form, which excluded the defendant from liability should the property be defective, was held to bind the plaintiff. It was significant, in Lynch J.'s view, that the exemption clause was prominently displayed just above the place of signature. These two cases provide evidence that the signature, ipso facto, will not necessarily incorporate the clause and, in general, this perspective is in line with the recent English and Canadian cases. Nevertheless the signature rule is not dead. In a proper context it has been described as a good general principle of law by a distinguished Australian court[56] and the signature rule will tend to be applied on a case-by-case basis.

7–20 This approach is not confined to consumer transactions. In *Western Meats Ltd v National Ice and Cold Storage Co*[57] a contract of bailment was allegedly concluded on the defendant's standard form conditions which provided, inter alia, that the company would not be answerable for any "delay, loss or damage caused by their own negligence or any cause whatsoever". The defendants negligently failed to label the plaintiff's goods so that when the plaintiff came to collect them they could not be easily retrieved, causing loss to the plaintiff's business. Barrington J. held that, while the parties were competent to agree on their own terms of contract, "a businessman, offering a specialist service, but accepting no responsibility for it, must bring home clearly to the party dealing with him that he accepts no such responsibility". In commenting on this case in *Sugar Distributors Ltd v Monaghan Cash and Carry Ltd*,[58] Carroll J. pointed out that the significant factors in the earlier case were that the service was a specialist one for which the specialist was taking no responsibility and that negotiations to commence the relationship between the parties did not involve mention of this sweeping clause, set out on a receipt. In *Sugar Distributors* the reservation of title clause, was a commonplace one

---

[54] [1990] 1 I.R. 278.

[55] [1991] I.L.R.M. 208; *Staunton v Toyota (Ireland)* [1996] 1 I.L.R.M. 171.

[56] *Toll (FGCT) Pty Ltd v Alphapharm Pty* (2003) 56 N.S.W.L.R. 662, affirmed by the High Court of Australia (*Toll (FGCT) Pty Ltd v Alphapharm Pty Ltd* (2004) 219 C.L.R. 165) on this point. *Scheps Fine Art Logistic Ltd* [2007] EWHC 541 (Q.B.) provides an interesting marginal situation on professional involvement and incorporation of terms. It should be contrasted with both the *British Crane Hire* case and *Laceys Footwear (Wholesale) Ltd v Bowler International Freight Ltd* [1997] 2 Lloyd's Rep. 369.

[57] [1982] I.L.R.M. 101. See O'Donnell J.'s treatment of this case in *James Elliott Construction Ltd v Irish Asphalt Ltd* [2014] IESC 74. The employees in question should be the kinds of employee that could be expected to form contracts. Marketing and accounts department personnel in the construction industry did not fall into such categories—see in particular *James Elliott Construction* at para.140, per O'Donnell J.

[58] [1982] I.L.R.M. 399.

couched in simple language and clearly visible on the face of the document. It was given effect.

(4) Incorporation by a course of dealing

7–21 The rules on incorporation present difficult issues of fact for the courts because a litigant who argues that he did not read the document cannot prove this contention very easily, and vice versa. If the parties contract with each other frequently and on a regular basis, however, the court has to balance the obvious injustice of holding one party bound by a term which he did not read (much less assent to) against the expectations of the proferens. If the parties contract regularly and the proferens issues documents which transfer risk to the other party he is entitled to assume that there is assent to the terms offered. Thus, in *Spurling v Bradshaw*[59] the owner of goods contracted to store his property with the defendant. These bailment contracts took place regularly. On each occasion the bailee handed over a document which limited the bailee's liability. The plaintiff at no time read the document or the conditions. This was not a ticket case—it was a contract freely negotiated. The English Court of Appeal held the plaintiff bound by this limiting clause: "by the course of business and conduct of the parties these conditions were part of the contract." If the clause in question is found in a particular trade or is commonly used in standard invoices, the term will be incorporated, even if utilised by a negligent defendant, certainly if there are as many as 11 previous instances of dealing between the parties; see *Circle Freight International v Medeast Gulf Exports*.[60]

7–22 For incorporation by a course of dealing to occur, the trade practice relied on by the proferens must be consistent. One or two isolated transactions do not constitute a course of dealing unless both parties are of similar bargaining strength and operate on terms which are acknowledged to be common within their industry; see *British Crane Hire Corp v Ipswich Plant Hire*.[61] This case was followed in *Lynch Roofing Systems (Ballaghaderreen) Ltd v Christopher Bennett and Son (Construction) Ltd*.[62] The parties were in dispute over a roofing contract; the plaintiff as a sub-contractor issued proceedings which the defendant sought to stay on the basis that the parties had agreed to an arbitration. Prior to the contract the defendant had notified the plaintiff of his intention to use an industry standard contract which contained an arbitration clause. The plaintiff argued he was not bound by such a clause because he had not agreed to it, nor had this been explained to him prior to commencement of work. Morris P. held that where both parties were engaged in the same business

---

[59] [1956] 1 W.L.R. 461.
[60] [1988] 2 Lloyd's Rep. 427. See also *Balmoral Group Property Ltd v Borealis UK* [2006] EWHC 1900 (Comm).
[61] [1975] Q.B. 303.
[62] [1999] 2 I.R. 450. *McCrory Scaffolding Ltd v McInerney Construction* [2004] IEHC 346. Post the Arbitration Act 2010 see *John G. Burns Ltd v Grange Construction and Roofing Co* [2013] IEHC 284 and *Mount Juliet Properties Ltd v Melcarne Developments Ltd* [2013] IEHC 286.

and of equal bargaining power, standard conditions habitually used would be part of the contract because of a common understanding that those conditions would apply. The basic impetus for this approach is not so much the course of dealing between the parties but a desire to give effect to expectations that have been created by commercial practice, where industry-wide, or created by the terms of a contract. A defendant who drafts the terms of the offer and acceptance, thus stipulating formalities and procedures to be followed, is unlikely to be able to rely on those terms being incorporated if the defendant fails to comply with his own prescribed formulae: *Jonathan Wren & Co Ltd v Microdec Plc*.[63]

7–23 The courts are less inclined to find a limiting clause has been incorporated if the transaction involves a large business and an individual consumer. In *Hollier v Rambler Motors*[64] the owner of a motor vehicle had left his car to be repaired with the defendants on three or four occasions over a number of years. He had then been given a receipt containing a limiting clause. On the occasion in question he left his car with the defendants again but he was not given a receipt containing the clause. The Court of Appeal held that the three or four isolated transactions between consumer and proferens did not incorporate the limiting clause into their last contract. The plaintiff was able to recover for the loss of his car when the garage burnt down.

7–24 In *Miley v R. & J. McKechnie Ltd*[65] the plaintiff left a garment to be cleaned. The defendants' employee gave her a receipt, marked "important", which set out on the face "all orders accepted without guarantee" and directed the attention of holders to conditions printed on the back. Miss Miley had contracted with the defendants regularly and had always been given such a receipt. She claimed that she at no time read the conditions but did know that the writing contained conditions. Judge Shannon held that display of conditions and the invariable practice of handing a ticket were sufficient to exempt the defendants from liability. The fact that Ms Miley had not read the conditions and that the ticket was given after the contract was concluded was unimportant given the course of dealing between the parties. *Miley* would be decided differently under the 1980 Act; s.40 requires a limiting clause be specifically brought to the attention of the consumer although Costello J., in *Carroll v An Post National Lottery Co*, held that this provision can be satisfied even if the party relying on a printed condition does not expressly draw the consumer's attention to the clause at the time of agreement. The Supreme Court in the two *Irish Asphalt* cases stressed that where the terms in question can be described as "onerous" the standard of reasonableness will involve a consideration of the degree of notice given. It can be deduced from the reasoning in these cases that if the terms are standard within a trade or industry, a cross reference to

---

[63] (1999) 65 Con. L.R. 157.
[64] [1972] 2 Q.B. 71.
[65] (1949) 84 I.L.T.R. 89.

those terms may suffice. In other cases, as Dunne J. said in *Noreside*, "the document relied on by the party asserting the terms and conditions should actually contain either the conditions themselves or in some other way identify the terms and conditions relied on."

(5) Web consent

7–25 Contracts and web access have raised issues of consent. In *Ryanair v Billigfluege de GmbH*[66] Hanna J. applied the traditional approach to inferred consent to a situation where Ryanair, through its terms and conditions that could be accessed by website users by clicking onto a link that was prominently displayed, sought to enforce terms, including an exclusive jurisdiction clause, on the defendant. The defendant had been "screenscraping" Ryanair's proprietary information, for its own commercial purposes, in breach of the terms and conditions. While no clicked consent could be shown, Hanna J. said that Ryanair's terms were clear and unambiguous and the defendant's consent was established, through access and use of the site. As between commercial entities the exclusive jurisdiction clause was contractually binding.[67] In contrast, terms and conditions in an online gaming contract were not binding in *Spreadex Ltd v Cochrane*.[68] In this case, standard terms in a clause imposed payment obligations on the defendant in a wide range of circumstances without requiring the terms to be read prior to hitting the "Agree" button:

> "[I]f, exceptionally, the defendant in fact chose to look at the documents, he would have been faced in the Customer Agreement alone with 49 pages containing the same number of closely printed and complex paragraphs. It would have come close to a miracle if he had read the second sentence of Clause 10(3), let alone appreciated its purport or implications, and it would have been quite irrational for the claimant to assume that he had."

Construction of the Exemption Clause

7–26 While it is no doubt paradoxical to adopt less than demanding rules on incorporation while at the same time requiring the proferens to draft the clause with great precision, Lord O'Hagan defended this position when he said in *McNally v Lancs & York Railway*[69]:

---

[66] [2010] IEHC 47 (appeal dismissed at [2015] IESC 11); *eBay International AG v Creative Festival Entertainment Pty Ltd* (2006) 170 F.C.R. 450.

[67] Distinguishing these facts from *Thornton v Shoe Lane Parking Ltd* and *Interfoto Picture Library Ltd v Stilleto Visual Programs Ltd*. The substantive issues in the *Ryanair* dispute remain to be decided: see *Ryanair v Club Travel Ltd* [2012] IEHC 165 and *Ryanair v On the Beach Ltd* [2013] IEHC 124.

[68] [2012] EWHC 1290 (Comm).

[69] (1880) 8 L.R. (Ir.) 81.

"There can be no hardship imposed by requiring companies to be clear and explicit in the framing of conditions designed for their own security. The humble and ignorant dealers who enter into transactions are at a disadvantage and at least they should be held strictly to the terms of the contracts deliberately prepared by their skilled advisors."[70]

In viewing an exemption clause restrictively the courts have developed several important rules or maxims of construction. However, the general approach sanctioned by the courts in relation to the interpretation of exemption clauses in recent years has inclined towards the view that where a commercial document is before the court, the court should strive towards a meaning that accords with business commonsense. Strained interpretation, or an interpretation that results in unreasonable results, must be eschewed or sidestepped, as the case may be. Most importantly of all is the context within which the clause was intended to operate: "construction is a composite exercise, neither uncompromisingly literal nor unswervingly purposive: the instrument must speak for itself, but it must do so *in situ* and not be transported to the laboratory for microscopic analysis."[71] The operation of this general approach is best illustrated by the decision of the Court of Appeal in *The Kleovoulos of Rhodes*.[72] The claimants insured a vessel against detention under a war risk policy, one of the exemptions being for "arrest ... by reason of infringement of any customs or trading regulations". The vessel docked in a Greek port where customs officers discovered cocaine in a chest. The vessel was detained for six months; the crew were tried but acquitted on drug smuggling charges. The claimants failed to recover on the insurance policy because the exempting provision was held to apply. The claimants sought to argue that "customs" related to import duties as the basis for detention. The Court of Appeal held that, in the context of an international contract of insurance, the wider interpretation was the norm. Further, earlier case law[73] had ruled on this point and contract draftsmen were to be taken as familiar with the case law and to have intended to adopt such a meaning. Absent such a clear and distinctive pedigree as the clause scrutinised in *The Kleovoulos of Rhodes*, the search for the ordinary meaning of the words used by the parties, judged in context, may lead a court to turn to these maxims or canons of interpretation. Although case law does not directly sanction this view, it may be that these canons of construction are more likely to be adopted in consumer transactions rather than arm's-length commercial contracts. But the starting point is the application of the ordinary meaning of the words. In *Insight Vacations Pty Ltd v Young*[74] the plaintiff was injured when the holiday coach she was travelling in braked suddenly. The plaintiff was retrieving items

---

[70] (1880) 8 L.R. (Ir.) 81 at 92.

[71] *Arbuthnott v Fagan* [1995] C.L.C. 1396 at 1400 per Bingham M.R., followed in *International Fina Services AG v Katarina Shipping Ltd* [1995] 2 Lloyd's Rep. 364.

[72] [2003] 1 Lloyd's Rep. 138. See also the "inherent vice" exclusion in *Global Process Systems Inc. v Berhad* [2011] UKSC 5.

[73] *The Anita* [1971] 1 Lloyd's Rep. 138.

[74] [2011] HCA 111; *Cleary v Rowland* [2009] NIQB 4.

from the overhead luggage rack at this time. The holiday company sought to rely on a clause requiring passengers to use fitted seatbelts. The High Court of Australia held that the contract did not require the passenger to remain seated at all times when the coach was in motion; "the provision of a lavatory at the rear of the coach shows that the operator accepted that a passenger could, and sometimes would, get out of his or her seat".

(1) The contra proferentem *rule*

7–27 If the exempting provision is ambiguous and capable of more than one interpretation then the courts will read the clause against the party seeking to rely on it. This rule is of general application in some contractual settings and it has recently been discussed in the interpretation of an option agreement: *Kramer v Arnold*.[75] The *contra proferentem* rule of interpretation, however, comes into its own in the context of exempting provisions in an agreement. In consumer transactions this will be an important rule, of benefit to the consumer, because it will generally be the seller who asserts that he is entitled to rely on the clause. In *Sproule v Triumph Cycle Co*[76] the seller of a motorbike tried to rely on a limiting clause excluding liability for breach of warranty. The purchaser argued that because s.14 of the 1893 Act implies a condition, this word "warranty" should be given its narrower meaning under that Act. The point was not decided by the Court of Appeal for Northern Ireland although there are several clear illustrations of the rule in English case law. For example, in *Wallis, Son and Wells v Pratt and Haynes*[77] a contract for the supply of "common English sanfoin" was formed, the seller contracting upon terms that he gave "no warranty, express or implied". A different variety of sanfoin was supplied so that the goods therefore failed to meet their description, with a resulting breach of s.13 of the 1893 Act. The obligation in s.13 is an implied condition, and by giving the word "warranty" as it appeared in the contract a narrow interpretation, the exclusion clause was held inapplicable. In *Andrews v Singer*[78] the contract was for the sale of a new Singer car. The vehicle delivered had 500 miles on the clock and could not be described as new. The contract purported to displace "any warranty (or condition) implied by common law statute or otherwise". The plaintiff successfully argued that the clause did not operate so as to displace express contractual obligations, only implied ones, and as the promise was to deliver a new car, this express term had not been complied with. Ultimately, the draftsman in *L'Estrange v F. Graucob*[79] managed to close these drafting errors and it was the fact that the judiciary became obliged to enforce unfair contracts that led to the development of the now largely discredited doctrine of fundamental breach of contract. The

---

[75] [1997] 3 I.R. 43.
[76] [1927] N.I. 83.
[77] [1910] 2 K.B. 1003.
[78] [1934] 1 K.B. 17.
[79] [1934] 2 K.B. 394. See, however, the tension between aggressive interpretation pre and post the *Photo Production* case, as evidenced by *The Mercini Lady* [2011] 1 Lloyd's Rep. 442 and *Air Transworld Ltd v Bombardier* [2012] EWHC 243 (Comm).

contra proferentem rule remains a useful but limited tool of interpretation. In the light of Lord Hoffmann's exposition in *West Bromwich*[80] on the relevant principles of interpretation of a contract, there is some doubt as to whether the interpretation of an exemption clause *contra proferens* remains an acceptable interpretative device. Certainly, the Irish Supreme Court approves of *contra proferens* interpretation of exclusion clauses. It seems also that the UK Supreme Court has continued to deploy this principle, notwithstanding Lord Hoffmann's strictures.[81] In *Société Générale London Branch v Geys*[82] the bank obtained the consent of Mr Geys to a contract of employment under which he agreed to accept a termination of contract payment in exchange for waiving all contractual and statutory claims he may have in the future. After deciding that the clause was ambiguous, Lord Hope said that in cases of ambiguity the exclusion clause, conceived in favour of the bank, was subject to ordinary *contra proferens* interpretation.

> "As Lord Dunedin said in *W & S Pollock & Co v Macrae* 1922 SC (HL) 192, 199, in order to be effective such clauses must be 'most clearly and unambiguously expressed'. In *Ailsa Craig Fishing Co Ltd. v Malvern Fishing Co Ltd.* [1983] 1 WLR 964, 969H Lord Fraser of Tullybelton said that it was an ordinary principle that such conditions must be construed strictly against the proferens. The principle is commonly applied in cases where the contract which the other party has entered into with the proferens is in a standard form or in terms set out by the proferens which were not negotiable. The more improbable it is that the other party would agree to excluding the liability of the proferens, the more exacting the application of the principle will be."

The *contra proferentem* rule is only one of interpretation and can be overcome by intelligent drafting. A court may find that the proferens has employed a lawyer who has designed a clause so as to eliminate all liability for "breach of all conditions and warranties express or implied under statute or common law, and all collateral warranties". In such a case the usefulness of this rule comes to an end; see *Tokn Grass Products Ltd v Sexton & Co.*[83] In this case the defendant, who had supplied a grain dryer to the plaintiff, was held entitled to rely on printed conditions which excluded implied conditions under the 1893 Act even after a *contra proferentem* interpretation of the clauses in question. As we shall see, there seems to be very little sympathy for treating limitation of damage clauses to a hostile interpretation, *contra proferentem*, although recent cases in England, Canada and Australia suggest that limitation of duty

---

[80] *Investors Compensation Scheme Ltd v West Bromwich Building Society* [1998] 1 All E.R. 98.
[81] See generally Ch.5.
[82] [2012] UKSC 63. In some instances *contra proferens* has no application. Common law rights of action and statutory rights may be limited by reference to international treaty obligations, some of which will be transposed into statute law. The judicial task will be to establish which takes priority: *Hennessey v Aer Lingus Ltd* [2012] IEHC 124 (Warsaw Convention).
[83] Unreported, High Court, October 13, 1983.

clauses are still to be read *contra proferentem*, as long as the interpretation placed upon the clause is not fanciful or disingenuous. For example, in the Manitoba case of *Caners v Eli Lilley Canada*[84] "vague" instructions for the use of a weedkiller were held not to point to contributory negligence by the plaintiff, a farmer, who sued for damage done to his crops by use of the defendant's product.

(2) The risk covered

7–28 Another approach advanced by the courts is to hold the words of an exempting clause inapplicable to certain eventualities. The words of the clause may not be viewed as excluding liability in several extreme cases. In *Ronan v Midland Railway Co*[85] the plaintiff agreed to ship his cattle with the defendants and he was given a receipt which said that the cattle were to travel "at owner's risk". The cattle were wilfully damaged and mutilated by the defendant's employees. The phrase "at owner's risk" was held not to exclude liability for deliberate acts of destruction. *Pearson v Dublin Corp.*[86] was to similar effect, the House of Lords holding that a limiting clause cannot be allowed to exclude liability for a fraudulent misrepresentation made by the defendant to the plaintiff.

7–29 The courts are reluctant to permit a proferens to exclude liability for the negligence of himself or his agents or employees, but if the clause is specific enough then this will be permitted; see *Millar v Midland Gt. W. Ry.*[87] If this happens the proferens will only be liable for wilful default. The judgment of Lord Morton in *Canada Steamship Lines v The King*[88] provides the best summary of the rules a court should follow where a cause of action in negligence is at issue:

(1) If the clause expressly exempts the proferens from liability for his own negligence the clause must be given effect.
(2) If the clause does not expressly refer to negligence the question is whether the words, given their ordinary meaning, cover negligence. The *contra proferentem* rule comes into play here. Phrases that do exclude liability for negligence include "liability for all loss,

---

[84] [1996] 5 W.W.R. 381.
[85] (1883) 14 L.R. (Ir.) 157.
[86] [1907] A.C. 351.
[87] (1905) 5 N.I.J.R. 202.
[88] [1952] A.C.192: *Spriggs v Sotheby Parke Bernet & Co* [1986] 1 Lloyd's Rep. 487; *Caledonia Ltd v Orbit Valve Co* [1993] 2 Lloyd's Rep. 418; *Mediterranean Freight Services Ltd v BP Oil International* [1994] 2 Lloyd's Rep. 506. See generally, Carter, "'Commercial' Construction and the Canada SS Rules" (1995) 9 J.C.L. 69. Recent English cases suggest a weakening of the influence of Lord Morton's guidelines; *HIH Casualty and General Insurance Ltd v Chase Manhattan Bank* [2003] 2 Lloyd's Rep. 61, and *Biffa Waste Services Ltd v Maschinenfabrik Ernst Hese GmbH* [2008] EWHC 6 (TCC); *Capita (Banstead 2011) Ltd v RFIB Group* [2014] EWHC 2197 (Comm); *Greenwich Millennium Village Ltd v Essex Services Group plc* [2014] EWCA Civ 960. Lord Hope, in *Société Générale London Branch v Geys* [2012] UKSC 63, nevertheless felt *Canada Steamship* remained a valid statement of the principle of interpretation vis-à-vis negligence.

howsoever caused is excluded" and "cars are driven at owner's sole risk" if the only liability possible is negligence; see *Rutter v Palmer*.[89]

(3) If the ordinary words are wide enough to exclude liability for negligence the court has to consider whether some other basis of liability—statutory or contractual, for example—can exist. If so, the proferens will be taken to have intended only to exclude liability for actions other than negligence. So in *White v Warrick*[90] the hirer of a bicycle was injured when the saddle slipped while he was riding the machine. The limiting clause was held to exclude strict liability in contract while leaving the owner liable in negligence.[91]

In contrast, however, stands the decision of Blayney J. in *Hughes v J.J. Power Ltd and Colliers Ltd*.[92] The plaintiff brought a damaged engine part to the premises of the second defendant in order to have the engine repaired. The process was a difficult one and the second defendant undertook the work at the plaintiff's risk. The work was carried out but damage resulted, and the issue was whether the second defendant was able to rely on the agreement that work would be undertaken at the plaintiff's risk. Blayney J. held that in this context, the duty imposed by the contract upon the second defendant was the same as that in tort, that is, to exercise the ordinary skill of an ordinary competent person engaged in the particular trade in question. "There was, accordingly, only a single duty imposed on Colliers, though arising both in contract and tort, and there was nothing that the exclusion could apply to other than a failure to comply with that duty." Blayney J. distinguished *White v Warrick* on the ground that, in the case before him, "there were not two heads of liability, but one, breach of a single duty of care, since it was the same duty that arose both in contract and in tort".

7–30 A very strong English Court of Appeal case has pointed out that the *Canada Steamship* principles are rules of construction, not rules of law and they are subject to significant qualifications. The principles are based upon the presumed intention of the parties: *Greenwich Millennium Village Ltd v Essex Services Group Ltd*.[93] Further, seen in the contractual setting of construction contracts where they are frequently encountered, the application of these principles results in consequences that are contrary to commercial common sense. Notwithstanding this deeper analysis, it is submitted that the Supreme Court in *McMullan Brothers Ltd v McDonagh*[94] can be said to have used *Canada Steamship* in a mechanistic manner, although findings of contributory negligence were able to produce an appropriate redistribution of loss between the plaintiff and the defendant.

---

[89] [1922] 2 K.B. 87.
[90] [1953] 1 W.L.R. 1285.
[91] See the remarkable "construction" process in *Casson v Ostley P.J. Ltd* [2003] B.L.R. 147.
[92] Unreported, High Court, May 11, 1988.
[93] [2014] EWCA Civ 960.
[94] [2014] IESC 22.

7–31 At one time the view was expressed that if there could be only one basis of liability then a very general limiting clause must be read so as to exclude that cause of action; this view, attributed to Lord Greene in *Alderslade v Hendon Laundry*,[95] has been rejected by members of the Court of Appeal in *Hollier v Rambler Motors*[96] and *Gillespie v Roy Bowles*.[97] These more recent cases, post-*Alderslade*, are in sympathy with the objective of protecting the consumer but at the risk of putting a narrow and sometimes disingenuous interpretation on the meaning of the clause.

7–32 Clauses that seek to exclude or limit liability often do so by conceding liability for direct loss while at the same time excluding or limiting liability for indirect or consequential loss. The meaning of each clause is to be gleaned from the words used and the intention of the parties, informed by any precedent that may be available to the court. The leading English case is *Deepak v ICI*,[98] where an industrial plant was destroyed by fire when the supplier provided services that did not meet the relevant standard, causing destruction of the plant itself. The limitation clause sought to exclude liability for "indirect or consequential" damage. Applying a line of authority[99] from the English Court of Appeal, it was held that the relevant question is whether the loss is direct or indirect; only indirect loss would be excluded. As lost profits were classified as being the direct result of destruction of a profit-earning resource (here an industrial production plant), the clause did not apply. Similarly, in *Ferryways NV v ABP*,[100] an employment contract that sought to exclude liability of an "indirect or consequential nature" arising out of the contract of employment was held not to prevent dependants from claiming for breach of duty which caused the death of the employee. Breach of the duty owed to the employee and the resulting death benefit and repatriation expenses were clearly direct losses that were not caught by the exclusion clause. Similarly, in *McCain Foods (GB) Ltd v Eco-Tec (Europe) Ltd*[101] the plaintiff purchased a waste water treatment system which, to the knowledge of the defendant suppliers, was to be used to produce biogas. The system was both defective and useless. A limitation clause excluding liability for indirect losses was held not to apply here as the losses fell under the first limb of *Hadley v Baxendale*, i.e. direct loss resulting from being deprived of an ordinary profit-earning chattel.

---

[95] [1945] K.B. 189.
[96] [1972] 2 Q.B. 71.
[97] [1973] Q.B. 400.
[98] [1999] 1 Lloyd's Rep. 387.
[99] *Millars Machinery v David Way* (1938) 40 Com. Cas. 204; *Croudace Construction v Cawoods* [1978] 2 Lloyds Rep. 55. This approach has not gone unchallenged: *ESL Consulting Ltd v Verizon (Ireland) Ltd* [2008] IEHC 369; *Fujitsu Services Ltd v IBM UK Ltd* [2014] EWHC 752 (TCC).
[100] [2008] EWHC 225 (Ch).
[101] [2011] EWHC 66 (TCC); *Elvanite Full Circle Ltd v AMEC Earth and Environmental (UK) Ltd* [2013] EWHC 1191 (TCC).

(3) The "main purpose" rule

7–33 This important rule of construction is designed to cut down the effect of a limiting clause which would produce undesirable consequences if the clause was read literally. The courts look to circumstances surrounding the transaction and, aided by the sometimes dubious premise that both parties are acting as reasonable men, the judges cut down general words in a contract. So in *Glynn v Margotson*[102] a general clause that gave the carrier of a cargo of fresh oranges the liberty to stay at any port in the Mediterranean, Black Sea or Adriatic was held not to exclude liability for damage to the cargo as a result of delay in proceeding directly from Malaga to Liverpool. The House of Lords presumed the main purpose of the contract was the safe transport of the goods. Lord Halsbury said: "looking at the whole instrument and seeing what one must regard as its main purpose one must reject words, indeed whole provisions, if they are inconsistent with what one assumes to be the main purpose of the contract." If the parties do intend to prevent the judges from imputing a main purpose they may do so but very clear evidence of intention and consent to such a term must be disclosed. Sometimes the main purpose, used to counteract the exemption clause, is identified from other express terms or from general contractual obligations. In *Sze Hai Tong Bank Ltd v Rambler Cycle Co*[103] a carrier of goods claimed to be able to rely on an exemption clause which released the carrier from liability after discharge of the goods in port. After discharge of the goods, the carrier's agent released the goods without production of a bill of lading to the consignee. The consignee never paid for the goods and the plaintiff sued the carrier. The carrier sought to rely on the exception clause. The Privy Council held that the exception clause was subject to modification in order to give effect to the main object of the contract, which in this case included an obligation on the carrier to deliver the goods only to a person entitled to deliver, that is, a person who is able to produce the bill of lading.

7–34 While it may be that the "main purpose" rule of construction may seem of limited value if the courts first of all use the exemption clause in order to establish what the contract actually provided for—in this situation the express clause may lead us to conclude that the implied obligation is in fact excluded from the contract (see *British Leyland Exports Ltd v Brittain Group Sales Ltd*[104])—it can still prove useful. In *Sperry Rand Canada Ltd v Thomas Equipment*,[105] Thomas Equipment purchased transmission equipment to be fitted to loading equipment manufactured and sold by it. It relied on Sperry Rand to select a suitable transmission system. The system selected and fitted turned out to be unsuitable as a system and Sperry Rand defended the action

---

[102] [1893] A.C. 351.
[103] [1959] A.C. 576; *Nissho Iwai Australia v Malaysian International Shipping* (1989) 86 A.L.R. 375.
[104] [1981] I.R. 35.
[105] (1982) 135 D.L.R. (3d) 197. See the Australian cases of *Sydney City Council v West* (1965) 114 C.L.R. 481 and *Van der Sterren v Cibernetics (Holdings) Pty* (1970) 44 A.L.J.R. 154.

brought against it for breach of contract by relying on a clause in the contract. La Forest J.A., in the New Brunswick Court of Appeal, held the contractual conditions inapplicable. The main purpose of the contract was to provide a system that was satisfactory as a system. The clauses in the contract limited liability for failures and defects in relation to individual units and not the system as a whole.

(4) The type of clause involved

7–35 In *Ailsa Craig Fishing Co v Malvern Fishing Co*[106] a distinction was drawn between a limitation clause (a clause limiting the remedy available to the injured party) and a clause of exemption (a clause which attempts to cut down the scope of the contractual duty). Because the former is usually clear and unambiguous in its terms it is less acceptable to give such a clause a secondary meaning than where the clause is an exemption clause. This approach has been followed in Canada in *Westcoast Transmission Co Ltd v Cullen Detroit Diesel Allison Ltd*.[107] That case involved the supply of generators by a third party to the defendant for incorporation with motors to be supplied and used by the plaintiff. The defendant settled a claim brought by the plaintiff when the generators and thus the motors failed. The defendant sought an indemnity from the third party but the third party sought to rely on a clause which excluded "liability for consequential damages in case of failure to meet conditions of any guarantee". The British Columbia Court of Appeal held the clause to be effective, holding that a clause of this kind is to be treated with less hostility than a clause which entirely excludes statutory obligations vis-à-vis performance.

(5) Entire agreement clauses

7–36 Entire agreement clauses are becoming increasingly common in standard form commercial contracts. Whether they are properly to be described as exemption clauses remains an open question. These clauses take a variety of forms. The clause may recite that no other contractual promise was given, or that any promise given was not relied upon. The clause may declare that the written contract forms the "entire" contract and that the contract may only be varied by a subsequent written agreement signed by both parties. Another variation is the use of a "merger" or "integration" clause in which the contract provides that all pre-contractual statements "merge" or are integrated into the written agreement. Whatever the form of words used, the intention is clear. The clause is a kind of express parol evidence rule which, the proferens hopes, confines the attention of the court to the four corners of the written contract. Will such a clause be effective? In general, the answer to this question involves a combination of factors including the construction of the words of the clause itself, the nature of the cause of action, and the possibility of statutory intervention.

---

[106] [1983] 1 W.L.R. 964; *BHP Petroleum v British Steel* [2000] 2 Lloyd's Rep. 277; and *Biffa Waste Services Ltd v Maschinenfabrik Ernst Hese GmbH* [2008] EWHC 6 (TCC).
[107] (1990) 70 D.L.R. (4th) 503.

7–37 The clause must cover the event. It may be that the clause may fail because of a failure to satisfy incorporation requirements. In *Beer v Townsgate I. Ltd*[108] purchasers of condominiums purchased on the basis of oral representations that the property was "risk-free", signing contracts that affirmed that no oral warranties had been made. The Ontario Court of Appeal held that because of the "frenzied atmosphere" in which the sale took place, failure to draw the attention of the buyers to the clause meant it was not binding on the purchasers. However, the leading English case on incorporation, *Inntrepreneur Pub Co v East Crown Ltd*[109] indicates that it is generally just such a situation that entire agreement clauses are intended to exclude or avoid:

> "[T]he purpose of an entire agreement clause is to preclude a party to a written agreement from threshing through the undergrowth and finding in the course of negotiations some (chance) remark or statement (often long forgotten or difficult to recall or explain) on which to found a claim such as the present to the existence of a collateral warranty ... the clause ... is to denude what would otherwise constitute a collateral warranty of legal effect."[110]

This appears to countenance the creation of a rule of law, but, it is suggested, the better view is that the clause creates a presumption against such a warranty being given, as the Australian courts appear to have indicated. It is also significant that in *Inntrepreneur* itself, Lightman J. went on to find that on the facts, no such warranty had been given.[111] The fact that *Inntrepreneur* does not create a rule of law has recently been affirmed by the English Court of Appeal in *Business Environment Bow Lane Ltd v Deanwater Estates Ltd*,[112] where, as in *Inntrepreneur* itself, an alleged oral warranty was found not to have been made or intended when negotiations were followed by further negotiations and the terms agreed, minus the alleged oral warranty, were set down in a written contract. In any case the words of the clause will have to cover the event. In *Deepak Fertilisers and Petrochemicals Corp v ICI Chemicals and Polymers Ltd*[113] one issue before the Court of Appeal was whether a clause excluding liability for "agreements, understandings, promises or conditions, oral or written, expressed or implied" could exclude liability for misrepresentations. The Court of Appeal held that the clause was not to be read so as to exclude misrepresentations made prior to the conclusion of the agreement; see also *Witter v TBP Industries Ltd.*[114] But each case will depend on the form

---

[108] (1997) 152 D.L.R. (4th) 671.
[109] [2000] 2 Lloyd's Rep. 611; in policy terms, particularly outside consumer or employment contracts, this approach has some judicial support, e.g. the English Court of Appeal in *North Eastern Properties Ltd v Coleman* [2010] EWCA Civ 277.
[110] [2000] 2 Lloyd's Rep. 611 at 614.
[111] [2000] 2 Lloyd's Rep. 611 at 617. This is also the case in *White v Bristol Rugby Ltd* [2002] 2 I.R.L.R. 204.
[112] [2007] EWCA Civ 622.
[113] [1999] 1 Lloyd's Rep. 387.
[114] [1996] 2 All E.R. 573.

of words used by the draftsperson. The clause must also address the cause of action and perhaps the specific remedy sought. Will an entire agreement clause exclude implied terms? In *Exxonmobil Sales and Supply Co v Texaco Ltd*[115] the purchasers of goods sought to persuade the court to imply a term based on custom and usage, but the words of the clause were held to be wide enough to exclude such an implied term. However, Deputy Judge Teare left open the issue whether, despite an entire agreement clause, a "business efficacy" implied term could be implied into a contract on the basis that it was mandated by other express terms in order to make the contract work.[116] The most important decision on entire agreement clauses is that of the English Court of Appeal in *Axa Sun Life Services Plc v Campbell Martin Ltd*.[117] An entire agreement clause that sought to displace "any prior representations" was held not to exclude liability in tort. Rix L.J., giving the leading judgment, said the word "representations", appearing in an entire agreement clause that spoke to contractual liability and contractual terms, meant that the word was "a word of contractual obligation". In Rix L.J.'s view, "misrepresentation and the exclusion of misrepresentation or liability for it are simply not the business of the clause at all". It should be noted that English courts have balanced this rigorous approach to contractual interpretation by deciding whether, nevertheless, the proferens can avoid liability by way of contractual estoppel.[118]

7–38 It is also possible that an entire agreement clause may have to satisfy a fair and reasonable test; this could arise by virtue of the provisions of s.46(1) of the 1980 Act. This provides that if any agreement contains a provision which could exclude or restrict any liability to which a party may be subject by reason of any misrepresentation made by him before the contract was made, or any remedy available to the other party, the provision shall not be enforceable unless it is shown to be fair and reasonable. The first English case in which the relevance of this provision, which is based on s.3 of the UK Misrepresentation Act 1967 (the "1967 Act"), was *Cremdean Properties Ltd v Nash*.[119] Here a strong Court of Appeal[120] found that the clause in question did not have the effect contended for on the facts but rejected the argument that the clause had the effect, in law, as if no misrepresentation had been made at all. In his judgment Bridge L.J., after giving an example of a clause that expressly mentioned the nullification of s.3, said that, "I should not have thought that the courts would have been ready to allow such ingenuity in forms of language to defeat the plain purpose at which section 3 is aimed".[121] Later English

---

[115] [2004] 1 All E.R. (Comm.) 435.
[116] [2004] 1 All E.R. (Comm.) 435 at para.27. See however *Hart v Macdonald* (1910) 10 C.L.R. 417 and *Mulvay v Henry Berry and Co Pty* (1938) 38 S.R.N.S.W. 389.
[117] [2011] EWCA Civ 133, approving the analysis of Ramsey J. in *BSkyb Ltd v HP Enterprise Services UK Ltd* [2010] EWHC 86 (TCC).
[118] *Springwell Navigation Corp v J.P. Morgan Chase Bank* [2010] EWCA Civ 1221. On estoppel by convention see *Mears v Shoreline Housing Partnership Ltd* [2015] EWHC 1396 (TCC).
[119] (1977) 244 *Estates Gazette* 547.
[120] Bridge, Scarman and Buckley L.JJ.
[121] (1977) 244 *Estates Gazette* 547 at 551.

cases have also followed the view that "the fair and reasonable test" as set out in the statutes in question are applicable[122] and that the proferens must run the gambit of a fair and reasonable test.[123] On the other hand, the view that entire agreement clauses, at least when they seek to exclude representations as distinct from remedies, do not exclude liability but serve to define the scope of the agreement, has significant support. In *McGrath v Shah*[124] Deputy Judge Chadwick said s.3 "was not apt to cover a contractual provision which seeks to define where the contractual terms are actually to be found," and this is also the central position in *Inntrepreneur*. English law appears to have resolved that where the plaintiff's claim is brought in tort, as distinct from contract, that is, for negligence or negligent misstatements, the courts will be free to apply s.3 of the 1967 Act,[125] vis-à-vis the tort claim or a claim under the UK equivalent of s.45(1) of the 1980 Act, that is, s.2(1) of the 1967 Act.

7–39 In any event, where the contract is an arm's-length contract between two parties of comparable bargaining power, the fair and reasonable test is likely to be upheld, as in *McGrath v Shah* itself. In *Watford Electronics Ltd v Sanderson CFL Ltd*[126] Peter Gibson L.J. took the view that contracts negotiated by experienced businessmen representing substantial companies of equal bargaining power should be the best judge of the fairness of an agreement.[127] Even *Cremdean Properties Ltd v Nash* does not gainsay this view because the Court of Appeal was not required to rule on the s.3 issue.

7–40 Doubts over the application of the 1967 Act to these clauses have now been dispelled.[128] In *Foodco UK v Henry Boot Developments Ltd*,[129] a clause that disclaimed liability for pre-contractual misrepresentations, other than those given by the defendant's solicitors in response to inquiries made by the plaintiff's solicitors, was held to pass the fair and reasonable test. Lewison J. found that the entire agreement clause strove to produce certainty; there was no contractual imbalance as between the parties, the clause was open to negotiation and the plaintiffs, if in doubt, had only to consult the defendant's solicitors to see if a statement was legally enforceable. This issue of the availability of a realistic remedy is very important[130] in evaluating a fair and reasonable disclaimer.

---

[122] *Witter Ltd v TBP Industries Ltd* [1996] 2 All E.R. 573; *Zanzibar v British Aerospace* [2000] 1 W.L.R. 2333.

[123] Section 3 of the Misrepresentation Act 1967 is now found in s.8 of the Unfair Contract Terms Act 1977 (UK).

[124] (1989) 57 P. & C.R. 452.

[125] *Leofelis SA v Lonsdale Sports* [2007] EWHC 451 (Ch); appeal allowed on another point: [2008] EWCA Civ 640; *Foodco UK v Henry Boot Developments Ltd* [2010] EWHC 358 (Ch); *AXA Sun Life Services plc v Campbell Martin Ltd* [2011] EWCA Civ 133.

[126] [2001] 1 All E.R. (Comm.) 696.

[127] See also *Grimstead (E. A.) & Son Ltd v McGarrigan* [1998–1999] Info. T.L.R. 384.

[128] *Springwell Navigation Corp v J.P. Morgan Chase Bank* [2010] EWCA Civ 1221.

[129] [2010] EWHC 358 (Ch).

[130] *Avrora Fine Arts Investment v Christie, Manson and Woods Ltd* [2012] EWHC 2198 (Ch).

7–41 The real issue that faces a court when an entire agreement clause is presented, either to a consumer or person with limited business expertise, is whether the view that the clause prevents the court from looking behind the clause is to prevail. It may be that the court may look into the contract and find that the obligation that the clause is seeking to exclude is an express term anyway.[131] The clause will not be able to exclude implied terms that are found in a statute[132] but depending upon the wording of the clause, custom and practice may be denied effect.[133] In *Mears v Shoreline Housing Partnership Ltd*[134] a contract was verbally agreed and in operation. A renegotiation took place but the terms as varied were not expressly amended so as to remove the effects of an entire agreement clause. Atkenhead J. held that the entire agreement clause could not operate in light of the ability of the representee to advance a right to invoke an estoppel (e.g. estoppel by convention). It is also clear that an entire agreement clause cannot be effective so as to exclude liability for fraud or deceit. This view is based upon the decision of the House of Lords in *Pearson v Dublin Corp.*[135] In *Witter Ltd v TBP Industries Ltd*[136] Jacob J. held that a clause that purported to exclude liability for all misrepresentations, including fraudulent misrepresentation, was not fair and reasonable under the statutory test because it had the potential to exclude liability for fraud, a strange result in the light of *Pearson*. Nevertheless, good drafting of entire agreement clauses makes it necessary to concede liability in fraud or deceit.

7–42 The closest the Irish courts have come in regard to giving a decision on entire agreement clauses is that of Birmingham J. in *McCaughey v Anglo Irish Bank Corp.*[137] Statements made by the defendants about the potential investment were followed by written provisions that sought to minimise the actionability of these prior statements by, *inter alia*, indicating that there had been no representations made to the plaintiff and that he had not relied on anything other than his own appraisal in deciding to proceed. These exemption clauses were held effective to deprive the plaintiff of any contractual claims, requiring the plaintiff to proceed via the more difficult cause of action in deceit. Birmingham J. distinguished both *Interfoto* and *Walsh v Jones Lang LaSalle Ltd*[138] on their facts from the case before him. The learned judge also said that in *Jones Lang LaSalle* a plea of contractual estoppel had not been

---

[131] *Leofelis SA v Lonsdale Sports* [2007] EWHC 451 (Ch), overruled on another ground: [2008] EWCA Civ 640.

[132] *Hart v Macdonald* (1910) 10 C.L.R. 417.

[133] *Exxonmobil v Texaco Ltd* [2004] 1 All E.R. 435. Employment contracts and contracts with inexperienced persons may also create difficulties. See *Cheverny Consulting Ltd v Whitehead Mann* [2006] EWCA Civ 1303. Clarke J.'s analysis in *Raiffeisen Zentralbank Österreich v RBS* [2010] EWHC 1392 (Comm) at paras 313–315 ("rewriting history") has been influential. See Loi, "Contractual Estoppel and Non-Reliance Clauses" [2015] L.M.C.L.Q.

[134] [2015] EWHC 1396 (TCC).

[135] [1907] A.C. 351; *HIH Casualty and General Insurance Ltd v Chase Manhattan Bank* [2003] 2 Lloyd's Rep. 61.

[136] [1996] 2 All E.R. 573.

[137] [2011] IEHC 546, affirmed at [2013] IESC 17.

[138] [2009] 4 I.R. 401.

put forward.[139] It is surprising that s.46 of the 1980 Act was not considered in relation to the exemption clauses as the investment opportunity was offered as a service.

The Core Obligation and Exclusion Clauses

7–43 Can a limiting clause be so widely drafted as to permit the proferens to avoid liability in cases which amount to non-performance of the promissory part of the contract? This proposition has troubled the English courts in particular for many years. The problem was identified in *L'Estrange v F. Graucob*[140] when the plaintiff was held bound by her signature to a contract for the purchase of a cigarette vending machine. The exempting provisions of the contract protected the seller in the event of any breach of contract short of non-delivery of the machine and outright refusal to service it.

7–44 The problem raised by "catch-all" exemption clauses may be one of definition; can a contract exist if the limiting provisions are so sweeping as to empty the contract of all promissory content? An airline that promises, "we will fly you from A to B" and then conditions this promise by adding, "we will not be liable if we cancel all flights from A to B" is creating an illusory contract; see *MacRobertson Miller Airlines v Commissioners of State Taxation*.[141] The difficulty here stems from the fact that the passenger will generally not be aware of this qualifying term or be in a position to negotiate an improved contract—he will be told to take it or leave it.[142]

7–45 It may be that both parties are prepared to agree that the risk of non-performance is to be taken by the purchaser. If each is free to agree to such a contract then the courts should enforce the contract because the core obligation of the contract must be taken to involve this allocation of risk. Indeed, in two Irish cases, *Western Meats Ltd v National Ice and Cold Storage*[143] and *Tokn Grass Products v Sexton & Co Ltd*,[144] Barrington J. and Doyle J. respectively pointed out that the intentions of the parties must be respected when they freely and voluntarily agree on the question of who is to bear a commercial risk. This is further illustrated by two Irish cases decided in the 1940s. In *O'Connor v McCowen & Sons Ltd*[145] the defendants sold turnip seeds to the plaintiff. Prior to the sale the defendants stated that they had not obtained the seeds from their usual source and could not guarantee them. The seeds produced a plant

---

[139] Birmingham J. cited with approval *Springwell Navigation Co v J.P. Morgan Chase Bank* [2010] EWCA Civ 1221 and *Peekay Intermark Ltd v Australia and New Zealand Banking Group Ltd* [2006] 2 Lloyd's Rep. 511.
[140] [1934] 2 K.B. 394.
[141] (1975) 133 C.L.R. 125.
[142] *Shea v Gt. S. Railway* [1944] Ir. Jur. Rep. 26.
[143] [1982] I.L.R.M. 101.
[144] Unreported, High Court, October 13, 1983.
[145] (1943) 77 I.L.T.R. 64.

that bore little resemblance to a turnip and was commercially worthless. The defendant argued that he was not liable because of his statement negativing a guarantee. Overend J. indicated that these words were not such as to amount to an agreement exempting the defendants from liability, following the leading English case of *Wallis, Son and Wells v Pratt & Haynes*.[146] Overend J. characterised this case as one where the purchaser was buying goods by description, the goods supplied not answering the description at all. If liability is to be excluded "the very clearest words must be used by the seller, such as: 'you may be purchasing seeds that are not turnip seeds at all'." Overend J. continued by observing that the obligation in this case did not arise under the 1893 Act: "the buyer, however, got something that was not turnip seed, and *quite apart from the Sale of Goods Act* he had a cause of action." In other words, the fact that a seller tries to exclude the terms implied under statute will not protect him in cases where he delivers goods different from those he contracted to sell. If, to use the facts of *O'Connor*, the purchaser is to take the risk of seeds not producing turnip plants at all he must be aware that this forms the basis of the contract. If the seeds sown had merely produced a poor crop of turnips then the seller may be protected, for this would not be the core obligation but a condition of warranty, then amendable to exclusion under s.55 of the 1893 Act. In *Wicklow Corn Co Ltd v Edward Fitzgerald Ltd*,[147] a Circuit Court case, Davitt J. held a corn factor to be protected by a clause excluding s.14 of the 1893 Act when seed wheat sold produced a poor crop. Here the defect was held to be one of quality only rather than an extreme case where another substance is supplied. In cases where a different substance is supplied it is better to treat this as a case of non-performance, to which the exempting clause is inapplicable except where the evidence suggests that the core obligation was speculative; a *spes*. A contract to sell peas is not performed by supplying beans. A contract to sell a tractor is not performed by supplying three horses. The same point was made by Dodd J. in *Fogarty v Dickson*[148] when he said, "[i]f a man orders a golf cloth cap, the order is not fulfilled by sending him a stylish silk hat". See also the case of *American Can Co v Stewart*.[149] The solution is different, however, if the contract gives the supplier the freedom to supply goods that may not meet the description and if, at the same time, an exemption clause limits liability for the loss occasioned by the supply of these goods, as in *George Mitchell (Chesterhall) Ltd v Finney Lock Seeds Ltd*,[150] when the House of Lords held that a limitation clause was effective at common law when the supplier of seeds provided cabbage seeds of the "wrong" variety which produced a commercially useless crop due to climatic conditions and incorrect crop husbandry.

---

[146] [1910] 2 K.B. 1003.
[147] [1942] Ir. Jur. Rep. 48; *Sholedice v Hurst Gunson Sope Tober Co*, unreported, High Court, July 28, 1972.
[148] (1913) 47 I.L.T.R. 281.
[149] (1915) 50 I.L.T.R. 132.
[150] [1983] 2 A.C. 803.

7–46 Notwithstanding the trend towards giving exemption clauses the meaning that the contracting parties must have intended (as judged on an objective basis) the fact that the judges have previously required such clauses to be precisely drafted retains some importance. The perception that general words in an exclusion clause seeking to displace "guarantees" or "warranties" will not be clear enough to exclude statutory implied conditions was recently reaffirmed by Rix L.J. in *The Mercini Lady*[151] on the basis that this "principle" of interpretation was deeply rooted in English law. In contrast, Cooke J., in a very forthright judgment has decided that where the language of the clause is capable of only one meaning, such a "principle" of English law must yield to the intention of the parties.[152] Cooke J. was comforted by this departure from more onerous drafting standards by the fact that by the end of the twentieth century statutory protection against unfair terms, even in business-to-business contracts, were in place. At this juncture, it is necessary to refer to what became known as the fundamental breach doctrine.

Fundamental Breach of Contract

7–47 During the 1950s and 1960s the response of many members of the English judiciary to the problem of exemption clauses that had been imposed by one party on another, or had been included in a contract to which the other party had not freely consented, was to develop a rule of substantive law, expressed by Denning L.J. (as he then was), in the following terms: "[e]xempting clauses of this kind, no matter how widely they are expressed only avail the party when he is carrying out his contract in its essential respects." So the supply of a car that was totally incapable of propulsion could not be excused by a sweeping clause; see *Karsales (Harrow) v Wallis*.[153] The supply of a tipping lorry that could not tip because of a defect in the hydraulic system was found to be a fundamental breach: *Astley Industrial Trust v Grimley*.[154] Theft by persons unknown of a carpet bailed for cleaning purposes may too constitute a fundamental breach of the cleaning contract, against which an exemption clause may not prevail; see *Levison v Patent Steam Carpet Cleaning Co.*[155] Cases that are decided by reference to such methods operate regardless of the intention of the parties and represent a belated, wrongheaded, but well-intentioned effort to redress doctrinal difficulties and protect persons from sweeping or draconian exemption clauses.

---

[151] [2011] 1 Lloyd's Rep. 442.
[152] *Air Transworld Ltd v Bombardier Inc.* [2012] EWHC 243 (Comm) applying dicta of Lords Wilberforce and Diplock from *Photo Production Ltd v Securicor* [1980] A.C. 827. *Air Transworld* was distinguished on the facts in *Dalmare SpA v Union Maritime Ltd* [2012] EWHC 3537 (Comm) (an "as is" case). Contrast the meaning attached to an "as is" clause in *Delmare* with Leggatt J.'s view in *Hirtenstein v Hill Dickinson LLP* [2014] EWHC 2711 (Comm). Leggatt J's view is to be preferred.
[153] [1956] 1 W.L.R. 936.
[154] [1963] 2 All E.R. 33.
[155] [1978] Q.B. 69.

7–48 This is the doctrine of fundamental breach of contract. The difficulty with this rule of law (as many critics have pointed out) is that it treats all exemption clauses and all parties as if they were alike; in fact there are cases where it may be reasonable to permit a limiting clause to operate so as to "shrink" the core obligation, thereby reallocating risk. The House of Lords in the *Suisse Atlantique*[156] case rejected this rule of substantive law, commenting obiter that the doctrine of fundamental breach was simply a rule of construction. In the later case of *Harbutt's Plasticine v Wayne Tank Corp*[157] the unsatisfactory nature of the fundamental breach doctrine was illustrated. The plaintiffs contracted with the defendants who were to install pipes into the plaintiffs' new factory where plasticine would be manufactured. Molten plasticine was to pass along the plastic pipes installed by the defendants, as per specification. Unfortunately the pipes were not strong enough for the task and the molten plasticine caused the pipes to melt, resulting in the total loss of the factory. The parties had agreed that for any loss caused by the defendants, damages payable would be limited to £15,000. Now this agreement was struck between two commercial concerns, both of whom had the right to consult lawyers. The agreement was obviously drafted by lawyers and the clause clearly covered the case. Insurance was to be arranged on the basis of this agreement but, because of the fundamental breach doctrine, reliance on the clause was denied to the defendants. The House of Lords in *Photo Production Ltd v Securicor Transport Ltd*[158] have overruled *Harbutt's Plasticine* as being a doctrine of law of doubtful parentage.

7–49 The facts of *Photo Production Ltd v Securicor Transport Ltd* concerned a contract for the supply of security services in respect of the plaintiff's factory premises, the main dangers to the property being fire and theft. Under the contract the defendant agreed to provide services by patrolmen but standard conditions excluded liability for the acts or omissions of employees unless these could have been foreseen and avoided by acts of due diligence by the employer, namely, the defendant. A patrolman started a fire which caused total destruction of the premises. It was not established that the patrolman intended to destroy the factory and there was no suggestion that the defendant had not exercised care in recruiting patrolmen in general, and this patrolman in particular. The court of first instance and the Court of Appeal held that the limiting clause could not be relied upon. In particular, Denning M.R. in the Court of Appeal considered whether the breach was fundamental and, after concluding that it was, held that the court could deprive the proferens of the exemption or limitation clause. The Court of Appeal's decision, in the view of the House of Lords, was insupportable, based as it was on *Harbutt's Plasticine*, a decision inconsistent with *Suisse Atlantique*. The issue for every court when

---

[156] *Suisse Atlantique Societe d'Armement Maritime SA v NV Rotterdamsche Kolen Centrale* [1967] 1 A.C. 361; see Brownsword, in Mitchell & Mitchell (eds), *Landmark Cases in the Law of Contract* (Oxford: Hart, 2008), p.299.
[157] [1970] 1 Q.B. 447.
[158] [1980] 2 W.L.R. 283.

interpreting an exception clause of any kind was said by Lord Wilberforce to rest entirely on principles of construction:

> "[T]he question whether, and to what extent, an exclusion clause is to be applied to a fundamental breach, or a breach of a fundamental term, or indeed to any breach of contract, is a matter of construction of the contract ... there are ample resources in the normal rules of contract law for dealing with these without the superimposition of a judicially invented rule of law."[159]

In the Commonwealth the *Photo Production* approach has been willingly followed by judges who are keen to reinstate an intelligible and coherent note into the common law. The Supreme Court of Canada in *Beaufort Realties (1964) Inc v Belcourt Construction (Ottawa) Ltd*[160] adopted *Photo Production*. The High Court of Australia has also abandoned the fundamental breach as a rule of law approach, holding in the case of *Nissho Iwai Australia v Malaysian International Shipping*[161] that a sweeping exception clause may operate even when defective performance of an obligation leads to the total loss, or self-induced frustration, of the contract in question.

Fundamental Breach in Ireland

7–50 It is instructive to compare the position in Ireland with that in Canada on fundamental breach. The Canadian courts, while following *Photo Production*, have developed a rather more dynamic perspective. In *Hunter Engineering Co v Syncrude Canada Ltd*[162] the Supreme Court of Canada rejected the fundamental breach doctrine because of the uncertainty it engendered, but the justices developed the view that an exempting clause could be struck down when there was unconscionability and inequality of bargaining power,[163] or, in the context of that particular breach, it was not fair and reasonable to enforce the clause.[164] Later cases have synthesized these two approaches.[165] However, because *Hunter Engineering* itself did not specifically overrule earlier fundamental breach cases relating to exemption clauses, the Canadian courts continued to strike down those clauses without undertaking a detailed analysis of what the clause sought to achieve. In *Tercon Contractors Ltd v Province of British*

---

[159] [1980] 2 W.L.R. 283 at 288–289; *Frans Mass (UK) Ltd v Samsung Electronics (UK) Ltd* [2004] EWHC 1502 (Comm).
[160] (1980) 116 D.L.R. (3d) 193.
[161] (1989) 86 A.L.R. 375.
[162] (1989) 57 D.L.R. (4th) 321. *Plastex Canada Ltd v Dow Chemical of Canada* (2004) 245 D.L.R. (4th) 650; *Prairie Petroleum Products v Husky Oil* [2006] 11 W.W.R. 606.
[163] Per Dickson C.J. and La Forest J.
[164] Per Wilson J. and L'Heureux—Dube J.
[165] *Fraser Jewellers 1982 Ltd v Dominion Electric Protection Co* (1997) 148 D.L.R. (4th) 496; *Carleton Condominium Corp No 32 v Camdev Corp* (1999) 47 C.L.R. (20) 224.

Columbia[166] the majority of the Supreme Court of Canada decided that the time had come to lay the doctrine of fundamental breach to rest. Nevertheless, all members of the Supreme Court of Canada believed that a role had to be reserved for some form of judicial discretion and the process outlined is to first consider whether the clause applies to the facts of the case. If the clause does apply, the court proceeds to the second stage which requires an analysis of the circumstances surrounding formation to test for unconscionability. If the contract is not unconscionable as formed, the third stage allows the court to consider whether the public interest in ensuring that contracts are enforced is outweighed by other policy factors (e.g. supply of dangerous goods or services to the public). This approach has led to some odd decisions. In *Tercon* itself, maintaining the integrity of public contracting mechanisms was at the root of the majority decision to strike down a clause excluding damages claims in respect of accepting non-compliant tenders. In contrast, waivers for death and personal injury occasioned by dangerous outdoor pursuits, even when the defendant has been negligent and the participant completely blameless, have been upheld: *Loychuk v Cougar Mountain Adventures Ltd.*[167] There is, of course, some truth in the argument that the English approach involves doing great violence to the words of a contract but the rather convoluted Canadian "solutions" appear even less satisfactory. One final point to make about the state of Canadian jurisprudence is that in one important case, *Solway v Davis Moving and Storage Co*,[168] the majority of the Ontario Court of Appeal struck down a clause limiting damages as "unconscionable" when goods owned by the plaintiff were stolen from the defendant, a courier. As this case, like the English bailment cases, can be viewed as sui generis, perhaps fundamental breach is not entirely dead: see Lewison.[169]

7–51 Such an approach might also help to sideline the leading Irish case of *Clayton Love v B + I Transport*.[170] The parties contracted to transport deep frozen scampi from Dublin to Liverpool. The loading was conducted at atmospheric temperature and this led to the scampi deteriorating to the extent that it was condemned when it arrived in Liverpool. The plaintiffs sued but were met by two exemption clauses, one of which was drafted widely enough to protect the defendants from liability. The second clause obliged the plaintiffs to claim within three days, otherwise the claim would be absolutely barred. Davitt P. at first instance relied on the substantive rule of law and (now discredited) dicta in two English cases, *Spurling Ltd v Bradshaw*[171] and *Smeaton Hanscomb & Co Ltd v Sassoon I. Setty*[172] and refused to apply the

---

[166] [2010] 1 S.C.R. 69.

[167] [2012] BCCA 122 (leave to appeal to the Supreme Court of Canada has been denied).

[168] (2002) 222 D.L.R. (4th) 251.

[169] *The Interpretation of Contracts*, 5th edn (London: Thomson Reuters, 2011), para.12.18. The cases and issues are well reviewed in *Astrazeneca UK Ltd v Albermarle International Corp* [2011] EWHC 1574 (Comm).

[170] (1970) 104 I.L.T.R. 157.

[171] [1956] 1 W.L.R. 461.

[172] [1953] 1 W.L.R. 1468.

first limiting clause. It is symptomatic of the confusion and complexity of this doctrine that Davitt P. then shifted ground and applied the second clause by holding that, "it was intended to, and does in fact cover the case of a clause arising from the breach of a fundamental term of the contract". This reasoning seems to be unsatisfactory because Davitt P. applied a rule of law to the first clause and a rule of interpretation to the other limiting clause. The Supreme Court eliminated this inconsistency by holding that the rule of law must apply to the second limiting clause, regardless of the intention of the proferens. A better approach to the problem in *Clayton Love* would have been to ask if the contract had been freely negotiated; did the shipper have a choice of terms upon which he could ship his goods (as in *Slattery v C.I.É.*, discussed above at para.7–14)? Most importantly, did the shipper know and consent to loading of such delicate frozen goods at atmospheric temperatures and did he know of the existence of this sweeping clause? It is probable that the Supreme Court would have still found in favour of the plaintiffs but it would have addressed the issues of freedom of contract and consent, factors that were not always considered by pro-fundamental breach judges.

7–52 While one must doubt whether the doctrine of stare decisis would be satisfied should an Irish High Court judge follow a decision of the House of Lords instead of a decision of the Irish Supreme Court, there are two cases in which the reasoning in *Photo Production* has been cited with approval. In *Western Meats*[173] Barrington J. stated obiter that he would be prepared to follow *Photo Production*. Similarly, in *Fitzpatrick and Harty v Ballsbridge International Bloodstock Sales*[174] O'Hanlon J. stated that the exemption clause in that case would be with certain exemptions wide enough to exclude a claim for damages or rescission and that a fundamental breach of contract would not be sufficient to defeat the exclusion clause unless a collateral contract could be proved. The most recent discussion of *Clayton Love* occurred in the case of *Parkarran v M & P Construction Ltd*[175] but the court, somewhat diplomatically, refrained from commenting on just that for which *Clayton Love* was authority! While this writer agrees that the reasoning of the House of Lords is to be preferred to "the rule of law" approach approved in *Clayton Love*, it is submitted that on this point (but not on other aspects of the *Photo Production* case: see O'Hanlon J. in *British Leyland Exports Ltd v Brittain Group Sales*) repudiation of *Clayton Love* must, of course, await a Supreme Court decision.

7–53 In the present uncertain climate it is hardly surprising to find that it remains a common practice for a litigant to plead that an exemption clause will be defeated by a finding of fundamental breach. In *Regan v The Irish Automobile Club Ltd*[176] the facts of which were that the plaintiff was injured while acting as a flag marshall for the Irish Automobile Club at a motor racing

---

[173] [1982] I.L.R.M. 101.
[174] Unreported, High Court, February 25, 1983.
[175] [1996] 1 I.R. 83.
[176] [1990] I.R. 278.

event in Phoenix Park, Dublin. She argued that the failure to provide safety barriers at the point where the accident occurred was a fundamental breach which disentitled the defendants from relying on an exemption clause that, on its construction, covered negligence of the defendants. While Lynch J. was able to avoid the fundamental breach plea by holding that there was insufficient evidence of a fundamental breach, the learned judge observed:

> "I am not to be taken as either accepting or rejecting the proposition that a fundamental breach of contract will necessarily have the results submitted on behalf of the plaintiff, having regard to cases decided since the decision in *Clayton Love*."

In *ESL Consulting Ltd v Verizon (Ireland) Ltd*[177] Finlay Geoghegan J. held that when the defendants suspended services provided under contract to the plaintiff, a business not a consumer purchaser, the plaintiffs had not committed a breach of contract because of limitation clauses in the contract. Finlay Geoghegan J. summarised the defendant's attempts to rely on the fundamental breach doctrine and the response of the defendant:

> "The plaintiff contends that such limitation clauses do not apply to the plaintiff's claim for damages by reason of the application of the doctrine of 'fundamental breach' or 'breach of fundamental obligation' as applied in this jurisdiction by the Supreme Court in *Clayton Love & Sons (Dublin) Ltd v The British and Irish Steam Packet Company Ltd* [1970] 104 I.L.T.R. 157. The defendants contend that the limitation clauses in the Agreements do apply and the Court should not disapply them in reliance upon the so-called doctrine of fundamental breach for a number of reasons. First, they contend that the breach which occurred in November 2006, was not a 'fundamental breach' within the meaning of the case law relied upon in *Clayton Love*. Secondly, the application by the Supreme Court of the doctrine of fundamental breach to the appeal in *Clayton Love*, was *obiter* as it was not in issue before it and therefore this Court is not bound by that decision to apply the doctrine of fundamental breach. Thirdly, assuming that this Court is free to determine the issue, even if it were to conclude that the breach which occurred was a fundamental breach, or breach of a fundamental obligation, that it should follow the approach of the House of Lords in *Photo Production Ltd v Securicor Transport Ltd* [1980] 2 W.L.R. 283, to this dispute. It is submitted that the Agreements at issue are agreements negotiated between two commercial entities and that the distribution of liability provided for in the Agreements should be upheld and applied by the Court."

After holding that the decision of the Supreme Court in *Clayton Love* was based on fundamental breach and was thus both the ratio decidendi of the case and binding upon her, Finlay Geoghegan J. continued:

---

[177] [2008] IEHC 369.

"I would add, that if I was free to decide the issue in the light of subsequent judgments in other jurisdictions, as has been observed already by a number of my colleagues in the High Court, there appear to be strong arguments in favour of the reconsideration of the application of the so-called doctrine of fundamental breach to agreements between two commercial entities for the reasons outlined by the House of Lords in *Photo Production*."

To summarise: the exemption clause which attacks the core obligation does not attack mere conditions or warranties but the foundation of the contract. If this is the case then the courts should consider whether the parties are contracting in circumstances which show that risk is being freely and voluntarily redistributed by the contract. The courts will lean against enforcement of unconscionable bargains and illusory promises by using the rules and principles specifically developed to deal with such agreements, but, at the end of the day, it may be apparent that the parties have effectively contracted in such terms as to make it clear that one party has freely agreed to take the entire risk. In the 1894 case of *Devitt v Glasgow, Dublin & Londonderry Steam Packet Co* a common carrier was held able to rely on his conditions of contract so as to avoid liability for the loss of part of a cargo he had contracted to transport from Dublin to Glasgow. Andrews J. stated:

"The law imposes on carriers by sea the liability of common carriers, but the obligations thus implied are all the subject of contract, and if the parties think fit to contract themselves out of these obligations, they can, no matter how hard the result may be."[178]

Fundamental Breach—Strained Interpretation OK?

7–54 Notwithstanding the apparent burial of the fundamental breach doctrine in *Photo Production*[179] there have been a number of recent English cases where a contracting party has sought to use express terms to limit either contractual duties or available remedies should that party perform the contract in a way that would disappoint the reasonable expectations of the other party. In *Internet Broadcasting Corp v Mar LLC*[180] a clause giving one party an apparent discretion to decline to perform a contract was said to be the subject of a presumption against being of application to cases of repudiatory breach. A later decision has directed that the courts should "strain against a construction which renders that party's obligation under the contract no more than a statement of intent and will not reach that conclusion unless no other construction is possible".[181] A similar result was achieved in *Kudos Catering*

---

[178] (1894) 29 I.L.T.R. 30 at 32.
[179] [1980] 2 W.L.R. 283.
[180] [2009] EWHC 744 (Ch); *Seadrill MSL v OAO Gazprom* [2010] EWCA Civ 691.
[181] *Astrazeneca UK Ltd v Albermarle International Corp* [2011] EWHC 1574 (Comm) at

(U.K.) Ltd v Manchester Central Convention Complex Ltd[182] where the English Court of Appeal read down a clause which purported to exclude loss of profits to cases where the contract was negligently performed but not instances of non-performance of the contract. Lord Justice Tomlinson, giving judgment for the Court of Appeal, repudiated a suggestion that this interpretation was to "resort to the discredited doctrine of fundamental breach". Tomlinson L.J. said:

> "I repudiate that suggestion. Rather it is, I hope, a legitimate exercise in construing a contract consistently with business common sense and not in a manner which defeats its commercial object. It is an attempt to give effect to the presumption that parties do not lightly abandon a remedy for breach of contract afforded them by the general law."

Refusal to Apply Exemption Clauses

7–55 An exemption clause will not be allowed to operate if someone assents to a clause, the terms of which are misrepresented by the proferens or his ostensible agent. It seems immaterial whether the misrepresentation is fraudulent or innocent. For an example where such an argument was raised see *Bolland v Waterford, Limerick & Western Railway.*[183] A disclaimer or limitation clause may also be denied effect if the evidence before the court suggests that custom and practice within the relevant sector relies upon a statement that the disclaimer seeks to nullify. In *Walsh v Jones Lang LaSalle Ltd,*[184] the plaintiff purchased a development property, the floor areas being represented as 23,057 square feet. The representation was made in a brochure which indicated that, "while every care has been taken in the preparation of these particulars, and they are believed to be correct, they are not warranted and intending purchasers/lessees should satisfy themselves as to the correctness of the information given". After completion the plaintiff discovered the floor area was only 21,248 square feet. The defendant sought to rely on the disclaimer. Quirke J. held that the disclaimer did not apply as evidence indicated that it was not the practice of commercial property purchasers to measure floor areas before completing a purchase. The court was also concerned to point out that there was no evidence that "every care had been taken" vis-à-vis accuracy.[185]

---

para.313 per Flaux J. See also *Shared Network Services Ltd v Nextiraone UK Ltd* [2012] EWCA Civ 1171.

[182] [2013] EWCA Civ 38. A distinction is to be drawn between instances where a clause does not seek to exclude liability but, rather, seeks to replace a common law remedy such as damages with a special contractual remedy such as a guaranteed supply of alternative goods: *Scottish Power UK plc v BP Exploration Operating Company Ltd* [2015] EWHC 2658 (Comm). Even if a breach of contract is deliberate Legatt J. held this should not affect the operation of a properly constructed clause of this kind vis-à-vis "persons" at arms-length.

[183] (1897) 31 I.L.T.R. 62.

[184] [2007] IEHC 28. The claim was brought in negligence.

[185] This point reflects the reasoning in *Esso Petroleum v Mardon* [1976] Q.B. 801.

7–56 If an oral undertaking is given by the proferens the courts will regard the oral undertaking as taking priority over the printed terms in a standard form agreement; see *Evans v Merzario*.[186] If, however, the oral undertaking is inconsistent with a document that was specifically drafted to record the agreement then it may be that the courts will feel compelled by the last vestiges of the parol evidence rule to give effect to the written terms.

7–57 An exemption clause which excludes "all warranties" may not be held applicable to "collateral warranties" unless "collateral warranties" are expressly negatived; see *Andrews v Hopkinson*[187] and *Gallagher Ltd v British Road Services Ltd*.[188]

7–58 Perhaps the most important basis upon which to justify a judicial refusal to apply an exemption clause is the equitable jurisdiction to provide relief against unconscionable bargains. While this doctrine is well established in the context of real property transactions and in several other contractual settings where the parties can be said to stand in a defined or fiduciary relationship to one another, there are only isolated instances where the doctrine has been considered relevant to exemption clauses. While Denning M.R. was prepared to canvass the adoption of such an expansion of the unconscionability doctrine in *Gillespie Bros & Co Ltd v Bowles (Roy) Ltd*,[189] the courts have tended towards the view that interference with contractual allocations of risk should be seen as a matter for legislative interference only. However, the use of the concept of fair dealing in the context of incorporation rules by Costello J. in *Carroll v An Post National Lottery Co* suggests that the day when an Irish court refuses to apply an exemption clause because the clause offends against this concept *as a matter of substantive result*, may not be far off. Indeed, in the Canadian case of *Atlas Supply Co of Canada Ltd v Yarmouth Equipment Ltd*[190] a one-sided franchising agreement was set aside as unconscionable. The stronger party had managed to negative certain warranties that he had given by way of exclusion clauses. This decision has been criticised because of the commercial uncertainty it is said to engender.[191]

Exemption Clauses and Third Parties

7–59 The principle known as privity of contract should, at first sight, provide a clear answer to the question of whether a third party can rely upon an exemption or limitation clause contained in a contract to which the third party

---

[186] [1976] 1 W.L.R. 1078. *Antorisa Investments v 172965 Canada Ltd* (2006) 82 O.R. (3rd) 437 (especially in consumer cases or pressurised sales situations).
[187] [1957] 1 Q.B. 229.
[188] [1974] 2 Lloyd's Rep. 440.
[189] [1973] Q.B. 400.
[190] (1991) 103 N.S.R. (2nd) 1.
[191] Da Re (1996) 27 C.B.L.J. 426.

is not privy. The answer should be in the negative, for it is axiomatic that only a party to a contract may enforce the contract or be the subject of obligations under it. Like most common law principles, however, the courts have tempered the doctrinal implications of the privity rule by reference to certain business realities and expectations. There are three areas of commercial activity where the privity rule has been drastically pruned back.[192]

7–60 First, in contracts of carriage, whereby goods or persons are transported for reward, it frequently occurs that part of the contractual obligations due may be performed on behalf of the carrier by others. It was decided in *Adler v Dickson*[193] that an exemption clause contained in a contract concluded between a shipping company and the plaintiff was not available to an employee of the shipping company when the plaintiff was injured by reason of the negligence of the employee on leaving the vessel in which he was sailing. The leading case is *Scruttons Ltd v Midland Silicones*.[194] The case concerned a contract of carriage under which the carriers limited their liability for damage to goods transported by the carriers under the contract. The goods were damaged by stevedores engaged by the carrier, and the stevedores, in an action brought against them by the owners, unsuccessfully sought to rely on the exemption clause in the contract of carriage. This decision is doctrinally sound and, on construction of the clause, is defensible, as the protection of the limiting clause was only available to carriers and persons bound by the bill of lading, which did not include the stevedores. It is not, however, the last word on this question. The Privy Council has decided that if the exemption clause is properly worded; the third party provides consideration under a separate contract; and due performance is intended by both contracting parties to entitle the third party to avail of the clause, then the limitation clause can be relied upon; see *The Eurymedon*.[195] The decision in *The Eurymedon* is a controversial one, although in some respects it merely re-instates the decision of the House of Lords in *Elder, Dempster & Co v Patterson Zochonis & Co*.[196] In this case, a unanimous House of Lords held that there were circumstances in which a third party could rely upon an exemption clause contained in a contract concluded between two other parties. More recent Commonwealth cases affirm the view that if third parties are intended to be protected, this commercial expectation will be given effect, notwithstanding the doctrinal niceties of the traditional common law theory of privity of contract. In *Glebe Island Terminals Property Ltd v Continental Seagram Property Ltd*[197] an exemption clause was held to apply to exclude both the carrier and terminal operator who were each in fundamental breach in making unauthorised delivery to an unauthorised

---

[192] As Ireland has no legislation like the Contracts (Rights of Third Parties) Act 1999 (UK), the case law remains important.
[193] [1955] 1 Q.B. 158.
[194] [1962] A.C. 446.
[195] *New Zealand Shipping Co Ltd v AM Sattherthwaite & Co Ltd (The Eurymedon)* [1974] 1 All E.R. 1015.
[196] [1924] A.C. 522.
[197] (1993) 40 N.S.W.L.R. 206.

person. The consignee was held bound by a clause that expressly stated there would be no liability for a fundamental breach. However, in a later case a court in Victoria stressed the need for the clause to be drafted in clear language, especially in cases of fundamental breach, if clauses are not to be "read down" or denied effect by a court when the proferens is trying to exclude liability for the deliberate wrongs of his employees.[198]

7–61 Secondly, the courts have recently provided an exception to the privity rule in respect of certain types of construction contract. The cases which develop this exception have a basic set of facts which, boldly and directly, raise the privity doctrine. A construction contract is concluded between an employer and a main contractor. The contract provides that neither the main contractor nor the sub-contractor, nor their servants or agents, shall be liable in respect of defects in the construction work. In the first decision on this particular aspect of the problem, *Southern Water Authority v Carey*,[199] the exclusion clause specifically referred to the defendant sub-contractor, and was concluded on the standard terms of the Institute of Mechanical Engineers/Institute of Electrical Engineers Model Contract Form A, which stated that the main contractor contracted on his own behalf and as trustee for his sub-contractors, servants or agents. The Official Referee, Judge Smout, held that in these circumstances the defendant could rely on the exclusion clause.

7–62 The decision of the Court of Appeal in *Norwich City Council v Harvey*[200] represents a significant extension of the *Carey* case because the exemption clause in the contract between employer and main contractor clearly protected the main contractor but did not expressly refer to sub-contractors and failed to specify that the main contractor acted as agent or trustee of the sub-contractor for the purpose of the exemption clause. Notwithstanding lack of privity of contract, the fact that the sub-contractor had contracted on the basis that the exemption clause would be available to him meant that it would not be just and equitable to deprive the sub-contractor of protection under the exemption clause. Again, the practice in the industry, when the Joint Contracts Tribunal Standard Form of Building Contract was used, as here, was to regard the employer as liable to bear the risk in question and for the employer to arrange insurance, regardless of the fact that the contract document itself did not reflect this reality.

7–63 Thirdly, the law of bailment provides a sui generis exception to the privity rule when a sub-bailee is sued in respect of loss of, or damage to, goods which have been bailed to the sub-bailee under a contract between bailee and sub-bailee. While in the case of *Morris v Martin & Sons Ltd*[201] Denning

---

[198] *Kamil Export (Australia) Property Ltd v PPL Australia Property* [1996] 1 V.R. 538.
[199] [1985] 2 All E.R. 1077; *The Pioneer Container* [1994] 2 All E.R. 250.
[200] [1989] 1 All E.R. 1180.
[201] [1966] 1 Q.B. 716; *Spectra International Plc v Hayesoak* [1997] 1 Lloyd's Rep. 153; *Frans Maas (UK) Ltd v Samsung Electronics (UK) Ltd* [2004] EWHC 1502 (Comm).

L.J. stated, obiter, that an appropriately worded clause could be effective, the issue has been directly confronted by Steyn J. in *Singer Co (U.K.) v Tees and Hartlepool Port Authority*.[202] The plaintiff company, Singer, had engaged another company, Bachman (U.K.) Ltd, to arrange to load a drilling machine owned by Singer onto a vessel. Bachman (U.K.) Ltd contracted as principals with the defendants in order to engage the defendants to load the machine. The machine was damaged by the defendants and when sued in negligence and bailment the defendants relied on standard conditions in the contract between themselves and Bachman (U.K.) Ltd Steyn J. held that the defendants, as sub-bailees, could rely on the terms in the contract between themselves and the bailee, even against a bailor who is not contractually linked with the sub-bailee. The fact that the bailor authorised the bailee to contract with a sub-bailee meant that the bailor was bound by terms found in that contract. While Steyn J. refused to rule on the scope of this bailment principle, the case is a significant one.

---

[202] [1988] 2 Lloyd's Rep. 164.

8 Consumer Protection

Introduction

8–01 In the previous chapter we considered the scope of the judicial power to control the use of exemption clauses. While no real dichotomy can be drawn between legislative and judicial attempts to control the possibilities of abuse of freedom of contract, when one party transfers a risk to another person through the medium of contract, the statutory provisions do provide a degree of protection for persons who do not contract "in the course of business". The need for greater legislative protection of the consumer than that afforded by the common law was recognised by Lord Reid in *Suisse Atlantique* when he considered the practical consequences of the substantive law doctrine of fundamental breach:

> "Exemption clauses differ greatly in many respects. Probably the most objectionable are found in the complex standard conditions which are now so common. In the ordinary way the customer has no time to read them, and if he did read them he would probably not understand them. And if he did understand and object to any of them, he would generally be told he could take it or leave it. And if he then went to another supplier the result would be the same. Freedom to contract must surely imply some choice or room for bargaining.
>
> At the other extreme is the case where parties are bargaining on terms of equality and a stringent exemption clause is accepted for a *quid pro quo* or other good reason. But this rule appears to treat all cases alike. There is no indication in the recent cases that the courts are to consider whether the exemption is fair in all the circumstances or is harsh and unconscionable or whether it was freely agreed by the customer. And it does not seem to me to be satisfactory that the decision must always go one way if, *e.g.* defects in a car or other goods are just sufficient to make the breach of contract a fundamental breach, but must always go the other way if the defects fall just short of that. This is a complex problem which intimately affects millions of people and it appears to me that its solution should be left to Parliament. If your Lordships reject this new rule there will certainly be a need for urgent legislative action but that is not beyond reasonable expectation."[1]

One is tempted to remark that the legislative reforms achieved in England and Ireland since the 1960s largely explain why the judiciary have felt able

---

[1] [1967] 1 A.C. 361 at 406. See generally *Chitty on Contracts*, edited by H.G. Beale, 32nd edn (London: Sweet & Maxwell, 2015), Vol.1, paras 15-001–15-169.

to discard the "fundamental breach as a rule of law" method of counteracting harsh exemption clauses.[2]

8–02 Although it must be conceded that the parties to a commercial contract still endeavour to carve out discretionary provisions that look, on the face of things, as if one party is reserving the right to either withdraw from the contract or avoid providing the other party with any meaningful remedy, judges have stressed that they will interpret such contracts as having such consequences as a matter of last resort.[3] In consumer contracts, however, the combined effect of national law and EU consumer law adjustments to contractual relationships means that straining the words of a consumer contract is generally unnecessary if a contract is to produce a fair result. In fact, the dichotomy between commercial contracts and consumer contracts can be inflexible and a source of some judicial discomfort. In *Robertson v Swift*,[4] the plaintiff, a doctor (described by Jackson L.J. "as an intelligent man well able to negotiate contracts which suit his interests") used the Distance Contracts Directive[5] to cancel a home removals contract, at a very late stage, which involved wasted and irrecoverable costs to the hapless removal firm, simply because he found a cheaper service provider. In holding that the cancellation right set out in the Directive could be used by Dr Robertson, Jackson L.J. observed that the facts of this case were inconsistent with the preamble to that Directive which speaks of the trader initiating negotiations and catching the consumer by surprise (here Dr Robertson began the process by inviting the removal firm to visit and provide a quotation). Jackson L.J. said:

> "I reach this decision with regret. For consumer protection regulations to apply in the circumstances of this case is, in my view, inappropriate. Many removal firms are small businesses. They necessarily visit customers at home in order to assess the proposed work. It must often happen that the remover and the customer enter into an agreement at the customer's home. Once the deal is done, the remover must incur costs in preparing for the move. He may also turn away other work during the relevant period. If the customer has seven days grace in which to cancel the contract, the remover is put in an impossible position."

While the English Court of Appeal held that the plaintiff could not recover his deposit, the UK Supreme Court[6] allowed the plaintiff's appeal on the ground that the plaintiff, as a consumer, was entitled to benefit from the Directive in

---

[2] See in particular the Sale of Goods and Supply of Services Act 1980.

[3] *Astrazenica U.K. Ltd v Albermarle International Corp* [2011] EWHC 1574 (Comm).

[4] [2012] EWCA Civ 1794.

[5] Directive 85/577 of December 20, 1985 to protect the consumer in respect of contracts negotiated away from business premises [1985] OJ L372/31. This Directive has been replaced by Directive 2011/83 of October 25, 2011 on Consumer Rights, effective from June 13, 2014. On transposition in Ireland, see the European Union (Consumer Information, Cancellation and Other Rights) Regulations 2013 (S.I. No. 484 of 2013).

[6] [2014] UKSC 50.

the light of the fact that "the overall purpose of the Directive is to enhance consumer protection" and the UK transposing regulations had to be construed to effect and advance this policy.

Basis Clauses

8–03 In the previous chapter we considered a slender line of authority[7] in which some express terms may be construed so as to define contracted obligations in a narrow way. The parties will seek to identify the basis of the contractual performance as resting upon a set of circumstances that may not be readily apparent on an objective basis. When this occurs the effect may be to prevent one contracting party from relying on an implied term or make out an action in tort. Statute law may acknowledge that the parties are entitled to do this, for example, Section 13(3) of the Sale of Goods and Supply of Services Act 1980 allows a written statement that a motor vehicle is sold without the vehicle being intended for use in the state it is delivered to be effective. It should logically follow that a vehicle sold on the understanding that it is to be cannibalised for spare parts will not benefit from implied statutory terms as to fitness for purpose/merchantability. There have been two contrasting decisions on the meaning of the phrase "sale, as is" in England. In *Dalmare SPA v Union Maritime Ltd*[8] it was said (obiter) that a good sold "as is" does not displace the statutory implied terms as to satisfactory quality and fitness for purpose but limits the buyers remedies for breach to damages only. In *Hirtenstein v Hill Dickinson LLP*[9] Leggatt J. doubted that this was correct on the basis that it was "most unlikely to reflect the expectations of ordinary business people or to be an interpretation that would occur to anyone other than an ingenious lawyer."

Standard Form Contracts

8–04 It is commonplace to find that the parties to a contract have reduced the terms of the bargain into written form, notwithstanding the fact that in most instances an oral bargain is enforceable without the need for its terms to be reduced into writing or evidenced by a memorandum. It is also by no means unusual to find that the offer itself is communicated by way of a standard form document which may have been drawn up by the offeror. It is also possible for the terms of the offer—which in turn will provide the parties with their contract unless the exceptions to the parol evidence rule come into play as in *Clayton Love v B + I Transport*[10]—to have been drawn up by the offeree and remitted to members of the public, traders and other commercial organisations. This indeed is normal practice in the insurance world where the company presents applicants with their own documentation by way of the proposal form which

---

[7] *McGrath v Shah* (1989) 57 P.C.R. 452; *Crestsign Ltd v National Westminster Bank* [2014] EWHC 3043 (Ch).

[8] [2012] EWHC 3537 (Comm).

[9] [2014] EWHC 2711 (Comm).

[10] (1970) 104 I.L.T.R. 157.

the applicant for insurance fills in, and, upon it being submitted to the company, an offer is made to the company on its own preferred terms. Similarly, tenders for the sale of goods or the provision of services are submitted on forms provided by the offeree.

8–05 The practice of formulating offers on standard form documents (often in tandem with a stipulation that the offer and any subsequent contract shall be determined only by reference to the standard form document and that no other statement, written or oral is to be operative) can be justified on economic grounds. Both sides benefit from the use of standard, printed conditions of contract. The cost of negotiating the contract is reduced; if the same forms and terms of contract are widely used throughout an industry or trade, the number of special conditions being kept to a minimum, then this helps each side to clarify their respective intentions and reduces the chance of mistakes or misunderstandings during the negotiation.[11]

8–06 The dangers, however, of allowing the standard form to invariably prevail are considerable. Standard forms are valuable simply because negotiations are truncated by virtue of their use; the possibility that persons may be able to negotiate favourable terms for themselves are substantially reduced if the contract is concluded on the terms proposed. While it is theoretically possible for the person who seeks to negotiate a particular contract to go elsewhere this option, in practice, is not always open. The terms used may be universal within a trade or industry; the bargaining position of the parties may, on the facts, be so disproportionate that the weaker party has no choice but to submit; more invidious still, the party presenting the terms may enjoy a monopoly, either by virtue of being the sole provider or market leader in an industry, or by way of statute. In these instances, where "freedom of contract" cannot be said to exist in any real sense, the contract is a contract of adhesion.[12] The terms are presented on a "take it or leave it" basis; the terms are drafted by one party who seeks to impose them on others in circumstances where negotiations to modify or alter them will not take place. The party is faced with a choice—contract on the terms proposed or not at all.

8–07 It is a mistake, however, to see all standard form contracts as being inherently unfair; it does not follow that because a contract is proposed and concluded on standard form that the bargain is at all suspect. In *Schroeder v Macaulay*,[13] Lord Diplock distinguished between two kinds of standard form document. The first consists of contracts which set out the terms on which mercantile transactions have traditionally been performed. Examples of such

---

[11] Llewellyn, "What Price Contract?—An Essay in Perspective" (1931) 40 Yale L.J. 704; see *British Fermentation Products Ltd v Compare Reavell Ltd* [1999] 2 All E.R. (Comm.) 389.

[12] Kessler, "Contracts of Adhesion—Some Thoughts About Freedom of Contract" (1943) 43 Col. L.Rev. 629. Contrast the observations of the Supreme Court on contract terms contained in agreements reached between individual health boards and pharmacies in *Collooney Pharmacy Ltd v North Western Health Board* [2005] IESC 44.

[13] [1974] 1 W.L.R. 1308.

transactions include bills of lading, charter parties, policies of insurance and contracts of sale in specialist commodity markets. Because these contracts have evolved over the centuries and have stood the test of time these contracts are not generally to be treated with suspicion; indeed, the terms of these contracts are to be presumed to be fair and reasonable. In contrast, the second type of standard form contract is not generally the result of negotiation but is the result of business activities being concentrated into a few hands. Contract terms are imposed by the party with stronger bargaining power. Lord Diplock gave as an example of this second type of contract the ticket cases by which railway companies in the last century obtained effective immunity from actions brought against them by members of the public.

8–08 In Ireland this analysis has been echoed in the Supreme Court. In *McCord v E.S.B.*[14] both Henchy J. and O'Higgins C.J., commenting on the General Conditions of Contract drawn up by the E.S.B. under their statutory obligations to provide an electricity supply, mentioned that customers must contract on the terms proposed, terms which are not only not open for negotiation but are subject to unilateral variation. Henchy J. said the real question in this case was whether the E.S.B. had the power to disconnect the supply of electricity to premises when the meter has been wrongfully interfered with (in this case without the knowledge of the occupier) and the occupier has refused to give a statement in writing setting out what he knows of the wrongdoing and giving an undertaking to pay by instalments for the electricity consumed but unrecorded. Henchy J. continued:

> "Before proceeding to answer this question, it is important to point out that the contract made between the plaintiff and the Board (incorporating the General Conditions relating to Supply) is what is nowadays called a contract of adhesion: it is a standardised mass contract which must be entered into, on a take it or leave it basis, by the occupier of every premises in which electricity is to be used. The would-be consumer has no standing to ask that a single iota of the draft contract presented to him be changed before he signs it. He must lump it or leave it. But, because for reasons that are too obvious to enumerate, he cannot do without electricity, he is invariably forced by necessity into signing the contract, regardless of the fact that he may consider some of its terms arbitrary, or oppressive, or demonstrably unfair. He is compelled, from a position of weakness and necessity *vis-à-vis* a monopolist supplier of a vital commodity, to enter into what falls into the classification of a contract and which, as such, according to the theory of the common law which was evolved in the *laissez-faire* atmosphere of the nineteenth century, is to be treated by the courts as if it had emerged by choice

---

[14] [1980] I.L.R.M. 153. See *Quinn v Honorable Society of King's Inns* [2004] IEHC 220, on the limits of this approach. In contrast to *McCord*, the Supreme Court, in *Viridian Power v Commissioners for Energy Regulation* [2012] IESC 13 treated a statutory supply agreement to ordinary principles of construction, within the *West Bromwich* line of case law.

from the forces of the market place, at the behest of parties who were at arm's length and had freedom of choice. The real facts show that such an approach is largely based on legal fictions. When a monopoly supplier of a vital public utility—which is what the Board is—force on all its consumers a common form of contract, reserving to itself sweeping powers, including the power to vary the document unilaterally as it may think fit, such an instrument has less affinity with a freely negotiated interpersonal contract than with a set of byelaws or with any other form of autonomic legislation. As such, its terms may have to be construed not simply as contractual elements but as components of a piece of delegated legislation, the validity of which will depend on whether it has kept within the express or implied confines of the statutory delegation and, even if it has, whether the delegation granted or assumed is now consistent with the provisions of the Constitution of 1937."[15]

If we confine our attention to the Statutory Conditions of Supply drafted and relied upon by the E.S.B., it is of interest to note that there has been one subsequent decision in which it was held that if the sweeping powers given to the E.S.B. are not exercised with due care and consideration for the consumer then there will be liability for breach of contract. In *Farrelly v E.S.B.*[16] the plaintiff's electricity supply was disconnected even though he had recently paid his electricity bill. The E.S.B.'s employees had acted unreasonably, ignoring the plaintiff's request to wait until the receipt could be produced. Ellis J. allowed the plaintiff's appeal from the Circuit Court and awarded a total of £600 damages. In truth the providers of public utilities can and at times do utilise their powers of cut-off in a relatively sensible way but for political reasons the powers of water authorities to discontinue supply have been constrained by legislation.[17]

8–09 There are a variety of techniques that can be utilised by the judges, who, alarmed at the possibility that superior bargaining power may be abused, are showing an increasing willingness to protect the weak from exploitation by the strong. One method is demonstrated by the House of Lords in *Liverpool City Council v Irwin*.[18] The Council drafted in standard form the conditions that tenants would be bound by if they became Council tenants. The express obligations imposed on the tenant were clearly set out but the document, hardly surprisingly, was silent on the obligations the Council was to undertake in respect of their tenants. Lord Wilberforce noted that it was necessary to imply terms into the contract in order to make what appeared to be a one-sided contract truly bilateral.

---

[15] [1980] I.L.R.M. 153 at 161.
[16] *The Irish Times*, March 10, 1983.
[17] Local Government (Delimitation of Water Supply Disconnection Powers) Act 1995. These disconnection provisions were repealed by the Water Services (No. 2) Act 2013.
[18] [1977] A.C. 239.

8–10 In *McCord v E.S.B.*,[19] Henchy J. indicated that in cases where the contract was presented on a "take it or leave it" basis, the courts will be vigilant in scrutinising the powers given under the terms of the contract to the party imposing those terms on the other. It must be said, however, that this approach is not universally endorsed. McCarthy J. in *Tradax (Ireland) Ltd v Irish Grain Board Ltd*[20] doubted whether the law of contract recognised a general principle that all contract terms should be read against the party who drafted them for in McCarthy J.'s view the only case where this can occur is when the *contra proferentem* rule is applied to exemption clauses. In this writer's view this broader view of the *contra proferentem* rule should apply where the standard form contract falls within Lord Diplock's second category of standard form contract. *Contra proferens* interpretation as a canon of construction is generally applicable, notwithstanding McCarthy J.'s view in *Tradax,* and Lewison[21] traces the maxim back to Coke. However, it is evident that while a court may be expected to deploy the maxim in favour of a consumer, the *West Bromwich* case[22] affords *contra proferentem* interpretation very little scope for application save in respect of exemption clauses.

8–11 Other methods of curbing reliance on standard conditions have surfaced within the context of exception clauses. If there is a conflict between a printed term and an oral statement, or typed or hand-written statement, then the printed form will generally not be applied.[23] The most revolutionary technique has been the direct attack mounted through the unconscionable bargain doctrine. If the contract has not been freely negotiated and the result achieved is seen as unfair then the transaction should, either in whole or in part, be denied effect. Lord Reid in *Schroeder v Macaulay*[24] said, "[i]f contractual restrictions appear to be unnecessary or to be reasonably capable of enforcement in an oppressive manner, then they must be justified before they can be enforced". Lord Denning M.R., on several occasions, asserted that such a common law power was available to the courts[25] and some other judges have approved this approach as desirable although these judges have stated that in the absence of legislation the unfairness or otherwise of a contract is irrelevant; see, for example, Kerr J. in *Gallaher v B.R.S.*[26] and O'Hanlon J. in *British Leyland Exports Ltd v Brittain Group Sales Ltd.*[27] A similar approach has been to

---

[19]   [1980] I.L.R.M. 153.
[20]   [1984] I.R. 1.
[21]   Lewison, *The Interpretation of Contracts*, 5th edn (London: Thomson Reuters, 2011), para.7.08.
[22]   *Investors Compensation Scheme Ltd v West Bromwich Building Society* [1998] 1 All E.R. 98. See also *McGeown v Direct Travel Insurance* [2004] 1 All E.R. 609.
[23]   *Evans v Merzario* [1976] 1 W.L.R. 1078.
[24]   [1974] 1 W.L.R. 1308.
[25]   *Gillespie v Roy Bowles* [1973] Q.B. 400; *Levison v Patent Steam Carpet Cleaning Co* [1978] Q.B. 69.
[26]   [1974] 2 Lloyd's Rep. 440.
[27]   [1981] I.R. 335. Canadian courts, however, have been more interventionist: see *Hunter Engineering Co v Syncrude Canada Ltd* (1989) 57 D.L.R. (4th) 321; *Atlas Supply Co of Canada Ltd v Yarmouth Equipment Ltd* (1991) 103 N.S.R. (2d) 1; *Solway v Davis Moving and Storage Inc* (2002) 222 D.L.R. (4th) 251.

emphasise that a broader duty of good faith will apply in relation to the use of standard conditions that the other contracting party may not reasonably expect to be present in the contract: see Bingham L.J. in *Interfoto Picture Library Ltd v Stilleto Visual Programmes Ltd.*[28] This general approach is particularly apposite in consumer contracts.[29]

8–12 Nevertheless, s.52(1) of the Sale of Goods and Supply of Services Act 1980 (the "1980 Act") empowers the Minister for Jobs, Enterprise and Innovation to, by order, require a person acting in the course of business who uses standard form contracts (within the scope of the 1980 Act) to serve notice on the public such information as the order may specify as to the user of this form and whether or not he is willing to contract on any other terms. No orders have been made under s.52(1).

8–13 The fact that Orders have not been made since 1980 does not mean that prescribing a minimum font size under s.53 of the 1980 Act is not an issue, as the Sales Law Review Group recommended that regulations relating to print size and other presentational issues in consumer contracts should be introduced.[30] In a recent Consultation Paper, *Consultation on the Regulation of Small Print in Consumer Contracts*,[31] two options have been outlined. The first, making an order under s.53 is one option. However, this is said to only address part of the broader problem of intelligibility and for this reason the Consultation Paper puts forward a second option, the enactment of detailed provisions on legibility and intelligibility in the forthcoming Consumer Rights Bill, "preparatory work for which is under way". However, the Scheme of Consumer Rights Bill, published in May 2015, does not contain any measures along these lines.

Irish Regulatory Policy and Mechanisms Protecting Consumers

8–14 In a book of this kind, which is concerned with the general principles that apply to the law of contracts, a full account of consumer law would be both difficult to deliver and somewhat inappropriate. Nevertheless, some general observations on Irish policy and institutions would not be out of place. The most significant driver of Irish consumer protection has been membership of the European Union. While the 1980 Act was, in essence, an updating exercise that provided for improved buyer and hire purchaser protection, as well as some other rights (e.g. for the purchaser of services), the more significant consumer protection measures relating to consumer credit, distance

[28] [1988] 1 All E.R. 548; *Montgomery Litho Ltd v Maxwell* [1999] ScotCS 246; *Finnegan v JE Davy* [2007] IEHC 18; *Kaye v Nu Skin* [2009] EWHC 3509 (Ch).

[29] *Carroll v An Post National Lottery Co* [1996] 1 I.R. 443; *Antorisa Investments Ltd v 172965 Canada Ltd* (2006) 82 O.R. (3d) 437.

[30] Prn. A 11/1576, para.13.50.

[31] Department of Jobs, Enterprise and Innovation (February 2013).

contracts, consumer guarantees, unfair contract terms, and so on, have been effected via the transposition of Directives. Consumers have been able to turn to some statutory agencies in order to obtain consumer advice and assistance, first, since 1998, from the Office of the Director of Consumer Affairs and subsequently through the National Consumer Agency. The important Consumer Strategy Group Report, *Make Consumers Count* (2005) drew attention to the fragmented structure of Irish consumer protection mechanisms and the absence of any accessible source of consumer information in any comprehensive sense. More importantly, the Consumer Strategy Group Report pointed out that Government policy was focusing on improving the quality of regulation generally, including statute law, subsidiary rules, consumer codes, and so on. Although it must be said that consumer interests are still addressed by a panoply of institutions looking at competition rules, food safety and financial services, for example, primary responsibility for "core" legislation rests in the Department of Jobs, Enterprise and Innovation. The Government has responded to such criticisms by amalgamating the functions of the National Consumer Agency and the Competition Authority so as to create one body, the Competition and Consumer Protection Commission under the Competition and Consumer Protection Act 2014. The functions of the Competition and Consumer Protection Commission are set out in s.10 of the Act, the first two of which are to promote competition and to promote and protect the interests and welfare of consumers. Other functions are broadly to be classified as enforcement powers under diverse legislative provisions as well as the Treaty on the Functioning of the European Union, arts 101 and 102. The Act makes several references to the Commission's role in promoting public awareness and information in relation to consumer protection and welfare. Section 10(3) (k) directs that the Commission

> "may, and shall when requested by the Minister, advise and, as appropriate, make recommendations to the Government, the Minister, any other Minister of the Government or any Minister of State, in relation to any proposals for legislative change, or any other policy matters concerning –
> (i) consumer protection and welfare, or
> (ii) competition,
> or both."

In terms of substantive law reform however, the work of the Sales Law Review Group, in its 2011 *Report on the Legislation Governing the Sale of Goods and Supply of Services*[32] has proved to be extremely important. The report drew attention to the need for one text in which all of the main provisions relating to Irish consumer law would be located. The Sales Law Review Group also suggested a number of structural reforms such as a broadening of the rights of consumers in relation to service contracts as well as a general updating of

---

[32] 2011 (Prn. A11/1576).

legal language, such as changing the merchantable quality implied term into a satisfactory quality implied term. Shortly after the Sales Law Review Group issued its report, the Consumer Rights Directive was adopted by the European Parliament and European Council[33] and the Consumer Rights Directive was subsequently transposed by virtue of the European Union (Consumer Information, Cancellation and Other Rights) Regulations 2013.[34] Further work on improving the coherence and accessibility of Irish consumer protection law by the Department of Jobs, Enterprise and Innovation has resulted in the publication of a text, *Scheme of Consumer Rights Bill* in May 2015. Pt 2 of the text sets out provisions in relation to the supply of goods while Pt 3 provides that the provisions in S.I. No. 484 of 2013 relating to digital content are re-enacted in primary legislation. Pt 4 expands on existing Irish law in relation to consumer contracts for the supply of a service (i.e. ss.39 and 40 of the Sale of Goods and Supply of Services Act 1980). Pt 5 re-enacts into primary legislation the unfair contract terms regulations, with some minor adjustments. Pt 5 also addresses the contentious subject of contracts for the supply of a gift voucher. Pt 6 makes a number of changes in relation to enforcement and declaratory orders. No Bill has appeared at the time of writing (July 2016).

Consumer Protection through the Criminal Law

8–15 The safety of foods is the primary responsibility of the Food Safety Authority of Ireland (the "Authority"), established under the Food Safety Authority of Ireland Act 1998. As the website of the Authority states, while food safety legislation dates back to the early nineteenth century, "most if not all of our national food legislation derives from Ireland's membership of the European Union". Powers to prosecute summary offences under food legislation are vested in the Authority under s.57 of the 1998 Act. The Authority in 2013 has taken the lead role in the testing and withdrawal of products contaminated by horse meat. A similar role is played by the Irish Medicines Board, established under the Irish Medicines Board Act 1995. In relation to drugs and substances used in human or veterinary medicine, information and safety advice is provided by the Irish Medicines Board. Other legislative provisions exist in order to prevent or control the extent to which chemical substances and drugs may be used in an attempt to ensure that such substances do not find their way into foodstuffs, for example, by way of chemical or antibiotic residue in meats, cereals and dairy products or providing notice to consumers of the presence of substances such as gluten in food.[35] The controversy over bovine spongiform encephalopathy, or "mad cow" disease, and the possibility that this could enter the human food chain, led to stringent measures[36] that are constantly reviewed and upgraded, as necessary. The

---

[33]   2011/83 of October 25, 2011. See [2011] OJ L 304/64.
[34]   S.I. No. 484 of 2013.
[35]   e.g. S.I. No. 556 of 2014; S.I. No. 389 of 2016.
[36]   e.g. S.I. No. 61 of 1989; S.I. Nos. 79 and 80 of 1997 and S.I. No. 253 of 2008.

Diseases of Animals Act 1966 is used to prescribe a number of controls on animal and poultry vaccines in order to protect the integrity of human health.[37] Legislation to protect foodstuffs from contamination by packaging is also an important means of protecting public health.[38] Related legislation such as the Abattoirs Act 1988 seeks to regulate the conditions under which animals are slaughtered, again for food safety reasons.

8–16 These enforcement mechanisms generally provide for direct enforcement of the law by State agencies or Government departments. An alternative route is by requiring growers and wholesalers to provide a method by which the consumer can identify the producer—under pain of a fine for failure to comply with the legislation—so as to give purchasers a greater opportunity of recovering in the civil courts by way of contract or tort. The obligation on potato growers and packers to register and identify themselves on packages sold by them is an example of this kind of provision, enacted under the Registration of Potato Growers and Packers Act 1984.[39] The use of the criminal law to protect consumers has a long history, with the Merchandise Marks Acts 1887–1931, as amended by the Consumer Information Act 1978, creating offences of applying a false trade description to goods and to services, and the 1978 Act also created the offence of placing false or misleading statements as to the price of goods, services and accommodation. This legislation was repealed by the Consumer Protection Act 2007, a statute that also created a new enforcement body, the National Consumer Agency. The National Consumer Agency has also been abolished and has reemerged as a part of the Competition and Consumer Protection Commission (the CCPC): see the Competition and Consumer Protection Act 2014. Section 39 of the 2014 Act transfers the functions held by the National Consumer Agency to the CCPC. The 2007 Act has at its core four provisions that prohibit the adoption, by traders, of unfair commercial practices (s.41), misleading commercial practices (ss.42–51), aggressive commercial practices (ss.52–54), and prohibited commercial practices (ss.55–63). Misleading commercial practices, as defined in the 2007 Act, are constituted by false information, as set out in the 2007 Act, which is likely to mislead or deceive the average consumer and make that consumer make a transactional decision that the average consumer would not otherwise make. Apart from giving the CCPC the consumer powers and remedies under the civil law, s.47 makes commercial practices that contravene some of the prohibition on misleading commercial practices criminal offences. Section 48 creates a criminal offence vis-à-vis traders who add surcharges to specific means of payment (e.g. more for credit cards than cash) while ss.50 and 51

---

[37] e.g. S.I. No. 289 of 2010, updating S.I. No. 528 of 2002.

[38] e.g. S.I. No. 587 of 2007, amended by S.I. No. 301 of 2010 and S.I. No. 105 of 2011 (polycarbonate infant feeding bottles). A very good example of the regulatory mechanisms that ultimately depend on criminal law sanctions is to be found in toy safety regulations: see S.I. No. 14 of 2011, as amended by S.I. No. 13 of 2013.

[39] See 1984 *Irish Current Law Statutes Annotated* (Dublin: Round Hall Sweet & Maxwell), p.84/24–01.

provide the CCPC with powers to direct that information be provided for goods and services, non-compliance by a trader being a criminal offence. Aggressive commercial practices—harassment, coercion or undue influence—may also lead to criminal proceedings (s.54), while prohibited commercial practices such as false trade authorisation or endorsements or persistent "spamming" are also criminal offences under s.56. The 2007 Act also is something of a consolidation measure because it also provides a prohibition on pyramid sales schemes, repealing the 1981 legislation in this regard (ss.64–66). With the exception of the pyramid selling offence, the 2007 Act provides a defence that the offence was due to a mistake or reliance upon information supplied to the accused, or an act or default by another person, or an accident or some other cause beyond the control of the accused, and the accused exercised due diligence and took all reasonable precautions to avoid the commission of the offence (s.78). The most widely publicised prosecutions in respect of the 2007 Act occurred in 2011. The first related to a "publicity stunt" operated by *The Mail on Sunday* in which it produced an edition of the newspaper that was made up in the style of *The Sunday Tribune* which had gone into receivership a few days before. Six summonses were issued in respect of various offences. Offences under ss.55 and 56 were held to involve a mens rea requirement while ss.43 and 47 were strict liability offences. The summons in respect of the ss.55 and 56 offences was dismissed because District Justice Gibbons found that the defendant had no intention of deliberately misleading or deceiving consumers. As the prosecution did not have to show mens rea in respect of ss.43 and 47, convictions were entered in respect of the other five summonses.[40] In the second 2011 prosecution, Tesco was found guilty of misleading labelling practices[41] and fined €600 plus costs and other expenses. It should be noted that in the Department of Jobs, Enterprise and Innovation document, *Scheme of Consumer Rights Bill* (May 2015), Pt 6 sets out a number of proposed amendments to existing enforcement provisions in the 2007 Act.

Statutory Protection and Civil Remedies

8–17 The 1980 Act is the most significant piece of consumer protection legislation since the founding of the State. The 1980 Act, in part, builds upon the Sale of Goods Act 1893 (the "1893 Act") and the Hire Purchase Acts 1946–1960 and it also extends some degree of protection into areas of commercial activity which have been ignored altogether by the legislature; this is particularly so when the contract involved a contract for the provision of a service rather than sale or hire purchase of goods. Part VI of the 1980 Act provides some degree of protection from commercial activities that are seen as unfair, for example, the despatch of unsolicited goods (s.47). The Hire

---

[40] Dublin Metropolitan District, *National Consumer Agency v Associated Newspapers (Ireland) Ltd*, decision of Gibbons J., January 25, 2011.
[41] National Consumer Agency, *Annual Report 2011*, p.12.

Purchase Acts, however, have been replaced by the provisions of Pt VI of the Consumer Credit Act 1995. It is also to be noted that in relation to credit agreements, s.42 of the 1995 Act not only does not prejudice the operation of the 1980 Act vis-à-vis suppliers, s.42 also gives the buyer recourse rights against the creditor in certain circumstances.

8–18 In relation to financial services, there is a significant body of statute law in the Central Bank Acts 1942 to 2013 which are intended to provide consumer protection measures in respect of financial institutions. The Regulatory Authority, under s.117(1) of the Central Bank Act 1989, has the power to draw up a code of conduct which licence holders shall observe, according to the statute. Some recent actions in which banks have sought to obtain possession of property against mortgage defaulters have been resisted on the basis that requirements of the code then in place were not met. In general the courts have found that while s.117 is silent on the status of (and consequences of not complying with) such a code, it is a factor that can be relevant in exercising any judicial discretion to grant an order of possession.[42] There has been an important ruling in relation to the code of conduct for mortgage arrears. The Supreme Court, in *Irish Life and Permanent plc v Dunne and Dunphy*[43] has ruled that a lender who seeks an order for possession without observing the moratorium provision in the code, may be denied such an order. Non compliance with that code in other respects will not affect a lender's rights in seeking possession.

Sale of Goods

8–19 The 1893 Act was never intended to apply as a comprehensive measure under which traders and suppliers were closely controlled, by statute, from dealing with consumers in such a way as to exploit their superior bargaining power. In fact the concept of the consumer was alien to the 1893 Act for it was a codifying statute which put into statutory form the law as it had evolved by way of mercantile practice. As these rules had evolved in the marketplace amongst traders it is difficult not to see the relevance of Lord Diplock's bifurcation of standard form contracts[44] being directly relevant here too; in such a case (i.e. where both parties are traders) there is little or no reason to hold that the statutory provisions are in any sense prima facie likely to lead to unfair results. Nevertheless the 1893 Act did amend the law in several respects; s.12, considered below, was not representative of the common law position, should the seller of goods not have title to them. Perhaps the most significant provisions in the 1893 Act are set out in ss.12–15, as amended by the 1980 Act.

---

[42] *Zurich Bank v McConnon* [2011] IEHC 75; *Stepstone Mortgage Funding Ltd v Fitzell* [2012] IEHC 142; *Irish Life and Permanent Plc v Duff* [2013] IEHC 43.
[43] [2015] IESC 46; *Danske Bank v Higgins* [2015] IEHC 371.
[44] In *Schroeder v Macaulay* [1974] 1 W.L.R. 1308.

These provisions are now only to be avoided by contrary express agreement, i.e. by an exemption clause, if it can be shown that the buyer does not deal as a consumer and it can be shown that the provision is fair and reasonable.[45]

Section 12

8–20 Section 12(1) of the 1893 Act sets out two obligations:

"(a) an implied condition in a contract of sale that the seller has the right to sell the goods and, in relation to an agreement to sell, that the seller will have the right to sell the goods, at the time property is to pass; and

(b) an implied warranty that the goods are, and will remain free until the time when property is to pass from any encumbrances not disclosed to the buyer and that the buyer shall enjoy quiet possession except in relation to encumbrances disclosed at the time of sale."

Section 12(1) is broken when the seller has no right to dispose of the property, not simply because the goods were stolen by the seller but also if the seller purchased stolen goods, in good faith, believing that thereby he acquired a good title to them; see *Rowland v Divall*[46] and *O'Reilly v Fineman*.[47] Section 12(1) is also broken if the buyer acquires a good title to the goods but a third party could have, at the time of the sale, obtained an injunction to restrain the sale because the labels attached to the goods infringed a trademark of that third party; see *Niblett v Confectioner's Materials Co*,[48] or infringed a patent held by another; see *Microbeads A.C. v Vinehurst Road Markings*.[49] Because s.12(1) is a condition there is a right to reject the goods and claim the purchase price back without the buyer being obliged to make an allowance for any benefits received. Consequential loss may also be recoverable; see *Stock v Urey*.[50] Section 12(2) enables the parties to limit the obligation in s.12(1) should the seller be unsure of his right to sell the goods. However, the words of the disclaimer must be clear. In *Great Elephant Corp v Trafigura Beheer BV*[51] a clause that merely recited that the contract was the entire agreement, along with a clause limiting remedies to the express terms of the contract, were ineffective. The fact that another clause sought to exclude statutory conditions and warranties relating to quality, fitness, and suitability under the 1893 Act, but not title, supported this conclusion. If the terms of s.12(2) are complied

---

[45] Section 55(4) of the 1893 Act, as inserted by s.22 of the 1980 Act.
[46] [1923] 2 K.B. 500.
[47] [1942] Ir. Jur. Rep. 36.
[48] [1921] 3 K.B. 387.
[49] [1975] 1 W.L.R. 218. On intellectual property rights and s.12 see Thomas, "Goods with embedded software: Obligations under Section 12 of the Sale of Goods Act 1979" (2012) 26 I.R.L.C.T. 165.
[50] [1957] N.I. 71.
[51] [2012] EWHC 1745 (Comm).

with and the buyer's quiet possession is disturbed at sometime in the future, the remedy sounds in damages only. However, in *Rubicon Computer Systems Ltd v United Paints Ltd*[52] the purchaser of a computer system was unable to use it because the seller, in a dispute over payment, had installed a time lock which disabled the system for six months, after which time the system was obsolete. The Court of Appeal agreed with the trial judge who held that there was both a breach of the implied term as to quiet possession and a repudiatory breach[53] which entitled the buyer to accept the breach and treat the contract as at an end.

Section 13

8–21 Section 13 enacts an implied condition that where goods are sold by description they will correspond with the description. While at first sight this implied condition simply appears to restate the obvious—that goods expressly described in the contract must meet the description—there are several advantages for the buyer in relying on s.13 rather than the general law. First, the term is labelled a "condition". Rescission is available under the 1893 Act. It is not necessary to show it is a condition expressly so agreed or under *Bentsen & Son v Taylor*.[54] Secondly, description under s.13(3) extends to "a reference to goods on a label or other descriptive matter accompanying the goods". The packaging of the goods may form part of the description; see *Re Moore & Co v Landauer & Co.*[55] It is also established by both English (see *Wren v Holt*[56]) and Irish (see *O'Connor v Donnelly*[57]) cases that the goods may be sold by description even if they are before the buyer, as long as the buyer relies on the description.[58] In the Irish case of *O'Connor v Donnelly* the plaintiff suffered injury when consuming a tin of salmon. While there was no reliance on the seller's skill and judgment so as to bring the case within s.14, both the Circuit Court and High Court affirmed the view that there can be a sale of goods by description even if the goods are shown to the buyer. Judge Davitt in the Circuit Court said that, in order to recover, the buyer must rely upon the description in establishing the essential characteristic of the goods and not simply a quality to be attributed to the goods. This distinction is brought out in *Ojjeh v Waller*[59] where oral promises that Lalique glass car mascots had been originally coloured by the manufacturer turned out to be false. While the

---

[52] (2000) 2 T.C.L.R. 453.
[53] Within *Hong Kong Fir* (see Ch.9); *Louis Dreyfus Trading v Reliance Trading Co* [2004] 2 Lloyd's Rep. 243.
[54] [1893] 2 Q.B. 274.
[55] [1921] 2 K.B. 519.
[56] [1903] 1 K.B. 610.
[57] [1944] Ir. Jur. Rep. 1.
[58] *Harlingdon and Leinster Enterprises v Christopher Hull Fine Art Ltd* [1990] 1 All E.R. 737; *Bolands Ltd v Trouw Ireland Ltd*, unreported, High Court, May 1, 1978; *O'Regan and Co v Micro-Bio Ltd*, unreported, High Court, February 26, 1980.
[59] English High Court, Buckley J., December 14, 1998, [1999] C.L.Y. 4405. For a discussion of this case and the broader context, see McKendrick (ed.), *Sale of Goods* (London: LLP, 2000), Ch.7.

mascots were Lalique glass they had been coloured subsequent to manufacture by persons unknown. Breach of s.13(1) was established and the measure of damages was the difference between the contract price and the value of similar clear Lalique pieces.

8–22 Section 13 is particularly valuable in respect of transactions in which the sale is a "private" sale in the sense that the seller is not a dealer or retailer in the goods in question. A further advantage of relying on s.13 follows from the fact that if the buyer does not deal in the course of business it is now impossible to exclude liability under s.13 for failure to provide goods that correspond with their description. In some of the cases the courts indicated that an appropriately worded exclusion clause may have enabled the seller to exclude liability in such a case; see Scrutton L.J.'s remarks in *Andrews v Singer*.[60] If, however, the buyer does not deal as consumer an exemption clause may operate as long as it is fair and reasonable.

Section 14

8–23 Section 14 of the 1893 Act, as amended, is in many respects the cornerstone of Irish consumer protection law where the quality of goods provided under a contract fall below the expected standard.

Section 14(2)

8–24 Section 14(2), as amended by the 1980 Act, provides that where a seller sells goods in the course of business there is an implied condition as to merchantability, as defined in s.14(3), except in regard:

"(a) to defects specifically drawn to the buyer's attention before contract; or

(b) if an examination is made prior to contracting, to defects the examination ought to have revealed."

In relation to the proviso in section 14(2) cases, it is not enough to point out to the buyer that the goods may be subject to some latent defect such as distemper in a dog.[61] If the goods are examined it may be that the inspection will still fail to transfer the risk from the seller to the buyer: *Bramhill v Edwards*.[62]

8–25 The definition of "merchantable" has troubled the courts for decades for it was not defined in the 1893 Act. The amended s.14(3) now provides a definition:

"… goods are of merchantable quality if they are as fit for the purpose or purposes for which goods of that kind are commonly bought and are as durable as it is reasonable to expect having regard to any description applied to them, the price (if relevant) and all the other relevant circumstances."

---

[60] [1934] 1 K.B. 17.
[61] *Wong Ng Kai Fung v Yau Lai Chu* (2006) 4 H.K.L.R.D. 134.
[62] [2004] EWCA Civ 403.

The importance of the statutory test has been recently addressed. In *James Elliot Construction Ltd v Irish Asphalt Ltd*,[63] the plaintiffs purchased crushed stone aggregate infill material from the defendants. The material included what Charleton J. described as "an abundance of pyrite" which, after use, "expanded and heaved upwards" in the buildings within which it was used, causing bulging and cracking in those buildings. Although expert testimony adduced was highly contentious, the learned judge found that because the foundations did not shift hardly at all, but the floor in which the infill material was used did, the infill material was the cause of the upward heave. Charleton J. found that the infill material was not of merchantable quality, holding that it was not possible to establish otherwise by showing that the goods in question were suitable for one of the purposes for which goods of that type are commonly bought. Thus, the fact that the aggregate might have been capable of use as the infill for a tarmacadamed car park did not make the material merchantable. Charleton J. approved decisions[64] which indicated that post-1893 legislative developments suggested the earlier, more pro-seller case law, was not reliable in relation to newer statutory provisions.

8–26 After a considerable amount of uncertainty it has been determined by the Court of Appeal that the seller sells goods in the course of a business if this is something that the seller does regularly or as an integral part of the business. In *Stevenson v Rogers*[65] it was held that when a fisherman sold his old fishing boat he did so in the course of a business even though his business was not that of a fishing boat factor. An example of someone who sells something regularly could be the sale by a mushroom grower of "spent" mushroom compost.

8–27 This flexible definition of "merchantable quality" has yet to be considered in Ireland in any reported case. There are several decisions from the UK which are of some assistance in fleshing out this concept. In many instances the problem arises in contracts for the sale of a motor vehicle. Even where a vehicle is new there are decisions which indicate that some defects are not such as to make the vehicle unmerchantable. In *Leaves v Wadham Stringer*[66] the vehicle supplied had a leaking boot, a defective bonnet light, a loose door, some rust and a defective fanbelt. The vehicle was nevertheless held merchantable. In contrast, in *Rogers v Parish (Scarborough) Ltd*,[67] a new Range Rover was supplied with a misfiring engine, excessive noise from the gearbox and transfer box, and substantial defects on the bodywork. The Court of Appeal held that a motor vehicle capable of being satisfactorily driven

---

[63] [2011] IEHC 269. Because the Supreme Court ruled on appeal that the exclusion clause was not incorporated into the contract, it did not address the merchantability/fitness for purpose issues: [2014] IESC 74.

[64] *Rogers v Parish* [1987] Q.B. 933 per Mustill L.J. at 942–943; *Cavalier Marketing (Australia) Pty v Rasell* (1990) 96 A.L.R. 375 per Cooper J. at 400–401.

[65] [1999] 2 W.L.R. 1064.

[66] [1980] R.T.R. 308.

[67] [1987] 2 All E.R. 232.

could nevertheless constitute a breach of the merchantable quality implied condition. Given the fact that the vehicle was a prestige model, a Range Rover, the description created expectations that would not necessarily arise in a less up-market marque; the price paid was also relevant and because the price paid here was greater than an average family saloon, the buyer had a right to expect a vehicle which surpassed that which was actually supplied to him. In general, however, motor vehicles which are defective will not be merchantable if the performance of the car is prejudiced, the defect cannot be easily remedied or repair will be expensive or take some time to perform; see *Bernstein v Pamson Motors (Golders Green) Ltd*[68] applying the leading case of *Bartlett v Sidney Marcus*.[69]

8–28 Where the vehicle is second-hand the traditional view of protection available to the consumer has been far from generous. In *Bartlett v Sidney Marcus*, Denning M.R. indicated that a vehicle is merchantable if it is in usable condition, even if not perfect. The standard has risen in relation to "exclusive" or prestige models, following *Shine v General Guarantee Corp*[70] and in a Northern Ireland case, the Denning M.R. test was denied a literal application. Carswell J., in *Lutton v Saville Tractors Ltd*[71] held in favour of the purchaser of a three-year-old Ford Escort XR3 who found the vehicle unsatisfactory and although the defects were minor, performance was clearly affected. Given the age, the price paid, the model involved, and the low mileage, the buyer could expect a better vehicle than that provided, particularly when given an express warranty in relation to the vehicle. Carswell J. indicated that if the vehicle was an older model, with higher mileage, sold at a lower price and did not create expectations of high performance, defects of the kind detected would not have rendered it unmerchantable. On the test of merchantable quality, Carswell J. indicated that the Denning M.R. test in *Bartlett v Sidney Marcus*,

"... is not universally valid in sales of second hand cars, nor would Lord Denning have intended it to be. At the end of the day a decision whether a car is of merchantable quality is a matter of fact and degree, and it is essential to take account of the factors specified in the statutory definition".[72]

In *Bramhill v Edwards*,[73] the English Court of Appeal had to consider whether the importation of a vehicle which rendered the buyer liable to prosecution as well as rendered it uninsurable meant the vehicle was not of satisfactory quality/unmerchantable. Finding that on the facts such vehicles were insurable

---

[68] [1987] 2 All E.R. 220. For an interesting Singapore decision on whether a Rolls Royce was of satisfactory quality see *KOH Wee Meng v TransEurokars Pte Ltd* [2014] 3 S.L.R. 663.
[69] [1965] 2 All E.R. 753.
[70] [1988] 1 All E.R 911.
[71] [1986] N.I. 327.
[72] [1986] N.I. 327 at 336.
[73] [2004] EWCA Civ 403; *Lamarra v Capital Bank* [2006] ScotCS CSIH 49.

and that the UK authorities had not prosecuted drivers of such vehicles, the Court of Appeal nevertheless upheld the claim that the vehicle was of "unsatisfactory quality". Some cases are much easier, as in situations where it is shown that the electrical system was defective, causing the vehicle to be destroyed by fire.[74]

8–29 Whether goods are of merchantable quality within this definition may depend on whether they meet a specification set down in a product manual, as in the case of computer hard drives.[75] Goods may be merchantable if found to be commercially saleable while not suitable for a given purpose but suitable for other purposes.[76] Certain kinds of product may not be merchantable at the time of delivery, the classical illustration of this being certain kinds of software[77] and goods of this kind will require the buyer to afford the seller a degree of time to render the product merchantable.[78] However, the issue of merchantability is one of fact and appellate courts can differ with a trial judge on the weight to be given in respect of evidence put before the trial judge; see *Clegg v Andersson*.[79]

8–30 The merchantable quality test can still produce some surprising results, as the case of *Harlingdon Ltd v Hull Fine Art Ltd*[80] shows. A painting, wrongly thought to be by a particular German expressionist, was sold for £6,000. When it was discovered to be a forgery the purchaser sought rescission as it was of a much lower value. The Court of Appeal, by a majority, held the painting still to be merchantable, mainly because the work could still be appreciated in an aesthetic sense even though its value was between £50 and £100.

Section 14(4)

8–31 In *The Mercini Lady*[81] the English Court of Appeal acknowledged that the statutory implied term as to merchantable, satisfactory quality may not be exhaustive and that there is room for argument that additional implied terms at common law may, in an appropriate case, be inferred. There is also Irish pre-1893 case law on implied warranties as to fitness—see *Sheils v Cannon*.[82] Section 14(4) of the 1980 Act gives added protection to the buyer.

---

[74] *Flynn v Dermot Kelly Ltd* [2007] IEHC 103.
[75] *Amstrad Plc v Seagate Technology* (1998) 86 B.L.R. 34, but not reported on this point; see [1998] C.L.Y. 4385.
[76] *Brown v Craiks* [1970] 1 W.L.R. 752; *Rotherham MBC v Frank Haslam Milan* (1996) 78 B.L.R. 10.
[77] *Saphena Computing v Allied Collection Agencies* [1995] F.S.R. 616, citing *Eurodynamics Systems Plc v General Automation*, unreported, English High Court, September 6, 1988.
[78] See also *Burnley Engineering Products Ltd v Cambridge Vacuum Engineering Ltd* (1994) 50 Con. L.R. 10.
[79] [2003] 2 Lloyd's Rep. 32 (a case on the UK satisfactory quality test). See also *Mitchell v B.J. Marine Ltd* [2005] NIQB 72.
[80] [1990] 1 All E.R. 737.
[81] [2010] EWCA Civ 1145.
[82] (1865) 16 I.C.L.R. 588.

This provision, the successor to s.14(1) of the 1893 Act, implies a condition into every contract for the sale of goods that where the buyer, expressly or by implication, makes known to the seller any particular purpose for which the goods are bought, the goods supplied should be reasonably fit for that purpose. While the seller must sell goods in the course of a business, this alone will not entitle the buyer to succeed for the section goes on to provide that the condition does not apply if the circumstances show the buyer did not rely on it, or it would have been unreasonable for the buyer to have relied on the seller's skill and judgment. The fitness for purpose condition in s.14(4) obviously overlaps with the merchantability condition in s.14(2). A copper detonator included in a bag of coal rendered the coal supplied both unmerchantable and unfit for its purpose; see *Egan v McSweeney*.[83] Foodstuffs which, unknown to the seller, are unsound at the time of sale are also both unmerchantable and unfit for their purpose. In the leading Irish case of *Wallis v Russell*[84] the plaintiff's granddaughter asked the defendant fishmonger for "two nice fresh crabs for tea". The defendant replied that he had no live crabs but that boiled ones were available; he selected two for the plaintiff's granddaughter who took them home. Both the plaintiff and her agent—the granddaughter—suffered food poisoning as a result of eating the crabs. The defendant indicated that he had inspected the crabs himself and would normally be able to detect (by their weight) if anything was wrong with them. Both the Court of Kings Bench and the Court of Appeal found for the plaintiff. Section 14(1) of the 1893 Act was not to be confined to manufactured goods; the intimation that the crabs were to be eaten was sufficient information disclosed to the defendant to signify the particular purpose for which they were required and it was no defence to say the defect was latent and could not be discoverable by inspection.

8–32 One problem that arises in relation to this aspect of s.14(4) follows on from *Wallis v Russell*—when does the buyer satisfy the requirement that a particular purpose be disclosed? In *Brady v Cluxton*[85] a woman purchased a fur coat with no intimation of the purpose for which it was required. The fur caused a skin disorder. The action for damages was dismissed because the plaintiff had not made known the particular purpose for which the coat was required; contrast the later English case of *Griffiths v Peter Conway Ltd*.[86] This approach has been relaxed when the goods have only one purpose: underpants are to be worn next to the skin, hot water bottles are to be used to pour water into, buns, beer and coal are to be "consumed". In the case of *Stokes & McKiernan v Lixnaw Co-op. Creamery Ltd*[87] the plaintiffs purchased alcohol to be used in testing milk. The defendants knew they were supplying a co-operative and that milk would be tested with it. The alcohol was of poor quality and gave misleading results. The purpose was held to have been made

[83]   (1955) 90 I.L.T.R. 40.
[84]   [1902] 2 I.R. 585.
[85]   (1927) 61 I.L.T.R. 89.
[86]   [1939] 1 All E.R. 685.
[87]   (1937) 71 I.L.T.R. 70.

known by implication; see also *Sproule v Triumph Cycle*.[88] On s.14(4) the issue in the pyrite case was whether the seller had made known the particular purpose for which the goods were being bought. On the evidence, Charleton J. found that visits by the seller's employees and communications between the parties would have communicated the intended purpose.[89]

8–33 Where the goods have a multiple purpose and are required to achieve a certain objective, or are intended for a particular use, then actual disclosure may be needed. If denim fabric is to be used to make denim jeans and the seller, unaware of this, provides cloth that is suitable for making dresses but not sturdy enough to make jeans then an action for breach of the merchantability and fitness for purpose obligations will fail; see *Brown (B.S.) & Son Ltd v Craiks Ltd*.[90] To similar effect is the decision of the Court of Appeal in *Rotherham M.B.C. v Frank Haslam Milan*.[91] Here a contract for the supply of steel slag, to be used as hardcore on building projects, was delivered to the buyer. The slag after use expanded causing damage to the building. The Court of Appeal held that the surrounding circumstances indicated that the employer did not rely on the skill and judgment of the contractor in this case. Similarly, if the risk is not a common one the implied term will not be triggered[92]: the essential issue is whether it is reasonable to imply the term, in all the circumstances of the case, and if the goods have a wide range of use specific knowledge may be required if the implied term is to arise.[93] This issue can really be considered to relate to causation. In *Balmoral Group Ltd v Borealis UK*[94] a polymer used in the manufacture of polyethylene storage tanks was found not to be unfit for purpose when the court found that the cause of tank failure related to the failure of the purchasers to redesign the manufacturing process so as to take account of the new polymer.

8–34 The seller may escape liability if it can be shown that the buyer did not rely on the skill and judgment of the seller. In *Slater and Slater (a firm) v Finning Ltd*[95] the defendant supplied a camshaft to be used on a fishing vessel, knowing that the camshaft would be used on that particular boat. The boat in question was liable to an unusual tendency to produce "excessive torsional resonance" so that the camshaft became badly worn. The defendants, not having been made aware of this factor, were in no position to exercise skill and

---

[88] [1927] N.I. 83. Efforts to draw distinctions between general and particular knowledge of the buyer's business in order to fix reliance are generally unsuccessful: *Kendall v Lillico* [1969] 2 A.C. 31; *Britvic Soft Drinks v Messer U.K. Ltd* [2002] 1 Lloyd's Rep. 20; *Webster Thompson Ltd v J.G. Pears (Newark) Ltd* [2009] EWHC 1070 (Comm), an important point when goods are sold on in a distribution chain.
[89] *James Elliot Construction Ltd v Irish Asphalt Ltd* [2011] IEHC 269.
[90] [1970] 1 W.L.R. 752.
[91] (1996) 78 B.L.R. 10, following *Young & Marten Ltd v McManus Childs Ltd* [1969] 1 A.C. 454.
[92] *Slater and Slater (a firm) v Finning Ltd* [1997] A.C. 473.
[93] *M/S Aswan Engineering Establishment Co v Lupdine Ltd* [1987] 1 W.L.R. 1.
[94] [2006] EWHC 1900 (Comm).
[95] [1996] 3 All E.R. 398.

judgment in dealing with that condition. Lord Steyn drew attention to the fact that consumer law had moved some way from the position of caveat emptor but observed that if the plaintiff recovered here, *caveat venditor* would be allowed to run riot. If, however, reliance is asserted it is established that reliance may be partial; if the buyer asks an animal foodstuffs manufacturer to produce food to the buyer's formula then if the food turns out to be unfit because one of the ingredients was of poor quality, thus rendering the food toxic, there will still be liability, the seller being relied upon to the extent that the buyer relied upon the seller to select ingredients of sound quality; see *Ashington Piggeries Ltd v Christopher Hill Ltd.*[96] Partial reliance upon the seller's skill and judgment is clearly possible and can be a source of both liability and a means of avoiding liability. In *Ashington Piggeries* the buyer gave the seller an order to make up a quantity of food to be fed to mink, as per the buyer's recipe. The seller was a manufacturer of animal foodstuffs but had never made up food for mink before. One of the ingredients was contaminated and poisoned the mink. The fact that the foodstuff was made up "to order" did not lead to the conclusion that there was no reliance; there was partial reliance in the sense that the seller was required to provide ingredients suitable to be fed to domestic animals and poultry. In *Jewsons Ltd v Boykan*[97] the plaintiffs, builders' merchants, were asked to recommend domestic heating boilers for installation in a block of flats to be converted by the defendant, an "occasional" property developer. They recommended a specific boiler which worked satisfactorily, but due to their failure to meet energy output requirements in regulations, the flats were difficult to sell. The Court of Appeal found that the defendant had partially relied upon the skill and judgment of the plaintiffs, who were bound to provide boilers that were fit for their purpose as boilers. This the sellers did. What they did not provide were boilers that met energy efficiency requirements because they were not asked to do so; the buyer relied upon other professionals in this respect and because the sellers had no background in property development it would be unreasonable to place reliance on them in this matter.

8–35 If in the *Lixnaw Co-op.* case the co-operative had tested the alcohol before purchasing, no liability under the fitness for purpose or merchantability conditions would arise. The most graphic example, however, is produced by *Draper v Rubenstein.*[98] A butcher who had 17 years' experience of buying cattle in Dublin Cattle Market was held to have relied upon his own skill and judgment and, accordingly, could not invoke s.14 when cattle turned out to be unfit for human consumption. The fitness for purpose condition is also broken if misleading instructions on the package make otherwise suitable merchandise less effective than would have been the case if used correctly; see *Wormell v R.H.M. Agricultural (East).*[99]

---

[96] [1972] A.C. 441.
[97] [2004] B.L.R. 31.
[98] (1925) 59 I.L.T.R. 119; *Southern Chemicals Ltd v South of Ireland Asphalt*, unreported, High Court, July 7, 1978.
[99] [1987] 3 All E.R. 75. On correct use instructions see *Kearney v Paul and Vincent Ltd*,

Section 15

8–36 This section, which was not amended in any way by the 1980 Act, enacts three implied conditions. First, if the goods supplied have been sold by sample there is an implied condition that the bulk will correspond with the sample. Secondly, the buyer must be given a reasonable opportunity to inspect the sample. Thirdly, if the goods supplied match the sample in every way but the sample and the bulk are defective and thus unmerchantable, there is to be liability in respect of this defect if it would not be apparent on reasonable examination of the sample. It is extremely difficult, even prior to the enactment of the new s.55 in the 1980 Act, to avoid liability under s.15; either the law of mistake[100] or a rule of construction (laid down in *Champanhac & Co Ltd v Waller & Co Ltd*[101]) may be invoked by the courts so as to short circuit any exemption clause.

The Consumer Guarantee Regulations

8–37 To this traditional scheme must be added the provisions of the consumer goods and guarantees regulations[102] which give additional rights and remedies to the consumer of goods that are not in accordance with the contract of sale.[103] Any lack of conformity, in addition to existing causes of action and remedies, will produce liability under reg.7(1) and the remedies available are an entitlement to have the goods brought into conformity free of charge by repair or replacement, or any appropriate reduction in price, or rescission of the contract with regard to those goods: reg.7(2). What is really innovative here is the consumer's right to require the seller to repair or replace the goods, free of charge, unless this is impossible or disproportionate: reg.7(3).

Hire-Purchase

8–38 If the transaction is a hire-purchase transaction rather than a contract of sale or an agreement to sell then the hirer cannot rely on the 1893 Act; witness the decision in the Irish case of *B.P. v Smyth*.[104] In 1946 the Oireachtas, through the Hire-Purchase Act 1946 (the "1946 Act"), gave consumers who found it necessary to obtain goods on hire-purchase a degree of protection from faulty

---

unreported, High Court, July 30, 1985. Incorrect use instructions were held to have been a factor in *Wright v AIB Finance Leasing* [2007] IEHC 409, a case where liability was fed down the chain of supply to the manufacturer.

[100] *Megaw v Molloy* (1878) 2 L.R. (Ir.) 530.

[101] [1948] 2 All E.R. 724.

[102] European Communities (Certain Aspects of the Sale of Consumer Goods and Associated Guarantees) Regulations 2003 (S.I. No. 11 of 2003), giving effect to Council Directive 1999/44.

[103] See generally (2001) 9 E.R.P.L. and specifically Bird (2001) 9 E.R.P.L. 279 on the impact on Irish consumer law.

[104] (1931) 65 I.L.T.R. 182.

and defective merchandise. While shadowing the 1893 Act, the 1946 Act in some respects went further than the 1893 Act.

(1) Implied terms

8–39 Section 9 of the 1946 Act implied into contracts of hire-purchase the same implied terms as were set out in ss.12–15 of the 1893 Act. In one respect protection afforded by s.9 was greater in relation to the fitness for purpose condition because this term could only be excluded if the hirer's attention had been specifically drawn to the existence of the express term in the contract which excluded the implied statutory condition. Section 2(4) of the 1980 Act repealed s.9 of the 1946 Act, but the implied terms were substantially re-enacted in ss.26–29 in the clarified and modified language applied to sale of goods by the 1980 Act.[105] The legislation that currently governs the hirer's rights in a hire-purchase contract is now set out in the Consumer Credit Act 1995 (the "1995 Act"); the 1946 and 1980 hire-purchase legislation has been repealed and substantially re-enacted in Pt VI of the 1995 Act. Section 74 of the 1995 Act sets out implied terms as to title and these cannot be displaced by contrary agreement: s.79(2). Implied conditions as to goods let by description, merchantability and fitness for purpose, and the letting of goods by sample, are found in ss.75, 76 and 77. The exclusion of these implied conditions may be made by agreement only if the excluding provision is fair and reasonable: s.79(3).[106] Section 82 of the 1995 Act reproduces the section 13 implied condition vis-à-vis the sale of motor vehicles and makes it equally applicable to hire-purchase letting of vehicles. While it is therefore clear that a person who takes goods on hire-purchase terms can rely on much the same set of rights in respect of those goods as an outright buyer of goods can, it will still be important to establish whether the contract is a contract of sale or one of hire-purchase in order to know which implied terms are to be pleaded; this will be particularly important if goods are bailed out to the hirer, through a dealer, the hirer's contract of hire-purchase being with a finance company rather than the dealer; see *Dunphy v Blackhall Motors*,[107] the effect of which is reversed by s.32 of the 1980 Act and re-enacted in s.80 of the 1995 Act.

(2) Other statutory terms

8–40 The hirer of goods obtains further protection under the 1995 Act; a copy of the terms of the agreement must be delivered or sent to the hirer within 10 days of the agreement, otherwise the contract may be unenforceable. If the hirer has paid one-third of the total hire-purchase price, the goods are protected goods and under s.64 cannot be repossessed without the appropriate court order, although this does not prevent the hirer from voluntarily giving

---

[105] *Butterley v UDT* [1963] I.R. 56.
[106] See *Sovereign Finance Ltd v Silver Crest Furniture* [1997] C.C.L.R. 76.
[107] (1953) 87 I.L.T.R. 128.

the property back; see *McDonald v Bowmaker (Ireland)*.[108] The consumer may be further protected by the courts from unreasonable default clauses.[109]

Hiring or Leasing

8–41 The rise of the leasing industry as a method of supplying moveable property to industry and commerce under an operating lease or a finance lease, has been a significant commercial development in recent years. However, because most operating leases do not give the lessee a right of purchase (a right of purchase during the lease or period of hire is inconsistent with a lease and an option to buy at the end of the leasing period does not create an agreement to buy),[110] the lessee did not enjoy any statutory rights should the moveables malfunction. Section 38 of the 1980 Act gave a lessee similar rights to those afforded to the hirer of goods under a hire-purchase contract; see *O'Callaghan v Hamilton Leasing*.[111] Even if the lessee loses rights to repudiate the leased property there may still be a remedy in damages; see *U.C.B. Leasing Ltd v Holtom*.[112]

8–42 Section 38 has been repealed by the 1995 Act and Pt VII of the 1995 Act provides the hirer of goods in a consumer hire agreement with rights that are based upon ss.75–83 of that Act; that is, such persons enjoy rights which parallel those of a hire-purchase letting. Where the hirer is a lessee acting in the course of a business there is a gap in the area of statutory protection, but the High Court has intervened by constructing a cause of action by way of collateral contract: *Flynn v Dermot Kelly Ltd*.[113]

Supply of Services

8–43 The most innovative aspect of the 1980 Act is found in Pt IV. There are implied terms—the 1980 Act does not say whether they are conditions or warranties in the technical sense—set out in s.39 which are to apply to contracts where the supplier is acting in the course of a business:

"(a) that the supplier has the necessary skill to render the service;
(b) that he will supply the service with due skill, care and diligence;
(c) that where materials are used, they will be sound and reasonably fit for the purpose for which they are required; and
(d) that, where goods are supplied under the contract, they will be of merchantable quality within the meaning of s.14(3) of the Act of 1893."

---

[108] [1949] I.R. 317.
[109] Particularly acceleration clauses: *Fernheath Developments Ltd v Malone* [2010] NI Ch 19.
[110] *Close Asset Finance Ltd v Care Graphics Machinery Ltd*, *The Times*, March 21, 2000.
[111] [1984] I.L.R.M. 146.
[112] [1987] R.T.R. 362.
[113] [2007] IEHC 103.

Section 39 has proved to be extremely useful in the context of holiday litigation where the tour operator will often fail to make clear express promises
about the quality of the holiday and incidental matters. In *O'Flynn v Balkan
Tours Ltd*[114] the scope of the duty of care incumbent upon a tour operator was
held to cover information about local ski runs within the ski resort. *McKenna
v Best Travel Ltd*[115] indicates that the section 39 duty extends to information
about the safety of a particular area or resort. So, when the plaintiff was injured
during a demonstration on the West Bank, the failure to advise the plaintiff, a
tourist to the Holy Land, of local conditions and suitable precautions was held
to break that duty.

8-44 The application of s.39 in *Irish Telephone Rentals Ltd v Irish Civil
Service Building Society Ltd*[116] illustrates how useful the section may
be in cases where the contract extends over a period of time. The plaintiff
contracted to install and maintain a telephone system in the premises of the
defendant. While the system seemed to function adequately in 1982, the time
of installation, by 1985 it was causing severe difficulties because it could not
cope with the increased volume of calls that resulted from the defendant's
greater volume of business, a volume of business that the telephone system
was supposed to handle adequately. Costello J. found that, under s.39, the
contract contained an implied term that goods would be of merchantable
quality. These goods installed as part of a leased telecommunications service
consisted of a switchboard, console and telephone sets; they were held not to
be fit for the purpose of providing a reasonably efficient telephone system.
On the facts of this case it would be likely that a common law duty would
also arise and, in a leasing contract, the implied conditions available under a
consumer hire contract would also be available to the lessee.

8-45 In practice the most problematical product that straddles the goods/
services boundary is computer software. Standard "shrink wrap" software
is regarded as a good and in most cases even software that is specifically
written ("bespoke") or adapted ("customised") for the buyer is regarded as
a good, even though it is the skill of the programmer(s) that is the core of
these transactions. Even if the software is directly loaded onto the buyer's
system the leading English case holds the software to be goods,[117] even under a
licence agreement, even though the licence agreement will not be a contract of
sale. In this case the view is also expressed that common law duties could arise
even if sale of goods legislation did not operate. Another possibility, especially

---

[114] Unreported, High Court, December 1, 1995, affirmed by the Supreme Court: unreported,
April 7, 1997.
[115] Unreported, High Court, December 17, 1996.
[116] [1991] I.L.R.M. 880. See also *Trebor Bassett Holdings Ltd v ADT Fire & Security plc* [2012]
EWCA Civ 1158.
[117] *St. Albans Council v International Computers Ltd* [1996] 4 All E.R. 481; contrast
Gammasonics Institute v Comrad [2010] NSWSC 267 and *Fern Computer Consultancy Ltd v
Intergraph Cordworx & Analysis Solutions Ltd* [2014] EWHC 2908 (Ch).

when a licence excludes a sale of goods, is that under the 1995 Act, implied terms might arise.

8–46 However, the concept of a service contract was given a narrow interpretation by Costello J. in *Carroll v An Post National Lottery Co.*[118] Section 39 was held not to apply when the plaintiff purchased a lottery ticket which was negligently processed by the staff at a post office, for the learned judge held that "the contract is to sell a ticket which confers rights and obligations on the parties to the contract". This appears a somewhat surprising conclusion. A contract of insurance can also be so described but no-one doubts that an insurance intermediary operates in the financial services sector. Similarly, ss.39 and 40 have been held not to be applicable on issues concerning the degree of notice required to incorporate an arbitration clause into a contract.[119]

Contracting out under the Sale of Goods and Supply of Services Act 1980

8–47 If the parties to the contract attempt to contract out of the implied terms inserted by the 1980 Act they will find that their right to do so is controlled by legislation. In the context of the Sale of Goods Acts 1893–1980, s.55(4) of the 1893 Act, as amended, renders ineffective any attempt to contract out of the implied conditions as to sales by description, merchantability, fitness for purpose, and the implied conditions as to sales by sample if the buyer deals as consumer. The 1893 Act also provides that an exemption clause shall in any other case not be enforceable unless it can be shown that the term is fair and reasonable. The "fair and reasonable" test also applies to attempts to contract out of s.13 (the implied term relating to motor vehicle sales), s.31 (the implied conditions in ss.27–29 which relate to non-consumer hire-purchase transactions), s.40 (implied terms relating to the supply of services) and s.46 (contractual attempts to limit or exclude liability for misrepresentation). Before the "fair and reasonable" test can operate, the person invoking the statutory rights conferred in relation to the sale or hire-purchase letting of goods by description, the sale or hire-purchase letting of goods alleged to be unmerchantable or unfit for their purpose, or the sale or hire-purchase letting of goods sold by sample, must show that they dealt as consumer.

8–48 Section 3 of the 1980 Act provides:

"1. In the Act of 1893 and this Act, a party to a contract is said to deal as consumer in relation to another party if—
    (a) he neither makes the contract in the course of a business nor holds himself out as doing so; and
    (b) the other party does make the contract in the course of a business; and

---

[118] [1996] 1 I.R. 443.
[119] *Carroll v Budget Travel*, unreported, High Court, December 7, 1995.

(c) the goods or services supplied under or in pursuance of the contract are of a type ordinarily supplied for private use or consumption.

2. On—
   (a) a sale by competitive tender; or
   (b) a sale by auction—
       (i) of goods of a type, or
       (ii) by or on behalf of a person of a class defined by the Minister by order,

the buyer is not in any circumstances to be regarded as dealing as consumer.

3. Subject to this, it is for those claiming that a party does not deal as consumer to show that he does not."

Section 3 has been considered on two occasions. In *O'Callaghan v Hamilton Leasing (Ireland) Ltd*[120] the lessee of a drinks vending machine to be used in his takeaway foods shop alleged the machine was defective within s.14 of the 1893 Act or, alternatively, s.38 of the 1980 Act. McWilliam J., allowing the lessor's appeal from a decision in the Circuit Court, held that the leasing agreement had effectively excluded liability for these defects. The plaintiff had not dealt as consumer—the goods were provided for the plaintiff's business use and s.3 did not require that the ultimate user of a product was always to be classified as a consumer. This approach was later followed in *Cunningham v Woodchester Investments Ltd*[121] when the acquisition of an automatic telephone system to be installed in an agricultural college was held to be a non-consumer sale, even though the college was run on a non-profit making basis.

8–49 While these two decisions of McWilliam J. are no doubt correct this approach is at odds with the decisions of the appellate courts in England, which, in two cases in particular,[122] have held that a degree of regularity in dealing is needed before the buyer will lose the status of a consumer. The net result in these English cases is to give a business purchaser the status of a consumer, even though the purchase is an incidental element in the purchaser's business activities (e.g. purchase of storage equipment). While the decision in *R. & B. Customs Brokers Co Ltd v U.D.T. Ltd* must be regarded as borderline, it is difficult not to agree with Pearce[123] that regarding business purchasers as consumers is a regrettable judicial development and a reversal of

---

[120] [1984] I.L.R.M. 146.
[121] Unreported, High Court, November 16, 1984; *British Fermentation Products Ltd v Compair Reavell Ltd* [1999] 2 All E.R. (Comm.) 389.
[122] *R. & B. Customs Brokers Co Ltd v U.D.T. Ltd* [1988] 1 All E.R. 847; *Davies v Sumner* [1984] 1 W.L.R. 1301.
[123] [1989] 3 L.M.C.L.Q. 371. For an interesting case in which an investor was permitted to amend his pleadings so as to rely on the Unfair Contract Terms Regulations, see *McCaughey v Anglo Irish Bank Corp* [2011] IEHC 546. This effort was ultimately in vain because the defence sought data on the plaintiff's financial affairs to establish if he was a private or personal investor and the amendment was withdrawn.

Parliamentary intention, which has taken place in isolation from a clear review of the policy issues invoked.

"Fair and reasonable"

8–50 The Schedule to the 1980 Act provides that a term is fair and reasonable if that term, in all the circumstances, was a term which was "or ought reasonably to have been known to or in contemplation of the parties when the contract was made". While this test looks to all the facts and requires the court to consider the reasonable expectations of the parties, given the industry or area of commercial activity concerned, the Schedule to the 1980 Act sets out factors that particular regard may be given to:

"(a) the relative bargaining position and the possibility of an alternative method of meeting the customer's requirements; or

(b) whether there was an inducement to enter this contract; could another supplier have provided the goods or service without the exception clause?; or

(c) whether the customer had actual or constructive knowledge of the existence of the term or its extent, having particular regard to a custom of trade or a course of dealing; or

(d) if the term imposed an obligation on the customer, to be met by him, was compliance practicable?; or

(e) whether the goods were manufactured, processed or adapted to the customer's special order."

Factor (a) is clearly designed to see if the customer had any real chance of negotiating a different contract. Even if the supplier holds a monopoly but the customer had a choice of contract options—whether to buy insurance, for example—this may still indicate the term was fair and reasonable; see *Slattery v C.I.É.*[124] In *Woodman v Photo Trading Processing*[125] a film processing service which excluded liability for loss and limited its liability to replacement of the reel of film, undertook to process the plaintiff's wedding photographs. Most of the photographs were lost. In considering whether the exclusion was fair and reasonable Clarke J. held that, within the industry, a code of practice recognised a two-tier level of service. The unavailability of a second level of service, under which the processor would be liable to exercise greater care (and be entitled to charge accordingly) meant that the processor could not show that the clause satisfied the statutory test of reasonableness. The issue seems to be whether the consumer could have obtained a similar service on

---

[124] (1972) 106 I.L.T.R. 71; *Moores v Yakeley Associates Ltd* [2000] T.C.L.R. 146. Contrast *Overseas Medical Supplies Ltd v Orient Transport Services* [1999] 1 All E.R. (Comm.) 981 with *Granville Oil and Chemicals Ltd v Davies Turner & Co* [2003] 1 All E.R. (Comm.) 819.
[125] (1981) 131 N.L.J. 933.

different terms either from the same supplier or another supplier. The fact that all suppliers shelter behind similar terms does not seem to have come before the courts other than in an oblique manner; see *Usher v Intasun*[126] and *Singer Co (U.K.) Ltd v Tees and Hartlepool Port Authority.*[127]

8–51 Factor (b) is similarly designed to consider whether the customer made a choice between one supplier as against another; if there was a collateral inducement—a "free gift" for taking one type of vehicle from dealer A when dealer B had the same vehicle but did not make this collateral inducement available—then the customer may be taken to have freely consented to that term. It is also relevant whether in practice another supplier could have been approached to provide the goods or services on other terms. It may be, for example, that the proferens has a degree of specialisation in the market—forwarding goods to Iran, for example—that makes it impracticable to seek related facilities such as insurance for those goods from someone other than the proferens.[128]

8–52 Factor (c) crosses the boundary from this notion of the substantive fairness of the transaction into the procedural fairness of using this particular term. Many of the comments made in relation to incorporation of exemption clauses are relevant here. If, however, the proferens has not on previous occasions relied upon the clause but has tried to negotiate a compromise of any claim—no doubt in order to retain the goodwill of his customers—this will indicate that the term was not fair and reasonable; see *Western Meats Ltd v National Ice & Cold Storage Co*[129] and *George Mitchell (Chesterhall) Ltd v Finney Lock Seeds Ltd.*[130] Consent is investigated, often by reference to the degree of expertise on each side, and even if the buyer finds that the seller is intransigent on a particular term, this fact may incline the court towards upholding the clause if the contract is between businesses contracting at arm's length.[131]

8–53 Factor (d) deals with limitation of liability clauses that require the customer to notify the seller or supplier within a set period of the risk of losing his cause of action; see cl.16 in *Clayton Love v B + I Transport*[132] for an example. Whether compliance was practicable is a question of fact. In *Stag Line Ltd v Tyne Ship Repair Group Ltd*[133] Staughton J. had to consider whether a limiting provision in respect of a ship repair contract could pass the reasonableness test. If the contract in question required the return of the vessel

---

[126] [1987] C.L.Y. 418.
[127] [1988] 2 Lloyd's Rep. 164.
[128] *St. Albans Council v International Computers* [1995] F.S.R. 686 (First Instance); *Overseas Medical Supplies Ltd v Orient Transport Services Ltd* [1999] 1 All E.R. (Comm.) 981.
[129] [1982] I.L.R.M. 101.
[130] [1983] 2 A.C. 803.
[131] *Watford Electronics Ltd v Sanderson C.F.L. Ltd* [2001] 1 All E.R. (Comm.) 696.
[132] (1970) 104 I.L.T.R. 157.
[133] [1984] 2 Lloyd's Rep. 211.

to the Tyneside ship repair yard in cases of defective work, such an impracticable obligation was said, obiter, not to be fair and reasonable given that the vessel could break down anywhere in the world.

8–54 Factor (e) seems to be ambivalent. Presumably, if the customer has laid down specific requirements this will point away from the clause being unfair or unreasonable. However, in *Edmund Murray Ltd v B P International Foundations*[134] an order placed by the plaintiffs for the supply of an oil rig, to specification, was given to the defendants because the defendants had specialist knowledge. In these circumstances the defendants' conditions, which excluded liability for the provision of a rig that was unsuitable *simpliciter*, were not fair and reasonable.

8–55 These factors are broad guidelines and may not be exhaustive in any sense. The view has been expressed that in cases where goods are sold under a finance arrangement whereby a finance house never possesses the goods, the clause may be more likely to be upheld,[135] but even if this has some validity, the decision in *Danka Rentals Ltd v Xi Software*[136] affords this factor very little weight if the clause is such as to remove any obligations from the shoulders of the seller.[137]

8–56 The leading English case of *George Mitchell (Chesterhall) v Finney Lock Seeds Ltd* indicates that other factors pertinent to the "fair and reasonable" test include whether the supplier could have insured against a claim without this materially affecting the price at which the goods or service could be provided. However, the cases suggest the issue is whether at the time of the formation of the contract, insurance was available to either or both parties and the terms upon which cover was available—the premiums paid and the exclusions applicable, for example. In *Singer v Tees and Hartlepool Port Authority*[138] Steyn J. held that it was irrelevant whether the parties were actually insured, and in *The Flamar Pride*[139] Potter J. held that, unless the evidence indicates that prior to the conclusion of the contract the existence or extent of cover was discussed, the law will not regard the insurance position of the parties as material in commercial or consumer contracts.

---

[134] (1992) 33 Con. L.R. 1; *St Gobain Building Distribution Ltd v Hillmead Joinery (Swindon) Ltd* [2015] EWHC B7 (TCC).

[135] *R&B Customs Brokers Co v U.D.T.* [1988] 1 W.L.R. 321; *Photoprint v Forward Trust* [1994] T.L.R. 146.

[136] (1997) 17 Tr. C.R. 74.

[137] It may also be argued that certain finance transactions may be traps for the unwary and thus enforceable; this is discussed in *Danka Rentals*; see *Lease Management Services Ltd v Purnell Secretarial Services* [1994] C.C.L.R. 127 and *Sovereign Finance v Silver Crest Furniture* [1997] C.C.L.R. 76.

[138] [1988] 2 Lloyd's Rep. 164.

[139] [1990] 1 Lloyd's Rep. 429.

8–57 It is suggested that, in practice, insurance is a most material factor. The *availability* of insurance, however, is a quite distinct matter and it was of critical importance in *St. Albans*.[140] Actual levels of cover may be relevant to the overall issues of reasonableness. In *Moores v Yakeley Associates Ltd*, cover of £500,000 in respect of building costs of half that amount (the balance being retained to cover potential legal costs) was held to be a reasonable amount of insurance. Dyson J. said of the argument that any "cap" below an average level of cover available to the supplier is per se objectionable:

> "[A]n architect might have insurance cover of £10 million, and be engaged to carry out a small project with an estimated contract value of £10,000. It would be absurd in such a case that any ceiling figure lower than £10 million would be unreasonable."[141]

If the limitation in question is out of line with levels found in other standard terms in the industry this can be a very relevant factor.[142]

8–58 The most important English decision on the reasonableness test is *Smith v Eric S. Bush (a firm)*.[143] The respondent applied to a building society for a mortgage in order to purchase a house. The building society engaged a firm of surveyors to carry out a statutory written report and valuation. The respondent paid a fee for the survey and obtained a copy of the report. The report was negligently compiled and failed to detect severe defects in the property. The purchaser relied upon the report and did not obtain a further report. The House of Lords indicated that a duty of care was owed in these circumstances to the intending purchaser by the surveyor. The surveyor was not allowed to rely upon a clause which purported to exclude liability for negligence. In cases where domestic property is purchased by an owner-occupier, it was unreasonable to allow a professional person to transfer risk to the owner-occupier given that the loss was caused by negligence and the loss could more reasonably be borne by the professional and his insurer. In contrast, a professional management contractor who limits liability for the provision of services may satisfy the "fair and reasonable" test if the contract is negotiated and not in standard form, the parties are seen as being at arm's length and there were others who could have been approached to contract on dissimilar terms. Both parties were able to obtain insurance against the risk so this factor was neutral in nature; see also *Chester Grosvenor Hotel v Alfred McAlpine Management*.[144] In recent cases the English Court of Appeal has emphasised that due consideration must be paid to the fact that the contract is between contracting parties who may be

---

[140] Here the actual cover was very low (it was increased after the claim was brought by the plaintiff) and higher cover was available at competitive rates.
[141] [2000] T.C.L.R. 146 at 156
[142] *Sonicare International Ltd v East Anglia Freight Terminal Ltd* [1997] 2 Lloyd's Rep. 48.
[143] [1989] 2 All E.R. 514.
[144] (1992) 56 B.L.R. 115; *W. Photoprint v F.T.E.* (1993) 12 Tr. L.R. 146; *Monarch Airlines v London Luton Airport* [1997] C.L.C. 698.

best able to look after their own interests and that the interests of justice are not served by giving limitation or exclusion clauses a "hostile" or artificial interpretation. Tuckey L.J. wrote that the "fair and reasonable" test,

> "[p]lays a very important role in protecting vulnerable consumers from the effects of draconian contract terms. But I am less enthusiastic about its intrusion into contracts between commercial parties of equal bargaining strength, who should generally be considered capable of being able to make contracts of their choosing and expect to be bound by their terms".[145]

Where the parties are not of equal bargaining strength, however, the "fair and reasonable" test should apply. In *Kingsway Hall Hotel Ltd v Red Sky IT (Hounslow) Ltd*[146] a hotel reservation booking system was supplied without meeting assurances as to effectiveness and without critical documents on use having been supplied. The buyer was relying upon the seller and had no expertise in information technology systems. The contract was on the seller's standard terms and was not negotiated, being "far removed" from a *Watford Electronics* scenario. Similarly, in *James Elliott Construction Ltd v Irish Asphalt Ltd*[147] construction aggregate was sold to buyers on foot of delivery notes containing very sweeping disclaimers of liability. The aggregate was laced with pyrite and did not meet construction industry standards despite being sold as being standard-compliant. Charleton J., obiter, found the disclaimer was not fair and reasonable. It would be unreasonable to expect the buyer to test the material as this was sold for multiple use on foot of the specification. The testing onus fell upon the owners of the quarry where the material originated. The purchaser's bargaining power vis-à-vis testing was "vastly different", with the buyer having no ability to test various products available to the buyer. Referring to factor (c) in the Schedule to the 1980 Act, Charleton J. said the term was not known to the buyer.

The test in relation to service contracts

8–59 Where the cause of action is rooted in s.39, the section 39 implied term can be excluded if the contract is a business-to-business transaction; if the buyer deals as a consumer the clause must be specifically drawn to the attention of the consumer and pass the "fair and reasonable" test. The first factor can in essence be satisfied by proof that the consumer was aware of the

---

[145] In *Granville Oil and Chemicals Ltd v Davies Turner & Co* [2003] 1 All E.R. (Comm.) 819 at 829; see also *Watford Electronics Ltd v Sanderson C.F.L. Ltd* [2001] 1 All E.R. (Comm.) 696; *Frans Maas (UK) Ltd v Samsung Electronics (UK) Ltd* [2004] EWHC 1502 (Comm).

[146] [2010] EWHC 965 (TCC); *Avrora Fine Arts Investment Ltd v Christie, Manson & Woods Ltd* [2012] EWHC 2198 (Ch), emphasises the importance of there being an effective remedy against the proferens.

[147] [2011] IEHC 269. The Supreme Court [2014] IESC 74 did not address this issue when rejecting Irish Asphalt's appeal.

existence of limiting provisions.[148] A recent English case gives an indication of judicial thinking in consumer contracts. In *Scheps v Fine Art Logistic Ltd*,[149] a contract of bailment under the terms of which the defendant was to store a Anish Kapoor sculpture on behalf of the plaintiff owner (the sculpture was subsequently destroyed by mistake while in the defendant's possession) was scrutinised by reference to the "fair and reasonable" test. While the court held that a limitation based upon weight and volume of the bailed object was not per se unfair or unreasonable, the clause had not been drawn to the attention of the plaintiff, nor had insurance matters been raised by the defendant with the plaintiff. The "fair and reasonable" test, in relation to the provision of services by an architect was considered in *Moores v Yakeley Associates Ltd*[150] The plaintiff retained the defendant to provide services on the basis of the Royal Institute of British Architects (RIBA) standard form agreement. The contract capped the liability of the architect to £250,000. Dyson J. held that the defendant had discharged the burden of showing the limitation clause was fair and reasonable. The figure was not arbitrary because the construction cost was estimated at £225,000. The defendant's fees were £20,000, so a cap of 10 times the fee was proportionate. The plaintiff was a wealthier man than the defendant and was in a stronger bargaining position, given the building recession. The plaintiff was in receipt of legal advice and had pronounced himself "happy" with the proposed agreement.

8–60 The earliest Irish case in which the substantive merits of an exemption clause were examined was the decision of Carroll J. in *McCarthy v Joe Walsh Tours Ltd.*[151] The contract in question was a package holiday agreement containing a standard arbitration clause which obliged the consumer to submit any dispute to compulsory arbitration before an Irish Travel Agents Association (ITAA) arbitrator. The ITAA scheme was both compulsory and a limitation of rights, because the maximum recoverable in any claim was £5,000. Carroll J. upheld the decision of Judge Murphy in the Circuit Court, deciding that the clause was a term which limited the implied term under s.39 and, accordingly, in a consumer contract, could only be enforced if specifically drawn to the attention of the consumer and if fair and reasonable. Carroll J. held that the clause could not be relied upon in this case because it was not specifically drawn to the attention of the consumer in question. However, it is arguable that the compulsory arbitration clause, if involving a limitation on liability, must be regarded as a clause limiting the rights of the consumer and that the "fair and reasonable" test cannot be satisfied in such circumstances. In an interesting

---

[148] *Carroll v An Post National Lottery Co* [1996] 1 I.R. 443; *Danka Rentals Ltd v Xi Software Ltd* (1998) 17 Tr. L.R. 74.

[149] [2007] EWHC 541 (Q.B.).

[150] [2000] T.C.L.R. 146, affirmed by the Court of Appeal: [2000] C.L.Y. 810. Similar reasoning appears in *Shepherd Homes Ltd v Encia Remediation* [2007] EWHC 70 (TCC). Contrast *West v Ian Finlay and Associates* [2014] EWCA Civ 316.

[151] [1991] I.L.R.M. 813.

comment on this case,[152] White argues that compulsory arbitration clauses may in general fall foul of the statutory test (presumably in consumer contracts at any rate) if it gives a proferens the right to unilaterally select an arbitrator on the basis of a risk of partiality.

8–61 There are two contrasting English cases which suggest that the Unfair Contract Terms Act 1977 does not generally operate against indemnity clauses which transfer risk as opposed to clauses which limit or exclude it.[153] Nor does the 1977 Act apply to agreements which, unfairly as it turns out, settle or compromise litigation; see *Tudor Grange Holdings v Citibank N.A.*[154] These decisions would also be applicable in Ireland under the 1980 Act.

8–62 The 1980 Act also provides additional protection for the buyer in respect of a manufacturer's or supplier's guarantee. Section 16 requires, inter alia, that the guarantee discloses information in relation to the person supplying the guarantee, the duration of the guarantee, plus the claim procedure involved, and discloses the carriage charges the buyer must meet; non-compliance with s.16 is an offence; see s.16(6). The seller may also be liable in respect of the manufacturer's or supplier's guarantee (s.17) and s.18 provides that rights given under the guarantee do not exclude or limit the buyer's rights under statute or common law. Section 18 declares that attempts to displace these rights, or impose additional obligations on the buyer, or reserve for the guarantor or his agent the right to be sole arbiter on whether goods are defective, "shall be void". Section 19 provides a right of action against the manufacturer or other supplier "as if that manufacturer or supplier had sold the goods to the buyer and had committed a breach or warranty". An extended definition of "buyer" and "manufacturer" is given under s.19.

8–63 Part VI of the 1980 Act also contains a series of additional measures designed to deal with directory entries that are made for trade or business purposes; trade directories have to be compiled according to criteria set out in s.48 and it is a criminal offence for the compiler to demand payment without satisfying the provisions of s.48. Other criminal offences are created by s.49—failure to meet prescribed terms in relation to the format to be employed in drafting invoices—or contracts or guarantees (s.51). Section 53 also empowers the Minister for Jobs, Enterprise and Innovation to prescribe the size or type to be used in printed contracts and guarantees; non-compliance renders the person who contravenes s.53 guilty of an offence. These provisions have not yet been employed for the Minister has yet to make any orders; see the discussion on the *Report of the Sales Law Review Group* and consultation exercise (2013) in Ch.4.

---

[152] (1991) 9 I.L.T. 92. See generally, Christou, *Boilerplate: Practical Clauses*, 7th edn (London: Sweet & Maxwell, 2015).

[153] *Phillips Products Ltd v Hyland* [1987] 2 All E.R. 620; *Thompson v Lohan (Plant Hire) Ltd* [1987] 2 All E.R. 631.

[154] [1991] 4 All E.R. 1.

Motor Vehicles

8–64 Section 13 of the 1980 Act (not to be confused with s.13 of the 1893 Act, as amended by the 1980 Act) sets out an implied condition which is of singular importance in contracts for the sale of motor vehicles. Section 13(2) states that, without prejudice to any other condition of warranty, there is an implied condition that at the time of delivery the vehicle is free from any defect which would render it a danger to the public, including persons travelling in the vehicle. The implied condition does not apply if the buyer is a dealer in motor vehicles, and subs.(3) provides that, if the vehicle is not intended for use in the State in which it is delivered, and a document to that effect is signed by both parties, and the agreement is fair and reasonable, the implied condition is inapplicable. The 1980 Act also provides a presumption of unfitness in certain circumstances and the implied condition cannot be excluded by contrary agreement. Another novel feature is that the condition is available for the benefit of persons travelling in the vehicle if they are injured as a result of the defect. In the first case under s.13, a decision of the High Court in *Glorney v O'Brien*,[155] a mini was sold in poor condition for £250. The vehicle crashed three weeks later when the suspension collapsed. The court brushed aside a claim that, given the low price, the vehicle was not intended for use but for spare parts:

> "[N]o matter how old or cheap a motor vehicle may be it must not be sold to an ordinary member of the public not in the motor trade in a condition which would render it a danger to the public including the occupants of the vehicle if driven on the road."

Damages totalling £18,650 were awarded to the driver and passenger in respect of the injuries suffered. The implied condition could presumably be used by a buyer to set aside a contract, even if the seller is not a dealer, so it provides a very useful additional remedy to motor vehicle buyers. The implied condition is also applicable to cases of hire-purchase and bailments, such as holiday car hire, fleet leasing or operating leasing of motor vehicles. However, if the contract is not a contract of sale, or a hire-purchase agreement, the person to whom the goods are let must deal as a consumer if the implied terms are to be available, including the s.13 implied condition. A tractor let to a farmer under a finance lease is outside s.13: *Flynn v Dermot Kelly Ltd*.[156]

Community Law

8–65 Title XV of the Treaty on the Functioning of the European Union (Lisbon), which consists of art.169, addresses the issue of consumer protection. Article 153.1 obliges the Community to "contribute to protecting the health,

---

[155] Unreported, High Court, November 14, 1988.
[156] [2007] IEHC 103.

safety and economic interests of consumers, as well as promoting their right to information, education and to organise themselves in order to safeguard their interests". Measures are to be adopted under art.114 of the Treaty in order to complete the Internal Market. Under the umbrella of consumer protection a significant body of Community contract *acquis* has built up and these measures have in turn sparked a debate on the desirability of a general harmonisation of European contract law, either in a sector—specific or general manner.[157] In the remainder of this chapter we will briefly outline the most important Directives, as transposed into Irish law.

(1) The Misleading Advertising Directive

8–66 This Directive,[158] adopted in September 1984, was implemented into Irish law on June 23, 1988 by Ministerial Order. The Directive, as implemented, afforded very useful additional powers to those given by the Consumer Information Act 1978 to the Director of Consumer Affairs, now the National Consumer Agency. The preamble to the Directive, after noting that the laws in force against misleading advertising differ widely and that the dangers that result include the distortion of competition within the Common Market, continues by declaring that consumer advertising affects the consumer's economic welfare and may cause the consumer to make prejudicial decisions when acquiring goods, property, or using services. The Directive, in art.2.1 defines "advertising" as "the making of a representation in any form in connection with a trade, business, craft or profession in order to promote the supply of goods or services", including immovable property. Article 2.2 defines "misleading advertising" as "any advertising which in any way, including its presentation, deceives or is likely to deceive". Article 4 requires Member States to ensure that adequate and effective means exist for the control of misleading advertising in the interests of consumers as well as competitors and the general public. The method of enforcement is to be resolved within each Member State. Article 4 allows the means of control to include legal provisions which enable persons having a legitimate interest in prohibiting misleading advertising to: (a) take legal action against such advertising; and/or (b) bring such advertising before an administrative authority to decide on complaints or initial proceedings. The Statutory Instrument which brings the Directive into force, the European Communities (Misleading Advertising) Regulations 1988,[159] gave the Director of Consumer Affairs the power to request any person engaging in misleading advertising, or proposing so to do, to discontinue or refrain from such advertising. Any person, including the Director, may seek an injunction in which the court may prohibit misleading advertising: the applicant is not

---

[157] Com (2003) 63, *Action Plan on European Contract Law: A More Coherent European Contract Law.* Von Bar and Swann (2003) 11 E.R.P.L. 595. See Gutman, *The Constitutional Foundations of European Contract Law* (Oxford: OUP, 2014).

[158] Council Directive 84/450 of September 10, 1984 relating to the approximation of the laws, regulations and administrative provisions of the Member States concerning misleading advertising [1984] OJ L250/17.

[159] S.I. No. 134 of 1988; *Dunnes Stores Ltd v MANDATE* [1996] 1 I.L.R.M. 384.

required to prove actual loss or damage, nor recklessness or negligence on the part of the advertiser. The question whether the advertisement is misleading or not is to be resolved by reference to art.3 of the Directive which requires the court to have regard to the characteristics of the goods and services such as availability, nature, execution, composition, method and date of manufacture or provision, fitness for purpose, quality, origin, price, rights and attributes of the advertiser, including any copyright or patent rights the advertiser may have.

8–67 The Misleading Advertising Directive has been amended so as to broaden the scope of regulation to include comparative advertising.[160] While comparative advertising, that is, the comparison of goods or services marketed, distributed or supplied by an enterprise by reference to the name, mark, reputation or image of a competitor, is the subject of industry self-regulation by way of the Advertising Standards Authority for Ireland, and while s.14(6) of the Trade Marks Act 1996 makes derogatory use of a competitor's mark a trade mark infringement, this Directive is intended to control comparative advertising throughout the EU, for in some countries such as Germany, such advertising is unlawful. The Directive permits comparative advertising if the practice meets a list of requirements, which can be paraphrased as requiring that the advertisement must not be misleading, is based on objectively verifiable factors, compares like with like, does not cause confusion in the market or denigrate the trade marks and other indicia of a competitor, or unfairly appropriate the mark or indicia of a competitor or his reputation. The Directive sets out a requirement that national laws afford appropriate remedies and legal procedures for rightholders.

(2) *The Directive on Contracts Negotiated Away from Business Premises*

8–68 This Directive, first proposed in 1977 and later amended in 1978, applies to contracts between a consumer and trader when negotiations have been initiated away from business premises—"doorstep contracts". The definition of "business premises" includes stalls at fairs and markets. Article 4 provides that the contract document must be signed by the consumer in his own hand and a copy given to him or forwarded immediately thereafter. The contract must contain specified information and the consumer is to have a seven-day cancellation period. The European Communities (Cancellation of Contracts Negotiated Away from Business Premises) Regulations 1989—implementing Directive 85/577[161]—came into effect on November 1, 1989.

---

[160] Directive 97/55 of October 6, 1997 amending Directive 84/450 concerning misleading advertising so as to include comparative advertising [1997] OJ L290/18.

[161] S.I. No. 224 of 1989: Directive 85/577 [1985] OJ L372/31. Directive 85/577 has been replaced by the Consumer Rights Directive (2011/83, [2011] OJ L304/64), the transposition date being December 13, 2013. The Consumer Rights Directive replaces the concept of a contract negotiated away from business premises with that of an off-premises contract that is wider in application (e.g. organised excursions) (see recitals 21 and 22 of the 2011 Directive). See S.I. No. 484 of 2013.

Under the terms of the Consumer Rights Directive[162] the Directive on Contracts negotiated away from business premises has been superseded by broader provisions relating to contracts concluded off business premises. Off premises contracts between a consumer and a trader require the trader to provide the consumer with stipulated information about a proposed transaction before and at the time of conclusion of the contract, as well as provision of a copy or confirmation of the contract. This includes information about cancellation rights which last for 14 days in most instances. These provisions have been transposed by S.I. No. 484 of 2013. The Department of Jobs, Enterprise and Innovation intend to integrate these provisions into one piece of primary legislation relating to Irish consumer law: see scheme of Consumers Rights Bill (May 2015).

(3) The Distance Selling Directive

8–69 This Directive[163] attempts to regulate the sale of products to consumers when the contract is concluded at a distance, that is, through direct marketing, telesales and internet-type sales, for example. The consumer of a good or service is to be given information about the name, address and type of product provided by the supplier and details concerning price, delivery charges or other fees, before the contract is concluded. Confirmation in writing is required and an ability to revoke the contract within seven days of supply of the goods is provided. Delivery of the goods, unless otherwise stated in the contract, must take place within 30 days of the conclusion of the contract. The Directive also addresses issues of inertia selling (see s.47 of the 1980 Act) and also regulates the use of automated dialling and fax machines and, generally speaking, prohibits "cold calling" of consumers. The Directive was transposed into Irish law by S.I. No. 207 of 2001, with effect from May 15, 2001 but the Directive has been replaced by the Consumer Rights Directive of 2011 – Directive 2011/83.[164] The Consumer Rights Directive stipulates that in relation to contracts under negotiation and concluded between traders, a consumer's information must be provided prior to conclusion of the contract and when a contract is concluded the consumer shall receive a copy or confirmation of that contract. Information to be provided includes information about 14 day cancellation rights. The Directive has been transposed by statutory instrument[165] but the provisions will be integrated into primary legislation in a forthcoming Consumer Rights Bill.[166]

---

[162] Directive 2011/83.
[163] Directive 97/7 [1997] OJ L144/19. Directive 97/7 has been replaced by the Consumer Rights Directive (2011/83 [2011] OJ L304/64). See S.I. No 484 of 2013.
[164] OJ L 304/64.
[165] S.I. No. 484 of 2013.
[166] A draft was circulated in May 2015.

(4) The Electronic Commerce Directive

8–70 Transposition of this Directive[167] has been effected by way of primary legislation, in the form of the Electronic Commerce Act 2000 and by S.I. No. 68 of 2003. Anti-spam measures are enforceable by the Data Protection Commissioner under enforcement powers afforded under the Data Protection Acts 1988 and 2003. The Directive must be read in conjunction with other Community texts on distance contracts. Perhaps the most important provisions relate to the limitation of liability that may be imposed upon internet service providers in respect of online services.

(5) The Online Sale of Financial Services Directive

8–71 This Directive,[168] which is a complimentary instrument to the Distance Selling Directive, must be transposed by October 9, 2004 in respect of the online sale of certain financial services to consumers. It was transposed with effect from February 15, 2005, by S.I. No. 853 of 2004.

(6) The Product Liability Directive

8–72 The most significant measure of consumer protection effected in tort law is the Product Liability Directive,[169] adopted by the Council on July 25, 1985. While the Directive does not affect any of the rights which are available through the laws in force relating to contractual and non-contractual liability (art.13), it is clear that the Directive is an important landmark in breaking down the distinction between consumer protection through contract (liability is stricter but extends only to the purchaser) and consumer protection in tort (liability of the defendant in negligence must be shown). In order to explain why Community legislation is necessary the Directive, in the preamble, refers to divergences in national law distorting competition, affecting the free movement of goods within the Community and entailing different degrees of protection for the consumer against damage caused to health and property from defective products. While the preamble identifies "liability without fault on the part of the producer" as the sole means of adequately solving the problem of products liability vis-à-vis technological methods of production, the Directive also acknowledges that liability should not be unlimited and that harmonisation will not be immediately obtained. The Directive in several respects is predicated on the assumption that implementation of the Directive is really a first step.

8–73 Article 1 declares that the producer shall be liable for damage caused by a defect in his product. "Product" is defined in art.2 as all moveables with

---

[167] Council Directive 2000/31, [2000] OJ L178/1.
[168] Council Directive 2002/65, [2002] OJ L271/16.
[169] Council Directive 85/374, [1985] OJ L210/29; see (1991) I.C.L.S.A. 91/28–02.

the exception of "primary agricultural products"[170] and game. "Primary agricultural products" means the products of the soil, stock-farming and fisheries, excluding products that have undergone initial processing. Thus tinned salmon would be covered by the 1985 Directive, as would probably a boiled crab, but whether fresh crabs or possibly even pasteurised milk would be covered may be open to some doubt. Article 2 also includes electricity as a product. "Producer" is defined in art.3 as:

"(a) the manufacturer of a finished product; or

(b) the producer of any raw material; or

(c) the manufacturer of a component part; or

(d) any person who by putting his name, trade mark or other distinguishing feature on the product thereby identifies himself as its producer."

Importers of goods into the Community are also responsible as producers; see art.3.2. A product is said to be defective when it does not provide the safety a person is entitled to expect having regard to the presentation, expected uses and time it was put into circulation; see art.6.

8–74 Liability under the Directive is not, however, strict. Article 7 provides the producer with six defences:

"(a) he did not put the goods into circulation; or

(b) it is probable that at the time of putting the product into circulation it did not have the defect; or

(c) the product was not manufactured by him for sale or distribution for an economic purpose nor in the course of business; or

(d) the defect was due to compliance with mandatory public authority regulations; or

(e) that, given the state of technical knowledge, it was not possible at the time of distribution to discover the defect; or

(f) if the product is a manufactured component the defect is the result of a design defect in the product into which the component has been fitted."

Liability is limited to the period of three years following the day the plaintiff became aware, actually or constructively, of the damage, defect and identity of the producer. Liability is also to extend only insofar as the damage occurs within 10 years of the product going into circulation by the producer unless the injured party has within that time issued proceedings. There may also be financial limits placed on the awards made under the national laws passed in order to implement the Directive; see art.16.

---

[170] However, Directive 1999/34 produced by the European Commission brought these products within the 1985 Directive, with effect from June 4, 1999.

8–75 Powers of derogation are given in relation to the scope of the definition of "product". Member States may include primary agricultural products and game, and the "state of knowledge" defence in art.7(e) may be omitted. Member States were obliged to bring the Directive into force not later than three years after notification. The Liability for Defective Products Act 1991 came into effect over three years late, on December 16, 1991. Section 2(1) sets out the basic liability of producers and s.2(2) defines a "producer" accordingly. The Act, despite Directive 1999/34, does not define "product" so as to include primary agricultural products which have not undergone initial processing because all Member States save for Luxembourg have excluded such products and to include primary agricultural products would disadvantage Irish farmers. Section 6(e) of the Act retains the "state of the art" defence despite art.15(1)(b) of the Directive. Damages below €435 are not recoverable and where damages exceed €435 the excess of that figure only is recoverable.[171] Exclusion clauses or notice are rendered inoperative by s.10, and s.11 provides that the Act does not affect any other rights at law which the injured person may have.

(7) The Directive on Consumer Guarantees

8–76 This Directive[172] is to be read with the Product Liability Directive for it sets out two guarantee rights. The first, a mandatory requirement, gives all consumers who shop anywhere in the EU a range of remedies for defective goods, including replacement rights, within two years of the sale. There is a second optional provision which must afford greater rights to the consumer than the minimum mandatory provisions. The Directive on Consumer Goods and Associated Guarantees[173] has been transposed into Irish law by S.I. No. 11 of 2003. The Directive gives consumers who purchase consumer goods rights in respect of contracts in which goods supplied are not in conformity with the contract. The consumer acquires rights to insist that the goods be either repaired or replaced. The Regulations also provide that consumer guarantees are legally binding upon the offeror of the goods and make provision for the form in which guarantees are to be made available, in paper or electronically.

(8) The Timeshare Directive

8–77 This Directive[174] was transposed into Irish law by S.I. No. 204 of 1997 and those Regulations came into operation on May 14, 1997. The Directive generally sets out contents requirements for timeshare contracts such as the name, address, domicile of the parties, state of construction and common parts details to be disclosed, as well as providing for language of the transaction requirements to be in the hands of the buyer. A 10-day cooling-off requirement is inserted. Statutory Instrument No. 73 of 2011 gives effect to Directive

---

171 Section 3.
172 See generally [2001] E.R.P.L. 157–483.
173 Council Directive 1999/44, [1999] OJ L171/12, replaced by Directive 2008/122/EC, [2008] OJ L33/10.
174 Directive 94/47, [1994] OJ L280/83.

2008/122, strengthening the buyer's rights (e.g. cooling-off period is now 14 days) in several respects.

(9) The Unfair Contract Terms Directive

8–78 This is undoubtedly the most important piece of consumer protection legislation to emanate from the European Community. While the Directive[175] at times appears to be quite familiar to UK and Irish contract lawyers, the philosophy behind the Directive is closer to French and German law insofar as the concepts of *bonne foi* and *Treu und Glauben* are essential parts of each contract regime and the Directive puts the concept of good faith at the centre of attention. The Directive is seen as an Internal Market measure,[176] giving consumers the assurance that they may conclude contracts anywhere within the Community and not find that their rights are prejudiced by virtue of each Member State providing varying degrees of consumer rights and remedies. The Directive has been transposed into Irish law by virtue of the European Communities (Unfair Terms in Consumer Contracts) Regulations 1995 (the "1995 Regulations")[177] which are applicable to all contracts concluded after December 31, 1994, as long as the contract is between a consumer and the seller of goods or supplier of services and the sale or supply is for purposes related to the seller or supplier's business. These provisions broadly shadow s.3(1) of the 1980 Act. Contracts relating to employment, succession rights, family law and company or partnership formation are not included within the scope of the 1995 Regulations. Mandatory or statutory provisions that must be included in a contract or international treaty are not covered, and where some provisions "shrink" the core of a contract in the sense that they define the main subject matter of the contract (e.g. a red Volkswagen Polo) or address the adequacy of the price (as distinct from permitting a price variation), those clauses are also not open for review under the 1995 Regulations. However these core exclusions must be set out in plain intelligible language for them to be immune from scrutiny and the UK Office of Fair Trading (OFT) has commented that for core exclusions to work, and thus avoid scrutiny under the Directive, core terms have to be brought to the attention to the consumer.[178]

8–79 The 1995 Regulations do not apply if the term in question has been individually negotiated and a term is always to be regarded as not having been individually negotiated where it has been drafted in advance and the consumer has thus not been able to influence its substance. Even if a specific term, or

---

[175] Council Directive 93/13, [1993] OJ L95/29.

[176] Article 100A; see opening recital to the Directive.

[177] S.I. No. 27 of 1995, as amended, by most notably S.I.s No. 307 of 2000, 160 of 2013 and 336 of 2014.

[178] OFT, *Unfair Contract Terms Bulletin* (No. 1), p.8. The uncertainty of core exclusions in respect of bank charges is highlighted by the decision of the UK Supreme Court in *OFT v Abbey National* [2010] 1 A.C. 696, a decision that is out of step with, for example, German law where bank charges are reviewable under the Directive. See the recent Court of Justice decision in *Jean-Claude Van Hove v CNP Assurances SA* Case C-96/14.

an aspect of that term, has been individually negotiated the 1995 Regulations may apply to the rest of the contract if it is assessed to be a pre-formulated standard contract. The onus of proof rests upon the seller or supplier to show the term was individually negotiated.[179]

8–80 The key to defining an "unfair contract term" is found in art.3(2) of the 1995 Regulations which provides:

> For the purpose of these Regulations a contractual term shall be regarded as unfair if, contrary to the requirement of good faith, it causes a significant imbalance in the parties' rights and obligations under the contract to the detriment of the consumer, taking into account the nature of the goods or services for which the contract was concluded and all circumstances attending the conclusion of the contract and all other terms of the contract or of another contract on which it is dependent.

The good faith requirement, when put into this context, appears to point to the circumstances surrounding the formation of the contract. It may be, for example, that a contract is one-sided in terms of the fairness of the exchange, but if the consumer is openly and fairly treated by the seller or supplier then it may be that the contract term in question will not be unfair; it remains possible, however, for a court to conclude that even if the consumer has entered into a contract without there being any hint of duplicity or oppression by the other party, the consumer's position is so out of balance with the other party, and so detrimental, that the clause is unfair. Whether good faith is present or absent is a matter for the courts and the 1995 Regulations, in Sch.2, set out four non-exhaustive guidelines for the courts, which are as follows:

> "In making an assessment of good faith, particular regard shall be had to
>
> - the strength of the bargaining positions of the parties,
> - whether the consumer had an inducement to agree to the term,
> - whether the goods or services were sold or supplied to the special order of the consumer, and
> - the extent to which the seller or supplier has dealt fairly and equitably with the consumer whose legitimate interests he has to take into account."

This statement broadly corresponds with the Schedule to the 1980 Act; the fourth factor in particular is something of an unconscionability catch-all provision which could make factors like degree of notice, availability of insurance, the risk to the consumer and the consumer's ability to avoid the harm, extremely relevant.

---

[179] Article 3 of S.I. No. 27 of 1995.

8–81 Once we move away from the good faith requirement, the 1995 Regulations give the issue a more specific focus by listing some 17 examples of terms in consumer contracts that may be unfair. This list, found in Sch.3 to the 1995 Regulations, is a grey-list and the 1995 Regulations require the specific clause to be set against the good faith requirement. The UK Office of Fair Trading, during its existence, classified the most common unfair terms encountered by it in the following way:

Entire agreement clauses—These exclude from the contract anything said or promised by a salesman or agent of the company.

Hidden clauses—Consumers are not bound by terms they could not get to know before signing a contract, but it is regrettably common for consumers not to have sight, or any notice, of the full terms and conditions until after they have signed a contract.

Penalty clauses—A number of consumer contracts have one-sided clauses which penalise consumers, for example by permitting a company to retain deposits with no counterbalancing penalties on the company if it does not comply with its obligations.

Exclusion clauses—These exclude liability for every possible eventuality, and are very common.

Variation clauses—Typically these give the supplier the right to put up prices with no realistic right for the consumer to withdraw without penalty.[180]

Some of the "grey-list" provisions are extremely beneficial to Irish consumers. Disclaimers in relation to physical injury or death caused while using a mode of transport or an amusement ride, for example, will now be rendered ineffective in most instances. The UK experience indicates that one-sided contracts for car hire, mobile phones, home installations like double-glazing and paving, satellite TV packages, and for some financial services, can be significantly re-addressed as long as the monitoring of such standard contracts is done effectively by the enforcement agency. In recent years the OFT[181] has been very active in explaining to tenants that contractual terms in letting agreements are covered by the Unfair Contract Terms Regulations, with clauses against assignment of the tenancy, late rental payment penalties and deposit retention featuring as unfair terms. Even clauses found in areas covered by other consumer legislation such as package holidays have been regarded by the OFT as coming within the Unfair Contract Terms Regulations. The previous consumer protection body that operated within the State, the National Consumer Agency and its predecessor, the Office of the Director of Consumer Affairs had, like the OFT in the UK, been critical of some sectoral agreements

---

[180] OFT, *Unfair Contract Terms Bulletin* (No. 1), p.9; *DGFT v First National Bank Plc* [2002] 1 A.C. 481.

[181] The OFT produces an *Unfair Contract Terms Bulletin* and Guidance Notes, available at: *http://www.oft.gov.uk.*

and practices. There have been complaints in both jurisdictions about both the format of mobile phone operator contracts—the print is just too small—as well as the open-ended nature of the contracts insofar as they bind customers to future terms or subject the customer to unfair treatment.[182] The consumer protection bodies that have operated in the State have, like the OFT and trading standards bodies in the UK, been critical of contractual terms found in certain kinds of contract as well as sectoral practices in specific industries. In its last Annual Report published just prior to its dissolution and reconstitution as a part of the Competition and Consumer Protection Commission, the Consumer Protection Agency reviewed terms and conditions in use in the domestic refuse industry and obtained undertaking from six operators that contracts would be amended to remove terms the agency considered to be unfair.[183] Similarly, the European Consumer Centre has reported significant levels of dissatisfaction with car rental operators, particularly on the question of misleading statements about price and the practice of loading extra charges onto the consumer.[184] In the 2011 *Annual Report* of the National Consumer Agency reference was made to unfair terms in respect of the Icelandic Ash Cloud cancellation compensation rules of one Irish airline, and in early 2013 the Agency sought to consider consumer rights under the Directive in respect of the HMV closure and HMV's gift voucher terms and conditions.

8–82 Note also that the 1995 Regulations also require clear and intelligible drafting of contract terms in standardised contract documents.

(10) Unfair contract terms litigation

8–83 Case law on the interpretation of the 1995 Regulations is sparse in Ireland. The only decision relates to an application brought by the Director of Consumer Affairs in relation to standard conditions of contract in common use in the construction industry. A declaratory order was obtained on December 5, 2001 preventing the use of some 15 sample standard conditions in building contracts; the clauses in question covering entire agreement provisions, builders' rights to rescind the contract, the limited right of customers to insist on remedial work and seek remedies for delay as well as staged payments and penalty clauses for late payment to the builder.[185] A review of the annual reports of the Office of the Director of Consumer Affairs reveals that a number of complaints about building practices have featured over the years and it is significant that UK litigation has also tended to focus on this sector.

8–84 In *Picardi v Cuniberti*,[186] an architect sought to rely upon an adjudication provision in the RIBA Conditions of Engagement. He was in dispute with the

---

[182] See Bray, "Communications and New Media: 3 Service Agreement—Unfair Conract terms" [2006] 12(6) C.T.L.R. 175.
[183] Annual Report (2013) p.18.
[184] See "Consumer centre calls for review of car rental deals", *Irish Times*, April 17, 2008.
[185] Dorgon, "Safe as houses?" [2002] *Law Society Gazette* 12.
[186] [2003] B.L.R. 487.

defendants, his clients, and the evidence indicated that these terms were not known to the defendants. Toulmin J. held they were not part of the contract, observing *obiter* that such a procedure as that set out might not be enforceable under the Unfair Contract Terms Regulations:

> "I conclude that a procedure which the consumer is required to follow, and which will cause irrecoverable expenditure in either prosecuting or defending it is something which may hinder the consumer's right to take legal action."[187]

Picardi v Cuniberti was distinguished in *Lovell Projects Ltd v Legg and Carver*,[188] where the defendants challenged the validity of an adjudication made in respect of a building contract concluded on the basis of the Joint Contracts Tribunal (JCT) Agreement for Minor Building Works. The defendants argued that their attention to the adjudication provisions had not been drawn to these terms. No imbalance, much less a significant imbalance, was held to exist in this contract and, further, the requirement of fair dealing was satisfied. The JCT Agreement was used at the behest of the defendant's architect; the defendants, though consumers, were experienced business people and they had the opportunity to consult their solicitors. In *Bryen & Langley v Boston*,[189] the consumer also invited tenders from builders on the basis of the JCT Agreement applying and because the consumer had the opportunity to influence the terms upon which the contract was to be concluded with the plaintiff bidder. Rimer J. stated *obiter* that it was arguable that the contract had been negotiated and that the consumer had, in practice, been able to influence the substance of the term: 1995 Regulations, reg.3(2) and (4). The question whether the clauses contravene the requirement of good faith was explored in *Westminster Building Co Ltd v Beckingham*[190]; a robust judgment from Judge Thornton Q.C. held they did not.

The First National *decision*

8–85 In the *Director General of Fair Trading v First National Bank*,[191] the House of Lords had occasion to provide guidance on how the Unfair Contract Terms Directive is to be interpreted and applied. The principle requirement of good faith was said by Lord Bingham to look to good standards of commercial morality and practice. The Directive itself (recital 16) requires that the assessment of the unfair character of unfair terms must be supplemented by an

---

[187] [2003] B.L.R. 452.
[188] [2003] B.L.R. 452, citing *Oceano Groupo Editorial S.A. v Rocio Musicano Quantiro,* Joined Cases C-240/98 to 244/98.
[189] [2005] B.L.R. 508, following *Westminster Building Co Ltd v Beckingham* [2004] B.L.R. 265.
[190] [2004] B.L.R. 265.
[191] [2002] 1 A.C. 481. Well-publicised litigation over penalties on unsanctioned overdrafts is in train: *OFT v Abbey National Plc and Others* [2008] EWHC 985 (Comm). The ultimate decision, however, proved to be somewhat disappointing: see *OFT v Abbey National plc and others* [2009] UKSC 6.

overall evaluation of all the interests involved; and that while the assessment is to be carried out as of the time of contract formation, the impact of the term on each party is also a legitimate constraint. The overlap between good faith and whether there is a significant imbalance between the parties was said to be substantial by Lord Steyn. In that case, the House of Lords found that provisions relating to the accrual of interest by a defaulting customer, post-judgment, were not unfair; their Lordships indicated that the real source of the "unsatisfactory" result that the term produced for consumers could more properly be visited as legislative and regulatory failures rather than the term itself. Apart from the *Picardi v Cuniberti* decision there is one other English case of interest on the JCT Terms. In *Domsalla v Dyason*,[192] the court followed earlier case law in holding that the jurisdiction provisions did not provide a significant imbalance, but His Honour went on to strike out provisions denying the consumer rights of set-off or counterclaim because the consumer had not been aware of the mechanisms that could have been used to reverse these prejudicial restrictions on his contractual remedies.

8–86 Irish case law has responded to the guidelines found in these English cases. In *Marshall v Capital Holdings*,[193] an arbitration clause found in a package holiday contract was held not to have been in breach of the good faith obligation, nor did it cause a significant imbalance as between the parties. In this case, Murphy J. contrasted the facts of the case with *Picardi* on the basis that in *Picardi* the clause sought to close off remedies that would otherwise have been available to the consumer.

8–87 In *West v Ian Finlay & Associates*[194] the English Court of Appeal gave an important ruling on the good faith requirement. The case concerned a net contribution clause in a construction contract. Such clauses are intended to permit a contractor to reduce any liability the contractor may have to meet where loss may be occasioned by virtue of a breach of contract caused by another contractor engaged on the construction project. In this case Mr and Mrs West sued their architect for defective construction work, the main contractor being insolvent. The English Court of Appeal felt that the words used were "crystal clear" and that, while there was an imbalance between the parties, the imbalance was not significant because Mr and Mrs West—experienced professional persons—could have renegotiated the clause or gone elsewhere for the services of an architect. They should have known of the existence of the clause, prominently displayed in the contract and it was not hedged with any particular restrictions.

---

[192] [2007] EWHC 1174 (TCC).
[193] [2006] IEHC 271.
[194] [2014] EWCA Civ 316.

The Package Holidays Directive

8–88 This Directive,[195] transposed into Irish law by the Package Holidays and Travel Trade Act 1995, adds to the existing law relating to misrepresentation and disclaimers in holiday contracts by setting out minimum standards for brochure content, pre-contractual disclosure, provision of information as well as obligations to be met before the package commences, a number of essential terms, a booking transfer right and restrictions on the right to vary prices. In *Scaife v Falcon Leisure Group*,[196] the Supreme Court has upheld the decision of the High Court in which a tour operator was held liable for personal injuries caused by the negligence of a hotel proprietor. While the Supreme Court held that the relevant standard is not one of strict liability, but one of reasonable care and skill, it was also held that the operator cannot avoid liability by delegating performance to another service provider. The operator is not an insurer vis-à-vis the consumer, but the tour operator cannot avoid liability simply by showing that the service provider or premises were respectively competent and safe at the time of selection.[197] Where, as in *Scaife* the consumer was injured by slipping on foodstuffs when taking a meal that she had contracted for, the breach of contract and injury were entirely foreseeable.

Future Reforms

8–89 Building upon the provisions in the Consumer Rights Directive which sets out provisions relating to the supply of digital content insofar as such contracts require consumer information and the cancellation right to be afforded to consumers, the European Commission on December 9, 2015 published two proposals for Directives that form part of the European Commission's Digital Single Market Agenda: see The Proposed Directive on Certain Aspects Concerning Contracts for the Supply of Digital Content.[198] In the case of contracts in which a supply of digital content—software, apps, streamed music for example—is provided to a consumer for a price or for consideration in the form of personal data, a set of mandatory rules that cannot be altered are to apply. Supply of the digital content must meet a standard that it be supplied "immediately after the conclusion of the contract". The digital contents must meet conformity standards such as fitness for purpose and be in conformity with intellectual property rights. Liability of the supplier and remedies are prescribed. The Proposed Directive Concerning Contracts for the Online and Other Distance Sale of Goods[199] does not apply to tangible items holding digital content such as DVDs and CDs, nor does the Proposed

---

[195] Council Directive 90/314 of June 13, 1990 on package travel, holidays and package tours, [1990] OJ L158/59. See generally Kilby [2005] E.L.R. 123.
[196] [2007] IESC 57.
[197] *Wong Me Wan v Kwan Kin Travel Services* [1996] 1 W.L.R. 38; *McKenna v Best Travel* [1998] 3 I.R. 57. See also *Lougheed v On the Beach Ltd* [2014] EWCA Civ 1538, followed in *Kerr v Thomas Cook Tour Operations Ltd* [2015] NIQB 9.
[198] Com (2015) 0634 final.
[199] Com (2015) 0635 final.

Directive apply to services. Embedded digital content built into goods like household appliances and toys in a subsidiary fashion are covered. Like the other Proposed Directive, the rules are mandatory and maximise harmonisation measures. Conformity standards are set out in the Proposed Directive as a range of remedies and provisions as to how the relevant remedy will be ascertained in a given case. In both Directives, Member States are required to provide for adequate and effective means to comply with the Directive.

9 Importance and Relative Effect of Contractual Terms

Introduction

9–01 Not all contractual terms are of the same weight and importance. At one time the common law position was different. All covenants were independent in the sense that if one party failed to perform or satisfy a covenant or condition, the contractual obligations of the other party subsisted; that other party could not use the failure of the condition as an excuse for his own non-performance. He was obliged to perform and sue the other for all loss occasioned by any breach of contract. If both parties broke the agreement and one party sued, the defendant could not plead that the plaintiff's own breach of contract excused the defendant. The defendant's remedy was a cross-action for damages. So, a promise by A to pay £1,000 for a piece of land owned by B was described in the language of the day as an independent covenant. Should B fail to convey land he could not excuse non-performance by asserting that A had broken his own covenant to pay £1,000 at a date prior to the agreed date for completion; B's remedy was an action for the £1,000. Lord Mansfield identified this as a source of some injustice; should A be unable to pay £1,000 this would oblige B to convey without giving him any realistic hope of obtaining the consideration promised by A. In *Kingston v Preston*[1] Lord Mansfield laid down that covenants could be broken down into three types:

"(1) conditions could be dependent; here B alleges a failure by A to show that a named event has occurred and that the event was a condition precedent, preventing B's obligation from accruing at all;

(2) covenants designed to be performed simultaneously with those of the other contracting party were described as concurrent conditions; this concurrent covenant was dependent in the sense that if the plaintiff alleged failure to perform by the defendant the plaintiff could not recover damages unless the plaintiff pleaded performance of his obligation or at least a willingness to perform;

(3) covenants could be independent. These covenants were actionable without reference to the obligations of the plaintiff."

---

[1] (1773) 2 Doug. 689. See *Chitty on Contracts*, edited by H.G. Beale, 32nd edn (London: Sweet & Maxwell, 2015), Vol.1, paras 2-15b (conditional agreements), 13-019 (classification of terms) and 13-106 (parol evidence).

9–02 While s.28 of the Sale of Goods Act 1893 (the "1893 Act") provides a statutory instance of a concurrent obligation—payment of price and delivery are concurrent obligations[2]—the issues raised are complicated indeed, and generally fall to be decided from first principles of common law rather than as the result of parliamentary guidance. Professor Corbin[3] provided the clearest explanation of this difficult area of law. Corbin explained that covenants have to be distinguished from promises. The old terminology of dependent/independent/concurrent covenant operated when one person tried to rely on the failure of another person to show that some stipulated event had not occurred and that the failure of this condition permitted that person from withholding the performance promised. In *Kingston v Preston* itself, it was held that the failure of the plaintiff to provide security in respect of a business owned by the defendant entitled the defendant to refuse to transfer the business to the plaintiff; the defendant did not wish to part with his business and stock-in-trade and become an unsecured creditor. The covenant was such that the defendant's obligation to transfer was dependent upon the plaintiff's obligation to provide adequate security.

9–03 The principle upon which the courts distinguished between dependent and independent covenants was the subject of the leading case of *Davidson v Gwynne*.[4] Lord Ellenborough observed:

> "... unless the non-performance alleged in the breach of the contract goes to the whole root and consideration of it, the covenant broken is not to be considered as a condition precedent, but as a distinct covenant for the breach of which the party injured may be compensated in damages."[5]

This approach was adopted in several nineteenth-century English and Irish cases. It was clearly held in *Cripps v Smith*[6] that a breach of warranty, or independent covenant, is to be the subject of a cross-action by the injured party and is not to be the basis for rescission of the contract. In *Garrick v Bradshaw*[7] the dichotomy between independent and dependent covenants was extensively considered and *Boone v Eyre*[8] was cited with obvious approval. In *Fearnley v London Guarantee Insurance Co*[9] May C.J. presented the issue in graphic terms:

> "... where, as in the present case, a defendant [who] sued for the non-performance of promises contained in an instrument relies on the breach by the plaintiff of some term in the same instrument to be performed by

---

[2] *MacAuley and Cullen v Horgan* [1925] 2 I.R. 1.
[3] (1919) 28 Yale L.J. 739.
[4] (1810) 12 East 381.
[5] (1810) 12 East 381 at 389.
[6] (1841) 3 Ir. L. Rep. 277.
[7] (1846) 10 Ir. L. Rep. 129.
[8] (1779) 1 Hy. Bl. 273; *Clements v Russell* (1854) 7 Ir. Jur. 102.
[9] (1881) 6 L.R. (Ir.) 219, 232, 394. The House of Lords disagreed: (1882) 5 App. Cas. 911.

him, as an answer to the action ... the point to be ascertained is, did the default of the plaintiff affect the essence of the contract between the parties?"[10]

9–04 In *Fearnley v London Guarantee Insurance Co* the issue was whether the plaintiff could enforce an insurance policy, a fidelity policy whereby the plaintiff sought an indemnity from his insurers because of fraudulent embezzlement by the plaintiff's employee. The defendant pleaded, inter alia, that a condition precedent to liability on the policy was that the plaintiff should diligently prosecute the employee in question. The Court of Exchequer and two members of the Court of Appeal held that on its true construction, the obligation was not a condition precedent to recovery on the policy because the obligation upon the insurer to indemnify the employer operated independently. While both Ball L.C. and Morris C.J. felt that the convenant was dependent, the members of the Court of Appeal stressed that the issue was one of construction of the contract.

9–05 A contrasting Irish appellate decision can be found in *Re Application of Butler*.[11] Under a valid contract for motor insurance Butler was required to give notice as soon as practicable of any motor accident in which he was involved. The policy declared that his covenant, inter alia, was a condition precedent. Butler failed to notify the company of an accident in which he was involved and the Supreme Court held that he was not entitled to recover on foot of the insurance policy for notification was a condition precedent to the insurer's obligation to pay out on the policy. The failure to notify was not of itself a breach of contract by Butler but it justified the company's refusal to pay. However, where a condition precedent to the existence of a contract is created, as in the case of an intellectual property licence agreement being subject to approval of the product being licensed, the courts may, in appropriate cases imply an obligation to notify the other party on the outcome of the test or pay the licence fee in default thereof; see *Stabilad Ltd v Stephens and Carter (No.2)*.[12]

9–06 While the insurer may waive the condition precedent there is no obligation to show non-compliance has been prejudicial; see Gannon J. in *Gaelcrann Teoranta v Payne*.[13] If the condition is independent the courts hold that, even if one of the conditions has not been met, this will not justify a refusal to satisfy the other condition. Corbin cites *Constable v Cloberie*[14] as the leading case. Here the plaintiff promised to sail with the next favouring wind. The defendant in turn promised to pay if the ship reached Cadiz and returned.

---

[10] (1881) 6 L.R. (Ir.) 219 at 242.
[11] [1970] I.R. 45: *Board of Ordnance v Lewis* (1854) 7 Ir. Jur. 17.
[12] [1999] 2 All E.R. (Comm.) 651. See also *O'Connor v Coady* [2004] IESC 54; *Decoma (UK) v Haden Drysys International* [2005] EWHC 2948 (TCC), on notice generally.
[13] [1985] I.L.R.M. 109.
[14] (1662) Palmer 397.

While sailing with the next wind was both a condition and a contractual promise it was not a dependent condition nor a contractual promise which, if broken, justified the defendant in withholding the promised sum.

9–07 One feature of dependent covenants, when they are external to the contract, is that the person bound by, or prejudiced by non-observance of the covenant, does not, as such, commit a breach of contract. See *Re Application of Butler*[15] for a clear illustration of this point. However, English and Irish judicial practice is to identify a dependent or independent covenant as part of the contractual nexus, that is, an obligation which is to be performed by one of the parties. In deciding whether an agreement is subject to the occurrence of an event, the non-performance of that event postponing the very existence of a contract, the practice within an industry or profession may be pertinent. The "subject to contract" cases in real property transactions are perhaps the best examples of such a process, for until the contract is signed or exchanged the majority of property sales do not have any legal force at all. The contract only comes into existence upon the contingent event. One of the most interesting features of "subject to contract" agreements is that it is entirely within the control of the parties to decide whether or not to proceed and execute the agreement: a capricious or unmeritorious decision not to sign the contract or to exchange contracts is not a basis for relief for the aggrieved party.

9–08 If, in particular, the condition fixed is something over which the parties can have no control—e.g. a statement that A will pay B £20,000 for an acre of farmland if the local authority grants B's application to re-zone the land for industrial use—it may be that A's statement will be held to be a condition and that until this event occurs there is no contract. In *Pym v Campbell*[16] an action brought upon an alleged agreement to pay for an interest in an invention failed when the defendant was able to show that the existence of the contract was conditional upon one Abernathie, an engineer, approving the invention. Abernathie failed to give his approval so no contract existed which could form the basis of the plaintiff's claim. In *Macklin & McDonald v Greacen & Co*[17] the defendant agreed to sell land to the plaintiffs providing the Northern Bank, who occupied the site, gave permission. This permission was not forthcoming. The plaintiffs' action for breach of contract failed; Griffin J. in the Supreme Court pointed out that because the defendant had not expressly or impliedly promised that the bank would give permission there could not be liability in contract. Even if the event in question is within the power of one party to secure, a condition precedent may still be held to exist; see *Myton Ltd v Schwab-Morris*.[18] In this case Goulding J. held that an agreement which required the purchase of land to pay a deposit involved a condition precedent and that until the payment was made no contract existed. The result in this

---

[15] [1970] I.R. 45.
[16] (1856) 6 El. & Bl. 370.
[17] [1983] I.R. 61.
[18] [1974] 1 W.L.R. 331.

case was, on the facts, a fair one for the defendant purchaser had registered a caution against the vendor's property and this result meant the caution could be removed. However, the reasoning of Goulding J. is open to criticism: the purchaser's duty to pay a deposit is part of the purchaser's contractual obligations, rather than an external condition upon which the contract's very existence will turn. If the event stipulated is within the power of one of the parties, it does not follow that there is an obligation to bring the stipulated event into being. Only if there is an express or implied obligation, or a duty, which requires one party to do, or abstain from doing, anything which may affect the happening of the stated event will the courts intervene.

9–09 As an example of this situation—that is, the court describes the obligation as contractual, rather than an external event—we can turn to *Reynolds v Altomoravia Holdings Ltd.*[19] A dispute between a landlord and prospective tenant was settled, with High Court approval, on the understanding that there would be completion of the contract on a set date. The defendants later postponed the closing date and prevaricated in order to wring further concessions from the landlord. Cregan J. held that the date of completion, as part of a contract and at the same time being binding on the parties, "is a condition of the contract". The learned judge appears to have regarded the term as a condition subsequent. Cregan J. characterised the defendant's conduct as a breach of the court order—a contractual obligation—thus entitling the plaintiff to damages and rescission of the contract. A condition subsequent may operate the other way where no contractual obligation is inferred. In *Thompson v ASDA-MFI Group Plc*[20] the plaintiff was a member of a pension scheme which gave him the option of increasing his shares. However, under the rules of the pension scheme, the option expired if the pensioner's employer ceased to be a member of the group. The defendants sold their shareholding in W. Ltd; the plaintiff's employer and the plaintiff therefore ceased to have any rights of purchase. Scott J. indicated that the plaintiff company was not bound by contract not to dispose of its shareholding in W. Ltd. *Thompson v ASDA-MFI Group Plc* is an illustration of a condition subsequent. Here the contract and contractual rights of the parties subsist until some stipulated, or contingent, event occurs. In this instance, the plaintiff had a right to purchase shares until his employer ceased to be a part of the ASDA-MFI Group. When this occurred the contractual right was terminated.

9–10 Conditions subsequent will be anticipated in situations where the buyer of goods takes delivery but wishes to have the goods inspected or examined to see if they comply with a description or statement about merchantability or fitness for purpose.[21] In contracts for the sale of land for potential development, the purchaser may stipulate that if the application for planning permission is

---

[19] [2015] IEHC 482.
[20] [1988] 2 All E.R. 722.
[21] *Head v Tattersall* (1871) L.R. 7 Exch. 7.

unsuccessful, the purchaser is to have the option of returning the property and obtaining the return of his purchase money.[22] Conditions subsequent may also be inserted so as to provide that an agreement may terminate if agreement is not reached between the parties on related matters. This use of a condition subsequent may have the effect of forestalling an argument that the contractual relationship in place is void for uncertainty: *Covington Marine Corp v Xiamen Shipbuilding Industry Co.*[23] Conditions subsequent are much less common than conditions precedent. Conditions precedent are more complex in effect. If a condition precedent is not met, this may prevent the contract itself from coming into existence, as in *Macklin & McDonald v Greacen & Co*, or it may simply control the remedies available to the parties. In *Gregg & Co v Fraser & Sons*[24] a contract provided that before an award of damages for breach of contract could be awarded by a civil jury there had to be a valid and enforceable award from an arbitrator or umpire. It was held that this clause was, implicitly, a condition precedent and that until it was satisfied a jury award could not be made.

9–11 It is common to find that the condition is held to also involve a promissory element. There may be an express promise that the condition will be fulfilled or it may be implied that efforts will be made to ensure that the condition precedent is satisfied as in *Rooney v Byrne.*[25] In this case, the purchaser of real property, under a contract subject to him obtaining satisfactory finance, was held to be under a duty to make efforts to find and accept satisfactory finance and not entitled to exercise a discretion to accept or refuse finance. Whether the condition precedent, to use Corbin's analysis, contains a promissory element is a question of construction. It may be that an express or implied statement to this effect can be detected. If the parties, or their agents, clearly considered the condition created an obligation then the condition is sometimes said to be a "fundamental term"; see *Damon Cia v Hapag Lloyd S.A.*[26]

9–12 The Irish case of *Tradax (Ireland) Ltd v Irish Grain Board Ltd*[27] illustrates that it will not be easy to find such an implied term if the condition itself is not stated in the contract. The majority of the Supreme Court, McCarthy J. dissenting, could not find an implied obligation upon the buyers of grain to open a letter of credit in favour of the seller. In distinguishing the facts of the case from the English cases (see, for example, *Ian Stach Ltd v Baker Bosley Ltd*[28]) the majority of the Supreme Court rejected the view that

---

[22] *Dorene Ltd v Suedes (Ireland) Ltd* [1981] I.R. 312.
[23] [2006] 1 Lloyd's Rep. 745. See the discussion in *O'Connor v Coady* [2004] IESC 54.
[24] [1906] 2 I.R. 545, 570.
[25] [1933] I.R. 609.
[26] [1985] 1 All E.R. 475; see also *United Yeast Co v Cameo Investments Ltd* (1995) 111 I.L.T.R. 13 and *O'Connor v McNamara* [2009] IEHC 190, examples where the Irish courts affirm that equity does not treat time obligations as being of the essence unless the agreement so provides or one party makes it so via a notice procedure.
[27] [1984] I.R. 1.
[28] [1958] 2 Q.B. 130.

this implied fundamental term could exist because it was inconsistent with the express terms of the contract.

9–13 So, where we use the term "condition" in the sense of contractual promise we can see that the courts face a difficult task of construction or interpretation; the principles of construction the courts have developed are of the utmost importance in resolving disputes over interpretation. In relation to express terms in the contract, s.11(2) of the 1893 Act, as amended by the Sale of Goods and Supply of Services Act 1980 (the "1980 Act"), provides:

> "… whether a stipulation in a contract of sale is a condition, the breach of which may give rise to a right to treat the contract as repudiated, or a warranty, the breach of which may give rise to a claim for damages but not to a right to reject the goods and treat the contract as repudiated, depends in each case on the construction of the contract. A stipulation may be a condition, though called a warranty in the contract."

The issue of whether an express term is a condition is not a matter of law but one of interpretation. The test for deciding whether a term is a condition or not, in cases where parties have not expressly so provided, is to be found in the words of Bowen L.J. in *Bentsen & Son v Taylor*[29]:

> "[T]here is no way of deciding that question except by looking at the contract in the light of the surrounding circumstances, and then making up one's mind whether the intention of the parties, as gathered from the instrument itself, will best be carried out by treating the promise as a warranty sounding only in damages, or as a condition precedent by the failure to perform which the other party is relieved of his liability."[30]

Therefore, the test for a condition requires the courts to look at the contract document and surrounding circumstances—at the time of contracting and not subsequent events—and try to fix the intention of the parties. A term may be held a condition even if the remedy of rescission is not affixed to the obligation.[31] In the decision of the House of Lords in *Total Gas Marketing v Arco British Ltd*[32] the designation of an obligation to be "conditional" upon the defendants entering a separate agreement was held to make that event a

---

[29] [1893] 2 Q.B. 274.

[30] [1893] 2 Q.B. 274 at 281. When a force majeure clause is inserted into a contract it is not uncommon for the clause to stipulate that when one party seeks to rely upon a force majeure event, notice must be given. Four recent English cases suggest notice provisions will not be conditions precedent: see *Mamidoil-Jetoil Greek Petideum Co SA v Okta Crude Oil Refines, AD* [2001] Lloyds 2 Lloyd's Rep. 76, affirmed on appeal at [2003] 1 Lloyd's Rep. 1; *The Azur Gaz* [2005] EWHC 2528 (Comm); *Great Elephant Corporation v Trafigura Beheer BV* [2012] EWHC 1745 (Comm); *Scottish Power UK plc v BP Exploration Co Ltd* [2015] EWHC 2658 (Comm).

[31] *Bunge Corp v Tradax S.A.* [1981] 1 W.L.R. 711.

[32] *The Times*, June 26, 1998.

condition precedent even in the absence of a stipulation entitling the plaintiffs, in the event of the default of the defendants, to regard their obligations as terminated or discharged for non-occurrence of the condition precedent.

9–14 If, however, the obligation was an implied obligation under the 1893 Act the situation becomes more complicated. If the goods sold were not the seller's to sell (s.12), did not meet the contract description (s.13), were unmerchantable or unfit for their purpose (s.14), or, having been sold by sample, did not accord with the sample (s.15), then the buyer had a right to reject the goods because these implied statutory obligations were statutory conditions for, as we have seen, the effect of this dichotomy was to provide a right of rescission if the obligation was a condition, but a right to damages only if the obligation was a warranty. This was graphically illustrated by *Re Moore & Co v Landauer*.[33] The contract was for the sale of 3,100 cases of Australian canned fruit packed 30 tins to a case. Some cases were delivered with fewer than 30 tins to a case, some with more. The total number of tins delivered met the contract requirement. No loss resulted for failure to meet the contract description yet the buyer was held entitled to rescind simply because s.13 (requiring goods to answer their description) was broken by defective packing of goods.

9–15 This rigid and inflexible result could be avoided by an exemption clause, but in the absence of such a clause the courts could not overturn the 1893 Act because (so it was thought prior to 1975) *all* contract terms, express or implied, in sale of goods cases were either conditions or warranties. After 1893, there was no room for an old approach in which the courts could sometimes ask, is the breach likely to go to the root of the contract? Is the innocent party to the contract likely to be substantially deprived of the fruits of the contract? *A fortiori*, the actual effects of breach were also not relevant.

9–16 The problem that bedevils this classification is this: who is to decide which category the obligation falls into? If the parties have taken the trouble to "label" each obligation then the courts will respect this, but, in the real world, persons are not so fastidious. As a result, obligations and their importance came to be an area for the exercise of judicial discretion. So, in *Ritchie v Atkinson*[34] a vessel left the Port of St. Petersburgh with a short cargo. Loading was broken off because of the danger of hostilities breaking out between Britain and Russia. On its arrival in Britain the merchant refused to pay the shipowners their freight, claiming that the obligation to deliver a full cargo was a condition precedent to the merchant's obligation. To uphold such a plea would have permitted the merchant to obtain free transportation of his goods. The Court of Kings Bench held the breach of contract had minor consequences for the merchant. The obligation to deliver a full cargo was independent and the merchant was obliged to pay freight on a pro rata basis; any loss suffered

---

[33] [1921] 2 K.B. 519.
[34] (1808) 10 East 295.

by the defendant as a result of the short cargo was to be actionable in damages. While some of the nineteenth-century decisions such as *Graves v Legg*[35] indicate that the nature of the term may change depending upon the consequences of breach, the issue of interpretation of the contract as a whole, and a search for the presumed intention of the parties ultimately became the basis upon which the contract term was classified. Palles C.B., in *Fearnley v London Guarantee Insurance Co*,[36] indicated that the classification given by the parties is not necessarily dispositive, for if the label given is inconsistent with the entire contract it will not be given effect. This is not to say, however, that the courts are free to ignore or override the clear intention of the parties, but rather the courts will infer that the entire agreement should be compatible with the classification adopted, for if doubts arise, the courts are likely to give effect to the most natural interpretation to be placed on the contract as a whole.

9–17 In the Irish case of *Knox v Mayne*[37] the Court of Exchequer upheld a plea of condition precedent. The sellers of a cargo of maize sued the defendant purchasers for non-acceptance. The purchaser was to have "privilege of having shipment to direct port" to be nominated by him. The sellers shipped the final cargo without requesting a port of discharge, whereupon the defendants took delivery but refused to pay for the final cargo. The plaintiffs argued that it was for the defendants to show loss resulted from the breach. It was held that the right of selection had to be given to the defendants. The failure was failure of a condition precedent, not a collateral or independent covenant. Two further examples serve to illustrate the difficulties encountered here. It is established that if a farmer acquiring land under an agistment or conacre agreement fails to pay the contract price this constitutes breach of a dependent covenant; the landowner may treat this failure as terminating his own obligation to permit use of the land; see *Carson v Jeffers*.[38] On the other hand, *Carson v Jeffers* must be contrasted with *Athol v Midland Gt. W. Ry. Co*.[39] The lessor convenanted to permit the plaintiff lessees use of a conduit for draining excess water from the land leased to them. The defendant lessor diverted the conduit. An action by the plaintiffs was met with the plea that they had not paid rent and that payment was a condition precedent to the defendant's obligation to permit use of the conduit. The plea failed; each obligation was held to be independent.

The Sale of Goods Act 1893

9–18 It is necessary to mention the effects of the 1893 Act on the common law rules outlined above. Although this Act should not have influenced the

---

[35] (1854) 9 Exch. 709.
[36] (1880) 6 L.R. (Ir.) 219, 232, 394; (1880) 5 App. Cas. 911.
[37] (1873) I.R. 7 C.L. 557.
[38] [1961] I.R. 44.
[39] (1867) I.R. 3 C.L. 333.

courts in non-sale of goods cases, it had a "spillover" effect which is only now being expunged from the common law.

Conditions and Warranties

9–19 The 1893 Act was not designed to be a radical measure of reform; it was primarily designed to codify the rules that had evolved at common law. But the difficulties surrounding the question of discharge of contractual obligations were met by invoking a new theoretical framework which, while it relied heavily on the dependent/independent convenant dichotomy, led to the temporary obliteration of the old common law rules, even in non-sale of goods transactions.

9–20 The 1893 Act divided obligations into conditions and warranties. Unfortunately, the draftsman did not define such obligations but contented himself with setting out the consequences of breach of each obligation. A condition is a term, breach of which entitles the innocent party to elect to rescind the contract and sue for damages or affirm the contract and sue for damages.[40] Under s.11(1)(c), the right to rescind was lost once delivery of goods had taken place and the contract executed. (The revised s.11 in the 1980 Act abandons this restriction on the right to rescind.) If the term is a warranty the innocent party has a remedy in damages only. A warranty is defined in s.62(1) as something "collateral to the main purpose of such contract". This technical use of the word "warranty", which connoted at common law a contractual representation, has been a source of some confusion and students should bear in mind that "warranty" may mean different things according to context.

The *Hong Kong Fir* Case

9–21 The first indication that the condition/warranty dichotomy was not all embracing was given by the English Court of Appeal in the *Hong Kong Fir* case.[41] A contract for the charter of a cargo ship for a period of two years was broken because the vessel was unseaworthy. Repairs were necessary and the vessel was out of service for 20 weeks. The charterers sought to rescind the contract claiming the obligation to provide a seaworthy vessel was a condition. (The charterers wanted to repudiate because a lowering of freight charges would permit the charterers to acquire another vessel at a lower cost). The Court of Appeal rejected this view of the bargain. The court looked to the pre-1893 case law and held that a seaworthiness obligation was not a condition in

---

[40] *White Sewing Machine Co v Fitzgerald* (1894) 29 I.L.T.R. 37.
[41] *Hong Kong Fir Shipping Co Ltd v Kawasaki Kisen Kaisha Ltd* [1962] 2 Q.B. 26.

the sense that failure to supply a seaworthy vessel discharged the charterer's obligation to take the vessel and pay freight or the cost of hire. Upjohn L.J. observed that to hold a seaworthiness obligation was a condition would lead to absurdities:

> "If a nail is missing from one of the timbers of a wooden vessel or if proper medical supplies or two anchors are not on board at the time of sailing, the owners are in breach of the seaworthiness stipulation. It is contrary to common sense to suppose that in such circumstances the parties contemplated that the charterer should at once be entitled to treat the contract as at an end for such trifling breaches."[42]

So, in non-sale of goods cases the condition/warranty dichotomy was challenged; unless there was conclusive evidence that the parties intended breach of such a term to lead to a right to rescission or damages only, the courts will now ask:

> "Does the breach of the stipulation go so much to the root of the contract that it makes further commercial performance of the contract impossible, or in other words is the whole contract frustrated? If yes, the innocent party may treat the contract as at an end. If nay his claim sounds in damages only."[43]

The problem with this approach is that it is very litigation-oriented. It has been attacked as inconsistent with the 1893 Act and undesirable because it leads to uncertainty and unpredictability of result. The *Hong Kong Fir* case was thought to be applicable only in contracts where the 1893 Act could not apply. Since the decision in *Cehave N.V. v Bremer Handelsgesellschaft*,[44] it is established that even in sale of goods cases the courts should not give the extreme remedy of rescission unless the parties have clearly so agreed or unless a precedent binds a court so to hold. In *Cehave N.V.* the Court of Appeal set out a series of questions that should be asked:

9–22 (1) Does the contract *expressly* confer a right of termination for such a breach? If so the courts must respect this and allow rescission even if loss resulting is minimal or non-existent.

9–23 (2) If "no" is the answer to question 1, does the contract impliedly give a right to rescission or only a right to damages? Again an affirmative answer will be conclusive, as *Schuler A.G. v Wickman Tools*[45] shows. However, it may be

---

[42] *Hong Kong Fir Shipping Co Ltd v Kawasaki Kisen Kaisha Ltd* [1962] 2 Q.B. 26 at 70. On seaworthiness generally, see *Golden Fleece Maritime Inc. v ST Shipping and Transport Inc.* [2008] EWCA Civ 584.
[43] [1962] 2 Q.B. 26 at 70 per Upjohn L.J.
[44] [1976] Q.B. 44.
[45] [1974] A.C. 235; *Rainy Sky SA v Kookmin Bank* [2011] UKSC 50.

that the unreasonableness of the result or absence of loss will point towards the next question coming into play.

9–24 (3) Does a statute or stare decisis point towards the obligation being a condition or warranty? The *implied* obligations under the 1893 Act (as amended by the 1980 Act) remain conditions or warranties so *Re Moore & Co v Landauer*[46] would still be decided in the same way; similarly, case law determines that a statement that a ship will be ready to load is a condition; see *Behn v Burness*[47]; so too is an expected date of arrival stipulation; see *The Mihalis Angelos*[48]; see also the decision in *Toepfer (Hamburg) v Verheijdens Veervoeder Commissiehandel (Rotterdam)*,[49] in which the Court of Appeal held an obligation to make prompt payment to be a condition, illustrating that if the court feels that commercial practice requires the obligation to be a condition the contract term will be so construed. See also *Gill & Duffus S.A. v Berger & Co*[50] in which the House of Lords held that failure by the buyer under a C.I.F. contract to pay the price when presented with documents constitutes a fundamental breach of contract entitling the seller to rescind and sue for damages. In *Barber v NWS Bank Plc*[51] the Court of Appeal held that an express term in a contract of hire-purchase which declared, wrongly, that the defendants were the owners of a car which was the subject of a conditional sale agreement was a condition. The term was fundamental to the contract and could be broken in one way only. The plaintiff could thus rescind the contract for breach of condition when the true state of affairs was discovered.

9–25 If we have another look at the facts of *Knox v Mayne*[52] it is likely that a modern Irish court, influenced by these English authorities, would not be so ready to hold the destination clause to be a condition and would now perhaps test the case by asking the fourth question posed in *Cehave N.V.*:

9–26 (4) Has the breach gone to the root of the contract so as to deprive the injured party of that which he contracted for? Unless this central or core obligation can no longer be obtained—several English judges and commentators call this *the fundamental term*—damages will be deemed to be the most appropriate remedy. This trend is only part of a broader movement towards conferring wide discretionary powers on the courts in the area of remedies.

9–27 The facts of *Laird Brothers v Dublin Steampacket*,[53] the leading Irish authority on this question, are instructive. The plaintiffs agreed to build a ship

---

[46]   [1921] 2 K.B. 519.
[47]   (1863) 3 B. & S. 751.
[48]   [1971] 1 Q.B. 164; *The Baleaes* [1993] 1 Lloyd's Rep. 215.
[49]   *The Times*, April 26, 1978.
[50]   [1985] 1 Lloyd's Rep. 621.
[51]   *The Times*, November 27, 1995.
[52]   (1873) I.R. 7 C.L. 557.
[53]   (1900) 34 I.L.T.R. 97.

to be delivered by August 1, 1897. Payment was to be made by instalments. The contract provided that the sixth and final instalment of £5,000 was not to be paid unless the vessel was completed on the agreed date. The vessel was not completed until September 1897. The defendants had not suffered loss but they argued that under the terms of the contract completion on the due date was a condition precedent to the payment of the last instalment. Andrews J. regarded the matter as one of construction and posed the following question:

> "[A]re the words of the clause … so precise, express and strong, when taken in connection with the entire contract, that the intention prima facie so unreasonable, is the only one compatible with the terms employed?"[54]

It would appear that the court was reluctant to give the contract term its plain and ordinary meaning—which would have favoured the defendants—because, as Andrews J. said, "[i]t is impossible to hold that this delay went to the root of the matter so as to render the performance of the rest of the contract by the plaintiffs a thing different in substance from what the defendants stipulated for". Yet, as we have seen, such a question can only be asked *after* the court has ascertained what the parties have agreed upon; a clear statement of intention must be given effect even if the result is unreasonable. It appears to this writer that Andrews J. went some way towards modifying the terms of this agreement by ruling that an unreasonable contract provision can only be given effect if an unreasonable result is the only possible interpretation that can be placed on the term. Viewed in the light of recent judicial developments in relation to the construction of commercial contracts, particularly the trend[55] towards holding that contracts are to be given a commercially sensible construction, this approach seems a very modern one. There is a lot of judicial support for taking a flexible approach by using *Hong Kong Fir* in a variety of disputes. In *Parol Ltd v Carroll Village (Retail) Management Services Ltd*[56] the High Court applied this test to the terms of a lease in which the lessor and lessee disputed whether breaches of the lessor's maintenance obligations in respect of the common parts of a shopping centre, individually or cumulatively, could have deprived the lessee of substantially the whole benefit of the contract. Clarke J. held the breaches by the lessor did not have any such consequence.

When will a breach go to the root of a contract?

9–28 The most important English judicial evaluation of how *Hong Kong Fir* is to be applied in a specific context is the judgment of Lewison L.J. in *Telford Homes (Creekside) Ltd v Ampurius New Homes Holdings Ltd*.[57] A contract for the development of four blocks of flats was delayed when the contractor

---

[54] (1900) 34 I.L.T.R. 97 at 100.
[55] *Rainy Sky SA v Kookmin Bank* [2011] UKSC 50 and *Dunnes Stores v Holtgen* [2012] IEHC 93 are just two examples.
[56] [2010] IEHC 498; see also *Gumland v Duffy Bros* [2008] HCA 10 (non-payment of rent).
[57] [2013] EWCA Civ 577; *Urban I (Blonk Street) Ltd v Ayres and Ayers* [2013] EWCA Civ 816.

experienced funding delays. This prevented the parties from concluding leasing arrangements under which the developer would grant 999 year leases to the defendant, a property developer. These delays led the developer to treat the contractor as being in fundamental breach of contract. The issue for Lewison L.J. was whether there were any repudiatory breaches of contract that would entitle the developer to terminate the contract. Lewison L.J. answered this question by reference to Diplock L.J.'s speech in *Hong Kong Fir* in which he said that the conduct of the party electing to treat the contract as at an end is to be judged by reference to the time when that election takes place. Lewison L.J. summarised the breach going to the cost of the contract test as involving three factors:

> "First, the task of the court is to look at the position as at the date of purported termination of the contract even in a case of actual rather than anticipatory breach. Second, in looking at the position at that date, the court must take into account any steps taken by the guilty party to remedy accrued breaches of contract. Third, the court must also take account of likely future events, judged by reference to objective facts as at the date of purported termination".

At the date of the contract being terminated the works had resumed. Given that the central objective was to complete the construction work in order to execute 999 year leases, any decision on the consequences of delay should have borne this in mind. In the context of a £18 million project, the losses to the developer, estimated at £100,000, were negligible. Termination was premature. Given that the contractor was pressing ahead to complete the work, and he did so several months after the target dates had passed, there were no breaches going to the heart or root of the contract.

The Shipping Cases

9–29 Most of the English decisions involve time and performance obligations in shipping cases.

9–30 In *Bunge Corp v Tradax S.A.*[58] the House of Lords upheld the decision of the Court of Appeal in which it had been held that an express obligation requiring the shippers of goods to give 15 days' notice of their date for the cargo to be available was a condition, breach of which entitled the owner to rescind the charterparty. While the contract did not expressly cede the remedy of rescission, this type of obligation—a time obligation—was held to be normally so important in commercial transactions that, for the sake of certainty, predictability and uniformity of approach, it will be interpreted as having been intended as a condition in the sense of an express promise which, if broken, gives the injured party the right to rescind the contract without reference to the actual effects of the breach. Nevertheless, each contract must

---

[58] [1981] 1 W.L.R. 71.

be construed as a whole. A term that requires a "readiness to load" notice is generally a condition, as is the term requiring the loading to take place before expiry of a set time. However, in *ERG Raffinerie Mediterranee SpA v Chevron USA*,[59] the Court of Appeal held that where the buyer has a right to shorten the "readiness to load" notice[60] (which will have a knock-on effect vis-à-vis the seller's obligation to load by a fixed date) it cannot have been the intention of the parties that the seller's obligation to load will be of the essence of the contract, i.e. a condition.

9–31 The movement towards holding that time obligations in mercantile contracts will generally be held to be conditions has been further emphasised by the House of Lords in *Cie Commercial Sucres et Denrées v Czarnikow Ltd, The Naxos*.[61] The contract was concluded on standard terms used exclusively between sugar dealers and incorporated rules of the Refined Sugar Association of London. Under the contract, the buyer was entitled to call upon the seller to load, the seller to be given not less than 14 days' notice that the buyer's vessels were expected to be ready to load. Due notice was given, but the seller failed to deliver the sugar. The buyer then rescinded the contract for breach, bought a replacement cargo and sued for consequential loss. The House of Lords had to consider whether the rules relating to boarding were contractual obligations which were binding on the seller once due notice was given by the buyer, and whether the obligation was in the nature of a condition. While both the Commercial Court and the Court of Appeal held in favour of the seller, the House of Lords reinstated the view of the arbitrators that the obligation in question was contractual and in the nature of a condition. In giving the leading judgment Lord Ackner followed *Bunge* and, classifying the contract as mercantile and the obligation as a time obligation, went on to consider the findings of the arbitrators. In the view of the arbitrators, the obligation was of the "utmost importance", because prompt performance of delivery obligations would be vital to both parties, and a prompt right to cancel for default would be essential to allow the buyer to mitigate loss by securing delivery from another source. The case is a compelling one because the rules in question, and the contract generally, were far from specific on the issue of remedies. Lord Brandon, dissenting, pointed out that similar time obligations were clearly warranties. The majority of the House of Lords, however, were clearly influenced by the arbitrators who had ruled that demurrage would not be an adequate remedy in such circumstances. The contract was therefore not symmetrical and, despite Lord Brandon's view that the result of the majority judgment was to create illogical consequences, the value of certainty and predictability of result was seen as of paramount importance.

---

[59] [2007] EWCA Civ 494.
[60] A so-called laycan provision: see Rix L.J. in *Tidebrook Maritime Corp v Vitoil SA* [2006] EWCA Civ 944.
[61] [1990] 3 All E.R. 641. Contrast the decision of Popplewell J. in *Spar Shipping AS v Grand China Logistics Holding (Group) Co Ltd* [2015] EWHC 718 (Comm) (failure to make payment of hire charges under a counterparty do not involve breaches of a condition).

9–32 These values have again prevailed in the recent case of *The Seaflower*.[62] This was a time charter in which the obligation placed on the owners was to obtain approval about the condition of the vessel from named oil companies. One company had not given permission and the contract provided that if approval was not obtained within 60 days of commencement of the charter the owners would be in breach. The owners gave notice that approval would not be obtained within time. Was this notice an anticipatory repudiatory breach or, in the alternative, a breach of condition when the 60-day period expired? Aikens J. at trial held that the term in the contract was innominate, holding, *inter alia*, that a statement about the physical state of the vessel was analogous to a seaworthiness clause and, absent an express right to terminate, it would be commercially nonsensical to view the term as a condition. The Court of Appeal unanimously reversed Aikens J.; the view that a statement in relation to the physical state of the vessel was analogous to a seaworthiness clause was rejected; such a term was characterised as relevant to the class of vessel (which is a condition). More critically, the Court of Appeal held that consistency required a time obligation to be regarded as a condition, *pace Bunge*. Jonathan Parker L.J. was of the view that Aikens J. had not afforded the virtue of legal certainty sufficient weight, noting that if the right to terminate depended on gauging the effect of the breach "the charter may be over before such a process would be completed by the parties".[63]

9–33 If we put to one side complicated transactions such as those in *Bunge* and *The Naxos*, and, bearing in mind Ormrod L.J.'s statement in *Cehave* that the courts should be slow to hold an express term in a condition, we can see that the *Hong Kong Fir* test means that the judges, apprised of all the facts and the results of the actual breach, are to have the power to determine which remedy is the most appropriate one in this particular dispute. While some flexibility of approach is sometimes demonstrated by the judges (*Regent O.H.G. Aisenstadt und Barig v Francesco of Jermyn St.*[64]) this will not always prove possible. There have been relatively few cases in which the fourth element or question in the *Hong Kong Fir* test has been applied, because the courts have tended to find that the obligation, expressly or by implication, has been intended to be a condition. However, the House of Lords in *The Gregos*[65] held that an obligation to redeliver a vessel at the end of a time charter was an innominate term; a short delay would not justify giving the obligation the status of a condition. Similarly, in one of the reported Irish cases in which *Hong Kong Fir* has been applied, Costello J. was able to hold that the obligation in question was to be tested by reference to the consequences of the breach in the case at bar. It is ironic that this area of jurisprudence, developed in the specialist world of maritime commercial law, has been more readily applied in more everyday

---

[62] [2001] 1 Lloyd's Rep. 341.
[63] [2001] 1 Lloyd's Rep. 341 at 353.
[64] [1981] 3 All E.R. 327.
[65] [1995] 1 Lloyd's Rep. 1.

contractual disputes. In *Anglo Group Plc v Winther Browne & Co*,[66] a computer system was delivered to the defendants. The system contained errors and "bugs", as all systems do; the buyers argued that the errors constituted a breach in the *Hong Kong Fir* sense. Toulmin J. held that the defects did not substantially deprive the buyers of the whole benefit of the contract and thus termination by the buyers was wrongful. Like the *Anglo Group* case, *Peregrine Systems Ltd v Steria Ltd*[67] concerned an alleged failure to install a satisfactory software application within a reasonable time. The Court of Appeal held there was no breach but went on to consider whether any breach, if it had occurred, was repudiatory. The Court of Appeal distinguished an obligation to complete a contract within a reasonable time from a term making "time of the essence". Only the latter entitles the injured party to terminate the contract for breach. The former classification will require the injured party to establish that the breach is repudiatory, that is, the breach is one "which will deprive the party not in default of substantially the whole benefit which it was intended he should obtain from the contract".[68] On the other hand, in *Rubicon Computer Systems Ltd v United Paints Ltd*[69] the purchaser of a computer system found that the supplier had wrongfully put a "time-lock" into the operating program because of a dispute over payment. The lock was in place for six months, after which period the system was obsolete. The Court of Appeal held that here the breach had deprived the buyer substantially of the whole benefit of the contract and was thus repudiatory under *Hong Kong Fir*.

9–34 In *Irish Telephone Rentals Ltd v Irish Civil Service Building Society Ltd*[70] the plaintiffs purported to rescind a contract for the supply of a telephone system on the ground that it malfunctioned. Costello J. found that the goods supplied were not in compliance with the implied term found in s.39 of the 1980 Act, and, specifically, that the goods were not of merchantable quality. It is important to note that s.39 obligations are implied terms—the 1980 Act does not assign them the status of condition or warranty in the context of supply of services even though merchantable quality is an implied condition in sale of goods, leasing and hire-purchase contracts. Costello J. cited the following extract from the judgment of Diplock L.J. in *Hong Kong Fir*:

> "The contract may itself expressly define some of these events, as in the cancellation clause in a charter party; but, human prescience being limited, it seldom does so exhaustively and often fails to do so at all. In some classes of contracts such as sale of goods, marine insurance, contracts of affreightment, evidenced by bills of lading and those

---

[66] (2002) 72 Con. L.R. 118; *Bedfordshire C.C. v Fitzpatrick Contractors Ltd* (1998) 62 Con. L.R. 64.

[67] [2005] EWCA Civ 259.

[68] Per Diplock L.J. in *Hong Kong Fir* [1962] 2 Q.B. 26 at 70, cited by Kay L.J. in *Peregrine Systems*.

[69] [2000] T.C.L.R. 453.

[70] [1991] I.L.R.M. 880; see also *Taylor v Smyth* [1990] I.L.R.M. 377.

between parties to bills of exchange, parliament has defined by statute some of the events not provided for expressly in individual contracts of that class; but where an event occurs the occurrence of which neither the parties nor parliament have expressly stated will discharge one of the parties from further performance of his undertakings, it is for the court to determined whether the event has this effect or not.

The test whether an event has this effect or not has been stated in a number of metaphors all of which I think amount to the same thing: does the occurrence of the event deprive the party who has further undertakings still to perform of substantially the whole benefit which it was the intention of the parties as expressed in the contract that he should obtain as the consideration for performing those undertakings?"[71]

Declaring that in his view this test was to be applied to the case before him, Costello J. held that the delays afforded in communications by virtue of the defective system were of a serious nature and justified giving the plaintiff the right to rescind.

9–35 This interesting application of *Hong Kong Fir*, however, is not free from difficulty. Costello J. also held that the defendants were in breach of an express term that the goods supplied would be provided and maintained in good working order. If express terms of this kind are, in any event, normally held to be conditions, even if the consequences of the s.39 breach had not been serious, the separate breach of an express condition should, arguably, have given the plaintiff a right to rescind anyway. The answer to this, of course, is that "good condition" express promises are normally characterised as innominate terms, after the decision in *The Hansa Nord*[72] and Costello J.'s decision should be seen in this context.

Two Restrictions on the Innominate Term

9–36 It has already been mentioned that the innominate term may have disadvantages that should not be understated. Litigation to decide what a term means should not be encouraged when commercial practices have proved to be a satisfactory means of resolving disputes. In a sequence of cases[73] involving a construction contract in Prince's Dock Belfast, Deeny J. held, first of all, that a contractual stipulation that the development should be completed on a particular date, while not being an obligation that made time of the essence, was nevertheless an innominate term or a condition which could trigger a right to rescind the contract. The Northern Ireland Court of Appeal[74] held that

---

[71] [1962] 2 Q.B. 26 at 65–66.
[72] [1976] Q.B. 44; *The Aktiou* [1987] 1 Lloyd's Rep. 283.
[73] [2012] NICA 58.
[74] *Hollowy v Sarcon (No. 177) Ltd* [2010] NI Ch 15; *Clear Homes v Sarcon (No. 177) Ltd* [2010] NI Ch 16; *Fitzpatrick v Sarcon (No. 177) Ltd* [2012] NICA 58.

this approach could not be upheld as there was clear judicial support for the view that in a contract of this kind, when the contract does not expressly or by implication make time of the essence, termination is only possible if there is either such an unreasonable delay that it constitutes repudiatory conduct or a notice has been served requiring completion within a reasonable time. Girvan L.J. said:

> "[T]he Respondents have not pleaded a case that the Appellant repudiated their contract by reason of such unreasonable delay as to evince an intention to repudiate. They did not make time of the essence in respect of a term in respect of which we have concluded time was not originally of the essence. We accept as correct the argument put forward by the Appellant that before a party could treat as repudiated a contract which was not subject to a time of the essence provision service of a notice making time of the essence was an essential step to be taken. There is clear authority for the requirement on a party to serve such a notice. See, for example, *Stickney v Keeble* [1950] AC 386, *United Scientific Holdings v Burnley Borough Council* [1978] AC 904 at 946, *British and Commonwealth Holdings Ltd. v Quadrex* [1989] 1 QB 842 at 857 and *Belzadi v Shaftesbury Hotels Ltd.* [1992] Ch 1 at 24. Such a notice must post-date the contractual completion date and must specify a reasonable time thereafter within which the contractual obligation of the party in default is to be completed."

A further example of judicial reservations being expressed about allowing the *Hong Kong Fir* or innominate terms approach to stray into an area of commercial law, that of itself is a sensitive one, is found in contractual conditions in insurance contracts. Insurance contracts generally require the insured to notify the insurer of claims that may be brought against the insured. These "claims made" provisions were regarded as being innominate terms, a serious breach of which would entitle the insurer to avoid the policy if the policy holder failed to comply.[75] In *Friends Provident Life and Pensions Ltd v Sirius International*[76] the English Court of Appeal saw this argument as unsound. Insurance companies could, the court said, label these obligations as conditions precedent and, in the absence of such a process, the court was reluctant to open up such an argument. Lord Justice Mance thought "claims made" clauses were ancillary provisions and that there was much to be said for the idea that in complex commercial transactions such as charter parties, each party "should be capable of looking after themselves". Mance L.J. observed, "English insurance law is strict enough as it is in the insurer's favour. I see no reason to make it stricter".

---

[75] *Alfred McAlpine Plc v BAI (Run-off) Ltd* [2000] L.R.I.R. 352; *The Mercandian Continent* [2001] L.R.I.R. 802.

[76] [2005] EWCA Civ 601. See Law Reform Commission, *Consultation Paper on Insurance Contracts* (LRC CP 65-2011).

Part 3

Invalidity

10 Mistake

Introduction

10–01 There are insuperable difficulties for any writer faced with the task of producing a neat and intelligible exposition of the law of mistake in contract.[1] The current law is beset with jurisdictional problems that can only be resolved by future decisions or legislation. Effective analysis of the law is hampered by the fact that judges do not use terms consistently: this is particularly true of the expressions "common", "mutual" and "unilateral". Cheshire and Fifoot[2] use this three-fold classification as the basis of their analysis, whilst conceding that the courts do not use these terms precisely. Several judges have used the terms "common" and "mutual" as synonyms: Dixon J. in *Nolan v Nolan*[3] even used the terms "mutual" and "unilateral" interchangeably, regarding any distinction as "largely one of phraseology". In the case of *O'Neill v Ryan*[4] Costello J. stressed that a preliminary problem of terminology can be an impediment to clear analysis, "for whilst the courts and text-book writers have used such descriptive terms as 'common', or 'mutual' or 'unilateral' to categorise the mistake which has affected the parties contract, unfortunately these adjectives have not been used consistently with the same meaning". Costello J. is clearly correct in pointing out the lack of uniformity, but the terms "common", "mutual" and "unilateral" can provide the student with a proximate, if at times unreliable, conceptual structure. We do not, however, intend to use the Cheshire and Fifoot classification which, even in an ideal world, would be unsatisfactory.

10–02 Instead, it is proposed that we look to what the courts do rather than what they say they do. We will first of all examine the case law in order to discover when a mistake will be operative, either at common law or in equity. As a second step we will consider the rules that have emerged in relation to the remedies of damages, rescission, rectification and specific performance. Students must bear in mind the fact that if a mistake is operative it does not follow that the party pleading mistake will be entitled to any or all of these remedies. An operative mistake may give rise to the remedy of rescission without allowing the court to change or rectify the contract. Further, even if a mistake is held not to prevent a contract coming into existence the court may

---

[1]   See, e.g. Stoljar, *Mistake and Misrepresentation* (London: Sweet & Maxwell, 1968); *Kerr on Fraud and Mistake* (1920) (reprinted 2010 Eale); MacMillan, *Mistakes in Contract Law* (Oxford: Hart Publishing, 2010); *Chitty on Contracts*, edited by H.G. Beale, 32nd edn (London: Sweet & Maxwell, 2015), Vol.1, paras 6-001–6-063.

[2]   *Cheshire, Fifoot and Furmston's Law of Contract*, 16th edn (Oxford: OUP, 2012), pp.292–337; Treitel, *The Law of Contract*, 14th edn (London: Sweet & Maxwell, 2015), pp.345–399.

[3]   (1954) 92 I.L.T.R. 94.

[4]   [1991] I.L.R.M. 672.

decline to award specific performance on the ground that the party labouring under the mistake should not be obliged to perform the contract—he may instead be held liable in damages.

Operative Mistake

(1) Mistake of law

10–03 One, or indeed both, of the contracting parties may mistakenly believe that a statute or an agreement has certain consequences; this may in turn produce an agreement based upon a misunderstanding of law. Once the true legal position is established an attempt may be made to avoid the contract by pleading its invalidity because of mistake. The legal maxim *ignorantia juris neminem excusat* may come into effect here. It would be inconvenient to allow persons to avoid contractual obligations because of a misunderstanding of the law, particularly in cases where the correct legal position could have been discovered quite easily. Thus it is often said that a mistake of law cannot be operative, either at common law or equity. In *O'Loghlen v O'Callaghan*[5] the plaintiff leased property to the defendant under an arrangement which permitted the defendant to deduct the rates and pay them to the local authority. *Both* plaintiff and defendant calculated the rate by reference to a section of the relevant Act which was later found to be inapplicable. As a result a lower rate than that calculated had been payable and the plaintiff sued for £100, being the difference between the rent actually paid and the rent payable had the rates been calculated correctly. It was held that at common law the defendant was not obliged to pay the difference; the mistake as a mistake of law was not operative.

10–04 The modern law of restitution, however, tends to skate over this distinction between mistakes of law and mistakes of fact. One specific example of this has surfaced in the Irish courts. If a local authority charges an excessive rate because of a misinterpretation of the rating legislation, or if the local authority charges an amount of money for a service or for the transfer of an interest in land which is in excess of the amount that should have been charged because of a misinterpretation of the enabling legislation, can the overpayment be reclaimed or used by way of set-off? While at first sight the older cases[6] suggest that this is not possible, the decision of the Privy Council in *Kiriri Cotton Co v Dewani*[7] has been followed. In *Dolan v Nelligan*[8] Kenny J. approved the speech of Lord Denning in *Kiriri Cotton* when his Lordship said: "If there is something more in addition to a mistake of law, if there is something in the defendant's conduct which shows that, of the two of them, he is the one primarily responsible for the mistake then it may be recovered

---

[5] (1874) I.R. 8 C.L. 116; *Gee v News Group Newspapers, The Times*, June 8, 1990.
[6] For a review of the old law, see Kerr, *Fraud and Mistake* (1954), pp.133–137.
[7] [1960] A.C. 192.
[8] [1967] I.R. 247.

back, they are not *in pari delicto*." In *Rogers v Louth County Council*[9] the Supreme Court also approved *Kiriri Cotton Co*. In the High Court decision in *Lord Mayor of Dublin v The Provost of Trinity College Dublin*,[10] Hamilton J. held that monies paid by the College in rates could be set off against monies due; the monies paid were in excess of the lawful rate. Hamilton J., after citing the above decisions said: "where money is paid, whether under a mistake of fact or law, justice requires that such money should be recoverable if the law so permits." While the Supreme Court later allowed an appeal there is nothing in the decision of the Supreme Court to suggest disapproval of Hamilton J.'s decision on this particular point. In *Avon C.C. v Howlett*,[11] the Court of Appeal was required to consider whether overpayments of salary could be recovered from an employee. The employee argued that the error arose due to a misinterpretation of his contract of employment and his entitlement to sick pay and was therefore a mistake of law. Slade L.J. in the leading judgment noted that since *Cooper v Phibbs* had been decided the courts had not been enthusiastic about upholding this distinction. The mistake was accordingly characterised as one of fact, and not of law. The overpayment was held irrecoverable on the grounds of estoppel and not because it was made under a mistake of law. This entire area has been definitively considered by the English Law Commission,[12] which recommended that the mistake of law rule should be abrogated by legislation.[13] However, in England reform has come from another direction.

10–05 The main criticisms of the distinction concerning the rule against recovery in respect of mistakes of law are, first, that the rule allows the payee to retain a payment which would not have been made but for the payer's mistake. Justice requires recovery by the payer unless there are special circumstances justifying retention. Secondly, the distinction itself is liable to yield results that are capricious, both in terms of the results of the distinction and the exceptions and qualifications to the rule.[14] This leads on to the third objection to the distinction: the consequences are so arbitrary that judicial efforts to manipulate the law in such a way as to avoid the rule leads to even greater uncertainty and unpredictability. The House of Lords, in a bold demonstration of judicial lawmaking, swept away the rule in *Kleinwort Benson Ltd v Lincoln City Council*.[15] This case concerned four currency swaps agreements of the kind declared illegal by the House of Lords in *Hazell v Hammersmith and Fulham CBC*,[16] agreements entered into before the decision in *Hazell* was handed down. It was acknowledged here that both Kleinwort Benson and the Council

---

9   [1981] I.L.R.M. 143.
10 [1986] I.L.R.M. 283.
11 [1983] 1 W.L.R. 605.
12 Law Com. No. 120, *Restitution of Payments made under a Mistake of Law* (1991).
13 Law Com. No. 227, *Mistakes of Law and Ultra Vires Public Authority Receipts and Payments* (1994), para.3.1.
14 See Law Com. No. 227, *Mistakes of Law and Ultra Vires Public Authority Receipts and Payments* (1994), paras 2.5–2.15.
15 [1998] 3 W.L.R. 1095.
16 [1998] 3 W.L.R. 1095.

contracted under a common mistake of law. While their Lordships took note of the public policy considerations that led to the evolution of the rule, namely fear of a flood of litigation, their Lordships opted to replace the rule against recovery of payments made under a mistake of law through a reformation exercise which would provide a right of recovery subject to specific defences and exceptions. In giving what is regarded as the leading judgment, Lord Goff of Chieveley distinguished private law payments from payments of taxation and other public charges, suggesting that public policy may more readily set its face against recoverability in the later situation. A majority of the House of Lords held that it was not necessary for Parliament to overturn the rule, along legislative lines as advocated by the Law Commission. We will return to the *Kleinwort Benson* case in Ch.20 in order to consider what exceptions and defences may be available to the general principle in favour of recovery of overpayments, whether made under a mistake of law or a mistake of fact.[17] The House of Lords in *Deutsche Morgan Grenfell v IRC*[18] has, by a majority of 4:1, held that the principle in *Kleinwort Benson v Lincoln City Council*,[19] whereby restitution of monies paid under a mistake of law will be available, may also apply to cases where the mistake of law relates to the payment of tax. The focus appears to be shifting away from considering the nature of the mistake to the issue whether the payment was made by a person who, expressly or impliedly, accepted the risk that the payment may be made in error.

10–06 However, a mistake of law is not the same thing as a decision to settle a damages claim based upon an earlier precedent which is subsequently overturned on appeal. The existence of a state of doubt on the law is not the same thing as a mistake of law and the solicitors acting for the claimant may be held to have impliedly accepted the risk that the law may changed by judicial interpretation: *Brennan v Bolt Burdon*.[20]

(2) Mistake of law in equity

10–07 In equity a distinction has been drawn between a mistake as to the general law, that is, the ordinary law of the country as found in public statutes, for example, and private law, the law as found in agreements, wills and Private Acts of Parliament. In *Cooper v Phibbs*[21] the plaintiff and defendant contracted to permit the plaintiff to lease a salmon fishery in Sligo. Both parties assumed that the defendant's father had earlier owned the Sligo fishery which had descended to them by will. In fact, a Private Act of Parliament made the plaintiff tenant for life. He sought to avoid the contract because in point of law he was already the owner. Lord Westbury, in giving judgment in the House of Lords declared:

---

[17] A mistake about the availability of a remedy, as distinct from liability to pay is within the new rule: *Nurdin and Peacock Plc v B. Ramsden & Co Ltd* [1999] 1 All E.R. 941.

[18] [2007] 1 All E.R. 449.

[19] [2008] 3 W.L.R. 1095.

[20] [2004] 3 W.L.R. 1321; *Futter v Revenue and Customs* [2013] UKSC 26.

[21] (1865) 17 Ir. Ch. R. 73; (1867) L.R. 2 H.L. 149.

"[P]rivate right of ownership is a matter of fact; it may be the result also of a matter of law; but if parties contract under a mutual mistake and misapprehension as to their relative and respective rights, the result is that the agreement is liable to be set aside as having proceeded upon a common mistake."[22]

10–08 In *Leonard v Leonard*,[23] Manners L.C. indicated that equity would not hold the plaintiff bound by an agreement to settle a dispute as to private ownership of land where the other party knew facts, unknown to the plaintiff, which influenced the plaintiff's decision to compromise an action. This decision, however, is based on fraud rather than a common or cross-purposes mistake.

10–09 In its review of the scope of the equitable jurisdiction to grant relief, the Court of Appeal, in *Great Peace Shipping Ltd v Tsavliris (International) Ltd*[24] countenanced that in *Cooper v Phibbs* the action was commenced in equity in order to "escape from an agreement that a court of law would hold binding"—per Phillips M.R. The Court of Appeal, however, did not develop this point so as to provide guidance on whether mistakes of law were treated differently at law and in equity, contenting themselves with the citation of Lord Chelmsford's dicta in *Earl Beauchamp v Winn*[25]:

"The cases in which Equity interferes to set aside contracts are those in which either there has been mutual mistake or ignorance in both parties affecting the essence of the contracts, or a fact is known to one party and unknown to the other, and there is some fraud or surprise upon the ignorant party."[26]

(3) Common mistake of fact

10–10 Not all mistakes of fact will justify rescinding a contract concluded under such a misapprehension, whether it be shared by both parties or not. The common law took a very restrictive view of such cases and the conventional wisdom holds that only if the mistake relates to the existence of the subject-matter of the contract, or to the existence of a person or a relationship essential to the whole transaction will it be fundamental enough to operate at common law. If parties contract to buy and sell corn which, unknown to both parties has perished, the transaction will be void[27]; if people who are not married enter into a separation agreement in the belief that they are married, the separation

---

[22] (1867) L.R. 2 H.L. 149 at 170; see Matthews, "A Note on *Cooper v Phibbs*" (1989) 105 L.Q.R. 599.
[23] (1812) 2 Ball & B. 171.
[24] [2002] 4 All E.R. 689; Reynolds, "Reconsider the Contract Textbook" (2003) 119 L.Q.R. 177; Hare, "Inequitable Mistake" (2003) 62 C.L.J. 29.
[25] (1873) L.R. 6 H.L. 223.
[26] (1873) L.R. 6 H.L. 223 at 233.
[27] *Couturier v Hastie* (1856) 6 H.L.C. 673.

agreement will be void.[28] A life insurance policy or annuity, taken out in the mistaken belief that the person in question is still alive, will be void; see *Strickland v Turner*.[29] In *Pritchard v Merchants and Tradesmans Mutual Life Assurance*[30] a life assurance policy had lapsed due to non-payment of the premium. The beneficiary sought to revive the policy by paying the premium, and while payment was made, both parties discovered that the assured, at the date of renewal, was in fact dead. An action to enforce the policy failed because the policy was void; the premium, however, was recoverable by action. Costello J. in *O'Neill v Ryan*[31] approved the decision in *Scott v Coulson*[32] which is of a similar effect. However, it must not be assumed that the parties will always be able to invoke a plea of common mistake for it may be that the agreement will, expressly or impliedly, transfer or allocate risk to one of the parties. The position is different if one party warrants the existence of the person or goods as in *McRae v Commonwealth Disposals Commission*[33] or is prepared to assume the risk that circumstances are otherwise; see *March v Pigot*.[34] This involved a colourful set of facts. Two young men resolved to contract that whoever was able to prove that his father lived longer than that of the other would pay a sum to the other—a contract to "run" the life of one father against that of the other. Unknown to the parties, one father had already died. The contract was not void for the parties were taken to have accepted that the risk of either parent already being dead was not to invalidate the contract.[35] In a more modern and everyday setting, the allocation of risk may be a matter of express or implied promise, or it may be the result of general rules of law such as *caveat emptor* in sale of goods cases or the rule that the vendor of land does not warrant the fitness for purpose of the land; see Hoffmann L.J. (as he then was) in *William Sindall Plc v Cambridgeshire C.C.*[36]

10–11 However, despite the narrow common law basis for holding contracts to be void *ab initio*, there are some judicial pronouncements that contemplate a broader role for the common law. In *Kennedy v Panama New Zealand and Australian Royal Mail Co*,[37] a case concerned with innocent misrepresentation, Blackburn J., borrowing from civil law systems the doctrine of error *in substantibus*, distinguished between (operative) mistakes of substance in the subject matter, and (inoperative) mistakes as to attributes, or quality. In using language that was also to be found in English jurisprudence on the vexed question of rescission for breach of obligation, Blackburn J. drew the common law and civil law position together when he wrote,

---

[28] *Galloway v Galloway* (1914) 30 T.L.R. 531.
[29] (1852) 7 Exch. 208.
[30] (1858) 3 C.B.N.S. 622.
[31] [1991] I.L.R.M. 672.
[32] [1903] 2 Ch. 249.
[33] (1951) 84 C.L.R. 377.
[34] (1771) 5 Burr. 2802.
[35] This wagering contract pre-dated the Gaming Act 1845.
[36] [1994] 3 All E.R. 932 at 952.
[37] (1867) L.R. 2 Q.B. 580.

"[T]he principle of our law is the same as that of the civil law; and the difficulty in every case is to determine whether the mistake or misapprehension is as to the substance of the whole consideration, going, as it were, to the foot of the matter, or only to some point, even though a material point, an error as to which does not affect the substance of the whole consideration."[38]

The usefulness of the civil law distinction between a mistake as to substance (operative) and a mistake as to attributes (inoperative) has been doubted in more recent English case law[39] on the basis that this distinction leads to a broader test of invalidity at common law than that countenanced in the leading decision. If this view prevails when tested in the highest UK appellate court, then a legislative response to the problem appears inevitable in that jurisdiction. Current English analysis is distinctly precedent-based. This writer believes that these lines of authority are not altogether incompatible but the cases are likely to reveal different approaches to a plea of common mistake, as a matter of legal philosophy. Some critics[40] view pleas of mistake with hostility because a valid plea leads to the contract being void, and it is not always evident that justice is served by transferring the entire loss from one person to another, particularly when an express clause could have been utilised to achieve the same result.

10–12 In the leading English case of *Bell v Lever Brothers*[41] Bell and another former employee of the defendants had negotiated "golden handshake" payments in the belief that Lever Brothers could not terminate the contract of employment in any other way, a belief also held by Lever Brothers. In fact, Bell was guilty of misconduct which would have justified summary dismissal. Lever Brothers claimed that this mistake was operative and that they could recoup the £50,000 paid. The House of Lords ruled that the mistake was not fundamental enough to justify rescission. Professor Waddams has argued in his *Law of Contracts*[42] that on the facts, the conclusion may be correct; a large part of the payment was reward for services rendered rather than being attributable to "buying out" the contract of employment. Nevertheless dicta in the Lords, particularly in the speech of Lord Atkin, suggests that a shared mistake as to the quality of goods will never be operative; if two parties contract to transfer a painting which they believe to be an old master and it turns out to be a modern copy, the mistake will not be operative unless there

---

[38] (1867) L.R. 2 Q.B. 580 at 589.

[39] Steyn J. in *Associated Japanese Bank (International) Ltd v Credit du Nord SA* [1988] 3 All E.R. 902, approved by the Court of Appeal in *Great Peace Shipping Ltd v Tsavliris (International) Ltd* [2002] 4 All E.R. 689.

[40] e.g. Atiyah and Bennion, (1961) 24 MLR 421. Even these commentators acknowledge there are often hard results (e.g. at 442), blaming Parliament for passing defective legislation in the context of *Solle v Butcher*.

[41] [1932] A.C. 161.

[42] 6th edn (Toronto: Canada Law Book, 2010), paras 389–390. See also MacMillan, "How Temptation Led to Mistake: An Explanation of *Bell v Lever Bros Ltd*" (2003) 119 L.Q.R. 625.

is an express warranty or a misrepresentation. There is oblique Irish authority supporting this view of the position at common law. In *Megaw v Molloy*[43] a mistake was held operative but in so concluding, Ball L.C. said that this "is not the case of a seller and purchaser intending to sell and buy the same horse with a misapprehension as to his soundness", thereby implying that such a mistake would not be fundamental enough to induce the common law courts to declare the transaction void.

10–13 In the most perceptive analysis of *Bell v Lever Brothers* made by an Irish Court, the strictness of the Atkin view has been maintained. In *Fitzsimons v O'Hanlon*[44] litigation over the estate of a deceased person was compromised on the basis that the contending factions agreed that the plaintiffs would be paid £60,500, with the balance of the estate (estimated at £150,000) going to the defendants. Efforts had been made prior to the settlement to identify and trace all the assets of the deceased—described by Budd J. as having been during his lifetime as "discreet, perhaps even secretive about the whereabouts of his assets". A further bank deposit of £58,000 came to light after the settlement. Budd J. upheld the settlement. On the facts, Budd J. observed that it was foreseeable that additional assets would be found even though all parties bona fide believed that all assets had been traced. In relation to issues of policy, Budd J. apparently speaking of both the common law and equitable jurisdictions said that in the interests of commercial convenience apparent contracts should, in general, be enforced. Budd J. also indicated that the error in the instant case related to the quality of the consideration and did not relate to an essential or integral element in the contract subject matter.

10–14 There are cases, however, which suggest that a fundamental mistake may, generally, render a contract void ab initio even though this approach is difficult to square with Lord Atkin's speech in *Bell v Lever Brothers*. The Privy Council in *Sheikh Brothers v Ochsner*[45] held that a contract, under which the lessee of agricultural land promised to deliver a minimum of 50 tons of sisal per month, was void for common mistake. Both parties wrongly thought the land in question was capable of producing that minimum figure. While attempts to limit the impact of *Sheikh Brothers* have in the main been successful—Cheshire and Fifoot simply footnote this case as turning entirely on a statutory provision,[46] an argument this writer cannot agree with—an Irish Circuit Court decision has endorsed this wider view of common mistake. In *Western Potato Co-operative Ltd v Durnan*[47] Judge Clarke held that a contract for the sale of seed potatoes was void because both parties erroneously believed the seed potatoes were sound. Judge Clarke approved the following statement in *Anson's Law of Contract*:

---

[43] (1878) 2 L.R. (Ir.) 530.
[44] [1999] 2 I.L.R.M. 551.
[45] [1957] A.C. 136.
[46] *Cheshire, Fifoot and Furmston's Law of Contract*, 16th edn (Oxford: OUP, 2012), p.302.
[47] [1985] I.L.R.M. 5: see Clark, "Of Potatoes and Pariahs" (1984) 19(1) Ir. Jur. 101.

"Where the parties contract under a false and fundamental assumption, going to the root of the contract, and which both of them must be taken to have in mind at the time they entered into it as the basis of their agreement, the contract may be void."[48]

An English application of *Bell v Lever Brothers* illustrates that the test, although difficult to satisfy, is not without vitality. In *Grains & Fourrages SA v Huyton*[49] the sellers and buyers of goods had these goods tested but being unhappy that the tests were perhaps not accurately carried out the parties agreed to read the test certificates in a particular way. Unfortunately both were in error about the same matter, the tonnage of the goods, and when this came to light the buyer sought to reopen the matter. Mance J. (as he then was) held that the common mistake was a fundamental one and that *Bell v Lever Brothers* was satisfied, citing Lord Atkin,[50] who observed whilst giving judgment in *Bell v Lever Brothers* that he agreed with counsel's submission that,

"… whenever it is to be inferred from the terms of the contract or its surrounding circumstances that the consensus has been reached on the basis of a particular contractual assumption and that assumption is not true, the contract is avoided".

If the parties have provided for the event by way of an express term and particularly an exemption clause, it would be inappropriate to apply a common mistake analysis. Similarly, where a foreseeable event materialises and the contract fails to provide for this, the fact that the party pleading common mistake has failed to anticipate the event may be a factor which militates against a plea of common mistake. Where the event is clearly a commercial risk and the law places an obligation on one of the parties vis-à-vis that risk, common mistake will not be available. In *Tony Investments Ltd v Kwan*,[51] the parties entered into an agreement to purchase a marine development, including a slipway. Unknown to both parties the vendor had no title to the slipway. Because the general law requires the vendor of land to make a good title, this obligation precluded reliance on a common mistake plea. Similarly, in *Mallett and Son (Antiques) v Rogers*,[52] the plaintiff sold an antique bookcase to the defendant. It transpired that the bookcase was stolen goods. The defendant was held liable in damages because s.12 of the Sale of Goods Act 1893 requires the seller of goods to provide a good title to the goods, this obligation being an implied condition in the contract. Fault has been identified by the High Court of Australia as a valid consideration when a plea of common mistake has

---

[48] Citing the 25th edn (Oxford: Clarendon Press, 1979), p.296.
[49] [1997] 1 Lloyd's Rep. 628.
[50] [1932] A.C. 161 at 225.
[51] [2006] 1 H.K.L.R.D. 835.
[52] [2005] IEHC 131.

been raised in *Pakullus v Cameron*.[53] As Costello J. in *O'Neill v Ryan*[54] said, however, "the circumstances in which a shared common mistake will nullify a contract are extremely limited ... a shared common mistake will not result in a void contract" save in exceptional circumstances. This view has been reiterated in *Fitzsimons v O'Hanlon*.

(4) Common mistake of fact in equity

10–15 The equitable rule in relation to shared or common mistake seems to have been wider and more flexible. The leading case of *Cooper v Phibbs*,[55] decided before the fusion of the common law and equity, is often said to be authority for the view that a common mistake can be relieved against on such terms as the court sees fit. In *Cooper v Phibbs* the House of Lords set aside the lease, declared the appellant the owner while ordering that the respondents were entitled to a lien on the property in respect of money paid improving it. The only difficulty that *Cooper v Phibbs* presents rests on the fact that the mistake in that case would probably have been operative, even at common law, by analogy with *Couturier v Hastie*.[56] This weakens the case if it is the primary support for the modern doctrine of equitable mistake. *Cooper v Phibbs*, however, does not stand alone as support for a broader equitable jurisdiction. The decision of the Court of Appeal in *Huddersfield Banking Co Ltd v Henry Lister & Co*[57] is a very substantial basis upon which to predicate a broader equitable approach. A mortgagee agreed that certain pieces of industrial machinery were not affected by a mortgage which included rights over fixtures and upon this basis the mortgagee and a receiver agreed to a sale of these items as chattels. It later transpired that the equipment should properly have been regarded as fixtures and the mortgagee sought a declaration that the mortgagee's consent was liable to be set aside for common mistake. Lindley L.J. regarded equity as being able to proceed in this case in much the same way as the courts of common law, citing, inter alia, *Strickland v Turner* and *Cooper v Phibbs*. Kay L.J. said that the equitable jurisdiction to set aside agreements can operate, "not merely for fraud, but in case [consent] was based upon a mistake of material fact which was common to all the parties to it".

10–16 This case can be regarded as really within the narrow line of cases anticipated as void at common law but it seems symptomatic of a more liberal equitable jurisdiction to *set aside* transactions rather than declare contracts void *ab initio*, and supporters of the common law approach, such as Lord Atkin,

---

[53] (1982) 43 A.L.R. 243.
[54] [1991] I.L.R.M. 672. In *Flynn v National Asset Loan Management Ltd* [2014] IEHC 408 Cregan J. held that a signature executed on a loan agreement was a mistake; as neither the lendor or the signatory intended that the signatory would be party to the loan, this prevented *consensus ad idem*. No cases were cited by Cregan J., nor was there any reference to *non est factum*.
[55] (1867) L.R. 2 H.L. 149.
[56] (1856) 6 H.L.C. 673.
[57] [1895] 2 Ch. 273; *Cue Club Ltd v Navaro Ltd, Irish Times Law Report*, February 17, 1997.

have asserted that *Huddersfield Banking* does not evidence a broader equitable doctrine, at least in an historical sense. Nevertheless a series of English Court of Appeal decisions establish that while the common law doctrine of mistake may not operate, equity can set aside a transaction on such terms as the court sees fit. In *Solle v Butcher*[58] a lease entered into when both parties believed the property not subject to rent restriction legislation was declared voidable and the contract was set aside on terms, the decree giving the tenant the option of leaving the flat or staying on at a rent that, in the view of the Court of Appeal, accurately reflected the value of the property. In *Grist v Bailey*[59] a contract to sell a house under the mistaken belief that a tenant was protected under the Rent Acts was also declared voidable, the purchaser being entitled to repudiate or take at a fair market value of £2,250 rather than the agreed price of £850. These cases have prompted Lord Denning M.R. to summarise the law as follows: "common mistake even on a most fundamental matter does not make a contract void at law but voidable in equity." Although the modern English case law has not been ruled on by the Supreme Court the Irish ancestry of the leading case of *Cooper v Phibbs* suggests that the Irish courts would decline to follow the narrower doctrine of mistake, as espoused in *Bell v Lever Brothers*, preferring instead the *Solle v Butcher* line of authority.

10–17 In *O'Neill v Ryan*[60] Costello J. provided a most useful summary of the English law on common mistake and, citing Denning L.J. in *Solle v Butcher*, apparently approved the proposition that:

> "[A] contract is also liable in equity to be set aside if the parties were under a common misapprehension either as to facts or as to their relative and respective rights, provided that the misapprehension was fundamental and that the party seeking to set it aside was not himself at fault."[61]

In *Associated Japanese Bank (International) Ltd v Credit du Nord SA*[62] Steyn J. attempted to reconcile the equitable and common law approaches to what the learned judge described as "common or mutual mistake". The defendant bank had guaranteed certain sale and lease-back transactions in which the plaintiffs purchased and leased back four machines, the seller/lessee being a Mr Bennett. In fact Bennett had defrauded the plaintiffs for the machines did not exist, and the issue was whether the guarantee of Bennett's obligations under the lease were enforceable by the plaintiff against the defendant. The

---

[58] [1950] 1 K.B. 671.
[59] [1967] Ch. 532. See however Hoffmann L.J. in *William Sindell Plc v Cambridgeshire County Council* [1994] 3 All E.R. 932 at 952.
[60] [1991] I.L.R.M. 672. In *Fitzsimons v O'Hanlon* [1999] 2 I.L.R.M. 551, Budd J. cited *Solle v Butcher* but found that neither the common law nor the equitable jurisdictions were triggered on the facts at bar.
[61] [1950] 1 K.B. 671 at 693.
[62] [1988] 3 All E.R. 902.

plea of common mistake gave Steyn J. the opportunity to examine the current state of English law and the learned judge held that the leading case of *Bell v Lever Brothers* was essentially concerned with common law mistake and that the equitable jurisdiction, set out in *Solle v Butcher*, "is not circumscribed by common law definitions". Steyn J., however, did not view *Solle v Butcher* as effecting the soundness of *Bell v Lever Brothers* when the issue is common mistake at common law. Steyn J. regarded the existing state of English law to be capable of coherent enunciation and application. Steyn J. argued that the first step to be taken is to look to see if the contract has made provision for the contingency; only if the contract is silent is there room for a plea of mistake. As a later step, a plea of common mistake at law must be considered and if the case can be accommodated within the narrow test, as found in Lord Atkin's speech in *Bell v Lever Brothers*, then the contract is void ab initio. If this is not possible the court may go on to consider whether the contract may be set aside in equity. On the facts before him Steyn J. held that the contract was void ab initio: the non-existence of the machines, the subject matter of the main contract, was of fundamental importance to the collateral guarantee, and the closeness to *res extincta* cases was also noted by the learned judge.

10–18 This layered approach is not, however, likely to be a precursor to widespread judicial acceptance of common mistake pleas. Steyn J. stressed that "the first imperative must be that the law ought to uphold rather than destroy apparent bargains", and even judges who have favoured the *Solle v Butcher* line of authority have been slow to intervene, as the case of *Amalgamated Investments v John Walker*[63] illustrates. In this case two parties were mistaken as to the likelihood of a building being declared a "listed building", which had the effect of reducing its value as a commercial property. The need for certainty and security of commercial transactions will be viewed as more important than the interests of one distressed litigant. In such cases the buyer should include a term that if at a later date the building is listed the buyer can rescind the contract. To similar effect is the decision of the Court of Appeal in *William Sindell Plc v Cambridgeshire County Council*.[64] The defendants sold land to the plaintiffs who intended to build on it. While the defendants had disclosed what they knew about the site, the plaintiffs discovered that a drain was incorporated into the site via an easement. When property values halved the plaintiffs sought to rescind, inter alia, on the ground of common mistake. The Court of Appeal held that the purchasers took the risk in accordance with the terms of the contract and settled principles of law. Evans L.J. pointed out that while the equitable rules were more likely to trigger rescission the fact that the contract dealt with this issue, allied to the relatively minor financial consequences for the builder, meant that the contract subsisted.

---

[63]   [1976] 3 All E.R. 509.
[64]   [1994] 3 All E.R. 932.

10–19 In England, the relationship between *Bell v Lever Brothers* and *Solle v Butcher* has been extensively reviewed in *Great Peace Shipping Ltd v Tsavliris (International) Ltd*.[65] The owners of a vessel, the Cape Providence, on learning that it was damaged and in danger of sinking, engaged the Great Peace to render assistance, chartering the Great Peace for five days in the belief that the Great Peace was much nearer to the distressed vessel than it was. The true facts came to light and the charterers refused to pay, invoking common mistake. The Court of Appeal, on the facts, found that the error was not such as to render it impossible for the Great Peace to perform the contracted services. More importantly, the Court of Appeal expressed the view that *Solle v Butcher* lacked any jurisprudential legitimacy. Denning M.R.'s view that contracts were no longer void for common mistake, but that contracts were liable to be voidable in equity, was simply inconsistent with *Bell v Lever Brothers*. The Court of Appeal indicated that in *Cooper v Phibbs*, Lord Westbury, in using the expression that a contract was "liable to be set aside", was stating that, on the facts, equity followed the law in considering the lease in that case as void and not merely voidable. Equity did not set forth a distinct jurisdiction from that identified by Lord Atkin in *Lever Brothers*. If this repudiation of *Solle v Butcher* in *Great Peace* is correct, the question arises whether an Irish court should also retrace this path. It is submitted that this would be unnecessary and counter-productive. The Court of Appeal, in *Great Peace*, was charged with the task of determining whether the decision of another Court of Appeal, in *Solle v Butcher,* could stand in the light of the 1932 decision of the House of Lords in *Lever Brothers*. For a post-1922 Irish court, no such exercise need be carried out, either as a matter of legal symmetry or legal policy. The reconciliation of the streams of authority effected by Costello J. in *O'Neill v Ryan*, viewed in the light of Steyn J.'s approach in the *Japanese Bank* case, affords a pragmatic and flexible solution. Reliefs granted in the equitable jurisprudence are more capable of doing justice than the absolutist common law remedy of a declaration that the contract is void ab initio. There is considerable support for the view that the "essential difference" tests are generally very restrictive, whether the common law or equitable jurisdiction is being invoked. *Great Peace* itself provides considerable support for the view that *Lever Brothers* in itself is not a satisfactory solution, for Phillips M.R. said, after effectively "overruling" *Solle v Butcher*:

> "We can understand why the decision in *Bell v Lever Brothers Ltd* did not find favour with Lord Denning. An equitable jurisdiction to grant rescission on terms where a common fundamental mistake has induced a contract gives greater flexibility than a doctrine of common law which holds the contract void in such circumstances. Just as the Law Reform (Frustrated Contracts) Act 1943 was needed to temper the effect of the common law doctrine of frustration, so there is scope for legislation

---

[65] [2002] 4 All E.R. 689.

to give greater flexibility to our law of mistake than the common law allows."[66]

Later English cases have rather enthusiastically embraced the *Great Peace* decision. In *Kyle Bay Ltd v Underwriters*,[67] the plaintiff and defendant agreed to settle an insurance claim brought by the plaintiff, both parties mistakenly believing that the principle of average applied. This led to the plaintiff receiving £108,000 less than it should have. An action to have the settlement declared void for common mistake failed. In the view of the judge, the mistake "did not render the settlement agreement impossible to perform. Nor did the mistake render the subject matter of the contract essentially and radically different from the subject matter that the parties believed to exist. It simply made it a rather poor deal from Kyle Bay's perspective".[68] Nor will settlement of a tort claim concluded on the basis that the plaintiff would be outside a limitation period be void for common mistake.[69] It is clear from these cases that the courts strive to uphold compromises of actual or threatened litigation wherever possible. The Singapore Court of Appeal cited *Great Peace* in its judgment in *Chwee Kin Keong v Digilandmall.com*,[70] and in Hong Kong, *Great Peace* was adopted in *Tony Investments Ltd v Kwan*.[71] The pattern set by the Irish judiciary has been to continue to uphold a narrow jurisdiction to hold contracts may be void for common mistake[72] while using equitable principles to set aside contracts. In *Intrum Justitia BV v Legal and Trade Financial Services*[73] the plaintiff purchased a company; when it emerged that there had been embezzlement of nearly half a million pounds the plaintiff sought rescission. O'Sullivan J. tested the facts by reference to both *Bell v Lever Brothers* and *Solle v Butcher* and held that the remedy of rescission for common mistake was not available, applying *O'Neill v Ryan*. It is clear that Irish judges favour the more flexible and pragmatic options that equitable principles applicable to common mistake may afford to a court.

10–20 There has been an echo of this approach in some Canadian provinces. The Ontario Court of Appeal, in *Miller Paving Ltd v B Gottardo Construction*

---

[66] [2002] 4 All E.R. 689 at 730. See also the comments of McMeel, "'Equitable' Mistake repudiated: the demise of *Solle v Butcher*? (The Great Peace)" [2002] L.M.C.L.Q. 449, Reynolds (2003) 119 L.Q.R. 177 and Hare (2003) 62 C.L.J. 29. MacMillan, *Mistakes in Contract Law* (2010), Ch.9 provides a good historical perspective.

[67] [2004] EWHC 607 (Comm).

[68] Per Deputy Judge Hirst Q.C. The Court of Appeal upheld the reasoning of Deputy Judge Hirst at [2007] EWCA Civ 57; *Dany Lions Ltd v Bristol Cars* [2013] EWHC 2997 (Q.B.).

[69] *Brennan v Bolt Burdon* [2004] 3 W.L.R. 1321.

[70] [2006] 1 L.R.C. 37. The Court of Appeal did so less enthusiastically than the trial judge. Online shopping enthusiasts and user groups often actively exploit errors and unintended consumer benefits. In one case mistakes in a three-for-£5 deal allowed customers to buy £36 of cider for £5. See "Cider worth £36 sells for £5 in latest Tesco price glitch", discussing the activities of members of Hot UK Deals—*Daily Telegraph*, April 25, 2013.

[71] [2006] 1 H.K.L.R.D. 835.

[72] *McMahon v O'Loughlin* [2005] IEHC 196.

[73] [2005] IEHC 190.

Ltd[74] has decided that a combination of the common law and equitable doctrines affords a useful means of resolving common mistake cases. After citing an influential article by McCamus[75] Goudge J.A. said:

> "*Great Peace* appears not yet to have been adopted in Canada and, in my view, there is good reason for not doing so. The loss of the flexibility needed to correct unjust results in widely diverse circumstances that would come from eliminating the equitable doctrine of common mistake would, I think, be a step backward."[76]

In this case the defendant was sued for construction materials sold and delivered to him. By mistake the parties believed all due sums had been paid and a signed acknowledgment was executed, but the monies claimed were for deliveries that the plaintiff had made but negligently overlooked. The Ontario Court of Appeal found there was no essential difference between the contract as struck and as it was performed. The mistake was that of the plaintiff and while there was a "windfall" to the defendant, the defendant was able to show that he had changed his position in purchasing new equipment when innocently discovering that profits on the construction project were higher than had been anticipated.

(5) Mistake as to the terms of the agreement

10–21 In these cases, which are often described as instances of mutual mistake, the parties are negotiating about different things. A wants to buy wheat; B wants to sell barley. At first sight there can be no contract. Indeed, Ball L.C. said in *Megaw v Molloy*[77] (see para.10–23 below) that a "dealing where the parties are not intending the same subject matter, evidently cannot be an agreement". This is not correct. The essential factor to be noted is whether the party pleading mistake has a reasonable expectation that the contract would include the contended terms. In *Stapleton v Prudential Assurance*[78] the plaintiff entered a life insurance contract believing that by paying two shillings a month for 11 years she would be paid £25 at the end of the period. In fact the contract provided that such a sum would be payable on her death; at the end of 11 years the policy was convertible into a free paid policy after 25 years. The plaintiff, when she learnt of the mistake sought to get back the premiums paid. Sullivan P. held that while Stapleton laboured under a bona fide mistake this would not justify rescinding the contract; see *Jameson v National Benefit Trust Ltd*[79] which also illustrates that self-induced mistakes as to the terms of a bargain will not ground relief for the mistaken party. The courts are concerned

---

[74] (2007) 285 D.L.R. (4th) 568; *Ahmadi v Fernbrook Homes* [2011] ONSC 7474.
[75] (2004) 40 Can. Bus. L.J. 46.
[76] In British Columbia, see *Yawney v Jehring* [2006] B.C.S.C. 1017 and *0707448 BC Ltd v Cascades Recovery Inc.* [2011] BCSC 1065.
[77] (1878) 2 L.R. (Ir.) 530.
[78] (1928) 62 I.L.T.R. 56.
[79] (1902) 2 N.I.J.R. 19.

to discover what the parties said and did during negotiations. If the intention of one party, objectively ascertained, indicates assent to a particular term, that term will be included in the bargain. The courts will not permit the reasonable expectations of one party to be defeated if they exist because of the conduct of the other party. This is often described as the rule in *Smith v Hughes*[80]:

> "… if whatever a man's real intention may be, he so conducts himself that a reasonable man would believe he was assenting to the terms proposed by the other and that other party upon that belief enters into a contract with him, the man thus conducting himself would be equally bound as if he has intended to agree to the other parties (*sic*) terms."[81]

If the agreement is clear in its terms then the defendant cannot avoid the agreement by pleading, or indeed convincing the court, that the defendant felt that the agreement would produce a quite different result. In *Mespil Ltd v Capaldi*[82] an action for possession of rented premises was commenced by the plaintiff lessor for breaches of covenant. Prior to these proceedings commencing the defendants had settled existing litigation in respect of the premises under an agreement which referred to a "full and final settlement of all matters". The defendants pleaded that they had intended to settle all matters outstanding, including all current disputes which were not the subject of proceedings. O'Hanlon J. held that the contract was not capable of having this extended application, and, citing *Smith v Hughes*, the learned trial judge held that because both sides were not under the same misapprehension as to the effect of the agreement, "there was an element of mutual mistake involved in the transaction", which could not, however, operate so as to defeat the plaintiff's legitimate expectations. On appeal, however, the Supreme Court held that the agreement was void for mutual mistake. While the Supreme Court upheld the distinction between a mistake as to the impact or effect of the bargain—which is not effective—and a mistake as to the true nature of the agreement—which may be effective—the Supreme Court characterised this mistake as falling into the second category. Henchy J. expressed the principles at issue here as follows:

> "When a person enters into an agreement, giving the other person the impression that he understands the nature and effect of the agreement, the general rule is that he will not be allowed to say later that he should not be bound by the agreement because he did not at the time under-stand its import or effect. That is undoubtedly correct law. Business relations would be thrown into undesirable uncertainty, if a party to an agreement who at the time gave no indication that he did not understand what he was doing, could later renounce the agreement on subjective considerations. If he freely and competently entered into the agreement

---

[80] (1871) L.R. 2 Q.B. 597.

[81] (1871) L.R. 2 Q.B. 597 at 607, per Blackburn J.; *Jennings v Carroll* (1849) 2 Ir. Jur. 275.

[82] [1986] I.L.R.M. 373; Maher (1987) 9 D.U.L.J. 113.

he will not normally escape being bound by it, by saying that he mis-understood its effect. The position is essentially different when, as in the case here, there was a mutual or bilateral mistake as to the true nature of the agreement. Different and more fundamental principles of the law of contract come to be applied in such circumstances. It is of the essence of an enforceable simple contract that there be a consensus *ad idem*, expressed in an offer and an acceptance. Such a consensus cannot be said to exist unless there is a correspondence between the offer and the acceptance. If the offer made is accepted by the other person in a fundamentally different sense from that in which it was tendered by the offeror, and the circumstances are objectively such as to justify such an acceptance, there cannot be said to be the meeting of the minds which is essential for an enforceable contract. In such circumstances the alleged contract is a nullity."[83]

The Supreme Court indicated that not only were the persons who had negotiated the settlement at cross-purposes, the written agreement itself was capable of being interpreted as a settlement of all disputes, but all surrounding circumstances justified the plaintiffs in their view that the settlement was limited: Henchy J. regarded the case as one in which there was "latent ambiguity and mutual misunderstanding".

10–22 The objective test can of course work the other way; if the agreement, objectively judged, cedes to the plaintiff a benefit which was unintended by the defendant, the defendant will not be able to claim that the contract should be enforced on the terms actually intended by the defendant. Two modern Irish cases provide clear illustrations of this particular aspect of this rule. In *Clayton Love v B & I Transport*[84] the appellants intended to contract with the respondents for the transport of frozen scampi. The appellants intended the scampi would be loaded at sub-atmospheric temperatures. The respondents intended loading would take place at atmospheric temperature. Applying *Smith v Hughes*, the Supreme Court held that because of the way the respondents had conducted themselves during negotiations they were bound to load the cargo on the terms anticipated by the appellants. They were therefore liable for the deterioration of the goods. In the important case of *Lucy v Laurel Construction*[85] Mr Lucy agreed to purchase a house to be built by Laurel Construction. The site plan indicated the plot would be 170 feet long. The plan was in error; the builders only intended to sell a plot 120 feet long. At no time was Mr Lucy ever told this and all he knew of the builders' intention was disclosed on the faulty site plan. When the builders discovered the mistake they sought to have the plan altered to reflect their intention. Mr Lucy was

---

[83] [1986] I.L.R.M. 373 at 376–377. Cited in *McGrath v Stewart* [2008] IEHC 348, but distinguished on the facts.

[84] (1970) 104 I.L.T.R. 157; *Diamond v Council for Catholic Maintained Schools* [1994] N.I.J.R. 77.

[85] Unreported, High Court, December 18, 1970.

held entitled to retain the bargain as initially struck. The site plan was the only objective manifestation of the other party's intentions; Mr Lucy had done nothing irregular or dishonest and Kenny J. declined to rectify the contract. While the objective principle will bind an offeror to the terms of the apparent bargain, there is an exception to this rule if the offeree knew or ought to have known of the error: *Centrovincial Estates Plc v Merchant Investors Assurance Co Ltd.*[86] *Centrovincial* was applied in *Redevco UK v WH Smith.*[87] The lessee was in occupation of premises in Belfast and at the end of the lease wrote a letter offering a renewal at an annual rent of £775,000 per annum. The lessor accepted the offer. The surveyor who had written the letter of offer, upon receipt of acceptance, realised he had made a mistake—he intended the figure to be £745,000. Rent had previously been fixed at £745,000 but in negotiations prior to the offer being made the lessor had pressed for a premium rent at £957,000. There was nothing to indicate that the lessor was aware of any error, nor was the lessor bound to make further inquiries. In this case, there was no unconscionability, Gillen J. observing that as a general rule, "the court is slow to introduce uncertainty into commercial transactions by over ready use of equitable concepts". Gillen J. held that offer and acceptance corresponded here.

10–23 There are cases in which the courts have held that no contract exists because of mistake. In *Megaw v Molloy*[88] the plaintiff employed a broker to sell maize for him. The maize he intended to sell had been imported on board the "Emma Peasant". The plaintiff had imported another cargo of maize on the "Jessie Parker", which was of a superior quality than that on board the "Emma Peasant". On the morning of the sale a sample purporting to be from the "Emma Peasant" was displayed but this sample was accidentally taken from the "Jessie Parker". The defendant purchased the cargo after inspecting the sample but later refused to take delivery when he discovered the true quality of the cargo. The plaintiff sued for non-acceptance. The defendant did not plead that the quality of the goods sold did not meet the sample for there was an express disclaimer of a warranty as to quality; he instead successfully argued that there was no contract at all. The vendor intended to sell the cargo on the "Emma Peasant"; the purchaser intended to buy the bulk out of which the sample had been taken, that is, the corn on the "Jessie Parker". Ball L.C. said there was "a misapprehension as to the very substance of the thing in contract, not as to any quality or incident or merit or demerit of it—*error in corpore*". This distinction between a mistake as to quality as against identity is often difficult to draw, as *Gill v McDowell*[89] shows, and it has been criticised as unsatisfactory in practice. Another way of looking at *Megaw v Molloy* would be to consider, who was responsible for the error? It would be monstrous to allow the party responsible for creating the mistake, whether by a deliberate falsehood or pure

---

[86] [1983] Com. L.R. 158 (see para.2–24 above for the facts).
[87] [2008] NIQB 116. Rectification was not sought by the lessee.
[88] (1878) 2 L.R. (Ir.) 530.
[89] [1903] 2 I.R. 463.

negligence, to compel the purchaser to take delivery of the wrong cargo and any express clause would hardly pass the "just and reasonable" test in the Sale of Goods and Supply of Services Act 1980. Contrast *Megaw v Molloy* with *Scott v Littledale*.[90] Here the defendants had sold tea "ex Star of the East". The sample provided was of a lower quality than the cargo and the defendants sought to plead mistake. The defence failed and they were held liable for non-delivery. In this situation the defendants had been careless and to allow a plea of mistake would not only deprive the plaintiffs of their bargain—albeit a bargain more advantageous than they thought—but also allow the defendants to ride free from the consequences of their own carelessness. Yet this approach is not always relied upon. If the remedy sought is specific performance the courts may refuse to grant the remedy against even the person responsible for the error if this would, on balance, work an injustice; see *Browne v Marquis of Sligo*.[91]

10–24 An interesting illustration of this discretionary aspect of mutual mistake is afforded by the *Minister for Education v North Star Ltd*.[92] The plaintiff sought specific performance of an agreement to sell a strip of land which was to provide vehicular access to a proposed development. The defendant agreed to the sale, but regarded it as essential that two other access points be provided. The plaintiff abandoned any attempt to develop these two other access points due to the hostility of local residents. Even though Lynch J. regarded this as a case of mutual mistake, and seemed of the view that the mistake itself was not known to the plaintiff, the change of intention was relevant to the remedy sought. "It is a fundamental principle of equity that he who seeks equity must do equity and the plaintiff is disqualified from the equitable remedy of specific performance by the plaintiff's abandonment of an intention to seek vehicular access via [the two other access points]."

(6) Mistake in executing a deed or contract

10–25 Three situations must be kept apart.

10–26 (i) The first is where one party at the time of the agreement assents to a term but notices that the other party has misstated the term when executing the contract document or memorandum of agreement. Here the error may favour the party who notices the slip of the pen. In *Nolan v Graves & Hamilton*[93] the plaintiff agreed to buy a row of houses sold by auction. Evidence showed that the plaintiff had agreed to pay £5,550; the auctioneer erroneously wrote the price to be £4,550. The plaintiff was not entitled to take at the lower price. The contract was rectified to reflect the bargain actually struck. Similarly, a separation agreement that gave income tax advantages to the wife when it was

---

[90] (1858) 3 E. & B. 815.
[91] (1859) 10 I.R. Ch. R. 1.
[92] Unreported, High Court, January 12, 1987.
[93] [1946] I.R. 377.

intended that these would accrue to the husband was rectified upon proof that the wife was aware that the agreement did not carry into effect the intent of both parties; see *Nolan v Nolan*.[94]

10–27 (ii) The second situation is where the contract is executed and one party later comes into court claiming that, as worded, the document does not accurately reflect the bargain struck. Here the party seeking relief will not always claim sharp practice on the part of the other. In unilateral mistake cases it has been held that knowledge may be actual knowledge or knowledge that is inferred. Knowledge may comprise of:

> "(i) actual knowledge;
> (ii) wilfully shutting one's eyes to the obvious;
> (iii) wilfully and recklessly failing to make such enquiries as an honest and reasonable [person] would make;
> (iv) knowledge of circumstances which would indicate the facts to an honest and reasonable [person]; or
> (v) knowledge of circumstances which would put an honest and reasonable [person] on enquiry."[95]

In *Peter Cremer GmbH v Cooperative Molasses Traders Ltd*[96] the applicants sought a declaration, inter alia, that a contract contained an agreement to arbitrate. While the contract document itself was silent on this point, Costello J. commented that, "once the terms actually agreed to have been established I do not think that an error in the preparation of a formal contract effects the legal consequences". A form of rectification occurred via the exceptions to the parol evidence rule: the contract document was held to be only part of the contract and was to be read with telex correspondence which referred to arbitration.

10–28 It will not always prove possible to avoid altering the contract document itself. The nineteenth-century Irish case of *Fallon v Robins*[97] provides a good illustration of this problem. Fallon agreed to take a lease from Robins. The lease, drafted by Fallon's solicitor, was to run for 31 years and it was intended that Fallon would have a right to terminate the lease after three years. The lease was ambiguously worded and Robins purported to take advantage of the termination clause. Smith M.R. held that unless the lease failed to accurately set out the intention of both parties it could not be *rectified*; as we shall see, however, an Irish court can order rescission on the authority of *Mortimer v*

---

[94] (1954) 92 I.L.T.R. 94: contrast *JD v BD* [1985] I.L.R.M. 688.
[95] Peter Gibson J. in *Baden SA v Société Générale SA* [1993] 1 W.L.R. 509 at 575–576, dealing with knowledge for the purposes of a constructive trusteeship (decided in 1983), followed in contract in *Hurst Stores Ltd v M.L. Europe Property Ltd* [2003] B.L.R. 391 at 407, appeal to the Court of Appeal dismissed: [2004] EWCA Civ 490.
[96] [1985] I.L.R.M. 564.
[97] (1865) 16 Ir. Ch. Rep. 422.

Shortall[98] in such cases. Nevertheless, in *Fallon v Robins*, Smith M.R. interpreted the ambiguous clause to permit Fallon a right of termination only. *Lucy v Laurel Construction*[99] illustrates this point too; unless the conduct and words of one party indicate assent on the terms now sought, a mistake which is not communicated to the other party will not be operative and the document will not be rectified.

10–29 The decision of the Supreme Court in *Irish Life Assurance Co Ltd v Dublin Land Securities Ltd*[100] will be of great assistance in delimiting the scope of rectification in mutual mistake cases. The plaintiff company wished to sell its portfolio of ground rents which totalled some 11,055 properties. The plaintiff company also owned lands at Palmerstown, Co. Dublin, which had been the subject of compulsory purchase orders and the plaintiff did not wish these properties to be included so as to later obtain compensation for compulsory purchase. In preparing the portfolio for sale the legal department of the plaintiff company failed to delete the Palmerstown lands from the portfolio. The defendant company acquired the portfolio but was not told that lands at Palmerstown were to be excluded; although an agent acting for the defendant was informed of the intention to exclude certain lands, this knowledge was not, in these circumstances, such as to give notice to the purchaser. When the error in the contract came to light, the plaintiff company sought rectification of the contract. Rectification was refused. The approach approved by the Supreme Court is that the court will not reform a contract made in writing in the absence of convincing proof that the contract, as the result of a mistake, has failed to give effect to the common intention of the parties previously manifested in outward accord.[101]

10–30 In contrast, however, stands the decision of Vice-Chancellor Chatterton in *Young v Halahan*.[102] The plaintiff assigned, by way of a lease, part of his land to a railway company. This was done by execution of two separate deeds in February and March 1871 respectively. The plaintiff subsequently sold part of the estate, including the land assigned to the railway company, by auction. The contract of sale failed to exclude all the land so assigned, and the defendant was only given express notification of the first lease executed in February. The purchaser brought proceedings at law for breach of covenant on the ground that part of the property sold to him had been already leased to the railway company. In equity, however, the defendant sought rectification of the contract so as to exclude the lands leased to the railway company. While this was a case in which the error was solely attributable to the defendants, equitable relief was granted. The crucial factor was the use and occupation of the lands in question by the railway company and the defendant's knowledge

---

[98] (1842) Connor & Lawson 417.
[99] Unreported, High Court, December 18, 1970.
[100] [1989] I.R. 253; *King v Ulster Bank* [2013] IEHC 250.
[101] [1989] I.R. 253 at 263 per Griffin J.
[102] (1875) I.R. 9 Eq. 70.

of this use and occupation. The real contract between the parties was held to be for the sale of an agreed parcel of lands, minus those lands occupied by the railway company, and the conveyance was rectified accordingly. In *Irish Life Assurance Co Ltd v Dublin Land Securities Ltd*[103] the purchaser had, in no sense, walked the lands, nor had he any substantial information about the Palmerstown lands.

10–31 (iii) The third situation is where the party pleading mistake shows that, despite the apparent assent of both parties to the written terms of the agreement, the document does not carry into effect what may be described as "the contract formula". Authority for this proposition stems from the unusual case of *Collen Brothers v Dublin County Council*.[104] The Council agreed to grant a construction contract to the plaintiffs, the price to be calculated on the defendants' bills of quantities minus a list or bill of reductions designed to lower costs. By a clerical oversight the contract price was £357 less than it should have been. The plaintiffs sought rectification. Ross J. was prepared to permit rectification, dismissing the claim of the Council that the plaintiffs were to bear the cost of the mistake; the intention of the parties, when analysed, was that the tender for the original amount of the priced section, less the amount of the priced bill of reductions, should be accepted. The sum of £167,000 was erroneously taken to be that figure and erroneously embodied in the contract. "In what way does this differ from an error in adding the figures? In no way." If, however, the parties complete the contract in the mistaken belief that they have actually agreed a price for the work, then the case goes beyond the realm of a miscalculation. In *Fanning v Wicklow County Council*[105] the plaintiffs claimed the balance due under an agreement to build houses for the defendant. The offer and acceptance did not correspond, and in this case O'Hanlon J. was constrained to hold that no contract had been concluded. The plaintiffs were, however, able to recover on a *quantum meruit* basis.

(7) Mistake as to title and the nature of an interest in real property

10–32 *Cooper v Phibbs*[106] establishes that equity will set aside on terms any leasing contract where both parties mistakenly believe that title to the land is vested in someone other than the prospective lessor. In *Gardiner v Tate*[107] a contract was held unenforceable at common law against a defendant who had been misled by the plaintiff's agent into believing that an interest purchased at an auction was a legal estate in land when in fact it was an equitable leasehold interest.

---

[103] [1989] I.R. 253.
[104] [1908] 1 I.R. 503.
[105] Unreported, High Court, April 30, 1984; *Lachhani v Destination Canada (U.K.) Ltd* (1997) 13 Const. L.J. 279; *KRG Insurance Brokers v Shaferon* (2009) 301 D.L.R. (4th) 522.
[106] (1867) L.R. 2 H.L. 149.
[107] (1876) I.R. 10 C.L. 460.

(8) Mistake as to identity

10–33 The Irish courts have not considered this problem to any great extent. For the sake of completeness the following propositions, based largely on English case law, can be advanced.

10–34 If one party contracts face-to-face with another, believing that other person to be someone else, the contract is voidable. In *Lewis v Averay*[108] a rogue obtained possession of a motor car by falsely representing that he was the television actor, Richard Greene, of the "Robin Hood" series. He showed a false pass from Pinewood Studios and apparently bore a strong resemblance to the actor. Convinced that he was dealing with the actor the owner took a cheque signed "R. A. Green". The cheque bounced. The car turned up with the defendant who had purchased it from the rogue. The Court of Appeal held that the initial owner could not successfully recover the vehicle on the ground of mistake. The contract between himself and the rogue conferred a voidable title upon the rogue which had been transferred to the defendant. This conclusion reached is a proposition of law. Denning M.R., citing *Corbin*, was prepared to follow American practice where "the courts hold that if A appeared in person before B impersonating C an innocent purchaser from A gets the property in the goods against C". The fraudulently induced mistake does not operate to make the transaction a nullity; a similar rule has been advanced and applied in the Irish cases of *Re French's Estate*[109] and in *Re Ambrose's Estate*.[110]

10–35 The rule is otherwise if the contract is concluded by post. The decision of the House of Lords in *Cundy v Lindsay*[111] was to hold the transaction void, thus preventing the purchaser from the rogue from obtaining a good title. Lord Cairns, in giving judgment, seemed persuaded by the view that if "minds do not meet", no "consensus" or contract can result, but this is not strictly true— see *Lucy v Laurel Construction* discussed above. Denning L.J. (as he then was) said in *Solle v Butcher*[112] that the "void" contract in *Cundy v Lindsay* would now be held to be voidable on terms. This seems on balance a preferable solution given that the court could adjust the rights of the parties under the terms of the decree. Legislation on this point is necessary. If it were possible for the original owner to recover damages in tort in such a case, s.34 of the Republic's Civil Liability Act 1961 would permit damages payable by the purchaser from the rogue to be reduced "by such amount as the court thinks just and equitable having regard to the degrees of fault of the plaintiff and defendant". Devlin L.J. in *Ingram v Little*[113] suggested a similar reform be initiated in England and *Cundy v Lindsay* has been held not to be authority for the proposition that

---

[108] [1972] 1 Q.B. 198.
[109] (1887) I.R. 2 Eq. 234.
[110] [1913] I.R. 506; [1914] I.R. 123.
[111] (1878) 3 App. Cas. 459.
[112] [1950] 1 K.B. 671.
[113] [1961] 1 Q.B. 31.

fraudulent transmission of documents between two innocent parties does not prevent a contract from being formed; see *Citibank NA v Brown Shipley & Co Ltd*.[114] The limitation of *Cundy v Lindsay* is to be very much welcomed, but *Cundy v Lindsay* still survives as a blot on the contractual landscape. The conflict between *Cundy* and the cases that champion the contracts *inter presentes* approach was addressed by the House of Lords in *Shogun Finance Ltd v Hudson*.[115] In this case, a rogue obtained the driving licence of a Mr Patel and forged the signature on the licence. The rogue signed a proposal form to obtain a motor vehicle from a dealer, the form being provided by Shogun Finance. The proposal form recited that the offer was made to Mr Patel and the rogue signed the proposal form, the signature matching that on the Patel driving licence. The rogue sold the vehicle to Hudson, a bona fide purchaser for value. In this case, two broad approaches were adopted. The majority, Lord Phillips, Lord Hobhouse and Lord Walker found that the case was governed by the principle *nemo dat quod non habet* and that because Shogun Finance only intended to deal with Mr Patel, no contract existed as between the rogue and Shogun Finance, thus making it impossible for the rogue to confer a voidable title on Hudson via a statutory exception to the *nemo dat* rule.[116] It should be noted that Lord Hobhouse in particular was at pains to stress that the case was not simply about resolving the conflict between common law rules; rather, the application of a statutory exception to the common law *nemo dat* rule, seen in the light of the particular contractual documents, was at the core of the approach of the majority. Nevertheless, Lord Hobhouse was of the view that Lord Denning's approach and dicta were "misplaced and wrong". In contrast, Lord Nicholl and Lord Millett were of the view that the conflict between the face-to-face approach and *Cundy* was to be resolved by overruling *Cundy* as well as the reasoning of the majority in *Ingram v Little*. Lord Millett also noted that German law opted for a solution that protected a purchaser in good faith from a rogue, expressing the view that a contrary approach in English law "would make the contemplated harmonisation of the general principles of European contract law very difficult to achieve".[117] In a 2002 Commonwealth decision, the South Australian case of *Papas v Bianca Investments Ltd*,[118] the approach in *Lewis v Averay* was expressly approved, the case having facts very similar to those in *Lewis v Averay*. Doyle C.J. followed the approach of Denning M.R.

10–36 The only Irish case in which the issue has been tested is the decision of the Supreme Court in *People (DPP) v Dillon*.[119] The Supreme Court was

---

[114] [1991] 2 All E.R. 690.
[115] [2004] 1 All E.R. 215.
[116] Specifically, s.27 of the Hire Purchase Act 1964 (UK), the Irish counterparts to which are, very loosely, s.9 of the Factors Act 1889, s.23 of the Sale of Goods Act 1893 and s.70 of the Consumer Credit Act 1995.
[117] [2004] 1 All E.R. 215 at 240.
[118] (2002) 82 S.A.S.R. 531.
[119] [2003] 1 I.L.R.M. 531.

required to answer the question whether a person who spoke to a garda on a mobile phone, the garda indicating that he was an associate of a suspect, was speaking to the garda by agreement. The Supreme Court, following Viscount Haldane in *Lake v Simmons*,[120] took the view that concealment of a person's true identity (as distinct from taking on the identity of another) will vitiate consent. Whether this view will prevail in the light of the attack mounted, albeit unsuccessfully, on *Cundy* in *Shogun Finance* remains to be seen. It is submitted that because contractual intention is objectively determined, criminal law decisions are unreliable in this context because of different policy considerations.

10–37 The mistaken identity cases have been declared to be inapplicable to situations where the contract is concluded in writing and the entire agreement is reduced into writing. In *Hector v Lyons*,[121] the contract was concluded in the name of an infant. The infant's father brought an action seeking specific performance, but was met with the objection that the person named in the contract was not the litigant. Infants cannot obtain the remedy of specific performance, so the infant's father, pleading the mistake *inter presentes* cases, sought a declaration that he was the contracting party. The submission was rejected on the ground that written documents should be regarded as conclusive and the identity of the vendor and purchaser is to be established by the names in the written contract.

10–38 Not all mistaken identity cases are instances where one party knows of the other's mistaken belief. For this reason the mistaken identity cases are not always instances of "unilateral mistake", to use Cheshire and Fifoot's classification. In *Smallman v O'Moore & Newman*[122] the two defendants carried on a partnership until 1954 when they converted the firm into a limited company. The plaintiff had dealt with the defendants as a partnership and although the defendants circularised their suppliers informing them of their change in legal status, the plaintiff failed to note the new position, even though the second defendant signed cheques in favour of the plaintiff in the company name. The plaintiff sued the defendants personally for the price of goods supplied, claiming that they were individually liable as if they remained partners in an unincorporated firm. The defendants successfully pleaded that the only contracts struck were between the company and the plaintiff even though the plaintiff thought he was contracting with someone else. Davitt J. held that the plaintiff could not rely on his own mistake in order to render the defendants personally liable. This decision should be contrasted with *Boulton v Jones*.[123]

---

[120] [1927] A.C. 487; *Sowler v Potter* [1940] 1 K.B. 271.
[121] *The Times*, December 19, 1988.
[122] [1959] I.R. 220.
[123] (1857) 2 H. & N. 564.

"Corrective Interpretation" or Lord Hoffmann's Fifth Principle

10–39 There has been a considerable amount of judicial[124] and academic commentary[125] on the principle of "corrective interpretation" and its relationship with the orthodox equitable remedy of rectification. Debate has centred upon the obiter parts of Lord Hoffmann's speech for the members of the House of Lords in *Chartbrook Ltd v Persimmon Homes Ltd*,[126] a case which one learned commentator has said is used to avoid some of the exclusionary rules of evidence and has little relevance other than in that context.[127] This point was made by Lord Nicholls of Birkenhead who said that in practice, many bogus rectification claims were mounted simply to bring negotiations before a court.[128]

10–40 It is clear, however, that rectification and corrective interpretation are distinct paths. Lord Hoffmann, in *Chartbrook Ltd v Persimmon Homes Ltd* said there were two exceptions to the exclusionary rule vis-à-vis prior negotiations. One exception is in cases of rectification. The principle of "corrective interpretation", on the other hand, is part of the general approach to giving contracts a "common sense" meaning and Principle 5 in *West Bromwich* (see above, para.5–08) is a part of that process. Coulson L.J., in a recent case has doubted that Lord Hoffmann's obiter observations in *Chartbrook* on mutual mistake are correct.[129] No less an authority than Lewison L.J. has said that rectification still has an important role to play,[130] drawing attention to the difficult theoretical effects on interpretation and rectification.[131] It is also evident that if the contract has omitted a key term a court could not "interpret" that contract so as to include that key term: in a practical sense the appropriate remedy would be to bring a suit for rectification. Burrows, echoing Lord Nicholls of Birkenhead[132] has said that rectification, not interpretation, would cure the problem.[133]

10–41 The Irish courts have on occasion been willing to regard obvious errors in the text of a contract as being mistakes that the court has the power to adjust or correct, examples being typographical errors or computational mistakes.[134]

---

[124] Buxton, "'Construction and Rectification after *Chartbrook*" [2010] 69(2) C.L.J. 253; Nicholls, "My Kingdom for a Horse: The Meaning of Words" (2005) 121 L.Q.R. 577.

[125] McLauchlan, "The 'Drastic' Remedy of Rectification for Unilateral Mistake" (2008) 124 L.Q.R. 608 and "Commonsense Principles of Interpretation and Rectification" (2010) 126 L.Q.R. 8.

[126] [2009] UKHL 38.

[127] McMeel, *Construction of Contracts*, 2nd edn (Oxford: OUP, 2011), para.1.23.

[128] (2005) 121 L.Q.R. 577 (i.e. rectification might be denied but the court has had the negotiations opened up for this purpose).

[129] *Daventry District Council v Daventry and District Housing Ltd* [2011] EWCA Civ 1153 at paras 173–178.

[130] *Cherry Tree Investments Ltd v Landmain Ltd* [2012] EWCA Civ 736.

[131] [2012] EWCA Civ 736 at para.122.

[132] (2005) 21 L.Q.R. 577.

[133] "Construction and Rectification", in Burrows and Peel (eds), *Contract Terms* (Oxford: OUP, 2007). See also McLauchlan (2014) 130 L.Q.R. 83 and Davies, "Rescission for Misrepresentation" [2016] 75(1) C.L.J. 15.

[134] *Collen Bros v Dublin County Council* [1908] 2 I.R. 503.

However, in *Investors Compensation Scheme Ltd v West Bromwich Building Society* Lord Hoffmann went further:

> "The 'rule' that words should be given their 'natural and ordinary meaning' reflects the common sense proposition that we do not easily accept that people have made linguistic mistakes, particularly in formal documents. On the other hand, if one would nevertheless conclude from the background that something must have gone wrong with the language the law does not require judges to attribute to the parties an intention which they plainly could not have had. Lord Diplock made this point more vigorously when he said in *Antaios Cia Naviera SA v Salen Rederierna AB, The Antaios* [1985] AC 191 at 201:
>
> > '... if detailed semantic and syntactical analysis of words in a commercial contract is going to lead to a conclusion that flouts business common sense, it must be made to yield to business common sense'."

The decision of Clarke J. in *Moorview Developments Ltd v First Active Plc* has been frequently cited and followed.[135] Here, a guarantee referred to the liabilities of "Moorview Properties Ltd". This entity did not exist, nor had it ever existed, although Moorview Developments Ltd was in existence and was actively negotiating loans with the lender. The mistake was obvious and the intended solution was obvious to Clarke J. who, in his own words, approved the Hoffmann fifth principle of the "correction of mistakes by construction". An even more striking example is to be found in the judgment of Wetherup J. in *Ulster Bank Ltd v Lambe*.[136] The defendant was in debt to Ulster Bank to the tune of £170,000. In order to effect a settlement there were ongoing negotiations which were unsuccessful. Eventually the bank wrote offering to settle the debt at €155,000, "being a reduction of almost one third of all interest accrued". The defendant immediately accepted in a letter sent by recorded delivery. The bank employee who wrote the letter (she had been settling accounts in the Republic of Ireland for euro customers) made two mistakes: the figure proposed was given in euro when sterling was intended and the settlement offer was made on bank stationary with a Dublin address. Significantly perhaps, the defendant did not give evidence. Despite the fact that rectification was not pleaded by the bank, Wetherup J. held that this was unnecessary because "the letter must be interpreted as offering to settle for a payment of £155,000 sterling". The most extensive review of the decision in *Chartbrook* is that undertaken by Edwards J. in *The Leopardstown Club Ltd v Templeville Developments Ltd*[137] a common mistake case in which rectification was allowed on conventional grounds without the court having to apply the

---

[135] [2010] IEHC 275; *Danske Bank v Coyne* [2011] IEHC 235 (rectification allowed); *Bank of Ireland v Fergus* [2012] IEHC 131; *Point Village Development v Dunnes Stores* [2012] IEHC 482; *Byrne v Killoran* [2014] IEHC 328.
[136] [2012] NIQB 31
[137] [2010] IEHC 152; appeal allowed but on the grounds of misrepresentation [2015] IECA 164.

obiter statements of Lord Hoffmann in *Chartbrook*. In *Boliden Tara Mines v Cosgrove* in 2010[138] the Supreme Court did not refer to *Chartbrook* but applied *Irish Pensions Trust Ltd v Central Remedial Clinic*[139] and *Irish Life Assurance Co Ltd v Dublin Land Securities Ltd*[140] perhaps preferring to rely on less problematic statements of principle in the hope that this will prevent an already difficult area of law from becoming virtually unintelligible.

Remedies Available for an Operative Mistake

10–42 A mistake operative at common law leads to the contract being declared void ab initio; see *Cundy v Lindsay*. Technically the party arguing mistake may seek a decree in the court in cases where the other party is pressing for performance, or title to goods or chattels transferred is in question. Equitable remedies in mistake cases prior to the Irish Union of Judicature Act 1877 were (and are) a good deal more sophisticated. Despite the fact that we no longer have separate courts of common law and equity, students should bear in mind that the remedies available have evolved from these distinct streams of law. At the risk of repetition we shall now turn to consider those remedies.

(1) Rescission—both at law and in equity

10–43 At law, a mistake which is common to both parties and which relates to a fundamental matter of fact, such as the continued existence of goods (see s.6 of the Sale of Goods Act 1893), or a person in insurance cases, will prevent a contract coming into being. The contract price paid will be returnable. Where parties are contracting at cross-purposes, that is where both persons contract to buy and sell different things, the contract may be invalid if the party pleading mistake reasonably but erroneously believes that a certain state of affairs exists: see *Megaw v Molloy*[141] and *Leonard v Leonard*.[142] If rescission is to be available, however, the mistake should refer to an essential or fundamental term in the contract and must not be an error in relation to the effect the contract will have. A mistake as to terms may ground relief but a mistake as to the results will most certainly not. In *Reen v Bank of Ireland Finance Ltd & Lucey's Garage (Mallow) Ltd*[143] an action for breach of contract was settled on terms which the plaintiff's solicitor erroneously believed would include all legal costs involved. This was incorrect, and, further, the solicitor for the defendant was aware that further expenses would accrue for the plaintiff. The plaintiff claimed the contract was liable to be set aside for mistake. McMahon J. dismissed the action remarking that the offer and acceptance corresponded and that there was no mistake as to the terms of the agreement:

---

[138] [2010] IESC 62.
[139] [2006] 2 I.R. 126.
[140] [1989] I.R. 253.
[141] (1878) 2 L.R. (Ir.) 530.
[142] (1812) 2 Ball & B. 171.
[143] [1983] I.L.R.M. 507.

"This is a case of a man entering into an agreement which he intended to make but which he would not have made but for a misunderstanding as to a matter extraneous the agreement, namely his client's position *vis-à-vis* other parties in the litigation."[144]

Had there been a unilateral mistake as to terms, e.g. the defendant's solicitor knew that the plaintiff was contracting in the belief that the defendant's solicitor had warranted or promised that the settlement would have the effect the plaintiff believed, then at common law the contract would be rescinded; see *Smith v Hughes*. One of the most important English decisions on this point is *Hartog v Colin and Shields*.[145] The plaintiff received an offer from the defendant offering to sell to the plaintiff Argentine hareskins at 10¼d a pound. In the trade, hareskins were sold by the piece, and, given that there are approximately three pieces to a pound, the offer was a most favourable one for the plaintiff. The plaintiff accepted but then sued for non-delivery. The defendant resisted the action by claiming that the offer was so obviously incorrect that the plaintiff must have realised that there was an error and sought to take advantage of it. The action for non-delivery failed. Singleton J. held that the offer was such that the plaintiff could not have reasonably supposed that it set out the offeror's real intention; the contract was invalid. *Chwee Kin Keong v Digilandmall.com*[146] is the leading internet mistake case. Due to an error in loading information onto a website, the defendants advertised laser printers for sale at $66. The intended price was $3,854. The six plaintiffs ordered 1,606 printers but the Singapore Court of Appeal held that the plaintiffs had actual or constructive knowledge of the error. The error was as to the terms of the contract and the error was a fundamental one. This was a clear case of unilateral mistake and, applying *Hartog v Colin and Shields*,[147] the contract was void. However, if the mistake in the offer, objectively ascertained, would not have been apparent to a reasonable offeree, and if the offeree reasonably interprets the agreement in another way the contract will not necessarily be liable to rescission; see *O'Neill v Ryan*.[148]

10–44 Rescission in equity is a much more fluid doctrine. The Sligo fishery case of *Cooper v Phibbs* illustrates, that mistakes that are operative at common law, can be treated differently in equity. Brady L.C. in the Court of Appeal in Ireland said that as a precondition to equitable relief, "there must be something

---

[144] [1983] I.L.R.M. 507 at 509–510.
[145] [1939] 3 All E.R. 566.
[146] [2006] 1 L.R.C. 37.
[147] [1939] 3 All E.R. 566.
[148] [1991] I.L.R.M. 672. In cases like *Hartog v Colin and Shields* the court holds that no contract exists because the mistake is obvious but the intended figure may not be apparent. As in *Ulster Bank v Lambe* [2012] NIQB 31, it may be that the intended figure is obvious and capable of being imposed via "corrective interpretation". This has the result of holding the parties to a bargain they did not make but few judges seem to consider this impermissible as the mistake is not an honest mistake—contrast *Ulster Bank v Lambe* with *VP Plc v Megarry* [2012] NIQB 22.

unconscientious on either one side or the other in order that the aid of this court should be called for". The modern English cases suggest that unconscientious dealing is not a precondition for relief, but rather, that ethical factors may help set the terms upon which rescission will be ordered.[149]

10–45 A decree of rescission may be given in cases where one party has sought rectification of the contract, the court refusing this relief. In *Mortimer v Shortall*[150] Sugden L.C. (later Lord St. Leonards) said, "a mistake on one side may be a ground for rescinding a contract but it is not a ground for taking from a man part of a property demised to him". So in *Gun v McCarthy*[151] Gun offered to let property to McCarthy for £33.10s. The offer was accepted but, as Flanagan J. later found, the figure was inserted by mistake. Gun intended the rent to be £55.10s. McCarthy knew the figure was so low that an error had been made. McCarthy did not know the intended figure. Flanagan J. refused to grant rectification and increase the rent. This would have obliged McCarthy to be bound by a contract which he had not assented to; instead Flanagan J. ordered rescission. In *Webster v Cecil*,[152] a similar English case, the court instead rectified the bargain, giving the purchaser the option of taking the property under the terms of the amended contract or rescinding the contract. This may not always be possible if there is no real contract struck; witness the decision of the House of Lords in *Cummins v Boylan*,[153] dismissing an appeal from the Court of Appeal in Ireland. In *Ferguson v Merchant Banking Ltd*[154] a case with facts very similar to *Irish Life Assurance Co Ltd v Dublin Land Securities Ltd*, discussed above, the error came to light before completion and the purchaser sought specific performance, leaving the defendant to counterclaim for rectification or, in the alternative, rescission. While the *Irish Life* case disposed of the rectification element in the counterclaim, Murphy J. considered the issue of rescission, a remedy not sought by the vendor in *Irish Life*. Murphy J. indicated that rescission would not be granted where the mistake is by one party and it is not shared or in any way contributed to by the other party, that other party being unaware that the agreement is not in its terms consensual.

---

[149] *Solle v Butcher* [1950] 1 K.B. 671.

[150] (1842) Connor & Lawson 417. There has been an explosion of case law in recent years on the basis of what in England is known as the rule in *Hastings–Bass v Inland Revenue Commissioners* [1975] Ch. 25. See also *Sieff v Fox* [2005] EWHC 1312 (Ch) and *Smithson v Hamilton* [2008] 1 All E.R. 1216. This is the jurisdiction to set aside voluntary transactions and deeds by settlors of occupational pension schemes: *Gibson v Mitchell* [1990] 1 W.L.R. 1304; *Gallagher Ltd v Gallagher Pensions Ltd* [2005] EWHC 42 (Ch); *Irish Pensions Trust v Central Remedial Clinic* [2005] IEHC 87, and *Boliden Tara Mines v Cosgrove* [2007] IEHC 60, overruled on another point at [2010] IESC 62. The leading English case is *Futter v Revenue and Customs* [2013] UKSC 26.

[151] (1884) 13 L.R. (Ir.) 304. After *Great Peace* the English courts have held there is no rescission jurisdiction in equity for unilateral mistake: *Statoil ASA v Louis Dreyfus Energy Services* [2008] EWHC 2257 (Comm). See Cartwright, "Unilateral Mistake in the English Courts" [2009] Sing. J.L.S. 226.

[152] (1861) 30 Beav. 62.

[153] (1901) 35 I.L.T.R. 170.

[154] [1993] I.L.R.M. 136 applied in *Murphy v Stewart* [2008] IEHC 348.

10–46 The remedy of rescission can be lost for a variety of reasons. If the parties cannot be returned to their pre-contractual position, the now superceded common law rule was that rescission would not be ordered. Equity would permit the rights of the parties to be adjusted by the decree. In *Cooper v Phibbs*[155] the House of Lords ruled that the defendants, who mistakenly believed they owned the fishery, possessed a lien against the land for improvements made; the plaintiff was ordered to pay rent for property he had enjoyed.

10–47 Rescission may be refused if there is a delay in seeking equitable relief: the facts of *Stapleton v Prudential Assurance*[156] illustrate this point graphically. Rescission will also be refused if the mistake renders the contract voidable, but before the contract is repudiated a bona fide purchaser acquires an interest in the goods. The Irish case of *Anderson v Ryan,*[157] discussed in the next chapter, is authority for this proposition.

(2) Rectification

10–48 Before the Judicature Acts, a court of common law, faced with a bargain that was not accurately recorded in a written instrument, was obliged to refer the case to a court of equity to enable rectification. Since 1877 the process is simpler. In *Borrowes v Delaney*[158] the Court of Exchequer, on discovering that a contract document contained a mistake, simply treated the contract as if it had been rectified. Dowse B. indicated that this remedy is available even though no express request for rectification had been made by either party. Once the true facts become known the courts will respond accordingly. It is possible to view this as an early example of constructive interpretation of contracts and deeds. However, rectification in modern times must be expressly pleaded.

10–49 The burden of proof resting on the party seeking rectification will be a heavy one. Although parol evidence is admissible Sugden L.C. in *Mortimer v Shortall*[159] suggested that parol evidence alone will not show conclusively that the written document is inaccurate:

> "There is no objection in law to rectify an instrument by parol evidence, when you have anything written to go by; but where you depend upon the recollection of witnesses, and the defendant denies the case set up by the plaintiff, to be the true one, there appears to be no remedy."

This onus demands rather too much of the plaintiff. The case of *Nolan v Graves & Hamilton*[160] suggests that if oral evidence shows conclusively that the instrument is defective, rectification will be ordered. But even this

---

[155] (1867) L.R. 2 H.L. 149.
[156] (1928) 62 I.L.T.R. 56.
[157] [1967] I.R. 34.
[158] (1889) 24 L.R. (Ir.) 503.
[159] (1842) Connor & Lawson 417.
[160] [1946] I.R. 377.

"conclusive" text sets the bar at too high a standard. In *Boliden Tara Mines v Cosgrove*[161] the Supreme Court specifically rejected an artificial standard of proof and endorsed "proof on the balance of probability". However, Hardiman J. approved a contextual approach to this test:

> "There is but one standard of proof (apart from criminal proceedings) which is the balance of probability, but in some cases that standard will be more easily met than in others. For example, a case where commercial parties have had their intentions expressed in a professionally drafted legal document, which document is later said not in fact to express the intentions of the parties, will naturally call for evidence which is clear, coherent and convincing if the onus of establishing on the balance of probability that the parties' intention was not correctly expressed is to be discharged. This is so obvious as to be almost a truism. The onus will, of course, be easier to discharge if the facts put forward are entirely un-contradicted notwithstanding that a representative of the class of persons interested in having the claim for rectification rejected was present and professionally represented, and did not cause the witness as to fact to be cross-examined."

The jurisdiction of a court to order rectification was succinctly stated by Kenny J. in *Lucy v Laurel Construction*[162] to exist:

"(a) where there is a shared or common mistake made by the two parties in the drafting of a written instrument which is to give effect to a prior oral agreement;

 (b) when one party sees a mistake in a written agreement and, aware that the other party has not seen it, he signs knowing it contains a mistake."

A good example of case (b) is provided by the facts of *Nolan v Graves & Hamilton*, which are related above.[163] This case also decides that if the instrument as it stood was sufficient to satisfy the Statute of Frauds 1695, the rectified instrument will also be deemed within the Statute. The actual decision in *Nolan v Graves & Hamilton* has been doubted by Professor Dowrick.[164] Instead of ordering specific performance of the rectified agreement, Mrs Nolan, who had tried to take advantage of the auctioneer's slip of the pen, was given the option of either taking the property under the terms of the amended instrument or rescinding. Professor Dowrick pointed out that under s.27(7) of the Union of Judicature Act 1877, specific performance of a rectified

---

[161] [2010] IESC 62; a similar statement of the relevant principles was made by Norris J. in *Forstater v Python (Monty) Pictures* [2013] EWHC 1873 (Ch) at para.86.

[162] Unreported, High Court, December 18, 1970. Recent discussions applying traditional rectification principles include *Moorview Developments v First Act Plc* [2009] IEHC 214; *O'Meara v Bank of Scotland Plc* [2011] IEHC 402.

[163] [1946] I.R. 377; see para.10–49 above.

[164] Irish Supplement to Cheshire and Fifoot's *Law of Contract* (London: Butterworth, 1954).

agreement can be ordered. Mrs Nolan should have been ordered to take the property; after all she had agreed to purchase on the terms of the rectified agreement, unlike the tenant in *Gun v McCarthy* (para.10–45 above). On the other hand, if the court cannot establish a common intention, as in *R McD v V McD*[165] where the parties to a settlement of a matrimonial dispute simply overlooked the question of whether liability to pay costs formed part of the agreement, rectification will not be possible.

10–50 The remedy of rectification is not dispensed liberally to litigants. In *McAlpine v Swift*,[166] Manners L.C. pointed out that equity will not rectify for mistake unless the court is sure that rectification will not work an injury. For this reason, the courts will not rectify a contract document if it appears that the parties have failed to reach a prior agreement on the terms to be inserted into the rectified instrument. As the contrasting cases of *Webster v Cecil* and *Gun v McCarthy* show, compulsory rectification in such a case compels one party to labour under a bargain he did not assent to and the judiciary view this as unacceptable. It is clear that this solution is often reached when the courts strike down exemption clauses, unconscionable bargains and insert implied terms into contracts. It may be that legislation which would permit the courts to vary or cancel contracts concluded by way of a mistake would provide a sensible solution to many mistake cases. The New Zealand Contractual Mistakes Act 1977, s.7 contains just such a provision as part of its discretionary remedy system.[167] One English judge has hinted that in cases of unconscionable conduct a court may be prepared to adopt a much more flexible approach to remedies. In *Commission for New Towns v Cooper*[168] Stuart Smith L.J. said, obiter:

> "I would hold that where A intends B to be mistaken as to the construction of the agreement, so conducts himself that he diverts B's attention from discovering the mistake by making false and misleading statements, and B in fact makes the very mistake that A intends, then notwithstanding that A does not actually know, but merely suspects that B is mistaken, and it cannot be shown that the mistake was induced by any misrepresentation, rectification may be granted. A's conduct is unconscionable and he cannot insist on performance in accordance to the strict letter of the contract; that is sufficient for rescission. But it may also not be unjust or inequitable to insist that the contract be performed according to B's understanding, where that was the meaning that A intended B should put upon it."[169]

---

[165] [1993] I.L.R.M. 717.
[166] (1810) 1 Ball & B. 285.
[167] See the cases of *Conlon v Ozolins* [1984] 1 N.Z.L.R. 489; *Engineering Plastics Ltd v Mercer* [1985] 2 N.Z.L.R. 72, and *Yeoh v Al Saffaf* [2005] NZHC 193.
[168] [1995] 2 All E.R. 929.
[169] [1995] 2 All E.R. 929 at 946. See also *George Wimpey UK v VI Construction* [2005] EWCA Civ 77.

A very compelling example of the kind of sharp practice that will invoke a judicial response is found in *Slattery v Friends First Life Assurance Co.*[170] In the course of protracted negotiations over a guarantee general counsel for the proposed guarantor amended drafts by inserting clause 2.2, a clause limiting the scope of the guarantee, emailing his client that, "I am adding the words … if the wording is accepted, (which it has every chance of not, but it is worth trying) then the guarantees will be recourse only". The client replied: "Any way to make [the wording] a bit more inconspicuous?" The other party did not spot the change included in what was assumed to be a "tidying up" exercise. McGovern J., after holding that the additional words had not been part of the negotiations, found that there was a unilateral mistake and that the appropriate remedy was rectification as a continuing common intention had been demonstrated by the plaintiff: even though there may not be a duty to negotiate in good faith the defendant and the defendant's legal team must,

> "… face the legal consequences of their conduct if they created a situation which gave rise to the defendant signing an agreement which did not represent the outcome of the negotiations, in circumstances where it would be inequitable or unconscionable to hold the defendant to that agreement, having regard to the surrounding circumstances and where there has been sharp practice, even if that falls short of outright and unambiguous dishonesty …
>
> Since I am satisfied the parties had reached broad agreement on the terms of the Deed of Pledge and that it was to ensure the provision of additional security, it seems to me that on the facts of this case, rectification is the more appropriate remedy so as to give effect to the real intention of the parties immediately before clause 2.2 was inserted".

In cases of this kind the court may be faced with the task of deciding whether justice requires that the court should side with a lawyer who has merely been negligent as opposed to a lawyer on the other side of the negotiations who has acted illegally or unethically, or has deployed sharp practice.[171]

10–51 Most cases can be regarded as mutual, not unilateral mistake cases. As such, the courts may seek to either interpret the contract or find some other way of giving effect to the bargain, objectively expressed.

---

[170] [2013] IEHC 136. An appeal, based upon McGovern J.'s errors in relation to findings on mistake and knowledge, has succeeded: [2015] IECA 149. Some cases mix together subjective evidence on what the legal teams intended, assessed on an objective basis in the light of the text agreed: *Equity Syndicate Management Ltd v GlaxoSmithKline plc* [2015] EWHC 2163 (Comm).

[171] *Daventry District Council v Daventry District Housing Ltd* [2011] EWCA Civ 1153, suggests that this answer may not be an obvious one. The trial judge and dissenting judge in the Court of Appeal sought to emphasise gross carelessness of one legal team while the majority in the Court of Appeal were swayed by the sharp practice of the other.

10–52 The prospect that judges will take a more creative, case-by-case approach to remedies and contractual mistake is a tantalising one. This much broader approach, in which issues such as comparative degrees of negligence and the unconscionable nature of the relief sought, seen in the light of "the balancing of equities" was demonstrated in the Manitoba case of *Orion Chevrolet Oldsmobile Ltd v Currie*.[172]

10–53 The leading Northern Ireland case of *Rooney & McParland v Carlin*[173] illustrates how limited the present remedy of rectification is. Carlin commenced nuisance proceedings against the plaintiffs who operated a quarry in County Armagh. The action was compromised by counsel for both parties. Counsel for the plaintiffs purchased land from Carlin believing that the land purchased was all the property Carlin owned in the vicinity. This belief was also shared by Carlin's counsel. The folio number and the map annexed to the agreement correctly identified and set out the property sold. In fact Carlin owned another field worth some £800 which was not included in the sale. The plaintiffs sought rectification so as to include this field, arguing that they were not obliged to pay further sums of money for this additional property. Kelly J. at trial permitted rectification. This decision was reversed by the Court of Appeal. Lord Lowry in his speech said that there was no mistake as to terms; neither counsel knew of the existence of the field and to talk of a mistaken common intention here was to confuse motive, object and belief with intention. Rectification was refused. Were the courts able to (a) reduce the price payable to reflect the lower value of the property purchased or (b) to order rectification upon condition a higher price is paid, a fairer result would ensue in such a case.

10–54 One important practical point that has fallen for extensive judicial consideration in recent years is this: is rectification available only in respect of a concluded legally enforceable contract, which pre-dates execution of the written document in respect of which rectification is sought? Alternatively, can rectification of a document be obtained, even though the document itself marks the formulation of an enforceable and binding contract? Until recently, Irish law tended to favour the first view. The leading case on this point was the decision in *Lucy v Laurel Construction Co*.[174] Kenny J., following *Rose v Pim*[175] and other English cases, held that a concluded oral contract must exist. The English Court of Appeal in *Joscelyne v Nissen*[176] have relaxed this requirement. It is sufficient for the party seeking rectification to show "a continuing common intention" to contract on particular terms, falling short of a concluded contract, and that the parties have outwardly expressed this. The

---

[172] (2000) 151 Man.R. (2d) 209.
[173] [1981] N.I. 138.
[174] Unreported, High Court, December 18, 1970.
[175] [1953] 2 Q.B. 451.
[176] [1970] 2 Q.B. 86.

Northern Ireland Court of Appeal, in *Rooney & McParland v Carlin*[177] has discussed and approved *Joscelyne v Nissen*. The Supreme Court, in *Irish Life Assurance Co Ltd v Dublin Land Securities Ltd*[178] also approved *Joscelyne v Nissen*, and overruled *Lucy v Laurel Construction Co* on this specific point. Both Keane J. and the Supreme Court approved the speech of Lord Lowry in *Rooney & McParland v Carlin* where his Lordship said that the following principles are applicable:

"1. There must be a concluded agreement antecedent to the instrument which is sought to be rectified; but

2. The antecedent agreement need not be binding in law (for example, it need not be under seal if made by a public authority or in writing and signed by the party if relating to a sale of land) nor need it be in writing: such incidents merely help to discharge the heavy burden of proof; and

3. A complete antecedent concluded contract is not required, so long as there was prior accord on a term of a proposed agreement, outwardly expressed and communicated between the parties, as in *Joscelyne v Nissen*."[179]

However, the onus resting upon the party seeking rectification can be problematical; that person must adduce convincing proof, manifested in some outward expression of accord, which shows that the common continuing intention of both parties was in favour of the term omitted from the written document. In the *Irish Life* case itself, the evidence admitted that the seller wished to exclude certain land, but the vagueness of the statements made by the seller could in no sense attribute the necessary continuing common intention upon both parties. This third requirement, however, may not always be strictly insisted upon. Particular difficulties of proof may arise where the error is committed by a solicitor acting for both parties, but if convincing proof from the solicitor can be adduced to show that a mistake was made, the fact that there is no outward expression of accord will not be fatal as long as there is convincing proof of the agreement or common intention; see *Mace v Rutland House Textiles*.[180]

10–55 The most interesting Irish case law in recent times has arisen in relation to claims for rectification of Deeds of Amendment that set out the rules applicable to occupational pension plans. Applications were made in *Irish Pensions Trust v Central Remedial Clinic*[181] and *Boliden Tara Mines*

---

[177] [1981] N.I. 138.
[178] [1989] I.R. 253.
[179] [1981] N.I. 138 at 146. Those are in fact the statements of principle by Russell L.J. in *Joscelyne v Nissen*.
[180] *The Times*, January 11, 2000.
[181] [2005] IEHC 87.

Ltd v Cosgrove.[182] In the most recent decision the application to rectify a Deed of Amendment was brought by the trustees to confine certain pension benefits to a defined class of worker. After holding that the Deed itself could not be construed so as to have that result, Finlay Geoghegan J. went on to consider the principles applicable in applications for rectification. While the court observed that the principles applicable to bilateral contracts, unilateral transactions and voluntary dispositions such as this were broadly the same, emphasis was placed upon the presumption that the signatory of a document intends to execute the document in that form "since the purpose of signing it is to make the document do the legal job it purports to do".[183] Finlay Geoghegan J. considered that, while in a bilateral transaction it may be appropriate to require the party seeking rectification to establish some "outward expression of accord", it appeared to her that such a requirement would be inappropriate in cases where there is no consent requirement; for example, where rules of a pension scheme merely provide a power to make or amend rules which can be exercised by the trustees of a pension scheme without the agreement of a principal employer. In such cases the party seeking rectification must adduce "cogent evidence" of the intention of the parties, such "cogent evidence" including an objective or outward manifestation of that common intention.[184] Finlay Geoghegan J. remarked that only in exceptional cases could an applicant succeed without adducing an external manifestation of that common intention. On the facts before her, Finlay Geoghegan J. could not find sufficient evidence to grant rectification. The Supreme Court overruled Finlay Geoghegan J. on the basis that the learned judge had concentrated on the negotiations that preceded the negotiation of the deed rather than the uncontested evidence of the lawyer who had drawn up the amendment to the deed as to the purpose behind the amendment. *Boliden*[185] is an extreme example of how in rectification actions evidence as to subjective intent can not only be admissible, but dispositive on a matter of contractual interpretation.

(3) Damages

10–56 If one party contracts under a mistaken belief as to the terms of the bargain a remedy in damages is not available unless the court can also find that a warranty or fraudulent or negligent misrepresentation was made. For this reason, the plaintiff, in the case of *Harlingdon Ltd v Hull Fine Art Ltd*[186] was constrained to plead misrepresentation and breach of implied condition when a painting which was thought to be an original by the German expressionist Munter turned out to be a forgery. A right to damages may also arise under the Sale of Goods and Supply of Services Act 1980 in limited cases. In

---

[182] [2007] IEHC 60.
[183] Rimer J. in *Lansing Linde Ltd v Alber* [2000] P.L.R. 15, para.124.
[184] Like Kelly J. in *Central Remedial Clinic*, Finlay Geoghegan J. preferred the decision of Lawrence Collins J. in *AMP (UK) Plc v Barker* [2001] P.L.R. 77, to that of Rimer J. in *Lansing Linde* on the "outward expression of accord" requirement.
[185] [2010] IESC 62.
[186] [1990] 1 All E.R. 737.

exceptional cases a court may be prepared to hold that the seller of goods who fails to disabuse a buyer of some mistaken belief may render the seller liable in damages for fraud. In *Gill v McDowell*[187] the seller of a hermaphrodite member of the oxen family—"when looked at from the back [it] appeared to be a heifer, but when looked at from certain other directions appeared to be a bullock"—was held liable in damages to the purchaser of the beast. The seller had taken the oxen to a market and sold it without informing the buyer of its unusual characteristics. This is something of a "rogue" decision because the Court of Appeal denied that a misrepresentation had been made; fraudulent intent seems to have provided the basis of the decision. The precedent value of *Gill v McDowell* is not high. The general principle of caveat emptor has been reaffirmed by the English Court of Appeal in *Sykes v Taylor-Rose*.[188] The plaintiffs purchased a house, which to the knowledge of the defendants had been the scene of a particularly gruesome murder prior to the defendants' purchase of the house. The defendants, who were similarly unaware of the murder at the time of purchase had been advised that they were not obliged to disclose this fact to the plaintiffs. Damages for the difference between the purchase price obtained by the plaintiffs upon resale (the plaintiffs felt in conscience bound to disclose the fact of the murder to their own purchaser) and the market value of the property without this history were refused.

10–57 It is possible for the parties to stipulate that any mistake in the contract is to be actionable in damages only and in *Phelps v White*[189] such a clause was upheld. If the cause of the mistaken belief is an actionable representation, however, it might be that any such clause will be seen as a limitation clause and thus subject to the "fair and reasonable" test under s.46 of the Sale of Goods and Supply of Services Act 1980, where applicable. It is foreseeable that some damages "caps" may be vulnerable under this test. This may also be more generally the case if a limitation on damages is combined with a bar on alternative reliefs and contractual liability is triggered by, for example, a unilateral mistake concerning the quality of goods on the part of the seller, the cause of action being breach of a statutory implied term.[190]

10–58 Submissions for statutory reform of the law of mistake have included suggestions that the courts be given a discretionary power to award damages in lieu of rescission or rectification. Again, the New Zealand Contractual Mistakes Act 1977 permits a court to grant relief by way of restitution or compensation.

10–59 It should be noted that both the Misrepresentation Act (Northern Ireland) 1967 and the Sale of Goods and Supply of Services Act 1980, reforming aspects of the law of misrepresentation in the Republic, permit

---

[187] [1903] 2 I.R. 463.
[188] [2004] EWCA Civ 299.
[189] (1881) 5 L.R. (Ir.) 318; 7 L.R. (Ir.) 160.
[190] e.g. *Jewsons Ltd v Boykan* [2004] B.L.R. 31.

the courts to grant damages in lieu of rescission. To extend this discretionary power into cases of mistake would seem a natural progression, one which would improve the remedial powers of a court faced with operative mistake.

(4) Specific performance

10–60 The fact that the defendant has made a mistake cannot, of itself, give him a defence to an action for specific performance. If there has been a misrepresentation or an ambiguity in the contract the court may decline to award specific performance; see *Tamplin v James*.[191] If the plaintiff has not acted equitably, specific performance may be refused as part of the overall discretionary nature of the remedy.[192]

Non Est Factum—"it is not my deed"

10–61 This plea was initially confined to cases where a blind or illiterate person signed the contract after its effect had been misrepresented to him. The plea expanded so as to become available to all persons who signed an instrument which turned out to be a different document to that which they had assumed or had been told they were signing. The plea is useful to the signor because if it is successful the contract is void and not merely voidable. Third parties cannot acquire title to goods where *non est factum* is successfully pleaded by the initial owner. Cherry C.J. in *Bank of Ireland v McManamy*[193] explained that:

> "The principle of the cases is not, however, that fraud vitiates consent, but rather that there is an entire absence of consent. That the mind of the party who signs under a fundamental error does not go with the act of signing, and that there is consequently no contract at all in fact."[194]

Bank of Ireland v McManamy establishes that fraud need not be shown although this will exist in most cases; see also *Siebel & Seum v Kent*.[195]

10–62 The facts of *McManamy* are worth recounting. The respondents, all 23 of them, were members of a co-operative creamery in Co. Roscommon. They were approached by the creamery manager who, so the defendants said, wanted them to sign forms to order manure and other creamery requirements. The documents were in fact bank guarantee forms. The jury found the defen-

---

[191] (1880) 15 Ch. D. 215.
[192] *Minister For Education v North Star Ltd*, unreported, High Court, January 12, 1987. See, however, the remarkable decision of Weatherup J. in *VP Plc v Megarry* [2012] NIQB 22, giving damages discounted in respect of an honest mistake made by the defendant, "applying" *Barrow v Scammell* (1881) 19 Ch. D. 175, an equitable relief case.
[193] [1916] 2 I.R. 161.
[194] [1916] 2 I.R. 161 at 173.
[195] Unreported, High Court, June 1, 1976.

dants were not negligent. An action for a new trial was refused on the ground that it was not necessary for the jury to find fraud; the jury had declined to answer this question.

10–63 Although the rationale for the plea is somewhat metaphysical—the mind of the signor did not accompany his hand—there are practical considerations here. As a matter of policy the plea is to be kept within narrow bounds. A party signing must show that the error was "fundamental" in nature. Signing a bank guarantee when one thinks the document is an application for a load of manure is a fundamental misconception; a guarantee of a debt for £100,000 when one thinks the sum was only £100 is also a fundamental error. *Saunders v Anglia Building Society*,[196] the leading English case, holds that to assign a house to X for £3,000 when the document is thought to be an assignment of the same house to Y by way of gift is not a fundamental enough error to ground *non est factum*. If the signor successively shows a fundamental error he must also show he has not been careless at the date of signing the contract. To sign a document without reading it is carelessness which will prevent the signor from relying on *non est factum*. In *U.D.T. v Western*,[197] the English Court of Appeal held that someone who signs a loan proposal form in blank, leaving another person to fill in the details, acts carelessly. There is one important exception to this rule. In the case of *Petelin v Cullen*[198] the High Court of Australia ruled that if A misrepresents a document's effect to B and B signs without reading it, then the document will not be valid if A tries to rely on it. Should A transfer his interest to C, an innocent third party, carelessness or negligence will be material here. *Saunders v Anglia Building Society*[199] illustrates this point well. The Building Society, an innocent third party, was not to bear the loss resulting from Mrs Gallie's negligence in signing a document unread. In *Bank of Ireland v McCabe and McCabe*[200] the defendants were held not to be able to utilise a *non est factum* defence in relation to a deed of guarantee when they claimed the guarantee was not applicable to a given transaction. Citing *Saunders v Anglia Building Society*, Flood J. said there was no evidence that the defendants had taken reasonable steps to have the document explained to them so as to acquire knowledge of its effect. The plea of *non est factum* also failed in *ADM Londis Plc v Arman Retail Ltd*,[201] where the signors of a guarantee were held bound by their signature, Clarke J. observing that the document was clearly on its face a guarantee and even a cursory reading of the document would have brought the nature of the instrument home to the defendants. To similar effect are obiter observations in *CF Asset Finance Ltd v Okonji*[202] where a solicitor signed hire purchase equipment orders provided

---

[196] [1971] A.C. 1004.
[197] [1976] Q.B. 813.
[198] (1975) 132 C.L.R. 355.
[199] [1971] A.C. 1004.
[200] Unreported, High Court, March 23, 1993.
[201] [2006] IEHC 306.
[202] [2014] EWCA Civ 870.

for her by the plaintiff's agent using the documents for fraudulent purposes. Because the defendant knew what she was putting her signature to, Patten L.J. was clearly of the view that *non est factum* could not be pleaded but the other two members of the English Court of Appeal were more reserved about what the Master of the Rolls described as "this difficult issue".

10–64 However, in *Lloyds Bank Plc v Waterhouse*[203] the Court of Appeal placed a somewhat interesting interpretation upon the lack of negligence element that the signor must satisfy. The defendant signed a bank guarantee in favour of the plaintiff in order to enable his son to buy a farm. The defendant believed the form was only applicable to the loan made in respect of the form when in fact it was a guarantee of all monies advanced to the defendant's son. The defendant was illiterate, but able to sign his name to the form. He did not advise the plaintiff of his disability. The Court of Appeal held *non est factum* could be pleaded. The defendant was under no duty to advise the bank of his disability and he was able to show that he had asked a series of questions in order to try and discover the implications of the guarantee, but the bank had been negligent in responding to these inquiries and this misled the defendant. This is a somewhat liberal application of *non est factum* which is attributable to the negligence of the plaintiff bank outweighing the lack of candour by the defendant, who was apparently "too shy" to inform the plaintiff of his disability.

10–65 The recent decision of Morris J. in *Ted Castle McCormack and Co v McCrystal*[204] also suggests that a temporary disability, as distinct from a lack of knowledge or cognitive incapacity, can possibly come within the defence. The defendant, proprietor of a garage business trading as a company, signed a personal guarantee in respect of petrol and oil supplied to the business by the plaintiff. The defendant claimed that he signed the document while suffering from anxiety and depression, believing that what he was signing was an exclusive supply or solus agreement. After summarising the requirements of *Saunders v Anglia Building Society*, Morris J. held that the document signed and the document believed to have been signed were radically different. More interestingly perhaps, in the light of evidence about the plaintiff's possible mental state and the circumstances in which signature was procured, Morris J. found the defendant was not negligent in signing the document put before him by the plaintiff.

10–66 There have been a variety of recent cases in which personal guarantees given as security for bank advances made to developers and entrepreneurs before the banking crash and subsequent economic downturn have been contested using *non est factum*. These cases have generally failed to attract

---

[203] [1991] Fam. Law 23.
[204] Unreported, High Court, March 15, 1999, an action seeking liberty to defend the action on the ground that there was a fair or reasonable probability of the defendant having a bona fide defence.

judicial sympathy on the basis that the factors set out in *Ted Castle*, applying *Saunders v Anglia Building Society*, have not been met. A person who executes a document without even reading it cannot expect to pass the *non est factum* tests on the basis that she was simply complying with practices in the family business. Nor will a court think it credible for the signor to have only had sight of the top sheet of a complex commercial document.[205] The most interesting case is that of one of the defendants in *AIB Plc v Higgins*,[206] a loan facility case. Tests indicated that the defendant had a reading age of seven years and a very low verbal comprehension score (less than three per cent of persons of his age would score so low), while the tests also revealed that in terms of non-verbal reasoning he was at least of average intelligence. Because the bank had not been informed of the defendant's disability the defendant failed to satisfy the requirement, taken from *Ted Castle*, that the person under the disability "take all reasonable precautions in the circumstances to find out what the document was".[207] Morris J. in *Ted Castle*, summarised the *Saunders* case thus:

> "I am satisfied that a person seeking to raise the defence of *non est factum* must prove:
> (a) That there was a radical or fundamental difference between what he signed and what he thought he was signing;
> (b) That the mistake was as to the general character of the document as opposed to the legal effect; and
> (c) That there was a lack of negligence, i.e. that he took all reasonable precautions in the circumstances to find out what the document was."

In *Friends First Finance Ltd v Lavelle*[208] Charleton J. has added a gloss to these recent cases on *non est factum* pleas when the guarantor is inexperienced in business and unwittingly provides security for a family commercial venture. Where the bank provides no cautionary advice and in fact studiously departs from standard practices, to the prejudice of the guarantor, *non est factum* may be available. In *Allied Irish Banks plc v Yates*[209] Noonan J. stressed that the facts of *Friends First Finance Ltd v Lavelle* were exceptional and that "mere assertions" of fact—in this case that the signature was obtained "for administrative purposes only"—will not dispense with the need to show a mistake was made in relation to the general character of the document.

---

[205] *Irish Bank Resolution Corp Ltd v Quinn* [2011] IEHC 470; *Bank of Scotland v Hickey* [2014] IEHC 202; *ACC Loan Management Ltd v Browne* [2015] IEHC 722.

[206] *AIB Plc v Smith* [2012] IEHC 381. See the wider principle expressed in *Hamilton v Judge* [2010] NICA 49.

[207] [2010] IEHC 219; affirmed on appeal at [2015] IECA 23; *Ulster Bank v Roche* [2012] IEHC 166; *Allied Irish Banks plc v Smith* [2012] IEHC 281.

[208] [2013] IEHC 250.

[209] [2016] IEHC 60.

11 Misrepresentation

Introduction

11–01 A misrepresentation is made when one contracting party has uttered a statement of fact which is untrue.[1] We have discussed in Ch.5 the extent to which the Irish courts are prepared to go in holding a pre-contractual statement to be a part of the contract. In such cases the injured party can sue for breach of a contractual term. The remedy available will depend on whether the promise takes effect as a warranty, condition or intermediate term. The misrepresentation may also produce a remedy in tort. Should a court refuse to hold the statement to be a contractual term, the injured party may still be able to recover damages or repudiate the contract if the misrepresentation can be deemed fraudulent, negligent or innocent. As we shall see, the remedy available depends largely on which category the statement falls into. As in the law of mistake equitable principles and remedies differ from those developed by the common law courts. Limited measures of statutory reform have come into operation in both parts of Ireland. As a result it is possible for a misleading statement to take effect in one of three ways; it can produce a remedy in contract; alternatively, the statement can produce a remedy in tort; thirdly, it could produce a remedy under Statute, e.g. Pt V of the Sale of Goods and Supply of Services Act 1980 (the "1980 Act"). In most cases a plaintiff will plead breach of contract, tortious misrepresentation, or breach of statute as alternative causes of action.

11–02 The Consumer Protection Act 2007 creates a new statutory framework in relation to the prohibition of unfair and misleading commercial practices in trader-to-consumer transactions. A commercial practice is defined in s.2 so as to include any representation by a trader, and a representation is defined so as to include:

> "(a) any oral, written, visual, descriptive or other representation by a trader, including any commercial communication, marketing or advertising, and
> (b) any term or form of a contract, notice or other document used or relied on by a trader in connection with a consumer transaction."

---

[1] On misrepresentation in tort, see McMahon & Binchy, *Law of Torts*, 4th edn (Dublin: Bloomsbury Professional, 2013). The leading text is Cartwright, *Misrepresentation, Mistake and Non-Disclosure*, 3rd edn (London: Thomson Reuters, 2012). See also *Chitty on Contracts*, 32nd edition, Vol.1, paras 7–001 to 7–181 (Sweet & Maxwell, 2015).

Section 42 of the Consumer Protection Act 2007 sets out a general principle whereby a trader is not to engage in misleading commercial practices, and ss.43–46 specify the various circumstances in which a trade practice will contravene this principle. The provision of false information is misleading under s.43, and s.43(3) sets out a list of factors such as the existence, nature of goods or services, its main characteristics, price, spare parts, as well as the nature or attributes of the trader. Section 44 also relates to product confusion as a misleading commercial practice, while s.45 relates to misdescription of the trader. Section 46 relates to the withholding of material information. Section 43(1) and (2) may give rise to criminal liability under s.47. Further clarity in respect of the express terms that a consumer may be able to rely on if goods or services turn out to be otherwise than stated in contracts and pre-contractual information requirements, are provided by the Consumer Rights Directive, Directive 2011/83, as transposed by the European Union (Consumer Information, Cancellation and Other Rights) Regulations 2013.[2]

11–03 In this chapter we will confine our attention to the contractual, tortious and statutory remedies available to someone who has entered a contract as a result of a misrepresentation.

The Statement

11–04 A very useful and influential summary of the law relating to the way in which statements are assessed has been provided by Christopher Clarke J. in *Raiffeisen Zentralbank Österreich AG v Royal Bank of Scotland*.[3]

> "whether any and if so what representation was made has to be judged objectively according to the impact that whatever is said may be expected to have on a reasonable representee in the position, and with the known characteristics of the acted representee ... the court may regard a sophisticated commercial party who is told that no representations are being made to him quite differently than it would a consumer.
>
> In the case of an express statement the court has to consider what a reasonable person would have understood from the words used in the context in which they were used ... [this] may depend on the nature and content of the statement, the context in which it was made, the characteristics [of the parties] and the relationship between them.
>
> In the case of an implied statement ... [the court] has to consider what a reasonable person would have inferred was being impliedly represented.[4]

---

2   S.I. No. 484 of 2013.
3   [2010] EWHC 1392 (Comm).
4   [2010] EWHC 1392 (Comm) at paras 81 and 82.

11–05 A statement of opinion will, in certain cases, be outside the law of misrepresentation. If the person uttering the statement knows it is false or had the opportunity to check its accuracy he will be bound, particularly if the representee was unable to investigate the facts for himself. If I say, "in my opinion, the car is sound" and I know the vehicle is only fit for the scrapheap, I have misstated my true opinion; this constitutes a misrepresentation of fact. In *Esso Petroleum v Mardon*,[5] the appellants were held to have made a misrepresentation when they told a prospective tenant that, in their opinion, a filling station would sell 200,000 gallons per annum at the end of a two-year period. The English Court of Appeal said Esso were liable for a misrepresentation nonetheless. The appellants were said to have misrepresented that they had exercised care and skill in calculating this figure. It should be noted that Esso was in the best position to estimate "throughput". However, a statement of intention is different from a promise; in *Mulcahy v Mulcahy*[6] a statement by a brother to his siblings that he wanted possession of family property because he intended to make it a home for both his family and his mother was held not to be a promise that, of itself, was either factually false or contractually binding: it was characterised as a "selling point" vis-à-vis securing the agreement of the siblings to release their interest in the family property but it was not characterised as fraudulent misrepresentation. This decision is marginal; given that the representor was not specifically examined on what his future intention was, and if it emerged in evidence that the representor had no such intention, the decision could easily go the other way. In *McCaughey v Irish Bank Resolution Corp*[7] the case concerned an argument about the alleged suppression of a material fact from an investment prospectus. The Supreme Court upheld the trial judge's decision that the investor would not have chosen another course of action if the facts had been disclosed. The facts were not material and non-disclosure was not a negligent act by the defendant. The trial judge's finding as to the investor's state of mind could be assessed objectively and subjectively. Hardiman J. said in the Supreme Court:

> "When one is assessing a statement of a person as to what he would have done, or not done, had matters developed differently to the way they actually developed, it is reasonable to consider, as a starting point, whether his claimed reaction would have been reasonable. It would be quite wrong, of course, to proceed on the basis that *only* a reasonable reaction was open to him because the Courts very often see instances where people react to particular developments in ways which are irrational, exaggerated, unduly bellicose or unduly timid, or otherwise improbable.

---

5   [1976] Q.B. 801. Later cases have said that statements of opinion contain an implied representation that the opinion is honestly held: *Parish v Danwood Group* [2015] EWHC 940 (Q.B.). See also *Walsh v Jones Lang LaSalle* [2007] IEHC 28. The decision in *McCaughey v Anglo Irish Bank Corp Ltd* [2011] IEHC 546 distinguishes *Walsh v Jones Lang LaSalle* on the facts. There is no discussion on this point in the Supreme Court: [2013] IESC 17.

6   [2011] IEHC 186, following *British Airways Board v Taylor* [1976] 1 All E.R. 65 at 68 per Lord Wilberforce.

7   [2013] IESC 17.

But the learned trial judge's finding here made every allowance for the capacity for odd reactions for subjective reasons and found that, though he did not accept Mr. McCaughey's evidence that 'I would not have invested', that this reaction was subjectively genuine and 'the product of hindsight and wishful thinking', not of deliberate falsehood."

The distinctions between statements of future intention, statements of opinion and actionable misrepresentations are extremely difficult to draw in situations where the contractual subject matter is itself speculative or aspirational. Many of the leading cases involve statements about the development potential of land, or a business venture, or a corporate body to be operated in the future. In general, the element of futurity can be exploited by the alleged misrepresentor as long as it can be shown that the intention or the opinion was held at the time of the statement being made. In *Buxton v The Birches Time Share Resort Ltd*,[8] the defendant read very attractive promotional material which painted a bucolic picture of a timeshare development which the plaintiff wished to undertake. The development, by way of chalet units, began and the defendant booked two weeks in that chalet unit. However, the contract document provided made it clear that the entire development of later units and certain facilities depended on successful completion of the staged development. The early phase was not a complete success. Some timeshare weeks remained unsold, and the defendant refused to proceed. Summary judgment was given against him and, on appeal, the judgment was upheld. Hardie Boys J. observed that, "a statement of intention will be a misrepresentation if the intention did not in fact exist when the statement was made but what appears to be a statement concerning the future may in reality be or it may imply a representation as to a present fact". The brochures clearly painted a brighter picture than the reality, but the learned judge did not find any basis for an implied misrepresentation of fact. At the legally significant date—entry into the contract—the full speculative nature of the venture was known: success "depended entirely on the success of the marketing of the project, a matter to a large degree beyond the control of the promoters. The risk involved was obvious, and those who purchased must have been prepared to run it. Mr Buxton having chosen to do so cannot now repudiate his contract when the risk appears to have materialised". For the purpose of assessing whether reliance on the alleged statement is appropriate the form in which the misrepresentation was allegedly made may also be relevant. Similarly, in *Spencer v Irish Bank Resolution Corp*[9] preliminary statements were made in a loose leaf brochure, this being followed by more detailed promotional material in which the statements were not carried over. Costello J. held that the plaintiff was not entitled to rely on the loose leaf text, this having been corrected by the subsequent documentation. Reliance on statements not in existence at the operative date is also not a tenable position for a plaintiff to assert.[10]

---

[8]   [1991] 2 N.Z.L.R. 641. See also *Lewin v Barratt Homes Ltd* (2000) 164 J.P. 182.
[9]   [2015] IEHC 395.
[10]   *Hunt v Optima (Cambridge) Ltd* [2014] EWCA Civ 714.

11–06 In the contrasting Ontario case of *447927 Ontario Inc v Pizza Pizza Ltd*[11] the plaintiffs, franchisees of a pizza restaurant, unsuccessfully sought damages in respect of a franchise agreement which the plaintiffs claimed had been concluded on the basis of misrepresentation and breach of warranty. The defendants, through their franchise sales manager, had stated the earnings level to be anticipated from a retail outlet, but the plaintiff knew of the risks and could not show any error of the kind disclosed in respect of the calculations and on this point *Esso Petroleum Co v Mardon* was distinguishable. In any event, the agreement executed contained an integration clause, that is, a clause that excluded pre-contractual statements and negotiations and made the written contract the entire contract. This express clause was operative and, in particular, negated the existence of any warranties by the defendant franchiser. In the Ontario High Court, Anderson J. specifically drew attention to this factual difference between the case at bar and *Esso Petroleum Co v Mardon*. Particular attention has been paid to integration clauses, or entire agreement clauses, in recent cases and the effect of this case law is summarised later in this chapter.

11–07 While this line of case law is supportable, there is the possibility of abuse by allowing advertising material to set out very laudatory claims which raise expectations that are then deflated, or negatived, by contract terms. No doubt the courts will strive to prevent fraud or negligently-made assertions and will require fairness during contract negotiations, but there remain some instances where *caveat emptor* will prevail. It is significant, for example, that in the *Harlingdon Ltd v Hull Fine Art Ltd*[12] case, the decision involving the forged Munter painting, the plaintiff did not pursue a claim of actionable misrepresentation, presumably on the ground that the statement about origin was a statement of opinion only. In contrast, in *Avrora Fine Arts Investment Ltd v Christie, Manson & Woods Ltd*[13] the terms and conditions upon which Christie's sold "Odalisque", a painting thought to have been the work of Kustodiev, contained a five-year warranty that it was "the work of a named author or authorship, is authentic and not a forgery". This warranty made reliance on negligent misstatement and the Misrepresentation Act 1967 (the "1967 Act") less important.

11–08 If neither party is in a position to verify the statement, an opinion that turns out to be wrong will not always be actionable. In *Smith v Lynn*[14] the plaintiff and defendant were both interested in buying the same house. The plaintiff outbid the defendant at auction. Both parties had read an advertisement stating that the property was "in excellent structural and decorative repair". Six weeks after the plaintiff bought the property he put it back on the market. The plaintiff used the same advertisement, and when asked by the defendant

---

[11] (1987) 44 D.L.R. (4th) 366, affirmed at (1990) 64 D.L.R. (4th) 160.
[12] [1990] 1 All E.R. 737.
[13] [2012] EWHC 2198 (Ch).
[14] (1954) 85 I.L.T.R. 57.

why the property was being resold, the plaintiff replied that the sale was due to personal reasons. The defendant purchased; after the sale it was discovered that the house was infested with woodworm. The defendant refused to proceed with the purchase pleading that the plaintiff had misrepresented that the house was sound. The defence failed. The advertisement was held to be a statement of opinion, an advertising "puff" not intended to have legal consequences. Both parties had inspected the premises and, in the view of the court, the defendant could not avoid the bargain. The case of *Hummingbird Motors v Hobbs*[15] is to similar effect. Here a statement by the defendant about the mileage of a motor vehicle sold to the plaintiff company was held not to be a warranty. However, statements of opinion that lack an objective quality, which are made by a person who has the facts upon which the opinion is based, cannot be made with impunity. In *Doheny v Bank of Ireland*[16] the defendant was held liable on a "glowing" reference it gave in respect of a bank customer whom the bank represented to be "respectable and trustworthy". The defendant had bounced several cheques written by the customer and knew that she had a record of dishonesty. The plaintiff, a landlord who had let property to the customer, was held able to recover damages for rent arrears and damage to property. Similarly, letting agents for units in a shopping centre who expressed the view that all units would be let by Christmas were held to have crossed the thin line between an aspirational "puff" and a statement of fact: see *Donnellan v Dungoyne Ltd*.[17]

11–09 In *Smith v Lynn* the court also formed the view that the defendant had not relied on the statements made. He purchased on the strength of his own examination of the building. Similarly, in *Intrum Justitia BV v Legal and Trade Financial Services*,[18] the plaintiff agreed to buy an Irish subsidiary company owned by the defendant. The defendants, prior to commencement of the usual due diligence process which investigates the state of the target company, assured the plaintiff that there were "no skeletons in the cupboard". There later emerged an admission of embezzlement of substantial sums of money. Rescission for misrepresentation was refused on the basis that there had been no reliance. The due diligence process was in no way affected and the plaintiffs relied upon this process, not the misrepresentation. A statement will not constitute a misrepresentation if it is not read or heard by the other party because of absence of reliance. In *Grafton Court Ltd v Wadson Sales Ltd*[19] the defendants took a lease in a shopping complex. They pleaded that the plaintiff developer had represented that the other tenants would be high quality commercial concerns. The defendants pleaded that the other tenants did not meet this standard. Finlay P. held that if this statement had been made,

---

[15]   [1986] R.T.R. 276.
[16]   *The Irish Times*, December 12, 1997.
[17]   [1995] 1 I.L.R.M. 388; *Shahid v College of Dermatologists* (2007) 72 I.P.R. 555.
[18]   [2005] IEHC 190; see also *Antorisa Investments v 172965 Canada Inc.* (2006) 82 O.R. (3d) 437.
[19]   Unreported, High Court, February 17, 1975.

the defendant had not relied on it. When the lease was signed the other units were occupied. The true facts were known to the defendants when the contract was entered into. In some cases the misrepresentor may purport to rectify the earlier misrepresentation; the onus upon the misrepresentor is to show that at the time of contracting, rectification of the misrepresentation was plainly brought to the attention of the representee. It is not enough to plead that the misrepresentation could have been discovered if a search had been undertaken, or that the misrepresentee was invited to verify the statement but declined to do so.[20] In practice many statements of apparent fact may be made but the actionability of these statements may be problematical. This is particularly the case in so-called "shut-out" agreements or during due diligence investigations. The first situation arises where one party or organisation is considering the acquisition of a business while in the later case a decision to acquire has already been made. The potential purchaser may be given statements of fact or intention which are then investigated, but the true state of affairs is not revealed. It has been held that these statements are made in the context of a non-binding "agreement to agree" rather than being misrepresentations of fact: see *Phoenix International Life Sciences Inc v Rilett*.[21] If this view is correct then it appears to be based on commercial expectations rather than the giving of constructive notice, considered below at para.11–15.

11–10 In *Sargent v Irish Multiwheel*[22] it was held that the representee does not have to inform the representor that he has seen the misleading statement; it is enough to show the fact of reliance. Sargent was therefore able to sue on an advertisement which represented that a van which he later purchased was English-assembled. A statement will also be actionable even if it is only one reason why the representee entered the contract. In *Edgington v Fitzmaurice*[23] the plaintiff purchased debentures partly due to a misrepresentation in the brochure and partly because of a self-induced mistaken belief that the debentures were such as to provide preferential creditor status in the event of the company failing. It was held sufficient to maintain an action on the misrepresentation to show that the misrepresentation was one of the reasons why the subsequent contract was entered into. However, the courts stop short of a test of total subjectivity. According to *Smith v Chadwick*[24] the misrepresentation must have been of a kind that would have induced a reasonable person to enter into the contract but this has been doubted in England,[25] the view being taken that the issue of whether a reasonable person would have been induced was relevant to issues of proof—did the representee act in

---

[20] *Redgrave v Hurd* (1881) 20 Ch. D. 1; *Buxton v The Birches Time Share Resort Ltd* [1991] 2 N.Z.L.R. 641.
[21] [2001] B.C.C. 115.
[22] (1955) 21–22 Ir. Jur. Rep. 42.
[23] (1885) 29 Ch. D. 459, *Loonam v Kenny* [2015] IEHC 545.
[24] (1884) 9 App. Cas. 187.
[25] Scott J. in *Musprime Properties Ltd v Adhill Properties Ltd* (1990) 36 E.G. 114.

reliance? In *McCaughey v Irish Bank Resolution Corp*[26] the Supreme Court appears to have favoured the broader combination of subjective and objective factors.

Implicit Representations and Third Party Materials

11–11 It is sometimes evident that a third party—often a professional— will furnish data to a client, that client passing this data on to an individual who may rely on it by entering into a contract with the client who has been provided with the data. What if the data is incorrect? Will the provision of that information be accompanied by an implied representation that the data being provided has been adopted. There is little clear authority on this but the English Court of Appeal has recently held, in *Webster v Liddington*[27] that when a professional clinician used brochures from a third party to explain how the treatment worked from a scientific point of view, the clinician became responsible for the statements made in the brochure because the clinician intended clients to contract with him to receive the treatment. Jackson L.J. wrote:

> "Let me now stand back from the authorities. When a person (X) passes information produced by another (Y) someone with whom X is hoping to contract (Z), a range of possibilities exist. In particular:
> i)   X may warrant to Z that the information is correct. X may thereby assume contractual liability to Z for the accuracy of the information. That liability may exist under the main contract or a collateral contract.
> ii) X may adopt the information as his own, thereby taking on such responsibility as he would have if he were the maker of the statement.
> iii) X may represent that he believes, on reasonable grounds, the information supplied by Y to be correct. That involves a lesser degree of responsibility than scenario (ii).
> iv) X may simply pass on the information to Z as material coming from Y, about which X has no knowledge or belief. X then has no responsibility for the accuracy of the information beyond the ordinary duties of honesty and good faith".

It seems clear that this set of possibilities will develop incrementally via case law.

Limiting or Excluding Liability for a Misrepresentation

11–12 It is at this point appropriate to consider the effect of express terms, inserted into a contract, which seek to negative or limit liability for pre-contractual statements of fact. This is an increasingly common contractual

---

[26] [2013] IESC 17.
[27] [2014] EWCA Civ 560, applying Toulson J.'s Analysis in *IFE Fund SA v Goldman Sachs International* [2006] EWHC 2887 (Comm) and *Foodco UK v Henry Boot Developments Ltd* [2010] EWHC 358 (Ch).

practice, being effected by the use of integration or entire agreement clauses, but the phenomenon is not new by any means. It is not unusual for the contract to attempt to place an obligation on the representee to verify all statements made to him. In *Pearson v Dublin Corp.*[28] the plaintiff was about to tender to the Corporation for a construction contract. He was told by the defendant's agent that a wall had been built on the construction site and that the foundations of the wall were nine-feet deep. This statement was untrue and it adversely affected the price contained in the tender, which the defendant accepted. The contract provided that the plaintiff had to verify all representations for himself and not rely on their accuracy. Palles C.B. held that this provision was effective and he refused to leave an issue to the jury, dismissing the action. The House of Lords granted a new trial. The statement was made by the agent fraudulently; several members of the House of Lords said that, in general, a person cannot avoid the effect of his or her agent's fraudulent statements by inserting a clause in the contract that the other party shall not rely on them. Any other rule would encourage fraudulent practices. The decision in *Pearson v Dublin Corp.* was discussed in *Dublin Port and Docks Board v Brittania Dredging Co Ltd.*[29] The defendants contracted to perform dredging work for the plaintiffs. The material to be dredged was stated in the contract to be of a particular quality but the survey upon which this representation was based was itself inaccurate. The material was much coarser and the cost of extraction was higher, thereby affecting the profitability of the contract. However, the contract provided that the defendants were deemed to have inspected the site and the plaintiffs were not liable for any misrepresentation. The Supreme Court characterised this misrepresentation as innocent, not fraudulent. The survey was provided honestly and in good faith. The clause could therefore be operative. More recently, Slade J. observed[30] that the rule "*caveat emptor* has no application to a case where a purchaser has been induced to enter the contract of purchase by fraud", but the general usefulness of exclusion clauses is outlined by *447927 Ontario Inc v Pizza Pizza Ltd*[31] where it was stated, obiter, that an exclusion clause could be relied upon to exclude liability for misrepresentations that did not find their way into the contract document. This proposition has been endorsed in the more recent English cases of *Inntrepreneur Pub Co v East Crown*[32] and *White v Bristol Rugby Ltd,*[33] where the view was expressed that such clauses, as a matter of law, negative the misrepresentation. Case law from

---

[28] [1907] A.C. 351.
[29] [1968] I.R. 136.
[30] *Gordon v Selico* [1986] 1 E.G.L.R. 71.
[31] (1987) 44 D.L.R. (4th) 366, affirmed at (1990) 64 D.L.R. (4th) 160.
[32] [2000] 2 Lloyd's Rep. 611; see also *McGrath v Shah* (1989) 57 P. & C.R. 452.
[33] [2002] I.R.L.R. 204. *Inntrepreneur* itself suggests that if the action is brought for a misrepresentation, as distinct from a claim in contract, "no reliance" clauses might be effective, subject to a "fair and reasonable" test under the Misrepresentation Act 1967 (s.46 of the Sale of Goods and Supply of Services Act 1980 in Ireland). See *Donnelly v Weybridge Construction* [2006] EWHC 2678 (TCC); *Foodco UK v Henry Boot Developments* [2010] EWHC 358 (Ch); and *Avrora Fine Art Investment Ltd v Christie, Manson and Woods Ltd* [2012] EWHC 2198 (Ch); Lloyd v Browning [2013] EWCA Civ 1637.

Canada and Australia, however, suggests that if the plaintiff can nevertheless make out the case that a false statement was made, which induced the plaintiff to enter into the contract, the entire agreement clause may not prevail.[34] In *Walsh v Jones Lang LaSalle*,[35] the defendants had misrepresented the floor area of a property to be sold at auction, but they sought to rely on a disclaimer that sought to require intending purchasers to inspect the details of the property themselves. The plaintiff was held entitled to damages on the basis that custom and practice in the Dublin commercial property market was to place reliance on the description made by the seller and seller's agent. Judicial hostility to this kind of clause is understandable even if the precise conceptual basis for counteracting such practices is not easy to articulate.[36]

11–13 However, some protection against exclusion clauses in sale of goods, hire-purchase, bailment and contracts for services is found in Irish statute law. Section 46 of the 1980 Act limits the effectiveness of such disclaimer clauses to cases where a clause is "fair and reasonable in the circumstances of the case". Although there is no compelling Irish case on this point, doubts have arisen in England on the applicability of this statutory provision to entire agreement clauses. It is argued that the UK equivalent of s.46—s.3 of the 1967 Act—does not apply to clauses that delineate the contract or indicate "where the contractual terms are actually to be found"[37] and the weight of judicial opinion[38] appears to be that the statutory "fair and reasonable" test is irrelevant to contract claims but applicable in tort actions.[39] Canadian cases, however, incline towards the view that an entire agreement clause will

---

[34] e.g. *Campbell v Backoffice Investments* [2009] HCA 25; *Alberta Treasury Branches v Gammell* (2011) 336 D.L.R. (4th) 378.

[35] [2007] IEHC 28.

[36] Perhaps this is one of those exceptional applications of the *Interfoto* principle whereby clauses that are not specifically brought to the attention of the other party are unenforceable because of basic unfairness: on the role of *Interfoto* in contractual documents see *JP Morgan Chase Bank v Springwell Navigation Corp* [2008] EWHC 1186 (Comm), upheld at [2010] EWCA Civ 1221. Contractual estoppel was identified as a relevant consideration in *McCaughey v Anglo Irish Bank Corp Ltd* [2011] IEHC 546; *Parsley Properties Ltd v Bank of Scotland plc* [2013] IEHC 624; *European Property Fund plc v Ulster Bank Ltd* [2015] IEHC 425.

[37] Deputy Judge Chadwick in *McGrath v Shah* (1989) 57 P. & C.R. 452 at 459. While this approach has been endorsed on several occasions it must be contextualised within arm's-length negotiations. Section 3 of the Misrepresentation Act 1967 has been held to lead to different results in cases where there is a complex commercial contract in which the parties are fully represented from contracts involving "the man in the street". See *Raiffeisen Zentralbank Osterreich AG v Royal Bank of Scotland Plc* [2010] EWHC 1392 (Comm); *Springhill Navigation Corp v JP Morgan Chase Bank* [2010] EWCA Civ 1221; *Avrora Fine Arts Investment Ltd v Christie, Manson and Woods Ltd* [2012] EWHC 2198 (Ch).

[38] e.g. *McGrath v Shah* (1987) 57 P. & C.R. 452; *Inntrepreneur Pub Co v East Crown Ltd* [2000] 2 Lloyd's Rep. 611; *White v Bristol Rugby Ltd* [2002] I.R.L.R. 204; *Watford Electronics Ltd v Sanderson CFC Ltd* [2001] 1 All E.R. (Comm.) 696.

[39] *Cremdean Properties Ltd v Nash* (1977) 244 E.G. 547; *Zanzibar v British Aerospace* [2000] 1 W.L.R. 2333. In any event the clause will be subject to hostile interpretation; if the language looks like contractual language, located in clauses that use contract terminology, the clause may be viewed as having nothing to do with tort liability: *Axa Sun Life Services Plc v Campbell Martin Ltd* [2011] EWCA Civ 133.

not operate if it is shown that there was an operative misrepresentation that involved the contract[40] or the operation of the entire agreement clause would be unconscionable.[41]

11–14 It will be important to establish when the representation was made. While, in general, representations made after a contract has been concluded cannot provide the misrepresentee with relief, in real property transactions there may be some ambiguity about when the contract is concluded for these purposes. In *Keegan Quarries Ltd v McGuinness*,[42] the vendor misrepresented that the land had been used as a quarry since 1958, having a significant impact on the ability of the purchaser to quarry the land vis-à-vis planning consents. These pre-contractual (i.e. pre-agreement) statements were made fraudulently, as were statements made by the vendor in response to specific requisitions on title (i.e. post-agreement but prior to conveyancing).

11–15 A representee who becomes aware of the untruth of a statement before he enters into the contract has no remedy; he has not relied upon the statement because he has notice of its falsity. Notice means actual and not constructive notice. In *Phelps v White*[43] the plaintiff was told that timber on land he intended to lease would be part of the property transferred. This was untrue. The plaintiff was furnished with documentation which would have revealed the misrepresentation. The Court of Appeal in Ireland refused to hold the plaintiff had notice of the misrepresentation. In *Gahan v Boland & Boland*[44] the defendants falsely but innocently represented that their property would not be affected by any new roads to be built in the area and, in reliance thereon, the representee purchased the property. After completion the plaintiff sought to rescind the contract of sale on the grounds of a contractual misrepresentation. The defendants argued that as the plaintiff was a solicitor and intending purchaser, he was obliged to pursue inquiries which would have led to him being informed of the true position. The Supreme Court granted rescission, holding that only actual and not constructive notice will debar a purchaser from repudiating a contract on the ground of misrepresentation. In *Peekay Intermark Ltd v Australia and New Zealand Banking*,[45] the plaintiff, who had a history of purchasing investment instruments through the defendant, purchased a number of Russian short-term bonds that carried a significant level of risk. The defendant's employee who sold the bonds misunderstood the nature of the instrument and the purchasers

---

[40] *Zippy Print v Pawliuk* [1995] 3 W.W.R. 324; *Foundation Co of Canada v United Grain Growers* (1997) 34 B.C.L.R. (3rd) 92. In Australia see *Karmot Auto Spares Pty Ltd v Dominelli Ford (Hurstville) Pty Ltd* (1992) 35 F.C.R. 560.

[41] *Founders Square Ltd v Nova Scotia* (2001) 192 N.S.R. (2d) 127.

[42] [2011] IEHC 453; see also *The Leopardstown Club Ltd v Templeville Developments Ltd* [2015] IECA 164.

[43] (1881) 7 L.R. (Ir.) 160; but see *Peekay Intermark Ltd v Australia and New Zealand Banking* [2006] EWCA Civ 386.

[44] Unreported, Supreme Court, January 20, 1984.

[45] [2006] EWCA Civ 386. The importance of *Peekay* is examined by Braithwaite at (2016) 132 LQR 120.

signed contract documents that clearly stated the nature of the instrument and levels of risk. One risk was that the Russian Government might default, which it did, thus rendering the bonds virtually worthless. The Court of Appeal found that the misrepresentation could not be relied upon because the final terms and conditions and the risk disclosure statements—documents signed by the plaintiffs—clearly corrected any error made. The plaintiffs were experienced investors and knew that the documents were important but they were barely glanced at. As these documents were contractual, and contained a statement that they had been read and understood, they effected a contractual estoppel which served to preclude liability under s.2(1) of the 1967 Act. This is a borderline decision based on specific commercial practices and suggests that properly worded contractual documents can themselves repair pre-contractual misrepresentations through the signature rule.[46] In *McBrearty v AIB Group (UK) Plc*[47] the ratio decidendi of *Peekay* was said to be that the promisor's statement in that case had not induced the promise to sign the documents and enter the contract. In contrast, in *McBrearty*, statements made about minimum investment returns were actionable in contract, negligent misstatement and breach of a collateral warranty.

11–16 In the Northern Ireland case of *Lutton v Saville Tractors Ltd*[48] an interesting point of law arose out of a contract for the sale of a second-hand motor vehicle. The plaintiff purchased the car, partly on the basis that the vehicle had not been involved in an accident, and the salesman innocently misrepresented that the vehicle had not been so involved. The plaintiff rescinded the contract because it proved defective. Shortly after proceedings commenced, the untruth of the assurance about involvement in an accident was discovered. Carswell J. nevertheless held that the innocent misrepresentation could be relied upon:

> "[I]t is a well established principle of the law of contract that a person who refuses to perform a contract on one ground, may, if that is inadequate, subsequently rely upon another ground which justifies his refusal to perform provided it in fact existed at the time of the refusal: *Benjamin's Sale of Goods*, 2nd Edition, paragraph 1725."[49]

In this case the learned judge also held that where an employee makes a representation in the course of employment this will be actionable against the

---

[46] See *Toll (FGCT) Pty Ltd v Alphapharm Pty Ltd* (2004) 219 C.L.R. 165.

[47] [2012] NIQB 12, following *National Westminster Bank v Binney* [2011] EWHC 694 (Ch) and *Evans v Merzario* [1976] 1 W.L.R. 1078. See also *Thinc Group Ltd v Armstrong* [2012] EWCA Civ 1227, on collateral warranties surviving *Peekay*, signature of the contract not being conclusive.

[48] [1986] N.I. 327.

[49] [1986] N.I. 327. Note the important decision in *Fitzroy Robinson Ltd v Mentmore Towers Ltd* [2009] EWHC 1552 (TCC), where, absent non-disclosure, the court found that breach of express and implied duties to co-operate in the performance of the contract could be relied upon, post-contract formation.

employer. On the question of whether an agent's knowledge of fraud can bind a principal, see the old Irish case of *Sankey v Alexander*,[50] and the more recent English case of *Stroves v Harrington*[51] in which Browne-Wilkinson V.C. considered the circumstances in which knowledge acquired by a purchaser's solicitor can be imputed to the purchaser, thereby effecting an estoppel. A novel application of estoppel by misrepresentation occurred in *Lease Management Services Ltd v Purnell Secretarial Services*.[52] Here a finance company used contract documents which deceived customers into thinking they were dealing with a company associated with an international trading group when there was no such link. The use of this misleading trade practice gave rise to an estoppel by representation so that it was bound by statements made by employees of the supplier of the goods. There are a number of recent English cases in which evidential estoppel arguments of this kind have prevailed, e.g., *E.A. Grimstead & Son Ltd v McGarrigan*.[53]

The Causes of Action

(1) Fraudulent misrepresentation

11–17 A fraudulent misrepresentation is actionable in the tort of deceit. In the leading English case of *Derry v Peek*,[54] Lord Herschell said "without proof of fraud no action of deceit is maintainable". In that case the House of Lords held that fraud is proved when it is shown that a false representation has been made knowingly, or without belief in its truth, or recklessly, without caring whether it is true or false. It is important that special care is taken to use language that does not unwittingly suggest that recklessness is a feature of negligence. Insofar as some judges stress the need to find "conscious knowledge and dishonesty"[55] such a standard is often at odds with other lines of authority that establish fraud through recklessness when there is no intention to defraud.

11–18 In *Fenton v Schofield*[56] the vendor of land represented that over the last four years a river running over the land had yielded 300–350 salmon a year and that he had spent £15,000 renovating the property. Both statements were untrue as the vendor well knew. A purchaser paid £17,000 for the land. The value of the property was calculated by assuming each statement to be true. When the purchaser learnt of their untruth he sued in deceit, recovering

---

[50] (1874) 9 Ir.Rep.Eq. 259.

[51] [1988] 1 All E.R. 769.

[52] [1994] C.C.L.R. 127.

[53] [1998–1999] Info. T.L.R. 384. See also *Walmsley v Acid Jazz Records* [2001] E.C.D.R. 49; *North Eastern Properties Ltd v Coleman* [2010] EWCA Civ 277.

[54] (1889) 14 App. Cas. 337. In Ireland see *Banco Ambrosiano SpA v Ansbacher* [1987] ILRM 669; *Michovsky v Allianz Ireland plc* [2010] IEHC 43; *Bergin v Walsh* [2015] IEHC 594..

[55] *Armstrong v Strain* [1951] 1 L.T.R. 871, cited by the Northern Ireland Court of Appeal in *Odyssey Cinemas Ltd v Village Theatres Three Ltd* [2010] NICA 25.

[56] (1966) 100 I.L.T.R. 69.

damages based on the difference between what the land was worth and what it was represented to be worth. In *Carbin v Somerville*[57] the vendor of a house in Clontarf misrepresented that the house was dry. The Supreme Court held the plaintiff, who purchased the house on the strength of this assurance, was entitled to rescind the contract.

11–19 The facts of *Pearson v Dublin Corp.*[58] show that fraud can exist even when the representor does not necessarily know that his statement is false. When the agent told the plaintiff that the foundations of a wall stood on the site, the agent did not know if this was true or false: the statement was nevertheless fraudulent. Signing a professional indemnity insurance proposal form after misrepresenting that the signor was a partner in a firm of solicitors was held to be a fraudulent misrepresentation in *McAleenan v AIG (Europe) Ltd.*[59] In this case the High Court found that the signor did not sign the document knowing of the misrepresentation and that she had not read questions put to her. But in signing the proposed form the signor was acting recklessly in the sense that she was careless as to whether the statements therein were true or false.

11–20 An action in deceit may lie even if the representor has no intention to cause loss to the representee. In *Delany v Keogh*[60] Keogh, an auctioneer, was employed by Bradley, a solicitor, to sell Bradley's interest in leasehold property. The conditions of sale stated that while the rent was £25 per annum the landlord had accepted £18. Before the sale Keogh was told by the landlord that the full rent of £25 would be charged to the purchaser of the lease. Bradley advised Keogh that, in his view, the landlord would be estopped from charging the full rent. Keogh was advised not to change the conditions of sale. The plaintiff purchased the lease. The Kings Bench Division refused to find Keogh liable in deceit because it could not be shown that Keogh intended to mislead. The Court of Appeal reversed this decision. Holmes L.J. found that the misrepresentation stemmed from a failure to make known that he had reason to believe that the landlord would charge the higher rent. While Keogh believed what Bradley had told him this would not absolve him. Keogh should have mentioned, after reading out the conditions, that while he had been informed by the landlord that a higher rent would be charged it was Keogh's solicitor's opinion that the landlord was legally estopped.

11–21 Holmes L.J. also distinguished the leading case of *Derry v Peek*:

> "The directors of a Tramway Co. that had authority to use steam power with the consent of the Board of Trade, believing that this consent would be given as a matter of course issued a prospectus in which it was stated that they had the right to use steam power without reference to

57   [1933] I.R. 227.
58   [1907] A.C. 351.
59   [2010] IEHC 128.
60   [1905] 2 I.R. 267.

any condition. It was held that this was not actionable, inasmuch as the statement was made in the honest belief that it was true. This is, I think old law; but if the directors had known, before they issued the prospectus that the Board of Trade had refused to consent or had announced its intention to refuse, the case would have been like this, and the directors would have no defence; nor in such a case would their position have been improved if their solicitor had assured them that there would be no difficulty in obtaining from Parliament an amending Act removing the condition."[61]

Keegan Quarries Ltd v McGuinness[62] provides a good example of how the court may establish, on the balance of probabilities, that a statement was made fraudulently. In this case the plaintiff purchased land on the basis of a representation that quarrying had taken place since 1958. This representation, the defendant said, had been made to him by the previous owner, who had since died. Finlay Geoghegan J. found, first, that statements made as between the parties and statements made for planning purposes were inconsistent and unsupported by contemporaneous documents in the form of diary entries. Secondly, planning documentation also communicated for planning purposes a number of inaccurate statements that were made recklessly "in the sense of being careless as to whether the information provided was true or false". A third inference was drawn from the general evidence given by the defendant in which he was held to be "untruthful as to certain matters ... it is a factor which must be taken into account".

(2) Negligent misstatement

11–22 In *Derry v Peek* the House of Lords ruled that there is no liability in deceit for a false statement made carelessly and without reasonable grounds for believing it to be true. In the absence of a contract, negligently made statements could be the subject of an award of damages only if a fiduciary relationship existed between the parties, such as solicitor and client. In 1963 the House of Lords declared that liability in the tort of negligence could arise from a negligent misstatement. In *Hedley Byrne v Heller*[63] a bank negligently represented a company to be on a sound financial footing. This caused the appellant to invest in the company which later collapsed. The Law Lords stated *obiter* that where a "special relationship" exists, a duty of care will arise between the parties. *Esso Petroleum v Mardon*[64] establishes that liability will arise under this cause of action where the misstatement results in a contract between the parties.

---

[61] [1905] 2 I.R. 267 at 290.

[62] [2011] IEHC 453. Contrast *Stephen Moffitt Ltd v Carla Scapa Group Ltd* [2012] IEHC 227.

[63] [1964] A.C. 465. For a colourful case including a bank guarantee and customer facilities for a casino account see *Playboy Club London Ltd v Banca Nazionale Del Lavoro SpA* [2014] EWHC 2613 (Q.B.); see McMahon & Binchy, *Law of Torts*, 4th edn (Dublin: Bloomsbury Professional, 2013), para.10.71.

[64] [1976] Q.B. 801.

11–23 The *Hedley Byrne* principle has been extensively considered by the courts in Ireland. In *Bank of Ireland v Smith*,[65] Kenny J. cited *Hedley Byrne* although the learned judge found the misrepresentation in that case would ground liability in contract. In *Stafford v Keane Mahony Smith*,[66] Doyle J. discussed the *Hedley Byrne* principle, as extended in *Esso Petroleum v Mardon*. Doyle J. noted that *Hedley Byrne* had been approved by Davitt P. in *Securities Trust Ltd v Hugh Moore & Alexander Ltd*[67] Doyle J. declared that:

> "In order to establish the liability for negligent or non-fraudulent misrepresentation giving rise to action there must first of all be a person conveying the information or the representation relied upon; secondly, that there must be a person to whom that information is intended to be conveyed or to whom it might reasonably be expected that the information would be conveyed; thirdly, that the person must act upon such information or representation to his detriment so as to show that he is entitled to damages."[68]

The action in *Stafford v Keane Mahony Smith* was brought against an estate agent who had represented that certain property would be a good investment. The plaintiff purchased the house but later had to resell it at a loss. The action failed because Doyle J. found that any representations made were not made to the plaintiff but to his brother.[69] In *Doolan v Murray*[70] the plaintiff entered into building work on property she had purchased from the first two defendants because she believed that a right of way was a pedestrian right of way only. The third defendant had assisted in bringing the plaintiff's belief into being but the right of way was more extensive than the third defendant had stated. The work had to be removed. Keane J. held that the plaintiff could not succeed against the first two defendants in either contract or tort, but that liability against the third defendant in negligent misstatement could be made out. This case is an interesting one because in most actions of this kind the defendant is a professional person or someone who holds themselves out as possessing special knowledge or skill: recent English and Irish case law has explored the issue of whether a solicitor, for example, will be in a special relationship with someone other than his immediate client and the courts hold that, exceptionally, this may be so.[71] Similarly, liability in tort has been visited upon auctioneers who, acting for a vendor, make careless statements to inexperienced or naive

---

[65] [1966] I.R. 646.
[66] [1980] I.L.R.M. 53; *Hazylake Fashions v Bank of Ireland* [1989] I.R. 601.
[67] [1964] I.R. 417.
[68] [1980] I.L.R.M. 53 at 64.
[69] Contrast *Irish Permanent Building Society v O'Sullivan and Collins* [1990] I.L.R.M. 598.
[70] Unreported, High Court, December 21, 1993.
[71] *White v Jones* [1995] 2 A.C. 207; *Doran v Delaney* [1998] 2 I.L.R.M. 1; *Woodward v Wolferstans (a firm), The Times*, April 8, 1997; *Rojack v Taylor & Buchalter* [2005] IEHC 28; Cartwright, *Misrepresentation, Mistake and Non-Disclosure*, 3rd edn (London: Thomson Reuters, 2012), para.6–41.

prospective purchasers about the development potential of the property; see *McAnarney v Hanrahan*[72] and *McCullagh v PB Gunne (Monaghan) Plc*.[73]

Banking Transactions

11–24 As the financial crisis of the last eight years created financial ruin for individuals and corporations worldwide, it is to be expected that investors in particular have sought to recover from unwise business decisions by seeking to transfer responsibilities to banks and other financial institutions.

> "It is well established law that a bank owes no general duty to advise its customers on the wisdom of their commercial projects".[74]

The situation where a bank does however decide to furnish information is pithily summarized by Mance J. in *Bankers Trust International plc v PT Dharmala Sakti Sejahtera*:[75]

> "in cases involving information which falls short of advice, a bank which undertakes to explain the nature and effect of a transaction owes a duty to take reasonable care to do so as fully and properly as the circumstances demand."

The Supreme Court in *Wildgust v Bank of Ireland*[76] has pushed the boundaries of liability for a negligent misstatement by holding that it is not necessary for a plaintiff who has suffered loss to show that the plaintiff had received the misrepresentation and acted upon it. Wildgust had assigned life insurance policies to a bank as security for a loan; he was obliged to pay the monthly premiums. The assignee, Hill Samuel, contacted the insurer and was told that the account was in order. Due to an error the premiums were not paid and the policies lapsed shortly before one of the insured persons died. Wildgust was never told of the misrepresentation and did not rely on it. The Supreme Court nevertheless held that there was a common interest between Wildgust and Hill Samuel in ensuring that the policies remained in force and it was enough that the insurer had induced reliance by Hill Samuel through the negligent misstatement. Kearns J. said that the proximity test in *Hedley Byrne*

> "must go further than [all representees] ... and include persons in a limited and identifiable class when the maker of the statement can reasonably expect, in the context of a particular inquiry, that reliance will be placed thereon by such person or persons to act or not act in a

---

[72] [1994] 1 I.L.R.M. 210.
[73] Unreported, High Court, January 17, 1997.
[74] Per Cregan J. in *Delaney v Allied Irish Banks plc* [2015] IEHC 52.
[75] [1996] CLC518, relied upon in *Crestsign Ltd. v National Westminister Bank* [2014] EWHC 3043 (Ch).
[76] [2006] 2 I.L.R.M. 28.

particular manner in relation to that transaction ... Mr. Wildgust and Hill Samuel had virtually an identical interest in preserving the policy and that both formed such an identical class, either of who could have acted to prevent Mr. Wildgust's loss."[77]

The Supreme Court also rejected the argument that the plaintiff could not invoke a claim in tort so as to overcome the fact that, by failing to pay the premium, the plaintiff was in breach of contract. The Supreme Court therefore maintains the position that concurrent liability in contract and tort is the general rule in Irish law.[78]

11–25 Irish case law also draws a distinction between the duty not to make a negligent misrepresentation and the duty not to make a negligent misstatement, Shanley J., in *Forshall v Walsh*,[79] describing negligent misstatement as being a wider tort. Whether this distinction is well founded in the light of judicial treatment of the distinction is open to doubt. In *King v Aer Lingus Plc*,[80] Kearns J. found that Aer Lingus had made an actionable misrepresentation to its employees and were liable for the tortious misrepresentation as distinct from negligent misstatement. Similarly, in *Carey v Independent Newspapers*[81] a failure to disclose all relevant facts surrounding the negotiations entered into with a view to the plaintiff accepting employment with the defendant was held to be an actionable misrepresentation, even though the line of authority that Gilligan J. followed was that of negligent misstatement *pace Hedley Byrne*.

11–26 In *Darlington Properties v Meath County Council*,[82] the plaintiffs were induced to buy a development site on the strength of the vendor's promise that the site could be developed, with permission to construct an access road being a key development objective. This promise was made negligently because the defendant had already given planning permissions for an adjoining site that made the construction of the intended road impossible. Kelly J. said this of *Hedley Byrne*:

> "The duty of care is not confined to professional persons expressing opinions or giving information. For example, a vendor has a duty to take reasonable care so as to ensure that statements he makes in seeking to induce a sale are true (see *Doran v Delaney* [1998] 2 I.R. 61). In *Gran Gelato Limited v Richcliff (Group) Limited* [1992] Ch. 560, it was common ground that the vendor owed a duty of care to a prospective purchaser and it was said that in the light of authorities such as *Esso*

---

[77] [2006] 2 I.L.R.M. 28 at 58.
[78] Following *Kennedy v AIB* [1998] 2 I.R. 48. See McMahon & Binchy, *Law of Torts*, 4th edn (Dublin: Bloomsbury Professional, 2013), paras 10.46–10.69.
[79] Unreported, High Court, June 18, 1997.
[80] [2002] 3 I.R. 481.
[81] *Irish Times Law Reports*, November 3, 2003.
[82] [2011] IEHC 70. Contrast *Stephen Moffitt Ltd v Carl Scarpa Group Ltd* [2012] IEHC 227.

Petroleum Company Limited v Mardon [1976] Q.B. 801, the contrary could not seriously be argued.

I am satisfied that a vendor, regardless of any other special relationship, is under a duty to take reasonable care to ensure that any representations made by him with a view to inducing contract are accurate.

In the present case, of course, the County Council was not any vendor.

It had a particular status and a particular means of knowledge. It was, after all, the planning authority. It itself granted the planning permission which rendered the building of the distributor road impossible. Yet it chose to market and offer the land for sale with explicit reference to the need for the distributor road to be built. Thus, even if it were necessary to show a special relationship (which it is not), I am satisfied that such special relationship existed having regard to the particular status of the County Council."

The boundary between negligent misrepresentation and negligent misstatement is certainly relevant to issues of remoteness of damage and quantum. It is also very relevant in cases where the statement in question does not induce the representee to enter into a contract with the respresentor, as in *Hedley Byrne* itself; but where a contract is induced as between the parties by the representation, cases such as *King v Aer Lingus Plc* and *Carey v Independent Newspapers* suggest that liability will readily be established under either or both torts as well as for breach of contract. The practical consequences for a plaintiff may well reside in the extent to which the plaintiff's cause of action may avoid a finding that the defendant was not negligent by pleading strict liability in contract, for example. It may be that the plaintiff may wish to select a particular cause of action in order to take advantage of more favourable remoteness of damage rules (e.g. pleading fraudulent misrepresentation[83] so as to recover all consequential loss) or the use of particular rules in relation to the assessment of damages, as in *Carey v Independent Newspapers* itself. In general terms the plaintiff is free to:

"... [t]ake advantage of the remedy which is most advantageous to him subject only to ascertaining whether the tortious duty is so inconsistent with the applicable contract that, in accordance with ordinary principle the parties must be taken to have agreed that the tortious remedy is to be limited or excluded."[84]

The general rule that in commercial negotiations there is no duty to communicate facts or intentions—no duty to speak—is subject to the exception,

---

[83] *Smith New Court Securities Ltd v Scrimgeour Vickers (Asset Management) Ltd* [1997] A.C. 254 or economic loss as in *Glencar Exploration Plc v Mayo County Council* [2002] 1 I.L.R.M. 481.

[84] Hamilton C.J. in *Kennedy v Allied Irish Banks Plc* [1998] 2 I.R. 48 at 56; *O'Donnell & Co Ltd v Truck and Machinery Sales Ltd* [1998] 4 I.R. 191; *McCaughey v Irish Bank Resolution Corp* [2013] IESC 17.

carved out in *Banque Keyser Ullman SA v Skandia (UK) Insurance Ltd*,[85] that if someone voluntarily assumes responsibility over a state of affairs, and there is reliance by others on this, then liability under *Hedley Byrne* may be made out. In the case of *Hamilton v Allied Domecq Plc*,[86] the House of Lords was unable to find that there was a representation simply because no assumption of responsibility could be made out. The House of Lords indicated that one negotiating party had no obligation to disabuse the other that he intended to follow a marketing strategy that the other party regarded as being essential to the success of a product launch.[87]

(3) Innocent misrepresentation

11–27 Prior to the *Hedley Byrne* decision it followed that all misrepresentations that were not fraudulent were classified as innocent misrepresentations. The fact that a misrepresentation was negligently made could not (in the absence of a fiduciary relationship[88]) avail the injured party. While *Hedley Byrne* has qualified this proposition it is still true to say that an innocent, non-fraudulent misrepresentation secures limited redress to the representee. It is at this point that jurisdictional factors become important. At common law the victim of an innocent misrepresentation could only repudiate the agreement if there was a total failure of consideration, that is, if the thing contracted for was not supplied at all or it was a totally different item from that envisaged at the time of agreement. The courts of equity permitted rescission upon proof that the misrepresentation was material in that it induced the contract. It was unnecessary to show a failure of consideration. This essential difference was overlooked in *Carbin v Somerville*[89] when Fitzgibbon J. in the Supreme Court held the vendor entitled to repudiate only if the statement was fraudulent or a total failure of consideration resulted. This proposition overlooks the equitable jurisdiction in which rescission would be ordered if an innocent misrepresentation was made. If the representation made is contractual in nature then the fact that the contract is executed is a barrier to rescission unless the barrier is removed by s.44 of the 1980 Act. Fitzgibbon J. may well have been alluding to this difficulty in *Carbin v Somerville*, a point we shall refer back to below.

11–28 Equity ordered the drastic remedy of rescission because historically an award of damages in lieu of rescission was not part of an equitable court's array of remedies. Because the common law courts took a restrictive view of

---

[85] [1990] 1 Q.B. 665.
[86] [2007] UKHL 33.
[87] Unlike *Ross River Ltd v Cambridge City Football Club* [2008] 1 All E.R. 1004, the written agreement in this case was silent on the matters alleged to have constituted the misrepresentation. The failure to explain signed commercial documents is not a basis for a misrepresentation claim: *JP Morgan Chase Bank v Springwell Navigation Corp* [2008] EWHC 1186 (Comm), affirmed at [2010] EWCA Civ 1221.
[88] *Nocton v Lord Ashburton* [1914] A.C. 932.
[89] [1933] I.R. 227. To make this observation accurate one has to add that the contract had been executed.

the cases in which an innocent misrepresentation would be operative, many victims of an innocent misrepresentation were denied a remedy in damages unless the statement could be elevated into a contractual term or a collateral warranty. In *Connor v Potts*[90] the plaintiff agreed to purchase two farms, innocently misrepresented to be 443 acres in all. The price was calculated at £12.10s. an acre. The farms fell 67 acres short of the figure represented. The plaintiff was held entitled to specific performance of the contract; the price payable by the plaintiff was reduced by calculating £12.10s x 67. Similarly in *Keating v Bank of Ireland*[91] an abatement of price was held to be allowable when the purchaser agreed to buy property following a misrepresentation. It was further held that the vendor could not insist upon the closing of the sale prior to the abatement being calculated under an arbitration clause which formed the basis of the agreement. In *O'Brien v Kearney*[92] the misrepresentee was able to counterclaim for specific performance at the abated price, using the misrepresentation as the successful basis for resisting the misrepresentor's action for specific performance, the misrepresentor seeking to have the issue of abatement being resolved subsequently.

(4) Negligence

11–29 If the boundary between negligent misrepresentation and negligent misstatement is uncertain, the boundary between pleading negligence in general (which will not readily be understood to constitute an allegation of negligent misstatement) and the *Hedley Byrne* cause of action has been recently examined by the Supreme Court in *Wildgust v Bank of Ireland*.[93] Whether a duty of care exists in tort is perhaps one of the most frequently litigated areas of civil law and often litigants push at the boundaries of tort in ways that underline economic trends and professional vulnerability. Some examples from recent Irish litigation include questions whether a financial institution can owe a duty to inform either an employee[94] or a customer[95] of some of the risks inherent in an investment or business decision. There are also instances in which lawyers acting in a negotiation on opposite sides might be said to owe a duty of care to professional counterparts.[96] However, in these cases if liability expands it tends to do so incrementally. The most common way in which the law advances here is by way of arguments about special relationships or fiduciary duties.[97]

---

[90] [1897] I.R. 534.
[91] [1983] I.L.R.M. 295. Often this remedy will be prescribed in lieu of rescission of the contract.
[92] Unreported, High Court, March 3, 1995; *Donnelly v Weybridge Construction* [2006] EWHC 2678 (TCC).
[93] [2006] 2 I.R.L.M. 28.
[94] e.g. *Friends First Finance Ltd v Cronin* [2013] IEHC 59.
[95] e.g. *Ulster Bank Ireland Ltd v Louis Roche* [2012] IEHC 166; contrast *BP Oil International Ltd v Target Shipping Ltd* [2012] EWHC 1590 (Comm) at para.203, Smith J.
[96] e.g. *Slattery v Friends First Life Assurance Co Ltd* [2013] IEHC 136 appeal approved on findings of fact [2015] IECA 149.
[97] In *Clements v Meagher* [2008] IEHC 258, Feeney J. cited with approval the definition of a fiduciary given by Millett L.J. in *Bristol and West Building Society v Mothew* [1998] Ch. 1

(5) Statutory right to damages

11–30 While pre-contractual statements are increasingly likely to be characterised as contractual terms (see Kenny J. in *Bank of Ireland v Smith*[98]) the Oireachtas has created a right to damages in cases of innocent misrepresentation. Section 45(1) of the 1980 Act provides:

> "Where a person has entered into a contract after a misrepresentation has been made to him by another party thereto and as a result thereof he has suffered loss, then, if the person making the representation would be liable to damages in respect thereof had the misrepresentation been made fraudulently, that person shall be so liable notwithstanding that the misrepresentation was not made fraudulently, unless he proves that he had reasonable ground to believe and did believe up to the time the contract was made that the facts represented were true."

This section is based upon s.2(1) of the English and Northern Ireland Misrepresentation Acts. It was seen as desirable to supplement the restrictive range of remedies available following an innocent misrepresentation which induces a contract because rescission is neither appropriate nor indeed possible in the majority of cases. Section 2(1) enables the representee to claim damages, as in *Gosling v Anderson*[99] when the Court of Appeal held the purchaser of a flat was entitled to damages when it was shown that planning permission to enable garages to be built had not in fact been obtained. The proviso to s.45(1) enables the misrepresentee to avoid liability if the court can be persuaded that the representee believed, and had a reasonable ground for believing, the truth of the statement. This defence is somewhat wide and in this writer's view it would be preferable to hold the mispresentor liable in damages simply upon proof that the statement was false. The New Zealand Contractual Remedies Act 1979, for example, provides an interesting contrast to the UK and Irish model, for s.6 of that Act provides a right to damages if the statement is false and was relied upon.

11–31 The proviso was interpreted narrowly on the one occasion when it was considered in detail by an English Court. In *Howard Marine & Dredging Co Ltd v A Ogden & Sons (Excavations) Ltd*[100] the plaintiffs were the owners of barges hired out to the defendant to enable it to dump excavated spoil at sea. The capacity of the barges was stated at 1,600 tonnes by the plaintiffs' marine manager, a figure based on recollection of the figure in Lloyd's Register. The Lloyd's Register was incorrect and the true capacity was 1,055 tonnes, a figure that was discernable by looking at the shipping documents, which

---

at 8; see also *Salthill Properties Ltd v Royal Bank of Scotland* [2009] IEHC 207, discussing *McMullen v Clancy (No. 2)* [2005] 2 I.R. 445; *AIB Plc v Diamond* [2011] IEHC 505.
[98] [1966] I.R. 646.
[99] (1972) 223 E.G. 1473.
[100] [1978] 2 All E.R. 1134; Brownsword (1978) 41 M.L.R. 735.

the marine manager had seen. In an action for non-payment, the defendant counterclaimed under s.2(1) of the 1967 Act. A majority of the Court of Appeal held the proviso inapplicable on the ground that the plaintiffs could not show that it was reasonable for their marine manager to rely on recollection rather than to consult the shipping documents in question. The case is also of interest because the Court of Appeal did not hold that a duty of care in tort is a *sine qua non* of liability—indeed, Denning M.R., dissenting, was of the view that the marine manager owed no duty of care and had not been careless. This point was clearly made by Moriarty J. in *O'Donnell v Truck and Machinery Sales*,[101] drawing attention to the fact that the English legislation was to govern disputes where no duty of care existed. Furthermore, Moriarty J. followed the earlier English case of *Gran Gelato Ltd v Richcliff (Group) Ltd*[102] in holding that even if there is fault on the part of the misrepresentee, liability will result; the fault of the misrepresentee may lead to damages being reduced under s.45(1) by way of a finding of contributory negligence under the Civil Liability Act 1961.

11–32 The remedy under s.45(1) was enacted in order to supplement the shortcomings of the range of remedies then otherwise available. It does not as such create a new statutory cause of action for persons who would otherwise have to satisfy other criteria. In *Resolute Maritime Inc v Nippon Kaiji Kyokai*,[103] Mustill J. held that the representee could not use s.2(1) of the 1967 Act to make an agent liable in damages under s.2(1) for any misrepresentation made by the agent within the scope of his authority. Mustill J. reasoned that the law of tort, through deceit and *Hedley Byrne*, conferred upon the misrepresentee a cause of action and that the law would develop along irrational lines if the misrepresentee could always side-step the "special relationship" requirement in *Hedley Byrne* by simply invoking the 1967 Act. Similarly, in *Phoenix International Life Services Inc v Rilett*[104] the receiver of a company made statements about the value of the company, subsequently found to be inaccurate in a due diligence exercise. Even if these statements could be held to have been statements of fact the receiver, as agent of the company, could not be held liable in damages under s.2(1) of the 1967 Act. These decisions suggest that in interpreting s.2(1), the court must examine the section in the general context within which it is to operate, specifically monetary remedies available at the time of the passing of the 1967 Act.

11–33 This approach has wider ramifications. The view previously held about the scope of s.2(1) of the 1967 Act and its relationship with the rule in *Bain v Fothergill*[105] has come under attack. According to *Watts v Spence*[106]

---

[101] [1997] 1 I.L.R.M. 466. Reversed by the Supreme Court at [1998] 4 I.R. 191 but not on this point.
[102] [1992] Ch. 560.
[103] [1983] 1 W.L.R. 857.
[104] [2001] B.C.C. 115.
[105] (1874) L.R. 7 H.L. 158, repealed in Ireland by s.53 of the Land and Conveyancing Law Reform Act 2009.
[106] [1976] Ch. 165.

all the victims of a misrepresentation (made in relation to the vendor of a real property's capacity to make a good title) had to do, in order to avoid the above rule (which limited damages to expenses incurred), was to invoke s.2(1). In *Sharneyford Supplies Ltd v Edge*,[107] Mervyn Davies J. refused to follow *Watts v Spence* on this point because the 1967 Act did not remove the requirement that, before *Bain v Fothergill* could be avoided, the vendor must be shown to have been in default. This aspect of s.2(1) of the 1967 Act is not germane to the Irish situation because s.43 confines s.45(1) to contracts for the sale of goods, hire-purchase and the supply of a service. In *Spencer v Irish Bank Resolution Corp*[108] Costello J. held that a life insurance bond, which the plaintiff had purchased after receiving what he claimed was misleading information, could not be regarded as leading to damages under section 45 of the Act. A preliminary brochure did contain inaccurate information but as it was not reasonable to regard the brochure as forming part of the loan contract, the defendants were successful in denying liability in tort and contract.

11–34 The usefulness of the statutory right to damages has been re-enforced by the decision of the Court of Appeal in *Production Technology Consultants v Bartlett*.[109] The defendant made an innocent misrepresentation in relation to land, the sale of which was made on the basis of the misrepresentation. The falsity of the representation became known to the plaintiff just prior to completion but the plaintiff still closed the purchase. The defendant submitted that in closing the sale, the plaintiff lost any right to damages by affirmation of the contract— the plaintiff must rescind and seek damages. The Court of Appeal rejected this submission. Affirmation of a contract may lead to loss of the right to rescind, but, following *Arnison v Smith*,[110] affirmation does not result in loss of a right to damages. However, s.2(1) of the 1967 Act has been held to be inapplicable to contracts uberrimae fidei unless there is a misrepresentation in the sense of an express statement rather than simple non-disclosure. The authority in question is the decision of the Court of Appeal in *Banque Financière de la Cité S.A. v Westgate Insurance Co Ltd*,[111] although the decision of the Court of Appeal was affirmed on other grounds by the House of Lords,[112] their Lordships declining to deal with this point, amongst others.

11–35 There remains one very important matter. What measure of compensation is available under s.45(1)? The section itself points to a tortious measure—"shall be so liable" seems to refer back to the measure in deceit. In *F & H Entertainments v Leisure Enterprises*[113] the tort measure was favoured.

---

[107] [1987] 1 All E.R. 588, reversing [1985] 1 All E.R. 976.
[108] [2015] IE HC 395, para.133.
[109] [1988] 1 E.G.L.R. 182. For proof of reliance and loss in relation to fraudulent misrepresentation and s.45(1), see the discussion in *Fitzroy Robinson Ltd v Mentmore Towers Ltd* [2009] EWHC 1552 (TCC) and cases cited therein.
[110] (1889) 41 Ch. D. 348 at 371 per Cotton L.J.
[111] [1989] 2 All E.R. 952.
[112] [1990] 2 All E.R. 947.
[113] (1976) 120 S.J. 331.

In *Davis & Co v Afa Minerva*[114] it was held that all consequential loss arising from the malfunctioning of a burglar alarm could be recoverable and it was not necessary to distinguish between the statutory cause of action and contractual warranties; see also Denning M.R. in *Jarvis v Swans Tours*.[115] Nevertheless, it is generally agreed that if the measure of compensation cannot include damages for loss of bargain, in appropriate cases, the statutory right to damages is not flexible enough. In contrast, s.6 of the New Zealand Contractual Remedies Act 1979 directs the contract measure will always be the measure of compensation! There is, as yet, no conclusive answer to this question in Ireland. In England, while *Watts v Spence*[116] indicates that damages for loss of bargain may be available, this case has not been followed in *Sharneyford Supplies Ltd v Edge*. Yet in that case Mervyn Davies J. expressly kept this point open: "I do not decide whether or not such damages for innocent misrepresentation embrace any element for loss of bargain." However, the matter seems to have been settled, for the moment, by a two-judge Court of Appeal, in *Royscot Trust Ltd v Rogerson*.[117] Here the Court of Appeal held that the tortious, rather than the contractual, measure should be awarded under the statutory cause of action. The Court of Appeal went on to hold that the relevant tortious measure is that for deceit rather than negligence. This means that the plaintiff is able to recover any loss which flowed from the defendant's fraud, even if it could not be foreseen.[118] So, in *Royscot Trust*, a finance company was held entitled to recover all losses incurred when financing a car-purchase agreement with a crooked dealer, even if the losses were unforeseeable.

Remedies

The Equitable Right of Indemnity

11–36 Although an action for damages is not permitted for an innocent misrepresentation, some limited pecuniary remedy is permitted to a representee where the terms of the contract have required the representee to make this expenditure. The courts have been careful to limit the right of indemnity for it is often difficult to distinguish expenditure required by the contract from expenditure envisaged by the contract. In the New Zealand case of *Power v Atkins*[119] the plaintiff agreed to purchase a hotel after an innocent misrepresentation had been made to him. The plaintiff repudiated the contract when he discovered the true facts. The plaintiff sued for the return of

---

[114] (1974) 2 Lloyd's Rep. 27; *Abbey National v McCann* [1997] N.I.J.R. 150; *Clef Aquitaine SARL v Laporte Materials (Barrow) Ltd* [2001] Q.B. 488.
[115] [1973] 2 Q.B. 233.
[116] [1976] Ch. 165.
[117] [1991] 3 All E.R. 294; *Naughton v O'Callaghan* [1990] 3 All E.R. 191; *Pankhania v Hackney* [2004] EWHC 323 (Ch).
[118] *Smith New Court Securities v Scrimgeour Vickers (Asset Management) Ltd* [1996] 4 All E.R. 769. Their Lordships were less than enthusiastic about the *Royscot* decision above. See also *GE Commercial Finance Ltd v Gee* [2006] 1 Lloyd's Rep. 337.
[119] [1921] N.Z.L.R. 763.

the deposit paid and expenses such as board and lodging, advertising, train fares, preliminary expenses, an accountant's fee for investigating the account, a valuer's fee, and the cost of investigating legal title. Salmon J. permitted recovery of the deposit as well as legal fees incurred in researching title. The accountant's fee was irrecoverable but a fee paid to a valuer of stock in trade was allowable on proof that the contract required this valuation be made. All other expenses were rejected as being appropriate to a claim in damages. The difficulty and uncertainty surrounding this doctrine is illustrated by the fact that another New Zealand judge, in the case of *Duncan v Rothery*,[120] also decided in 1912, held legal fees to be irrecoverable in the equitable action for an indemnity. The leading English case is *Whittington v Seale Hayne*.[121] The defendants leased farm premises to the plaintiff, representing that the premises were in sanitary condition. The lease required the plaintiff to carry out any repairs required by the local council. The water supply was polluted, causing an outbreak of disease which wiped out the commercial value of the plaintiff's poultry and made the farm manager and his family ill. The local authority required the drains to be repaired and the house made fit for human habitation. The plaintiff sought to recover the value of stock, consequential loss in the form of lost sales and loss of the breeding potential of the stock, and medical and removal expenses. Because the only payment rendered necessary by the lease was for the repairs done to the premises, the amounts recoverable were limited to such repairs, the other items being, in reality, a claim for damages.

11–37 Section 43 of the 1980 Act, does not permit an action for damages under s.45(1) when real property forms the subject matter of a contract.

Rescission—When will the Right to Rescind be Lost?

(i) When the contract is executed

11–38 In *Legge v Croker*[122] the defendant innocently misrepresented that a leasehold interest he was about to sell to the plaintiff was not subject to any public right of way. The transfer was executed. Manners L.C. held that an executed lease could not be set aside, even under the wider equitable jurisdiction to rescind, unless there is a fraudulent misrepresentation. This statement was taken up by later courts and forged into a doctrine commonly known as the doctrine in *Seddon v North Eastern Salt*[123]; this rule provides that where a contract has been executed, it will only be set aside in equity where there has been equitable fraud. The rule was not confined to cases where land formed the subject-matter of the contract. In *Lecky v Walter*[124] the plaintiff purchased bonds, issued by a Dutch company. The plaintiff had been told that the bonds were secured and that in the event of a liquidation his claim would

---

[120] [1921] N.Z.L.R. 1074.
[121] (1990) 82 L.T. 49.
[122] (1811) 1 Ball & B. 506.
[123] [1905] 1 Ch. 326.
[124] [1914] I.R. 378.

take priority as a security. The bonds were not so secured and were in fact virtually worthless. The plaintiff's action for rescission failed. It was held that an executed contract can only be repudiated if the representation is fraudulent or if the plaintiff has suffered a total failure of consideration. In *Lecky v Walter* the plaintiff could not make out a case under either of these exceptions.

11–39 The rule has been attacked: see, in particular, the English Court of Appeal's decision in *Leaf v International Galleries*.[125] Section 1(b) of the 1967 Act, giving effect to the Law Reform Committee's recommendation for reform, provides that no matter what the subject matter of the contract may be, the fact that a contract has been executed should not impede rescission. Section 44(b) of the 1980 Act is based on the desire to sweep away the rule but, again, s.43 of the 1980 Act prevents this. Most of the cases that arise under *Seddon* are cases involving land and such contracts are outside the 1980 Act. Even the decision in *Lecky v Walter* would not be different—shares are choses in action and cannot be goods—see *Lee & Co (Dublin) Ltd v Egan (Wholesale) Ltd*[126]— so further reforms are necessary here too.

(ii) Affirmation

11–40 Should the misrepresentee obtain full knowledge of the facts and the existence of a misrepresentation, and if the misrepresentee is aware of his right to rescind,[127] then any declaration of intent to proceed, or any action which is evidence of such an intention, will be held to be an affirmation of the contract. The misrepresentee thus loses any right to rescind the contract. However, in *Lutton v Saville Tractors Ltd*[128] Carswell J. held that the right to rescind is only lost if the misrepresentation is known to the misrepresentee, so, the fact that the plaintiff was unaware of the existence of a misrepresentation at the time he retained the defective motor vehicle (the alleged acts of affirmation) could not constitute an affirmation: loss of the right of rescission, due to affirmation of the contract by the misrepresentee, does not prevent the misrepresentee from obtaining a remedy in damages; see *Production Technology Consultants v Bartlett*.[129]

(iii) Delay in seeking relief or "laches"

11–41 Because rescission will generally be sought in equity, the equitable doctrine that litigants should seek equitable relief promptly may operate here.

---

[125] [1950] 2 K.B. 86.
[126] Unreported, High Court, December 18, 1979. This point may well have been overlooked in *Donnellan v Dungoyne Ltd*, [1995] 1 I.L.R.M. 388. In *Darlington Properties v Meath County Council* [2011] IEHC 70, Kelly J. left open "the interesting topic of whether the remedy of rescission is available in cases of contracts induced by negligent misrepresentation". Presumably the argument would be that *Seddon* arose at a time when negligent misstatement/ negligent misrepresentation was not a cause of action.
[127] *Peyman v Lanjani* [1984] 3 All E.R. 703.
[128] [1986] N.I. 327.
[129] [1988] 1 E.G.L.R. 182.

The doctrine of laches, as well as the Statute of Limitations 1957 may prevent equitable relief. The courts have shown a willingness to hold that the victim of a fraudulent misrepresentation need not be as prompt as someone who has contracted on the strength of an innocent misrepresentation. In *O'Kelly v Glenny*[130] the plaintiff, in ignorance of the full value of her interest in her deceased father's estate, sold the interest to her solicitor who fraudulently misrepresented her position. Ten years later an action setting the transfer aside was brought. Laches was held not to prevent rescission; see also *Murphy v O'Shea*.[131] If the defrauded party, on learning of the fraud, fails to rescind within a reasonable time, however, acquiescence will be imputed; delay of 27 and 54 years would clearly be fatal to a claim of rescission; see *Hovenden v Lord Annesley*.[132]

11–42 The victim of an innocent misrepresentation is not treated so indulgently. In *Leaf v International Galleries*[133] an innocent misrepresentation that a picture, "Salisbury Cathedral", was painted by the famous Romantic painter John Constable was made at the time of sale. Five years later the purchaser learnt this was untrue. He claimed rescission on the ground of innocent misrepresentation. The Court of Appeal held the action must fail. By analogy with other sale of goods cases the right to rescind is lost if it is not sought within a reasonable time after the sale. Five years was not a reasonable time. Jenkins L.J. noted that the proper remedy was breach of warranty and not rescission; it may be that the plaintiff sued for rescission to avoid a finding that the statement as to the identity of the painter was not a contractual term; see also *Mihaljevic v Eiffel Tower Motors*.[134]

11–43 In *Dillon Leech v Maxwell Motors Ltd*[135] the plaintiff purchased a car on the basis of an oral representation that the vehicle was reliable and suitable for long journeys; these statements were untrue. There were several incidents in which the vehicle demonstrated its unreliability, yet the plaintiff retained the vehicle. While this delay no doubt prejudiced his equitable right to rescind, Murphy J. was able to hold that the defendants had subsequently accepted the purchaser's offer to effect a return of the vehicle. The courts have also been obliged to consider in sale of goods cases whether a right to rescind can be lost through acceptance of the goods. *Lutton v Saville Tractors Ltd*[136] seems to indicate a broader view of this issue for Carswell J. held that s.35(1) of the

---

[130] (1846) 9 Ir.Eq.R. 25.

[131] (1845) 8 Ir.Eq.R. 329.

[132] (1806) 2 Sch. & Lef. 637. These are extreme situations involving fraud/unconscionable bargains. Although not a misrepresentation case, there is a useful discussion in *McGrath v Stewart* [2008] IEHC 348; and see also *Pierson v Keegan Quarries Ltd* [2010] IEHC 404.

[133] [1950] 2 K.B. 86. The correctness of *Leaf v International Galleries* has been doubted by the English Court of Appeal in *Salt v Stratstone Specialist Ltd* [2015] EWCA Civ. 745. For a comment on the *Salt* decision see [2016] C.L.J. 15.

[134] [1973] V.R. 545.

[135] [1984] I.L.R.M. 624.

[136] [1986] N.I. 327.

Sale of Goods Act 1979 did not operate against the buyer when the buyer co-operates with the seller in seeking to have the goods repaired.

11–44 It should also be noted that, in Ireland, a second ground in *Leaf v International Galleries* for refusing rescission would have been the rule in *Seddon's* case; the Republic's 1980 Act would now remove such an objection if *Leaf v International Galleries* was an Irish case occurring after 1980; see s.44(b).

(iv) Third party rights

11–45 Although one early Irish case holds a fraudulent conveyance by A to B to be void and not merely voidable—*O'Connor v Bernard*[137]—it is now established that fraud renders a contract voidable and not void unless the party seeking to invalidate the transfer of property can show that the misrepresentation had the further effect of rendering the contract void at common law, as in *Cundy v Lindsay*,[138] as limited by the decision in *Citibank NA v Brown, Shipley & Co Ltd*.[139]

11–46 Rescission will not be available if a third party acquires an interest in the property and can show he is a bona fide purchaser for valuable consideration. The leading Irish case is *Anderson v Ryan*.[140] Davis owned a mini. He answered a newspaper advertisement offering a Sprite motor car for sale. The parties agreed to swap vehicles, no money changing hands. The Sprite was a stolen vehicle. Davis was dispossessed of the Sprite but the gardaí eventually returned the Mini to Davis. The Mini had been the subject of two subsequent deals. The defendant purchased the vehicle from a person representing himself to be Davis. This person was, in all probability, the person who had misrepresented that he owned the Sprite. The defendant in turn sold the Mini to the plaintiff, Anderson, who was dispossessed by the gardaí. Anderson sued Ryan claiming that under ss.12(1) and 21(1) of the Sale of Goods Act 1893 (the "1893 Act"), Ryan lacked title to the goods at the time of the transfer of the property to him, Anderson. The Circuit Court judge found for Anderson. The decision was reversed on appeal to the High Court. Henchy J. found the essential issue to be whether Ryan had a good title to the car when he sold it to Anderson. Davis, the original owner had parted with the vehicle as a result of a fraudulent misrepresentation but this rendered the contract voidable. Because the contract between Davis and the rogue had not been avoided before the sale between Anderson and Ryan had been concluded, Ryan had, under the terms of s.23(1) of the 1893 Act, a valid, if voidable, title. This title was transferred to Anderson. As Henchy J. observed, the seizure of the Mini by the gardaí was a wrongful act and redress should be sought from that direction. *Anderson v Ryan* was distinguished in

---

[137] (1838) 2 Jones 654.
[138] (1878) 3 App. Cas. 459.
[139] [1991] 2 All E.R. 690.
[140] [1967] I.R. 34.

Mallett and Son (Antiques) Ltd v Rogers.[141] Here the plaintiff purchased an antique bookcase from the defendant. Unknown to both parties the bookcase had been stolen. The defendant sought to avoid liability to, inter alia, return the consideration, pleading *Anderson v Ryan*. Quirke J. held that *Anderson v Ryan* concerned a case where the purchaser obtained a good albeit voidable title. In this situation, however, there was no title transferred—the contract was void—and s.12 of the 1893 Act, as well as the fact that consideration had totally failed, gave the plaintiff rights to restitution and damages.

11–47 If property is transferred to a person who subsequently cannot be traced, rescission can be effected by informing the police of the fraud in the hope that property can be recovered; this will prevent further transactions involving the property from passing a good title to the transferee, even if he is an innocent third party; see *Car and Universal Finance Co v Caldwell*.[142]

11–48 In *Crystal Palace FC (2000) v Dowie*,[143] the importance of the parties being able to effect restitution was highlighted. The plaintiff sought to obtain a liquidated damages sum of £1 million when it negotiated a settlement agreement to rescind the defendant's contract of employment. The rescission was obtained by fraudulent misrepresentation and the £1 million was stipulated in that settlement agreement as being due compensation should the defendant take up employment with a Premiership club, which he did. The plaintiff argued that setting aside the settlement agreement would revive the contract of employment, but, even allowing for this, the remedy of rescission would not be available because the defendant could not be returned to his previous job with the plaintiff by the plaintiff, nor was the defendant free to resume employment with the plaintiff. Third-party rights made restitution impossible so Tugendhat J. ordered an inquiry into damages instead.

(v) Rescission—total or partial?

11–49 Where a person has been induced into giving a guarantee for past and future debts on the basis of an apparently fraudulent misrepresentation that the guarantee relates to future debts only, the High Court of Australia held in *Vadasz v Pioneer Concrete (SA) Pty Ltd*[144] that rescission in equity would not extend to the guarantee entirely. Rescission in part was ordered because the guarantor had the benefit of performance by the misrepresentor and the effect of the High Court's order was to leave the guarantor in the position represented. Nevertheless, the English Court of Appeal has recently reaffirmed the general view that partial rescission for misrepresentation is not generally possible; see *De Molestina v Ponton*.[145]

---

[141] [2005] IEHC 131.
[142] [1965] 1 Q.B. 525.
[143] [2007] I.R.L.R. 682.
[144] (1995) 184 C.L.R. 102; contrast *TSB Bank v Camfield* [1995] 1 All E.R. 951.
[145] [2002] 1 All E.R. (Comm.) 587. See also *ICDL GCC Foundation FZ–LLC v European Computer Driving Licence Foundation Ltd* [2012] IESC 55, where the contract could not be interpreted to give partial termination rights.

(vi) Power to award damages in lieu of rescission

11–50 Section 45(2) of the 1980 Act permits a court to declare a contract subsisting and award damages in lieu of rescission if the court is "of opinion that it would be equitable to do so". This statutory restriction on the right to rescind seems sensible given the restrictions developed by the courts on the right to rescind; see *Cehave N.V. v Bremer Handelsgesellschaft GmbH.*[146] It should be noted that until recently it was thought that the court may award damages in lieu of rescission only if the remedy of rescission was still available to the representee. If rescission has been lost because of lapse of time, affirmation or waiver, it is not possible to award damages under s.45(2). This is unfortunate; the discretion should not be so limited, particularly in cases where the doctrine of laches applies. In *Lutton v Saville Tractors Ltd*[147] Carswell J., *obiter*, considered whether the case could have been an appropriate instance in which damages should have been awarded in lieu of rescission. Carswell J. did not, however, give any guidance on the factors that will lead a court to award damages in lieu of rescission. Nor did the learned judge provide any indication of the appropriate measure of damages under s.2(2), for it is by no means certain that the deceit measure found in s.2(1) is also recoverable under s.2(2). However, guidance on both these points has been provided in two English cases. In *Thomas Witter Ltd v TBP Industries Ltd*[148] Jacob J. held that the right of a judge to grant damages under s.2(2) would survive the loss of any right to grant rescission. The same view was expressed by Jack J. in *Zanzibar v British Aerospace Ltd.*[149] However, in *William Sindall Plc v Cambridgeshire County Council*[150] doubts were expressed about this, and in *Floods of Queensferry Ltd v Shand Construction (No. 3)*,[151] the decision in *Thomas Witter* was disapproved, the view being taken that at the time of the hearing of an application for damages in lieu, rescission should still be a "live" remedy. Less controversy surrounds the second point. In *William Sindall Plc v Cambridgeshire County Council*[152] two members of the Court of Appeal indicated that the measure of damages under s.2(2) is rooted in the notion of indemnity for a breach of warranty and that to award all consequential loss, the s.2(1) measure, would be inappropriate in such situations. The first instance decision of Deeny J. in *Odyssey Cinemas Ltd v Village Theatres Three Ltd*[153] provides an interesting illustration of the circumstances in which damages in lieu of rescission might be awarded as part of the exercise of judicial

---

[146] [1975] 3 All E.R. 739.
[147] [1986] N.I. 327.
[148] [1996] 2 All E.R. 573.
[149] [2000] 1 W.L.R. 2333.
[150] [1994] 3 All E.R. 932.
[151] [2000] B.L.R. 81. It is not entirely clear what the English Court of Appeal decided on this point in *Salt v Stratstone Specialist Ltd* [2015] EWCA Civ. 745; see case-note at [2016] C.L.J. 15.
[152] [1994] 3 All E.R. 932.
[153] [2010] NI Ch 1.

discretion, but as the decision of Deeny J. was held to be wrong in principle by the Northern Ireland Court of Appeal, it is only an interesting exercise.[154]

(vii) Specific performance

11–51 Should the plaintiff be responsible for making a misrepresentation the defendant may avoid an action for specific performance by pleading the plaintiff's misrepresentation. This is discussed by Delany.[155] The representee may be permitted to obtain an injunction preventing the representor from continuing an action. Such an injunction was awarded to a misrepresentee in *Costello v Martin*.[156]

Section 46—the Exemption Clause

11–52 Section 46 attempts to control the extent to which persons may make false statements and then attempt to avoid or limit liability by way of an exemption clause. While *Pearson v Dublin Corp.*[157] is authority for the proposition that a fraudulent misrepresentation cannot be negatived by an express disclaimer from liability for false statements, there were no special rules governing the use of exemption clauses where one party was responsible for a misrepresentation. Section 46 provides:

> If any agreement (whether made before or after the commencement of this Act) contains a provision which would exclude or restrict (a) any liability to which a party to a contract may be subject by reason of any misrepresentation made by him before the contract was made, or (b) any remedy available to another party to the contract by reason of such a misrepresentation, that provision shall not be enforceable unless it is shown that it is fair and reasonable.

The "fair and reasonable" test has been considered above,[158] and the factors set out are of general application.

11–53 Of special interest under s.46 are the English decisions which consider the English counterpart to s.46. In *Walker v Boyle*[159] the vendor of land misrepresented that there were no disputes in relation to the boundaries of the

---

[154] The issue of contributory negligence may influence the decision of a court on whether to grant rescission or award damages in lieu of rescission. The court should hear evidence on the principles governing the award of damages for breach of warranty and s.45(2) before deciding on this point: *Odyssey Cinemas Ltd v Village Theatres Three Ltd* [2010] NICA 25. The law in the UK and Ireland on contributory negligence in contract is quite different.
[155] [1951] Ir. Jur. 51. See Delany, *Equity and the Law of Trusts in Ireland*, 6th edn (Dublin: Round Hall, 2016), Ch.14.
[156] (1867) 1 Ir.Rep.Eq. 50.
[157] [1907] A.C. 351.
[158] See Ch.8.
[159] [1982] 1 W.L.R. 495: contrast *McGrath v Shah* (1989) 57 P. & C.R. 452.

land to be sold. This was an incorrect statement. The contract provided that "no error, mis-statement or omission in any preliminary answer concerning the property ... shall annul the sale". This exclusion clause, despite the fact that it was a term in the English Law Society Standard Conditions of Sale for many years, was denied effect. In *Southwestern General Property Co v Marton*[160] the misrepresentation appeared in an auctioneer's particulars of sale and gave readers of the particulars the impression that planning permission would be available in relation to a site if a suitable development were proposed. The catalogue attempted to exclude liability for any misrepresentation contained therein. The exclusion clause was denied effect. Here the sale was concluded by auction and the purchaser had bid for the property at short notice. There was no possibility of the purchaser making the normal inquiries before he was bound. A similar conclusion was reached in *Production Technology Consultants v Bartlett*.[161] In Ireland, s.46 cannot operate within the context of contracts for the sale of land and it remains possible for the agreement itself to control the misrepresentee's range of remedies following certain innocent misrepresentations. See the provisions of Condition No. 21 of the 1978 edition of the *General Conditions of Sale of the Incorporated Law Society of Ireland*, discussed in *Keating v Bank of Ireland*.[162]

The Duty to Disclose and Silence as a Misrepresentation— *Uberrimae Fidei*

11–54 In the early part of this chapter we talked of a misrepresentation in terms of being a false "statement". Can silence constitute a statement? It is generally held that silence or failure to disclose a material fact may constitute a misrepresentation only in exceptional cases. If I have made a statement which, while true at the time it was uttered, is subsequently rendered false by subsequent events, my failure to advise of the change will constitute a misrepresentation.[163] This duty arises out of the fact that in making a positive statement, particularly at the commencement of negotiations, any subsequent alteration of those facts prior to either the abandonment of the negotiations or the conclusion of the contract must be disclosed. So, in *Spice Girls Ltd v Aprilia World Service B.V.*[164] a company approached Spice Girls Ltd with a view to concluding a year-long sponsorship deal. Prior to the contract being concluded Spice Girls Ltd became aware that one member of the group intended to leave within the sponsorship period. Failures not only to disclose this fact, but the making of repeated promises about the composition of the group, were held to be actionable misrepresentations. Even if there is no appreciable time lag, silence may distort other statements made. So, in *Carey v*

---

[160] (1982) 263 E.G. 1090.
[161] [1988] 1 E.G.L.R. 182.
[162] [1983] I.L.R.M. 295. The current version dates from 2009.
[163] *Davies v London and Provincial Marine Ins. Co* (1878) 8 Ch. D. 469.
[164] [2002] EWCA Civ 15. *Fitzroy Robinson Ltd v Mentmore Towers* [2009] EWHC 1552 (TCC).

Independent Newspapers Ltd[165] the editor of a newspaper offered the plaintiff an employment contract, but failed to disclose that senior management had expressed reservations about the working conditions negotiated by the plaintiff. Failure to disclose this material fact was both an actionable misrepresentation and breach of contractual warranty. It may be that conduct may be viewed as involving a misrepresentation. In the interesting Hong Kong case of *Green Park Properties Ltd v Dorku Ltd*[166] it was held that the vendor's action of taking a prospective purchaser of a flat into a yard was to be taken to constitute a representation that the yard was part of the property to be sold when in fact it was a common part. On the other hand, if I agree to sell goods there is no obligation on me, the seller, to advise the buyer of material facts which may influence his decision to purchase. The case of *Gill v McDowell*[167] conditions this second proposition somewhat. The purchaser of the hermaphrodite animal thought he was buying either a cow or a bull. The seller failed to disclose the true facts. Because the animal was sold in a market where cow or bulls were sold, the seller was held to be under a duty of disclosure. The decision may have been different had the buyer purchased the animal while visiting the seller's property. The fact that the Irish courts have developed a duty of disclosure in the context of contracts to sell animals, a not unreasonable development in a primarily agricultural society, is further illustrated in *Kennedy v Hennessy*.[168] Gibson J. there declared that to sell a yearling heifer in calf without disclosing this fact—such an animal being less valuable because of the dangers of such an early pregnancy—may be actionable if the seller has knowledge of this. The parties may themselves create a contractual duty to make full disclosure of all material facts and if this subsequently turns out not to have been done the contract may be avoided; see *Munster Base Metals Ltd v Bula Ltd*.[169] In *Geryani v O'Callaghan*[170] the purchaser of property rescinded a contract of purchase upon discovery that certain defects had not been disclosed. While Costello J. held that the general law did not make such disclosure obligatory, the conditions of contract, specifically the Law Society General Conditions of Sale, made disclosure necessary under the terms of the contract. A similar issue arose in the English Court of Appeal in *Sykes v Taylor-Rose*.[171] The defendants discovered that the house they had purchased had been the scene of a gruesome murder and sought advice from their solicitor on whether they had any remedy. The advice given was that the vendor had no duty to disclose and that the defendants, in turn, would have no duty to disclose when they sold the property on. The defendants sold on the property to the plaintiffs, responding to a question from the plaintiffs' solicitor that they did not know any other

---

[165] *Irish Times Law Reports,* November 3, 2003.
[166] [2001] H.K.L.R.D. 139.
[167] [1903] 2 I.R. 463. If the seller is a trader and the buyer a consumer, see now the Consumer Protection Act 2007 s.46.
[168] (1906) 40 I.L.T.R. 84.
[169] Unreported, High Court, July 27, 1983.
[170] Unreported, High Court, January 25, 1995.
[171] [2004] EWCA Civ 299.

information which the buyer may have had a right to know. The Court of Appeal had to consider whether there was a misrepresentation in the form of the response to this question, but after expressing considerable sympathy for the plaintiffs, held that no misrepresentation had been made, the defendants having given an honest answer to the question.

11–55 The obligation to disclose has been considered in the context of sale of leasehold property which is subject to restrictive covenants. In *Power v Barrett*[172] the plaintiff, lessee of premises in Abbey St, Dublin, wanted to sell his lease, which was to his knowledge subject to a covenant that the lessee would not carry on any dangerous, noxious or offensive trade. He sold his interest to a chandler, who wanted to store oil on the premises. This would breach the restrictive covenant. The defendant pulled out of the contract when he learnt of the covenant. Chatterton V.C. refused to order specific performance against the chandler: "if a purchaser states the object which he has in purchasing and the seller is silent as to a covenant in a lease prohibiting or interfering with that object, his silence would be equivalent to a representation that there was no such prohibitory covenant." This rule applies to sales of leasehold interests only. The duty of disclosure applies even to clauses the "representor" is unaware of; see *Flight v Barton*.[173] Equity has required the vendor of property to disclose any unusual defects in title, a proposition laid down in 1885 and reaffirmed in *Rignall Developments Ltd v Hill*.[174] A more celebrated example of a duty of disclosure in a property context is found in the New York case of *Stambovsky v Ackley*.[175] The plaintiff sought the return of a deposit paid by him to the defendant in order to purchase a large Victorian house. The plaintiff withdrew from the contract when he discovered that the house was haunted by three ghostly figures attired in colonial dress. On appeal, it was held that there was a duty of disclosure and that silence constituted misrepresentation on the part of the defendant. This decision turns upon equitable rescission and is thus distinguishable from that reached by the English Court of Appeal in *Sykes v Taylor Rose*[176] on the basis of there being no disclosure by the defendant here as distinct from the partial disclosure in *Stambovsky v Ackerley*. In the Ontario case of *Dennis v Gray*[177] a motion was brought seeking to dismiss a claim that the defendants, vendors of a house, were liable in respect of non-disclosure of a "latent defect" relating to that property when failing to inform the purchasers that a person living on the opposite side of the street had convictions in respect of child pornography. This was a matter of common knowledge in the neighbourhood. While the decision is inconclusive in the sense that the court found the plaintiff's case was not such as to disclose no cause of action,

---

[172] (1887) 19 L.R. (Ir.) 450.
[173] (1832) 3 My. & K. 282.
[174] [1988] Ch. 190.
[175] 572 N.Y.S. (2d) 672 (1991).
[176] [2004] EWCA Civ 299.
[177] (2011) 333 D.L.R. (4th) 376.

situations of this kind are being increasingly litigated on the boundaries of mistake and misrepresentation.

11–56 A general duty to disclose does apply to fiduciary relationships. It has been said that the most fundamental obligation that the law can place upon a partner is the duty to display good faith towards his co-partners in all partnership dealings and transactions.[178] Each partner in negotiations concerning partnership assets must place before the others all material facts and must not conceal what that partner alone knows.[179] The English Court of Appeal has recently extended this duty into non-disclosure of material facts during negotiations leading up to the conclusion of a partnership. In *Conlon v Sims*[180] the defendant solicitor was negotiating with the plaintiffs with a view to forming a partnership. He failed to disclose acts of dishonesty in relation to the conduct of his legal practice, these acts emerging later in disciplinary proceedings. The Court of Appeal held that the duty to disclose arose as between prospective partners and that where there was a duty to disclose, non-disclosure was tantamount to an implied representation that there was nothing relevant to disclose and that where fraud is made out, damages in default may be recoverable. A failure to disclose material facts was held fatal in *Dunbar v Tredennick*[181] where the transfer was between agents and trustees on the one hand, and principal and beneficiary on the other. Members of a family are also under an obligation to disclose all material facts; see *Leonard v Leonard*,[182] and the obligation is imposed in a diverse range of transactions, such as agreements to vary the terms of a will, or settle or transfer property. In some instances the duty to make full and frank disclosure will operate within a family context because statute requires it. The leading English cases involve agreements struck during matrimonial proceedings. Should an agreement be made, one spouse failing to disclose to the other party, and the court, some material circumstance, such as an intention to remarry, then the settlement may be liable to amendment; see *Livesy v Jenkins*.[183] In certain types of commercial contracts, exceptional circumstances may need to be disclosed. For example, in suretyship contracts, the creditor may be under a duty to disclose to a guarantor facts of which the creditor is aware which make the risk to which the guarantor is to be exposed an unusual one, or a risk materially different to that which the surety would normally expect. So, in *Levett v Barclays Bank Plc*[184] the plaintiff was not told that the arrangements between the debtor and the bank made the plaintiff's treasury stock—the property being put up by

---

[178] *Lindley and Banks on Partnership*, 19th edn (London: Sweet & Maxwell, 2010), para.10–92; Twomey, *Partnership Law* (Dublin: Butterworths, 2000), para.15.14.
[179] *Law v Law* [1905] 1 Ch. 140 at 157 per Cozens-Hardy L.J.
[180] [2007] 2 All E.R. 802
[181] (1813) 2 Ball & B. 304.
[182] (1812) 2 Ball & B. 171.
[183] [1985] A.C. 424; *Border v Border* [1986] 2 All E.R. 918.
[184] [1995] 2 All E.R. 615; the duty is limited to unusual features as in *North Share Ventures Ltd v Anstead Holdings* [2011] EWCA Civ 230.

the plaintiff—virtually worthless. The contract was set aside. In an important recent judgment, the English High Court has stretched the duty to disclose beyond partnerships and fiduciaries by concentrating on duties of good faith in joint venture situations that are underpinned by a contract. *Ross River Ltd v Cambridge City Football Club*[185] concerned a contract to sell the freehold of a football ground in order to develop the land for residential housing. The transaction meant that the sellers, the football club, stood to gain considerable amounts if the number of housing units were maximised during the planning process. The sale agreements contained mutual co-operation covenants. The buyer's agent gave false assurances, misleading statements and failed to disclose material facts. While Briggs J. said that duties of good faith will not lightly be implied in commercial contracts, especially where there are detailed contractual arrangements in place between parties of comparable bargaining power, an analysis of the contract indicated that it was a joint venture analogous to that of a partnership. Although Briggs J. preferred to describe the duty as being rooted in an implied duty of good faith, as distinct from a fiduciary duty,[186] it was said to be an implied term that had something of the fiduciary duty embedded in it.

11–57 The most common instances of actionable non-disclosure concern insurance contracts. It is often said that when the prospective insured makes an application for insurance he is in the best position to know the circumstances surrounding the application.[187] This is certainly true in cases of life assurance and health insurance. The applicant is in the best position to know his age, health, and plans for the future. A failure to answer truthfully *and* disclose all material facts may each invalidate the insurance policy. If the contract is one of marine insurance, the Marine Insurance Act 1906 (the "1906 Act") still has effect in Ireland. This Act, largely a codification of mercantile practice, states the general duty, in s.18(1), as follows:

> Subject to the provisions of this section, the assured must disclose to the insurer, before the contract is concluded, every material circumstance which is known to the assured, and the assured is deemed to know every circumstance which, in the ordinary course of a business, ought to be known by him. If the assured fails to make such disclosure, the insurer may avoid the contract. Every circumstance is material which would influence the judgement of a prudent insurer in fixing the premium, as determining whether he will take the risk.

There are provisions within the 1906 Act that have recently been held to apply to both marine and non-marine insurance policies. The decision of a

---

[185] [2008] 1 All E.R. 1004.
[186] [2008] 1 All E.R. 1004 at 1055.
[187] See generally Bennett [1999] L.M.C.L.Q. 165.

very strong English Court of Appeal in *PCW Syndicates v PCW Reinsurers*[188] deals extensively with the relationship between the pre-1906 common law and provisions of the 1906 Act, particularly s.18. On the issue of materiality, it is material, for example, that the vessel to be insured has grounded[189] or that the cargo is to be carried on deck, a circumstance which is unusual and renders the cargo vulnerable.[190] In the case of *Seaman v Fonereau* the insured was held bound to disclose rumours that the vessel was leaking, and missing the next day, even though no actual proof was known to the insured, and it matters not that the report is in fact inaccurate.[191] In *The Elena G*,[192] David Steel J. said that the duty extends to rumours or reports of which the insured is aware, as long as they are not "mere speculations, vague rumours or unreasoned fears". Even if the insured bona fide believes the report is incorrect, this will not excuse non-disclosure.[193] Despite a recent case to the contrary,[194] it is clear that if at the time of placement of the application for insurance, a material fact of this kind is not disclosed, the insurer's right to subsequently avoid the policy is not inhibited by knowledge that the rumour or report was not well founded, e.g. because the insured brings forward evidence that the report, for example, was false and the court cannot overturn an avoidance on the basis of facts that come to light after the avoidance has been made by the insured.[195] The duty of disclosure is mutual, and applies both to insurer and insured, but it is not ipso facto a basis for the award of damages.[196] Fortunately for the assured there are limits on the duty, for the basis of the duty to disclose is an assumption that the assured is in the best position to know material circumstances. The assured does not have to disclose matters of common knowledge for, as s.18(3)(b) puts it, "the insurer is presumed to know matters of common notoriety or knowledge, and matters which an insurer in the ordinary course of his business, as such, ought to know ...". For this reason O'Hanlon J. in *Brady v Irish National Insurance Co Ltd*[197] held that a boat-owner's failure to inform his insurers of his intentions to lay up the boat over the winter and effect maintenance and repairs and cook in the galley during this time, did not entitle the company to avoid the policy. It was a matter of "common notoriety" that this occurred within the boat-owning fraternity. The decision was affirmed by the Supreme Court on this point. The decision of the Supreme Court[198] is noteworthy for the fact that both Finlay C.J. and McCarthy J. were critical of the use by the

---

[188] [1996] 1 W.L.R. 1136. See more recently *Brit UW Ltd v F&B Trenchless Solutions Ltd* [2015] EWHC 2237 (Comm) in which a contractor's liability policy was avoided for material non-disclosure and broker misrepresentation.

[189] *Russell v Thornton* (1860) 6 H. & N. 140.

[190] *Alluvials Mining Machinery Co v Stowe* (1922) 10 Lloyd's L.R. 96.

[191] (1723) 2 Stra. 1183; *Lynch and Jones v Hamilton* (1810) 3 Taunt. 37.

[192] [2001] 2 Lloyd's Rep. 378.

[193] *Shirley v Wilkinson* (1781) 3 Doug. 41.

[194] *The Grecia Express* [2002] 2 All E.R. (Comm.) 213.

[195] *Drake Insurance v Provident Insurance* [2003] 1 All E.R. (Comm.) 759; Midwinter [2003] L.M.C.L.Q. 158.

[196] *Westgate Insurance Co Ltd v Banque Financiere de la Cité SA* [1990] 2 All E.R. 947.

[197] [1986] I.L.R.M. 669.

[198] [1986] I.R. 698.

insurer of a marine insurance contract in the context of a pleasure craft in use on the Shannon and other inland waterways. This observation, however, has to be seen in the light of recent case law in which the courts have drawn attention to the fact that the 1906 Act, in many respects, does not create a regime that only operates in marine insurance cases: some of these provisions are declaratory of the common law also. One English case, decided within the spirit of the line of Irish cases that begin with *Aro Road*, discussed below, is particularly welcome. In *Economides v Commercial Insurance*[199] the Court of Appeal held that the duty of disclosure involves only a duty to be honest. In satisfying the test of subjectivity which is found in s.20(5) of the 1906 Act, the representor does not have to go further and impliedly represent that there are objectively reasonable grounds in existence which justify that belief. Further, it is only actual knowledge that is relevant to the duty of disclosure. Constructive knowledge is not imposed on the representor.

11–58 A proposal form may broaden or abridge the duty of utmost good faith by requiring the proposer to only disclose a range of information "to the best of the proposer's knowledge and belief", or a similar standard of knowledge.[200] The proposal form may also contain a restriction on the insurer's right to avoid the policy, in recognition that avoidance is an extreme remedy capable of operating harshly. The clause in *McAleenan v AIG (Europe) Ltd*[201] is a good example. Here, the insurer undertook not to avoid or modify the policy if the "alleged non-disclosure, misrepresentation or untrue statement was innocent and free of any fraudulent intent. The onus of proving otherwise shall be on the insurers". Cases of this kind are often standard in consumer or small business insurance but this is a concession made by the insurer, absent which, the insurer's rights to avoid are still heavily weighted in the insurer's favour.[202]

11–59 In many insurance contracts, however, the insurer may seek to place an even heavier duty on the shoulders of the insured. The insured, when completing the proposal form, may be asked questions, often about matters of fact which the insured may not be in a position to answer authoritatively or accurately, and will then be obliged to warrant that the answer is factually correct. The accuracy of all replies is said to be "the basis of the contract" and gives the insurer a possible ground for repudiation of the policy should the answer subsequently turn out to be inaccurate. However, the courts seek to narrow these "basis of contract" clauses wherever possible, either by denying the clause the character of a promissory warranty, as in *Fearnley v London Guarantee Insurance Co*,[203] or by reading any ambiguous warranties *contra proferentem*. In *Brady v Irish National Insurance Co Ltd*[204] the majority of the

---

[199] [1997] 3 W.L.R. 1066; Clarke [1998] C.L.J. 24.
[200] See *Synergy Health U.K. v CGU Insurance Plc* [2010] EWHC 2583 (Comm).
[201] [2010] IEHC 128.
[202] Marine Insurance Act 1906 s.18.
[203] (1882) 5 App. Cas. 911.
[204] [1986] I.R. 698.

Supreme Court held that use of a gas cooker in a galley while the vessel was laid up was within the concept of customary overhaul of the vessel and thus did not represent breach of an express warranty that the vessel would not be available for use during the laid-up period. The "basis of contract" clause can operate very harshly if the promise made relates to some matter about which the promisor has no special knowledge. In life assurance policies a warranty that the insured is in good health may be obtained. Should the insured not be in good health and the condition or illness manifests itself later, the insurer could repudiate the policy if the facts indicate that the latent condition or illness must have existed, unknown to all, on the date the warranty was given. Again, the Supreme Court has been protective of the insured when an insurer asserts the existence of an absolute warranty.

11–60 In *Keating v New Ireland Assurance Co Plc*[205] the defendant sought to avoid a life insurance policy on the ground, inter alia, that the policy contained an absolute warranty by the insured that he was in good health, when, unknown to the insured, he was suffering from angina (the insured believed he was suffering from a gastric disorder of no importance). In this case the alleged warranty was to be found in the policy and a declaration in the proposal form that the answers given "are true and complete". The Supreme Court held that the words used did not create the warranty claimed. McCarthy J., with whom Finlay C.J. and Hederman J. concurred, rejected the interpretation placed upon this contract of insurance by the insurers. In interpreting the words found in the contract itself—"the policy is conditional upon full and true disclosure"—McCarthy J. stated that the principles which govern the interpretation of a contract of insurance include the proposition that "if insurers desire to found the contract upon any particular warranty, it must be expressed in clear terms without any ambiguity", and, further, that "if there is any ambiguity, it must be read against the persons who prepared it".[206] Disclosure required disclosure of facts known to the insured and, in this case, the insured was unaware of his medical condition so the warranty was not breached. The case represents a considerable improvement in terms of consumer protection, for the Supreme Court now, essentially, requires the "basis of contract" warranty to be absolutely explicit before it will be enforced. McCarthy J. posed the following rhetorical question:

> "If the proposal form were to contain a statement by the proposer that the statements and answers written in the proposal together with the written statements and answers made to the company's medical examiner shall form the basis of the proposed contract 'even if they are untrue and incomplete for reasons of which I am totally unaware,' would there be any takers for such a policy?"[207]

---

[205] [1990] I.L.R.M. 110.
[206] [1990] I.L.R.M. 110 at 119.
[207] [1990] I.L.R.M. 110 at 119–120.

In *Coleman v New Ireland Assurance Plc*[208] the High Court has followed *Keating* in holding that avoidance for material non-disclosure in Ireland is available to an insurer only when the proposer knew of material facts which were not disclosed. The proposer failed to disclose medical tests for problems with her eyesight some years before. She was not told at that time that there was a chance that she would develop multiple sclerosis, a condition that unfortunately did materialise. Although two inaccurate answers were given on completing the proposal form, Clarke J. said that the essential question was whether there was a material failure to disclose matters within the knowledge of the proposer so as to lead the answer, for failure to disclose, as being properly described as untruthful.

11–61 If there is no "basis of contract" clause, or no warranty, however, it will be extremely difficult to avoid a policy concluded in good faith. In *Manor Park Homebuilders Ltd v AIG Europe (Ireland) Ltd*,[209] the defendants were insurers of a building that was the subject of a fire insurance policy. It had been represented that the building was secured by steel shutters and that there was a burglar alarm in place. In fact, the building had been largely bricked up and, at the time of the contract, the alarm was working but disconnection of the electricity caused the alarm to cease to function. In the context of insurance cover that was not followed up by any policy document, McMahon J. held that these statements were not warranties. Even if they were warranties, the alarm was operative upon the date of the contract and the defendant had failed to satisfy the onus of showing that the plaintiffs were giving a continuing representation that the alarm would continue to function[210]; putting a question or statement in the present tense may negate an intention to make it speak to future conduct or obligations.

11–62 However, if a "basis of contract" clause is made out, the answers given must be accurate. It is not necessary for the misstatement to be material in the sense that it would be an important factor which would influence the terms upon which risk would be assessed or the premium fixed. A graphic illustration is afforded by *Keenan v Shield Insurance Co Ltd*.[211] The policy was a household building and contents policy. The proposal form asked whether there had been any previous claim; the householder answered in the negative. In fact a claim for £53 in respect of fire damage to a pump had been made in the previous year. While this was a trivial and non-material misstatement, the plaintiff had warranted that the particular answers were true and complete in every respect, and as Blayney J. observed, even if the answer given was a trivial inaccuracy, "that would be no obstacle to the defendant repudiating the policy in view of the inaccuracy of the answers in the proposal form having

---

[208] [2009] IEHC 173.
[209] [2008] IEHC 174.
[210] Applying *Re Sweeney and Kennedy's Arbitration* [1950] I.R. 85 and *Hussain v Brown* [1996] 1 Lloyd's Rep. 627.
[211] [1987] I.R. 113. An appeal to the Supreme Court failed: [1988] I.R. 89.

been warranted by the plaintiff". Another very hard case, which illustrates the unfairness of the rule, is *Farrell v S.E. Lancs. Insurance Co Ltd.*[212] Farrell purchased a bus. An insurance broker filled in the proposal form on Farrell's behalf, misstating that Farrell had paid £800 for the vehicle when in fact only £140 was paid. The "basis of contract" clause invalidated the application. Although "basis of contract" clauses operate harshly and are generally not widely used in consumer contracts, there are many examples where they still operate in business insurance. One learned Irish commentator has used such clauses to illustrate the shortcomings in self-regulation and "soft law" solutions to disparity of bargaining power.[213]

11–63 It is often difficult to disentangle cases where the insured has falsely and fraudulently answered a question or has falsely and fraudulently failed to correct an impression created by an earlier, untruthful answer. Care should be taken to consider whether the facts of the case involve uttering a falsehood rather than a clear case of non-disclosure. An example of the former is provided by *Abbot v Howard.*[214] An applicant for life insurance was asked if he had been treated for certain diseases. He replied "No". The answer was false. The contract of insurance was held void because of the misrepresentation. If the insurer discovers that a fraudulent misrepresentation has been made and that the applicant has received payment, the Supreme Court's decision in *Carey v W.H. Ryan Ltd*[215] suggests that the insurer can seek a declaration that the contract is avoided and may trace the monies paid out on foot of the policy.

11–64 Where, however, the case involves simple non-disclosure of a material fact, fraud is not always material to the inquiry at all. The test is not intention to defraud but whether the misrepresentation related to a material fact. The duty to disclose all facts that a reasonable insurer would think material to the risk requires a lot of the insured; he is required to know what the insurer thinks material.

11–65 Nevertheless, Kenny J. in the Supreme Court, in *Chariot Inns Ltd v Assicurazioni Generali S.P.A. & Coyle Hamilton, Hamilton Phillips*[216] stated the test thus:

> "It is not what the person seeking insurance regards as material, nor is it what the insurance company regards as material. It is a matter or circumstance which would reasonably influence the judgment of a prudent insurer in deciding whether he would take the risk and, if so, in determining the premium which he would demand. The standard by which materiality is to be determined is objective, not subjective. The

---

[212] [1933] I.R. 36.
[213] Buckley, *Insurance Law*, 3rd edn (Dublin: Round Hall, 2012), para.1.20; [2005] C.L.P. 10.
[214] (1832) Hayes 381.
[215] [1982] I.R. 179.
[216] [1981] I.L.R.M. 173.

matter has, in the last resort, to be determined by the court: the parties to the litigation may call experts in insurance matters as witnesses to give evidence of what they would have regarded as material but the question of materiality is not to be determined by the parties."[217]

The *Chariot Inns* case represents the approach taken by Irish and English courts for decades, but in *Pan Atlantic Insurance Co v Pine Top Insurance Co*[218] the majority of the House of Lords, in a marine insurance case, reformulated the test so as to require that the information not disclosed be material in the sense that the prudent insurer would like to know this fact, even if it did not ultimately influence the decision to take the risk. This broadening of materiality is immediately countered by another requirement, that the insurer should be required to show that the non-disclosure induced the insurer into entering the contract. The post-*Pan Atlantic* cases indicate that the first factor, objective materiality, has a low threshold. The majority of the House of Lords posited this question: was the information that was not disclosed the kind of information that a prudent insurer would have wished to know? The second factor, subjective inducement, requires the underwriter to show that the facts presented via the non-disclosure were an effective cause of the decision to provide cover. So if the court holds that the insurer would have provided cover anyway, even if all the facts were before the insured, no inducement will be made out.[219] The *Pan Atlantic* decision has not been considered by an Irish court, and two Law Lords dissented strongly, and it may be that *Pan Atlantic* would not be followed here.

11–66 In *Chariot Inns* the Supreme Court held that a prudent insurer, in relation to an application for insurance on a building, would expect the applicant to disclose that a fire had occurred in a building owned by an associated company less than two years prior to the application. Similarly, an application for household insurance may be avoided if the applicant fails to disclose that he has criminal convictions; see *Schoolman v Hall*.[220] Sometimes, however, the applicant may feel a sense of grievance for it has been held that there may be no obvious correlation between the fact not disclosed and the risk to be covered. An obvious example of this is found in *Lambert v Co-operative Insurance Society Ltd*.[221] The policy was an "all risks" policy which provided cover in respect of jewellery owned by the plaintiff and her husband. When completing the proposal form the plaintiff failed to disclose that her husband, some years earlier, had been convicted of a dishonesty offence, and, later, her husband was convicted again of dishonesty offences but this was not disclosed at renewal of the policy. When a claim was made in respect of

---

[217] [1981] I.L.R.M. 173 at 174.
[218] [1994] 3 All E.R. 581; *Drake Insurance Plc v Provident Insurance Plc* [2004] 2 All E.R. (Comm.) 65; *North Star Shipping Ltd v Sphere Drake Insurance* [2006] EWCA Civ 378.
[219] *Assicurazioni Generali SpA v Arab Insurance Group* [2003] 1 All E.R. (Comm.) 140. See, in particular, Clarke L.J.'s judgment.
[220] [1951] 1 Lloyd's Rep. 139.
[221] [1975] 2 Lloyd's Rep. 485.

lost or stolen items the defendant refused to meet the claim. Because the test of materiality is that which the prudent insurer, not the reasonable insured, thinks material, the defendants were held to be entitled to refuse to meet the claim. McKenna J. found the law to be unsatisfactory, and seemed to be of the view that a reasonable insured would, like Mrs Lambert, think her husband's convictions to be irrelevant, and it must be conceded that the courts have, traditionally, been most accommodating to insurers in non-marine insurance cases. Refusal by another company to take a fire insurance application when the applicant sought car insurance has been held material in *Lockyer & Woolf Ltd v Western Australian Insurance Co.*[222] In *London Assurance v Mansel*[223] failure to disclose that other companies had turned down an application for life cover was held material to an application for life assurance. In *Mansel* it was also held that it did not matter that the applicant did not think the refusal was material because he felt the applications were turned down on grounds other than the state of his, the applicant's, health. The position of the insured is made all the more difficult by virtue of the fact that the Supreme Court, in *Carna Foods Ltd v Eagle Star Insurance Co*[224] has emphatically reaffirmed that there is no implied obligation on the insured to explain why an application for a new policy, or a renewal, has been turned down.

11–67 Many cases on materiality are straightforward. In life policies, it is relevant for the insurer to know the medical history of the assured as in *Kelleher v Irish Life Assurance Co Ltd*,[225] when a life policy was avoided on the ground that the insured failed to disclose that he had previously suffered from cancer and had suffered radiation damage as a result of treatment. Similarly, in *Curran v Norwich Union Life Insurance Society*[226] an incorrect declaration made by an applicant that he was in good health, when shortly before the application being made the applicant suffered a minor epileptic attack, probably as a result of a head injury the year before, rendered the policy unenforceable at the option of the insurer. However, the issue of materiality is a matter for the judge to rule on. There can be evidence, adduced by the insurer in the form of testimony given by other underwriters, but essentially the materiality of the fact withheld is to be decided by the judge. In *Aro Road and Land Vehicles Ltd v The Insurance Corp of Ireland Ltd*,[227] the facts of which are set out below at para.11–71, the Supreme Court overruled the judge at first instance, who had indicated that, while she did not feel that the fact withheld was material, expert testimony to the contrary was to be adopted. McCarthy J. observed that to defer to expert testimony is incorrect, for it is the judge who is "the sole and final arbiter" on materiality. This reluctance to allow "expert" testimony to prevail is to be welcomed. In *Manor Park Homebuilders Ltd v AIG Europe*

---

[222] [1936] 1 K.B. 408.
[223] (1879) 11 Ch. D. 363.
[224] [1997] 2 I.L.R.M. 499.
[225] Unreported, High Court, December 16, 1988.
[226] Unreported, High Court, October 30, 1987.
[227] [1986] I.R. 403.

(Ireland) Ltd,[228] McMahon J. found that there had not been a failure to disclose material facts—that a burglar alarm was not functioning and that the building insured was bricked up—simply because they were not material facts. In a fire-only policy the fitting or otherwise of a burglar alarm was not material while bricking up a building rather than installing metal shutters was held to provide greater protection against the risk of a fire being caused by an intruder than mere installation of metal shutters.

11–68 In cases where a life assurance contract is taken out where the insured misstates his age, the common law renders the contract void. The courts could not form an opinion as to the terms upon which the policy would have been effected if there had not been a misrepresentation, and permit limited recovery: see *Irish National Assurance Co v O'Callaghan.*[229] The Oireachtas stepped in to pass the Insurance Act 1936, s.64 of which permits such a calculation in contracts of industrial assurance, defined as life assurance contracts; see, on the 1936 Act, *McCarthy v New Ireland Assurance Co.*[230] If, however, the policy is a policy for health cover which involves the insurer making payments in order to replace lost earnings while the insured is out of work, the policy may require the insured to give a full disclosure of his medical condition. In *Harnedy v Century Insurance*[231] the court had to consider whether this kind of obligation is material or not. Harnedy failed to disclose that he was suffering from a heavy cold; this cold in fact was a symptom of a more serious condition that eventually led to him claiming on a disability insurance policy. Evidence from brokers suggested that the practice would have been to suspend the policy. McWilliam J. held the insurer had not established materiality.

11–69 The insurance companies are given other advantages by the courts over the insured, over and above the use of "basis of contract" clauses. In *Farrell's Case,*[232] the broker was seen as agent of the insured, not the insurer, thereby fixing the insured with the loss occasioned by the broker's mistake. Knowledge of surrounding circumstances will bind the insurance company's agents only in relation to facts made known while the agent is employed by the insurance company; see *Taylor v Yorkshire Insurance.*[233] If the broker acts as agent for the applicant and he fills in the application form incorrectly or fails to disclose a material fact the policy will not bind the insurance company. The applicant will be able to recover in an action against the broker; see *Chariot Inns Ltd v Coyle Hamilton, Hamilton Phillips.*[234] Should the insured's broker fail to inform the insurer when, after effecting the insurance, the broker learns of facts which may render the insurance contract invalid for material non-disclosure,

---

[228] [2008] IEHC 174.
[229] (1934) 68 I.L.T.R. 248.
[230] (1941) 75 I.L.T.R. 225.
[231] Unreported, High Court, February 22, 1983.
[232] [1933] I.R. 36.
[233] [1913] 2 I.R. 1.
[234] [1981] I.L.R.M. 173.

the broker may be liable to his client. In *Latham v Hibernian Insurance Co Ltd and Peter J. Sheridan and Co Ltd*[235] the second defendant obtained building insurance on behalf of the plaintiff, his client, from the first defendant. Shortly afterwards the second defendant discovered that the plaintiff had been guilty of dishonesty offences which rendered the insurance, in respect of a retail grocery and tobacconist shop, potentially invalid. In failing to inform the insurer the second defendant was in breach of the contractual duty owed to the plaintiff. The plaintiff lost the opportunity to consider whether to continue to trade, without insurance in all likelihood, or close the business altogether, thereby avoiding the loss of the premises as a result of fire. In general, constructive knowledge of the falsity of a representation made to an insurance company will not bind them. In *Griffin v Royal Liver Friendly Society*[236] the applicant for a burial insurance policy falsely stated he was in good health. The insured was examined by a doctor who failed to notice the true medical condition of the applicant. The company was held not to have constructive knowledge so as to estop it from declaring the policy void. The fact that an employee or agent of the insured obtains knowledge of the true facts from someone other than the insured or the insured's agent may be enough to sustain the insurance contract as long as that information is received in the course of that person's duty and employment; see *Woolcott v Excess Insurance.*[237] If information is obtained by the employee or agent purely in the course of socialising with friends, Blayney J. has held, in *Latham v Hibernian Insurance Co Ltd and Peter J. Sheridan and Co Ltd,*[238] that this knowledge will not generally suffice to impute knowledge to the insurer, although it is submitted, this must be a very general rule to be viewed in the light of each individual case.

11–70 On the other hand, an applicant is not obliged to do the insurance company's job for it. If the insured informs the company of all the circumstances surrounding an application and the company fails to pursue the matter and inquire further, the policy may still be valid; see *Kreglinger and Fernau Ltd v Irish National Insurance Co Ltd.*[239] In *Manor Park Homebuilders Ltd v AIG Europe (Ireland) Ltd,*[240] the insurers had been fully furnished with details of the property, the risk and the previous relationship between the applicant and insurers of the property. Yet no inspection took place, no documents were furnished; in particular, no policy was issued. After observing that the duty of the disclosure is "balanced by a reciprocal duty on the insurer to make its own reasonable inquiries", McMahon J. went on to hold that the insurer had failed to do so, observing rather pithily that "'uberrimae fidei' is not a charter

---

[235] Unreported, High Court, March 22, 1991; for restitution of premiums paid to the company, see *Byrne v Rudd* [1920] 2 I.R. 12. For the broker's liability in damages to the insurer, see *HIH Casualty and General Insurance Ltd v Chase Manhattan Bank* [2003] 2 Lloyd's Rep. 61.
[236] (1842) 8 Ir. Jur. Rep. 29.
[237] [1979] 1 Lloyd's Rep. 231.
[238] Unreported, High Court, March 22, 1991.
[239] [1956] I.R. 116.
[240] [2008] IEHC 174.

for indolent insurers". It is critical to note that the insured acted openly and honestly in this case. In contrast, the plaintiff in *Griffin v Royal Liver Friendly Society* was guilty of a fraudulent misrepresentation. The court was obviously reluctant to permit an estoppel to work in such a case.

Modification of the Standard of Disclosure in Ireland

11–71 The standard fixed by the courts over the last 150 years is onerous; the insured must disclose every material circumstance within the knowledge of the assured, and the proper question is, whether any particular circumstance was in fact material, and not whether the party believed it to be so.[241] From time to time suggestions for reform have centred around a revised definition of "material", such as a fact which would be considered material to a reasonable insured: see Law Reform Committee *5th Report*, 1957 (UK). While no movement has been made on the legislative front either in Ireland or the UK, the Supreme Court, in two cases, has substantially modified the standard of disclosure. In *Aro Road and Land Vehicles Ltd v Insurance Corp of Ireland Ltd*[242] the policy in question, property insurance in respect of goods being transported by road from Dublin to Maize, Co. Antrim, was negotiated over the phone between the insured and an agent of the insurer. No proposal form was completed—no details were requested other than identity of the goods and destination. After the goods had been destroyed by armed gunmen who burned the vehicle, the insurer sought to avoid the policy because it had not been revealed that the managing director of the plaintiff company had been convicted of receiving stolen goods some 19 years before. In holding the policy valid the Supreme Court reaffirmed that the general duty of disclosure is based upon the standard of that which a reasonable and prudent insurer would consider material in deciding to take the risk and on what terms. Henchy J., however, said that the rule has exceptions. In particular, "over-the-counter" insurance, effected by way of intermediaries such as airlines, shipping companies and travel agents, are insurance contracts where full disclosure is not a practical or reasonable possibility, and in these instances, the company is willing to provide insurance without requiring full disclosure. Henchy J. found that, looking at the circumstances in which this policy was concluded, the insurer's agent was "indifferent" about matters such as the personal circumstances of the managing director of the insured company. McCarthy J., with whom Walsh and Hederman JJ. agreed, was even more forthright in qualifying the standard of disclosure in cases of "one-off" or over-the-counter insurance concluded with a minimum of formality. McCarthy J. indicated that where there is no proposal form, and relevant questions are

---

241 Per Kenny J. in *Chariot Inns* [1981] I.L.R.M. 173.
242 [1986] I.R. 403. On the duty to disclose criminal convictions and Irish law, see Kilcommins (2002) 37 *Irish Jurist* 167. On the need for reform, see Kilcommins and O'Donnell (2003) 51 *Administration* 73, L.R.C. Report 84–2007. Under the terms of the Criminal Justice (Spent Convictions and Certain Disclosures) Act 2016, natural persons who were at least 18 years of age at the time of the commission of the offence may benefit from that Act if at least seven years have elapsed since the effective date of conviction and other elements in the Act are satisfied.

not asked to spur the memory, materiality may be tested by a standard other than that of the prudent insurer:

> "[I]f the judgement of an insurer is such as to require disclosure of what he thinks is relevant but which reasonable insured, if he thought of it all, would not think relevant, then, in the absence of a question directed towards the disclosure of such a fact, the insurer, albeit prudent, cannot properly be held to be acting reasonably. A contract of insurance is a contract of the utmost good faith on both sides."

McCarthy J. returned to this theme of the mutuality of the good faith obligation later in his judgment when he observed that the managing director's criminal conviction many years before had been forgotten by him. It was no longer a factor influencing his behaviour. The learned judge observed that the test remains one of "utmost good faith":

> "[H]ow does one depart from such a standard if reasonably and genuinely one does not consider some fact material; how much the less does one depart from such a standard when the failure to disclose is entirely due to a failure of recollection?"[243]

It is important to note that both Henchy and McCarthy JJ. considered these observations to be applicable to cases of honest failure to recollect: the concession would not be available in cases of fraudulent concealment of material facts. The Supreme Court returned to this area in *Keating v New Ireland Assurance Co Plc*.[244] Because the insured was unaware of the nature of his medical condition he was held not to be in breach of the duty of disclosure. McCarthy J. again emphasised that the duty of disclosure was based on good faith and the superior knowledge of the insured:

> "[O]ne cannot disclose what one does not know, albeit that this puts a premium on ignorance. It may well be that wilful ignorance would raise significant other issues; such is not the case here. If the proposer for life insurance has answered all the questions asked to the best of his ability and truthfully, his next-of-kin are not to be damnified because of his ignorance or obtuseness which may be sometimes due to a mental block on matters affecting one's health."[245]

The approach outlined above and the restrictions placed on the "basis of contract" clause in *Keating's* case are very much to be welcomed. Insurers should be required to be specific and efficient when insurance contracts are under negotiation: basic fairness so requires. Most recently, the Supreme Court,

---

[243] [1986] I.R. 403 at 413–414.
[244] [1990] I.L.R.M. 110.
[245] [1990] I.L.R.M. 110 at 116.

in *Kelleher v Irish Life Assurance*[246] held that the defendants had abridged the duty to make full disclosure from the way in which they had formulated the proposal form and presented the package to a large group of potential customers via a special promotional deal. However, these decisions are not unprecedented. Two Irish judges from the last century adopted forthright positions on this issue and it is to be welcomed that the Supreme Court has rediscovered this kind of radicalism. In *Rose v Star Insurance Co*[247] Richards B. said:

> "[I]t is most unjust to allow a company to disturb insurances after having taken the money of the party. The parties ensuring [*sic*] are frequently country gentlemen, ladies, and other persons knowing nothing about the law. The papers are generally filled in in the office of the company, and signed merely as a matter of form."

Earlier still, Smith B., dissenting in *Abbott v Howard*,[248] wrote:

> "Here, *ex hypothesi*, are two innocent parties; the Company and the Insured. Of these, which is in default? Which has been, in some degree negligent and remiss? Those who have not made an enquiry which they could have made; and which might have produced information, that we will assume to have been material? Or he, who innocently, (keep this in mind,) having answered the questions asked, happens to stop there, without any fraudulent motive for so doing? Where, if any, is the negligence or default? I should say, on the part of the innocent Company. And on whom is the loss and penalty to attach? On the found to be not less innocent Insured. Is this conformable to the rules usually applied to the case of two innocent persons, one of whom must suffer?"[249]

However, the duty of utmost good faith extends to all facets of the insurance contract. In *Fagan v General Accident*[250] the duty was held to extend even to the making of a claim and where the insured inflated the claim by 100 per cent, Murphy J. held this to constitute a breach of duty entitling the insurer to repudiate the contract.

11–72 The existence of the continuing duty of good faith is controversial and while it clearly subsists during the period within which the insurer has a right to repudiate the contract for breach,[251] it does not exist once proceedings have been issued, the rules of court regulating such matters.[252]

---

[246] [1993] I.L.R.M. 643.
[247] (1850) 2 Ir. Jur. 206.
[248] (1832) Hayes 381.
[249] (1832) Hayes 381 at 410–411.
[250] Unreported, High Court, February 19, 1993. See now *The Star Sea* [2001] 1 All E.R. 743; Eggers [2003] L.M.C.L.Q. 248 and Yeo (2003) 66 M.L.R. 425.
[251] *K.S. Merc-Skandia v Lloyds Underwriters* [2001] Lloyd's Rep. I.R. 802.
[252] *The Good Luck* [1989] 3 All E.R. 628; *The Star Sea* [2001] 1 All E.R. 743.

Contra proferentem

11–73 Two Irish cases provide clear guidance on the position to be adopted in the interpretation and construction of insurance contracts. In *Rohan Construction Ltd and Rohan Group Plc v Insurance Corp of Ireland Ltd*[253] Keane J. observed:

> "It is clear that policies of insurance, such as those under consideration in the present case, are to be construed like other written instruments. In the present case, the primary task of the court is to ascertain their meaning by adopting the ordinary rules of construction. It is also clear that, if there is any ambiguity in the language used, it is to be construed more strongly against the party who prepared it, *i.e.* in most cases against the insurer. It is also clear that the words used must not be construed with extreme literalism, but with reasonable latitude, keeping always in view the principal object of the contract of insurance. (See *MacGillvray and Parkington on Insurance Law* (7th ed.), pp.433 *et seq.*)"[254]

In *Brady v Irish National Insurance Co Ltd*[255] Finlay C.J. also reaffirmed the proposition that where an express warranty is vague it is to be construed against the party relying upon it.

11–74 In *Re Sweeney & Kennedy's Arbitration*[256] the High Court used the *contra proferentem* rule to facilitate the insured's claim on a motor vehicle insurance policy. The proposal form asked: "Are any of your drivers under 21 years of age or with less than 12 months of driving experience?" The applicant answered "No". While this was true at the date of application the insured later hired a driver below 21 years of age who had less than 12 months' experience. Kingsmill Moore J. refused to hold that the "basis of contract" clause could operate here; in cases of ambiguity the question in a motor insurance proposal form should be drafted precisely. It was possible for the insured to ask whether the applicant intended to use young inexperienced drivers and, in the absence of specific questions, the insurer should bear the loss. The *contra proferentem* rule may not always be used. In *Young v Sun Alliance*[257] the English Court of Appeal refused to read an exclusion from cover *contra proferentem*, preferring instead to adopt a "plain and ordinary meaning" approach.

11–75 In *HIH Casualty and General Insurance Ltd v Chase Manhattan Bank*,[258] the House of Lords has indicated that the interpretation of clauses

---

[253] [1986] I.L.R.M. 419.
[254] [1986] I.L.R.M. 419 at 423. The Supreme Court allowed an appeal in part but this principle was not doubted: [1988] I.L.R.M. 373.
[255] [1986] I.R. 698.
[256] [1950] I.R. 85, applied in *Manor Park Homebuilders Ltd v AIG Europe (Ireland) Ltd* [2008] IEHC 174.
[257] [1976] 3 All E.R. 561; contrast *Gaelcrann Teo v Payne* [1985] I.L.R.M. 109 with *Capemel v Lister* [1989] I.R. 319.
[258] [2003] 2 Lloyd's Rep. 61. On the interpretation of warranties the English Court of Appeal, in *The Resolute* [2009] EWCA Civ 1314 has endorsed general *West Bromwich*

must take place against the factual matrix and that where it is clear that a waiver clause in respect of a duty of disclosure was intended to apply to the insured, it may not readily be interpreted as being available to the broker also. The influence of the *West Bromwich*[259] approach to interpretation of insurance contracts in Ireland remains to be seen, but it has triggered certain hostility to *contra proferens* construction in England. Nevertheless, the Supreme Court in *Analog Devices BV v Zurich Insurance Co,*[260] interpreted exclusions from the scope of protection in a policy classified as an "all risks policy" relating to manufacturing by reference to *contra proferens* principles. Geoghogan J. referred to the discussion on *contra proferens* interpretation in relation to insurance contracts in the fourth edition of this book with approval. McMahon J., in *Manor Park Homebuilders* also used a *contra proferentem* analysis.

Future Developments in Insurance Contracts

11–76 The Law Reform Commission in its 2011 Consultation Paper, *Insurance Contracts,*[261] has made some recommendations on how the law may be amended. The Commission favours bringing insurance contract law into line with regulatory mechanisms such as the Financial Services Ombudsman's adjudications and the principles found in the Central Bank Consumer Code, with the statutory Codes of Practice being admissible in evidence, applicable in consumer disputes, consumer disputes being defined so as to include business insureds with a turnover of €3 million per annum or less. On the duty of disclosure the Commission favours a redacted duty to volunteer special facts known to the proposer to be highly relevant to the risk. This is to be offset with a duty on the insurer to explain both the duty and the consequences of non-disclosure. Differences between innocent, negligent and fraudulent non-disclosure, or misrepresentation should be recognised with avoidance for misrepresentation only being available in cases of fraud or where the insurer can show that the proposal would not have been accepted in any circumstances. Remedies in damages should be given to compensate the insurer, measured on a restitutionary basis. The Commission also recommends that warranties should not be permitted to form the basis of a contract and that warranties as to the future should be drafted in plain intelligible language and subject to review under the Unfair Contract Terms Regulations.[262]

---

principles but has also approved *Hussain v Brown* [1996] 1 Lloyd's Rep. 627. Continuing warranties that may have draconian results must not be interpreted literally and can be diluted by reference to the other terms of the contract, as well as read *contra proferens*. Thus, in *AC Ward & Son Ltd v Catlin (Five) Ltd* [2009] EWCA Civ 3122, Faux J. limited burglar alarm warranties to the alarm system in place at the time insurance commenced. McMahon J. arrived at the same conclusion in *Manor Homes* by a more direct route.
[259] *Investors Compensation Scheme Ltd v West Bromwich Building Society* [1998] 1 All E.R. 98.
[260] [2005] IESC 12.
[261] LRC CP 65-2011 has made a number of recommendations in respect of insurance contract law generally. Attention here is concentrated on the non-disclosure, misrepresentation and warranty provisions.
[262] S.I. No. 27 of 1995; S.I. No. 307 of 2000; S.I. No. 160 of 2013. See the decision of the CJEU in *Jean-Claude Van Hove v CNP Assurances SA* Case C-96/14.

11–77 In the Law Reform Commission Report on *Consumer Insurance Contracts*, published in July 2015,[263] most of the recommendations made in the Consultation Paper have been endorsed although the Report confines the recommendations to consumers and the small business insured (i.e. turnover of €3 million per annum or less). The Report emphasises that insurers should be required to pose specific questions to proposers to assist in identifying issues the insurer would think material. As in the Consultation Paper, repudiation of the policy for innocent or negligent misrepresentation, or non-disclosure, should be replaced by a system of proportionate remedies. Other recommendations in the Report on Consumer Insurance Contracts are considered elsewhere in this book.

---

[263] LRC 113–2015.

12 Duress

Introduction

12–01 Despite the recent spate of decisions which establish the concept of economic duress, these decisions continue to demonstrate that duress will be kept within narrow limits by the judges. It is invoked by a party to a contract who claims that he was forced into entering the contract or modifying a term contained in a contract. This is, of course, consistent with the restrictive circumstances in which duress will succeed as a defence to a criminal charge.[1] The Privy Council, in the case of *Barton v Armstrong*,[2] an appeal from the High Court of Australia, has ruled that duress may render a contract void. In that case threats to the safety of a man or his family were sufficient to vitiate consent to the contract. While it may seem that duress can only operate at common law where the danger apprehended is assault or injury to the person, it is suggested that the courts of equity have taken a more liberal position on the plea of duress, although the cases are isolated instances of duress. For an interesting discussion on the development of duress from cases of violence or threats of violence into overbearing conduct, see the judgment of Charleton J. in *ACC Bank v Dillon*.[3] In a domestic or family context, general allegations of pressure are likely to be regarded as instances of undue influence rather than duress.[4]

12–02 In *Lessee of Blackwood v Gregg*[5] an old man of 92 was abducted by relatives. He later executed a deed in favour of one of the captors. The deed was not read over to the old man. The trial judge was held by the Court of Exchequer to have correctly left it for the jury to decide whether the personal restraint imposed on the old man constituted duress. In *Rourke v Mealy*,[6] Palles C.B. indicated that a person threatened with the prosecution of a near relative unless he or she undertakes to pay a debt owed by the relative, may, in certain instances, be able to plead duress in equity. There are also English cases which

---

[1] *DPP v Lynch* [1975] A.C. 653, overruled in *R. v Howe* [1987] A.C. 417; *R. v Gotts* [1992] 1 All E.R. 832. See LRC 95–2009, *Defences in Criminal Law*. See *Chitty on Contracts*, edited by H.G. Beale, 32nd edn (London: Sweet & Maxwell, 2015), Vol. 1, paras 8-001 to 8-056.
[2] [1976] A.C. 104; the view now is that the contract is voidable not void; see *Byle v Byle* (1990) 65 D.L.R. (4th) 641 and *Cockerill v Westpac Banking Corp* (1996) 142 A.L.R. 227.
[3] [2012] IEHC 474.
[4] *Lambert v Lyons* [2010] IEHC 29; *Burin Peninsula Community Business Development Corp v Grandy* (2010) 327 D.L.R. (4th) 752.
[5] (1831) Hayes 277; *Armstrong v Gage* (1877) 25 Grant Ch. Cas. 1.
[6] (1879) 13 I.L.T.R. 52; *Williams v Bayley* (1866) L.R. 1 H.L. 200.

support the operation of a duress plea in this context. In *McClatchie v Haslam*[7] the plaintiff's husband, employed as the secretary of a building society, misappropriated funds. Fearing a prosecution of her husband, she executed a mortgage of her own property to provide security; although she was not sure that a prosecution would commence, the mortgage was set aside. Kekewich J. expressed the view that:

> "[T]his lady, though in one sense she executed this deed freely and voluntarily, did not execute it so freely and voluntarily as to defeat her right now to say that she did it under duress, and in order to free her husband from the criminal prosecution which she believed under the circumstances to be imminent."[8]

Other cases where equity has refused to enforce bargains concluded under duress include instances where the legal process itself is abused. Attempts to detain persons in order to extract payments through bogus legal claims, as in *Scott v Scott*,[9] have not been tolerated in equity, and in *Nicholls v Nicholls*[10] Lord Hardwicke stated that:

> "... though a man is arrested by due process of law, if a wrong use is made of it against the person under such arrest, by obliging him to execute a conveyance which was never under consideration before, this Court will construe it as duress, and relieve against a conveyance executed under such circumstances."[11]

This concept of abuse of process has been used in several cases. In *Borrelli v Ting*[12] the liquidators of a company sought to bring proceedings for a scheme of arrangement which was opposed by Ting for no good reason other than to conceal suspected wrongdoing on his part. Ting had not cooperated with the liquidators who were found to agree not to investigate Ting's affairs in exchange for Ting's withdrawal of opposition to the proposed scheme of arrangement. Of this settlement agreement, Lord Saville of Newdigate said:

> "An agreement entered into as the result of duress is not valid as a matter of law. Duress is the obtaining of agreement or consent by illegitimate means. *Director of Public Prosecutions for Northern Ireland v Lynch* [1975] AC 653; *Universal Tankships Inc of Monrovia v International Transport Workers Federation* [1983] 1 AC 366. Such means include what is known as '*economic duress*', where one party exerts illegitimate economic or similar pressure on another. An agreement obtained

---

7   (1891) 17 Cox C.C. 402.
8   (1891) 17 Cox C.C. 402 at 406; *Northern Bank Ltd v McCarron* [1995] N.I. 258.
9   (1846) 9 Ir.Eq.R. 451.
10 (1737) 1 Atk. 409.
11 (1737) 1 Atk. 409.
12 [2010] UKPC 21.

through duress is invalid in the sense that the party subject to the duress has the right to withdraw from the agreement, though that right may be lost if that party later affirms the agreement or waives the right to withdraw from it."

In this case Ting was not only suspected of misconduct, he had been able to oppose the proposed scheme of arrangement by forgery of documents. Ting had the liquidators "over a barrel" and used illegitimate means to obtain consent of the liquidators to the settlement agreement. While the Privy Council considered the law relating to duress to provide a solution—Lord Saville said the conduct of Ting was criminal and represented bad faith, and enforcement of the settlement agreement would offend justice—it could also be said that Ting had engaged in an abuse of the legal process. In *Reynolds v Altomoravia*[13] the parties to a property dispute obtained a court order and settlement agreement. The defendants failed to complete the transaction on the date set out in the court order. For several months thereafter they raised a number of issues and, in effect, sought to delay and re-negotiate the transaction, acting generally in "an unconscionable and inequitable manner." The plaintiff secured an order to set aside the settlement and Cregan J. held, citing Finnegan J. in *O'Sullivan v Weisz*[14]:

> "a compromise may be set aside on the ground that it was illegal as against public policy, or obtained by fraud, or misrepresentation, or non disclosure, or was concluded under a mutual mistake of fact. Specifically a compromise can be set aside on the ground that it was obtained by duress: *Cumming v Ince* (1847) 11 Q.B. 112. Thus the compromise and the agreement sought to be set aside by the Plaintiff in these proceedings can be set aside on the grounds of duress. Duress can encompass economic duress."

12–03 Perhaps the broadest and most frequently established plea of duress operates in the context of marriage contracts. In *Griffith v Griffith*[15] a young man was threatened with imprisonment and dishonour unless he married a young girl he was alleged to have made pregnant while on a camping holiday on Howth Head. His father and the local priest joined with the girl's mother in pressing him into a contract of marriage. When it became known that the plaintiff was not the father of the child he successfully claimed that his contract of marriage was void for duress. The court indicated that if he were the father a petition for a decree of nullity would not have been successful. The Irish civil courts in recent years have adopted a more expansive view of the situations in which a marriage will be declared void ab initio for duress and *Griffith v Griffith* has been disapproved by O'Hanlon J. in *MK (McC) v*

---

[13] [2015] IEHC 482
[14] [2005] IEHC 74.
[15] [1944] I.R. 35.

McC.[16] A marriage took place between the petitioner (who was pregnant by the respondent) under extreme pressure from both parents. O'Hanlon J., taking a broader view of the civil law jurisdiction in relation to duress, held "the will, not merely of one partner but of both husband and wife, was overborne by the compulsion of their respective parents and that they were driven unwillingly into a union which neither of them desired". An extensive review of the many recent Irish marriage cases would be out of place in a book devoted to general principles of contract and readers should examine specialist works on family law, and the Supreme Court decision in *DB v N O'R.*[17] The law has been comprehensively reviewed by Kinlen J. in *OB v R and OB,*[18] the High Court setting out the applicable principles where a marriage is alleged to be a nullity due to the petitioner's inability to give consent due to coercion by force of circumstances.

12–04 The most important Irish decision on duress is *Smelter Corp of Ireland v O'Driscoll.*[19] The plaintiff company sought specific performance on an option agreement which gave it a right to purchase O'Driscoll's land in Co. Cork. The option had been given reluctantly. The agent of the plaintiff company believed that if O'Driscoll did not sell to the company directly, the County Council intended to make a compulsory purchase order. When the agent communicated this to O'Driscoll he felt he had no alternative but to give the option. In fact, the County Council did not intend to purchase the land. O'Higgins C.J. in the Supreme Court said, "in these circumstances it appears to me that there was a fundamental unfairness in the transaction". The unfairness stems from O'Driscoll's belief that he was going to lose his land, one way or another. He could not be said to have consented to the agreement. Specific performance was refused. The case is perhaps to be regarded as an illustration of the reluctance of equity to grant specific performance of a contract which is struck in circumstances of substantial unfairness, or where the enforcement of the contract would be oppressive to the defendant, or where consent cannot be said to have been given; see *P.M.P.S. Ltd v Moore.*[20] As such, it must be conceded that these isolated instances of equitable jurisdiction do not constitute a coherent, unified system of jurisprudence. However, the law of restitution, and, in particular, the action for money had and received, has been a fruitful source of legal principle that can transcend the narrow, factual constraints on the development of the law of duress. One such example is found in cases where money payments are made as a result of coercion.

---

[16] [1982] I.L.R.M. 277.
[17] [1991] 1 I.R. 289. See also *UF v JC* [1991] I.R. 330; *BC v L O'F*, unreported, High Court, November 24, 1994.
[18] [2000] 1 I.L.R.M. 306; *C v S* [2008] IEHC 463.
[19] [1977] I.R. 305.
[20] [1988] I.L.R.M. 526; see also *O'Reilly v Minister for Industry and Commerce* [1994] E.L.R. 48.

12–05 In *Great Southern and Western Railway Co v Robertson*[21] a railway company was under statutory obligation to transport soldiers and their equipment at a rate of two pence per ton per mile. It charged the plaintiff, a carrier who had agreed to act as agent for the military, a higher rate. The plaintiff paid the excess, some £601, under protest. He was held entitled to recover the excess as money had and received to his use. In these cases the party exercising duress often does so because of some misinterpretation of the legal position. This will not justify the exercise of coercion and, further, restitution will be ordered even though it is generally true to state that a mistake of law will not be operative. The oppressive conduct of the payee will justify an award of restitution even if the mistake of law was shared by both parties. In *O'Loghlen v O'Callaghan*[22] and *Jackson v Stopford*[23] this rule against holding money paid under a mistake of law to be recoverable was affirmed[24]; this position is under review. There seems to be a trend towards widening the circumstances in which recovery of money paid under a mistake of law will be ordered. In *Rogers v Louth County Council*[25] money was paid to the defendants in order to redeem an annuity. This figure was calculated in good faith according to guidelines distributed by the then Department of Local Government. After payment was made the Supreme Court ruled this basis of assessment inaccurate. The plaintiff sought to recover £953.53 as an overpayment. On a case stated to the Supreme Court by the Circuit Court it was held that the sum was recoverable. Despite the fact that both parties knew the (albeit erroneous) calculation was the result of advice from an independent source the Supreme Court declared the parties not to be *in pari delicto*. This, it is submitted, is beside the point. The case relied upon in *Rogers* is an authority on illegality, not mistake of law, *viz. Kiriri Cotton Co v Dewani*.[26] The factors that will justify a court refusing to follow the rule against non-recovery were stated in *O'Loghlen v O'Callaghan*[27] to be "mala fides … fraud or imposition" per Whiteside C.J. It is hardly accurate to describe a demand for payment made by a local authority in the mistaken belief that this payment is due as a case of "imposition" but, nevertheless, the Supreme Court in *Rogers v Louth County Council*[28] broadened the notion so as to include such payments. Indeed in that case Griffin J. said overpayment could be recoverable in an action for money had and received where it was paid involuntarily, "that is, as the result of some extortion, coercion and compulsion". The facts of *Rogers and Dublin Corp v Trinity College Dublin*[29] suggest that the implicit sanction— fear of proceedings such as an execution against property—may satisfy the

---

21   (1878) 2 L.R. (Ir.) 548; *Scott v Midland Gt. W. Ry. Co* (1853) 6 Ir. Jur. 73.
22   (1874) I.R. 8 C.L. 116.
23   [1923] 2 I.R. 1.
24   See Law Com. No. 120 (1991).
25   [1981] I.L.R.M. 143; *Woolwich Equitable Building Society v I.R.C.* [1993] A.C. 70.
26   [1960] A.C. 192.
27   (1874) I.R. 8 C.L. 116.
28   [1981] I.L.R.M. 143.
29   [1985] I.L.R.M. 283.

"compulsion" element, even though the payment itself may not have been made under protest. See generally, Ch.20.

12–06 Apart from isolated instances where coercion was able to ground relief by way of restitution, or could be a contributory factor in showing that the bargain was unconscionable, very few jurisdictions acknowledged a distinct doctrine of duress in contracts. The courts in the US and, to a lesser extent, those in Australia and Canada, have often acknowledged that contracts negotiated or re-negotiated under a practical compulsion may not be enforceable if the party coerced seeks to have the transaction declared void.[30] It is only within the last 40 years that the English courts have, somewhat hesitantly, acknowledged that coercion of the will may provide a distinct basis for holding a contract invalid. The first instance decision of Kerr J. in *The Siboen and the Sibotre*[31] has provided the basis for this development. A contract for the charter of a ship was re-negotiated on the strength of fraudulent misrepresentations about the perilous economic position of the charterer. Although the case was decided on the basis of fraud, Kerr J. emphatically rejected the view that English law restricted its doctrine of duress to threats of the imposition of violence, and duress of goods. In *North Ocean Shipping v Hyundai Construction*,[32] Mocatta J. also approved the view that coercion may be operative if the coercion means that the will of the person promising is overborne. Mocatta J. was willing to hold that a promise to pay an additional sum of money in order to secure the completion of a ship which was being built by the defendant company could be procured by duress; to threaten to break the contract unless the payment is made or promised would possibly create serious financial difficulties for the party threatened and may involve the breach of some further contract entered into by that party on the strength of the delivery dates set out in that contract, dates that will not be met if the contract is broken. The Privy Council approved of these developments in *Pao On v Lau Yiu Long*[33] although in all three of these cases no complete case for relief had been made out, indicating perhaps that it will be difficult to set out a case for relief via duress. In a later case, however, the House of Lords, by a majority of three to two, upheld the view that a payment obtained by a trade union by threatening industrial action, specifically the "blacking" of a cargo on board a ship, constituted duress. In *Universe Tankships of Monrovia v International Transport Workers Federation*[34] the union threatened to "black" the appellant's vessel unless it was paid a sum of money which the union would disburse amongst seamen

---

[30] Sutton, "Duress by Threatened Breach of Contract" (1974) 20 McGill L.J. 254; Beatson, "Duress as a Vitiating Factor in Contract" (1974) 33 C.L.J. 97; Ogilvie, "Economic Duress: An Elegant and Practical Solution" [2011] J.B.L. 229. The fact that the contract procured by duress is voidable and not void does not afford an argument that the contract may be valid if restitution is not possible: *Borrelli v Ting* [2010] UKPC 21.

[31] [1976] 1 Lloyd's Rep. 293.

[32] [1979] Q.B. 705.

[33] [1980] A.C. 614.

[34] [1982] 2 All E.R. 67.

employed on "flag of convenience" ships. Lord Diplock, giving the leading judgment for the majority, declared of duress:

> "… the rationale is that his apparent consent was induced by pressure exercised on him by that other party which the law does not regard as legitimate, with the consequence that the consent is treated in law as revocable unless approbated either expressly or by implication after the illegitimate pressure has ceased to operate on his mind. It is a rationale similar to that which underlies the avoidability of contracts entered into and the recovery of money enacted under colour of office, or under undue influence or in consequence of threats of physical duress."[35]

Lord Scarman, dissenting, took a more structured view; while the *threat* may indeed be coercive it can be "legitimated" by looking at the broader question: is the *demand* made an acceptable one? Can pressure within this context be upheld as a justifiable use of bargaining power? Lord Scarman indicated that four factors were relevant as evidential matters[36]:

"(1) Did the person protest?

(2) Was there an alternative course open to him?

(3) Was he independently advised?

(4) After entering the contract did he take steps to avoid it?"

The traditional hostility of English judges to trade union objectives and the use of industrial action in support of collective bargaining is no doubt a narrower issue than that raised by the facts of *Universe Tankships*—the workers to benefit were not even members of the Union—but there is a danger that the "overborne will" theory may intrude into industrial relations law generally. The House of Lords, in *The Evia Luck (No. 2)*[37] has reaffirmed the application of the "overborne will" theory, holding that the threat to "black" a vessel may be illegitimate, even if the threat is not tortious or even unlawful under the law of the place where the "blacking" is to be implemented, in this case the law of Sweden. Hostility to the "overborne will" theory has surfaced in some jurisdictions, particularly in Australia where many of the leading cases that are shaping the restitutionary character of this cause of action have formed a distinctive jurisprudence. A New South Wales court, in *Crescendo Management Property v Westpac Banking Co*[38] and a Victoria court have presented a test of illegitimate pressure in contra-distinction to "overborne will". In the Victoria case of *Deemcope Property v Cantown Property*[39] the court stressed the need

---

[35] [1982] 2 All E.R. 67 at 75–76.
[36] [1982] 2 All E.R. 67 at 88. This analysis was adopted by Tipping J. in *Shivas v Bank of New Zealand* [1990] 2 N.Z.L.R. 327; see also *Gordon v Roebuck* (1989) 64 D.L.R. (4th) 568.
[37] [1991] 4 All E.R. 871.
[38] [1988] N.S.W.L.R. 40.
[39] [1995] 2 V.R. 44.

to locate conduct other than ordinary commercial pressures and leverages; in the absence of unlawful threats of unconscionable conduct the transaction will be sustained.

12–07 The English courts have shown a ready facility for applying duress to other kinds of industrial action, when taken by workers in a concerted manner and at a time when the employer in question has little option but to agree to the demands made by the workforce. In *B & S Contracts v Victor Green Publications*[40] the plaintiffs agreed to pay an additional sum to the defendants, who had been engaged to erect an exhibition stand. The sum would be used to pay the defendants' workers who were demanding increased payments for the work. The defendants indicated that if the sum was not paid they would cancel the contract under a cancellation clause. The Court of Appeal held the cancellation clause could not have been available in these circumstances and that the payments obtained had been paid under duress. The clearest English decision in which a plea of economic duress has been sustained in favour of a contracting party who has been coerced into re-negotiating a contract is *Atlas Express Ltd v Kafco (Importers and Distributors) Ltd*.[41] In June 1986 the defendant company engaged the plaintiff company to deliver cartons on behalf of the defendant to branches of Woolworths. The estimated contract price payable to the plaintiff proved uneconomic, due to a miscalculation by the plaintiff's depot manager, and the plaintiff in November 1986 obtained the defendant's consent to a new higher rate. The defendant agreed to the new rate because it was dependant upon the contract with Woolworths, was unlikely to find another carrier, and feared that if the plaintiff company refused to deliver the cartons the defendant would be sued by Woolworths. In holding that the defendant's consent to the November 1986 agreement had been given unwillingly and under compulsion, Tucker J. further held that the defendant's apparent consent to the agreement was induced by pressure which was illegitimate. Tucker J. also held that the defendant's November 1986 agreement was unenforceable for lack of consideration. Most English cases indicate that it will be difficult to establish duress and the "coercion of the will so as to vitiate consent" theory has been described by Atiyah as "unsatisfactory" because it deflects attention away from the central issue, "the permissible limits of coercion in our society".[42] If the pressure is the result of outside pressure by third parties, such as a bank, then coercion will not be present according to Deputy Judge Millett in *Alec Lobb (Garages) Ltd v Total Oil*.[43]

12–08 More recent English cases suggest that the "overborne will" theory is yielding to an "illegitimate pressure" test. Although most of these decisions are not appellate cases, they represent a very clear statement of principle. In

---

[40] [1984] 1 I.C.R. 419.
[41] [1989] 1 All E.R. 641; *The Alev* [1989] 1 Lloyd's Rep. 138.
[42] (1983) 99 L.Q.R. 356.
[43] [1985] 1 W.L.R. 173.

DSND Subsea Ltd v Petroleum Geo-Services ASA,[44] Dyson J. (as he then was) put forward the following propositions as being an accurate statement of the law:

> "The ingredients of actionable duress are that there must be pressure, (a) whose practical effect is that there is compulsion on, or a lack of practical choice for, the victim, (b) which is illegitimate, and (c) which is a significant cause inducing the claimant to enter into the contract: see *Universe Tankships of Monrovia v ITWF* [1983] AC 336, 400B-E, and *The Evia Luck* [1992] 2 AC 152, 165G. In determining whether there has been illegitimate pressure, the court takes into account a range of factors. These include whether there has been an actual or threatened breach of contract; whether the person allegedly exerting the pressure has acted in good or bad faith; whether the victim had any realistic practical alternative but to submit to the pressure; whether the victim protested at the time; and whether he affirmed and sought to rely on the contract. These are all relevant factors. Illegitimate pressure must be distinguished from the rough and tumble of the pressures of normal commercial bargaining."[45]

Although in *DSND* it was held that the alternatives available negatived duress, Dyson J. had occasion to apply this test in *Carillion Construction Ltd v Felix UK Ltd*,[46] a most instructive decision which promises to be influential in the application of economic duress to construction contracts. Carillion engaged Felix to provide cladding for use in the construction of an office building. Felix fell behind with the work, breaching "best efforts" provisions and a delivery timetable fixed by the contract. Differences arose between the parties on performance and price and Felix indicated that further deliveries were dependent upon settlement of these differences. Negotiations were concluded on terms favourable to Felix; Felix knew that further delays would hold up other sub-contractors and that Carillion was facing penalty clauses in the event of late completion. On the day of the settlement, Carillion wrote a letter of protest and when the work was completed, Carillion claimed that the settlement had been procured by economic duress and was not binding. Dyson J. held that Carillion had to show the presence of pressure or a threat, such pressure or threat being illegitimate, the practical effect of which being that Carillion had no practical alternative but to enter the agreement and that the pressure or threat was a significant cause in inducing the contract. It is interesting to note that Carillion, as a very large civil engineering company, had considerable commercial muscle, but the focus in these cases is on the individual circumstances surrounding the negotiation. On the facts, Dyson J. held that threats to break the contract had been made and the fact that the

---

[44] [2000] B.L.R. 530; Bigwood, "Economic Duress by (Threatened) Breach of Contract" (2001) 117 L.Q.R. 376.

[45] [2000] B.L.R. 530 at 535.

[46] [2001] B.L.R. 1. *Capital Structures Plc v Time and Tide Construction Ltd* [2006] EWHC 591 (TCC).

settlement agreement afforded a benefit in the form of legal certainty did not answer the point. On the critical issue of the legitimacy, or otherwise, of the pressure, Felix knew it had no right to make such threats or withhold further performance and arbitration was available to Felix under the sub-contract. Felix also knew of the importance of timely completion, the penalty clauses and that Carillion could not find another supplier of what were custom-built materials. The question of practical choice was also resolved in favour of Carillion. Not only was there no alternative supplier, there had been consultations with Carillion's lawyers on whether Felix could be the subject of injunctive reliefs, but this course of action was regarded as being unrealistic. The removal of pressure by Felix caused Carillion to immediately contest the validity of the agreement so the causal element required to make out a case of economic duress was satisfied.

12–09 The question of what constitutes illegitimate pressure was discussed extensively by Cooke J. in *Progress Bulk Carriers Ltd v Tube City IMS*.[47] The claimants chartered a specific vessel, to be available on April 30, 2009. The owners nevertheless chartered that vessel to another party, this being found to be a repudiatory breach of contract. The owners gave assurances that the claimants would be provided with another vessel and compensation. As time elapsed the owners made a number of requests for concessions from the charterers, ultimately, as the arbitrators found, putting a settlement agreement to the charterers absolving the owners of liability for their earlier repudiatory breach on a "take it or leave it" basis. The charterers accepted the proposal in order to secure access to the substitute vessel but later sued for damages in respect of the repudiatory breach and late arrival of the substitute vessel. Cooke J. upheld the decision of the arbitrators who found that the settlement had been obtained by economic duress. The owners made a primary submission which asserted that economic duress required illegitimate pressure and that this involved a finding of illegal conduct. The arbitrators had not found illegality on the owner's part. Cooke J. pointed to earlier case law in which the fact that a demand for payment accompanied by a threat to do a lawful act did not preclude economic duress. Cooke J. found that illegitimate pressure could consist of past and future conduct. In this case the repudiatory breach and subsequent assurances that compensation would be paid (which were not honoured) could ground the claimant's action for damages:

> "What however the Owners' submissions overlook is the fact that their repudiatory breach was the root cause of the problem and that their continuing conduct thereafter was, as described by the Arbitrators, designed to put the Charterers in a position where they had no option but to accept the settlement agreement in order to ship the cargo to China and avoid further huge losses on the sale contract to the Chinese

---

[47] [2012] EWHC 273 (Comm); Lee [2012] L.M.C.L.Q. 478; see also *Adam Opel GmbH v Mitras Automotive UK Ltd* [2007] EWHC 3481 (Q.B.).

receivers. As the Charterers submitted, it would be very odd if pressure could be brought about by a threatened breach of contract, which did amount to an unlawful act but not by a past breach, coupled with conduct since that breach, which drove the victim of the breach into a position where it had no realistic alternative but to waive its rights in respect of that breach, in order to avoid further catastrophic loss."

Several judges have been concerned to distinguish economic duress from commercial pressure which is not sufficient to vitiate consent.[48] An excellent case which distinguishes between these two situations is *Walmsley v Christchurch City Council*.[49] Here the plaintiff had been engaged to produce a souvenir programme for a Golden Jubilee airshow organised by the defendant. Due to production difficulties, the programme was substandard and rejected by the defendant, who then pressed the plaintiff to provide and pay for a reprinting, the plaintiff to be entitled to any profits over and above a guaranteed minimum amount. Weeks after the airshow, the plaintiff sought to claim that consent to the new arrangement was coerced. Hardie Boys J. rejected this plea. Even though the defendant had obtained the consent of the plaintiff by a threatened breach of contract, in refusing to accept the programme, the proof-reading errors were such that the defendant was in law entitled to reject the programme. Further, the fact that the plaintiff had time to consult his business partner and legal advisers pointed away from duress. Delay in rescinding the contract was also relevant here.

12–10 If the payment is made or promised "under protest" this will not be essential and the presence or absence of protest is not conclusive: per Lord Scarman in *Pao On*. If the person making the promise has an alternative course of action—the possibility of quick and effective legal action to remove the threat of pressure, for example—this may signify consent and the absence of duress.[50] Perhaps the most controversial issue is motive. Mocatta J. in *North Ocean Shipping* held it immaterial whether the person making the demand and uttering the threat was aware that the person addressed had no effective alternative because the person making the demand had full knowledge of the difficulties the threatened action would produce. It is submitted that if we are concerned with notions of legitimacy and the motive of the person threatening, rather than simply the will of the party threatened, then this factor should be of great importance. It was clearly material in *D & C Builders v Rees*[51] that the builders were known to be in a difficult financial position when they "agreed"

---

[48] *Magnacrete Ltd v Douglas Hill* (1988) 48 S.A.S.R. 565; *Alec Lobb (Garages) Ltd v Total Oil* [1985] 1 W.L.R. 173.

[49] [1990] 1 N.Z.L.R. 199; *Haines v Carter* [2001] 2 N.Z.L.R. 167, appeal to the Privy Council dismissed: [2002] UKPC 22; *Teat v Willcocks* [2013] NZCA 162

[50] Per Griffiths L.J. in *B&S Contracts v Victor Green Publications* [1984] I.C.R. 419.

[51] [1966] 2 Q.B. 617; see a prescient comment by Winder, "The Equitable Doctrine of Pressure". (1966) 82 L.Q.R. 165 and an earlier comment at "Undue Influence and Coercion" (1940) 3 M.L.R. 97 by the same writer.

to accept a reduced settlement of their claim; see also *Osorio v Cardona*.[52] It is, however, clear that if the person threatened does not immediately seek relief once the pressure is removed, then he is likely to be held to have consented to the demand; see *North Ocean Shipping v Hyundai Construction*[53] and *Walmsley v Christchurch City Council*.[54] Much play was made of the importance of this factor in *Carillion Construction Ltd v Felix (UK) Ltd* where, on the facts, the plaintiffs protested and challenged the settlement on the very day it was agreed.

12–11 The discussion in the English Court of Appeal in *CTN Cash and Carry v Gallaher Ltd*[55] concerned a threat to refuse the buyers the use of credit facilities that the sellers had extended to the buyers, as a privilege, unless the buyers paid a disputed sum of money. Although it later transpired that the buyers were not liable in law to pay this money, the Court of Appeal held that the payment made was not improperly obtained. The sellers were bona fide of the view that the sums were due and the threat to discontinue the credit facility, while coercive, was not unlawful. However, the Court of Appeal, in a refreshing discussion of the boundaries of duress, conceded that in certain circumstances a threat to do something that was coercive could be improper even though not in its own terms being unlawful. The presence of a bona fide belief that the demand was a proper one was dispositive in the Ontario Court of Appeal's decision on legitimacy, in *Techform Products v Wolda*.[56] A demand by an employer that an independent contractor should transfer intellectual property rights in an invention was held to have been a legitimate threat in the light of the belief that the employer was entitled to ownership.

12–12 One English judge has indicated that in his view the likelihood of an employer–employee agreement being voidable for economic duress must be remote indeed; see Popplewell J. in *Hennessy v Craigmyle*,[57] in which it was held that the court had no jurisdiction to hear an unfair dismissal claim because the claim had earlier been settled by agreement. In the Ontario case of *Stott v Merit Investment Corp*,[58] the Ontario Court of Appeal provided a compelling illustration of just how difficult it will be to make out a claim of economic duress in this context. The plaintiff, a financial securities salesman employed by the defendant, was obliged to meet shortfalls on his customer accounts and after pressure was brought to bear by his supervisor, he signed a document acknowledging his indebtedness, fearing that otherwise he could not find employment in the industry. He was at this time financially embarrassed and in

---

[52] (1985) 59 B.C.L.R. 29. On the impact of duress vis-à-vis an arbitrator's jurisdiction see *Capital Structures Plc v Time and Tide Construction Ltd* [2006] EWHC 591 (TCC).
[53] [1979] Q.B. 705.
[54] [1990] 1 N.Z.L.R. 199; contrast *Byle v Byle* (1990) 65 D.L.R. (4th) 641.
[55] [1994] 4 All E.R. 714; Smith (1997) 56 C.L.J. 343.
[56] (2001) 206 D.L.R. (4th) 171. Contrast *Hobbs v TDI Canada Ltd* (2005) 246 D.L.R. (4th) 43.
[57] [1985] I.R.L.R. 446; *McConville v ESB* [1995] E.L.R. 46.
[58] (1988) 48 D.L.R. (4th) 288.

no position to terminate his employment. The majority of the Ontario Court of Appeal found that even if his consent was coerced, the plaintiff had remained in employment and thus approbated the agreement. In his dissenting judgment, Blair J.A. drew a quite different inference from the plaintiff's apparent inactivity: "it is unrealistic to suggest that at all times [Stott] had the option of resigning, exposing himself and his family to the hazards of unemployment, bankruptcy and litigation which he could not afford." It is also evident that in *Techform Products v Wolda*, sharp differences were entertained between the trial judge and the Ontario Court of Appeal over whether it was realistic[59] to expect the defendant to resign or challenge his employer to the point of offering his resignation.[60]

12–13 Even in the most coercive of employments, duress is likely to fail as a plea. In *Attorney-General for England and Wales v R*,[61] the New Zealand Court of Appeal held that an agreement between the Crown and a serving SAS officer that he would not publish his account of the Bravo Two Zero patrol was not procured by duress. While the Court of Appeal acknowledged that the relationship between a serving officer and his superiors is one of compulsion, there was an unpalatable alternative available to the respondent in the form of a transfer back to his unit. The central issue, however, was whether the pressure brought to bear upon the respondent to agree not to publish was "illegitimate pressure". Even though the pressure brought to bear was such as to abridge the important human right of freedom of expression, it was brought to bear, in good faith, in order to preserve the operational effectiveness of the UK Special Forces. As such, duress was not made out. The Privy Council has upheld this decision.[62]

12–14 In this case the New Zealand courts also examined key aspects of consideration in the context of duress. The relationship between the adequacy of consideration and economic duress was also explored in *South Caribbean Trading v Trafigura Beheer BV*.[63] South Caribbean agreed to sell fuel oil to Trafigura from a specific source but later proposed to buy in fuel oil from elsewhere, a proposal that was unacceptable to Trafigura. While much of the argument covered the interpretation of the contract—Colman J. held that South Caribbean had committed a repudiatory breach by proposing substitution of the fuel product—the court had to consider whether there had

---

[59] See also *Hall v Woolaston Hall Leisure Ltd* [2001] 1 W.L.R. 225 for similar observations in an illegality case.
[60] In this case Wolda was in law an independent contractor which, a priori, made the economic duress argument more difficult for him to sustain. For an interesting analysis of economic duress in which an "illegitimate pressure" test has been rejected, see *NAV Canada v Greater Fredericton Airport Authority* (2008) 290 D.L.R. (4th) 405; *Bell v Levy* [2011] BCCA 417 charts a more conventional path. See also *Process Automation Inc. v Norstream Intertec Inc.* (2010) 341 D.L.R. (4th) 724.
[61] [2002] 2 N.Z.L.R. 91.
[62] [2003] UKPC 22; O'Sullivan (2003) 65 C.L.J. 554.
[63] [2004] EWHC 2676 (Comm).

been an agreed extension of the delivery date in favour of South Caribbean which was supported by consideration. While Colman J., reluctantly, followed *Williams v Roffey Bros Ltd*,[64] on the consideration point, the threat to withhold performance was held to be analogous to economic duress and thus an invalid consideration within the *Roffey Bros* analysis.

Restitutio in integrum

12–15 On the question whether duress is available to a party who cannot offer the other party *restitutio in integrum*, see *Halpern v Halpern*.[65]

---

[64] [1990] 1 All E.R. 512.

[65] In particular, Carnwath L.J. at [2007] EWCA Civ 291, discussing Deputy Judge Teare's judgment in *Halpern v Halpern (No. 1)* [2006] 3 W.L.R. 946. Both Judge Teare and the Court of Appeal inclined towards holding that general principles relating to counter restitution should apply to contracts vitiated by undue influence and other vitiating factors, including duress.

Part 4

Equitable Intervention

13   Equitable Intervention

Introduction

13–01 Equitable intervention in contracts is a very broad and sometimes ill-defined notion. Equity may intervene by imposing evidential requirements or substantive obstacles to the enforcement of a promise when the conduct of one of the parties to the contract is regarded as unconscionable—take, for example, several of the estoppel reliefs and, in particular, promissory and proprietary estoppel considered in Ch.2. The remedy of part performance in relation to land transactions is increasingly being ascribed to judicial reluctance to condone unconscionable conduct. Equitable reliefs such as the constructive trust may be viewed in the same light. However, traditional methods of overturning transactions that are vulnerable to review by a court of equity centre around undue influence, unconscionable bargain and the improvident transaction jurisdictions, and these form the basis of this chapter. It is important to note that these jurisdictions have not influenced the freedom of a court to take into account inequality of bargaining power in determining whether the words in a contract must be interpreted only in the way expressed. The leading case of *Autoclenz Ltd v Belcher*[1] concerned a "sham" transaction in which a contract for services was reclassified as an employment contract by the UK Supreme Court. While this decision is not an example of the doctrine of undue influence, the overlaps are obvious. Case law in Northern Ireland is already under way on *Autoclenz*.[2]

Undue Influence

13–02 The doctrine of undue influence enables a court to set aside contracts, transfers of property inter vivos and dispositions by will whenever it appears that one party has not freely consented to the transaction. The doctrine is designed to discourage victimisation and sharp practice, particularly on the part of persons who are in positions of trust and confidence and who may abuse the power they acquire over other persons.

---

[1]   [2011] UKSC 41. *Autoclenz* and its context is discussed in *Chitty on Contract*s, edited by H.G. Beale, 32nd edn (London: Sweet & Maxwell, 2015), Vol. 2, paras 40 to 025. For undue influence see *Chitty on Contracts* Vol. 1, paras 8-057 to 8-129.
[2]   *Watson v Carter Clothing Ltd* [2012] NIIT 00839; *Orr v Department of Employment* [2012] NIIT 01629; *Department for Employment and Learning v Morgan* [2016] NICA 2.

(1) The presumption of undue influence

13–03 Persons who acquire a considerable amount of influence over others often do so because of the very nature of the relationship that exists between them. A patient may place trust and confidence in his physician: *Aherne v Hogan*.[3] A trustee who employs an agent to carry out his obligations places that agent in a fiduciary relationship vis-à-vis the beneficial owner of the property; see *Murphy v O'Shea*[4] and *King v Anderson*.[5] A solicitor will normally hold some degree of influence and dominion over a client; see *Lawless v Mansfield*.[6] In these cases it goes without saying that the solicitor, trustee, or physician should not misrepresent or trick the other party into conveying property to him or her. Equity also requires all transactions between these persons to be justified by the party in whom trust and confidence is placed. In certain cases the courts go so far as to say that there is an absolute incapacity to contract. In *Atkins v Delmege*[7] a purchase of property was set aside when the purchaser turned out to be the legal representative of the estate, the sale being ordered by a court. The solicitor in such circumstances was declared to be incapable of purchasing. The general rule is that once the purchaser falls into a category of person in whom trust and confidence is reposed he is obliged to show that the sale was fair and freely assented to. In *Molony v Kernan*[8] it was held that before an agent could take a lease from his principal the agent must show that full information was given to the principal and that the contract was entered into in good faith.

13–04 Undue influence will also be presumed where property is transferred to a religious association by a devotee. In *White v Meade*[9] the plaintiff, then aged 18, entered a religious establishment as a lodger. It was envisaged that if the plaintiff decided at a later date to take holy orders she could do so after being allowed to consult with friends. The defendants prevailed on her to take holy orders while actively preventing her from seeking guidance from her brother. The order also managed to get the plaintiff to transfer £1,100 and a large amount of realty to the order. The transfer was set aside. It is not necessary to show that the religious order practised coercion. It is enough to show that the religious devotee was unable to freely consent to the transaction because he or she was incapable of exercising independent judgment. *Allcard v Skinner*[10]

---

[3] Dru. *temp*. Sug. 310: Bigwood, *Exploitative Contracts* (Oxford: OUP, 2003); Clark, *Inequality of Bargaining Power* (Toronto: Carswell, 1987); Sheridan, *Fraud in Equity* (London: Pitman, 1957); Keane, *Equity and the Law of Trusts in the Republic of Ireland*, 2nd edn (Dublin: Bloomsbury Professional, 2011), Ch.28.

[4] (1845) 8 Ir.Eq.R. 329.

[5] (1874) 8 Ir.Eq.R. 625; *Tate v Williamson* (1886) L.R. 2 Ch. 55.

[6] (1841) 1 Dr. & War. 557.

[7] (1847) 12 Ir.Eq.R. 1.

[8] (1832) 2 Dr. & War. 31; *Patten v Hamilton* [1911] 1 I.R. 46.

[9] (1840) 2 Ir.Eq.R. 420.

[10] (1887) 36 Ch. D. 145. For more modern examples, see *Azaz v Denton* [2009] EWHC 1759 (Q.B.); *Curtis v Curtis* [2011] EWCA Civ 1602, affords a more humanist perspective.

shows that even if a court does not impute improper motive or unconscionable behaviour to the party taking under the contract or transfer, the transaction will be set aside unless it can be shown to be fair and freely consented to. The facts of *Allcard v Skinner* were as follows: the plaintiff, a woman in her mid-thirties, was introduced by the spiritual adviser to the defendant, a lady superior of a Protestant enclosed sisterhood. There was a similar link between the charitable body and the spiritual adviser. After some years, the plaintiff entered the sisterhood and, in furtherance of vows, gave property to it which was used for charitable purposes. Under the rules of the sisterhood, obedience to the defendant was a central tenet. After eight years, she left the sisterhood. Some six years later, she sought the return of that portion of her donated property that was unspent on the date of her departure from the sisterhood. While no pressure had been placed upon the plaintiff other than the ordinary rules and vows of poverty and obedience, and no improper use had been made of the monies, undue influence was presumed. Lindley L.J. explained the basis of the doctrine in the following terms:

> "What is the principle? Is it that it is right and expedient to save persons from the consequences of their own folly?—or is it that it is right and expedient to save them from being victimised by other people? In my opinion the doctrine of undue influence is founded upon the second of these two principles. Courts of Equity have never set aside gifts on the ground of folly, imprudence or want of foresight on the part of the donor."[11]

A presumption in appropriate cases is seen as a useful foil to victimisation. Nevertheless, delay in seeking relief, and acts of affirmation carried out during the six-year interval, together prevented the plaintiff from succeeding in *Allcard v Skinner*. There are, however, some instances in which gifts to religious bodies have been held to be freely and voluntarily given. In *Kirwan v Cullen*[12] a gift to the Catholic Church was upheld. The executor of the donor's estate alleged that one of the trustees of the property conveyed had been the religious confessor of the donor; the transaction was upheld when it was shown that the trustee in question had ceased to be the donor's confessor two years before the gift was made. It remains of course possible for the court to hold that, while the religious mentor did not have a confidential relationship with the donor in a formal sense, undue influence was in fact exercised. In *Murphy v O'Neill*[13] the jury found that undue influence was exercised by a priest over a member of the Church although the priest had not been the confessor of the victim and the victim was resident in the next parish.

---

[11] (1887) 36 Ch. D. at 182–183.
[12] (1854) 2 Ir. Ch. Rep. 322.
[13] [1936] N.I. 16.

13–05 Other relationships the courts view with suspicion include parent and child, and guardian and ward. In *Wallace v Wallace*[14] and *Croker v Croker*[15] transfers of property by a son in favour of his father were set aside because the father was unable to show that the transfers were freely made. In *McMackin v Hibernian Bank*[16] a guarantee signed by a young girl living with her mother was set aside because of the undue influence of the mother. This presumption also applies to instances of guardian and ward. *Mulhallen v Marum*[17] is a very colourful illustration of the presumption in this context. The plaintiff, a young man of 18 years, went to live with his married sister and her husband. The plaintiff was supplied with horses, clothing, money and other essentials by his sister's husband. He was then effectively placed in the custody of his sister's husband and upon his reaching full age was persuaded to transfer lands, including valuable mining rights, to him. These transactions were set aside on the basis that the transfers had been made to a person standing in the position of guardian, receiver of rents of the plaintiff's land, agent and tenant of the plaintiff, all of which separately could be viewed as a basis for imputing undue influence in a proper case.

13–06 The most compelling modern cases in which transactions have been re-opened as a result of undue influence have involved music artists who, while unknown and unsuccessful, and under the influence of advisers who have a fiduciary relationship with the artist, have entered into recording contracts, music publishing contracts and have executed copyright assignments. In *O'Sullivan v Management Agency & Music Ltd*[18] the artist Gilbert O'Sullivan was able to successfully set aside publishing and recording contracts which were entered into by the artist following advice of his manager, the contracts in question being unduly restrictive and concluded with recording and publishing companies with whom the manager was closely linked. In *John v James*[19] Elton John and Bernie Taupin were also able to successfully plead the existence of a fiduciary relationship between themselves and music publishers, so when the agreements were not exploited by the publishers in a manner which was conscientious and fair to the artists, there could be an account ordered of profits made by the fiduciary. In *Wadlow v Samuel*,[20] a management contract between the plaintiff and the defendant, the artist Seal, was found to have been struck in circumstances where the artist placed his reliance and trust in the hands of

---

[14] (1842) 2 Dr. & War. 452: persons in loco parentis; *O'Connor v Foley* [1905] 1 I.R. 1.
[15] (1870) 4 I.L.T.R. 181.
[16] [1905] 1 I.R. 296.
[17] (1843) 3 Dr. & War. 317.
[18] [1984] 3 W.L.R. 448.
[19] [1991] F.S.R. 397; see Tatt, "Music Publishing and Recording Contracts in Perspective" [1987] 9 E.I.P.R. 132; Woolcombe, "Fairness versus Certainty—Pop the Music Contract" [1987] 9 E.I.P.R. 187. On account of profits see *Warman International Ltd v Dwyer* (1995) 182 C.L.R. 544.
[20] [2007] EWCA Civ 155. A separate analysis of a settlement agreement was held not to have required explanation and the court observed that if it had, the onus was discharged via independent legal advice.

the plaintiff. The court also examined the agreements and found that clauses that gave the manager rights to perpetual post-termination commissions and additional commissions on publishing agreements were provisions that were not readily explicable by the ordinary motives behind such agreements. The evidential burden, therefore, shifted to the manager who, on the facts, was held to have discharged the burden of proof.

13–07 There are other instances where the courts may eventually hold that the burden of showing the propriety of the transaction rests upon the party seeking to uphold it. The value of the presumption is that it results in the transaction being set aside if the onus is not discharged. This is a reversal of the burden of proof in most civil actions where it normally rests on the person impugning the transaction. This evidentiary matter was considered by the Northern Ireland Court of Appeal in *R. (Proctor) v Hutton, Re Founds Estate*.[21] An action was brought by executors of Mrs Found's estate to set aside legacies on the ground of undue influence having been exerted by a niece of the deceased. Jones L.J. said:

> "The presumption of undue influence may arise in two sorts of cases. The evidence may show *a particular relationship* for example that of solicitor and client, trustee and *cestui que trust*, doctor and patient or religious adviser and pupil. Those cases or some of them, depending on the facts, *may of themselves* raise the presumption. Such examples, as regards undue influence, have much in common with the doctrine of *res ipsa loquitur* in relation to negligence. But then there is the other sort of case, the precise range of which is indeterminate, in which *the whole evidence,* when meticulously considered, may disclose *facts* from which *it should be inferred* that a relationship is disclosed which justifies a finding that there is a presumption of undue influence. In other words the presumption enables a party to achieve justice by bridging a gap in the evidence where there is a gap because the evidence is impossible to come by."[22]

Lord Lowry L.C.J. agreed:

> "The relationships which raise the presumption are left unlimited by definition, wide open for identification on the facts and in all the circumstances of each particular case as it arises ... it is a common but not a necessary feature of the relationship that the person on whose part undue influence is alleged assumed a responsibility for advising the donor even managing his property. There are certain relationships which are recognised as giving rise to the presumption, but there are also those which, upon a consideration of the particular facts, may raise the same presumption."[23]

---

[21] [1978] N.I. 139.
[22] Unreported, Court of Appeal, April 30, 1979, affirming Lowry L.C.J. in [1978] N.I. 139; emphasis added.
[23] Unreported, Court of Appeal, April 30, 1979. Discussed in *Carroll v Carroll* [2000] 1 I.L.R.M. 201.

This second instance of a presumption operating in favour of the party seeking to invalidate the transaction can be illustrated by peripheral family relationships which may give one person the opportunity to gain dominance over the other. Brother and brother: *Armstrong v Armstrong*[24]; brother and sister and uncle and nephew: *Gregg v Kidd*[25]; brother-in-law and sister-in-law: *Evans v Elwood*.[26] These are all cases where the presumption may come into effect after evidence has been given to show that a relationship of trust and confidence developed between these persons. In the case of *McGonigle v Black*[27] this second instance of a presumption arising on the facts was held to operate by Barr J. An elderly farmer, living alone following the death of relatives, contracted to sell his property to a near-neighbour and the transaction was set aside, Barr J. citing with approval the speech of Lord Lowry L.C.J. in *R. (Proctor) v Hutton, Re Founds Estate*. After looking at all the facts, Barr J. concluded that this was "a grossly improvident transaction which was brought about by undue influence persistently exercised by the defendant over Mr McGonigle who, because of a combination of bereavement, inability to cope, loneliness, alcoholism and ill-health, was vulnerable to manipulation and was so manipulated by the defendant to the vendor's obvious disadvantage". In *McGonigle v Black* the facts disclosed that not only was there a trust and confidence relationship, triggering the presumption, there was also the exercise of undue influence as of fact. The importance of the presumption, however, has been reaffirmed in three recent cases. In *Carroll v Carroll*[28] a transfer of a public house from an elderly man to his son was impugned on the basis of undue influence. Evidence before the High Court from members of the family seeking to overturn the transfer indicated that undue influence had not in fact been exercised and the trial judge also found that the donor possessed a clear mind at the time of the transaction. Nevertheless, undue influence was present because the presumption had not been rebutted. In cases where the presumption arises, the court does not have to find a wrongful act but, rather, the court intervenes in order to prevent an abuse of influence possessed by one over the other. To similar effect is *Pesticcio v Huet*.[29] An elderly man, of significantly lower intelligence than the average, while recovering from illness, made a deed of gift in favour of a donee, his sister, following advice from a solicitor who had been contacted by the donee. The English Court of Appeal upheld a decision to declare the transfer void as between donor and donee, brushing aside the donee's objection that she had done nothing wrong. Mummery J. explained that public policy rather than proof of wrongdoing lay behind the operation of

---

[24] (1873) I.R. 8 Eq. 1. A presumption of undue influence will not arise simply by virtue of the fact that a guarantor and the debtor are siblings: *ACC Loan Management v Sheehan* [2015] IEHC 818. Some notice of reliance/dependency will be necessary.

[25] [1956] I.R. 183. *Naidoo v Naidu, The Times*, November 1, 2000, like *Gregg v Kidd*, also addresses the situation where a third party exercises undue influence.

[26] (1874) 8 I.L.T.R. 118.

[27] Unreported, High Court, November 14, 1988.

[28] [2000] 1 I.L.R.M. 210.

[29] *The Independent*, April 7, 2004. See also *Hammond v Osborn* [2002] EWCA Civ 885, noted by Scott [2003] L.M.C.L.Q. 145; *Randall v Randall* [2004] EWHC 2258 (Ch).

the presumption and that it was the nature of the continuing relationship rather than specific conduct of the donee that was scrutinised by the court. Similarly, Laffoy J. has held that undue influence may arise in the *Gregg v Kidd* context of blood relationships, such as siblings, when the actual relationship gives rise to a presumption of undue influence. In *Mulcahy v Mulcahy*[30] this was said to be satisfied when the plaintiffs effectively delegated aspects of financial affairs relating to family property to their mother who relied upon the defendant, the plaintiff's brother, to manage those affairs.

13–08 Particular difficulties arise in relation to pleas of undue influence when a husband and wife relationship is under scrutiny. It has been held in several cases that no presumption of undue influence arises out of the simple fact of the relationship created by way of marriage (e.g. *Bank of Montreal v Stuart*,[31] cited by Murnaghan J. in *Northern Banking Co v Carpenter*).[32] If, however, the person seeking relief can show that one spouse was under the dominion of the other, then the party holding power over the other will be required to show that the transaction was the result of the exercise of free will and independent judgment. The same proposition applies in relation to the banker–customer relationship. In *Lloyds Bank v Bundy*[33] the Court of Appeal held that, while in most cases a bank will only be involved in a creditor–debtor relationship with its customers, there may be situations in which there may be obligations placed upon the bank to ensure that customers have a full and complete explanation of a transaction when they enter into a financial transaction with the bank. The scope of this duty of fiduciary care remains as yet undefined. While Peter Pain J. in *Horry v Tate & Lyle Ltd*[34] held that an insurance company settling an accident compensation claim with an employee of the insured was obliged to disclose all relevant information, and perhaps ensure the employee obtained independent advice, or run the risk of the settlement being overturned, it has been held in *O'Hara v Allied Irish Banks*[35] that *Lloyds Bank v Bundy* does not create a right to damages if a bank fails to ensure that a guarantor receives a full and comprehensive explanation of the nature of, and circumstances affecting, a guarantee. It is, however, safe to say that if a bank does not provide a full and detailed explanation of a guarantee given by one of its customers in favour of another customer the instrument may not be enforceable. In *Midland Bank Plc v Cornish*[36] a wife executed a mortgage in favour of a bank, in order to provide security for her husband's business debts, without having been given a clear explanation of the impact of the mortgage. The Court of Appeal held that the bank, having chosen to provide advice to a customer, was under

---

[30] [2011] IEHC 186; *Hackett v CPS* [2011] EWHC 1179 (Admin).
[31] [1911] A.C. 120.
[32] [1931] I.R. 268; *F v F*, unreported, High Court, October 24, 1985.
[33] [1975] Q.B. 326. See Herbert J.'s view, in *Friends First Finance Ltd v Cronin* [2013] IEHC 59, that it was arguable that the fact that the borrower was both a customer and an employee raised a *Bundy* special relationship for the purpose of providing advice.
[34] [1982] 2 Lloyd's Rep. 416.
[35] *The Times*, February 7, 1984.
[36] [1985] 3 All. E.R. 513.

an obligation to provide a full explanation, and, upon proof that an unfair advantage had been taken, a presumption of undue influence arose.[37] While the Court of Appeal found that no unfair advantage could be shown and, following *National Westminster Bank v Morgan*,[38] no presumption could thus arise, the bank was liable in damages under *Hedley Byrne*. Until very recently, English courts took a very restrictive view of the obligation a financial institution has resting upon it to ensure that a full explanation of the nature *and* advisability of a transaction is given to persons with whom the institution deals. There are much stronger Canadian and Australian lines of authority which require financial institutions to ensure that guarantors, particularly elderly persons or other persons who are keen to help the customer of that institution (typically a son of the guarantors) are given an adequate explanation of the instrument; see *Morrison v Coast Finance*[39] and the High Court of Australia's decision in *Commercial Bank of Australia v Amadio*.[40] In *Amadio* two members of the High Court of Australia in particular were anxious to explain that when a bank knows that the proposed guarantor is potentially at a disadvantage—here, elderly parents without a good command of English, guaranteeing business debts of their son, the dominant member of the family, in circumstances where the bank feared that the business activities were not likely to succeed—the institution extracting the guarantee is vulnerable. Mason J. indicated that the bank will be guilty of unconscionable conduct if it does not disclose to would-be guarantors such facts as to enable them to form a judgment for themselves and advise them to seek independent advice. Dean J. observed that at least the bank, in this case, was bound to inquire whether the transaction had been adequately explained. This line of reasoning has been consolidated by *National Australia Bank v Noble*.[41] The respective parents of a married couple, of Italian extraction with limited powers of understanding English, gave security for a building company run by their son. They gave a guarantee and mortgaged land without being told that the bank had formed the view that the building company was in a poor financial condition. The documents, however, were explained fully by the bank manager. Applying *Amadio*, the Federal Court of Australia held the mortgage invalid for the unconscionable behaviour of the bank in not explaining the full facts of the background to the securities provided to the bank.

13–09 One English case takes a similar line. In *Avon Finance Co v Bridger*[42] the parents of a young man signed a legal charge over their property in order to guarantee loans made by a licensed moneylender to their son. They had not

---

[37] On related pleas of *non est factum* and negligent misstatement, see *Lloyds Bank Plc v Waterhouse* [1991] Fam. Law 23; *Friends First Finance Ltd v Lavelle* [2013] IEHC 201.

[38] [1985] A.C. 686.

[39] (1965) 55 D.L.R. (2d.) 710.

[40] (1983) 151 C.L.R. 447. For an imaginative use of *Amadio*, albeit an unsuccessful one, see *Kakavas v Crown Melbourne Ltd* [2013] HCA 25; *Bigwood* (2013) 37 M.U.L.R. 463.

[41] (1991) 100 A.L.R. 227.

[42] (1979) 123 S.J. 705; *Asia Pacific International Property v Dalrymple* [2000] 2 Qd R. 229.

received an explanation of the instruments signed from either the lender or their son. Lord Denning held the case fell within the inequality of bargaining power principle he had earlier enunciated in *Bundy* itself. The son's failure in particular to explain the instrument was a risk that could most appropriately be taken by the lender—a kind of *de facto* agency arose here. While a later Court of Appeal, in *Coldunell Ltd v Gallon*[43] attempted to confine *Avon Finance* to its own facts, the Court of Appeal, in *Midland Bank Plc v Shephard*[44] has endorsed the view that when a creditor, pressing for a security for a debt, gives the task of explaining an instrument to a person who is in a position to obtain consent to that instrument by fraud or misrepresentation, and there is fraud or misrepresentation, the instrument will not be enforced in favour of the creditor. However, both *Midland Bank v Shephard* and *Bank of Baroda v Shah*[45] indicate that creditors and their solicitors are only required to advise a surety that it would be desirable to seek independent advice. It is only when the creditor leaves the surety in the hands of a person who, to the knowledge of the creditor, may exercise some influence over the surety, that the security may be in danger through this agency principle. The Commonwealth cases go further by making the security vulnerable when it is an oppressive or unconscionable transaction even if the creditor advises the surety to seek independent advice. The operation of the agency concept is graphically illustrated by *Barclay's Bank Plc v Kennedy*.[46] The Court of Appeal held that where a husband charges the matrimonial home after the creditor permits the husband to obtain his wife's consent, the husband in law will be held to act as agent for the creditor. The creditor must not be in any better position than the husband, so if the husband exercises undue influence or induces signature by misrepresentation, the creditor will suffer the consequences.

13–10 In 1993 the House of Lords took a new tack, deciding that concepts of agency, or the possible evolution of a "special equity" for spouses providing security for a business debt out of the family home, did not afford a coherent basis for regulating suretyship transactions. In *Barclay's Bank v O'Brien*[47] the House of Lords reformulated the evidentiary requirements of undue influence and, allied with the concept of notice, sought to balance the interests of the financial services industry with the need for transactions to be procedurally irreproachable. In *O'Brien* Lord Browne-Wilkinson indicated that the following classification of undue influence, laid down by the Court of Appeal in *Bank of Credit and Commerce International v Aboody*[48] was to be adopted:

> "Class 1: actual undue influence. Here the claimant must affirmatively show the undue influence alleged.

---

[43] [1986] 1 All E.R. 429.
[44] [1988] 3 All E.R. 17.
[45] [1988] 3 All E.R. 24.
[46] *The Financial Times*, November 15, 1988.
[47] [1993] 4 All E.R. 417; *Smith v Bank of Scotland*, *The Times*, June 23, 1997.
[48] [1990] 1 Q.B. 923.

Class 2: presumed undue influence. This class breaks into two parts. First, Class 2A under which the relationship itself raises the presumption (e.g. solicitor and client). Secondly, Class 2B under which the presumption arises when the facts prove, *de facto*, repose of trust and confidence by the complainant in the wrongdoer and the transaction is manifestly disadvantageous to the complainant."

Building upon this classification (which is mirrored in Irish case law) their Lordships reaffirmed the view that a husband and wife, or a cohabiting couple, do not come within Class 2A. However, if one spouse can show that financial decisions were left by that party for the other to address, then a Class 2B presumption may be made out, and the transaction may be rendered voidable as between those persons. However, if the issue is whether a transaction between the dominated spouse and a third party—classically a bank and a married woman—is liable to be invalidated, the analysis becomes more complex. Should the bank be aware of undue influence as of fact then the transaction will not be enforceable; but, in the absence of such knowledge, is the bank to be denied the right to enforce any security interest it has vis-à-vis the dominated spouse? The decision of the House of Lords, in *Canadian Imperial Bank of Commerce Mortgages Plc v Pitt*[49] makes it clear that if the transaction is an everyday transaction, of some benefit to the spouse, and that it has no unusual provisions or surrounding circumstances (a remortgage ostensibly to obtain funds to buy a holiday home, for example) the bank can enforce its interest even if the wife is the victim of actual, i.e. Class 1 undue influence, for in such a case it is the husband who is the wrongdoer. However, if the parties are known to be closely linked by marital, sexual or other strong emotional ties and the transaction involves the use of property as security for existing or future indebtedness, such circumstances will fix the bank with constructive notice that undue influence exists: in such a case,

> "... unless the creditor who is on inquiry takes reasonable steps to satisfy himself that the wife's agreement to stand surety has been properly obtained, the creditor will have constructive notice of the wife's rights"
> [i.e. to have the transaction set aside for misrepresentation or undue influence].[50]

The House of Lords was given the opportunity to refine aspects of the *O'Brien* decision in *Royal Bank of Scotland Plc v Etridge (No.2)*.[51] Their Lordships reduced the Class 2A and 2B categories of presumed undue influence into one, the test of manifest disadvantage in Class 2B being identified as having given

---

[49] [1993] 4 All E.R. 433, followed in *O'Neill v Ulster Bank* [2015] NICA 64.
[50] [1993] 4 All E.R. 433. *O'Brien* has been approved in Canada; see *Gold v Rosenberg* (1997) 152 D.L.R. (4th) 385; *C.I.B.C. Mortgagee Corp v Rowatt* (2002) 220 D.L.R. (4th) 139; Ogilvie, "The Reception of Etridge (No.2) in Canada" [2008] J.B.L. 191. In New Zealand, see *Lee v Damesh Holdings Ltd* [2003] 2 N.Z.L.R. 422 and *Gardiner v Westpac New Zealand Ltd* [2015] 3 N.Z.L.R. 1.
[51] [2001] 3 W.L.R. 1021.

rise to difficulties of interpretation and application. The presumption of undue influence as between persons in *O'Brien* "husband and wife" relationships will not arise where a family home is simply the subject of a charge, but it will arise where the family home is offered as surety for a husband's business debts or in respect of the indebtedness of a business in which each partner has a shareholding. These commercial purposes will put the lender on inquiry and the lender is required to ensure that, because the transaction of itself calls for some explanation, the lender is required to guard against the possibility that the wife does not understand the transaction, so as Lord Scott of Foscote said in *Etridge (No.2)*, the lender is put on inquiry:

"… not about the existence of undue influence, for how could any inquiry reasonably to be expected of a bank satisfy the bank that there was no undue influence? 'On inquiry', in my opinion, as to whether the wife understood the nature and effect of the transaction she was entering into."[52]

While this view appears to suggest that suretyship cases within *O'Brien* are the subject of a distinct ground of invalidity, apart from misrepresentation and undue influence, their Lordships located the analysis within undue influence by stressing that if the lender is aware that the transaction is so exceptional that it cannot be explained solely on the grounds of natural love and affection as between the debtor and surety, then, following *Allcard v Skinner*,[53] the burden is on the bank to support the transaction.

13–11 Thus, the bank should have clear procedures to ensure that the transaction is clearly understood by the "wife". A private meeting in the bank, with the "husband" being excluded will satisfy this "reasonable steps" test. Merely sending documents to the home of the parties without ensuring that they are explained will not suffice (the facts of *O'Brien* itself). Current practice appears to be to make sure that documents are sent to a reputable firm of solicitors, the lender obtaining from the solicitor a certificate that the transaction has been adequately explained to all the parties to the transaction. Even if there are irregularities in the way in which the clients are advised, as in *Massey v Midland Bank Plc*,[54] where the firm was selected by the dominant spouse and he was present at the time the transaction was explained, the bank will avoid constructive notice of the dominated spouse's equity for it can rely on the professional competence of the client's solicitor and any certificate provided: *Banco Exterior v Mann*.[55] As Hoffmann L.J. put it in *Bank of Baroda v Rayarel*,[56] the "bank's legal department is not obliged to commit the

---

[52] [2001] 3 W.L.R. 1021 at 1072–1073.
[53] (1887) 36 Ch. 145, especially at 185 per Lindley L.J.
[54] [1995] 1 All E.R. 929.
[55] [1995] 1 All E.R. 936.
[56] [1995] 2 F.L.R. 376, approved in *Barclays Bank v Thomson* [1997] 4 All E.R. 816. The bank's legal department is required to ensure a reply is given by the nominated solicitor: *Cooke v National Westminster Bank, The Times*, July 27, 1998.

professional discourtesy of communicating directly with the solicitor's client and tendering such advice itself. Nor is it obliged to inform the solicitor of his professional duties".

13–12 While most cases involve suretyship, some cases involve new loans which are not on their face to the advantage of the spouse, the duty of inquiry still arising according to *Allied Irish Bank Plc v Byrne*[57] and *Halifax Mortgage Services v Stepsky*.[58] Nor is the relationship necessary to trigger the duty one of marriage or cohabitation: emotional links created by virtue of being the parents of a child sufficed in *Massey*, while in the most radical of these cases, *Credit Lyonnais v Burch*,[59] a complex relationship between an older man and a female employee was able to come within the *O'Brien* mechanism. It will not be necessary to show that an emotional link of some kind exists within the context of the relationship after *Etridge (No. 2)* because the whole thrust of that decision was to dispense with individual inquiries into factors of that kind and require the court to focus on whether the transaction was understood. Even a transaction between an elderly man and a son may be attributed to natural love and affection and be a transaction that may not be so exceptional as to put the bank on inquiry; see *Portman Building Society v Dusangh*.[60] One of the consequences of the decision in *Etridge (No. 2)* to dispense with the category 2B form of undue influence is the removal of any clear guidance on how undue influence is to be shown in non-husband-and-wife transactions of the kind that *Dusangh's* case represents. Presumably, actual proof of undue influence will be required if the facts of *Dusangh* were not of themselves persuasive on the undue influence plea. In this case a man of 72, illiterate in English and with a large family, mortgaged his house to 75 per cent of its value to finance the purchase of a supermarket for his son. The lender left the explanation of the transaction to the son and a solicitor was engaged for this purpose. Despite findings of improvidence and the "poor and ignorant" status of the father, the Court of Appeal upheld the trial judge's view that undue influence by the son had not been made out and that the lender was not "on inquiry". Absent actual proof of undue influence, the exceptional nature of the transaction will have to be extremely exceptional if non-marital transactions are to trigger the duty to take reasonable steps to ensure the transaction is understood, at least in cases where undue influence is being pleaded against a financial institution, whether under suretyship or otherwise.

13–13 It is evident that the *O'Brien* case means that difficulties that may arise when family property is used as a finance tool have been addressed by the

---

[57] [1995] 2 F.L.R. 325.
[58] [1996] 2 All E.R. 277.
[59] [1997] 1 All E.R. 144; *Hooley and O'Sullivan* [1997] L.M.C.L.Q. 17; contrast *Banco Exterior v Thomas* [1997] 1 All E.R. 46; *Trustees of Beardsley Theobalds Retirement Benefit Scheme v Yardley* [2011] EWHC 1380 (Q.B.).
[60] [2000] 2 All E.R. (Comm.) 221; *Chater v Mortgage Agency Services (No.2) Ltd* [2003] EWCA Civ 490; *Bradley v Bank of Ireland* [2016] NI Ch 11.

adoption of new practices that make it likely that the transaction will stand, in the absence of some omission by the lending institution. Some commentators favour the view that *O'Brien* does not recognise the special position of the family home and that it does not go far enough as a protective mechanism. Fehlberg,[61] in particular, criticises the post-*O'Brien* decisions, saying that there is an overemphasis on suretyship being for the "common good" and that the cases tend to underestimate the degree of pressure under which a "dependant spouse" within the post-*O'Brien* schema may actually be. More protective laws like Canadian "homestead" legislation, or consumer credit-type "cooling off" and explanatory document legislation would also be useful. Fehlberg's arguments are brought home by a careful reading of *Northern Bank Ltd v McCarron*.[62]

13–14 In *Etridge (No. 2)* the House of Lords was critical of some of the post-*O'Brien* decisions in which the quality of the legal advice proffered clearly fell short of ensuring that the "wife" did indeed understand the transaction. Their Lordships set out a three-fold approach. First, the bank should communicate directly with the "wife" and may only proceed after an appropriate response. Secondly, the "wife" must be afforded financial information either directly from the bank if the bank undertakes to explain the transaction, or it must be furnished to the solicitor acting for the "wife". Lord Nicholls indicated that the information should usually be the purpose behind the facility, the current amount of the husband's indebtedness and a copy of the application. Unfortunately their Lordships recognised that even these steps would not necessarily guard against the "unscrupulous husband", nor would proof that the "wife" did not understand the transaction lead to the transaction being set aside. This is particularly the case in situations where the same solicitor acts for the "husband", the "wife" and the lender, a situation that the House of Lords in *Etridge (No. 2)* did not set its face against. Nor will evidence that the solicitor failed to properly advise the "wife" be imputed to the bank unless the bank knew or had cognisance of facts that should have alerted the bank. The third requirement that the solicitor certify the transaction has been explained does not entitle the solicitor to in any way "veto" the transaction. *Etridge (No. 2)* refocuses the attention of the court to issues of comprehension rather than victimisation[63] so it looks rather like a decision that addresses the improvidence of a transaction rather than undue influence. While *Etridge (No. 2)* broadens the *O'Brien* analysis, it is still being criticised as erring too far in terms of protecting the financial institution rather than the surety.[64]

13–15 Returning to the issue of non-coercive transactions we should note that it is easier to make an allegation of undue influence than to sustain it as a

---

[61]   (1994) 57 M.L.R. 467; (1996) 59 M.L.R. 675.
[62]   [1995] N.I. 258. Carswell L.J. applies the law with all the probity one would expect from such a good judge, but the result in the case still seems shocking to this writer.
[63]   See O'Sullivan (2002) 118 L.Q.R. 337 at 349.
[64]   Wong [2002] J.B.L. 439 at 456; O'Sullivan (2002) 118 L.Q.R. 337 at 349.

defence. The leading English case of *National Westminster Bank v Morgan*[65] is most frequently cited for Lord Scarman's observations on the doctrine of inequality of bargaining power and his Lordship's questioning of the need for such a general principle in English law. What is often overlooked is the application of principles of undue influence to the facts of the case. Mrs Morgan was in no sense "victimised": the financial arrangement made by the bank in that case offered her the best prospect available of salvaging the family home and was struck on the kind of terms a borrower, in the perilous condition of the Morgans, could expect from a respectable lender. The contrast between *Morgan* and *Amadio* lies in the unconscionable behaviour of the bank in the latter case and the absence of any such unconscionable behaviour in *Morgan*. The decision of the Court of Appeal in *Woodstood Finance Ltd v Petrou*[66] confirms the view that in the absence of undue influence between husband and wife, proved by way of dominion or victimisation by one over the other, a normal loan transaction made by a bank, as part of a general banker–customer relationship, will be upheld, as between the wife and lender, absent some factor putting the bank on notice. In *O'Neill v Ulster Bank Ltd*[67] Weir L.J. said that "the threshold" at which a lender is placed on inquiry will vary according to the particular acts on a continuum between the absence of any such obligation, as in the holiday home example of Pitt,[68] and the obligation that will almost certainly arise in a normal surety case.

O'Brien *and* Etridge (No.2) *in Irish law*

13–16 Even though the decisions of the House of Lords could have been regarded as rather opaque and at times less than helpful on a range of issues— see, in particular, the reluctance of Australian judges to jettison earlier jurisprudence developed by the High Court of Australia—Irish judges have, in general terms, drifted towards endorsing persuasive authority from other jurisdictions, without attempting to develop an overarching analysis of the equitable rules. At the core of these cases stands a financial institution that wishes to enforce contractual rights against customers and third parties.

13–17 There is little direct Irish authority on whether this duty to explain, or ensure that an explanation is given, exists. The decision of the majority of the Supreme Court in *Northern Banking Co v Carpenter*[69] at first sight seems applicable but in that case (in which a husband lodged title deeds of his wife's property as security for loans made to him) the bank simply failed to show that the wife knew of or signed any instrument relating to her property. In *Bank of*

---

[65] [1985] A.C. 686.
[66] [1986] F.L.R. 158.
[67] [2015] NICA 64.
[68] *Canadian Imperial Bank of Commerce Mortgages Plc v Pitt* [1994] A.C. 200 (money advanced ostensibly for purchase of a holiday home used by husband to gamble on stockmarket. The husband's actual undue influence did not prejudice the lender.)
[69] [1931] I.R. 268.

Nova Scotia v Hogan[70] the Supreme Court cited with approval the reasoning in *O'Brien* but on the facts there was no evidence of undue influence or misrepresentation, actual or presumed. The Supreme Court also referred to the Australian approach with approval so a definitive view is yet to emerge in Ireland. The concern of the Irish courts to see that transactions are concluded on equal terms (see *Grealish v Murphy*[71] and *Macken v Munster & Leinster Bank*[72]) suggests that the broader equitable approach favoured in Canada and Australia will prevail in Ireland.

13–18 This is borne out by two contrasting recent Irish cases. In *Ulster Bank v Fitzgerald*[73] the suretyship cases like *O'Brien* were distinguished on both the facts and the application of relevant legal principles. Here the second-named defendant signed a guarantee for the existing and future debts of a family-run company in which she had a share, the company being operated by her husband, the first-named defendant. Judgment in an action for a money amount, as distinct from possession of the family home, was sought and granted by O'Donovan J. On the facts, O'Donovan J. found that the wife had signed the guarantee in an interview with the manager of the branch, at which the husband was not present and the guarantee had been explained to her, and although she had been advised by the manager to seek independent legal advice, she signed the documents there and then. The argument that the bank manager should have advised the wife that her family home was potentially at risk and that the bank should have ensured she obtained that advice was rejected on the ground that this was not a family home suretyship situation, as in *O'Brien*. Further, no presumption of undue influence arose here, even though O'Donovan J. was prepared to accept the possibility that the husband may well have exercised undue influence over the wife. Critically, the nature of the transaction did not raise constructive notice of the possibility that the wife had been the victim of undue influence, given her clear financial interest in the business and lack of evidence that the bank had in any way been given information on the relationship between husband and wife. This is a robust application of traditional undue influence principles, but the precedential value of the case is limited because of certain gaps in the evidence (the husband did not give testimony) and the findings of fact made concerning the nature and circumstances surrounding the transaction. One may, however, take exception to O'Donovan J.'s observation that in advising the wife to seek independent legal advice, the bank manager was going "above and beyond the call of duty". Such advice would appear to be a prudent step for the bank to take, even in the light of earlier case law pre-*O'Brien*. It is the fact that the bank manager explained the guarantee personally to the wife in a one-to-one interview that saved this transaction and this is, in this writer's experience, exceptional business practice.

---

[70]   [1997] 1 I.L.R.M. 407.
[71]   [1946] I.R. 35.
[72]   [1959] I.R. 313.
[73]   [2001] IEHC 159; see Mee (2002) 37 *Irish Jurist* 392.

13–19 In *Ulster Bank Ireland Ltd v Louis Roche*[74] Clarke J. refused to follow O'Donovan J.'s decision in *Ulster Bank v Fitzgerald*, remarking that:

> "A regime which places no obligation on a bank to take any steps to ascertain whether, in the presence of circumstances suggesting a non-commercial aspect to a guarantee, the party offering the guarantee may not be fully and freely entering into same, gives insufficient protection to potentially vulnerable sureties."

Clarke J. went on to say that he approved the general principle which underlies *Etridge (No.2)* that "a bank is placed on inquiry when it is aware of facts which suggest, or ought to suggest, that there may be a non-commercial element to a guarantee". There are some other isolated decisions[75] that suggest that *O'Brien/Etridge (No.2)* is proving of assistance. However, on the general distinction between instances when a financial institution is put on notice, the High Court, in *GE Capital Woodchester Home Loans Ltd v Reade and Reade*[76] has endorsed the distinction between undue influence in cases where a spouse or partner agrees to stand as surety for the debts of another partner from cases where there is a loan to a couple, secured against property, for the benefit of both and secured on family property owned by both. In this case, the defendants represented that they wished to jointly obtain a loan of €230,000 in place of an existing loan of €160,000 with another financial institution. Laffoy J. held there was nothing on the facts of that case to put the bank "on inquiry". Laffoy J. contrasted the "joint advance" case from instances of surety transaction. The learned judge's summary of the decision in *Ulster Bank Ireland Ltd v Roche*[77] could not be bettered so it is reproduced below in full. Laffoy J. said:

> "Recently, in [*Roche*], which was a case in which the second defendant, Ms. Buttimer, had acted as surety for Louis Roche Motors Ltd, a business owned by Mr. Roche, who was her partner in the personal sense of that term, under a guarantee given by Mr. Roche and Ms. Buttimer to Ulster Bank, the decision of the House of Lords in the *Etridge* case was considered by the High Court (Clarke J.). Clarke J. stated (at para.5.14) that he was satisfied that 'the general principle, which underlies *Etridge*, is to the effect that a bank is placed on inquiry where

---

[74] [2012] IEHC 166.

[75] On the scope of *O'Brien/Etridge (No.2)* applying beyond personal relationships into commercial partners, see *Bank of Ireland (U.K.) Plc v Crawford* [2012] NI Master 6. Laffoy J. has also considered the relevance of *Etridge (No.2)* to a case where a bank sought to obtain security for a loan it was advancing to one party to a joint deposit account in *O'Meara v Bank of Scotland Plc* [2011] IEHC 402. For an interesting, if inconclusive, extension of *O'Brien* and the extent to which a bank can shelter behind independent advice to a third party, see *Tynan v County Registrar of Kilkenny* [2011] IEHC 250.

[76] [2012] IEHC 363; *ACC Bank v McEllin* [2013] IEHC 454; *Bank of Scotland plc v Hickey* [2014] IEHC 202.

[77] [2012] IEHC 166.

it is aware of facts which suggest, or ought to suggest, that there may be a non-commercial element to a guarantee'. Clarke J. found that the general principle went far enough to cover the facts of the case before him, so that Ms. Buttimer had a defence to the claim of Ulster Bank under the guarantee, the oral evidence having established that there had been 'undoubted undue influence' exercised over her by Mr. Roche, by virtue of the failure of Ulster Bank to take any steps to ensure that she was acting freely when it was on inquiry. However, he had noted earlier (at para. 5.11) that, in his speech in *Etridge,* Lord Nicholls had –

'... distinguished between cases where the surety guaranteed the debts of a spouse or partner from a case where the monies were advanced to the spouses or partners jointly (the lender not being on inquiry in the latter case unless it was known to the bank that the loan was for the benefit of one person only) ...'

Accordingly, while it is true to say, albeit at the risk of oversimplification, that the decision in *Ulster Bank Ireland Ltd v Roche* does represent a development of the law in this jurisdiction, it has no bearing on the factual situation with which the Court is concerned in this case."

(2) Undue influence as of fact

13–20 If the presumption does not arise automatically and if the court does not feel that the facts shown raise an inference that the transaction was not freely consented to, it is necessary to convince the court that the transaction should not stand. The courts will not presume that undue influence exists if, at first sight, one person is in no position to hold dominion over another. In a sense the courts presume that the parties deal on an equal footing. In the case of *Mathew v Bobbins*[78] the English Court of Appeal ruled that the relationship of employer/employee does not give rise to the presumption that the employer stands in a dominant position vis-à-vis the employee. The Court of Appeal reasoned that twentieth-century employment protection legislation has readjusted an imbalance that clearly existed in the last century. Mr Bobbins was held not to have been prevailed upon by his employer when he "agreed" to sign a document which changed his status from a tenant into a licensee of accommodation provided by his employer. It is open to doubt whether employment legislation, either in Ireland or in Great Britain, has reached the level of sophistication or effectiveness contemplated in this case. Other

---

[78] *The Times,* June 21, 1980; contrast the Canadian decision in *Blackmore v Cablenet Ltd* [1995] 3 W.W.R. 305. Principles of interpretation, as expressed under Lord Hoffmann's *West Bromwich* guidelines (see Ch.5) are increasingly diluting the impact of the earlier principles and presumptions relating to equitable intervention. Employment contracts which the courts classify as "sham" transactions so as to allow one party certain taxation or other advantages by exploiting inequality of bargaining power may be reclassified (e.g. a contract of employment rather than a contract for services): *Autoclenz Ltd v Belcher* [2011] UKSC 41. But note the impact of inequality of bargaining power as an aid to interpretation in employment contracts, in contrast to "arm's length" commercial contracts.

status-based relationships are problematical. In *Attorney-General for England and Wales v R*,[79] the New Zealand Court of Appeal held that, absent an order to sign a contract, a serving officer does not become subject to actual undue influence, nor does *O'Brien* Class 2A or 2B undue influence arise. The Court of Appeal overturned the trial judge's view that the Army command structure and position of enlisted soldiers led to a Class 2B presumption arising on the basis that the facts demonstrated that the respondent had in fact lost faith or confidence in his superior officers vis-à-vis the transaction in question. This is clearly a borderline decision and does not sit easily with the kind of "institutional dominion" approach that finds expression in *Allcard v Skinner*. In affirming this case, the Privy Council[80] stressed that signature of the agreement was not a direct order, but this seems beside the point.

13–21 Similarly, the Privy Council in *Glover v Glover*[81] held that debtor/creditor and mortgagor/mortgagee relationships do not give rise to a presumption. Lord Porter said that in cases where no presumption ordinarily arises:

> "… certain matters are always regarded as relevant and sometimes conclusive, amongst which the following are worthy of special mention:
>
> (1) that the transaction in question was a voluntary gift;
> (2) that the transaction, if amounting to a contract was for a manifestly inadequate consideration;
> (3) the existence of a marked disparity in age and position between the parties to the transaction."[82]

Because the House of Lords has recently emphasised that "victimisation" is the essence of undue influence it will be difficult to grant relief if, as in *National Westminster Bank Plc v Morgan*[83] itself, there is proof that the transaction was understood by the person allegedly influenced (even if no full explanation was given) and the transaction itself, in its substantive terms, is not unfair.

13–22 There is no presumption of undue influence vis-à-vis personal guarantees within a family business solely by virtue of the signor being a housewife and mother: *Irish Bank Resolution Corp Ltd v Quinn*.[84] After finding that there was no presumption of undue influence in those family circumstances, Kelly J. went on:

> "The absence of the presumption does not mean that there could not be actual undue influence. But if there was such actual undue influence,

---

[79] [2002] 2 N.Z.L.R. 91.
[80] [2003] UKPC 22.
[81] [1951] 1 D.L.R. 657.
[82] [1951] 1 D.L.R. 657 at 664–665.
[83] [1985] A.C. 686; *Macklin v Dowsett* [2004] EWCA Civ 904.
[84] [2011] IEHC 470.

there would have to be, at least, some evidence demonstrative of such impropriety. There is no evidence of any sort to support such a contention. There is no suggestion of Mrs. Quinn suffering from any intellectual disability, mental illness, feebleness of mind or cognitive impairment. Neither is there any evidence of any threats of bullying or such behaviour towards her by Mr. Quinn. There is not the slightest evidence to suggest any allegation of actual undue influence could be sustained."

However, the facts of each individual case may produce a compelling basis for judicial intervention, possibly through *non est factum* or duress.

13–23 In *O'Flanagan v Ray-Ger Ltd*[85] an agreement between two sole share-holders of a company, transferring property to the defendant, was set aside for undue influence. There was a marked disparity in terms of business acumen, the defendant being dominant and the more astute. Negotiations took place away from business premises in circumstances where the very considerable persuasive powers of the defendant partner could freely operate. The agreement was improvident, virtually a gift transaction because of the poor health of the transferor who, to the knowledge of both parties, was terminally ill. In these circumstances Costello J. held that the plaintiff, executor of the estate of the transferor, had proved undue influence as a fact. Indeed, in this writer's view, the facts are so compelling that it would have been possible to hold that the whole evidence would raise the presumption of undue influence in the second sense in which Jones L.J. talked of the presumption arising in *R. (Proctor) v Hutton, Re Founds Estate*, as well as coming within Class 2B in *Barclay's Bank v O'Brien*.[86] The more recent English case of *Daniel v Drew*[87] also contains a colourful set of facts in which a young and "forceful" nephew "cornered" his elderly aunt into executing a deed by misrepresentation and making "threatening" statements that he would have to take her to court. Ward L.J. described his conduct as "unconscionable".

13–24 Family transactions are often problematical because it may be difficult to regard these arrangements as being truly contractual. Members of a family are often motivated by love and affection and a desire to assist persons who are in need of financial support. Nevertheless, the presumption will be important because there may be an absence of any evidence upon which undue influence can be found as a fact. Before the onus of proof will shift to require the party who is seeking to uphold the transaction to provide an explanation about it, the court may decide that there are no unusual circumstances so as to warrant any shifting of the evidential burden. It must be said that, at times, too much is made of the role of the so-called presumption. The desire to protect people

---

[85] Unreported, High Court, April 28, 1983; *Loonam v Kenny* [2015] IEHC 545 (financial advisers to person with intellectual disability, undue influence as of fact).

[86] [1978] N.I. 139, Court of Appeal judgment of April 30, 1979.

[87] [2005] EWCA Civ 509.

from being forced, tricked or misled in any way into parting with property (per Lindley L.J. in *Allcard v Skinner*) is the underlying objective, regardless of which class of undue influence is under review. Even if trust and confidence are reposed by one party it may be that the transaction is so unexceptional that it is the kind of everyday familial event that does not have to be justified in order to understand. The court will of course need to make findings of fact on the core issues. In *Turkey v Awadh*[88] the English Court of Appeal was faced with an unusual case where the appellants, daughter and son-in-law of the respondent, agreed to sell property to the respondent for a large cash sum and his agreement to pay off the mortgage (which would take nine years). The parties at no time sought to value the property by reference to market value, giving the respondent the possibility that he was acquiring a property at a bargain price. It was likely that if the presumption, that is, the evidential burden, was on the respondent, then the transaction would be set aside as no independent legal advice had been obtained by the sellers. The question that the Court of Appeal presented to itself was whether the transaction could not be explained by reference to the ordinary motives by which people are accustomed to act.[89] If the answer was in the affirmative then the evidential burden would shift to the respondent. The Court of Appeal, however, agreed with the County Court judge that the presumption did not arise. This was not an ordinary commercial transaction. It was largely a family arrangement. The fact that the property had not been valued was unusual but the fact that a large part of the price was paid up front, with the sellers being able to live in the property for a further nine years, was significant. Further, the appellants had received the cash in order to pay off debts—a hole that the appellants had dug for themselves—and meant that entering a bargain of this kind could well be explained by reference to the motives that ordinary persons, in the position of the appellants, would be driven by. The transaction did not call for the respondent to give an explanation. The decision is, therefore, very similar to that reached in *National Westminster Bank Plc v Morgan*.

(3) Discharging the onus of proof

13–25 Once the presumption operates, the party seeking to uphold the transaction must show that consent was freely given and that the party with whom he contracted did so with his eyes open. The cases suggest that this can be done by advising that independent advice be sought from a respectable source. In *McMackin v Hibernian Bank*[90] a bank was denied enforcement of a bank guarantee because the guarantor, its client's daughter, should have obtained legal advice; the case where the guarantor is also a client of the bank is considerably a fortiori; see *Lloyds Bank v Bundy*.[91] The case of *Smyth v Smyth*[92] holds that it is enough if the party seeking to enforce the bargain shows

---

[88] [2005] EWCA Civ 382; *Hart v Burbidge* [2014] EWCA Civ. 992.
[89] Lord Scott of Foscote's test in *Etridge (No.2)* [2002] 2 A.C. 773 at 854.
[90] [1905] 1 I.R. 296.
[91] [1975] Q.B. 326.
[92] Unreported, High Court, November 22, 1978; *Noonan v O'Connell*, unreported, High Court, April 10, 1987.

that it was contemplated that independent legal advice would be given before the contract was completed. This may be a dangerous precedent to rely on. The best advice would be to advise the other person to seek and obtain independent legal advice. Even where independent legal advice has been given, the advice may be tested and if the solicitor was acting for both parties, but in substance was instructed by the transferee and it is not shown that the instrument was read over to the transferor, this may point away from the presumption being displaced; see *Carroll v Carroll*.[93] However, each case turns upon its own facts. If the advisor turns out to be a trusted friend or respected member of the community this may suffice.

13–26 In fact, sales in which no advice was sought or given have been upheld. What the doctrine boils down to is the protection of persons who are not able to freely consent to a transaction. If, after hearing the evidence, the court feels that the bargain should stand, no a priori test will stand in the way. This is shown vividly by *Smyth v Smyth*. In *McCrystal v O'Kane*[94] there was evidence of a sale at a substantial, but not gross, undervalue, and in the absence of other vitiating factors Murray J. held that there was not a sufficient basis for finding undue influence as of fact, particularly when the defendant vendor was advised twice to obtain independent advice by the solicitor acting for both vendor and purchaser.

13–27 However, in cases where the presumption arises, it will not be enough to show that the mental state of the vendor or donor, as the case may be, was satisfactory, or that the purchaser or donee had done nothing wrong.[95]

13–28 In *McCormack v Bennett*[96] Finlay P. upheld a transfer of farm property made by an elderly couple to a daughter, who in return, agreed to look after them for the rest of their lives. The disposition was challenged on the ground that no independent advice was given. The action was dismissed:

> "The presence of full and satisfactory independent advice is not the only way of proving that a voluntary deed even though it may be on the face of it improvident resulted from the free exercise of the donor's will ... I think it is a reasonable inference from the evidence which I have heard that he was a sufficiently astute man to know that no form of bargain or commercial transaction was likely to secure for himself what they really needed and that was personal care and attention granted largely through affection and kindness by a member of their family."

---

[93] [2000] 1 I.L.R.M. 210; *Lynn v O'Hara* [2015] IEHC 122. For a case where the quality of the solicitor's advice was found wanting, see *Vale v Armstrong* [2004] EWHC 1160 (Ch).

[94] [1986] N.I. 123.

[95] *Carroll v Carroll* [2000] 1 I.L.R.M. 210; *Pesticcio v Huet, The Independent,* April 7, 2004.

[96] Unreported, High Court, July 2, 1973; *Provincial Bank v McKeever* [1941] I.R. 471.

As a general rule it is more difficult for administrators of an estate to convince a court that the deceased was unable to freely consent, particularly if the deceased later seems to have approved the consequences of her action: see *Kirwan v Cullen*.[97] This reluctance to "second guess" the deceased, particularly when he or she seems mentally competent, is evident in *McCormack v Bennett* also. However, if the facts are equivocal the disposition may be overturned. In *Carroll & Carroll v Carroll*[98] the elderly transferor of a family pub appeared to the court to have been misled by his son, the transferee, and his assurances to his daughters that they would "have a home" were compatible with lack of knowledge that he had actually executed a transfer of property as well as an act of concealment by the transferor. In these circumstances the presumption of undue influence was not rebutted.

(4) Delay in seeking relief

13–29 A party who later approves and seeks to take advantage of a bargain will be bound by it, even if it was suspicious at the time it was entered into; see *De Montmorency v Devereux*,[99] affirmed by the House of Lords.

13–30 In cases where the presumption operates but there is no evidence of fraud or overbearing conduct, relief must be sought promptly. In *Carroll v Carroll*, where proceedings were commenced within one year of the true circumstances emerging, the Supreme Court held that defences of laches or acquiescence could not be made out. In *Allcard v Skinner*[100] relief was refused because of a delay of six years in seeking relief. Where fraud or overbearing conduct exists as of fact a delay of 12 years was held not to be fatal in *O'Kelly v Glenny*.[101] Time begins to run from the date of emancipation from the dominion of the other party. In *Wadlow v Samuel*[102] a settlement agreement in respect of music publishing contracts was challenged some 11 years after it was struck. In the intervening period registration of title for the purpose of collecting royalties had taken place on the basis of these agreements being valid. The defences of acquiescence and laches were successfully mounted to negate undue influence. It is important to note that undue influence ceased after the settlement agreement was signed.

13–31 In many of these cases, the agreement has been carried into effect, often over a period of many years. Where land has been exploited, for

---

[97] (1854) 2 Ir.Ch.R. 322. *Randall v Randall* [2004] EWHC 2258 (Ch).

[98] [2000] 1 I.L.R.M. 210. In *Pathania v Adedeji* [2010] EWHC 3085 (Q.B.), a presumption of undue influence was in part refuted for some transactions by evidence that the client was an astute sophisticated medical practitioner who had signed a promissory note that benefitted his solicitor, acknowledging in writing that he had taken independent legal advice prior to executing the note.

[99] (1840) 2 Dr. & Wal. 410.

[100] (1887) 36 Ch. D. 145.

[101] (1846) 9 Ir.Eq.R. 25.

[102] [2006] EWHC 1492 (Q.B.), affirmed at [2007] EWCA Civ 155; *Davies v AIB Group (U.K.) Plc* [2012] EWHC 2178 (Ch).

example, the court may order an account of profits and may allow the person who has benefited from the undue influence some degree of remuneration, or an allowance for improvements made; see *Mulhallen v Marum*.[103] In the more recent English cases[104] in which recording and publishing contracts were overturned, several years after these contracts had been in operation, an inquiry into profits made was ordered and the court allowed the deduction of reasonable out-of-pocket expenses incurred in exploiting these works, as well as an allowance for skill and labour exercised on behalf of the artist, including a profit element. Considerable flexibility in the granting of equitable reliefs is available, the concept of fair compensation in equity being available as well as an inquiry into an account of profits.[105] There is recent English authority in which a contract for the sale of property was held to be voidable for undue influence and unconscionable bargain but because an innocent third party had advanced monies to the purchaser, on foot of a charge, the High Court could not order restitution of the property. Because the third party interest intervened, the purchaser was ordered to pay damages on an indemnity basis: *Bank of Scotland v Hussain*.[106] In Canada, the Supreme Court of Canada, in *Rick v Brandsema*[107] has made an important decision in setting aside a separation agreement obtained by a husband who did not disclose important financial details whilst exploiting the emotional vulnerability of his spouse. The Supreme Court of Canada could not effect rescission but reinstated an award of $690,000 (Cdn) as being either damages/equitable compensation/a statutory remedy under British Columbia statute law. There appears to be no reason why an Irish court could not, in similar circumstances, be required to provide a compensatory remedy where traditional equitable reliefs such as rescission are not available.[108]

Unconscionable Bargains

13–32 The Irish courts of equity have intervened in unconscionable bargains by setting aside the transaction or amending the terms in order to produce what the court sees as a fairer transaction. Historically the courts, both here and in England, have protected persons who mortgaged or sold an interest in family property by obliging the mortgagee or purchaser to show the bargain to be a fair one.[109] This jurisdiction extended into cases where an aged or illiterate

---

[103] (1843) 3 Dr. & War. 317.
[104] e.g. *O'Sullivan v Management Agency and Music Ltd* [1984] 3 W.L.R. 448; *John v James* [1991] F.S.R. 397; *Walmsley v Acid Jazz Records* [2001] E.C.D.R. 29; *Wadlow v Samuel* [2006] EWHC 1492 (Q.B.), affirmed at [2007] EWCA Civ 155.
[105] Contrast *Cheese v Thomas* [1994] 1 All E.R. 35 with *Mahoney v Purnell* [1996] 3 All E.R. 61.
[106] [2010] EWHC 2812 (Ch) (see the 2001 Order in this remarkable case and [2012] EWCA Civ 1661).
[107] [2009] 1 S.C.R. 295.
[108] See the loss of profits claim in *Keating v Keating* [2009] IEHC 405 (an improvident bargain case).
[109] The doctrine is traced in Ch.1 of Clark, *Inequality of Bargaining Power* (Toronto: Carswell, 1987). The leading Irish cases are *Scott v Dunbar* (1828) 1 Moll. 457; *Woodroffe v Allen*

person, for example, sold property, of which he or she was in possession, for an inadequate consideration.[110] The equitable doctrine relating to expectant heirs and reversioners, as these persons came to be known, has, in part, produced a wider equitable jurisdiction.

13–33 In the case of *Slator v Nolan*,[111] Sullivan M.R. after reviewing the early cases declared:

> "I take the law of the Court to be that if two persons—no matter whether a confidential relation exists between them or not—stand in such a relation to each other that one can take an undue advantage of the other, whether by reason of distress or recklessness or wildness or want of care and where the facts show that one party has taken undue advantage of the other, by reason of the circumstances I have mentioned—a transaction resting upon such unconscionable dealing will not be allowed to stand."[112]

In *Slator v Nolan* itself, a young man, in want of money because of his youthful excesses, was able to set aside a sale of his inheritance. In more recent times the unconscionable bargain jurisdiction was invoked to set aside a gift of the family home by the owner to his daughter, largely motivated by an obsessional fear that, should the Australian Labor Party come to power, the Party would take the home and the pension of the donor. Invoking the Australian "special disability" concept, as well as the fact that the solicitor acting for donor and donee was not specifically advised as to all surrounding circumstances, the New South Wales Court of Appeal found the gift both improvident and unconscionable: *Aboody v Ryan*.[113] Allsop P. referred to the fact that across the common law world, an unconscionable bargain jurisdiction, based on equity's "norms and values" could be found:

> "[T]here is an underlying general principle, the applications or exemplifications of which are impossible to describe fully. Thus, one should always be careful not to dwell over-technically or textually on individual expressions of general principle of normative values rooted in the remedying of injustice. It is general principle, not a precisely expressed rule, that operates. The principle is wide, and the danger in further textual definition (as opposed to exemplification or illumination) is that inaccuracy or undue restriction may be brought about: I C F Spry, *Equitable Remedies*, 8th ed."

(1832) Hayes & Jo. 73; *Cook v Burtchaell* (1842) 2 Drur. & War. 165; *Ormsby v Lord Limerick* (1849) 2 Ir. Jur. 301.

[110] e.g. *Garvey v McMinn* (1846) 9 Ir.Eq.Rep. 526.

[111] (1876) I.R. 11 Eq. 367.

[112] (1876) I.R. 11 Eq. 367 at 409.

[113] [2012] NSWCA 395; see generally Capper, "The Unconscionable Bargain in the Common Law World" (2010) 126 L.Q.R. 403. On unconscionability and gifts see *Prendergast v Joyce* [2009] IEHC 199 and *Evans v Lloyd* [2013] EWHC 1725 (Ch).

These cases proceed on a finding that the parties were not equal at the time the contract was struck, largely as a result of the individual circumstances into which one of the parties has fallen. In *Rae v Joyce*[114] a pregnant woman who mortgaged a reversionary interest in real property at an undervalue was held entitled to set the transaction aside. The mortgagee, a Dublin moneylender, was clearly the more commercially astute; the delicate medical condition of the mortgagor and her needy circumstances, allied to a rate of interest fixed at 60 per cent, convinced the Irish Court of Appeal that the bargain should be set aside, a rate of interest of five per cent being substituted instead. The mortgagee was unable to show that the bargain was not a hard one.

13–34 Although sharp practice, misrepresentation and collusion often appear in these cases, the basis of relief is not fraud in any real sense of a fraudulent misrepresentation. If a bargain is harsh in its terms and if one party is clearly in a stronger bargaining position, equity will intervene. The hardness of the bargain was stressed to be the foundation of intervention in *Benyon v Cook*[115] but it is not clear whether this is of general application and whether it is compatible with Selborne L.C.'s speech in *Aylesford v Morris*[116] when the Lord Chancellor stressed that equitable intervention "depended on an unconscientious use of the power arising out of these circumstances and conditions". A further retrenchment has occurred in the Privy Council. In *Hart v O'Connor*,[117] it was emphasised that a contract will not be overturned simply because the bargain is on its terms unfair if there is no evidence of unconscionable dealing. To put it another way, a bargain that is one-sided cannot be interfered with if the conscience of the party benefiting most is not affected. This is graphically illustrated by the more recent decision of the English Court of Appeal in *Portman Building Society v Dusangh*.[118] An improvident transaction entered into by an elderly father, in English (which he did not understand) brought the unconscionable bargain jurisdiction into operation, but relief was denied on the grounds that while the lending institution had not followed its own guidelines it had not acted in a morally reprehensible manner. It is noteworthy that the Court of Appeal seem to have regarded this jurisdiction as turning upon misconduct as distinct from the parties coming to the transaction on an unequal footing and this English case should be contrasted with *Carroll v Carroll*.[119] All members of the Supreme Court stressed the need for adequate and independent legal advice to be given, absent which, the contract will not be allowed to stand. While the English courts arguably incline towards upholding the transaction where a lending institution is concerned, Canadian judges, for example, do not hesitate to overturn the transaction if acceptable standards of commercial morality, or sound lending practices, are not met; e.g.

---

[114] (1892) 29 L.R. (Ir.) 500; contrast *Secured Property Loans v Floyd* [2011] IEHC 189.
[115] (1875) L.R. 10 Ch.App. 389.
[116] (1873) L.R. 8 Ch.App. 484.
[117] [1985] 2 All. E.R. 880.
[118] [2000] 1 All E.R. (Comm.) 221; see also *Jones v Morgan* [2001] EWCA Civ 995.
[119] [2000] 1 I.L.R.M. 210.

CIBC v Ohlson.[120] Some novel applications of the principle have been thrown up by recent decisions, such as penalties imposed on trade union members by the constitution of their trade union.[121]

Unconscionable bargains and family property

13–35 In transactions involving family property, Laffoy J. has asked whether, by virtue of lack of transparency in respect of providing detailed information and relevant documentation, a transaction can be unconscionable or improvident because the beneficiary can thus be said to act in "a morally culpable manner". In *Mulcahy v Mulcahy*[122] there were shortcomings but the transactions that resulted were neither overreaching nor oppressive and the payments made to the plaintiffs were, on the evidence before the court, satisfactory. In contrast, in *Keating v Keating*[123] Laffoy J. set aside a sale made by an elderly farmer, who due in part to illness was unable to either understand or obtain independent advice.

13–36 The Irish courts are extremely protective of elderly persons who sell or dispose of farmland outside the family unit. In *Buckley v Irwin*,[124] McVeigh J. in the Northern Ireland Chancery Division refused to grant a decree of specific performance in favour of the plaintiff who had purchased the defendant's farm at undervalue. The parties were not equally competent in business matters; the plaintiff was described as "sharp-eyed and experienced", the defendant characterised as "a person who would require protection and guidance in carrying out business affairs". In *Grealish v Murphy*[125] a transfer of land made by an elderly, intransigent and illiterate farmer, again at undervalue in favour of a younger man, was set aside by Gavan Duffy J. on the ground that the parties were not on an equal footing.

13–37 At this point we should consider whether the basis of invalidity is always a finding that the weaker party has been "overreached". Many cases turn upon the fact that one party, while he or she cannot be said to be clinically insane, is unable, for reasons of intellectual impairment or disability, senility, illness or lack of business acumen, to understand the implications of the contract. *Grealish v Murphy* is such a case. Here the transaction was drafted and explained to the old man by his lawyer. While Gavan Duffy J. held that the lawyer had not done everything he could have done to bring home to his client the implications of the transaction, it is difficult to see how this would

---

[120] (1997) 154 D.L.R. (4th) 33.
[121] *Birch v Union of Taxation Employees* (2008) 305 D.L.R. (4th) 64; contrast *Graham v Inpark* (2010) ONSC 4982 (parking penalty fees).
[122] [2011] IEHC 186. The plaintiffs here were educated young women, not the "feckless middle-aged women" referred to in *Grealish v Murphy*. See also *Pitt v Holt* [2011] EWCA Civ 197 per Lloyd L.J.
[123] [2009] IEHC 405, an important case as neither duress nor undue influence was present.
[124] [1960] N.I. 98; *Stronge v Johnston* [1997] N.I.J.B. 56.
[125] [1946] I.R. 35.

be possible if the old man was incapable of grasping the consequences of the contract. In these situations invalidity results from the fact that the bargain is so improvident that no reasonable person would enter into it. Some of the best modern authorities are provided by *Lyndon v Coyne*[126] and *JH v WJH*.[127] In *Lyndon v Coyne* the aged owner of land transferred the property to his nephew in return for a promise by the nephew to permit the old man and his wife to remain on the property for their lives, and for periodic payments of cash. Given the health and age of the old man the instrument was a foolish and improvident one. There was no revocation clause included in the instrument; payments were likely to end at an early date—the old man died three months later—and the instrument as a whole was curiously drafted, suggesting to the court that it was not understood by the old man. O'Byrne J. set the deed aside. More pertinent still is the decision in *Rooney v Conway*.[128] An elderly man sold his farm outside the family at undervalue to a young man who had befriended and helped him in his old age. The sale was set aside even though there was no evidence of improper or unconscionable behaviour. It was expressly stated that in cases where the sale is at gross undervalue and between persons not on equal footing, and the transaction is thus improvident, it is not necessary to show improper behaviour or equitable fraud by the stronger party before the relief can be granted. Improvidence, in many of these cases, is used to describe a contract that may not of itself be one-sided. Indeed, many improvident transactions are gift transfers which are unsupported by consideration. The transfer has a speculative nature about it and it is the fact that events may change the shape of the transaction that brings the equitable jurisdiction into play. So the execution of deeds without cancellation provisions or conditions subsequent may be the real basis of the "improvidence" analysis; see *Carroll v Carroll*.[129] Similar decisions can be found in English law but the equitable jurisdiction seems to be more frequently utilised in Ireland. The traditional equitable jurisdiction to grant relief against unconscionable bargains in England is summarised in *Fry v Lane*[130] as depending upon three factors; the poverty and ignorance of the plaintiff, the consideration being at undervalue and the lack of independent advice. In *Cresswell v Potter*[131] a matrimonial home was held by both husband and wife. When the marriage broke down, the wife was persuaded to execute a conveyance of her interest in the property to her husband, in return for an indemnity against liability under the mortgage and for nothing else. The wife claimed that she believed the document was necessary in order to realise her interest in the matrimonial property, by enabling it to be sold. There was no fraud, no misrepresentation, and no undue

---

[126] (1946) 12 Ir. Jur. Rep. 64.

[127] Unreported, High Court, December 20, 1979.

[128] Unreported, March 8, 1986, a decision of the Northern Ireland Chancery Division. *Macklin v Dowsett* [2006] EWCA Civ 904, is a recent English parallel.

[129] Especially at [2000] 1 I.L.R.M. 210 at 221.

[130] (1888) 40 Ch. D. 312, applied by the Privy Council in *Boustany v Piggot* [1993] UKPC 17. See also *Crédit Lyonnais v Burch* [1997] 1 All ER 144; *Pitt v Holt* [2011] EWCA Civ 197.

[131] [1978] 1 W.L.R. 255.

influence. Megarry J. held that all three *Fry v Lane* factors existed. The wife was a member of the "lower income groups" and thus poor and ignorant. The sale was at an undervalue and, finally, made without independent advice. A more principled approach has emerged in Canada. Canadian case law has, at the highest level, stressed the need for full and frank disclosure by both sides when separating spouses are negotiating separation agreements. While in *Miglin v Miglin*[132] the case concerned agreements upon divorce, the Supreme Court of Canada, in *Rick v Brandsema*[133] stressed that the parties to a marital breakdown are vulnerable at such a time and that, while the courts are obliged to respect the rights of the parties to decide for themselves what bargain they are prepared to make, Abella J., giving judgment for the Supreme Court of Canada, said:

> "... contractual autonomy, however, depends on the integrity of the bargaining process ... a duty to make full and honest disclosure of all relevant financial information is required to protect the integrity of the result of negotiations undertaken in these uniquely vulnerable circumstances. The deliberate failure to make such disclosure may render the agreement vulnerable to individual intervention ..."

While each case will turn on its own facts, this broad duty of disclosure is an important part of an overall unconscionability-based process in Canadian family law.

13–38 Unconscionable bargains are sometimes concluded by commercial organisations with persons of little or no business experience. The Canadian courts, for example, have utilised this jurisdiction to set aside settlements of insurance claims when the bargain is unfair. An illustration of this is afforded by *Doan v Insurance Corp of British Columbia*.[134] A loss adjuster settled a claim on behalf of an insurance company and the plaintiff, a road accident victim, for $60,000(Cdn). The injury was a serious one and the plaintiff and his family were unsophisticated and relied entirely on the advice of the loss adjuster. The injury worsened and an application was brought to set aside the settlement. Paris J. cited the leading case of *Harry v Kreutziger*[135] where McIntyre J. had held that:

> "Where a claim is made that a bargain is unconscionable, it must be shown that there was inequality in the position of the parties due to the ignorance, need or distress of the weaker party which would leave him in the power of the stronger, coupled with proof of substantial unfairness in the bargain."[136]

---

[132] [2003] 1 S.C.R. 303.
[133] [2009] 1 S.C.R. 295.
[134] (1987) 18 B.C.L.R. (2d) 286; contrast *Gindis v Brisbourne* (1999) 183 D.L.R. (4th) 430.
[135] (1978) 95 D.L.R. (3d) 231.
[136] (1978) 95 D.L.R. (3d) 231 at 237, applying, inter alia, *Waters v Donnelly* (1884) 9 O.R. 391.

Paris J., following this test, held the settlement to be unconscionable and set it aside, assessing damages at a total figure of $312,000(Cdn).

13–39 It will be difficult to obtain relief from an allegedly unfair bargain if the transaction is struck between commercial organisations. If improper pressure is imposed then economic duress may be relevant but, in general terms, the courts take the view that a predominantly market economy does not require that unsound business decisions should be amended by allowing one party to invoke the unconscionable bargain jurisdiction unless there existed a duty of fiduciary care (*Lloyds Bank v Bundy*).[137] Nevertheless, Costello J. in *O'Flanagan v Ray-Ger Ltd*[138] indicated that even business transactions are not sacrosanct, when, in the context of an agreement between the two sole shareholders in a company, he considered *Grealish v Murphy* to be potentially applicable although, on the facts, undue influence was established. In *McCoy v Greene & Cole*,[139] Costello J. reiterated the view that unconscionable bargains may exist within the context of commercial transactions (albeit within the context of a family business) but that the onus of showing that the contract is unfair rests upon the person seeking relief.

13–40 Recent Commonwealth decisions uphold the view that the jurisdiction is relevant to situations other than real property cases[140] and that the meeting of a board of company directors[141] could well be held in the context of "surprise" within *Evans v Llewellyn*.[142] In the case of a very large construction project between a government department and a construction company it has been held that the *Amadio* decision may be invoked to overturn a dispute settlement.[143] The Canadian courts, in particular, have championed the use of the jurisdiction to strike down sweeping exemption clauses or entire agreement clauses having unconscionable effects.[144] Even "homemade" agreements made outside a commercial context are vulnerable. In *Pitcher v Downer*,[145] the Supreme Court of Newfoundland and Labrador struck down a liability release executed between the parties to a road traffic accident which sought to settle the cost of repairing the damage to the plaintiff's vehicle whilst at the same time preventing a subsequent claim for personal injuries from arising in favour of the plaintiff. The plaintiff signed the release form without reading it. In all circumstances "There was an inequality of bargaining power arising out of the ignorance, need or distress of the weaker party".

---

[137] [1975] Q.B. 326.
[138] Unreported, High Court, April 28, 1983.
[139] Unreported, High Court, January 19, 1984.
[140] *Aqua-Max Property Ltd v MT Associates Pty* [2001] 3 V.R. 43.
[141] *Aqua-Max Property Ltd v MT Associates Pty* [2001] 3 V.R. 43.
[142] (1787) 1 Cox C.C. 333.
[143] *Minister for Industrial Affairs v Civil Tech. Pty* (1998) 70 S.A.S.R. 39; the case could also be the subject of analysis via economic duress.
[144] e.g. *Hunter Engineering Co v Syncrude Canada Ltd* (1989) 57 D.L.R. (4th) 321; *Tercon Contractors Ltd v Province of British Columbia* [2010] 1 S.C.R. 69.
[145] [2013] CanLII 43387, applying *Howell v Reitmans (Canada) Ltd* [2002] CanLII 540722.

Upholding the unconscionable bargain

13–41 *Rae v Joyce*[146] suggests that in cases of the sale of a reversionary interest the purchaser must show that the bargain is, in point of fact, fair, just and reasonable. *Kelly v Morrisroe*[147] decides that where an eccentric and elderly owner of property sells to a younger person, the onus of showing that the bargain was fair rests on the purchaser. As in cases of undue influence the purchaser will discharge this onus by convincing the court that the vendor contracted with his eyes open and was given the market value of the property. The prudent purchaser will advise the vendor to seek independent advice before contracting. In cases where the presumption of unconscionable bargain is raised, and no independent advice has been sought, or the party seeking to support the bargain has not advised the weaker party to obtain independent advice, the bargain can be upheld if the contract can be shown to be fair and reasonable, both as regards the circumstances in which it was struck, and the relative mutuality or fairness of the exchange.

13–42 In *Smyth v Smyth*[148] the trustee of real property purchased part of the land from the beneficial owner, a young man who suffered from a drink problem. The young man had first raised the question of a sale. The sale took an "inordinate" length of time to complete, so there was no question of the bargain being concluded without giving the vendor time for reflection. Costello J. refused to find the bargain invalid. He rejected evidence that the consideration paid was inadequate and despite the fact that no independent solicitor was consulted—one solicitor acting for both parties—the transaction was, in the learned judge's view, neither unconscionable nor improvident.

13–43 It is clear that the judges will take radically different positions on the implications to be drawn from the evidence—witness the old but seminal case of *O'Rorke v Bolingbroke*,[149] an appeal to the House of Lords from the Court of Chancery in Ireland, and the English Court of Appeal decision in *Re Brocklehurst (deceased)*.[150] Many academic commentators are critical of the unconscionability doctrine because of the uncertainty surrounding its application to individual cases, yet it is sometimes difficult to see how else the courts could deal with the cases in which unconscionability is pleaded other than allow injustice to prevail.

---

[146] (1892) 29 L.R. (Ir.) 500.
[147] (1919) 53 I.L.T.R. 145.
[148] Unreported, High Court, November 23, 1978; *Lynn v O'Hara* [2015] IEHC 689.
[149] (1877) 2 App. Cas. 814.
[150] [1978] 1 Ch. 14.

Part 5

Public Policy

14 Illegal Contracts

Introduction

14–01 A contract may be rendered invalid because the transaction runs into conflict with some important value or principle which must be upheld, at the cost of rendering a bargain void or unenforceable.[1] These cases are often divided into two categories: the first category is reserved for cases which are illegal in the purest sense; these transactions infringe a statutory or common law rule to the extent that the whole contract is rendered invalid. Cases falling into the second category, often described as void contracts, do not produce the cataclysmic effects that attend illegal contracts. It is possible for the courts to remove or "sever" the unpalatable or void term while enforcing the rest of the transaction. This distinction seems well established, particularly in English law.[2]

14–02 Many writers regard the distinction with distrust but, in general, the cases fall into line with the classification. A further consequence of the distinction concerns collateral transactions which may also be invalid if the main contract is illegal. Megarry J. observed in *Spector v Ageda*,[3] "[a] transaction may simply be void, or it may be unenforceable, and in either case other connected transactions may nevertheless be perfectly valid and enforceable. But illegality is another matter; for it may be contagious".[4] Where an illegal contract is made out, the traditional effect has been to deny either party any contractual relief. However, the draconian consequences of this view have been recognised as being undesirable, both in relation to instances of common law and statutory illegality, and some recent cases demonstrate judicial unwillingness to apply older lines of authority with the full force of the law. Indeed, in *Soteriou v Ultrachem*,[5] the English High Court rejected a powerful argument that English law, in denying reliefs to a party to a contract which was illegal by performance, was incompatible with art.6 of the European Convention on Human Rights. It was implicitly recognised that more recent case law has adopted a more flexible approach than was the case previously:

---

[1] See, generally, Winfield, "Public Policy in the English Common Law" (1928) 42 Harvard L.R. 76; Grodecki, "In pari delicto potior est conditio defendentis" (1955) 71 L.Q.R. 254; Furmston, "The Analysis of Illegal Contracts" (1966) 16 U.T.L.J. 267; Buckley, *Illegality and Public Policy,* 2nd edn (London: Sweet & Maxwell, 2009).

[2] *Bennett v Bennett* [1952] 1 K.B. 249; *Lee v Showmans Guild* [1952] Q.B. 329; *Goodinson v Goodinson* [1954] 2 Q.B. 118.

[3] [1973] 1 Ch. 30.

[4] [1973] 1 Ch. 30 at 42.

[5] [2004] EWHC 983 (Q.B.).

Hall v Woolston Hall Leisure Ltd.[6] In the aftermath of the House of Lords decision in *Tinsley v Mulligan*,[7] the English Law Commission[8] has opted to recommend the replacement of the *in pari delicto* rule and the consequences flowing therefrom with a legislated discretion for the courts. Remedies and reliefs would be based upon a consideration of factors such as:

(i) the seriousness of the illegality;

(ii) knowledge and intention of the party seeking the relief;

(iii) the policy objectives behind deterring illegal conduct;

(iv) whether refusal or enforcement would further such objectives; and

(v) the proportionality of the result.

Only if a statute expressly provides for the impact that illegality has upon the contract would such a statutory discretion be unavailable to the court.

14–03 The Recommendations of the English Law Commission have not been adopted in that jurisdiction and it appears to be unlikely that discretion of this kind will be enacted. Recent decisions of the UK Supreme Court have suggested that various manifestations of a discretionary approach are not acceptable alternatives to the existing rules of law. Some flexibility is desirable but uncertainty in the law is not. In Ireland the Supreme Court, in *Quinn v Irish Bank Resolution Corporation (In Special Liquidation)*[9] has charted a course which seeks to build upon the approaches of the Australian and UK appellate courts in recent years. In setting out the position for a unanimous five-judge Supreme Court, Clarke J. drew attention to the way in which society has increasingly found the illegality principle being called into play in circumstances where no rule of the criminal law, or principle of morality, has been infringed. Early cases in which the English courts developed the rule that "no court will lend its aid to a man who founds his cause of action upon an immoral or an illegal act" appeared to Clarke J. to be inapposite in many contemporary situations:

> "Since the early case law on illegal contracts was developed, the extent of regulation by statute has expanded to an exceptional extent. The number of regulatory regimes is significant. The areas of life which are subject to regulation are correspondingly large. The number of ways in which a party might be said to be in breach of some element of a regulatory regime is many and varied. Furthermore, the range of

---

6 [2001] 1 W.L.R. 225.
7 Lord Goff called for a review of the law; see [1993] 3 All E.R. 65 at 80. See also Lord Sumption's views expressed at [2012] R.L.R. 1.
8 *Illegal Transactions: The Effect of Illegality on Contracts and Trusts* (1999) Consultation Paper No. 154; *The Illegality Defence* (2007) Consultation Paper No. 189. In 2012 the UK Government announced it would not implement the Law Commission proposals.
9 [2015] IESC 29.

breaches which can arise stem across a spectrum from the minor and technical to the substantive and extremely grave. At one end of the spectrum, a party may simply not have a licence to conduct a particular activity in circumstances where they were clearly entitled to the licence. Strictly speaking, the carrying on of the activity concerned may well, in those circumstances, be illegal, for the relevant statute may well specify that it is unlawful to carry on the activity concerned without the relevant licence. At the other end of the spectrum, there may be a deliberate and serious breach of important obligations imposed in the public interest by the relevant regime."

As we shall see, the Supreme Court has stressed that the court is to examine the statutory context, not whether an individual case merits the contracting parties to be treated in a particular way: "the proper approach is … statute specific, not case specific."

In *Quinn v Irish Bank Resolution Corporation (In Special Liquidation)*, the judgment of McHugh J.A. in *Nelson v Nelson*[10] was highly influential in shaping the new Irish approach, considered below.

Illegal Contracts at Common Law

(1) Contracts to commit a crime or tort

14–04 Contracts which are *contra bonos mores* are absolutely illegal. So, contracts to publish libellous material, knowing the material has this character,[11] to commit a physical assault on a third party[12] or a criminal conspiracy to defraud investors,[13] are clearly illegal. Sometimes the guiding principle is expressed somewhat differently; a person is not to benefit from his or her wrong, even if the level of moral guilt is minimal. So, persons who have been convicted of manslaughter have generally not been permitted to recover under the will of the deceased and even social welfare widows' pensions have been denied when widowhood was the consequence of the unlawful killing by a wife of her husband.[14] The principle was extended to cover the personal representatives of the deceased in *Beresford v Royal Insurance Co.*[15] Here the insured took his own life. A life assurance policy was in existence, but the policy did not contain a clause which prevented payment if the insured took his own life and therefore the policy should have been payable to the estate of the

---

[10] (1995) 184 C.L.R. 538. The Law Commission, *The Illegality Defence*, Law Com. 320 (2010) has suggested that the common law should be allowed to develop incrementally but that courts be encouraged to explain policy issues that underpin decisions. A limited statutory discretion in trust law is recommended. Legislation will not be adopted however.

[11] *Apthorp v Neville & Co* (1907) 23 T.L.R. 575.

[12] *Allen v Rescous* (1676) 2 Lev. 174.

[13] *Scott v Brown Doering* [1892] 2 Q.B. 724.

[14] *Re Giles* [1972] Ch. 544; *R. v N.I.C., Ex p. O'Connor* [1980] Crim. L.R. 579.

[15] [1937] 2 K.B. 197.

deceased for the benefit of relatives and creditors. While the House of Lords held the policy valid for certain purposes, the payment of the assured sum to the estate was not sanctioned. Suicide, as a criminal act, would have been committed for the benefit of the wrongdoer's estate and it was not considered desirable that such wrongful acts be permitted or encouraged, even indirectly. Furmston[16] has argued that contracts of insurance which indemnify the insured for his unlawful acts should, in certain instances, be enforceable. Nevertheless, the English case of *Gray v Barr*[17] takes the rule of public policy even further. The defendant was convicted of manslaughter but was acquitted of murder. The widow of the deceased sued the defendant in negligence for causing the death of her husband. The Court of Appeal refused to allow the defendant to rely on an insurance policy covering "home accidents". This seems to be both undesirable and improper. If the defendant had already been acquitted of the intentional offence of murder the Court of Appeal acted irregularly when it imputed intentional improper conduct to him. However, the rationale for such an extreme position is found in the dictum that "a man is not to be allowed to have recourse to a court of justice to claim a benefit from his crime, whether under a contract or a gift".[18] Nevertheless, there are certain kinds of insurance policies that will indemnify individuals who are convicted of criminal offences. There has been controversy in the UK over the extension of insurance cover to motorists who lose their licence in connection with speeding—the banned motorist can claim up to £6,000 to pay for transport costs incurred during the period of the ban. Road safety organisations have been critical of this policy on the ground that it constitutes an endorsement of speeding.[19] In cases where no crime has been established, the party pleading illegality will have to discharge the onus of proof. So, in *Gray v Hibernian Insurance Co*[20] a publican was acquitted of arson, despite two alleged accomplices giving testimony that the publican had commissioned them to set fire to a public house in order to extract insurance. In the Circuit Court during malicious injuries proceedings the accomplices again gave evidence but meanwhile the publican had died. The Circuit Court judge indicated that the accomplices were probably telling the truth; on this basis an insurance settlement with the widow of the publican was repudiated. In the High Court Barron J. held that the onus rested on the defendant to prove the illegal bargain and that the burden of proof was, on

---

[16] (1966) 16 U. of Toronto L.J. 267.

[17] [1971] 2 Q.B. 554; Fleming, "Insurance for the Criminal" (1971) 34 M.L.R. 176. It is clear that this application of public policy prejudices innocent third parties and is undesirable for this reason. Public policy considerations in cases where one person causes the death of another, which may result in benefits accruing from the estate of the deceased, are provided for in s.120 of the Succession Act 1965, codifying the common law. In *Cawley v Lillis* [2011] IEHC 515, Laffoy J. considered that a legislative response was required in relation to the question whether the manslaughter by one co-owner triggers under the forfeiture rule automatic severance or a constructive trust vis-à-vis jointly owned property. In England and Wales, see the Forfeiture Act 1982 and the Estates of Deceased Persons (Forfeiture Rule and Law of Succession) Act 2011.

[18] Per Lord Atkin in *Beresford v Royal Insurance Co* [1937] 2 K.B. 197.

[19] See "Speed Ban 'insurance' condemned", *The Times*, January 27, 2004.

[20] Unreported, High Court, May 27, 1993.

these facts, a heavier standard of proof than the balance of probabilities, given the fact of the initial acquittal and the non-availability of the deceased to rebut the "accomplice" evidence in the later proceedings. The settlement was held to be enforceable. It may be particularly difficult for the party pleading illegality to make out a specific crime merely from the facts that may indicate a dubious commercial practice and generalised allegations of conspiracy to injure are unlikely to be effective: *AL Barnes Ltd v Time Talk UK Ltd.*[21] A sharply divided House of Lords, in *Stone & Rolls Ltd v Moore Stephens (a firm)*[22] had to consider whether the liquidator of an insolvent company, S, being the sole directing mind and beneficial owner of that company, could bring proceedings against the auditors of the company for negligence. S and the insolvent company had operated a giant fraud on its bank who obtained judgment for deceit which could not be met by the insolvent company, hence the liquidator's action. Assuming the auditors had been negligent, could the liquidator's claim be met by a plea of ex turpi causa? By way of a three to two majority their Lordships held that because the directing mind and will of the company was also the owner of the company, that person, S, should be treated as carrying on the business of the company. Both S and the company could not resist an ex turpi causa defence. There were two dissenting speeches: Lord Scott in particular argued that ex turpi causa was a rule of public policy that in his view should not bar a cause of action for negligence when an insolvent third party has lost out because of that negligent action and the fraudster would not benefit if the action was not discontinued on these tenuous public policy grounds.

14–05 Nor will the courts award a contractual remedy to a plaintiff when enforcement of a contract would, directly or indirectly, lead the defendant into doing something prohibited by the law then being in force. So, in *Namlooze Venootschap De Faam v Dorset Manufacturing Co*[23] the plaintiff company sought to recover in an action for goods sold and delivered. While the contract was itself unexceptional, the Emergency Powers (Finance) (No. 7) Order 1941 prohibited the transfer of foreign exchange beyond the State without the permission of the Minister for Finance. The contract provided for payment abroad in Dutch guilders but permission was not sought by the defendants for the transfer. Dixon J. felt unable to award the contract price for to do so would be to compel the defendants to perform an act prohibited by law and would be contrary to public policy. This reasoning was subsequently approved by the Supreme Court in *Fibretex (Societe Personnes Responsibilite Ltd) v Beleir Ltd.*[24] However, in *Westpac Banking Corp v Dempsey*[25] Morris J. noted

---

[21] [2003] B.L.R. 331.
[22] [2009] 4 All E.R. 431. Dissatisfaction with the majority reasoning in *Stone & Rolls Ltd* is profound: see in particular *Jetivia SA v Bitta (UK) Ltd* [2015] UKSC 23, especially the speech of Lord Neuberger at para.30. For an overview of the recent UKSC decisions see *Strauss* (2016) 132 L.Q.R. 236.
[23] [1949] I.R. 203.
[24] (1955) 89 I.L.T.R. 141.
[25] Unreported, High Court, November 19, 1992.

that exchange control legislation did not make acts done in contravention of these statutes a nullity. All the legislation did was make payment in circumstances where exchange controls were not satisfied temporarily prohibited. So, upon evidence that exchange control legislation after the decision in *Namlooze* and *Fibretex* had been effectively dismantled, the learned judge permitted enforcement of a foreign judgment obtained in England because Irish enforcement proceedings had started shortly after the removal of all EC controls.

(2) Contracts prejudicial to the administration of justice

14–06 It should be noted that a person who protects or shelters a felon is at common law guilty of a criminal offence. Contracts which serve to subvert the cause of justice, while not of themselves criminal, are illegal and cannot give rise to enforceable contractual obligations. In *Brady v Flood*[26] the defendant was paid a sum of money to get criminal charges of conspiracy dropped. Brady C.B. refused to hear litigation arising from this transaction because it was clearly illegal.

14–07 As a matter of public policy it is of the utmost importance that criminal proceedings, once commenced, should be completed without interference from persons who may have some personal interest in the case. Although the courts view agreements to compromise civil suits favourably, agreements relating to a criminal offence are viewed differently. The public interest requires persons accused of criminal offences to be prosecuted, particularly if the offence committed is serious. In the leading English case of *Keir v Leeman*[27] an agreement to compromise criminal proceedings arising from a riot was held to be illegal; Lord Denman indicated, however, that if the criminal proceedings commenced can also be the subject of a civil action it will be possible to execute a valid compromise. In cases of assault, which has the dual characteristic of being a tort and a crime, a compromise of proceedings will be enforceable. The decision in *Nolan v Shiels*[28] illustrates that this exception will be viewed restrictively. The plaintiff, victim of an indecent assault, was given a cheque for £50 in return for her promise not to prosecute the defendant's friend who had committed the offence. Judge Pigot refused to allow an action on the cheque; he noted that if the offence committed had been the less serious offence of common assault, *Keir v Leeman* would have allowed an action to succeed on the dishonoured cheque. An extremely vivid illustration of this principle is found in *Parsons v Kirk*.[29] Here a payment of money was agreed in return for an undertaking by a petitioner to withdraw his petition. The petition had questioned the election of a member of Parliament, alleging that there had been bribery of voters. The consideration was held to be void. Clearly the

---

[26] (1841) 6 Circuit Cases 309.
[27] (1846) 9 Q.B. 371; *Edgcomb v Rodd* (1804) 5 East 294; *Australia and New Zealand Banking Group v Naga* [2007] 1 Lloyd's Rep. 487.
[28] (1926) 60 I.L.T.R. 143.
[29] (1853) 6 Ir. Jur. (N.S.) 168.

investigation of such an important issue was in the public interest and could not be made the subject of a private bargain.

14–08 If no prosecution has commenced and the promissory note is given in exchange for a promise not to take the matter further, the case of *Rourke v Mealy*[30] suggests that an action may succeed. The plaintiff held a negotiable instrument which he suspected had been forged by a relative of the defendant. He informed the defendant of his suspicions, whereupon the defendant made himself personally liable on the instrument in consideration for the plaintiff's promise not to charge the relative with forgery. The plaintiff was held entitled to sue the defendant on the instrument. This was not an agreement to stifle a prosecution for no proceedings were in progress; nor did the public interest require the truth of an allegation of forgery to be ascertained. Similarly, in the 1885 case of *Re Boyd*,[31] a grocer, who had been both customer and agent of Leatham and Howard, owed them considerable sums of money. They received notice of Boyd's impecuniosity and approached him with a view to settling accounts. Boyd, in the face of pressure, transferred goods and gave an equitable mortgage over property to Leatham and Howard; there was a suspicion on their part that Boyd had embezzled monies belonging to them. The three members of the Court of Appeal allowed an appeal against a finding that this agreement was illegal. There was no agreement to stifle a prosecution; as Sullivan L.C. said: "a threat of prosecution will not invalidate a security thereupon given, if there was no agreement to abandon the prosecution ultimately."[32] These Irish cases reflect quite a benign view of this matter. In recent times the approach found in cases like *Kier v Leeman*,[33] in which a strict rule against the enforceability of promises was laid down, has waned in favour of allowing such promises to be enforced unless some public interest can be shown to take priority. Private prosecutions are less frequent and restitution by the perpetrators of crime is a more acceptable response to crime than it was in former times. It is significant that when the Oireachtas amended the law in relation to the reporting of offences of theft and dishonesty[34] as well as abolishing the distinction between felony and a misdemeanour,[35] no recommendations on this issue were set out in the legislation. It is to be hoped that the more liberal approach found in jurisdictions[36] where the law relating to illegal contracts has been reformed by statute will prevail in Ireland.

14–09 A person who fraudulently abuses judicial proceedings to obtain the benefits of bankrupt status should be brought to justice; an agreement between

---

[30]   (1879) 4 L.R. (Ir.) 166.
[31]   (1885) 15 L.R. (Ir.) 521; *Brook v Hook* (1871) L.R. 6 Ex. 89.
[32]   (1885) 15 L.R. (Ir.) 521 at 542, citing *Ward v Lloyd* (1843) 7 Sc. N.R. 499.
[33]   (1846) 9 Q.B. 371.
[34]   Criminal Justice (Theft and Fraud Offences) Act 2001.
[35]   Criminal Law Act 1997.
[36]   See the New Zealand Illegal Contracts Act 1970, as interpreted in *Polymer Developments Group Ltd v Tiliato* [2002] 3 N.Z.L.R. 258 and the English Law Commission Consultation Papers No. 154 (1999) and No. 189 (2009).

a creditor and the defrauding debtor, in which proceedings to set aside a discharge as fraudulently obtained are compromised for a promise to pay the debt, is illegal: *Daly v Daly*.[37] An alternative way of rationalising these decisions is to hold that there is a failure of consideration, for an unlawful consideration is not recognised in the eyes of the law.

14–10 A rather surprising result was reached in *Bagot v Arnott*.[38] The plaintiff had lent large sums of money to S, who, in return for a further advance, gave bills of sale to the plaintiff as security, instructing the plaintiff to sell the property covered by the bills to realise the security. Bagot knew that S had committed forgery and would use the advance to flee abroad and avoid prosecution. The goods were seized by other creditors. The plaintiff successfully sued in tort to recover the goods. The Court of Common Pleas held that, notwithstanding Bagot's knowledge that S intended to use part of the funds to evade prosecution, *the purpose* behind the advance was to obtain security for earlier bona fide debts, not to enable S to leave the country. The case is best regarded as an authority on the enforceability of monies lent in order to discharge illegal contracts, considered below.

14–11 The common law judges have also viewed contracts which encourage speculative litigation as undesirable. Where the effect of a transaction, such as an assignment of causes of action, is to make litigation uncertain or unworkable, public policy requires these transactions to be void; see *Investors Compensation Scheme Ltd v West Bromwich B.S.*[39] Both the common law and several ancient statutes have sought to suppress arrangements that constitute trafficking in litigation by way of maintenance and champerty. If a third party lends assistance to a litigant in circumstances which are viewed as improper he is guilty of the crime of maintenance. Lord Denning M.R. defined maintenance as:

> "Improperly stirring up litigation and strife by giving aid to one party to bring or defend a claim without just cause of excuse."[40]

In *Uppington v Bullen*,[41] Bullen, a solicitor, took a conveyance of lands from Fleming, a client, the conveyance being for £400. However, by a separate agreement it was provided that the £400 would be made up of £100 cash, the balance being the costs of an action being run by Bullen on behalf of Fleming, as plaintiff. The conveyance was set aside, Sugden L.C. observing that this was unlawful maintenance.

---

[37] (1870) I.R. 5 C.L. 108.

[38] (1867) I.R. 2 C.L. 1.

[39] [1998] 1 All E.R. 98.

[40] *Re Trepca Mines Ltd* (N.Z.) [1963] Ch. 199 at 219. See generally Leonowicz, "Maintenance and Champerty" (2005) 12(6) C.L.P. 157. On "trafficking in litigation", see *Operation 1 Inc. v Phillips* (2004) 248 D.L.R. (4th) 349.

[41] (1842) 2 Dr. & War. 184. Execution of an assignment is the prudent cause of action: *Waldron v Herring* [2013] IEHC 294.

14–12 Where, however, a person other than the litigant stands to gain from the litigation—by agreeing to pay legal fees in return for an agreed portion of the damages awarded, if any, the contract is described as champertous. Strictly speaking, lawyers who agree to fund litigation on a contingency fee basis are guilty of champerty. In *Littledale v Thompson*,[42] Whaley was a party to a dispute concerning the right to a clerical living or advowson. Thompson agreed that if Whaley continued to press his claim to the advowson, Thompson would pay legal fees if Whaley would in turn convey the advowson to him, if successful. Littledale, Whaley's executor, sued Thompson when he failed to pay the fees. The action was dismissed as being part of a champertous contract. An agreement to assist a litigant to recover property, via litigation, is tainted it seems. The policy behind this prohibition is the danger that a lawyer, or a person who provides assistance in the context of litigation such as an accountancy firm providing specialist services[43] or a "paralegal" with language skills[44] may not do so honestly or objectively because of the prospect that his financial rewards will be fixed by reference to the result of the litigation. Clearly, an expert witness who is to be paid by reference to the outcome of the case will certainly be party to a champertous contract and it has recently been reaffirmed that such a payment would not be recoverable.[45] However, the danger that a lawyer may at the worst be tempted to pervert the course of justice in order to ensure that he or she is going to be paid has to be counterbalanced with a competing policy objective, the interests of society in ensuring that citizens will have access to justice and cases may turn on their own special facts.[46] In *Greenclean Waste Management v Leahy*[47] an insurance product, after the event legal cost insurance, was held not to be champertous for the reason that it funded third party litigation in which the funder had no interest or legitimate concern. Trafficking in litigation may still be a policy that the Irish courts seek to discourage, Hogan J. observed, but constitutional and societal changes must be kept in mind when assessing each case. Products of this kind for example may serve a public purpose in facilitating access to the courts and to justice. The danger that this product might simply be a disguised form of speculative contingency fee litigation funding was outweighed by the fact that this form of insurance also provides cover for an insured who loses in the litigation.

---

[42] (1878) 4 L.R. (Ir.) 43.

[43] *R (Factortame Ltd) v Secretary of State*, *The Times*, July 3, 2002.

[44] *Mohamed v Alaga* [1999] All E.R. 699.

[45] *R (Factortame Ltd) v Secretary of State*, *The Times*, July 3, 2002.

[46] *R (Factortame Ltd) v Secretary of State*, *The Times*, July 3, 2002; *Dal-Sterling Group Plc v WSP South and West Ltd* [2002] T.C.L.R. 428.

[47] [2014] IEHC 314, following *Thema International Fund plc v HSBC International Trust Services Ireland Ltd* [2011] IEHC 654. Hogan J.'s approach was criticised on appeal: [2015] IECA 97. Despite the attractiveness of Hogan J.'s reasoning, it has not been followed in a landmark case. In *Persona Digital Telephony Ltd v Minister for Public Enterprise* [2016] IEHC 187 Donnelly J. reviewed the law relating to maintenance and champerty but rather than finding that public policy considerations were to prove dispositive, Donnelly J. found that because the Statute Law Revision Act 2007 retained these torts on the statute book, and because the ingredients of these torts could be made out, professional third party funding was caught by the torts of maintenance and champerty.

14–13 In *McElroy v Flynn*[48] the plaintiff sought a declaration that a contract between himself and the defendants was valid. The plaintiff, a specialist in tracing next-of-kin, contacted the defendants after seeing an advertisement which requested information on the whereabouts of the relatives of a deceased person, the advertisement being placed by the British Treasury Solicitor in an attempt to dispose of the estate: the defendants were cousins of the deceased. The agreement provided that 25 per cent of the shares in the estate would be paid to the plaintiff in consideration of the plaintiff informing the defendants of their entitlement. Blayney J. held the agreement void as being champertous:

> "[T]he real agreement here was that the plaintiff should do more than merely inform the defendants of the name of the deceased. I consider that the plaintiff agreed in addition to assist actively in the recovery of the defendant's shares in the estate and that the agreement accordingly is void."

This distinction between contracting to provide information, which is lawful, and contracting to assist in prosecuting the claim and procuring evidence, which is unlawful, was affirmed by the Supreme Court in *Fraser v Buckle*.[49] O'Flaherty J., in particular, indicated that Irish law had not changed on this point for over a century, and that heir locator contracts, as a particularly speculative enterprise that is clearly open to abuse and fabricated claims, are viewed with hostility in England and in many US jurisdictions, and are not to be encouraged. However, despite several recent English cases in which legal aid "collateral" contracts have been held unenforceable[50] it is evident that some changes in judicial attitude to these common law policies are taking place to avoid apparently sensible arrangements being invalidated because legal proceedings are in danger of being scandalised. Even if the contingency fee arrangement is tainted by illegality, it may be possible for services to be remunerated via a quantum meruit claim. In *Mohamed v Alaga*[51] the plaintiff promised to provide interpreter services to a law firm and to introduce clients to the firm from the Somali community in return for a promise to share legal aid fees to the firm. This agreement was clearly illegal as involving the promise by a solicitor to share fees. However, a separate claim for reasonable remuneration for work done was sustainable.

---

[48] [1991] I.L.R.M. 294. The fraud of the plaintiff in concealing material facts should be seen as an essential element in the *ratio* of this case.

[49] [1996] 2 I.L.R.M. 34; applied in *SPV Osus Ltd v HSBC International Trust Services (Ireland) Ltd* [2015] IEHC 602. Capper (1997) 60 M.L.R. 286.

[50] *Joyce v Kammac (1988) Ltd, The Times*, October 16, 1995; *Norglen Ltd v Reeds Rains Prudential Ltd, The Times*, December 1, 1997; *Thai Trading Co (a firm) v Taylor, The Times*, March 6, 1998; *Spencer v Wood, The Times*, March 30, 2004; *Sibthorpe v Southwark* [2011] EWCA Civ 25. These cases involve conditional fee regulations for solicitors in England. In Ireland see *O'Keeffe v Scales* [1998] 1 I.L.R.M. 393.

[51] [1999] 3 All E.R. 699.

14–14 If, however, the proceedings cannot be said to be proceedings in a court of law, or are proceedings which are not in the nature of litigation, an agreement in relation to such proceedings may be enforceable. In *Pickering v Sogex Services (UK) Ltd*[52] a contingency fee payable to surveyors who had achieved a considerable reduction in local authority rate charges was held recoverable because negotiations before a local valuation court were not part of a process of litigation; nor was a district valuation court a court of law. If, however, legislation has been passed to relax the prohibition against maintenance and champerty, as is the case in relation to permitting trustees in bankruptcy and liquidators to conclude certain types of agreements enabling litigation to be pursued for the benefit of creditors, some unusual arrangements that are not embraced by the statutory exemption may still fall foul of these common law proscriptions. In *Grovewood Holding Plc v James Capel and Co*[53] Lightman J. held that while insolvency law allowed the sale of bare causes of action, the sale of interests in the fruits of litigation were still unlawful. In England there is a strong line of authority which has cast doubt on the future of these concepts in a closely regulated modern society.[54] The House of Lords, in *Norglen Ltd v Reeds Rains Prudential Ltd*[55] has held that an assignment of a cause of action by a company to an individual is not to be rendered invalid by virtue of the underlying intention, namely to support the litigation by obtaining legal aid, the view being taken that abuses of legal aid were to be counter-manded by the relevant regulatory agencies, not the common law concept of public policy. Furthermore, in *Thai Trading Co (a firm) v Taylor*[56] the Court of Appeal upheld an arrangement to finance litigation on a contingency fee basis as long as the successful solicitor was only seeking normal fee levels and disbursements rather than, say, 50 per cent of damages obtained.

14–15 In Ireland the bare assignment of a cause of action, without there being in existence any property right or interest that stands apart from the assignment of the cause of action is champertous: *SPV OSUS v HSBC International Trust Services Ireland Ltd.*[57] It matters not that the proper law of the contract is not Irish law. Litigation in Ireland will not be entertained.

(3) Agreements which serve to defraud the Revenue

14–16 Attempts are sometimes made to reduce the tax liability of the vendor of real property by misstating the purchase price. In *Starling Securities v*

---

[52] (1982) 263 E.G. 770; *Porter v Kirtlan* [1917] 2 I.R. 138.
[53] [1994] 4 All E.R. 417. On the distinction between a liquidator's right to sell a bare cause of action and an assignment of the fruits of an action (the latter being champertous) see *Ruttle Plant Ltd v Secretary of State for Environment, Food and Rural Affairs (No. 3)* [2009] 1 All E.R. 448, following dicta in *Grovewood Holdings*.
[54] *Giles v Thompson* [1994] 1 A.C. 142; *Kain v Wynn Williams Co* [2013] 1 NZLR 498.
[55] *The Times*, December 1, 1997.
[56] *The Times*, March 6, 1998, overruling *Aratra Potato Co Ltd v Taylor* [1995] 4 All E.R. 695. In *Smits v Roach* (2002) 55 N.S.W.L.R. 166, *Thai Trading* was preferred to the decision in *Awwad v Geraghty and Co* [2001] Q.B. 570.
[57] [2015] IEHC 602.

Woods[58] the plaintiff purchased real property under an oral contract which would have been enforceable had it not become apparent to McWilliam J. that the consideration had been misstated in order to defraud the Revenue Commissioners. In *Whelan v Kavanagh*,[59] however, Herbert J. advised that a plea of illegality should not be readily entertained in the absence of statements, facts or circumstances which tend to show that an illegal act was intended by both parties. Collusive arrangements between employers and employees in which the employee is given "expenses" in order to reduce his liability to PAYE or PRSI contributions are also illegal. Indeed, an employee party to such an agreement has been held unable to recover arrears of wages and unable to bring an action for redundancy payments or unfair dismissal; see the English cases of *Napier v N.B.A.*[60] and *Tomlinson v Dick Evans "U" Drive.*[61]

14–17 In the first edition of this book the author expressed the hope that the *Tomlinson case* would not be followed in Ireland. The Employment Appeals Tribunal (EAT) has, however, adopted the reasoning in *Tomlinson* in *Lewis v Squash Ireland Ltd.*[62] Lewis was employed as managing director of the respondent company. Apart from his £14,000 annual salary Lewis was paid annually £2,000, as "expenses". Following his dismissal Lewis sued for compensation for an alleged unfair dismissal under the Unfair Dismissals Act 1977. The EAT expressed concern about the £2,000 element in the salary paid to the plaintiff and formed the view that the payment was in fact remuneration, though described as expenses, in order to minimise the PAYE obligations of the employee. Applying the earlier English cases, the EAT found that Lewis knew that his salary was being misdescribed and that PAYE returns made by the employer would not refer to the £2,000 as remuneration. The scheme was therefore illegal and while severance of the illegal portion of the salary was mathematically possible, the fact that the parties knowingly incorporated this term into the contract made it impossible to sever this illegal term and enforce the rest of the contract. Even though the employee may be seeking to enforce a statutory cause of action and not a common law cause of action, i.e. unfair dismissal and not wrongful dismissal—the EAT refused to limit the illegality doctrine, holding that culpability vis-à-vis the contracting parties would no doubt be taken into account by the Revenue Commissioners when they decided whether both parties were to be prosecuted for tax evasion. The *Tomlinson* position at common law is unacceptable; the method of payment in these cases is, generally, the sole responsibility of the employer. The employer can also benefit from the wrongful act—often more so than the employee— for PRSI contributions, levied as a proportion of the employee's salary are often reduced for the employer as well as the employee, to say nothing of the

---

[58] Unreported, High Court, May 24, 1977.
[59] Unreported, High Court, January 29, 2001.
[60] [1951] 2 All E.R. 264.
[61] [1978] I.C.R. 638.
[62] [1983] I.L.R.M. 363. The decision was reversed by s.7 of the Unfair Dismissals (Amendment) Act 1993, amending s.8 of the 1977 Act.

fact that payments "under the table" may be made to discourage other workers from making claims for increases in salary. The basic fear of comparability claims was alleged to be at the heart of the *Lewis* stratagem itself. In the case of *Hayden v Sean Quinn Properties Ltd*[63] the employee was given a tax free "expenses" top up, to bring his income up to the level obtained in his previous employment and even though the court seemed to have decided that the employer was the prime mover, the *Napier* case was followed and the defendant was denied a remedy for wrongful dismissal because "the plaintiff allowed himself to agree to something which would benefit the defendant at the expense of the Revenue": per Barron J. Finally, the position of the court is fundamentally unfair for the penalty smacks of double jeopardy. A worker who has worked for many years in one job could find statutory redundancy or unfair dismissal rights prejudiced by the fact that the worker recently worked weekends on a "tax-free" basis by being paid out of petty cash. The question whether illegal payments made during the currency of a contract of employment may render statutory claims and common law causes of action unenforceable arose in *Red Sail Ltd (In Receivership)*.[64] During a receivership process the receiver discovered that several employees had been paid "under the table", avoiding tax and PRSI in the process. The then Department of Enterprise, Trade and Employment had paid employee claims under the Minimum Notice and Terms of Employment Act 1973, the Unfair Dismissals Act 1977, and the Protection of Employees (Employer's Insolvency) Act 1984 and the point raised by the receiver was whether the Department, as a preferential creditor, should be entitled to exercise rights of subrogation vis-à-vis these employees. Did the employees participate in the illegality? Laffoy J. noted that after the *Lewis v Squash Ireland* case the Oireachtas had intervened to provide that contravention of the Income Tax Acts or Social Welfare Acts will not preclude resort to an unfair dismissal action.[65] A similar statutory solution was held to arise in relation to the Minimum Notice and Terms of Employment Act 1973.[66] However, in relation to claims for arrears of wages and holiday pay, claims that the Department had settled in the knowledge that the contracts of employment were tainted with illegality, it was submitted that as there were no statutory provisions[67] the common law barrier should be imposed. Laffoy J. declined to discriminate between employees, all of whom had been treated uniformly by the Department and while Laffoy J. accepted that this was not a principled approach to the problem, the judge accepted the "pragmatic" solution adopted by the Department. The decision of the Court of Appeal in *Hall v Woolston Hall Leisure Ltd*[68] suggests that this principle

---

[63] Unreported, High Court, December 6, 1993.

[64] [2007] 2 I.R. 361.

[65] Unfair Dismissal Act 1977 s.8(11), as inserted by the Unfair Dismissals (Amendment) Act 1993.

[66] Minimum Notice and Terms of Employment Act 1973 ss.12 and 13. See now Workplace Relations Act 2015, s.49.

[67] The controlling legislation for wage arrears and holiday pay, the 1984 legislation, is silent on this point.

[68] [2001] 1 W.L.R. 225; *Addey and Stanhope SGB v Vakante* [2003] I.C.R. 290.

of public policy may have to yield in the light of EU legislation that requires workers to enjoy sanctions that ensure real and effective judicial protection in the context of a claim for sex discrimination contrary to the Equal Treatment Directive.[69] The Court of Appeal noted that the Directive did not permit Member States to legislate for any derogation from the Directive, even on the ground of public safety,[70] but no final opinion was given in respect of the question whether such considerations precluded resort to public policy in all instances. This case is also significant because the Court of Appeal took a more realistic view of the *in pari delictu* rule. A perfectly lawful employment contract was performed by an employer who deducted income tax and national insurance against part of the wages of the employee only; when she challenged this practice she was told that this was the way the employer did business; Mance L.J. remarked that the employee "may have had little real choice but to submit to the employer's act of deception". While *Woolston Hall* effects an exception to the common law rule in specifically applying to statutory claims for sex discrimination, a reassessment of the common law on issues such as the difference between knowledge and participation, and relative degrees of guilt may be overdue. *Hall v Woolston Hall Leisure Ltd* has eased the severity of the illegality test by requiring a court to consider three kinds of situations:

(1) where a contract is entered into with the intention of committing an illegal act;

(2) where the contract is expressly or impliedly prohibited by statute; and

(3) where the employee knows facts that indicate the performance is illegal and the employee actually participates in it.

While classes (1) and (2) are clearly instances of illegality, class (3) at least allows some room for manoeuvre vis-à-vis differing levels of culpability. This test was considered in *Wheeler v Quality Deep Ltd*.[71] A Thai national was employed in a Thai restaurant for three years, payment being made in cash without deduction of tax and national insurance contributions. The Employment Tribunal held she could not pursue remedies for dismissal because she and her husband "must have known something was wrong" and acquiesced in it. The Court of Appeal held the Tribunal had applied the wrong test. The test requires proof of knowledge of the illegal performance and participation. The court should not assume illegality, however. On this point, the English tribunals and courts have provided useful assistance in cases where students have sought to recover unpaid wages whilst working in breach of visa conditions. In *Blue Chip Trading Ltd v Helbawi*[72] the appellant engaged Helbawi as a security guard but paid him less than the minimum wage.

---

[69] Directive 76/207.

[70] *Johnston v RUC* [1987] I.C.R. 983; *Draehmpaehl v Immobilien-Service* [1998] I.C.R. 164.

[71] [2005] I.C.R. 265. See also *McEwing v Samoa Ltd* [2004] EAT 0813/13 (UK) and *Delaney v McMahon* [2013] NICA 65, distinguishing participation from acquiescence.

[72] [2009] I.R.L.R. 128; *San Ling Chinese Medicine Centre v Ji* [2010] UKEAT 1370-09-2501. Contrast *Vakante v Addey and Stanhope School* [2004] EWCA Civ 2004.

Helbawi's claim was resisted on the grounds that there had been breaches of visa conditions limiting employment of the student in term time to 20 hours per week. The President of the UK EAT, Elias P., held that the EAT was incorrect in offsetting breach of immigration law with a statutory policy of enforcing minimum wage legislation. The courts could not condone deliberate breaches of immigration law in those weeks where Helbawi worked for more than 20 hours. But severance was possible and Helbawi could recover for work done in vacation periods (when no restrictions were in place) and for hours worked in those weeks where the 20-hour limit was observed. The application of the ex turpi causa rule in cases where the employee is the subject of employment as a domestic servant that shades into people trafficking has been considered by the UKSC to fall on the side of the *Hall* case rather than *Vakante v Addly* and *Stanhope School*: see *Hounga v Allen*.[73] In *Hounga v Allen* the claim did not require disclosure of the employment contract and the claim was brought in tort, not contract. In *Red Sail Ltd (In Receivership)*,[74] Laffoy J. thought that for the purposes of the case at bar, "it is reasonable for present purposes to adopt the requirement of active participation in addition to knowledge of the facts to render a contract of employment unenforceable", so, it is by no means clear whether, in a case of wrongful dismissal, an Irish court would accept the more flexible test found in *Woolston Hall* or stick to the *Hayden v Sean Quinn/ Napier* line of authority.

(4) Agreements which serve to corrupt public officials

14–18 In *Lord Mayor of Dublin v Hayes*[75] the defendant was appointed Marshall of the City of Dublin, a position which also gave him the post of Registrar of Pawnbrokers. This entitled the defendant to collect fees which he agreed to transfer to the City Treasurer. It was clear that the appointment was made in exchange for the defendant's promise. The promise was held unenforceable because such a contract would tend to encourage corrupt practices amongst public officials.

14–19 The desire to encourage public officials to discharge their duties conscientiously and without hope for a separate reward has been seen as a principle of public policy and morality that transcends national borders. For this reason, an English court has held that a contract governed by English law, but which would have the effect of corrupting public officials of a foreign state, is not enforceable in England in appropriate circumstances.[76]

(5) Contracts tending to encourage immorality

14–20 Even if the conduct contemplated by the contract is not itself illegal, as would be the case in an arrangement to procure the seduction of a girl below

---

[73] [2014] UKSC 47; See *Bogg & Green* (2015) 44 I.L.J. 101.
[74] [2007] 2 I.R. 361.
[75] (1876) 10 I.R.C.L. 226.
[76] *Lemenda Trading Co Ltd v African Middle East Petroleum Co Ltd* [1988] 1 All E.R. 513.

the age of consent, a contract that promotes some illicit sexual behaviour is illegal. Illicit sexual behaviour simply means sexual intercourse which takes place outside the confines of marriage. The older common law cases draw an important distinction; a contract that contemplates an obligation to provide future sexual intercourse is illegal while a contract that is made in consideration for sexual favours already conferred is not illegal; it may be invalid for want of consideration. This can be overcome if the promise is in a deed under seal. In *Reade v Adams*[77] a deed was executed providing an annuity to any children of an illicit union should the woman marry another man. The annuity was held enforceable; the deed did not require the woman to continue illicit sexual intercourse in order to retain the annuity; contrast the badly reported case of *Quidihy v Kelly*.[78]

14–21 The English courts, faced with the trend towards stable relationships being formed outside marriage, have decided to respond by permitting one partner to acquire rights in the other partner's property through the doctrines of estoppel, contractual licence, and constructive trust; see, in particular, *Tanner v Tanner*[79] and *Pascoe v Turner*.[80] The words of Sable J. in *Andrews v Parker*,[81] a Queensland decision, are instructive:

> "Are the actions of people to-day to be judged in the light of the standards of the last century? As counsel for the plaintiff said, cases discussing what was then by community standards sexual immorality appear to have been decided in the days when for the sake of decency the legs of tables wore drapes ... I do not accept that immoral today means precisely what it did in the days of *Pearce v Brooks*. I am, I believe entitled to look at the word under modern social standards."[82]

This dictum was cited with approval in the New South Wales case of *Seidler v Schallhofer*.[83] An agreement made between a cohabiting couple, who were contemplating a trial run for a future marriage, involved the joint purchase of a house as joint tenants, the female party borrowing money from the male party to enable her to pay her part of the consideration. The agreement provided that if at the end of a fixed period the parties decided that it was best that they not marry then the male party would buy out the female party's interest. The agreement was upheld. Given that community standards of morality had changed (both statute law and law reform agencies in Australia were referred to so as to provide evidence that quasi-marital relationships are common in Australia) an agreement of this kind was not to be denied legal effect on grounds of public policy.

---

[77] (1855) 2 Ir. Jur. (N.S.) 197; *Zapletal v Wright* [1957] Tas. S.R. 211.
[78] (1788) Vern. & Scriv. 515.
[79] [1975] 1 W.L.R. 1346.
[80] [1979] 2 All E.R. 945.
[81] [1973] Qd. R. 93.
[82] [1973] Qd. R. 93 at 104.
[83] [1982] 2 N.S.W.L.R. 80.

14–22 It is evident that this head of public policy is perhaps the one that is in the greatest state of flux. Denying individuals the right to enter into legally enforceable contracts because of sexual orientation and lifestyle or marital status (or lack of it) appears to be out of step with equality legislation and certain provisions in both the Irish Constitution and the European Convention on Human Rights.[84] The Law Reform Commission, in a recent consultation paper,[85] suggested that cohabiting couples, including same-sex couples, should enjoy rights of access to the courts to arbitrate on property rights and maintenance issues if the relationship ends. The consultation paper has been followed by legislation in relation to civil partnership and later marriage as between same-sex couples but the issue of contractual arrangements which are directly intended to secure sexual services has not been addressed. While social mores have changed there are still sexual taboos in contract law: a prostitute would nevertheless have extreme difficulty in recovering a fee if he or she performed his or her part of a bargain to provide sexual favours on credit terms.[86]

14–23 This interesting area of private morality and public policy was extensively reviewed by the New South Wales Supreme Court in *Ashton v Pratt (No. 2)*.[87] What survives of the public policy considerations that render promises given in return for the benefits of sexual contact appear to be confined to contracts for prostitution and contracts for "meretricious sexual services", defined by Brereton J. in *Ashton v Pratt (No. 2)* as "a contract treating a woman as if she were a prostitute".[88] Thus, cases where the parties maintain separate homes and perhaps marital relationships but for which sexual acts are contractually stipulated for are still contractually beyond the pale. Cases where the parties are in a relationship that involves cohabitation outside traditional marriage are clearly no longer contrary to public policy and the law has long recognised that when the parties seek to "regularise" a relationship of cohabitation outside marriage then the effect may be that such an agreement can actually be supported in public policy terms,[89] and similar conclusions have long been reached in respect of child maintenance contractual arrangements between parents of a child born outside marriage. Stable relationships between contracting parties that are cemented by way of cohabitation agreements, marriage and civil partnerships, agreements and collateral arrangements as between persons who are sharing their life together can no longer be viewed with the same "anti-social" or immoral gaze as in earlier times. Brereton J. also saw this shift in social attitudes as being gender neutral. Of tainted contracts

---

[84] See *Mendoza v Ghaidan* [2004] 3 All E.R. 411.
[85] *Rights and Duties of Cohabitees*, LRC CP 32–2004.
[86] See *Theakston v Mirror Group Newspapers* [2002] E.M.L.R. 22.
[87] [2012] NSWSC 3 (appeal to the NSWCA dismissed but on other grounds [2015] NSWCA 12).
[88] Citing *Marvin v Marvin* 18 Cal. 3d 660 (1976) and contrasting it with *Nicols v Nicols* (NSWC, December 6, 1986) and *Markulin v Drew* (NSWSC, August 12, 1993).
[89] *Fender v St. John – Mildmay* [1938] A.C. 1.

for "purely meretricious sexual services" Brereton J. said, "in this modern age it may be that it is the woman who is rewarding the man for sexual services he provides from time to time".[90] In *Ashton v Pratt (No. 2)* itself the plaintiff sought to recover on a promise given by a former client that if she discontinued to work as an "escort" he would give her $500,000 a year, set up multi-million dollar trust funds for the plaintiff's children (who were not fathered by the promisor), and support the plaintiff's business enterprises in return for sexual and emotional supports for the one or two nights a week the promisor was in Sydney. No cohabitation was intended. Brereton J. held that the existing state of the law in Australia led to the conclusion that this contract was contrary to public policy and unenforceable.[91] On the other hand, in the earlier Australian case of *Barac v Farnell*,[92] the plaintiff broke her arm while employed as a receptionist in a brothel. It was held that there was no public policy interest in existence which prevented her from recovering compensation for her injuries. On appeal, the contract was held to be void for uncertainty, the New South Wales Court of Appeal declining to take a position on the illegality issue. Incidental transactions may also be invalid. In *Pearce v Brooks*[93] a contract for the hire of a carriage to a prostitute who, to the knowledge of the owner intended to use it in furtherance of her "immoral vocation", was breached when the carriage was returned in a damaged condition. The owner's action failed; his knowledge of the immoral purpose behind the contract meant he "participated" in the illegality. However, in *Armhouse Lee Ltd v Chappell*[94] the defendants had provided a telephone sex line service to the public, placing advertisements for their services with the plaintiffs. The defendants refused to pay, calling in aid a defence that to allow recovery would be to encourage sexual immorality over the telephone line at a price. The defence was rejected, the English Court of Appeal stating that no general moral code condemned these sex line services. Contracts should be upheld and it was not for judges to impose their standards of morality onto the public in the area of a civil law dispute.

14–24 A contract designed to promote unlawful gambling is just as illegal as one aimed at furthering illicit sexual activity. In *Devine v Scott and Johnston*[95] the plaintiff let premises in Belfast to Johnston who intended to carry on an unlawful bookmaking business. The plaintiff's agent was fixed with knowledge which bound the principal. An action to recover arrears of rent was dismissed. In contrast, the EAT in *Donohue v Simonetti*[96] found the applicant to have been dismissed without the requisite notice from her employment as a cashier in an

---

[90] Quoting from Young J. in *Markulin v Drew* (NSWSC, August 12, 1993).
[91] According to the plaintiff in *Ashton v Pratt (No. 2)* she was told, "[y]ou know the position of mistress is now available" and this announcement started the negotiations between the parties: *Zapletal v Wright* [1957] Tas. S.R. 211.
[92] (1994) 125 A.L.R. 241.
[93] (1866) 1 Ex. 213.
[94] *The Times*, August 7, 1996.
[95] (1931) 66 I.L.T.R. 107.
[96] U.D. 639/1981.

amusement arcade. The EAT rejected as a defence the defendant's claim that its gaming activities were probably unlawful because, at that time, litigation concerning illegal gaming machines was pending before the Supreme Court.

14–25 Even so, it is submitted that the contract of employment would not be rendered unlawful by the fact that the employer ran his business in such a way as to commit a criminal offence, for the Gaming and Lotteries Act 1956, considered below, does not prohibit contracts of employment but certain activities that may themselves be committed by the employer through the employee. A contract to hire a room for illegal gambling directly raises an illegal mutual purpose; a licensed gaming machine proprietor who employs persons who, following the employer's instructions may break the criminal law, does not necessarily, even indirectly, taint the contract of employment. If, however, both employer and employee are aware that the employer's business is itself illegal—the employee knows that the employer's business activity or objective is itself contrary to the criminal law—then the employee cannot enforce any rights under that contract. The employee cannot, for example, recover social security pensions for his illegal employment was not insurable, even if deductions have in fact been made and remitted to the Revenue (*McHugh v Ministry of Labour for Northern Ireland*[97]) unless there is statutory guidance on this point.

(6) Contracts to trade with enemies of the State

14–26 A contract between nationals and enemy "aliens" is contrary to public policy. In *Ross v Shaw*[98] a contract to purchase yarn to be supplied from a mill in Belgium could not be lawfully performed once the mill was occupied by German troops during World War I. The plaintiff's action for non-delivery failed. However, where currency restrictions are in place in order to regulate commercial transactions in enemy territory, legislation may be passed in order to buttress common law prohibitions on contracts to trade with the enemy. In a relatively recent English case the Court of Appeal has both reaffirmed the public policy dimension to such legislation and indicated that such legislative rules are proportionate within human rights legislation.[99]

(7) Contracts that breach foreign law

14–27 The courts refuse to enforce a contract that is illegal according to the law of the place where it is to be performed. In *Stanhope v Hospitals Trust*

---

[97] [1940] N.I. 174 (e.g. a courier who is a "mule" being employed by a "drugs baron").

[98] [1917] 2 I.R. 367. Related transactions include contracts which involve performance in another country of acts contrary to law in that country or public policy in that country: *Regazzoni v K C Sethia (1944) Ltd* [1958] A.C. 301; *Lemenda Trading Co Ltd v African Middle East Petroleum Co Ltd* [1988] 1 All E.R. 513; see generally Binchy, *Irish Conflicts of Law* (Dublin: Butterworth, 1988).

[99] *Al Kishtaini v Shanshal* [2001] 2 All E.R. (Comm.) 601, applying *Boissevain v Weil* [1950] A.C. 327.

Ltd[100] the plaintiff in Natal posted Irish sweepstake tickets to the Dublin office where the draw was to take place. The tickets were not included in the draw. Sweepstakes were illegal in Natal; the contract was illegal according to the law of the place where the contract was formed; it was not illegal under Irish law and could be enforceable in Ireland. A joint enterprise to violate foreign and domestic customs laws will be illegal and unenforceable by both parties; see *Whitecross Potatoes v Coyle*.[101]

The categories of public policy are not closed

14–28 The fact that contemporary societies are likely to be closely regulated by legislation does not mean that the categories of common law illegality are to be viewed as anachronistic or likely to be overtaken by changes in mores. While there may be grounds for viewing contracts that spring out of changes in lifestyle (persons living together outside of marriage and pre-nuptial arrangements that have property implications, for example) as being more likely to attract wider public support in the twenty-first century than previously, novel contractual arrangements may still fall to be examined by public policy and the categories of contracts which are void as being contrary to public policy are not closed.

14–29 One interesting illustration of this point is found in the Australian case of *Taylor v Burgess*.[102] Taylor claimed to be the son of a man, now deceased, who at the birth of Taylor entered into a deed with Taylor's mother in which the man promised to support the child, a condition of which being that the mother would not make allegations of paternity against the promisor. Taylor sought to have his mother provide evidence of paternity and the promisor's estate sought an injunction based on the deed. Barrett J. reasoned that this case did not fall within any of the accepted heads, but, agreeing with an earlier Australian judge who had observed that "public policy is a variable thing ... new heads of public policy come into being and old heads undergo modification",[103] he held that such an agreement was contrary to public policy. After noting that distinctions based upon the wedlock of parents have been rejected by the legislators, Barrett J. wrote: "the civil rights of children born out of wedlock are today, exactly the same as those of children born to married parents. There is not only a species of human right for any individual to know their true identity, subject only to statutory constraints but also a need for matters going to the very root of society—matters regulating procreation in a civilised society—to be capable of being known."[104]

---

[100] (1936) Ir. Jur. Rep. 25.

[101] [1978] I.L.R.M. 31.

[102] [2002] 29 Fam. L.R. 167, following, inter alia, *G v H* (1994) 181 C.L.R. 387.

[103] Sir Frederick Jordan in *Re Morris (decd.)* (1943) 43 S.R. (NSW) 352 at 356; see also *Evanture v Evanturel* (1874) L.R. 6 P.C. 1 at 29 per Colville J. See also Browne-Wilkinson J. in *Coral Leisure Group Ltd v Barnett* [1981] I.C.R. 503 at 507.

[104] (2002) 29 Fam. L.R. 167 at 174.

14–30 In contrast, however, Halsbury L.C. in *Janson v Driefontein Consolidated Mines Ltd*[105] denied the power of a court to invent new heads of public policy. In a more recent case,[106] however, Brown J. in the English High Court held that a person who provided information to the Revenue about tax defaulters could not recover on an alleged contract for reward on the basis that public policy would not countenance such a bargain if it existed. While this might be seen as a case related to champertous transactions it is not in fact a champertous contract, so the case may provide further support for identifying new heads of public policy and thus tainted agreements.

Statutory Illegality

14–31 Rules of public policy, whether designed to further social or economic objectives, are articulated by the legislature in the Acts of the Oireachtas or Statutory Instruments. Contractual arrangements that fall foul of these policy objectives may be invalidated by legislation, either expressly or impliedly. The distinction drawn by the courts between a void and an illegal contract is not always relied upon by the legislature.

14–32 Legislation expressly proscribes contracts in many situations. In the Republic, the now repealed Moneylenders Acts 1900–1989 made contracts entered into by unlicensed moneylenders unenforceable; charging of compound interest was also unlawful. The Family Home Protection Act 1976 s.3(1) provides: "[W]here a spouse, without the prior consent in writing of the other spouse, purports to convey any interest in the family home to any person except the other spouse, then, [subject to legislative exceptions] the purported conveyance shall be void." The Consumer Credit Act 1995 requires hire-purchase contracts to be evidenced in writing; otherwise the transaction is unenforceable: *Henry Forde & Son Finance Ltd v John Forde & General Accident Fire & Life Assurance Co.*[107] In employment contracts the Holidays (Employees) Act 1973 makes contracts to give up rights to holiday pay void; so too are contracts to give up rights to minimum periods of notice under the Minimum Notice and Terms of Employment Act 1973 s.5(3), as applied by the EAT in *Foley v Labtech Ltd.*[108] In this case the employee was entitled to compensation under s.4 following failure by the employer to give the statutory minimum notice, notwithstanding a term in the contract entitling either side to terminate the contract without notice after the first four months of employment. An employer cannot contract with employees to bargain away

---

[105] [1902] A.C. 484.
[106] *Robinson v Customs Excise, The Times*, April 28, 2000. In *Kelly v Simpson* [2008] IEHC 314, Charleton J. declined to award specific performance of a contract to sell land on the basis that the price was an inflated one, the transaction being intended to undermine planning legislation and environmental protection measures. Illegality was not pleaded but false disclosures to the planning authority were a key part of the development process, as evidenced by correspondence between the parties.
[107] Unreported, High Court, June 13, 1986.
[108] M 259/1978.

redundancy payments and compensation for unfair dismissal; attempts to avoid equal pay legislation are also rendered void by legislation—see s.8 of the Employment Equality Act 1998. Interpretation of contracts can involve anti-abuse conclusions—*Autoclenz Ltd v Belcher*[109]—in cases where employers have been resourceful in seeking to discover methods of avoiding statutory prohibitions against contracts that effectively limit statutory entitlements. See, in particular, *Marshalls Clay Products Ltd v Caulfield*[110] on payments under agreements that make provision in respect of holiday pay.

14–33 Licensing legislation of various kinds is a fruitful source of examples of statutory invalidity. Section 36(1) of the Road Transport Act 1933 provided that "it shall not be lawful for any person to enter into an agreement for the carriage for reward of merchandise by any other person unless such other person is a licensee under a merchandise licence". In *O'Shaughnessy v Lyons*[111] the plaintiff agreed to train as well as transport the defendant's greyhounds to and from race meetings. Justice O'Briain refused to permit an action to recover the agreed fee for this work because such a contract was in breach of s.36(1). Similarly, s.11 of the Moneylenders Act 1933 provided protection for lenders which, if not observed, led to the loan being unenforceable as against principal debtor and surety; see *Handelman v Davies*.[112] In contrast, however, the legislature may expressly provide that, notwithstanding the illegality, the entire contract is not to be rendered unenforceable. This is necessary where the legislation creates rights for individuals who would otherwise have to run the gauntlet of showing that a statute has not worked an implied prohibition. Two examples should suffice. The Consumer Information Act 1978 in s.25 provided: "A contract for the supply of any goods or the provision of any services shall not be void or unenforceable by reason only of a contravention of any provision of the [Merchandise Marks Acts 1887–1970] or this Act." Section 73(1) of the Social Welfare Consolidation Act 2005 enables the Minister for Social Protection to direct that the employment is to be insurable for the purposes of entitling a worker injured as the result of an accident arising out of, and in the course of, his employment to occupational injuries benefits "notwithstanding that, by reason of a contravention of or non compliance with [a statute] passed for the protection of employed persons or of any class of employed person the contract ... was void or the employed person was not lawfully employed". This section, in a piece of legislation designed to supplant the old Workmen's Compensation Acts, stands in contrast to cases where unlawful employment originally prevented the worker from recovering workmen's compensation should the worker be injured; see *Pountry v Turton*,[113] applied in *McHugh v Ministry of Labour for Northern Ireland*.[114]

---

[109] [2001] UKSC 41.
[110] [2003] I.R.L.R. 552.
[111] [1957] Ir. Jur. Rep. 90.
[112] (1937) 71 I.L.T.R. 268.
[113] (1917) B.W.C.L. 601.
[114] [1940] N.I. 174; *Barac v Farnell* (1994) 125 A.L.R. 241.

14–34 An Act may go further than rendering an agreement unlawful. In *Gray v Cathcart*[115] the defendant had taken a lease of an insanitary house in Belfast. The Belfast Corporation Acts made it an offence to occupy insanitary premises. The landlord's action to recover arrears of rent failed; Johnston J. said:

> "Everyone commits a misdemeanour who does any act forbidden by a statute: accordingly when these parties entered into an agreement to occupy a house which had been condemned it was a contract to do that which the statute says you could not do. It was a contract to do an illegal thing, and though the parties might go through the form yet such a contract is not binding and cannot be sued upon."[116]

It does not follow, however, that simply because conduct is by statute made a criminal offence any contract in which one party acts in breach of such a statute will automatically render the contract illegal. Johnston J. was in error if the above reasoning is advanced as the modus operandi to be invariably followed by the courts. If the statute expressly makes such contracts void the courts have no option but to follow this provision. If, however, the legislature has not spelt out the consequences of entering into a contract it is not to be assumed that a contract will be invalid. The courts must ask: does this statute impliedly prohibit a contract of this nature? The court should inquire into the purpose behind the statute; licensing arrangements are often designed simply to raise revenue for the Government or to regulate an industry. Changing social and religious values may lead to a statutory prohibition being changed or repealed; see the Statute of Frauds 1695 forbidding Sunday trading repealed by the Statute Law Revision (Pre–Union Irish Statutes) Act 1962 and *Brady v Grogan*.[117]

14–35 In *Smith v Mawhood*[118] a statute prohibited the sale of tobacco by unlicensed dealers. The plaintiff was an unlicensed dealer and in an action brought against the defendant for tobacco sold and delivered, the defendant pleaded that the contract was illegal. Parke B. said "the question is, does the Legislature mean to prohibit the act or not?" The Court of Exchequer held that this was not the legislative intention but the prohibition was merely a revenue-raising measure. In *O'Brien v Dillon*[119] the exceptional nature of *Smith v Mawhood* was recognised and the general rule was stated to be, in the words of Lord Ellenborough in *Langton v Hughes*[120] that, "what is done in contravention

---

[115] (1899) 33 I.L.T.R. 35.
[116] (1899) 33 I.L.T.R. 35.
[117] (1842) *Armstrong* 278.
[118] (1845) 14 M. & W. 452.
[119] (1858) 9 Ir. C.L.R. 318. For specific statutory control of corruption amongst office-holders, see *Fitzgerald v Arthure* (1839) 1 Ir.Eq.R. 184.
[120] (1813) 1 M. & S. 593.

of the provisions of an Act of Parliament cannot be made the subject matter of an action".[121]

14–36 In fact, even this approach is now recognised as being too broad. If the Act is clear and declares the contract to be illegal, then there is little room for doubt that illegality in the strict sense will be intended; see Megarry J. in *Spector v Ageda*.[122] But the trend in recent years has been marked by a reluctance to readily infer a legislative intention to prohibit contracts.

14–37 The leading English decision on statutory illegality is *St. John Shipping Corp v Joseph Rank*.[123] The plaintiffs sued for freight owed by the defendants who had contracted for the plaintiffs to transport their cargo. The master of the vessel overloaded the vessel contrary to statute, calculating that even after paying the maximum fine a profit would still be made by carrying excess cargo. Devlin J. held for the plaintiffs. This contract was lawful at the time it was entered into. The breach of statute, which occurred during performance, did not run foul of any express or implied provision invalidating contracts. The matter is one of construction of the statute; Devlin J. said that the test is not whether there is an illegal act during performance of the contract but rather, does the illegal performance thereby turn the contract into one which is prohibited by statute? The test here is determined by reference to the statute in question. If the statute expressly or implicitly prohibits the contract being sued upon here, then the intention of the parties is not material to the issue. As Devlin J. pointed out, a contract to actually overload the ship with bunkering may have been illegal but a contract to carry a cargo in circumstances in which the vessel was thus overloaded would not be unlawful. In the latter case of *Archbolds (Freightage) Ltd v Spanglett Ltd*[124] an action brought by the owner of goods for their value when lost while in the possession of the defendant haulier was met with a plea that the contract of carriage was illegal because here the haulier was not suitably licensed under the Road Traffic Acts. The defendants tried to rely on the argument that the contract was illegal under statute but, noting the distinction in *St. John Shipping*, the Court of Appeal rejected the defence. While the Road Traffic Acts may prohibit the use of an unlicensed vehicle on the highway and may indeed prohibit all contracts for the use of unlicensed vehicles, it did not follow that statute impliedly prohibits contracts for the carriage of goods by unlicensed vehicles, for this kind of transaction is seen as collateral in character. As Pearce L.J. pointed out, if this defence was to succeed it would affront common sense. A taxi driver operating without a licence could dump a passenger in the middle of nowhere at dead of

---

[121] (1813) 1 M. & S. 593 at 596.
[122] [1973] 1 Ch. 30.
[123] [1957] 1 Q.B. 267; *SCF Finance v Masri (No. 2)* [1987] 2 W.L.R. 58.
[124] [1961] 1 Q.B. 374; *Cotronic (U.K.) v Denzione* [1991] B.C.C. 200. Contrast the unlicensed estate agent case of *RTA (Business Consultants) Ltd v Biallwell* [2015] EWHC 630 (Q.B.) where wider interests in counteracting money laundering and terrorism were advanced.

night and in an action brought by the passenger for breach of contract could plead in defence the "status" of unlicensed carrier. The public policy interest that would be served by such a situation was stated by Pearce L.J. to be non-existent, and such a solution would "injure the innocent, benefit the guilty and put a premium on deceit". This observation was cited with approval by Morris J. in *Westpac Building Corp v Dempsey*.[125]

14–38 In *Hortensius Ltd and Durack v Bishop*[126] the trustees of the Trustee Savings Bank, Dublin, used depositors' funds in order to purchase investment opportunities from the plaintiffs, the use of such funds not being a business use recognised by the Trustee Acts 1863–1979. The plaintiffs built upon this fact to argue that a contract and certain mortgages and charges entered into were void and unlawful, as being illegal contracts. Costello J. held that there was no question of statutory illegality on the facts of this case. The prohibition found in s.15 of the Trustee Act 1863 did not make illegal contracts for the purchase of loans, it prohibited the trustees from entering into such contracts. Costello J. held that there was an important distinction between a statutory provision which made it illegal for a trustee to enter into certain types of contract and a statutory provision which made certain kinds of contract illegal. The prohibition in s.15 was in the former category and the intention of Parliament was to make trustees liable in the law relating to breach of trust and not make unlawful any such contracts entered into by a trustee in breach of statutory duty. As Costello J.'s approach illustrates, the issue is essentially one of construction of the statute in the light of surrounding circumstances; the courts lean against finding that the Act, on its construction, has this effect because it means treating persons who intend to break the law in the same way as persons who do so unwittingly. The possibility that a lawbreaker will not only be fined but lose the fruits of a contract also contributes towards a restrictive approach to the implied prohibition problem; such a conclusion punishes a person twice over.

14–39 The Supreme Court's decision in *Gavin Lowe Ltd v Field*[127] is instructive. The plaintiff sued on a dishonoured cheque which had been given to them by the defendant who had purchased a cow from the plaintiff. The beast was bought after it had been put on the market in such a way as to be "exposed for sale"; public health legislation made it an offence to "expose for sale" a diseased animal; the cow had later to be destroyed because it was tubercular. The legislation did not in terms make it an offence to sell diseased livestock; it was therefore possible to buy cattle that were diseased as long as the transaction did not involve an act of "exposure for sale". The plaintiff argued that he was entitled to recover on the dishonoured cheque; he argued that the purpose behind the legislation was not to make contracts for the sale of diseased livestock illegal but to protect the public health by

---

[125] Unreported, High Court, November 19, 1992.
[126] [1989] I.L.R.M. 294.
[127] [1942] I.R. 86.

making it an offence to expose for sale diseased meat. The majority of the Supreme Court accepted this argument and permitted recovery on the cheque. Sullivan C.J. held that because the Acts did not make it an offence to sell, the defence of illegality would only succeed if the unlawful act of exposure and the sale amounted "to a unity of design". In the Chief Justice's view this was not so. Murnaghan and Geoghegan JJ. concurred. A more satisfactory view is advanced by the dissenting members of the Supreme Court. Meredith J. held it to be "an absurdity" to reach such a conclusion; the prohibition of an act preparatory to sale was designed to preclude the sale itself from being legal. "Prohibition of the bud is then prohibition of the blossom."[128] O'Byrne J. agreed: "It seems difficult to justify such a construction as would recognise the validity of a contract arising out of exposure for sale, though the exposure itself is made a criminal offence."[129]

14–40 The "unity of design" approach favoured by the majority is not of any great value for it seems to this writer to be far too vague. A more recent approach to problems of statutory illegality, in contrast, however, is blessedly simple for it requires the legislature to spell out the implications of a statute for any contracts that may arise in the course of some illegal activity. In *Yango Pastoral Co Property v First Chicago (Australia) Ltd*[130] a mortgage granted in favour of the mortgagee bank by the mortgagor was alleged to be void because the bank, as an unlicensed body, was committing criminal offences for which a daily maximum fine could be imposed upon conviction. The mortgagor claimed the mortgagee could not enforce the security. The High Court of Australia rejected this, even though the activity prohibited was clearly central and not collateral to the bank's primary trading activity—lending money on security. Mason and Aickin JJ. opined that there is much to be said for the view that once a statutory penalty has been provided for an offence, the role of the common law in determining the legal consequences of the commission of the offence is thereby diminished.

14–41 This issue later came before the High Court of Australia again in *Fitzgerald v FJ Leonhardt Pty Ltd*.[131] A driller, licensed under statute, entered into a contract to bore for water. The landowner inadvertently failed to obtain the necessary permits so some of the wells drilled were created illegally under statute and the landowner was thus guilty of criminal offences. The issue before the court was whether the contract was illegal. In the view of the High Court the driller was entitled to recover the contract price. In their joint opinion, McHugh and Gummow JJ. noted that the statute in question prescribed a penalty:

---

[128] [1942] I.R. 86 at 100.
[129] [1942] I.R. 86 at 107.
[130] (1978) 139 C.L.R. 411; *Fitzgerald v F.J. Leonhardt Property* (1997) 189 C.L.R. 215.
[131] (1997) 189 C.L.R. 215, following *Yango,* and *Nelson v Nelson* (1995) 184 C.L.R. 538. See also *Corradini v Lovrinov Crafter Pty* (2000) 77 S.A.S.R. 125 and *Sutton v Zollo Enterprises* [2000] 2 Qd. R. 196.

"In such a case the role of the common law in determining the legal consequences of commission of the offence may thereby be diminished because the purpose of the statute is sufficiently served by the penalty. Here, the imposition of an additional sanction, namely inability of the driller to recover moneys otherwise owing by the owner, would be an inappropriate adjunct to the scheme for which the Act provides. The contrary decision would cause prejudice to an innocent party without furthering the objects of the legislation."[132]

In *Master Ed Services v Ketchell*[133] the High Court of Australia considered whether non-compliance by a franchiser with provisions requiring that franchisees be supplied with details of codes of practice rendered claims for payments under the contract unenforceable due to statutory illegality. The High Court of Australia indicated that, in policy terms, this was essentially an exercise in statutory interpretation. Flexibility in terms of remedies that could be imposed was held to be an important factor in this process. Because the statute provided a wide range of franchisee reliefs where loss had occurred, and because the statute was intended to protect franchisees, a conclusion that a franchisee's bargain would be struck down in every case made no sense. The High Court of Australia observed:

"A preferable result, and one for which the Act provides, is to permit a franchisee to seek such relief as is appropriate to the circumstances of the case."

While decisions like *Master Ed Services* should be seen in the light of movement in Australia towards a more flexible assessment of the appropriate remedy, as Irish law currently stands, one should treat the view that illegality principles contain a discretionary element with considerable caution.

The unpredictability of the nuanced approach—three recent examples.

14–42 There is a considerable degree of agreement on the relevant issues as between appellate courts in the UK, Ireland and Australia. *Tinsley v Milligan*[134] remains the leading decision in the UK because in the three recent cases decided by the UK Supreme Court, it was not invited to consider or review *Tinsley v Milligan*.[135] In *Quinn v Irish Bank Resolution Corporation* the Irish Supreme Court clearly rejected *Tinsley v Milligan*; Clarke J. took the view that Australian case-law provided clearer guidelines but it must be open to doubt

---

[132] (1997) 189 C.L.R. 215 at 227. On the purpose of the legislation see the judgment at p.222 (guarding against undue depletion of ground water in the Northern Territories).

[133] (2008) 236 C.L.R. 101.

[134] [1993] 3 All E.R. 65.

[135] *Tinsley v Mulligan* generally stands for the proposition that if a claim can be mounted without disclosing facts which involve illegality, a claim may succeed. English judges tend to reason around this notion so as to produce a more intellectually satisfying position, e.g. see all judgments in *Patel v Mirza* [2014] EWCA Civ. 1047.

whether any of the three jurisdictions have resolved these difficult issues in a coherent manner. Three examples come to mind, each taken from the three most relevant jurisdictions.

Example 1: Quinn v Irish Bank Resolution Corporation[136]: *the new Irish Approach*

14–43 In this case Clarke J., writing for a five judge supreme court, has built upon the earlier Australian case law, as well as finding much assistance from English case law, in order to set out a principled approach to resolving issues of statutory interpretation presented to a court if the Oireactas has not expressly ruled that a contract should be illegal and unenforceable. Citing Lord Sumption in *Les Laboratoires Services v Apotex Inc.*[137] Clarke J. rejected arguments that sought to turn the principle of illegality from a rule of law into a power that can be judicially exercised by a court on a discretionary basis. Observing that "whatever may be the disadvantages of the rule of law approach ... leaving the question of enforceability up to a very broad consideration by a trial judge on the facts of any individual case would arguably be worse". The exercise is one of statutory interpretation and the court is required to decide whether public policy requires contracts to be treated as unenforceable to ensure that the courts do not enforce contracts tainted by illegality and thus fail to discourage illegal activities. Each particular statutory provision must be assessed in order to determine whether public policy requires a related contract to be void or unenforceable in addition to any sanctions found in the relevant legislation. In this regard the undesirability of allowing courts to become involved in the enforcement of contracts tainted by illegality should be afforded appropriate weight unless there is significant counter weight to be gleaned from the language or policy of the statute concerned. Clarke J. also said that the fact that the Oireachtas has had the opportunity to direct that the relevant contracts were to be void or unenforcable (but did not) must be regarded, although this will not of course be decisive.

14–44 Clarke J. went on to make an assessment of the factors that the implied prohibition problem raised in the instant case. In so doing stress was laid on the need to adopt a more nuanced approach, on the basis that this was needed in order to comply with modern requirements of policy in a highly regulated age. Clarke J. stressed that the context is important: the transaction type before the court was a lending transaction involving serious allegations of criminality. Clarke J. wrote:

> "When considering the broad category of underlying transaction which is under consideration in this case, being a lending transaction, it is possible to envisage a very wide range of circumstances, in which such a transaction might be said to be tainted with illegality. There might,

---

[136] [2015] IESC 29.
[137] [2014] UKSC 55.

for example, be money lent to a drug dealer in circumstances where it was known to the lender that the money was to be used for trafficking in drugs. At the other end of the spectrum, there might be lending which is connected with a transaction where the transaction concerned is in technical breach of a complex regulatory regime and where the lender, although aware of the facts, might not appreciate that there was a technical problem with the transaction for which the lending was provided. A whole range of intermediate cases can be envisaged."

14–45 The first matter that a court should consider is whether the contract in question is designed to carry out the very act which the relevant legislation is designed to prevent. In doing so the court should look to the language of the statute to glean any intention to imply that the remedies or consequences found in the statute are sufficient to carry out the statutory objective.

The court must also seek to discern an intention that the prohibition be directed at only one party to the transaction or to all parties. Citing from the overloaded shipping cases and statutes regulating consumer transactions, parliament may have intended to impose a regulatory burden on one person alone.

It follows therefore that imposing a sanction on an innocent party or a person who was intended to be protected by the statute might mean that the imposition of voidness or unenforceability would be counterproductive to the statutory objective itself.

14–46 Clarke J. went on to make some further "tentative" suggestions taken from the range of administrative sanctions that may flow from infringement of a statute. Where the statute contains "an elaborate, significant and proportionate scheme of adverse consequences" this may indicate that the illegality principle and the void or unenforceable consequences are not to operate. Conversely, a "light" range of sanctions could suggest that public policy requires that the contracts in question be void and unenforceable. It may also be arguable that a proportionality test is relevant, Clarke J. quoting from McHugh J.A.'s speech in *Nelson v Nelson*. Clarke J. went on to stress that in lending transactions and instances where guarantors are concerned, underlying facts as to knowledge and participation in legality may affect the process of statutory interpretation.[138]

14–47 The above observations represent a brief paraphrase of Clarke J.'s speech[139] and as the learned judge observed, the lending transaction context in which these comments were made may not be readily replicated in other contexts. It is also possible to say that some of the more tentative observations look rather like a formula for taking account of the underlying circumstances of a given case. Although Clarke J. did not say as much, it is possible to view these guidelines as leading to the conclusion that it will only be in the most egregious cases—serious criminality, morally reprehensible conduct or

---

[138] [2015] IESC 29 at paras 8:45 to 8:47.
[139] At [2015] IESC29, para.8:55, Clarke J. provided a useful summary of his analysis.

cases where a statute expressly prohibits a contract—that a court will hold a connected contract will be void and/or unenforceable. In these cynical times it may be that the courts will actually conclude that infractions of the law do not readily engage the public interest so as to call into play the ex turpi causa principle, even if certain criminal statutes (e.g. intellectual property statutes) are blurring the line between the civil law and the criminal law.

Example 2: Patel v Mirza *in the English Court of Appeal.*

14–48 A most enlightening analysis of the statutory purpose approach is provided by Gloster L.J. in *Patel v Mirza*.[140] The parties intended to use Mirza's spread betting account in order to invest on the stock exchange. Patel transferred £620,000 into Mirza's account for this purpose. The parties intended to use insider information for this to be achieved, a criminal offence under statute. The Government changed its policies in respect of the company in question so the insider dealing plan was frustrated. Patel did not recover his funds and sued for their return. The trial judge held the monies irrecoverable because of the legal arrangement. In the English Court of Appeal an appeal was allowed unanimously but in her judgment Gloster L.J. gave a clear example of how the statute could be read, noting that this was not an action seeking to enforce an agreement for an illegal purpose. The statutory provision, s.52 of the Criminal Justice Act 1993 was reviewed. Starting from the principle of law that an investor who enters into a contract of agency with a broker (Patel and Mirza respectively) may enforce the contract and require the agent to account to the investor for monies received, her ladyship said:

- Section 52 is aimed at countering market abuse—here, the transaction never took place;
- Section 63(2) of the 1993 Act specifically provided that no contract is to be void or unenforceable by reason only of s.52;
- The claim is not to enforce a criminal conspiracy but recover deposited funds;
- The trial judge did not find Patel knew of the illegality. The scheme originated with Mirza;
- In her view the criminal conduct was not proximate to the investment transfer to Mirza, who as an agent had no right to retain the funds;
- Controversially perhaps, the plaintiff's loss was a serious one and the agent's gain was, as the more blameworthy party, disproportionate, applying *Saunders v Edwards*.[141]

Example 3: The High Court of Australia and Statutory Purpose

14–49 In *Gnych v Polish Club Ltd*[142] the appellants entered into an oral lease for five years. No documentation was executed, resulting in the appellants

---

[140] [2014] EWCA Civ 1047.
[141] [1987] 2 All E.R. 651.
[142] [2015] HCA 23.

being outside licensing legislation intended to prevent potentially improper persons from being involved in the management and supervision of licensed premises. Significantly, the lessee appellants only discovered that licensing provisions had not been met when the respondents sought to terminate the lease. The New South Wales Court of Appeal held that the relevant public policy considerations directed that the licensing authority required the right to license persons in the position of the appellants. The lease was therefore void and unenforceable. The High Court of Australia reversed this decision. While an agreement by both parties that an oral lease would be entered into, sidestepping the licensing authority, would have been such as to render the lease unenforceable, the case was very different. The statutory purpose was a flexible one; the lessor, not an intending lessee, committed an offence and the statutory provisions, to be used by the licensing authority, were flexible and discretionary. The authority in question for example could declare the lease to be cancelled, suspended or subject to a stated condition. The lessees could be awarded damages for unlawful termination of the lease by the lessor.

14–50 If the legislature, however, gets the drafting of the statute wrong then unfortunate consequences will follow. *Phoenix General Insurance Co of Greece S.A. v Administratia Asigurarilor de Stat*[143] is a decision that must now be regarded as providing the definitive statement on how pleas of statutory illegality relating to insurer licensing must be approached. The Insurance Companies Act 1974, intended as a piece of protective legislation, required the insurance business to be carried on only by authorised insurers. Phoenix, prior to January 1978, were authorised insurers. However, in that year, new regulations were introduced which reclassified the various kinds of insurance. These regulations were very complex and Phoenix continued to underwrite in the same way. Phoenix entered into reinsurance contracts with the defendants and when claims were submitted by Phoenix, the defendants refused to pay. The defendants claimed that the contracts of reinsurance were illegal because Phoenix had not obtained the necessary authorisation. The Court of Appeal, however, held that under transitional arrangements Phoenix were, in fact, authorised, reversing Hobhouse J. on this point. The Court of Appeal went on to consider what the position would have been had the insurer not been authorised. The Court of Appeal noted that public policy would be best served by holding that the illegality would not render the contract void because the purpose behind the legislation was very much one of protecting the unwitting consumer who would not be in a position to know if the insurer was authorised or not, but in the context of this statute there was no room for public policy. The unilateral prohibition of unauthorised insurers did not simply prohibit the business of effecting contracts of insurance for which the insurer had no authority, it extended to "carrying out contracts of insurance". As Kerr L.J. noted:

"[T]his extension of prohibition has the unfortunate effect that contracts made without authorisation are prohibited by necessary implication

---

[143] [1987] 2 All E.R. 152.

and therefore void. Since the statute prohibits the insurer from carrying out the contract (of which the most obvious example is paying claims) how can the insured require the insurer to do an act which is expressly forbidden by statute?"[144]

Parliament amended the Statute by way of the Financial Services Act 1986 s.132.[145]

14–51 This case illustrates how poor drafting can unwittingly subvert the very objective behind a statute itself. Fortunately, this case is, as the Court of Appeal observed, a decision based very much on its own facts, and most statutes, when not expressly providing for the consequences of illegality on contracts, do leave room for a more purposive interpretation, as in *Archbolds (Freightage) Ltd v Spanglett Ltd*.[146] In *Marrinan v O'Haran*[147] Pringle J. followed the *Spanglett* case. The issue before the Court in *Marrinan v O'Haran* was whether the plaintiff would be prevented from obtaining a commission payable for services rendered in introducing to the defendant a property owner who gave the defendant sole agency rights to sell property which the owner was anxious to sell. The defendant was not a licensed house agent, and was thus acting contrary to s.7 of the Auctioneers and House Agents Act 1947 which provided that it was a criminal offence to carry on, hold out or represent oneself as a house agent, or act as a house agent without a licence. Pringle J. indicated that he would not have prevented the plaintiff from recovering "as there was no evidence that he knew that the defendant had no auctioneer's licence and the contract itself was not expressly forbidden by statute". Even if the party pleading illegality can point to some default by the defendants or their agents or employees, the protection afforded by statute and the underlying policy will be closely scrutinised and, in the absence of a clear express prohibition of the contract under statute, the underlying policy will be given effect.[148]

Gaming and Wagering Contracts

14–52 The regulation of gaming is something that any modern democratic State may have a legitimate interest in promoting and developing, given that commercial interests may seek to exploit the vulnerable in ways that would not be consistent with contemporary views on consumer protection. Gaming laws in Ireland, even after the enactment of the Betting (Amendment) Act 2015 are archaic, particularly in the light of electronic gaming and remote gaming through the use of the internet, e-mobile technology and even interactive

---

[144] [1987] 2 All E.R. 152 at 176.
[145] See now the Financial Services and Markets Act 2000 ss.26 to 30 (UK).
[146] [1961] 1 Q.B. 374.
[147] Unreported, High Court, June 17, 1971.
[148] *Hughes v Asset Managers Plc* [1995] 3 All E.R. 669; *Anandh v Barnet Primary Health Care Trust* [2004] EWCA Civ 5.

broadcast technology. Many governments have identified the taxation and other revenue streams that may be lost unless the legal system in question recognises and regulates activities such as online casino-style gaming and online betting, mobile phone betting, in particular, being seen as a huge area of growth in the years ahead. In the UK a policy of simplification of gambling regulation, under the control of a Gambling Commission, has been outlined in a White Paper,[149] produced following a Parliamentary Select Committee Report on gaming. The UK Parliament legislated in 2005.

14–53 The Gaming and Lotteries Acts 1956–2003 are the most important Acts regulating the way in which gambling is carried on within the Republic. While an analysis of this legislation is outside the scope of this book, s.36 of the Gaming and Lotteries Act 1956 (the "1956 Act") governs the consequences of the contractual relationship created by gaming and wagering. For an exhaustive analysis of the law, see Smith and Monkcom, *The Law of Gambling*.[150]

14–54 It is widely agreed that the 1956 Act is generally inappropriate and largely unenforceable in modern day Ireland. The body charged with the most recent investigation of a large area regulated by the 1956 Act, that of casino gaming,[151] was directed by the Government to specifically legalise casinos and associated areas of activity and provide for the regulation of these casinos. That body, the Casino Committee, looked at gaming as conducted in fairs and amusement arcades, as well as the legislation governing, and regulation of, casinos, and the Casino Committee made a number of recommendations directed at effective regulatory structures that seek to observe three public policy objectives, namely:

"(a) to ensure that gaming is conducted in a verifiably fair and open fashion in order to protect the interests of the consumer;

(b) to ensure that, to the greatest extent possible, children and other vulnerable persons are protected from harm or exploitation by gaming;

(c) to prevent gaming in casinos being or becoming a source of crime or disorder."[152]

---

[149] *A Safe Bet for Success* (2001), Cm 5397; see Miers, "The Gambling Review Report: Redefining the Social and Economic Regulation of Commercial Gambling" (2003) 66(4) M.L.R. 605. UK law is exhaustively covered in Smith & Monkcom, *The Law of Gambling*, 3rd edn (Haywards Heath: Tottel, 2009).

[150] 3rd edn (Haywards Heath: Tottel, 2009). See also Corbet and Bollard, "Ireland" in Harris and Hagan (eds), *Gaming Law* (London: European Lawyer Reference Series, 2012).

[151] *Regulating Gaming in Ireland* (2006), available at: *http://www.justice.ie/en/JELR/casino*.

[152] *Regulating Gaming in Ireland* (2006), available at: *http://www.justice.ie/en/JELR/casino*, para.1.4.1. Even though the Casino Committee Report suggested that in the future betting should be regulated so as to provide for protection of vulnerable consumers and children, in *Sporting Index Ltd v O'Shea* [2015] IEHC 407 MacEochaidh J. held that s.36(2) of the 1956 Act still directed that it would be manifestly contrary to public policy to enforce a judgment obtained in England and Wales for the recovery of a gambling debt of over €180,000, the debt being incurred in the course of spread betting activities engaged in by the defendant, an account holder with the plaintiff company. The judge was perhaps concerned with the way the

The Casino Committee did not recommend that betting or wagering should be regulated in the same way, but it did suggest that certain machines located on bookmaker's premises should be regulated by the mooted new Gaming Regulatory Authority. The Casino Committee also suggested that, in relation to Internet betting, or remote gaming as it was called, a full impact study should be carried out.

14–55 The Betting (Amendment) Act 2015 is based upon several reviews of betting legislation. While the Betting (Amendment) Act 2015 updates existing legislative provisions in respect of the licensing of bookmakers and suitable persons rules, as well as allowing for the licensing of bookmakers and betting exchanges that operate remotely (e.g. over the internet), no effort is made to address broader aspects of betting. For example, the 2015 Act does not enact specific rules declaring what consequences would follow if bets are placed with an unlicensed remote bookmaker. More specifically, there is no adjustment to the well established rules on the recovery of stakes or the enforceability of winning bets. The consequences of winning bets placed by minors in breach of the Betting (Amendment) Act 2015 s.27 for example is not addressed but one could speculate that the Oireachtas would impliedly direct that such a wager is void and unenforceable because the minor commits an offence in misrepresenting his true age for betting purposes.

(1) Wagering

14–56 The legislation does not define a "wager" but case law has produced the following definition, taken from *Cheshire, Fifoot and Furmston's Law of Contract*:

> "Staking something of value upon the result of some future uncertain event such as a horse race, or upon the ascertainment of the truth concerning some past or present event, such as the population of London, with regard to which the wagering parties express opposite views."[153]

It is of the essence of a wager that one party is to win and the other to lose upon the determination of the event. For this reason a bet placed with "the Tote", that is, the Racing Board established by the Totalisator Act 1929, is not a wager. This was decided by Pringle J. in *Duff v Racing Board*.[154] Because the Racing Board is legally bound to pay all the money received to successful ticketholders it follows that the Board can neither win nor lose.

---

debt arose. Consumer protection policies are frustrated by the fact that the European Union distance contracts and consumer rights Directives, as well as the e-commerce Directives, do not apply to gambling contracts as a matter of subsidiarity. It is understood that in the new consumer protection legislation there was an initial intention to include distance gaming contracts with consumers, but the bill has not been published (July 2016).

[153] 13th edn (London: Butterworth, 1996), p.334.

[154] Unreported, High Court, November 19, 1971 applying *Tote Investors Ltd v Smoker* [1968] 1 Q.B. 509.

14–57 English case law establishes that multipartite arrangements are not wagers: *Ellesmere v Wallace*.[155] The Alberta case of *Breitmeier v Batke*,[156] on the other hand, suggests that an arrangement between three persons may be a wager. Fridman, author of the leading Canadian text, suggests that the Canadian authority is to be preferred for "the true test surely is whether one person can win and others lose".[157] Irish cases should follow this test in this writer's view. Nevertheless a tripartite wager may often be a lottery.

14–58 Trading ventures which induce subscribers to join a venture may fall foul of the pyramid selling legislation and a number of highly publicised cases in England, such as *One Life Ltd v Roy*,[158] the *Titan* case[159] and *Re Vanilla Accumulation Ltd*[160] indicate that many dubious product marketing ventures are illegal. The National Consumer Agency provides useful guidance on the more common kinds of pyramid schemes and advises consumers to "be scam savvy"[161] and a code of practice is in place to protect consumers. Even apparently innocent promotional ventures may fall foul of the law against unlawful lotteries. In *Flynn v Denieffe and Independent Newspapers*[162] the Supreme Court struck down a game of no skill as being a lottery, notwithstanding that all participants did not have to purchase a newspaper and thus they did not provide a payment when playing the "Scoop" game.

14–59 Many transactions resemble a wager; a contract of insurance is "a bet on the outcome of a future uncertain event". It is not a wager if the assured has an insurable interest in the subject matter; to insure a ship's cargo against destruction during a voyage is a valid contract of insurance if the assured has an interest in the cargo. It is a wager if not.[163] Stockbroking arrangements often fall into the category of wagers. "Contracts for differences" involve an agreement between two persons who agree that they will ascertain the difference in price of certain shares on one day and their price at a later date. If the parties do not intend that the shares will be purchased the "contract for differences" will be void. Similarly in *Byers v Beattie*[164] the plaintiffs agreed to purchase and sell shares which were owned by the defendants. The agreement provided that if the price for which the shares were later sold was greater than that paid

---

[155] [1929] 2 Ch. 1.
[156] (1966) 56 W.W.R. 678.
[157] Fridman, *The Law of Contract*, 5th edn (Toronto: Thomson, 2006), p.357.
[158] *The Times,* July 12, 1996.
[159] *Re Senator Hanseatische Verwaltungsgesellschaft* [1997] 1 W.L.R. 515.
[160] *The Times*, February 24, 1998.
[161] *http://www.nca.ie*. See also *The Irish Times*, March 21, 1998; "Investors in Pyramid Scheme lose their case", *The Irish Times*, December 5, 2002. See Consumer Protection Act 2007 ss.64–66 for legislation.
[162] *Irish Times Law Report*, February 23, 1993, following *Imperial Tobacco Ltd v A.G.* [1981] A.C. 718.
[163] See *Church and General Insurance Co v Connolly and McLoughlin*, unreported, High Court, May 7, 1981; *Fuji Finance v Aetna Life Insurance* [1996] 4 All E.R. 608 illustrates how new insurance products must be carefully structured to avoid this trap.
[164] (1867) I.R. 1 C.L. 209.

by the defendants, the defendants would pay the difference plus any charges and commission to the plaintiffs. The plaintiffs sued for sums due under this agreement. The arrangement was held a wager.

(2) Gaming

14–60 At common law gaming was legal if the element of chance was negligible and the outcome of the game turned upon the skill of the players. The present legislation defines "gaming" as "playing a game (whether of skill or chance or partly of skill and partly of chance) for stakes hazarded by the players".[165] Section 4 of the 1956 Act makes gaming unlawful if:

    (a) the chances of all of the players, including the banker, are not equal; or
    (b) if a portion of the stakes are retained by the banker otherwise than as winnings; or
    (c) gaming is conducted by way of slot machines.

Later sections make gaming at a circus, travelling show, carnival, public house, amusement hall and funfair lawful gaming in specific instances.

(3) Lotteries

14–61 Section 21(1) of the 1956 Act provides that "[n]o person shall promote or assist in promoting a lottery". Private lotteries, lotteries at dances and concerts, carnivals and other events, as well as lotteries under permit or licence are lawful. Lotteries on football games are outside the terms of the 1956 Act; see s.32 of the Betting Act 1931. The Irish Hospitals Sweepstakes, before its dissolution,[166] was a lawful agreement under the Public Hospitals Act 1933 and was enforceable in the Republic's courts (*Stanhope v Hospitals Trust Ltd (No.2)*)[167] as is the National Lottery; see the National Lottery Act 2013.

Consequences of a Gaming or Wagering Contract

14–62 Section 36 of the 1956 Act provides:

    (1) Every contract by way of gaming or wagering is void.
    (2) No action shall lie for the recovery of any money or thing which is alleged to be won or have been paid upon a wager or which has been deposited to abide the event on which a wager is made.
    (3) A promise express, or implied, to pay any person any money paid by him under or in respect of a contract to which this section applies or to pay any money by way of commission, fee, reward or otherwise

---

[165] 1956 Act, s.2. On netting contracts see the Netting of Financial Contracts Act 1995 discussed by Foy at (1996) 3 C.L.P. 72 and Ch.5 of Foy, *The Capital Markets: Irish and International Laws and Regulations* (Dublin: Round Hall Sweet & Maxwell, 1998). The Act is fully annotated by Hoy in *Irish Current Law Statutes Annotated*.
[166] By the Public Hospitals (Amendment) Act 1990.
[167] [1936] Ir. Jur. Rep. 25.

in respect of the contract or of any services connected with the contract is void and no action shall lie for the recovery of any such money.

Subsection (4) allows the winner of a lawful game to sue for the prize provided it is not a stake. The section is based in part upon s.18 of the Gaming Act 1845 (the "1845 Act"), which is repealed in Ireland by the Schedule to the 1956 Act. The following points must be made about the meaning of the 1956 Act, as gathered from litigation on s.18 of the 1845 Act.

14–63 By declaring every contract by way of gaming or wagering void the Oireachtas has reaffirmed that, while the transaction is not illegal, no rights can accrue to either party. Thus in *Pujolas v Heaps*[168] a bookmaker, licensed under betting shops legislation, refused to pay out to a punter who had won his bet. The punter was unable to recover his winnings in an action. If the loser pays by cheque and then cancels it, no action will lie on the dishonoured cheque. The legislation confers a privilege upon the loser; if he choses to waive this privilege by paying the winner, the loser has no right to recover the money paid; see also the badly reported case of *Phelan v Stewards of the Kilmacthomas Races*.[169]

14–64 The opening limb of s.36(2) produces an interesting problem of construction. One view of this subsection holds that it adds nothing to s.36(1); as a result, a subsequent contract to pay the sum due on a wager may be enforceable if given for good consideration. In *O'Donnell v O'Connell*[170] the defendant owed debts to the plaintiff, a bookmaker. The plaintiff said he would list the defendant as a defaulter, which would have damaged his creditworthiness at the track. The plaintiff compromised his admittedly hopeless action on the debt and refrained from listing the defendant in return for a promissory note. The plaintiff successfully sued on the promissory note. The trial judge, Molony C.J., following the now overruled[171] English Court of Appeal decision in *Hyams v Stuart King*,[172] held that the 1845 Act did not invalidate an action brought on a promise given for some act of forbearance. The better view of the legislation is that subsequent transactions are rendered unenforceable by what is now s.36(2). The House of Lords so ruled in *Hill v William Hill (Park Lane) Ltd*.[173] It is to be hoped that the flagrant evasion of the policy underlying the Act leads to a future Supreme Court overruling *O'Donnell v O'Connell*. In any event, *O'Donnell v O'Connell* is certainly inconsistent with two earlier Irish

---

[168] (1938) 72 I.L.T.R. 96.
[169] (1896) 30 I.L.T. 36.
[170] (1923) 57 I.L.T.R. 92.
[171] In *Hill v William Hill (Park Lane) Ltd* [1949] A.C. 530.
[172] [1908] 2 K.B. 696.
[173] [1949] A.C. 530.

cases: *O'Donnell v O'Sullivan*[174] and *Walker v Brown*.[175] Mac Eochaidh J, in *Sporting Index Ltd v O'Shea*[176] has held that s.36 has the effect of making it possible to prevent a foreign gaming or wagering service provider to enforce a contract debt incurred by way of a spread betting account, even on the foot of a judgment obtained in the courts of that other jurisdiction.

14–65 The second part of s.36(2) has also received a narrow interpretation. At first sight it should mean that where money has been deposited with a stakeholder no action will succeed. In *Graham v Thompson*[177] money was deposited with a stakeholder. The plaintiff repudiated the agreement before the money was paid but after the result of the event was known. It was not clear whether the plaintiff was the winner or loser. It was held that whenever the loser of an illegal wager repudiates at any time before the wager is paid he can recover his part of the stake in an action for money had and received. The second part of s.36(2) prevents any person, whether he be winner or loser, from recovering the other person's part of the stake: *McElwain v Mercer*.[178] This interpretation of the words of s.18 of the 1845 Act has carried over into the 1956 Act as the case of *Crean v Deane*[179] shows.

14–66 Section 36(3) deals with the case of a contractual arrangement in which a principal engages an agent to place bets on his behalf. If the agent advances his own money to cover the stake and he is promised, expressly or impliedly, recompense, he cannot recover in an action against the principal. Nor is the principal liable to pay a commission, fee or reward to the agent. Section 36(3) substantially recites s.1 of the Gaming Act 1892, which prevents the ordinary rule that an agent is liable to be indemnified for all lawful acts from extending into wagering transactions. In *Close v Wilson*[180] the English Court of Appeal had to consider whether an advance made by a principal to an agent (or perhaps a loan made by a lender to a borrower), the money to be spent on placing bets, could be recoverable if diverted to other users by the payee. On the assumption that the transaction was one in which the borrower/agent was to repay the loan from winnings, the Court of Appeal held that it did not matter whether such terms existed as in essence the contract in question was one to repay money in respect of bets which were to be placed and was therefore void under s.1 of the Gaming Act 1892 (repealed in Ireland by the 1956 Act and replaced by s.36(3) of that Act). It is only sums advanced that *may* be used for betting purposes (as distinct from

---

174 (1913) 47 I.L.T.R. 253.
175 (1897) 31 I.L.T.R. 138.
176 [2015] IEHC 407, ruling that Article 34 of Regulation 34 of Council Regulation (EC) No. 44 of 2001 provided a basis for refusing to enforce an English judgment. It would be manifestly contrary to public policy allow the enforcement of a betting transaction contrary to section 36.
177 (1867) I.R. 2 C.L. 64.
178 (1859) 9 I.C.L.R. 13.
179 [1959] I.R. 347.
180 [2011] EWCA Civ 5.

sums advanced that are to be used as a matter of contractual obligation) that are recoverable.[181]

14–67 On the other hand, the principal may have the right to recover if the agent places the bet but refuses to pay over the winnings; see *Griffith v Young*.[182] If the agent fails to place the bet and the wager would have been successful the principal has no remedy for breach of contract; see *Cohen v Kittell*.[183] However, a complete departure from the contractual purpose is a different matter. The interrelationship between restitutionary reliefs and the proscription against recovery of monies advanced for betting or gaming purposes was recently explored in *Close v Wilson*.[184] Close advanced £20,000 to Wilson with the intention that this be expended on betting transactions; most of the sum appears to have been lost with Betfair. However, Close traced some of the money into Wilson's building society account and sought recovery of this sum. After pointing out that the statutory prohibitions do not preclude an action to recover from an agent any *winnings* that the agent receives[185] the Court of Appeal reasoned that if part of the money was used by Wilson for his own purposes, outside of the scope of the agreement, the unenforceable nature of any claim brought on the agreement itself could not defeat a restitutionary action. To put it another way, any claim to restitution is *not* based on an express or implied promise, the subject matter of s.36(3) of the 1956 Act.

14–68 If money is paid to a stakeholder the stakeholder becomes an agent for both parties; as we have seen the stake is recoverable if the agent's authority to pay is revoked before payment is made. The agent will be liable if he then pays the stake to the other party. No action will lie for the recovery of sums actually paid to the winner, in breach of the stakeholder's authority. In *Toner v Livingston*,[186] A made a bet with B regarding the weight of a bullock owned by A. A deposited £20 with a stakeholder to abide the result. The bullock was never weighed but the stakeholder paid the £20 to B. A sued B for money had and received; the action failed, being caught by the words of what is now s.36(3) of the 1956 Act.

Money lent for gaming and wagering

14–69 In *Anthony v Shea*,[187] Anthony lent Shea £43 knowing Shea was to use it for gaming. Even though it was not proved that the money was so used Anthony was unable to recover from Shea's estate. The gaming transaction

---

[181] *MacDonald v Green* [1951] 1 K.B. 594; *Al Tamimi v Khadari* [2009] EWCA Civ 1109.
[182] (1810) 12 East 513.
[183] (1889) 22 Q.B. 680.
[184] [2011] EWCA Civ 5. A retrial on factual issues was ordered.
[185] e.g. *De Mattos v Benjamin* (1894) 63 L.J.Q.B. 248; *Jeffrey v Bamford* [1921] 2 K.B. 351.
[186] (1896) 30 I.L.T.R. 80.
[187] (1951) 86 I.L.T.R. 29.

in question may have been lawful gaming but this point was not made; the English textbooks state that money lent for lawful gaming is recoverable.[188]

Cheques and other securities.

14–70 The party who takes a negotiable instrument which has been given for a gambling debt can sue upon it if he can show he is a "holder in due course".[189]

The Consequences of Common Law and Statutory Illegality

14–71 The common law rules which circumscribe the remedies available to persons who have entered a contract which is illegal at common law also apply where the contract is illegal under statute. Legislators do not frequently resolve the problems which arise here by stipulating that such and such an illegal contract is to give rise to the following consequences. This often leads to unfortunate results as we shall see. Three situations must be distinguished.

(1) Where the contract is unlawful on its face

14–72 A contract which creates an illegal consideration is unlawful on its face. When the plaintiff in *Littledale v Thompson*[190] promised to convey a right to an advowson in return for the defendant's promise to pay the costs of the plaintiff's litigation the contract was champertous on its face. All parties to such an agreement are prevented from suing to enforce any promise under that contract. If a contract is illegal on its face the contract is said to be illegal at its inception. In *Gray v Cathcart*[191] the landlord was held unable to recover arrears of rent because the insanitary premises could not be lawfully let. Similarly, under s.44 of the Land Act 1936, a sub-lease of certain lands could only be lawful if the consent of the Land Commission was obtained. No such consent was sought or given. The landlord was held unable to recover arrears of rent because the lease was illegal; the landlord sought to avoid the illegality by invoking estoppel, but the High Court held that estoppel cannot be used to avoid an illegal contract.[192] The leading case is *Murphy & Co Ltd v Crean*.[193] The plaintiffs agreed to lease premises to Crean who was to carry on the business of publican, taking all the stout needed for this purpose from the plaintiffs. The licence necessary was transferred, with the consent of the local justices, to the defendant. The contract, however, also contained

---

[188] See *Cheshire, Fifoot and Furmston's Law of Contract,* 16th edn (Oxford: OUP, 2012), pp.422–423, especially *CHT Ltd v Ward* [1965] 2 Q.B. 63. The Gaming Act 1892 was repealed by the 1956 Act thus clearing the way for an application in Ireland of the dictum in *CHT Ltd v Ward* [1965] 2 Q.B. 63.
[189] Bills of Exchange Act 1882 s.29(1).
[190] (1878) 4 L.R. (Ir.) 43.
[191] (1899) 33 I.L.T.R. 35.
[192] *Dempsey v O'Reilly* [1958] Ir. Jur. Rep. 75; *O'Kane v Byins* [1897] 2 I.R. 591.
[193] [1915] 1 I.R. 111.

a provision which later obliged the defendant to transfer the licence to any person in another public house nominated by the plaintiffs. Irish licensing legislation does not permit transferability of a liquor licence to a person not in occupation of the premises. This rule is designed to prevent someone whom the licensing justices have deemed a fit person from transferring the licence to someone who may not be of good character. This illegal covenant rendered the whole agreement unenforceable. The plaintiffs were held unable to prevent the defendant from selling stout manufactured by another company. The Supreme Court, in *Macklin & McDonald v Greacen & Co*,[194] reaffirmed this general approach by refusing to grant specific performance in relation to a contract for the sale of a liquor licence, the sale to be independent from the sale of premises. The leading English case of *Re Mahmoud and Hispani*[195] shows that in this situation the rule can operate harshly. The plaintiff agreed to sell linseed oil to the defendant who falsely represented that he, the defendant, had a licence to purchase the oil. Such a licence was necessary under statute. The defendant refused to take delivery and was sued for non-acceptance. The action failed. The innocent party was held unable to sue on a contract unlawful at its inception. *Re Mahmoud* was followed in the Queensland case of *Olsen v Mikkelsen*.[196] The plaintiff purchased seeds from the defendant who supplied them without giving an invoice, an offence under statute. The seeds failed to germinate. The contract was held illegal at formation so the plaintiff could not sue for breach of warranty. *Anderson v Daniel*[197] also points to how far-reaching statutory illegality can be. The plaintiff sued for the price of fertilisers sold and delivered to the defendant. The defendant pleaded non-compliance with legislation which made it necessary to deliver to the buyer a notice indicating the composition of the fertilisers. The Court of Appeal held that the legislation in question was not revenue legislation, and had as its objective the protection of the public. There was no legislative basis for upholding the vendor's submission that analysis was on these facts extremely burdensome and thus, an apparently unmeritorious purchaser was able to retain the goods without having to pay for them.

14–73 There are comparatively few Irish cases in which a statute has been held to declare that a particular transaction is not to be actionable. In *Irvine v Teague*[198] loans made to the defendant and secured by way of mortgage were held to infringe the provisions of s.24 of the Charitable Loan Societies Act 1843 which declared that "it shall not be lawful" to lend more than £10 to one borrower at one time. This infringement prevented the Treasurer of the Society from enforcing the mortgage.

---

[194] [1983] I.R. 61.
[195] [1921] 2 K.B. 716.
[196] [1937] Qd. R. 275.
[197] [1924] 1 K.B. 138.
[198] (1898) 32 I.L.T.R. 109.

14–74 In the English case of *Ashmore v Dawson*[199] the plaintiffs owned a piece of heavy engineering equipment which had to be transported by lorry. The defendant hauliers agreed to transport the machinery, a perfectly valid agreement. The defendants, to cut costs, intended to use a particular lorry which did not meet the capacity requirements set out in legislation. The plaintiff's transport manager was present when the machinery was loaded onto the vehicle; he was held to know that the statutory restrictions were being broken. In the view of the majority of Lord Justices in the Court of Appeal the knowledge and acquiescence of the transport manager meant that he "participated" in the illegal performance. Phillimore L.J. went further; he found that the contract was deliberately given to the defendants knowing that it would be performed in this manner, rendering the agreement unlawful at its inception. The decision in *Devine v Scott and Johnston*[200] provides another Irish example of this type of illegal contract.

(2) Where the contract is lawful on its face but one person only intends to perform unlawfully

14–75 Again, *Ashmore v Dawson*, above, is in point. Had the transport manager not been present, or if it had been shown that he did not know of the restrictions on transporting goods by lorry, the plaintiffs would have been able to sue on the contract for the rule is that the party intending illegal performance is unable to avoid the rule, ex turpi causa non oritor actio, but the innocent party, that is a party who does not know or participate in the illegality, has the full range of remedies available for him because, from his perspective, the contract was lawful. The burden of proving a joint illegal intent lies upon the party pleading the illegality.

14–76 The decision of Finlay P. in *Whitecross Potatoes v Coyle*[201] emphasises the importance of distinguishing contracts which one party only intends to perform illegally. Coyle, a farmer in Meath agreed to sell potatoes to the plaintiffs, a company in England who intended to use the potatoes in their chain of fish and chip shops. Each party suspected that the UK and Irish Governments were about to impose restrictions on the export and import of potatoes. The agreement provided that if this occurred a higher price would be payable. This clause was consistent with two modes of performance; the plaintiffs explained that Coyle was going to purchase potatoes in Northern Ireland and deliver these to them, thereby getting around the problem of import restrictions. This would be perfectly lawful. The defendant, however, explained that he intended no such thing; he intended to smuggle the potatoes into Northern Ireland, the higher price covering transport costs. Finlay P. held that Coyle alone intended to perform the contract in an illegal manner. The plaintiffs were therefore entitled to recover for non-delivery of the potatoes.

---

[199] [1973] 1 W.L.R. 828.
[200] (1931) 66 I.L.T.R. 107.
[201] [1978] I.L.R.M. 31, applied in *Da Silva v Rosas Construcoes Gabriel A.S. Couto SA* [2016] IEHC 152.

14–77 These distinctions are not always drawn. In *Martin v Galbraith*[202] the Supreme Court had to consider whether an employee could recover for overtime worked in breach of legislation limiting hours worked in excess of 48 hours a week. The majority of the Supreme Court held such an action must fail; statute made it an offence for the employer to require this work to be done, although the employee did not commit an offence. Murnaghan J. stated: "parties to a contract which produces illegality under a statute passed for the benefit of the public cannot sue upon the contract unless the legislature has clearly given a right to sue."[203] This analysis is too simplistic for if the contract is illegal in relation to overtime an employee could not sue to recover unpaid wages earned during the 48-hour period of lawful employment! The correct questions to ask would be, have the parties agreed at formation that unlawful overtime would be worked? If not, has the employer exacted unlawful performance from the employee who knew of the breach of statute? Are the parties equally at fault?

(3) Where the contract is lawful on its face but both parties intend to perform it unlawfully

14–78 A contract to buy and sell a painting is clearly lawful on its face, but if the painting is owned by a third party and it will be acquired by A through burglary in order to sell it to B, B having commissioned the burglary, the contract will be void and unenforceable. Where statutory illegality is concerned, *Patel v Mirza*[204] now suggests that the statutory purposes within legislation may allow restitutionary claims. The most important guidelines that have evolved in Irish case law are afforded by the Supreme Court decision in *Quinn v Irish Bank Resolution Corporation Ltd (In Special Liquidation)*.[205] A number of financial share transactions were entered into by Sean Quinn and Anglo Irish Bank. Those transactions were allegedly illegal, involving the Bank in providing loans to allow Sean Quinn and related companies to purchase shares in the Bank, contrary to s.60 of the Companies Act 1963 and the Market Abuse Regulations.[206] In furtherance of these funding transactions the Quinn children executed guarantees and share charges which they sought to have declared invalid on the basis that these subsequent guarantees and charges were tainted by statutory illegality. The Quinn children were assumed to be unaware of the underlying illegality for these purposes. Charleton J. held that the statutory provisions in the 1963 Act and the Market Abuse Regulations did not prevent a court from using illegality principles so as to enable the Quinn children to have the guarantees and share charges declared invalid, unenforceable and having no legal effect.

---

[202] [1942] I.R. 37.
[203] [1942] I.R. 37 at 54.
[204] [2014] EWCA Civ. 1892 (ch).
[205] [2015] IESC 29.
[206] Directive 2003/6/EC, transposed by S.I. No. 342 of 2005. For sanctions and offences see the Investment Funds Companies and Miscellaneous Provisions Act 2005.

The Supreme Court unanimously allowed an appeal brought by Anglo Irish Bank. On s.60 Clarke J. followed the reasoning in a number of Australian lending cases, noting in particular that s.60(14) of the Act provided that loans made were valid unless the Bank itself sought to set the transaction aside against a party with notice. Under the Market Abuse Regulations Clarke J. found that the regulations were intended to counteract the manipulation of markets via false or misleading information and practices. The regulations contained criminal offences and penalties of a substantial nature as well as administrative sanctions. The regulations were intended to support investor confidence and assist in maintaining share values for the benefit of shareholders. To deprive shareholders of the value of the guarantees and share charges that the Quinn family sought to invalidate would be counterproductive to the central purpose behind the regulations.

Judicial Attitudes to Illegality

14–79 The general attitude of the courts when faced with an illegal transaction was succinctly stated by Lindley L.J. in *Scott v Brown Doering*,[207] an English case followed in several Irish decisions:

> "*Ex turpi causa non oritur actio* … No court ought to enforce an illegal contract or allow itself to be made the instrument of enforcing obligations alleged to arise out of a contract or transaction which is illegal if the illegality is duly brought to the notice of the court and if the person invoking the aid of the court is himself implicated in the illegality."[208]

It is clear that damages will not be awarded for breach of an illegal contract; indeed, in *McDonnell v Grand Canal Co*[209] an injunction preventing a company from carrying into effect an intention to enter an illegal contract was issued. It is less clear why the courts go further by preventing restitutionary relief in cases where property has been transferred as part of the illegal transaction; Lindley L.J. said in *Scott v Brown Doering* that any legal rights a party has apart from the illegal contract may be recognised. The case of *Brady v Flood*[210] suggests that ownership alone may not be enough to permit restitution. Brady sued Flood for the recovery of banknotes which Flood had been given in return for a promise to get criminal charges against Brady's sons dropped. This agreement was illegal as interfering with the administration of justice. Brady C.B. said: "I will not try this case. You are parties to an illegal contract and whoever has got the money I will allow him to keep it."[211]

---

[207] [1892] 2 Q.B. 724.
[208] [1892] 2 Q.B. 724 at 726.
[209] (1853) 3 Ir. Jur. (N.S.) 197.
[210] (1841) 6 *Circuit Cases* 309.
[211] (1841) 6 *Circuit Cases* 309 at 311. See also *Taylor v Chester* (1869) L.R. 4 Q.B. 309.

14–80 The judges shelter behind another Latin maxim—*In pari delicto potior est conditio possidentis*—which means that where both parties are equally in fault the condition of the possessor is best. Nevertheless, there are signs that if the contract is illegal and the illegality is neither socially nor morally reprehensible—as in a case where the contract is illegal because one party fails to get a licence or complete a document—restitution and/or damages may be ordered. See the controversial case of *Bowmaker v Barnet's Instruments*.[212] Here Smith sold three machine tools under a contract to the plaintiffs, who then let them to the defendants on hire-purchase. The initial sale to the plaintiffs was illegal. The defendants wrongly sold machine tools one and three to third parties and failed to pay hire charges due under the contract in respect of machine tool two. The plaintiffs sued for conversion; the defendants resisted the action on the ground that the initial illegal contract also attached to the hiring contracts. The Court of Appeal noted that neither the plaintiffs nor the defendants were aware of the technical illegality, but there was an illegality. Nevertheless, the action in conversion succeeded. The wrongful sale of tools one and three had the effect in law of terminating the defendants' right to possession and, because it was conceded that ownership passed to the plaintiffs from Smith notwithstanding the initial illegality, the plaintiffs could, fortunately, rely on their rights of ownership and were not constrained to plead the illegal contract. Du Parq L.J. indicated that there was no public policy objection to allowing the owner of goods to recover in conversion, even if there were unlawful dealings in the goods at some time in the past. *Bowmakers Ltd v Barnets Instruments* is a difficult case because the agreement in respect of machine tool two was not concluded with a clause giving an automatic right of repossession to the owner for non-payment of hire charges, and non-payment of rental is not a basis for liability in conversion simpliciter. Hamson[213] has argued that *Bowmakers Ltd v Barnet Instruments* would, on this point, now permit recovery of possession under an illegal lease for non-payment of rent, as long as a clause to that effect were contained in the lease. *Bowmakers Ltd* has its defenders both in respect of the practicality and justice of the result and legal principle.[214]

14–81 The *in pari delicto* rule has unfortunate consequences. First of all, the party responsible for the illegality may use it to his advantage in circumstances which are quite unfair. In *Daly v Daly*[215] the defendant, a discharged insolvent debtor, had obtained his discharge through fraud. The plaintiff, one of his creditors, learned of the fraud and upon confronting the defendant obtained a promise that the defendant would pay the initial debt in full, even though the discharge extended to this sum. The plaintiff dropped proceedings to set the discharge aside for fraud. The action on the new promise failed.

---

[212] [1945] K.B. 65.
[213] (1949) 10 C.L.J. 249.
[214] e.g. Coote (1972) 35 M.L.R. 38.
[215] (1870) I.R. 5 C.L. 108.

14–82 The application of the rules on illegality may conflict with other policy considerations, particularly when a statute is the source of the initial prohibition. In *Martin v Galbraith*[216] the statute prohibiting excessive overtime was designed to ensure, inter alia, the payment of wages at fair rates to employees. As O'Byrne J., dissenting, pointed out, the interpretation placed on the legislation defeated the intention of the Oireachtas. A similar US decision has been criticised by Furmston.[217] The judges are often aware that the effect of holding the contract to be illegal is to prejudice the very class of persons that public policy has identified as worthy of protection. In *Phoenix General Insurance Co of Greece SA v Administratia Asigurarilor de Stat*[218] Kerr L.J. stressed that each case must turn upon distinct factual and policy considerations.

> "[O]ne merely has to contrast moneylending contracts with a contract of insurance to see why it is good public policy to refuse to enforce the former but bad policy in the case of the latter. In both cases the legislation is designed to protect the customer, but the protection he requires is wholly different. In cases of moneylending the contract leaves virtually every subsequent obligation to be performed by the borrower, whereas in contracts of insurance the position is precisely the opposite."[219]

Kerr L.J. went on to contrast food legislation which is also intended to protect consumers: if food is purchased on foot of an illegal contract and the food causes illness, the policy of the law would also be subverted if there could be no liability in contract due to illegality. However, as in *Phoenix* itself, the statute, in cases of express prohibition, leaves no room for flexibility. In cases of implied prohibition under statute, or instances of common law illegality, many judges are alive to this issue. One legislative improvement that could be considered by the Oireachtas would be to vest in the judiciary a general residual discretion to depart from the ex turpi causa rule, where an application produces unfortunate consequences, as it did in the *Phoenix* case.

Exceptions to Ex Turpi Causa and *In Pari Delicto*

(1) Where the parties are not equally at fault

14–83 The first "exception" is not really an exception at all. In the Northern Ireland case of *Sumner v Sumner*[220] Megaw J. accepted that if one party to the illegal contract entered into the bargain because of fraud, duress or undue

---

[216] [1942] I.R. 37. On the knowledge and participation elements in respect of employment contracts lawful on their face but which are intended to be performed illegally, see *Conaghan v McGurk and Moore* [2012] NIIT 00188, one of 11 Northern Ireland Industrial Tribunal cases decided on February 28, 2012. On appeal see [2014] NICA 3.

[217] (1966) 16 U.T.L.J. 267 at 288, criticising *Coules v Pharris* (1933) 250 N.W. 404.

[218] [1987] 2 All E.R. 152; *Byrne v Rudd* [1920] 2 I.R. 20.

[219] [1987] 2 All E.R. 152 at 175.

[220] (1935) 69 I.L.T.R. 101.

influence on the part of the other he may have a remedy. The courts will generally permit recovery of money paid. So too, participation in the illegal contract will not be a bar to relief if the participator can show that he was a member of *the class* which the statute was designed to protect; see the old English case of *Browning v Morris.*[221] In *Martin v Galbraith,*[222] Meredith J., dissenting, was in favour of holding the employee entitled to recover because the employee was not *in pari delicto*; he did not commit an offence. It can also be argued that an employee who refused to work in an illegal manner may fear dismissal so he is not *in pari delicto*: see *Mathew v Bobbins.*[223] In one case the English Court of Appeal permitted a person innocently breaking exchange control regulations to recover in an action for deceit, if a successful plea of illegality would permit the rogue to retain the benefits of his fraudulent conduct; see *Shelley v Paddock.*[224] Contrast cases where the plaintiff was aware of the illegality, e.g. *Thackwell v Barclays Bank Plc.*[225]

14–84 Two important English cases indicate that there is a considerable movement afoot in respect of judicial attitudes to the *in pari delicto* rule. The fact that one party only is to benefit from the disgraceful act may be a powerful indicator in future cases that the parties are not *in pari delicto*, even if the non-benefiting contracting party is aware of, or even assists in, furthering the illegal purpose. In *Saunders v Edwards*[226] the plaintiffs agreed to purchase a flat from the defendant, acting upon a fraudulent misrepresentation which induced the contract. In order to minimise their stamp duty on the purchase of the property, the plaintiffs obtained the defendant's participation in a conveyance which valued the contents at £5,000, thereby reducing the liability of the plaintiffs for stamp duty. The contents were worth between £500 and £1,000, at most, and the misdescription was an attempt to defraud the revenue. The plaintiffs' action was brought in the tort of deceit, the plaintiffs realising that enforcement of the contract itself would not be available but, on the merits, the plaintiffs were held entitled to damages for the tort of deceit. The moral culpability of the plaintiffs was outweighed by the fraud perpetrated by the defendant; the misrepresentation was an unanswerable tort and unconnected to the contract. Even if there had been no subsequent arrangement to mislead the Revenue, the loss to the plaintiffs would still have been occasioned by the defendant's fraud. *Sweetman v Nathan,*[227] however, takes this exception even further because the fraudster was a partner in a firm of solicitors and it was the innocent partners that were being used by the plaintiff. The Court of Appeal did not think that this changed the applicability of *Saunders v Edwards*.

---

[221] *Browning v Morris* (1778) 2 Comp. 790; *Kiriri Cotton Co v Dewani* [1960] A.C. 192.
[222] [1942] I.R. 37.
[223] *The Times*, June 21, 1980.
[224] [1980] 2 W.L.R. 647.
[225] [1986] 1 All E.R. 676.
[226] [1987] 2 All E.R. 651; *Standard Chartered Bank v Pakistan National Shipping Corp (No. 2)* [2000] 1 Lloyd's Rep. 218; *Sweetman v Nathan* [2003] EWCA Civ 1115.
[227] [2003] EWCA Civ 1115.

14–85 In *Euro-Diam Ltd v Bathurst*[228] the Court of Appeal went even further by holding that an insurance contract was enforceable in favour of the plaintiff, even though the plaintiff had assisted in enabling a customer to defraud the German revenue authorities. Euro-Diam Ltd had sold diamonds to a German company on foot of invoices that misstated the price and led to a lower rate of German import tax being levied. Euro-Diam Ltd effected a related contract of insurance but did not rely on the lower figure and had declared the full value of the goods to the insurers. The diamonds were stolen and the contract of insurance sought to be relied upon. While the issue of the invoice was reprehensible, the related contract of sale was not being sued upon; the false invoice did not assist Euro-Diam Ltd, and involved no deception of the insurers. There was no public policy consideration which required the contract of insurance in this particular case to be caught by the ex turpi causa defence.

14–86 A further illustration of the exceptional circumstances which may cause the courts to relax the *in pari delicto* rule is afforded by the facts of *Howard v Shirlstar Container Transport Ltd*[229] where a pilot who took an aircraft from Nigeria, in breach of air traffic control regulations, was held entitled to recover his previously agreed fee for doing so, because the acts were committed in order to escape from an apparently life-threatening situation to the pilot and his wireless operator. The Court of Appeal held that the conscience of the court would not be affronted by allowing recovery in such exceptional circumstances.

(2) Repentance

14–87 If the transaction is illegal at formation but has yet to be performed, repudiation of the illegal transaction may permit the repudiating party to recover property transferred. A person who parts with property in an attempt to defraud creditors may recover those assets if he repents before any creditors are affected. In *Tribe v Tribe*[230] a father transferred assets as a pre-emptive move to put those assets out of the reach of creditors. The transfer, to his son, was part of a bogus sale. When the anticipated litigation with the creditors did not materialise the father asked for the assets back but the son refused to comply, arguing that for the father to succeed he would have to reveal the illegal purpose. The Court of Appeal held that because no creditors had been defrauded the father could "repent" and be reimbursed, notwithstanding the illegality. *Patel v Mirzan*[231] clarifies the basis of this exception to the rule whilst broadening its scope. Repentance in the sense of the claimant being required to withdraw from the transaction before it is carried into effect is not the basis of the exception; the case of *Tribe v Tribe* did not involve remorse but

---

[228] [1988] 2 All E.R. 23. See also *Kavanagh v Caulfield* [2002] IEHC 67.
[229] [1990] 3 All E.R. 366.
[230] [1995] 4 All E.R. 236; Creighton, "The Recovery of Property Transferred for Illegal Purposes" (1997) 60 M.L.R. 102.
[231] [2014] EWCA Civ. 1047.

a realisation by the plaintiff that the shifting of assets was no longer needed. In *Patel v Mirzan* the illegal purpose could not be realized by frustration of the illegal purpose by shifting circumstances. As a restitution case in which the parties did not implement the illegal purpose in any direct sense, restitution was possible. The position is uncertain if the illegal purpose is not carried into effect after the transfer of property has taken place because the illegal purpose is detected by law enforcement or regulatory agencies, for example. There are no Irish cases on these points of law.

(3) Independent cause of action

14–88 Case law exists which suggests that property in goods passes when parties to a contract for the sale of goods (the contract being illegal) transfer physical possession to the purchaser; see *Singh v Ali*,[232] a decision of the Privy Council. Indeed, property may pass under an illegal contract even if a third party holds the goods according to *Belvoir Finance Co v Stapleton*,[233] an English Court of Appeal decision. In *Hortensius Ltd & Durack v Bishop*,[234] the decisions in *Singh v Ali* and *Belvoir Finance v Stapleton* were cited with approval by Costello J. Thus, if the loan purchase transactions in *Hortensius Ltd* had been illegal contracts which could not have been enforced by the trustees in question, "once the consideration provided in them has been paid, and the property referred to in them transferred to the trustees, they are not void contracts". Execution of the illegal agreement gave good title to choses in action and properties transferred to them by the agreements, thereby allowing the trustees rights of enforcement albeit by a somewhat circuitous route. An action in detinue, a tort independent of contract, will be possible if the transferor later interferes with goods. The Privy Council has decided that the registered owner of land who lets property under an illegal landlord and tenant agreement can rely upon his title to recover possession. The tenant would not be able to plead the illegal contract as a defence to an action in trespass based on the plaintiff's ownership: *Amar Singh v Kulyubya*.[235] Contrast *Brady v Flood*[236] if banknotes are transferred. The English courts have frequently had to consider the ex turpi causa rule in the context of claims brought against the innocent partners of defendants who have participated with the plaintiff in a fraud,[237] companies wronged by a defendant who has acted in cahoots with a company employee who bribed public officials,[238] and auditors whose fraud or negligence in failing to identify wrongdoing by a company employee injured the company.[239] Generally, the ex turpi causa rule will only preclude a claim if a reliance test is satisfied. Should the plaintiffs claim be "founded on", or arise

---

[232] [1960] A.C. 167.
[233] [1971] 1 Q.B. 210.
[234] [1989] I.L.R.M. 294.
[235] [1964] A.C. 142.
[236] (1841) 6 *Circuit Cases* 309.
[237] *Sweetman v Nathan* [2003] EWCA Civ 1115.
[238] *Marlwood Commercial Inc v Kozeny* [2006] EWHC 872 (Comm).
[239] *Stone & Rolls Ltd v Moore Stephens* [2007] EWHC 1826 (Comm), upheld at [2009] UKHL 39.

from an illegal act, or the illegal act must necessarily be pleaded or relied upon in order to sustain the claim, the ex turpi causa rule may be operative.[240]

(4) Quantum meruit

14–89 In a radical departure from earlier case law, the Court of Appeal in *Mohamed v Alaga*[241] held that even if a fee sharing agreement between a solicitor and another person is illegal, an action in quantum meruit for the value of work undertaken at the request of the solicitor may be maintained.

Separate Transactions

14–90 In order to permit a limited remedy the courts may view a transaction as divisible into separate contracts, thereby isolating or limiting the effects of the illegality. In *McIlvenna v Ferris and Green*[242] the defendants ordered construction of a building. Under Emergency Powers legislation such work could only be lawfully carried out under licence. No licence was obtained. The plaintiff's action for work performed under the written contract failed; the court permitted the plaintiff to recover for additional work ordered just after the regulation had been rescinded on the basis that this was the subject of a separate contract. Another Irish decision in point is *Sheehy v Sheehy*.[243]

14–91 It is common in building contracts for the parties to expressly covenant that all necessary planning permission has been obtained by the owner of the site. In *Strongman (1945) Ltd v Sincock*[244] a similar agreement was held to give rise to a remedy in damages when it transpired that the necessary permission had not been obtained. The action here was brought upon a collateral contract, separate and distinct from the illegal construction contract. In *Namlooze Venootschap De Faam v Dorset Manufacturing Co*,[245] Dixon J. held that the free transfer of foreign exchange was prohibited under statute. While an award of damages could not be made, for this would result in the statute being ignored, it remained possible for the plaintiff to establish a right to damages by showing a failure by the defendant to use due diligence in obtaining the consent of the Minister for Finance to a transfer of foreign exchange out of the jurisdiction.

---

[240] *Stone & Rolls Ltd v Moore Stephens* [2007] EWHC 1826 (Comm) per Langley J. at para.43, upheld at [2009] UKHL 39. But dissatisfaction with the majority reasoning in *Stone & Rolls Ltd* is profound: see in particular *Jetivia SA v Bitta (UK) Ltd* [2015] UKSC 23, especially the speech of Lord Neuberger at para.30. For an overview of the recent UKSC decisions see *Strauss* (2016) 132 L.Q.R. 236.

[241] [1999] 3 All E.R. 699. See also *Patel v Mirza* [2014] EWCA Civ 1047 on restitution.

[242] [1955] I.R. 318.

[243] [1901] 1 I.R. 239.

[244] [1955] 2 Q.B. 525.

[245] [1949] I.R. 203.

Contracts of Loan

14–92 Loans made in order to enable the borrower to make or perform an illegal contract, or to pay a debt contracted under an illegal contract, are also illegal if the lender is aware of the purpose for which the loan is sought.[246] If a loan is sought in order to discharge a loan which itself was illegal, then that second transaction will also be tainted and unenforceable if the earlier illegality was known to the second lender; see *Spector v Ageda*.[247] However, the fact that the lender knows that the loan may be used to evade lawful creditors which is not itself unlawful, does not bring the case within this principle, at least when the loan is made in order to obtain security for an earlier bona fide debt; see *Bagot v Arnott*.[248]

Contracts of guarantee

14–93 If the main contract between A and B is illegal in circumstances which make it impossible for A to sue B, can a contract of guarantee be enforceable by A, the creditor, against C, the guarantor? The question was answered in the negative in *Devine v Scott and Johnston*.[249] Devine, landlord under an illegal letting to Johnston, was held unable to recover rent from either Johnston or Scott, the guarantor of Johnston's indebtedness.

Severance

14–94 In *Devine v Scott and Johnston* only a part of the demised premises was used for the illegal purpose. The plaintiff suggested that the court could permit recovery of a portion of the rent, calculated by reference to the proportion of the property used in a lawful manner. The court rejected the view that such a power exists at common law. Furthermore, if a covenant contained in the contract is illegal this is said to taint the entire contract. The case of *Murphy & Co Ltd v Crean*[250] illustrates this. The plaintiffs were not attempting to enforce the illegal covenant requiring Crean to transfer the licence but this illegal clause precluded enforcement of other covenants which, taken alone, were unobjectionable. The weight of authority, both in England and Ireland, is against extending the doctrine of severance beyond cases which are in restraint of trade. Specifically in *Taylor v Bhail*[251] an argument that an illegal transaction in the form of a criminal conspiracy could be divided up in respect of the legal and illegal parts of the performance was rejected. Severance in a statutory illegality case is a possibility but will not be permitted in instances of common law illegality.

---

[246] *Cannan v Bryce* (1819) 3 B. & Ald. 179; *Fisher v Bridges* (1854) 3 E. & B. 642.
[247] [1973] 1 Ch. 30.
[248] (1867) I.R. 2 C.L. 1.
[249] (1931) 66 I.L.T.R. 107; *Rooney v Armstrong* (1847) 10 Ir. L. Rep. 291.
[250] [1915] 1 I.R. 111.
[251] (1995) 50 Con. L.R. 70; *Shafron v KRG Insurance Brokers* (2009) 301 D.L.R. (4th) 522.

14–95 There is support for the other view, however. In *Carolan v Brabazon*[252] the plaintiff sought specific performance of a lease which contained a covenant requiring the tenant to pay poor law rates. This covenant was illegal by Act of Parliament. Sugden L.C. said, obiter, that it may have been possible to grant specific performance of the lease minus the term as to payment of the poor law rate. In *Furnivall v O'Neill*,[253] O'Neill, an arranging debtor, entered into a secret arrangement in 1879 with Furnivall, a creditor, under which Furnivall was promised payment in full. This agreement was illegal. In 1880 this promise was repeated and a contract executed reciting the obligation. This contract also recorded other debts due to O'Neill which were legitimate. O'Neill sought to recover on the 1880 instrument. Andrews J. held that the promise to pay the illegal sums formed the main and operative consideration for the 1880 deed, and was thus fatal to the action. Had the illegal promise been incidental or peripheral then, like *Carolan v Brabazon*, severance may have been possible.

14–96 One English case decides that severance may be possible in cases of statutory illegality; see *Ailion v Spiekermann*.[254] Templeman J. in that case refused to follow the practice of other judges by "washing" his hands of the illegal contract because he said that such a solution was particularly unsatisfactory where one party is an unwilling victim. This case is to be welcomed; if severance is a legitimate device to do some measure of justice in restraint of trade cases, there is no reason why it should not be available in other contracts where public policy is infringed. Indeed, *Ailion v Spiekermann* and the Court of Appeal's decision in *Shelley v Paddock*[255] are indicative of a new and refreshing trend towards illegality cases; the English courts now seem reluctant to readily brand each party equally at fault, thereby making a restitutionary remedy available to the less culpable party. Indeed, the Privy Council in *Carney v Herbert*[256] established that severance is possible where the illegal promise forms a collateral or incidental part of the transaction and no compelling social, economic or moral imperative would be subverted by enforcement of the rest of the transaction. In an important decision on arbitration awards made in contravention of statutory restrictions, the New Zealand Court of Appeal, in *Gallaway Cook Allan v Carr*[257] has stressed that there are "no set or absolute rules for determining whether severance of an invalid provision from the balance of an agreement is appropriate. The primary inquiry must focus on the contractual provisions within their factual or statutory setting and the nature of the invalidity". The court was particularly persuaded that the result of allowing severance produced a just result, with the rights of appeal of both parties being unaffected. It is no longer possible to generalise and state that severance of statutory infractions contained in a

---

[252] (1846) 9 Ir.Eq.R. 224.
[253] [1902] 2 I.R. 422.
[254] [1976] Ch. 158.
[255] [1980] 2 W.L.R. 647.
[256] [1985] A.C. 301; *Nielson v Stewart* [1991] UKHL 13, per Lord Jauncey of Tullichettle.
[257] [2013] NZCA 11.

contract are more likely than in the case of common law illegality: the New Zealand approach has the benefit of approving a flexible solution.

14–97 While the spirit of *Carney v Herbert* is to be welcomed it would not lead an Irish court into adopting a different approach to *Lewis v Squash Ireland Ltd.*[258] The employee would still not be able to recover for wrongful dismissal or a redundancy payment, or compensation for unfair dismissal. Nor is it likely that the facts of *McHugh v Ministry of Labour for Northern Ireland*[259] would go the other way after *Carney v Herbert*.

Flexible Remedies—Possible Reforms

14–98 Some English judges have argued the need for the evolution of a public conscience test to give the courts a more discretionary power to react to any illegal purpose that the court takes note of: *Thackwell v Barclays Bank.*[260] Lords Goff and Keith, dissenting in *Tinsley v Milligan*,[261] championed this approach but the majority of the House of Lords in that case regarded such reforms as a matter for statutory reform. While some statutory reforms have given the courts a very broad power to adjust remedies where appropriate— witness the New Zealand Illegal Contracts Act 1970, s.7 of which gives the courts the power to grant relief "by way of restitution, compensation, variation of the contract, validation of the contract in whole or in part for any particular purpose, or otherwise howsoever as the court in its discretion thinks just"—it is not likely that, in the absence of statutory reform, such a public conscience test would evolve through case law in Ireland. However, not all judges are as timorous as the majority in *Tinsley v Milligan*. In *Nelson v Nelson*,[262] *Tinsley v Milligan* was not followed by the High Court of Australia, that court adopting a novel approach involving the surrender by the wrongdoer of the value illegally obtained in order to give practical effect to the purpose behind the statute and the "clean hands" doctrine.

14–99 After the decision of the unanimous Supreme Court in *Quinn v Irish Bank Resolution Corporation Ltd (In Special Liquidation)*[263] a unanimous Supreme Court has laid down some guiding principles and a number of factors that should be used in order to test whether public policy objectives behind a specific statute would be best served by allowing the loss to lie where it falls (i.e. do nothing) or permit a transaction to be enforceable, or allow restitution. The factors and criteria set out by Clarke J., whilst based on existing case law,

---

[258] [1983] I.L.R.M. 363.
[259] [1940] N.I. 174.
[260] [1986] 1 All E.R. 676.
[261] [1993] 3 All E.R. 65. See the comments of Enonchong, "Title Claims and Illegal Transactions" (1995) 111 L.Q.R. 135. See also *Lowson v Coombes* [1999] 2 W.L.R. 720, criticised by Cotterill, "Property and impropriety—the *Tinsley v Milligan* problem again" [1999] L.M.C.L.Q. 465.
[262] [1996] 184 C.L.R. 538.
[263] [2015] IESC 29; see also *Bank of Scotland v Mallon* [2015] NICh. 13-9: "a wrongdoer should no longer benefit from his own wrongdoing."

leave the law open to case-by-case incremental erosion and countermanding of the ex turpi causa rule. An increasing number of judgments not only stress that while the process involves statutory interpretation, there is a significant emphasis on different levels of participation and knowledge as well as the proportionality of the result. As Hogan J. stressed in *Greenclean Waste Management v Leahy*,[264] rules formulated at some time in the past should be accommodated "to modern social relatives" and be assessed by reference to Irish constitutional law norms which might cast the impugned provisions or practices in a new light. In any event, high judicial authority in Ireland has speculated on how open-ended the new principles, guidelines and criteria are, especially under a nuanced approach which will require the balancing of complex issues.

14–100 In *Quinn v Irish Bank Resolution Corporation Ltd (In Special Liquidation)* the Supreme Court was careful to observe that the Quinn children were assumed not to have knowledge of the underlying illegal transactions entered into by Sean Quinn and Anglo Irish Bank. If this were not the case then the application to invalidate the guarantees and share charges would have raised the issue whether all parties intended the guarantees and share charges to be in furthermore of an illegal purpose involving serious criminality. Clarke J. opened up the possibilities when he said:

> "An analysis of the appropriate criteria might result in the conclusion that public policy requires that the underlying transaction between two guilty parties should nonetheless be enforced, notwithstanding its connection with illegality. But it would not necessarily follow that an entirely innocent guarantor should suffer to the benefit of a party who was directly engaged in the illegality concerned. On the other hand, different considerations might well apply, where the guarantor was, whether innocently or otherwise, designed to benefit from the very transaction itself or from closely connected transactions. In such circumstances it might be difficult to see how public policy required that such a party should potentially gain the benefit of an illegal transaction without having to comply with obligations entered into as part of the very same series of transactions."

Clarke J. went on to say the application of observations of this kind "must await a case in which the appropriate acts squarely arise" for determination.

14–101 Even if more flexibility were introduced into the law, it is doubtful that the courts would allow compensation to conscious wrongdoers. There has been a tentative exploration of this point in relation to legislation directed at identifying money laundering by suspected criminals.

---

[264] [2014] IEHC 314 (a champerty case); Hogan J.'s approach to the contract was heavily criticised in the Court of Appeal: [2015] IECA 97.

In *Vehicle Tech Ltd v AIB Plc*[265] the High Court declared that s.31(8) of the Criminal Justice Act 1994, a provision which gave the Gardaí the right to effectively freeze monies held in a bank account as part of an investigative process into suspected criminal activities, was unconstitutional. Such a direction infringed constitutional rights to fair procedures.[266] The legislation in question did not specifically provide the person responding to the direction with any civil law defence or immunity. On the issue whether the plaintiff was entitled to damages against the bank for an alleged breach of contract or conversion, Laffoy J, decided that such an issue would await the outcome of the criminal investigation. Laffoy J. said:

> "If the monies in the accounts in the Ashbourne branch of the Bank in the name of the plaintiff are, or represent, the proceeds of criminal conduct, then it would have been an offence on the part of the Bank under s. 31(1) of the Act of 1994 to operate the account after it had become aware that the monies were the proceeds of criminal conduct, irrespective of the existence of the July 2008 Direction. It seems to me that the significance of that is that, if it is the case that the monies are, or represent, the proceeds of criminal conduct, then the plaintiff cannot establish any loss or damage as a result of the existence of the direction. Therefore, if such is the case, the plaintiff cannot establish any entitlement to an award of damages. That is so irrespective of whether it would be appropriate to make an award of damages on the basis that s. 31(8) has been found to be unconstitutional if it were otherwise and the plaintiff could establish loss. However, it is important to emphasise that the issue was not addressed in any depth by the parties, although in the plaintiff's written submissions there is a reference to those who suffer discrete losses on account of the application of unconstitutional legislation being entitled to be compensated, citing *Blascaod Mór Teo v Commissioners of Public Works in Ireland (No. 4)* [2000] 3 I.R. 565."

Pleading Illegality

14–102 If the illegality appears on the face of the contract document it is not necessary that illegality be pleaded as a defence. The courts will not enforce the agreement; see *Murphy & Co Ltd v Crean*.[267] If the agreement is not illegal on its face the party seeking to resist the action should plead illegality if he wishes to avoid liability on this basis; see *Whitecross Potatoes v Coyle*.[268] A person may be reluctant to do this, for obvious reasons; a confession of illegality often invites a prosecution later. If, however, illegality is not pleaded

---

[265] [2010] IEHC 525.
[266] See now s.4 of the Criminal Justice (Money Laundering and Terrorist Financing) Act 2010.
[267] [1915] 1 I.R. 111.
[268] [1978] I.L.R.M. 31.

but during the course of the trial it becomes clear to the trial judge that an illegal contract is disclosed, he is not obliged to disregard the illegality. In *Starling Securities v Woods*,[269] McWilliam J. refused to enforce a contract formed with an illegal object in mind, even though illegality was not expressly pleaded as a defence; see also *Lewis v Squash (Ireland) Ltd*.[270]

---

[269] Unreported, High Court, May 24, 1977.
[270] [1983] I.L.R.M. 363; see also *Kelly v Simpson* [2008] IEHC 314.

15 Void Contracts

Introduction

15–01 A contract may be held to be void, or declared to be void, by virtue of a common law policy imperative or because a statute declares that the contract is void. On occasion, both the common law and statute law produce similar results: take, for example, the common law restraint of trade doctrine and statutory competition law. But enforcement may take very different paths. In historical terms, many practices that traders engaged in to inflate prices, for example, were common law offences and later proscribed by statute. But in the case of contracts in restraint of trade, the criminal law had no role to play in counteracting economically undesirable practices. In contrast, anti-competitive practices are difficult to identify and establish as participants in such conduct are unlikely to come forward without some incentive or a promise of immunity. Specialist investigations by agencies are essential if consumers are to be protected so the role of traditional private law litigation, and declarations that contracts are void under statute do not represent a meaningful enforcement mechanism or deterrent to anti-competitive practices. There appears to be a reluctance to use Competition Act damages as a distinct award, even by the most experienced competition law judges.[1]

15–02 The declaration in s.4(1) of the Competition Act 2002, which sets out that all agreements between undertakings that have as their object or effect anti-competitive practices, "are prohibited and void", is an important provision, but the real strength of Irish competition law, in terms of the deterrent effects of the prohibition is extra-contractual; see the criminal sanctions set out in ss.6–8 of the Competition Act 2002, as strengthened by the Competition (Amendment) Act 2012. In *DPP v Duffy*,[2] McKechnie J. set out the sentencing factors that are to be observed by a court in considering the appropriate sentence to be imposed upon a convicted person.

---

[1] Cooke J. in *Island Ferries Teo v Minister for Communications* [2012] IEHC 256. Non-compliance with public procurement rules may also lead to declaration that a contract is ineffective but other reliefs such as novation of the contract may apply also so declarations of ineffectiveness are uncommon. See e.g. European Communities (Public Authorities Contracts) Review Procedures Regulations 2010 (S.I. No. 130 of 2010): *Henderson v 305 2775 Nova Scotia* [2006] UKHL 21; *Lightways (Contractors) Ltd v Inverclyde Council* [2015] Scot CS CSOH 169. See *Chitty on Contracts*, edited by H.G. Beale, 32nd edn (London, Sweet & Maxwell, 2015), Vol.1, paras 11–151 to 11–052.
[2] [2009] IEHC 208.

Void Contracts under Statute—Recent Examples

15–03

(a) The law relating to fraudulent conveyances has been updated by s.74 of the Land and Conveyancing Law Reform Act 2009, replacing the Statute of Fraudulent Conveyances of 1634. Section 74(3) provides that any conveyance of property made with the intention of defrauding a creditor or any other person is voidable by any person thereby prejudiced. While s.74(4)(a) provides that s.74(3) is not to apply to good faith conveyances for valuable consideration to persons with no notice of any fraudulent intention, the courts are nevertheless vigilant in policing fraudulent conveyances.[3] In *Keegan Quarries Ltd v McGuinness*,[4] the defendant, locked in litigation over an alleged fraudulent misrepresentation by himself, transferred land to his wife. He was not in good health due to a serious accident. There was no consideration paid for the conveyance. Finlay Geoghegan J. said the primary purpose behind the transfer was to defeat any possible claim. Although the plaintiff was not at the date of the conveyance a debtor, the plaintiff was a "person thereby prejudiced" by the transfer under s.74(3). The transfer between Mr and Mrs McGuinness was declared void under s.74.

(b) A recent example of a direct statutory prohibition on contracts is afforded by s.32 of the Multi-Unit Developments Act 2011, an Act which seeks to regulate contracts between multi-ownership entities and owners/tenants in respect of maintenance of common parts. The Act seeks to limit the duration of contracts on the basis that long-term contracts may not be in the best interests of owners/tenants. Section 32 provides:

> "An owners' management company shall not, after enactment of this Act, enter into a contract for the provision of a service or the purchase of goods—
>
> *(a)* which is expressed to run for a period in excess of 3 years from the date the contract is entered into by the owners' management company, or
>
> *(b)* which provides for a penalty to be imposed on or damages to be paid by the owners' management company if the contract is terminated by it after a period of 3 years from the date the contract is entered into by the owners' management company."

(c) The Property Services (Regulation) Act 2011 provides another recent example. Section 90(1) provides that any express or implied term in a contract in respect of the sale or a letting of land that requires an agent's fees or expenses to be met by the purchaser or tenant "shall be void, and

---

[3] Leading cases are *Re Moroney* (1887) 21 L.R. Ir. 27; *McQuillen v Maguire* [1996] 1 I.L.R.M. 394; and *MIBI v Stanbridge* [2008] IEHC 389.

[4] [2011] IEHC 453.

any monies paid pursuant to such a provision shall be recoverable as a simple contract debt in a court of competent jurisdiction".[5]

(d) Contractual provisions that seek to exclude or limit maintenance and attachment of earnings provisions in respect of civil partnerships are void under s.67 of the Civil Partnership and Certain Rights and Obligations of Cohabitants Act 2010. This section reflects earlier marital legislation.

(e) Implied prohibition—It will be obvious, perhaps, that in certain kinds of transactions the fact that the legislation makes provision for criminal offences will not exhaust the possible effects of common law illegality: contracts for the sale of drugs and other similar substances provide an example. The Criminal Justice (Psychoactive Substances) Act 2010 was intended to prohibit contracts facilitating substance abuse although sellers and importers are identified as the persons who commit offences under that Act. Issues of implied prohibition will also arise in the future in regard to betting transactions under the Betting (Amendment) Act 2015. It is likely that bets placed by minors for example will be void although the Act is silent on this point.

Contracts Void at Common Law

15–04 As we saw in the previous chapter, there are instances where the judiciary may refuse to enforce a contract on the ground that the contract, or an individual clause or objective, is contrary to public policy. Where the contract is held to be illegal at common law, the entire contract is incapable of grounding a cause of action, even if the obligation which is being relied upon by the plaintiff is itself unobjectionable. Further, while the courts are increasingly discriminating in respect of using the principle of severance if the source of the illegality is a statute, or if the party resisting severance has been guilty of fraud, there is still a substantial difference between cases in which contracts are illegal at common law and contracts which are held to be void because they infringe public policy. In a leading English case the distinction was stated thus:

"There are two kinds of illegality of differing effect. The first is where the illegality is criminal, or *contra bonos mores*, and in these cases, which I will not attempt to enumerate or further classify, such a provision, if an ingredient in a contract, will invalidate the whole, although there may be many other provisions in it. There is a second kind of illegality which has no such taint; the other terms in the contract stand if the illegal portion can be severed, the illegal portion being a provision which the court, on grounds of public policy, will not enforce."[6]

---

[5] Section 90(2) does not affect recovery where the purchaser or tenant retains the agent when that agent is not also retained by the vendor or landlord.

[6] Per Somervell L.J. in *Goodinson v Goodinson* [1954] 2 Q.B. 118 at 121, citing *Bennett v Bennett* [1952] 1 All E.R. 413.

It is generally accepted that there are three kinds of contract which fall into the second category referred to in the above quotation. There are some isolated *sui generis* examples of void transactions that have been reappraised and either diluted by judicial decisions or the legislature. One such example is the rule in *Pigot's Case* which renders altered deeds void ab initio.[7]

(1) Agreements to oust the jurisdiction of the courts

15–05 Persons who seek to become members of a professional or trade association may find that part of the agreement dictates that in the event of a dispute the decision of the association shall be final. Such a provision is invalid; attempts to uphold agreements and at the same time deny recourse to the ordinary courts are also invalid; the public interest requires that disputes be amenable to the jurisdiction of the courts; see *Lee v Showman's Guild of Great Britain*.[8] The basic distinction that must be observed is between clauses that attempt to reserve issues of law for the sole decision of a private tribunal or arbitrator, and clauses which give the private tribunal or arbitrator sole competence on issues of fact. The right of the parties to seek review of an arbitration on the basis of an error of law must be upheld, and any clause to the contrary will be void.

15–06 In contrast, there is a venerable line of authority which holds that the parties can make provision for a tribunal to seek to establish the salient facts and, to this end, a clause making the arbitration a condition precedent will be upheld as long as the clause does not seek to close off the ordinary courts altogether. The leading case is *Scott v Avery*,[9] a decision of the House of Lords in 1856, and, while *Scott v Avery* has been followed in Ireland on numerous occasions,[10] the Irish courts have sometimes been reluctant to extend this decision. In *Mansfield v Doolin*[11] a clause provided that if a dispute broke out over a building contract the award of an architect was to be a condition precedent to any proceedings. The arbitrator's award was held not to constitute a condition precedent but the clause was classified as being simply an agreement to refer a dispute to arbitration which did not take away the right to sue in the ordinary courts immediately. The distinction is generally agreed to be a somewhat elusive one. When the question of the impact of the decision in *Scott v Avery* came directly before the Irish Court of King's Bench,

---

[7] *Pigot's Case* (1614) 11 Co.Rep. 26B; *Caldwell v Parker* (1869) I.R. 3 Eq. 519; *Raiffeisenzentralbank Österreich v Cross Seas Shipping* [2000] 3 All E.R. 274; *Northern Bank v Laverty* [2001] NI Ch 9; *Anglo Irish Bank v Collins* [2011] IEHC 385. In Northern Ireland the rule in *Pigot's Case* has been abolished since 2005 by Statutory Instrument (February 1, 2005): see *Swift 1st Ltd v McCourt* [2012] NI Ch 33.

[8] [1952] 2 Q.B. 329; *Burnett v Hamilton Toa Radio Cabs* [2010] CSOH 97.

[9] (1856) 5 H.L. Cas. 811; *Jagger v Decca Music Group Ltd* [2005] F.S.R. 582.

[10] *Mansfield v Doolin* (1868) 4 I.R.C.L. 17; *Gregg & Co v Fraser & Sons* [1906] 2 I.R. 545.

[11] (1868) 4 I.R.C.L. 17. On the effectiveness of such clauses to bind the parties see *Uniform Construction Ltd v Cappawhite Contractors Ltd* [2007] IEHC 295 and *Irishenco Construction v Dublin City Council* [2009] IEHC 325.

and then the Court of Appeal, in *Gregg & Co v Fraser & Sons*,[12] it was said by both Lord Chief Barron Palles and Fitzgibbon L.J. to lay down nothing new. Fitzgibbon L.J. said *Scott v Avery* laid down that "[i]t is lawful for parties to contract that no action shall be brought upon until arbitrators have decided, and that effect must be given to a contract which amounts to that". Indeed, the Arbitration Act 1980 s.5, enabled a court to restrain proceedings brought in the courts when it is established that an arbitration clause had not been observed,[13] thereby strengthening a similar provision in s.12 of the Arbitration Act 1954. Furthermore, under the Arbitration Act 1954 s.35(1), the High Court was given a supervisory jurisdiction; in particular, the arbitrator "may, and shall if so directed by the court", state questions of law or the terms of an award for decision by the court as a special case. This section re-affirms the inability of parties to absolutely prohibit recourse to the courts at least on questions of law. Indeed, in *Winterthur Swiss Insurance Co v I.C.I.*,[14] O'Hanlon J. indicated that in certain instances the court may exercise its discretion to refuse to stay proceedings before a court on the ground that arbitration may not prove the best method of resolving a dispute between the parties. The power of the parties to a contract to make arbitration a condition precedent to an action in the ordinary courts may be restricted in many instances, as a result of the decision of Carroll J. in *McCarthy v Joe Walsh Tours Ltd*.[15] The arbitration clause in question was found in a holiday contract, concluded on the industry standard form contract, and sought to make arbitration a binding element of the contract. Carroll J. held that because the clause and the arbitration scheme provided only limited relief, the clause was a limitation clause which could not be relied upon because it had not been specifically drawn to the attention of the consumer and did not meet the requirements of s.40 of the Sale of Goods and Supply of Services Act 1980. It remains open to a court to hold that such a clause is also not "fair and reasonable", even if incorporated into the contract. The Arbitration Act 2010 repeals the Arbitration Acts 1954 to 1998 giving effect to a number of international agreements on arbitration. This purely domestic perspective, therefore, will cease to determine arbitration agreements[16] on this point.

15–07 Several of the leading English cases concern the issue of whether a spouse may give up a statutory right to maintenance payments. The tendency has been to hold that such clauses are invalid because such a clause would force the separated spouse onto social security and thus oblige the taxpayer to provide support.[17] However, a recent Court of Appeal decision has introduced greater flexibility. In *Soulsbury v Soulsbury*,[18] the plaintiff was the first wife

---

12 [1906] 2 I.R. 545.
13 See *Mitchell v Budget Travel* [1990] I.L.R.M. 739; *Parkarran Ltd v M. & P. Construction Ltd* [1996] 1 I.R. 83; *Doyle v Irish National Insurance Co Plc* [1998] 1 I.L.R.M. 502.
14 [1990] I.L.R.M. 159; *Greyridge Developments v McGuigan* [2006] IEHC 441.
15 [1991] I.L.R.M. 813.
16 See Dowling-Hussey and Dunne, *Arbitration Law* (Dublin: Round Hall, 2008), para.7–18.
17 *Hyman v Hyman* [1929] A.C. 60; *Bennett v Bennett* [1952] 1 All E.R. 413.
18 [2007] EWCA Civ 969.

of the deceased. Divorce proceedings resulted in the courts giving financial support obligations in the plaintiff's favour. The deceased tried to persuade the plaintiff not to enforce these orders promising to give her £100,000 in his will. The deceased's marriage to the defendant shortly before his death revoked the will. Could the plaintiff recover in contract? After reciting the principle in *Hyman v Hyman*,[19] namely that a wife cannot contract out of a statutory right to maintenance and that an agreement to that effect is an agreement to oust the jurisdiction of the court, and citing the exception forged in *Goodinson v Goodinson*,[20] Ward L.J. concluded that:

> "[T]his was an agreement to pay £100,000 subject to conditions subsequent, namely, (1) the death of the deceased and (2) the claimants not having enforced any arrears nor applied for further matrimonial relief. Those events have been fulfilled. Thus the obligation crystallised on the death of the deceased. Nothing in the agreement, express or implied, prevented her from applying to the court for relief. She could have gone back to court at any time without being in breach of any promise that she would not do so. There was no promise not to apply to the court."[21]

In Ireland the scope of such clauses has been discussed by Walsh J. in *HD v PD*.[22] In considering whether a contractual separation agreement under s.8 of the Family Law (Maintenance of Spouses and Children) Act 1976 is final, Walsh J. stated "it is not possible to contract out of the Act by an agreement made after the Act came into force or by an agreement entered into before the legislation was enacted". This judgment was followed by Barr J. in *JH v RH*,[23] allowing a wife to make an application for revision of maintenance under the 1976 Act, notwithstanding a full and final settlement clause in the separation agreement. Barr J. held that this power operates even in regard to matters arising under the Judicial Separation and Family Law Reform Act 1989. The test in operating such a revision power is whether the husband has failed to provide maintenance which is proper in all the circumstances.

(2) Contracts which subvert the sanctity of marriage

15–08

(a) It is said to be a matter of public interest that persons enter into contracts of marriage and affiliated transactions for reasons which are likely to produce satisfactory marriages. Marriage brokerage contracts, in which a fee is paid to a marriage bureau in return for an undertaking to find a wife or husband, are void; see the English case of *Hermann v Charlesworth*.[24] In the old

---

[19] [1929] A.C. 60; [1954] 2 Q.B. 118.

[20] [2007] EWCA Civ 969, para.22. Contrast *Gallaway Cook Allan v Carr* [2013] NZCA 11.

[21] See Longmore L.J.'s unilateral contract analysis [2007] EWCA Civ 969 at paras 48–50.

[22] Unreported, Supreme Court, May 8, 1978. See Crowley, *Family Law* (Dublin: Round Hall, 2015) at paras 11-56 to 11-64.

[23] *Irish Times Law Report*, October 30, 1995.

[24] [1905] 2 K.B. 123.

Irish case of *Williamson v Gihan*,[25] Williamson, an impecunious young man, obtained the help of his friend Gihan in spiriting away a young heiress to Scotland where Williamson married the young lady. He promised Gihan £500, payable from his wife's property for services rendered. Williamson was held not entitled to fetter his wife's estate in these circumstances. It seems that the court frowned upon contracts of marriage that resulted from elopement—despite the fact that the then Lord Chancellor Lord Eldon had procured his wife in this manner—fearing that even collateral transactions between the groom and others would lead to fortune-hunting.

15-09

(b) Unilateral contracts in which one person promises not to marry any person other than the promisee are void; see *Lowe v Peers*.[26] However, this line of authority is not to be taken too far. The Supreme Court of Canada in *Caron v Caron*[27] upheld a separation agreement which made financial provision for the female spouse until she either remarried or cohabited as man and wife with any person for a period of more than 90 days. Wilson J., who gave the leading judgment, observed that although the clause may have had the effect of discouraging remarriage, it was not to be seen as analogous to a promise not to marry or a promised payment if the promisor marries a particular person.

15-10

(c) Contracts for Future Separation. Prior to the removal of the constitutional prohibition in Art.41.3.2° against divorce in the Republic of Ireland, the petition for a decree *a mensa et thoro*, or judicial separation, was (and is) an important but frequently expensive way in which the parties to a marriage may get the courts to make financial and property adjustments when a marriage has broken down. The parties may instead wish to make their own arrangements. Nevertheless a contract which provides that one party is to pay a certain sum to support the other in the event of future separation will be void as weakening the marriage bond; see *Marquess of Westmeath v Marquess of Salisbury*.[28] A more recent illustration is provided by the English case of *H v H*.[29] The litigation arose out of an agreement between two couples who, as part of a spouse-swapping arrangement, divorced their respective spouses and then married the eligible spouse of the other couple. Prior to the remarriage it was agreed that each man would support and provide a home for the new partner. Ewbank J. refused to enforce an agreement of this kind for it involved the breaking up of two marriages. Recent appellate case law has drawn a clear distinction between pre-nuptial and post-nuptial agreements and

---

[25] (1805) 2 Sch. & Lef. 357.
[26] (1768) 4 Burr. 2225.
[27] (1987) 38 D.L.R. (4th) 735.
[28] (1830) 5 Bli.(N.S.) 339; *H v W* (1857) 3 K. & J. 382.
[29] (1983) 127 S.J. 578.

there have been two landmark decisions. The first of them concerned post-nuptial contracts. Baroness Hale, giving judgment for the Privy Council in *McLeod v McLeod*,[30] has given a very full account of the important historical and policy perspectives that distinguish pre-nuptial and post-nuptial agreements. Agreements for post-nuptial separation are based upon the supposition that there exist enforceable duties on a husband and wife to live together. As this duty no longer exists—a "husband's right to use self help to keep his wife at home has gone. He can now be guilty of the offences of kidnapping and false imprisonment"—so the Privy Council held that separation agreements should be enforceable when executed between married persons, and should be valid regardless of at what point in the marriage the agreement was executed. Safeguards in the form of judicial discretion vis-à-vis financial terms and the retention of public policy considerations when the agreement seeks out the jurisdiction of the courts should remain as important anti-abuse mechanisms. Different considerations apply to agreements struck before a marriage.

15–11 These kinds of agreements, so called pre-nuptial contracts, are becoming increasingly common, particularly in relation to the marriage of the wealthy and/or the famous. The traditional view is that these agreements undermine the institution of marriage as a life-long institution, but this is often countered by the argument that, but for the legal certainty that these agreements create, the marriage would not take place in any event. This of course is a circular argument because what has to be established is whether the pre-nuptial is legally enforceable. The evidence from recent English case law and practice is that pre-nuptial agreements are no longer per se void. In *K v K*[31] the plaintiff signed a pre-nuptial agreement limiting her claim to her husband's property to £120,000. The circumstances surrounding the agreement were that the plaintiff became pregnant and through her own father pressed the father of her child into marrying, the understanding being that should the marriage fail the plaintiff would limit her claim to the agreed figure. Both parties to the marriage were independently wealthy. Hayward Smith J. upheld the agreement. Both parties had been legally advised independently, all relevant facts were known or disclosed and there was no duress. Further, the claim made was excessive and only deemed appropriate for a wife who had made a significant contribution to a marriage over a long period of time, as distinct from here where the marriage had not been a happy one for its 14-month duration. The decision in *K v K* has been welcomed[32] as providing a useful checklist of relevant factors, but the English courts have insisted that these agreements do not displace the jurisdiction of the courts to make the final determination on the distribution of family assets on separation or divorce.

---

[30] [2009] 1 All E.R. 851; the *Marquis of Westmeath* case was not followed.
[31] Deputy High Court Judge Hayward Smith Q.C, "Pre-nuptial deals gain validity as wife loses £1.6m claim", *The Independent*, April 14, 2003.
[32] Deputy High Court Judge Hayward Smith Q.C, "Pre-nuptial deals gain validity as wife loses £1.6m claim", *The Independent*, April 14, 2003.

15–12 In the second landmark decision the UK Supreme Court in *Radmacher v Granatino (No. 4)*[33] did not follow the earlier decision of the Privy Council in *McLeod v McLeod* on the distinction between pre-nuptial and post-nuptial agreements: no distinction could be discerned.[34] The majority judgment said:

> "The question should be tested by comparing an agreement concluded the day before the wedding with one concluded the day after it. Nuptial agreements made just after the wedding are not unknown and likely to become more common if the law distinguishes them from ante-nuptial agreements".

Even if the view that the pre-nuptial agreement is no longer void per se takes root, close judicial scrutiny of such agreements will be expected via duress or unconscionable bargain concepts, by analogy with the established principles that apply to separation agreements.[35] In the many jurisdictions where pre-nuptial agreements are valid in contractual terms, they are strictly policed in order to ensure that the parties have freely entered into them, on an informed basis. The terms of the agreement provide valuable evidence of the hopes, beliefs and expectations of the parties, which can have compelling evidentiary value for the court, often placed in the difficult position of doing justice many years removed from the marriage itself. The retention of the broad discretion in respect of the distribution of the assets of the marriage, and the fact that the terms that become inappropriate (e.g. in relation to confidentiality or custody of any children of the marriage) may be ignored or varied, should ensure that pre-nuptial agreements receive overt judicial recognition in Ireland in the years ahead.[36]

15–13 Some change in the law in this area is imminent in the UK. The Lord Chancellor's Department and the Cabinet have approved the introduction of legally binding pre-marriage contracts under which the parties contract on asset distribution should the marriage later break down. In a 2014 Report,[37] the Law

---

[33] [2011] 1 A.C. 534. *D v E* [2013] NI Master 13 is an interesting Northern Ireland decision which affected property located in Dublin. In some jurisdictions a prenuptial agreement may not be void but may be tested by reference to unconscionability or be struck down as a penalty: see the Manitoba case of *Dundas v Schafer* (2014) 377 DLR (4th) 485.

[34] In some cultures the pre- and post-nuptial distinction does not really work. Case law from Canada and Australia has determined that pre-nuptial and post-nuptial agreements under Sharia law are justiciable, such agreements to pay a dowry or making payments upon divorce or separation (Moakar Sadak) being continuing obligations. These agreements are to be respected and enforced as long as they are compatible with marriage legislation: *Nasin v Nasin* (2008) ABQB 219; formal defects may not be a barrier to enforcement: *Khanis v Noormohamed* [2009] O.J. No. 2245 (Ont. S.C.J.); *Mohamed v Mohamed* [2012] NSWSC 852, citing *Black and Sadiq* (2011) 17 N.S.W.L.J. 82.

[35] *Mundinger v Mundinger* (1969) 3 D.L.R. (3d) 338.

[36] See Shannon, "To have and to hold" [2003] *Law Society Gazette* (June) 12.

[37] Matrimonial Property, Needs and Agreements: Law Com No. 342. No legislation has been enacted in the UK, but for judicial support and an interesting set of facts see *WW v HW* [2015] EWHC 1844 (Fam).

Commission of England and Wales recommended that the law should facilitate legislation relating to "qualifying nuptial agreements" for two reasons:

> "they will be an important source of legal certainty for high net worth couples who want to make clear and reliable arrangements for their wealth... qualifying nuptial agreements will be helpful in circumstances where the parties to a marriage or civil partnership have been in a relationship before and wish to safeguard a house or other assets for their children from that previous relationship".

The debate in the UK has also informed Irish developments. Following on from a Pre-Nuptial Agreements motion in Seanad Éireann on October 18, 2006, the then Minister for Justice, Equality and Law Reform established an expert group[38] that reported on April 24, 2007. The Report called for agreements to be enforceable in law but that the judiciary should be free to depart from the terms of the agreement, especially where the circumstances of the spouses have altered since the making of the agreement.[39]

15–14 If, however, the parties are not living together but they decide to resume cohabitation, agreeing that if the reconciliation thereby effected should later break down then the wife will be paid a certain sum, this will be enforceable. In *MacMahon v MacMahon*,[40] Holmes L.J. said of such an agreement, "far from endangering the unity of the family, it restored it". But for this clause the initial separation would have continued. These agreements preclude further action for financial support, even if the defendant who relies upon the agreement is guilty of adultery; see *Ross v Ross*[41] in which Andrews J. distinguished actions for a decree *a mensa et thoro* from cases where adultery precludes reliance on a provision restraining divorce actions.

15–15 Separation agreements which unwittingly tend to encourage immoral practices are not per se void; see *Lewis v Lewis*.[42]

15–16
(d) Contracts for Foreign Divorces. Prior to the passing of the Fifteenth Amendment to the Constitution, contracts to obtain a divorce outside the jurisdiction may also have been in conflict with Irish public policy because of the constitutional ban on divorce. An illustration of public policy being utilised to enforce the marriage contract, albeit in a rather mechanical fashion, is afforded by *Dalton v Dalton*.[43] An application to have a separation agreement made a rule of court under s.8 of the Family Law (Maintenance of Spouses and Children) Act 1976 ran into difficulty

---

38   184 *Seanad Debates* Cols 1751–1770.
39   Chaired by Inge Clissmann S.C.
40   [1913] 1 I.R. 428.
41   [1908] 2 I.R. 339.
42   [1940] I.R. 42; contrast *Jackson v Cridland* (1859) 10 I.C.L.R. 376.
43   Unreported, High Court, September 9, 1981.

because the contract contained a clause whereby the parties agreed to obtain a divorce *a vinculo* outside the jurisdiction. Because both spouses were domiciled in Ireland, the divorce would not then be recognised in Irish law. The application failed because to grant the application would be contrary to public policy. Upon a later application by the parties, the court deleted the clause and the agreement was accepted under s.8 in this amended form.[44]

15–17

(e) Cohabitation Agreements. Cohabitation agreements, whether in contemplation of marriage or not, are contrary to public policy and void. In *Ennis v Butterly*[45] the parties were married, but not to each other. The plaintiff alleged a contract whereby she would move into a house bought by them, give up her employment and take on the role of home-maker. She also alleged an agreement to marry upon the granting of a divorce to each of them. Dealing with the contract to marry argument first, Kelly J. held that such a contract was statute-barred by s.1 of the Family Law Act 1981, which abolished this cause of action. Further, at common law, such contracts, by married persons, are void; see *Wilson v Carnley*.[46] Irish law, Kelly J. held, did not recognise cohabitation contracts where the provision of "wifely services"[47] is the consideration. Kelly J. followed the English case of *Windeler v Whitehall*[48] in which Millett J. had declared cohabitation or "palimony" contracts contrary to public policy in England. Kelly J. observed:

"Given the special place of marriage and the family under the Irish Constitution, it appears to me that the public policy of this State ordains that non-marital cohabitation does not and cannot have the same constitutional status as marriage. Moreover, the State has pledged to guard with special care the institution of marriage. But does this mean that agreements, the consideration for which is cohabitation, are incapable of being enforced? In my view it does since otherwise the pledge on the part of the State, of which this Court is one organ, to guard with special care the institution of marriage would be much diluted. To permit an express cohabitation contract (such as is pleaded here) to be enforced would give it a similar status in law as a marriage contract. It did not have such a status prior to the coming into effect of the Constitution, rather such contracts were regarded as illegal and

---

[44] See reporter's note to the above unreported judgment.
[45] [1997] 1 I.L.R.M. 28.
[46] [1908] 1 K.B. 729.
[47] [1997] 1 I.L.R.M. 28 at 31. While in *Ennis v Butterly* the bargain envisaged sexual relations as between the parties and cohabitation, it is doubtful that these services were "meretricious sexual services" within *Ashton v Pratt (No.2)* [2012] NSWSC 3. See the decision of the New South Wales Court of Appeal at [2015] NSWCA 12. *Ennis v Butterly* should not be followed in this writer's view.
[48] [1990] 2 F.L.R 505.

unenforceable as a matter of public policy. Far from enhancing the position at law of such contracts the Constitution requires marriage to be guarded with special care. In my view, this reinforces the existing common law doctrines concerning the non-enforceability of cohabitation contracts. I am therefore of [the] opinion that, as a matter of public policy, such agreements cannot be enforced."

With respect, views of this kind make it essential that legislative changes to contract and property law are made soon. The regulation of private morals should not be undertaken by the courts in this negative way. Patterns of behaviour and social order that may well have had some resonance in the mind of a Victorian chancery judge seem quite at odds with the everyday experiences of persons living in the third millenium. The Law Reform Commission, in its consultation paper on this subject,[49] suggests that *Ennis v Butterly* does not go so far as to invalidate all cohabitation agreements. In *Ennis* the agreement sought to operate as a marriage contract and not merely as an agreement regulating the financial and property interests of the parties. The Law Reform Commission drew a distinction between those aspects of the contract relating to the agreement to marry and the agreement to cohabit, and remarked that while this particular agreement was struck down, it did not follow that all cohabitation agreements are void in Irish law. This must of course be so, but *Ennis* would still be a significant obstacle to enforcement of rights where a sexual relationship outside marriage is at the heart of such a property arrangement.

15–18 In the Law Reform Commission's Report, *Rights and Duties of Cohabitees* (2006),[50] a contractual model was proposed as the basis for legislation and this occupies a large amount of the reform mechanism. The Report found against a need to create parallel institutions such as civil partnership and opted for solutions that offer vulnerable cohabitees effective methods of redress when a relationship breaks up. The parties can choose the terms of the agreement either directly through cohabitation agreements or indirectly via co-ownership agreements and wills but the courts are to be able to adjust the terms of any agreement to avoid injustice on the termination of the relationship. The Law Reform Commission also recommended that cohabitation agreements should be written, signed and witnessed, and that the parties should receive separate legal advice before execution of the agreement. Failure to comply with these formal requirements should render the agreement unenforceable.

15–19 Notwithstanding this compromise effected by the 2006 Law Reform Commission Report, the Oireachtas, by enacting the Civil Partnership and Certain Rights and Obligations of Cohabitants Act 2010 has gone a considerable distance towards enacting gender-free rules in respect of contractual rights and

---

[49] *Rights and Duties of Cohabitees,* LRC Consultation Paper 32–2004.
[50] LRC 82–2006. See *www.blueblindfold.gov.ie,* [2015] NSWCA 12.

obligations in respect of property and other rights that have been afforded in respect of such rights in orthodox marriages. The Marriage Act 2015 closes the gender discrimination/same sex marriage debate in Ireland by validating same sex marriages in Ireland and recognising foreign marriages entered into by same sex couples.

15–20

(f) The protection of vulnerable persons.

That such persons may be targeted for human trafficking purposes, particularly in relation to prostitution, makes it necessary to consider whether public policy requires that transactions in which sexual services are provided should be criminalised in the sense that the recipient of the service should be liable to a criminal prosecution.[51] There is a debate about this in several jurisdictions but in the main the matter is not, in Ireland at least, something that has been a factor in any litigation relating to public policy.

Contrast the New South Wales Court of Appeal's decision in *Ashton v Pratt*.[52] In this case a wealthy businessman informed a female from whom he had previously obtained escort services that "the position of mistress is now available". Arrangements were made on the provision of sexual services in exchange for promises of money, property and a trust fund. The trial judge noted that this was not a cohabitation case, in which sexual contact was a feature of a wider relationship—Australian case law had found such agreements to be enforceable many decades earlier—but held that contracts for the provision of meretricious sexual services were still contrary to Australian public policy and thus void and illegal. As the New South Wales Court of Appeal was able to hold the contract was void for uncertainty and there was an absence of legal intent, the Court found it unnecessary to make a ruling in respect of illegality. Clearly, Ms Ashton was far from being a vulnerable person but difficult issues of policy will arise in such instances.

15–21

(g) Miscellaneous.

Other family or analogous transactions that have been scrutinised under a contractual prism but which in reality raise fundamental rights issues, include the enforceability of contractual arrangements made as between a sperm donor and a female donee,[53] the ability of persons to contract polygamous marriages[54] and challenges to legislation prohibiting services aimed at effecting assisted suicide.[55]

---

[51] See *www.blueblindfold.gov.ie.*
[52] [2015] NSWCA 2
[53] *MD v L* [2008] IEHC 96.
[54] *H v A* [2010] IEHC 497.
[55] *Fleming v Ireland* [2013] IEHC 2; [2013] IESC 19.

(3) Contracts in restraint of trade

15–22 This venerable common law doctrine has been succinctly stated by Diplock L.J. in the English Court of Appeal in the following terms:

> "A contract in restraint of trade is one in which a party (the covenantor) agrees with any other party (the covenantee) to restrict his liberty in the future to carry on trade with other persons not parties to the contract in such manner as he chooses."[56]

The Irish judiciary have followed this approach, most notably in the case of *John Orr Ltd and Vescom B.V. v John Orr*[57] where Costello J. summarised the restraint of trade doctrine in these terms:

> "All restraints of trade in the absence of special justifying circumstances are contrary to public policy and are therefore void. A restraint may be justified if it is reasonable in the interests of the contracting parties and in the interests of the public. The onus of showing that a restraint is reasonable as between the parties rests on the person alleging that it is so. Greater freedom of contract is allowable in a covenant entered into between the seller and the buyer of a business than in the case of one entered into between an employer and an employee. A covenant against competition entered into by the seller of a business which is reasonably necessary to protect the business sold is valid and enforceable. A covenant by an employee not to compete may also be valid and enforceable if it is reasonably necessary to protect some proprietary interest of the covenantee such as may exist in a trade connection or trade secrets. The courts may in some circumstances enforce a covenant in restraint of trade even though taken as a whole the covenant exceeds what is reasonable, by the severance of the void parts from the valid parts."[58]

One problematical issue about the scope of the restraint of trade doctrine remains unresolved, notwithstanding the deliberations of the Supreme Court in *Kerry Co-operative Creameries Ltd v An Bord Bainne Co-operative Ltd.*[59] Does the doctrine only operate if an express covenant of a restrictive nature is before the court, or can the doctrine be applicable in relation to a contractual provision that has the effect of restraining freedom to trade? The argument arose in the context of a proposed rule change which required the members of a co-operative society to trade with the society or run the risk that non-trading members would find that shareholdings would be diluted by being excluded from bonus share distributions, by termination from membership of the society

---

[56] *Petrofina (Great Britain) Ltd v Martin* [1966] Ch. 146 at 180; cited with approval by Lords Hodson and Morris in *Esso Petroleum Co Ltd v Harpers Garage (Stourport) Ltd* [1986] A.C. 269.
[57] [1987] I.L.R.M. 702.
[58] [1987] I.L.R.M. 702 at 704.
[59] [1991] I.L.R.M. 581.

and by loss of voting rights. McCarthy J. favoured the view that the restraint of trade doctrine could be applicable to such a situation, and he rejected the view that the doctrine is only applicable to express covenants or conditions in a contract. O'Flaherty J. took the opposite view and held that there had to be a covenant in restraint of trade, or something akin to a covenant. Finlay C.J. declined to state his views on this point. Whatever the final outcome of this point it is sufficient, for present purposes, to state that the modern doctrine of restraint of trade is designed to strike at commercial and professional practices which unduly restrict the covenantor's freedom to carry on a business or profession; not all restrictive covenants operate in such a way as to incur the wrath of the judges.

Historical antecedents

15–23 Restrictive commercial practices were not unknown in late medieval times. Commercial arrangements between traders designed to artificially inflate prices—known as badgering, forestalling, regrating and engrossing—were made criminal offences under statute. The Elizabethan desire to control food prices made the prohibition of such transactions necessary. When commercial attitudes changed these offences were repealed in 1844 under 7 & 8 Vict. c.24, which extended into Ireland. The establishment of Guilds, Craft Associations and Corporations also led to restrictive practices designed to regulate and protect members of those associations. An Act of 1846, 9 & 10 Vict. c.76, also attempted to bring these older medieval practices into step with the needs of laissez-faire capitalism by abolishing the privileges held by trading organisations in Ireland; the Act provides that it shall be lawful for any person to carry on any lawful trade or profession and take apprentices. Fines and penalties could not be extracted by the Guilds.[60]

15–24 These isolated pieces of legislation serve the same policy objectives as the common law restraint of trade doctrine. The courts, however, had to struggle with the problem, often unaided by statute. In the landmark case of *Mitchel v Reynolds*[61] it was laid down that a general restraint was bad; partial restraints were valid. Thus a covenant not to carry on trade throughout England was invalid; a provision limiting the prohibition to a town or district was valid if good and adequate consideration was provided.

15–25 This general/partial distinction began to wear a little thin when commercial and industrial innovations meant that the consequences of carrying on trade in a remote part of England, or indeed the world, could have severe implications for persons some distance away. The *Mitchel v Reynolds* doctrine was revised in a series of decisions handed down between 1893 and 1916, the most important of which was *Nordenfelt v Maxim Nordenfelt*.[62] In this

---

[60] See generally, Holdsworth, *History of English Law* (London: Sweet & Maxwell, 2003), Vol.8., pp.56–62.
[61] (1711) 1 P.Wms. 181.
[62] [1894] A.C. 535.

case Nordenfelt, the vendor of a business, in which guns and other munitions were manufactured, agreed that, upon the sale of the business to a company formed to purchase the munitions business, he would not, for a period of 25 years, carry on business, or be engaged, directly or indirectly, with any other manufacturer of guns, mountings, or munitions. This agreement entered into in 1886 was revised two years later when the purchasing company merged with another company to form Maxim Nordenfelt. During this time, the original vendor had been engaged as managing director at a handsome salary; the evidence indicated that Nordenfelt had freely consented to the changes wrought by the 1888 re-arrangement. Despite the worldwide nature of the covenant, it could be justified.[63] Lord Macnaghten restated the law of restraint of trade so as to abandon the general/partial distinction, preferring instead to hold that all interference with liberty of action in trading, and all restraints of trade in themselves are contrary to public policy and void. To this general rule exceptions may arise if a restriction can be held to be reasonable "in reference to the interests of the parties concerned and reasonable in reference to the interests of the public".

The modern doctrine
15–26 In the leading case of *Esso Petroleum Co Ltd v Harpers Garage (Stourport) Ltd*[64]—hereafter "*Esso*"—the House of Lords gave a comprehensive analysis of the existing rules of restraint of trade. Lord Reid in his speech stressed that the following questions are to be asked:

"(1) Does the restraint go further than to afford adequate protection to the party in whose favour it was granted? If so, the covenant is *prima facie* void.

 (2) Can it be justified as being in the interests of the party thus restrained?

 (3) Is the covenant contrary to the public interest?"[65]

The onus of showing the restraint to be in the interests of the party thus restrained, or, to put it another way, that the covenant is reasonable as between the parties, is upon the person seeking to uphold the transaction. If the agreement is alleged to be unenforceable because it is contrary to the public interest, notwithstanding its reasonableness inter partes, the burden of proof is upon the party alleging the invalidity of the covenant.[66]

---

[63] Lord MacNaghten observed of the original Nordenfelt business: "His customers were comparatively few in number, but his trade was worldwide in extent. He had upon his books almost every monarch and almost every state of any note in the habitable globe"; [1894] A.C. 535 at 559. For a more recent munitions case see *Societa Esplosivi Industriali SpA v Ordnance Technologies UK* [2004] 1 All E.R. (Comm.) 619. For a worldwide restraint in the pharmaceutical industry see the Northern Ireland case of *Norbrook Laboratories Ltd v Smyth*, unreported, N.I. High Court, September 30, 1986.

[64] [1968] A.C. 269; *Leeds Rugby v Harris* [2005] EWHC 1591 (Q.B.) is instructive.

[65] See [1968] A.C. 269 at 300.

[66] See [1968] A.C. 269 at 319 per Lord Hodson.

15–27 It should be stressed that while public policy is at the heart of this doctrine two separate policy considerations are at issue here; first of all, the courts view it as being a cardinal rule of public policy that a person be held to a contract freely entered into: *Murphy v O'Donovan*.[67] On the other hand a man is not to be permitted unduly to fetter his freedom to contract and earn a living for himself and his family; see *Langan v Cork Operative Bakers T.U.*[68] The desire of the courts to uphold both of these often conflicting objectives means, as Lord Morris said in *Esso*, that "a certain adjustment is necessary". Lord Pearce, in the same case, stressed the essentially pragmatic nature of the doctrine.

> "The rule relating to restraint of trade is bound to be a compromise, as are all the rules imposed for freedom's sake. The law fetters traders by a particular inability to limit their freedom of trade so that it may protect the general freedom of trade and the good of the community."[69]

This adjustment of diverse interests is achieved by way of a reasonableness test. In *TFS Derivatives Ltd v Morgan*,[70] Mrs Justice Cox explained that in assessing reasonableness the court undertakes a three-stage process. First, the court must decide what the clause means when properly construed. Secondly, the covenantee must be shown to have legitimate business interests requiring protection. Thirdly, the clause must be shown to be no wider than is reasonably necessary for the protection of those interests.[71] In assessing reasonableness this is undertaken against the factual matrix, and factors such as the level of consideration paid and other contractual matters are relevant thereto.

Restraints outside the doctrine of restraint of trade

15–28 Not all contracts that restrain or prevent a contracting party from entering into agreements must be tested by reference to the restraint of trade doctrine.

15–29 Exclusive dealing arrangements between commercial traders are valid if they are commonplace and incidental to everyday trading activities; a contract by a restaurant owner to take all the Beaujolais he may require from one retailer does not fall within the doctrine.[72] The practice, in former times common in the Cork area, of trading in a public house as a tenant, agreeing to take all the stout and beer from the landlord company, may no doubt be

---

[67] [1939] I.R. 457.

[68] [1938] Ir. Jur. Rep. 65. On coercive practices between a trade union and a worker, being contrary to common law and under the Irish Constitution, see Ryan J. in *O'Connell v BATU* [2014] IEHC 360.

[69] [1968] A.C. 269 at 324.

[70] [2004] EWHC 3181 (Q.B.); *White Digital Media v Weaver* [2013] EWHC 1681 (Q.B.).

[71] Followed in *Dyson Technology Ltd v Ben Strutt* [2005] EWHC 2814 (Ch); *Beckett Investment Management Group Ltd and Others v Hall* [2007] EWHC 241 (Q.B.); *Norbrook Laboratories (GB) Ltd v Adair* [2008] EWHC 978 (Q.B.).

[72] *Servais Bouchard v Princes Hall Restaurant* (1904) 20 T.L.R. 574.

restrictive of the freedom of the tenant to obtain supplies from other companies but is not an arrangement that must be justified as reasonable as between the parties and the public interest. In *Murphy & Co v O'Donovan*[73] the defendant took an assignment of a lease, the lease containing a covenant that the premises would be operated as a public house that would only take supplies of stout and porter from the plaintiff lessors. The defendant sought to avoid the covenant by arguing that as it was a restraint on competition, the covenant was void. The covenant, entered into by a person of full age and competent understanding, was enforceable and was not, in the view of Johnston J., to be equated with the *Nordenfelt* case. Indeed, the marketplace, by evolving its own rules relating to fair trading, requires that freedom of contract be upheld when no anti-competitive practice is evident.

15–30 Restrictive covenants in which the purchaser of an interest in land agrees that he will not use the land for a particular commercial or industrial purpose are also per se enforceable.[74] There are similar lines of authority in respect of restrictions found in leasehold property transactions, the general view being that the lessee of property who takes property under a lease which contains a restrictive covenant, does not come within the restraint of trade doctrine because the freedom to carry on the trade is only acquired under the lease, and it is not contrary to public policy for such transactions to be left unscrutinised, save in exceptional circumstances.[75] In *Sibra Building Co v Ladgroves Stores Ltd*[76] a covenant in a contract for the sale of land prevented the buyers from erecting on the site a public house or licensed premises. A supermarket was built on the site, which sold beer and spirits. The vendor objected, invoking the covenant and the purchasers argued that the covenant was in restraint of trade. The Supreme Court upheld the judgment of Keane J. at first instance in which he granted an injunction restraining the purchasers from selling beer and spirits. The restraint of trade doctrine did not apply, *pace Harper's Garage*, to an ordinary negative covenant relating to use because at the time of the sale or lease the purchaser or lessee had no right to be there at all, and, in agreeing to the covenant, he gave up no right or freedom he previously had. Although it is difficult to distinguish these cases from other transactions which fall under the restraint of trade doctrine, Lord Wilberforce in *Esso* explained these exceptions as due to the fact that they have "passed into the accepted and normal currency of commercial or contractual or conveyancing relations". This test has been described as the "trading society" test and is often contrasted with the "existing freedom" test. In Australia, Lord Wilberforce's analysis of when the doctrine of restraint of trade does not apply has been approved in *ACT v Munday*,[77] latterly applied by the Federal Court

---

[73] [1939] I.R. 457; *Murphy Co v Crean* [1915] 1 I.R. 111.
[74] Wylie, *Irish Land Law*, 4th edn (Dublin: Bloomsbury Professional, 2010), Ch.19.
[75] e.g. *Clegg v Hands* (1890) 44 Ch. D. 503; *Ravenseft Properties v Director General of Fair Trading* [1978] Q.B. 52.
[76] [1998] 2 I.R. 589.
[77] (2000) 99 F.C.R. 72; *Peters (W.A.) Ltd v Petersville Ltd* (2001) 52 I.P.R. 289.

of Appeal in *Hospitality Group Pty v Australian Rugby Union Ltd.*[78] The issue here was whether restrictions that the defendants placed on the resale of tickets for rugby matches played in the defendant's stadium could be challenged as being in restraint of trade. Under either test the Federal Court of Appeal upheld the view that the doctrine could not be invoked. The test that was most frequently used to explain why the restraint in question is not within restraint of trade is Lord Pearce's speech in *Esso*, where he explained that the restraint doctrine applies where an individual who has an existing freedom to trade in a particular way contracts to give or fetter that freedom. The restriction placed in a contract that confers upon an individual the right to trade, on the other hand, is not within the restraint of trade doctrine; see Costello J. in *Irish Shell Ltd v Elm Motors.*[79]

15–31 Covenants in employment contracts that restrict or deter an employee from working for a rival concern when he leaves employment are within the doctrine; covenants that restrict an employee while in employment are not. In *McArdle v Wilson*[80] the contract of workmen employed in a factory in Tyrone obliged them to give two weeks' notice if they wished to terminate employment. The contract provided that if more than five employees gave notice then the notice of other employees would not be accepted. The provision was clearly designed to reduce the effectiveness of strike action; failure to observe the covenant was to result in the docking of one week's wages. An action to recover wages retained failed; the Court of Exchequer found the covenant valid; Palles C.B. went further and held the doctrine of restraint of trade inapplicable. So, too, a provision obliging an employee to repay training expenses incurred should he terminate his contract of employment has been held outside the doctrine of restraint of trade because no restriction operated once the employee had left work; see *Schiesser International (Ireland) Ltd v Gallagher.*[81]

15–32 The House of Lords decision in *Schroeder Music Publishing Co Ltd v Macauley*[82] did not involve a contract of employment, but one for exclusive services, the agreement unduly restricting the freedom of one party during the currency of the agreement. *Schroeder Music Publishing Co Ltd v Macauley* has commenced a line of case law in which little-known composers and musicians have been able to have publishing agreements, copyright assignments and management contracts declared to be invalid as unreasonable restraints of trade. These cases include *Silverton Records Ltd v Mountfield*[83] in which the

---

[78] (2001) 110 F.C.R. 157, applied in *Kosciuszko Thredbo Pty Ltd v ThredboNet Marketing Pty Ltd* [2014] FCAFC 87.
[79] [1984] I.R. 200.
[80] (1876) 10 I.L.T.R. 87.
[81] (1971) 106 I.L.T.R. 22.
[82] [1974] 1 W.L.R. 1308.
[83] [1993] E.M.L.R. 152; see also *Zang Tumb Tuum v Johnson* [1993] E.M.L.R. 61; contrast *Panayiotou v Sony* [1994] E.M.L.R. 229 and *Leeds Rugby v Harris* [2005] EWHC 1591

Stone Roses were able to overturn recording agreements because the terms were one-sided and capable of operating for many years due to extension option clauses. A publishing agreement that could also operate indefinitely was also set aside, the publisher's rights to alter and adapt the works being substantively unfair. This line of cases may, by analogy, lead to a decision in which restrictions operating during a contract of employment may be held within the restraint of trade doctrine.[84]

15–33 The most recent illustration of the restraint of trade doctrine being held to be applicable in exclusive services contracts can be found in *Wadlow v Samuel*.[85] Here a dispute between the recording artist Seal and a former manager over the enforceability of a management contract and a dispute settlement agreement required the court to consider whether a clause giving the manager commission for post-termination engagements was in restraint of trade because it was open-ended as to time. An earlier unreported decision, *Armatrading v Stone*,[86] favoured Seal but the "evil" that the clause constrained inherently within it—the artist being unable to get a new manager—was neither a likely nor an unreasonable outcome. Perhaps the best-known decision on restraint of trade and management contracts is *Watson v Prager*.[87] Here the boxer Michael Watson sought to avoid an exclusive services contract between himself and his manager. The plaintiff pleaded that the agreement which tied him to the defendant was potentially very prejudicial because the defendant was seen to be subject to several conflicts of interest, as he also promoted boxing events. Scott J. held that because *Nagle v Feilden*[88] decided that the current rules of a sporting association could be scrutinised by reference to the restraint of trade doctrine, the analogous manager/boxer contract was also to be tested.

15–34 While the restraint of trade doctrine may be invoked so as to overturn a transfer of copyright the context of the bargain is all-important. A settlement of a dispute over intellectual property rights by way of a negotiated agreement will not easily be challenged subsequently by one of the parties by way of the restraint of trade doctrine. The courts will take account of the countervailing policy interest in ensuring that freely negotiated contracts will be enforced. In *World Wildlife Fund v WWF Entertainment Ltd*,[89] the parties negotiated a settlement over the rights to use the initials WWF, a settlement that WWF Entertainment sought to later invalidate via invoking the restraint of trade doctrine. The Court of Appeal upheld the trial judge's view that before the restraint of trade doctrine can apply to the settlement of such a dispute the

---

(Q.B.).

[84] Heydon (1969) 85 L.Q.R. 229 at 235.
[85] [2006] EWHC 1492 (Q.B.).
[86] Unreported, High Court, September 17, 1984.
[87] [1991] 3 All E.R. 487.
[88] [1966] 1 All E.R. 689; *Macken v O'Reilly* [1979] I.L.R.M. 79.
[89] [2002] F.S.R. 530; *Educational Co of Ireland v Fallon* [1919] 1 I.R. 62.

settlement must go beyond any reasonably arguable scope of the intellectual property right that is the subject of the settlement. Carnwath L.J. said that this does not exclude the doctrine altogether; a threshold requirement is being set in order to reflect the factual context of the agreement.

> "[T]he parties, with proper legal advice, are the best judges of what is reasonable in their respective trading interests: and that agreement between them is normally the fairest and most efficient way of drawing the boundaries."[90]

Where doubts arise as to the meaning to be extracted from an express clause the standard rules that have evolved in relation to contractual interpretation will apply: *Prophet plc v Huggett*.[91] The courts in particular will not readily infer that something must have gone with the language, nor will it be permissible to read into the contract words that will modify the term in question.

Contracts traditionally within the doctrine

15–35 The courts have consistently reaffirmed the view that the categories of restraint of trade are not closed. So, if the court takes the view that a plaintiff has a legitimate proprietary interest then a covenant will be upheld even if the plaintiff falls outside the category of a traditional "restraint" plaintiff. So, in one recent English case[92] a restraint covenant could be subjected to the scrutiny of the doctrine, the contract relating to a joint venture even though no employment relationship or business transfer was involved.

(i) Employment contracts

15–36 The freedom of an employee to carry on an activity which adversely affects a former employer may be circumscribed by agreement. In fact the common law furnishes some degree of protection to an employer, and in several Irish cases the conduct of the employee breached a common law rather than a contractual duty. The common law, through the implied obligation to serve an employer faithfully, makes it a breach of contract for an employee to prepare a list of customers while intending to use this list after the contract of employment has ended. An employee who solicits orders from his employer's customers, intending to meet the orders personally rather than *qua* employee, also breaches this implied term. The facts of *Arclex Optical Corp v McMurray*[93] and *Stanford Supply Co Ltd v O'Toole*,[94] (in which employees solicited orders to be met by their own concerns while still employed by the plaintiff companies), are in point. Some contracts may seek to impose duties of faithful

---

90 [2002] F.S.R. 530 at 543, applying *Apple Corp v Apple Computers Ltd* [1991] 3 C.M.L.R. 49.
91 [2014] EWCA Civ 1013; *Carewatch Care Services Ltd v Focus Caring Services Ltd* [2014] EWHC 2313 (Ch).
92 *Dawnay Day & Co v D'Alphen* [1998] I.C.R. 1068.
93 [1958] Ir. Jur. Rep. 65.
94 Unreported, High Court, December 11, 1972.

service by way of express terms[95] or the employee may occupy a position which places the employee under a fiduciary duty.[96] So in *Shepherd Investments Ltd v Walters*,[97] former directors of a company who set up a competing business after diverting business opportunities and abusing confidential information were held to have breached implied duties of faithful service and fiduciary duties. But an employee is not bound to forgo preparatory acts of research pursuant to an intention to compete unless there are express restrictions that clearly close off such activities: *Integrated Systems Ltd v Tunnard*.[98]

15–37 It is sometimes said that the common law implied term is not the most accurate explanation for judicial protection being made available here. Sometimes the courts consider that on the facts there exists a confidential relationship between the parties and that this relationship creates an obligation for one person not to abuse trust or confidence, to the prejudice of the other. While these cases may involve employment contracts—which in part helps explain why the implied contract is sometimes advanced as the basis of the jurisdiction—the duty not to abuse confidential information can operate as between business partners too. The leading Irish case must be considered to be *House of Spring Gardens Ltd v Point Blank Ltd*.[99] In that case a licensee of bullet proof vests breached an agreement by manufacturing a similar product, thereby infringing the plaintiff's copyright and breaking the licensing agreement. Costello J., in a judgment approved by the Supreme Court who dismissed the licensee's appeal, stated that the court must consider whether a confidential relationship exists and whether the information imparted can properly be described as confidential information. In considering these facts it is relevant to consider the degree of skill, time and labour involved in compiling the information. If the owner has expended skill, time and labour in compiling this information, use of this information may be treated as confined for a specific purpose, and for that purpose only, if the court holds a confidential relationship exists. Even if the information could be gleaned from other sources there may still be a breach of duty if the information has been compiled by the plaintiff, although in this context the decision of McWilliam J. in *Nu Glue Additives and Bika (Ireland) Ltd v Burgess Galvin & Co*[100] suggests the remedy may be limited to damages rather than injunctive relief. This proposition cannot be supported because there are many cases in which not only has such relief been given[101] but the information itself has been delivered up; see *NP Generations Property Ltd v Feneley*.[102]

---

[95] *Integrated Systems Ltd v Tunnard* [2007] I.R.L.R. 126.
[96] *British Midland Tool Ltd v Midland International Tooling Ltd* [2003] 2 B.C.L.C. 523.
[97] [2007] I.R.L.R. 110.
[98] [2007] I.R.L.R. 126.
[99] [1985] F.S.R. 327.
[100] [1983] I.L.R.M. 372.
[101] Lavery, *Commercial Secrets* (Dublin: Round Hall Ltd, 1996), pp.233–240.
[102] (2002) 53 I.P.R. 563; Lavery, *Commercial Secrets* (Dublin: Round Hall Ltd, 1996), pp.240–241.

15–38 In these cases the employer may seek an interlocutory injunction restraining the employee until the merits of the action can be heard. The injunction is the primary remedy here although an account for profits made, or payment of damages, can also be ordered.

15–39 An employer may also wish to extract an express covenant from his employees. The many advantages for the employer may include greater predictability—the employee *knows* that he cannot solicit—and certainty of remedy. More importantly, the employee may not be able to carry on his trade or profession for a period after leaving employment. It is essential that the employer shows he has a legitimate commercial interest capable of protection; he must also show that the covenant goes no further than is necessary in order to protect that interest. In a modern commercial context it is often quite difficult for the employer to establish that the express covenant has been broken. In *Meadox Medicals Inc v V.P.I. Ltd*[103] the defendant company had been formed by two former employees of the plaintiff in order to manufacture and market medical equipment. The employees were researchers who marketed products which rivalled those manufactured by the plaintiff company. McWilliam J. found that while the defendant's product was an improved product it had been made by using trade secrets, know-how and other information, in breach of their contractual undertaking not to use this kind of knowledge within one year after leaving employment.

15–40 If the employee has acquired trade or professional secrets which would prejudice the employer's business if, upon termination of employment, these secrets could be used by the employee, either for his own or another's benefit, the employer can prevent the employee from entering future employment in that field or industry. The secret need not be expensive or complex. In *Forster & Sons v Suggett*[104] the works engineer for the plaintiff company who manufactured glass bottles knew the correct proportion of gas and air to be introduced into the furnaces during the manufacturing process. He was successfully prevented from working in the glass-making industry for a period of five years after leaving employment; the restraint covered the whole of the UK. An employer cannot by contract prevent an employee from using the skill he ordinarily employs in his trade, even if the employer has contributed towards developing this talent; so in *Arthur Murray Dance Studios of Cleveland Inc v Witter*[105] the plaintiffs could not prevent the defendant from working for a rival studio simply because they taught the defendant to become a proficient dance instructor. No "secret" information or skill was conferred upon the defendant.

---

[103] Unreported, High Court, April 22, 1982.
[104] (1918) 35 T.L.R. 87.
[105] (1952) 105 N.E. 2d. 685; contrast *Pastor v Chen* (2002) 19 C.P.R. (4th) 206. *Thomas v Farr Plc* [2007] EWCA Civ 118: a non-compete clause might be justifiable if the boundary between protectable and non-protectable post-termination information is difficult to draw. Non-solicitation clauses have recently been held to be given greater latitude than non-compete clauses: *Coppage v Freedom Security Ltd* [2013] EWCA Civ 1176.

Where, however, the employee acquires information that may be confidential even if the information can be recalled from memory; there is no need for the employee to commit the information to memory for the purpose of illicit later use as long as the information can still be seen as objectively proprietory and vested in the employer; see *SBJ Stephenson Ltd v Mundy*.[106] Problems arise where the information acquired is not a trade secret. Unless the information is used in such a way as to breach the implied duty of fidelity owed by an employee to the employer (as in *A.F. Associates v Ralston*[107] when employees, on resignation, took confidential customer files with a view to using them to start a rival business by soliciting customers of the employer) confidential information may be used by former employees for their own purposes even if such use directly harms the business of their former employer. In *Faccenda Chicken Ltd v Fowler*[108] the defendants, former employees of the plaintiff company, started to directly compete in the business of selling fresh chickens from refrigerated vans. The defendants knew the pricing policy of the plaintiff and the routes, delivery days and names and addresses of the plaintiff's customers as a result of their former employment and, using this knowledge, began to undercut the plaintiff company. Because this case did not involve the deliberate copying of lists or other documents and because no employment relationship existed at the time of use the plaintiff could not invoke the implied contractual term to serve the employer faithfully. Further, the fact that no express term had been included in the contract was held not to be material for the Court of Appeal held that even where confidential information that is not a trade secret (i.e. knowledge of a process, method of manufacture or the like) may prove commercially harmful to the employer if used by a former employee, former employees may not be prevented from using it for their own advantage even by an express covenant. The Court of Appeal left open the question whether such information can be protected from use if the former employee seeks to sell it to a third party for gain rather than use it himself in order to earn a living. In principle there should be a difference because the restraint of trade doctrine is directed at permitting an individual to carry out a trade, not cash in on confidential information. But it is dangerous for an employer to rely on the implied term argument. It has been held, for example, that a solicitor is free to use confidential information about the clients of a law firm from which the solicitor has recently departed in order to solicit those customers; see *Wallace Bogan & Co v Cove*.[109] The protection of the customer connection is not generally enough, absent an express term.

15–41 The most common interest an employer can advance as worthy of protection has been described as his "customer connection". Businessmen,

---

[106] [2000] I.R.L.R. 233.
[107] [1973] N.I. 229.
[108] [1985] I.C.R. 589; *Baker v Gibbons* [1972] All E.R. 759; *European Paint Importers Ltd v O'Callaghan* [2005] IEHC 280.
[109] [1997] EWCA Civ 973. Nor is use of information within the public domain restrainable under *Faccenda Chicken*; see *Brooks v Olyslager OMS (UK) Ltd* [1998] I.R.L.R. 590.

partnerships and corporations view customers and clients as part of their assets and, as such, the former employee who solicits orders may imperil the stability of the venture. If the employee has a close working relationship with members of the public the chances of the customers "following" the employee are substantial. It is legitimate to try and prevent this. Instances where the "customer connection" may be shown to exist include travelling salesmen (*Arclex Optical Corp v McMurray*[110]); warehouse manager (*Waterworth v Eaton*[111]); laundry manageress (*Franklin Steam Laundry Co v Anderson*[112]); solicitor (*Mulligan v Corr*[113]); hairdresser (*Oates v Romano*[114]); and milk roundsman (*Home Counties Dairies v Skilton*[115]).

15–42 If the employee does not have close contact with the public a restraint will not be allowed to operate. The position of a laundry manageress who has close contact with the public can be contrasted with a menial employee who works in the laundry pressing clothes. Even if there is some degree of contact with the public it does not follow that the employee will have sufficient "pull" to entice away former customers; a law firm would not expect to find its business falling away if a receptionist left to work for a rival firm. Nor will members of the public move with an auctioneer if he leaves one place of employment for another. The customers will be interested in the quality of the goods under the hammer and be indifferent as to who actually invites bids: see *Winnipeg Livestock Sales Ltd v Plewman*.[116] In *Dosser v Monaghan*[117] the defendants were musicians who had formerly played in a band owned by the plaintiff. They had agreed not to enter into similar employment within 50 miles of Great Yarmouth, Redcar, Southport, New Brighton and Belfast, towns in which the band played regularly. Best L.J. refused to grant an interlocutory injunction preventing the defendants from breaching the covenant; given the fact that the defendants were obscure members of the band the covenant was not reasonable. "It would be different if the musicians were famous." Similarly in *Levinwick Ltd v Hollingsworth*[118] the plaintiff failed to obtain an injunction enforcing a 24-month covenant under which the defendant agreed not to do similar work as a pharmacy manager within two miles of the plaintiff's pharmacy after leaving employment. Evidence was not adduced that bore out the plaintiff's claim that the defendant was "the force" behind the pharmacy. There were other employees who had closer customer contacts and the defendant had a large number of administrative duties. McGovern J. appears to have also had reservations about the length of the restraint.

---

[110] [1958] Ir. Jur. Rep. 65.
[111] (1905) 40 I.L.T.R. 27.
[112] (1903) 3 N.I.J.R. 85.
[113] [1925] I.R. 169.
[114] (1950) 84 I.L.T.R. 161.
[115] [1970] 1 All E.R. 1227.
[116] (2000) 192 D.L.R. (4th) 525.
[117] [1932] N.I. 209.
[118] [2014] IEHC 333.

15–43 The courts will extend the limited protection available to employees via the restraint of trade doctrine to persons who are not, strictly speaking, engaged under a contract of employment. "Employment-like" relationships such as an auctioneer engaged under a contract for services[119] are also within the doctrine as are consultancy agreements outside an employment contract.[120]

(ii) Covenants on the sale of a business
15–44 Again, certain obligations are implied upon the sale of a business. The rule which dictates that a man must not derogate from his grant prevents the vendor of a business from directly soliciting his former customers; see *Trego v Hunt*,[121] per Lord MacNaghten. If the vendor wishes to open up a shop next door to his former business, trading in exactly the same product, he can do so. As a result, the purchaser of a business will include a term in the contract limiting the freedom of the vendor to compete. Again, a covenant must be shown to be reasonable as between the interests of the parties and in the public interest. In *Nordenfelt*, the House of Lords upheld a worldwide covenant preventing the vendor of a munitions firm from trading for a period of 25 years. On the other hand, if the covenant is designed to go further and prevent the vendor from competing with the purchaser it may be rejected. In *British Reinforced Concrete v Schieff*[122] the plaintiffs, manufacturers of road reinforcements used throughout the UK, purchased a business which made steel road reinforcements. The owner of the business sold covenanted not to act as servant of any person concerned in the business of manufacturer or sale of road reinforcements in any part of the UK. The covenant was held too wide; the defendant dealt only in a particular kind of reinforcement; he manufactured the product and was not responsible for retail activities. Younger L.J. observed that it is only the business *sold* which is the legitimate subject of protection. In Ireland *Trego v Hunt* was extended in *Gargan v Ruttle*[123] to prevent a former partner soliciting customers of the old "firm".

15–45 The consideration paid for goodwill may be regarded as of vital importance. Care should be taken in relation to sale and purchase agreements which negate the consideration, because if a restraint is set out in another document, such as a deed of conveyance of the business, the consideration being absent from the deed, this omission will require the court to examine the reasonableness of the restraint clause without resort to the goodwill payment. In *Helsby v Oliver*,[124] as a general rule of thumb, it was remarked that the more the purchaser paid for goodwill, as a proportion of the purchase price of the business, the more likely it would be that a restraint would be held

---

[119] *Winnipeg Livestock Sales Ltd v Plewman* (2000) 192 D.L.R. (4th) 525.
[120] *Lapthorne v Eurofi Ltd* [2001] U.K.C.L.R. 996.
[121] [1896] A.C. 7; *Gargan v Ruttle* [1931] I.R. 152.
[122] [1921] 2 Ch. 563; *Allied Dunbar (Frank Weisinger) Ltd v Frank Weisinger, The Times,* November 17, 1987.
[123] [1931] I.R. 152; *Oswald Hickson Collier & Co (a firm) v Carter-Ruck* [1984] 2 All E.R. 15.
[124] [1999] 1 N.Z.L.R. 77.

to be enforceable. In general, the position of a professional person or trader who has been a partner in a professional or business organisation is seen as being governed by the "sale of a business interest" line of authority, as distinct from being an employee covenant. So, in cases where a solicitor, a doctor, an accountant, a designer, or other professional person, becomes a partner, then the partnership deed may validly seek to prevent the partner from competing, or taking the firm's clients when leaving the partnership. While in some cases there may be some nice issues of fact, such as who were the firm's customers,[125] the general view is that these agreements are to be more readily enforceable than employment covenants.[126] There may, however, be other considerations which make the covenant unenforceable, as in *Kerr v Morris*[127] where the Court of Appeal had to consider whether a medical partnership which limited the power of a retiring partner to practice infringed legislation regulating the National Health Service, but as long as the activity of the professional concerned is seen as a partnership activity, the covenant will not be as closely scrutinised as an employee restraint. However, in the case of a salaried partner who does not participate fully as a partner, i.e. does not share fully in the profits, or losses, of the partnership, the courts may regard the partner as being, in reality, an employee and thus may deprive the covenant of the benefit of the arm's length presumption that attaches to goodwill covenants. So, in *Briggs v Oates*[128] the defendant was held, as a salaried partner, to be an employee.

15–46 Another problematical contemporary development in this context is the advent of profit sharing, or share transfers in a company to employees as part of their remuneration. Does this sharing element put the employee in the same kind of position as the vendor of a business for the purpose of enforcement of a restraint clause? There is an English case which indicates that this will be so in appropriate circumstances.[129]

(iii) Franchise agreements
15–47 In the case of franchise agreements the courts have been required to classify them in some way: are they to be regarded as being closer to employment contracts or to vendor–purchaser transactions? In most cases they have been regarded as vendor–purchaser transactions although it must be said that certain modest franchise operations may not fall into this category if the franchisee makes a modest financial investment, so cases may not always be treated in this way. In the leading English cases the franchise agreement has been seen as a lease of the franchisor's goodwill.[130]

---

[125] *Whitehill v Bradford* [1952] Ch. 236; *Deacons (a firm) v Bridge* [1984] 2 All E.R. 19; *John Mitchell Design Plc v Cook* [1987] I.C.R. 445; *Clarke v Newland* [1991] 1 All E.R. 397.
[126] *Kerr v Morris* [1986] 3 All E.R. 217.
[127] [1986] 3 All E.R. 217.
[128] [1991] 1 All E.R. 407.
[129] *Systems Reliability Holdings Plc v Smith* [1990] I.R.L.R. 377.
[130] *Kall-Kwik Printing (UK) v Bell* [1994] F.S.R. 684; *Dyno-Rod Plc v Reeve* [1998] F.S.R. 148; *Vendo Plc v Adams* [2002] N.I. 95; *O'Brien's Sandwich Bars v Byrne* [2008] IEHC 466; *Carewatch Care Services Ltd v Focus Care Services Ltd* [2014] EWHC 2313 (Ch).

(iv) Exclusive dealing arrangements

15–48 Members of an industry may decide to amalgamate in order to support and protect their common interests. In the agricultural community it is common for producers to form co-operative ventures, the rules of which may have to satisfy the restraint of trade doctrine. The leading case is *McEllistrem v Ballymacelligott Co-operative Agricultural and Dairy Society*,[131] a decision of the House of Lords on appeal from the Court of Appeal in Ireland. The appellant was a member of a co-op. in Kerry, the co-op. being formed to develop and improve dairy farming in the district. Members of the society were bound by its rules which provided that while the society was bound to take and market all the milk produced by its members, the members were precluded from selling milk to any other local creamery. Members could not resign from the creamery unless the co-op.'s committee consented. The Court of Appeal in Ireland felt bound by two earlier decisions and upheld the rules; these cases, *Athlacca Co-operative Creamery v Lynch*[132] and *Coolmoyne & Fethard Co-operative Creamery v Bulfin*[133] were overruled. The House of Lords reasoned that while the respondents were entitled to protect their venture by ensuring stability, both of supply and in the lists of their customers, the restraint went further than was necessary to ensure this; it was no answer to say that the restraint operated locally and that the appellant could carry on farming in another part of Ireland:

> "[I]n a sparsely inhabited agricultural neighbourhood, with scanty means of communication, a prohibition of trade in every township within a radius of ten miles, might have precisely the same effect upon the business of a small trader, as if the preclusion extended to the remotest corners of Donegal …"[134]

In *Kerry Co-operative Creameries v An Bord Bainne Co-operative Ltd*[135] the plaintiffs, members of the first defendant, a co-operative society established for the purpose of assisting Irish dairy farmers, inter alia, by arranging for the export sale of dairy produce, proposed to change its rules so as to dilute the shareholding and related rights of members who declined to trade with Bord Bainne, but marketed export sales products themselves. The proposed rule change obtained the necessary two-thirds majority at a special general meeting, but the plaintiffs objected and sought to have the rule change declared an unlawful restraint of trade. Costello J., holding the doctrine applicable, found the changes to be reasonable. The new rules required members to make a commercial decision as to the benefits of trading with Bord Bainne or otherwise. Further, the duty to trade with Bord Bainne was of a limited nature—indeed it replaced a broader duty to provide all produce to the Board—and,

---

[131] [1919] A.C. 548.
[132] (1915) 49 I.L.T.R. 233.
[133] [1917] 2 I.R. 107.
[134] [1919] A.C. 548 at 562 per Lord Birkenhead L.C.
[135] [1991] I.L.R.M. 851.

given Bord Bainne's legitimate interest in securing continuity of supply, the rule changes did not fall within *McEllistrem*. The Supreme Court also upheld the restraint as reasonable, although O'Flaherty J., as mentioned above, was not persuaded that the doctrine applied in the absence of a restraint covenant.[136] McCarthy J., utilising Art.45 of the Constitution in interpreting the common law, concluded:

> "I am satisfied that the restraint as I have outlined it is also a reasonable one; indeed, I have difficulty in understanding any argument that it is unreasonable that a co-operative dairy society may not use any legitimate means available to it, to secure that those of its members who trade through it will benefit and greatly benefit by such trading as compared with those of its members who decide to go it alone, in whole or in part. As to the second consideration of public good, it is clear as a legitimate opinion to be held by the majority of the members that the national interests are best served by the promotion and expansion of Bord Bainne."[137]

(v) Solus agreements

15–49 The most frequently litigated exclusive dealing arrangement in the late twentieth century involved contracts between petroleum wholesalers and retailers, the arrangement obliging retailers to take all the petrol and motor oils they may require from one particular wholesaler. These contracts, known as "solus" agreements, are common, both in the Republic and Northern Ireland. There are important formal differences between the law on each side of the border.

15–50 A solus agreement typically involves a promise given by a wholesaler who undertakes to keep retailers supplied with petrol if the retailer in turn agrees to take all the petrol he will require from the wholesaler alone. The retailer may also promise to keep his filling station open at all reasonable hours and to take a minimum gallonage. The retailer may in return be given a rebate on petrol supplied, as well as interest-free loans and help in purchasing petrol pumps. There are substantial advantages to the wholesaler under such agreements. Distribution costs are kept down and the wholesaler can better predict customer demand in the future. The retailer, apart from the financial advantages, is also guaranteed some degree of security of supply.

15–51 In the Republic the solus agreement was investigated by the Fair Trade Commission, predecessor of the Restrictive Practices Commission,[138] who

---

[136] O'Flaherty J. distinguished *Stenhouse Australia Ltd v Phillips* [1974] A.C. 391; *Wyatt v Kreglinger* [1933] 1 K.B. 793; and *Bull v Pitney Bowes* [1966] 3 All E.R. 384. See also the case of *Sadler v Imperial Life Assurance* [1988] I.R.L.R. 388.

[137] [1991] I.L.R.M. 851 at 871.

[138] Now replaced by the Competition and Consumer Protection Commission by s.9 of the Competition and Consumer Protection Act 2014.

reported in 1961[139] that, while the solus system was generally of benefit to the public, the profitability of the retail trade led to an undesirable proliferation of outlets that could not then be controlled under existing planning legislation. A statutory instrument was passed in order to discourage the expansion of the solus system. The maximum period an agreement could run was for five years; retailers could not obtain price advantages under a solus agreement for the instrument made it unlawful for wholesalers to, directly or indirectly, discriminate as between retailers although rebates are paid to retailers who sign solus agreements.[140]

15–52 The Statutory Instrument of 1961 produced a change in policy on the part of petrol distributors in the Republic. Wholesalers decided not to invest in retailers, who could obtain substantial advantages and ride free of the tie after a relatively short time. This led to wholesale distributors purchasing their own retail outlets. Statutory Instrument No. 294 of 1961 was modified in 1972 so that a solus agreement could run for a maximum period of 10 years.[141] A ban on the acquisition of retail outlets by wholesalers, known as company-owned outlets, was also imposed. The Commission in its 1979–1980 Report[142] recommended no change be made in the maximum period of 10 years and that restrictions on the acquisition of outlets by companies remain, with some modifications. While the author cannot give here a detailed outline of the effects of the legislation it should be noted that in S.I. No. 70 of 1981 the Minister continued the 10-year maximum period for the duration of solus agreements but altered the terms and conditions a solus agreement may contain. While the wholesaler was not entitled to discriminate between solus and non-solus retailers, wholesalers could provide training facilities for solus retailer staff, advance loans to rebuild, repair or extend stations and any similar service or facility, without being obliged to provide these facilities to non-solus retailers. Statutory Instrument No. 70 of 1981 also entitled the wholesaler to charge a lower price to solus retailers as long as the differential was "reasonable and justifiable" in the circumstances. Limitations on the acquisition of company-owned retail outlets remained in force.

15–53 In its last report on this question the Fair Trade Commission considered that while the 10-year maximum period was long and had anti-competitive aspects, there was a net benefit to the public in the form of wholesaler investment in independent outlets which would otherwise not be made. However, given the fact that the European Communities[143] in 1983 had passed legislation in the form of a Regulation which gave petrol outlets a

---

[139] Pr. 6000.
[140] S.I. No. 294 of 1961.
[141] Following a second inquiry into the motor spirit distribution trade (I Prl. 1931) (1971): S.I. No. 150 of 1972.
[142] The Fair Trade Commission Inquiry was published in 1990 (Pl. 7951).
[143] Regulation 1984/83; see now the Competition Authority Vertical Restraints Declaration (Decision No. D/10/001 (effective December 1, 2010)).

similar exemption under (old) art.85(3) of the Treaty, there was no real point in continuing to regulate solus agreements under domestic law. This report was not implemented directly *in toto*, but the repeal of the Restrictive Practices Acts by the Competition Act 1991 meant that the Statutory Instruments governing solus agreements are no longer in force. While Council Regulation No. 330/2010, reflected in the Competition Authority Decision D/10/001 reduces valid restraints to five years, it is conceivable that the common law doctrine could, in an exceptional case, lead to some kind of contractual challenge. If other factors make a tie oppressive it may still be held an unreasonable restraint of trade, notwithstanding that it is to last for under five years. Factors that are important here are the duration of the tie, mutuality of obligation and the position of the wholesaler in the industry. There are signs that a court may permit a new wholesaler, attempting to establish himself in the market, to extract slightly better terms for himself. The desire to stimulate new competition explains this factor. While it is possible for the courts to look forward and anticipate future events like inflation and international fuel price increases—see *Amoco Australia Property v Rocca Brothers*[144]—a solus agreement that is fair and reasonable at the time of agreement cannot be unenforceable if subsequent events produce this result; see *Shell U.K. v Lostock Garage*.[145]

15–54 The leading Irish case is the decision of Kenny J. in *Continental Oil Co of Ireland Ltd v Moynihan*.[146] Moynihan, a retailer, entered into a solus agreement in 1970 agreeing to take petrol at the plaintiff's scheduled prices. The agreement was to run for five years; Moynihan was obliged to buy all his petrol from the plaintiffs and to give 48 hours' notice of his requirements. He was to take the largest possible consignments, not less than 800 gallons. The station was to be kept neat and clean and the number of pumps was not to be reduced. Moynihan benefited from the agreement by purchasing pumps on interest-free hire-purchase terms. Moynihan refused to take any further supplies from the plaintiffs when they operated a differential pricing scheme that threatened Moynihan's already slender profit margins. Kenny J. upheld the plaintiff's claim for an injunction to restrain the defendant from taking supplies from elsewhere. Viewed at the date of agreement Kenny J. held the agreement reasonable as between the parties and refused to find that enforcement of this agreement was against the public interest. While this may be correct, a later decision of the Court of Appeal in England puts a new light on *Moynihan*; if the differential pricing scheme operates harshly it is possible to deny an injunction on the grounds that the wholesaler has not acted fairly and should thus be denied an equitable remedy.[147]

15–55 While it is material to the question of reasonableness to decide if there is a prohibition on the retailer selling or leasing the premises to a third party

---

[144] [1975] A.C. 561.
[145] [1977] 1 All E.R. 481.
[146] (1977) 111 I.L.T.R. 5.
[147] *Shell U.K. v Lostock Garage* [1977] 1 All E.R. 481.

without the wholesaler's consent (see *Irish Shell Ltd v Burrell*[148]) the duration the tie has to run is perhaps the most important factor in determining reasonableness; in *Esso* the House of Lords held a 21-year tie unreasonable but a four-year and five-month tie valid; the Ontario Court of Appeal, however, upheld a 10-year tie, with an option to renew for a further 10 years, on the particular circumstances of the case before it; see *Stephens v Gulf Oil Canada Ltd.*[149] Many of the cases involving solus agreements have been cases in which the company taking the benefit of the "tie" has sought interlocutory relief, e.g. *B.P. Ireland Ltd v Shreelawn Oil Co Ltd*[150] and *Irish Shell Ltd v Dan Ryan Ltd*[151] and it is clear that the English cases are influential, notwithstanding the legislative gloss in Ireland that results from the Competition Act 1991, now replaced by the Competition Act 2002. Indeed, in the only Irish case in which the limits of the restraint of trade doctrine have been thoroughly examined, Costello J. gave his view of the correct solution to a question that has troubled academic lawyers and judges since *Esso Petroleum Co Ltd v Harpers Garage (Stourport) Ltd*[152] was decided. According to a majority of the Law Lords in *Esso Petroleum* the doctrine of restraint of trade does not apply to cases where, at the time of contracting, the trader does not enjoy the freedom to carry on the trade in question. If, therefore, a lease is executed under which X *acquires* from the company a lease of a station as well as the freedom to carry on the trade of petroleum retailer, and the lease also contains a solus tie, it is arguable that the doctrine does not apply for only by signing the lease does the trader *acquire* the freedom to carry on the trade; at that time, that is, just prior to signing, he has no freedom to trade. While this dogmatic proposition has been affirmed as a *prima facie* rule in *Cleveland Petroleum Co v Dartstone Ltd*[153] by the Court of Appeal, the Privy Council, in *Amoco Australia Property v Rocca Brothers*[154] (mindful that this proposition could provide a neat method of evading the restraint of trade doctrine altogether) held that the reasonableness of the covenant had to be established even in such a case. In *Irish Shell Ltd v Elm Motors*,[155] Costello J., after considering these three decisions, distinguished *Esso* from *Amoco* on the ground that in the former case the garage proprietor never owned the land leased to him while in *Amoco* the proprietor had earlier owned the land. Holding that the case before him fell outside the restraint of trade doctrine (even though the site was partly owned by the lessee proprietor before the lease containing the tie was granted to the lessee proprietor), Costello J. said:

> "As a general principle the common law doctrine of restraint of trade does not apply to restraints on the use of a particular piece of land

---

[148] Unreported, High Court, June 17, 1981.
[149] (1976) 65 D.L.R. (3d.) 193.
[150] [1983] I.L.R.M. 372.
[151] Unreported, High Court, April 25, 1985.
[152] [1968] A.C. 269.
[153] [1969] 1 W.L.R. 116.
[154] [1975] A.C. 561.
[155] [1984] I.R. 200.

when imposed by a conveyance or lease of the land in question. This exemption would not, however, apply if the restriction is contained in a demise when the lessor has obtained the land as part of a transaction which enables the restriction to be imposed. If such a transaction takes place the restraint must pass the test of reasonableness laid down in the doctrine."[156]

It does not seem to have been argued that the tie in *Irish Shell Ltd v Elm Motors Ltd* requiring the lessee to purchase motor fuels from the lessor for the duration of the lease—42 years—was unenforceable by virtue of S.I. No. 70 of 1981.

15–56 The Competition Authority, in Authority Decision No. 25 on motor fuels,[157] granted a licence in respect of the purchase of motor fuels under certain conditions. This licence has been supplanted by the Competition Authority Vertical Restraints Declaration (Decision No. D/10/001, effective December 1, 2010).

(vi) "Bad Leaver" clauses in employment contracts and partnership agreements
15–57 A covenant that terminates an employee's rights to salary bonus payments in the event that the employee leaves employment[158] may be struck down as a disguised covenant in restraint of trade. In *Finnegan v JE Davy*[159] a stockbroker had in previous years been paid a significant annual bonus based entirely on the trading activities of the firm and his own performance. When he left the defendant's employment to work for another stockbroking firm, he was informed that payment of his bonus would be withheld for some time, the defendant having developed a "loyalty" rule that operated against a departing employee who left to work for a rival. Apart from holding that insufficient notice was given so as to trigger invalidity under *Interfoto Picture Library Ltd v Stiletto Visual Programmes Ltd*,[160] T.C. Smyth J. also held the practice to be in restraint of trade[161] as there was no proprietary interest that required the restraint to be imposed. T.C. Smyth J. clearly felt that the defendants were seeking to prevent competition, something the restraint of trade doctrine studiously guards against. *Imam-Sadeque v BlueBay Asset Management*

---

[156] [1984] I.R. 200 at 213.
[157] Decision of July 1, 1993 under s.4(2) of the Competition Act 1991. Compliance with the Competition Authority licence was stressed by Clarke J. as an injunction pre-requisite in *Irish Shell Ltd v J.M. McLaughlin (Balbriggan) Ltd* [2005] IEHC 304.
[158] "Bad leaver" terminology is used in *Greck v Henderson Asia Pacific Equity Partners* [2008] Scots CSOH 2.
[159] [2007] IEHC 18. Contrast *Lichters v DEPFC Bank Ltd* [2012] IEHC 10, distinguishing *Finnegan v Davy* on the facts and holding that deferral of bonus provisions are not caught by the restraint of trade doctrine.
[160] [1988] 1 All E.R. 348.
[161] Following *Wyatt v Kreglinger* [1933] 1 K.B. 793; *Bull v Pitney Bowes* [1966] 3 All E.R. 384; and *Marshall v NM Financial Management Ltd* [1995] 4 All E.R. 785.

(Services) Ltd[162] provides a shorthand analysis of repudiatory breach of a contract of employment within the context of "bad leaver" clauses.

(vii) "Garden Leave Clauses"

15–58 Clauses that allow an employer to leave a departing employee on salary on condition he or she does not work are strictly speaking not restrictive covenants. It is an increasingly common feature of employment contracts in which a professional person or a key employee who leaves employment may be entitled to continue to be paid but is obliged to refuse to take alternative employment. Where this obligation to remain idle is imposed for long periods of time, there is the possibility of abuse. The former employee cannot work and may run the risk of losing skills or reputation while the former employer may purchase protection from competition from that former employee or the person who engages him or her. It may also dissuade the employee from giving notice to leave employment. "There is a public policy against the compulsory sterilisation and potential atrophy of skills".[163] Injunction sought will be tailored accordingly.

Resale Price Maintenance and Restrictive Commercial Practices

15–59 Agreements between producers or retailers which keep the price of goods or services at a certain level are not invalid at common law unless the person challenging the agreement is able to show the price level maintained is unreasonable or is designed to produce a monopoly. In *Cade v Daly*[164] an agreement between members of the South of Ireland Mineral Water Manufacturers and the Bottlers Trade Protection Association that no member would sell beer and minerals below a scheduled price was upheld; the agreement operated within one district of Cork and was to run for a short period.

15–60 This position reflects a reluctance to protect consumers against artificial pricing arrangements. In the Republic, prices of many essential goods have in the past been controlled by legislation; see, e.g. the Prices Act 1958 and statutory instruments limiting the price payable for milk. The Restrictive Trade Practices Acts 1953–1987 made it the task of the Commission established by the Acts to establish fair trading rules in relation to the supply and distribution of goods and services.[165] The legislation was upgraded in 1972 by the passing of the Restrictive Practices Act 1972 and later, in 1978, the Mergers, Take-overs and Monopolies (Control) Act 1978 added a further level of control.

---

[162] [2012] EWHC 3511 (Q.B.).
[163] Per Warby J. in *Elsevier Ltd v Munro* [2014] EWHC 2648 (Q.B.), applying inter alia, *JM Finn & Co Ltd v Holliday* [2013] EWHC 3450 (Q.B.) and *William Hill Organisation v Tucker* [1999] ICR 291. Where a restraint clause is struck down as excessive in seeking to stifle fair competition, a related gardening leave clause may also fail; *Bartholomews Agri Food Ltd v Thornton* [2016] EWHC 648 (Q.B.), distinguished in *Pickwell v Pro Cam CP Ltd* [2016] EWHC 1304 (Q.B.).
[164] *Cade v Daly* [1910] 1 I.R. 308.
[165] *Report on Travel Companies and Tour Operators* (1984), Pl. 2601.

15–61 The Restrictive Practices Acts were used to counteract certain anti-competitive practices, most notably through the use of a statutory order prohibiting below-cost selling as a means of combating the trend towards the increasing control of the grocery trade by a small number of multiple super-market outlets.[166] While the Below-cost Selling Order has been repealed by the Consumer Protection Act 2007, most of the pricing orders under the 1958 and 1978 legislation are retained by ss.92 and 93 of the 2007 Act. The restrictive practices legislation was repealed by the Competition Act 1991. The 1991 Act was supplanted by the Competition Acts 2002–2012, although the central features of both pieces of legislation were not changed as Lucey has pointed out.[167] The basic model for the 1991 and 2002 legislation was provided by the (old) arts 85 and 86 of the Treaty of Rome, now set out at arts 101 and 102 of the Treaty on the Functioning of the European Union (TFEU). The Competition Acts 2002–2012 have now been supplemented as a result of the enactment of the Competition and Consumer Protection Act 2014. The 2014 Act created the Competition and Consumer Protection Commission, replacing the dissolved National Consumer Agency and Competition Authority.

15–62 Article 85 of the original EEC Treaty (now Article 101 TFEU) applies to anti-competitive agreements and practices which may affect trade between Member States within the European Community, and in a number of recent Irish cases, the Irish courts have been required to consider whether art.85 has been infringed. Similarly, art.86 of the original EEC Treaty (now art.102 TFEU), which provides a means of counteracting practices which affect trade between Member States and constitute abuse of a dominant position, has been considered by Irish courts, most notably in *Kerry Co-operative Creameries Ltd v An Bord Bainne*.[168] In cases where the agreement or practice does not have an EU competition dimension because it does not involve trade between Member States, Irish competition law, prior to the implementation of the Competition Act 1991, was heavily dependent upon public agencies for investigation and enforcement. The 1991 Act, however, took a different tack by giving the relevant agency, the Competition Authority, certain powers of scrutiny, investigation, licensing of agreements and certification of agreements and practices, but the Act envisaged that recourse to the courts in respect of anti-competitive practices and agreements, and any abuse of a dominant position, would generally be the prerogative of aggrieved persons. Section 6 of the Act conferred a cause of action for relief against any undertaking which is a party to the offending agreement upon any aggrieved person—generally a competitor, trader or consumer, but the expression was not defined.[169]

---

[166] Restrictive Practices (Groceries) Order 1987 (S.I. No. 142 of 1987); Restrictive Practices (Confirmation of Order) Act 1987.
[167] (2003) 25 D.U.L.J. 124; see Annotation to the Competition (Amendment) Act 2012 at I.C.L.S.A. 2012.
[168] [1991] I.L.R.M. 851.
[169] Lucey (2003) 25 D.U.L.J. 124.

15–63 The most important section in respect of competition rules is s.4 of the Competition Act 2002. Section 4(1) provides that

> "… all agreements, decisions or concerted practices between undertakings or associations of undertakings which have as their object or effect the prevention, restriction or distortion of competition in trade in any goods or services in the State or in any part of the State are prohibited and void."

Section 4(1) goes on to specify particular examples of prohibited and void agreements, decisions or concerted practices. These are agreements, decisions or concerted practices which:

"(a) directly or indirectly fix purchase or selling prices or any other trading conditions;

(b) limit or control production, markets, technical development or investment;

(c) share markets or sources of supply;

(d) apply dissimilar conditions to equivalent transactions with other trading parties, thereby placing them at a competitive disadvantage; or

(e) make the conclusion of contracts subject to acceptance by the other parties of additional obligations which by their nature or according to commercial usage have no connection with the subject of such contracts."

Section 4(1) catches price-fixing, production-fixing, market-sharing, exclusive purchasing and distribution agreements, franchising agreements, intellectual property licensing agreements, and agreements which contain restrictive covenants, amongst others. Under the 1991 Act the Competition Authority could licence and therefore exempt anti-competitive agreements if the agreement met criteria fixed by the legislation. This power has been dropped in the 2002 Act, the Authority instead being given the somewhat less extensive right to issue Category Declarations. However, the Category Declaration does not confer any immunity from an action in damages under the 2002 legislation and it is to be anticipated that litigation in the years ahead will force the Irish courts to effect some kind of reconciliation of the common law and statutory competition requirements. In *O'Brien Sandwich Bars Ltd v Byrne*,[170] however, a franchise agreement was challenged on the basis of competition law rather than via the restraint of trade doctrine. Relying upon expert testimony and decisions of the Competition Authority, Laffoy J. held a geographical and time restriction not to infringe competition law.

15–64 While the Act was based on art.85 of the Treaty of Rome, s.5 of the 1991 Act was a rough approximation of the art.86 abuse of a dominant position provision found in the Treaty of Rome. Examples of abuse were

---

[170] [2008] IEHC 466. See also *Hyland v Dundalk Racing (1999) Ltd* [2014] IEHC 60.

found in s.5 and these include the imposition of unfair purchase or selling prices, imposition of unfair trading conditions, limitations on production, markets or technical developments, but the precise identification of abuse will be a matter for the Minister and the Authority, under s.14, or the courts, following a section 6 action brought by an aggrieved person. One of the first instances of ministerial action was the reference of the proposed purchase of the *Sunday Tribune* by Independent Newspapers; Independent Newspapers, in the event of the acquisition proceeding, would control three of Ireland's (then) five Sunday newspapers. The Competition Authority recommended that the acquisition should be permitted. A ministerial order prohibiting the transaction was subsequently made.[171] In its first decision on whether certain agreements are designed to prevent, restrict or distort competition, the Authority ruled that a non-competition clause in a partnership sale agreement, which bound the seller not to engage in a similar business for three years within a 20-mile radius, would have no effect on competition in the circumstances of the case.[172] Following on from the merger of the Competition Authority and the Consumer Protection Agency[173] to form the Competition and Consumer Protection Commission (CCPC), there has been a restatement of the statutory competence of CCPC for competition law and the role of the CCPC in relation to civil competition enforcement. The website of the CCPC contains details on civil cases and settlements reached with organisations as diverse as the Irish Medical Organisation and importers of branded footwear on matters such as the termination of services and resale price maintenance.[174] The interface between restraint of trade and the Competition Acts remains somewhat ill-defined. There is some evidence that the courts are sticking to certain basic tenets of restraint of trade while the Competition Authority is evolving an approach which is closer to EU competition law and more directly influenced by economic theory. For example, in *Sibra Building Co v Palmerstown Centre Development Ltd*,[175] Keane J. reaffirmed the view that covenants to fetter a future freedom are outside the scrutiny of the doctrine; the Competition Authority takes no such view. Also, in *Apex Fire Protection Ltd v Murtagh*[176] the Competition Authority, while upholding a confidentiality covenant in an employment contract, struck down non-competition clauses imposed upon a former employee who intended to enter the market. The Authority also took a very strict view of duration restraints, opting for an "absolute necessity" test rather than a reasonableness test. The basis upon which injunctive relief may be available for breach of the Competition Acts has been tentatively explored[177]

---

[171] Report, March 1992, Pl. 8795.

[172] Decision of April 9, 1992, Nallen/O'Toole Agreement.

[173] Competition and Consumer Protection Act 2014.

[174] *www.ccpc.ie*. The CCPC have recently warned the Approved Tour Guides of Ireland that minimum price recommendation rates were likely to breach the law. See *The Irish Times* "Consumer body warns over minimum pricing" January 9, 2016.

[175] Unreported, High Court, November 24, 1992.

[176] [1993] E.L.R. 201; see generally the Competition Authority, *Employee Agreements and the Competition Act, Iris Oifigiúil*, September 18, 1992.

[177] *Premier Dairies v Doyle* [1996] 1 I.L.R.M. 363.

by the Supreme Court, and the possibility of an award of damages for breach of the provisions of the Competition Acts is a very real option for the Irish courts; see *Blemings v David Patton Ltd*[178] and *Carna Foods Ltd v Eagle Star Insurance*,[179] even if the plaintiff in such an action is party to a contract that would otherwise be enforceable.

Restraint of trade and EU competition law

15–65 Where the doctrine of restraint of trade is invoked within the context of Community law, recent European case law suggests that Community law should take priority over domestic competition laws: the coexistence of the restraint of trade doctrine with EU competition law has been the subject of a careful examination by Dr Mary Catherine Lucey.[180] This approach was applied by Langley J. in the English case of *Days Medical Aids Ltd v Pihsang Machinery Manufacturing*.[181] A distributorship agreement was held not to be in conflict with art.81(1) of the Treaty of Rome but was likely to be too long to satisfy the restraint of trade doctrine. It was held that where Community law did not apply but restraint of trade did, the court was required to disapply the restraint of trade doctrine to the extent that it was otherwise applicable.

Trade union rules affecting union members[182]

15–66 It is established that because the relationship between a trade union and its members is based on contract, the rules of a union which control or restrict the freedom of union members to earn a living are subject to the restraint of trade doctrine; see *Doyle v Trustees of the Irish Glaziers and Decorative Glass Workers T.U.*[183] In the leading case of *Langan v Cook Operative Bakers Trade Union*[184] a trade union gave financial assistance to members who wished to emigrate and find work abroad. The rules provided that a member who returned to the district was bound not to work as a baker in that locality. The plaintiff was held able to repudiate the agreement upon making restitution of the sums advanced, the agreement being an unreasonable restraint of trade. While these decisions would appear to be incompatible with the spirit of s.3 of the Trade Union Act 1871, for that section effectively excluded all union agreements from the restraint of trade doctrine, it is easy to endorse the justice of the result in *Langan's* case.

---

[178] Unreported, High Court, January 15, 1997.
[179] [1997] 2 I.L.R.M. 499; *Island Ferries Teo v Minister for Communications* [2012] IEHC 256.
[180] (2014) 52 Irish Jurist 115.
[181] [2004] 1 All E.R. (Comm.) 991; Lucey [2007] E.R.P.L. 419.
[182] Wedderburn, *The Worker and the Law,* 3rd edn (Harmondsworth (Middlesex): Penguin, 1986), pp.788–817; Forde and Byrne, *Industrial Relations Law*, 2nd edn (Dublin: Round Hall, 2010), paras 8–17 to 8–18.
[183] (1926) 60 I.L.T.R. 78.
[184] [1938] Ir. Jr. Rep. 65; *O'Connell v BATU* [2014] IEHC 380.

Expansion of the Restraint of Trade Doctrine—Sports Stars

15–67 While employment and sale of a business contracts are the classical instances in which the restraint of trade doctrine will operate, the categories of restraint of trade are never closed; English case law has held the rules of the Football Association,[185] Pharmaceutical Society of Great Britain[186] and the Test and County Cricket Board,[187] to be subject to review under the doctrine. These cases involve persons who complain about rules to which they did not consent. Indeed, the rules of the Irish Football League, which laid down maximum signing-on fees and wages for part-time professional footballers, were held an unreasonable restraint of trade in *Johnston v Cliftonville Football & Athletic Club Ltd*,[188] even though these rules, agreed between the football club and the Irish league were, in a formal sense, consented to by the plaintiff when he registered as a league player with the club. In *Watson v Prager*[189] the rules of the British Boxing Board of Control, which regulated contracts between managers and boxers, were not only held to be subject to the restraint of trade doctrine, *pace Schroeder Music Publishing Co Ltd v Macaulay*,[190] but the contract between the boxer and the manager could also be regulated during the currency of the agreement.

15–68 In the field of equestrian sports, the rules of the Jockey Club were scrutinised by reference to the restraint of trade doctrine in *Nagle v Fielden*[191] and a decision to refuse a trainer's licence to the plaintiff on the ground of her sex were held an unlawful restraint of trade. *Nagle v Fielden* is a fairly conventional application of the rules of restraint of trade but the decision of the Supreme Court in *Eddie Macken v O'Reilly*[192] breaks new ground in several respects. The plaintiff, a world famous show jumper, complained that the rules of the Equestrian Federation of Ireland, which obliged Irish competitors to ride only Irish-bred horses, constituted an unreasonable restraint of trade. The rules were protective measures designed to promote the Irish horse-breeding industry. Hamilton J. held that the rules, because they denied Macken the opportunity to compete on the best available horses, Irish or otherwise, constituted an unreasonable restraint of trade. In the Supreme Court, O'Higgins C.J. and Kenny J., the only judges who found it necessary to discuss the restraint of trade doctrine, ruled that even if the rules did prejudice the plaintiff, they were still to be enforced because the wider public interest required that Macken's individual interests be overridden. O'Higgins C.J. ruled:

---

[185] *Eastham v Newcastle United Football Club* [1964] Ch. 413.
[186] *Pharmaceutical Society of Great Britain v Dickson* [1970] A.C. 403.
[187] *Greig v Insole* [1978] 1 W.L.R. 302.
[188] [1984] N.I. 9.
[189] [1991] 3 All E.R. 486.
[190] [1974] 1 W.L.R. 1308.
[191] [1966] 2 Q.B. 633.
[192] [1979] I.L.R.M. 79.

"The trial judge disregarded entirely the undisputed evidence as to the effect a change of policy would have on the horse breeding industry and on equestrian sport in Ireland. This ought to have been considered as a balance to the harm or inconvenience caused to the plaintiff."[193]

With respect, the rules on restraint of trade as they stand do not require such a "balancing process"; if the rule is unreasonable inter partes it is unnecessary to consider the public interest; indeed most cases are decided entirely on reasonableness inter partes. The view that individual interests which are unreasonably prejudiced must be sacrificed if they conflict with wider public interests is a novel doctrine. The general approach to the common law doctrine of restraint of trade is largely individualistic; if the agreement is not shown to be reasonable inter partes then the restraint falls at the first hurdle and there is no room for a balancing process of this kind. However, there are signs of a modified Irish doctrine emerging, as a result of the *Eddie Macken* case and the observations of McCarthy J. in *Bord Bainne*[194] where, it will be recalled, the learned judge observed that Art.45 of the Constitution could influence the interpretation of the restraint of trade doctrine. While McCarthy J. held that the rules of Bord Bainne were reasonable *inter partes* and that the public interest would best be served by the development of Bord Bainne, McCarthy J. may well have been prepared to uphold the rules, even if unreasonable inter partes because of the greater public interest that the Bord Bainne rules supported.

15–69 In *Proactive Sports Management Ltd v Rooney*,[195] the Court of Appeal was asked to consider whether an image rights management contract executed by Wayne Rooney, at the beginning of his career, could be vitiated by way of the restraint of trade doctrine. The High Court had held that the doctrine applied. One attack mounted on the first instance decision was that a restraint of trade could be effective upon contractual provisions that sterilised a person's ability to carry on a trade or profession. In this case, the trade or profession was that of professional footballer. The contract between Rooney and the management company did not affect that activity, it related to an ancillary or incidental aspect of Rooney's trade or profession. As such, the doctrine of restraint of trade simply did not apply. The Court of Appeal disagreed; public policy is generally concerned with the manner in which a person is able to properly realise his economic potential. Product endorsement is an economic activity and it is in the public interest that these rights be "fully realisable for this economic purpose". The Court of Appeal also dismissed a second argument that because the contract allowed Rooney to realise his commercial potential rather than sterilise that potential, the doctrine did not apply. This decision represents a significant expansion of the restraint of trade doctrine.

---

[193] [1979] I.L.R.M. 79 at 91.
[194] [1991] I.L.R.M. 581.
[195] [2011] EWCA Civ 1444.

Construction of Covenants in Restraint of Trade

15–70 While it is true to say that covenants in restraint of trade are to be read and interpreted by reference to the ordinary rules of construction found in leading English and Irish cases (see Ch.5) it cannot be denied that before this process begins there are some preconceptions that many judges will articulate. Employment restraints are viewed with greater judicial circumspection than contracts for the sale of a business. Franchise agreements involving inexperienced franchisees and large corporations are treated as being closer to the former rather than the latter. *Contra proferens* interpretation of clauses will also be readily resorted to in relation to employment restraints. These statements must therefore condition our view on what the words found in the restraint provision will mean.

The process of construction seeks to view the words used in the light of the objectives sought to be achieved by the agreement. If the clause seeks to protect the covenantee's customer base or trade secrets, for example, the words should not be viewed as applicable to activities that, at the time of the agreement, the parties would not have considered to pose a threat to the goodwill or business connections of the covenantee. The courts should also not strive to give the clause a meaning which enables the clause to take effect if the words used do not, as a matter of construction, reasonably support that meaning. The court:

> "... must steer a course between giving to the clause a meaning which is extravagantly wide and giving to the clause a meaning which is artificially limited. The task of the court, in construing the contractual term is simply to ask itself: 'what did these parties intend by the bargain which they made in the circumstances in which they made it?'"[196]

However, there is authority for the view that if a clause is ambiguous in the sense that the words may equally support an interpretation that would lead to the clause being an unreasonable restraint of trade, while the other interpretation would not, the court should favour the latter interpretation "on the basis that the parties are to be deemed to have intended their bargain to be lawful and not to offend against the public interest".[197]

15–71 It is often said that employment restraints, because they are "negotiated" between persons who are in unequal bargaining positions, are viewed restrictively; it is clear that an employer and employee restraint is treated with greater suspicion than a restraint imposed on the sale of a business. In *John Orr Ltd and Vescom B.V. v John Orr*[198] Costello J. observed that "greater freedom of contract is allowable in a covenant entered into between the seller and the buyer of a business than in the case of one entered into between an

---

[196] Per Chadwick L.J. in *Arbuthnot Fund Managers v Rawlings* [2003] EWCA Civ 513.
[197] *TFS Derivatives Ltd v Morgan* [2004] EWHC 3181 (Q.B.) per Cox J. at para.43.
[198] [1987] I.L.R.M. 702 at 704.

employer and employee". In *Murgitroyd and Co Ltd v Purdy*,[199] the defendant was a patent agent, a specialist profession with only some nine or 10 firms in the State. His contract of employment with the plaintiff firm contained a non-competition clause for 12 months after leaving employment. In breach of this covenant the defendant began to practice in the intellectual property field. While the nationwide restraint was reasonable, the blanket anti-competition provision was not. Such clauses are more likely to be operational where the identities are of the covenantee's customers are unknown but in this situation the plaintiff's customers were readily identifiable. Clarke J. held the restraint to be unenforceable as against an employee: a non-solicitation clause would have been enforceable.

15–72 In contrast, in the case of franchise agreements, express covenants that lock the outgoing franchisee from competing in a geographical area appear to be strictly construed against the franchiser, but the franchiser can, however, protect the goodwill built up by the ongoing franchisee by way of a non-solicitation clause; see *Vendo Plc v Adams*.[200]

15–73 The courts recognise that goodwill covenants may be a reasonable means of permitting the purchaser to enjoy the benefits of the business acquired, while in employment cases all the employer purchases is the services of the employee and, further, the deeper pocket of the employer is more likely to be able to fund litigation than that of the employee. While in some instances the employee may possess considerable clout—Lord Denning observed that "a managing director can look after himself"[201]—there are reasons which indicate that the restrictive interpretation of employment covenants is perhaps a sound policy. Employers sometimes rely on provisions which exceed protection of their legitimate interests and the courts should not help an employer who has not drafted the covenant with precision. Two Irish cases support this view; the first is *Oates v Romano*.[202] The second, *Coleborne v Kearns*,[203] concerned an employee who worked in a shop which involved him in close contact with the community. The employer extracted a covenant that prevented him from working in a similar shop within 15 miles of the employer's shop for seven years should he "leave" employment. The court refused to interpret "leave" as also covering dismissal by the employer.

15–74 If, however, the employer can show he has a legitimate interest to be protected the courts often permit the employer to enforce the covenant, even if it, literally construed, would cover less meritorious cases. The employee will

---

[199] [2005] IEHC 159, following *Kores Manufacturing Co Ltd v Kolok Manufacturing* [1959] Ch. 108.
[200] [2002] N.I. 95.
[201] *Littlewoods Organisation v Harris* [1978] 1 All E.R. 1026 is illustrative of the difference between key employees and other workers.
[202] (1950) 84 I.L.T.R. 161.
[203] (1911) 46 I.L.T.R. 305.

often place an extended, quite fantastic and literal interpretation on a covenant hoping that this will lead the court to strike the covenant as invalid. In *Home Counties Dairies v Skilton*[204] an employer was able to enforce a covenant against a milk roundsman who worked as a roundsman for a rival concern, even though literally construed the covenant against working as a dairy produce salesman would prevent him from selling cheese in a grocer's shop. The Court of Appeal ruled that the covenant must be construed by reference to the commercial background in which the contracting parties operated. A useful exercise is to compare *Oates v Romano*[205] with *Marion White v Francis*.[206] In the first case the covenant was interpreted literally and held to be too wide because it would have precluded the defendant, a hairdresser, from working as a receptionist or having even a financial interest in the plaintiff's business. In *Marion White v Francis*, on the other hand, the clause indicated that the employee could not be engaged as agent, servant or assistant or in any other capacity whatsoever in the business of ladies' hairdresser. The Court of Appeal rejected the contention that the clause could prevent the employee from working as a bookkeeper in a back-room, or be a shareholder or director in a hairdressing company. The covenant was held to be directed at active participation which was directly connected to the hairdressing business and had to be read in such a context.

15–75 The same principle is applicable to restraints in general, regardless of the kind of relationship involved. In *Clarke v Newland*[207] two general practitioners engaged in a partnership executed a deed which obliged a retiring partner "not to practise within the practice area" within three years. The defendant argued that the covenant was too wide because it prevented him from practising in a hospital or as a consultant. This interpretation was rejected in favour of an interpretation limiting the covenant to practising as a general practitioner, because the objective behind the clause was the protection of one partner against rivalry in trade and, further, the clause had to be construed by reference to the context and factual matrix at the time when the agreement was made.

Severance of Void Provisions and Reasonableness—Basic Principles

15–76 Even if the courts place a very liberal interpretation on covenants in restraint of trade the court may well decide to limit the scope of a restraint by strict application of the doctrine of severance.[208] The doctrine of severance is

---

[204] [1970] 1 All E.R. 1227.
[205] (1950) 84 I.L.T.R. 161.
[206] [1972] 1 W.L.R. 1423.
[207] [1991] 1 All E.R. 397; *Norbrook Laboratories Ltd v Smyth*, unreported, High Court, September 30, 1986; *PAT Systems v Neilly* [2012] EWHC 2609 (Q.B.).
[208] See generally Heydon, *The Restraint of Trade Doctrine* (London: Butterworths, 1971), pp.122–136. The limited scope of severance in English law has been reaffirmed in *Francotyp*

not intended to give the courts a free hand to redesign or reshape a covenant that fails to meet a test of proportionality. As Younger L.J. said in a leading case, the doctrine is "permissible in a case where the covenant is not really a single covenant but is in effect a combination of several distinct covenants. In that case and where the severance can be carried out without the addition or alteration of a word, it is permissible but in that case only".[209] This principle is strictly adhered to in employment cases, but seems to be relaxed somewhat in sale of business cases. In *John Orr Ltd and Vescom B.V. v John Orr*[210] Costello J. had to consider the enforceability of a restraint clause which bound the defendant who had sold his interest in the first plaintiff company to the second plaintiff company. The share transfer agreement obliged the defendant to enter into a service agreement, and for one year after leaving employment, not to compete with the business of the second defendant, on a worldwide basis, and not to solicit customers of either the first or second plaintiff. Costello J. found this covenant to be too wide and, holding that it was legitimate to protect the purchaser from solicitation of the first plaintiff's customers by the defendant, the learned judge severed that part of the solicitation clause that operated vis-à-vis the acquiring company, Vescom B.V. However, the finding of the court in relation to the competition clause is inconclusive because counsel for the plaintiffs submitted that the restraints were reasonable and did not suggest that the court had a power to redraft covenants which were too wide. Costello J. held the restraints, as worldwide restraints covering business activities of the second defendant, were excessive and in these circumstances were unenforceable. Each case will be considered on its merits by reference to the time the agreement was made. In *Allan Jones LLP v Johal*,[211] an express covenant that prevented a solicitor from canvassing clients of the solicitor's firm for which she had worked for one year, post-employment, was upheld. While the court observed that reasonableness is a matter of fact and that each case needs to be considered on its merits, the fact that the covenant was not limited to clients of the firm with whom the employee solicitor had worked did not render it unreasonable as the post was a senior one that could have been expected to ripen into a partnership. The marketing and promotion of the firm as a whole would have led the employee solicitor into contact with clients outside her practice area.[212]

– *Postalia Ltd v Whitehead* [2011] EWHC 367 (Ch). A severance clause of the standard type was said to simply reflect a common law "blue pencil" test.

[209] *Attwood v Lamont* [1920] 3 K.B. 571 at 593; *N.I.S. Fertilizers Ltd v Neville*, unreported, N.I. High Court., February 10, 1986; *Marshall v NW Financial Management, The Times*, June 24, 1997. For an interesting trio of Canadian cases on severance, see *Canadian American Finance Corp v King* (1989) 36 B.C.L.R (2d) 257; *Sterling Fence Co v Steelguard Fence* [1992] 36 A.C.W.S. (3d) 644; and *Restauronics Services v Forster* (2000) 13 C.P.R. (4th) 1. A most perceptive judicial analysis of severance is to be found in the Singapore case of *Lee Gwee Noi v Humming Flowers & Gifts Pte Ltd* [2014] 3 SLR 27.

[210] [1987] I.L.R.M. 702.

[211] [2006] EWHC 286 (Ch).

[212] The court also advised against following earlier decisions, such as *Fitch v Dewes* [1921] 2 A.C. 158, on the basis that public policy has changed radically. On a recent trend in Ireland towards threatening or joining prospective employers, see *Net Affinity Ltd v Conaghan and*

15–77 If the restraint is too wide in relation to the geographical area to be covered the court may limit the scope of the covenant by cutting down the area, insofar as this can be done by eliminating towns, districts or even countries through a "blue pencil" test. In *Mulligan v Corr*[213] the defendant, a solicitor's apprentice, agreed that when he left the plaintiff's employment he would not practice (a) within 30 miles of Ballina and Charlestown; and (b) within 20 miles of Ballaghaderreen. The Supreme Court considered reducing the geographical area by severing (b), leaving covenant (a) enforceable. It was held that even if severance were performed the area covered by covenant (a) was still excessive.

15–78 The issue of geographical scope is a very difficult issue that can only be decided on a case-by-case basis. In an important English case a restraint preventing the branch manager and a consultant employed by an employment agency was held excessive even though it operated within 1,000 metres of their previous place of employment. The area covered was, in effect, most of the city of London and, as such, an impermissible restraint.[214] Even a relatively small geographical area may be excessive, depending on circumstances. Twenty miles was too wide where the customers constituted a static group that was unlikely to move away from the former district in any large numbers; see *N.I.S. Fertilizers Ltd v Neville*.[215] Individual trading patterns will have to be considered. In *Vendo Plc v Adams*[216] the business in question was a truck washing franchise, which required the franchisee to travel to various premises of customers rather than operate his business from his own fixed premises. Girvan J. regarded a clause which prevented a franchisee from working within that defined territory as excessive and going beyond what would be reasonable; the nature of the business would permit both the outgoing franchisee and the incoming franchisee to operate successfully in such a wide geographical area.

15–79 The duration of the restraint is also of cardinal importance, non-solicitation clauses of former customers being probably more likely to be reasonable than blanket "sterilisation" clauses. Again, each case will turn on its own facts. In *Societa Esplosivi Industriali SpA v Ordnance Technologies UK*,[217] a clause in a joint venture agreement in which design assistance was provided in respect of the development of missiles prevented the designers from working in the field for nine-and-a-half years. Lewison J. held the restraint to be reasonable:

Another [2012] E.L.R. 11 and *Hernandez v Vodafone Ireland Ltd* [2013] IEHC 70.

[213] [1925] I.R. 169; *Sadler v Imperial Life Assurance* [1988] I.R.L.R. 388; *Ronbar Enterprises Ltd v Green* [1954] 1 W.L.R. 815.

[214] *Office Angels Ltd v Rainer Thomas, The Times*, April 11, 1991; *Spence v Marchington* [1988] I.R.L.R. 392.

[215] Unreported, High Court, February 10, 1986 (N.I.).

[216] [2002] N.I. 95; *Convenience Co v Roberts* [2001] F.S.R. 625.

[217] [2004] 1 All E.R. (Comm.) 619.

"A period of 9 and a half years is not a long one in the context of a defence project using cutting edge technology … the [evidence indicated] the research phase of such a project could take up to 15 years, and the development phase could take 7. Even the bid phase could take several years. A decade in the pop music business by contrast, is a very long time indeed."[218]

In *Proactive Sports Management Ltd v Rooney*,[219] the English Court of Appeal has adopted a very sweeping approach to the reasonableness of a restraint question. The contract was signed by Wayne Rooney at the age of 17. Neither he nor his parents were commercially sophisticated and they were, despite recitals to the contrary, not furnished with independent legal advice. The contract lasted for eight years, effectively the lifetime of the average footballer. The decision of the first instance judge that the contract here was oppressive was upheld by the Court of Appeal.

15–80 In *Skerry, Wynne & Skerry's College Ireland Ltd v Moles*[220] a teacher who agreed not to teach within seven miles of Belfast, Dublin and Cork when he left employment with the plaintiffs as a shorthand typing instructor was held bound. The court severed the geographical restraint by deleting Dublin and Cork. It was also argued that the covenant was too wide in terms of duration. The "evil" the plaintiffs were entitled to protect themselves against was the possibility that when the teacher left he would take his students with him. The defendant argued that the restraint, to apply for three years, was indefensible because the courses offered by the plaintiffs ran for 12–18 months; Barton J. dismissed this argument. It is suggested that the case is wrongly decided on this point. If the employer can show he has a legitimate interest to protect, but the covenant is excessively long, a court cannot substitute a reasonable period for the unreasonable period. There are isolated situations, however, where this appears to have been done: in *Lennon and Pakatak Ltd v Doran and Corrigan*,[221] Carroll J. appears to have held that the contract in which a business was sold and which contained a two-year non-compete clause would be enforceable for one year. If, however, the plaintiff seeks an injunction the same result may follow from the way in which the courts implement this discretionary remedy. In *Cussen v O'Connor*,[222] the plaintiff employed the defendant as a commercial traveller, obliging him not to work for any rival business for either (a) 10 years after commencement of employment in 1889; or (b) two years after termination of employment. The defendant left employment in 1892; the covenant therefore had seven years to run, an unduly long time. Andrews J. instead of striking down the restraint, ruled that the court had a discretion to determine how long the injunction was to run; in the view of the

---

[218] [2004] 1 All E.R. (Comm.) 619 at 655.
[219] [2011] EWCA Civ 1444.
[220] (1907) 42 I.L.T.R. 46.
[221] Unreported, High Court, February 20, 2001.
[222] (1893) 32 L.R.(Ir.) 330.

learned judge a reasonable period would be two years. So, although the court could not reduce the plaintiff's substantive rights to reasonable proportions it could limit the scope of the primary remedy available.

15–81 There is a suggestion in the judgment of McWilliam J. in *E.C.I. European Chemical Industries Ltd v Bell*[223] that the courts may now be prepared to "tailor" a restraint which is clearly too wide in terms of area and duration, once the employer can show he has a legitimate interest worthy of protection. In that case the plaintiffs had inserted an excessively wide covenant, adding that if the covenant was held invalid "the said covenant shall be given effect to in its reduced form as may be decided by any court of competent jurisdiction". After noting the conflict between the English cases of *Commercial Plastics v Vincent*[224] and *Littlewoods v Harris*, McWilliam J. expressed obiter a preference for the later decision. While one can sympathise with McWilliam J. who was clearly concerned that the employee should not use trade secrets to the positive detriment of the former employer, in principle the courts should not allow the employer "two bites at the cherry", i.e. draft a wide restraint which will no doubt discourage employees from engaging in quite acceptable and lawful activities after leaving employment, and then invite the courts to redraft the contract when one employee challenges through the courts the validity of the covenant; see *Davies v Davies*.[225]

15–82 The American courts take a more adventurous view of the doctrine of severance and openly admit that they have the jurisdiction to shape and restrict area, duration and activity restraints to reasonable proportions. It may be, however, that the Irish courts may, of necessity, be required to develop wider powers to reshape and redraft covenants via radical reassessment of the severance doctrine. Under the Competition Act 2002 it is exclusively for the courts to adjudicate on the enforceability of covenants and s.4(6) of the 2002 Act empowers the courts to apply any "relevant rules of law as to the severance of those terms". Because the Competition Authority has the capacity to negotiate and thus shape covenants, particularly in relation to declarations of compliance under s.4(3) of the 2002 Act, a more flexible severance power would seem appropriate if the statutory competition regime and the common law are to be reconciled.

15–83 There is one final point which should be mentioned. Most employment restraints are governed by reasonableness inter partes, as are covenants for the sale of a business. The question of reasonableness in the public interest does not generally arise. In the English case of *Hensman v Traill*[226] a covenant

---

[223] [1981] I.L.R.M. 345: contrast *John Orr Ltd and Vescom B.V. v John Orr* [1987] I.L.R.M. 702.
[224] *Commercial Plastics v Vincent* [1965] 1 Q.B. 623; *Littlewoods v Harris* [1978] 1 All E.R. 1026, criticised by Phillips (1978) 13 Ir. Jur. 254.
[225] (1887) 36 Ch. D. 359, followed in *Days Medical Aids Ltd v Pihsang Machinery Manufacturing* [2004] 1 All E.R. (Comm.) 991.
[226] *The Times*, October 22, 1980; *Kerr v Morris* [1987] Ch. D. 90.

preventing a doctor from competing was struck down as being unreasonable in regard to the public interest and inter partes; had the covenant been reasonable inter partes it would still have been defeated, it being contrary to the public interest to prevent a doctor practising in such circumstances. In *Johnston v Cliftonville Football & Athletic Club Ltd*[227] an attempt to justify maximum wage payments as being in the public interest was made by the Irish League: if wages could be freely negotiated there was, the League argued, a danger that the two biggest and wealthiest clubs would attract the best players through lucrative contracts and this would lead smaller clubs to overreach themselves financially in an attempt to retain their best players. Murray J. held that this consequence was not established by the defendants, on the evidence.

Repudiatory Breach and Enforceability

15–84 The enforceability of a restraint clause may also be in doubt in cases where the party seeking enforcement has been guilty of a repudiatory breach of contract. So, where an employee has a fixed-term contract and the company employing him is compulsorily wound up, thereby effecting a wrongful dismissal, the employer is not entitled to the benefit of the restraint by virtue of the repudiation of the contract of employment.[228] This principle was further applied in *Briggs v Oates*.[229] The defendant was employed by a firm of solicitors for a fixed period. The partnership came to an end and the employment of the defendant accordingly terminated. A restraint preventing the defendant from practising for five years within five miles of the partnership office was held unenforceable. The breach must, however, be repudiatory.[230] *Briggs v Oates* was used as the foundation for an argument that where the restraint purported to operate when a repudiatory breach took place on the part of the employer, the entire clause was unenforceable even if the event that brought the clause into play was innocuous (e.g. the resignation of the employee).[231] In *Rock Refrigeration Ltd v Jones*[232] the Court of Appeal has rejected this argument. In *Hospitality Group Pty Ltd v Australian Rugby Union Ltd*,[233] the Australian Federal Court of Appeal indicated that the public interest in suppressing ticket "scalping" could justify contractual restrictions on the resale of tickets. If the restraint seeks to prevent pioneering research work in the area of medical science the deleterious effects of such a covenant in the public interests are obvious and the clause will not readily be upheld. In *Dranez Anstalt v Hayek*,[234] the inventor of a medical ventilator contracted not

---

[227] [1984] N.I. 9.
[228] *Measures Bros. Ltd v Measures* [1910] 2 Ch. 248.
[229] [1991] 1 All E.R. 407; *Stone v Fleet Mobile Tyres Ltd* [2006] EWCA Civ 1209.
[230] *Spence v Marchington* [1988] I.R.L.R. 392.
[231] *D v M* [1996] I.R.L.R. 192. The English and Canadian case law has been extensively reviewed in *Globex Foreign Exchange Corp v Kelcher* (2011) 337 D.L.R. (4th) 207 (Alberta C.A.).
[232] [1997] 1 All E.R. 1.
[233] (2001) 110 F.C.R. 157.
[234] [2002] EWCA Civ 1729.

to apply his skills in the future, such a promise being given in respect of the sale of an invention. While the restraint was too long in terms of duration, given that patent rights expire after 20 years, the Court of Appeal went further in observing that:

> "[I]t must be a wholly exceptional case in which the imposition of such restraints on a pioneer in a field of medical science—in the development of which there is, at least prima facie, such an obvious public benefit— can be justified."[235]

However, the principle has been held not to apply to cases where the restraint arises by way of a duty of confidence and the contract is one for services; see *Campbell v Frisbee*.[236]

Interlocutory Injunction and Enforcement

15–85 The facts of *Hernandez v Vodafone Ireland Ltd*[237] are unusual insofar as the plaintiff sought an interlocutory injunction against his former employer requiring the employer not to prevent the plaintiff from taking up employment with O₂ and from interfering with the plaintiff's new contract of employment with O₂. The plaintiff disputed the enforceability of a six-month post-termination provision against taking up a post with an entity that "competes or conflicts (or is likely to compete or conflict) with any business interest or commercial activity of Vodafone". This clause does indeed look too wide but as the case was one in which an interlocutory injunction was sought and the defendant argued that the core issue of enforceability of the clause could not appropriately be dealt with in such proceedings, Laffoy J. considered that such an issue could only be dealt with at trial. However, as the plaintiff was bound by both a non-solicitation clause and confidentiality restrictions, in the light of financial hardship to the plaintiff caused by his being deprived of an income for several months, the injunction was granted. However, should the parties adduce oral evidence on the issue of enforceability in interlocutory proceedings, then the court will give a ruling.[238] The court also has jurisdiction to "invite" the parties to a mediation process under Ord.56A of the Rules of the Superior Courts.[239]

---

[235] Per Chadwick L.J.
[236] [2002] E.M.L.R. 656.
[237] [2013] IEHC 70.
[238] *Murgitroyd v Purdy* [2005] IEHC 110; *Net Affinity Ltd v Conaghan and Another* [2012] E.L.R. 11.
[239] S.I. No. 502 of 2010: *Irish School of Yoga v Murphy* [2012] IEHC 218.

Part 6

Capacity to Contract

16 Contractual Capacity

Introduction

16–01 Most systems of law seek to protect persons falling into particular categories of "disability" by rendering them unable to contract freely. When this occurs, the individual bargain is thereby invalid although it may be that some limited remedy may still be available. For example, s.2 of the Sale of Goods Act 1893 provides an exception to the general rule that capacity to buy and sell is regulated by the general law concerning capacity to contract and to transfer and sell property. When necessaries are sold and delivered to an infant or minor or a person who by reason of drunkenness is incompetent to contract, that person must pay a reasonable price therefore.[1] In the case of a person who lacks capacity to enter into a contract for the sale of goods or services, s.137 of the Assisted Decision-Making (Capacity) Act 2015 provides that such a person shall pay the supplier a reasonable sum for goods or services supplied at the request of that person. In both sections the goods or services—services may be necessaries under section 2 of the 1893 Act and at common law—must be suitable for the condition in life and actual requirements of the incapacitated person at the time of actual supply. As we shall see the Assisted Decision-Making (Capacity) Act 2015 brings about a radical restructuring of contractual capacity provisions for a wide and diverse range of persons.

Infants or Minors

16–02 The possibility that a young person may enter into a contract which may be unconscionable or improvident has already been considered in Ch.13, but the common law has always afforded protection to persons through the status of infancy, and statute law has supplemented this protection in various ways. While the law is widely and correctly regarded as in serious need of reform, there are no obvious signs of development in Ireland at this time. In fact, modern commercial and media practices have had to address the difficulty that the rules relating to infant contracts present, particularly in relation to young sports stars and entertainers. Periodic press coverage[2] of 14-year-old soccer players entering into million-dollar sportswear contracts and three-

---

[1]   Contrast the position in British Columbia where even contracts for necessaries are unenforceable: Infants Act [RSBC 1996] s.19. An exception is made in relation to student loans vis-à-vis contractual capacity of minors; see *Chitty on Contracts*, edited by H.G. Beale, 32nd edition (London, Sweet & Maxwell, 2015) Vol. 1, paras 9.001 to 9.074.

[2]   "Sport's Bright Young Things", *The Times*, April 3, 2004.

year-old basketball players being used in sports commercials reflect both the commercial potential of young people of exceptional talent and the legal difficulties that enforcement may bring. The singer Charlotte Church famously settled an action brought against her for repudiatory breach of a management contract concluded when she was 12 years old.[3] The same artist, at the time she came of age, contracted a memoirs book deal for a £500,000 advance.[4]

16–03 At common law a person attained the age of majority at 21 years of age: this age was selected because it was felt to be the age at which it became possible to expect a youth to be able to wear and carry a full set of armour.[5] Following upon the Law Reform Commission's *Report on the Age of Majority, the Age for Marriage and some Connected Subjects*,[6] the Oireachtas enacted the Age of Majority Act 1985 (the "1985 Act"). The 1985 Act follows a strong international trend towards reducing the age of majority.[7] Section 2(1) provides:

> "Where a person has not attained the age of twenty-one years prior to the commencement of this Act, he shall attain full age—
> (a) on such commencement if he has attained the age of eighteen years or is or has been married, or
> (b) after such commencement when he attains the age of eighteen years, or in case he marries before attaining that age, upon his marriage."

The 1985 Act came into force on March 1, 1985. Therefore, s.2 provides that any person who was aged 18 years or was a married person on that date, or had been married before that date, attained full age on March 1, 1985. Where a person married after that date, or attained full age after March 1, 1985, then such a person will attain full age on marriage or his or her eighteenth birthday, as the case may be.[8]

16–04 While the decision to reduce the age of majority to 18 has attracted wide agreement, as the Law Reform Commission's Report pointed out, and is compatible with developments elsewhere, the decision to confer full age upon

---

[3] "Mother's greed ended dream for Charlotte", *The Times*, November 22, 2000. In a recent High Court decision the *Harry Potter* actor Devon Murray was held liable to pay unpaid fees to his former agent Neil Brooks for work done while Devon Murray was a minor. Moriarty J. obviously held the agency contract was valid, presumably as a contract for necessary services or a beneficial contract of service: see "Irish Harry Potter actor ordered to pay agent €260,000" *Irish Times*, April 8, 2016.

[4] "Child star signs £500,000 book deal", *Sunday Times*, November 26, 2000.

[5] Harland, *The Law of Minors in Relation to Contracts and Property* (Sydney: Butterworths, 1974), s.106.

[6] (1977) L.R.C. 2. In the UK see the *Report of the Committee on the Age of Majority* (Cmnd. 3342) (1969), and Law Commission Report No. 134.

[7] See generally, Hartwig (1996) 15 I.C.L.Q. 780; Hartland, *The Law of Minors in Relation to Contracts and Property* (1974) in Ch.2 examines the general position in common law jurisdictions. The law in Canada is based on the common law and various provincial statutes, each of which sets the age at either 18 or 19 years.

[8] In the UK the age of majority fell from 21 to 18 as from January 1, 1970: Family Law Reform Act 1969 s.1.

a person by virtue of marriage was described by one commentator as arguably a policy of debatable merit.[9] As this commentator points out, the policy of encouraging banks and other institutions to deal with young persons may be a laudable one but there are still difficulties of definition and it is arguable that the 1985 Act may expose immature and inexperienced young persons to legal liabilities at a time when they require more protection rather than less. The 1985 Act does not, however, alter any of the rules relating to an infant's liability in contract and it is to this (as the law stands) quite unsatisfactory area of the law of contract that we now turn.

16–05 Professor Treitel points out that the law relating to infants' contractual liability attempts to strike a balance between two conflicting objectives; first of all, the courts seek to protect an infant from the consequences of his own inexperience in commercial matters. On the other hand, the judges seek to protect commercial men who unwittingly contract with infants, particularly if the infant has misrepresented that he is of age.[10] However, the position under the Infants Relief Act 1874, and the general case law surrounding infants' contracts, is generally agreed to favour the infant unduly. While in Ireland the 1874 Act continues to present an obstacle to a rational reappraisal of the law, in the UK, the Minors Contracts Act 1987 has adjusted many of the worst features of the law, in particular providing sweeping and largely discretionary relief against a minor who has had property transferred to him on foot of a contract.[11] We will consider the 1987 Act below.

16–06 The general rule at common law is that an infant's contract is voidable; voidable in this context bears two meanings. First of all, certain contracts are valid unless repudiated by the infant. Other contracts are voidable in the sense that unless the infant affirms the transaction within a reasonable time after coming of age the transaction does not bind him. Certain contracts are valid at common law; these are contracts for necessaries and beneficial contracts of service.

Necessaries

16–07 The following statement, found in *Coke upon Littleton*, a seventeenth-century English text, is perhaps one of the most enduring propositions in the common law:

> "An infant may bind himself to pay for his necessary eat, drink, apparel, necessary physic, and such other necessaries, and likewise for his good teaching or instruction, whereby he may profit himself afterwards, but

---

[9] Commentary to the Age of Majority Act 1985, in *Irish Current Law Statutes Annotated*, at 85/2–11 (Binchy).

[10] Treitel, *The Law of Contract*, 14th edn (London: Sweet & Maxwell, 2015), paras 12–002, 12–025, and 12–033 to 12–036.

[11] Section 3(1).

if he bind himself in an obligation or other writing, with a penalty for the payment of any other, that obligation shall not bind him."

Necessaries are defined in s.2 of the 1893 Act as "goods suitable to the condition in life of such infant or minor ... and to his actual requirements at the time of the sale and delivery". Many of the old cases were decided before juries, who favoured the interests of the trader, by giving an extended meaning to necessaries. It is now the role of the judge to say first of all whether an item is capable of being classified as a necessary. Certain items are incapable of being necessaries. In *Skrine v Gordon*[12] the defendant, who represented himself to be a member of the Surrey Staghunt, agreed to buy a hunter from the plaintiff for £600. The price was never paid. Lawson J. ruled that the issue of whether this was a necessary or not should never have been left to a jury: "luxuries or amusement are quite different from necessaries". So, in the leading English case of *Ryder v Wombwell*[13] jewelled cuff-links were held incapable of being classified as necessaries. One Australian case holds that a bicycle may be a necessary if used to convey the infant to and from his place of work 11 miles away; see *Scarborough v Sturzaker*.[14] Early Canadian case law suggests that a motor car cannot be a necessary even if used for business purposes; see *Nobles v Bellefleur*.[15] However, in *First Charter Financial Bank v Musclow*[16] Craig J. found that in more recent times the access to a motor vehicle must generally be regarded as a necessary and this view must be correct, certainly if the vehicle is to be used for essential activities such as travel, whether work-related or for general domestic purposes. Whether a flashy sports model or a racing car would be caught by the argument that these are items of luxury or amusement must, however, remain an open question. Vehicles which are to be used for entrepreneurial business activities must, however, be regarded as incapable of being necessaries, for the common law does not regard trading contracts to be enforceable, even if apparently for the benefit of the infant.[17] It is clear that a heavy lorry cannot be a necessary; see *Mercantile Union v Ball*,[18] not least because of the traditional reluctance of the common law to allow an infant to enter trade, thereby running the risk of financial ruin. The necessaries test will vary depending upon the circumstances of the infant. While a motor boat may not be a necessary for most infants—see *Prokopetz v Richardsons Marina*[19]—it is conceivable that a young person supplied with such a boat in a remote lakeland region may come within the rubric of an infant supplied with necessaries. The Law Reform Commission Report[20] contains an example which

---

[12] (1875) I.R. 9 C.L. 479.
[13] (1868) L.R. 4 Ex. 32.
[14] (1905) 1 Tas. L.R. 117.
[15] (1963) 37 D.L.R. (2d.) 519.
[16] (1974) 49 D.L.R. (3d.) 138.
[17] *Cowern v Nield* [1912] 2 K.B. 419.
[18] [1937] 2 K.B. 498.
[19] (1979) 93 D.L.R. (3d.) 442; Clark, "Property Passing Under a Void Contract—Minor Difficulties" (1980) 26 McGill L.J. 110.
[20] (1985) L.R.C. 15.

readers may find enlightening. A computer supplied to a 17-year-old who uses the machine in pursuit of his studies in computer science at the university may be a necessary (after all, books supplied to students are necessaries, according to *Soon v Wilson*[21]) but the same computer, supplied to a 17-year-old who uses the machine to play computer games, will not be a necessary. Similarly, a set of encyclopaedias sold to an infant television researcher, blogger or journalist may be a necessary but, in general, would not be if supplied to an infant with a mere thirst for knowledge. Guns supplied to an infant game-keeper may, according to the case of *Dickson v Buller*,[22] be necessary goods.

16–08 If the goods can be classified as necessaries the supplier must go further and show that the infant was not adequately supplied with such goods; this will be a difficult burden to discharge. In *Nash v Inman*[23] 11 fancy waistcoats supplied to an Oxford undergraduate were held not to be necessaries, the father of the infant being able to show to the court that his son was adequately supplied with clothing. As a general rule:

> "If a man satisfies the needs of the infant or lunatic by supplying to him necessaries, the law will imply an obligation to repay him for the services so rendered, and will enforce that obligation against the estate of the infant or lunatic. The consequence is that the basis of the action is hardly contract. Its real foundation is an obligation which the law imposes on the infant to make a fair payment in respect of needs satisfied. In other words, the obligation arises *re* and not *consensu* ... the sum he recovered was based on a *quantum meruit* ... this is very ancient law, and is confirmed by the provisos of section 2 of the Sale of Goods Act 1893—an Act which was intended to codify the existing law ... the plaintiff has to shew, first, that the goods were suitable to the condition in life of the infant; and, secondly, that they were suitable to his actual requirements at the time—or, in other words, that the infant had not at the time an adequate supply from other sources."[24]

The words of s.2 of the 1893 Act indicate that an infant can only be liable for necessary goods if they have been supplied; even then, the section provides the infant is only liable to pay a "reasonable price" for such goods. A contract to purchase goods which will be used to carry on a trade are not necessaries as the English case of *Whittingham v Hill*[25] and the Nova Scotia case of *Jenkins v Way*[26] show. Contracts for necessary services are also valid. An infant widow

---

[21] (1962) 33 D.L.R. (2d.) 428. The use of the Web for information, instruction and interaction raises the question if web access is a necessary service? Is a Twitter or Facebook account a necessary service?

[22] (1859) 9 I.C.L.R. (Appendix).

[23] [1908] 2 K.B. 1.

[24] Fletcher-Moulton L.J., [1908] 1 K.B. 1 at 8, and see the same judge in *Re J* [1909] 1 Ch. 574 at 577. Contrast Buckley L.J. in *Nash v Inman* [1908] 1 K.B. 1 at 12.

[25] (1619) Cro. Jac. 494.

[26] (1881) 14 N.S.R. 394.

will be liable on a contract to obtain funeral services for her deceased husband; see *Chapple v Cooper*.[27] A contract to enable an infant to gain instruction and earn his living as a professional billiards player will be enforceable, even if partly executory in nature; see *Roberts v Gray*.[28] Legal advice which results in substantial benefits to an infant may also be a necessary service; see *Helps v Clayton*.[29]

16–09 If the service or goods provided are made available to the infant upon terms that are not universally favourable the contract may not be enforceable, even though the goods or service, viewed in isolation, are undoubtedly a necessary. In *Fawcett v Smethurst*[30] a contract for the hire of a motor vehicle was held in the circumstances to be one for necessaries but because the hire was concluded on terms which included an express term placing the responsibility for loss or damage to the vehicle on the infant hirer in all circumstances, this was held to make this particular contract unenforceable because the contract, viewed as a whole, was not advantageous to the infant.

Beneficial Contracts of Service

16–10 This category of enforceable contract has evolved relatively recently. It seems to have originated in the nineteenth century when the courts began to view contracts of apprenticeship and related transactions as enforceable at common law: contrast *Horn v Chandler*[31] with *De Francesco v Barnum*.[32] Many cases that are treated as beneficial contracts of service are difficult to disentangle from the category of necessary services. A contract of service will bind the infant if, viewed as a whole, the contract is seen as beneficial to the infant. The fact that one or more terms may be to the disadvantage of the infant will not be conclusive. In *Shears v Mendeloff*[33] an infant boxer appointed the plaintiff to be his manager. The agreement provided that the manager would get 25 per cent of the infant's earnings. The manager had not expressly covenanted to obtain fights for the plaintiff and the infant had to pay his own expenses. Avory J. in the English High Court held this contract of service not to be beneficial to the infant; it may be different if the infant receives instruction as a boxer; see the Australian case of *McLaughlin v D'Arcy*.[34] The provision of education and instruction will not be dispositive, even if no alternative source of instruction was available on improved terms.

---

27 (1844) 13 M. & W. 252.
28 [1913] 1 K.B. 520; see Mathews (1982) 33 N.I.L.Q. 148.
29 (1864) 17 C.B.(N.S.) 553.
30 [1914] 84 L.J.K.B. 473.
31 (1670) 1 Mod. 271.
32 (1890) 45 Ch. D. 430. The first edition of *Simpson on Infants* (London: Stevens and Haynes, 1875) does not contain an analysis of any such separate category.
33 [1914] 30 T.L.R. 342.
34 (1918) S.R.N.S.W. 585.

In *Toronto Marlboro Hockey Club v Tonelli*[35] a young hockey player signed a standard form contract which tied him to a junior hockey club. This method of recruitment to the lucrative world of North American ice hockey was the only established method of advancement and the terms offered were the only terms available, for all junior clubs used the same terms. There were penalty provisions and compensation clauses which obliged Tonelli to pay over a percentage of his earnings to the plaintiffs when his contract expired, should he be signed by a senior professional team. The Ontario Court of Appeal, by a majority of two to one, held Tonelli was not bound by this contract.

16–11 Management contracts involving young sports personalities and entertainers are amenable to challenge as contracts of service that are not beneficial to the interests of the young person. It appears that most contractual challenges to the enforceability of these agreements will raise a multiplicity of potential vitiating factors such as infancy, unconscionable bargain, improvidence and breach of fiduciary duty.[36] A further complicating factor is that such contracts often involve adult third parties such as parents or guardians, with the parent or guardian often providing warranties or "best endeavour" undertakings (which themselves could be legally uncertain under the doctrine of undue influence). Some of the most recent manifestations of litigation in the English courts involve interlocutory proceedings involving Lisa Stansfield[37] and the settlement of a repudiatory breach action brought by the dismissed manager of Charlotte Church.[38]

16–12 If the contract in question is incidental to the means whereby an infant earns his living it may be enforceable. In *Doyle v White City Stadium*,[39] Jack Doyle, then an infant, obtained a licence to box from the British Boxing Board of Control. The terms of the licence provided that should the licensee be disqualified in a contest his purse would be forfeited. Doyle, never the most scientific of pugilists, was disqualified for a low blow during a title fight. He challenged the rules, alleging that they could not bind him. The English Court of Appeal upheld the rules. It was generally in Doyle's interest to uphold the rules prohibiting or discouraging illegal blows, even if on this occasion the rules operated against him.[40] In *Douglas v Kinger*[41] the owner of a holiday

---

[35] (1979) 96 D.L.R. (3d.) 135. The law in some USA States permits minors' entertainment and sports contracts to be enforceable if there is court approval, e.g. in California: see *Warner Bros Pictures v Brodel* (1948) C 2d 766.

[36] "Faxed letter that fired manager", *The Times*, November 22, 2000.

[37] *Stansfield v Sovereign Music Ltd* [1994] E.M.L.R. 224.

[38] "Faxed letter that fired manager", *The Times*, November 22, 2000.

[39] [1935] 1 K.B 110.

[40] Hanworth M.R. said the rule "is applicable on both sides and cannot be looked at merely from the particular point of view of one person such as the plaintiff in this case".

[41] [2008] ONCA 452. The case was concerned mostly with a negligence action. The Ontario Court of Appeal gave a compelling argument why, as a matter of policy, *Lister* should not be followed in subrogation claims against employees, short of wilful misconduct by the employee. See LRC CP 65–2011, paras 10.65 to 10.101.

cottage hired a local 13-year-old boy to carry out routine chores around the property. The boy accidentally caused a fire, damaging the property. Using the principle in *Lister v Romford Ice and Cold Storage Co Ltd*,[42] the insurance company that had settled a claim brought by the property owner, sought, via subrogation, to recover against the boy for breach of contract vis-à-vis his employment contract with the property owner. The Ontario Court of Appeal considered that as the contract as a whole was not for the benefit of the minor, it was not binding on him.

16–13 The most significant examination of this category of potentially enforceable contract is the decision of the Court of Appeal in *Chaplin v Leslie Frewin (Publishers) Ltd*.[43] The plaintiff, a son of Charlie Chaplin, had fallen out with his father and, while marrying during his infancy, was dependent solely upon national assistance payments for the support of himself and his wife. He entered into an agreement with the defendants whereby the defendants would publish a ghost-written autobiography of the plaintiff in which the plaintiff would make revelations about his famous father and his family life. The plaintiff was paid a substantial advance and he co-operated with the writers. After the book was written it proved to be a most unflattering work about the Chaplin family, and the plaintiff, prior to publication, sought to have the publishing contract, including an assignment of copyright, declared unenforceable as being a contract of service which was not to his benefit because it was potentially libellous. The Court of Appeal held that the contract was to be viewed as akin to a beneficial contract of service and that the general test of substantial benefit could be satisfied. The royalties payable and the advance already made, in the view of the majority of the Court of Appeal,[44] outweighed the negative aspects of the agreement, namely the potential for litigation it created and the adverse publicity that would attach: as one judge observed, "the mud may cling but the profits will be secured".[45] The contract enabled the plaintiff to make a start in the world of journalism and it mattered not that the work was scurrilous and lacked literary merit. The English cases suggest that beneficial contracts of service, as a category of contract that may be enforceable against an infant, must be capable of being viewed as analogous to a contract of apprenticeship, education or employment. Although the case was one in which summary judgment was being sought, *Proform Sports Management Ltd v Proactive Sports Management Ltd*[46] is the most recent case in which the boundaries of such a category were

---

[42] [1957] A.C. 555.

[43] [1966] Ch. 71.

[44] Denning M.R. at 88 dissented:

> "I cannot think that a contract is for the benefit of a young man if it is to be a means of purveying scandalous information. Certainly not if it brings shame and disgrace on others; invades the privacy of family life; and exposes him to claims of libel … it would be better for him to take his mother's advice: 'Get a job and go to work.'."

[45] Per Danckwerts L.J. at 95.

[46] [2007] 1 All E.R. 542. Rooney became embroiled in litigation with Proactive Sports in later years: see *Proactive Sports Management v Rooney* [2011] EWCA Civ 1444.

tested. While aged just over 15 years of age, Wayne Rooney entered into a management contract for a two-year period with Proform. He was already contracted with Everton Football Club who provided him with instruction and training as well as playing opportunities. Within six months of expiry of that management contract the defendant, Proactive, secured Rooney's agreement to a management contract, with immediate effect. Proactive defended this case on the basis that the Rooney/Proform contract was a trading contract and was thus void, and that, even if they were wrong on this point, the contract was not beneficial to Rooney. Following *Shears v Mendeloff*,[47] and an observation in *Chitty on Contracts*[48] that "a minor's trading contracts are not binding on him, even if beneficial",[49] Judge Hodge Q.C. said that this contract did not fall within the categories of apprenticeship, education or employment, nor was it a contract that allowed the infant to earn his living. The judge observed that all these "benefits" enured to Rooney under his contract with Everton Football Club. The management contract did not necessarily secure for Rooney any benefits over and above those already provided by his club. Judge Hodge Q.C. was clearly persuaded that under Football Association rules, Rooney was bound to his club on schoolboy forms and those rules prevented Rooney from concluding a full contract of employment until he was 17 years of age, and that any such contract would be voidable at Rooney's election. The judge was not going to allow Proactive to side-step centuries of case law designed to protect the vulnerable (when Rooney signed the contract with his parents' consent at the age of 15 no independent legal advice was given). Having found that the contract was not analogous to that in *Doyle v White City Stadium*[50] it was unnecessary for Judge Hodge Q.C. to rule on whether, viewed as a whole, it was for the benefit of the infant.[51]

16–14 In *Keays v Great Southern Railway*[52] the plaintiff, a child of 12, held a season ticket, issued at a reduced rate, which exempted the defendants from liability for injuries caused by their negligence. The season ticket was purchased to enable the plaintiff to travel to and from school. The plaintiff was injured while travelling on the defendants' line, the injuries being the result of negligence. Hanna J., after construing the contract as a whole, ruled that the terms of the contract were so harsh as to entitle the infant to repudiate it:

> "The contract in this case is very unfair to the infant because it deprives her of practically every common law right that she has against the

---

[47] (1914) 30 T.L.R. 342.
[48] 29th edn (London: Thomson Sweet & Maxwell, 2004), para.8–028.
[49] On the disadvantageous nature of image rights contracts see *Proactive Sports Management v Rooney* [2011] EWCA Civ 1444.
[50] [1935] 1 K.B. 110.
[51] The court did not have to rule on the status of the schoolboy forms agreement. It should be noted that the Football Association fined Paul Stretford, the person behind Proactive, some £300,000 and suspended him for 18 months for a number of irregularities, including procuring his agency agreement with Wayne Rooney.
[52] [1941] I.R. 534: contrast *Clements v London and North Western Railway* [1894] 2 Q.B. 482.

railway company in respect of the negligence of themselves or their servants. For that reason, I think it is not for her benefit."

Even a contract entered into by an infant which does not as such enable the infant to obtain schooling, instruction or a living may fall into this category. In *Harnedy v National Greyhound Racing Association*[53] an exemption clause which purported to prevent an infant greyhound owner from suing in respect of injuries to the dog was held not to be beneficial and could be repudiated.

Voidable Contracts

16–15 The common law courts recognised that contracts in which an infant was capable of being subjected to a series of recurring obligations were voidable in the sense that the infant was bound unless he repudiated the contract within a reasonable time.[54] These contracts fall into five distinct categories.

16–16 (i) There is Irish support for the proposition that an insurance contract which involves a periodic obligation to pay premiums is a voidable contract; see *Stapleton v Prudential Assurance*.[55] If the premium has been paid and the risk has begun to run, the infant cannot repudiate the contract and obtain the return of premiums paid.[56] If the contract is void, for infringing the Life Assurance Act 1774, for example, premiums will be repayable.[57]

16–17 (ii) An infant is also liable on contracts to take shares or to meet "calls" made upon shareholders. This obligation was explained by Parke B. in the leading English case of *North Western Railway Co v McMichael*[58] as turning upon the fact that the infant acquires an interest in something of a permanent nature rather than a mere chattel. The exception may implicitly rest on the need to facilitate the development of joint stock companies in general and railways in particular. *McMichael's* case was followed in *Midland Railway v Quinn*.[59] If the infant is to avoid liability he must show and plead that he repudiated the contract within his infancy or a reasonable time thereafter; *Dublin and Wicklow Railway Co v Black*.[60] An action to recover money paid by the infant on foot of such an obligation will fail unless the infant can show a total failure of consideration; see *Steinberg v Scala (Leeds) Ltd*,[61] followed in *Stapleton's* case.

---

[53] [1944] I.R. 160.
[54] *Carter v Silber* [1892] 2 Ch. 278, affirmed at [1893] A.C. 360.
[55] (1928) 62 I.L.T.R. 56.
[56] (1928) 62 I.L.T.R. 56; see also *Ritchie v Salvation Army Assurance* [1930] I.A.C. Rep. 20.
[57] *Gardner v Hearts of Oak Assurance* [1928] I.A.C. Rep. 20.
[58] (1850) 5 Ex. 114.
[59] (1851) 1 I.C.L.R. 383.
[60] (1852) 8 Exch. 181.
[61] [1923] 2 Ch. 452.

16–18 (iii) An infant who agrees to enter a partnership will be bound by that contract unless he repudiates openly within a reasonable time; *Griffiths v Delaney*,[62] however, establishes that the supplier of goods delivered to the partnership cannot recover the price from an infant partner. Should an infant partner sue other partners for specific performance the action will fail for want of mutuality—the courts do not award specific performance against an infant. The infant will be able to sue should he affirm the partnership agreement upon coming of age; see *Shannon v Bradstreet*.[63]

16–19 (iv) Family settlements and those made by an infant in contemplation of marriage may be avoided within a reasonable time after coming of age. Indeed, in *Paget v Paget*[64] the plaintiff agreed with his father upon the terms of a resettlement of family property. At the time of the transaction the plaintiff, unknown to himself, was only 20 years of age. Ten years later he learnt that he was an infant at the date of execution of the settlement and repudiated immediately. He was held to have done so in time. Any delay after learning the true facts would have been fatal to the right to repudiate; see *Allen v Allen*.[65] Contrast the position where an infant spouse signs a consent form permitting the other spouse to sell the family home; under s.10(1) of the Family Law Act 1981, the consent is not voidable on the grounds of infancy alone.

16–20 (v) A lease taken by an infant is voidable. If the infant repudiates within a reasonable time after coming of age he will not be liable to pay rent due in the future. The case of *Blake v Concannon*[66] is authority for the view that if the infant has used and enjoyed the property before repudiation he will be liable to pay for the use and enjoyment of the demised property; the desire to prevent unjust enrichment of the infant is evident in *Mahon v Farrell*[67] which supports the view that an infant assignee is liable in similar circumstances. However, the view advanced in *Blake v Concannon* has not been accepted in other jurisdictions and, in particular, Jessel M.R. declined to accept it in one English case.[68] The view that is advanced in the leading English case of *North Western Railway Co v McMichael*[69] is contradictory. Parke B. indicated that the rule applicable in cases where an infant waives or repudiates the permanent interest is that the interest is at an end, as is any liability due upon it, even though avoidance of the contract may not have taken place before liability accrued. In the present writer's view, the Irish rule is preferable, at least when use and enjoyment of property has

---

[62] (1938) 4 Ir. Jur. Rep. 1.
[63] (1803) 1 Sch. & Lef. 64; *Milliken v Milliken* (1845) 8 Ir.Eq.R. 16.
[64] (1882) 11 L.R. (Ir.) 26.
[65] (1842) 2 Dr. & War. 307.
[66] (1870) I.R. 4 C.L. 323.
[67] (1847) 10 I.L.R. 527.
[68] *Re Jones* (1881) 18 Ch. D. 109 at 118.
[69] (1850) 5 Ex. 114.

occurred. *Cheshire, Fifoot and Furmston's Law of Contract*,[70] however, favours the view of Parke B. There are decisions the other way. In *Kelly v Coote*[71] a lease which devolved to an infant by operation of law was held to make an infant liable to pay rent even though the infant tenant had not moved into possession.

16–21 There are other kinds of contract which have been described as voidable contracts. In these contracts the transaction is not binding until it is affirmed. Most of the cases involve transactions which were not within the category of necessary goods and services and, for all practical purposes, this category of voidable contract did not survive the Infants Relief Act 1874 (the "1874 Act").

Infants Relief Act 1874

16–22 This statute, still in force in Northern Ireland and the Irish Republic, is a controversial piece of legislation; Treitel calls it: "a somewhat mysterious statute. No convincing reason has ever been advanced to explain exactly why it was passed".[72] One may add that few convincing observations have been advanced to conclusively show what it achieves.

Section 1

16–23

> All contracts, whether by specialty or by simple contract, henceforth entered into by infants for the repayment of money lent or to be lent, or for goods supplied or to be supplied (other than contracts for necessaries), and all accounts stated with infants shall be absolutely void …

Section 1 goes on to except contracts valid under statute and contracts valid at common law or in equity.

16–24 Several points must be made about s.1.

16–25 (i) Contracts in which money is lent to an infant and in which goods are supplied to an infant are rendered "absolutely void" by this section; cases in which the infant supplies goods or lends money are outside the section. It has been argued by Treitel[73] that the exception in favour of contracts for necessaries includes money-lending contracts in which the infant borrows money in order to purchase necessaries. In *Bateman v Kingston*[74] the

---

[70]   16th edn (Oxford: OUP, 2012).
[71]   (1856) 5 I.R.C.L. 469; *Slator v Brady* (1863) 14 I.C.L.R. 61.
[72]   (1957) 73 L.Q.R. 194.
[73]   (1957) 73 L.Q.R. 194 at 198–199.
[74]   (1880) 6 L.R. (Ir.) 328.

plaintiff sued upon a promissory note given by the defendant; the money lent upon the note was used to purchase necessaries. Lawson J. refused to allow an action on the notes *which bore interest*. It was suggested by Lawson J. that if notes were given to a trader in return for necessaries an action on the note may lie in such a case. The view that s.1 validates a loan to purchase necessaries seems inconsistent with *Bateman v Kingston* and Treitel has since withdrawn this argument.

16–26 (ii) It is doubtful whether an infant can sue upon such a contract. Although the common law rule was otherwise, the wording of s.1 on this point—"absolutely void"—seems to be irrefragable. English textbook writers, however, tend to favour the view that an infant can sue on the "absolutely void" contract.

16–27 (iii) The orthodox view is that an infant cannot recover property transferred under an "absolutely void" contract. In order to recover the infant must show that there has been a total failure of consideration. In *Pearce v Brain*[75] the infant plaintiff exchanged a motorcycle for a motor car. The car broke down four days later. The plaintiff sought to recover his motorcycle. The action failed; the plaintiff had used the car and was thus unable to show a total failure of consideration.

16–28 (iv) A mortgage given in respect of property partly owned by an infant[76] and the infant's parents will be binding on the infant's parents and may bind the infant, even if "absolutely void" under statute. In *Horvath v Commonwealth Bank of Australia*,[77] money was advanced to co-owners on foot of a mortgage, one of them being an infant, the bank manager failing to advert to the issue of the age of the plaintiff, who then claimed the mortgage was "absolutely void" as against him under the Victorian equivalent of s.1. Phillips J.A., obiter, remarked that the legislation did not invalidate the security, particularly in cases of co-ownership involving adults, but the Court of Appeal for the State of Victoria held, applying *Nottingham Permanent Benefit Building Society v Thurstan*,[78] that because the monies advanced had been applied to pay the purchase price owed by the infant to the vendor, the lender, via subrogation, could obtain such lien as the vendor was entitled to assert against the infant purchaser.

16–29 (v) The English case of *Stocks v Wilson*[79] is authority for the proposition that property will pass under an "absolutely void" contract. The Supreme Court of British Columbia, on the other hand, has ruled that property will

---

[75] [1929] 2 K.B. 310; *Valentini v Canali* (1889) 24 Q.B.D. 166.
[76] Under the Settled Land Acts a trustee of infant's property may be appointed; see *Re Locke* (1913) 47 I.L.T.R. 147; Land and Conveyancing Law Reform Act 2009 s.18(1)(c).
[77] [1999] 1 V.R. 643.
[78] [1903] A.C. 6; *Orakpo v Manson Investments Ltd* [1978] A.C. 95.
[79] [1913] 2 K.B. 235.

not pass under an "absolutely void" contract to an infant buyer unless the infant has paid the purchase price; see *Prokopetz v Richardson's Marina*.[80] The English view, because it protects innocent purchasers from an infant, is to be preferred.

16–30 (vi) A guarantee of a loan made to an infant, which is "absolutely void", is itself unable to create a liability for an adult guarantor, according to the English case of *Coutts & Co v Brown-Lecky*.[81] This decision has not escaped criticism and in the British Columbia case of *First Charter Financial Bank v Musclow*[82] Craig J. thought the decision to be wrong. The 1874 Act was designed to protect infants and it is difficult to see why an adult should be able to avoid a guarantee simply because the principal debtor can plead the 1874 Act as a defence. In fact the injustice of the decision in *Coutts & Co v Browne-Lecky* has been recognised by the UK Parliament. Section 2 of the Minors Contracts Act 1987 now provides that where a guarantee is given in respect of another's obligation under a contract, and the obligation is unenforceable by virtue of the minority of the contracting party, "the guarantee shall not for that reason alone be unenforceable against the guarantor".

16–31 (vii) In cases where an infant trader acquires goods, those goods are not classifiable as necessaries. It appears from the Irish case of *Re Rainey*[83] that the infant cannot be adjudicated a bankrupt in respect of non-necessary goods caught by s.1 of the 1874 Act, even if the infant has suppressed the fact of infancy in order to induce others to contract with him.

Section 2

16–32 This obscure section provides:

> No action shall be brought whereby to charge any person upon any promise made after full age to pay any debt contracted during infancy, or upon any ratification made after full age of any promise or contract made during infancy, whether there shall or shall not be any new consideration for such promise or ratification after full age.

Most of the reported cases deal with persons who contract to marry whilst an infant, and who make a new contract, not merely a ratification of the old, upon coming of age.[84] Section 2 has been considered in the Irish case of *Belfast Banking Co v Doherty*.[85] Doherty was sued upon a bill of exchange drawn by Wilson in consideration for a loan made to Doherty while Doherty was an

---

[80] (1979) 93 D.L.R. (3d.) 442; Clark (1980) 26 McGill L.J. 110.
[81] [1947] K.B. 104.
[82] (1974) 49 D.L.R. (3d.) 138.
[83] (1878) 3 L.R. (Ir.) 459.
[84] *Coxhead v Mullis* (1878) 3 C.P.D. 439; *Northcote v Doughty* (1879) 4 C.P.D. 385; *Ditcham v Worrall* (1880) 5 C.P.D. 410.
[85] (1879) 4 L.R. (Ir.) 124.

infant. Doherty accepted the bill of exchange when he attained his majority. Wilson indorsed the bill of exchange to the plaintiffs who took without knowledge of the circumstances surrounding acceptance by Doherty. The Queen's Bench Division held that while s.2 would have prevented Wilson from recovering upon a promise to pay for a debt contracted during infancy, it was not to be extended so as to prejudice a bona fide holder for value. The decision in *Belfast Banking Co v Doherty* is not, however, of any great significance following the enactment of s.5 of the Betting and Loans (Infants) Act 1892. This section declares that a fresh promise given after the coming of age to pay a loan contracted during infancy, that loan being void at law, and any negotiable instrument given in respect of such a loan, is to be void as against all persons. So, while the *Belfast Banking* case would still be effective in relation to an adult acceptor of a bill of exchange in respect of necessaries supplied to the acceptor while still an infant, the case would be decided differently today.

Miscellaneous

(i) An infant's liability in tort

16–33 It was held in *O'Brien v McNamee*[86] that an infant over the age of seven may be liable in tort so long as the tort in question (a) does not require malice to be shown; and (b) does not arise out of a breach of contract. As we have seen, many incidents can produce liability in tort as well as contract.[87]

16–34 The test developed to distinguish viable tort actions against an infant from those that are too closely linked to contract has been summarised by Pollock; the minor:

> "... cannot be sued for a wrong, when the cause of action is in substance *ex contractu*, or is so directly connected with the contract that the action would be an indirect way of enforcing the contract [but if the act is] independent of the contract in the sense of not being an act of the kind contemplated by it, then the infant is liable."[88]

The test is artificial in the extreme. The cases of *Jennings v Rundall*[89] and *Burnard v Haggis*,[90] discussed in the leading English texts, illustrate this point. One obvious way in which an infant might be held liable in tort, where he has fraudulently misrepresented his age or creditworthiness, for example, would be to sue in deceit. It was held in the Irish case of *Bird v Wilson*[91] that an infant does not "misrepresent" that she is of age simply by signing a contract.

---

[86] [1953] I.R. 86.
[87] See Ch.11.
[88] *Pollock's Principles of Contracts*, 12th edn (London: Stevens, 1946), p.63.
[89] (1799) 8 Term Rep. 335. On the liability of adults for minors' torts, see Law Reform Commission Report No. 17 (1986).
[90] (1863) 14 C.B.N.S. 45; *Ballet v Mingay* [1943] K.B. 281.
[91] (1851) 4 Ir. Jur. Rep. 58.

16–35 Even if an infant positively asserts that he is of age, thereby inducing an adult to contract with him, the decision in *R. Leslie v Sheill*[92] suggests that, because the statement is directly linked to the contract, no liability in deceit can arise. Irish case law, such as it is, suggests that the same rule will apply. In *Bateman v Kingston*[93] the plaintiff pleaded that he had taken promissory notes from an infant, the infant fraudulently misrepresenting that he was of age. Lawson J., following the English case of *Bartlett v Wells*,[94] held that the infant could not be liable in deceit. The only Irish authority the other way is a dictum of Crompton J. in *McNamara v Browne*[95] where it was observed that an infant who gave a bond after holding himself out as of age may be liable on the bond.

16–36 If the infant retains property transferred the court will order restitution; see *R. Leslie v Sheill*, above. However, if the infant does not retain the property but has, for example, sold the property and merely has in his possession the proceeds of sale, then restitution is not possible on the ground that restitution stops where repayment begins.[96] Nor can the infant be ordered to make restitution in respect of the value of goods consumed. In the UK s.3(1) of the Minors Contracts Act 1987 confers a broad discretion upon the courts, in cases where a contract is unenforceable by virtue of the minority of one party, when just and equitable to do so, to require the minor to transfer to the other party property acquired under the contract, or any property representing it. This power stops short of ordering the infant to pay compensation out of funds that have not been obtained by selling property transferred to the infant under the contract, for example, but it marks a significant expansion of proprietary relief in order to counteract unjust enrichment.

(ii) An infant's liability in quasi-contract

16–37 An action brought for the recovery of money paid or property transferred to an infant will be successful if the infant retains possession of the banknotes or chattel, even if property in the goods has passed to the infant. In cases like this there can be no question of the infant being forced to perform a contract; all the adult seeks is a limited restitutionary remedy. The cause of action, however, is, in substance, contractual.

16–38 In *Stocks v Wilson*,[97] Lush J. suggested that if the infant has obtained property by way of fraud then equity will require the infant to account for the proceeds should he part with the goods. This observation was rejected by the

---

92 [1914] 3 K.B. 607.
93 (1880) 6 L.R. (Ir.) 328.
94 (1862) 1 B. & S. 836.
95 (1843) 5 I.L.R. 460.
96 (1843) 5 I.L.R. 460 per Lord Sumner. The case of *Stocks v Wilson* [1913] 2 K.B. 235 indicates that proceeds of sale may be disgorged from the infant but this decision is out of step with established authority.
97 [1913] 2 K.B. 235.

Court of Appeal in *R. Leslie v Sheill*[98] a year later. *R. Leslie v Sheill* has been followed in other jurisdictions but the matter has still to be ruled upon by an Irish court. It is suggested that a fraudulent infant should be liable to account in such situations. There is an Australian case in point. In *Campbell v Ridgely*[99] an infant fraudulently misrepresented that he was of age, thereby inducing the plaintiff to do work for him and also supply building materials. The plaintiff sued claiming (a) the value of the materials, £382; or, in the alternative (b) return of so much of the materials still in the infant's possession; and (c) an inquiry into the value of the goods not in possession. The defendant challenged ground three as an impermissible basis of relief. Although the later case of *R. Leslie v Sheill* would suggest the defendant's challenge should have succeeded, the Supreme Court of Victoria rejected the view that an account for the value of property fraudulently obtained and disposed of cannot be ordered against an infant.

16–39 It is hoped that this wider view of equitable restitution prevails in Ireland.[100]

(iii) Estoppel

16–40 Fraud by an infant will not operate an estoppel; see *Levene v Brougham*.[101]

(iv) Inducing a breach of contract

16–41 In an action for inducement of breach of contract it has recently been held that if a contract with an infant is voidable at the option of the infant, persuading the infant to exercise that option does not come within that tort because the infant does not commit a wrong by exercising that right: *Proform Sports Management Ltd v Proactive Sports Management Ltd*.[102]

Infants—Suggestions for Reform

16–42 The law relating to an infant's liability in contract and tort is generally recognised as being fraught with anachronistic and extremely irrational distinctions, distinctions which at times seem to ignore the underlying policy objective of preventing young persons from being exposed to liabilities that may unduly prejudice them—witness *Coutts & Co v Brown-Lecky*, above. Indeed, it is certainly arguable that the law is so complex that reforms

---

[98] [1914] 3 K.B. 607.
[99] (1887) 13 V.L.R. 701.
[100] *Peters v Tuck* [1915] 11 Tas. S.R. 30 suggests that an infant can be ordered to pay the value of banknotes bailed with him.
[101] (1909) 25 T.L.R. 265.
[102] [2007] 1 All E.R. 542, following Slade J.'s dictum in *Greig v Insole* [1978] 3 All E.R. 449 at 486.

may necessitate the complete repeal of all statutes which attempt to grant immunities from suit to infants. Protection from improvident, unconscionable or unfair transactions is available from the courts on equitable grounds, and, so this argument runs, with a modern expansion of the unconscionable bargain jurisdiction it may be that specific rules on infants' contracts are unnecessary and that the power of a court to protect young persons from unconscionable or oppressive bargains may produce more satisfactory solutions. In the Ontario case of *Toronto Marlboro Hockey Club v Tonelli*[103] the majority of the Ontario Court of Appeal, using *Schroeder v Macauley*,[104] decided an infant's contract dispute on unconscionability grounds. In fact readers should note that two old Irish cases, *Aylward v Kearney*[105] and *Dawson v Massey*,[106] suggest that equity will protect young (not necessarily infant) persons from oppressive bargains. While this argument in favour of total repeal may at first sight seem an attractive one, it has not found favour with any of the law reform agencies, nor has it provided the basis for legislation. The Irish Law Reform Commission's *Report on Minors' Contracts*[107] considered this course of action undesirable, primarily because it was likely to lead to considerable uncertainty in the law until the courts developed a coherent set of principles in relation to such contracts. After an expansive review of solutions enacted or proposed in several jurisdictions the Law Reform Commission recommended that legislation should seek to implement a policy "of qualified enforceability, which seeks to impose contractual responsibility on minors to the extent that it would be fair to do so, but no further". The Law Reform Commission proposed that legislation should introduce a general principle of restitution whereby a contract made by a minor with an adult party would be enforceable by the minor against the adult, but unenforceable by the adult against the minor. The parties would be entitled to apply to the court for compensation based on restitutionary rather than contractual principles. Restitution is to be interpreted widely, and, while the main objective is to reform the existing law which generally precludes an adult from recovering property or receiving compensation, it is also the intention of the Law Reform Commission to enable infants to obtain restitutionary relief in circumstances in which the law currently denies the infant a remedy—see *Stapleton v Prudential Assurance*.[108] The legislation should, in the Commission's view, include a power to grant to any party such relief by way of compensation or restitution as is proper, and upon doing so, to discharge the parties from further obligations specified by the contract if the court considers it proper to do so. The Report specifies that in making such orders the court should have regard to:

(a) the subject-matter and nature of the contract;

---

[103] (1979) 96 D.L.R. (3d.) 135.
[104] [1974] 1 W.L.R 1308.
[105] (1814) 2 Ball & B. 463.
[106] (1809) 1 Ball & B. 219.
[107] LRC 15–1985.
[108] (1928) 62 I.L.T.R. 56.

(b) the nature and value of property involved in the transaction;

(c) age, mental capacity and experience of the minor, when contracting, and at the time of the hearing;

(d) experience and knowledge of the minor relative to the contract;

(e) relative economic circumstances of the parties, at the time of contract and hearing;

(f) circumstances surrounding the transaction and the reasonableness or fairness of the bargain;

(g) value of actual benefits obtained under the contract;

(h) the amount of any benefit retained at the date of the hearing;

(i) the expenses or losses sustained or likely to be sustained; and

(j) all other relevant circumstances.

The Commission, in the Report, went on to recommend the abolition of the concept of necessaries because it was felt that the concept is a difficult one that is not easily or readily understood or justifiable. The restitutionary principle, in the view of the Law Reform Commission, is able to accommodate transactions involving necessaries, but the Report recommended that specific reference be made in the legislation to whether the goods or services were suitable to the condition in life and actual needs of the minor, so that the courts can take account of such factors when determining an appropriate compensatory or restitutionary award.

16–43 The Report also set out a series of specific recommendations. The Law Reform Commission recommended that no action upon any debt contracted during infancy should be possible—even if a new promise "to pay" the debt is made when of full age—and the same rule should apply vis-à-vis loans made to infants even for necessaries. Ratification of undertakings made during infancy, however, should be possible if the infant comes of age. A validation procedure should be available which would enable a court to approve contracts entered into by minors upon an application by any party to the contract—but not the parents of the minor—if the court thinks it correct to do so. Factors the court should have particular regard to are:

(a) the age of the minor;

(b) the nature, subject-matter and terms of the contract;

(c) the reasonable likelihood of performance by each party;

(d) the requirements of the minor;

(e) the financial resources of the minor; and

(f) the wishes of the guardians of the minor.

This validation procedure would probably be used by young entertainers—rock musicians, sports stars and the like—and must be seen in context; the Law Reform Commission recommended that employment contracts should bind infants if for their benefit. It would be anomalous if this closely related kind of transaction could not bind the infant in any circumstances. The Report also suggested legislation to clarify the existing law in relation to certain matters. Property should pass when the infant seller of goods or property transfers such property to the adult, even if the adult is aware of the infancy of the seller (subject to the restitutionary principle vis-à-vis the infant seller and the immediate purchaser). The restitutionary principle should apply to cases of misrepresentation as to full age but the existing law in relation to tort liability should remain. The Law Reform Commission also favoured the view that an adult guarantor should not be able to avoid liability simply upon proof that the infant principal debtor was a minor.

16–44 While one may quibble with one or two of the recommendations—total abolition of the concept of the contract for necessaries, for example—the Report of the Law Reform Commission represents an admirable and balanced attempt to remedy some of the worst inequities that arise in the entire law of contracts and the general thrust of the Report—the restitutionary principle—is a coherent basis for reforming legislation.

Convicted Persons

16–45 Section 8 of the Forfeiture Act 1870 rendered a convict incapable of making any contract, express or implied.[109] The Law Reform Commission, in 1989, recommended the abolition of this provision on the basis that it caused difficulties for prison inmates in disposing of property unrelated to crime.[110] Schedule 3 to the Criminal Law Act 1997 repealed the entire Act. This is in line with a more enlightened set of legislative measures that reflect human rights values.[111]

Mental Incapacity

16–46 The modern authorities in England favour the view that a contract entered into by someone who is insane is voidable. Such a person has contractual capacity and may be bound by a contract unless he was known to be insane by the other party, who, accordingly, took advantage of the other's infirmity. This rule, requiring knowledge of insanity, can be traced to the old

---

[109] *O'Connor v Coleman* (1947) 81 I.L.T.R. 42.
[110] LRC Report 30–1989.
[111] e.g. the Electoral (Amendment) Act 2006; see in general Whelan, *Mental Health Law and Practice* (Dublin: Round Hall, 2009).

common law cases. There is, however, authority for the view that a contract entered into by a person who, unknown to the other, was insane at that time, will be invalid in equity. The insane person must show that, at the time, he was so insane as to be incapable of understanding the contract. The Australian case of *Gibbons v Wright*[112] and the British Columbia case of *Moore v Confederation Life Association*[113] are in point.

16–47 The first approach, adopted by the English common law courts in the latter part of the nineteenth century, is at first sight irrational; how can a person consent to a bargain when it is established by the evidence that the transaction was not understood by that mentally ill person? The answer lies not so much in the rejection of the consensus theory, but in the need for commercial certainty. Bargains fully performed would be liable to be subsequently overturned in circumstances where persons dealing with the mentally disturbed could not be expected to know of that other's illness and inability to consent. In fact the view that an executed contract cannot be overturned on the ground that one party was so insane as to be incapable of understanding what was being done was later, in *Imperial Loan Co v Stone*,[114] extended to all transactions, executed or executory, although the inconvenience that would result if the contract was declared void (in this writer's view) does not justify the extension effected by *Imperial Loan Co v Stone*.[115]

16–48 It is, however, clear that *Imperial Loan Co v Stone* simply sets out the modern common law approach to pleas of mental incompetency and that the cases of *Gibbons v Wright* and *Moore v Confederation Life Association* are representative of a more venerable common law and equitable doctrine. Those cases establish that it does not follow that the *Imperial Loan Co* case—even though it was decided by the Court of Appeal after the Union of Judicature Acts—delimits the situations in which a transaction involving a mentally unsound person will be overturned. The decision of the Privy Council in *Hart v O'Connor*[116] recognises that all transactions struck with a person who, by virtue of mental illness, is unable to understand and thus consent to the transaction, will have to be tested by reference to unconscionability, in addition to *Imperial Loan Co*. Therefore, there now exist alternative grounds for relief. However, the Privy Council has adopted criteria that indicate that before the bargain can be overturned it must be unfair in two senses. There must be procedural unfairness—sharp practice, victimisation, pressure and the like—as well as substantive unfairness or "contractual imbalance" as Lord Brightman described it. Their Lordships all agreed with Lord Brightman that

---

[112] (1953) 91 C.L.R. 423.

[113] (1918) 25 B.C.R. 465.

[114] [1892] 1 Q.B. 559. See also *Dunhill v Bergin* [2014] UKSC 18 and *Josife v Summertrot Holdings Ltd* [2014] EWHC 996.

[115] For a more considered view of the law, see the present writer's work, *Inequality of Bargaining Power* (Toronto: Carswell, 1987), pp.111–142.

[116] [1985] 3 W.L.R. 214.

"equity will not relieve a party from a contract on the ground that there is contractual imbalance not amounting to unconscionable dealing". So, when old Mr O'Connor, being of unsound mind, sold trust property at undervalue, on unusual terms, without fully independent advice, the sale was not to be subsequently overturned because the buyer was unaware of Mr O'Connor's condition and the buyer had not acted in any way unfairly. The Privy Council overruled *Archer v Cutter*[117] and the decision of the New Zealand Court of Appeal, below, in *O'Connor v Hart*[118] on the ground that the wider view—that a contract to buy property from a mental incompetent can be overturned because the price is a substantial undervalue—is not truly representative of equitable practice.

16–49 In Ireland there is authority for the wider view that did not prevail in *O'Connor v Hart*. In *Hassard v Smith*[119] an action to set aside a lease on the ground that the lessor was of unsound mind failed. While it was clear that the lessee believed the lessor to be of sound mind, Chatterton V.-C. declared that for a contract with a person in the condition of the plaintiff to be upheld in equity the defendant lessee must show it was "fair and bona fide"; more importantly, Chatterton V.-C. accepted that the disparity between price paid and market value may itself provide proof that the transaction was not honest, that the buyer may know that the price is so unrealistic that the purchase is not a fair exchange and that the seller has been victimised.

16–50 This wider protective approach—it is akin to protection from improvident bargains—represents a reasonable compromise between promoting commercial certainty and general contractual principles, and it is to be hoped that the "fair and bona fide" test is not subjected to the same interpretation in Ireland as it was in *Hart v O'Connor*. The Irish courts have gone further than the English courts in holding that persons of diminished intellectual capacity are to be protected from entering into improvident bargains even if there is no proof of unfair dealing by the other; see *Grealish v Murphy*[120] and *Rooney v Conway*.[121]

16–51 Where goods or services have been supplied to a person who lacks capacity to enter into such a contract the Assisted Decision-Making (Capacity) Act 2015 provides in s.137 that payment of a reasonable sum must be made by that person when the goods or services have been provided at his or her request. The goods or services must have been suitable for the condition in life and actual requirements of that person at the time of supply.[122]

---

[117] [1980] 1 N.Z.L.R. 386.
[118] [1983] 1 N.Z.L.R. 280; Hudson [1984] Conv. 32.
[119] (1872) I.R. 6 Eq. 429.
[120] [1946] I.R. 35. See generally, Ch.13 above.
[121] Unreported, N.I. High Court, March 8, 1982.
[122] Section 2 of the Sale of Goods Act 1893 is amended to delete the reference to "mental incapacity" in s.2. The 2015 Act has not been commenced (July 2016).

Drunkards

16–52 Contracts struck with persons who are so drunk as to be incapable of understanding the bargain are voidable. It is also said that the other, sober party must be shown to have known of this condition. It is likely that this will be far easier to prove than in cases of insanity. In *Kurth v McGavin*,[123] a recent New Zealand case, Priestley J. observed that, while drunkenness which deprives a party of all powers of reason may be void, in practice the courts tend to hold such contracts to be voidable. Priestley J. found that a vendor who subsisted in a state of habitual drunkenness and who was so drunk at the time of agreeing to sell land that he lacked "business sense", could not avoid the contract because this condition was not known to the other contracting party. Specific performance was refused but the purchaser was held entitled to damages. However, in cases where the contract is negotiated in writing, or possibly at an auction,[124] there is the prospect of more difficult issues presenting themselves; should the contract not be promptly repudiated when sobriety returns, the contract will be binding.[125] If the degree of intoxication falls short of the required standard the contract will also be viewed as potentially unconscionable according to the case of *White v McCooey*.[126] A drunkard, like an infant and a person who lacks capacity due to intellectual disability, is bound to pay a reasonable price for necessaries supplied: see s.2 of the 1893 Act.[127]

Married Women

16–53 The Married Women's Status Act 1957 swept away in the Republic the rules and concepts that conferred upon married women limited contractual and property rights. Section 2(1) declares that the capacity of a woman to contract is unchanged upon marriage. The Act does give a married woman additional advantages in terms of extended contractual capacity.[128]

Legislative Changes—The Assisted Decision-Making (Capacity) Act 2015

16–54 In historical terms the ability of persons to manage their own affairs has been inextricably linked to the concept of legal capacity. We each have

---

[123] [2007] 3 N.Z.L.R. 614. See generally *Chitty on Contracts*, edited by H.G. Beale, 32nd edn (London: Sweet & Maxwell, 2015) paras 9-105 to 9-106.

[124] *Hawkins v Bone* (1865) 4 F. & F. 311.

[125] *Nagle v Baylor* (1842) 3 Dr. & War. 60; *Bawlf Grain Co v Ross* (1917) 37 D.L.R. 620.

[126] Unreported, High Court, June 24, 1976; *Black v McGonigle*, unreported, High Court, November 14, 1988; *McCrystal v O'Kane* [1986] N.I. 123.

[127] *Re Byrne* [1941] I.R. 378. Section 137 of the Assisted Decision-Making (Capacity) Act 2015 restates the necessaries rule in respect to persons lacking capacity to make a decision under that Act.

[128] Sections 7 and 8.

different levels of intelligence and competences but legal capacity may be denied to certain individuals who are perceived to be incapable of making decisions and looking after their own affairs. Limited intellectual capacity has been seen as requiring State intervention, which has involved denial of legal capacity in certain instances. For example, capacity to marry is in part regulated by the Marriage of Lunatics Act 1811. General issues of capacity to contract for persons with intellectual disabilities are governed by the Lunacy Regulation (Ireland) Act 1871. This paternalistic but archaic body of law removed the capacity of an individual who in turn would have their affairs dealt with by a guardian who would seek an appointment from the High Court under a wardship order. Intellectual impairments occur for a variety of reasons such as genetic causes, illness, accidents, or may be age related, for example, but the wardship model imposed legal incapacity on the individual. Starting from the position established under Article 12 of the UN Convention on the Rights of Incapacity Disabilities (2006) which states as a basic principle "that persons with disabilities enjoy legal capacity on an equal basis with others in all aspects of life", it was essential for Ireland to move towards an entirely new approach to legislating for intellectual disability. Legal safeguards, not incapacity to contract, must be put in place. The guiding principles set out in s.8 of the Assisted Decision-Making (Capacity) Act 2015 are:

(a) a person is presumed to have capacity in respect of the matter concerned unless the contrary is shown;

(b) a person shall not be considered as unable to make a decision unless all practicable steps have been taken to help him or her do so;

(c) a person shall not be considered as unable to make a decision merely because the decision made or likely to be made is an unwise decision;

(d) intervention should only take place on the basis of necessity and individual circumstances;

(e) intervention must be made in accordance with human rights, be proportionate and limited in duration;

(f) the intervenor must make maximum efforts to meet the wishes of that individual and take account of other specified requirements and interests.

In terms of the way in which the individual concerned will be enabled to exercise their right to personal autonomy over decision making when it is established that a person lacks the capacity to make a decision—see s.3—the Act provides for a statutory framework of decision-making assistance agreements. These are formal agreements whereby the individual can appoint a trusted person to act as a decision-making assistant. The assistant is just that: he or she is charged with obtaining information and assisting the individual to understand, make or express a decision (ss.9–15). The Act also contains co-decision-making provisions intended to enable persons with more profound intellectual disabilities to appoint a co-decision-maker to jointly make decisions with the individual who has appointed him or her. The Act provides for the making of a co-decision-making agreement, in writing, the agreement to be registered in the register of co-decision-making agreements, maintained by the Director of the Decision Support Service (ss.16–24 and s.94). The Director has extensive supervisory and governance functions in respect of co-decision-making agreements. In cases of profound inability to make a decision the Circuit Court may appoint a decision-making representative (s.38).

Persons with intellectual disabilities may even under traditional common law rules enter into contractual arrangements in circumstances where a failure to provide services to that person might attract liability for a breach of duty. In *Haughey v JE Davy*[129] investment decisions made by the defendant on behalf of a young man who suffered intellectual impairment from a series of strokes starting when he was eight years of age turned out badly when the defendants failed to assess the needs, background and knowledge of the client and to tailor the advice appropriately.

It is suggested that while the 2015 Act is an important advance there are a number of other issues that need to be addressed.

16–55 It is important to bear in mind the overlap between capacity issues and undue influence.[130] As case law from other jurisdictions attests, particular attention should be paid to limitation periods, a difficult issue at the best of times. There are other cautionary tales to consider. In *Seaton v Seaton*[131] issues of laches and contractual capacity arose. The plaintiffs were the surviving members of Musical Youth, a band that had a phenomenal success in 1982 with "Pass the Dutchie". They sued their former manager alleging breach of contract and breach of trust. One plaintiff was mentally ill for a considerable period of time and limitation periods are the subject of statutory presumptions in such cases. While Roth J. examined the issues of disability and incapacity under both the UK Limitation Act 1980 and the Mental Capacity Act 2005 respectively, this particular plaintiff was unable to establish a sufficiently arguable case to continue proceedings alleging, inter alia, breach of contract.

---

[129] [2014] IEHC 206.
[130] *Gorjat v Gorjat* [2010] EWHC 1537 (Ch) is instructive.
[131] [2012] EWHC 735 (Ch).

Part 7

Third Party Rights

17 Privity of Contract

Introduction

17–01 The doctrine of privity of contract prevents a contract from being enforceable in favour of, or against, someone who is not a party to that contract. While this is, in general, the basic rule, the English Law Commission, in Consultation Paper No. 121,[1] emphasised that there are three aspects to the doctrine:

(i) a person cannot enforce rights under a contract to which he is not a party;

(ii) a person who is not a party to a contract cannot have contractual liabilities imposed on him; and

(iii) contractual remedies are designed to compensate parties to a contract, not third parties.

The doctrine resembles the rule (already considered in Ch.2) requiring consideration to move from a promisee before a promise can be enforced by that person. Furmston[2] has convincingly argued that these two propositions are in fact two different ways of saying the same thing. A "stranger to the consideration" (i.e. a person who has not rendered himself liable upon the contract) does not provide consideration for any promise addressed to him. By the same token, the fact that a gratuitous promise is addressed to a person does not make that person a promisee; the test used to identify persons who are privy to a bilateral contract is whether that person is bound to do anything under the contract. Nevertheless, the weight of authority is in favour of regarding the law as having two distinct rules:

> "My Lords, in the law of England certain principles are fundamental. One is that only a person who is a party to a contract can sue on it ... A

---

[1] *Privity of Contract: Contracts for the Benefit of Third Parties* (1991); the final Report is *Contracts for the Benefit of Third Parties* (1996). These reports were the basis of the Contracts (Rights of Third Parties) Act 1999. See generally on the 1999 Act, Merkin (ed.), *Privity of Contract* (London: LLP, 2000); Furmston and Tolhurst, *Privity of Contract* (Oxford UP, 2015). Periodical literature includes Mitchell, "Privity Reform and the Nature of Contractual Obligations" (1999) 19 L.S. 229; Dean, "Removing a dot on the Landscape—The Reform of the Doctrine of Privity" [2000] J.B.L. 143; and Stevens, "The Contracts (Rights of Third Parties) Act 1999" (2004) 120 L.Q.R. 292. Reform of the privity rule in Hong Kong has followed the same path as the 1999 UK legislation: see Mason, "Enforcing Contracts for the Benefit of Third Parites: Recent Reform of the Doctrine of Privity" (2015) 45 H.K.L.J. 13. No Irish Bill has been circulated despite LRC 88-2008 being a non-contentious Law Reform Commission report. See generally, *Chitty on Contracts*, edited by H.G. Beale, 32nd edn (London: Sweet & Maxwell, 2015), Vol. 1, paras 18-001 to 18-153.

[2] (1960) 23 M.L.R. 373.

second principle is that if a person with whom a contract not under seal has been made is to be able to enforce it, consideration must have been given by him to the promisor or to some other person at the promisor's request."[3]

Indeed, in the case of *Coulls v Bagot's Trustee*[4] the High Court of Australia confirmed the view that there are two distinct rules, indicating that a promise made to two promisees makes the promisees each contracting parties, and that a promise thus made is enforceable by both separately, even if only one promisee furnishes consideration. Although the decision has been criticised,[5] it does represent an example of a judicial desire to ensure that the expectations of parties to a contract are not frustrated by technical rules that do not serve the interests of justice.

Origins

17–02 The cases of *McCoubray v Thompson*[6] and *Barry v Barry*,[7] discussed in Ch.2, indicate that the doctrine is designed to prevent persons who are simply the objects of a gratuitous promise from suing others in contract. The doctrine is not popular and many writers have argued that it is in fact a common law doctrine of fairly recent origin. The leading English case is the decision of the Court of Queen's Bench in *Tweddle v Atkinson*.[8] An action was brought by a son-in-law to recover a sum of money from the estate of his deceased father-in-law. The sum had been promised in return for a similar promise given by the plaintiff's own father upon the plaintiff's marriage. The action failed. *Tweddle v Atkinson* stands in marked contrast to a series of earlier English cases, particularly *Dutton v Poole*[9] where similar family arrangements were held to be enforceable by third parties. These older cases are to be regarded as having been overruled by *Tweddle v Atkinson* and the later case of *Dunlop v Selfridge*,[10] a House of Lords decision in which the plaintiff company, which had sold its tyres to a wholesaler under the terms of a contract which provided that the tyres would not be resold at a price below the recommended retail price, was held not to be entitled to enforce the term against the defendant retailer for reason of lack of consideration and the privity rule.

17–03 The most important Irish common law decision is probably *Murphy v Bower*.[11] The plaintiffs, railway contractors, undertook construction work

---

[3]   Viscount Haldane L.C. in *Dunlop Pneumatic Tyre Co Ltd v Selfridge & Co* [1915] A.C. 847.
[4]   (1967) 40 A.L.R. 385; (1967) 119 C.L.R. 460.
[5]   Coote [1978] C.L.J. 301.
[6]   (1868) 2 I.R.C.L. 226.
[7]   (1891) 28 L.R. (Ir.) 45.
[8]   (1861) 1 B. & S. 393.
[9]   (1678) 2 Lev. 210; *Carnegie v Waugh* (1823) 1 L.J.(o.s.) K.B. 89.
[10] [1915] A.C. 847.
[11] (1868) I.R. 2 C.L. 506. See also *Waugh v Denham* (1865) 16 I.C.L.R. 405; *Corner v Irwin* (1876) 10 I.R.C.L. 354.

for a railway company. The company employed Bower as an engineer to supervise the work. The construction contract stipulated that Bower would issue certificates as work was completed, thereupon entitling the plaintiffs to payment. Bower refused to certify the work. The Court of Common Pleas dismissed the plaintiffs' action against Bower. It should be noted that the plaintiffs had not engaged the engineer; nor was Bower's employer, the railway company, a plaintiff in the action. Monahan C.J. observed: "it has been decided that where the foundation of the right of action is rested upon contract, no one can maintain an action who is not a party to the contract."[12]

Equity's Response to Actions Brought by Third Parties

17–04 The courts of equity adopted a characteristically flexible position. In the early case of *Shannon v Bradstreet*[13] a tenant for life with a power to lease entered into an agreement to execute a lease in favour of Shannon. Shannon entered into possession but no lease was formally executed (which prevented the possibility of the lease binding successors as a covenant running with the land). On the death of the tenant for life the remainderman sought ejectment claiming the lease did not bind him. Lord Redesdale gave judgment for Shannon, holding that in equity a remainderman is bound by a leasing agreement made by a predecessor in title.

17–05 This isolated example of equity recognising that a third party may be bound by a contract pales into insignificance when contrasted with the line of authority commencing with the English case of *Tomlinson v Gill*,[14] in which a decision of Hardwicke L.C., Gill promised a widow that if she would appoint him administrator of her deceased husband's estate he would personally meet any debts the estate could not discharge. An action brought by a creditor on this promise succeeded: "the plaintiff ... could not maintain an action at law, for the promise was made to the widow; but he is proper here, for the promise was for the benefit of the creditors and the widow is a trustee for them."[15]

17–06 While traditionally the equitable concept of the trust does provide a right of action to a beneficiary who may sue the trustee should he not discharge his duties, it has been said that, in this context, the trust is not apparent. In *Tomlinson v Gill* there was no express intention to create a trust; nor was a trust fund established. Corbin, in his exhaustive review of these early cases,[16] observed of this case that "there was merely a contract between two persons in which one promised to pay a debt owed to a third party; the promisee—the widow—was called a trustee of the promise merely to allow the action in equity to succeed against the promisor".[17]

---

[12] (1868) I.R. 2 C.L. 506 at 512.
[13] (1803) 1 Sch. & Lef. 64.
[14] (1756) Amb. 330; *Les Affréteurs Reunis SA v Leopold Walford Ltd* [1919] A.C. 801.
[15] (1756) Amb. 330 at 335.
[16] (1930) 46 L.Q.R. 12.
[17] (1930) 46 L.Q.R. 12 at 21.

17–07 The trust concept has been discussed in several Irish cases. In *Drimmie v Davies*[18] a father and son agreed to establish a dental practice. The partnership deed obliged the son to pay annuities to his mother and his siblings in the event of the father predeceasing him. The executor of the deceased partner's estate and the beneficiaries sued to enforce the promise. The executor's action succeeded; Chatterton V.C., in a judgment upheld by the Court of Appeal, ruled that the defence of privity between promisor and beneficiaries did not prevail in equity and, following the Judicature Act, the equitable rule prevailed, namely, "the party to whose use or for whose benefit the contract had been entered into has a remedy in equity against the person with whom it was expressed to be made". Note also Holmes L.J.'s judgment in the Court of Appeal. The fact that the trustee himself—the executor—was prepared to sue makes this statement obiter dictum: see *Beswick v Beswick*.[19] If the executor/ promisee is unwilling to bring proceedings such a dictum may be invaluable.

17–08 In *Kenney v Employer's Liability Insurance Corp*[20] a bank, mortgagees of Kenney's estate, appointed B as a receiver to hold and pay over to it rents and profits. B took out insurance with the defendant to cover acts of default. B defaulted and Kenney, who had paid out to cover B's default, sued on the insurance policy. The majority of the Court of Appeal held Kenney entitled to sue on the contract. Holmes L.J. for the majority said the case fell within the trust principle established in *Drimmie v Davies*. Walker L.J., dissenting, said that B did not intend to confer a beneficial right on the mortgagor, nor did B intend to make himself a trustee for the mortgagor. In general, however, the courts, by the early years of this century, had carved out a most subversive doctrine. The intention to benefit a third party, once demonstrated, led the courts to readily infer a trust to benefit that third party. The House of Lords, in *Les Affréteurs Reunis SA v Leopold Walford Ltd*,[21] gave such a development its approval, holding that a broker who had negotiated a charterparty could enforce a promise contained therein whereby the owners of the vessel promised to pay the broker a commission, even though the broker was not privy to the contract.

17–09 There is one nineteenth-century Irish case that goes the other way. In *Clitheroe v Simpson*,[22] John Simpson, father of both the defendant and Alice Clitheroe, late wife of the plaintiff, agreed by deed with the defendant that in consideration of the defendant agreeing to pay Alice Clitheroe £100, John Simpson would convey land to the defendant. The sum was not paid; the plaintiff, executor of his wife's estate, sued but the action failed. Morris

---

[18] (1899) 1 I.R. 176. For a modern Canadian case in which it was held that the death of the promisor did not affect the liability of the heirs to perform obligations that were not a personal kind, see *Benzie v Kunin* (2012) 357 DLR (4th) 255.
[19] [1968] A.C. 58.
[20] [1901] 1 I.R. 301; *Walsh v Walsh* [1900] 1 N.I.J.R. 53.
[21] [1919] A.C. 801.
[22] (1879) 4 L.R. (Ir.) 59.

C.J. observed that even if a trust had been pleaded, which it was not, he did not think any circumstances existed which would bring the case within that exception to the privity rule. Lawson and Harrison JJ. concurred. This case (decided by judges from a predominantly common law background) was described by Corbin as one in which the judges looked for a trust fund, "and finding none denied the plaintiff a remedy. The possibility of regarding the promisee as a trustee of the contract right did not occur to the Court".

17–10 While the primacy of the *Drimmie v Davies* line of authority has not been directly challenged in the Irish courts, the practice of utilising the concept of the trust as a means of avoiding the privity doctrine has fallen into disfavour. Lord Wright described it as "a cumbrous fiction" when used in this context.[23] The Privy Council in *Vandepitte v Preferred Accident Insurance Corp of New York*[24] refused to allow a third party to sue on an insurance contract because it could not be shown that the insured intended to benefit the third party. In fact the position taken in *Vandepitte* closely resembles that of Walker L.J. dissenting in *Kenney*, above. In the case of *O'Leary v Irish National Insurance Co Ltd*[25] the court left open the question whether an intention to create a trust must be shown before a third party can recover but Barrington J., in *Cadbury Ireland Ltd v Kerry Co-op Creameries Ltd*,[26] held that such an intention must be present. In that case a promise contained in a document agreed between the defendant company and the State, made when the defendant company sought to acquire a semi-state company in the Kerry district, was not actionable by the plaintiff company even though the interests of the plaintiff company were intended to be protected by the State when agreeing to sell the semi-state company to the defendant. If at the time of the promise the beneficiary does not exist, it may sometimes be more difficult to persuade the court to uphold the trust concept than would otherwise be the case. In *Inspector of Taxes Association v Minister for the Public Service, Ireland & the Attorney-General*,[27] Murphy J. refused to hold that the plaintiff Association could avail of a conciliation and arbitration scheme. Following the *Kerry Co-op* case the judge found it impossible to infer "that the various Staff Associations who were parties to the original C. & A. agreement purported to contract by implication as trustees on behalf of other associations which might be formed hereafter". There are nevertheless individual employment cases where relatives of an employee have been held entitled to recover benefits payable under the rules of their deceased relative's trade union.[28] The trust exception to the privity rule was invoked in *Dalton v Ellis: Estate of Bristow*.[29] The first

---

[23] (1939) 55 L.Q.R. 189 at 208.
[24] [1933] A.C. 70; *Green v Russell* [1959] 2 Q.B. 226.
[25] [1958] Ir. Jur. Rep. 1.
[26] [1982] I.L.R.M. 77.
[27] Unreported, High Court, March 24, 1983, affirmed by the Supreme Court: [1986] I.L.R.M. 296.
[28] Contrast *Kelly v Larkin* [1910] 2 I.R. 550 with *Rooney v T.O.S.I.* (1913) 47 I.L.T.R. 303.
[29] (2005) 65 N.S.W.L.R. 134.

plaintiff was involved in a relationship with Bristow and became pregnant by Bristow. Shortly before the birth of their child the first plaintiff and Bristow executed a deed under the terms of which Bristow promised to make a will favouring the child. Bristow died without having made any will. After holding that under statute an unborn child may not sue on a deed, the court upheld the child's right, as second plaintiff to invoke the trust exception and thereby allow the second plaintiff to sue in her own name. The requisite intent to create a trust, as distinct from a mere intention to benefit a third party, was present as the deed itself specifically referred to the first plaintiff as holding the promise as trustee.

17–11 This application of the trust concept is not, however, very common. The trust concept is out of favour, both in England and Ireland, because it strikes many judges as intellectually dishonest. More importantly, perhaps, the use of this "cumbrous fiction" can unduly interfere with perfectly sensible arrangements by preventing the parties from being able to rescind or vary them by agreement. This occurs because the "beneficiary", as the possessor of an equitable interest, must often consent to a variation; see *Re Schebsman*.[30] It is important that donor and beneficiary are both litigants. In *Kuzmanovski v New South Wales Lotteries Corp*[31] a purchaser of a lottery ticket who gave the ticket to her husband as a birthday present was held to have assigned her rights in the ticket to her husband, including rights to any prize. As both the assignor and assignee were before the court, the assignee could recover monies due on the ticket. Judicial innovation will be the exception, not the rule. In *Marks v CCH Australia Ltd*,[32] the defendant funded an endowed Chair at the University of Melbourne, the plaintiff being the holder of the Chair until, inter alia, retirement. The defendants repudiated the contract and the university exercised an option it had in its contract with the plaintiff to terminate his employment contract for non-payment of monies by the defendant. The plaintiff sought to argue that he could sue the defendant because the University held the defendant's promise in trust for the plaintiff. No such express or constructive trust was held to exist. The contract between the University and the defendant was executed under the common seal of both parties and the term in the agreement giving the University the power to terminate the agreement if funding stopped was inserted for the benefit of the University alone. Nevertheless it is suggested that the case of *McKay v Jones*[33] (the facts of which are given in Ch.3) should be considered as wrongly decided. The possibility that the boy's parents were trustees of the contract promise does not seem to have been argued.

---

[30] [1944] Ch. 83.
[31] [2010] FCA 876.
[32] [1999] 3 V.R. 513.
[33] (1959) 93 I.L.T.R. 177.

Agency

17–12 If an agent is appointed and given the authority to contract on behalf of a principal then any transaction within the scope of such authority will bind the principal. Before the agency exception can operate there must normally exist an intention to create the relationship of principal and agent; see *Sheppard v Murphy*.[34] The doctrine of the undisclosed principal, however, allows enforcement of a promise by a principal if the contract has been made by an agent within the agent's authority, even if the agent has, to all intents and purposes, contracted in his own name and for his own benefit. Commercial convenience is the most obvious explanation for such a rule. In most agency cases, however, the link between the agent and principal will be apparent or established through a long line of custom and usage. In the area of insurance, commercial convenience will establish that, as between brokers, an agent and sub-agent are in a direct contractual relationship, and that even if there exists a contractual relationship between the sub-agent and the principal of the other agent (which is unlikely), this will not exclude the privity of contract as between agent and sub-agent; see *Prentis Donegan & Partners Ltd v Leeds and Leeds Co*.[35] The precise status of brokers and agents in insurance transactions can be contentious. The Insurance Act 1989 s.51 does not so much as create an exception to the privity of contract rule but, rather, it provides that an insurance agent will be deemed to be acting for the insurer vis-à-vis completion of a proposal for insurance when there are errors or omissions in so doing. The section also renders the insurer responsible for any act or omission of a tied agent in respect of any matter as if the tied agent were an employee.[36] Attempts to avoid the common law rule are often based upon alleged "custom and practice", but even in areas such as banking law the privity doctrine remains strong. It has been held that there is no privity of contract between the payee/customer of a bank, which is remitting a cheque, and the collecting bank, as a sub-agent is not in privity with the principal.[37] A recent attempt to invoke an international banking code in support of relaxing the privity doctrine failed in *Grosvenor Casinos Ltd v National Bank of Abu Dhabi*.[38] This case illustrates that while an agent may delegate performance to a sub-agent, the sub-agent will not necessarily come into a contractual relationship with the principal.[39]

17–13 In *Pattison v Institute for Industrial Research and Standards*[40] a trade union negotiating on behalf of its members obtained a promise from the defendant to pay an additional allowance to the plaintiff, an employee of the

---

[34] (1867) 1 Ir.R.Eq. 490.
[35] [1998] 2 Lloyd's Rep. 326; *Calico Printers Association v Barclays Bank* (1931) 36 Com. Cas. 71.
[36] On liability in tort and under the Contracts (Rights of Third Parties) Act 1999 in England and Wales, see *Crowson v HSBC Insurance Brokers* [2010] Lloyd's Rep. 441.
[37] *Calico Printers Association v Barclays Bank* (1931) 36 Com. Cas 71; *Henderson v Merrett Syndicates Ltd* [1995] A.C. 145.
[38] [2008] EWHC 511 (Comm).
[39] *New Zealand and Australian Land Co v Watson* (1881) 7 Q.B.D. 374.
[40] Unreported, High Court, May 31, 1979; *Keighley, Maxsted & Co v Durant* [1900] A.C. 240.

defendant. McWilliam J. held that the plaintiff could enforce this promise. The decision can only be explained as resting on a finding that the union negotiated as agent for its members.

17–14 The agency exception has produced a controversial series of decisions in recent years. In *The Eurymedon*[41] machinery was to be transported by ship from England to New Zealand. The consignors in England contracted with a carrier, the contract providing that liability of the carriers, their employees, agents and independent contractors would be limited. The carriers employed the defendant stevedores to unload the machinery, which was damaged due to the stevedores' negligence. The majority of the Privy Council held the stevedores entitled to rely on a limitation clause even though it was contained in a contract between consignor and carrier. The Privy Council, following the earlier case of *Scruttons Ltd v Midland Silicones*,[42] held if the following four conditions can be satisfied the third party will take the benefit of such a clause:

(1) the contract must make it clear that the stevedore is intended to be protected;

(2) the contract clearly provides that the carrier has the status of agent for the purpose of obtaining the benefit of the contract for a principal;

(3) the carrier has the authority to contract on the stevedore's behalf; and

(4) there are no difficulties in relation to consideration.

The minority in *The Eurymedon* were unable to find that the contract also contained an offer addressed to the stevedore; the dissenting members of the Privy Council expressed misgivings about using a legal fiction to avoid the privity doctrine (in much the same way as their predecessors had in *Vandepitte* when faced with the trust argument). Nevertheless *The Eurymedon* has been followed in *The New York Star*,[43] also a Privy Council decision. The classical analysis in *Midland Silicones* was reaffirmed by the English Court of Appeal in *Borvigilant v Romina G*.[44] The tanker, Romina G, was damaged on colliding with a tug, the Borvigilant, when berthing at an Iranian oil terminal. The Romina G was being afforded tug services on foot of a contract with Iranian Oil. That contract, signed by the master of the Romina G, afforded the benefit of protective conditions to vessels hired by Iranian Oil to provide tug services, the *Borvigilent* being owned by Borkan. Could Borkan obtain the benefit of these clauses? It was conceded that factors 1 and 4 were satisfied, but were the other two? Factor 2 was held not to require that the contract must expressly state that the carrier must contract as agent for the stevedore and on the facts, because a trust was not intended, an agency relationship clearly was. The intention to benefit Borkan was conclusive. It was also held that Iranian Oil

---

[41] *New Zealand Shipping Co Ltd v AM Satterthwaite & Co Ltd (The Eurymedon)* [1975] A.C. 154.
[42] [1962] A.C. 446.
[43] [1980] 3 All E.R. 257; see, however, *International Technical Operators Ltd v Miida Electronics Inc* (1986) 28 D.L.R. (4th) 641.
[44] [2003] 2 All E.R. 736.

had actual authority to contract for Borkan given the absence of opportunity for a direct contract, custom and practice in the industry as well as a previous course of dealing between the parties. In *Borvigilant v Romina G*, the Court of Appeal was at pains to stress the commercial undesirability of allowing standard agreements of this kind to be side-stepped when giving Himalaya clauses too narrow an interpretation.[45] *The Eurymedon* has, as a general exception, also found favour in areas of law that go beyond the carriage of goods. The principle has been applied recently in relation to the negotiation of an insurance contract; see *National Oilwell (UK) Ltd v Davy Offshore Ltd*.[46] However, the most striking illustration of the principle is the use made of it by O'Sullivan J. in the controversial litigation in *Hearn and Matchroom Boxing Ltd v Collins*.[47] One of the issues facing the court was whether an agreement made between the second plaintiff and Stephen Collins could be the subject of enforcement by the first plaintiff, a defence of privity being raised by the defendant. After mentioning the four elements set down by the majority in *The Eurymedon*, O'Sullivan J. found that all four factors were satisfied. As a management contract the parties were aware that only a human person could manage a boxer and Matchroom Boxing, in the judge's view, was contracting as agent for Barry Hearn. The company clearly acted within the scope of its authority and the "consideration which moved from Barry Hearn as an individual was his undertaking to extend the management agreement and also of course to be bound by its terms and provide appropriate services to Stephen Collins thereunder". While *The Eurymedon* is normally seen as a decision on bailment and the law relating to exclusion clauses in contract and tort, O'Sullivan J.'s decision gives it a broader application. However, we should return to the law of bailment for a moment. We have seen earlier in this book specific illustrations of how the law of bailment produces a *sui generis* example of a contracting party, the bailor, being held to impliedly consent to the terms of a later contract entered into with sub-bailees by the original bailee.[48]

17–15 In *Fox v Higgins*,[49] Gibson J. also encountered difficulties when confronted with a contractual arrangement intended to bind persons outside the original bargain. The plaintiff was employed by the Rev. Busby, school manager, as a teacher in a national school. The Rev. Busby resigned; the defendant Higgins replaced him as school manager. Before the defendant was confirmed as manager Fox fell ill and was away from work for several months. Fox, on his return to work, was told that his contract of employment ended when the Rev. Busby resigned. Gibson J. found that Higgins was bound by the

---

[45] [2003] 2 All E.R. 736 at 744, citing Lord Goff in *The Mahkutai* [1996] 3 All E.R. 502 at 509. See also Lord Steyn's dissent in *The Starsin* [2003] 1 All E.R. (Comm.) 625 at 645.

[46] [1993] 2 Lloyd's Rep. 582.

[47] Unreported, High Court, February 3, 1998.

[48] *Morris v C. W. Martin & Sons Ltd* [1966] 1 Q.B. 716; *Singer (U.K.) v Tees and Hartlepool Port Authority* [1988] 2 Lloyd's Rep. 215; *Spectra International Plc v Hayesoak* [1997] 1 Lloyd's Rep. 153.

[49] (1912) 46 I.L.T.R. 22.

National Board rules to enter into a contract with all teachers employed at the commencement of his own service as school manager; this was described as "a kind of triangular pact" by which in certain circumstances the new manager is bound "in the same way and to the same effect as if he had signed the contract".

17–16 These tripartite contracts are exceptional; see *Halpin v Rothwell & U.D.T.*[50] It is a matter of construction whether an arrangement binds all parties equally or whether the relationship between contracting parties subsists in a series of separate transactions; the speech of O'Higgins C.J. in *Henley Forklift (Ireland) Ltd v Lansing Bagnall & Co Ltd*[51] is instructive.

Covenants Running with the Land

17–17 Conveyancing practice and a wealth of case law establishes that covenants that "touch and concern" real property may be enforced against, and indeed be enforced by, persons who are not parties to the original transaction. Considerations of space do not permit an extensive review of this exception to the privity doctrine. The law is discussed with great clarity in Wylie, *Irish Land Law*.[52] An illustration of the *Tulk v Moxhay*[53] principle is afforded by the decision of Murphy J. in *Whelan and Whelan v Cork Corp*.[54]

The De Mattos *principle*

17–18 *De Mattos v Gibson*[55] lays down a broad principle of equity which indicates that a person with notice of a right or interest, who acquires property, whether movable or immovable, will not be able to ignore that right of a third party if the third party has given valuable consideration for the interest. The precise scope of the principle is in doubt but the existence of this principle is not: see *Law Debenture Corp v Ural Caspian Ltd.*[56] In *Welltec APS v Precision Drilling Corp*,[57] Madame Justice Kent trenchantly observed that "the *De Mattos* principle is an equitable principle restricted to instances where equitable relief is sought, not a vehicle available to impose contractual obligations where none exist". Hoffmann J., in *Law Debenture*, held that *De Mattos* only applies to give a negative injunction to restrain the person with notice from acting in a way that is inconsistent with the rights of the third party.

17–19 There are no Irish cases dealing with the applicability of such covenants to contracts for the sale of chattels. *De Mattos* was considered by Laffoy J. in

---

[50] [1984] I.L.R.M. 613.
[51] Unreported, Supreme Court, December 3, 1979; *Herlihy v Sullivan* (1896) 30 I.L.T. 536.
[52] 5th edn (Dublin: Bloomsbury Professional, 2013), Part VIII.
[53] (1848) 2 Ph. 774.
[54] [1991] I.L.R.M. 19.
[55] (1859) 4 De G. & J. 276; *Lord Strathcona S.S. v Dominion Coal Co Ltd* [1926] A.C. 108; *Swiss Bank Corp v Lloyds Bank* [1979] Ch. 548.
[56] [1993] 2 All E.R. 355, citing *Barker v Stickney* [1919] 1 K.B. 121.
[57] [2004] 10 W.W.R. 587.

Moylist Construction v Doheny,[58] a case arising out of a contractual licence dispute following receivership of a development company.

Limitation clauses—A Canadian exception

17–20 A majority of the Supreme Court of Canada, in *London Drugs Ltd v Kuehne & Nagel International Ltd*[59] has identified a separate exception to the privity doctrine based upon the intention of the parties, fairness, business and insurance practices. Where a limitation clause was intended to benefit a third party—an employee of a contracting party, for example—the courts will allow the benefit of the clause to defeat or restrict liability in tort or contract. While this exception may operate in *The Eurymedon* context, the Supreme Court of Canada preferred a method that did not involve the artificiality of *The Eurymedon* reasoning. In developing the application of this line of authority it has been held that a Provincial Government has been entitled to avail of a promise not to sue under a settlement agreement reached between a patient and a publicly funded hospital, the Government not being a party to the settled litigation or the settlement.[60] It has also been held that the exception to the privity doctrine is to be used defensively—as a shield and not a sword—and cannot be invoked to create liability as an ersatz cause of action.[61] The British Columbia Court of Appeal, in *Holmes v United Furniture*,[62] has refused to allow purchasers of furniture seeking to claim on a sales contract voucher system a right to claim in an asset transfer agreement when the seller's business was subsequently purchased by the defendant, the defendant undertaking to meet the seller's liabilities. Groberman J. said if such a claim were to succeed, this exception,

> "... would represent a monumental change in the law in at least two respects: first (and most importantly), it would do away with any requirement that a third party seeking to take advantage of the contract be a person that the contracting parties intended to benefit; and second, it would extend rights to third parties to sue under the contract, rather than simply using it as a defence".

Dunlop v Lambert

17–21 Some of the exceptions created by case law are, of course, transaction-type specific. In the area of the carriage of goods by sea, the consignor of specific goods may recover substantial damages if the goods are lost in transit even though ownership in the goods may have passed to the consignee. This

---

58 [2010] IEHC 162.
59 (1992) 97 D.L.R. (4th) 261; Waddams, "Privity of Contract in the Supreme Court of Canada" (1993) 109 L.Q.R. 349.
60 *Marble v Saskatchewan* [2004] 7 W.W.R. 580.
61 *Kitimat v Alcan Ltd* (2006) 256 D.L.R. (4th) 462.
62 (2012) 32 B.C.L.R. (4th) 161.

is known as the rule in *Dunlop v Lambert*.[63] Although this exception has been extended into the area of construction contracts,[64] it has been held in *Alfred McAlpine Construction Ltd v Panatown Ltd*[65] that the exception in *Dunlop* will not apply where, on the facts, it was intended that the third party received or was able to use some other cause of action. Nor will the exception apply in the case of a franchisee who repudiates a franchise contract and thus fails to sell goods supplied by a party other than the franchisor because of lack of evidence that the franchise agreement was intended to benefit third party suppliers.[66] The reluctance of first instance judges to develop the rather sketchy exceptions that the *Panatown* judgments *may* authorise is well summed up by Seymour J. in *Rolls Royce Power Engineering Plc v Ricardo Consulting Engineers Ltd*,[67] a case dealing with several privity issues. After conducting a thorough review of the *Dunlop v Lambert* case law, the court observed that, in the light of differing judicial utterances and the fact that the exceptions contended for were either contrary to principle or difficult to apply: "In these treacherous waters I prefer to navigate by already published charts and to seek to apply the law as it has already clearly developed, rather than to speculate as to how it may develop in the future."[68]

Deeds

17–22 Share purchase transactions are also, in practice, a fertile area for the privity doctrine to take root in; the need for the parties to execute collateral agreements leaves open potential promissory gaps. The law relating to the execution of documents as deeds rather than simple contracts has recently opened up another potential argument which may enable a third party to enforce a promise even though that person was not a signatory of the deed. In *Moody v Condor Insurance Ltd*,[69] the plaintiffs sold their shares in a company to Group Ltd Group Ltd arranged a contract of guarantee between itself and Condor, the terms of which were held to require Condor to pay sums due to the sellers should Group Ltd default in payment, as Group Ltd did. The plaintiffs were not signors of the deed. Park J. held that the plaintiffs could enforce the guarantee in their own name. The distinction between deeds poll and deeds *inter partes* was called in aid by the plaintiffs: a deed poll allows non-signatory beneficiaries to enforce the deed directly, and Park J. was of the view that the critical issue was whether the deed and related documents evidenced an intention that the beneficiaries were to be entitled to enforce the

---

[63] (1839) 6 C.I. & F. 600; *The Albazero* [1977] A.C. 744.
[64] *Linden Gardens Trust Ltd v Lenesta Sludge Disposals Ltd* [1993] 3 All E.R. 417; *Darlington B.C. v Wiltshier Northern Ltd* [1995] 3 All E.R. 895.
[65] [2001] 1 A.C. 518.
[66] *And So To Bed Ltd v Dixon* [2001] F.S.R. 935.
[67] [2003] EWHC 2871 (TCC).
[68] [2003] EWHC 2871 (TCC), para.130.
[69] [2006] EWHC 100 (Ch).

guarantee directly. After finding a considerable body of evidence that this was indeed the case, Park J. followed earlier cases that allowed building societies[70] and creditors[71] to enforce payment obligations set out in deeds to which those beneficiaries were not a party.

Statutory Exceptions to the Privity Doctrine

17–23 In England the Law Revision Committee recommended in a 1937 Report[72] that legislation be enacted conferring sweeping rights of action upon third party beneficiaries. This Report was ignored by the UK Parliament until the Contracts (Rights of Third Parties) Act 1999 (the "1999 Act") but it did help to stimulate legislative action in 1957 in Ireland.

17–24 The first recommendation builds upon s.11 of the Married Women's Property Act 1882. By adopting the trust concept, discussed above, Parliament in 1882 gave widows and children of a deceased man the right to sue upon a policy of life insurance. Section 7 of the Married Women's Status Act 1957 (the "1957 Act") extends this right of action to endowment policies also. This right of action applies to policies whether the policy is "expressed to be for the benefit of" or "by its express terms purporting to confer a benefit upon the wife, husband or child of the insured".[73]

17–25 More importantly, perhaps, s.8 of the 1957 Act creates a cause of action in all contracts other than those covered by s.7 if the contract is expressed to be for the benefit of a wife, husband or child of one of the contracting parties, or if the contract purports to confer a benefit upon such a third party. As a result the contract will be enforceable by the third party in his or her own name.

17–26 The facts of *Jackson v Horizon Holidays*[74] illustrate the usefulness of s.8. Jackson booked a holiday in Ceylon for himself and his family. The accommodation provided was unsatisfactory so on his return to England Mr Jackson sued to recover damages for the disappointing holiday. He recovered damages to compensate not only himself but all members of the family. *Jackson* makes good sense but the Court of Appeal's reasoning has been attacked as incorrect in law[75] and was disapproved by the House of Lords in *Woodar Investment v Wimpey Construction*.[76] However, in *Linden Gardens Trust Ltd v Lenesta*

---

[70] *Chelsea and Waltham Green Building Society v Armstrong* [1951] 1 Ch. 853.
[71] *Re A&K Holdings Pty Ltd* [1964] V.R. 257.
[72] Cmd. 5449.
[73] See Dowrick (1958) 21 M.L.R. 98.
[74] [1975] 1 W.L.R. 1468.
[75] Wylie (1975) 26 N.I.L.Q. 326.
[76] [1980] 1 All E.R. 571, cited with approval by Finlay C.J. in *Burke v Lord Mayor of Dublin* [1990] 1 I.R. 18.

Sludge Disposals Ltd[77] the House of Lords indicated that there are exceptional situations in which a plaintiff may recover damages for breach of contract even though the recoverable loss may be that of a third party. Lord Griffiths in particular canvassed a very broad right of recovery on behalf of third parties and his judgment sets out a very sound and commonsense approach to the issue of third party rights. In *Alfred McAlpine Construction Ltd v Panatown Ltd*,[78] the dicta of Lord Griffiths were confined to situations where the promisee had paid for the performance or that promisee would be liable to pay over the damages received to the third party, the two judges in the majority on this point, Lords Clyde and Jauncey, observing that unless this was an element in the test for recovery, the promisee would be recovering damages when the promisee had not suffered any loss. As Coote points out[79] the characterisation of who has suffered loss is problematical and he prefers the reasoning of Lord Millett, the dissenting Law Lord. However, the status of the *Jackson* case in English law remains uncertain. In Ireland the 1957 Act provides a clear solution. Under s.8 the wife and children of a contracting party would, on similar facts, be able to sue in contract in their own name. Section 8 does permit the contract to be rescinded by the contracting parties at any time before the beneficiary adopts it; the third party is also bound by any defences the defendant may have against the other contracting party. So in *O'Keeffe v Ryanair Holdings*,[80] damages were awarded in favour of the plaintiff and her husband (even though at the time of the plaintiff's success in winning free flights for life for herself and her companion, she was unmarried). Clearly, the plaintiff alone provided consideration and the application of s.8 seems problematical.

17–27 If a tenancy agreement between a male tenant and a landlord envisages that the tenant's wife is to live on the premises it may be that the wife will fall within the scope of s.8, depending of course on the terms of the letting agreement. If the wife of the tenant is injured because the premises turn out to be defective she should in such a case be able to sue the landlord under s.8. This point does not seem to have been argued in either *Chambers v Cork Corp*[81] or *Coughlan v Mayor of Limerick*.[82] However, in *Burke v Lord Mayor of Dublin*[83] the first plaintiff, a minor, sought damages to compensate for aggravation of his asthma condition, his condition being the result of living in unfit housing conditions, the tenants being his parents. The plaintiff's counsel argued that because local authority differential rents were calculated by reference to the number of children resident therein, it was possible to argue that the contract was expressed to be for the benefit of, or, by its express terms, purported to

---

[77] [1993] 3 All E.R. 417; *Darlington B.C. v Wiltshier Northern Ltd* [1995] 3 All E.R. 895.
[78] [2000] 3 W.L.R. 946; *And So To Bed Ltd v Dixon* [2001] F.S.R. 935.
[79] (2001) 117 L.Q.R. 81.
[80] [2003] 1 I.L.R.M. 14. See also the wedding reception case of *Dinnegan v Ryan* [2002] 3 I.R. 178.
[81] (1959) 93 I.L.T.R. 45.
[82] (1977) 111 I.L.T.R. 114.
[83] [1990] 1 I.R. 18.

benefit, the infant plaintiff. The argument was rejected by the Supreme Court. The need for an express reference is a considerable barrier to the operation of s.8, but the words of s.8 seem to permit no other result in a case such as *Burke v Lord Mayor of Dublin*. However, the alternative argument, based upon *Jackson v Horizon Holidays*, suggests that family holiday contracts, contracts for restaurant services, taxi services, and the like, will be capable of giving a right of action to persons envisaged as being recipients of the service, even if the consideration and the contract involve one of the recipients only. McCarthy J., while holding *Jackson v Horizon Holidays* to be inapplicable, approved the idea that these situations call for special treatment, citing Lord Wilberforce in *Woodar Investment v Wimpey Construction*.

17–28 Section 76(1) of the Road Traffic Act 1961 gives a person claiming against an insured motorist certain remedies against the insurer. If judgment is obtained against the insured, s.76(1)(b) and (c) provide that an application to execute judgment against the owner or user may be brought; see *Herlihy v Curley*.[84] Should the claimant not recover judgment against that person then s.76(1)(d) essentially provides that the claimant may apply to institute proceedings against the insurer or guarantor, in lieu of the owner or user of the vehicle, if:

(1) the owner or user is outside the State, or cannot be found or is immune from process; or

(2) for any other reason it is just and equitable that the application be granted.

Case law indicates a considerable overlap between these two provisions, e.g. *Norton v General Accident*.[85]

17–29 In *Hayes v Legal Insurance Co Ltd*[86] and in *O'Leary v The Irish National Insurance Co*,[87] Budd J. expressly left open the question of whether this provision confers a right of action on third parties against insurance companies in the same way that English statute law did. This argument has the advantage of sidestepping the trust doctrine which, as we have seen, was disapproved of by the Privy Council in *Vandepitte v Preferred Accident Insurance*.[88] Whatever the doubts are about the old law under the Road Traffic Act 1933, it is clear that under s.76 of the Road Traffic Act 1961 the insurer can in essence be proceeded against directly.[89]

---

[84] [1950] I.R. 15. See Buckley, *Insurance Law*, 3rd edn (Dublin: Round Hall, 2012), paras 8-93 to 8-105.
[85] (1941) 74 I.L.T.R. 123; *Hayes v Legal Insurance Co Ltd* [1941] Ir. Jur. Rep. 40.
[86] (1941) Ir. Jur. Rep. 40.
[87] [1958] Ir. Jur. Rep. 1.
[88] [1933] A.C. 70.
[89] *Sinnott v Quinnsworth* [1984] I.L.R.M. 523; for uninsured persons, see *Bowes v MIBI* [2000] 2 I.R. 79.

17–30 Section 62 of the Civil Liability Act 1961 provides that where an insured effects a policy of insurance in respect of a wrong, should that person, or a company, become bankrupt or insolvent, as the case may be, any monies payable to the insured are not to be assets for bankruptcy or insolvency purposes: see *Dunne v PJ White Construction Co Ltd (In Liquidation)*.[90] As Peart J. said in a recent case, citing from an earlier analysis of Laffoy J., "the insurance monies are 'ring fenced' to meet the claim made on the policy, and does not disappear into the general fund for the benefit of other creditors". Hu was injured at work and sued his employer who subsequently went into liquidation. Hu obtained judgment against the employer. Unknown to Hu, the employer had failed to pay an excess sought by the insurer who accordingly repudiated the policy. Hu sought to join the insurer as a defendant to the proceedings but Pearl J. held that there was no privity of contract between Hu and the insurer. Section 62 could not be availed of because repudiation of the policy by the insurer meant that no monies were payable by the insurer to the insured. The decision in *Hu v Duleek Formwork Ltd* suggests that the Oireachtas should consider legislative amendments along the lines of the Third Parties (Rights Against Insurers) Acts 1930 and 2010 in the UK.[91] In *Hu*, most of the plaintiff's difficulties were caused by delays in establishing the factual position between the insured and the insurer: the UK legislation of 2010 contains rights of access to information for third parties but the repudiation problem remains. The Law Reform Commission, in its 2015 *Report on Consumer Insurance Contracts*,[92] makes a specific recommendation regarding third party consumers who are or may be entitled to benefit under the terms of a contract of insurance. In the event that the insured person dies, cannot be found, is insolvent, or where it appears to the court to be just and equitable to do so, the High Court may declare the third party consumer should enjoy the rights vested in the contract of insurance and be able to enforce those rights directly against the insurer, notwithstanding, *inter alia*, the doctrine of privity of contract.[93]

17–31 The privity of contract doctrine has also proved to be very problematical in another commercial context. Where goods, typically a motor vehicle, have been "sold" on hire-purchase terms, the hirer, often unaware of the complex legal nature of the transaction into which he has entered, attempts to obtain a contractual remedy from the wrong source. Because the hirer's contractual arrangements are generally with a finance company rather than the dealer, there have been cases in which the dealer has escaped liability in respect of

---

[90] [1989] I.L.R.M. 803; *Hu v Duleek Formwork Ltd* [2013] IEHC 50; *Stewart v McKenna* [2014] IEHC 301; *Murphy v Allianz Plc* [2014] IEHC 692.

[91] [2013] IEHC 50. See Bullimore, "The Third Parties (Right Against Insurers) Act 2010: unanswered questions and rights of set-off" [2012] L.M.C.L.Q. 382, who explains why the legislation is no panacea for third party insurance claims.

[92] LRC 113 2015.

[93] Paragraph 6.35; a number of other recommendations are made which borrow heavily from the UK 1930 and 2010 Rights of Third Parties legislation.

defective goods by pleading the privity doctrine; see *Dunphy v Blackhall Motors*.[94] The Hire-Purchase Acts 1946–1980, subsequently supplanted by the Consumer Credit Act 1995, closed this gap in the law. Section 80 of the 1995 Act provides that, in respect of agreements where the antecedent negotiations were conducted by another person, that person, along with the owner of the goods shall be deemed to be a party to the agreement. That person and the owner are jointly and severally liable to the hirer for any misrepresentation made in the course of the antecedent negotiations.

17–32 The Sale of Goods and Supply of Services Act 1980, by s.13(2), enacts an implied "condition" in sales by a dealer of a motor vehicle to the effect that the vehicle is, at the time of delivery, free from any defect which would render it a danger to the public including persons travelling in the vehicle. The provision goes further by providing in subs.(7) that a person using the vehicle with the consent of the buyer, who suffers loss as a result of breach of subs.(2), "may maintain an action for damages against the seller in respect of the breach as if he were the buyer".[95] Section 34 extends the s.13 implied "condition" to contracts involving the hire-purchase of motor vehicles. Section 14 of the 1980 Act also makes a finance house liable for breach of contract and a dealer's misrepresentations if goods are sold by a dealer to a consumer, the dealer being paid the purchase price by a finance house, the purchaser repaying the finance house.

17–33 In relation to data processing the need to ensure that personal privacy is respected has led to a specific obligation requiring that personal data transferred outside the European Economic Area for processing operations must take place on foot of a contract which affords data subjects guarantees about the level of privacy and security to be obtained. In the event that these obligations are not met the data subject has a right to enforce these contractual obligations directly, notwithstanding that the data subject is not a party to the processing contract.[96]

Further Reforms?

17–34 Apart from the piecemeal legislative reforms sketched out in the above paragraphs, the doctrine of privity of contract remains in force in Ireland although we shall see that the Law Reform Commission is actively considering the subject of legislative reform. In England, Wales and Northern Ireland there has been an important review of the topic in the form of a Consultation Paper[97] and a Report from the Law Commission.[98] In these texts the Law Commission

---

[94] (1953) 87 I.L.T.R. 128.
[95] See *Glorney v O'Brien*, unreported, High Court, November 14, 1988.
[96] Data Protection (Amendment) Act 2003 s.12, amending s.11 of the Data Protection Act 1988.
[97] Consultation Paper No. 121 (1991); Adams and Brownsword (1993) 56 M.L.R. 722.
[98] Report No. 242 (1996); Reynolds, "Privity of Contract" (1997) 113 L.Q.R. 53; Andrews,

suggested that the law should be amended so as to give effect to the intention of the parties to a contract; where it appears that the parties intended that a third party was to be able to enforce the contract term directly, that person should be able to do so. The principle is easy enough to state in abstract terms, but the means of implementation are not free from difficulty. Nevertheless, the 1999 Act has implemented the Law Commission's recommendations and the Irish Law Reform Commission in its own recent deliberations has been strongly influenced by the 1999 Act.

17–35 Section 1 of the 1999 Act provides that a person who is not a party to a contract may enforce a term of the contract if—

> (i) the contract expressly provides that he/she may do so; or
> (ii) the term purports to confer a benefit upon that person.

This second factor is likely to prove difficult to apply in cases where it is clear that an individual was intended to benefit from the largesse of another but as a matter of common sense it is difficult to see how a third party entitlement can be justified. For example, if a landlord lets a commercial property which requires the tenant to sell only beer and wine, if the tenant breaches the covenant and starts to sell groceries,[99] can the local brewery who no longer receives orders for beer from the tenant enforce the contract? If X employs a solicitor to draft a will but this is done negligently, can a disappointed legatee sue for breach of contract? The UK legislation tends to duck this kind of issue by virtue of a presumption that the third party is entitled to enforce the term[100] unless, as a matter of construction, it appears that the parties did not intend the term in the contract to be enforceable by a third party.[101] The third party must be named in the contract, or be a member of a class or meet a description found in the contract, but the third party need not be in existence at the time the contract is entered into.[102] The third party is entitled to all remedies that would have been available if he or she was a party to the contract[103] and specific provision is made in respect of the enforceability of exemption clauses.[104] The impact of s.1 becomes evident in s.2(1). The parties to the agreement may not rescind, vary, or extinguish the entitlement of the third party if the third party has communicated his or her assent to the promise, the promisor is aware of reliance, or such reliance is shown and was foreseeable by the promisor.

"Reform of the Privity Rule in English Contract Law: The Law Commission's Report No.242" [1997] C.L.J. 25; Hemsworth, "Life Assurance and the Cohabitant: The Law Commission's Reforms on Privity" [1998] 57(1) C.L.J. 55.

[99] *And So To Bed Ltd v Dixon* [2001] F.S.R. 935; *Nisshen Shipping Co Ltd v Cleaves & Co* [2001] 1 All E.R. (Comm.) 481.

[100] *Nisshen Shipping Co Ltd v Cleaves & Co* [2001] 1 All E.R. (Comm.) 481.

[101] Section 1(2).

[102] Section 1(3).

[103] Section 1(5).

[104] Section 1(6).

Rescission or variation will be possible if the contract expressly provides.[105] The promisor may avail of certain defences that were available in respect of the promisee and rights of set-off are also applicable vis-à-vis the third party as if he or she was a party to the contract.[106] The promisee may continue to enforce the contract[107] notwithstanding s.1, although provision is made in order to protect the promisor from double liability.[108] Certain contracts are exempted from the scope of the 1999 Act (e.g. contracts of employment). The 1999 Act has been considered by the English courts on several occasions. In *Laemthong International Lines v Artis*,[109] the Court of Appeal interpreted the requirements of s.1 in such a way as to hold that a letter of indemnity issued by the receivers of a consignee to charterers of a vessel in order to secure delivery of goods was intended to be available to the owners of the vessel as "agents". In *Avramides v Colwill*,[110] the defendant had purchased a construction company that had carried out building work for the plaintiff who was dissatisfied with the work. The transfer agreement as between the two companies was held not to have permitted the plaintiff, as a former customer of the transferor, any rights that could be utilised by way of the 1999 Act. In particular, s.1(3) required the third party to be identified by name, by class or by description, and the transfer agreement did none of these things.

The Law Reform Commission's Proposals

17–36 In 2006 the Law Reform Commission issued a Consultation Paper, *Privity of Contract: Third Party Rights.*[111] In reviewing the existing law in the context of developments in other jurisdictions, both in the common law world and elsewhere, the Law Reform Commission noted that where the privity doctrine was operative, it has been recognised as problematical and capable of having a negative impact across a wide range of contractual agreements. The various means used in order to grant rights to third parties were described as "confusing and unnecessary"[112] and the Commission concluded that unless the rule was reformed it still had the "potential for injustice, inconvenience and expense".[113] The provisional recommendation of the Law Reform Commission was for reform so as to allow third parties to enforce rights under contracts made for their benefit. The preferred option to effect this reform was a legislative text that would preserve the existing exceptions to the privity doctrine and allow third parties access to existing remedies available thereunder.

---

[105] Section 2(3)(a).
[106] Section 3.
[107] Section 4.
[108] Section 5.
[109] [2005] 2 All E.R. (Comm.) 167.
[110] [2005] EWCA Civ 1533; *Holding and Management (Solitaire) Ltd v Ideal Homes NW* [2005] EWCA Civ 59.
[111] LRC CP 40–2006. See Kelly (2007) 14(1) C.L.P. 8.
[112] LRC CP 40–2006, para.1.168.
[113] LRC CP 40–2006, para.1.169.

17–37 The Consultation Paper has been followed by a Report, *Privity of Contract and Third Party Rights*.[114] The Report contains a draft Bill, Contract Law (Privity of Contract and Third Party Rights) Bill 2008, which sets out the essence of the reform proposals in nine sections. Section 1 sets out the short title and commencement provisions while s.2 is the definition section, providing, as it does, definitions of "promise", "promisor" and "third party". Section 3 provides that, subject to the Bill, a third party may enforce a term of a contract in his or her right if:

"(a) the contract expressly provides that he or she may, or
(b) subject to subs.(2), the term expressly confers a benefit on him or her."

Section 3(2) denies the right to a third party if, following the construction of the contract, interpreted by reference to surrounding circumstances, the parties did not intend the contract to be enforceable by the third party.

17–38 Section 3(3) provides that in relation to terms excluding or limiting liability, the reference in s.3(1) to enforcing the term means that term is to be available to the third party.

17–39 Section 3(4) requires the third party to be expressly identified by name as a member of a class or as answering a particular description.

17–40 Section 3(5) provides that the Bill does not require the third party to be in existence at the time of contract or at the time of assent, by another third party.[115] The Consultation Paper itself did not take a position on this point.

17–41 Section 3(6) provides that without prejudice to the consideration requirement vis-à-vis the promisor and promisee, consideration need not be a sine qua non to the third party rights.

17–42 Section 3(7) provides that the s.3(1) right is subject to and exercisable in accordance with any other relevant terms of the contract.

17–43 Section 3(8) gives the third party a right to the full range of remedies including damages and specific performance in the same circumstances as if that person were a party to the contract.

17–44 Section 4 deals with the issue of variation and termination of a contract which is intended to be enforceable by a third party. The section envisages that this entitlement cannot be extinguished or altered where the third party has assented to the contract, to the knowledge of either party (s.4(1)). Section 4(2)

---

[114] LRC 88–2008.
[115] See *Dalton v Ellis: Estate of Bristow* (2005) 65 N.S.W.L.R. 134.

provides for the means of manifesting effective consent, while s.4(3) qualifies s.4(1) by providing that the contracting parties may still, by way of an express term in the contract, either rescind or vary the agreement or alter the consent provisions in s.4(1). Section 4(3), (4) and (5) would enable either the High Court or the Circuit Court to dispense with those various consents, although adding a power to fix terms, including a right to compensation to the third party where that consent is dispersed with (s.4(6)). Section 4(7) deals with multiple third party beneficiaries and allows one third party to assent on behalf of another third party when deemed appropriate by the court.

17–45 Section 5 provides the promisor with the range of defences and right of set-off that the promisee would have had (including rights to counterclaim) had the action been brought by the promisee rather than a third party, while s.6 provides that s.3 does not affect any right of the promisee to enforce any term of the contract, subject to double liability provisions in s.7. Sections 8 and 9 contain provisions relating to specific contracts and exceptions to the Bill. The Bill is to apply to deeds, is not to prejudice the insurable interest requirement in insurance contracts, and the Bill is also to apply to consumers without prejudice to the European consumer *acquis*. Section 9 excludes from the Bill negotiable instruments and commercial credits, Companies Act 1963 s.25 contracts, and carriage of goods contracts. The section also preserves third party rights and remedies that subsist independently of the Bill. Section 9(6) and (7) binds third parties to terms relating to enforcement of contractual terms by arbitration and in a particular jurisdiction.

17–46 It remains to be seen how the Oireachtas will respond to the Consultation Paper and the Report but it is believed to be some way off the Government's list of legislative priorities at the present time (July 2016).

17–47 Issues of privity of contract in relation to mortgage protection policies,[116] as well as so-called house construction bonds or guarantees are extremely contentious. In Ireland, in recent months[117] the Government has been concerned with the enforceability of builder's insurance and construction industry guarantees given to house purchasers and whether such guarantees are enforceable against a structural guarantee provider or insurer in respect of pyrite contamination of building materials. Ad hoc solutions based on remediation schemes rather than privity clarifications are, wisely, to be put in place to deal with the pyrite issue.

---

[116] *Thompson v Lloyd's Undertakings* [2008] 443 A.R. 164.
[117] See the *Report of the Pyrite Panel* (June 2012), p.112, available at: *http://www.environ.ie*. Tort claims have been successful when purchasers rely on assurances in construction industry guarantee cases: *Brennan v Flannery* [2013] IEHC 145. However, problems of accountability ultimately led the government to legislate for a remediation scheme as a matter of last resort. See the Pyrite Resolution Act 2013.

Part 8

Discharge

18 Discharge of Contractual Obligations

Introduction

18–01 Contracts may be discharged in a variety of ways. The most obvious method will be through performance but disputes about what was required by the contract and whether the relevant standard was attained will be foreseeable. The contract may be discharged as a result of breach of contract by one party, but in many cases the contract survives notwithstanding the breach. The contract may be terminated by operation of law through the frustration doctrine. The contract may also be terminated by agreement or, exceptionally, by waiver or estoppel of a legal right.

Discharge of a Contract through Performance

Entire contracts

18–02 Before a contract may be discharged by performance it must be established that performance complies exactly with the terms of the contract. Only the most insignificant deviations imaginable will be excused under the maxim *de minimis non curat lex*.

18–03 Two picturesque examples of the general position were given by Jessel M.R. in *Re Hall & Baker*[1]:

> "If a man engages to carry a box of cigars from London to Birmingham, it is an entire contract, and he cannot throw the cigars out of the carriage half-way there, and ask for half the money; or if a shoemaker agrees to make a pair of shoes, he cannot offer you one shoe and ask you to pay half the price."[2]

Re Moore & Co v Landauer & Co[3] illustrates how demanding this obligation may turn out to be. In this case the seller delivered tinned fruit to the buyer. The contract description indicated that the tins were to be packed 30 tins to each case. While the correct number of tins in total were delivered, some cases contained only 24 tins. The seller was held not to be entitled to

---

[1] (1878) 9 Ch. D. 538. For performance and discharge of contracts in general see *Chitty on Contracts*, edited by H.G. Beale, 32nd edn (London: Sweet & Maxwell, 2015), Vol. 1, paras 21-001 to 25-034.
[2] (1878) 9 Ch. D. 538 at 545.
[3] [1921] 2 K.B. 519.

payment, for the breach of the obligation to deliver in cases of 30 tins was a basis for repudiation of the contract by the buyer, inter alia, on the ground of breach of s.13 of the Sale of Goods Act 1893. Normally, however, the issue of whether a contract is entire or not will arise when the party who has provided less than full performance is subject to a series of obligations, often over a period of time. In the Irish case of *Nash & Co v Hartland*[4] it was pointed out that whether a contract is entire or not is a matter of construction. If the contract, expressly or impliedly, sets out that precise and exact performance by one party must be rendered before any obligation accrues to the other, the contract is entire.

18–04 The leading English case is *Cutter v Powell*.[5] Cutter was engaged as a second mate to serve on a voyage from Jamaica to Liverpool. He was given a promissory note for 30 guineas, payable 10 days after the vessel arrived in Liverpool, should he serve faithfully in that post. Cutter died en route. His widow sued, claiming entitlement to a proportionate part of the sum on a quantum meruit basis. The action failed. The normal rate of pay for a second mate on such a voyage was £8. The higher rate was explained as being "a kind of insurance": per Kenyon M.R. The bargain here was an exceptional one. If Cutter served and arrived in Liverpool he would be paid nearly four times the normal rate; if not, he would recover nothing.

18–05 In the case of *Brown v Wood*[6] the Irish Court of Exchequer distinguished *Cutter v Powell* from the case at bar. The plaintiff agreed to take yarn from the defendant and manufacture cloth from it. Under the terms of the agreement, the plaintiff gave monies as security for the defendant's yarn and undertook to deliver the cloth as it was completed, whereupon the plaintiff would be paid manufacturing expenses and a profit element. While several consignments of cloth were delivered, the plaintiff failed to convert all the yarn, and he disposed of it. While the plaintiff had not completed all the work set by the contract, it was held that the plaintiff was entitled to payment for that part of the work actually completed and delivered, as well as the monies advanced as security for the defendant's yarn. The defence was one of entire contract. As a matter of construction and justice, the contract was held not to be entire. The plaintiff was held entitled to recover for completed goods delivered, and to be entitled to the return of the monies paid by him as security for the yarn; the defendant was held entitled to retain monies given as security for the yarn not processed and to an action for non-delivery of the work not completed.

18–06 The entire contract, as Beck has pointed out,[7] has been confused with a lump-sum contract. The courts all too readily presume that if it is agreed that a lump-sum will be payable after performance the parties had made an entire

---

4   (1840) 2 Ir. L.R. 190.
5   (1795) 6 *Term Reports* 320; *Vigers v Cook* [1919] 2 K.B. 475.
6   (1854) 6 Ir. Jur. 221; *Taylor v Laird* (1856) 1 H. & N. 266.
7   (1975) 38 M.L.R. 413.

contract. This, Beck argues, is a non sequitur; it is possible that the parties also intend that periodic payments or payment for partial completion can be claimed while work is in progress. This view is illustrated by the judgment of Whiteside C.J. in *Collen v Marum*,[8] a case in which a builder agreed to construct a house for a fixed sum. Whiteside C.J. said in such a case the contract is entire and indivisible and that "the employer is not bound to pay for half or quarter of a house for the court and jury can have no right to apportion that which the parties themselves have treated as entire".[9]

18–07 The courts hold that a lump-sum building contract and an entire contract are synonymous; despite Beck's comments[10] it is understandable that this should be so, otherwise a builder would be encouraged to abandon work in progress should a more lucrative contract come along, safe in the knowledge that he can recover for the work completed. Before the courts will permit this it must be shown that the employer has acquiesced to the deviation from precise performance: per Whiteside C.J.[11] The case of *Coughlan v Moloney*[12] takes the test a little further by requiring the builder to show an implied agreement to pay for the work done. The plaintiff there agreed to build a house for the defendant for £200, to be completed by Christmas 1902. No provision for periodic payments was made. The work was left incomplete and in October 1903 the defendants wrote asking for an account to be submitted so that "the matter should be finally wound up". No reply came; the builder sued for the value of work completed, the defendants having engaged another builder to finish the work. The action for work completed failed; if the employer has a half-completed structure on his land he has no choice whether to accept or reject the work. It would be absurd to require the employer to leave the structure in that condition; so, if he used materials left on the site he impliedly promises to pay for their value; he does not impliedly pay for work completed. In *Coughlan v Moloney* the letter of October 1903 was held not to be a new contract for the builder did not provide consideration for this new promise.

18–08 The English case of *Sumpter v Hodges*[13] provides a clear statement of the relevant legal principles. Here a builder undertook to build two houses and a stable on the defendant's land for a lump sum. The builder indicated that he was unable to complete the work due to a cash shortage. The trial judge found that the plaintiff had abandoned the work and was not entitled to recover on a quantum meruit basis. A.L. Smith L.J. indicated that the trial judge was correct: "the law is that, where there is a contract to do work for a

---

8   (1871) 5 Ir. C.L.R. 315.
9   (1871) 5 I.C.L.R. 315 at 319.
10 (1975) 38 M.L.R. 413.
11 (1871) 5 Ir. C.L.R. 315 at 320.
12 (1905) 39 I.L.T.R. 153.
13 [1898] 1 Q.B. 673. The notion that restitution for value of abandoned materials might be possible but that work undertaken is not to be remunerated has been affirmed in *Cleveland Bridge UK Ltd v Multiplex Constructions Ltd* [2010] EWCA Civ 139. *Sumpter v Hedges* thus survives recent expansion of restitution.

lump sum, until the work is completed the price of it cannot be recovered."[14] If the work completed is adopted by the person who initially commissioned it, in circumstances where there is an option to adopt or reject the work, it may be possible to infer a new contract in appropriate circumstances. However, if the commissioner has no option but to accept the work, then no inferred new contract is possible. Both Chitty and Collins L.JJ. agreed. Chitty L.J. noted that the mere fact that a person remains in possession of land does not give rise to an inference that half-completed works on the land will be paid for. The commissioner is not obliged to keep unfinished buildings on his land for such a construction would be a nuisance on the land.

18–09 The position taken in *Coughlan v Moloney* and *Sumpter v Hedges* is a harsh one; after all, the employer gets a substantial benefit which he does not have to pay for. Nevertheless, the rule in *Sumpter v Hedges* has been defended in a recent article[15] on the basis that criticisms of the rule, which often focus on the perceived "unfairness" or "unconscionability" of the rule, as well as the element of unjust enrichment that may result, are misplaced. The authors point to a number of cases in which similar consequences follow on from the failure of one party to a contract to perform entire promissory and contingent conditions and they make the argument that the plaintiff failed in *Sumpter*, not because he was in breach of contract, but because he failed to meet conditions set out in the contract which were a sine qua non to performance of the defendant's obligation to make any payment. The rule itself is not the problem; rather, it is the over-eagerness of the courts to classify the obligation as entire that is the cause of difficulty. So while *Sumpter* creates a strict rule, there are exceptions established by case law as in the case of acceptance of the varied performance,[16] waiver or estoppel,[17] and the case of deviation in a contract for the carriage of goods[18] which may trigger a quantum meruit claim by the carrier. To mitigate the effects of the general rule the courts have developed a doctrine called "substantial performance". If the work has been carried out in its essential respects the party rendering substantial performance will be entitled to the contract price, subject to the employer being able to set off all sums necessary to engage another person to complete the work. Two factors are important here:

(1) the nature of the defects; and

(2) the cost of remedying the defects as against the contract price.

In *Hoenig v Isaacs*[19] a builder agreed to redecorate the defendant's flat for £750; work was not completed and the cost of remedying the defects was £55. The

---

[14] [1898] 1 Q.B. 673 at 674.
[15] McFarlane and Stevens, "In Defence of *Sumpter v Hedges*" (2002) 118 L.Q.R. 569.
[16] *Steele v Tardiani* (1946) 72 C.L.R. 386; *GEC Marconi Systems v BHP—IT* (2003) 128 F.C.R. 1.
[17] *Steele v Tardiani* (1946) 72 C.L.R. 386; *Tufton v Dilmun Shipping* [1992] 1 Lloyd's Rep. 71.
[18] *Hain v Tate & Lyle* (1934) 39 Com. Cas. 259.
[19] [1952] 2 All E.R. 176.

English Court of Appeal held that because the defects were insignificant—a bookcase had to be completed—the builder was entitled to total payments of £695. In *Hoenig v Isaacs* Denning L.J. expressed the law in the following way:

"[T]he first question is whether, on the true construction of the contract, entire performance was a condition precedent to payment. It was a lump sum contract, but that does not mean that entire performance was a condition precedent to payment. When a contract provides for a specific sum to be paid on completion of specified work, the courts lean against a construction of the contract which would deprive the contractor of any payment at all simply because there are some defects or omissions. The promise to complete the work is, therefore, construed as a term of the contract, but not as a condition. It is not every breach of that term which absolves the employer from his promise to pay the price, but only a breach which goes to the root of the contract, such as an abandonment of the work when it is only half done. Unless the breach does go to the root of the matter, the employer cannot resist payment of the price. He must pay it and bring a cross-claim for the defects and omissions and is usually calculated by the cost of making them good."[20]

In contrast it has been held that where a central heating system was installed improperly, payment being agreed at £560, the system emitting fumes and working inefficiently, these defects, which would cost £124 to put right, meant that the deviation fell short of substantial performance; see *Bolton v Mahadeva*.[21]

18–10 There is authority for the view that substantial performance will not apply if the builder refuses to complete or abandons work he acknowledges to be due; only if the parties genuinely dispute whether the work completed meets the contract standard can the compromise of substantial performance operate. In *Kincora Builders v Cronin*,[22] the only Irish case in which substantial performance has been considered, Pringle J. held that where a builder refused to insulate an attic this would constitute an abandonment, denying him a remedy under substantial performance.

18–11 The English Law Commission in a Working Paper[23] pointed out that the result of the present law is to create a strong possibility of an employer being unjustly enriched if a builder, through lack of funds, is unable to complete work. Sweeping restitutionary changes were proposed if it could be shown that one party to a lump-sum contract has conferred substantial advantages on the other. The Law Commission in its final Report[24] agreed that where a builder conferred a benefit on the other party, payment should be made unless

---

20 [1952] 2 All E.R. 176 at 180; *Dunnes Stores v Holtglen Ltd* [2012] IEHC 93.
21 [1972] 2 All E.R. 1322.
22 Unreported, High Court, March 5, 1973.
23 Working Paper No. 65 (1975).
24 Law Comm. No. 121 (1983).

the contract excludes this. The dissent of one member of the Commission to such a proposal draws attention to the danger of allowing compensation where the builder refuses to complete for no good reason. The dissenting member had this to say of the proposal that a party in breach of an entire contract should be entitled to some payment if a net benefit has been conferred on the other contracting party, unless the contract expressly provides to the contrary:

> "Experience has shown that it is all too common for such builders not to complete one job of work before moving on to the next. The effect of the report is to remove from the householder almost the only effective sanction he has against the builder not completing the job."[25]

If money is paid in advance under an entire contract and some benefit has been conferred upon the party making advance payment, restitution of the total price paid is not possible, for there will not have been a total failure of consideration. Damages will be awarded, calculated by reference to the cost of having the work completed by a third party.[26]

(1) Statutory modifications

18–12 The position reached in *Coughlan v Moloney*, a building contract, is echoed by s.30(1) of the Sale of Goods Act 1893 which provides that while the buyer of goods who takes delivery of a quantity of goods which are less than he consented to take may reject them, he is obliged to pay for them at the contract rate should he accept the goods; see s.31 and *Norwell & Co v Black*.[27] If certain services have already been rendered by A to B, A then terminating the contract without having been paid on a quantum meruit basis, there can be no question of B electing to accept or reject partial performance. The Apportionment Act 1870 does give some limited redress. Under the combined effect of ss.2 and 5 "rents, annuities, dividends and other periodical payments", including "salaries and pensions", shall be considered as accruing from day to day. A lump-sum payment for one period of employment is not a periodical payment so *Cutter v Powell* would be outside this Act; see also *Creagh v Sheedy*,[28] which seems to have been decided *per incuriam*.

18–13 If the claimant *terminates* employment his termination does not prevent him from relying on the Act. In *Treacy v Corcoran*,[29] Treacy was employed as a clerk, the remuneration being payable half-yearly. In April 1872 he resigned. Corcoran took over the job and at the end of the half year Corcoran was paid £115, the sum payable for the whole of the period. Treacy was held entitled to a proportion of that sum, based on the 34-day period he was in employment. *Treacy v Corcoran* has been followed in the English Court of Appeal decision

---

[25] Brian Davenport Q.C., at p.36.
[26] *Whincup v Hughes* (1871) L.R. 6 C.P. 78.
[27] (1930) 65 I.L.T.R. 104.
[28] [1955–1956] Ir. Jur. Rep. 86. For a more recent English case illustrating the operation of the Act, see *Taylor v East Midlands Offender Employment* [2000] I.R.L.R. 760.
[29] (1874) I.R. 8 C.L. 40.

in *Item Software (UK) Ltd v Fassihi*.[30] An employee, paid on a monthly basis on the last day of each month, was dismissed on June 26 for misconduct. The employee sought payment for June 1–26, but the claim was resisted on the basis that earlier authority had held that where a dismissal for misconduct occurred, that conduct amounting to fraud, no proportion of salary which is to accrue later is recoverable.[31] Holding that the language of the statute was clearly in favour of recovery, the Court of Appeal observed that in the *Boston* case[32] the Apportionment Act 1870 had not been cited, with Lady Justice Arden in particular characterising the common law rule as unjust while the 1870 Act was remedial in nature.[33]

18–14 It should be noted that the Construction Contracts Act 2013 introduces a mechanism whereby parties to a construction contract, or contracts ancillary thereto, shall fix interim payments and final payments amounts and dates, thereby addressing lack of clarity issues that are a feature of the Irish construction industry. There are default provisions in the Schedule to the Act for contracts and subcontracts that are not compliant in this regard. Contractors benefit from a payment notice procedure and rights to payment when there is no contest as to payment, that is, there is no dispute about the contractor causing loss or damage. Suspension of work for non-payment is a remedy and where there is a dispute about payment, the Act creates an adjudication system, to be discharged by a panel selected by the Minister for Public Expenditure and Reform. The Act will come into operation on 25 July 2016 and the Act will apply to construction contracts entered into after that day.[34] This Act, where it applies, rebalances the law relating to construction contracts by ending the basic disparity in economic power which directed that contractors would be paid only when the developer or main contractor has been paid.

(2) Divisible contracts

18–15 If a contract is held to be made up of a series of separate obligations, the contract providing that payment is to be due during the process of performance, the contract is divisible. In the building industry contracts are generally drafted so as to entitle the builder to payment as certain stages are completed; to ensure performance the contract normally provides that a proportion of the total price—15–20 per cent—will be retained until some time after the work has been completed.

---

[30] [2004] EWCA Civ 1244.
[31] On the background to the Act and services see Williams, "Partial Performance of Entire Contracts" (1941) 57 L.Q.R. 373 and Matthews, "'Salaries' in the Apportionment Act 1870" (1982) 2 *Legal Studies* 302. Matthews argued the Act is relevant to officeholders in the main, not employees. The wider view has prevailed. The Act has most recently been considered in the context of striking teachers e.g. *Hartley & Ors v King Edward VI College* [2015] EWCA Civ 455, although that case does not resolve issues about the sections 2, 3 and 7 issues at all.
[32] *Boston Deep Sea Fishing & Ice Co v Ansell* (1888) 39 Ch. D. 339.
[33] e.g. *Clapham v Draper* (1885) Cab. & El. 484.
[34] S.I. No. 165 of 2016.

18–16 If work is to be done on part of a building or some other structure a presumption may arise in favour of the contract being divisible rather than entire. A trade custom in favour of a shipwright being entitled to call for repair work to be payable in instalments explains the leading case of *Roberts v Havelock*.[35] In the case of *Verolme Cork Dockyard Ltd v Shannon Atlantic Fisheries Ltd*[36] the plaintiffs claimed for £28,000, alleged to be due for repair work performed on the defendants' fishing boat. The defendants pleaded that the work was not completed and that the contract was entire. Finlay P. on the evidence held that the contract contained a term requiring a substantial payment on account to be made when a reasonably high proportion of the work had been carried out.

(3) Fault of one party preventing performance

18–17 While an entire contract must be performed precisely there will be a remedy available in quantum meruit should one party fail to perform his obligations because of some act or default on the part of the other. In the case of *Arterial Drainage Co Ltd v Rathangan River Drainage Board*[37] contractors agreed to drain land for the defendant Board, the contract being entire. The contract provided that if the contractors failed to carry out work with due diligence the employer could terminate the contract. The defendant purported to exercise this right. It appears that the work was not performed as quickly as envisaged because the defendant had failed to make land and plans available to the contractors. The Court of Common Pleas, distinguishing *Cutter v Powell*, held that the defendant's default prevented the plaintiffs from performing their obligations. The plaintiffs were therefore entitled to treat the contract as rescinded and sue for the value of work completed.

(4) Tender of performance

18–18 When one party unsuccessfully attempts to render performance this is known as a tender. The effects of a tender differ according to the nature of the outstanding obligation.

18–19 If the obligation is to pay a sum of money, the creditor refusing to accept the sum, this does not discharge the debtor's obligation to pay. Should the debtor pay the sum into court the creditor may recover the sum by way of action but interest will not be payable; the debtor will recover his costs.[38]

18–20 Even if the obligation is an obligation to pay money and the contract does not make provision for the form in which payment is made, one party may accept a cheque, or credit card payment as the method of payment. Should the payment be dishonoured there may be either an action for the recovery

---

[35] (1832) 3 B. & Ad. 404.

[36] Unreported, High Court, July 31, 1978.

[37] (1880) 6 L.R. (Ir.) 513; *Planché v Colburn* (1831) 8 Bing. 14.

[38] *Griffiths v Board of Ystradyfodwg* (1890) 24 Q.B.D. 307; Rules of the Superior Courts 1986 Ord.22.

of the original debt or an action on the dishonoured payment. Whether such actions are available is a matter of interpretation. In *P.M.P.S. Ltd v Moore*[39] the question arose as to whether acceptance of a bill of exchange operated as a conditional or absolute acceptance. While the general presumption is that the acceptance is conditional only, thereby making a tender of the bill incapable of discharging the underlying debt in the case of dishonour, Murphy J. indicated that an exception will arise where the bill tendered is drawn by the creditor himself and endorsed back to the creditor.

18–21 The debtor must meet any contractual terms set as to the place, time and manner of payment. The Northern Ireland case of *Morrow v Carty*[40] establishes that attempted payment of a deposit required in cash by offering a cheque will not be sufficient. In the Republic of Ireland the Decimal Currency Act 1969 defined legal tender within the State as follows; silver coins were legal tender up to the sum of £10 (s.8(1)); a tender of bronze coins and silver coins up to a value of 10p. was legal tender for any sum up to £5 (s.8(2)); bronze coins were legal tender up to a sum of 20p. Irish Central Bank banknotes were legal tender up to any amount. UK banknotes and coins are not legal tender in the Republic because they are not issued under the Coinage Acts 1926–1950, or the Decimal Currency Act 1969. The Economic and Monetary Union Act 1998 outlined the repeal of these provisions by June 30, 2002 (ss.9 and 10), and from the beginning of January 1999 the currency of the State was declared to be the euro, the Irish pound being a subdivision thereof (s.6). See also the Euro Changeover (Amounts) Act 2001.

18–22 If the tender consists of an attempt to perform actions other than payment of money, the delivery of goods for example, non-acceptance may discharge the obligations of the promisor. Thus if goods are due and they are tendered during a reasonable hour, a refusal to accept may amount to a repudiation entitling the seller to treat the contract as discharged: Sale of Goods Act 1893 ss.29(4), 31(2) and 37. The essential issue is whether the tender gives the buyer the opportunity to adequately inspect the goods.

(5) Time of performance

18–23 While at common law any time fixed for the performance of a contract was held to be "of the essence of the contract", failure to perform entitling the other party to terminate and sue for damages,[41] the equitable rule which now prevails makes it clear that normally time for performance is not of the essence; see the Judicature Act 1877 s.28(7) and *Maye v Merriman*.[42] In Ireland, time will be of the essence if the contract so provides; this is frequently

---

[39] [1988] I.L.R.M. 526; Gill (1987) 6 I.L.T. 81.
[40] [1957] N.I. 174.
[41] *Bowes v Shand* (1877) 2 App. Cas. 455. This rule was particularly strong in cases of delivery of goods: *Clements v Russell* (1854) 7 Ir. Jur. 102.
[42] Unreported, High Court, February 3, 1980.

done in conveyancing. In *Crean v Drinan*[43] the plaintiff purchaser stipulated a completion date in connection with the purchase of property. It had also been stipulated that an assignment of an interest held by third parties would be obtained by the closing date. While it was held that the failure to close on the completion date did not itself discharge the agreement, the failure to obtain the deed of assignment by that date did discharge the contract. Applying the leading case of *Aberfoyle Plantations v Cheng*,[44] Barrington J. held that where a conditional contract of sale fixes the date by which the condition must be met the date so fixed must be strictly adhered to. The contract accordingly was discharged when the defendant failed to obtain the assignment stipulated by the plaintiff. The plaintiff was entitled to the return of his deposit. However, each agreement will turn on its own facts. In *Sepia Ltd and Opal Ltd v M. & P. Hanlon Ltd*[45] the defendants agreed to sell two parcels of land, Block A and Block B, to the plaintiffs. Block A was the subject of a contract which expressly fixed the closing date and expressly made time of the essence. The agreement was subject to the plaintiffs obtaining planning permission. Should the permission not be obtained by the closing date, the defendant vendor would have been able to treat the contract as at an end and the purchaser's deposit would have been forfeited. In this case the planning permission difficulty was not such as to excuse non-performance of the obligation to close the Block A contract.

18–24 The English courts have recently restated the view that where a contract expressly makes time of the essence equitable principles cannot be used to overlook non-compliance with the literal terms of the bargain. In *Union Eagle Ltd v Golden Achievement Ltd*[46] a contract for the conveyance of a flat in Hong Kong provided for completion on or before 17.00 on a given day. Non-compliance would give the vendor a cancellation right and the right to forfeit the deposit. The purchaser was 10 minutes late. Proceedings by the purchaser to obtain specific performance ultimately failed in the Privy Council, equity not intervening to absolve the purchaser from the effects of the "time of the essence" clause and the cancellation provision; there was nothing in the nature of a penalty involved here and the Privy Council refused to evolve an unconscionability remedy on the ground that such relief would cause uncertainty and fly in the face of the contract itself. In *Ochre Ridge Ltd v Cork Bonded Warehouses and the Port of Cork Co*,[47] a contract for the purchase of a leasehold interest specifically made the completion date "of the essence". That date passed without completion. The intended lessee's action claiming bad faith and breach of contract failed on the basis that no such duties existed

---

[43] [1983] I.L.R.M. 82.
[44] [1960] A.C. 115. In some commercial property sales time may be of the essence as a matter of implication: *O'Brien v Seaview Enterprises*, unreported, High Court, May 31, 1976.
[45] Unreported, High Court, January 23, 1979.
[46] [1997] A.C. 517, applying *Steedman v Drinkle* [1916] 1 A.C. 275. See Stevens, "Having your Cake and Eating it? *Union Eagle Ltd v Golden Achievement Ltd*" (1998) 61 M.L.R. 255.
[47] [2006] IEHC 107.

and that the passing of the completion date meant the contract was discharged. Smyth J. indicated that where time is of the essence:

"... the date so fixed must be strictly adhered to, and the time allowed is not to be extended by reference to equitable principles".

If the contract does not originally make time of the essence, one party may subsequently serve a notice that as from a stated date, time shall be of the essence. In *Nolan v Driscoll*[48] the plaintiff, in December 1975, agreed to purchase the defendant's house; due to problems relating to registration of title the sale was still incomplete two years later; on March 2, 1977 the defendant, being of the view that a sufficient title had been shown, served notice that he now wished to make time of the essence, and that completion should take place at the end of the month. McWilliam J. upheld the defendant's view that he was entitled to terminate when the plaintiff failed to meet the closing date and refused to order specific performance against him. However, if there is a date fixed for closing, it may be that the parties will subsequently extend or in some way alter the closing date. In *Sepia Ltd and Opal Ltd v M.&P. Hanlon Ltd*,[49] while the contract in respect of Block A contained an express term making time of the essence, the later contract for Block B, which was silent on this point, superseded the original closing date in the Block A contract, and provided that the closing date for both contracts was to be one of two fixed dates, at the option of the purchasers. When both dates passed, the defendant vendors wrote a letter making time of the essence and giving three months' notice of the closing date fixed. Costello J. stated the applicable principles as follows:

"If a stipulation as to time is not of the essence of a contract, then when one party has been guilty of undue delay the other may give notice requiring the contract to be performed within a reasonable time specified in the notice. In considering the reasonableness of the time so limited the court will consider not merely what remains to be done at the date of the notice but all the circumstances of the case, including the previous delay of the purchaser and the attitude of the vendor to it. If the notice is a reasonable one the vendor may at its expiration treat the contract as at an end if the purchaser refuses to complete."[50]

In this case the purchasers had been dilatory in order to progress their application for planning permission to the stage of grant of the permission prior to closing. The notice period was reasonable, given that the delays in respect of the planning permission were also in part due to the plaintiffs' tardiness and the fact that the defendants had no hand or part in this process and the very consistent attitude of the defendants. They had been sympathetic

---

[48] Unreported, High Court, April 25, 1978. See generally Stannard, "The Contractual Last Chance Saloon: Notices Making Time of Essence" (2004) 120 L.Q.R. 137.

[49] Unreported, High Court, January 23, 1979.

[50] Citing *Stickney v Keeble* [1915] A.C. 386; *Ajit v Sammy* [1967] 1 A.C. 259.

to the plaintiffs but had pressed for closing on the dates fixed. More recently, the English courts have been presented with the opportunity to further refine these principles. For example, when the closing date arrives, the purchaser may, if it is apparent that there will be a delay, be immediately presented with a notice making time of the essence. The vendor is not obliged to wait for a reasonable period before serving the notice. However, the time set must be a reasonable one.[51] In accordance with the rules on tender, the duty to complete by tendering the purchase price is strict and cannot be excused by, for example, a dispute over the monies due under the contract.[52] A further basis upon which the contract may be terminated, even in the absence of an express notice, either at the time of contracting or following a delay, is where the purchaser or vendor has been guilty of a frustrating delay. The vendor or purchaser, if innocent of fault, is entitled to treat the contract as discharged by operation of the doctrine of frustration. The decision of the Supreme Court in *O'Connor v Coady*[53] extends the principles laid down in *Aberfoyle Plantations v Cheng* into conditional contracts where the obligation is not a time obligation but is one whereby the contract is conditional upon the grant of planning permission. O'Connor agreed to sell land to Coady, subject to Coady obtaining planning permission within four months from the date of the contract. Planning permission was not granted within that time and no significant contact took place until almost one year after the expiry of the four-month deadline when the purchaser's solicitor wrote to inform the vendor's solicitor that planning permission was likely to be issued soon. The vendor's solicitor immediately replied that it was the vendor's view that the contract was at an end. In the High Court, Carroll J. held that the contract remained in existence on the basis that the vendor had failed to serve a notice making time of the essence, thus giving the purchaser 28 days to meet the condition set or waive the need for planning permission, by analogy with the reasoning in *Sepia Ltd and Opal Ltd v M.&P. Hanlon Ltd*. The Supreme Court allowed the vendor's appeal. In the view of all three judges the completion notice[54] proce-dure referred to in the contract was irrelevant as it was only to be triggered when the planning permission was granted. The Supreme Court held that, in this case, the four month condition was not a promissory condition but it was an absolute obligation that, as in *Aberfoyle Plantations*, could not be extended by reference to equitable principles. All three members of the Supreme Court viewed the contract as being voidable once the four-month period had elapsed, unless the person for whose sole benefit the planning permission provision had been inserted chose to waive it. In this case the condition was for the sole

---

51 *Behzadi v Shaftesbury Hotels Ltd* [1991] 2 All E.R. 477, disapproving *Smith v Hamilton* [1950] 2 All E.R. 928. The decision in *British and Commonwealth Holdings v Quadrex Holdings Ltd* [1989] 3 All E.R. 492 is something of a transitional decision after the *Behzadi* case. In Northern Ireland see *Fitzpatrick v Sarcon (No.177) Ltd* [2012] NICA 58.

52 *Carne v Debono* [1988] 3 All E.R. 485.

53 [2004] 3 I.R. 271.

54 Completion notices are considered in a number of recent Irish cases, e.g. *Tyndarius v O'Mahony*, unreported, High Court, March 3, 2003, following *Viscount Securities Ltd v Kennedy*, unreported, Supreme Court, May 6, 1986. See also *Birmingham v Coughlan* [2004] IEHC 211.

benefit of the purchaser. Because the contract was voidable the Supreme Court held that there was a need to communicate an intention to avoid the contract, and the Supreme Court held that the vendor's solicitor's letter of response in which the opinion was expressed that the contract was at an end was sufficient for this purpose. The Supreme Court expressed the view that a waiver may be effective either during the period within which the condition is to be satisfied or before an intention to avoid the contract is communicated. McCracken J. stated obiter[55] that it had not been argued that the contract came to an end automatically when the condition set was not fulfilled, and the learned judge was clearly of the view that this argument was sustainable although he was prepared to accept the opinion held by counsel on both sides (as well as Geoghegan J.)[56] that the contract was voidable. With respect, it is difficult to see how a condition that is not promissory can render a contract voidable (after all, there is no breach of contract) and it would be more consistent to follow McCracken J.'s dicta on this point, should the matter arise for decision.

18–25 In a subsequent case[57] in which the contract was said to be unenforceable unless the planning permission has been obtained within the requisite period, it has been reaffirmed that a waiver is possible but the waiver must be communicated before the other party communicates an intention to avoid the contract. In landlord and tenant cases the House of Lords has indicated that the attitude to all time obligations, whether the property is commercial or otherwise, will be governed by the general rule that, in the absence of an express term, time is not of the essence. The decision in *United Scientific Holdings Ltd v Burnley Borough Council*[58] is to be seen as the leading case on time covenants generally.

18–26 In commercial contracts the courts are reluctant to hold time of the essence unless the contract so requires; see s.10(1) of the Sale of Goods Act 1893. Due to the nature of the commodity sold time will be of the essence in contracts for the sale of a business as a going concern. Non-observance of time obligations in a commercial contract may permit the innocent party to regard the other party as being in breach, thereby entitling the innocent party to treat the contract as at an end, if the obligation is a condition or the obligation, as an intermediate stipulation, has been broken in a way that goes to the root of the contract.[59]

(6) Human rights legislation and contractual termination rights

18–27 The inter-relationship between human rights legislation and private law is still very much in its infancy but the decision of the European Court of

---

[55] [2004] 3 I.R. 271 at 293–294.
[56] McGuinness J. issued a judgment concurring with the judgments of both McCracken J. and Geoghegan J.
[57] *Hand v Greaney* [2004] IEHC 391.
[58] [1977] 2 All E.R. 62, followed in *Hynes v Independent Newspapers* [1980] I.R. 204.
[59] *Hong Kong Fir Shipping Co v Kawasaki Kishen Keisha* [1962] 2 Q.B. 26.

Human Rights in *McCann v UK*,[60] handed down on May 13, 2008, suggests that privacy rights may abridge many contractual rights. Here, the plaintiff successfully invoked art.8 of the European Convention on Human Rights, the right to family life and privacy, arguing that the termination of a tenancy agreement in accordance with procedures set out in the contract were incompatible with art.8. The Supreme Court, in *Donegan v Dublin City Council*,[61] has found that the statutory ejectment provisions in s.62(3) of the Housing Act 1966 do not afford a tenant the right to question the decision of the housing authority to seek ejectment of the tenant. Section 62(3) only allows a review of the proofs set out in the section. Section 62 is incompatible with art.8; the possibility of judicial review is not an effective remedy for a tenant in all cases and does not repair the breach.

Discharge through Agreement

18–28 Post-contractual representations which purport to have the effect of abrogating or modifying contractual terms present acute difficulties, due in the main to a failure on the part of judges to use and define terms like "rescission", "variation" and "waiver" with any degree of precision; the term "waiver", for example, bears at least six meanings.[62] Additional difficulties are presented by jurisdictional factors; modern equitable lines of authority provide solutions which differ from those developed by the courts of common law.

(1) Rescission through accord and satisfaction

18–29 For a contract to be terminated by mutual agreement (accord), consideration (satisfaction) must be present. No difficulty arises where the transaction is executory on both sides; mutual promises not to sue for non-performance generate consideration from both parties. Even if the agreement is partly executed on both sides the same rule applies. In general, the form in which the contract is discharged is not relevant. A deed may be rescinded by a simple contract and need not be contained in a deed. However, if there is a written instrument which records the terms of the executory or partly executed contract in order to make the agreement enforceable as a matter of statute law, as in s.2 of the Statute of Frauds 1695, then it may be necessary to record the terms of any agreement which is intended to vary or supplement any prior agreement in the same way as the initial agreement. If these oral terms are not recorded in a memorandum in writing, to use the example of the Statute of Frauds, then the agreement continues and the oral variation will not be enforceable.[63] In contrast, if the oral agreement is intended to extinguish

---

[60] [2008] ECHR 385.
[61] [2012] IESC 18.
[62] Dugdale and Yates (1976) 39 M.L.R. 680; see generally, Wilken and Ghaly, *The Law of Waiver, Variation and Estoppel*, 3rd edn (Oxford: OUP, 2012).
[63] *McQuaid v Lynam* [1965] I.R. 564; *Morris v Baron & Co* [1918] A.C. 1; *Scott v Midland Great Western Railway* (1853) 6 Ir. Jur. 73; *Ruck v Brownrigg* (1849) 2 Ir. Jur. 142.

or abrogate an executory or partly executed contract for the sale of land, this can be done by an oral agreement. If the intention is to abrogate the written contract, which does comply with statutory formalities, and replace it with an entirely oral agreement which is incompatible with the earlier agreement, then both the earlier and later agreements are unenforceable for different reasons. In relation to the first, it is rescinded verbally but the second is unenforceable for failure to comply with the statute in question.[64] If the intention is simply to supplement or vary orally a written agreement, then the written agreement will remain enforceable.[65] These strict rules may be relaxed by way of the notice of waiver.[66]

18–30 If one party has completely performed his part of the contract a promise given by that person will not rescind the contract. So, if A has delivered wheat to B and B has yet to pay for the goods, a promise by A not to sue B is ineffective unless recorded in a deed under seal or B gives some nominal consideration for A's promise.[67] In *Compagnie Noga d'Importation et d'Exportation SA v Abacha (No. 2)*[68] the parties to a dispute settlement which was unperformed executed a later document reciting similar terms. In drawing the distinction between the continuation of an agreement with a variation, as opposed to the rescission of an earlier agreement which is executory, Tuckey L.J. wrote of the consideration requirement in both contexts:

> "The essential difference between rescission and variation for present purposes is that a contract comes to an end when it is rescinded but continues if it is varied. If the rescinded agreement is replaced by a new agreement containing the same obligations, it is not the old agreement which compels the performance of those obligations, but the new agreement. It follows that the principle in *Stilk v Myrick* has no application to this situation because it is premised on the continuation of the obligations in the old agreement … consideration is however necessary for the agreement to rescind the old contract. There is no difficulty about this in the present case where at the time of rescission the [earlier agreement] was executory on both sides."[69]

It suffices for the purpose of the discharge of the initial cause of action, if the satisfaction agreed upon—for example, a cash debt of £500—is to be satisfied by the debtor transferring to the creditor a motor vehicle owned by the

---

64 *Morris v Baron & Co* [1918] A.C. 1; *Jackson v Hayes* [1939] Ir. Jur. Rep. 59; *Travers Construction Ltd v Lismore Homes Ltd*, unreported, High Court, March 9, 1990.
65 *UDT Corp (Jamaica) Ltd v Shoucair* [1969] 1 A.C. 340.
66 See the discussion in *Wright v Griffith* (1851) 3 Ir. Jur. 138, in which *Goss v Nugent* (1833) 5 B. & Ad. 58 is examined in the context of waiver.
67 *Drogheda Corp v Fairtlough* (1858) 8 Ir. C.L.R. 98; *Foakes v Beer* (1884) 9 App. Cas. 605.
68 [2003] 2 All E.R. (Comm.) 915.
69 [2003] 2 All E.R. (Comm.) 915 at 931; contrast *Antons Trawling Co v Smith* [2003] 2 N.Z.L.R. 23, discussed by Coote at [2003] N.Z.U.L.R. 361; *Teat v Willcocks* [2013] NZCA 162.

debtor in full satisfaction of the cash debt—is promised without the actual performance having been executed.[70] This is subject, of course, to qualification. The creditor may make the discharge conditional upon actual receipt of the satisfaction promised by the debtor.

18–31 Section 62 of the Bills of Exchange Act 1882, in force in both parts of Ireland, provides that no satisfaction is necessary for the renunciation of a debt owed to the holder of a bill of exchange or promissory note. So a straight-forward way of avoiding the general rule would be for the creditor to take a bill or note in satisfaction of the debt and then renounce the debt.[71]

(2) Variation

18–32 Consideration must also be present if a contractual term is deleted or altered, leaving the rest of the contract untouched; see *Fenner v Blake*.[72]

18–33 The variation, to be effective, may have to overcome certain evidentiary hurdles. Section 2 of the Statute of Frauds 1695 and s.4 of the Sale of Goods Act 1893 come into play here. A variation may have to be recorded in writing. The leading Irish case is *McQuaid v Lynam*[73]; Kenny J. said:

> "It is essential to distinguish between the case in which the parties to an agreement intend that agreement to find expression in a written contract and that in which the parties make an oral contract which is intended to be binding. If in the latter case a memorandum or note in writing is required by the Statute of Frauds, that memorandum or note does not become the contract."

After reading s.2, Kenny J. continued:

> "[W]here the parties intend their agreement to find expression in a written document, a subsequent oral variation of the contract is not effective unless it is evidenced by a memorandum or note in writing … But in the other type of case, where the oral agreement is intended to be the contract, evidence may be given of an agreed variation even if there is a memorandum or note of the contract but not of the variation."[74]

However, if no formal requirement to reduce the contract into writing exists then an oral variation of the contract can be proved in the usual way; see *Saphena Computing Ltd v Allied Collection Agencies*.[75]

---

[70] *Cartwright v Cooke* (1832) 3 B. & Ad. 701; *British Russian Gazette Ltd v Associated Newspapers Ltd* [1933] 2 K.B. 616.
[71] See Treitel, *The Law of Contract* 13th edn (London: Sweet & Maxwell, 2011), para.3–061.
[72] [1900] 1 Q.B. 427.
[73] [1965] I.R. 564.
[74] [1965] I.R. 564 at 573.
[75] [1995] F.S.R. 616.

18–34 There is, however, a developing line of New Zealand authority for the view that consideration is not necessary to render a variation of a contract enforceable unless policy reasons support such a position: *Antons Trawling Co v Smith*.[76]

(3) Waiver

18–35 If a contractual term is subject to a variation then as a matter of contract the terms of the agreement are altered. If, however, there is a request for some degree of forbearance, such request being agreed to, no change occurs vis-à-vis the contractual obligation. In this context it is common to describe the conduct of the party granting the concession as waiver of a contractual right. Even entire agreements may be the subject of a waiver but it is necessary that the conduct of the party who is alleged to have waived the obligation in question should either unequivocally dispense with the need for entire performance or engage in conduct which makes it clear that no further service is required from the claimant; see *Tufton v Dilmun Shipping*.[77] Perhaps the most enlightening discussion of waiver of contractual rights and the relationship between waiver, contractual and promissory estoppel is the decision of the High Court of Australia in *Agricultural and Rural Finance Property Ltd v Gardiner*.[78] The leading judgment spoke of efforts to classify various types of waiver, the court observing that it "is not necessary to consider whether such classifications are useful. Rather, it is important to identify the principles that are said to be engaged in the particular case".[79]

18–36 Again the Statute of Frauds 1695 becomes material to the discussion. Waiver of a contractual right does not have to be evidenced in writing unlike a variation, because in strict theory the right continues to exist while it may be unenforceable—a jurisprudential oddity.

18–37 The case of *McKillop v McMullen*[80] illustrates the effect of a waiver on a contractual obligation. The defendant agreed to sell land to the plaintiff subject to the defendant acquiring a right of way over a road to be built upon the land; planning permission was to be a condition precedent to the sale. When the closing date agreed upon arrived the defendant vendor failed to rescind; in fact he later requested performance. Shortly after this he, without notice, rescinded the contract. Planning permission was granted shortly after. Murray J. held that when the defendant allowed the date for completion to pass, insisting that the parties complete at some later date, that this was a waiver of his right to terminate for failure to obtain planning permission at

---

[76] [2003] 2 N.Z.L.R. 23; *Teat v Willcocks* [2013] NZCA 162.
[77] [1992] 1 Lloyd's Rep. 71 at 80.
[78] [2008] HCA 57.
[79] Gummow, Hayne & Kiefel JJ., citing Potter J. in *The Happy Day* [2002] 2 Lloyd's Rep. 487 at 506 and Wilken and Ghaly, *The Law of Waiver, Variation and Estoppel*, 3rd edn (Oxford: OUP, 2012).
[80] [1979] N.I. 85; *O'Connor v Coady* [2004] 3 I.R. 271.

the date of completion; the waiver was not unqualified, however. The right to terminate could be exercised upon giving reasonable notice of a new date; failure to give such notice meant that the waiver remained effective.

18–38 Waiver may also affect the range of remedies available to the party forbearing to enforce his rights. In *Car & General Insurance Corp v Munden*[81] the plaintiffs, insurers of the defendant's motor vehicle, required in cl.2 of the contract that no admission, offer, promise, payment or indemnity would be given by the insured without the consent of the plaintiffs who were also to have a right to sue in respect of an accident involving the insured. The insured's vehicle collided with a bus injuring the insured and damaging the vehicle. The insured signed a release note issued by the bus company who paid compensation for his personal injuries. The plaintiffs believed that this broke cl.2; the right of subrogation was thereby extinguished. The plaintiffs therefore claimed to be entitled to recover £130 paid in respect of damage to the vehicle. It was held that while cl.2 may have been broken, payment of the £130 constituted a waiver of the right to refuse to indemnify the defendant. The waiver only prevented the plaintiffs from terminating the agreement and obtaining restitution; they were entitled to recovery damages, which, because of difficulties of proof, were nominal in this case.

18–39 This result seems a curious one. It is difficult to see how waiver may be possible in cases of this nature where that person is unaware that the right to terminate has come into play: when the insurance company paid out it was unaware of Munden's non-observance of cl.2. In contrast, the Court of Appeal in *Peyman v Lanjani*[82] held that before a contracting party can be held to have affirmed an agreement and waived a right to rescind it, knowledge of the right to elect whether to affirm the contract or rescind must be shown. If there is simply knowledge of the facts without knowledge that, on these facts, rescission is possible, then waiver cannot be said to take place if that party simply refrains from a particular course of action. The decision of Carswell J. in *Lutton v Saville Tractors Ltd*[83] is to similar effect. The purchaser of a motor car obtained a warranty that the vehicle had not been involved in a motor accident. After taking delivery of the vehicle, it proved unsatisfactory and the purchaser took the vehicle back on several occasions to have it repaired. Eventually, he returned the vehicle on the basis of unsatisfactory performance. After rescission, the purchaser discovered that the vehicle had been involved in an accident. The purchaser could not have affirmed the contract in respect of this misrepresentation because he had no knowledge of the true state of affairs at the time of the alleged affirmation.

---

[81] [1938] I.R. 584.
[82] [1985] 2 W.L.R. 154.
[83] [1986] N.I. 327.

18–40 It is not an act of waiver to intimate that one may be prepared in certain circumstances to waive some contract right: per Barrington J. in *S.A. Fonderies Lion M.V. v International Factors (Ireland) Ltd.*[84]

18–41 On the waiver of constitutional rights and, in particular, constitutional fundamental freedoms in employment contracts see *Murphy v Stewart*[85] and the general discussion in Hogan and Morgan, *Administrative Law.*[86]

(4) Estoppel

18–42 It may be that the equitable doctrine of promissory estoppel will, in time, present a universal doctrine which will eliminate the distinctions between variation and waiver; Denning L.J. in *Charles Rickards Ltd v Oppenheim*[87] described forbearance, waiver and variation as "a kind of estoppel". This thematic approach was reiterated by Lord Denning M.R. in *Crabb v Arun District Council,*[88] a dictum later approved by Finlay P. in *Smith v Ireland.*[89]

(5) Reform

18–43 Dugdale and Yates[90] have suggested that post-contractual statements should be analysed in two ways: first, consensual agreements altering terms of the contract shall be effective without consideration; secondly, conduct which the representor knows should induce a change in position should, if the statement is unambiguous, affect the remedies available to the representor. This scheme seems eminently sensible and would eliminate most of the sterile distinctions that plague this area. More recently, in the context of a valuable analysis of estoppel as a cause of action, Helliwell has argued that where a person has induced another into an expectation that a particular state of affairs will or does exist, and it would be unconscionable for the inducer to go back on the words or conduct that has had this effect, then a remedy should be available.[91] The remedy in question should be proportionate.[92] The consideration requirement, however, stands as a firm obstacle to such a development at this time.[93]

---

[84] [1985] I.L.R.M. 66.
[85] [1975] I.R. 97.
[86] 4th edn (Dublin: Round Hall, 2012), paras 14.06–14.07 and 11.96–11.100.
[87] [1950] 1 K.B. 616.
[88] [1976] Ch. 179.
[89] [1983] I.L.R.M. 300; the extension of the public law concept of legitimate expectation into contractual matters such as the employment contract will accelerate this process in Ireland, e.g. *Duggan v An Taoiseach, Members of the Government and Thomas Gerard Fahy* [1989] I.L.R.M. 710. See generally *Lett & Co v Wexford Borough Council* [2012] IESC 14.
[90] Dugdale and Yates, "Variation, Waiver and Estoppel: A Re-Appraisal" (1976) 39 M.L.R. 680.
[91] Halliwell, "Estoppel: unconscionablity as a cause of action" (1994) 14 L.S. 15.
[92] See also Pawlowski, "Satisfying the equity in estoppel" (2002) 118 L.Q.R. 519 at 522.
[93] On estoppel and entire agreement clauses see *Walmsley v Acid Jazz Records* [2001] E.C.D.R. 29 and *J.P. Morgan Chase Bank v Springwell Navigation* [2010] EWCA Civ 1221.

18–44 However, the movement towards viewing the various estoppels as being rooted in unconscionability and/or detrimental reliance suggests that the judiciary are moving far beyond making modest inroads into orthodox contract principles. In *Courtney v McCarthy*[94] Geoghegan J. endorsed the estoppel by convention principles as set out in *Amalgamated Property Co v Texas Bank*.[95] McCarthy had rescinded a contract for the sale of land and had forfeited Courtney's deposit. A subsequent conversation led McCarthy to promise to close the transaction if certain conditions were met. There was a "volte face" on the part of McCarthy's representatives. Geoghegan J. in particular doubted the conventional wisdom, remarking that the "shield and sword" metaphor had long since been honoured more by the breach than the observance. The "artificial assumption" that formed the basis of the estoppel by convention was that "the contract was still alive and enforceable if the sale was completed on a particular date and time". Finnegan J. also used estoppel to provide the remedy of specific performance to Courtney but was less specific on the nature of the estoppel, citing *Dolan v Thompson Ltd*[96] and *Ryan v Connolly*.[97] Conduct or reliance upon either the promise or the conventional or assumed state of facts, to the detriment of the person seeking relief, as well as the unconscionable consequences of not intervening, lie at the root of all estoppels.[98] While underlying principles in relation to estoppel by convention are clear enough, application to specific cases will be heavily fact-dependant: *Durkan New Homes v Minister for the Environment, Heritage and Local Government*.[99]

Discharge Following a Breach of Contract

18–45 It is generally accepted that a breach of contract does not of itself terminate a contract. Such a result would be unsatisfactory because a person could, by his own act, put an end to his contractual obligations. The innocent party has an option when a breach of contract occurs; he may elect to treat the breach as discharging his contractual duties as well as the primary obligations of the other party to perform. He may also decide to waive the right to repudiate, choosing instead to treat the contract as remaining in existence. In this second situation the innocent party may recover damages for any loss occasioned by the breach. However, upon a failure to accept the breach as one which terminates the contract, the innocent party is obliged to provide the agreed price should the party in breach perform obligations due under the contract, after making provision for any damages occasioned by the breach of contract.[100]

---

[94] [2008] 2 I.R. 376. In *McMullan Brothers Ltd v McDonagh* [2015] IESC 19 Charleton J. observed that the case of *Courtney v McCarthy* was a case of estoppel by representation rather than estoppel by convention..

[95] [1982] 2 Q.B. 84.

[96] [1978] I.R. 223.

[97] [2001] 1 I.R. 627.

[98] See also *NAMA v MIK Properties* [2012] IEHC 397.

[99] [2012] IEHC 265.

[100] *Sim v Rotherham M.D.C.* [1987] Ch. 216. See para.2–27 of *Carter's Breach of Contract* (London: LexisNexis, 2011).

18–46 Of course the right to terminate does not arise in every case. If the term broken is a warranty, the remedy of termination is not available.[101] Any statutory power given to an agency may have to be exercised reasonably; see *Zockoll Group v Telecom Éireann*.[102] If the basic claim is for termination of the contract following upon a misrepresentation, under certain circumstances the court may have a statutory discretion to award damages in lieu of rescission; see the Sale of Goods and Supply of Services Act 1980.

18–47 Although academics and judges are at variance on the correct terminology to apply, the right to terminate will arise in three situations:

(1) where the breach amounts to a repudiatory breach of contract;

(2) where the breach is a fundamental breach; that is, it goes to the root of the contact so as to deprive the innocent party of the commercial benefits envisaged; and

(3) where the term broken is such as to amount to breach of a condition.

(1) Repudiatory breach

18–48 A party may be in breach of contract, but the breach will not be held repudiatory. In many cases the terminology applied by the judges will be inconsistent, with the focus being upon the consequences of breach as distinct from seeking to discern whether the party allegedly in breach intended to repudiate his or her contractual obligations. This first situation is to be distinguished from the second one although a neat division is impossible. In relation to the first usage, a repudiatory breach involves a decision by one party that he will not perform his contractual obligations. In *Mersey Steel and Iron Co v Naylor Benzon*[103] the purchaser of goods refused to pay for goods delivered by a company that was the subject of winding-up proceedings, the purchaser being wrongly advised that effective payment was only possible with leave of a court. The evidence disclosed that the plaintiffs were in fact anxious to discharge the debt. The House of Lords refused to find a repudiatory breach. In contrast, the House of Lords held, in *Athlone Rural District Council v A. G. Campbell & Son (No. 2)*[104] that the appellants were guilty of repudiatory breach. Contractors agreed to excavate a well under the terms of a contract which made the issue of an engineer's certificate a condition precedent to payment for their work. After the work was completed in part, the contractors (following an unsuccessful action for damages) wrote indicating their willingness to complete their work. The local authority replied that it would not

---

[101] *Cripps v Smith* (1841) 3 Ir. L. Rep. 277; *Garrick v Bradshaw* (1846) 10 Ir. L. Rep. 129; see the discussion of *Poussard v Spiers and Pond* (1876) 1 Q.B.D. 410 and *Bettini v Gye* (1876) 1 Q.B.D. 183 in *Fearnley v London Guarantee* (1880) 5 App. Cas. 911 and in the lower court at (1880) 6 L.R. Ir. 219.

[102] [1998–1999] Info. T.L.R. 349.

[103] (1884) 9 App. Cas. 434.

[104] (1913) 47 I.L.T.R. 142.

require the work to be done. This letter of reply was held to be a repudiatory breach of contract. The contractors were held entitled to recover damages for breach of contract or mount a claim in quantum meruit. Particularly in the case of construction contracts, the cases turn on their own facts. On repudiatory breach each case will frequently turn on "the terms of the contract, the breach of contract, and all the facts and circumstances of the case. The question is not capable of a simple answer, as a matter of general principle".[105]

18–49 Landlord and tenant disputes are subject to the same approach. Similar observations were made by Clarke J. in *Parol Ltd v Carroll Village Retail (Management) Services Ltd*[106] when a tenant unsuccessfully argued that breaches of contract by the landlord were repudiatory:

> "A landlord who either fails to comply with the landlord's obligations under a lease or acts otherwise in a manner to a sufficient extent so as to substantially prevent a lessee from using the lessee's premises in the manner contemplated by the lease in question, renders the lease open to being regarded as having been repudiated by the landlord concerned. What amounts to such conduct will depend on the facts of each individual case. Some actions on the part of the landlord may be one off but nonetheless so serious as to meet that test. On the other hand, a persistent failure on the part of the landlord (particularly when called upon to desist) might also amount, in principle, to circumstances justifying the lessee as treating the lease as having been repudiated, even though such action for a brief period of time or on a relatively small number of occasions, might not be sufficient."

Where the scale of the performance expected is onerous it will be expected to allow the party in breach a degree of latitude when no intention to abandon the contract, or refuse performance is evident, particularly if the defects are promptly addressed when drawn to the attention of the party in breach.[107] A contracting party who incorrectly regards the conduct of the other party as repudiatory and accepts the "repudiation" as terminating the contract will of course be held to have wrongfully repudiated the contract.[108] The decision in *Decro-Wall International SA v Practitioners in Marketing Ltd*[109] provides an instructive statement on the relevant principles. Here the defendants

---

[105] *Mayhaven Heathcare Ltd v Bothma* [2009] EWHC 2634 (TCC) per Ramsey J. holding that if a contractor breaches a construction contract by wrongfully suspending the works such conduct does not, as a matter of law, constitute repudiatory breach. See also an earlier decision in relation to these parties at [2007] EWCA Civ 527.

[106] [2010] IEHC 498.

[107] *South Oxfordshire DC v Sita UK Ltd* [2007] Env. L.R. 13.

[108] The cases are legion but three recent illustrations are found in *Hadley Design Associates Ltd v Westminster CC* [2004] T.C.L.R. 1; *Stone v Fleet Mobile Tyres Ltd* [2006] EWCA Civ 1209; and *Seadrill Management Services Ltd v OAO Gazprom* [2009] EWHC 1530 (Comm).

[109] [1971] 2 All E.R. 216.

were appointed sole distributors of the plaintiffs' goods within the UK. The defendants, as the plaintiffs knew, were short of working capital and relied upon payment from customers to meet the plaintiffs' invoices. Payment was consistently late, but it was never in doubt that payment would at some time be made. Instead of charging the defendants with the consequential loss incurred, namely bank interest charges on monies borrowed, the plaintiffs terminated the distributorship. The defendants alleged wrongful repudiation; the plaintiffs alleged that the late payment by the defendants was repudiatory. The Court of Appeal reiterated that the test was whether the breach goes to the root of the contract. This, as a matter of degree, obliges the court to consider all the facts of the case. Here the loss was minor; some £20 on each unpaid bill. The delay in payment was, on average, an eight-day delay. The contract did not make time of the essence in respect of payment, and the plaintiffs did not give notice that if late payment continued the contract would be terminated. The decision of the Court of Appeal in *Nottingham Building Society v Eurodynamics Systems Plc*[110] is to similar effect. Here the defendants provided computer software to the plaintiff but a dispute about the contract developed. The plaintiff refused to pay invoices and the defendants purported to accept this repudiation. The Court of Appeal held that in no sense could the plaintiff be taken to have repudiated the contract through a refusal to pay disputed invoices. This case and others indicate that conduct which may be alleged to be a repudiatory breach may not be a breach of contract at all.[111] On the other hand, there may be serious and continuous breaches that leave little room for doubt. A senior employee who assists in the setting up of a rival company whilst in employment, assists that rival in recruiting workers from his employer for that rival company, and provides employment documents from the employer for the use of that rival company, was held to be, individually and collectively, in repudiatory breach of both express terms as to non-competition when in employment, and implied duties of fidelity: *Imam Sadeque v BlueBay Asset Management (Services) Ltd.*[112]

18–50 The breach may be characterised as a breach of an innominate term as in *Valilas v Januzaj*.[113] The plaintiff was permitted to use dental equipment and services under a contractual arrangement requiring him to pay monthly fees. Differences between the parties arose and although the plaintiff withheld three payments the majority of the Court of Appeal decided that at no stage had he demonstrated an intention not to pay as distinct from an intention to delay payment—as such the breach did not go to the root of the contract. The plaintiff was held entitled to claim fees due as the defendant had wrongfully terminated the contract. In contrast, had the contract expressly stipulated that payment would be required to be timely,[114] or where the due payment is late for many

---

[110] [1995] F.S.R. 605.
[111] e.g. *Martin-Smith v Williams* [1999] E.M.L.R. 571.
[112] [2012] EWHC 3511 (Q.B.).
[113] [2014] EWCA Civ 436.
[114] *Withers v Reynolds* (1831) 2B & Ad 822.

months, being appropriately described as "repeated and persistent, perhaps also unexplained".[115]

18–51 A more controversial decision is presented by the case of *Woodar Investment v Wimpey Construction*.[116] A contract for the sale of land to Wimpey by Woodar was subject to a condition that should the property *later* become subject to compulsory purchase proceedings the purchaser would have the right to terminate; land prices fell dramatically and Wimpey, who was anxious to re-negotiate the price, purported to rescind because part of the land was later compulsorily purchased, even though these particular proceedings were in progress when the contract of sale was concluded. Woodar's agent indicated that his company would not accept the rescission, indicating that: "We will retire to our battle stations and it goes without saying I am sure that you will abide by the result as I will". All members of the House of Lords held the rescission to be wrongful but by a majority (three to two) it was held that there was no repudiatory breach; while the fall in land prices provided a motive for termination, the conduct of Wimpey did not of itself manifest an intent to breach the contract—termination was purportedly effected under the agreement itself. As Lord Wilberforce said in the leading speech for the majority: "unless the invocation of that provision were totally abusive, or lacking in good faith, the fact that it has proved to be wrong in law cannot turn it into a repudiation."[117] A similar view applies in Ireland. In *Continental Oil Co v Moynihan*[118] it was argued that a differential pricing arrangement, introduced by the plaintiffs during the currency of a solus agreement, was a breach entitling the defendant retailer to treat the contract as discharged. Kenny J. dismissed this argument by holding that the conduct of the plaintiffs did not evidence an intention to repudiate the contract.[119] While this may be so, it is clear that there are other grounds upon which termination may be available. Kenny J.'s judgment seems incomplete on the question of discharge of a contract, as we shall see. In *House of Spring Gardens Ltd v Point Blank Ltd*[120] the Supreme Court upheld the decision of Costello J. in which the learned judge decided that a repudiatory breach of contract had occurred. The defendants attempted to redesign a bulletproof vest in such a way as to create

---

[115] Per Floyd L.J. in *Valilas v Januzaj*, describing the central facts in *Alan Auld Associates v Rick Pollard Associates* [2008] EWCA Civ 655, referring to Tuckey L.J.'s speech in which he said the late payments there were "substantial, persistent and cynical" and thus repudiatory in nature. In *Warren v Burns* [2014] EWHC 3671 (Q.B.) late payments were serious, created a poor record and did no credit to the obligor but stopped short of being repudiatory.

[116] [1980] 1 All E.R. 571; contrast *Federal Commerce and Navigation Co Ltd v Molena Alpha Inc.* [1979] A.C. 757; *Woodar* was applied in *Orion Finance Ltd v Heritable Finance* [1997] EWCA Civ 1080.

[117] [1980] 1 All E.R. 571 at 574.

[118] (1977) 111 I.L.T.R. 5.

[119] Intention is judged objectively: *Nottingham Building Society v Eurodynamics Systems Plc* [1995] F.S.R. 605.

[120] [1985] F.S.R. 327; [1985] I.R. 611. For a not dissimilar instance of repudiatory breach by provision of false information see *Yam Seng PTE Ltd v International Trade Corporation Ltd* [2013] EWHC 111 (Q.B.).

a product that did not infringe the plaintiffs' copyright. Had this exercise been successful the defendants would not have been in breach of contract. Counsel for the defendants argued, however, that the breach could not be repudiatory because the defendants had evinced an intention not to infringe the copyright; rescission should not therefore be available. This argument was rejected. Griffin J., in the Supreme Court, found that misleading correspondence written by the defendants, allied to suppression of information by the defendants, to the prejudice of the plaintiffs, indicated an intention to defraud the plaintiffs. These facts led to an irresistible inference that the defendants had no intention to perform their contractual obligation to pay royalties to the plaintiffs.

18–52 If the contract is one involving exclusivity, as, for example, a contract in which a foreign manufacturer agrees to supply goods to only one Irish retailer, it will be a repudiatory breach of contract to supply competitors of that Irish retailer.[121] Similarly, if a franchise agreement obliges a retailer to stock only products approved by the franchisor, non-observance of this obligation after being served notice of a breach will be repudiatory.[122] In both these cases the term broken was critical to the success of the joint venture. The court may be prepared to draw an inference that silence may be indicative of repudiatory breach, at least in cases where the breach is continuing or recurring and the party in breach has at an earlier time evinced an intention not to perform certain obligations.[123]

18–53 While a repudiatory breach may occur during performance of the agreement it is less obvious that such a breach may also occur before performance is due. Further, the innocent party may immediately sue and recover damages even though at the date of judgment the agreed time for performance may be months or even years away.

18–54 In the famous case of *Hochster v De La Tour*[124] the defendant engaged the plaintiff to work as a courier. Agreement was struck on April 12; the plaintiff was to start work on June 1. On May 11 the defendant informed the plaintiff that his services would not be required. The plaintiff immediately sued. Counsel for the defendant argued that the announcement was only an offer to rescind and that until the date of performance the offer may be retracted. Further, until that date arrives there can be no breach of contract. The argument failed. The view that the plaintiff was obliged to remain inactive until June 1 and that he could not find alternative employment for that period, without sacrificing his right to sue, proved unattractive to the court. The plaintiff should be encouraged to mitigate his loss and the best way of doing this is to characterise a statement of intent not to perform as itself a breach of

---

[121] *Bob Bushell Ltd v Luxel Varese SAS*, unreported, High Court, February 20, 1998.
[122] *And So To Bed Ltd v Dixon* [2001] F.S.R. 935.
[123] *Stocznia Gdanksa SA v Latvian Shipping (No. 3)* [2002] 2 All E.R. (Comm.) 768.
[124] (1853) 2 E. & B. 678.

contract; the innocent party loses a right to expect the contract to be kept open for performance.[125] While this may be so, it is difficult to see why the plaintiff should be able to immediately sue, particularly when granting an immediate right to action makes the assessment of damages speculative.[126]

18–55 The doctrine in *Hochster v De La Tour* is known as the doctrine of anticipatory breach. It has been accepted in Ireland. In *Leeson v North British Oil and Candle Co*[127] the defendants contracted to supply the plaintiff's nominees with up to 300 casks of paraffin over a winter season. In January the plaintiff was told that due to a strike it would not be possible to supply the paraffin for about two months, by which time, of course, demand would be negligible. The plaintiff refused to take further orders from his own customers fearing that if his own supplier could not meet orders the plaintiff would possibly leave himself open to actions for breach of contract. The plaintiff sued recovering damages for orders already submitted as well as for loss of orders that he would have accepted but for the defendants' statement that he would not be able to meet future orders. The defendants argued on appeal that the plaintiff's refusal to accept orders was precipitous; he should have placed the orders with the defendant on the chance that supply of paraffin might be obtained elsewhere. The Court of Queens Bench dismissed the appeal holding that the statement made entitled the plaintiff to immediately rescind the contract and recover all profits lost.

18–56 Until recently it was thought that, upon an anticipatory breach, a positive act of acceptance was required by the non-repudiating party. This could consist of bringing a claim for damages or some form of communication to the repudiating party. Mere inactivity was thought never to be an act of acceptance. After *Vitol SA v Norelf Ltd*[128] this question depends on individual circumstances. The point here is that if the breach is not accepted, the injured party may not be successful in obtaining damages if the court says communication of acceptance of the breach was not made.[129] The recent decision in *South Caribbean Trading Ltd v Trafigura Beheer BV*[130] contains an interesting discussion on whether acceptance by the innocent party of the repudiatory breach has been communicated.

18–57 In *Stocznia Gdanksa v Latvian Shipping (No. 3)*[131] the Court of Appeal had to consider whether an election to accept an anticipatory breach could be final and conclusive, the point being that if the basis of the acceptance was a

---

[125] *Frost v Knight* (1872) L.R. 7 Ex. 711. See generally Liu Qiao, *Anticipatory Breach* (Oxford: Hart, 2011).
[126] *Melachrino v Nicholl and Knight* [1920] 1 K.B. 693.
[127] (1874) 8 I.R.C.L. 309.
[128] [1996] 3 All E.R. 193.
[129] *Johnstone v Milling* (1886) 16 Q.B.D. 460.
[130] [2005] 1 Lloyd's Rep. 128.
[131] [2002] 2 All E.R. (Comm.) 768.

contractual right to terminate, the measure of compensation under the contract was less generous to the innocent party than damages for a common law anticipatory breach. Professor Treitel[132] has urged that in cases of recurring breach any election should not prejudice the innocent party in later exercising termination rights unless some hardship to the party in breach can be shown, and in *Latvian Shipping (No. 3)* Rix L.J., obiter, appears to have accepted that an "affirmation *prima facie* relates only to the past".[133]

18–58 If communication of acceptance is made, the fact that damages may be difficult to assess is not a bar to relief. As in all contract actions the plaintiff will have to prove a loss and in some anticipatory breach claims there may be no loss. Nevertheless, in *White & Carter (Councils) Ltd v McGregor*[134] the House of Lords, by a majority of three to two, held that upon an anticipatory breach the injured party may elect to affirm the contract, in which case the contract remains in full effect and the injured party will thus be able to sue for the full contract price. This is seen as wasteful[135] and at odds with a duty to mitigate loss. Lord Reid, one of the majority judges, was prepared to admit that there could be exceptional cases where the injured party could not recover the contract price (e.g. where there was no legitimate interest to be served such as generating enhanced publicity for the injured party by performance), but the precise scope of these exceptions are uncertain.[136] Not all "anticipatory" breaches will give rise to a right to accept the contract is at an end.[137] Minor breaches will not suffice whether for damages or rescission: the "substantial failure of performance" test is used but this seems to cover fundamental breach and breaches of condition.

18–59 The law of partnership can provide some interesting illustrations of the law of repudiatory breach. While a partnership deed will no doubt contain clauses permitting withdrawal from, or termination of, the partnership, there may arise differences which make continued co-operation impossible. In *Bothe v Amos*[138] the partners, a married couple, found that differences arose between them in their married life together and the wife left her husband. It was held that by her departure she had abandoned her marriage and the partnership. In a more recent Irish case[139] all the members of an accountancy firm fell out

---

132 Treitel, "Affirmation After Repudiatory Breach" (1998) 114 L.Q.R. 22.

133 [2002] 2 All E.R. (Comm.) 768 at 795. Tuckey and Aldous L.JJ. delivered concurring judgments.

134 [1961] 3 All E.R. 1178; Liu, "The *White & Carter Principle*: A restatement" (2011) 74 M.L.R. 171.

135 Nienaber, "The Effect of Anticipatory Repudiation: Principle and Policy" (1962) 20 C.L.J. 213; contrast Furmston, "Notes of Cases: The Case of the Insistent Performer" (1962) 25 M.L.R. 364.

136 *Ministry of Sound (Ireland) Ltd v World Online Ltd* [2003] 2 All E.R. (Comm.) 823.

137 See Treitel, *The Law of Contract*, 14th edn (London: Sweet & Maxwell, 2015), paras 21-012 to 21-015.

138 [1975] 2 All E.R. 321.

139 *Larkin v Groeger and Eaton*, unreported, High Court, April 26, 1988. Counsel used the idea that conduct may "repudiate the partnership" but Barrington J. did not adopt this expression.

and effectively ignored their obligations under the partnership agreement. Barrington J. held that while the agreement was not terminated under the terms of the deed, or as a result of any of the standard causes, such as death, bankruptcy, expulsion or completion of the joint venture, the partnership can be terminated by conduct which is inconsistent with the continuance of the partnership. *Hurst v Bryk*,[140] however, underlines that while the partnership may be terminated via repudiatory breach, obligations due may survive the ending of the partnership.

(2) Fundamental breach

18–60 In this context "fundamental breach" is used to describe a breach of contract which is sufficiently serious to entitle the injured party to repudiate the contract; this has nothing to do with the vexed question of the applicability of an exception clause after a fundamental breach; see *Clayton Love v B. + I. Transport*.[141]

18–61 Certain breaches of contract are so cataclysmic that the innocent party may regard himself as free to terminate the contract. In *Robb v James*[142] the plaintiffs purchased fabrics at an auction, the conditions of the sale requiring payment of the price and collection within 24 hours. They failed to comply with these terms and the defendants sold the goods to a third party. The plaintiffs failed in an action for breach of contract. Their failure to pay the price and collect was described by May C.J. as a breach of "the most essential term of the contract . . . under such circumstances, the seller may treat the contract as abandoned by the purchaser, and may detain and resell the goods".[143] Even if there is a breach by one party, that breach stopping short of being repudiatory, the conduct of the other may constitute a fundamental breach. So in *Rubicon Computer Systems Ltd v United Paints Ltd*[144] the supplier of a computer system responded to the customer's failure to pay a bill by "time-locking" the system for a period of six months making the system useless and ultimately obsolete. This reaction by the supplier was held to be a repudiatory breach which the customer was entitled to treat as terminating the contract. The modern law relating to a fundamental breach entitling the innocent party to treat the breach as discharging him or her from any obligation to render further performance is *Hong Kong Fir Shipping Co Ltd v Kawasaki Kishen Kasha Ltd*.[145] While the Lords Justices tended to focus on the issue of whether the performance rendered was radically different from that contracted for, the approach of Sellers L.J. also considered when defective performance would not constitute a fundamental breach:

---

[140] [2000] 2 All E.R. 193.
[141] (1970) 104 I.L.T.R. 157; see generally Ch.7.
[142] (1881) 15 I.L.T.R. 59.
[143] (1881) 15 I.L.T.R. 59 at 60.
[144] (2000) 2 T.C.L.R. 453.
[145] [1962] 2 Q.B. 26.

"... if what is done or not done in breach of the contractual obligation does not make the performance a totally different performance of the contract from that intended by the parties it is not so fundamental as to undermine the whole contract."[146]

This dictum was applied by Laffoy J. in *Uniform Construction Ltd v Cappawhite Contractors Ltd.*[147] Here a sub-contractor was held entitled to regard late payment of fees and efforts to impose obligations that had not been specified in the contract as a fundamental breach of contract. In these cases the court is required to determine what the contractual obligations are rather than attribute any particular intention to the parties vis-à-vis performance or an intention to breach or abandon the contract. Laffoy J. specifically endorsed Salmon L.J.'s test for determining the presence of a fundamental breach, confining the term to breaches "such as reasonably to shatter the plaintiff's confidence in the defendant's ability to pay for the goods with which the plaintiff supplied them".[148]

18–62 In this context, the question of the objectively ascertained intent of the party in breach is irrelevant; hence the present writer's reservations about Kenny J.'s dictum in *Continental Oil Co v Moynihan*, discussed on p.627. This is illustrated graphically by the judgment of Finlay P. in *Dundalk Shopping Centre Ltd v Roof Spray Ltd.*[149] The plaintiffs engaged the defendant company to spray a waterproof substance over the roof of a shopping centre. Due to various delays, and the defendants' negligence, the work was carried out inefficiently. Water seeped into the building. It was held that failure to make the roof watertight was a breach of a fundamental term of the contract, namely "to provide an effective waterproofing of this roof within a reasonable time". This breach entitled the plaintiffs to terminate the contract and obtain damages for consequential loss. Far from evidencing an intent to break the contract, the conduct of Roof Spray Ltd showed it intended to perform the contract; however, its defective performance was sufficiently serious as to entitle the employer to treat the contract as discharged through breach.

18–63 The two most important factors in identifying a fundamental breach are:

(1) the seriousness of the breach and the effect of the breach; and

(2) the likelihood of this recurring in the case of contracts with future obligations to be performed by the party in breach.

---

[146] [1962] 2 Q.B. 26 at 59.
[147] [2007] IEHC 295; *Airscape Ltd v Heaslon Properties Ltd* [2008] IEHC 82.
[148] *Decro-Wall International SA v Practitioners in Marketing Ltd* [1971] 2 All E.R. 216 at 222.
[149] Unreported, High Court, March 21, 1979. Contrast with *Airscape Ltd v Heaslon Properties Ltd* [2008] IEHC 82, where Edwards J. indicated breaches were fundamental breaches "as a matter of fact and of law".

Other factors that will be significant include whether damages may be an adequate remedy, and the motive behind the desire to terminate. If termination is sought to avoid a bad bargain, the claim will be less meritorious.[150] In essence, the issue is the same, and the test to be applied is the same as that which arises when the court concludes that an express term is neither a condition nor a warranty, *strictu sensu*.[151]

18–64 An excellent application of this approach is demonstrated by Lardner J. in *Taylor v Smyth*.[152] The plaintiff, owner and lessor of business premises, agreed to compromise a complex set of proceedings which he had brought in 1981 against the various defendants in respect of an earlier 1975 agreement to purchase the premises by the first defendant and resolve other points of disagreement, such as arrears of rent due to the plaintiff, the release of debts alleged to be payable by the plaintiff to other defendants and securing the vacation of a *lis pendens* registered in respect of the property, this latter obligation resting upon the plaintiff. However, the plaintiff was unable to obtain the consents required and Lardner J. held that the delay was an unreasonable one. However, did the unreasonable delay in respect of completion of the sale by Taylor allow the defendants to regard the contract as repudiated? Lardner J. ruled that the obligation to transfer the freehold was not severable, and had to be seen in the light of the other, diverse obligations, which the vendor could observe:

> "… a consideration of the nature of this contract and of its terms leads me to conclude that its various provisions were intended to be a settlement or compromise agreement which comprehended them all, that they were interdependent and were intended to constitute an entire contract."[153]

After noting that it was not contended that the vendor's breach made the entire contract repudiatory, the defendants insisting that certain obligations survived the delay and were binding, the learned judge advanced the view that, where a delay in an entire contract which consists of a number of heterogeneous obligations occurs, the question of whether the innocent party can treat the contract as discharged is to be tested by reference to the *Hong Kong Fir* test. Lardner J. said the court, in this context, must consider the effect of the breach upon the contract as a whole and whether the effect of the delay deprived the innocent party of substantially the whole benefit of the contract. Lardner J. held the breach here

---

[150] *Hong Kong Fir Shipping Co Ltd v Kawasaki Kishen Kaisha Ltd* [1962] 2 Q.B. 26.
[151] Consider *Telford Homes (Creekside) Ltd v Ampurius Nu Home Holdings* [2013] EWCA Civ 577 and *Valilas v Januzaj* [2014] EWCA Civ 436, cases in which the HCA decision in *Koompahtoo Local Aboriginal Land Council v Sanpine Pty Ltd* [2007] HCA 61 was heavily relied upon for guidance on the practical importance of the breach "going to the root of the context" phrase and what it means.
[152] [1990] I.L.R.M. 377; *Clarke v Kilternan Motor Co*, unreported, High Court, December 12, 1996. *Force India Formula One Team Ltd v Etihad Airways PJSC* [2010] EWCA Civ 1051 follows a similar approach. This case is also very instructive on the overlap between express termination clauses and the common law, especially on remediation notices.
[153] [1990] I.L.R.M. 377 at 388.

did not entitle the defendants to treat the contract as discharged. Because no loss had been occasioned, the defendants were held not entitled to damages.

(3) Breach of condition

18–65 Any term which the parties or statute has deemed to be sufficiently important to entitle the innocent party to repudiate the contract when that term is broken may conveniently be described as a condition (sometimes it is called a fundamental term). As we have seen in Ch.9 on the nature of express obligations, the classification of express terms into conditions, warranties and innominate terms is universal. In *Gold Group Properties Ltd v BDW Trading Ltd*[154] the parties entered into a joint venture under which the plaintiffs would provide land while the defendant, an arm of the Barrett Group, would develop the site. Ramsey J. had ample material on which to find that the defendants had failed to commence, carry out and complete the development works. Ramsey J. found that those terms were conditions, not innominate terms. The defendants told the plaintiffs that they considered that certain practical difficulties meant the contract was potentially discharged by operation of law, returning the keys to the site some two months later, "a sure sign that they did not intend to comply further with this Agreement". In *Rubicon Computer Systems Ltd v United Paints Ltd*[155] the conduct of the supplier of a computer system in "time-locking" or disabling the system was held to be a breach of the implied statutory condition of quiet possession. In instances where the obligation broken is an implied term, the court may have to classify the term if breach of the term per se is to trigger the right to rescind; see *Bridgesoft Systems Corp v British Columbia.*[156] Even if the contract, in express terms, identifies that a right of termination exists for breach of certain obligations, there is recent English authority for the proposition that the clause will not be read literally and the court may require the injured party to establish that the breach is serious[157] or material. Even if a breach of an express term is made out, if the term requires that rescission is to be available only if a "material or irremediable breach" takes place, the party seeking rescission will have to satisfy the court that such a breach has taken place.[158]

18–66 The right to rescind for breach of an express term may be lost via the operation of estoppel principles, affirmation or delay in seeking relief. Even a statute may intervene. Section 11(1)(c) of the Sale of Goods Act 1893 prevented a purchaser from rescinding the contract:

(1) if the contract was non-severable and the buyer accepted the goods or a part thereof; or

---

[154] [2010] EWHC 323 (TCC).
[155] [2000] 2 T.C.L.R. 453.
[156] (1998) 60 B.C.L.R. (3rd) 246 (obligations classified as fundamental terms).
[157] *Rice v Great Yarmouth B.C.* (2001) 3 L.G.L.R. 4.
[158] *Glolite Ltd v Jasper Conran Ltd, The Times*, January 28, 1998.

(2) if the contract was for the sale of specific goods, property having passed to the seller.

In the Irish Republic the Sale of Goods and Supply of Services Act 1980 has repealed ground (2): s.11(3). In all other cases a breach of condition by the seller may be waived by the buyer or he may elect to treat the breach as a breach of warranty and not as a ground for treating the contract as repudiated: s.11(1).

(4) Material breach

18–67 The contract itself may include provisions that constrain the injured party in respect of termination. There may be a requirement to give notice of breach and an opportunity to remedy the breach within a period of time. Whether these requirements have been met is an issue of fact and non-compliance may render termination by the injured party repudiatory.[159] The contract may also permit termination by the injured party if the breach is a "material breach". The tests for material breach are objective and the intention fixed, on that basis, appears to be to allow termination when the breach is not minimal or trivial, but the breach does not have to be repudiatory. Again, the circumstances of the breach and reasons behind the breach are relevant.[160]

(5) Employment contracts

18–68 While a breach of contract may entitle the innocent party to rescind the contract it does not follow that the contract is discharged by the breach alone. The innocent party may affirm the contract in the hope that precise performance may later be rendered. In contracts of employment the position is somewhat different. Because specific performance of a contract of employment is traditionally unavailable, the innocent party has often no practical option but to accept the breach. An employee wrongfully dismissed must take alternative employment should it come along.[161] However, in some cases the employee may wish to keep the contract alive for certain purposes, such as establishing social welfare, redundancy or pension entitlements, and in *Thomas Marshall (Exports) Ltd v Guinle*[162] Megarry V.-C. indicated that repudiation of the contract by an employee does not terminate the contract but, rather, gives the employee the usual choice to accept or reject repudiation. If the employee takes alternative employment, the employee will be taken to have accepted the

---

[159] *ICDL GCC Foundation FZ – LCC v European Computer Driving Licence Foundation Ltd* [2012] IESC 55.

[160] *Dalkia Utilities Services Plc v Celtech International* [2006] 1 Lloyd's Rep. 599; *Fitzroy House v Financial Times Ltd* [2006] EWCA Civ 329; *Mid Essex Hospital Services NHS Trust v Compass Group* [2013] EWCA Civ 200; *Scottish Power UK Plc v BP Exploration Operating Co* [2015] EWHC 2658 (Comm); *C&S associates UK Ltd v Enterprise Insurance Company Plc* [2015] EWHC 3767 (Comm).

[161] This, however, is a practical requirement because the employee is obliged to mitigate loss.

[162] [1979] Ch. 227; Rose, "The Effects of Repudiatory Breaches of Contract" [1981] 34(1) *Current Legal Problems* 235.

option to rescind the contract,[163] but if the employee does not, then damages may be reduced because of failure to mitigate.[164] Not every breach of the contract of employment will entitle termination. The test advanced in the English case of *Pepper v Webb*[165] by Karminski L.J. has been influential in Ireland: "A person repudiates the contract of service if he wilfully disobeys the lawful and reasonable orders of his master."[166] Not all acts of disobedience justify termination by the other party. In the case of *Brewster v Burke*[167] an employee's refusal to bury a dead horse was held not to be a sufficient act of misconduct as to justify summary dismissal. A tour bus courier who works for a rival concern in his own time should be disciplined but not dismissed; see *Mullen v C.I.É.*[168] The impact of email messaging and social networking sites on employment law was brought home in *Kiernan v A Wear Ltd*.[169] The appellant was dismissed for gross misconduct when an email complaining about her employers that contained a number of rather choice expletives was posted onto a Bebo site by a friend. The Employment Appeals Tribunal (EAT) held that while the appellant's conduct merited strong censure, dismissal was a disproportionate response.

18–69 In any event, the common law affords an employer the right to terminate a contract of employment (absent an express or implied term to the contrary) upon the giving of a reasonable period of notice.[170] It may be, however, that either constitutional or statutory considerations will require procedures to be in place. In the case of academic staff within Irish universities, it was held in *Cahill v Dublin City University*[171] that the provisions of s.25(6) of the Universities Act 1997 do not entitle a university to terminate the employment of tenured staff unless statutory provisions have been provided and complied with, which provisions are to regulate the termination of an employment contract.

18–70 Certain breaches of contract are sufficiently serious so as to entitle the employer or employee to treat the contract as discharged. Refusal to pay wages would entitle an employee to terminate the contract; the issue of strike notice may entitle the employer to regard this as a breach of contract, although Irish law differs from the English authorities on this point. This point has been considered by the Court of Appeal in *Cantor Fitzgerald International v Callaghan*.[172] The employer arranged a bonus package for his workforce

---

[163] *Dietman v Brent LBC* [1987] I.C.R. 737.
[164] *Gunton v Richmond Upon Thames London Borough* [1980] 3 W.L.R. 714.
[165] [1969] 2 All E.R. 216.
[166] [1969] 2 All E.R. 216 at 218, followed in *Brewster v Burke* (1985) 4 J.I.S.L.L. 98; *Harrington v Irish Life and Permanent*, unreported, High Court, June 18, 2003; *Berber v Dunnes Stores* [2009] IESC 10.
[167] [1985] 4 J.I.S.L.L. 98; *Lyons v Johnson* UD 579/1983.
[168] UD 54/1979.
[169] UD 643/2007; see "Expletive-laden Bebo message led to dismissal", *Irish Times*, June 6, 2008.
[170] *Sheehy v Ryan* [2008] IESC 14; *Higgins v Bank of Ireland* [2013] IEHC 6.
[171] [2007] IEHC 20.
[172] [1999] 2 All E.R. 411.

involving the payment of tax at a future date. The employer then changed his mind and refused to honour the commitment. Some employees left their employment. It was held that the employer's conduct was repudiatory. A deliberate refusal to pay wages or a remuneration package is to be distinguished from a failure or delay in making such a payment. The first is repudiatory, the second case not necessarily so.[173] In *Simmons v Hoover Ltd*[174] an English EAT held that participation in a strike was a fundamental breach of contract entitling the employer to dismiss an employee without notice. On the other hand, the Supreme Court in *Becton Dickinson Ltd v Lee*[175] held that issue of a strike notice, if the period of notice was sufficiently long to comply with the notice requirements necessary to terminate the contract, would not entitle the employer to treat the employee as guilty of a fundamental breach. Walsh J. in his speech expressly approved of Lord Denning M.R.'s theory, advanced in *Morgan v Fry*,[176] in which the Master of the Rolls argued that due notice and participation in a strike suspend a contract of employment.

18–71 There is also Irish authority for the view that in certain cases a fundamental breach of an employment contract may automatically terminate the contract. In *Carvill v Irish Industrial Bank*,[177] O'Keeffe J. said:

> "There can be some breaches of contract so fundamental as to show that the contract is entirely repudiated by the party committing them, and that such an act might be relied upon in an action for wrongful dismissal, not as justifying the dismissal, but as supporting the plea that the dismissed servant had himself put an end to the contract."[178]

Indeed, one English commentator has argued that a breach of contract automatically terminates that contract unless the innocent party chooses to waive the breach.[179] This theory must be regarded as unsound given the leading decision of the House of Lords in *Photo Production Ltd v Securicor Transport Ltd*.[180] Their Lordships expressly overruled *Harbutt's Plasticine*[181] and Lord Wilberforce observed that the "deviation" case of *Hain Steamship Co Ltd v Tate & Lyle Ltd*,[182] in which a similar rule is enunciated, must be regarded as sui generis. Thomson's thesis was based on the correctness and general applicability of these two cases. In Ireland the decision of Costello J. in *Industrial Yarns Ltd v Greene*[183] puts the matter beyond doubt. Claims

---

[173] *Adams v Charles Zub Associates Ltd* [1978] I.R.L.R. 551.
[174] [1977] I.C.R. 61.
[175] [1973] I.R. 1; *Bates v Model Bakery Ltd* [1993] 1 I.R. 359.
[176] [1968] Q.B. 710.
[177] [1968] I.R. 325.
[178] [1968] I.R. 325 at 345.
[179] Thomson (1975) 38 M.L.R. 346 and "The Effect of a Repudiatory Breach" (1978) 41 M.L.R. 137.
[180] [1980] 2 W.L.R. 283.
[181] *Harbutt's Plasticine v Wayne Tank Corp* [1970] 1 Q.B. 447.
[182] [1936] 41 Com. Cas. 350.
[183] [1984] I.L.R.M. 15.

for redundancy payments were challenged by an employer on the ground that there had been no dismissal or lay-off by reason of redundancy; rather, the claimants had terminated their own contracts of employment by resignation. Costello J. emphatically rejected this argument and, in so doing, re-integrated the rules relating to discharge of contracts of employment with the ordinary principles of repudiatory breach:

> "If there is no contractual power (express or implied) in the contract of employment to suspend the operation of the contract for a limited period then by ceasing to employ an employee and refusing to pay him wages the employer has been guilty of a serious breach of contract amounting to a repudiation of it. At common law that repudiation would not automatically bring the contract of employment to an end; the employee is free to accept that the repudiation has terminated the contract or not to do so (see: *Gunton v Richmond-upon-Thames London Borough* [1980] 3 W.L.R. 714 for a recent view on the effect of an employer's repudiation of the contract of employment). If he accepts the repudiation of the contract then there has been a constructive dismissal of the employee at common law and the contract has been terminated by the employer. But if the employee responds to the employer's lay-off notice and adopts the lay-off procedures (instead of immediately accepting the employer's repudiation of the contract) and it is shown that the statutory condition for their initiation by the employer did not exist, then, it seems, the employee is entitled to treat the repudiation of the contract (which occurred when the cesser of employment began) as having terminated the contract of employment, and to base his claim for redundancy payment on that fact."[184]

In *Pickering v Microsoft Ireland Operations Ltd*,[185] the plaintiff had been a senior employee in the defendant company but after being bypassed for promotion she felt that her position in the company had been undermined and she had been isolated within the company by other managerial staff. Following a period of sick leave the plaintiff refused to be transferred to a disability benefits scheme and she claimed that she had been constructively dismissed by the defendant. Esmond Smyth J. viewed the defendant's conduct as being in fundamental breach of express terms entitling the plaintiff to participate in senior management processes and consultations. After citing both this book and Costello J. in *Industrial Yarns* the learned judge held that an employee is free to accept that the repudiation has terminated the contract or not to do so. Although there is a lack of clarity on whether Esmond Smyth J. was holding that all repudiatory breaches by an employer will not per se end the employment contract, this, it is submitted, is the better view of this decision. Nevertheless, the view that a contract may be automatically terminated by virtue of the conduct of the party in breach has been repeated by O'Sullivan J. in *Hearn and*

---

[184] [1984] I.L.R.M. 15 at 20–21.
[185] Unreported, High Court, December 21, 2005.

Matchroom Boxing v Collins.[186] This was not a contract of employment, but a contract for management services and the statements were delivered obiter. Irish law would appear to require the Supreme Court to overrule O'Keeffe J.'s observation in *Carvill* before the automatic termination by breach theory is finally put to rest.

18–72 While the point therefore appears still to be open in Ireland, the scope of an argument which puts forward an automatic termination perspective in relation to contracts of employment must be in doubt after the decision of the UK Supreme Court in *Societe Generale, London Branch v Geys*.[187] In that case, Geys was summarily dismissed and "escorted from the building". He refused to accept the termination. Contractual entitlements depended on the effective date of termination—the date of dismissal or a much later date, to be calculated by reference to a contractual termination formula. The Supreme Court divided four to one on the question and after noting that there was a division of opinion and that English case law was inconsistent, the majority opted for endorsing the general elective theory rather than the automatic termination theory; Lord Wilson, Lady Hale and Lord Hope were persuaded that the general principle should prevail. Lord Hope said:

> "I find it helpful to stand back and to remind myself of the overall effect of the automatic theory. It is to reward the wrongful repudiator of a contract of employment with a date of termination which he has chosen, no doubt as being, in the light of the terms of the contract, most beneficial to him and, correspondingly, most detrimental to the other, innocent, party to it. We must, I suggest, be very cautious before turning basic principles of the law of contract upon their head so that, in this context, breach is thus to be rewarded rather than its adverse consequences for the innocent party negatived. It is, says Professor Freedland in *The Personal Employment Contract*, 2003, at p390 'a matter of concern if the common law of wrongful dismissal functions so as to invite opportunistic breach of contract'."

(6) Consequences of breach

18–73 In general, the innocent party must act promptly and decisively. In *An Bord Iascaigh Mhara v Scallan*[188] the plaintiffs supplied the defendant with a fishing boat on hire-purchase terms, the agreement specifying that a particular type of winch would be fitted to the vessel. No such winch was provided but in July 1967 the defendant took possession, nevertheless. Some attempts were

---

[186] Unreported, High Court, February 3, 1998. This should be contrasted with the decision in *Cantor Fitzgerald International v Callaghan* [1999] 2 All E.R. 411, another fundamental breach case where affirmation was pleaded—irrelevant if fundamental breach by the employer terminates the contract.

[187] [2012] UKSC 63. Lord Sumption dissented while Lord Carnwath had doubts on aspects of the case which he did not feel merited a dissenting judgment.

[188] Unreported, High Court, May 8, 1973.

made to bring the winch into a satisfactory state, but these efforts came to nothing; the defendant continued to use the vessel until October 1968 when he abandoned it in Wexford harbour. While the plaintiffs were clearly in breach of s.9(2) of the Hire-Purchase Act 1946, Pringle J. held that the defendant should have repudiated the contract shortly after it became clear the winch could not be made to work satisfactorily; the defendant approbated the contract and thus could not rescind. Contrast *Dillon-Leech v Maxwell Motors Ltd*[189] and *Lutton v Saville Tractors Ltd*.[190] In relation to defective motor vehicles, case law establishes that where the defect is clear and accepted (to exist as a breach of condition, for instance) the injured party may lose the right to rescind within a matter of months of taking delivery: *Jones v Gallagher*.[191]

18–74 The need for the innocent party to elect to affirm the contract or rescind it, any delay being seen as being affirmatory, causes difficulties in practice because in many situations the injured party may be hoping for a change of heart by the wrongdoer. It is commonly said that the injured party has no right to suspend performance for breach, but this is not the case if a contractual term so provides or future performance by the injured party is held to be unnecessary because the injured party has obligations that are dependent or concurrent on those of the party in breach. This is an area of the law where there is little clear authority.[192] In *Stocznia Gdanska v Latvian Shipping (No. 3)*,[193] however, the injured party was held not to have lost common law rights to rescind. The Court of Appeal held that there could be a middle course[194] between rescission and affirmation for the period in which the innocent party is making up his mind what to do:

> "If he does nothing for too long, there may come a time when the law will treat him as having affirmed. If he maintains the contract in being for the moment, while reserving his right to treat it as repudiated if his contract partner persists ... then he has not yet elected."[195]

While some degree of prevarication by the injured party may be permitted, in general terms the termination must be of the contract *in toto*. Partial termination of a contract has been held by the Irish courts to be the exception rather than the rule. In *ICDL GCC Foundation FZ–LCC v European Computer Driving Licence Foundation Ltd*,[196] the parties to an educational training licence agreement were in dispute over the licensor's right to terminate the

---

[189] [1984] I.L.R.M. 624.
[190] [1986] N.I. 327.
[191] [2005] 1 Lloyd's Rep. 377, following *Clegg v Andersson* [2003] 2 Lloyd's Rep. 32.
[192] See Carter, "Suspending Contract Performance for Breach" in Beatson and Friedmann (eds), *Good Faith and Fault in Contract Law* (Oxford: Clarendon Press, 1995), p.485. See generallly *Carter's Breach of Contract* (London: LexisNexis, 2011), Ch.11.
[193] [2002] 2 All E.R. (Comm.) 768.
[194] See *Bentsen v Taylor* [1893] 2 Q.B. 274 at 279 per Escher M.R.
[195] [2002] 2 All E.R. (Comm.) 768 at 792 per Rix L.J. See also *GEC Marconi Systems v BHP-IT* (2003) 128 F.C.R. 1.
[196] [2011] IEHC 343.

licence for breach by the licensee. The licence operated in several jurisdictions in the Middle East but the licensor purported to terminate the licence in respect of the Saudi Arabia "part" of the licensed area only. Clarke J., citing academic opinion[197] on partial termination as a contractual remedy, apparently approved the proposition that partial termination arose via an express term in the contract or through severance. There was no express term in the contract, and severance was inappropriate—"the parties' contractual entitlements were specified by reference to a single target across the region. In those circumstances, it is difficult to see how the contract could be severable"—particularly in the light of the fact that Saudi Arabia was a large part of the licensed area. If the licensor wished to terminate for breach, the licensor had to terminate the entire licence. Although the Supreme Court divided on certain aspects of this case, all three judges found the contract did not provide for partial termination.[198]

18–75 The consequences of a breach which entitles one party to terminate the contract and its effect upon certain contractual obligations have been clarified by the *Photo Production* case.[199] Photo Production engaged Securicor to provide a security service for its factory. Securicor engaged a worker who maliciously burned down the premises. The contract contained an exculpatory clause absolving Securicor from the actions of its employees unless the conduct could have been foreseen and avoided by the exercise of due diligence on its part. The House of Lords reversed the decision of the Court of Appeal, rejecting the view that because the fire automatically terminated the contract, the limiting provision was unavailable to Securicor. Their Lordships explained that a limiting clause may operate so as to qualify or exclude liability for what would otherwise be a breach of contract. Lord Diplock in his speech described each party's obligation to perform as "primary legal obligations". These obligations may be the result of express agreement or through implication of law (statutory or otherwise). Upon breach, the innocent party may elect to terminate his own primary obligation to perform and in certain cases he may also terminate these obligations which the party in breach has yet to perform. This does not mean that all obligations are at an end. This is particularly true of an exemption clause. Lord Diplock argued that when primary obligations are discharged they are replaced by secondary obligations, the most obvious of which is the obligation to pay monetary compensation. Further, the decision to terminate the contract leads to the discharge of the unperformed primary obligations of the party in breach. While these primary and secondary obligations may be modified they cannot be eliminated or controlled if this would lead to the contract being deprived of all promissory content.

18–76 It should be mentioned that some contractual obligations only become effective after an alleged failure to perform a primary obligation; choice of

---

[197] Carter, "Partial Termination of Contracts" (2008) 24 J.C.L. 1.
[198] [2012] IESC 55. On suspension under the contract see *ESL Consulting v Verizon (Ireland) Ltd* [2008] IEHC 369.
[199] [1980] 2 W.L.R. 283.

forum clauses and arbitration clauses are examples; see Lord Diplock in *Photo Production*. In *Doyle v Irish National Insurance Co Plc*[200] Kelly J. addressed the issue whether an insurance company, which had repudiated a policy of motor insurance for non-disclosure of a material fact, could invoke an arbitration clause in that self same contract. Kelly J. affirmed the leading case of *Heyman v Darwins*[201] where it was said that a repudiated contract "survives for the purpose of measuring the claims out of the breach, and the arbitration clause survives for determining the mode of their settlement". Kelly J. held that these observations hold true in cases of rescission for misrepresentation or non-disclosure also. It should also be mentioned that the Irish courts have not endorsed the view advanced in *Boston Deep Sea Fishing and Ice Co v Ansell*[202] which permits an employer who terminates a contract of employment on inadequate grounds to rely on other sufficient grounds for termination even though those grounds were unknown at the date of termination.

18–77 In *And So To Bed Ltd v Dixon*[203] the *Boston* case was held to permit an innocent party to rely upon a repudiatory breach when he had earlier relied upon a contractual power to terminate the contract. The view that an employer would thus be able to successfully defend an action for wrongful dismissal was examined in *Carvill v Irish Industrial Bank*.[204] O'Keeffe J. held that only where the wrongful act amounts to a repudiation of the contract of employment will the *Boston* principle hold good in Irish law. In *Glover v B.L.N.*,[205] Kenny J. went further, arguing that the *Boston* principle should be expunged from Irish law. This view is to be supported; further, the English courts have rejected this rule in cases of unfair dismissal; see *W. Devis & Sons Ltd v Atkins*,[206] a decision of the House of Lords. The EAT in the Republic may permit an employer, who becomes aware after the dismissal of facts which support the decision to dismiss, to use these new facts, if they indicate misconduct similar to the grounds relied on at the date of dismissal.[207] It is still not clear whether a fundamental breach ends a contract outside employment, without more contracts: *Hearn and Matchroom Boxing Ltd v Collins*.[208] Here the court found that the first plaintiff had breached his contract with the defendant by seeking to persuade the World Boxing Organisation (WBO) to provide one of his clients, Chris Eubank, with a particular status, the effect of which would

---

[200] [1998] 1 I.R.L.M. 502.
[201] [1942] A.C. 356.
[202] (1888) 39 Ch. D. 339.
[203] [2001] F.S.R. 935. There is no sign in England that *Boston Deep Sea Fishing* is likely to be revised: *Imageview Management Ltd v Jack* [2009] 2 All E.R. 666 (a secret profit by an agent case); *Stupples v Stupples & Co* [2012] EWHC 1226 (Ch) (breach of fiduciary duty); *Cavenagh v William Evans Ltd* [2015] EWCA Civ 697; *Williams v Leeds United Football Club* [2015] EWHC 376 (Q.B.) (use of company email to send pornographic images).
[204] [1968] I.R. 325.
[205] [1973] I.R. 388.
[206] [1977] A.C. 931.
[207] *Loughran v Rights Commissioner*, UD 206/1978.
[208] Unreported, High Court, February 3, 1998.

have been to cause substantial loss of earnings to Stephen Collins in relation to a title defence. Because the plaintiffs were still contractually bound to Collins, as well as Eubank, this represented a fundamental breach of contract by the first plaintiff. Apart from this breach, the first plaintiff had conducted himself at a purse bid ceremony in such a way as to undermine the financial merits of the fight in question, a separate fundamental breach. On this basis the defendant regarded the contract as at an end; the Hearn/WBO correspondence was unknown to the defendant and in fact only came to light after trial of the action had commenced. In his judgment O'Sullivan J. seems to have given the *Boston* case some renewed life. After observing that there are different legal consequences "where there have been breaches of an agreement as distinct from fundamental breaches", and citing *Carvill* and *Glover*, the learned judge observed:

> "If a fundamental breach comes to light after dismissal it may still be relied upon by the employer to make a claim, not that this subsequently known ground was relied upon as a reason for or otherwise justified the dismissal, [*sic*] but rather that the contract at the time of the dismissal had already been repudiated."

Note that the facts of the case do not disclose an employment contract but a services contract, so the *Carvill* case is being given a broader application than before. Furthermore, this observation is clearly obiter because the subsequently known ground actually occurred after the fundamental breach that the defendant actually relied upon, took place.

Judicial Review

18–78 The powers of a statutory body, when that body has been given powers to enter, vary, or terminate contractual relationships with others are said to be subject to certain responsibilities. The courts have held that this is so in relation to the powers of the Voluntary Health Insurance Board,[209] Telecom Éireann[210] and Bus Éireann,[211] for example. Professional bodies are similarly constrained to exercise powers in accordance with constitutional requirements[212] and the public nature of these duties, whether statutory or otherwise, can be challenged by way of judicial review. Judicial review procedures have the advantage of greater speed but the courts do attempt to limit[213] judicial review to matters that are public law in nature and matters of a private nature derived solely from contract are excluded.[214] The courts

---

[209] *Callinan v VHI*, unreported, High Court, April 22, 1993, reversed in part by the Supreme Court, July 28, 1994.

[210] *Zockoll Group Ltd v Telecom Éireann, Irish Times Law Report*, January 19, 1998.

[211] *Rafferty v Bus Éireann*, unreported, High Court, November 21, 1996.

[212] *Geoghegan v Institute of Chartered Accountants* [1995] 3 I.R. 86.

[213] *Beirne v Commissioner of An Garda Síochána* [1993] 1 I.L.R.M. 1.

[214] *Beirne v Commissioner of An Garda Síochána* [1993] 1 I.L.R.M. 1; *Healy v Fingal County*

also indicate that judicial review applications are not to be used to challenge or second guess properly constituted decisions of statutory bodies.[215] Public law remedies are discretionary and not available as of right.[216] In the light of decisions such as *Dellway Investments Ltd v National Asset Management Agency*[217] and *Treasury Holdings v National Asset Management Agency*,[218] and the review of contracts concluded by public tender (see Ch.1), judicial review case law appears destined to explode as a remedial mechanism.

Discharge by Operation of Law—The Doctrine of Frustration

18–79 This modern doctrine has evolved in order to deal with cases where contractual obligations can no longer be performed as a result of circumstances beyond the control of either party. The common law required a person who had agreed to perform contractual obligations to discharge those obligations; the fact that it was extremely difficult or even impossible to do so did not excuse non-performance. Thus in *Leeson v North British Oil and Candle Ltd*[219] the fact that the defendants could not obtain paraffin from their own supplier because of a strike did not excuse their failure to supply the plaintiff. Similarly in *Gamble v The Accident Assurance Co*[220] the executor of the estate of Gamble sued upon a life insurance policy which provided that if the insured met with an accident he should inform the insurers within seven days. Gamble died in a drowning accident and could not of course meet this obligation. The Court of Exchequer held that the agreement envisaged that Gamble, in his lifetime, was to arrange for a third party to notify the insurers if he met with an accident which caused his immediate demise. Pigot C.B. in his judgment expressly approved the leading English case of *Paradine v Jane*.[221]

18–80 In *Paradine v Jane* the plaintiff had let lands to the defendant under the terms of a lease which required the lessee to pay rent on a quarterly basis. The lessee was ejected from possession by armed force, the lands then being occupied by the military during the English Civil War. In an action for arrears of rent the lessee pleaded that these circumstances excused non-payment of rent. The plea was rejected. A distinction was drawn between a general duty imposed by law upon a lessee and a duty taken on by way of contract. In this latter case:

Council, unreported, High Court, January 17, 1997. See the unusual case of *Reynolds v Altomoravia Holdings Ltd* [2015] IEHC 482 where both parties to an unexecuted lease were seeking specific performance. Cregan J held the tenant's conduct was repudiatory.

[215] *Radio Limerick One Ltd v Independent Radio and Television Commission*, unreported, High Court, October 14, 1996.

[216] *Bane v Garda Representative Association* [1997] 2 I.R. 449.

[217] [2011] IESC 14.

[218] [2012] IEHC 297.

[219] (1874) 8 I.R.C.L. 309.

[220] (1869) I.R. 4 C.L. 204.

[221] (1647) Aleyn 26; Simpson, "Innovation in Nineteenth Century Contract Law" (1975) 91 L.Q.R. 247.

"… when the party by his own contract creates a duty or charge upon himself he is bound to make it good, if he may, notwithstanding any accident by inevitable necessity because he might have provided against it by his contract."[222]

However, if the transaction is an executory one, and premises are destroyed by fire, there is early Irish authority, in the form of *Re Walter John Carew*,[223] for the proposition that the purchaser is not obliged to pay the price and take a conveyance; the risk falls upon the vendor. This, however, is not a decision which represents a direct attack on *Paradine v Jane*, but it provides an illustration of judicial awareness of the harshness of the doctrine of absolute contractual obligations, at least when viewed from the perspective of the party who is faced with the prospect of being bound by the contract. It is, however, not a reliable decision because it is now accepted that risk passes to the buyer upon signature, not completion, of a contract of purchase, and insurance should be organised accordingly.

18–81 The view that contractual obligations were absolute in the sense that supervening events could never provide a lawful excuse for non-performace was questioned in *Taylor v Caldwell*.[224] The defendants agreed to let a music hall to the plaintiffs for four days. Just before the first day arrived the music hall was destroyed by fire, the accident occurring without the fault of either party. The plaintiffs sued to recover money spent in advertising the scheduled performances. Blackburn J. held that the destruction of the music hall discharged the contract, viewing the agreement as subject to an implied condition that the building remained in existence. The licensor was excused from failing to provide a music hall and the licensee was excused from payment of fees due to the licensor. In so holding, Blackburn J. used the analogy of a contract involving a person who dies after agreeing to write a book. Such a contract is thereby discharged; the executors cannot be liable upon a personal contract of this nature. The point is illustrated by *Kean v Hart*.[225] The plaintiff and one Lyster were appointed agents. The contract provided for notice of termination of six months. Shortly after the commencement Lyster died. The plaintiff was then given notice that the agency would end six months hence. He claimed the period of notice was insufficient. The Court of Exchequer Chamber dismissed the action, Whiteside C.J. observing that, regardless of notice, Lyster's death itself terminated the contract.

18–82 Because these cases do not seem very easy to reconcile, it is important to establish the rationale for judicial intervention in frustration cases. Lord

---

[222] (1647) Aleyn 26 at 27. See generally, Treitel, *Frustration and Force Majeure*, 3rd edn (London: Sweet & Maxwell, 2014).
[223] (1851) 3 Ir. Jur. 232; contrast *Paine v Meller* (1801) 6 Ves. 349.
[224] (1863) 3 B. & S. 826. See MacMillan in Mitchell and Mitchell (eds), *Landmark Cases in the Law of Contract* (Oxford: Hart Publishing, 2008), p.167.
[225] (1869) I.R. 3 C.L. 388.

Hailsham has observed that five theories of the basis for the doctrine have been advanced at various times.[226] On the theoretical basis of this doctrine, Blackburn J. in *Taylor v Caldwell* said:

> "When from the nature of the contract it appears that the parties must from the beginning have known that it could not be fulfilled, unless when the time for the fulfilment of the contract arrived some particular specified thing continues to exist, so that when entering into the contract they must have contemplated such continued existence, as the foundation of what was to be done, then, in the absence of any express or implied warranty, that the thing shall exist, the contract is not to be considered a positive contract but subject to the implied condition that the parties shall be excused, in case, before breach, performance becomes impossible, from the perishing of the thing without the default of the contractor."[227]

This dictum was approved by O'Connor M.R. in 1912 in the case of *Cummings v Stewart (No. 2)*[228] in which it was held that the lapse of patent rights held by the plaintiff patentee discharged the defendant, who held an exclusive licence to work the patents, from an obligation to pay royalties to the plaintiff. However, the implied term theory is no longer widely supported, as we shall see.

(1) Frustration of the business venture

18–83 The cases of impossibility of performance (because of the physical destruction of a person, an object or structure) present difficulties when they are invoked so as to justify non-performance because subsequent events, while they do not make performance impossible, make it impossible to secure the commercial benefits envisaged at the date of agreement. In these cases of unanticipated difficulty, if it threatens to destroy the basis of the contract or make the contract as performed something fundamentally different to that envisaged at the time of agreement, then the contract may be treated as discharged.[229]

18–84 The English "coronation" cases are the best examples of this situation. When the coronation procession of Edward VII had to be cancelled due to the illness of His Royal Highness, many arrangements in which persons obtained the right to view the procession from hotels and rooms overlooking the route came before the English courts. In *Krell v Henry*[230] the plaintiff let his flat to

---

[226] *National Carriers Ltd v Panalpina (Northern) Ltd* [1981] 1 All E.R. 161 at 165, citing Lord Wilberforce in *Liverpool City Council v Irwin* [1976] 2 All E.R. 39.

[227] (1863) 3 B. & S. 826.

[228] [1913] 1 I.R. 95.

[229] See *Jackson v Union Marine Insurance Co Ltd* (1874) L.R. 10 C.P. 125 for the origins of the test in this particular context.

[230] [1903] 2 K.B. 740.

the defendant in order to enable him to view the procession. A £25 deposit was paid, the defendant owing £50 which was to be paid on the very morning the ceremony was cancelled. The plaintiff sued for the outstanding sum. The rooms were still available; the defendant could have used the rooms but, of course, because the procession had been cancelled the purpose implicit in the arrangement would not be attained. The Court of Appeal held the contract frustrated; Vaughan-Williams L.J. in his speech observed that the basis of the contract was the position of the rooms in relation to the coronation procession. The cancellation prevented performance and thus discharged the defendant's obligation to pay the outstanding sum of £50.

18–85 The fact that the test advanced in these cases can produce seemingly incompatible results is illustrated by the contrasting case of *Herne Bay Steam Boat Co v Hutton*.[231] The defendant had chartered a steamboat in order to view the Naval Review on two set days, and to sail around the fleet. The Naval Review was cancelled due to the illness of Edward VII. The fleet, however, remained at anchor. The defendant was sued for the balance due on the charter and pleaded the King's illness discharged the contract. The Court of Appeal held that this was not a defence. The court found that the Naval Review was not the foundation of the contract. Sterling L.J. pointed out that while the Naval Review was cancelled, there remained the opportunity to view the fleet and enjoy the cruise, notwithstanding. While the boundary between these cases may be a narrow one, it is clear that the hire contract in *Herne Bay* was not tied to the presence of the monarch—it was expressed to be basically a contract to hire a boat—in the same way that the room-hire agreement in *Krell v Henry* was only entered into because of the anticipated procession. In general terms, the fact that property or goods cannot be used for the anticipated purpose is not sufficient to discharge the contract unless an express term so provides. So, the fact that goods intended to be exported by the buyer to a country that prohibits the importation of those goods will not necessarily frustrate the contract.[232]

18–86 The courts have emphasised that a contract will not be frustrated simply because increased costs or labour disputes make it impossible for one party to perform the contract without incurring serious financial losses. It would be undesirable for a businessman to agree to perform a contract for a fixed amount and permit him to seek relief through the doctrine of frustration if, during performance, unanticipated difficulties arise.[233] In the old case of *Revell v Hussey*,[234] Manners L.C. expressed the point thus:

---

[231] [1903] 2 K.B. 683.

[232] *Congimex Companhia Geral de Comercia Importadora e Exportadora Sarl v Tradax Export SA* [1983] 1 Lloyd's Rep. 250.

[233] This sentence was cited with approval in *Zuphen v Kelly Technical Services (Ireland) Ltd* [2000] E.L.R. 277; *Galway CC v Samuel Kingston Construction* [2008] IEHC 429.

[234] (1813) 2 Ball & B. 280.

"Suppose a case that very frequently occurs of a colliery, where the company has contracted to supply iron works at a price agreed on; surely it can be no ground to rescind it that subsequent circumstances have occurred to render it very prejudicial; that the coals may have greatly increased; that the expenses working the mine may have been considerably increased."[235]

In *Zuphen v Kelly Technical Services (Ireland) Ltd*[236] the plaintiffs were a number of copper jointers recruited from South Africa by the defendants, a recruitment agency, to provide services to Eircom in respect of telecommunications network installation. These workers were recruited on 12-month contracts, but Eircom discontinued giving work to the defendant agency. The defendants claimed that Eircom's withdrawal of work frustrated the employment contracts between itself and the plaintiffs. Murphy J. rejected the argument because the contracts of employment could have made continued engagement of the plaintiffs conditional on the Eircom contracts, which they did not, and, on the evidence, work had been made available to some of the plaintiffs. On the application of relevant principles, Murphy J. said:

"It is not hardship or inconvenience or a material loss which calls the principles of frustration into play. There must be such a change in the significance of the obligation that the thing undertaken would if performed, be a different thing from that contracted for."[237]

The so-called Suez Canal cases are perhaps the best known illustrations of the principle that a contract will not be frustrated simply because of a supervening event which results in extra expense or inconvenience for a contracting party. In *Tsakiroglou & Co v Noblee and Thorl*,[238] the sellers of ground nuts agreed to ship the goods *CIF* from Port Sudan to Hamburg. Freight charges if the journey was undertaken via the Suez Canal were £7 10s. a ton. Because of war conditions, the Canal was later closed to shipping, thereby necessitating a journey via the Cape of Good Hope at £15 a ton. The closure of the Canal, and the extra time and cost involved, were held by the House of Lords not to frustrate the contract. There was no basis for an implied term that the Canal was the only permissible route; nor did the extra time involved cause any deterioration in the goods shipped, nor did the delay result in loss of any seasonal market.

18–87 In the leading English case of *Davis Contractors v Fareham U.D.C.*[239] contractors agreed to build houses for a sum of £94,000. The work, expected to take eight months to complete, took some 22 months, mainly due to materials

---

[235] (1813) 2 Ball & B. 280 at 284.
[236] [2000] E.L.R. 277.
[237] [2000] E.L.R. 277 at 291.
[238] [1961] 2 All E.R. 179.
[239] [1956] A.C. 696.

shortages and labour difficulties. The work cost £115,000. The contractors claimed that these events terminated the contract, entitling them to claim for the value of the work on a quantum meruit basis, which was greater than the contract price. The House of Lords dismissed the claim. Lord Radcliffe in his speech remarked that hardship or material loss does not of itself bring the doctrine into play. "There must be as well such a change in the significance of the obligation that the thing undertaken would, if performed, be a different thing from that contracted for."[240] Additionally, it must be pointed out that these ordinary commercial risks may be covered by contract terms; a failure to provide for these contingencies should not readily be rectified by invoking a plea of frustration. In *Amalgamated Investments v John Walker*[241] a building which was sold as a warehouse was listed as a historic building. This event, which occurred shortly after contracts were exchanged, prevented commercial development of the building and reduced its value from £1,710,000, the contract price, to £200,000. While it may be possible to explain the Court of Appeal's refusal to hold the contract frustrated as in part due to the purchasers' failure to show that this listing could not be revised, there was a reluctance to reallocate ordinary commercial risks when the contract draftsman had failed to do so. To similar effect is the decision of the majority of the New Zealand Court of Appeal in *Karelrybflot AO v Udovenko*.[242] Fishermen were engaged on fixed-term contracts. The employer knew that proceedings for illegal fishing were in progress and that forfeiture of the vessels was possible. The vessels were detained but the contracts of engagement were not frustrated because the employer "elected to offer the crew contracts and must be taken to have assumed the risk of loss of the vessels by forfeiture".[243]

18–88 This approach was endorsed by McWilliam J. in *McGuill v Aer Lingus and United Airlines*.[244] The plaintiffs booked internal holiday flights within the US with the second defendants. At the time of booking the second defendants were aware that their employees had served strike notice, but, fearing that if they disclosed this the plaintiffs would book flights with another carrier, the defendants did not tell the plaintiffs or insert an exception clause into the agreement. When the strike commenced the plaintiffs had to be carried on other flights with other airlines and, as a result, their holiday itinerary was cut short. The defendants pleaded frustration. While McWilliam J. refused to hold that a strike may never constitute a frustrating event, it could not be pleaded on the facts of this case.

---

[240] [1956] A.C. 696 at 729.
[241] [1977] 1 W.L.R. 164; *E. Johnson & Co (Barbados) Ltd v NSR Ltd, The Times,* July 24, 1996; *Des Forges v Wright* [1996] 2 N.Z.L.R. 758.
[242] [2000] 2 N.Z.L.R. 24.
[243] [2000] 2 N.Z.L.R. 24 at 33–34 per Blanchard J.
[244] Unreported, High Court, October 3, 1983. McWilliam J. laid down seven principles that neatly summarise the law. The *McGuill* principles were approved in *Collins v Gleeson* [2011] IEHC 200.

18–89 *McGuill* also illustrates the point that in some senses the frustrating event may exist, in an undiscovered state, at the time the contract is formed. An even more striking instance of this is provided by *Gamerco SA v ICM/Fair Warning Agency*.[245] Here a rock concert in Madrid was cancelled when it was found that building materials used in the construction of the stadium made this unsafe. The condition only came to light after the concert had been arranged. A more surprising conclusion was that the local concert promoters were able to plead frustration at all, for it is arguable that local agents should impliedly warrant that the venue they find for the band is satisfactory, but Garland J. declined to allocate a foreseeable risk of this kind to the concert promoter so that, when Madrid City Council cancelled the permit, the cancellation was held a frustrating event.

18–90 It is sometimes said that the event in question should have been unforeseen or unexpected. However, in *Ocean Tramp Tankers Corp v O Sovracht, The Eugenia*,[246] Denning M.R. pointed out that, essentially, this means that the parties should not have made provision for the event in the contract. It is by no means necessary to prove that the event in question was not foreseen by the parties because frustration is a flexible enough doctrine to apply in a proper case. The decision in *Neville and Sons Ltd v Guardian Builders Ltd*[247] is in point. The defendant purchased a plot of land in order to develop it. The land bordered two local authorities, and in order to obtain satisfactory access to the development, planning permissions and the goodwill of adjoining property owners had to be secured. The defendant agreed to give building work to the plaintiff. The site ran into difficulties in respect of access and the plaintiff obtained the contractual right to carry out the work. However, the parties knew at the time of the agreement that satisfactory access could only be obtained if Dublin County Council sold a strip of land to the defendant; for compensation reasons the sale did not occur. As Murphy J. said, at the time of the agreement, the site was landlocked and both parties believed the vital strip of land would be sold, so as to facilitate the developer, at some time in the near future. "The change that took place between the date of the contract and the time for its performance was the frustration of this expectation." The failure of a contemplated event may just as much frustrate a contract as a cataclysmic occurrence. The crucial fact to note is that even though the parties, objectively, could have anticipated difficulties in obtaining permission, the contract did not contain a provision dealing with the contingency. The Supreme Court, however, overturned Murphy J., holding that there was no frustrating event. Using principles of risk allocation the Supreme Court took the view that the plaintiff was entitled to damages. This is one of those cases that straddles the law relating to frustration, mistake and implied terms[248] and in his judgment

---

[245] [1995] E.M.L.R. 263.
[246] [1964] 1 All E.R. 161.
[247] [1995] 1 I.L.R.M. 1; for a similar Canadian case see *John E. Dodge Holdings Ltd v 805062 Ontario Ltd* (2003) 223 D.L.R. (4th) 541.
[248] Smith (1994) 110 L.Q.R. 400; *Drocarne Ltd v Seamus Murphy Properties* [2008] IEHC 99.

Blayney J. echoed *Davis Contractors* by observing that the access difficulties made the contract "more onerous but that was all".

18–91 A contract cannot normally be discharged through the doctrine of frustration if a contract term covers the events which are alleged to constitute frustration. In *Mulligan v Browne*,[249] Dr Browne was employed as a physician by the trustees of a charity established to provide a hospital in Ballyshannon, Co. Donegal. His contract of employment provided that if there were insufficient funds to allow the hospital to continue in operation then the contract could be discharged by giving three months' notice. The hospital ran into severe difficulties and in 1974 the trustees purported to terminate Dr Browne's employment. Dr Browne argued that his employment was permanent in the sense that it could not be terminated except in specific cases which had not occurred. Gannon J. held that the severe difficulties into which the hospital had fallen discharged the plaintiff's contract. The Supreme Court overturned Gannon J. on this point; Kenny J. pointed out that in this case the contract expressly provided for the contingency: "if it is dealt with in the contract then it was within the contemplation of the parties and the doctrine [of frustration] cannot apply." Cases of delay that "the relevant market" provides for are unlikely frustration situations.

18–92 In *The Sea Angel*[250] the "event" was the detention of a tanker by a port authority following the virtual completion of a 20-day charterparty, the vessel being urgently required to assist in the unloading of crude oil from a large tanker that had foundered within the port. The *Sea Angel* was caught up in a dispute between the port authority and the owners of the stricken vessel, an event which the Court of Appeal regarded as an event which is foreseeable, a "risk of the salvage industry", but not one that was actually foreseen by the parties. As the risk of unreasonable detention is normally borne by the charterer, Rix L.J., in the leading judgment, found that the dictates of justice pointed away from upholding that the charterparty was frustrated.

18–93 If, however, the events are literally within the scope of the provision it remains open for a court to hold that the events that have occurred are so cataclysmic that the parties could not have intended the clause to cover such a profoundly different set of circumstances. In one English case a clause in a charterparty obliging the vessel to sail "with all possible despatch, dangers of navigation excepted" was held inapplicable when the vessel ran aground, the ship being under repair for over six months. The delay was held to frustrate the commercial purpose behind the charter; see *Jackson v Union Marine Insurance Co Ltd*.[251]

---

[249] Unreported, High Court, July 9, 1976; unreported, Supreme Court, November 23, 1977; *Ringsend Property Ltd v Donatex Ltd* [2009] IEHC 568.
[250] [2007] 1 All E.R. (Comm.) 407.
[251] (1874) L.R. 10 C.P. 125.

(2) Theoretical basis of frustration

18–94 Despite the approval of the implied contract theory in the 1912 Irish case of *Cummings v Stewart (No. 2)*[252] it is now generally recognised that there are alternative explanations for the frustration doctrine. Indeed the implied contract theory seems distinctly out of favour today and is, in reality, a convenient explanation, cobbled together by the judges at a time when the judges were keen to preserve the twin illusions that the judges do not make law and that the judges do not interfere in bargains struck. The only Irish case in which the theoretical basis of frustration has been extensively discussed is *Mulligan v Browne*.[253] In his judgment Kenny J. said of the concept of frustration:

> "During the past seventy years it has been developed and refined by many decisions of the House of Lords and the Privy Council. The expression 'the contract is frustrated' so commonly used to-day is misleading: the doctrine relates, not to the contract but to the events or transactions which are the basis of the contract. It is these which make performance of the contracts impossible. This aspect of the doctrine was explained by Lord Wright in *Constantine Line v Imperial Smelting Corporation* [1942] A.C. 154:
>
> > 'In more recent days, the phrase more commonly used is "frustration of the contract" or more shortly "frustration." "Frustration of the contract" however is an elliptical expression. The fuller and more accurate phrase is "frustration of the adventure or of the commercial or practical purpose of the contract." The change in language corresponds to a wider conception of impossibility, which has extended the rule beyond contracts which depend on the existence, at the relevant time of a specific object ... to cases when the essential object does indeed exist, but its condition has by some casualty been so changed as to be not available for the purposes of the contract, either at the contract date or if no date is fixed, within any time consistent with the commercial or practical adventure.'
>
> There has been considerable judicial controversy as to its foundation. At least three possible bases for it have been suggested each of which can claim emminent judicial support. The first is that it depends upon an implied term in the contract (Viscount Simon in *Constantine Line v Imperial Smelting Corporation* [1942] A.C. 154) or upon 'the presumed common intention of the parties' (Viscount Maugham in the same case). The second rejects wholly the implied term theory and rests the doctrine on the true construction of the contract.

---

[252] [1913] I.R. 95.

[253] Unreported, High Court, July 9, 1976; unreported, Supreme Court, November 23, 1977. The most extensive and illuminating discussion of this in recent years can be found in the New Zealand appellate courts' decisions in *Planet Kids Ltd v Auckland Council* [2012] NZCA 562, and [2013] NZSC 147; see Roberts (2014) 26 N.Z.U.L. Rev. 350 and [2014] L.M.C.L.Q. 305.

'It appears to me that frustration depends, at least in most cases, not on adding any implied term but on the true construction of the terms which are, in the contract, read in light of the nature of the contract and of the relevant surrounding circumstances when the contract was made.'

Lord Reid in *Davis Contractors v Fareham U.D.C.* [1956] A.C. 696:

'So perhaps, it would be simpler to say at the outset that frustration occurs whenever the law recognises that, without default of either party, a contractual obligation has become incapable of being performed because the circumstances in which performance is called for would render it a thing radically different from that which was undertaken by the contract'

(per Lord Radcliffe in the same case). The third theory—associated with Lord Wright—is that where the dispute between the parties arises from an event which they never thought of, the court imposes the solution that in the circumstances is just and reasonable (Lord Wright's *'Legal Essays and Addresses'* at p.258 and *Denny Mott and Dickson Ltd v Fraser and Co. Ltd* [1944] A.C. 265 at p.275)."

While on the facts it was not necessary for Kenny J. to select any of these three theories it is fair to say that subsequent dicta in the House of Lords tend to favour the second and third theories. In *National Carriers v Panalpia (Northern) Ltd*, the most recent case in which the juristic basis of frustration was considered by their Lordships, both Lord Hailsham L.C. and Lord Roskill favoured the view of Lord Radcliffe in *Davis Contractors*, as quoted above by Kenny J. in *Mulligan v Browne*. Indeed, in *Neville and Sons Ltd v Guardian Builders Ltd*[254] Murphy J. also cited Lord Radcliffe's dictum as proof of the extent to which the courts have moved away from the implied term theory "to an objective test based on the construction of the contract". This tendency to favour Lord Radcliffe's view of the juristic basis of frustration has continued in the decision of Murphy J. in *Zuphen v Kelly Technical Services (Ireland) Ltd.*[255]

(3) Frustration and illegality

18–95 Several of the cases can be explained as being decided in this way because any attempted performance would involve a breach of either the civil or the criminal law. Gannon J. used this reasoning to support his view in *Mulligan v Browne*. If the trustees continued to operate the charity this would involve them in a breach of their duties as trustees.

---

[254] [1995] 1 I.L.R.M. 1.
[255] [2000] E.L.R. 277.

18–96 In *O'Cruadhlaoich v Minister for Finance*[256] the plaintiff had been appointed a judge by the first Dáil Éireann. The appointment was for life. These courts were later abolished by statute passed by the Government of Saorstát Éireann. O'Cruadhlaoich sued for salary due to him under the contract of employment. The action was dismissed. Following the leading case of *Reilly v R*.[257] it was held that the abolition of the post by statute discharged the contract of employment. The Supreme Court of Canada, in *Wells v Newfoundland*,[258] has undermined the influence of *Reilly v R*. A senior civil servant was appointed to a Government of Newfoundland Board to serve until the age of 70. Before that date the post was abolished by statute. The legislation in question did not give compensation to the civil servant and he sought damages for breach of contract. The Government of Newfoundland pleaded that the contract had been frustrated. In distinguishing *Reilly* as turning on the specific statutory provision, the Supreme Court of Canada held that the Government had entered into a contract with the plaintiff and public policy required contracts to be upheld. Frustration was not available to the Government of Newfoundland because the Government had passed the legislation and thus the situation was one of self-induced frustration.[259]

18–97 In *Ross v Shaw*[260] it can be argued that the German occupation of Belgium operated so as to make lawful performance impossible, thereby frustrating the contract. The boundary between illegality and frustration can be narrow indeed. A reluctance to award damages for a breach of contract when statute renders the transaction void was demonstrated by Dixon J. in *Namlooze Venootschap De Faam v Dorset Manufacturing Co.*[261] A more recent illustration is provided by the dissenting judgment of Costello J. in *Dunne v Hamilton*.[262] The Supreme Court was required to consider whether the enactment of the Family Home Protection Act 1976 prevented a conveyance, signed without his wife's consent but not executed by the husband prior to the enactment of the 1976 Act, from being specifically enforceable. The majority of the Supreme Court allowed the purchaser's appeal against Gannon J.'s decision that s.3 of the 1976 Act meant that any conveyance in consequence of a decree of specific performance would be void. While the case really turns on principles of statutory interpretation, Costello J. agreed with Gannon J., holding that the 1976 Act discharged the vendor from his obligations under the contract. By the exercise of the wife's power to stop the sale, the contract was discharged by operation of law and, further, these new facts (the 1976 Act) did not expose the vendor to liability in damages.

---

[256] (1934) 68 I.L.T.R. 174.
[257] [1934] A.C. 176.
[258] (1999) 177 D.L.R. (4th) 77.
[259] Citing *National Trust Co v Wang Aviation Ltd* (1969) 3 D.L.R. (3rd) 55.
[260] [1917] 2 I.R. 367.
[261] [1949] I.R. 203.
[262] [1982] I.L.R.M. 290.

18–98 While legislation may have the effect of discharging entirely private transactions such as a contract for the sale of land, if the legislation is enacted for the convenience of the State, which is party to the contract, *Wells v Newfoundland*[263] suggests that it may be difficult to rely on frustration, and the same may be true of legislative charges that can impact on public entities such as utility companies. This is evident from New Zealand case law in which the impact of time upon long-term contracts could make a contract extremely burdensome for one party. In *Gore v The Power Company*[264] a 1927 contract to supply electricity to the Gore District Council became less financially desirable over the decades as inflation and other factors increased the cost of electricity. The New Zealand Court of Appeal held that increased costs would not invoke frustration principles and, further, the court expressed doubts over whether frustration was at all appropriate in relation to contracts involving public agencies where the exercise of executive or legislative powers provide an obvious means of dealing with unexpected changes in long-term contracts.

(4) Self-induced frustration

18–99 It is essential that the event or events is/are outside the control of either party. It is not essential that it be conclusively shown that the only explanation for the event does not involve carelessness or fault. In *Constantine Line v Imperial Smelting Corp*[265] a vessel on charter exploded and sank. Three possible causes of the accident were advanced, one of which involved a finding of negligence by the shipowners. The Court of Appeal held that it was incumbent on the shipowners to show that the accident occurred without default. The House of Lords rejected the view that such a heavy burden of proof rests on the party pleading frustration. Where the loss is unexplained, fault will not be attributed to either of the parties. The burden of proof rests upon the party alleging self-induced frustration. Their Lordships held the contract automatically discharged by the explosion.

18–100 The leading Irish authority on the doctrine of self-induced frustration is *Herman v Owners of S.S. Vicia*.[266] The plaintiffs were engaged for a round-trip voyage from the US to Britain and back again. Due to war conditions it was necessary for the owners of the vessel to obtain "travel warrants" in order to ensure safe access to British ports. The vessel docked in Dublin on the way to Britain. The owners of the vessel failed to obtain the necessary documentation from the British authorities. The owners pleaded that this frustrated the contracts of employment entered into with the plaintiffs. It is clear that failure to obtain the necessary documentation was due to the neglect of the defendants themselves; this is, then, a perfect example of "self-induced"

---

[263] (1999) 177 D.L.R. (4th) 77.
[264] [2003] 1 N.Z.L.R. 697.
[265] [1941] 2 All E.R. 165.
[266] [1942] I.R. 304.

frustration. It is possible to view *Gamble v The Accident Assurance Co*[267] in a similar light.

18–101 In *Byrne v Limerick Steamship Co Ltd*[268] the defendants engaged the plaintiff to serve on board a ship going to England. The British authorities refused to allow Byrne a war permit. The defendants claimed that this frustrated the contract. The submission failed; the party pleading frustration in these circumstances must show that he took reasonable steps to have the decision reversed. There was no evidence that the employer had pointed out additional factors which may have caused the British authorities to reverse the decision. To this extent, then, the refusal was "self-induced". In the context of failure to secure permissions, it is important to recall that the frustrating event must be an external event. The fact that one party exercises a contractual right against the other party which is prejudicial to the self-interest of the other is not an external event: *Collins v Gleeson*[269] per Feeney J., or, to put it another way, this is a case of "self-induced frustration" which is not a repudiatory or any other breach of contract.

18–102 The standard of conduct insisted upon by the courts in a plea of frustration can be extremely high. In *Maritime National Fish Ltd v Ocean Trawlers Ltd*[270] the defendant chartered a fishing vessel from the plaintiff but in order to utilise the vessel as a trawler, a licence to use an otter trawl had to be obtained from the then Minister for Fisheries. The licence was obtained on an annual basis from 1928–1932, but when the defendant sought five licences for his five trawlers for the 1935 season the Minister indicated that only three licences would be issued and the defendant was asked to name the three vessels in question. The plaintiff's trawler was not one of them. In an action for hire charges, the defendant pleaded frustration. The Privy Council held that the contract was not frustrated. It was the decision of the defendant not to include the relevant vessel of its own election, and not the decision of the Minister, which was the basis of the failure to obtain a licence for that particular vessel. Similarly, if goods are to be shipped to a particular country where they are to be weighed, the fact that the foreign law later prohibits the landing of the goods will not necessarily frustrate the contract, if, for example, it would be possible to weigh the goods in another jurisdiction.[271]

(5) Contracts of employment

18–103 Events which have been held to discharge a contract automatically include the sinking of a vessel upon which the employee serves; see *Kearney v Saorstát and Continental Shipping*[272]; conscription has also been held to effect

---

[267] (1869) I.R. 4 C.L. 204.
[268] [1946] I.R. 138.
[269] [2011] IEHC 200.
[270] [1935] A.C. 524.
[271] *Congimex Companhia v Tradax Export* [1983] 1 Lloyd's Rep. 250.
[272] [1943] Ir. Jur. Rep. 8.

the discharge of a contract of employment as has a prison sentence; see *Hare v Murphy Brothers*.[273] While the sentence must of course have the effect of making performance of the contract of employment impossible, it has been held that the sentence itself does not automatically bring the contract to an end. In *Chakki v United Yeast*,[274] Chakki was sentenced to a term of imprisonment. His wife telephoned his employer to inform the employer that her husband would not be coming into work. A replacement driver was engaged. On appeal the sentence was suspended but the employer refused to re-engage Chakki. It was held that the employer had acted precipitously, especially when Chakki was about to start his annual holidays when the sentence was imposed. The employer should have waited for some days before engaging a replacement. However, *Chakki* has been said to be of doubtful authority by Kilner Brown J. in *Morris v Southampton City Council*.[275] Here a prison sentence prevented the employee from carrying out his contract. The fault of the employee in deliberately doing something which led to an inability to carry out his contract was said to be repudiatory conduct and thus incapable of bringing the contract into the frustration concept. These contrasting decisions were confronted by the Court of Appeal in *F. C. Shepherd & Co Ltd v Jerrom*.[276] An apprentice was sentenced to not less than six months' borstal training when he was halfway through a four-year apprenticeship. The Court of Appeal had to consider whether the contract of the apprenticeship was repudiated and, if not, whether the case was one of self-induced frustration. The contract was held to have been frustrated because of the length of the sentence in the context of the length of the apprenticeship. The employee was held not to be able to plead self-induced frustration in order to assist him in establishing a right to compensation for unfair dismissal. Thus, *Chakki v United Yeast*[277] remains good law. Because the doctrine of frustration operates automatically, without reference to the intention of the parties, Irish EAT authority holds that even if the employee becomes available for work shortly after the employer asserts that the contract has been frustrated by virtue of a prison sentence, frustration will still be upheld. In *Gallagher v Eircom Ltd*[278] the claimant received an eight-year prison sentence in 1988. On March 1, 2004 the respondent communicated its view that the contract had been frustrated and declined to allow the claimant to resume his employment one week later following his release from prison. The EAT found in favour of the respondent. Should the prison sentence rather than the criminal condition be the disabling event that prevents the employee's performance, a successful appeal cannot "undo" the frustrating event.[279]

---

[273] [1974] I.C.R. 603.
[274] [1982] 2 All E.R. 446; *Song v Patrick McDermott* [2008] NIIT 71.
[275] [1982] I.C.R. 177.
[276] [1986] 3 All E.R. 589; *Alghussean Establishment v Eton College* [1991] 1 All E.R. 267.
[277] [1982] 2 All E.R. 446.
[278] UD 955/2004. See also *Boyle v Marathon Petroleum (Ireland) Ltd* [1995] E.L.R. 200.
[279] See *Harrington v Kent C.C.* [1980] I.R.L.R. 353, followed in Ireland in an anonymous EAT decision: UD 181/2007.

18–104 The courts have frequently been troubled by the possibility that illness of the employee may discharge the contract of employment. In *Flynn v Great Northern Railway Co*[280] a van driver's contract of employment was held to have been frustrated when medical evidence was introduced to show that his medical condition was such as to make it impossible for him ever to return to his job; see also *Donovan v Murphy & Sons*.[281] The position differs if the evidence does not conclusively show a return to work is out of the question. In *Nolan v Brooks Thomas*,[282] a decision of the EAT Nolan claimed compensation for unfair dismissal and, in the alternative, redundancy or wrongful dismissal. Nolan was employed as a woodcutter/machinist from October 1969, suffering a severe injury at work in July 1973. He was only fit for work after prolonged treatment in March 1978. In August 1977 the employer purported to discharge Nolan. The work reduced his capacity for normal manual work considerably; the employment in question was potentially dangerous even to a fully-fit person; the period of absence from work was considerable—almost five years. Applying the test evolved in the leading English cases of *Marshall v Harland and Woolf*[283] and *Egg Stores v Leibovici*,[284] the nature of the employee's incapacity viewed at the date of purported dismissal (August 1977) made it appear likely that further performance of Nolan's obligations in the future would be impossible, or at least radically different from those undertaken by him. Similarly, in *Mulvaney v Riversdale Concrete Products Ltd*[285] the contract of employment of the plaintiff, a labourer, was held to have been discharged by law. He had last worked in 1974 and at the time of the employer going into liquidation, March 1981, he was still unfit for work. The EAT held the contract had been frustrated "long before the respondent company went into liquidation". No redundancy payment was payable, the employer having discharged the onus to show frustration.

18–105 The most exhaustive Irish examination of the frustration concept is the decision of the EAT in *Donegal County Council v Langan*.[286] The employee, a general labourer, was employed since 1974. In 1985 he was incapacitated due to lumbar pain and was still on sick leave, submitting certificates, when, in April 1988, the Council wrote that it did not intend to re-employ him. In July 1988 he was medically certified as fit. In an action for unfair dismissal, the employer pleaded frustration. The EAT indicated that among the matters to be taken into account in deciding if a contract is frustrated are:

"(i) the length of the previous employment.
(ii) how long it has been expected that the employment would last.

---

[280] (1953) 89 I.L.T.R. 46.
[281] UD 184/1977.
[282] UD 379/1979.
[283] [1972] 1 W.L.R. 899.
[284] [1976] I.R.L.R. 376.
[285] UD 457/1981; *Sweeney v Glanbia Fresh Pork Ltd* UD 200/2005.
[286] UD 143/89. See also *Lafreniere v Leduc* (1990) 60 D.L.R. (4th) 577 on the issue of proof.

    (iii) the nature of the job.

    (iv) the nature, length and effect of the illness or disabling event.

    (v) the need of the employer for the work to be done.

    (vi) whether wages have continued to be paid.

    (vii) the actions of the employer in relation to the employment.

  (viii) whether consideration was given to retaining the employee on the books if not in employment.

    (ix) whether the employer discussed with the employee and his trade union the employee's problems and prospects.

    (x) whether adequate medical investigation was carried out (*e.g.* employers should ask their own or their employee's doctor for reports to establish the real medical facts and if there is conflicting medical evidence, to seek an independent source).

    (xi) whether, in all the circumstances a reasonable employer could be expected to wait any longer."

In this case Langan was not a key worker. He had been paid only for the first 12 weeks of absence. There was no consultation with him or his union, nor was a medical examination undertaken prior to termination, and he was fit for work within three months of termination. In these circumstances, frustration had not been established by the employer.

18–106 It has been held that extraneous factors such as an increase in an employer's insurance premiums due to an employee's disability may lead to the contract being discharged through frustration, even if the worker is able to perform his duties satisfactorily; see *Duggan v Thomas J. O'Brien and Co Ltd*.[287] This case should be regarded as wrongly decided on this point because it is a factor outside the test advanced in *Egg Stores*, as approved in *Nolan v Brooks Thomas*.

18–107 In the case of *Mooney v Rowntree Mackintosh Ltd*[288] the EAT indicated that the doctrine is inappropriate in cases where an employee is intermittently absent from work due to a series of minor ailments. Frustration may also be unsuitable in cases where a short-term periodic contract cannot be performed due to a serious illness of the employee.[289] More generally, Murphy J. in *Zuphen v Kelly*[290] observed that:

> "It seems to me to be inappropriate … to apply a strict contract law approach to employment disputes. Attempts to so apply tend to obscure the social implications of certain kinds of conduct or events by reducing them to legalistic principles."[291]

---

[287] UD 156/1978.

[288] UD 473/1980.

[289] *Notcutt v Universal Equipment Co (London) Ltd* [1986] 3 All E.R. 582.

[290] [2000] E.L.R. 277.

[291] [2000] E.L.R. 277 at 288.

This point is strengthened by observations in *G.F. Sharp and Co v McMillan*[292] where concern was expressed about the impact that frustration has on statutory rights and "contractual" practices where the doctrine has terminated the employment relationship. In cases where illness or disability has reduced or altered the capacity of an employee to discharge contractual duties envisaged prior to the incapacity occurring, the traditional notion that the contract of employment is terminated automatically is no longer tenable. In *Warner v Armfield Retail and Leisure Ltd*[293] an employer was found to be liable to make reasonable adjustments to the contractual arrangement to allow the employee to return to work.

(6) Frustration of a lease

18–108 The concept of a leasehold interest in land has caused difficulties in relation to the doctrine of frustration. Because a lease creates an estate or interest in land it is argued that while a building situated on the land may perish in a fire or earthquake the *estate* itself endures. In Ireland the Landlord and Tenant Law Amendment Act (Ireland) 1860 (Deasy's Act) creates contractual rights to enter onto an estate in favour of a tenant; Deasy's Act does not confer an estate in land upon the tenant.[294] Deasy's Act provides a statutory solution to many frustration problems by enacting that, in the absence of any express covenants to repair, a tenant may surrender his tenancy if the premises are destroyed or rendered uninhabitable by fire or some other inevitable accident: s.40.

18–109 If, however, the premises are rendered uninhabitable by some event which is outside s.40 it is by no means clear that the theoretical differences between English and Irish leasehold interests would lead to the doctrine of frustration being held more readily applicable in Ireland. The majority of the House of Lords in the *Cricklewood* case[295] held a lease could not be frustrated, no matter how cataclysmic the event. In *National Carriers Ltd v Panalpina (Northern) Ltd*[296] their Lordships have clearly overruled *Cricklewood*. Frustration of a lease will rarely occur, however. In *National Carriers* the appellants were lessees of a warehouse under a 10-year lease, commencing in January 1974. Due to the danger of an adjoining building collapsing the local authority closed the main access road in May 1979, thereby preventing the appellants from using the building as a warehouse. It was estimated that the street would be reopened in January 1981. The appellants claimed the lease was frustrated. While the House of Lords, by four to one, held that frustration may occur, the facts of this case did not disclose a change of circumstances

---

[292] [1998] I.R.L.R. 632.
[293] [2014] IRC 239.
[294] Lyall, *Land Law in Ireland,* 3rd edn (Dublin: Round Hall, 2010), pp.580 and 658.
[295] *Cricklewood Property and Investment Trust Ltd v Leighton's Investment Trust Ltd* [1945] A.C. 221.
[296] [1981] 1 All E.R. 161, following *Highway Properties Ltd v Kelly Douglas & Co Ltd* (1971) 17 D.L.R. (3d) 710.

grave enough to justify holding the lease frustrated. *Panalpina* was applied in the case of a residential tenancy in the Hong Kong decision of *Ching v Xuan Yi Xiong.*[297] The outbreak of the potentially deadly SARS virus in Hong Kong in 2003 meant that the tenant could not have access to his leased apartment for 10 days. It was held that 10 days out of a two-year lease did not warrant holding the lease was frustrated. In Ireland many of the situations that came within potential frustrating events are regulated under the Residential Tenancies Act 2004.

18–110 There is an unreported Irish case in which O'Higgins C.J. held that a lease may be frustrated. The reasoning of the Chief Justice is not entirely satisfactory in this case of *Irish Leisure Industries Ltd v Gaiety Theatre Enterprises Ltd.*[298] The defendant lessors agreed to let theatre premises to the plaintiff for three years, the lease to commence six months from the date of execution of the lease. However, the existing tenant obtained a six-year extension of the lease by making an application under the Landlord and Tenant Act 1921. This prevented the plaintiff from obtaining use of the theatre. O'Higgins C.J. held the plaintiff's lease to be frustrated. Judgment on this question was given orally; the only report of the case deals with assessment of damages. This suggests that the case is one in which the defendant lessor was in fact in breach.

18–111 It is suggested that the Oireachtas should declare the doctrine of frustration applicable to leases generally.[299]

18–112 Statutory provisions which are intended to regulate the rights and duties of parties to a contract when subsequent events make performance of that contract something seriously different to that envisaged at the time of entry into the contract now include contracts under which the supply of foodstuffs and intoxicating liquors are made to grocery goods undertakings, i.e. sales exceed €50 million per last year worldwide: see the Consumer Protection Act 2007 (Grocery Goods Undertakings) Regulations 2016.[300] Where the non-performance of a supply contract takes place due to factors that are beyond the reasonable control of a party to the contract, Regulation 7 provides:

> "7. (1) A party to a grocery goods contract shall not be liable for a delay or failure to perform the contract concerned resulting from circumstances beyond the reasonable control of the party concerned.

---

[297] [2004] 1 H.K.L.R.D. 754. See also the lease of an advertising signage site in *Ooh! Media Roadside Property Ltd v Diamond Wheels Property Ltd* [2011] VSCA 116.

[298] Unreported, Supreme Court, February 12, 1975.

[299] The dispute resolution provisions in the Residential Tenancies Act 2004 will produce decisions revolving around frustration-type issues.

[300] Made under s.63B of the Consumer Protection act 2007, inserted by s.83 of the Competition and Consumer Protection Act 2014.

(2) A party affected by circumstances referred to in paragraph (1) shall notify, in accordance with the terms specified in the contract, the other party of—

  (a) the specific circumstances which caused the delay or failure in the performance of the contract,

  (b) the date and time in relation to which the circumstances causing the delay or failure in the performance arose, and

  (c) where applicable, the date and time in relation to which the circumstances causing the delay or failure in the performance of the contract ceased.

(3) Where the circumstances referred to in paragraph (1) continue for a specified continuous period as provided for in the grocery goods contract, either party may terminate the grocery goods contract by written notice in accordance with the terms specified in the contract."

Clearly, a standard of "circumstances beyond the reasonable control" of a party is less onerous than the frustration standard "an event (without default of either party and for which the contract makes no sufficient provision)".[301]

(7) Effects of the doctrine of frustration

18–113 If a contract is frustrated the common law courts decreed that all future obligations are thereby discharged. So in *Kearney v Saorstát and Continental Shipping*,[302] Mr Kearney's contract of employment ended with the sinking of his ship, thereby preventing his widow from obtaining compensation under the Workmen's Compensation Acts when he later died.

18–114 In *Krell v Henry*[303] the licensee was discharged from an obligation to pay the balance of £50 because that obligation had not fallen due before cancellation of the procession. It should be noted that the licensee's cross-action to recover the sum already paid was discontinued: because that obligation had arisen before cancellation, frustration could not provide a right to restitution on the ground that the licensee would ever enjoy the benefits of the contract. Indeed, if the licensee's obligation to pay had occurred before frustration an action to recover this sum would have been successful; see *Chandler v Webster*[304] where the Court of Appeal held that in frustration cases, the loss lies where it falls at the date of frustration. In cases where hire charges had been pre-paid prior to the cancellation of the coronation procession, actions to recover the monies were unsuccessful.[305] The injustice that this may cause is

---

[301] Blayney J, giving judgment for the Supreme Court in *Neville & Sons Ltd v Guardian Builders Ltd* [1995] 1 I.L.R.M. 1, citing Lord Simon in *National Carriers Ltd v Panalpina (Northern) Ltd* [1981] 2 All. E.R. 161.

[302] (1943) Ir. Jur. Rep. 8.

[303] [1903] 2 K.B. 740.

[304] [1904] 1 K.B. 493, applying the earlier case of *Blakeley v Muller & Co* [1903] 2 K.B. 760.

[305] *Blakely v Muller & Co* [1903] 2 K.B. 760; *Civil Service Co-operative Society Ltd v General Steam Navigation Co* [1903] 2 K.B. 756.

particularly striking in cases where the contract is entire. In *Appleby v Myers*[306] the plaintiff agreed to install machinery on the defendant's premises and to maintain the machinery for two years after installation. A price of £459 was agreed. When installation was almost complete, a fire destroyed the premises and the installation. The plaintiff brought an action for £419 for work done and materials sold and delivered, but the action failed. While the contract was discharged as a result of *Taylor v Caldwell*, the obligation to pay the price had not fallen due at the date of the fire and no payment of any kind was available to the plaintiff.

18–115 A right that has come into existence before frustration then cannot be discharged by the event itself; frustration is only prospective in its effects. So in *Herman v Owners of S.S. Vicia*[307] the obligation to repatriate the seaman was an "accrued right" that could not be discharged through frustration. In that case Hanna J. observed that a successful plea of frustration would only prevent the employer from being liable in damages for wrongful termination.[308] Section 40 of Deasy's Act also makes this clear; the accident which entitles the tenant to surrender the lease serves to discharge the tenant from all *future* obligations.

18–116 The common law position is far from satisfactory. The decision in *Chandler v Webster* obliged the hapless licensee to produce the sum due even though he had no chance of obtaining even a partial benefit. The House of Lords in the *Fibrosa* case[309] overruled *Chandler v Webster* and held that if a party to a frustrated contract can show that no tangible benefit has resulted from the contract then restitution of money paid will be ordered.[310] This result is almost as unfair as *Chandler v Webster* for the payee may have spent a considerable amount of time and/or money in furtherance of the contract— witness *Fibrosa* itself where the respondents were ordered to repay £1,000 to the appellants, even though the respondents had incurred costs in respect of the manufacture of specialist machines which could not be delivered to Poland, a country occupied by an enemy power.

18–117 The Law Reform (Frustrated Contracts) Act 1943 (the "1943 Act"), the principles of which are applicable in Northern Ireland, permits some degree of apportionment in these cases; the Act has been adopted in several jurisdictions in the Commonwealth and similar legislation is in force within the US. In Ireland the courts have not as yet been faced with choosing between *Chandler v Webster* and *Fibrosa*; it is desirable that the Law Reform Commission and the Oireachtas provide some legislative guidelines on this

---

[306] (1867) L.R. 2 C.P. 651.
[307] [1942] I.R. 304.
[308] *Flynn v Great Northern Railway Co (Ir.)* (1953) 89 I.L.T.R. 46.
[309] *Fibrosa Spolka Akcyjnia v Fairbairn Lawson Combe Barbour Ltd* [1943] A.C. 32.
[310] The various Commonwealth statutes are critically examined by Stewart and Carter, "Frustrated Contracts and Statutory Adjustment: The Case for a Reappraisal" [1992] C.L.J. 66 who find all of them seriously flawed.

question, perhaps by adding an amendment to the Civil Liability Acts 1961–1964. It is notable that in the only English case in which the 1943 Act has been exhaustively considered, Robert Goff J. adopted a somewhat critical position. The learned judge pointed out that the 1943 Act does not give a general power to apportion loss between the parties. Nor is the statute designed to either put the parties in the position they would have been in if the contract had been performed or restore them to their pre-contractual position. The judge's reasoning in this case, *B.P. Exploration Co (Libya) Ltd v Hunt (No. 2)*,[311] was approved by the House of Lords.[312] In the only other English case in which the 1943 Act was discussed, *Gamerco SA v ICM/Fair Warning Agency Ltd*[313] the discretion to allow the payee to retain some monies for out-of-pocket expenses was not exercised by the court even though some loss was suffered. When the Law Reform Commission and/or the Oireachtas ultimately consider the law of frustration it is hoped that the 1943 Act is not utilised in its present raw state.

18–118 In the Republic of Ireland, s.7 of the Sale of Goods Act 1893 remains in force. The common law rules on contracts of insurance, carriage of goods by sea and voyage charters (which are excluded from the 1943 Act) remain applicable in the Republic. It cannot, however, be disputed that some kind of general legislative measure is overdue. The choice seems to be between a measure which is similar to the 1943 Act, or some more radical legislative initiative. Section 265 of the US Restatement of Contracts (1981) empowers the courts to "grant relief on such terms as justice requires, including protection of the parties reliance interests". Such a measure is an improvement on the 1943 Act in one significant way. The 1943 Act does not give the court the power to order one party to transfer a monetary amount to the other party, in order to compensate the transferee for wasted expenditure if, for example, the transferee was only to be paid at the end of the contract, which has been frustrated prior to completion.[314]

No Temporary or Partial Frustration

18–119 There can be instances where distinct and severable obligations, if frustrated, can be severed from the contract and the remainder of the contract enforced (e.g. an arbitration clause names a specific individual as arbitrator but that person dies). But, in general, the plea of frustration, if it succeeds, renders the entire contract at an end. The common law concept does not recognise partial or temporary frustration on account of partial or temporary impossibility. In *Ringsend Property Ltd v Donatex Ltd*[315] Kelly J.

---

[311] [1982] 1 All E.R. 925.
[312] [1982] 1 All E.R. 986.
[313] [1995] E.M.L.R. 263.
[314] It is doubtful whether *Appleby v Myers* (1867) L.R. 2 C.P. 651 would be decided differently under the 1943 Act; see *Parsons Brothers Ltd v Shea* (1965) 53 D.L.R. (2d) 86.
[315] [2009] IEHC 568.

parodied counsel's efforts to argue that one clause could be frustrated whilst the remainder of the contract remained in force. Indeed, counsel went further to argue that the clause "would at some stage in the future, through some unexplained and, I suspect, inexplicable alchemy, revive itself ... the proposition is clearly devoid of substance".

Part 9

Remedies Following Breach of Contract

19 Damages

Remedies in General

19–01 While the judges are at times said to be concerned with the interpretation and enforcement of contractual obligations rather than the creation of new obligations for contracting parties, in this particular context, the enforcement of contractual rights by way of a binding judicial pronouncement that one contracting party must perform a contractual obligation is not, in fact, the primary remedy available to the victim of a breach of contract to which that victim is privy.[1] The remedy of specific performance is not freely available and even when the contract in question falls within the traditional ambit of specific performance, the best example being contracts for the sale of an interest in land, there are a variety of discretionary or residual factors that may deny the plaintiff the promised performance. Further, there are instances where the contract in question involves an obligation or range of obligations that are traditionally seen as inappropriate subjects for specific performance, such as contracts of employment and contracts for the sale of goods. The common law system of remedies is at times quite out of kilter with the expectations of ordinary citizens. For example, when consumer goods malfunction, most consumers are concerned about having the goods adequately and promptly repaired by the seller or manufacturer, but the common law and the Sale of Goods and Supply of Services Act 1980 do not give the consumer any such right.[2] The remedy available in respect of breach of a particular obligation often depends on the condition/warranty/innominate term classification addressed elsewhere in this book.

19–02 Where the contract is wholly or partly executory, the primary remedies of damages or specific performance may not be realistic propositions. The loss to the plaintiff may not be capable of calculation, particularly in a speculative venture such as a business franchise, and specific performance may not be available at all. The plaintiff may still, however, seek a remedy in the form of a declaration that the contract has been rescinded, and this may be valuable if property has been transferred or a third party interest makes the situation somewhat complicated. We have already considered rescission as a remedy

---

[1] On the remedy of an injunction see Kirwan, *Injunctions*, 2nd edn (Dublin, Round Hall, 2015). See also Farrell, *Irish Law of Specific Performance* (Dublin, Bloomsbury Professional 1995). On damages generally see McGregor, *McGregor on Damages*, 19th edn (London: Sweet & Maxwell, 2014); Dorgan and McKenna, *Damages* (Dublin: Round Hall, 2015), Ch.11.

[2] There is a movement towards establishing replacement or repair as a primary remedy under s.53 of the Sale of Goods Act 1893 (amended by s.21 of the Sale of Goods and Supply of Servcies Act 1980). This is particularly the case in EU consumer law, reflecting the reluctance of most sales laws in the EU to allow a buyer to reject non conforming goods.

in the context of mistake and misrepresentation. It remains possible, however, for a contract to deny to the injured party the right to rescind or treat the contract as terminated for breach by the other by way of an exemption clause; many contracts seek to address both the consequences of agreement and the consequences of breach, and the skills of the contract lawyer must include an awareness of how the interests of the client can best be protected. For example, the contract may require payment of a deposit; the contract should specify the consequences of breach or non-performance on whether, for example, that deposit is forfeited or refundable. Care must be taken to avoid the rules on penalties. Other matters that will obviously occupy the contract lawyer will be the availability, or otherwise, of damages for consequential loss, for the express terms of the contract may be a useful way of narrowing, or broadening, the common law rules on recovery, in particular the rules on remoteness of damage. It is of course necessary for the plaintiff to establish both a breach of contract by the defendant and that, on the balance of probabilities, the fact that the breach occasioned the loss: *Steward v Harmonstown Motors Ltd*.[3]

Restitutionary Damages

19–03 While *Hickey & Co Ltd v Roches Stores (Dublin) Ltd (No. 1)*[4] countenances a broad restitutionary principle, developments in England should also be carefully noted. In the landmark decision of the House of Lords in *Attorney General v Blake*[5] Lord Nicholls indicated that "exceptionally, an account of profits may be the most appropriate remedy for a breach of contract".[6] *Blake*, an infamous spy, sold his memoirs to a publisher in breach of a contractual undertaking to stay silent. The Crown sought to stop the publisher from paying Blake's profits to him, the Crown relying before the House of Lords on breach of contract as the cause of action. However, the Crown had not proved any loss to the Crown. Building upon cases in which damages for infringement of intellectual property and other property rights has led to the award of damages even though the property owner had suffered no loss, in particular *Wrotham Park Estate Co v Parkside Homes*,[7] Lord Nicholls, with whom three other Law Lords concurred, thought it a "modest" step to expand this exceptional remedy into the contract arena. This decision confines *Bredero Homes*[8] to the scrapheap, but *Blake* itself raises as many problems as it solves. Lord Nicholls indicated that an account of profits—he preferred this terminology to restitutionary damages—should be awarded only where the usual remedies are inadequate and the plaintiff has a legitimate interest in seeking to disgorge from the defendant his gains. But it is not clear whether

---

[3] [2005] IEHC 83; *Re–Source America International Ltd v Platt Site Services* [2005] 2 Lloyd's Rep. 50.
[4] [1980] I.L.R.M. 107.
[5] [2001] 1 A.C. 268.
[6] [2001] 1 A.C. 268 at 285.
[7] [1974] 1 W.L.R. 798.
[8] *Surrey County Council v Bredero Homes Ltd* [1993] 1 W.L.R. 1361.

the case requires the plaintiff to establish a subjective intention to break the contract.[9] Many commentators remain uncomfortable with this approach because it looks very like the development of an approach which is intended to punish a wrongdoer rather than compensate the victim of a breach of contract, and some of the comments of Lord Hobhouse, who dissented in *Blake*, are noteworthy. In Lord Hobhouse's view many of the persuasive authorities in the property field that Lord Nicholls relied upon were compensatory damages cases and he saw the account of profits award as a departure from principle. In the later case of *Experience Hendrix LLC v PPX Enterprises Inc*,[10] a case in which the plaintiffs sought damages for breach of licensing agreements, the Court of Appeal adopted a measure of compensation based upon a reasonable licence fee, a head of loss that shades into *Blake* but which stopped short of allowing the plaintiff to recover *all* the profits earned by the defendant.[11] The Court of Appeal has also departed from its earlier decision in *Bredero Homes* in *WWF – World Wildlife Fund for Nature v World Wrestling Federation*,[12] a case in which the reasonable licence fee measure of damages was classified as being compensatory in nature. That case suggests that *Wrotham Park* damages are available at common law, even if an injunction is not available to the plaintiff or the plaintiff has not sought an injunction in the first place. While no Irish court has considered this topic, the Law Reform Commission examined this issue, amongst others, in its 2000 Report, *Aggravated, Exemplary and Restitutionary Damages*[13] and while this Report now looks rather dated in the light of subsequent English developments, it should be noted that the Law Reform Commission indicated that damages for equitable wrongs should be available on compensatory principles (and even exemplary damages) if decisions from other jurisdictions were followed and that the Law Reform Commission approved of the award of restitutionary damages under *Hickey*, suggesting that the development of this area should be left to the common law.[14] *Blake* has not been followed in Australia on the ground that *Robinson v Harman*, accepted by the High Court of Australia as holding that a plaintiff is entitled to compensation only,[15] is inconsistent with the reasoning in *Blake* and Australian case law as it currently stands:

---

[9]   See Beatson, "Courts, Arbitrators and Restitutionary Liability for Breach of Contract" (2002) 118 L.Q.R. 377; Campbell and Harris, "In Defence of Breach: A Critique of Restitution and the Performance Interest" (2002) 22 L.S. 208.

[10] [2003] 1 All E.R. (Comm.) 830; Jaffey, "Disgorgement and 'Licence Fee Damages' in Contract" (2004) 20 J.C.L. 57.

[11] If the claim is for infringement of copyright, punitive damages are available under the Copyright and Related Rights Act 2000 s.128(3).

[12] [2007] EWCA Civ 286; see also *Lunn Poly Ltd v Liverpool and Lancashire Properties* [2007] L. & T.R. 6 (quiet enjoyment).

[13] LRC 60–2000.

[14] LRC 60–2000, para 6.48. For substantial *Wrotham Park* damages for breach of a confidentiality agreement, see the decision of the Privy Council in *Pell Frischmann Engineering Ltd v Bow Valley Iran Ltd* [2009] UKPC 45. The exceptional circumstances that make an award of Wrotham Park damages appropriate are highlighted in *Morris-Garner v One Step (Support) Ltd* [2016] EWCA Civ 180.

[15] e.g. *Wenham v Ella* (1972) 127 C.L.R. 454 and *Commonwealth v Amann Aviation Pty Ltd* (1991) 174 C.L.R. 64.

"… it would be inconsistent with the current principles laid down by the High Court to confer a windfall on a plaintiff under the guise of damages for breach of contract."[16]

Purpose Behind an Award of Damages

19–04 An award of damages following a breach of contract is designed to compensate the injured party and not necessarily to punish the party in breach. The motive underlying such an award should be contrasted with the measure of compensation; this was explained by Parke B. in *Robinson v Harman*[17] as being designed to put the plaintiff "so far as money can do it … in the same situation … as if the contract had been performed". While this maxim will not always explain the precise measure of damages in every case, it should be noted that it is designed to secure for the innocent party compensation in excess of money spent in furtherance of the contract.

The ruling principle set out in *Robinson v Harman* was recently reaffirmed by a majority of the High Court of Australia in *Clark v Macourt*.[18] The purchaser of a business—an assisted reproduction facility—spent $381,000 (Australian) to acquire the business and its assets including straws of human sperm. The sperm was in part unusable. The purchaser had to purchase replacement sperm from the only alternative source in the US. The purchaser sued the vendor for breach of warranties given in the deed of transfer. Applying the guiding principle, Hayne J., relying on first principles, observed that it is important to identify what loss is being compensated for, as well as the time at which the loss is to be assessed. Furthermore, Hayne J. stressed that there is a primary objective that the law seeks to promote, observing that "the loss which is compensated reflects a normative order in which contracts must be performed". The damages awarded would be the difference in value at the time of the asset transfer (breach) and their value had they been compliant with the contract. These were proved by reference to the replacement cost of $1.2 million (Australian). It is the monetary value of faithful performance that should be the primary objective when a plaintiff seeks to recover expectation damages. After noting that the vendor was seeking to refer to the difference between the cost of the purchase price and the damages sought, Keane J said:

> "This is the complaint of any vendor in breach of a contract in which the purchaser made the better bargain. The fundamental value protected by the law of contract is that *pact sunt servanda*, bargains are to be kept. That the contract crystallizes a state of affairs in which the purchaser's

---

[16] Per Hill and Finkelskein JJ. in *Hospitality Group Pty Ltd v Australian Rugby Union Ltd* (2001) 110 F.C.R. 157 at 196. For "restitutionary heresy" see Brennan, "The Beautiful Restitutionary Heresy of a Larrikin" [2011] Syd. L. R. 209.

[17] (1848) 1 Ex. 850 at 855, followed in Ireland by Palles CB in *Hamilton v Magill* (1883) 12 L.R.Ir. 186 at 202.

[18] [2013] HCA 56.

gain is the vendor's loss is a characteristic of commerce in a capitalistic economy."[19]

19–05 In contrast, damages assessed in tort actions are generally designed to return the injured party to his or her position before the tort occurred: *restitutio in integrum*.[20]

19–06 A simple example may make this clear. A purchases a book for €200 from B who misrepresents that it is worth €500. The book is in fact worth €150. The measure of damages in tort will be €50. B's tort has resulted in A parting with €200; A retains a book worth €150; an award of damages of €50 is necessary to return A to the pre-tort position. In contrast an action brought in contract for breach of warranty will produce an award of €350. A has a book worth €150; A, because of B's promise, thought the book was worth €350 more than this. A is therefore entitled to be put in this position through an award of €350, the difference between the actual value of the book and the value as warranted.

19–07 This distinction is not always kept clear; witness Finlay P.'s observation in *Hickey & Co Ltd v Roches Stores (Dublin) Ltd (No. 1)*.[21] The rationale for differing rules as between contract and tort are in part explained by the fact that contractual liability is generally strict and can in several cases be adjusted by the parties, while in tort the duty of care is shaped by considerations of public policy and the presence or absence of ethical factors such as carelessness and fraud. There are, of course, cases in which the measure of damages will be the same regardless of the cause of action, as the English Court of Appeal case of *Esso Petroleum v Mardon*[22] indicates. Nevertheless the rules on remoteness of damage, mitigation of loss and the possibility of an award of punitive damages are not identical in contract and tort, thereby increasing the chances of differing awards being made, depending on the cause of action. This is particularly likely in litigation surrounding a misrepresentation or breach of an express term. In *Archer v Brown*[23] this point was re-emphasised by Peter Pain J. when he stated that while damages in the tort of deceit may allow the plaintiff to recover all damages that flow directly from the fraudulent misrepresentation, the same facts, if an action is brought in contract, may produce a different measure of compensation, for damages are limited by the "reasonable contemplation" test, as set out in *Hadley v Baxendale*.[24] The House of Lords, in *Smith*

---

[19] [2103] HCA 56 at para.135.
[20] See the excellent explanation given of these principles by Costello J. in *McAnarney & McAnarney v Hanrahan & T.E. Potterton* [1994] 1 I.L.R.M. 210; McMahon & Binchy, *Law of Torts*, 4th edn (Dublin: Bloomsbury Professional, 2013), Ch.44.
[21] Unreported, High Court, July 14, 1976; [1993] R.L.R. 196; Clark, "Damages and Unjust Enrichment" (1978) 29 N.I.L.Q. 128.
[22] [1976] Q.B. 801.
[23] [1985] Q.B. 401, applying *Doyle v Olby (Ironmongers)* [1969] 2 Q.B. 158; see also *Royscot Trust Ltd v Rogerson* [1991] 3 All E.R. 294.
[24] (1854) 9 Ex. 341.

New Court Securities Ltd v Scrimgeour Vickers (Asset Management) Ltd[25] has held that in cases of fraudulent misrepresentation the defendant will be liable for all loss flowing from the fraud, as long as the plaintiff has acted so as to mitigate the loss.

19–08 In *Keegan Quarries Ltd v McGuinness*[26] the High Court has approved the seven principles set out in the speech of Lord Browne-Wilkinson in *Smith New Court Services Ltd v Scrimgeour Vickers Assets Management Ltd*,[27] where the noble Lord said:

> "In sum, in my judgment the following principles apply in assessing the damages payable where the plaintiff has been induced by a fraudulent misrepresentation to buy property: (1) the defendant is bound to make reparation for all the damage directly flowing from the transaction; (2) although such damage need not have been foreseeable, it must have been directly *caused* by the transaction; (3) in assessing such damage, the plaintiff is entitled to recover by way of damages the full price paid by him, but he must give credit for any benefits which he has received as a result of the transaction; (4) as a general rule, the benefits received by him include the market value of the property acquired as at the date of acquisition; but such general rule is not to be inflexibly applied where to do so would prevent him obtaining full compensation for the wrong suffered; (5) although the circumstances in which the general rule should not apply cannot be comprehensively stated, it will normally not apply where either (a) the misrepresentation has continued to operate after the date of the acquisition of the asset so as to induce the plaintiff to retain the asset or (b) the circumstances of the case are such that the plaintiff is, by reason of the fraud, locked into the property; (6) in addition, the plaintiff is entitled to recover consequential losses caused by the transaction; (7) the plaintiff must take all reasonable steps to mitigate his loss once he has discovered the fraud."

19–09 In *Keegan Quarries* the measure of the loss was the difference between the contract price and the value of the land purchased at the time of sale. As the land was valued at €1.5 million but the purchase price was €7 million, damages in fraud were computed at €5.5 million with other additional losses being awarded such as stamp duty, legal costs and interest paid on monies to borrow the purchase price (these items being discounted to take account of the fact that the plaintiffs retained the land purchased). The quantum awarded for breach of warranty was computed in the same way. Note that causation principles operated to deny recovery on other "heads of loss". However, if the plaintiff can only show that the defendant was negligent then the degree of culpability of the defendant is less and the appropriate measure of recovery

---

[25] [1996] 4 All E.R. 769; *Clef Aquitaine SARL v Laport Materials (Barrow) Ltd* [2001] Q.B. 488.
[26] [2011] IEHC 453.
[27] [1996] 3 W.L.R. 1051.

will be the indemnity measure. Whether the s.2(1) deceit measure in cases of statutory misrepresentation (see s.45(1) of the Sale of Goods and Supply of Services Act 1980) is the correct measure is now in some doubt: in *Smith New Court* the House of Lords was noticeably tepid in its support for *Royscot Trust Ltd v Rogerson*.[28]

Classification of the Measure of Compensation

19–10 Fuller and Purdue, in an extremely influential article, "Reliance Interest and Contract Damages",[29] advanced the view that while damages in contract are compensatory, three distinct types of loss are commonly involved:

(1) The expectation loss

19–11 If P purchases goods on a rising market, the seller subsequently deciding not to deliver to P but sell elsewhere, it would be unsatisfactory simply to entitle P to claim back the purchase price for, as the terminology involved here indicates, P's expectation that the contract will be performed is seen as a legitimate area of compensation. If the price of the self same goods has risen P should be able to buy substitute goods. The measure of damages here will be the difference between the contract price and the price of the substitute goods at the later relevant date—normally the date of breach. Compensating the buyer on this basis also has the advantage of discouraging the seller from breaking the contract for if the courts in effect take away the profit to be made from breach of contract there will be little or no reason for the seller (other than malice) to refuse delivery to the buyer.

(2) The reliance loss

19–12 A purchaser who hires a lorry from a third party in order to collect goods may find that the goods are unavailable; the cost of hiring the vehicle from the third party would also be a legitimate head of loss which the purchaser may seek to recover. It must be said that such loss—reliance loss—will most frequently be recovered in cases where the court cannot estimate expectation loss because of the impossibility of finding that the plaintiff has or was likely to suffer loss. The plaintiff may elect to recover reliance loss in cases where expectation loss has not occurred as a result of the plaintiff making a bad bargain. It may be that where promissory estoppel succeeds as a plea the courts may elect to award reliance loss rather than expectation loss; justice may require the promisee recovering only the value of what he or she has lost rather than that which was promised.[30]

---

[28] [1991] 3 All E.R. 294; their Lordships were enthusiastic about Hooley's criticisms of *Royscott*: (1991) 107 L.Q.R. 547. See more recently *Spice Girls Ltd v Aprilia* [2001] E.M.L.R. 174.

[29] (1936) 46 Yale L.J. 52, 573.

[30] See s.90 of the US Restatement of Contracts (2d.) and *Hoffman v Red Owl Stores Inc* 133 N.W. 2d. 267 (1965). For an excellent discussion of this principle see the New Zealand case of *Wilson Parking Ltd v Fanshaw 136 Ltd* [2014] 3 N.Z.L.R. 564.

(3) Restitution loss

19–13 If P has paid €500 to a seller who refuses to deliver the goods as promised, P will be entitled to claim the return of the consideration paid to the seller. This is to be seen as necessary in order to prevent the unjust enrichment of the seller. Restitution loss differs from reliance loss in that reliance loss may result from transactions involving third parties. In general there is a considerable overlap between restitution and reliance loss. The importance of selecting the appropriate head of loss should not be under-estimated. Where the contract has been fully performed on one side and the other party defaults *in toto*, on a falling market, an action for restitution, special damages and loss of interest will be preferable for the plaintiff: *Durkan New Homes v Minister for the Environment, Heritage and Local Government.*[31]

(4) Other heads of loss

19–14 Other factors may justify an award of damages. Consequential loss may result from the breach of contract. Suppose a case where non-acceptance of goods constitutes a breach of contract by the buyer; the seller is unable to arrange an immediate resale. The seller's loss, if forced to make the sale for less than the agreed price, will be recoverable if it is not too remote. While this illustration may in fact also be an illustration of "expectation loss"—the resale price will provide evidence of value at the date of breach—other cases of consequential loss cannot fall into this category. A splendid illustration of this point is provided by the facts of *Stoney v Foley.*[32] Ten ewes, warranted sound, were sold by the defendant to the plaintiff. A few days after the sale, scab developed on the sheep and the plaintiff's land was proclaimed unfit from February until June. Besides compensation for the loss of sheep the plaintiff recovered damages for being unable to let the land for that period. In *Leahy v Rawson*[33] the defendant undertook to build an extension but carried out the work so negligently that the extension had to be demolished. Apart from compensation in respect of the cost of demolition and rebuilding, the plaintiff was held entitled to consequential loss in the form of loss of income that would have accrued by using the premises as a bed and breakfast business. In *JP Morgan Chase Bank NV v Springwell Navigation Corp.*[34] Chase was charged with managing Springwell's investment portfolio which was to be used to invest in acquiring replacement vessels for Springwell's shipping business. Chase allegedly carried out its duties negligently causing a $280 million loss so instead of buying 20 vessels, Springwell only purchased two. Chase sued for loss on its portfolio and profits lost on its shipping business due to only having two new ships instead of 20. Chase argued unsuccessfully that the claim was one in which there was double recovery. Wall L.J. observed that he was unable to accept this argument:

[31] [2012] IEHC 265.
[32] (1897) 3 I.L.T. 165.
[33] Unreported, High Court, January 14, 2003.
[34] [2006] EWCA Civ 161, an early decision in a protracted piece of litigation.

"On Springwell's case, had all gone according to plan, it would have used the portfolio to purchase the ships which would then have made the profits. Chase's actions, by reducing the value of the portfolio, had deprived it of the capacity to purchase the ships and to earn profits from them. On this argument, I think it properly arguable that the measure of damage is (1) the loss of value of the portfolio and (2) the loss of the shipping profits which would have followed from the purchase of the ships."[35]

The defendant may be liable to reimburse the plaintiff for "incidental" losses, for example, the expense involved in arranging to buy substitute goods when a defendant vendor refuses to perform the contract, or, in cases of non-acceptance, warehouse costs incurred prior to effecting a resale at a higher price than that fixed by the contract.[36] In *Bob Bushell Ltd v Luxel Varese SAS*[37] wasted expenditure in seeking to find another supplier, the defendants being in repudiatory breach, was recoverable along with lost profits. Similarly, in *Mallett and Son (Antiques) Ltd v Rogers*[38] the plaintiff purchased an antique bookcase that needed a degree of restoration. The plaintiff spent £31,533 in preparing the bookcase for resale. It transpired that the bookcase had been stolen and it was returned to the original owner. Because the defendant was aware that the plaintiff intended to resell it, the defendant was held liable to return both the purchase price and the cost of the remedial work in an action for breach of s.12 of the Sale of Goods Act 1893, as amended.

(5) The performance interest

19–15 Recent case law[39] and academic comment have drawn attention to the need for the recognition of a performance interest.[40] In many of these cases the courts are asked to compensate the plaintiff for the cost of remedying any defective performance by the defendant under the contract. This is often described as a "cost of cure" measure and it is to be distinguished from the diminished value of property that the plaintiff experiences due to defective performance or the reliance loss occasioned by the breach, or the consequential loss that results from the breach. Performance loss is illustrated by Professor Coote's example of a contract to build a folly which the builder repudiates before commencement. The "economic" measure of loss might be the fall in

---

35 Paragraph 18 of the judgment.
36 *Baker Perkins Ltd v C.J. O'Dowd*, unreported, High Court, April 13, 1989.
37 Unreported, High Court, February 20, 1998.
38 [2005] IEHC 131.
39 *Ruxley Electronics Ltd v Forsyth* [1995] 3 All E.R. 268 is the leading case. For an interesting if inconclusive discussion of *Ruxley* see *Consolidated Development Co Ltd v Evariste M. Diotte and E.M. Diotte Construction Inc* (2014) N.B.R. (2d) 271.
40 Coote, "Contract Damages, *Ruxley*, and the Performance Interest" [1997] 56(3) C.L.J. 537; Friedmann, "The Performance Interest in Contract Damages" (1995) 111 L.Q.R. 628. The use of extra-contractual remedies to vindicate the performance interest is forcefully advocated by Turner, "Proprietary Modes of Protecting the Performance Interest in Contract" [2012] L.M.C.L.Q. 549.

value of the building site (which will be zero if work is not commenced) or the reduction in value that the site bears if the folly is incomplete. But, Coote argues, if the disappointed landowner is able to obtain substituted performance elsewhere "damages must be based on the cost of getting the work done or completed" even if the folly is an eyesore that has a neutral or even a negative financial implication for the landowner. Indeed, Coote argues forcefully that the protection and vindication of the performance interest should be seen as a "primary object" of the award of damages in contract. In *Ruxley Electronics* damages for "loss of amenity" were modest, some £2,500. In *South Parklands Hockey and Tennis Centre Inc v Brown Falconer Group Property Ltd*,[41] the defendants installed a playing surface for hockey and tennis in 1994–1995. Soil movement made the surface erratic in terms of bounce and ball movement. The evidence indicated that it was reasonable for the plaintiffs to wait until the soils below the surface "settled down", a situation that was reached in 2003, before replacement work would commence. General damages for disturbance and inconvenience, including having to put up with erratic ball movement, in the sum of $30,000 (Australian) were awarded.

Punitive Damages

19–16 It is often said that there is no scope for an award of damages designed to punish a party who deliberately breaches a contract. Nevertheless if a cause of action arises both in contract and tort it is clear that punitive damages may be awarded by placing stress on the tortious aspect of the defendant's conduct. In *Drane v Evangelou*[42] the English Court of Appeal awarded punitive damages against a landlord who was held liable in trespass for the unlawful eviction of tenants.

19–17 In *Garvey v Ireland*[43] the plaintiff, a Garda Commissioner, was summarily dismissed from his post. Applying the classification advanced by Lord Devlin in *Rookes v Barnard*[44] this action was held to be arbitrary and unconstitutional conduct on behalf of the Government which was seen as meriting the award of exemplary damages against the State. Decisions from other jurisdictions provide support for this approach; the Canadian provinces have all produced decisions in which employees have recovered punitive damages for the manner in which they have been dismissed. These cases go further than *Garvey* for it is clear that punitive damages are available even against private sector employers; it is essential for the plaintiff to show that the contract "has been breached in a high-handed, shocking and arrogant fashion

---

[41] [2004] SASC 81.
[42] [1978] 1 W.L.R. 459; *Whelan v Madigan*, unreported, High Court, July 18, 1978.
[43] Unreported, High Court, December 19, 1979. For other issues see [1981] I.R. 75.
[44] [1964] A.C. 1129; *Bradford Metropolitan City Council v Arora* [1991] 3 All E.R. 545. In Northern Ireland see *Breslin v McKevitt* [2011] NICA 33 and *Crawfords Burn Inn Ltd v Graham* [2013] NIQB 79.

so as to demand condemnation by the Court as a deterrent"; per Linden J. in *Brown v Waterloo Regional Board of Commissioners of Police*,[45] applied in *Pilato v Hamilton Place Convention Centre*.[46] The Ontario Court of Appeal in *Brown* stressed the need for bad faith to be shown. And in a landmark decision, *Whiten v Pilot Insurance Co*,[47] the Supreme Court of Canada has given an exhaustive statement of the availability of punitive damages in Canadian law. In some instances the courts have taken the view that damages may be awarded to compensate the plaintiff for the distress and upset that can result from violent, aggressive or insensitive conduct by the party acting in breach of contract, and some judges distinguish clearly between damages which are intended to punish or mark the court's disapproval of the defendant's conduct on the one hand, and instances where the objective is to compensate the plaintiff. In this latter situation, often described as instances where aggravated damages are payable, the issue is regarded, increasingly, as an aspect of remoteness of damage. There are several Canadian cases that go further than this. While punitive damages are not generally available in breach of contract cases, there are decisions which indicate that where a contracting party acts with shocking disregard for the safety of others, for example, by letting a property to tenants while suppressing information that the water supply is unsafe to drink, punitive damages are available.[48] In contrast, the Australian courts incline towards the compensatory principle with punitive damages for breach of contract not being available for breach of contract; see *Hospitality Group Property Ltd v Australian Rugby Union Ltd*.[49] The Irish Supreme Court seems to have set its face against the award of punitive or exemplary damages, leaving open the possibility that if a claim is mounted in negligence, nuisance or trespass, then damages for aggravated loss (i.e. damages that are intended to compensate the plaintiff rather than punish the defendant) may be possible; see *Conway v I.N.T.O.*[50] as explained in *Swaine v Commissioners for Public Works*.[51] This approach is evident in *Irish Ferries Teoranta v Minister for Communications, Energy and National Resources*.[52] The defendant was ordered to pay damages for reputational loss and commercial embarrassment caused to the plaintiff by *ultra vires* conduct but Cooke J. resisted counsel's claim to punitive damages. The Law Reform Commission, in an important Report, *Aggravated, Exemplary and Restitutionary Damages*,[53] has indicated that, in general, the Commissioners do not welcome the use of exemplary

---

45 (1983) 103 D.L.R. (3d.) 748.
46 (1984) 45 O.R. (2d.) 652.
47 (2002) 209 D.L.R. (4th) 257.
48 *MacDonald v Sebastian* (1987) 43 D.L.R. (4th) 636; also where a party acts with cynical disregard for the rights of others, as in *D.K. Investments Ltd v S.W.S. Investments Ltd* (1986) 6 B.C.L.R. (2d.) 291; *Brown and Root Services Corp v Aerotech Herman Nelson Inc* (2002) 167 Man. R. 100.
49 (2001) 110 F.C.R. 157.
50 [1991] 2 I.R. 305.
51 [2003] 2 I.L.R.M. 252.
52 [2012] IEHC 256.
53 LRC 60–2000.

damages in breach of contract claims, conceding, however, that the boundary between punitive damages and aggravated damages is a difficult one to draw.[54]

Unjust Enrichment

19–18 There is Irish support for the view that persons who deliberately break contracts because they calculate that they will make a profit from so doing, even after calculating damages payable for loss suffered by the victim, are to be deterred from considering this kind of conduct. In *Hickey & Co Ltd v Roches Stores (Dublin) Ltd (No. 1)*[55] the defendants broke a contract to allow the plaintiffs to sell fabric in their store, calculating that even after paying agreed damages they would profit from carrying on the business themselves. Finlay P. stated obiter that where a wrongdoer calculates that by breach of contract or through tortious conduct he will profit thereby, such mala fide conduct should lead the courts to look at both the injury suffered by the victim and the profit or gain unjustly obtained by the wrongdoer. If the wrongdoer would still obtain a profit after quantifying the victim's loss, damages should be increased to deprive the wrongdoer of this profit. However in *Surrey County Council v Bredero Homes*[56] the Court of Appeal awarded only nominal damages for breach of contract when the defendants built five homes more than the planning permission obtained allowed for. The Court of Appeal found there was no authority at common law for a measure of damages that was not compensatory in nature.

19–19 The decision in *Bredero Homes* has been doubted by the House of Lords in *Attorney-General v Blake*, discussed above, and the decision of the House of Lords in sanctioning an expanding view of damages that *Bredero Homes* set its face against will lead to considerable litigation to test the limits of restitutionary or "disgorgement" damages. This movement towards compensation for non-economic loss is operative on several fronts and it has had a subtle impact in Ireland, with *Hickey & Co Ltd v Roches Stores (Dublin) Ltd (No. 1)* being an important harbinger of cases to come. There are no Irish cases in which the court has actually applied this principle of assessment. The most recent case in which the *Hickey* decision was considered is *Vavasour v O'Reilly and Windsor Motors Ltd*,[57] a decision of Clarke J. The plaintiff was party to a motor vehicle franchise agreement that was to run for three years, the plaintiff having an option to extend his participation in the venture for a further year. Approximately 15 months into the agreement the other parties excluded

---

[54] In some statutes punitive and aggravated damages may both be recoverable in addition to economic loss; see the Copyright and Related Rights Act 2000 s.128(3); Consumer Protection Act 2007 s.74.
[55] Unreported, High Court, Finlay P., July 14, 1976. See also *Hanley v I.C.C. Finance* [1996] 1 I.L.R.M. 463.
[56] [1993] 1 W.L.R. 1361; *Jaggard v Sawyer* [1995] 1 W.L.R. 269.
[57] [2005] IEHC 16.

the plaintiff from participating in the franchise. The plaintiff was held entitled to 50 per cent of the profits denied to him for the four-year period and he was awarded damages for loss of opportunity to participate in a profit-earning venture for the rest of the period in which the agreement operated (with a 40 per cent discount in recognition of the "significant risk" that the plaintiff may not have continued to participate in the venture after year four), applying *Philp v Ryan*.[58] Mr Vavasour also advanced a claim to damages under *Hickey*, Clarke J. clearly distinguishing *Hickey* damages[59] as being "additional" damages, as distinct from compensatory damages. After noting that the arrangement between the parties involved a 50/50 division of profits and that the defendant O'Reilly had been found liable in damages, Clarke J. held the *Hickey* case had no application where there was no difference between the gains made by the defendant and the losses incurred by the plaintiff.

19–20 The decision in *Blake* has also had an impact on the deliberations of Irish reform agencies. The Law Reform Commission, in the Consultation Paper on *Aggravated, Exemplary and Restitutionary Damages*[60] has taken a very conservative position on unjust enrichment, taking the view that while restitutionary damages should be available at least in cases of deliberate wrongdoing and perhaps for all torts and equitable wrongs, such awards should not be available in cases of breach of contract. However, in the report on civil damages in Irish law[61] the Law Reform Commission recommended that the availability of restitutionary damages should continue to be possible for all torts and in breach of contract, with the application of the law being left to the judiciary via the common law. Legislation was not felt to be necessary at this time.

"Speculative" Damages

19–21 In many situations the courts are placed in the invidious position of having to calculate damages in relation to events that will happen at some time in the future, as in cases of anticipatory breach, or according to a formula that must depend on a hypothetical set of circumstances. In *Hickey & Co Ltd v Roches Stores (Dublin) Ltd (No. 2)*[62] a claim for loss of profits was sustained on the assumption that Hickeys would suffer loss of business even after the contract could have been lawfully terminated and that the repercussions would

---

[58] [2004] IESC 105.
[59] See further judicial approval in the copyright infringement case of *Duhan v Radius Television Production Ltd* [2007] IEHC 292 (Herbert J.).
[60] April 1998, LRC 12–1998.
[61] *Aggravated, Exemplary and Restitutionary Damages*, LRC 60–2000, Ch.6. Judicial developments may open up new lines of argument based on legislative changes. It is possible to envisage the award of aggravated damages should an insurer or defendant resist a personal injury claim in bad faith: *Lackey v Kavanagh* [2013] IEHC 341; *Seleh v Moyvalley Meats (Ireland) Ltd* [2015] IEHC 762.
[62] [1980] I.L.R.M. 107. See also *Bob Bushell Ltd v Luxel Varese SAS*, unreported, High Court, February 20, 1998.

last (at a diminishing volume) for a further two years. Finlay P. in particular showed a considerable degree of willingness to estimate loss of profits figures once it can be shown that loss of profits are certain to result; in a memorable passage in *Grafton Court Ltd v Wadson Sales*[63] the learned judge observed that a court "should be alert, energetic and if necessary ingenious to assess damages where it is satisfied that a significant injury has flowed from breach". In *Callinan v Voluntary Health Insurance Board*[64] Keane J. at first instance declined to award damages in favour of the plaintiffs when certain payments were discontinued, causing contraction of the nursing services provided by the plaintiff nursing order. The Supreme Court[65] remitted the case back to the High Court, observing that it was clear that loss had been occasioned by the defendant's breach of contract. Blayney J. held that Keane J. had fallen into error when he took the view that "because the plaintiffs had not established the full extent of the loss they were claiming, they had not discharged the onus of proving that they had not suffered any damage. In my opinion this does not follow".

19–22 A court may also be persuaded to award damages if it can be shown that a particular event was almost certain to occur. In *McGrath v Kiely*[66] the plaintiff who had been injured in a motor accident sued her doctor and solicitor, both of whom had negligently failed to bring to counsel's attention the full extent of her injuries. She claimed that this failure adversely affected the damages recovered. Henchy J. formed the view that this injury would have resulted in additional damages of £100 being awarded. In *O'Keeffe v Ryanair Holdings*[67] the process of calculating the plaintiff's loss of the right to free flights with Ryanair for life was fraught with uncertainty. Kelly J. had to calculate the average cost of booking a flight and estimate the frequency with which the facility would have been taken up by the plaintiff and her husband. Loss to the date of trial was estimated at €7,500[68] with the capital value of those flights for the remainder of the life of the plaintiff and her husband at €60,000. An even more extreme situation arises when a plaintiff claims loss of opportunity to earn a prize in a competition as the English case of *Chaplin v Hicks*[69] shows. In the remarkable Irish case of *Hawkins v Rogers*[70] the plaintiff purchased a racehorse "plus engagements", thereby entitling him to run the horse in a series of Irish "classic" races. The defendant, however, maliciously withdrew the horse from the races after the sale, thereby denying the plaintiff the opportunity to win prize money. Even though it was clearly impossible to determine the likelihood of the horse winning all or any of the races Dixon J.

---

[63] Unreported, High Court, February 17, 1975.
[64] Unreported, High Court, April 22, 1993.
[65] Unreported, Supreme Court, July 28, 1994.
[66] [1965] I.R. 497.
[67] [2003] 1 I.L.R.M. 14.
[68] €1,500 of this sum was awarded under *Jarvis v Swan Tours* [1973] 2 Q.B. 233 in respect of "unpleasant and shabby treatment" of the plaintiff on a given occasion.
[69] [1911] 2 K.B. 786.
[70] (1951) 85 I.L.T.R. 129.

awarded damages "calculated" in part by reference to the horse's performance in later races. In contrast Pringle J. in *Afton v Film Studios of Ireland*[71] refused to award damages for lost future profits because he was unable to hold that it was probable that a net profit would result from the venture.

19–23 The normal practice in cases where the expectation loss is so uncertain that damages cannot be recovered under this head is to award reliance loss; in *Hawkins v Rogers* the court could have awarded the plaintiff the price paid plus any expenses incurred in maintaining the race horse had the plaintiff wished to treat the contract as discharged through breach. The plaintiff wished to retain the race horse, however, so Dixon J. seems to have awarded damages simply to punish the defendant rather than compensate the plaintiff for ascertainable loss; Dixon J. felt that "the law might justly be accused of futility if the plaintiff were in such circumstances left without any legal remedy".

Date of Assessing Loss

19–24 In cases where a contract has been broken, and the breach is treated as putting the contract to an end, the assumption is that the injured party will go into the market place and obtain identical goods or services, or sell identical goods or services, as the case may be. However, where the subject matter of the contract has shifted in value, it will be necessary to fix the dates upon which the goods or services are to be valued in order to assess the plaintiff's loss. The normal contractual measure is the difference between the contract price and the value of the goods at the time of due delivery, but in real property transactions the courts are increasingly permitting the plaintiff to submit that a different time be selected. Because the plaintiff may reasonably seek specific performance it may be that the plaintiff can obtain damages based upon the value of the property at the time when it was clear that specific performance was going to be unsuccessful, or even the date of judgment.[72] In accordance with this approach, should the vendor obtain a specific performance decree which cannot be enforced, it is possible to obtain damages based upon the valuation at the date of the order being aborted.[73] *Darlington Properties Ltd v Meath County Council*[74] provides a very good example of the importance of post-breach damages assessment criteria. The plaintiff purchased development land from the defendant in April 2006 for €4.51 million, based upon misrepresentation about development potential. N. Ltd, who owned development land adjoining the site, had bid €2.225 million. Unknown to the plaintiffs, the development potential was much diminished by planning permissions already granted to N. Ltd by the planning department

---

[71] Unreported, High Court, July 12, 1971; *Powerbeat Canada Ltd v Powerbeat International Ltd* [2002] 1 N.Z.L.R. 820.

[72] *Malhotra v Choudhury* [1980] Ch. 52.

[73] *Johnson v Agnew* [1980] A.C. 367.

[74] [2011] IEHC 70; see also *Vandeleur & Moore v Dargan* [1981] I.L.R.M. 75.

of the defendant. Kelly J., applying *Golden Strait Corp v Nippon*[75] and *Duffy v Ridley Properties Ltd*[76] said that in these circumstances damages were to be awarded "on the basis of the monies actually expended by Darlington less credit being given for the value of the lands retained". Darlington would not have entered into the contract at all if the misrepresentation had not been made. While the parties were agreed that the market value of the lands as at April 2006 was in the region of the price paid of €4.51 million, there were sharp differences on subsequent valuations, but Kelly J. preferred the valuations arrived at by the plaintiffs. At the date of breach, the actual value of the (impaired) lands was around €2.31 million (in line with the N. Ltd tender price) so had the measure been the difference between price paid and value at the date of breach, damages would have been €2.22 million. But as the court decided that the compensatory principle required the adoption of a different date for assessment, value at the date of trial had fallen to €0.5 million and by the date of judgment the value had fallen by a further €50,000. Thus, damages awarded were €4.06 million. The general rule, that damages in respect of services are to be calculated by reference to the cost of obtaining a replacement service, or another employer, can be found in *Hoenig v Issacs*.[77] However, in *Corrigan v Crofton & Crofton*[78] a contract for building work was completed negligently. In an action for breach of contract in respect of workmanship and materials, O'Hanlon J. held that damages could be calculated by reference to the date of judgment rather than an earlier date, the date when a schedule for remedial work was drawn up. The fact that completion of the work was delayed because of the plaintiff's impecuniosity, because it was a substantial job, and the defendants had denied liability, made it reasonable for the plaintiff to postpone the work until he knew the outcome of the legal action. In *Scheps v Fine Art Logistic Ltd*,[79] the plaintiff purchased a sculpture in June 2004 for $35,000 (US). The art work was bailed with the defendants but it was lost and, in all likelihood, thrown into a skip. The court found that at this time the sculpture was worth much more, around £135,000. The plaintiff was also held to be entitled to damages reflecting the increased value of the sculpture in the period between breach of contract (September 2004) and the date of judgment (March 2007). This figure by way of consequential damages was estimated at £219,375. Teare J. held that the sharp rise in value of the works of the sculptor, Anish Kapoor, was not too remote, rejecting an argument that this increase

---

[75] [2007] 2 A.C. 353.
[76] [2008] 4 I.R. 282, a pre-Celtic Tiger collapse case. See also *McGrath v Stewart* [2008] IEHC 348. These are both damages in lieu of specific performance situations. Where the buyer is in default the English Court of Appeal has held that the breach date is the right date only where there is an immediately available market for the sale of the relevant asset: *Hooper v Oates* [2013] EWCA Civ 91.
[77] [1952] 2 All E.R. 176.
[78] [1985] I.L.R.M. 189, following *Dodd Properties (Kent) Ltd v Canterbury City Council* [1980] 1 All E.R. 928; *Perry v Sidney Phillips & Son* [1982] 3 All E.R. 705. See also *James Stewart Ltd v Callaghan*, unreported, Supreme Court, July 28, 1982; *Doran v Delaney* [1999] 1 I.L.R.M. 225; *Leahy v Rawson*, unreported, High Court, January 14, 2003.
[79] [2007] EWHC 541 (Q.B.).

in value could be compared to the particularly lucrative dying contracts that were too remote in *Victoria Laundry*. The plaintiff was held entitled to "date of judgment" damages because any delay in prosecuting the claim was attributed to efforts made to find the missing artwork. Students should also refer to the discussion of the recent UK case law at paras 19–48 to 19–54 for the importance of determining whether the date of breach rule is a guiding principle or merely a point of departure.

19–25 The measure of damages in relation to sale of goods actions is considered below.

Relationship between the Heads of Loss

19–26 In principle the plaintiff should not be able to recover both wasted expenditure —reliance loss—and lost profits—expectation loss. If P has hired a lorry in order to collect goods which the seller now refuses to sell, P should not be able to recover the cost of hiring the lorry *and* profits lost because a resale of those goods has now fallen through; had the seller not broken the contract the hire charges would have been necessary in order to realise the profits on resale.

19–27 Nevertheless the injured party may choose between the various heads of loss; see the English Court of Appeal decision in *Cullinane v British Rema Manufacturing Co*[80] followed by the Supreme Court in *Waterford Harbour Commissioners v British Rail Board*.[81] In *Waterford* the defendants repudiated a statutory obligation to provide a shipping service between Waterford and Fishguard. The plaintiffs, in anticipation of the service continuing, spent £300,000 in building a new wharf, which, at the time of trial, did not produce any income because of the termination of the service. Henchy J., giving judgment for the majority on the question of quantum of damages, observed that the plaintiffs in this case could not sell the building because of its unique nature and situation. If this were possible, Henchy J. continued, the plaintiffs would have the choice of claiming damages either for their net capital loss after the sale or for loss of profit.

19–28 In England the plaintiff who opts for lost expenditure has been held able to recover for expenditure incurred before the contract was struck or before the contract became legally binding; see *Anglia Television v Reed*[82] and *Lloyd v Stanbury*.[83] The plaintiffs may on occasion seek to recover heads of

---

[80] [1954] 1 Q.B. 292; *Anglo Group Plc v Winther Browne & Co* (2000) 72 Con. L.R. 118 at 163. See however the formula developed in *T.C. Industrial Plant Pty v Robert's Queensland Pty* (1963) 180 C.L.R. 130.
[81] Unreported, Supreme Court, February 18, 1981.
[82] [1972] 1 Q.B. 60; *Salvage Association v Cap Financial Services* [1995] F.S.R. 654.
[83] [1971] 2 All E.R. 267.

damages that are mutually exclusive as in *Fitzpatrick v Frank McGivern Ltd.*[84] The court must be vigilant in guarding against over-compensating the plaintiff in this manner. Thus in the *Waterford* case the Supreme Court by a majority were of the view that Costello J. at trial had in effect permitted recovery for net expenditure and loss of profits, reversing the decision on this point.

19–29 The decision in *Anglia Television v Reed* has recently been qualified both in Canada and in England. The plaintiff cannot recover reliance loss if it is clear that the plaintiff had initially entered a bad bargain and it can be established that, but for the breach of contract by the defendant, the commercial venture would have proved an even greater financial disaster for the plaintiff. In *Bowley Logging Ltd v Domtar Ltd*[85] the plaintiff employed the defendants to haul logs by trailer. The defendants failed to provide the agreed number of vehicles and were sued for breach of contract, the plaintiff (the liquidator of the company) seeking to recover all wasted expenditure. It was shown that the initial contract entered into by the plaintiff company was itself the cause of the company going into liquidation. They were selling logs for $7 a ton less than it cost to produce and, in a sense, the defendants' failure to provide the requisite number of trailers actually kept the losses down; the British Columbia Court of Appeal upheld the trial judge's conclusion that damages were not available in this case. In *C.C.C. Films Ltd v Impact Quadrant Films Ltd*,[86] Hutchison J. held that if the plaintiff seeks to recover damages for wasted expenditure, the onus is upon the defendant to prove that the expenditure would not have been recovered had the defendant performed his contract. Because the defendant could not show that the films, which the defendant had failed to deliver to the plaintiff, would not have enabled the plaintiff to break even, the defendant was liable to compensate for wasted expenditure. In *Milburn Services Ltd v United Trading Group*,[87] another case in which a wasted expenditure claim was made in relation to a loss-making project, the court observed that if the plaintiff could show he would have made less of a loss had the defendant performed the contract, the plaintiff is to be put in the position of having made that smaller loss.

Loss of Chance

19–30 The law draws a distinction between a loss of chance based upon existing facts—did something occur or not—as opposed to a loss of chance or loss of opportunity. In the first situation, the plaintiff is required to establish

---

[84] Unreported, High Court, February 10, 1977.

[85] [1978] 4 W.W.R. 105, affirmed at (1982) 135 D.L.R. (3d.) 179; *Re–Source America International Ltd v Platt Site Services* [2005] 2 Lloyd's Rep. 50. The *Bowlay Logging* principle was also adopted in *Omak Maritime Ltd v Mamola Challenger Shipping* [2010] EWCA Civ 2026. On restitutionary remedies in a contractual context, see Jaffey (2013) 76 M.L.R. 429.

[86] [1984] 3 All E.R. 298; see also *C. & P. Haulage v Middleton* [1983] 3 All E.R. 94. Contrast *Times Newspapers Ltd v Wiedenfeld & Nicholson Ltd* [2002] F.S.R. 463.

[87] (1995) 52 Con. L.R. 130.

that, on the balance of probabilities, a particular loss was suffered.[88] In the second situation, where an event clearly has not occurred, the plaintiff argues that, but for the defendant's breach of contract, a benefit may have accrued to the plaintiff. In this case, the standard of proof requires some degree of proof of possible losses, the test being whether the chance or possibility was substantial enough to warrant some award of damages.[89] These claims do involve some element of combining distinct heads of loss, often allowing tort and contract claims to merge together.[90] As the decision of the House of Lords in *Jackson v Royal Bank of Scotland*[91] attests, this process is far from being an exact science.Note the contrasting approach between the High Court and the Supreme Court in assessing damages in *Lett and Co Ltd v Wexford Borough Council*[92] which, although a legitimate expectation case, was one in which the Supreme Court reduced the award by nearly half and cautioned against speculative awards for future loss.

Quantification of Damages

19–31 Few problems arise where the plaintiff is seeking damages for reliance loss or restitution; money spent or the estimated value of services rendered will be the basis of the award. If the claim is for expectation loss the court may, in certain cases, have to consider whether the plaintiff should recover compensation for deterioration in the value of the property or the cost of remedying the defect. For example, a house that is insulated by poor quality or pungent cellulose foam may reduce the value by €2,000; it may cost €10,000 to pull down the walls and remove the offending substance. Which measure is to apply? In general the courts award the measure that seems most appropriate; cost of curing the defect applies in building contracts; see *Kincora Builders v Cronin*.[93] It may be that the construction work is executed so poorly that demolition of the structure and rebuilding, as distinct from merely correcting the deficiencies in the structure, will be the appropriate measure; see *Leahy v Rawson*.[94] In the Republic the measure of damages recoverable against a tenant for non-repair is the fall in the value of the reversion that results: s. 55 of the Landlord and Tenant Act 1931, considered extensively in *Groome v Fodhla Printing Co*[95] and *Gilligan v Silke*.[96] *Gilligan v Silke* was subsequently applied

---

[88] *Davies v Taylor* [1974] A.C. 207; *C. & P. Haulage v Middleton* [1983] 3 All E.R. 94. See generally Poole [2006] L.M.L.Q. 63.
[89] *Allied Maples Group Ltd v Simmons & Simmons* [1995] 1 W.L.R. 1602; *Vavasour v O'Reilly and Windsor Motors Ltd* [2005] IEHC 16.
[90] e.g. *4 Eng Ltd v Harper, Times Law Report*, June 23, 2008.
[91] [2005] 1 W.L.R. 377; *Ball v Druces & Atlee* [2004] EWHC 1402 (Q.B.).
[92] [2012] IESC 14.
[93] Unreported, High Court, March 5, 1973.
[94] Unreported, High Court, January 14, 2003.
[95] [1943] I.R. 380.
[96] [1963] I.R. 1.

in *Trustees of St. Catherine's Parish v Alkin.*[97] In cases where the covenant is a covenant to repair and it is the landlord who is in breach, the Court of Appeal, in the leading case of *Hewitt v Rowlands*,[98] has indicated that the measure is the diminution in market value of the premises created by the lack of repair. This may be an appropriate measure in commercial lettings, but in residential lettings the trend is towards the cost of cure and consequential loss,[99] such as damage to personal effects.[100] This issue was graphically explored by the House of Lords in *Ruxley Electronics Ltd v Forsyth.*[101] The defendant engaged the plaintiffs to build a swimming pool to a depth of 7 foot 6 inches. On completion the pool depth varied from 6 foot to 6 foot 9 inches and he refused to pay, counterclaiming for cost of cure. At the trial the judge found that the pool was not reduced in value by the breach and awarded £2,500 damages for loss of amenity. On appeal, the Court of Appeal increased damages to cost of cure at £21,560 although it was unlikely that Forsyth would demolish and rebuild. The House of Lords allowed the appeal by Ruxley, accepting that while in this kind of case cost of cure is the normal measure, the court is not constrained to order either cost of cure or the diminution in value measure. A median path, the lost amenity value, was a further option and the House of Lords opted to restore the trial judge's decision on this point.

19–32 When the issue of the appropriate measure of compensation arises within the context of a contract of insurance (typically a contract insuring a building against destruction by fire) an additional premium may normally be payable in order to obtain the cost of reinstatement rather than market value, but, in the absence of this additional payment, the insured, it seems, may recover reinstatement costs if there is an intention to rebuild; see *Murphy v Wexford County Council*,[102] applied by the Supreme Court in *St. Alban's Investment Co v Sun Alliance.*[103]

Sale of Goods

19–33 The rules relating to the assessment of damages under ss.49 to 54 of the Sale of Goods Act 1893 are considered in the Report of the Sales Law Review Group[104] where a number of reforms are suggested. It should be pointed out

---

[97] Unreported, High Court, Carroll J., March 4, 1982; *Fetherstonhaugh v Smith*, unreported, High Court, February 12, 1979.
[98] (1924) 93 L.J.K.B. 1080: but see *Olympia Productions v Olympia Theatre*, unreported, High Court, February 25, 1980. The High Court of Australia has recently approved the cost of cure quantum where a commercial tenant breaks a covenant not to alter premises without consent: *Tabcorp Holdings Ltd v Bowen Investments Pty Ltd* (2009) 136 C.L.R. 272.
[99] *Calabar Properties v Stitcher* [1984] 1 W.L.R. 287.
[100] *Siney v Dublin Corp* [1980] I.R. 400; *Burke v Dublin Corp* [1990] 1 I.R. 181.
[101] [1995] 3 All E.R. 268; Coote [1997] C.L.J. 537.
[102] [1921] 2 I.R. 230.
[103] [1984] I.L.R.M. 50. On the measure of damages in respect of fire loss due to non-repair of leasehold premises, see *Taylor v Moremiles Tyre Services*, unreported, High Court, June 6, 1978.
[104] Prn. A11/1576 (2011).

however that contracting parties to a contract for the sale of goods may decide to provide for a self-contained system of remedies, which may involve the displacement of either common law rules or the statutory defendant rules provided in the Sale of Goods Acts 1893–1980 as long as the contract contains clear provisions to this effect: *Scottish Power UK Plc v BP Exploration Operating Company Ltd.*[105]

19-34 In cases where the seller fails to deliver goods, the buyer, it will be assumed, can go into the market to buy identical goods at the market price. Damages will be the amount by which the market price at the date of breach, that is, the time when delivery should have been made,[106] exceeds the contract price: s.51(3) of the Sale of Goods Act 1893. In *Cullen v Horgan*[107] a wool merchant in Cahirciveen agreed on October 26 to sell and deliver wool to the plaintiffs in Dublin. No date was fixed for delivery. The defendant declined to answer the plaintiff's letters seeking delivery: meanwhile the market price of wool rose steadily until the following March. The plaintiff was held entitled to recover damages based on the difference between the contract price and the market price in the following January, the date by which delivery (in the view of the court) should have taken place. It should be noted that no evidence was introduced to show an available market in Cahirciveen at the date of breach. The court instead heard evidence of the market price in Dublin—some £100 more than the contract price—and after deducting transport costs of £50 saved, awarded £50 in damages.

19-35 The rule found in s.51(2), that the measure of damages is the estimated loss directly and naturally resulting, in the ordinary course of events, from the seller's breach of contract, is a restatement of the first limb in *Hadley v Baxendale*. The measure of damages can be broadened so as to include consequential loss, such as loss of an exceptional profit made by agreeing a resale of the goods prior to the buyer taking delivery, at higher than market rates, but in order to do so the person suing for non-delivery must show that the seller had knowledge of these exceptional circumstances. In general, a resale is irrelevant in fixing market value[108] and the resale price will not be available to reduce damages (where the resale price is lower than the market price at the date of delivery) or increase damages (where the resale is at a price higher than the market price at the date of delivery). If there is no available market, however,[109] then a resale price will be utilised to fix market value.[110] If the buyer does not obtain the same goods because there is no available market, the buyer may purchase goods of a superior quality, if, for example, goods are

---

[105] [2015] EWHC 2658 (Comm).
[106] Section 51(3) provides that where no time for delivery is fixed the relevant time is the time of refusal to deliver.
[107] [1925] 2 I.R. 1.
[108] *Williams Bros. v Agius* [1914] A.C. 510.
[109] For a definition of "available market", see *Charter v Sullivan* [1957] 2 Q.B. 117 at 128 per Jenkins L.J.
[110] *Patrick v Russo-British Grain Export Co* [1927] 2 K.B. 535.

needed urgently to complete a contract. The extra expense involved in such a case will be recoverable; see *Blackburn Bobbin Co v Allen*.[111]

19–36 In cases of late delivery of goods the measure of loss is the fall in the value of goods from the agreed date until the date of actual delivery; this rule will also apply if an immediate resale was contemplated.[112] However, it does not follow that this measure will inevitably be employed, for in a case where a builder is deprived of materials which are delivered late but used by the builder, additional costs rather than a shift in the value of the materials would appear to be the appropriate measure.[113]

19–37 If goods are sold in breach of the condition that the seller had the right to sell, s.53(2) provides that the correct measure of damages is the difference between the ordinary retail price and the contract price. In *O'Reilly v Fineman*[114] the plaintiff buyer was prevented from obtaining a Chesterfield which he had purchased in a sale for £21; the sofa had been initially priced at £24. The plaintiff was awarded £3 in damages. This measure of compensation may include any improvements made to the goods by the dispossessed purchaser, such as repair or renovation of the property. The leading case is *Mason v Burningham*.[115] The plaintiff purchased a typewriter for £20, and spent £11 to repair it. The typewriter had been stolen, and was repossessed. Damages of £31 were awarded.

19–38 Where the cause of action is breach of condition or breach of warranty, s.53(2) and (3) apply. Section 53(2) again re-emphasises the first limb in *Hadley v Baxendale*, and s.53(3) indicates that the measure under s.53(2), in relation to quality, is, prima facie, the difference between the value of the goods at the time of delivery and their value if in accordance with the contract. This measure also applies to breach of fitness for purpose and description obligations. Again, sub-contracts are generally ignored.[116]

19–39 Where the loss is due to non-acceptance of goods by the buyer, the measure of damages found in s.50, in cases where there is an available market, is said in s.50(2) to be governed by the first limb in *Hadley v Baxendale*. Section 50(3) states this to be the difference between the contract price and the market price at the date when the goods ought to have been accepted or, if no time was fixed, the date when the buyer refused to accept the goods.

---

[111] [1918] 1 K.B. 540.

[112] *Heron II* [1969] 1 A.C. 350; *Victoria Laundry (Windsor) Ltd v Newman Industries Ltd* [1949] 2 K.B. 528.

[113] *Croudace Construction v Cawoods Concrete Products* [1978] 2 Lloyd's Rep. 55.

[114] [1942] Ir. Jur. Rep. 36; *Stock v Urey* [1955] N.I. 71.

[115] [1949] 2 K.B. 545.

[116] *Slater v Hoyle & Smith Ltd* [1920] 2 K.B. 11. But see *Bence Graphics International Ltd v Fasson U.K. Ltd* [1997] 1 All E.R. 979; *Louis Dreyfus Trading Ltd v Reliance Trading Ltd* [2004] 2 Lloyd's Rep. 243.

19–40 In cases of so-called lost volume sales, that is where the seller is a dealer in goods who finds that a purchaser has not accepted the goods, the dealer is entitled to claim that a resale of the goods on the market does not prevent a claim for the lost profit, for the dealer has, at the end of the day, sold one less car, or caravan, or telephone than he would otherwise have sold. In *W.L. Thompson Ltd v Robinson (Gunmakers) Ltd*[117] the defendant failed to take delivery of a standard Vanguard car from the plaintiff dealers. The plaintiff returned the car to their suppliers, who did not charge for the lost sale. The price was fixed by the supplier and the profit on each for the dealer was £61. The defendant claimed that loss was non-existent because the plaintiff could either resell the vehicle or return it, which the plaintiff had done. Given that the demand for these vehicles was less than the supply available within the plaintiff's region, the prima facie rule in s.50(3) was inapplicable. There was no available market for these cars—they could not be readily re-sold—and the loss of profit was in this case a tangible loss. If, however, demand outstrips supply then it will be assumed that a re-sale will be effected and only nominal damages will be recoverable; see *Charter v Sullivan*.[118]

19–41 In hire-purchase and leasing contracts, where the goods are defective, the measure of damages is calculated by reference to the hire charges due under the contract, subject to a deduction for the hirer's use of the goods.[119] However, the prima facie rules found in ss.50, 51 and 53, by mirroring the first limb of *Hadley v Baxendale*, are similarly displaced by the second limb of *Hadley v Baxendale*. Section 54 of the Sale of Goods Act 1893 makes this clear by stating that other losses are recoverable if within the reasonable contemplation of the parties at the time of the contract. The leading case remains *Victoria Laundry (Windsor) Ltd v Newman Industries Ltd*,[120] considered below.

Remoteness of Damage

19–42 A party in breach is not liable to compensate for all loss resulting from the breach of a contract. In a contemporary context, Lord Reid, in *The Heron II*,[121] indicated that not every type of damage that is foreseeable will be recoverable in contract. The loss must be "of a kind which the defendant, when he made the contract, ought to have realised was not unlikely to result from the breach".[122] The rules determining the extent to which damages are recoverable

---

[117] [1955] Ch. 177; *Glencore Energy UK Ltd v Cirrus Oil Services Ltd* [2014] EWHC 87 (Comm).

[118] [1957] 2 Q.B. 117; contrast second-hand vehicles: *Lazenby Garages Ltd v Wright* [1976] 2 All E.R. 770.

[119] *Charterhouse Credit Co v Tolly* [1963] 2 Q.B. 683; *U.C.B. Leasing v Holtom* (1987) 137 N.L.J. 164.

[120] [1949] 2 K.B. 528.

[121] [1969] 1 A.C. 350.

[122] [1969] 1 A.C. 350 at 382–383.

are in the main set out in the leading case of *Hadley v Baxendale*.[123] The plaintiffs owned a mill. A shaft broke and had to be despatched for replacement or repair, the defendants being employed to carry the shaft. It was returned at a date later than could have been expected, the defendants being less than diligent in transporting it. The plaintiffs' mill was stopped for the entire period because they could not operate without the shaft. They sued the defendant carriers for loss of profits. Alderson B. observed:

> "[W]here two parties have made a contract which one of them has broken, the damages which the other party ought to receive in respect of such breach of contract should be such as may fairly and reasonably be considered either arising naturally, *i.e.* according to the usual course of things, from such breach of contract or such as may reasonably be supposed to have been in the contemplation of both parties, at the time they made the contract, as the probable result of the breach of it."[124]

Although it is not clear whether the rule in *Hadley v Baxendale* consists of one rule with two limbs or is in fact two rules the point is largely irrelevant.[125] What is important is the fact that different factors are material to each of the separate rules or limbs. While *Hadley v Baxendale* is the cornerstone of the law on contractual remoteness of damage, the clearest statement of principle is found in the judgment of Asquith L.J. in *Victoria Laundry (Windsor) Ltd v Newman Industries Ltd.*[126] The injured party is only entitled to recover that part of the loss which occurred, and, at the time of the contract, was reasonably foreseeable.[127] In turn, foreseeability depends on the knowledge possessed by the party in breach. Asquith L.J. indicated that for this purpose, knowledge possessed is of two kinds:

> "Everyone, as a reasonable person is taken to know the 'ordinary course of things' and consequently what loss is liable to result from a breach of contract in that ordinary course. This is the subject matter of the 'first rule' in *Hadley v Baxendale*. But, to this knowledge, which a contract-breaker is assumed to possess whether he actually possessed it or not, there may have to be added in a particular case knowledge which he actually possesses of special circumstances outside the 'ordinary course of things,' of such a kind that a breach in those special circumstances

---

[123] (1854) 9 Ex. 341.

[124] (1854) 9 Ex. 341 at 354–355.

[125] Ogus, *The Law of Damages* (London: Butterworths, 1973), pp.72–73. Robertson (2008) 28 L.S. 172 sees the remoteness risk as a "gap saving device" rather than based on intention of the parties.

[126] [1949] 2 K.B. 528.

[127] The test of reasonable foreseeability was criticised by the House of Lords in *The Heron II* [1969] 1 A.C. 350 as likely to confuse the contract and tort remoteness principles: Lord Reid in particular favoured the view that the common knowledge and contemplation of the parties, rather than reasonable foreseeability, should determine remoteness of damage issues in contract.

would be liable to cause more loss. Such a case attracts the operation of the 'second rule' so as to make additional loss also recoverable."[128]

Asquith L.J. went on to stress that knowledge is the knowledge that would be attributed to a reasonable man. Under the first limb it is clear that loss will be recoverable if it can be said to flow naturally from certain breaches of contract; a diseased animal may render the land upon which it grazes unsafe for some agricultural purposes; see *Stoney v Foley*.[129] Animal fodder laced with lead pellets will fail to meet the contract description and, in the ordinary course of things, injure animals that feed upon it; see *Wilson v Dunville*.[130] In that case the supplier pleaded that such loss was outside its reasonable contemplation. Palles C.B. pointed out that under the rule in *Hadley v Baxendale* if the consequences of a breach of contract "result solely from the act in question, and an usual state of things, they are the ordinary and usual consequences of that act". The state of knowledge or expectation of the parties is irrelevant under the first limb. So, in *Stock v Urey*[131] the defendant sold to the plaintiff a car registered in the Republic, the sale taking place in Northern Ireland. The car had in fact been smuggled into the North. The vehicle was seized by the UK customs authorities and the plaintiff was obliged to pay £68 to get it back. This constituted a breach of the implied condition and warranties under s.12 of the Sale of Goods Act 1893. The court held that payment of this sum to the authorities was loss naturally resulting from breach of s.12 for which the defendant was liable.[132] Similarly, in *Lee and Donoghue v Rowan*[133] a farmer was held able to recover the amount of money required to complete the construction of a drying shed from builders, who, in breach of contract, had refused to complete the work. Costello J. held this loss to be recoverable under the first limb.

19–43 If, however, loss does not arise in the ordinary course of things from the breach it must be shown that the defendant in particular was possessed of such knowledge that would enable an ordinary man, at the time of contracting, to foresee that extraordinary loss would ensue from the breach of contract. In *Waller v The Great Western Railway (Ir.) Co*[134] the defendant failed to supply horse boxes to transport the plaintiff's hunters to a sale in Dublin. The horses had to be ridden to the sale where they were sold at a lower price due to their deteriorated condition. The plaintiff indicated that the horses suffered on the journey because of an earlier change in diet; but for this change the journey would have been undemanding. Morris C.J. in his speech indicated

---

[128] [1949] 2 K.B. 528 at 539–540.
[129] (1897) 31 I.L.T. 165.
[130] (1879) 6 L.R. (Ir.) 210.
[131] [1955] N.I. 71.
[132] Contrast *Maye v Merriman*, unreported, High Court, February 13, 1980, discussed at (1981) 16 Ir. Jur. 28.
[133] Unreported, High Court, November 17, 1981.
[134] (1879) 4 L.R. (Ir.) 326.

that loss arising naturally would be the deterioration in the condition of the horses that were fit to make the trip, such loss being nominal. The second limb of *Hadley v Baxendale* was not satisfied because the defendants were unaware of the extraordinarily delicate condition of the horses. Fitzgibbon L.J. observed that the only loss recoverable was the expense of using riders to transport the horses plus any fatigue and inconvenience resulting to both riders and horses. Similarly, in *Diamond v Campbell-Jones*[135] the purchaser of a leasehold property in Mayfair sued the vendor for wrongful repudiation of the contract. He sought to obtain damages based on the profit he, as a dealer in property, would have made in converting the house into offices and maisonettes. Buckley L.J. held that the only damages recoverable were based on the ordinary measure of difference between contract price and market value at the date of repudiation: "special circumstances are necessary to justify imputing to a vendor of land a knowledge that the purchaser intends to use it in any particular manner."[136]

19–44 If we return to the facts of *Hadley v Baxendale* we can also see that the first limb would not be satisfied for it was possible, for example, that a spare shaft was available to the plaintiff. Nor would the second limb be satisfied for the law report indicates that the defendants were unaware that the mill was stopped. The leading English cases provide very good illustrations of the limits of the "reasonable contemplation" test which is often said to form the basis of the second limb. In *Victoria Laundry (Windsor) Ltd v Newman Industries Ltd*[137] the defendants delivered a boiler five months after the agreed date had expired. They knew the plaintiffs intended to use it immediately in their laundry business and were held liable for lost profits that would ordinarily result from being deprived of its use; the defendants were not liable for profits lost as a result of having to pass up exceptionally profitable government contracts, for in the absence of knowledge of the existence of these specific contracts they could not have reasonably contemplated their existence. In *The Heron II*[138] a shipowner who was transporting a cargo of sugar to the port of Basrah, aware that a market for sugar existed in that port, arrived in Basrah nine days late. The owner, who, unknown to the shipowner, intended to sell immediately on arrival lost £4,000 by having to sell on a falling market. This loss was held recoverable. A reasonable man would, in the view of the House of Lords, have regarded an immediate sale as "not unlikely" or a "serious possibility"; when this very real possibility was prevented by the delay, thereby occasioning loss, the owner was able to recover for loss of bargain. Similarly, in *Lee and Donoghue v Rowan*[139] a farmer was obliged to plough under crops grown on his land when a drying shed, to be built under the terms of a contract, was not completed in time for the harvest. Costello J. held that while the builders

---

[135] [1961] Ch. 22.
[136] [1961] Ch. 22 at 35–36.
[137] [1949] 2 K.B. 528.
[138] [1969] 1 A.C. 350; *Kpohraror v Woolwich B.S.* [1996] 4 All E.R. 119.
[139] Unreported, High Court, November 17, 1981.

knew that a failure to complete the shed would require the farmer to incur the cost of transporting his crops to some other farmer's drying sheds they could not have contemplated that a shortage of drying facilities would lead to the loss of the farmer's entire crop. The farmer was held to be able to recover the estimated cost of putting his crops into storage and the transport costs that would have been involved if storage could have been obtained. Nor can the purchaser of real property recover the cost of storing furniture when the vendor refuses to complete the sale unless knowledge can be attributed to the vendor.[140] It is evident, therefore, that some profits will be recoverable under the first limb if loss of profits is a direct result of breach. The general dichotomy between direct loss as "first limb" and indirect or consequential loss as "second limb" is particularly unreliable.[141] The distinction between loss of "ordinary" profits under the first limb, as distinct from profits over and above "ordinary" profits (and which requires knowledge, or a special contract) was explored in *Mayhaven Healthcare Ltd v Bothma*.[142] Construction work on a care home was delayed, causing loss of profits. The rate charged for elderly persons was a lower rate than that charged for younger persons but no information on these residents was given to the defendants. Care home losses were recoverable under the first limb but, absent knowledge, the defendant was not liable under the second limb. A most useful illustration of both limbs in an everyday situation is afforded by the decision of the Court of Appeal in *Kemp v Intasun Holidays Ltd*.[143] The plaintiff's wife booked a family package holiday in Spain. On arrival, their chosen hotel was full and they were billeted in the staff quarters of another hotel. The room was filthy and dusty, triggering off the plaintiff's asthma for several days. The plaintiff's wife on booking the holiday had not informed the travel company of his asthma condition. In the County Court, £400 was awarded for inconvenience and discomfort, loss of enjoyment and disappointment, and £800 for the consequences of the plaintiff's asthma attack. The Court of Appeal held that this second amount should not have been awarded. The condition, asthma, was not so common as to be within the reasonable contemplation of the tour company as a necessary or natural consequence and, in the absence of special knowledge of the plaintiff's condition, the second limb of *Hadley v Baxendale* was not satisfied.

---

[140] *Malone v Malone*, unreported, High Court, June 9, 1982; *Pilkington v Wood* [1953] Ch. 770.

[141] *Croudace Construction v Cawoods Concrete Products* [1978] 2 Lloyd's Rep. 55; *Deepak v ICI* [1999] 1 Lloyd's Rep. 387; *Hotel Services Ltd v Hilton International Ltd* [2000] B.L.R. 235; *McCain Foods GB Ltd v Eco-Tec (Europe) Ltd* [2011] EWHC 66 (TCC). There have been some recent English cases in which the direct and indirect loss dichotomy in the context of profits has been criticised: *Fujitsu Services Ltd v IBM UK Ltd* [2014] EWHC 752 (TCC); *Scottish Power UK Plc v BP Exploration Operating Company Ltd* [2015] EWHC 2658 (Comm).

[142] [2009] EWHC 2634 (TCC). This is a contentious drafting issue on which there is no clear Irish authority. Finlay Geoghegan J., in *ESL Consulting Ltd v Verizon (Ireland) Ltd* [2008] IEHC 369, referred to criticisms in Australia (*Environmental Systems Property Ltd v Peerless Holdings Pty Ltd* [2008] VSCA 26) of the English approach to classifying loss of profits but did not reach any clear conclusion on the point.

[143] [1987] 2 F.T.L.R. 234.

The Achilleas

19–45 The decision of the House of Lords, in *Transfield Shipping Inc v Mercator Shipping Inc, The Achilleas*,[144] represents the most important decision on contract damages in the last 40 years. Although all five members of the House allowed the appeal, Lord Hope of Craighead and Baroness Hale of Richmond were of the view that the issue of remoteness was finely balanced, with the latter observing that, in the case before her, "there is no obviously right answer". The charterers of a vessel under a time charter had hired a vessel for seven months at a daily rate of $16,700. Shortly before the charter was to expire the vessel went on a specific voyage but, due to delays, the ship was returned almost nine full days after the expiry of the charter: this was a breach of contract. It was agreed that if the market value of the daily rate was the relevant figure, then the owners were entitled to $158,301 (overrun damages). However, unbeknownst to the charterers, the owners had hired out the vessel for a follow-on charter at a rate of $39,500 daily. When it was clear that the vessel would be late for its follow-on engagement, the owners informed the follow-on charterers, who used a power to cancel the vessel for late delivery to leverage a reduction in the daily rate from $39,500 to $31,500. Freight rates had fallen dramatically in this volatile market. The reduction of $8,000 per day over the life of the follow-on charter, a loss of profit occasioned by the late redelivery, cost the owners $1.3 million which they sought to recover from the defendant. The majority of a three-panel arbitration, the High Court[145] and the Court of Appeal[146] held that loss of profits, not "overrun" damages, were recoverable. This kind of loss, the possibility that a follow-on engagement might be cancelled, was found to be an event that might be within the first limb in *Hadley v Baxendale*, and, following the reasoning in *Parsons v Uttley Ingham*,[147] once the type of loss was likely to arise naturally, the fact that the scale of the loss was larger than might have been anticipated did not matter. The Court of Appeal in particular accepted that while shipping lawyers would have anticipated the overrun measure was the appropriate quantum, *Hadley v Baxendale* did not require a court to look to the expectations of players in a particular market.

19–46 The House of Lords allowed the appeal, but the ratio decidendi of the case is far from clear. At one extreme Lord Hoffmann and Lord Hope of Craighead were of the view that loss arising out of a breach of contract did not depend upon a literal application of a test whether the loss was foreseeable or not unlikely to occur. Lord Hoffmann regarded this as being a prima facie assumption that could be rebutted "in cases in which the context, surrounding circumstances or general understanding in the relevant market shows that a party would not reasonably have been regarded as assuming responsibility for

---

[144] [2008] UKHL 48.
[145] [2007] 1 Lloyd's Rep. 19.
[146] [2007] 2 Lloyd's Rep. 555.
[147] [1978] 1 All E.R. 525.

such losses".[148] Lord Hoffmann said that before a court sets about the task of calculating damages upon a *Robinson v Harman* basis, the court must ask whether the loss for which compensation is sought is of a "kind" or "type" for which the contract breaker ought fairly to have assumed responsibility. Lord Hope of Craighead also endorsed an "assumption of loss" test, and both Law Lords found that expectations within a specialist market, the exceptionally volatile nature of this market, and the fact that the appellant charters had no knowledge of the details of the follow-on engagement, meant that imposing liability upon the charterer would, in Lord Hope's words, produce "a real risk of serious commercial uncertainty which the industry as a whole would regard as undesirable". Lord Rodger of Queensferry took a more restrained view, declining to deal with the voluntary assumption of risk and the type of loss argument, and he was anxious to stress that the delay was an "innocent" breach of contract (perhaps bearing in mind disgorgement damages in cases of deliberate breach, a factor that clearly lay behind the Court of Appeal's reasoning). Lord Rodger also stated that if the charterer was advised of a lucrative follow-on engagement, then lost profits might be recoverable, and he was also of the view that if the facts indicated that the market knew that a loss of profit might be a natural result then, following *Victoria Laundry*, an award for a general sum, based on being deprived of a profit-earning chattel, may occur.[149] Baroness Hale concurred with Lord Rodger. Lord Walker of Gestingthorpe appears to have held that it was not proper to decide that the common intention of the parties was to impose an extraordinary level of loss at the feet of a charterer who was responsible for a relatively short delay in effecting re-delivery of the vessel.[150]

A New "Assumption of Responsibility" Test of Remoteness?

19–47 To the extent that *The Achilleas* was thought to have laid down a new test of remoteness of damage (particularly in the speech of Lord Hoffmann) later cases have, so to speak, steadied the ship by emphasising that their Lordships were divided and that Lord Hoffmann's perspective was a minority view on this point: per Flaux J. in *The Amer Energy*,[151] cited with approval by Cooke J. in *Classic Maritime Inc v Lion Diversified Holdings Berhad*.[152] The English Court of Appeal, in *Supershield Ltd v Siemens Building Technologies FE Ltd*[153] has observed that:

---

[148] [2008] UKHL 48 at para.9.
[149] [2008] UKHL 48 at paras 58 and 59.
[150] [2008] UKHL 48 at para.84, following Lord Reid in *The Heron II* [1969] A.C. 350 at 385.
[151] [2009] 1 Lloyd's Rep. 293.
[152] [2009] EWHC 1142 (Comm); *The Sylvia* [2010] EWHC 542 (Comm).
[153] [2010] EWCA Civ 7; *John Grimes Partnership v Gubbins* [2013] EWCA Civ 37. See also Beatson L.J.'s somewhat caustic comments on the lack of clarity engendered by *The Achilleas* in *SC Confectia SA v Miss Mania Wholesale Ltd* [2014] EWCA Civ. 1484: "the effect of that case on the understanding of remoteness of damage in the law of contract has of course been profound. Law students up and down the country are probably set the task of identifying the ratio of that case".

"*Hadley v Baxendale* remains a standard rule but it has been rationalised on the basis that it reflects the expectation to be imputed to the parties in the ordinary case, ie that a contract breaker should ordinarily be liable to the other party for damage resulting from his breach if, but only if, at the time of making the contract a reasonable person in his shoes would have had damage of that kind in mind as not unlikely to result from a breach. However, *South Australia* and *Transfield Shipping* are authority that there may be cases where the court, on examining the contract and the commercial background, decides that the standard approach would not reflect the expectation or intention reasonably to be imputed to the parties."

There is debate[154] about whether the Hoffmann approach can be ignored, whether the assumption of responsibility issue is an adjunct to existing principles, or confined to limited and exceptional circumstances.[155]

The *Golden Strait* Decision

19–48 *The Achilleas* is not the only recent decision in which the House of Lords has limited recovery of damages, but, unlike *The Achilleas*, the decision engenders commercial uncertainty as distinct from avoiding it. In *Golden Strait Corp v Nippon Yusen Kubishika Kaisha (The Golden Victory)*[156] the contract related to a time charterparty, to run from 1998 to 2005. The charterers repudiated the charterparty by redelivering the ship to the owner in December 2001, the owners accepting the repudiation that same month and issuing proceedings for damages. Clause 33 of the charterparty afforded the charterers a right of cancellation in the event of a war between named countries, including Iraq, the UK and the US, and the charterers used the outbreak of the Second Gulf War in March 2003 to limit damages, arguing that because they would have exercised the clause 33 option, damages for the period from March 20, 2003 were irrecoverable. In a critical finding, the arbitrator held that, looking at the situation in December 2001, "a reasonably well informed person" would have formed the view that a war was "merely a possibility", so the value of what they lost in December 2001 was a four-year charterparty with slightly less than four years to run. Following *The Mihalis Angelos*,[157] the arbitrator, Langley J. in the High Court, and the Court of Appeal, held the argument to be open to the charterer. By a majority of three to two the House of Lords held that it was possible for a court, in assessing damages, to take account of the March 2003 hostilities and the strong likelihood that the charterers would have exercised their clause 33 cancellation right. The majority view opined

---

[154] Peel, "Remoteness Re-visited" (2009) 125 L.Q.R. 6.
[155] It is arguable that an Irish court should decline to follow *The Achilleas* on the basis that greater predictability and ease of application are facilitated by following earlier decisions.
[156] [2007] UKHL 12.
[157] [1970] 3 All E.R. 125.

that the basic rule, that damages are assessed as at the date of breach is not an inflexible one, and that the search should focus on most fairly compensating the injured party, pointing to cases such as *Dodd Properties v Canterbury City Council*,[158] as one of the many exceptions and qualifications of the date of breach rule. The majority view indicated that because post-termination events such as total loss of the ship (frustration) could be brought into consideration, so should post-breach but pre-assessment events of this kind in order to avoid the danger of over-compensating the plaintiff. Lord Bingham and Lord Walker vigorously dissented, observing that departure from the standard position offended principle, represented a misapplication of *The Mihalis Angelos*, and, citing Treitel,[159] injected into an area of commercial law a level of unwanted uncertainty of result.

19–49 After *Golden Strait*, it is clear that the plaintiff must show that the breach of contract, on the balance of probabilities, would have resulted in a net loss and in this regard the court is entitled to look to post-breach events. In *Tele2 International Card Co SA v Post Office Ltd*[160] an Irish phonecard company sought to recover lost profits following a repudiatory breach of contract. The English Court of Appeal took account of the fact that had the repudiatory breach not occurred, the contract would have been performed by two other entities and the plaintiff would not have received a fee and would not have incurred any costs. Aikens L.J. said:

> "[I]t was certain that Tele 2 Ireland would neither have received the fee nor incurred any costs if the Agreement had continued to be performed. Therefore, applying the 'compensatory principle', the judge was right to conclude that Tele 2 Ireland had suffered no substantial loss."

Nominal damages only were awarded.[161]

"Type" of Loss and "Degree" of Loss

19–50 Once the species of loss is held to arise naturally it is unnecessary for the defendant to be able to reasonably contemplate the degree of loss that results. So, in *Parsons Ltd v Uttley Ingham*,[162] the plaintiff was able to

---

[158] [1980] 1 W.L.R. 443.
[159] Treitel, "Assessment of Damages for Wrongful Repudiation" (2007) 113 L.Q.R. 9.
[160] [2009] EWCA Civ 9; *Dalwood Marine Co v Nordana Line A/S* [2009] EWHC 3394 (Comm).
[161] Related issues may arise where there is a repudiatory breach of a contract that affords to the defendant latitude on how the contract is to be performed, e.g. *Durham Tees Valley Airport Ltd v BMI Baby* [2010] EWCA Civ 485; *Dhanani v Crasnianski* [2011] EWHC 926 (Comm). The court is required to undertake a factual inquiry about what the plaintiff would have done if the plaintiff had not accepted the repudiatory breach by the defendant. A price on offer might have led to orders being placed: *Jet2.com Ltd v SC Compania Nationala De Transporturi Aeriene Romane Tarom SA* [2014] EWCA Civ 87.
[162] [1978] 1 All E.R. 525; *Wilson v Dunville* (1879) 6 L.R. (Ir.) 210.

recover for the loss of a herd of pigs that had been poisoned when the plaintiff fed mouldy pignuts to the animals, the condition being caused by a defect in the pig hopper supplied by the defendant. Even though the consequences of feeding these foodstuffs could not be foreseen—the strain and severity of infection was quite unprecedented—the Court of Appeal held that it was sufficient for the plaintiff to show that a natural consequence of defective feed being given to animals was illness. It did not matter, under the first limb, if the illness was of an extreme kind unknown to veterinary science at that time. If, however, the loss arises under the second limb it may be possible to argue that where the degree of loss is outside the reasonable contemplation of the parties this may truncate the defendant's liability. In *Hickey (No. 2)*,[163] Finlay P. held that while the defendants could reasonably contemplate that loss as a result of inflation may occur they would not be able to anticipate that the effects and consequences of inflation would be felt for a period of six years; the defendants were therefore not liable to compensate the plaintiffs for this head of damage suffered. Similarly, in *Malone v Malone*[164] the defendant agreed to sell a boarding house to the plaintiff but failed to complete, in breach of contract. The plaintiff had borrowed money to pay for the property, intending to meet the interest due on the loan from the profits made by the boarding house. Because the sale did not proceed these profits did not accrue and additional interest on the loan accumulated. Costello J. held that while the defendant could contemplate that the plaintiff would borrow funds to pay for the property it could not be contemplated, nor was the defendant aware that the plaintiff was not in a position to pay interest to the bank if the defendant did not complete the sale. There are, however, contrasting English cases in which the impecunious plaintiff has been, on the facts, entitled to recover additional finance charges.[165]

19–51 In cases where the subject matter has a fluctuating value and the ability of the buyer to resell is hampered by breach of contract, remoteness principles may come into play. Loss of opportunity to resell property on a rising market, the market later shifting downwards, may be too remote to found a claim for breach of contract, but will not necessarily preclude recovery in tort; see *Cadoks Pty Ltd v Wallace Westley and Vigar Pty Ltd.*[166]

Bunge SA v Nidera—the UK Supreme Court affirms Golden Strait

19–52 It is a mark of the current uncertain state that English law occupies that in the most important recent decision, *Bunge SA v Nidera BV*,[167] a specialist first tier arbitration Board, the GAFTA Appeal Board, Hamblen J in

---

[163] [1980] I.L.R.M. 107.
[164] Unreported, High Court, June 9, 1982.
[165] *Wadsworth v Lydall* [1981] 1 W.L.R. 598; *Bacon v Cooper (Metals) Ltd* [1982] 1 All E.R. 397. In Ireland see also *Brohan v Crosspan Developments Ltd*, unreported, High Court, February 26, 1985.
[166] (2000) 2 V.R. 569.
[167] [2015] UKSC 43. See also *Novasen SA v Alimenta SA* [2013] EWHC 345 (Comm).

the English High Court and a unanimous Court of Appeal, should all find for the sellers while, on appeal to the UK Supreme Court, a unanimous Supreme Court allowed the appeal in favour of the buyer. *Bunge SA v Nidera BV* itself reaffirms the predominance of the compensatory principle in *Robinson v Harman*[168] but continues to stress that the valuation of the injured party's loss at the date of breach provides no final answer to the question of what the plaintiff may recover in damages. All of the circumstances known to the court or tribunal at the date of judgment may be relevant. So, if the plaintiff does not go into the market to buy substitute performance as of the date of breach this may be relevant. Similarly, if after breach the party in default makes a reasonable offer to reinstate the contract this too may be relevant. Conversely, if a contractual termination provision or frustration would have entitled the party in breach to effect lawful termination or a right to treat the contract as terminated by operation of law then it may be that the injured party to the contract will have suffered no loss. In *Bunge* itself the buyer was awarded nominal damages of $5(US) because immediately following on from the sellers' breach the sellers offered to reinstate the contract, an offer which the buyers declined. Furthermore, the sellers would have exercised contractual rights of termination, applying *Mihalis Angelos*.[169] The mitigation principle and the contractual termination provision respectively meant that the buyers had suffered no loss. So, despite criticisms, it is clear the date of breach rule is now, in English law at least, only the starting point and it is difficult to say what is the rule and what are the exceptions.[170] In *Bacciottini v Gotelee*[171] the defendants negligently failed to identify a planning restriction in property purchased by their clients, the plaintiffs. When the oversight was detected the diminution in value caused by the restriction was estimated at £100,000 (in May 2007). The plaintiffs in late 2009 made an application to the local authority seeking to remove the restrictions, the application being successful with an application fee of £250 being the only cost. Proceedings were issued in 2013. Both the High Court and the Court of Appeal found that the only damages that could be recovered here were based on the late fee of £250. It is possible to see this case as a mitigation case[172] as much as an illustration of the exceptional circumstances in which the breach rule will not be applicable.

19–53 The date of breach approach to measuring damages, as a ruling principle, has been stoutly defended by one Australian judge[173]:

---

[168] (1848) 1 Ex. 850.

[169] [1971] 1 Q.B. 164.

[170] See Dyson and Kramer, "There is no 'breach date rule': mitigation, difference in value and date of assessment" (2014) 130 L.Q.R. 259, and Carter and Tolhurst, "Contract damages following discharge for repudiation—revisiting later events" (2016) L.Q.R. 1.

[171] [2016] EWCA Civ 170.

[172] Although imposing mitigation obligations on a plaintiff two and a half years after the breach is rather exceptional.

[173] Keane J. in *Clark v Macourt* [2013] HCA 53 at para.10.

"The application of the ruling principle to measure value lost at the date of breach of contract serves the important end of bringing finality and certainty to commercial dealings. It ensures that whatever might befall the purchaser after the date of breach, for good or ill, and whether by reason of the purchaser's acumen, or lack of it, in dealing with other persons who were not party to the contract, and whatever movements may occur in the market, these developments have no bearing on the entitlement of the purchaser and the liability of the seller".

Cases in which *Hadley v Baxendale* does not Apply

19–54 While the test of reasonable contemplation seems well established, there are several situations where the test would appear to point to recovery of damages but, nevertheless, the courts are reluctant to apply the logic of the reasoning in *Hadley v Baxendale*; often this can be seen as the result of historical or policy considerations. However, a discernable trend towards rationalisation of the law is evident in many of these special situations. A foremost illustration is provided by recent case law on the payment of interest, considered in detail below, but traditional views are still influential. The fact that a person may have to borrow monies due to breach by another contracting party, or be financially ruined, or lose out on a business opportunity does not in general give the plaintiff any prospect of compensation for such loss.[174]

19–55 Where the failure to pay a sum of money involves a breach of contract the measure of damages recoverable is limited to the sum in question plus interest; see *Fletcher v Tayleur*.[175] The common law judges departed from this rule in cases of a banker's refusal to honour a cheque drawn by a customer, the account having sufficient funds to meet it. The resulting damage to the reputation and creditworthiness of the customer was thought worthy of compensation; see *Rolin v Steward*.[176] This principle was extended by the Court of Exchequer in Ireland against a mercantile agent who failed to pay a money order submitted to him for payment by a customer of the principal; see *Boyd v Fitt*.[177] If however the cheque is presented by the customer himself but the bank refuses to meet it this is outside the "commercial trader" exception established in *Rolin v Steward*; even if third parties overhear the conversation between cashier and customer the sole recourse is an action in defamation; see Kennedy C.J. in *Kinlan v Ulster Bank*.[178] These common law rules are unaffected by ss.57 and 89(1) of the Bills of Exchange Act 1882; see s.97(2). However, in a spirited attack upon this rule the Court of Appeal in *Kpohraror*

---

[174] See *Wallis v Smith* (1882) 21 Ch D 243; there are signs that the position is not so fixed as it was: *Trans Trust S.P.R.L. v Danubian Trading Co* [1952] 2 Q.B. 297.
[175] (1855) 17 C.B. 21.
[176] (1854) 14 C.B. 595.
[177] (1863) 14 Ir. C.L. Rep. 43.
[178] [1928] I.R. 171.

v Woolwich Building Society[179] has decided that credit ratings and credit reputation are important for all citizens and that the trader exception should go. Thus, general damages under the first limb of *Hadley v Baxendale* should be available in all cases of wrongfully dishonoured cheques. However, liability for unforeseeable trading losses under the second limb was not established against the defendants even though the defendants were aware that the plaintiff was a small trader.

19–56 A further exception is provided by *MacKenzie v Corballis*.[180] The plaintiff was engaged as a servant in South Africa by the defendants who brought her back to Ireland, agreeing that upon leaving their employment the plaintiff would be paid her fare to return to South Africa. The defendants refused to pay the fare and the plaintiff was obliged to stay in Dublin pending the outcome of the litigation. She was held entitled to the fare and the cost of lodgings for this period. Andrews J. explained this case as coming within the second limb of *Hadley v Baxendale*; the agreement "may reasonably be supposed to have brought it within the defendant's contemplation that the plaintiff might suffer damage through being detained by reason of not having any funds to return to South Africa".[181]

19–57 The general rule in *Fletcher v Tayleur* was not framed by reference to *Hadley v Baxendale*, however; it was designed to prevent juries from awarding damages on an arbitrary basis; this view of the origins of the rule is supported by observations made in *Parker v Dickie*.[182] The same institutional conflict— the judges devising a rule of remoteness that took this head of loss out of the reach of the jury—explains too the old common law rule denying damages for any distress, disappointment, frustration or loss of enjoyment resulting from a breach of contract. While there are old Irish cases that go the other way—in *French v West Clare Railway Co*,[183] for example, the plaintiff recovered £10 by way of damages for missing a concert because a train was delayed as a result of the defendant's negligence—the rules laid down in *Hobbs* case[184] were accepted by the Supreme Court in *Kinlan v Ulster Bank*.[185]

19–58 In England these older cases have been swept away in recent years. In *Jarvis v Swans Tours*[186] the Court of Appeal compensated the plaintiff for a disappointing holiday that failed to meet up to the warranties given in the holiday brochure. This case has been followed in Ireland also. MacMahon J. in

---

[179] [1996] 4 All E.R. 119.
[180] (1905) 39 I.L.T.R. 28.
[181] (1905) 39 I.L.T.R. 28.
[182] (1879) 4 L.R. (Ir.) 244.
[183] (1897) 31 I.L.T. 140. The plaintiff later immortalised the railway company in the song, "Are Ye Right There Michael".
[184] *Hobbs v L.S.W.R.* (1875) L.R. 10 Q.B. 111.
[185] [1928] I.R. 171.
[186] [1973] 2 Q.B. 233; *Jacobs v Thomson Travel* [1986] C.L.Y. 975.

Johnson v Longleat Property[187] indicated that where a builder fails to provide a house which meets the standards set out in the contract, damages for physical discomfort, loss of enjoyment and inconvenience will result; see also *Murphy v Quality Homes*.[188] Those damages for physical inconvenience and discomfort may be considerable. In *Leahy v Rawson*[189] some £30,000 to cover a six-year period during which building work remained incomplete was awarded, and the Irish courts, on the whole, shadow the approach of the Australian courts in awarding significant damages[190] in these cases. There have been several ex tempore Circuit Court and District Court decisions. In one case damages followed when children suffered distress when viewing a DVD labelled as a "My Little Pony" film but which turned out to be adult pornography.[191] A software defect which wrongly suggested to mobile phone subscribers that the plaintiff was sending them pornography was also the subject of a damages award,[192] but, perhaps surprisingly, a plaintiff who wasted eight hours trying to assemble a defective flat-pack wardrobe was not awarded damages for the aggravation and frustration engendered by his experience.[193] Most of the case law, however, revolves around situations in which damages have been awarded against travel firms who have failed to provide satisfactory holidays and it is clear from newspaper accounts that compensation has included compensation for inconvenience and disruption, for example: *Hynes & Hynes v Happy Holidays Ltd*.[194] The *Irish Times* of May 17, 2006, reports a typical case in which the District Court, exercising jurisdiction as a Small Claims Court, has allowed damages awards for either distress, physical discomfort, injury, misrepresentation or loss of amenity arising out of package holidays that go badly wrong. Under the headline, "Family awarded compensation for holiday ordeal", the newspaper reports that the Furlong family were subjected to "a litany" of problems such as a three-and-a-half-hour flight delay, construction work going on until the early hours around the pool, physical injury through broken glass being left around the pool area, as well as rowdy parties in the complex. Damages to the maximum financial limit of €1,269 were awarded. In *Scaife v Falcon Leisure Group*,[195] the Supreme Court has held that hotel

---

[187] Unreported, High Court, May 19, 1976: noted in (1978) 13 Ir. Jur. 186.

[188] Unreported, High Court, June 22, 1976.

[189] Unreported, High Court, January 14, 2003. In *Mitchell v Mulvey* [2014] IEHC 37, Hogan J. said the defects and physical discomfort and distress was more acute than in *Leahy v Rawson*. The plaintiffs were awarded damages of €20,000 per annum for physical discomfort, distress and inconvenience.

[190] *Bonchristiano v Lohmann* [1998] 4 V.R. 82. On quantum in England see *AXA Insurance UK Plc v Cunningham Lindsay UK* [2007] EWCA Civ 3023; *West v Ian Finlay & Associates* [2014] EWCA Civ 316 (£2,500 per annum).

[191] "DVD turned out to be porn film", *The Irish Times*, July 26, 2006.

[192] *The Irish Independent*, March 28, 1985; "Woman awarded €7,500 for phone bug", *The Irish Times*, April 31, 2004.

[193] *Artis v MFI Ltd* [2006] C.L.Y. 1013.

[194] *The Irish Independent*, 28 March 1985 (Circuit Court). See also "Family forced to abandon holiday settles case", *The Irish Times*, April 25, 2006; "Holidaymaker awarded €1,300", July 27, 2005.

[195] [2007] IESC 57.

proprietors, both at common law and under the Package Holiday Directive, owe a duty to exercise reasonable care and skill vis-à-vis facilities to be provided, and that if these obligations are not met, then the consumer is entitled to sue the organiser of the holiday; although the Package Holiday Directive is silent on the definition of damages, European Court of Justice case law supports the award of non-economic loss under the Directive.[196] In one Circuit Court case[197] damages of £10,235 were awarded in respect of the late cancellation of a luxury cruise which the plaintiffs were to enjoy as their honeymoon, the defendant substituting a much inferior package at a very late stage in the booking. While this award may seem high, the consideration paid for the cruise was around £13,000. At the other end of the scale, four women on a disastrous holiday weekend to Blackpool were awarded a cash refund of £168.[198] There are some privity of contract issues here.[199] The most significant discussions of principle are found in *Baltic Shipping Co v Dillon*[200] and *Farley v Skinner*.[201]

19–59 In *Farley*, the House of Lords considered the availability of damages in respect of negligent advice given by a surveyor to the prospective purchaser of property, the property having a high degree of amenity which the plaintiff intended to use during his retirement. A high volume of noise from a nearby airport was not identified by the surveyor, thus disturbing the buyer's use and enjoyment of the property. Non-pecuniary damages were awarded. "It is sufficient if a major or important object of the contract is to give pleasure, relaxation or peace of mind"[202] and it matters not that the defendant gave no guarantee concerning the state of affairs the defendant was engaged to investigate or bring about. Negligent execution of skills by a professional person will breach the contract and as long as the case can be fitted into the "exceptional category", non-pecuniary loss will be recoverable. This case contains a number of observations on the characterisation of loss such as distress or disappointment, vexation or disappointment, physical inconvenience, tension or aggravation, with most of their lordships describing the plaintiff's loss here as being one of disappointment or inconvenience, while Lord Scott and Lord Hutton stressed the level of discomfort occasioned by the noise. Lord Scott observed, *obiter*, that in contract cases the threshold of remoteness is higher than in negligent surveyor actions in tort. Damages for mental distress will not be automatically awarded to every plaintiff who can show that the breach of contract resulted in this head of loss. In *Kelly v Crowley*[203] the plaintiff

---

[196] The leading case is *Simone Leitner v TUI Deutschland* [2002] E.C.R. I-2631.
[197] *The Irish Times*, July 2, 1997. For English appellate authority, see *Milner v Carnival Plc* [2010] EWCA Civ 389.
[198] *The Irish Times*, January 15, 1998.
[199] See *Wilkes v Jessop* [2007] C.L.Y. 795.
[200] (1992) 176 C.L.R. 345.
[201] [2001] 3 W.L.R. 899.
[202] Per Lord Steyn, citing Capper (2000) 116 L.Q.R. 553 at 556.
[203] Unreported, High Court, March 5, 1985; modest damages for breach of contract causing distress and disappointment may be awarded even in conveyancing transactions: see the decision in *Young v Hamilton* [2012] NI Ch 4 (negligent solicitor).

purchased licensed premises. His solicitor failed to investigate whether the premises had a satisfactory licence and was held in breach of contract. The plaintiff suffered mental distress when he discovered the licence was a hotel licence and not a public house licence. Murphy J. held "damage of that nature is not reasonably foreseeable. No doubt all commercial ventures carry a considerable stress … but I do not think it gives rise to any additional claim for damage". If the contract involves the provision of services of a recreational or social nature, then damages for distress and disappointment will be available. Several cases have arisen in the context of contracts to provide services at a wedding reception. If a hotel cancels a reception due to a double booking, transferring the reception to cramped accommodation with a cold buffet rather than the full meal contracted for, the guests having nowhere to dance, the father of the bride may recover damages for the very real inconvenience that will result.[204] If the band fails to show up[205] or the mobile disco fails to arrive,[206] leaving the guests to entertain themselves, the embarrassment, loss of status and aggravation that result can also be compensated. If the white Rolls Royce and the photographer, both to be provided by the defendant, fail to arrive and the resulting audiovisual and photographic record "rivals a low grade comedy film", in the words of the judge, very substantial damages may be awarded.[207] In *Dinnegan and Dinnegan v Ryan*[208] the plaintiffs had engaged the defendants to provide a modest buffet in their public house after the plaintiffs' marriage ceremony, but on arrival the plaintiffs and their guests were asked to leave the premises, causing considerable distress and humiliation to the plaintiffs who were awarded damages of €6,000 each by Murray J., upholding the decision of the Circuit Court on the issue of liability. If the contract is intended to secure peace of mind but this does not result, then again damages can include anxiety and disappointment as heads of loss, as in *Heywood v Wellers*[209] where the defendants failed to perform legal services intended to obtain an injunction to prevent a third party from molesting the plaintiff. In *Hamilton-Jones v David & Snape (a firm)*[210] the defendants failed to renew a notice to the Passport Office informing it not to issue passports in the name of the plaintiff's children and/or her estranged husband, with the effect that the husband was able to remove the children to Tunisia in breach of a court order. No liability for this head of loss in tort was available, but Neuberger J. held that this would not preclude recovery in contract. Noting that the English courts had recently adopted a more "liberal" approach to exceptions to *Addis v Gramophone Co Ltd*,[211] Neuberger J. followed in particular *Heywood v Wellers*[212] holding that

---

[204] *Hotson and Hotson v Payne* [1988] C.L.Y. 1047.

[205] *Dharni v Dhami* [1989] C.L.Y. 409.

[206] *Dunn v Disc Jockey Unlimited Co* (1978) 87 D.L.R. (3d.) 408.

[207] See "£13,000 award for wedding day miss", *The Irish Times*, March 2, 1995.

[208] [2002] 3 I.R. 178.

[209] [1976] 1 All E.R. 300.

[210] [2004] 1 W.L.R. 924. On the compensatory principle and a solicitor's breach of duty in not serving a court order see *Stewart v Patterson* [2014] NIQB 103.

[211] [1909] A.C. 488.

[212] [1976] Q.B. 446; see also *McLeish v Amoo-Gottfried & Co* (1993) 10 P.N. 102 and *Rey v*

this case was one in which the plaintiff was contracting for a degree of peace of mind and that the plaintiff was therefore entitled to damages for mental distress.[213] Other professionals who fail to observe duties of confidence may also be liable in damages for injury to feelings, compensation being assessed on a fair and reasonable basis.[214] It has also been held that an insurance contract may be one in which an important object is securing peace of mind or that aggravated damages may be recoverable under this head.[215] However, if the contract is an ordinary conveyance of a dwelling house, damages for distress, annoyance and inconvenience will not be recoverable according to *Smyth v Huey & Co*,[216] *a fortiori* if the plaintiff is a company.[217] Injury to the pride and dignity of a businessman in connection with a conveyancing transaction in which that businessman's company suffered loss due to the breach of duty by the conveyancer is not recoverable; see *Johnson v Gore Wood and Co*.[218] In contrast, damages were awarded in the Dublin Circuit Court[219] in respect of a hair restoration product that misleadingly referred to a "strand by strand" hair procedure when the Circuit Court found that what the purchaser received was effectively a hairpiece, to be glued on at monthly intervals. The Circuit Court awarded €5,100 in damages for breach of contract, including a modest sum for general damages, the award recognising distress and anxiety caused to the plaintiff: the hairpiece had cost the purchaser €3,600.

19–60 Inconvenience and loss of enjoyment damages were extended by Hogan J in *Browne v Iarnród Éireann (No.2)*[220] in which the defendants reneged on an agreement to allow Mr Browne early retirement. Mr Browne worked on for another three years. He suffered no economic loss—indeed his extra income and additional pension plan contributions enhanced his pension and lump sum payments—but there was a loss which Hogan J. valued at €20,000 per year for each of the three years in question:

"The type of loss and inconvenience suffered by the plaintiff is undoubtedly intangible and very difficult to measure. It is nevertheless a real one. Who, for example, contemplating a difficult and taxing day at work as he or she set out from their house in teeming rain on a cold winter's morning, would not long for the leisurely life of the retired? Mr Browne must surely have wistfully reflected on this from time to time as he continued in the workforce. This loss can really be regarded as a

---

Graham & Oldham [2000] B.P.I.R. 354.
[213] Measured by reference to "a broad brush approach" at £20,000.
[214] *Cornelius v De Taranto* [2001] E.M.L.R. 329; *Archer v Williams* [2003] E.M.L.R. 869.
[215] *McIssac v Sun Life Assurance* (1999) 173 D.L.R. (4th) 649.
[216] [1993] N.I. 236.
[217] *Firststeel Cold Rolled Products v Anaco Precision Pressings, The Times*, November 21, 1994.
[218] [2002] 1 A.C. 1.
[219] "Hairpiece Client awarded €5,000 over 'misleading, unclear' contract", *Irish Independent*, May 19, 2012.
[220] [2014] IEHC 117. Contrast actions based in negligence: *Walter v Crossan* [2014] IEHC 377 and *Murray v Budds* [2015] IECA 269.

form of inconvenience and lost expectation, inasmuch as Mr. Browne was deprived of an important benefit—a restful and less stressful life—associated with the early retirement contract."

19–61 In cases of wrongful dismissal the older Irish cases hold that damages cannot be recovered for the high-handed or arbitrary manner in which a servant[221] or an apprentice[222] is dismissed. While an oblique attack was mounted on this rule in England in *Cox v Phillips Industries*[223]—a demotion and not a dismissal case—McWilliam J. in *Garvey v Ireland*[224] accepted that the sole remedy a dismissed employee has (subject to he or she being employed by the State, in which event punitive damages may be awarded) is an action in defamation. In fact, the English position is now realigned with the traditional view after the decision of the Court of Appeal in *Bliss v South East Thames Regional Health Authority*.[225] Dillon L.J. observed that until the House of Lords reconsiders the *Addis* case, the rule preventing damages for injured feelings in wrongful dismissal cases is too firmly fixed. *Cox v Philips Industries* was overruled by a unanimous Court of Appeal. In contrast several Canadian decisions establish the proposition that, while damages are not to be awarded for the mental distress occasioned by a dismissal per se, damages may be awarded for mental distress caused by the employer's failure to give proper notice.[226] In the Supreme Court of Canada, *Addis* has not prevented the award of damages for humiliation and distress where it is established that the employer, in bad faith, terminated the contract of employment; see *Wallace v United Grain Growers*.[227] The New Zealand courts have not continued to follow *Addis*[228] but *Addis* survives in Australia,[229] and the House of Lords has recently declined to overrule *Addis* in termination of contract of employment cases. In *Johnson v Unisys*[230] the plaintiff failed to dislodge *Addis* in a case where he was seeking damages for mental distress caused by the manner of dismissal, their Lordships pointing to difficulties in relation to proof of causation and the fact that the creation of statutory rights in relation to unfair dismissal made the development of common law reliefs in respect of the manner of dismissal unnecessary and undesirable in the majority of cases, and in *Carey v Independent Newspapers Ltd*[231] Gilligan J. cited *Johnson v Unisys* but felt it unnecessary to express any view on the issue. In *Malik v Bank of Credit and*

---

[221] *Breen v Cooper* (1869) 3 I.R.C.L. 621.

[222] *Parker v Cathcart* (1866) 17 I.C.L.R. 778.

[223] [1976] 3 All E.R. 161.

[224] Unreported, High Court, December 19, 1979.

[225] [1987] I.C.R. 700.

[226] e.g. *Brown v Waterloo Regional Board of Commissioners of Police* (1983) 103 D.L.R. (3d.) 748; *Fitzgibbon v Westpress Publications Ltd* (1983) 30 D.L.R. (4th) 366.

[227] (1997) 152 D.L.R. (4th) 1.

[228] *Stuart v Armourguard Security* [1996] 1 N.Z.L.R. 484.

[229] *Baltic Shipping Co v Dillon* (1992) 176 C.L.R. 345; *Aldersea v Passenger Transport Corp* [2001] 3 V.R. 499.

[230] [2001] 2 All E.R. 801; *Orr v Zomax Ltd* [2004] IEHC 47.

[231] Unreported, High Court, August 7, 2003. On the expansion of stigma damages into racial documentation cases, see *Chagger v Abbey National Plc* [2009] EWCA Civ 1202.

Commerce International[232] the plaintiffs were able to sidestep *Addis* by pleading that the defendant, their employer, had breached the implied duty of trust and confidence in operating its business dishonestly and corruptly, causing the plaintiffs difficulty in obtaining new employment when the defendant bank collapsed. These stigma damages were characterised as financial loss, not injured feelings, and thus, by distinguishing both the cause of action and the head of loss, the *Addis* case was removed from the equation. All *Addis* decides is that the "loss of reputation in that particular case could not be compensated because it was not caused by a breach of contract", per Lord Steyn. Lord Steyn also took a very narrow view of the decision in *Addis* in giving his concurring judgment in *Johnson v Unisys*. Following the decision of the House of Lords in *Eastwood and Williams v Magnox Electric Plc*[233] the aggrieved employee has tended to argue that a distinction is to be drawn between the employer's breach of duty during the currency of the contract and the termination of the contract itself. Damages for distress etc. caused by breaches during the contract (bullying of the employee,[234] failure to afford the employee suitable employment,[235] inappropriate treatment during a period of suspension for alleged misconduct[236]) may fall outside the *Addis/Unisys* prohibition on the availability of distress or stigma damages. Irish judges have followed *Johnson v Unisys* in a number of cases[237] and the effect is that if the plaintiff claims that breach/dismissal has had significant effects on his/her physical or mental wellbeing, damages will only be available if the medical evidence establishes some psychological injury that goes beyond ordinary occupational stress, such as clinical depression.[238]

Breach of Confidence

19–62 While *Hadley v Baxendale* may constitute a bar to damages directed at emotional distress caused by breach of a commercial contract, this is not the final word. Irish law has developed in recent years from the implied term

---

[232] [1997] 3 All E.R. 1.
[233] [2004] 3 W.L.R. 322; *Berber v Dunnes Stores* [2009] IESC 10.
[234] *Quigley v Complex Tooling* [2005] IEHC 278. In *Ruffley v Board of Management of St. Anne's School* [2015] IECA 287 the Court of Appeal divided on the issue of whether the conduct of the defendant could be held to constitute bullying but were agreed on the recoverability of damages for an identifiable psychiatric injury.
[235] *Cronin v Eircom Ltd* [2006] IEHC 380.
[236] *Eastwood and Williams v Magnox Electric Plc* [2004] W.L.R. 322.
[237] *Orr v Zomax Ltd* [2004] IEHC 47; *McGrath v Trintech* [2004] IEHC 342. If there is no breach of contract by the employer then it may be necessary to consider a breach of duty claim in tort: *Berber v Dunnes Stores Ltd* [2009] IESC 10.
[238] *Maher v Jahil Global* [2005] E.L.R. 233; *Pickering v Microsoft*, unreported, High Court, December 21, 2005; *Berber v Dunnes Stores* [2009] IESC 10. Contrast *Carroll v Dublin Bus* [2005] IEHC 278. There may be powerful public policy considerations to bear in mind. For damages awards in respect of failed sterilisation procedures, see *Byrne v Ryan* [2009] 4 I.R. 542 and *Hurley v Moore* [2013] IEHC 72, following the "mainstream" principles in *McFarlane v Tayside* [2000] 2 A.C. 59.

approach to the duty of confidentiality that is owed by a bank to its customer vis-à-vis unauthorised disclosure of the state of a customer's account. *Tournier v National Provisional and Union Bank of England*[239] has broadened via judicial interpretation into a general equitable jurisdiction that extends beyond banking transactions[240] into protecting commercial secrets as between co-operating parties engaged in a joint venture[241]; often there may be a professional relationship or a fiduciary duty or fiduciary relationship as between parties and their representatives. The broad duty of confidence is recognised by cases such as *National Irish Bank Ltd v RTÉ*[242] and *Herrity v Independent Newspapers Ltd*,[243] as well as via constitutional right to privacy considerations that have not been fully articulated in a commercial setting. In *Slattery v Friends First Life Assurance Co*[244] McGovern J. said:

> "[I]t is clear that the law recognises a duty of confidentiality such as would apply in this case, whether framed in contract, in tort, in equity or on a constitutional basis, and that this court is possessed of the jurisdiction to award damages on foot of a breach thereof."

In *Slattery* the defendants improperly disclosed confidential information, undermining the plaintiff's negotiating position in a commercial transaction. McGovern J. explored the principles upon which damages could be assessed. Compensatory damages were available but these could include aggravated damages, notwithstanding that special loss had not been shown by the plaintiffs. Citing with approval the definition found in an earlier Law Reform Commission Consultation Paper,[245] *Aggravated, Exemplary and Restitutional Damages*:

> "Aggravated damages are classified as a species of compensatory damages, which are awarded as additional compensation where there has been intangible injury to the interests or personality of the plaintiff, and where this injury has been caused or exacerbated by the exceptional conduct of the defendant."

McGovern J. went on to characterise the conduct of the defendant as:

> "... a quite improper use of information gathered in the course of a fiduciary relationship. The plaintiff is entitled to be compensated for the deliberate and conscious breach of his right to confidentiality, involving

---

[239] [1924] 1 K.B. 461.

[240] *Walsh v NIB* [2007] IEHC 345, applying *Haughey v Moriarty* [1999] 3 I.R. 1.

[241] *House of Spring Gardens v Point Blank Ltd* [1985] I.R. 611; *Caldwell v Mahon* [2007] 3 I.R. 542. On springboard injunctions in respect of breach of contract or breach of fiduciary duties see the decisions of Clarke J. in *Pulse Group Ltd v O'Reilly* [2006] IEHC 50 and *Allied Irish Bank Plc v Diamond* [2011] IEHC 505.

[242] [1998] 2 I.R. 465 per Shanley J.; see the Supreme Court judgment at [1998] 2 I.R. 480.

[243] [2009] 1 I.R. 216; *Giller v Prokopets* [2008] VSCA 236.

[244] [2013] IEHC 136.

[245] LRC CP 12 (1998); see also LRC 60–2000; *Conway v INTO* [1991] 2 I.R. 305. Contrast *Hollybrook (Brighton Road) Management Co Ltd v All First Property Management Co* [2011] IEHC 375.

an extraordinary, wilful and totally inappropriate dissemination of this information."

On the facts, however, the Court of Appeal has reversed McGovern J.[246] on the basis that the information disclosed by Friends First was not financial information relating to the duty of confidence owed by a bank to a customer but information about the conduct of the plaintiff vis-à-vis the transaction in question. There is nothing however to suggest that McGovern J.'s analysis of the compensatory issues contains any errors or omissions.

Contracts for the Sale of Land

19–63 Four rules of particular importance here are:

(1) The rule in Bain v Fothergill[247]

19–64 This rule, which developed as a result of the particular difficulties a vendor had in showing title to land, limited damages in cases where the vendor, without deceit or wilful default, was unable to make a good title to the sums paid by the purchaser including costs of preparing the conveyance. While the rule may have been valid at earlier periods of time it is unnecessary today. Nevertheless it has been accepted in *Kelly v Duffy*[248] and *McDonnell v McGuinness.*[249] The courts have refused to extend the rule into areas other than real property; see *Lee & Co (Dublin) Ltd v Egan Wholesale.*[250] The Law Reform Commission in its *Report on Land Law and Conveyancing Law: (1) General Proposals*[251] commented on the rule in *Bain v Fothergill* and recommended that it be abolished by statute.[252] This course of action was again endorsed in Law Reform Commission Consultation Paper 34–2004,[253] and again in the *Report on the Reform and Modernisation of Land Law and Conveyancing Law.*[254] Section 53(1) of the Land and Conveyancing Law Reform Act 2009 provides:

> "The rule of law restricting damages recoverable for breaches of contract occasioned by defects in title to land (known as the Rule in *Bain v. Fothergill*) is abolished."

---

[246] *Slattery v Friends First* [2015] IECA 149
[247] (1874) L.R. 7 H.L. 158; the case of *Flureau v Thornhill* (1776) 2 Wm. Bl. 1078 marks the origin of the rule and was applied in Ireland, e.g. *Buckley v Dawson* (1854) 6 Ir. Jur. R. 374.
[248] [1922] 1 I.R. 82; O'Driscoll, "A Note on the Rule in Bain v Fothergill" (1975) 10 Ir. Jur. 203.
[249] [1939] I.R. 223.
[250] Unreported, High Court, December 18, 1979.
[251] LRC 30–1989.
[252] LRC 30–1989, paras 30–32.
[253] LRC 34–2004, paras 576–579.
[254] LRC 74–2005.

The section came into operation on 1 December 2009[255] and affects contracts made after that date.

(2) Damages following breach of (or an award of an unenforceable decree of) specific performance

19–65 English authorities until recently held that a person who had elected to sue for and obtain a writ of specific performance was bound by this election; if the decree was unenforceable the holder could not collect damages in lieu of specific performance. This peculiar state of affairs was established in cases like *Horsler v Zorro*.[256] The House of Lords have now overruled this line of authority in *Johnson v Agnew*[257] and it is firmly established in Irish law that damages in such a situation are recoverable: McWilliam J. so held in *Murphy v Quality Homes*[258] and *Vandeleur & Moore v Dargan*.[259] In the more recent decision McWilliam J. expressly approved and applied rr.4 and 5 in Lord Wilberforce's speech in *Johnson v Agnew*. As we have seen, damages may not always be valued as of the date of breach. Damages calculated by reference to the difference between the contract price and the value of the contractual subject matter at the date of judgment were held to be appropriate in *Duffy v Ridley Properties Ltd*.[260] Duffy agreed to purchase lands on May 7, 2003 for €520,000. The parties fell out over the construction of a wall on the lands. The contract required the vendor to build prior to completion and after litigation it was established that the plaintiff was not entitled to damages in lieu; the trial judge[261] awarded €880,000 in damages, being the difference between the contract price and the value of the lands, some €1.4 million as of the date of judgment in the specific performance action. The Supreme Court, applying *Wroth v Tyler*[262] (in which McGarry J. held that a court could select a valuation date other than date of breach or date of judgment where to do so would do justice in the individual case) held that it would not be appropriate to value the property at any intervening date because there was no evidence of any delay on the part of the plaintiff in prosecuting his claim and there was ample evidence of unreasonable conduct by the defendant.

---

[255] Land and Conveyancing Law Reform Act 2009 (Commencement) Order 2009 (S.I. No. 356 of 2009).

[256] [1975] Ch. 302; Oakley, 'Pecuniary Compensation for Failure to Complete a Contract for the Sale of Land" (1980) 39 C.L.J. 58.

[257] [1980] A.C. 367.

[258] Unreported, High Court, June 22, 1976.

[259] [1981] I.L.R.M. 75.

[260] [2008] 4. I.R. 282.

[261] [2005] IEHC 314 per Finlay Geoghegan J.

[262] [1970] 1 Ch. 30; the Supreme Court distinguished the instant case from *Suliman v Savari* [1989] 2 All E.R. 460. In *McGrath v Stewart* [2008] IEHC 348, damages in lieu of specific performance were not awarded due to the delay of the plaintiff in seeking a remedy. See the additional damages claim for delay in completing the contract in *Mount Kennett Investment Co v O'Meara* [2010] IEHC 216.

(3) Deposit

19–66 Irish law traditionally allowed the vendor of property to bargain for a deposit—often 10 per cent of 25 per cent of the price—and forfeit that deposit in the event that the sale did not proceed to completion by virtue of the purchasers' default. Section 54 of the Land and Conveyancing Law Reform Act 2009 provides that:

> "Where the court refuses to grant specific performance of a contract for the sale or other disposition of land, or in any action for the return of the deposit, the court may, where it is just and equitable so to do, order the repayment of the whole or any part of any deposit, with or without interest."

(4) Purchaser receives incorrect advice on the value of the property

19–67 If the purchaser of real property pays more for the property than it is really worth as the result of incorrect advice from a professional adviser—a solicitor, estate agent, valuer, surveyor or architect, for example—the English case of *Ford v White & Co*[263] holds that the measure of compensation must be the difference between (1) the market value of the property at the date of the purchase; and (2) the price actually paid. This proposition was endorsed by Finlay P. in *Taylor v Ryan & Jones*[264] as generally applicable although on the facts a slight modification was made. The decision in *Taylor v Ryan & Jones* was applied by Murphy J. in *Kelly v Crowley*.[265] In cases where a lender acts upon a negligent valuation, lending monies to purchasers who default on the loan, leaving the lender to try to resell property that is worth less than the sum advanced due to the collapse of the property market, the House of Lords has held that the measure of loss is the difference between the valuations made and the figure a careful valuer, using the information available at the time, would have come up with.[266]

(5) Purchaser receives negligent legal services in breach of contract

19–68 In a falling property market the question whether the purchaser who specifically instructs a solicitor to provide services that will guard against certain foreseeable risks from materialising has been a contentious one. Where the purchaser can show that, but for the breach of contract, the transaction would not have been entered into, and steps to mitigate loss would have been successful, expectation damages may be recoverable: *KBC Bank Ireland Ltd v BCM Hanby Wallace*.[267]

---

[263] [1964] 1 All E.R. 885.

[264] Unreported, High Court, March 10, 1983; Clark (1984) D.U.L.J. 279.

[265] Unreported, High Court, March 5, 1985.

[266] *South Australia Asset Management Corp v York Montague Ltd* [1996] 3 All E.R. 365.

[267] [2012] IEHC 120, following *Bristol and West Building Society v Rollo, Steven and Bond* [1998] S.L.T. 9. Appeal allowed on other grounds [2013] IESC 32. See also *ACC Bank v Johnston* [2011] IEHC 376. More broadly, see *John Grimes Partnership v Gubbins* [2013] EWCA Civ 37.

Mitigation of Damage

19–69 It has recently been said while it is a general principle that the plaintiff is bound to mitigate loss occasioned by a breach of duty, "the standard by which a claimant is judged in this regard is not an unduly harsh one because it is the defendant, as wrongdoer, who has put the claimant into that difficult position".[268] There are broader considerations, however, that may come into play.

19–70 It is economically desirable that the resources "released" by the breach of contract be used by the innocent party to minimise the damage that results from breach. In *Bord Iascaigh Mhara v Scallan*[269] the owners of a fishing vessel which had been abandoned by the hirer were held obliged to retake possession when the hirer wrongfully repudiated the contract. They could not sit by while the vessel was deteriorating and recover for physical damage that resulted. Further, had a prospective hirer come along they would have been obliged to hire it out to him if possible; see *M.C.B. (N.I.) Ltd v Phillips (Coleraine) Ltd*.[270] Similarly the buyer of goods which the seller refuses to deliver cannot sit by and watch the market rise, choosing to sue when the goods in question reach an optimum price. The court in *Cullen v Horgan*[271] said that, in the case of non-delivery of goods, the buyer must at some reasonable point after breach regard the contract as at an end and seek to mitigate his loss by purchasing substitute goods elsewhere.

19–71 The duty to mitigate may even extend to requiring the injured party to contract with the party in breach. In *Payzu Ltd v Saunders*[272] the defendant had agreed to supply silk to the plaintiff on monthly credit terms but after some delays in payment, the defendant demanded payment on delivery: this was a breach of contract and constituted a repudiatory breach which the plaintiff accepted. However, the plaintiff was held not to be entitled to damages. The market had risen considerably and no alternative source of supply was available to the plaintiff. The plaintiff should have accepted the defendant's offer to supply the silk on cash terms. There are limits, however. If the plaintiff is offered re-employment by an employer who has previously dismissed the employee in a high-handed manner, or accused the employee of theft, a reasonable person

---

[268] Jackson J. in *Shepherd Homes Ltd v Encia Remediation* [2007] EWHC 1710 (TCC), following *McGlinn v Waltham Contractors* [2007] EWHC 149 (TCC). On mitigation in construction contracts and the reasonableness question, see the survey of the authorities by Akenhead J. in *Linklaters Business Services v McAlpine Ltd* [2010] EWHC 2931 (TCC). Mitigation steps taken prior to the collapse of the property market in Ireland in 2008 are considered in *Greenband Investments v Bruton* [2011] IEHC 109 and *Darlington Properties Ltd v Meath County Council* [2011] IEHC 70.

[269] Unreported, High Court, May 8, 1973.

[270] Unreported, N.I. High Court, December 17, 1974.

[271] [1925] 2 I.R. 1.

[272] [1919] 2 K.B. 581; Bridge, "Mitigation of Damages in Contract and the Meaning of Avoidable Loss" (1989) 105 L.Q.R. 398.

would not require the employee to accept the offer of re-employment. Also in *Lennon v Talbot (Ireland) Ltd*[273] the plaintiffs were motor dealers who sought damages from the defendant who had wrongfully terminated their dealerships and had appointed the Gowan Group, a large garage group, to be the sole distributor of Talbot cars in the Republic. The issue arose whether the plaintiffs should have limited their loss by ordering vehicles and parts from the Gowan Group. Keane J. indicated that where the terms presented in the revised offer are both prejudicial and substantially different to those in the contract which has been breached, *Payzu Ltd v Saunders* is not applicable.

19–72 Under Irish law there can be a close relationship between a duty to mitigate and the statutory rules on liability and contributory negligence considered below. In *Hyland v Dundalk Racing (1999) Ltd No. 2*[274] the defendant sought contributions from licensed bookmakers towards the cost of refurbishing the racetrack at Dundalk. The licensed bookmakers, correctly, asserted there was no basis for seeking such a contribution and that the defendant was in breach of contract. The defendant sought to persuade the defendants to make a payment, on a without prejudice basis and seek a declaratory judgment. The bookmakers rejected this proposal and for some years were not able to take up their "pitches" at the track. In rejecting this offer, had the plaintiffs acted reasonably? Hogan J said that initially, in the context of a protracted and heated dispute, a reluctance to embark on litigation after making the payment, with possible implications in relation to access to other racetracks, was understandable. Hogan J went on:

> "I am driven to the conclusion that, viewed objectively, it became unreasonable after a certain point for the plaintiff to refuse to take up a pitch offered by Dundalk. This was especially so once it became clear that the protests had been ineffective, that the dispute was not going to be quickly resolved, and that the issue would have to be judicially determined".

Damages were reduced by 20 per cent for each of the years following on the end of the first year in which the impasse commenced to take effect.

19–73 A similar rule entitles the party in breach to plead that certain benefits which have accrued to the plaintiff should be taken into account in order to reduce the damages payable. Here the object is not to encourage the efficient use of resources but to prevent over-compensation of the plaintiff; a plaintiff should not be in a better position as a result of breach than would have been the case had the contract been performed. In *O'Brien v White Spunner*[275] the plaintiff was awarded a decree of specific performance entitling him to enforce

---

[273] Unreported, High Court, December 20, 1985.
[274] [2015] IEHC 57: contrast *Browne v Iarnród Éireann (No. 2)* [2014] IEHC 117.
[275] Unreported, High Court, November 23, 1979.

a contract for the purchase of a house. The defendant vendors who had refused to complete were held liable to pay the rental value of the property from the agreed date for completion and the date of actual entry into possession. The amount of interest that had accrued to the plaintiff as a result of having the unpaid balance of the purchase price on deposit was offset against the plaintiff's damages however. In *Malone v Malone*[276] damages were not awarded to compensate the purchaser of real property for additional interest charged against him by a bank in respect of a loan taken out to pay for the property; Costello J. held the plaintiff should have mitigated his loss by repaying the money to the bank. If the innocent party has a choice of two methods of mitigating damage, both of which are reasonable in the circumstances, it is not possible to say that the innocent party acts unreasonably because it transpires that the loss would have been less had the innocent party adopted the other method; see *Gebruder Metelmann GmbH & Co v N.B.R. (London) Ltd*.[277] The guiding principle, as stated by Lord MacMillan in *Banco de Portugal v Waterlow and Sons Ltd*[278] was followed by Keane J. in *Lennon v Talbot Ireland Ltd*:

> "Where the sufferer from breach of contract finds himself in consequence of that breach placed in a position of embarrassment, the measures which he may be driven to adopt in order to extricate himself ought not to be weighed in nice scales at the instance of the party whose breach of contract has occasioned the difficulty. It is often easy after an emergency has passed to criticise the steps which have been taken to meet it, but such criticism does not come well from those who have themselves created the emergency. The law is satisfied if the party placed in a difficult situation by reason of the breach of a duty owed to him has acted reasonably in the adoption of remedial measures, and he will not be held disentitled to recover the cost of such measures merely because the party in breach can suggest that other measures less burdensome to him might have been taken."[279]

In cases of anticipatory breach by the seller of goods, if the innocent party accepts the breach and terminates the contract, the duty to mitigate will lead to damages being assessed as at the date of the purchase. If the innocent party does not purchase, then damages will be based on the value on the date when the goods ought to have been delivered.[280] If the anticipatory breach is not accepted, mitigation does not arise until breach occurs.[281] In cases where

---

[276] Unreported, High Court, June 9, 1982. As *Darlington Properties Ltd v Meath County Council* [2011] IEHC 70 demonstrates, a court will look unfavourably upon a defence that the plaintiff has failed to mitigate its loss when steps taken to try to re-negotiate a contract that the defendant has breached were met by "an ostrich-like approach" to liability and the plaintiff's genuine efforts to repair the situation.

[277] [1984] 1 Lloyd's Rep. 614.

[278] [1932] A.C. 452.

[279] [1932] A.C. 452 at 506.

[280] *Melachrino v Nicholl and Knight* [1920] 1 K.B. 693.

[281] *White and Carter (Councils) Ltd v McGregor* [1962] A.C. 413.

the seller of property seeks damages from a defaulting buyer, a resale at an increased price will result in nominal damages or damages for incidental expenses. In *Baker Perkins Ltd v C.J. O'Dowd*[282] the defendants refused to take delivery of bakery equipment ordered from the plaintiffs. The equipment was sold for £60,359 more than the price agreed with the defendants. The plaintiffs could recover warehousing charges incurred pending disposal by way of a resale, for such loss was contemplated by the parties arising out of the breach.

19–74 Where the injured party has received compensation from another source—an insurance policy or a gift from friends or relatives—the common law rules prohibit those advantages from reducing the damages payable to the defendant: *Bradburn v Great Western Railway*.[283] In *Hamilton-Jones v David & Snape (a firm)*[284] financial help from the plaintiff's mother in the cost of travelling to see the plaintiff's children who had been unlawfully taken abroad due to the negligence of the defendant was ignored in computing the damages payable to the plaintiff. In the Irish Republic the Employment Appeals Tribunal deduct employment benefits paid from any award of compensation for unfair dismissal or redundancy but not from wrongful dismissal claims under the Minimum Notice and Terms of Employment Act 1973. In Northern Ireland the leading case of *Hill v Cunningham*[285] holds unemployment benefit deductible from damages for breach of contract, but Barrington J., in *Irish Leathers Ltd v Minister for Labour and Foley*,[286] has rejected this argument, preferring instead to deny a contract breaker the advantage of deducting social welfare payments from compensation payable to a worker following implementation of a redundancy agreement. Statute law often provides that certain social welfare benefits are not deductible—see the Civil Liability (Amendment) Act 1964 s.2, which provides that State and other benefits payable upon the occurrence of a non-fatal injury are not deductible. However, s.96(1) of the Social Welfare Consolidation Act 2005 provides that occupational injuries benefits are deductible in part: an employee who recovers damages for breach of contract which has caused an occupational injury will find damages reduced by occupational injuries benefits for a period of five years after the cause of action arose. Section 286 of the Social Welfare Consolidation Act 2005 similarly requires the deduction of disability benefit or invalidity pension payable for five years in respect of injuries received following the use of a motor vehicle when damages are awarded to the injured person, regardless of whether the cause of action is contract or tort. In *Dennehy v Nordic Cold Storage Ltd*[287] the defendant employer was held to be entitled to take advantage of any insurance payments made to the plaintiff on the foot of a private insurance contract that

---

[282] Unreported, High Court, April 13, 1989; contrast *Hussey v Eels* [1990] 2 W.L.R. 234.
[283] (1874) L.R. 16 Ex. 1.
[284] [2004] 1 W.L.R. 924.
[285] [1968] N.I. 58.
[286] Unreported, High Court, March 12, 1986.
[287] Unreported, High Court, May 8, 1991.

the defendant employer had taken out in respect of the employer's liability, s.2 of the Civil Liability (Amendment) Act 1964 not operating within that context. In *Greene v Hughes Haulage Ltd*,[288] however, s.2 was held to come into play when the payment was the result of a contract of insurance effected by the plaintiff's employer, who paid the premiums. These insurance provisions were held to be part of the plaintiff's remuneration package although in the nature of a disability payment calculated by reference to the plaintiff's salary levels. Other collateral benefits may not be used to offset damages on basic grounds of public policy.[289]

Contributory Negligence

19–75 In England it has been decided that, save in cases where liability in contract and negligence are the same,[290] contributory negligence is not material in actions based on a breach of contract. Apportionment of liability under s.1(1) of the Law Reform (Contributory Negligence) Act 1945 is only possible in respect of tortious liability.

19–76 The provisions of the Civil Liability Act 1961 lead to a quite different conclusion in Ireland. Section 2 of that Act defines "wrong" so as to include "a tort, breach of contract or breach of trust". The Act is the basis upon which a defence of contributory negligence is made available to the defendant. In *Lyons v Thomas*[291] the purchaser of real property sought damages for the deterioration in the condition of property between the date of the agreement and closing of the sale. While the vendor was clearly liable, Murphy J. held that a deduction of 10 per cent should be made. The plaintiff was aware of the deterioration but failed to notify the vendor of this fact. In *O'Flynn v Balkan Tours Ltd* the level of assessment was 75 per cent.[292] On the other hand, in *KBC Bank Ireland Ltd v BCM Hanby Wallace*[293] a solicitor was instructed to ensure that his client's purchase of property was fully secured vis-à-vis title but the solicitor failed to do this. A defence of contributory negligence—there was a failure to investigate the true state of affairs—was rejected. McGovern J. said:

> "… no bank which retains the services of a professional, such as a firm of solicitors, should have to check into those assurances before releasing the funds".

---

[288] *Irish Times Law Report*, September 29, 1997; *Monahan v Dunnes Stores* [2013] IEHC 79.

[289] *McKenna v Best Travel Ltd*, unreported, High Court, December 17, 1996. See *Deductability of Collateral Benefits from the Award of Damages* (LRC CP15–1999) (Consultation Paper) and the final Report LRC 60–2000 for a discussion of this subject.

[290] *Forsikringsaktieselskapet Vesta v Butcher* [1988] 2 All E.R. 43. See Law Commission, *Contributory Negligence as a Defence in Contract* No.219 (1993).

[291] [1986] I.R. 666.

[292] Unreported, Supreme Court, April 7, 1997, affirming High Court judgment of December 1, 1995.

[293] [2012] IEHC 120. The Supreme Court has remitted the contributory negligence issue back to the High Court for reconsideration: [2013] IESC 32.

19–77 Recent cases[294] have stressed that "fault" in s.34 of the Civil Liability Act 1961 involves a departure from the standard of behaviour to be expected from a reasonable man or woman in the circumstances. This does not involve a moral assessment. Declarations of 30 per cent have been made in respect of a franchising dispute[295] and a 50 per cent deduction was made when the plaintiff's carrying out of electrical work in his home without contacting the ESB and the shoddy nature of the job contributed to the outbreak of a fire at that home.[296]

Taxation

19–78 Although the *Gourley*[297] principle was approved and applied by Kenny J. in *Glover v BLN (No. 2)*,[298] and considered to be good law by the same judge in *Browne v Mulligan*[299] and by Pringle J. in *Afton v Film Studios of Ireland*,[300] its general applicability in the Republic remains uncertain outside cases of wrongful dismissal. Finlay P. in *Hickey (No. 2)*[301] was reluctant to apply *Gourley* in a loss of profits case, preferring instead to find that the damages themselves should in principle be subject to taxation; indeed the learned judge went further by holding "that the rule or principle followed by Mr Justice Kenny in *Glover v B.L.N. (No. 2)* applies only to damages for wrongful dismissal and breach of a contract of service and is so expressly to be confined".[302] The Supreme Court has approved this approach in *Marah & Marah v O'Mahony*.[303] However, it must be established that the damages recoverable by the plaintiff are exempt from tax and in two recent cases, *Allen v O'Suilleabháin*[304] and *Sullivan v Southern Health Board*,[305] the courts have been unwilling to impute a tax liability exemption for the damages in question in the absence of proof.

---

[294] *KBC Bank Ireland Ltd v BCM Hanby Wallace* [2013] IESC 32; *McMullan Brothers Ltd v McDonagh* [2015] IESC 19, applying *Carroll v Clare County Council* [1975] I.R. 221, at 227 per Kenny J.

[295] *ADM Londis Plc v Ranzett Ltd (No. 2)* [2014] IEHC 659.

[296] *Nolan v Electricity Supply Board* [2015] IEHC 765.

[297] *British Transport Commission v Gourley* [1956] A.C. 185.

[298] [1973] I.R. 432.

[299] Unreported, Supreme Court, November 23, 1977.

[300] Unreported, High Court, July 12, 1971.

[301] [1980] I.L.R.M. 107.

[302] [1980] I.L.R.M. 107 at 124. See Dorgan and McKenna, *Damages* (Dublin: Round Hall, 2015), p.365.

[303] [1985] IESC 12. On VAT and damages, see *Durkan New Homes v Minister for the Environment, Heritage and Local Government* [2012] IEHC 265.

[304] Unreported, High Court, July 28, 1995. See the Supreme Court judgment of March 11, 1997.

[305] Unreported, Supreme Court, July 30, 1997. In a recent review of the law relating to taxation of damages in dismissal cases, the position has been described as "unsatisfactory": *Nerney v Thomas Crosbie Holdings* [2013] IEHC 127; see Taxes Consolidation Act 1997 s.123.

Interest

19–79 Under the provisions of the Debtors (Ireland) Act 1840 (the "1840 Act"), it is possible for the courts to award interest upon judgment debts; s.26 of the 1840 Act, as amended in the Republic by the Courts Act 1981 (the "1981 Act") s.19(1), obliges the debtor to pay interest of 11 per cent from the time of entering up the judgment until satisfaction of the judgment. Section 20(1) of the 1981 Act gives the Minister for Justice and Equality the power to keep this rate in line with current interest rates. A 1989 Statutory Instrument reduces the interest rate to eight per cent.[306] Whether interest can be awarded to cover the period between breach of contract and the date of judgment is controlled by s.53 of the 1840 Act. The sum in question must be a liquidated or certain amount and the creditor must have served notice in writing of intention to claim interest at the current rate as from the date of demand. In the absence of such a notice damages cannot attract interest; see *East Cork Foods v O'Dwyer Steel Co*,[307] as applied in *Incorporated Food Products Ltd v Minister for Agriculture*.[308] The 1981 Act seems to have superseded s.53 of the 1840 Act by providing that where money, including damages, is payable as a result of the decree of the court, the judge may "if he thinks fit" award the rate of interest in force under s.26 of the 1840 Act, as amended by the 1981 Act, "on the whole or any part of the sum in respect of the whole or any part of the period between the date when the cause of action accrued and the date of the judgment". This discretion to award interest on damages under s.22 must depend on the facts of each particular case and Finlay P. has stated that it does not follow that recovery of interest on arrears in regard to a liquidated demand will follow automatically; see *Mellowhide Products Ltd v Barry Agencies Ltd*.[309]

19–80 The common law position in respect of the charging of interest, other than when following on a judgment given against a creditor, was extensively reviewed in *President of India v La Pintada Compania Navigacion SA*.[310] The House of Lords considered whether it was possible for interest to be charged in cases where proceedings have commenced but the debtor pays before their conclusion, or where the debtor pays late but before proceedings have commenced. While there are exceptional circumstances where interest is awarded in the field of admiralty law and equity, the common law position was established by the House of Lords in *London, Chatham and Dover Railway Co v South Eastern Railway Co*.[311] In the absence of agreement or statutory authority, a court has no power to award interest, simple or compound, by way of damages for late

---

[306] Courts Act 1981 (Interest on Judgment Debts) Order 1989 (S.I. No. 12 of 1989).
[307] [1978] I.R. 103.
[308] Unreported, High Court, June 6, 1984.
[309] [1983] I.L.R.M. 152. In England and Wales see *West v Ian Finlay & Associates* [2014] EWCA Civ 316.
[310] [1985] 1 A.C. 104; Mann, "On interest, compound interest and damages" (1985) 101 L.Q.R. 30.
[311] [1893] A.C. 429, reaffirmed by the Supreme Court in *O'Donnell & Co Ltd v Truck and Machinery Sales Ltd* [1998] 4 I.R. 191.

payment of a debt. The House of Lords, in *La Pintada*, reaffirmed this rule. In *Sempra Metals Ltd v IRC*[312] the House of Lords have held that an English court has jurisdiction at common law to award compound and simple interest on claims in contract to pay a debt, subject to remoteness of damage and other limiting factors such as any duty to mitigate. *La Pintada* was disapproved as being incompatible with the *Hadley v Baxendale* "first limb".

19–81 It is possible for the parties to agree to provide interest upon a certain event as a term of the agreement; this is particularly common in cases where a sale of land is not completed on time; see *Lappen v Purcell*.[313] A stipulated rate of interest of 20 per cent was upheld in *Treacy v Dwyer Nolan Investments*.[314] The Prompt Payment of Accounts Act 1997 allows the supplier of goods or services to State bodies—identified in the Act to cover Government departments, agencies and hospitals as well as universities, inter alia—to obtain interest on overdue accounts of just over 11 per cent per annum.[315] The European Communities (Late Payment in Commercial Transactions) Regulations are also in point.[316]

Damages in Foreign Currency

19–82 It is possible for an Irish arbitrator or Irish court to order payment of damages in a foreign currency.[317]

Penalty Clauses and Liquidated Damages Clauses

19–83 Lewison defines a penalty clause as:

"... a clause which, without commercial justification, provides for payment or forfeiture of a sum of money, or transfer of property by one party to the other, in the event of a breach of contract, the clause being designed to secure performance of the contract rather than compensate the payee for the loss occasioned through the breach."[318]

---

[312] [2007] 4 All E.R. 657.
[313] [1965] Ir. Jur. Rep. 1.
[314] Unreported, High Court, October 31, 1979; such clauses are standard in finance leases where the lessee is in default of payments.
[315] See the Annotation by Hoy in *Irish Current Law Statutes Annotated*.
[316] European Communities (Late Payment in Commercial Transactions) Regulations 2012 (S.I. No. 580 of 2012); European Communities (Late Payment in Commercial Transactions) (Amendment) Regulations 2013 (S.I. No. 74 of 2013) ; European Communities (Late Payment in Commercial Transactions) (Amendment) Regulations 2016 (S.I. No. 281 of 2016). In cases of contracts for grocery supplies between Suppliers and grocery goods undertakings see S.I. No. 35 of 2016, Regulation 10.
[317] *Cremer (Peter) GmbH v Co-operative Molasses Traders Ltd* [1985] I.L.R.M. 564.
[318] *The Interpretation of Contracts*, 5th edn (London: Thomson, 2011), para.17.01.

In modern times, the issue of commercial justification is the guiding principle. So, a clause in a share purchase agreement which bound the seller not to engage in competing activities adversely impacting on the value of the shareholding acquired from the seller, upon pain of not being able to recover outstanding payments due, was held not to involve a penalty in *Cavendish Square Holding BV v EI Makdessi*.[319] Nor was a related share purchase clause, triggered in the event of the activities in question occurring. Such activities would be a breach of contract on the part of the seller. Each clause had a legitimate function, the clauses were not intended to punish the party in breach and, as standard commercial clauses that were extensively negotiated by properly advised commercial entities, of equal bargaining power, the clauses could be enforced.

Although there are, as we shall see, a number of guidelines taken from cases decided in the early twentieth century, this definition stresses that the search is for commercial justification of the clause. In historical terms, both the common law courts and the courts of equity viewed these covenants with suspicion, being of the view that a clause which could oblige a party to pay a measure of compensation grossly disproportionate to the injury produced by the breach, should not be enforceable.[320] A fundamental distinction has been drawn in the modern cases. A clause will be valid if it is a genuine pre-estimate of the damage which will probably result from a breach of contract. Such a clause is called a liquidated damages clause. If the clause is designed to deter one party from breaking the contract by stipulating that breach will result in the payment of a fixed amount the courts will refuse to enforce the clause by holding it to be a penalty. The burden of showing that the sum is a penalty rather than liquidated damages is upon the proferens. While penalty clauses are normally found to exist where the party in breach of contract is required to pay a sum of money upon breach, it has been recognised that where non-monetary obligations arise following a breach of contract, the law relating to penalties may still be invoked. In *Ringrow Pty Ltd v BP Australia Pty Ltd*,[321] R purchased a filling station from BP, the transaction involving a five-year solus tie in favour of BP. In breach of this agreement R took petroleum products from another supplier. The transaction included a provision that gave BP an option to purchase back the property upon breach of contract by R. Under the option agreement the price was to be fixed by a valuer but the valuer was not to make an allowance for goodwill and the option clause was cumulative in the sense that the contract also contained a liquidated damage clause (which

---

[319] [2015] UKSC 67.

[320] Ibbetson, *A Historical Introduction to the Law of Obligations* (Oxford: OUP, 1999), pp.72–73; Holdsworth, *A History of English Law*, Vol.2, p.177 (Sweet & Maxwell, 1972 Reprint).

[321] [2005] HCA 71. If the sum is payable, not on breach, but by virtue of the exercise of a termination right, the weight of opinion is inclined towards viewing the law relating to penalties as having no application: *Interstar Wholesale Finance Pty Ltd v Integral Home Loans Pty Ltd* [2008] NSWCA 310, applying *Export Credit Guarantee Department v Universal Oil Products Co* [1983] 2 All E.R. 205. The High Court of Australia, however, in *Andrews v Australia and New Zealand Banking Group Ltd* [2012] HCA 30 has rejected this limitation. See Peel, "The Rule against Penalties" (2013) 129 L.Q.R. 152, who criticises the penalty jurisdiction and doubts that it is worth retaining.

was not challenged by R). The High Court of Australia held that the option provision was not extravagant or unconscionable, particularly in the light of evidence that goodwill in this context was unlikely to be of any value. In this case the High Court of Australia adopted a very traditional view of the law relating to penalties and this approach stands in stark contrast to the more recent "commercial purpose" approach canvassed in the English courts.

19–84 The case of *Toomey v Murphy*[322] presents a simple illustration of a liquidated damages clause. The defendant agreed to complete construction work by an agreed date. If the work was then incomplete he agreed to pay "a penalty as liquidated damages" of £5 per week. The plaintiff sued for £160, being 32 weeks at £5 per week. The Queens Bench Division held the sum to be liquidated damages. The operation of a penalty clause has been graphically illustrated by the case of *Giraud UK Ltd v Smith*.[323] The plaintiff company engaged the defendant as a driver under a contract of employment, requiring the driver to give four weeks' notice of intention to leave employment. The contract provided that the driver would lose a day's wages for each day in respect of which inadequate notice was given. Further, any actual loss would be independently recoverable. The clause was struck down as a penalty because replacement drivers were available, the clause did not genuinely pre-estimate the loss that was likely to occur and because the clause did not limit recovery to the monies nominated in the clause it clearly operated oppressively. As Maurice Kay J. said, the clause functioned on a "heads I win, tails you lose" basis.

19–85 Whether the clause is a penalty or liquidated damages depends on the intention of the parties at the date of agreement; in this context the words used to describe the clause will provide some indication of their intention. In *Toomey v Murphy* the words "penalty" and "liquidated damages" were used so the terminology was equivocal; if the parties describe the clause as a penalty this will provide evidence that the clause is to be held *in terrorem* over the head of one party. There are many cases in which a clause has been described as a penalty but has been held a valid liquidated damages clause, for example *Gerrard v O'Reilly*.[324] The converse is also true.[325] The fact that a clause may be of a kind that ordinary commercial contracts have contained as standards terms for many years will not necessarily provide that clause with immunity from scrutiny. In *M&J Polymers Ltd v Imerys Minerals Ltd*,[326] the parties negotiated a three-year supply contract for chemicals giving the buyers a promise of continuity of supply in return for agreeing a "take or pay" clause requiring the buyers to pay monthly for a minimum amount, even if that quantity was not ordered. Burton J. held that even though such a clause was

---

[322] [1897] 2 I.R. 601; *French v Macale* (1842) 4 Ir.Eq.Rep. 573.
[323] [2000] I.R.L.R. 763.
[324] (1843) 2 Connor and Lawson 165; *Alder v Moore* [1961] 2 Q.B. 57.
[325] (1829) 6 Bing. 141.
[326] [2008] EWHC 344 (Comm).

generally unexceptional in commercial contracts, it still had to be tested: the clause was upheld as being commercially justifiable.

19–86 Although, as we shall see, several influential statements in the early twentieth century stressed that any impungned clauses should be characterised as penal in nature, this is no longer the case. In *Cavendish Square Holding BV v El Makdessi*[327] the majority judgment of Lords Neuberger, Sumption and Carnwath eschewed references to "penal", "unconscionable" or extravagant, saying that:

> "The true test is whether the impugned provision is a secondary obligation which imposes a detriment on the contract breaker out of all proportion to any legitimate interest in the enforcement of the primary obligation. The innocent party can have no proper interest in simply punishing the defaulter. His interest is in performance or in some appropriate alternative to performance ..."

In this observation their Lordships were clearly endorsing the commercial justification test as it has evolved from *Lordsvale Finance Plc v Bank of Zambia*.[328]

Lord Dunedin's Four Factor Test

19–87 It is generally accepted that the best summary of the presumptions to be applied in testing whether a clause is valid or invalid is to be found in the speech of Lord Dunedin in *Dunlop Pneumatic Tyre Co v New Garage & Motor Co*[329]:

> "(a) The sum will be held to be a penalty if the sum stipulated for is extravagant and unconscionable in amount in comparison with the greatest loss that could conceivably be proved to have followed from the breach ..."

In *Durkan New Homes v Minister for the Environment, Heritage and Local Government*,[330] Charleton J. held that a clause in special conditions of sale, which required the vendor to pay damages, on an ascending scale, of €20,000 to €50,000 per week from the closing date to the date of actual transfer, infringed the first of Lord Dunedin's presumptions. This is generally the most important test. In cases where there is only one obligation, the chance of this test being operative in a way which strikes down the clause is less pronounced than in cases of multiple obligations, for here the clause, if it strikes at a variety

---

[327] [2015] UKSC 67.
[328] [1996] Q.B. 752.
[329] [1915] A.C. 79 at 86–87.
[330] [2012] IEHC 265. This is a heterodox decision as the court looked at post-contractual events in viewing and judging the clause.

of possible breaches, in the same way, will probably be held to be a penalty. In *Irish Telephone Rentals Ltd v Irish Civil Service Building Society Ltd*[331] Costello J. had to consider a clause which obliged a subscriber who repudiated a contract for the hire of telephone equipment to pay all accrued charges plus all remaining rentals due under the contract, a five per cent allowance being made for receiving rentals immediately and not over future years, and a 25 per cent discount being made because of the saving to the owner on maintenance costs. Costello J., after citing the above rule, concluded that the discounting process was not sufficient to prevent the acceleration clause from infringing the rule. Wages of maintenance staff and other costs were not included in the 25 per cent discount. The profit figure estimated by the plaintiffs, 71.25 per cent of the gross rent, seemed to be excessive, and because the exercise undertaken by the plaintiffs did not attempt, in any methodically consistent way, to identify actual loss, this standard provision was held to be a penalty. See also *Bradshaw v Lemon*[332] where a sum payable upon non-repair of premises was held a penalty because the loss that could result from breach would not in any case match the sum stipulated: the repairer could breach the contract in a variety of ways. A Singapore case,[333] which is of considerable interest, has held that when an employment contract provided that any breach of a non-competition clause would result in an obligation to pay liquidated damages calculated as one year's salary, that clause was unenforceable by reference to Lord Dunedin's first test. The sum was said to be an arbitrary figure plucked from the air and was by no means a genuine pre-estimate of damage.

> "(b) The sum will be a penalty if the breach consists only in paying a sum of money, the sum stipulated being greater than the sum which ought to have been paid."

Thus if the clause obliges a person to pay €200 upon failure to pay a rental of €50 the clause will be penal; see the dictum of Lawson J. in *Wright v Tracey*.[334] In the leading Irish case of *O'Donnell & Co Ltd v Truck and Machinery Sales Ltd*[335] the Supreme Court held that where the breach consists of a failure to pay a fixed sum, the damages payable will be that sum plus commercial rates of interest. Should the contract provide for payments in excess of this formula then the "agreed rate" will be regarded as a penalty and not a genuine pre-estimate of loss. An "acceleration clause" has been held not to infringe this rule. These clauses (which operate in contracts where a debtor repays sums of money in instalments) provide that upon failure to pay any of the instalments the whole balance will become immediately due. Even though the obligation to pay the entire sum will generally be more expensive to the party in breach

---

[331] [1991] I.L.R.M. 880, following *Robophone Facilities Ltd v Blank* [1966] 1 W.L.R. 1428.
[332] [1929] N.I. 159.
[333] *HR net One Pte Ltd v Adrian* [2006] SGDC 202.
[334] (1873) I.R. 7 C.L. 134.
[335] [1998] 4 I.R. 191.

the validity of such a clause was upheld in *Protector Loan Co v Grice*,[336] a decision of the English Court of Appeal; see a similar clause in *National Telephone Co v Griffen*.[337]

19–88 The acceleration clause will be carefully policed however. In *U.D.T. Ltd v Patterson*[338] the plaintiff advanced £900 to the defendant, repayable with interest by 36 equal monthly instalments. It was a term of the agreement that immediately upon default the whole amount would be due and payable. The defendant paid one instalment and then defaulted. The plaintiffs claimed £1,137.50 being the sum lent minus one instalment paid and interest over the period at 10 per cent per annum. McGonigal J. ruled the clause penal. It was noted that if the loan was repaid at an early date the contract provided that no interest would be payable for the period after repayment; in this instance the default clause did not provide for payment of interest calculated up to the date of repayment of the principal only. McGonigal J. distinguished *Grice's* case by holding:

> "The amount to be paid on default is a larger amount than the amount actually due if calculated on the basis of the balance still outstanding and interest to that date and a larger sum than the amount which would have to be paid if the borrower had elected to pay at that point of time during the currency of the loan."[339]

It may be that the party in default will seek to discharge the duty to show the clause is penal by giving the clause an extreme interpretation. Just such an attempt failed in the case of the *Angelic Star*.[340] The acceleration clause, found in a shipbuilding contract, required the purchaser in default of instalment payments, to pay immediately "the loan together with all other monies due". While Donaldson M.R. was prepared to accept that a clause in a long-term loan contract which provided that on any breach the capital sum and interest for the full term would be a penalty, this agreement did not have this effect. The words "together with all monies due" referred simply to all monies due at the time of the default. Conversely, in *Trustee Savings Bank Dublin v Maughan*[341] Costello J. held that unless the alleged clause is a genuine pre-estimate, agreed between the parties, the clause will be liable to be considered a penalty clause.

19–89 Acceleration clauses aside, caution must be exercised in relation to this presumption. Even a substantial discrepancy between the sum forfeited and the loss occasioned by breach—in *General Trading Co (Holding) Ltd*

---

[336] (1880) 5 Q.B.D. 529.
[337] [1906] 2 I.R. 115; *Azimut Bennetti v Darrell Marcus Healey* [2010] EWHC 2234 (Comm).
[338] [1975] N.I. 142.
[339] [1975] N.I. 142 at 145.
[340] [1988] 1 Lloyd's Rep. 122.
[341] Unreported, High Court, October 8, 1981.

v Richmond Corp Ltd[342] the figures were £540,000 and £200,000 respectively—can be upheld under the broader approach to penalty clauses in recent years. At the time the contract was made, in the *General Trading* case, the clause was commercially justifiable, did not amount to oppression and was freely negotiated between parties of comparable bargaining powers. Most importantly, there was no predominant purpose of deterring a breach of contract. Mere presumptions, as distinct from statutory rules, are at the core of Lord Dunedin's four factors, particularly this one.

19–90 The decision of Finlay Geoghegan J. in *ACC Bank plc v Friends First Managed Pensions Funds*[343] follows *Lordsvale* in holding that any surcharge that is added to loan repayments after an act of default must be a modest amount if it is to reflect the fact that a default will create adverse financial implications for a lender. The judge clearly felt that a default rate of 6 per cent, as set out in the contract, could be anything other than a penalty intended to dissuade the borrower from breaching the contract. No commercial justification had been advanced by the lender and the fact that the increase was only prospective, not retrospective as well, could not save this particular provision from being penal.

19–91 However, if the breach of obligation has already occurred, any subsequent agreement may avoid the law relating to penalties. In *Cameron v UBS AG*[344] the appellant had been found liable by a Swiss court to pay $8.4 million (AUD) to the respondent. The respondent sought to enforce the judgment in an Australian court whereupon the parties, by deed, agreed that if the appellant paid $1 million (AUD) in five instalments, this would discharge the debt, but if not, then the respondent could seek the entire $8.4 million. The appellant failed to pay the first instalment. The Victoria Court of Appeal held that the terms of the deed did not disclose a penalty. This was not the case of an illegal acceleration clause,[345] but rather a case where "the sum payable upon default is already due and owing and the chance to pay a lesser sum or on terms is being afforded as a privilege or indulgence".[346]

> "(c) There is a presumption that a clause is penal when a single lump sum is payable on the occurrence of one or more or all of several events, the events occasioning varying degrees of loss."

The unusual case of *Jobson v Johnson*[347] is perhaps to be seen as illustrative. Here the defendant had purchased shares in a football club. The contract

---

[342] [2008] EWHC 1479 (Comm).
[343] [2012] IEHC 435. *ACC Bank Plc v Friends First Managed Pensions Funds* has been followed in *AIB Plc v Fahy* [2014] IEHC 244 and in *Sheehan v Breccia* [2016] IEHC 67 and *Flynn v Breccia* [2016] IEHC 68.
[344] (2000) 2 V.R. 108.
[345] See *O'Dea v Allstates Leasing System (WA) Pty* (1983) 152 C.L.R. 359 and *Acron Pacific Ltd v Offshore Oil NL* (1985) 157 C.L.R. 170.
[346] Per Phillips J.A. at 115, following *Thompson v Hudson* (1869) L.R. 4 H.L. 1.
[347] [1989] 1 All E.R. 621.

provided for a price of £351,688 payable by a down-payment of £40,000 and six equal half-yearly payments of the balance. The contract provided that upon default, the buyer would be obliged to reconvey the shares for a fixed consideration of £40,000. The clause was penal because the repurchase was to be effected at £40,000 regardless of whether the defendant defaulted on the second or last instalment, for example. The clause also operated prejudicially by requiring the repurchase for less than £40,000 if the default of the purchaser occurred on the first of the six instalments. Similarly, in *CMC Group v Zhang*,[348] Z settled a claim brought against the defendant for alleged breach of contract. The settlement agreement sought to provide that if Z continued to harass CMC staff, a sum of $40,000 (US) would be payable. The Court of Appeal held that this was a penalty as it could be a term that could be broken in different ways—a solicitor's letter from Z, for example—and because the clause also operated with another provision entitling the plaintiff to damage for loss of business occasioned by breach, the English Court of Appeal found this came within factor (c).

19–92 *Re An Arranging Debtor*[349] presents an illustration of how this rule can be avoided. Patentees installed equipment into premises under a contract which obliged the hirers not to allow others to use, repair or purchase the machinery, £30 being payable if any of these events occurred. The clause was held not to be penal; the covenants were held to import obligations of equal, not varying, importance. This rule seems to best explain the case of *Schiesser International (Ireland) v Gallagher*.[350] The defendant went to Germany to be trained as a textile cutter. He agreed that if he left the employment of the plaintiff within three years of his return to Ireland he would reimburse it for travelling expenses and training expenses incurred. The clause was struck down as a penalty. It was pointed out that if the defendant had left employment one day after his return from Germany or one day before expiry of the three-year period the same sum would be payable.

> "(d) If the consequences of breach are difficult to estimate in financial terms this, far from being an obstacle to the validity of the clause, will point in favour of upholding it, the courts taking the view that it is better for the parties themselves to estimate the damages that will result."

Factor (d) makes it increasingly likely that arm's-length clauses will be upheld. In *Philips Hong Kong Ltd v AG of Hong Kong*,[351] Lord Woolf M.R. stressed that "what the parties have agreed should normally be upheld. Any

---

[348] [2006] EWCA Civ 408.

[349] (1916) 51 I.L.T.R. 68.

[350] (1971) 106 I.L.T.R. 22.

[351] (1993) 61 B.L.R. 49. The uncertainty that might lead a court to uphold an agreed damages clause might well be the result of judicial decisions such as the *Golden Strait* decision, as long as the intention of the parties is clear: *Novasen SA v Alimenta SA* [2013] EWHC 345 (Comm).

other approach will lead to considerable uncertainty especially in commercial contracts". Other recent English cases have stressed the importance of observing the maxim, *pacta sunt servanda*.[352] Indeed, the use of a clause may be such as to save a court from having to embark upon a valuation exercise, particularly in relation to contracts that may be difficult, if not impossible, to value for the plaintiff. One such case of notoriety is presented by auction sales when the seller engages in sharp practice by "puffing up" bids. In *Tkachuk Farms Ltd v Le Blanc Auction Service Ltd*,[353] a clause requiring a defaulting seller to pay fixed compensation of 14 per cent of a fixed commission was upheld, the Saskatchewan Court of King's Bench specifically rejecting an argument that the sum was a penalty. A calculation made in good faith to settle litigation will not be struck down just because it turns out badly.[354]

19–93 While the best illustration of this rule is to be gleaned from contrasting the *Dunlop Pneumatic Tyre* case with *Ford Motor Co v Armstrong*[355] Irish students should note that this rule was used to "explain" the difficult case of *Smith v Ryan*[356] by the majority in *Dickson v Lough*.[357]

Penalty Clauses—The "Dominant Commercial Purpose" Test

19–94 Lord Dunedin's four tests have proved to be a very useful benchmark and although there has been a degree of judicial reworking in recent years, Lord Dunedin's speech is still authoritative. However, there is authority for the view that because the penalty clause jurisdiction is an exception to the rule that commercial agreements should be upheld, wherever possible, the courts should look beneath the agreement, in order to test whether the clause is commercially justifiable. In *Lordsvale Finance Plc v Bank of Zambia*,[358] Colman J. said that:

> "... the jurisdiction in relation to penalty clauses is concerned not primarily with the enforcement of inoffensive liquidated damages clauses but rather with protection against the effect of penalty clauses. There would therefore seem to be no reason in principle why a contractual provision the effect of which was to increase the consideration payable under an executory contract upon the happening of a default should be struck down as a penalty if the increase could in the circumstances be explained as commercially justifiable, provided always that its dominant purpose was not to deter the other party from breach."[359]

---

[352] *Murray v Leisureplay Plc* [2005] EWCA Civ 963.
[353] [2007] 2 W.W.R. 66.
[354] *CFW Architects v Cowlin Construction Ltd* [2006] EWHC 6 (TCC).
[355] (1915) 31 T.L.R. 267.
[356] (1843) 9 I.L.R. 235.
[357] (1886) 18 L.R. (Ir.) 518.
[358] [1996] Q.B. 752; *Re Brown and Another* [2003] NI Ch 1.
[359] [1996] Q.B. 752 at 764, cited with approval by the Court of Appeal in *Euro London Appointments v Claessens International* [2006] 2 Lloyd's Rep. 436.

This "dominant commercial purpose" test allows a court to ascribe to the contract objectives other than oppressive conduct or a desire to inhibit parties from breaching contracts. It may be that the clause will only be struck down in cases where there is a significant gap between the damages likely to be suffered and the sums stipulated in the contract.[360]

In *Parking Eve v Beavis*[361] a straightforward example of the new approach is evident. A standard provision in a retail park advised shoppers who park their cars that overstays on the maximum parking period would result in an £85 parking charge. The charge was not imposed to provide a genuine pre-estimate of the loss that will be occasioned by a breach but it nevertheless has two legitimate functions, namely (1) the efficient use of parking spaces for the benefit of retail outlets by deterring commuters and other long stay users, and (2) to help to finance the parking facilities that were otherwise free to compliant users. The UK Supreme Court found the penalties rule was engaged but the charge was not a penalty:

> "the trial judge, Judge Moloney QC, found that the £85 charge was neither extravagant nor unconscionable having regard to the level of the charges imposed by local authorities for overstaying in car parks on public land. The Court of Appeal agreed and so do we".

Application

19–95 In the area of employment law, the decision of the English Court of Appeal in *Murray v Leisureplay Plc*[362] brings together these new approaches. Murray was the Chief Executive of a financial services company that sought to acquire other financial institutions. Murray was himself involved in other businesses and was engaged by Leisureplay to work for three days a week. His draft contract provided that upon wrongful termination of his contract, he was to be given up to three years' salary, although this was later revised down to require one year's compensation. Murray was dismissed with seven and a half weeks' notice and claimed to be entitled to pocket both the salary paid during that seven and a half weeks, plus one year's salary under the liquidated damages clause. Leisureplay claimed that the clause was a penalty; in particular, Leisureplay pointed out that under the clause Murray had no obligation to mitigate his loss and, given his other business interests, Leisureplay argued that it was likely on breach that Murray would find employment elsewhere. The comparison between the stipulated sum and the

---

[360] *Alfred McAlpine Capital Projects Ltd v Tilebox Ltd* [2005] B.L.R. 271. Standard demurrage clauses may also be held to be penal if they give the carrier a right to keep the contract alive so as to recover demurrage indefinitely, notwithstanding the absence of any loss to a reasonable carrier: *MSC Mediterranean Shipping Company SA v Cottonex Anstalt* [2015] EWHC 283 (Comm).

[361] [2015] UKSC 67, followed in *Paciocco v Australia and New Zealand Banking Group* [2015] HCA 28.

[362] [2005] EWCA Civ 963; *Steria Ltd v Sigma* [2008] B.L.R. 79.

sums recoverable in a common law action resulted in the stipulated sum being more favourable to Murray, but this did not mean the sum was a penalty. The sum need not be an accurate statement of the loss. Buxton L.J. said the contract terms were generous but not unconscionable.

19–96 On the "broader" issue of what the agreement sought to do, Buxton L.J. took judicial notice of the fact that a company in this area would need to offer a package that gave "generous reassurance" against the eventuality of dismissal. The contract contained restrictions against Murray working in a competing environment after departure. The clause precluded any right to claim arrears of pension contribution. The contract injected certainty and averted possible disputes and unwanted publicity. The mitigation point was met by remarking that *at the time of contract* it was by no means clear that Murray would get other employment and the absence of any statement in the contract, vis-à-vis duty to mitigate, was intended to avoid disputes about whether Murray was acting reasonably. On the *in terrorem* point, the Court of Appeal found that Murray had no interest in deterring breach but, objectively, the clause was there to compensate for the loss to other business interests that followed from his employment with Leisureplay. The Court of Appeal stressed the importance of ensuring that contractual agreements should be upheld and that the onus rests upon the party invoking the penalty jurisdiction to satisfy the court that the clause is penal. The dominant purpose here was to compensate Murray in respect of loss to other business interests due to his contract with Leisureplay, and no deterrent function was evident. The law relating to penalty clauses in employment contracts was reviewed by Popplewell J. in *Imam Sadeque v BlueBay Asset Management (Services) Ltd*.[363] Contingent rights such as acquiring the benefit of bonus payments if the employee observed the terms of the contract of employment were held to be outside the penalty doctrine. The court also considered deferred bonus payments of this kind to be both commercially sustainable and "common place throughout the City of London and elsewhere".

19–97 An obligation to pay for goods even if not ordered will be upheld when registered against a background of previous dealing when the goods are scarce and the buyer is seeking to acquire the commercial advantage of security of supply.[364]

Penalty Clauses in Agricultural Lettings

19–98 It is clear that the modern case law on penalty clauses has produced different results to those that could have been anticipated under the earlier rules; McGregor observes that the nineteenth-century cases on penalties were

---

[363] [2012] EWHC 3511 (Q.B.).
[364] *M&J Polymers Ltd v Imerys Minerals Ltd* [2008] EWHC 344 (Comm).

often confused and difficult to reconcile and he concludes that, "perhaps today they are of real value only as illustrations of type-situations".[365] This is particularly true of clauses in agricultural leases in which a tenant was bound not to plough land or take away meadowing or grass (*Smith v Ryan*[366]); not to raise a stone weir (*Gerrard v O'Reilly*[367]); nor sublet premises (*Boyle v McGovern*[368]) upon pain of having to pay double the rent due. In these early cases the sums were held not to be a penalty, either at common law (*Hubbard v Grattan*[369]) or in equity (*Smith v Ryan*). Since then the Irish courts have moved towards holding these clauses to be penalties by holding the leading case of *Smith v Ryan* to depend on rule (d) above; see *Dickson v Lough*[370] and the Northern Ireland case of *Bradshaw v Lemon*.[371]

Sums Payable on Termination Not Breach

19–99 It should be noted that in the *Schiesser* case the clause was designed to deter the defendant from lawfully terminating his employment rather than from breaking the contract. The clause then could not be an agreed damages clause in the orthodox sense unless the contract there was for a fixed period of at least three years; no such finding appears in the law report however. Nevertheless the rules applicable to penalties upon breach were held applicable.[372] The rights of the hirer of goods to terminate a hire-purchase contract and the capping of the liability of the hirer have been removed from the penalty clause arena by the Consumer Credit Act 1995, specifically s.63.

19–100 Section 63 applies to consumer credit agreements entered into after May 13, 1996, and it replaces the earlier Hire Purchase Act 1946. The 1946 Act, unlike the 1995 Act, was not confined to consumer credit agreements so much of the law relating to termination of breach of non-consumer hire contracts must be resolved by common law rules rather than the statutory regime. Section 63 of the 1995 Act basically allows for termination of a consumer credit agreement by the hirer, who becomes liable to pay one-half of the hire-purchase price to the owner. Where the contract is terminated for reasons other than s.63 (e.g. hirer's breach, contractual termination rights) there is no clear authority whether the law relating to penalties applies,

---

[365] *McGregor on Damages*, 19th edn (London: Sweet & Maxwell, 2015), para.15.007.

[366] (1843) 9 I.L.R. 235.

[367] (1843) 2 Connor and Lawson 165.

[368] (1841) 6 *Circuit Cases* 308.

[369] (1833) *Alcock and Napier* 389.

[370] (1886) 18 L.R. (Ir.) 518.

[371] [1929] N.I. 159; *McGregor on Damages*, 19th edn (London: Sweet & Maxwell, 2015), para.15.051, says of the English cases that they "trail in a desultory way into the twentieth century: the result is always penalty".

[372] *Schiesser International (Ireland) v Gallagher* (1971) 106 I.L.T.R. 22; compare *Alder v Moore* [1961] 2 Q.B. 57 and *Export Credits Guarantee Department v Universal Oil Products Co* [1983] 2 All E.R. 205 with *Schiesser*.

although in *Bridge v Campbell Discount*[373] Lords Denning and Devlin thought that the law of penalties still applied. Recently, there has been some English case law which suggests that the law is uncertain on this point.[374] In *Berg v Blackburn Rovers Football Club*[375] Berg was recruited as a manager of the club. A clause in the contract providing that in the event that the club exercised a right of early termination a fixed sum would be payable to Berg. The club tried to avoid having to make the payment on the basis that it was a penalty. The clause was held not to be a penalty because it was not a payment that fell due upon breach of a contract.

19–101 The Berg decision applies the orthodox view. In contrast, in *Volkswagen Financial Services (UK) v Ramage Cambridge (County Court)*,[376] a hire contract provided that, upon early termination, the hirer would pay "as compensation or agreed damages", the total amount of rental (36 months) less amount of rentals paid. This clause was held to be a penalty. No account was taken of the benefit of early return of a profit-earning chattel, and certain savings to the owner under the agreement (breakdown service), as well as the fact that there was no effort to estimate the loss in any genuine way.

19–102 If the concern of the Oireachtas is to provide a degree of consumer protection, then hire-purchase and leasing transactions must be scrutinised at some future date in order to counteract the effect of contractual terms which attempt to secure for the owner compensation for loss of future instalments, in the form of minimum percentage or acceleration clauses as well as the return of the contractual subject matter. This is highlighted by attempts to evade a decision[377] of the Court of Appeal which held that any contractual term which seeks to allow the owner to claim damages for loss of future instalments following the owner's decision to terminate for breach will not be successful. Damages will be limited to instalments unpaid at the time of the owner's decision to rescind. It has been held, however, that if the contract contains a clause which makes prompt payment of the essence of the contract, then any breach will go to the root of the contract and entitle the owner to terminate at common law, independently of the terms of the contract.[378]

---

[373] [1962] A.C. 600.
[374] The High Court of Australia, in *Andrews v Australia and New Zealand Banking Group Ltd* [2012] HCA 30, has applied the rules on penalties to banking charges that could not be described as payment on breach fees. See Peel, "The rule against Penalties" (2013) 129 L.Q.R. 152. This question will be decided on a case by case basis: *Paciocco v Australia and New Zealand Banking Group* [2016] HCA 28.
[375] [2013] EWHC 1070 (Q.B.).
[376] [2007] C.T.L.C. 119. See 2007 *Current Law* and Freemann (2007) *In-house Lawyer* 152 (July/August) 39–41. See statements at para.89 of Herbert J.'s judgment in *Irish Bank Resolution Corporation Ltd v Drumm* [2013] IEHC 378.
[377] *Financings Ltd v Baldock* [1963] 2 Q.B. 104.
[378] *Lombard North Central Plc v Butterworth* [1987] 1 All E.R. 267.

Effects of the Penalty Clause

19–103 If the clause is held to be a penalty clause it is unenforceable. If the plaintiff can prove actual loss he will be limited to the amounts proved; see *Schiesser*.[379] If the clause is a penalty, which, because of subsequent events, does not cover the loss suffered, it is said that the plaintiff can opt to rely on the clause or sue for the actual loss suffered; see *Wall v Rederiaktiebolaget Lugudde*.[380] In cases where the actual loss exceeds the amount fixed by the unenforceable penalty clause, it may be that the amount recoverable will be set by the penalty clause and cannot be exceeded, but McGregor doubts this proposition[381] and, on principle, if the clause is unenforceable as a penalty it should not interfere with ordinary rules of assessment. Where the obligation struck down is not an obligation to pay money, but to perform some agreed act, such as transfer property,[382] the process of determining the remedies available to the injured party can be difficult indeed.

---

[379] *Schiesser International (Ireland) v Gallagher* (1971) 106 I.L.T.R. 22; *Irish Telephone Rentals Ltd v Irish Civil Service Building Society* [1991] I.L.R.M. 880; *O'Donnell & Co Ltd v Truck and Machinery Sales Ltd* [1998] 4 I.R. 191.

[380] [1915] A.C. 79.

[381] 17th edn (London: Sweet & Maxwell, 2003), para.15–027.

[382] *Jobson v Johnson* [1989] 1 All E.R. 621.

20 Quasi-Contractual or Restitutionary Relief

Introduction

20–01 "The Law of Restitution is the law relating to all claims, quasi contractual or otherwise, which are founded upon the principle of unjust enrichment. Restitutionary claims are to be found in equity as well as at law. But the common law of quasi contract is the most ancient part of restitution."[1]

20–02 Traditional legal scholarship has tended to regard the categories of tort and contract as the two primary sources of liability in private law. The impact of this bifurcation for legal theory has in England been profound. Apart from attempts by Lord Mansfield, primarily in *Moses v McFerlan*,[2] to establish a third category, that of unjust enrichment—a category that would both cut across contract and tort and at the same time establish a third or quite self-contained area of private law within which the judiciary could operate—there was until recently a tendency to argue that restitutionary relief could only be available if the plaintiff's cause of action fell within contract, tort or possibly the equitable concept of the fiduciary relationship; see *McNeill v Millen & Co*.[3] Both judicial and academic opinions have shifted from the position taken by the nineteenth-century judges who repudiated *Moses v McFerlan*, primarily because of the authoritativeness of the modern view that the old causes of action should not rule us from their graves, and also because it is realised that unjust enrichment—rather than implied contract, for example—provides a more realistic and coherent basis for explaining the cases, particularly the mistake of fact cases. Judicial activism and academic scholarship—using *Moses v McFerlan* as the starting point—have produced a very sophisticated set of principles and rules and the work of the American Law Institute has been very influential.[4]

20–03 In Ireland the courts have until very recently tended to resist the

---

[1] Burrows, *Restatement of the English Law of Unjust Enrichment* (Oxford: OUP, 2012); Goff and Jones, *The Law of Unjust Enrichment*, 8th edn (London: Sweet & Maxwell, 2011); Baloch, *Unjust Enrichment and Contract* (Oxford: Hart, 2009); Virgo, *The Principles of the Law of Restitution*, 3rd edn (Oxford: OUP, 2015); Stoljar, *The Law of Quasi-Contract*, 2nd edn (North Ryde, New South Wales: Law Book Co, 1989).

[2] (1760) 2 Burr. 1005; see Gummow, "*Moses v Mcfelan*: 250 Years on" (2010) 84 A.L.J. 756 on the decision in *Moses v McFerlan* and its influence in Australia and elsewhere; Birks (1984) 37 C.L.P. 1.

[3] [1907] 2 I.R. 328.

[4] Perillo, "Restitution in the Second Restatement of Contracts" (1981) 81 Col. L.R. 37. See generally, ALI, *Restatement of the Law Third, Restitution and Unjust Enrichment* (2010).

temptation to consider whether the principle of unjust enrichment forms an essential element in Irish law. While there are isolated cases in which the unjust enrichment doctrine has surfaced—witness *Hickey v Roches Stores (No. 1)*[5]—there has been a tendency to decline to accept counsel's invitation to consider a broad application of *Moses v McFerlan*; see Morris J. in *Leader v Leader*.[6] There are, however, cases where the unjust result of not allowing an action for recovery to succeed has contributed to the reasoning, e.g. *Carse v Taylor*,[7] without in any way suggesting that this forms the basis of a cause of action. Twentieth-century Irish judges considered either unjust enrichment or fault to be possible explanations for a successful action in restitution—witness Judge O'Briain in *O'Connor v Listowel UDC*[8] and the Supreme Court in *Rogers v Louth County Council*.[9] More recently, however, see *O'Callaghan v Ballincollig Holidays*.[10]

It has been argued[11] very persuasively that not only is Irish law very underdeveloped in this area, the jurisprudential basis upon which Irish law currently purports to sanction a broad and contemporary approach to restitution, that is, unjust enrichment as a cause of action that sits alongside contract and tort, is actually very tenuous given the doctrine of stare decisis.

Modern Irish Cases

20–04 The most significant Irish development on the jurisprudential basis upon which restitutionary relief is founded is the treatment of the topic by Keane J. in *Dublin Corp v Building and Allied Trade Union*.[12] Inspired perhaps by recent English case law that had rejected *Sinclair v Brougham*[13] but relying heavily on a creative interpretation of Irish case law, the learned judge declared, in the context of a claim for the return of compulsory purchase monies paid in order to allow the defendant to rebuild premises, such work not being done:

> "It is clear that, under our law, a person can in certain circumstances be obliged to effect restitution of money or other property to another where it would be unjust for him to retain the property. Moreover, as Henchy J. noted in *East Cork Foods Ltd v O'Dwyer Steel Co. Ltd*, this principle no longer rests on the fiction of an implied promise to return the property which, in the days when the forms of action still ruled English law, led to its tortuous rationalisation as being 'quasi-contractual' in nature.

---

[5] Unreported, High Court, July 14, 1976; [1993] R.L.R. 196.
[6] (1874) I.R. 6 C.L. 20.
[7] (1858) 5 I.C.L.R. 451.
[8] [1957] Ir. Jur. Rep. 43.
[9] [1981] I.R. 265; [1981] I.L.R.M. 144.
[10] Unreported, High Court, March 31, 1993.
[11] Cleary, "Restitution of Mistake of Law in Ireland" (2016) 55 *Irish Jurist* 25.
[12] [1996] 2 I.L.R.M. 547.
[13] [1914] A.C. 398.

The modern authorities in this and other common law jurisdictions, of which *Murphy v Attorney General* [1982] I.R. 241 is a leading Irish example have demonstrated that unjust enrichment exists as a distinctive legal concept, separate from both contract and tort, which in the words of Deane J. in the High Court of Australia in *Pavey & Matthews Pty. Ltd v Paul* (1987) 162 C.L.R. 221 at pp.256–257:

'... explains why the law recognises, in a variety of distinct categories of cases, an obligation on the part of a defendant to make fair and just restitution for a benefit derived at the expense of a plaintiff and which assists in the determination, by the ordinary process of legal reasoning, of the question of whether the law should, in justice, recognise the obligation in a new or developing category of case.'

The authorities also demonstrate that, while there is seldom any problem in ascertaining whether two essential preconditions for the application of the doctrine have been met—*i.e.* an enrichment of the defendant at the expense of the plaintiff—considerably more difficulty has been experienced in determining when the enrichment should be regarded as 'unjust' and whether there are any reasons why, even where it can be regarded as 'unjust', restitution should nevertheless be denied to the plaintiff.

As to the first of these difficulties, the law, as it has developed, has avoided the dangers of 'palm tree justice' by identifying whether the case belongs in a specific category which justifies so describing the enrichment: possible instances are money paid under duress or as a result of a mistake of fact or law or accompanied by a total failure of consideration. Whether the retention by the union of the entire compensation in the present case falls within such a category or not, however, it would in any event be necessary to consider whether restitution is precluded because of other factors."[14]

In *Criminal Assets Bureau v J.W.P.L,*[15] Feeney J. cited these observations of Keane J. but added some very useful observations of his own. Restitution applies to cases even where the person who receives the benefit may have done nothing wrong.[16] Restitution is not concerned with compensation for losses but rather with the return of unjust enrichments. The civil law here is:

---

[14] [1996] 2 I.L.R.M. 547 at 557–558. The earlier Irish cases, both direct and oblique, are well collected and put into context in O'Dell (1993) D.U.L.J. 27. These factors could include a desire to uphold the contract as the basis upon which the commercial relationship should be assessed, as well as anomalous consequences arising from the fact that compensation for breach of contract and compensation based on restitutionary principles are not the same: *Costello v MacDonald* [2011] EWCA Civ 930.

[15] [2007] IEHC 177.

[16] For an example, see subrogation cases such as *Primlake Ltd v Matthews Associates* [2006] EWHC 1227 (Ch) (wife blameless).

"... based upon reversing unjust enrichment on the part of a defendant. In doing that it involves removing from the defendant some accretion to his wealth which, in the eyes of the law, he should not be entitled to retain, or making the defendant pay for some non-money benefit on the basis that it would be wrong to allow him to retain it for nothing."[17]

Feeney J. noted that while restitution and compensatory principles overlap— e.g. a fiduciary buys trust property at undervalue (loss to the trust and gain to the wrongdoer will be the same)—the law is somewhat uncertain in scope where there is no loss to the claimant but there is a clear breach by the defendant which produces a benefit. While Feeney J. regarded the case cited to him, *AG v Blake*[18] as "exceptional", no mention was made of Irish case law that appears to sanction the disgorgement of gains that may not have caused any loss to the claimant.[19]

20–05 The most recent Irish decision not only regards *Dublin Corporation v Building and Allied Trade Union* as countenancing unjust enrichment as sweeping away much of the old law, it affords a six-fold classification of unjust enrichment.

The law of restitution recognises certain categories of "unjust" enrichment which may be categorised as follows:

    (a) mistake, where an enrichment is conferred on the defendant by reason of the plaintiff's mistake;

    (b) contracts discharged by breach, where the plaintiff seeks to recover a benefit that was conferred by him as part of his contractual performance, the contract itself having been discharged by breach of either the plaintiff or the defendant;

    (c) contracts discharged by frustration, where the plaintiff seeks to recover a benefit that was conferred by him as part of his contractual performance, the contract itself having been discharged by frustration;

    (d) legally recognised transactions which are void, voidable or otherwise ineffective where the plaintiff seeks to recover a benefit that was conferred by the plaintiff but where the transaction becomes unenforceable in law;

    (e) claims for the recovery of money or the recovery of a non money benefit and where the plaintiff has discharged the defendant's debt;

    (f) restitution for "wrongs".

---

[17] [2007] IEHC 177, para.3.2.

[18] [2001] 1 A.C. 268.

[19] See the discussion at (1978) N.I.L.Q. 128 of the *Hickey v Roches Stores* decision, as later discussed in *Vavasour v O'Reilly & Windsor Motors* [2005] IEHC 16 and *Duhan v Radius Television Production* [2007] IEHC 292. See also *Conneran and O'Reilly v Corbett & Sons Ltd* [2006] IEHC 254.

20–06 In this case, *Vanguard Auto Finance Ltd v Browne*,[20] the defendants were each involved in a development project undertaken by Browne Corporate Finance Ltd, the second defendant. Paula Browne, the first defendant, and Bairbre Wall, the third defendant, were involved in a transaction under which invoices were generated ostensibly to purchase goods to be used in fitting out the development, a responsibility undertaken by the third defendant. The invoices against which the bank paid advances to the third defendant were described by Barton J. as "a fiction": no goods of the description attached to either the invoices or the bank's payment printout had been purchased. The second defendant went into liquidation, and so the bank sought to obtain restitution from the first and third defendants, the third defendant having fed the cheque she received into the accounts of the second defendant via her own business account. Barton J. held that there had been a total failure of consideration in this case; further, the third defendant at the stage when the cheque was received must have been aware that the proceeds were intended for purposes to which they were not put.[21] Payments were recoverable as money had and received to the use of the plantiff.[22]

Recent English Decisions

20–07 In *Rowe v Vale of White Horse D.C.*[23] Lightman J. summarised the law of restitution in the following way:

"It is now authoritatively established that there are four essential ingredients to a claim in restitution:
  i) a benefit must have been gained by the defendant;
  ii) the benefit must have been obtained at the claimant's expense;
  iii) must be legally unjust, that is to say there must exist a factor (referred to as an unjust factor) rendering it unjust, for the defendant to retain the benefit;
  iv) there must be no defence available to extinguish or reduce the defendant's liability to make restitution."

20–08 The UK Supreme Court has endorsed this four-factor test in its most recent ruling in the *Menelaou* case. In *Bank of Cyprus UK Ltd v Menelaou*[24] Menelaou received a gift in the form of a property that was purchased for her by her parents. The purchase was financed by the bank agreeing to release charges of £2.2 million over the family home, that family home then being sold. £750,000 of the proceeds of sale were actually paid to the bank, reducing

---

[20] [2014] IEHC 465.
[21] *Bluestation Ltd v Kamyab* [2007] EWCA Civ 1073 applied.
[22] Following *Jones v Churcher* [2009] 2 Lloyd's Rep. 94.
[23] [2003] 1 Lloyd's Rep. 418.
[24] [2015] UKSC 66, applying *Benedelti v Sawiris* [2013] UKSC 50.

the £2.2 million debt with the balance owed of £1.45 million being charged against Menelaou's gifted property. Menelaou was registered as the proprietor but she did not sign the documents registering the charge—this was done by the conveyancing solicitor. Menelaou discovered the existence of the charge some 18 months later. Menelaou challenged the validity of the bank's charge against her property. The bank responded by seeking to obtain, via subrogation, an unpaid vendor's lien in relation to the purchase price paid by Menelaou's parents to the vendor of the acquired property (some £875,000). Lord Clarke considered that four questions must be asked:

"(1) Has the defendant been enriched?
(2) Was the enrichment at the claimant's expense?
(3) Was the enrichment unjust?
(4) Are there any defences available to the defendant?"

As Menelaou was unaware of the existence of the charge at the time of its creation, she could not be held to have acted unconscionably or fraudulently, but she was not a purchaser for value; she was a mere donee. As Lord Neuberger observed, the reason why the enrichment was unjust is attributable to the fact that the donee,

"received the freehold as a gift from her parents. Had she been a bona fide purchaser for full value, it may very well have been impossible to characterise her enrichment as unjust, especially if she had no notice of the Bank's rights. If she had paid a small sum to her parents for her acquisition, a difficult question might have had to be faced, although, as at presently advised, I think that her enrichment would still have been unjust, but the extent of any unjust enrichment would be reduced by the small sum. But she paid nothing, and she therefore cannot, in my view, be in any better position than her parents so far as the Bank's claim is concerned."

The exposition of the law in *Rowe v Vale of White Horse D.C.* has been cited and followed by the English courts on several occasions[25] and it is submitted that benefit-based claims of this kind have long been a part of Irish law. Thus, to sum up, Irish law recognises an independent cause of action in unjust enrichment. The "triggering" issue is whether the defendant has been enriched at the expense of the plaintiff. If so, the court proceeds to consider if such enrichment is unjust, by reference to determined categories into which the case at bar falls. The final issue is whether, notwithstanding the unjust enrichment, there are broader issues that point away from requiring the defendant to disgorge those ill-gotten gains.

---

[25] e.g. *Chief Constable of Greater Manchester v Wigan Athletic* [2009] 1 W.L.R. 1580; *Amin v Amin* [2009] EWHC 3356 (Ch); *Mahmood v Mitsubishi Europe B.V.* [2013] EWHC 44 (Ch).

20–09 For the sake of ease of exposition restitution will be broken into two parts: quasi-contractual claims on the one hand, and *quantum meruit* on the other.

Quasi-Contracts—Typically Restitution of Moneys Transferred by the Plaintiff

20–10 Efforts will often be made to defeat an unjust enrichment claim by seeking to argue that the case before the court will not fall within one of the accepted categories. The courts will resist such arguments in most cases. The category may be defined in a purposive or liberal fashion. But the weight of opinion appears to still favour the view that:

> "My lords, there is no general doctrine of unjust enrichment recognised in English law. What it does is to provide specific remedies in particular cases of what might be classified as unjust enrichment in a legal system which is based upon the civil law."[26]

In *Gibb v Maidstone & Tunbridge Wells NHS Trust*[27] Laws L.J. was concerned with what could be described as the ambiguity of the law when the court is faced with a search for legal principle and a desire to avoid injustice: after citing conflicting views on a court's jurisdiction vis-à-vis unjust enrichment jurisprudence, he went on:

> "There is, I think, something of a tension underneath this reasoning. It is between these two propositions. (1) The categories of unjust enrichment claims cannot be closed, for if they were this branch of the law would be condemned to ossify for no apparent reason; and nothing could be further from the common law's incremental method. But (2) such a claim must fall 'within one of the hitherto established categories of unjust enrichment' which suggests (at least) that the categories rather than any overriding principle are paramount. The authorities' reluctance to assert first principles may be ascribed to the justified fear of the palm tree: if the principle of unjust enrichment does no more than to invite one judge after another, case by case, to declare that this or that enrichment is inherently just or unjust, it is not much of a principle."

(1) Mistake of fact and law

20–11 Earlier in this book, through the leading Irish mistake cases, one central proposition was established to which we now return. Payments made on the basis of a mistaken belief are generally recoverable if the mistake is fun-

---

[26] Per Lord Diplock in *Orakpo v Manson Investments* [1978] A.C. 95 at 104.
[27] [2010] EWCA Civ 678.

damental and relates to the terms of the contract. The general rule was stated thus by Parke B. in *Kelly v Solari*[28]:

> "Where money is paid to another under the influence of a mistake, that is, upon the supposition that a specific fact is true which would entitle the other to the money, but which fact is untrue and the money would not have been paid if it had been known to the payer that the fact was untrue, an action will lie to recover it back."[29]

This dictum was endorsed in Ireland by Budd J. in *National Bank Ltd v O'Connor & Bowmaker Ireland Ltd*[30] and it provides an important exception to the general rule that payments voluntarily made are irrecoverable. There are, however, some important restrictions on this restitutionary principle.

20–12 In an important article[31] which explores the basis upon which Irish courts have provided restitution for mistaken payments, Cleary argues that Irish judges have proceeded upon two distinct routes. The first, where the mistake is described as a liability mistake, requires the payor to be mistaken about a factual matter that, if true, would render the payor to be liable to the payee for the sums so paid. The second route requires the court to characterise the mistake as being "fundamental" or a "basic" error. In contrast, most common law jurisdictions have shifted towards a more flexible causative mistake test—but for the error the money would not have been paid—and Cleary concludes that the future adoption in Ireland of a causative mistake test is no panacea.[32] Cleary also points out that as Irish law currently stands, mistakes of law cannot trigger restitution until the Supreme Court reverses earlier case law. In historical terms, if the mistake could be characterised as one of law, then it was not possible to order restitution. A mistake as to the interpretation of a Public General Act is a mistake of law—see *O'Loghlen v O'Callaghan*[33] and *Jackson v Stopford*[34]—as is a mistake based upon the misinterpretation of delegated legislation; see *Holt v Markham*.[35] The Supreme Court's decision in *Casey v Irish Sailors and Soldiers Land Trust*[36] is illustrative. A trust was established under statute to provide and administer a scheme for the provision of cottages for ex-servicemen. The trustees charged rent for the cottages provided but in *Leggett v Irish Sailors and Soldiers Land Trust*[37] the Supreme Court held that the plaintiffs in that action should not have paid rent. Casey and others brought

---

[28] (1841) 9 M. & W. 54.
[29] (1841) 9 M. & W. 54 at 58; *Rover International Ltd v Cannon Film Sales (No. 3)* [1989] 3 All E.R. 423.
[30] (1966) 103 I.L.T.R. 73.
[31] (2016) 55 Irish Jurist 25.
[32] (2016) 55 Irish Jurist 25 at 28–29.
[33] (1874) I.R. 8 C.L. 116.
[34] [1923] 2 I.R. 1.
[35] [1923] 1 K.B. 504.
[36] [1937] I.R. 208.
[37] Unreported, Supreme Court, 1923, cited in [1937] I.R. 208.

actions to recover the rent paid under their illegal tenancy agreement with the trustees. The Supreme Court, applying *Sharp Brothers & Knight v Chant*,[38] affirmed that "the rule that money paid under a mistake of law cannot be recovered back is founded upon principles of convenience as well as justice. The rule has been so long and so firmly established that it cannot be called into question."[39]

20–13 In *Kleinwort Benson Ltd v Lincoln City Council*,[40] the majority of the House of Lords held that there is a general right to recover money paid under a mistake, whether that mistake be one of fact or law. Their Lordships also resisted an argument that in cases of mistake of law, restitution should not be possible if the mistake related to a settled understanding of the law, particularly in relation to private law transactions as distinct from the payment of taxes, for example. Their Lordships also rejected a further defence of honest receipt of the payment[41] and declared that restitution will still be possible under a void contract notwithstanding the fact that the contract has been fully performed.[42] The Irish Supreme Court will have to consider whether it will follow the lead given by the House of Lords in judicially abrogating the rule, but until then the rule is one that is binding on Irish courts. Notwithstanding the weight of authority underpinning the distinction, the Supreme Court, in *Harris v Quigley and Irwin*,[43] has indicated that it will be prepared to formally overrule the earlier line of authority when the opportunity presents itself. In this case the issue before the Supreme Court was one of statutory interpretation: did s.934(6) of the Taxes Consolidation Act 1997 require the Revenue Commissioners to refund income tax that the Appeal Commissioners had ruled to have been overpaid, pending the outcome of a case stated brought by the Revenue Commissioners? While much of the judgment of the Supreme Court concentrated on issues of statutory interpretation, the Supreme Court found that the statute did not close off a common law action. In delivering the Supreme Court judgment, Geoghegan J. observed that Keane J.'s judgment in *O'Rourke v Revenue Commissioners*[44] correctly represented Irish law. Thus, it is clear that Irish law has recognised that a mistake of law will not preclude restitution of taxes or other charges that are the result of a misinterpretation of a statute, for example. *Harris v Quigley and Irwin* goes further in holding that

---

[38] [1917] 1 K.B. 770.
[39] [1937] I.R. 208 at 222 per Murnaghan J. However, if money is paid under ultra vires tax demands, a general restitutionary principle may operate: *Woolwich Building Society v I.R.C.* [1993] A.C. 70.
[40] [1999] 2 A.C. 349. Cleary points out that the Supreme Court has not overruled the mistake of law obstacle to granting restitutionary reliefs and, in a rather perverse way, some Irish judges regarded the *Kleinwort Benson* ruling in the House of Lords as establishing a general defence of mistake of law in Ireland: (2016) 55 Irish Jurist 25 at 42–44.
[41] Based on Brennan J.'s suggestion in *David Securities Pty Ltd v Commonwealth Bank of Australia* (1992) 175 C.L.R. 353.
[42] [1999] 2 A.C. 349 at 385 per Lord Goff.
[43] [2006] 1 I.L.R.M. 401.
[44] [1996] 2 I.R. 1.

interest as well as principal sums will also be caught by the unjust enrichment and the duty to make good (in Geoghegan J.'s words the "over-retention of tax"[45]), but a mistake of law remains problematical.

20–14 Even if a mistake of law was successfully established, there were often ways of avoiding the full force of this arbitrary rule. In *Casey's* case counsel for the various plaintiffs argued that the statutory authority vested in the trustees created, vis-à-vis their tenants, a fiduciary relationship. The Supreme Court rejected this argument, holding that there existed only a statutory tenancy. The argument was made in order to avail of certain English cases which establish that restitution may be ordered even following a mistake of law when there has been a breach of trust by the defendant. The Privy Council, in *Kiriri Cotton Co v Dewani*[46] affirmed *Rogers v Ingham*[47] in which James L.J. indicated that equity sometimes provided relief by way of restitution if the case involved something more than a mere mistake of law. Lord Denning in *Kiriri Cotton* indicated that if the obligation to observe the law is to be placed on the shoulders of one of the parties, as against the other, the parties to the contract are not *in pari delicto*. While in this case Lord Denning also stressed that the duty imposed by law should be imposed in order to protect the other person, this requirement, it is submitted, has been quietly dropped in later cases (e.g. *Shelley v Paddock*[48]). As a result it can be confidently stated that where the parties are not equally situated and, in particular, when the payee has either a duty vis-à-vis the plaintiff, or perhaps is simply in a better position to ascertain the true state of the law, or indeed is primarily responsible for making the error in interpretation (negligently or otherwise), then the payee may be obliged to make restitution. The Irish cases which adopt this approach, like *Kiriri Cotton* itself, do not actually require a fiduciary relationship to be shown. In *Dolan v Neligan*[49] overpayments made by the plaintiff to the Revenue as a result of an incorrect interpretation of ss.30 and 31 of the Customs Consolidation Act 1876 were held to be recoverable within *Kiriri Cotton*. No fiduciary relationship existed between the payee and the plaintiff importer, but Kenny J. in the High Court held that the defendant, a collector of customs, had been responsible for making the incorrect demand. While the Supreme Court in *Dolan v Neligan* did not find it necessary to consider the decision in *Kiriri Cotton*, the dictum of Lord Denning was later endorsed in the Supreme Court in *Rogers v Louth County Council*.[50] An overpayment made by the plaintiff in order to redeem an annuity was held recoverable even though at the time of payment both parties believed the sum calculated was correctly estimated by the defendant council in accordance with guidelines provided by the then Department of Local Government. The error only came to light after the demand had been

---

[45] [2006] 1 I.L.R.M. 401 at 404.
[46] [1960] A.C. 192.
[47] (1876) 3 Ch D 351.
[48] [1980] 2 W.L.R. 647.
[49] [1967] I.R. 247.
[50] [1981] I.L.R.M. 144.

made, as a result of a Supreme Court decision on the correct interpretation of the relevant statutory provision, s.99 of the Housing Act 1966. These facts were held to be sufficient to bring the case within *Kiriri Cotton*: "the plaintiff's solicitor could not be expected to know the redemption price. He relied on the defendants to give him the correct figure."[51] Hamilton J. in the High Court in *Dublin Corp v Trinity College Dublin*[52] has also endorsed the view that *Kiriri Cotton* means that a mistake of law for which one person is "primarily responsible" can oblige that person to make restitution. Hamilton J.'s decision was later reversed by the Supreme Court but on another ground.

20–15 The House of Lords in *Woolwich Building Society v IRC*[53] suggested that the mistake of law rule could be given a narrow interpretation. In *O'Rourke v Revenue Commissioners*,[54] Keane J. cited the following extract from Lord Goff's judgment with approval:

"I would therefore hold that money paid by a citizen to a public authority in the form of taxes or other levies paid pursuant to an *ultra vires* demand by the authority is prima facie recoverable by the citizen as of right. As at present advised, I incline to the opinion that this principle should extend to embrace cases in which the tax or other levy has been wrongly exacted by the public authority, not because the demand was *ultra vires* but for other reasons, for example, because the authority has misconstrued a relevant statute or regulation. It is not, however, necessary to decide the point in the present case, and in any event cases of this kind are generally the subject of a statutory regime which legislates for the circumstances in which money so paid either must or may be repaid. Nor do I think it necessary to consider for the purposes of the present case to what extent the common law may provide the public authority with a defence to a claim for the repayment of money so paid: though for the reasons I have already given I do not consider the principle of recovery should be inapplicable simply because the citizen has paid the money under a mistake of law."

The House of Lords, in *Deutsche Morgan Grenfell v IRC*,[55] has held that where tax is demanded and paid by a taxpayer on the foot of a statutory provision that is contrary to Community law, the taxpayer may seek restitution on the basis of either a claim for the repayment of tax unlawfully demanded or by pleading mistake of law. In this situation the claimant was entitled to take advantage of

---

[51] [1981] I.L.R.M. 144 per Kenny J. at 148.
[52] [1985] I.L.R.M. 283.
[53] [1993] A.C. 70. If a person makes a payment taking the risk that the view taken by him or her might be wrong, this is not a payment made by virtue of a mistake: *Brennan v Bolt Burdon* [2005] Q.B. 303; *Marine Trade SA v Pioneer Freight Futures Co Ltd* [2009] EWHC 2656 (Comm).
[54] Unreported, High Court, December 18, 1996.
[55] [2006] UKHL 49; on interest see *Sempra Metals Ltd v IRC* [2007] 4 All E.R. 657 and *Harris v Quigley and Irwin* [2006] 1 I.L.R.M 401; Yip, "Use Value of Money" (2010) 30 L.S. 586.

the longer limitation period available in relation to a mistake of law claim. For a common law claim to be available to the claimant, however, any statutory provisions must be construed in order to consider whether Parliament intended to limit or exclude any common law remedy.[56] If the intention of Parliament is clearly intended to have such an exclusionary effect it matters not that the claim is dressed up as a mistake of law or another cause of action such as the *ultra vires* demand under the *Woolwich Building Society* case.[57]

20–16 In the most recent decision of the UK Supreme Court on financial issues, *Pitt v Holt*[58] a case in which a carer for her mentally incapacitated husband agreed to proposals for a voluntary disposition of property put to her by her tax advisers in order to reduce inheritance tax liability, the Supreme Court set aside the special needs trust instrument in question because the advisers had not framed the instruments correctly. The UK Supreme Court endorsed a general conscience test (at least in relation to voluntary dispositions) made on the basis of mistaken facts and law. Unconscionability is to be evaluated on an objective basis. Their Lordships said[59]:

> "The gravity of the mistake must be assessed by a close examination of the facts, whether or not they are tested by cross-examination, including the circumstances of the mistake and its consequences for the person who made the vitiated disposition. Other findings of fact may also have to be made in relation to change of position or other matters relevant to the exercise of the court's discretion. Justice Paul Finn wrote in a paper, Equitable Doctrine and Discretion in Remedies published in *Restitution: Past, Present and Future* (1998):
>
>> 'The courts quite consciously now are propounding what are acceptable standards of conduct to be exhibited in our relationships and dealings with others …. A clear consequence of this emphasis on standards (and not on rules) is a far more instance-specific evaluation of conduct.'
>
> The injustice (or unfairness or unconscionableness) of leaving a mistaken disposition uncorrected must be evaluated objectively, but with an intense focus (in Lord Steyn's well-known phrase in *In re S (A Child)* [2005] 1 A.C. 593. Para.17) on the facts of the particular case."

While in Ireland *Kiriri Cotton* has triggered a subtle change in the area of restitution there are other, perhaps more soundly based, exceptions to the general rule that a mistake of law cannot ground restitution of overpayments made. If there is a misrepresentation by the defendant there is a possibility of

---

[56] *Johnson v Unisys* [2001] 2 All E.R. 801; *Deutsche Morgan Grenfell v IRC* [2006] UKHL 49; *Monroe v Commissioners for HM Revenue and Customs* [2008] EWCA Civ 306.
[57] *Monroe v Commissioners for HM Revenue and Customs* [2008] EWCA Civ 306.
[58] [2013] UKSC 26.
[59] [2013] UKSC 26, para.126.

restitution by virtue of the misrepresentation. In *Carse v Taylor*[60] the plaintiff paid money to the defendant on the basis of a statement that the defendant was the administrator of the deceased, Mary Scott. The plaintiff made the payment fearing that civil execution was about to be levied against him. It later transpired that Mary Scott was not dead and the defendant was not able, in law, to be the administrator of a living person's estate. The defendant argued, distinguishing the annuity case of *Strickland v Turner*,[61] that this was a mistake of law. The Irish Court of Queen's Bench held that the misrepresentation entitled the plaintiff to recover the payments made. This case would seem to come within the test propounded by Whiteside C.J. in *O'Loghlen v O'Callaghan*[62] in which it was said that restitution of moneys overpaid may be ordered if "mala fides ... fraud or imposition" is practised. An example of *mala fides* (suppression of facts which may have led the plaintiff to refuse to make the payment) is provided by *Leonard v Leonard*.[63]

20–17 The other important exception to the position established by, inter alia, *Casey v Irish Sailors and Soldiers Land Trusts Co*[64] stems from a dictum of Lord Westbury in *Cooper v Phibbs*,[65] when he observed that the private right of ownership is a matter of fact even though it may also be the result of a matter of law: "If parties contract under a mutual mistake and misapprehension as to their relative and respective rights, the result is that the agreement is liable to be set aside as having proceeded upon a common mistake."[66] While this dictum is clearly in step with the decision of the Irish Court of Chancery,[67] it provides difficulties in reconciling the cases. It is clear that whenever the boundary between fact and law becomes pertinent the courts endeavour to characterise the mistake as one of fact or title. In *Platt v Casey's Drogheda Brewery*,[68] overpayments made to debenture holders on foot of a mistaken interpretation of their rights under statute were held to be recoverable as made on a mistake of fact, not law; see *National Pari Mutuel Association Ltd v R.*[69]

20–18 If the plaintiff overcomes the hurdle presented by the aphorism, "money paid under a mistake of fact may be recovered but money paid under a mistake of law cannot", described by Kenny J. in *Rogers v Louth County Council* as "grossly inaccurate",[70] there are two other obstacles to recovery. First, it is by no means clear whether the mistake of fact is operative if, when the payment

---

[60] (1858) 5 I.C.L.R. 451.
[61] (1852) 7 Exch. 208.
[62] (1874) I.R. 8 C.L. 116.
[63] (1812) 2 Ball & B. 171. See *Vanguard Auto Finance Ltd v Browne* [2014] IEHC 465 in which fraud was negatived.
[64] [1937] I.R. 208.
[65] (1867) L.R. 2 H.L. 149.
[66] (1867) L.R. 2 H.L. 149 at 170.
[67] (1865) 17 Ir.Ch.R. 73.
[68] [1912] 1 I.R. 271.
[69] (1930) 47 T.L.R. 110.
[70] [1981] I.L.R.M. 144 at 148.

was made, the person making the payment knew that he was not in law liable to make the payment to the payee. The distinction is illustrated by a simple example, taken from *Cheshire, Fifoot and Furmston's Law of Contract*.[71] A has given B a sum of money in the erroneous belief that B is pursuing a particular piece of research or has no means of subsistence. Can A sue B in quasi-contract when he discovers his error? There is a clear mistake of fact but the payment, according to at least one nineteenth-century case,[72] is irrecoverable because the payment was made voluntarily without the belief that there existed a legal liability. More recent cases, however, adopt a more liberal approach,[73] and it is now established that money mistakenly paid will be recoverable if paid in order to discharge a liability owed by the person making the payment. Thus, if a bank makes a payment to the defendant in circumstances where the payment was gratuitous (i.e. consideration is absent) recovery is still possible by the bank (see Budd J. in *National Bank Ltd v O'Connor & Bowmaker Ireland Ltd*[74]) if the mistake is a "fundamental" one.

20–19 The second obstacle to recovery arises when the payment involves more than two parties. Despite some English authorities which favoured the view that the payment must be made to a person to whom the payer is obliged as against a third party, Budd J. in *National Bank Ltd v O'Connor & Bowmaker Ireland Ltd* indicated that the mistake need not apply inter partes. Budd J. summarised his conclusions thus:

"It is not easy to reconcile all the decisions with regard to the recovery of money paid under a mistake of fact. It is therefore difficult to arrive at a precise statement as to when in law money thus paid is recoverable. Reviewing the authorities cited and others it can however, I think, safely be said that it can be so recovered in the following circumstances. First where it has been proved that it has been paid under a mistake of fact. It must be a fundamental mistake but no question really arises here as to that because such mistakes as arose were obviously of that nature in this case. It is of course necessary in order to establish a mistake of fact to show that the fact supposed to be true was untrue, and that the money would not have been paid if it was known that the fact was untrue. Secondly, it must be shown that the mistake was as to a fact, which, if true, would make the payer either liable or under a duty to pay the money. Having regard to the decision in *Waring and Gillow Ltd* I am satisfied, however, that the mistake has not been shown to be a mistaken belief on the part of the payer that he was under a liability to pay the payee. It is sufficient if it be shown that the payer was under a mistaken belief that he was under an obligation to pay someone and that

---

[71] 14th edn (London: Butterworth, 2001), p.738. This chapter was dropped from the 15th and 16th editions.
[72] *Aiken v Short* (1856) 1 H. & N. 210 at 215 per Bramwell B.
[73] *Larner v London County Council* [1949] 1 All E.R. 964.
[74] (1966) 103 I.L.T.R. 73.

payment to the actual payee would be appropriate and would discharge the obligation.

There is then another matter to be considered. It is urged on the part of the defendant O'Connor that the mistake must be inter partes and there is a good deal to support this in the cases cited. But just what it means is difficult to say. I am not satisfied that it must necessarily exist as between payer and payee exclusively. There seems to be no logical reason why it should be so confined. There would seem no logical reason why a mistake between the payer and the person to whom the supposed obligation exists should not also involve a mistake as between payer and payee. In other words why a mistake between the payer and the other two parties should not be equally well a mistake inter partes as regards both.

Moreover the case of *Jones Ltd v Waring and Gillow Ltd* indicates that where the supposed obligation is to pay someone and a person to whom such supposed obligation does not exist, but who it is supposed can give a discharge, is paid, the money is recoverable."[75]

(2) Unlawful demands for tax to be paid

20–20 This head of unjust conduct was created in 1992 by the House of Lords in *Woolwich Equitable Building Society v IRC*,[76] as a way around the rule preventing mistakes of law per se to ground a restitutionary claim. A distinction has been drawn between this situation and cases where a taxpayer files a tax return and makes the payment, absent a demand: *NEC Semi-Conductors Ltd v Revenue and Customs Commissioners*.[77] Case law from Canada[78] and the *FII Group* decision of the UK Supreme Court[79] now clearly rejects this dichotomy. Lord Sumption,[80] in reviewing the *Woolwich line*, said that:

"The word 'demand' as it was used in the speeches in *Woolwich Equitable* referred in my view simply to a situation in which payment was being required by the taxpayer without lawful authority. Nothing in the principle applying the decision turned on the mechanism by which that requirement was communicated to the taxpayer."

(3) Total failure of consideration

20–21 Where one contracting party has not received any part of that contracted for, it is said that there is a total failure of consideration. In this context consideration takes on a narrower meaning than that utilised for the

---

75 (1966) 103 I.L.T.R. 73 at 96; *Jones Ltd v Waring and Gillow* [1926] A.C. 670.
76 [1992] 3 All E.R. 737.
77 [2006] EWCA Civ 25.
78 *Air Canada v British Columbia* (1989) 59 D.L.R. (4th) 161, per Wilson J., endorsed by the Supreme Court of Canada in *Kingstreet Investments Ltd v New Brunswick (Finance)* [2007] 1 S.C.R. 3.
79 *Test Claimants in the FII Group Litigation v Inland Revenue* [2012] UKSC 1.
80 [2012] UKSC 1, para.174.

purpose of determining whether a contract has been formed. As Lord Simon put it in the *Fibrosa* case:

> "In the law relating to the formation of contract, the promise to do a thing may often be the consideration, but when one is considering the law of failure of consideration and of the quasi-contractual right to recover money on that ground it is, generally speaking, not the promise which is referred to but the performance of the promise."[81]

So, if there is defective performance by one contracting party in circumstances entitling the other party to rescind the contract (breach of an express or implied condition, for example), the injured party may pursue whatever contractual remedies are available or elect instead to claim restitution. If, however, there has not been a total failure of consideration the quasi-contractual remedy will not be available, and if the defendant has a valid defence in contract to the plaintiff's action (frustration, for example) the plaintiff may not have any financial remedy at all. Monies paid over and retained in respect of an illegal licence fee may be recovered by the payer in an action for restitution; in such a case there may be a failure of a distinct and severable part of the consideration; see *Roxborough v Rothmans of Pall Mall Australia Ltd*.[82]

20–22 Examples of total failure of consideration can be found in several Irish cases. In *Hayes v Stirling*[83] the plaintiff made a payment to the defendant, a putative director of a company to be formed in the future. The payment was made in order to secure shares in the company. The company was never established. The Court of Exchequer held the money recoverable on the basis of a consideration that had wholly failed. Similarly, in *P v P*,[84] money was paid in consideration of marriage. The marriage was a nullity. The money paid was recoverable for total failure of consideration. The terms of the bargain, however, should be closely scrutinised, for if it is clear that one person is taking the risk that the shared venture will not result in a tangible benefit accruing to that person, then recovery in quasi-contract may not be possible. Witness cases where the buyer of real and personal property knows and accepts that there is a possibility that the property is not the seller's to dispose of; see *Griffin v Caddell*[85] and s.12 of the Sale of Goods Act 1893, as amended by the Sale of Goods and Supply of Services Act 1980.

20–23 If the plaintiff seeks restitution of money paid it will be fatal to the claim for the court to conclude that the plaintiff received any part of the promised consideration. *Hayes v Stirling*[86] should be contrasted with *Lecky*

---

[81] *Fibrosa Spolka Akcyjna v Fairbairn Lawson Combe Barbour Ltd* [1943] A.C. 32.
[82] (2001) 208 C.L.R. 516, criticised by Jaffey, "Failure of Consideration: *Roxborough v Rothmans*" (2003) 66 M.L.R. at 284.
[83] (1863) Ir. C.L.R. 277.
[84] [1916] 2 I.R. 400.
[85] (1875) I.R. 9 C.L. 488.
[86] (1863) Ir. C.L.R. 277.

v Walter.[87] In the latter case the plaintiff purchased shares on the basis of a misrepresentation. The shares were virtually worthless. It was nevertheless impossible to say the consideration had wholly failed. In *Robertson v Swift*[88] the English Court of Appeal rejected a claim to the return of a deposit initially paid by a consumer to a home removals company, the consumer cancelling the contract under the UK Regulations governing contracts concluded away from business premises. The basis of the restitutionary claim was total failure of consideration but because the service provider had made urgent arrangements and entered external financial commitments to carry out the work, at the claimant's request, there was not a total failure of consideration. Similarly, in *Stapleton v Prudential Assurance*[89] restitution of insurance premiums paid by the plaintiff on foot of a voidable contract was denied because there was no failure of consideration; while no claim on the policy had been made, she was covered by the policy throughout the duration of the period in which the contract was valid.

20–24 In contrast, it does not follow that because the plaintiff received some tangible benefit a court will be constrained to hold that a total failure of consideration did not result. While the leading English case is *Rowland v Divall*,[90] the Irish case of *Chartered Trust Ireland Ltd v Healy & Commins*[91] illustrates this point. Healy hired a truck on hire-purchase terms. The transaction was financed by the plaintiff finance company. It later transpired that the truck was illegally brought into the State and was not in fact the vehicle it was represented to be. Barron J. held the contract was null and void and awarded Healy the return of all moneys paid by way of hire-purchase instalments and all other payments made in pursuance of the agreement, following *United Dominions Trust (Ireland) v Shannon Caravans Ltd.*[92] The fact that Healy had used the truck for over a year did not mean that he had received any part of the consideration; in contracts of sale, title to the property, and in hire-purchase cases, the option to purchase, is seen as the consideration. Because the action is not brought for damages for breach of contract, but rather in quasi-contract, there is no allowance made for the benefits that have accrued under the contract. The view that appears to be gaining ground is that the fact that the plaintiff has received some benefit (e.g. payment of interest but not capital on a voidable loan) is not payment of consideration, but, even if it were, the fact that the plaintiff can restore the benefit conferred, will keep the plaintiff within this exception: contrast *Baltic Shipping Co v Dillon*[93] with *Goss v Chilcott*.[94]

---

[87]   [1914] I.R. 378.
[88]   [2012] EWCA Civ 1794. Reversed at [2014] UKSC 50 on a point of statutory interpretation.
[89]   (1928) 62 I.L.T.R. 56.
[90]   [1923] 2 K.B. 500; *Rover International Ltd v Cannon Film Sales Ltd* [1989] 3 All E.R. 423.
[91]   Unreported, High Court, December 10, 1985.
[92]   [1976] I.R. 225.
[93]   (1992) 176 C.L.R. 345; *Wilmot-Smith* [2013] C.L.J. 414.
[94]   [1996] A.C. 788.

(4) Money paid under a conditional contract

20–25 When a contract is conditional upon a stated event occurring and the event does not occur it is possible to maintain an action for the recovery of money paid in furtherance of the conditional contract, unless there is an express clause to the contrary. In *Lowis v Wilson*[95] the plaintiff agreed to purchase the defendant's land "subject to contract". She declined to proceed with the sale and successfully maintained an action for the return of the deposit paid to the defendant on the ground that it was money paid without consideration. Recovery depends on the terms of the contract and nature of the consideration. However, a non-returnable deposit, if clearly stipulated for, may not be the subject of restitution. This has been the subject of some quite extensive litigation in England and Wales in recent years.[96]

(5) Money paid or property transferred in consequence of a void contract

20–26 While it is clear that restitution of money paid under a void contract will be recoverable, either as being paid under a mistake of fact of a fundamental nature (see *National Bank Ltd v O'Connor & Bowmaker Ireland Ltd*[97]) or of law, or because there is a total failure of consideration (see *Chartered Trust Ireland Ltd v Healy & Commins*[98]) there are difficulties when the contract is void because of some statutory provision; readers should refer to the discussion on the effects of s.1 of the Infants Relief Act 1874.[99] Nevertheless, the House of Lords in *Kleinwort Benson Ltd v Lincoln City Council*[100] rejected the view that restitution was not possible under a void contract, even if the contract has been fully performed. Equitable relief may be available in relation to the exercise of contractual or similar powers that may render a legal act void or voidable. Irish courts have discussed the possibility of holding that where a trustee exercises a discretion in relation to powers, in good faith, but the exercise of those powers may not produce the results expected, then it may be that any instrument may be held to be void (and thus give rise to restitutionary reliefs). The leading case in England is *Hastings–Bass v Inland Revenue Commissioners*,[101] as developed in *Sieff v Fox*[102] in which a parallel jurisdiction to set aside gifts for mistake was discussed.[103] More recent English cases[104] are reading *Hastings–Bass* as being a narrow interventionary equitable

---

[95] [1949] I.R. 347.

[96] See the case law discussed in *Sharma v Simposh Ltd* [2011] EWCA Civ 1383. Section 54 of the Land and Conveyancing Law Reform Act 2009, however, shadows s.49(2) of the Law of Property Act 1925 (UK) to allow a court to override a contract and allow return of a deposit where "just and equitable so to do".

[97] (1966) 103 I.L.T.R. 103.

[98] Unreported, High Court, December 10, 1985.

[99] Chapter 16.

[100] [1999] 2 A.C. 349.

[101] [1975] Ch. 25.

[102] [2005] 3 All E.R. 693.

[103] e.g. *Ellis v Ellis* (1909) 26 T.L.R. 166; *Gibbon v Mitchell* [1990] 3 All E.R. 338.

[104] *Smithson v Hamilton* [2007] EWHC 2900 (Ch); *Thorpe v Commissioners for Her Majesty's Revenue and Customs* [2008] UKSPC SPC 00683.

principle, and Finlay Geoghegan J. in *Boliden Tara Mines Ltd v Cosgrove*[105] declined to exercise this broader jurisdiction; the courts are clearly conscious of using a jurisdiction that can be criticised as allowing rectification "by the back door" in too liberal a manner. In *Futter v Revenue and Customs*[106] the UK Supreme Court has sought to restrict the impact of *Hastings–Bass* by holding that where relief is given, the effect is to render the transaction voidable, not void, thus making the relief subject to other factors such as intervening third party rights. The UK Supreme Court also drew distinctions between instances where a trustee commits an error going beyond the scope of a power (excessive execution), and an error in failing to give proper consideration to matters prior to making a decision (inadequate deliberation). The effect of this distinction is that for the rule to apply in cases of inadequate deliberation the conduct of the trustees must amount to a breach of fiduciary duty. The Supreme Court did not overrule the leading void contract case of *Cloutte v Storey*[107] on fraudulent appointments but said this may have to be "revisited one day".

20–27 Payments made on a void agreement have been held to provide the factual basis for an unjust enrichment: *Eastbourne B.C. v Foster*[108] and *Gibb v Maidstone and Tunbridge Wells NHS Trust*.[109]

(6) Money paid or property transferred on foot of an illegal contract

20–28 Return of money or property transferred under an illegal contract is recoverable if there can be some cause of action utilised which does not require disclosure of the illegal purpose contemplated by the illegal performance, but this method of avoiding the *in pari delicto* rule is not always likely to lead to success; see *Taylor v Chester*.[110] Where the source of the illegality is some compelling moral imperative, restitution will be denied. In *Brady v Flood*[111] money paid to secure the discontinuance of criminal charges brought against the plaintiff's sons was held irrecoverable. Similarly, if the source of the illegality is a statutory provision the statute itself may declare whether there is to be restitution. If statute declares a moneylending transaction illegal it is unlikely that an action upon the contract or for restitution of the principal moneys advanced will succeed.[112] Unrelated instances of misuse, however, may ground restitution for unjust enrichment. In *Close v Wilson*[113] money was transferred by the plaintiff to the defendant for the express purpose of funding betting. The transaction was void but when the defendant diverted part of the

---

[105] [2007] IEHC 60, following *Irish Pensions Trust Ltd v Central Remedial Clinic* [2005] IEHC 87.
[106] [2013] UKSC 26.
[107] [1911] 1 Ch. 18.
[108] [2003] I.C.R. 234.
[109] [2010] EWCA Civ 678.
[110] (1869) L.R. 4 Q.B. 309. Contrast *Patel v Mirza* [2014] EWCA Civ 1047.
[111] (1841) 6 *Circuit Cases* 309.
[112] *Irvine v Teague* (1898) 32 I.L.T.R. 109; *Handelman v Davis* (1937) 71 I.L.T.R. 268.
[113] [2011] EWCA Civ 5.

fund for his own use, the English Court of Appeal ordered an inquiry, by way of a new trial, into the amount of the funds that were misused in order to allow restitution of that amount.

20–29 The exceptions to the *in pari delicto* rule should also be remembered; if the parties are not *in pari delicto* or if one party has perpetrated a fraud on the other, as in *Shelley v Paddock*,[114] for example, or if there has been repentence before the illegal objective has been substantially performed, then there exists the possibility of restitution for the more deserving party to the illegal contract. In *Byrne v Rudd*[115] the plaintiff entered into an illegal insurance contract following the fraudulent misrepresentations of an insurance agent. The insurance company was held not to be entitled to retain the premiums obtained from the plaintiff, for, in these circumstances, they were not to benefit from the fraud of a third party, i.e. the agent.

(7) Restitution from a wrongdoer

20–30 As we have seen in relation to cases of pre-contractual misrepresentation, whether the claim is brought for a breach of contract or in tort such as the tort of deceit,[116] the wrongdoer will be obliged to make restitution should the claimant select such a head of loss. A misrepresentation on the part of the defendant may give rise to a mistake on the part of the claimant.[117] In *Mallett and Sons (Antiques) Ltd v Rogers*,[118] the plaintiff purchased an antique bookcase on the strength of a representation that it was owned by the defendant. The item had in fact been stolen. Restitution was ordered of the purchase price. Into this well-established area of law comes the relatively vitiating factor of duress. English case law suggests *obiter* that rescission for duress should be based upon the rules applicable to undue influence.[119]

20–31 Suppose the plaintiff pays money or transfers property to the defendant because the defendant has made an unwarranted demand which the plaintiff is in no position to resist. The emerging doctrine of economic duress suggests that the plaintiff can seek the return of his property or money even if the threat made, if carried out, would not be independently actionable; see *Universe Tankships of Monrovia v International Transport Workers Federation*.[120] The possibility of restitution by way of an action for money had and received has long existed in English law; witness the dictum of Willes J. in *Great Western Railway Co v Sutton*:

---

[114] [1980] 2 W.L.R. 647.
[115] [1920] 2 I.R. 12, applying *Hughes v Liverpool Victoria Friendly Society* [1916] 2 K.B. 482.
[116] *London Allied Holdings Ltd v Lee* [2007] EWHC 2061 (Ch) is a remarkable recent example.
[117] *Blue Station Ltd v Kamyab* [2007] EWCA Civ 1073.
[118] [2005] IEHC 131, also an important decision on damages.
[119] *Halpern v Halpern (No.2)* [2007] 3 All E.R. 478.
[120] [1982] 2 W.L.R. 803; *Kolmar Group AG v Traxpo Enterprises PVT Ltd* [2010] EWHC 113 (Comm).

"I have always understood that when a man pays more than he is bound to do by law for the performance of a duty which the law says is owed to him for nothing, or for less than he has paid, there is a compulsion or concession in respect of which he is entitled to recover the excess by *conditio indebiti*, or action for money had and received. This is every day's practice as to excess freight."[121]

This dictum, later restated by Reading C.J. in *Maskell v Horner*,[122] was applied in the Irish case of *Great Southern and Western Railway Co v Robertson*.[123]

20–32 An action for money paid to the defendant's use was successful in *Midland Great Western Railway v Benson*.[124] The defendant transferred a consignment of butter to Kelly via the plaintiff company. The defendant, being dissatisfied with the financial arrangements made between himself and Kelly, wrongfully secured the return of the butter before it reached Kelly. Kelly had paid £40 on account for the butter and upon the threat of legal action the plaintiff paid £40 to Kelly. Monahan C.J. in the Court of Common Pleas indicated that in these circumstances the law would imply that the defendant promised to repay the company that which it was bound to pay to Kelly, who could maintain an action against the company.

20–33 The *Benson* case leads us on to examine one further requirement, apart from the requirement that the plaintiff make the payment because of the existence of some element of practical compulsion. There should be an obligation in law upon the defendant to pay the money due. It is possible that the defendant may have promised to make restitution to the plaintiff, in which case an action will be brought upon the express promise[125] but an implied promise will not be imposed upon the defendant unless the defendant was bound to make the payment; see *Brooks Wharf v Goodman Brothers*.[126] So in *Irish National Insurance Co v Scannell*[127] the defendant, a licensed auctioneer, and the plaintiff company executed a professional indemnity bond which obliged the company to meet any claims brought against members of the Irish Auctioneers and Estate Agents Association, of which the defendant was a member. The company met certain lawful debts and liabilities incurred by Scannell. The plaintiff company was held to be able to recover these moneys as money paid for and on behalf of the defendant. In cases where there is a joint liability on both plaintiff and defendant, e.g. the plaintiff stands as surety for another, upon payment of the debt due to a third party the surety can sue his

---

[121] (1869) L.R. 4 H.L. 226 at 249.
[122] [1915] 3 K.B. 106.
[123] (1878) 2 L.R. (Ir.) 548. In a different context see *Hanley v I.C.C. Finance Ltd* [1996] 1 I.L.R.M. 463.
[124] (1875) Ir. C.L. Rep. 52.
[125] e.g. *Cook v Wright* (1861) 1 B. & S. 559.
[126] [1937] 1 K.B. 534.
[127] [1959] Ir. Jur. R. 41.

co-sureties, if any, for a contribution or seek reimbursement from the principal debtor; see *Gore v Gore*.[128] Where liability is imposed by a court upon one of several tortfeasors the tortfeasor held liable may also seek to obtain a contribution from the other tortfeasors; see the Civil Liability Act 1961 s.21, discussed in *East Cork Foods Ltd v O'Dwyer Steel Co*.[129]

(8) Money paid by the plaintiff for the defendant's use

20–34 When payment has been made by the plaintiff in circumstances where the defendant has benefited therefrom—typically the plaintiff makes a payment and in so doing he discharges a legal liability imposed upon the defendant— there exists the possibility of recovery through an action for money paid by the plaintiff to the defendant's use. There are few cases, however, in which the plaintiff has been successful in such an action and it is generally accepted that at common law the plaintiff will generally be treated as having voluntarily paid the sums in circumstances where restitution will not be ordered.

20–35 If, however, the plaintiff has been obliged by force of circumstance to make the payment because failure to do so will seriously prejudice the plaintiff, restitution may be possible. In *Beresford v Kennedy*[130] the defendants owned farmland in Waterford. The plaintiff, who farmed adjoining land, discovered that the poor-rate collector had seized some of his cattle which had strayed on to the Kennedys' land, the defendants having failed to pay the poor rate. The plaintiff paid the rates due in order to obtain the return of his stock and then sued the defendants for the sums paid, seeking to rely on the English case of *Exall v Partridge*.[131] Andrews J. distinguished *Exall v Partridge* on the ground that in that case Exall paid Partridge's landlord arrears of rent due from Partridge in order to prevent distress being levied on his carriage, which he had left on Partridge's premises. Andrews J. held that in the case before him Beresford's cattle were not lawfully on the defendants' land whereas Exall had lawfully bailed the carriage with Partridge. Andrews J. said: "there is no authority in the books to show that where property is unlawfully on defendants' premises, the wrongdoer can recover against the defendant."[132]

(9) Money had and received from a third party to the use of the plaintiff

20–36 There is authority[133] for the view that where money is received by the defendant for the use of the plaintiff, the payment being made by a third party with instructions to the defendant to pay the sum over to the plaintiff, the plaintiff can maintain an action in quasi-contract to secure payment. A quasi-contractual action is necessary here because the contract, if any exists, is between the defendant and the third party and, further, the plaintiff rarely

---

[128] [1901] 2 I.R. 269.
[129] [1978] I.R. 103; Kerr, *The Civil Liability Acts*, 4th edn (Dublin: Round Hall, 2011).
[130] (1887) 21 I.L.T.R. 17.
[131] (1799) 8 Term Rep. 308.
[132] (1887) 21 I.L.T.R. 17 at 19. See also *Gormley v Johnston* (1895) 29 I.L.T.R. 69.
[133] *Stevens v Hill* (1805) 5 Esp. 247.

provides consideration in these circumstances. Sometimes the doctrine of privity of contract intrudes into this area, witness the Irish cases of *Leader v Leader*[134] and *Sweeney v Moy*,[135] but because the claim is quasi-contractual the doctrine of privity of contract should not properly intrude.

20–37 Recent English case law extends this cause of action from cases where the defendant is obliged to administer a specific amount of money or a particular fund for the third party to cases where the defendant is simply under an obligation vis-à-vis the transferor to administer a monetary liability.[136] The action for money had and received, as a common law conception, was a personal claim. Until recently, in the absence of a constructive trust or a fiduciary relationship it was thought that only this common law action could be available to a plaintiff. However, in *Lipkin Gorman (a firm) v Karpnale Ltd*[137] and in *F.C. Jones & Sons v Jones*[138] principles of tracing at common law have been utilised to allow the legal owner of property to trace his property to the property into which it has been transformed, and also allow the owner to obtain any profits that the wrongful use of his property has produced. While two members of the House of Lords, in *Foskett v McKeown*[139] called for unitary principles of tracing, it should be noted that Lord Hoffmann stressed the differences between unjust enrichment and property rights.

(10) Payment by one surety of more than the due proportion

20–38 Where two or more persons stand as guarantors of a debt, and one of the guarantors pays a sum of money which exceeds the rateable proportion of the debt, a restitutionary right to seek the other surety to contribute arises. This right, according to O'Brien J. in *Gardiner v Brooker*[140] "comes, in equity, originally and absolutely, by the payment and discharge of a common burthen, and has no existence inchoate or complete, until the payment is made".[141] While normally the right to a contribution does not arise until the excess amount is paid, the right may arise if there is litigation in train against one co-surety only, that defendant being able to seek an indemnity for instance from another surety.[142] This right of contribution can be asserted against the co-surety even though the creditor's right of action against the surety has become time-barred. In *Roche v Wymes*[143] a case arising out of the Bula/Tara

---

[134] (1874) I.R. 6 C.L. 20; *Murnaghan v McCreevy*, unreported, High Court, December 21, 1981.

[135] [1931] L.J. Ir. 42.

[136] *Shamia v Joory* [1958] 1 Q.B. 448.

[137] [1991] 2 A.C. 548. Speculative academic writings on the identification of possible new restitutionary claims abound, e.g. O'Dell, "Restitution, Rectification and Mitigation: Negligent Solicitors and Wills, Again" (2002) 65 M.L.R. 360.

[138] [2000] 3 All E.R. 97.

[139] [1996] 4 All E.R. 721.

[140] [1897] 2 I.R. 6, following *Dering v Earl of Winchelsea* (1787) 1 Cox Eq. C. 318.

[141] [1897] 2 I.R. 6 at 12.

[142] *Wolmershausen v Gullick* [1893] 2 Ch. 514; *Gore v Gore* [1901] 2 I.R. 269.

[143] [2008] IEHC 141. The High Court also held that as the defendant had benefited from the payment by having legal charges removed from his land he had ratified the settlement and could not thus complain of lack of notice.

Mines controversy, the plaintiffs were subject to a judgment obtained against them in their capacity, along with the defendant, as guarantors of a debt. The claimant paid the debt in 2004 and then successfully sued for a contribution. The same principle will apply in regard to a payment made by one debtor to a creditor which clears or reduces a debt owed to the same creditor by a fellow debtor. In *McCarthy v McCarthy & Stone Plc*[144] the claimant successfully obtained the reimbursement (on the basis of monies paid to the use of the claimant) of income tax and social insurance payments that the claimant had made to the relevant authorities when the defendant had left the claimant's employment. Because the defendant had the primary liability to meet these obligations, independent of any contract, the claimant could seek restitution of these payments from the defendant.

Defences

20–39 Even if the defendant has been unjustly enriched a number of defences, or obstacles to restitution may exist. These include estoppel[145] and change of position[146] as well as the fact that there may be a bona fide purchaser for value involved. If counter-restitution is impossible then in principle the court will not order restitution in favour of the claimant, although it has recently been doubted whether counter-restitution will ever be impossible.[147] Of course restitution by both parties may not be possible.[148] Restitution may be defeated by the defence of a change of position.[149] If an overpayment is made and the payee uses the money in a certain way, restitution may not be ordered. However, the mere discharge of a debt such as paying off a mortgage (unless the mortgage contained exceptionally low interest rates) will not be a change of position.[150] Overpayments that lead to a change of lifestyle such as overspending may lead to a change of position defence; see *Philip Collins Ltd v Davis*.[151] A change of position defence does not depend upon the expenditure of money: it is enough if the defendant can show that it acted in accordance with the regulatory requirements laid down by law, so in *Abou–Rahmah*

---

[144] [2006] 4 All E.R. 1127.

[145] *Avon C.C. v Howlett* [1983] 1 W.L.R. 605.

[146] *Lipkin Gorman (a firm) v Karpnale Ltd* [1992] 4 All E.R. 512.

[147] *Halpern v Halpern (No.2)* [2007] 3 All E.R. 478.

[148] *Crystal Palace FC (2000) Ltd v Dowie* [2007] EWHC 1392 (Q.B.).

[149] *Lipkin Gorman (a firm) v Karpnale Ltd* [1992] 4 All E.R. 512; *David Securities Pty v Commonwealth Bank of Australia* (1992) 175 C.L.R. 353; *Miller Paving Ltd v B. Gottardo Construction Ltd* [2007] 285 D.L.R. (4th) 568; *Jones v Churcher* [2009] EWHC 722 (Q.B.); *MGN Ltd v Horton* [2009] EWHC 1680 (Q.B.). See generally, Bant, *The Change of Position Defence* (Oxford: Hart, 2009). The most impressive judicial account of the change of position defence can be found in the various judgments of the High Court of Australia in *Australian Financial Services and Leasing Pty Ltd v Hills Industries Ltd* (2014) 253 CLR 560.

[150] *Scottish Equitable Plc v Derby* [2001] 3 All E.R. 818.

[151] [2000] 3 All E.R. 808; *National Bank of Egypt International Ltd v Oman Housing Bank* [2002] EWHC 1760 (Comm).

v Abacha,[152] customers of the defendant bank defrauded claimants. It was held that the claimants could not recover those losses from the bank on the basis that it had informed banking regulators of its suspicions, even though the defendant had continued to allow the fraudsters to use its services. The defence will succeed if the person pleading it can show he/she has suffered a "disenrichment".[153] This defence has effectively been allowed to abrogate the defence of estoppel by representation in the sense that in both change of position and estoppel by representation cases the court may allow a defence to the restitution claim to the extent that an overpayment will not be fully recoverable if it would be unconscionable to do so.[154] The defence of change of position is not available to a wrongdoer; see *Garland v Consumers Gas Co*.[155] The scope of the defence of payment in settlement of an honest claim remains uncertain. The fact that Parliament has apparently not intervened on the issue and the broader public policy that a matter has been decided—res judicata—is at the heart of the decision of the Supreme Court in *Dublin Corp v Building and Allied Trade Unions* not to order the return of at least part of the monies paid, citing Henchy J. in *Murphy v A.G.*[156]:

> "Over the centuries the law has come to recognise, in one degree or another, that factors such as prescription (negative or positive), waiver, estoppel, laches, a statute of limitation, *res judicata*, or other matters (most of which may be grouped under the heading of public policy) may debar a person from obtaining redress in the courts for injury, pecuniary or otherwise, which would be justiciable and redressable if such considerations had not intervened."

The converse position is also true when legislation has been enacted. Restitution may be excluded as a private law claim when it is clear that Parliament intended to create a watertight system of recovery for unpaid sums due under statute: *R (Child Poverty Action Group) v Secretary of State for Work and Pensions*.[157]

Quantum Meruit

20–40 We now turn to examine the converse situation to that just considered; suppose the plaintiff has transferred property or performed some service for the defendant without a price having been paid or expressly agreed upon; can

---

[152] [2006] EWCA Civ 1492.
[153] *Commerzbank AG v Price Jones* [2003] EWCA Civ 1663; *City Index Ltd v Gawler* [2008] 2 All E.R. (Comm.) 950.
[154] *National Westminster Bank Plc v Somer International* [2002] 1 All E.R. 198.
[155] (2004) 237 D.L.R. (4th) 385.
[156] [1982] I.R. 241 at 314. The *Dublin Corporation* case ([1985] I.L.R.M. 283) also suggests that the courts are aware of the implications for the Exchequer on follow-up claims, as does *O'Rourke v Revenue Commissioners* [1996] 2 I.R. 1.
[157] [2010] UKSC 54; *Legal Services Commission v Loomba* [2012] EWHC 29 (Q.B.).

the plaintiff succeed in an action either for some consideration, in which case the claim is really contractual, or, otherwise, in quasi-contract for the value of the benefit conferred upon the defendant? Sometimes the generic term of quantum meruit is applied to both situations. When the claim is really contractual in nature the plaintiff often seeks to recover a price for goods delivered or property sold under the terms of an agreement which did not itself fix the amount. The measure of compensation is generally the amount the defendant would expect to pay in order to obtain the benefit which has been duly conferred; where this process is open to a court a reasonable price will be fixed, either by reference to general principles[158] or statute.[159] In *Fanning v Wicklow County Council*[160] building work was completed in the mistaken belief that a contract had been negotiated. There was no contract because the price had not been agreed beforehand, as was the common intention of the parties. O'Hanlon J. held the builder entitled to recover the value of the work on a quantum meruit. In *Rover International Ltd v Cannon Film Sales (No. 3)*[161] both Kerr and Nicholls L.JJ. were of the view that where *quantum meruit* is sought in respect of work done under a supposedly valid contract, it was incorrect to assess the *quantum meruit* by placing a ceiling on the amount due by reference to a maximum amount set by the invalid contract. The appropriate measure is equitable restitution as between the parties, regardless of their respective positions if the contract had been valid. As the courts are essentially being asked to measure market value of the goods or services rendered, however, an agreed price will be important and while it might appear obvious that any agreed remuneration should constitute the award, this may not be effective should there be evidential difficulties.[162] The question of how to evaluate the award to be made on a quantum meruit has been considered by the English Court of Appeal in *Benedetti Sawiris*[163] which contains useful guidelines on any trade usage and consensual factors such as a formula set out in an inchoate agreement; market value of services (calculated on a liberal basis at the top-end of the scale) appears to be expressly sanctioned in this case. In an appropriate case the award may be satisfied by a transfer of shares of some other commodity.[164] In *Benedetti* the trial judge was criticised for taking into account a post-services offer to settle the dispute although the Court of Appeal approved flexibility in respect of the date of valuation, such an offer providing no evidence as to market value. Exceptional value of the services to the beneficiary may also be an appropriate reference point in a limited number of cases.[165]

---

[158] e.g. *Hillas v Arcos* [1932] Comm. Cas. 23.
[159] e.g. *Hillas v Arcos* [1932] Comm. Cas. 23.
[160] Unreported, High Court, April 30, 1984.
[161] [1989] 3 All E.R. 423.
[162] *Proactive Sports Management Ltd v Rooney* [2011] EWCA Civ 1444 at paras 119–124.
[163] [2010] EWCA Civ 1427, affirmed at [2010] UKSC 50.
[164] Per Arden L.J. at para.73.
[165] Etherton L.J. discussed the theoretical basis of unjust enrichment, i.e. failure of consideration or free value; Etherton L.J.'s views were endorsed at [2013] UKSC 50.

20–41 The most enlightening series of Irish cases involve claims in *quantum meruit* brought by auctioneers and estate agents seeking reasonable remuneration for work completed. While we have considered the general position in relation to actions brought upon an implied contract,[166] two contrasting decisions indicate that quasi-contract may provide the auctioneer or estate agent with an alternative to the implied contract argument. In *Stokes & Quirke Ltd v Clohessy*[167] the plaintiff auctioneers were instructed by the defendant to find a buyer for his house. They introduced a buyer prepared to purchase at a satisfactory figure but the sale did not proceed when, prior to execution of the formal contract, the defendant received a higher offer from a third party. Nothing had been said about the plaintiff's commission. Their action in contract failed as did their action in quantum meruit. McLoughlin J. held it was not evident that the plaintiffs were to be paid simply upon introduction of someone willing to buy, even if the sale did not ultimately proceed. In contrast in *Henehan v Courtney & Hanley*[168] an estate agent was held entitled to recover on a *quantum meruit* when instructed by an intending purchaser to find a farm for him. The estate agent did find a farm which was suitable and, more to the point, the purchase was closed. Even though nothing had been said about the commission Teevan J. quoted *Bateman on Auctions*:

> "It is the employment of a professional agent to perform duties of the kind usually undertaken by members of his profession which gives rise to an implied promise to pay him reasonable remuneration."

Therefore if one engages an architect to undertake planning work of a kind normally undertaken by members of the profession a quantum meruit will lie for reasonable remuneration.[169] Similarly, in *Chieb v Carter*[170] the plaintiff had been appointed sole agent by the defendant to arrange the shipment of cattle from Ireland to Egypt, the plaintiff being required to liaise with the Egyptian authorities for an agreed commission. The sale did not proceed at the time anticipated, but the defendant later independently arranged for shipment without the assistance of the plaintiff, nevertheless building upon the work that the plaintiff had done as sole agent. The Supreme Court upheld the decision of the High Court, finding that the plaintiff's work and expenditure subsequently utilised by the defendant entitled him to payment quantum meruit. In contrast, where there is no clarity on what the nature of the contractual duties are and the professional status of the claimant is uncertain, the necessary contractual context may be absent to anchor a quantum meruit: *Donnelly v Woods*.[171] Purely voluntary services that could be explained away as being dictated by

---

[166] Chapter 6.
[167] [1957] I.R. 84.
[168] (1966) 101 I.L.T.R. 25.
[169] *Devaney v Reidy*, unreported, High Court, May 10, 1974; *McCarthy v VHI*, unreported, High Court, July 24, 1984.
[170] Unreported, Supreme Court, June 3, 1987.
[171] [2012] IEHC 26. Contrast *Bergin v Walsh* [2015] IEHC 594.

"ties of friendship and neighbourliness" will be similarly outside a quantum meruit claim: *Coleman v Mullen*.[172]

20–42 When the claim is brought in quasi-contract the case often proceeds on the assumption that no valid contract subsists. For example, the contract may have been discharged by frustration and the plaintiff, who has nevertheless afterwards conferred a valuable benefit upon the defendant, may seek to recover the value of the benefit actually conferred, which may or may not be higher than any price fixed by the contract which has been discharged by operation of law; see *Davis Contractors v Fareham UDC*.[173] However, the fact that the performance is rendered more expensive by virtue of circumstance or additional costs incurred is not generally sufficient to ground a quantum meruit, for the courts are reluctant to allow contracting parties to seek to pick and choose which obligations they will observe and those for which they will seek relief via quantum meruit. For this reason, in *Travers Construction Ltd v Lismore Homes Ltd*[174] Gannon J. held that, where a contract had been voluntarily terminated by the agreement of both parties, one party could not subsequently seek a *quantum meruit* remedy, for the rights of the parties had to be governed by their agreement.

20–43 It may also be possible to bring quantum meruit on the basis of a contract that has been wrongfully discharged by the defendant. The old Irish case of *Lawlor v Alton*[175] indicates that where the plaintiff is wrongfully deprived of his employment but work has been carried out a remedy in damages may also be available.[176]

20–44 In contrast, where the contract is void there may be no alternative but to sue in quasi-contract. The principle stated in the leading English case of *Craven-Ellis v Canons Ltd*[177] is that recovery turns upon a rule of law imposed by virtue of the work done rather than an inference of fact arising from acceptance of services or goods. This case and the reasoning therein were expressly accepted by Judge Ó Briain in *O'Connor v Listowel UDC*.[178] The plaintiff had been appointed engineer and town surveyor by the defendant council but the appointment was invalid. The plaintiff, before the invalidity came to light, had rendered services for six months. It was held that the plaintiff was not entitled to recover in contract, for the transaction was invalid, but that he was entitled to a reasonable remuneration for such services requested and accepted by the defendants.

---

[172] [2011] IEHC 179.
[173] [1956] A.C. 696.
[174] Unreported, High Court, March 9, 1990.
[175] (1873) I.R. 8 C.L. 160.
[176] *De Barnardy v Harding* (1853) 3 Exch. 822; *Brown v Wood* (1854) 6 Ir. Jur. 221.
[177] [1936] 2 K.B. 403.
[178] [1957] Ir. Jur. R. 43.

20–45 The law will not, however, impose the obligation to pay reasonable remuneration to the plaintiff when the plaintiff fails to complete an entire contract. In *Creagh v Sheady*[179] a labourer left his employment before the agreed period of employment—an annual hiring—had run. He was held not entitled at common law to bring quantum meruit. Nor is a claim sustainable when the plaintiff has committed a civil wrong; see *Beresford v Kennedy*.[180] Where the contract is unenforceable, e.g. there is a failure to satisfy the writing requirements of the Statute of Frauds 1695, it is well established that an action in quantum meruit can be brought to recover the value of benefits conferred upon the defendant on foot of the unenforceable contract.[181]

20–46 When negotiations which are intended to produce a contract are in train it is by no means unusual to find that the parties undertake preparatory work, or indeed commence to perform the contract, in the optimistic belief that the negotiations will be successful. If the negotiations break down it is clear that any benefits conferred by the plaintiff upon the defendant can be compensated for through quantum meruit. In *British Steel Corp v Cleveland Bridge & Engineering Co*[182] the plaintiff delivered a quantity of steel nodes to the defendants, to be used in building a bridge. The steel was ordered on foot of a "letter of intent" which indicated that while negotiations were still in progress the defendants would like performance to commence pending preparation and issue of a formal sub-contract. Each sides refused to accede to the other's terms vis-à-vis delivery and quality of the goods. Robert Goff J. held that there was no contract for there was a failure to agree on essential terms but, notwithstanding this: "the law simply imposes an obligation on the party who made the request to pay a reasonable sum for such work as has been done pursuant to that request, such an obligation sounding in quasi-contract, or as we now say, in restitution."

20–47 It is also established that a quantum meruit may entitle the plaintiff to recover for preparatory work so requested even if the defendant receives no benefit (unlike *British Steel* when some of the materials were actually delivered). The Irish case of *Folens & Co v Minister for Education*[183] provides an excellent illustration. The plaintiff entered into negotiations with the Department of Education with a view to publishing a children's encyclopaedia in Irish for the Department. While negotiations progressed the plaintiff undertook preparatory work on the publication with the approval of the Department. The Department eventually decided not to proceed with the publication. The company sought to recover expenses incurred. While McWilliam J. found it impossible to hold that a concluded contract had resulted from the negotiations, relying on the leading English case of *Brewer*

---

[179] [1955–1956] Ir. Jur. R. 86; contrast *Brown v Wood* (1854) 6 Ir. Jur. 221.
[180] (1887) 21 I.L.T.R. 17.
[181] *Deglman v Guarantee Trust* [1954] 3 D.L.R. 785.
[182] [1984] 1 All E.R. 504.
[183] [1984] I.L.R.M. 265.

Street Investments Ltd v Barclay's Woollen Co,[184] McWilliam J. found for the plaintiff company in quasi-contract:

> "I have no doubt that had the Department said: 'we want you to put this work in hand but we are only going to pay for it provided we eventually agree upon the terms of a contract between us,' the plaintiff would not have done the work at its own risk as to cost. On this basis, I am of opinion that the plaintiff is entitled to be paid for all the work which had been done with the approval or at the direction of the Department."[185]

Similarly, in *Premier Dairies v Jameson*,[186] the *Brewer St.* case was again relied upon by McWilliam J. when he awarded quasi-contractual relief to the plaintiff when it became apparent that both parties to a contract mistakenly believed that a binding and enforceable contract had been concluded. It appears from the *Folens* decision that the court is not confined to assessing the costs incurred by the plaintiff alone; McWilliam J. also awarded the plaintiff company compensation for an element of lost profits. It is submitted that this was speculative on the facts before the court and to this extent the decision may be unsound.

Constructive Trust and Other Equitable Reliefs

20–48 "A constructive trust will arise when the circumstances render it inequitable for the legal owner of property to deny the title of another to it. It is a trust, which comes into existence irrespective of the will of the parties and arises by operation of law. The principle is that where a person who holds property in circumstances which in equity and good conscience should be held or enjoyed by another he will be compelled to hold the property in trust for another."[187]

This concept of the new model constructive trust has been extra-judicially sanctioned by Chief Justice Keane, writing in his text, *Equity and the Law of Trusts in the Republic of Ireland*,[188] and in *Kelly v Cahill*,[189] Barr J. imposed a constructive trust on the beneficiary of a will which unwittingly did not give effect to the intention of the testator due to the inadvertence of the solicitor who drew up the will. The law relating to constructive trusts and other means of acquiring proprietary interests in property has been restated by the House

---

[184] [1953] 3 W.L.R. 869.

[185] [1984] I.L.R.M. 265 at 276.

[186] Unreported, High Court, March 1, 1983.

[187] Per Costello J. in *HKN Invest OY v Incotrade PVT Ltd* (*In Liquidation*) [1993] 3 I.R. 152 at 162, citing *Hussey v Palmer* [1972] 1 W.L.R. 1286.

[188] 2nd edn (Haywards Heath: Bloomsbury Professional, 2011), paras 13–57 to 13–60; see also Delany, *Equity and the Law of Trusts in Ireland*, 6th edn (Dublin: Round Hall, 2016), Ch.8.

[189] [2001] 2 I.L.R.M. 205. *Thorner v Major* [2009] 1 W.L.R. 776 has been followed in *Coyle v Finnegan* [2013] IEHC 463 and *Finnegan v Hand* [2016] IEHC 255.

of Lords and the Supreme Court in the UK.[190] It is to be expected that these decisions will be influential in both parts of Ireland.[191]

20–49 In *Bank of Cyprus UK Ltd v Menelaou*[192] the remedy awarded by the English Court of Appeal and the Supreme Court was an equitable charge by way of an unpaid vendor's lien over real property that had been acquired by the donee of property as a consequence of the bank surrendering valid legal charges over other property in favour of less valuable security interests which, in the event, were void and unenforceable.

---

[190] *Stark v Dowden* [2007] UKHL 17; *Jones v Kernott* [2011] UKSC 53.
[191] Clearly binding on Northern Ireland courts—see *Gracey v Beck* [2009] NI Ch 59 and *Bank of Scotland Plc v Brogan* [2012] NI Ch 21. In the Republic, see *C v S* [2008] IEHC 463 and *Stanley v Kieran* [2011] IESC 19. See generally, Delany, *Equity and the Law of Trusts in Ireland*, 6th edn (Dublin: Round Hall, 2016); Keane, *Equity and the Law of Trusts in the Republic of Ireland*, 2nd edn (Dublin: Bloomsbury Professional, 2011), Ch.13.
[192] [2015] UKSC 66.

Index